WORLDCOMP'13
July 22-25, 2013
Las Vegas Nevada, USA
www.world-academy-of-science.org

PROCEEDINGS OF
THE 2013 INTERNATIONAL
CONFERENCE ON
SECURITY & MANAGEMENT

SAM 2013

Editors

Kevin Daimi
Hamid R. Arabnia

Associate Editors

Michael R. Grimaila
Kathy Liszka
George Markowsky
Ashu M. G. Solo

(An Imprint of Laxmi Publications Pvt. Ltd.)
An ISO 9001:2008 Company
BENGALURU • CHENNAI • COCHIN • GUWAHATI • HYDERABAD
JALANDHAR • KOLKATA • LUCKNOW • MUMBAI • RANCHI • NEW DELHI
BOSTON (USA) • ACCRA (GHANA) • NAIROBI (KENYA)

This volume contains papers presented at The 2013 International Conference on Security & Management (SAM'13). Their inclusion in this publication does not necessarily constitute endorsements by editors or by the publisher.

Branches

	Branch	Phone	
✆	Bengaluru	080-26 75 69 30	
✆	Chennai	044-24 34 47 26,	24 35 95 07
✆	Cochin	0484-237 70 04,	405 13 03
✆	Guwahati	0361-254 36 69,	251 38 81
✆	Hyderabad	040-27 55 53 83,	27 55 53 93
✆	Jalandhar	0181-222 12 72	
✆	Kolkata	033-22 27 43 84	
✆	Lucknow	0522-220 99 16	
✆	Mumbai	022-24 91 54 15,	24 92 78 69
✆	Ranchi	0651-220 44 64	

Published in India by

An ISO 9001:2008 Company
113, GOLDEN HOUSE, DARYAGANJ,
NEW DELHI - 110002, INDIA
Telephone : 91-11-4353 2500, 4353 2501
Fax : 91-11-2325 2572, 4353 2528
www.laxmipublications.com info@laxmipublications.com

C—
Printed at:

Foreword

It gives us great pleasure to introduce this collection of papers to be presented at the 2013 International Conference on Security and Management (SAM'13), July 22 through 25, 2013, at the New Tropicana Hotel, Las Vegas, USA.

The conference was sponsored and or supported by the US Chapter of World Academy of Science (http://www.world-academy-of-science.org/); Computer Science Research, Education, and Applications Press (CSREA); Aldebaran Robotics Inc., USA; Taylor & Francis, United Kingdom. In addition, a number of university faculty members and their staff (names appear below and also on the cover of the proceedings), several publishers of computer science and computer engineering books and journals, chapters and/or task forces of computer science associations/organizations from 5 countries, and developers of high-performance machines and systems provided significant help in organizing the conference as well as providing some resources.

An important mission of World Congress in Computer Science, Computer Engineering, and Applied Computing (a federated congress to which this conference, SAM, is affiliated with) includes "Providing a unique platform for a diverse community of constituents composed of scholars, researchers, developers, educators, and practitioners. The Congress makes concerted effort to reach out to participants affiliated with diverse entities (such as: universities, institutions, corporations, government agencies, and research centers/labs) from all over the world. The congress also attempts to connect participants from institutions that have **teaching** as their main mission with those who are affiliated with institutions that have **research** as their main mission. The congress uses a quota system to achieve its institution and geography diversity objectives."

The program committee would like to thank all those who submitted papers for consideration. About 40% of the submissions were from outside the United States. Each paper was peer-reviewed by at least two experts in the field (occasionally by three) for originality, significance, clarity, impact, and soundness. The only exception to the above evaluation process was for papers that were submitted directly to chairs/organizers of approved sessions/workshops; in these cases, the chairs/organizers were responsible for the evaluation of such submissions.

We are very grateful to the many colleagues who helped in organizing the conference. In particular, we would like to thank the members of the SAM'13 Program Committee who we hope will offer their help again in organizing the next year's conference (SAM'14). The SAM'13 Program Committee members were:

- *Dr. Iftikhar Ahmad, Department of Software Engineering, King Saud University, Saudi Arabia*
- *Prof. Wasim Al Hamdani, Department of Computer Technology Sciences, Kentucky State University, USA*
- *Prof. Nizar Al Holou, Chair, Department of Electrical and Computer Engineering, University of Detroit Mercy, USA*
- *Prof. Hamid R. Arabnia, (Vice Chair and Coordinator, SAM'13), Elected Fellow, ISIBM; Editor-in-Chief, The Journal of Supercomputing (Springer); University of Georgia, Georgia, USA*
- *Dr. Shadi Banitaan, Computer Science and Software Engineering, University of Detroit Mercy, USA*
- *Dr. Rita Barrios, Computer and Information Systems, University of Detroit Mercy, USA*
- *Dr. Clive Blackwell, Computing and Communication Technologies, Oxford Brookes University, UK*
- *Dr. Violeta Bulbenkiene, Department of Informatics Engineering, Klaipeda University, Lithuania*
- *Dr. Juan V. Capella, Department of Computer Engineering, Technical University of Valencia, Spain*
- *Dr. Feng Cheng, Chair of Internet Technologies and Systems, Hasso-Plattner-Institute, University of Potsdam, Germany*

- *Prof. Hung-Min Sun, Director of Information Security, Department of Computer Science, National Tsing Hua University, Taiwan*
- *Dr. Alok Tongaonkar, CTO's Office, Narus Inc., USA*
- *Prof. Woei-Jiunn Tsaur, Department of Information Management, Da-Yeh University, Taiwan*
- *Dr. Gregory Vert, Department of Computer Information Systems, Texas A&M University, USA*
- *Dr. Montri Wiboonrat, College of Graduate Study in Management, Khon Kaen University, Bangkok Campus, Thailand*

We express our gratitude to keynote, invited, and individual conference/tracks and tutorial speakers - the list of speakers appears on the conference web site. We would also like to thank the followings: UCMSS (Universal Conference Management Systems & Support, California, USA) for managing all aspects of the conference; Dr. Tim Field of APC for managing the printing of the proceedings; and the staff of the New Tropicana Hotel in Las Vegas for the professional service they provided. Last but not least, we would like to thank the Co-Editors and Associate Co-Editors of SAM'13: Prof. Kevin Daimi, Prof. Hamid R. Arabnia, Prof. Michael R. Grimaila, Prof. Kathy Liszka, Prof. George Markowsky, and Ashu M.G. Solo.

We present the proceedings of SAM'13.

Steering Committee,
2013 World Congress in Computer Science, Computer Engineering and Applied Computing
http://www.world-academy-of-science.org/

Contents

SESSION: SECURITY MANAGEMENT, SECURITY EDUCATION, AND HARDWARE SECURITY I

SESSION: BIOMETRIC AND FORENSICS

SESSION: COMPUTER SECURITY I

SESSION: INFORMATION ASSURANCE

SESSION: CRYPTOGRAPHIC TECHNOLOGIES I

SESSION: NETWORK SECURITY I

SESSION: NETWORK SECURITY II

SESSION: CYBERSECURITY EDUCATION

SESSION

SECURITY MANAGEMENT, SECURITY EDUCATION, AND HARDWARE SECURITY I

Chair(s)

Dr. Dusan Stevanovic

Most Successful Vulnerability Discoverers: Motivation and Methods

Abdullah M. Algarni, and Yashwant K. Malaiya
Computer Science Department, Colorado State University, Fort Collins, CO 80523, USA
{Algarni, Malaiya}@cs.colostate.edu

Abstract— *In this paper, we investigate the factors that motivate and enable successful vulnerability discovery and the role of vulnerability markets. This is done by studying the career, motivation and methods of the most successful vulnerability discoverers. Vulnerability discovery takes considerable expertise. Some vulnerabilities, if exploited, can cause enormous damage to an organization, a segment of the economy, or even national security. Software developers, security organizations and government agencies are continuously engaged in efforts to prevent improper disclosure of vulnerabilities that can lead to zero-day exploitations. We observe that a major percentage of vulnerabilities are discovered by individuals external to software development organizations. We identify the top vulnerability discoverers throughout the past 12 years, and examine their motivation and methods. We observe that financial reward is a major motivation, especially to discoverers in Eastern Europe.. The paper studies the actual vulnerability market, rather than the hypothetical markets often studied in recent literature.*

Keywords – Software security; vulnerability discovery model; risk management; vulnerability market; vulnerability patching

1 Introduction

Potential exploitation of software security vulnerabilities has now emerged as a major security threat to organizations, some of the economic sectors, and national defense. Software vulnerability can be defined as a software defect or weakness in the security system that could be exploited by a malicious user causing loss or harm [1]. The number of unremedied vulnerabilities in a system represent the degree of security risk. It is important during the software lifecycle development process to evaluate and manage the risk, in order to assess how it will impact users, organizations, and the society.

Vulnerability discovery models that attempt to model the vulnerability discovery process have been recently proposed [2,3]. However there has not been a study of actual vulnerability discoverers and what motivates them. The individuals who discover the vulnerabilities (termed *discoverers* here) and those who exploit them (*exploiters*) are two separate groups. Discovering a vulnerability takes a much higher degree of technical skill and insight. The exploiters do not require a comparable skill—in fact, in the presence of an exploit (code that exploits one or more vulnerabilities), a patient hacker may achieve a security breach largely mechanically. The vulnerability discoverers represent a critical source of risk, should they choose to sell the vulnerability to malicious organizations or individuals. For example, Google has twice paid a $60,000 reward for details on a single vulnerability [4], suggesting that the potential damage caused by these vulnerabilities could have been enormous.

Many vulnerability discoverers seek to preserve the right to their claim of having discovered a vulnerability, since it serves to acknowledge the discoverer's expertise. For example, the well known University of Cambridge researcher Ross Anderson mentions a vulnerability he and his student discovered in 2003 [5]. A mid-year peak in vulnerability discovery, specifically in Microsoft products, can be explained by the coinciding date of a major conference, wherein security experts often present their vulnerability findings [6].

As presented here, a large percentage of vulnerabilities are found by experts external to the actual software development organizations. They are free to disclose the vulnerabilities they discover in any way they like. The hackers who are vulnerability exploiters are often classified as *white hat*, *black hat*, and *gray hat* [7,8]. These classifications do not apply to the security researchers engaged in finding vulnerabilities. However, the vulnerability markets may be classified as *legitimate*, where the transactions are properly recorded and disclosed; *black*, where the transactions are not disclosed; or *gray*, where the transactions are at the borderline. The current software vulnerability reward programs are a major part of the legitimate markets that attempt to attract the vulnerability discoverers who might otherwise resort to selling their findings on the black market. Those programs are relatively new and sometimes limited. They attempt to bring a discovery to the legitimate market, which significantly reduces the risk to the society. It is possible that some groups, such as government defense agencies, may be willing to pay a much higher price in the black or gray market [9].

There are several vulnerability databases organized by government-affiliated or private organizations. They include the National Vulnerability Database (NVD), Open Source Vulnerability Database (OSVDB), the vulnerability data collected by Frei et al. [10] (FVDB), Exploit Database, and IBM X-Force Vulnerability Database. In this paper, we have used OSVDB frequently for our investigations. As implied by its name, OSVDB is an open-source, community-organized

TABLE I
SUMMARIZE THE IMPORTANT INFORMATION ABOUT SOME CURRENT VULNERABILITY REWARDS PROGRAMS

Program	# VULN TYPE	Max reward	Min reward	# of beneficiaries	Trend
Vulnerability Reward Program for Google web properties	5	$20,000	$100	2010: 51 2011: 122 2012: 189	Increase
Chrome Vulnerability Reward Program	Any security bug	>= 10,000	500	494	N/A
CCBill Vulnerability Reward Program	7	500	300	42	Hold
Secunia Vulnerability Coordination Reward Program (SVCRP)	Most bugs depending on some criteria	Most Valued Contributor & Most Interesting Coordination Report	N/A	N/A	N/A
The Mozilla Security Bug Bounty Program	Certain bugs depending on some criteria	$3000 (US) cash reward and a Mozilla T-shirt.	500	N/A	N/A
ZDI Rewards Program(TippingPoint)	Particular bugs depending on some criteria	$25,000	$1000	N/A	N/A
Facebook	7	No maximum	$500	Prior to 2011: 43 2011: 46 2012: 111	Increase
WordPress Security Bug Bounty Program	11	$1000	$25	N/A	N/A
iDefense (Verisign)	N/A	N/A	N/A	Significant number	N/A

database associated with the Open Security Foundation, with the stated aim being to provide "accurate, detailed, current, and unbiased technical information". It contains more than 90,377 vulnerabilities found by 4,735 researchers [11].

The first section of this paper provides some background about vulnerability markets and the current reward programs. The next section identifies the top vulnerability discoverers, using the OSVDB database, and examines their careers. We examine the data for well-known open-source browsers in order to determine how many vulnerability discoverers were discovered internally by the browser development teams, and to assess the relative significance of external vulnerability finders. We show the specific questions that we have posed to several top discoverers and present what we have discovered. Finally, we discuss our findings and present our conclusions along with suggestions for future work.

2 Background

Any unpatched vulnerabilities in a software program can allow hackers to attack the system, harming an organization or compromising sensitive information. Therefore, remedying any newly discovered vulnerabilities before they are exploited is critical. While many discoverers are likely to be responsible professionals, they need to be provided the opportunity to use their skills in a positive, productive way in order to avoid passing the information to those who might exploit the vulnerabilities. If there is a lack of incentives from organizations in the field, they might be tempted to sell the information in the vulnerability black market, resulting in possible exploitation of systems.

2.1 Vulnerability markets

Vulnerability discoverers seek rewards for their capabilities. This gives rise to vulnerability markets, which may be termed legitimate markets, black markets or gray markets. Vulnerabilities discovered within a developer organization do not enter the market. Those discovered within a security company are used for demonstrating the company's capabilities to potential customers, and perhaps providing customers early remediation. Freelance discoverers will attempt to maximize their reward by selling their vulnerabilities in the vulnerabilities markets [12,13]. Vulnerabilities have significant economic value [14] because they can lead to zero-day exploits that might harm organizations, the economy, and ultimately, society [15]. Some exploits have been sold for as much as $250,000 [16]. In addition to money, many discoverers find the fame generated by the disclosure also attractive, as it can be translated into further economic opportunities.

In legitimate markets the buyers are original software developers, the third-party security organizations follow proper practices for disclosing the vulnerabilities, and the transactions are well documented. Several international government organizations are also said to have been significant buyers [16], but their policies are not generally disclosed. In a few countries, the government may be the only major buyer. Selling and buying software vulnerabilities should ideally be done through a well-regulated market [17, 18]. The software vulnerability reward programs discussed below are a major part of the vulnerability market [19]. Such markets should be efficient, legal, and attractive for both discoverers and buyers, and should involve policies that will protect the society. A few commercial organizations that serve as brokers now exist [20,21]. In the black market, the vulnerabilities could be sold to the highest bidder, some of whom may attempt to use them maliciously. Some vulnerability discoverers may consider the black market an attractive option for selling their discovered vulnerabilities [22]. They may find the vulnerability reward programs unattractive because they pay significantly less. The reward programs are still new, and their rewards may often pale in comparison with prices in the black market, which can pay a significant amount depending on the vulnerability's severity. Some organizations, such as Google, have acknowledged the importance of freelance discoverers, and offer a significant monetary award in addition to the possible inclusion in their 'discoverers hall of fame'. A good example of a vulnerability discoverer who has taken advantage of such a reward program is Sergey Glazunov, a Russian student and security researcher who earned $60,000 by discovering a new exploit in Google's Chrome browser [23].

2.2 Vulnerability reward programs

Rewarding security researchers and others who make software products more secure is important. Providing rewards to motivate people to find software defects or weaknesses before they are exploited by black hat exploiters is critical to improving computer security.

There are only a few current vulnerability reward programs, and most of them were created a few years ago. The idea of reward programs is still quite new, and needs more development and improvement.

The current reward programs include these listed below. The key information about them is provided in Table 1:

• Vulnerability Reward Program for Google web properties [24]: This program was created in November 2010. People who discover one of five types of vulnerabilities, such as remote code execution, SQL injection, and other common web flaws, are rewarded from $100 to $20,000. The number of discoverers who have received approval from the reward panel has ranged between 53 winners in the fourth quarter of 2010 to 39 winners in the fourth quarter of 2012.

• Chrome Vulnerability Reward Program (Chromium Security Reward) [25]: All vulnerabilities are considered in this program, provided the vulnerability is identified as being of sufficiently high severity. The rewards range from $500 to $10,000 and up.

• Secunia Vulnerability Coordination Reward Program (SVCRP) [26]: There are two special awards: most valued contributor and most interesting coordination report.

• The Mozilla Security Bug Bounty Program [27]: The rewards range from $500 to $3,000 depending on the severity rating of the vulnerability, and the reward includes a Mozilla t-shirt.

• ZDI Rewards Program [28]: The Zero Day Initiative (ZDI) provides reward points each time a vulnerability submission is purchased. These points determine the ZDI status, which are bronze, silver, gold, platinum, and diamond. The rewards range from is $1,000 to $25,000.

• Facebook [29]: This program is similar to most other reward programs. It offers a bounty for certain qualifying security bugs. The reward has a minimum of $500 with no specified maximum, and is based on severity and creativity.

• WordPress Security Bug Bounty Program [30]: This program has two different bounties: one for WordPress and another for WordPress Plugins. The minimum reward is $25, and the maximum reward is $1,000.

• CCBill Vulnerability Reward Program [31]: CCBill is an Internet billing service. The rewards range from $300 to $500, depending on the types of vulnerabilities found, such as SQL Injection, DoS, and persistent XSS. This program has been temporarily placed on hold due to corrections needed in the reported bugs.

• iDefense Vulnerability Contributor Program: This is one of the oldest reward programs, and a few of the top discoverers mention working with iDefense. However the detailed reward information is not available.

Notably, Microsoft has been steadfast in not offering a reward program, although it works with discoverers and acknowledges their discoveries [32]. Microsoft does use outside consultant organizations to test their software on a contract basis, however [33].

3 The vulnerability discoverers

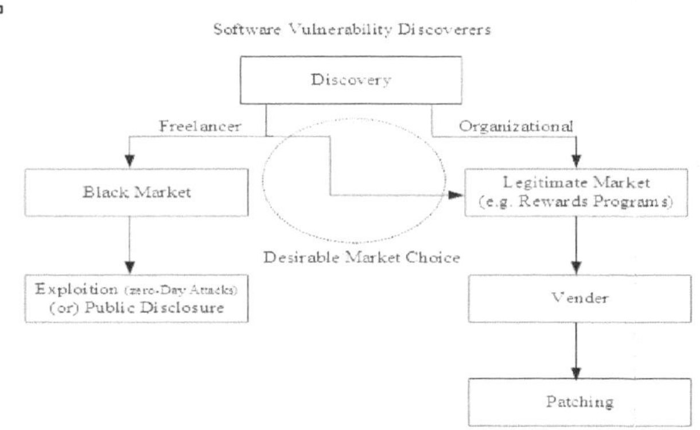

FIG. 1. THE EVENTS IN THE VULNERABILITY LIFE CYCLE

The motivation for vulnerability discoverers has been considered briefly by researchers in the past [34], but has never been studied using actual data. The discovery and disclosure of vulnerabilities are processes that are significantly impacted by the economics involved [35]. A few researchers have considered theoretical modeling of the vulnerabilities market. This paper asks these questions: who are the actual vulnerability finders, and what motivates them?

As shown in Figure 1, vulnerability discovery is done by organizational researchers—who generally follow proper disclosure policies—and freelance researchers, who may sell their findings, either in the legitimate or the black market. Some vulnerabilities are sold in the legitimate market via vulnerability reward programs, or by contacting venders directly. The developers get a chance to develop software patches for the vulnerabilities before the vulnerability is disclosed. On the other hand, when the vulnerabilities are sold on the black market, they are likely to be exploited before public disclosure. The key strategy would be to encourage the researchers to sell their discovered vulnerabilities in the legitimate market instead of the black market (dotted circle on the figure). This will reduce trading in the black market and more vulnerabilities will enter the legitimate market.

Software development organizations such as Google or Microsoft have divisions dedicated to security-related work. They are responsible for the development of security patches. They also discover some of the vulnerabilities in their own products. However as Figures 2 and 3 show, a large fraction of the vulnerabilities, perhaps a majority of them, are discovered by outside discoverers. These external discoverers have their own motivation, which may be different from the motivation

TABLE 2
VULNERABILITY DISCOVERERS FROM JULY. 1, 2012 TO DECEMBER 31, 2012: INSIDERS OR OUTSIDERS

DISCOVERERS	SAFARI'S VULNERABILITIES	PERCENTAGE	CHROMIUM'S VULNERABILITIES	PERCENTAGE
PRODUCT'S COMPANY DISCOVERERS	17	20%	0	0%
PRODUCT'S COMPANY DISCOVERERS AND OTHERS	0	0%	35	35%
OUTSIDE DISCOVERERS	66	80%	63	64%
UNKNOWN DISCOVERERS	0	0%	1	1%

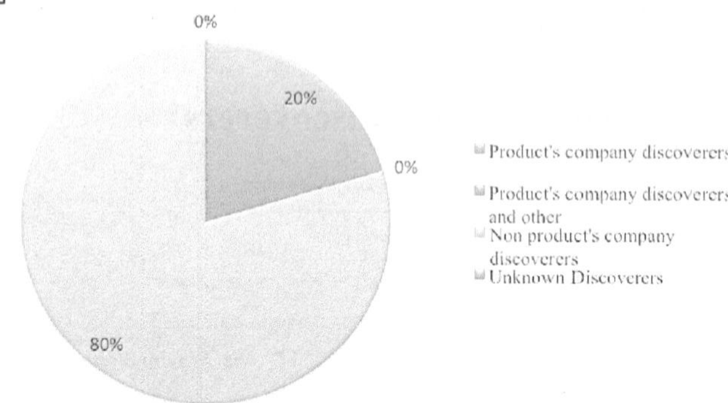

FIG. 2. VULNERABILITY DISCOVERERS IN SAFARI

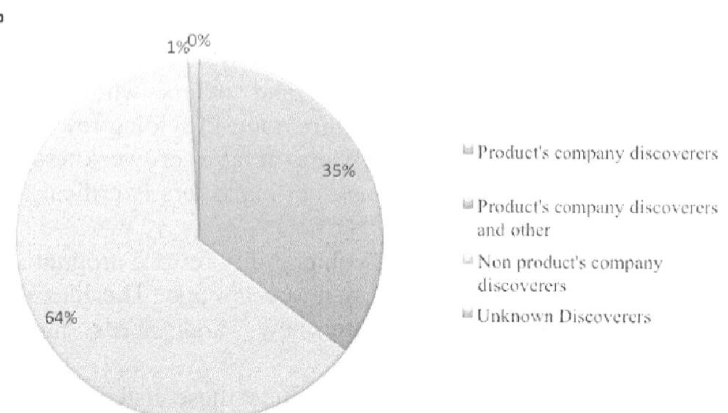

FIG 3. VULNERABILITY DISCOVERERS IN CHROMIUM

of those engaged in discovering vulnerabilities internally in a software development organization. Many external discoverers are freelancers either working on their own or on contract basis. Some of the external discoverers are part of organizations that provide security services.

3.1 Top discoverers

To understand the vulnerability discovery process, we examine the records of the top vulnerability discoverers. Since each of them has successfully discovered quite a large number of vulnerabilities, we can presume that they did not just get lucky—rather, they have a system that has been demonstrated to work. To find the top vulnerability discoverers, we obtained data from the OSVDB database created in 2002. We identified the following ten vulnerability discoverers in the database who found the most vulnerabilities. The actual names are not identifiable in some cases; they are generally known by the login identifier that they use in their blogs.

• r0t: He is a Latvian associated with a group named Unsecured Systems [36]. He discovered 810 vulnerabilities between Aug. 9, 2005 and Sept. 16, 2010. No additional information about him could be located.

• Lostmon Lords: He is a security researcher from Spain [37]. He discovered 279 vulnerabilities between June 20, 2004 and Aug. 15, 2009, as recorded by OSVDB. According to his blog [38], he continued to discover vulnerabilities from Nov. 2009 to July 2012, but apparently disclosed them in such a manner that he is not identified as the discoverer in OSVDB.

• rgod: He is Andrea Micalizzi from Catania, Italy. He was 36 years old when he died in 2006 [39]. However, one of his friends has continued to use rgod login. Together they discovered 277 vulnerabilities between June 6, 2005 and Aug. 29, 2012. According to rgod's website [40], rgod's friend is still discovering vulnerabilities but rgod is not identified as the creditee in OSVDB.

• James Bercegay: He is the owner of GulfTech Security Research and Development [41], which was started in 2002. He discovered 200 vulnerabilities between June 3, 2003 and Sept. 20, 2008.

• Aliaksandr Hartsuyeu: He is the owner of eVuln [42], a security company, which was started on Nov. 14, 2005 [43]. He discovered 229 vulnerabilities between Dec. 28, 2005 and Feb. 03, 2011.

• Kacper: He was a part of the Devil team [44]. He is from Poland. He discovered 199 vulnerabilities between May 12, 2006 and Aug. 10, 2007.

• Luigi Auriemma: He is from Milan, Italy [45]. He discovered 267 vulnerabilities between July 8, 2000 and Mar. 16, 2013.

• Janek Vind, or "waraxe": He runs an interactive software vulnerability and security website [46]. Janek is from Estonia and his collaborators are from Australia, Turkey, Argentina, and other countries. They discovered 319 vulnerabilities between Aug. 08, 2003 and Mar. 21, 2013.

• Luny: The little information provided in the database records states that he discovered 142 vulnerabilities between May 18, 2006 and July 13, 2006.

• Russ McRee: He is a senior security analyst, researcher, and the founder of holisticinfosec.org in the United States [47]. He found 237 vulnerabilities between Jan. 14, 2008 and Mar. 2, 2012.

3.2 Outsider and insider discoverers

One key question in understanding the vulnerability discovery process is whether a discoverer of vulnerabilities is a part of the software product team or an outsider. This will help us to understand what motivates discoverers to find and report software vulnerabilities. To address this question we examined two well known open-source software products: Safari and Google Chromium (Table 2, Figures 2,3). The period we

TABLE 3
SUMMARIZES TOP VULNERABILITY DISCOVERERS' ANSWERS TO SPECIFIC QUESTIONS ABOUT THEIR VULNERABILITY DISCOVERING AND VULNERABILITY REWARD PROGRAMS.

DISCOVERER	MOTIVATING FACTORS	STOP DISCOVERING	IMPACT OF REWARDS PROGRAMS	APPLYING TO REWARDS PROGRAMS
DISCOVERER 1	HOBBY AND LIFESTYLE CHOICE	NO.	N/A	NO
DISCOVERER 2	MAKE HIS WEBSITE MORE POPULAR	NO.	LIMITED IMPACT	NO
DISCOVERER 3	CURIOSITY	NO. HE HAS A COMPANY	NOT MUCH IMPACT	ZDI AND IDEFENSE.
DISCOVERER 4	ENJOYMENT	YES. NOT ENOUGH TIME	MOSTLY, YES.	NO
DISCOVERER 5	FUN, PROFIT, AUDITING	NO.	YES	ZDI AND IDEFENSE.

investigated was from July 1, 2012 to December 31, 2012, and we used the Open Source Vulnerability Database OSVDB as the data source.

As shown in Table 2, for these two products, the majority of the vulnerabilities discovered were found by outsiders. This demonstrates the importance of outsider discoverers and the potential significance of providing discoverers with more enticing vulnerability reward programs, or other forms of a legitimate market. It is definitely worth knowing what would motivate the discoverers to participate in such reward programs.

3.3 Questions for top discoverers

In order to gain insight into their thinking, we decided to contact the top discoverers and ask them some questions. We were able to locate contact information for most of them. We then contacted them and asked some key questions, including the following:

1. What motivates you to discover software vulnerability?
2. How and when did you start?
3. What specific tools do you use for discovering vulnerability?
4. Did you stop working as a vulnerability discoverer? If so, when and why did that happen? If not, why not?
5. Do you think that vulnerability reward programs will help reduce black market transactions and encourage the use of legitimate markets? Please explain.
6. Did you apply to one of the current vulnerability reward programs, and if so, why?
7. Do you have any other comments?

Considering that freelance vulnerability discoverers can sometimes be secretive, we were pleasantly surprised when several of them actually responded. The following section includes some of the answers to the above questions. To ensure their privacy, we have replaced the discoverers' names with aliases. Table 3 summarizes the responses.

- Discoverer 1: He uses his own tools, "specifically his hands and mind, in preference to automated tools". He has not sold a vulnerability in the past ten years. Rather than sell or exploit a vulnerability, he prefers to help developers make a patch available for it. He does not find the reward program to be attractive.
- Discoverer 2: The main reason he became a vulnerability discoverer is that it made his own website more popular and enabled him to offer a source code review service. He only uses his own tools, which are offered on his organization's website. He is also of the opinion that vulnerability reward programs are of limited use, as the black markets offer more money. Like Discoverer 1, he does not apply for any reward programs.
- Discoverer 3: He started in 2002 while following Bugtraq and other mailing lists. He uses various public and proprietary tools to discover vulnerabilities. Although he now runs his own company, he still finds the time for discovery work. In his opinion, vulnerability reward programs do not help to reduce black market transactions substantially and encourage the use of legitimate markets. He states that reward programs pay very little for exclusive information and bug patches, which can be sold for much more on the black market. Nevertheless, he has submitted some vulnerabilities to the ZDI and iDefense reward programs in the past.
- Discoverer 4: He started in 2008 and focuses entirely on web application security flaws, largely specific to free and open source applications. To discover vulnerabilities, he uses a combination of tools such as Burp Suite, OWASP ZAP, and a number of Firefox plugins (Tamper Data), as well as simple manual testing. He thinks that, for the most part, vulnerability reward programs will help to reduce black markets and encourage legitimate markets. He acknowledges that money is always a motivator and if vulnerability discoverers are paid well via the legitimate market, hopefully they will be less likely to sell the bug on the black market. He mentions that he does not sell vulnerabilities. He always coordinates his findings with Secunia but does not take any further action regarding the vulnerability.
- Discoverer 5: He believes that the most profitable option for a vulnerability discoverer like him is to offer software security auditing services. His first 'hacks' were done many years ago, between 1992 and 1993. The tools that he uses for discovering vulnerabilities are Notepad++ for PHP and other scripting languages, which allow him to search specific text strings through multiple files and color coding. He also uses Apache/PHP/MySQL on his home PC, and all of his web application research is done using @localhost. Discoverer 5 usually works manually, without automatic vulnerability scanners. Moreover, he believes that vulnerability reward programs will surely lessen damage, and mentions that he is aware of hundreds of zero-day findings sold to ZDI and other vulnerability reward programs. He has worked with ZDI and iDefense because they pay for findings, arrange all communications with developers, and give him credit in the public advisory.

3.4 Discussion

Upon investigating the factors that influence vulnerability discovery and disclosure, we summarize our findings as follows.

We note that freelance discoverers play a significant role in vulnerability discovery. In some cases, they have even formed their own companies or groups. An unusually high number of successful vulnerability discoverers are from Eastern Europe, a region also known for its sophisticated vulnerability exploiters [48]. That may be attributable to a high degree of technical skill combined with weaker local economies. The rewards for finding vulnerabilities often come from international software organizations based in the United States.

Discovering vulnerabilities requires considerable technical and research skills. Some of the discoverers have an extensive background in software security. The responses by the top discoverers to our questions suggest that they tend to rely on their expertise and intuition rather than just the tools. The discoverers, like other well paid software professionals or researchers, expect to be fairly compensated for their services. With a few critical, high-severity vulnerabilities in hand, they may be in a position to bargain.

An attractive reward program based on vulnerability criticality can provide a significant alternative to the black market. A few software developers and security organizations now run a small number of such programs. These programs ensure time for patch development before a disclosure. Some of the top discoverers that we contacted suggest that sometimes the reward programs do not pay enough, and a better reward may be obtained on the black market, but none of them admitted to selling any vulnerabilities on the black market.

We note that after a few years of very successful vulnerability discovery, many of the top discoverers apparently disappear from the scene as credited discoverers. Some of them suggest that they find it more profitable to contract out their security auditing services to software developers.

The black market may often provide better rewards for some individual vulnerabilities than current legitimate programs. The black market might sometimes be more attractive because applying to reward programs may be tedious or slow. Limited awareness of reward programs may also contribute to the attractiveness of the black markets. The reports suggest that many of the buyers in the black market may be affiliated with various governments [16], bringing a significant amount of money to the black market.

Companies and organizations need to design attractive vulnerability reward programs for their products. This will allow the legitimate markets to compete with the black market. Some reward programs, such as the one for Google Chrome, appear to have been successful. Google has a good reputation in technology as well as management, and has recognized the discoverers as high-achievement professionals. While the amount of money committed to the reward programs is only a tiny part of the company's revenues, Google is giving out some of the best monetary rewards.

A significant part of the global vulnerabilities market is quite opaque. Even the emerging legitimate markets have not been studied in detail, although some mathematical studies based on the classical market theories have appeared. There is a need to examine actual data and practices in order to understand the vulnerability discovery and disclosure.

4 Conclusion and future works

This paper has examined the motivation and methods of vulnerability discoverers by studying the motivation and the methods of discoverers and the vulnerability market. The most successful vulnerability discoverers are identified, and their motivation and techniques have been examined.

While vulnerability discoverers use some tools— including those that they have developed themselves—they rely on their expertise and insight to a considerable extent. It must be kept in mind that tools for finding known vulnerabilities are completely different, and are not of use for discovering new vulnerabilities.

We find that a large fraction of the discoverers are from outside of the software development organizations, and their key motivation is a monetary reward. The vulnerabilities are disclosed in a proper and responsible way when they are traded though the legitimate markets. Reward programs and contract-based software review services are the major components of the legitimate markets. Organizations that act as vulnerability brokers may deal in either the legitimate or the black market. The vulnerability discoverers acknowledge that the black markets can often be attractive. Reports suggest that government agencies may make up a significant part of the black market buyers. This suggests a need for expanded and more attractive legitimate markets.

The research reported in this paper needs to expanded further by looking at a larger number of individual discoverers. There is a need to study the legitimate and the black markets so that the processes can be modeled accurately. Because this is a dynamically changing field, studies such as this need to be repeated in order to see if there are any observable trends in terms of the vulnerabilities that end up in the legitimate and black market periodically, and the subsequent risks to society.

Acknowledgement

We would like to thank all of the top discoverers who took the time to answer our questions. Their answers and comments have provided us with a much clearer understanding of the field. This work was partly supported by a scholarship from King AbdulAziz University in Saudi Arabia.

5 References

[1] C. P. Pfleeger and S. L Pfleeger. Security in Computing, 3rd ed. Prentice Hall PTR, 2003.

[2] O. H. Alhazmi and Y. K. Malaiya, "Application of Vulnerability Discovery Models to Major Operating Systems," IEEE Trans. Reliability, March 2008, pp. 14-22

[3] S.-W. Woo, H. Joh, O. H. Alhazmi and Y. K. Malaiya, "Modeling Vulnerability Discovery Process in Apache and IIS HTTP Servers", Computers & Security, January 2011, Pages 50-62.

[4] "Teen Exploits Three Zero-Day Vulns for $60K Win in Google Chrome Hack Contest | Threat Level | Wired.com," Threat Level. [Online]. Available: http://www.wired.com/threatlevel/2012/03/zero-days-for-chrome/. [Accessed: 01-Apr-2013].

[5] R, Anderson, University of Cambridge, Home page. [Online]. Available: http://www.cl.cam.ac.uk/~rja14/ [Accessed: 27-Apr-2013].

[6] H.-C. Joh and Y. K. Malaiya, "Seasonal variation in the vulnerability discovery process," in Software Testing Verification and Validation, 2009. ICST'09. International Conference on, 2009, pp. 191–200.

[7] "White hat," Search security. [Online]. Available: http://searchsecurity.techtarget.com/definition/white-hat [Accessed: 01-Apr-2013].

[8] "HacK, CouNterHaCk | New York Times Magazine," [Online]. Available: http://www.nytimes.com/library/magazine/home/19991003mag-hackers.html. [Accessed: 01-Apr-2013].

[9] Andy Greenberg, Meet The Hackers Who Sell Spies The Tools To Crack Your PC, Forbes, March 21, 2012, bit.ly/11cbLC6

[10]M. Shahzad, M. Z. Shafiq, and A. X. Liu, "A large scale exploratory analysis of software vulnerability life cycles," in 2012 34th International Conference on Software Engineering (ICSE), 2012, pp. 771–781.

[11]The Open Source Vulnerability Database. [Online]. Available: http://www.osvdb.org. [Accessed: 01-Apr-2013].

[12]Karthik Kannan and Rahul Telang, Market for Software Vulnerabilities? Think Again, Management Science, Vol. 51, No. 5 (May, 2005), pp. 726-740.

[13]Arora, A.; Rahul Telang, "Economics of software vulnerability disclosure," Security & Privacy, IEEE, vol.3, no.1, pp.20, 25, Jan.-Feb. 2005.

[14]R. Böhme, "Vulnerability markets," Proc. of 22C3, vol. 27, p. 30, 2005.

[15]R. Anderson, C. Barton, R. Böhme, R. Clayton, M. J. van Eeten, M. Levi, T. Moore, and S. Savage, "Measuring the cost of cybercrime," in 11th Workshop on the Economics of Information Security (June 2012), 2012.

[16]"Shopping For Zero-Days: A Price List For Hackers' Secret Software Exploits - Forbes," Forbes. [Online]. Available: http://www.forbes.com/sites/andygreenberg/2012/03/23/shopping-for-zero-days-an-price-list-for-hackers-secret-software-exploits/. [Accessed: 01-Apr-2013].

[17]C. Miller, "The legitimate vulnerability market: the secretive world of 0-day exploit sales," in Workshop on the Economics of Information Security (WEIS), 2007, pp. 7–8.

[18]D. McKinney, "Vulnerability Bazaar," IEEE Security Privacy, vol. 5, no. 6, pp. 69–73, 2007.

[19]A. Ozment, "Bug auctions: Vulnerability markets reconsidered," in Third Workshop on the Economics of Information Security, 2004.

[20]Ryan Gallagher, "Cyberwar's Gray Market- Should the secretive hacker zero-day exploit market be regulated?" Slate, Jan. 16, 2013.

[21]Michael Riley and Ashlee Vance "Cyber Weapons: The New Arms Race" BloomsbergBusinessWeek, July 20, 2011.

[22]S. Ransbotham, S. Mitra, and J. Ramsey, "Are markets for vulnerabilities effective?," MIS Quarterly-Management Information Systems, vol. 36, no. 1, p. 43, 2012.

[23]"Google throws stacks of cash at hackers to publicly crack its Chrome browser," VentureBeat. [Online]. Available: http://venturebeat.com/2012/03/08/hackers-crack-chrome-in-publi/. [Accessed: 01-Apr-2013].

[24]Vulnerability Reward Program for Google web properties. [Online]. Available: http://www.google.com/about/appsecurity/reward-program/. [Accessed: 01-Apr-2013].

[25]Chrome Vulnerability Rewards Program. [Online]. Available: http://www.chromium.org/Home/chromium-security/vulnerability-rewards-program. [Accessed: 01-Apr-2013].

[26]Secunia Vulnerability Coordination Reward Program (SVCRP). [Online]. Available: http://secunia.com/community/research/svcrp/. [Accessed: 01-Apr-2013].

[27]The Mozilla Security Bug Bounty Program. [Online]. Available: http://www.mozilla.org/security/bug-bounty.html. [Accessed: 01-Apr-2013].

[28]ZDI Rewards Program. [Online]. Available: http://www.zerodayinitiative.com/about/benefits/. [Accessed: 01-Apr-2013].

[29]Facebook rewards program. [Online]. Available: https://www.facebook.com/whitehat/bounty/. [Accessed: 01-Apr-2013].

[30]Wordpress rewards program. [Online]. Available: http://www.whitefirdesign.com/about/wordpress-security-bug-bounty-program.html. [Accessed: 01-Apr-2013].

[31]CCBill Vulnerability Reward Program. [Online]. Available: http://www.ccbill.com/developers/security/vulnerability-reward-program.php. [Accessed: 01-Apr-2013].

[32]Dennis Fisher "As Bug Bounty Programs Mature, Still More Room For Growth", August 17, 2012, threatpost.com

[33]Dennis Fisher, "Microsoft Says No to Paying Bug Bounties", July 22, 2010, Threatpost.com

[34]Alhazmi, O.H.; Malaiya, Y.K., "Quantitative vulnerability assessment of systems software," Reliability and Maintainability Symposium, 2005. Proceedings. Annual, vol., no., pp.615, 620, Jan. 24-27, 2005.

[35]Ross Anderson and Tyler Moore, The Economics of Information Security, Science, 27 October 2006: 314 (5799), 610-613.

[36]Blog of r0t. [Online]. Available: http://pridels-team.blogspot.com. [Accessed: 01-Apr-2013].

[37]Facebook's account of Lostmon. [Online]. Available: https://www.facebook.com/lostmon. [Accessed: 01-Apr-2013].

[38]Blog of Lostmon Lords. [Online]. Available: http://lostmon.blogspot.com. [Accessed: 01-Apr-2013].

[39]Personal website of rgod. [Online]. Available: http://retrogod.altervista.org. [Accessed: 01-Apr-2013].

[40]Blog of rgod. [Online]. Available: http://retrogod.altervista.org. [Accessed: 01-Apr-2013].

[41]The website of James Bercegay. [Online]. Available: http://gulftech.org. [Accessed: 01-Apr-2013].

[42]The website of Aliaksandr Hartsuyeu. [Online]. Available: http://evuln.com. [Accessed: 01-Apr-2013].

[43]StatsCorp.com Evuln.com security audit [Online]. Available: http://www.statscrop.com/www/evuln.com. [Accessed: 01-Apr-2013].

[44]Personal website of kacper. Available online at: http://www.devilteam.yum.pl

[45]Personal website of Luigi Auriemma. [Online]. Available: http://aluigi.altervista.org. [Accessed: 01-Apr-2013].

[46]Personal website of Janek Vind "waraxe". [Online]. Available: http://www.waraxe.us. [Accessed: 01-Apr-2013].

[47]Personal website of Russ McRee. [Online]. Available: http://holisticinfosec.org. [Accessed: 01-Apr-2013].

[48]Report: Eastern European Hackers More Sophisticated Than Asian Counterparts. [Online]. Available: http://blogs.wsj.com/digits/2012/09/18/report-eastern-european-hackers-more-sophisticated-than-asian-counterparts/. [Accessed: 01-Apr-2013].

About the Authors

Abdullah M. Algarni is a Ph.D. student in the Department of Computer Science at Colorado State University. He received his MS in Software Systems Engineering from the University of Melbourne in Australia in 2008. He is interested in software engineering and computer security.

Yashwant K. Malaiya is a Professor in the Computer Science Department at Colorado State University. He received his MS in Physics from Sagar University, MScTech in Electronics from BITS Pilani, and PhD in Electrical Engineering from Utah State University. He has been published widely in the areas of fault modeling, software and hardware reliability, and testing and quantitative security. He has also been a consultant to industry. He has served as a General Chair and a Program Chair for several international meetings, including as the General Chair of 2003 IEEE International Symposium on Software Reliability Engineering. He is a Golden Core member of IEEE Computer Society and a recipient of the IEEE Third Millennium Medal.

Using Client-Side JavaScript to Mitigate Drive-by-Downloads

Abner Mendoza, and Narasimha Shashidhar
Department of Computer Science, Sam Houston State University, Huntsville, TX, USA

Abstract - *The prevalence of web-based malware distribution has exploded in recent years, with malicious enterprises continuously devising new ways of exploiting vulnerabilities. Security professionals have found themselves in an arms race in an attempt to contain the spread of malware. Drive-by-downloads, as coined by Google in 2007, is a particularly insidious form of malware distribution that uses browser exploits to automatically install malware on unsuspecting end-user machines. To gain maximum exposure, developers of drive-by-download malware have continuously infiltrated unsuspecting websites that are trusted by many users, and have recruited these websites into their malware distribution network without the consent or knowledge of the website owners. Websites that have been hacked in this manner often go unnoticed for long periods of time by their owners who are oblivious to the malware that their websites are serving. Often, website developers will include third-party widgets, or other features that introduce vulnerabilities to their website that often lead to these types of attacks on their websites. There are many server-side solutions that scan and protect websites from such attacks. In this paper, we propose a JavaScript solution that could be applied directly into the website code in an effort to add security enhancements from the client-side perspective.*

Keywords: iframes, drive-by-downloads, html5 sandboxing, web-based malware, widget vulnerability.

1 Introduction

In recent years, drive-by-downloads have become the most popular delivery method used by malicious enterprises to compromise and infect host computers with malware [1,15]. Web-based malware attacks are able to target vulnerabilities not only on the internet browser, but on a large number of plugins attached to the browser. Cyber-criminals continue to exploit the many opportunities available on the Internet as a delivery mechanism for their malware payload. Security professionals and malware developers have found themselves in an arms race of sorts where new evasive measures are continuously devised as new detection techniques are developed. In recent years, one of the more crafty techniques used to distribute malware has been drive-by-downloads [1], [7]. Gone are the days where you could avoid infection by taking measures such as only visiting trusted websites or not downloading files over the Internet. The prevalence of drive-by-downloads today means that even the most trusted websites can deliver malware to their unsuspecting users. Additionally, vulnerabilities on browser plugins means that attacks are not limited to any single browser vendor, but affect any browser that supports the vulnerable plugin. Most browsers that support plugins such as Adobe PDF, Flash, QuickTime, and others, are in some way currently or have previously been vulnerable to attacks from web-based malware [1,7,11]. The success of web-based attacks traditionally depended on a bit of social engineering to entice the user to perform an action on the client-side that launches the attack. A drive-by download, on the other hand, occurs when malware is automatically downloaded and installed on a host machine when a user visits what is usually a trusted website, requiring no further action or consent from the user. These types of attacks are particularly evasive, and are used to download, store, and install a wide variety of malware payloads to victim machines [1]. Through this method, a user's computer can become infected with malware in mere seconds by simply visiting an infected website. There are some particularly alarming aspects of such an attack, and there is a larger eco-system at work that allows this attack to occur in the way that it does. In this paper, we will explore the general anatomy of a drive-by-download attack, and propose a simple method that can be used to mitigate such attacks from a web developer point of view. Specifically, we explore the attacks that are delivered primarily through the use of JavaScript and html iframes. JavaScript is a popular client-side scripting language used extensively in many modern websites to enhance user experience, and iframes are html components that are used to embed external content into an existing browser window or website. We will introduce some defensive JavaScript code that web developers can embed into their website code to thwart such attacks by taking advantage of iframe security features introduced in the newly introduced HTML5 framework.

2 Related Work

Previous research and detection techniques have been primarily developed from the perspective of protecting the network infrastructure, or tools that are executed either on the client operating system or the web server software. BLADE [2], for example, is a client-side detection and prevention system that implements a series of operating system kernel extensions which detect and block drive by downloads at the point when the downloaded binary files are about to be executed on the local system. BLADE is installed on the host operating system and effectively intercepts file downloads and imposes execution restrictions based on whether it detected user consent to the download or not. Solutions such as WebJail [12], and ConScript [13], seek to enforce restrictions on script execution using least-privilege policies. These solutions, however, rely on modification of the browser kernel and could also introduce overhead to the browser execution time. Cujo [14] is a solution implemented through a web proxy that automatically and transparently inspects and detects malicious JavaScript code before it reaches the client machine. This is also an effective approach which relies on the user being connected through a web proxy to ensure that all ingress traffic is inspected and perhaps sanitized before it gets to the user.

An example of a successful drive-by-download campaign was investigated in a paper by Stone-Gross, et al. titled "Peering through the iframe" [15]. In this paper the authors describe their extensive investigation into the Mebroot drive-by-download campaign over the period of one year. During that time, they were able seize control of part of the infrastructure used by the criminals. Mebroot is described as a sophisticated piece of malware that infected the Master Boot Record of a victim's PC. The initial payload was used to download and bootstrap additional malware plugins used to harvest targeted information from user machines. In a period of 5 months, the investigators observed over 1 million requests to just the portion of the infrastructure that they infiltrated. These requests mapped to over 201 countries around the world. This illustrates the far-reaching capabilities of an attack launched through a drive-by-download campaign. Consider also that these statistics are merely from a portion of the larger infrastructure used in the Mebroot attack. In a 2011 attack discovered on a server belonging to the Massachusetts Institute of Technology, hackers commandeered a server in a campaign that infected over 100,000 websites with code that delivered a drive-by-download attack. As recently as May 2012, the well-known Amnesty International website was hacked and infected with code that delivered the Gh0st Rat Trojan malware to visitor's websites via drive-by-download. A simple Google search reveals frequent occurrences of such attacks on a wide variety of trusted websites. As shown in [15], a large majority of these attacks are dependent on the use of iframes. Our work is motivated by this assertion, and our solution is an approach that dynamically inspects iframes just before they are fully processed by the browser.

Most related research works have all proven in some way to be effective in mitigating the threat from malicious third party content. There has also been extensive research in exposing the prevalence of drive by downloads used to spread malware [1,4,7,15]. Most frameworks and solutions devised from previous work require additional software to be installed on either the client or server side. For example, in the model used by BLADE, processes are installed on the client system that monitors file downloads. Using BLADE, the malware payload is allowed to download to the host system before it is analyzed by the BLADE extension. In such a scenario, the drive-by-download attack has completed half of its intended purpose which is to download the malware executable to the victim computer. Nevertheless, BLADE and other solutions have been proven to be effective to some degree. However, while previous works have been effective, none has totally eliminated the threat. In this paper, we will introduce a model that is intended to complement existing solutions by adding a purely client-side solution which requires no additional software or kernel extensions. The goal of our approach is to add defensive JavaScript code on websites that may be compromised so that there is an additional layer of defense that is executed in the context of the client browser before any malicious payload is fetched from an external source.

3 Anatomy

Drive-by downloads have been in existence since as early as 2000. As techniques for utilizing this method have matured, it has become increasingly prevalent and widespread. The term "drive-by-download" was coined in 2007 through a paper from Google titled "The Ghost in the Browser" by Neil Provos, et. al.[1]. In that paper, the authors gave a specific definition of the term as it relates to malware that is automatically installed through a browser flaw or a flaw in a browser plugin. Inline frames, called "iframes", are one of the critical components of a successful drive-by download attack. An iframe allows external content to be embedded into an existing browser document. While an iframe is inherently isolated from its parent browsing context, there is generally no restriction on the type of content that may be embedded into an iframe. An iframe can be invisibly embedded into a website and cause the browser to download resources from any third-party source on the internet.

Exploits that utilize iframes are usually embedded into trusted websites that have been compromised by the cyber criminals to enable the drive-by-download attack. By infecting trusted websites, malware distributors instantly attain a huge user base that may not be wary of infection by virtue of the trust associated with the infected website. As an example, the Symantec Internet Threat Report [11] indicates that the likelihood of malware infection is quite higher on religious websites than on pornographic websites.

In addition to an iframe, another important component of the drive-by download is the use of scripting. Attackers usually use JavaScript, but there have been some exploits that use other forms of ECMA-based scripting languages. JavaScript, however, is the most widely used scripting language, especially since the web 2.0 explosion. Additionally, JavaScript support is an integral part of the new HTML5 standards that are now supported on most major browsers. As the HTML5 standard moves closer to completion and full adoption, it has been suggested that JavaScript use will become even more ubiquitous. Because JavaScript objects are allocated on a browser's memory heap, they all have access to the same memory contents [4]. This, together with the elevated privileges of browser plugins, makes them a prime target for use in malware distribution.

The general characteristics of the different variants of drive-by downloads is that no consent is required of the user other than visiting a website. Merely loading the infected website in a browser causes the malware code to execute and infect the host. The steps for infection can be roughly outlined as the following [5]:

A. *Browser loads infected website.*
B. *Injected exploit code executes, which causes execution of shell code.*
C. *Browser downloads payload and writes it to disk.*
D. *Browser executes malware installer.*

There are several preliminary steps that an attacker must perform in order to launch a successful drive-by-download campaign. Chief among this is to distribute the exploit code through trusted websites. There are various ways by which attackers are able to inject exploit code into a trusted website. One of the most prevalent methods involves SQL injection attacks which modify website back-end databases with specific code that is then inserted into any website whose content is derived dynamically from the database. Another method employed my attackers is to gain access to a web server through FTP vulnerabilities and modify the website code by inserting minimal and unobtrusive exploit code. The goal of the attacker in these cases is to remain undetected, and so there are no particularly visible changes made to the infected websites. Additionally, if the attack is launched from a piece of JavaScript code, that code is usually obfuscated in an effort to thwart detection from users or website developers scanning their code.

4 How Browsers Render Websites

While the attack process can be generalized for most attacks, we also know that the specific procedure for executing a drive by download does not always follow the same pattern [5]. In the drive-by-cache variant [5], for example, the malware executable is downloaded to the browser cache immediately after the page is loaded. This demonstrates some of the ingenious ways that attackers employ to circumvent detection systems. What is consistent in most cases, however, is the first step where the browser has to initially load an external URL to the iframe. It is therefore important to consider the process by which browsers render websites, and the order in which different resources are loaded. Tali Garsiel [6] published a comprehensive research on the internal operation of modern web browsers titled "How Browsers Work: Behind the Scenes of Modern Web Browsers". The paper describes details of the common work-flow or protocol that is employed by web browsers for rendering and ultimately presenting a web page to an end user. The rendering engine of a browser does most of the heavy lifting as far as painting the visual representation of the html code on the browser. The rendering engine employs a parser whose job is to parse the code and transform it into some logical tree structure that is representative of the code. The output of the parser is called the DOM, or Document Object Model. The DOM is a hierarchical representation of the html document, and it is the main interface to the JavaScript scripting language. Before any JavaScript code is executed, the DOM must be initialized. JavaScript is then able to manipulate the DOM structure in order to add interactivity to the web page.

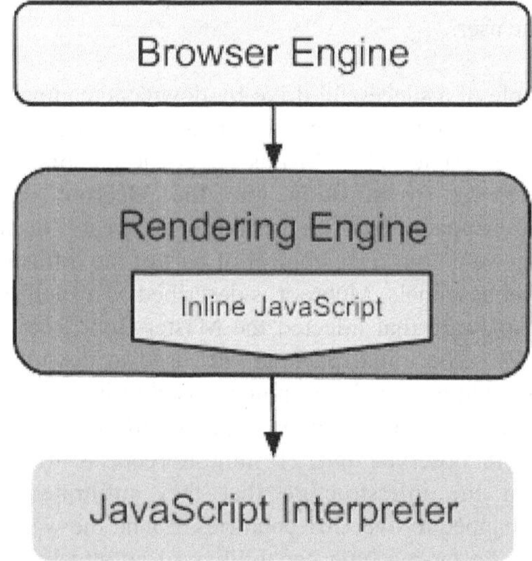

Figure 1: Flow of Browser Rendering

Malicious JavaScript is usually injected into a web page as in-line JavaScript. This means that the JavaScript is executed as soon as the parser in the rendering engine encounters the code. Non-inline JavaScript is otherwise marked as deferred, and executed until after the parser is finished creating the DOM. In the particular exploits that we have targeted in this work, we specifically consider injected inline JavaScript that ultimately cause an iframe element to be inserted into the DOM. An iframe element will contain a "src" attribute that contains a URL that usually points to an external third party resource which is usually where the malware executable is hosted. Alternatively, the URL may point a series of script files that eventually points to the executable hosted at either the same or another third party web server.

There are various techniques used by cyber-criminals in an effort to obfuscate their actions. However, despite the particular obfuscation techniques used, the iframe URL starts a chain that eventually leads to the malware payload source. You will recall that this process is transparent to the user visiting the compromised trusted site. At the point where the iframe is loaded to the DOM by the parser, the actual content of the external URL is not yet loaded. When the parser is finished parsing all the code, the document is finally marked as interactive, at which point deferred JavaScript code is also executed. In the final step of the parsing process, the document is marked as complete and a "load" event is fired [6]. In analyzing these steps, we note that the iframe which is involved in the drive-by-download is visible on the DOM before the contents the exploit URL are fetched to the browser. This is exactly the point at which there is an opportunity to neutralize the iframe. Neutralizing an iframe means that we would restrict its capability as far as executing scripts and browser plugins. Additionally, if we can determine that an iframe's URL points to a malicious domain or is a known source of attack, we could remove the iframe node altogether before any content is fetched to the client browser.

5 Neutralizing iFrames

In software development, it is often said that all input is evil. In other words, external content should never be trusted and all precautions should be taken when dealing with external input. The iframe attacks described here all introduce external content to a website, without the knowledge of the website owner or the end user. The iframe element exists for legitimate reasons, and as such, there are often conflicts that arise when considering restrictions on content served through an iframe. For example, many advertisement networks use iframes to syndicate their content to third party websites all over the Internet. In fact, malicious users have been known to infiltrate these advertisement networks to introduce what is known as "malvertisement". This is basically just another variant of the drive-by-download technique. In a 2008 paper published by Google titled "All Your iFRAMEs point to us", the authors contend that while Ad-delivered malware are not long-lived, their effects are widespread given the nature of the advertisement syndication [7]. They also observed that most advertisement networks utilized long delivery chains to serve the actual advertisement campaigns. As such, advertisers will most likely contend that unrestricted iframes are a necessary evil despite the risks. We could also appreciate the point of view from a website owner who may derive revenue through third party advertisements on their websites. Nevertheless, there is also the large number of instances in which iframes are of no use, or where neutralized iframes would not affect the usability of the website. This is the segment for which our solution is targeted and would be most useful.

Our proposed solution for mitigating iframe-based attacks is a simple, yet novel approach to the problem. At the most basic level, we introduce a deferred script into an html page that is guaranteed to execute as soon as the browser engine is done parsing the document, but before it loads resources which include third-party content from embedded iframes. At this precise moment in the rendering workflow, we can use JavaScript to inspect the DOM and find all iframes, even those dynamically added through inline JavaScript. We don't need to be concerned with the malicious scripts being obfuscated, or how many delivery chains are involved, because at the point that our defensive JavaScript executes, the maliciously injected code would have at least inserted the iframe into the DOM together with the value of the "src" attribute which most likely points to a url that serves the malicious content. The malicious JavaScript does not have any advantage at this point, because any third party resources referenced through the iframe would still not have been downloaded. Conversely, our defensive script now holds an advantage because we now know the un-obfuscated URL to which the iframe points. At this point we can take the URL value and submit a query to the Google Safe Browsing API to determine if the domain has already been flagged by Google as being malicious. If it turns out that the URL is flagged as malicious, we can remove the value from the iframe or remove the iframe element altogether from the DOM. In instances where the URL is not flagged as malicious, we can attempt to neutralize the iframe so that scripts and plugins are disabled in the iframe browser context. We must preface this discussion by noting that this proposed neutralization is largely dependent on a feature included in the yet to be released HTML version five specifications (HTML5) [8]. However, while the specifications have not yet been officially released, most browsers already support most of the features. HTML5 includes specification for a sandboxing feature to be included with iframes. Sandboxing, as specified in the HTML5 draft, would include a "sandbox" attribute on an iframe that would enable an extra set of restrictions to the content hosted in an iframe element. The restrictions applied to an iframe that uses the sandboxing attribute are specified as follows:

- *All markup is treated as being from a unique origin*
- *All forms and scripts are disabled*
- *All links are prevented from targeting other browsing contexts*
- *All features that triggers automatically are blocked*
- *All plugins are disabled*

Fine grained controls are allowed in cases where it is necessary to enable or disable each of these features individually. The HTML5 specifications describe the details of such fine grained controls [8] which simply require the addition of a value to the sandbox attribute such as sandbox="allow-scripts".

Enabling such restrictions on a malicious iframe would effectively neutralize the iframe and disable a number of attacks. As of this writing, this feature is currently only supported in the latest version of Google's Chrome browser. Microsoft Internet Explorer includes support for a similar "security" attribute on iframes [9]. While not as strict, this will enforce similar restrictions on certain versions of Internet Explorer. We suspect that support for the iframe sandboxing will eventually be available in all major browsers, but that is pure speculation at this point.

An alternative to simply adding security restrictions to iframe elements would be to remove the iframes altogether. This scenario would be useful in cases where the developer knows that no iframes are used in his website. In many instances, a web developer will have intricate knowledge of the functionality of any of his websites and would know whether iframes are used or not. Another use-case for removing iframes that are dynamically added would be in instances where there is an active attack and the responders need to keep the website online but avoid additional users from being attacked while they discover and fix the exploit on the server side.

Finally, while we propose the use of the Google Safe Browsing API as an added step, we must also note that this approach does introduce additional overhead and could result in false negatives. In our solution, we suggest the use of this API to do quick lookups on iframe target URL's, and effectively leverage the work done by server-side detection technology, while at the same time neutralizing the code on the website before it is executed by the browser. This technique could aid in preventing both known and unknown attacks that utilize iframes as a delivery method. It is also worth noting that our solution uses the Google Safe Browsing API as a black box for detecting known malware URL's. Our approach can be abstracted into two paradigms where we can use the additional Google API features or bypass the additional URL detection and only implement the basic html5 security features. By using the Google Safe Browsing API, we accept its quirks and the additional overhead that may be introduced. The use of this API, however, is not essential to our solution and is suggested more as a black box enhancement. As such, if a new service is made available in the future that offers better detection rates and increased efficiency, we can easily switch to the new service without any effect to the core features of our solution.

6 Sample Implementation

To implement the techniques described, we can use the jQuery JavaScript library to hook to the browser events and manipulate the DOM elements [10]. jQuery is a lightweight and very robust JavaScript library that can be leveraged in any webpage simply by adding a script tag to the header with a "src" attribute that points to the jQuery script source. By using such a library in our implementation, we avoid having to reinvent the wheel, so to speak, in terms of hooking to events and dealing with browser compatibility and other issues. Using jQuery, we can call the .ready() function which is guaranteed to execute as soon as the DOM is registered in the browser, which is before external content is loaded. The jQuery library also provides methods to find and manipulate DOM elements. Figure 2 illustrates the flow basic flow of the algorithm which executes before external resources are fetched by the browser.

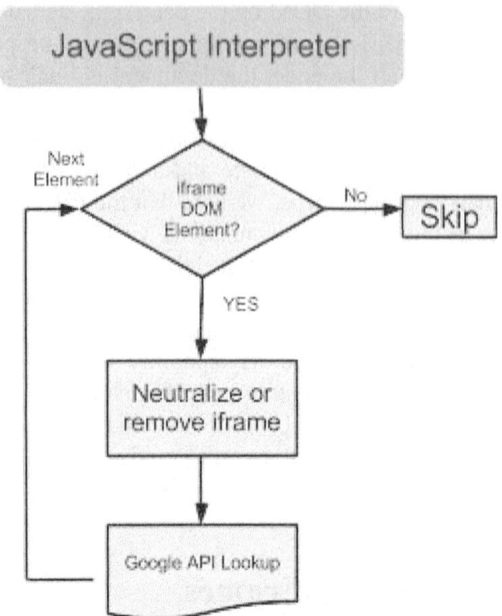

Figure 1: Flow of Algorithm

Below is a sample script that has been tested to work in Google Chrome version 15+:

```
$(document).ready(function () {
//for each iframe, add SECURITY and sandbox attributes
  $("iframe").each(function () {
  var frameSrc = escape(unescape($(this).prop("src")));
     var myFrame = $(this);
     $(this).prop("SECURITY", "restricted");
     $(this).prop("sandbox", "");
     //check google safe browsing api lookup
     $.ajax({
        type: "GET",
        async: false,
        url: "googleAPI_Proxy.url?" + frameSrc,
        success: function (proxyResponse) {
          // handle proxy response
         if (proxyResponse.malicious == "true") {
              $(myFrame).prop("src", ""); }
        }
     });
  });
});
```

The sample code enumerates all the iframes found in the DOM, and inspects each one of them and appends the sandbox and security attributes described earlier. This implementation could be further modified to include other techniques that would further restrict code that may run against the DOM. Additionally; our sample code makes an HTTP request to a proxy that we setup on the same server hosting this sample site. We must use a proxy method to query the Google Safe Browsing API since this would constitute a security violation in the browser if we try to do a request directly to the Google service from within our JavaScript. Our proxy is a web service that runs on the server and communicates with the Google API on the back-end. Our proxy returns a JSON object that we can parse for a custom value of a variable called "malicious" that is either true or false depending on the results of the lookup to the Google Safe Browsing API.

7 Case Study

In one case study, we implemented a revised version of the above sample code without the Google API lookups. The code was added to a website belonging to a small regional printing company that used WordPress as its content management engine to manage their website. Wordpress is a popular content management engine used by thousands of websites across the Internet. As such, it has become a prime target for attack by many of the exploit kits used by malware distributors. In this case study, the ftp service on the server hosting the website was eventually found to have been targeted by the Blackhole exploit kit. The company was alerted to the problem by customers using the Google Chrome browser who received alerts from the Google Safe Browsing service that the website was found to contain malware. The web developer at the company quickly found that an iframe was added to the code on one of the Wordpress files that caused it to show up on every page of the website. As discussed in [15], this is a common method used when websites are compromised. The web developer promptly removed the code, but found that it reappeared again every few days. It took several weeks for the source of the compromise to be identified. In the interim, the company was faced with an embarrassing situation. We were able to implement our solution on this website, and modified the iframe inspection code so that it would remove any iframes found since it was determined that no iframes were to be used on that website. Subsequent monitoring of this website showed that while the website was still continuously hacked, our solution effectively mitigated the attack while the source of the web server compromise was still being investigated.

8 Future Work

We believe that this novel solution to mitigating drive-by-downloads could be of some value to smaller website developers. Future work on enhancing this solution could include revisions that take advantage of new features that may be introduced in future HTML5 enhancements. Additionally, future work on this solution will include cases studies to show the effectiveness of the solution across different scenarios that the one case study done. The above sample implementation worked to restrict iframes regardless of the techniques used to insert the iframes into the DOM. Future work could explore issues such as attacks that could override our .ready() to execute after our code has run. This is a promising result, and more testing needs to be done on real world data to develop a more robust technique.

9 Conclusion

We have explored the general anatomy of a typical drive-by download, and identified some possibilities in mitigating these attacks by inserting "good" script into the website code itself to aid in detecting and preventing iframe attacks from executing. While this is by no means presented to be a complete solution with regards to drive-by-download attacks injected into trusted website, it is a technical solution that could complement existing solutions that exist on server-side technologies and client anti-virus engines. The HTML5 specifications currently propose some promising security features that would help in hardening website code to utilize built-in security features of modern browsers. We specifically investigated the sandboxing feature and proposed a solution that would ensure that all third-party iframes are forced to implement this feature. We contend that this could help in preventing the spread of zero-day attacks that utilize iframes on a compromised site that previously implemented our techniques in their website code. Furthermore, we showed how the Google Safe Browsing API could be utilized in a website to do real-time checking of iframe destination URL's in an effort to detect rogue iframes that may have been injected into a website. While additional data gathering and testing is required for our proposed solution, we believe that it is a simple approach that could be implemented today and further refined and optimized as an added security layer for websites.

10 References

[1] Provos, N., McNamee, D., Mavrommatis, P., Wand, K., and Modadugu, N. The Ghost in the Browser: Analysis of Web-based Malware. In Proceedings of the first USENIX workshop on hot topics in Botnets (HotBots'07). (April 2007).

[2] Lu, L., Yegneswaran, V., Porras, P., & Lee, W. BLADE : An Attack-Agnostic Approach for Preventing Drive-By Malware Infections. interactions, pp. 440-450. ACM Press (2010)

[3] Google Safe Browing API, Google Inc, (Online) Available: See http://code.google.com/apis/safebrowsing/.

[4] Egele, M., Kirda, E., & Kruegel, C. Mitigating Drive-by Download Attacks : Challenges and Open Problems. Ifip International Federation For Information Processing, pp 52-62. Springer (2009)

[5] Wayne Huang, Newest Adobe flash 0-day used in new drive-by download variation: drive-by cache, targets human rights website, Armorize Malware Blog, (Online) Available: http://blog.armorize.com/2011/04/newest-adobe-flash-0-day-used-in-new.html

[6] Tali Garsiel, Paul Irish, How Browsers Work: Behind the Scenes of Modern Web Browsers, Html5Rocks.com, August 2011 (Online) Available: http://www.html5rocks.com/en/tutorials/internals/howbrowserswork/

[7] N. Provos, P. Mavrommatis, M. Rajab, and F. Monrose. All Your iFRAMEs Point to Us. In Proceedings of the USENIX Security Symposium, 2008.

[8] HTML5, A vocabulary and associated APIs for HTML and XHTML, Editor's Draft , Ian Hickson, Google Inc., W3C. (Online) Available: http://dev.w3.org/html5/spec/Overview.html

[9] SECURITY Attribute, Microsoft MSDN Library, Microsoft Corporation, (Online). Available: http://msdn.microsoft.com/en-us/library/ms534622(VS.85).aspx

[10]jQuery Javascript Library, John Resig, The jQuery Project (Online). Available: http://www.jquery.com

[11]Symantec Internet Threat Report 2011, Symantec Corporation

[12]Meyerovich, L., and Livshits, B. ConScript: Specifying and enforcing fine-grained security policies for Javascript in the browser. In IEEE Symposium on Security and Privacy (2010).

[13]Acker, S. V., et. al., Webjail: Least-privilege integration of third-party components in web mashups. In Annual Computer Security Applications Conference (ACSAC) (2011)

[14]Konrad Rieck, Tammo Krueger, and Andreas Dewald. 2010. Cujo: efficient detection and prevention of drive-by-download attacks. In Proceedings of the 26th Annual Computer Security Applications Conference (ACSAC '10). ACM, New York, NY, USA, 31-39.

[15] B. Stone-Gross, M. Cova, C. Kruegel, and G. Vigna, "Peering through the iframe", Proceedings of IEEE International Conference on Computer Communications (INFOCOM) Mini-Conference Shanghai, China April 2011

Secure NAND Flash Architecture Resilient to Strong Fault-Injection Attacks Using Algebraic Manipulation Detection Code

Pei Luo
Reliable Computing Lab
Electrical and Computer Engineering
Boston University
Email: luopei@bu.edu

Zhen Wang
Mediatek Wireless, Inc
Email: wang.zhen.mtk@gmail.com

Mark Karpovsky*
Reliable Computing Lab
Electrical and Computer Engineering
Boston University
Email: markkar@bu.edu

***Abstract*—Multi-level cell (MLC) NAND flash memories are widely used because of their high data transfer rate, large storage density and long mechanical durability. Linear error correcting codes (ECC) such as Reed-Solomon (RS) codes and Bose-Chaudhuri-Hocquenghem (BCH) codes are often used for error correction. Although linear codes can efficiently detect and correct random errors, they are not sufficient for protecting NAND flash memories used in cryptographic devices against malicious fault injection attacks. In this paper, we will present an architecture based on the combination of RS codes and Algebraic Manipulation Detection (AMD) codes which can correct any four byte errors and detect any malicious injected errors with a high probability under the strong attack model. This proposed architecture can significantly improve the security level of the MLC NAND flash memories used in cryptographic devices at the cost of only slightly larger latency and area overhead.**

***Keywords*-MLC NAND Flash, Reed-Solomon code, Algebraic Manipulation Detection Code, Error Correction, Fault Injection Attack, Hardware Security**

I. INTRODUCTION

NAND flash memories are widely used in cell phones, digital cameras, USB devices due to the high data transfer rate, low power consumption, large storage density and long mechanical durability [1]. Different from NOR flash and single-level cell (SLC) NAND flash memories, MLC technology is implemented in MLC NAND flash memories to increase the capacity. While MLC technology can increase the capacity of the devices, it will reduce the voltage margin separating the states and thus result in the possibility of more errors. In order to increase the reliability of the MLC NAND flash devices, ECC are often used in the devices to detect and correct the errors.

Most of the works on protecting NAND flash devices against random errors are based on linear codes. In [2], the authors analyzed the error characteristics of MLC flash memory and proposed an error control coding using non-binary low-density parity-check (LDPC) codes. In [3], the authors proposed a high speed architecture based on $(4148, 4096)$ BCH codes correcting quadruple $(t = 4)$ errors. In [4], the authors proposed product codes which use RS codes along rows and Hamming codes along columns which have reduced hardware overhead.

The security of modern devices can be broken by malicious attackers via side channel attacks such as fault injection attacks [5], [6], [7]. While linear error correcting codes are very useful for the detection and correction of random errors, they are not enough against advanced attacks.

In order to improve the security of the system against advanced fault injection attacks, non-linear codes have been used. In [1], the authors proposed two general constructions of nonlinear multi-error correcting codes and compared the architectures to those based on BCH codes and RS codes. In [8], [9], [10], the authors proposed Robust Codes to detect the side channel fault injection attacks. Robust codes can provide nearly equal protection against all error patterns. The error masking probabilities for robust codes are upper-bounded by very small numbers for all non-zero errors [11]. But the limitation of robust codes is that it is assumed that the output of the device is almost uniformly distributed and is not controlled by the attacker [11]. So robust codes can provide protection against weak attacks but it's not good enough against strong attacks.

In order to protect the devices against strong attacks, the authors of [11] implemented AMD codes based on nonlinear encoding functions to detect the fault injection attacks. AMD codes can provide a guaranteed high error detecting probability even if the fault-free outputs as well as the error patterns of a device-under-attack are controlled by the attacker [11], [12].

In this paper, we will present an architecture for MLC NAND flash based on the combination of RS and AMD codes. This architecture is not only able to correct any four byte errors, it can also detect the errors injected by the strong attackers with a very high probability. The results show that the proposed architecture can significantly improve the security of MLC NAND flash devices with minor timing and resource overhead. The simulation results show that while the attacker can inject random errors into the common RS architecture MLC NAND flash memories with probability of miscorrection

*The work of the third author is sponsored by the NSF grant CNR 1012910.

about 4.092%, the proposed architecture can detect most of these miscorrections with a probability $1 - 1.77 \times 10^{-8}$.

The rest part of this paper is organized as follows. We describe the MLC NAND flash memory model and the advanced attack model in Section II. In Section III, we present the definition and construction of AMD codes. In Section IV, the construction of the encoder and decoder based on the combination of RS and AMD codes are presented. In Section V, we present the synthesis and the fault-injection simulation results for the proposed architecture, and compared them with the architecture based only on RS code.

II. MLC NAND Flash Memory and Attack Model

Multi-level cell is able to store multiple bits by separating the threshold voltage into four parts or more, this will increase the bit error rate in the memories because electrons stored in adjacent levels tend to shift more easily from one level to another. Besides such random errors, memories may also be threatened by fault injection attacks. In this section, we will describe MLC NAND flash memories and the attack model we use in this paper.

A. MLC NAND Flash Memory

The threshold voltage of the whole memory array satisfies a Gaussian distribution due to random manufacturing variations [1]. Figure 1 illustrates the threshold voltage distribution of a 2 bits multi-level cell [13], [14], [15], [16].

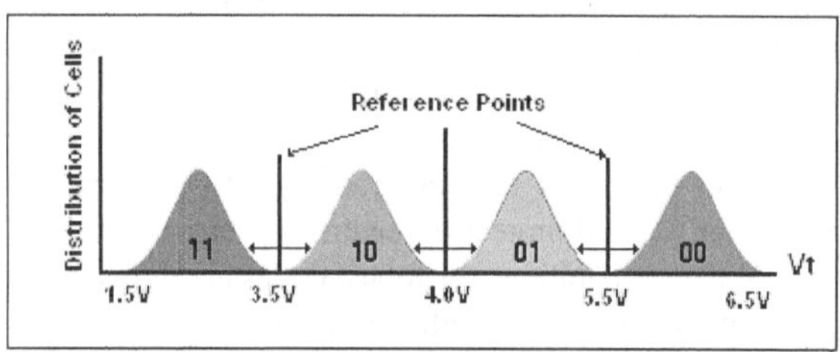

Fig. 1: Voltage threshold of MLC NAND flash

The NAND Flash array is grouped into a series of blocks, which are the smallest erasable entities in a NAND flash device. Each block is composed of some pages, which are the smallest read and program unit [17]. Each page is composed of storage area plus spare area. For example, the page size is 8,936 bytes in MT29F512G08CUCBB from Micron, in which 8,192 bytes are used for storage with extra 744 bytes as the spare area [18].

Because the page size is very large nowadays, the storage area is always divided into several sections to increase the processing speed and decrease the encoding and decoding complexity. For the memory architecture, we assume that the page size of the memory is 2,112 bytes (16,896 bits) in the model we use in this paper, and the storage area is divided into four main sections, spare area are also divided into four parts, each for one main section, as in the Figure 2 [19], [20], [21]. Thus each section will be 512 bytes. We will build our error correcting architecture based on this size.

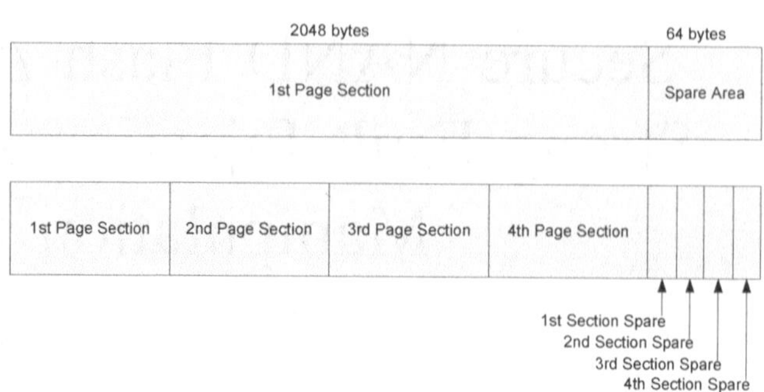

Fig. 2: Section structure of one page

B. Attack Model

We assume an advanced attack model in this paper. Under this model, the attacker knows every detail of the memory, including the error control codes used. The attacker is able to choose the specific inputs to the device during fault injection. At the same time, we assume the attacker has the ability to inject any errors at the output of the device. Thus the attacker will have full control of the fault-free output y, and the faulty output $\tilde{y} = y \oplus e_y$ where e_y is an error pattern and $\oplus$ stands for component wise addition in finite field. Under such a strong attack model, all the previous error correcting codes architectures will be insufficient [1], [11], [12].

Architectures which can provide a guaranteed fault detection probability under such a strong attack model are called strong secure architectures. In this paper, we will describe a strong secure architecture for MLC NAND flash memories based on the combination of RS and AMD codes. We will show that under the strong attack model described in this section, the proposed architecture will still provide a high error (fault) detection probability.

III. AMD codes

Throughout the paper we denote by $\oplus$ the component-wise modulo addition in $GF(q), q = 2^r$. All the results presented in the paper can be easily generalized to the case where $q = p^r$ (p is a prime). An code V with codewords $(y, x, f(y, x))$, where $y \in GF(2^k)$ are the information bits, $x \in GF(2^m)$ are the random bits, and $f(y, x) \in GF(2^r)$ are the redundant bits, will be referred to as a (k, m, r) code.

Definition 3.1: (**Security Kernel**) [11] For any (k, m, r) error detecting code V with the encoding function $f(y, x)$, where $y \in GF(2^k), x \in GF(2^m)$ and $f(y, x) \in GF(2^r)$, the **security kernel** K_S is the set of errors $e = (e_y, e_x, e_f), e_y \in GF(2^k), e_x \in GF(2^m), e_f \in GF(2^r)$, for which there exists y such that $f(y \oplus e_y, x \oplus e_x) \oplus f(y, x) = e_f$ is satisfied for all x.

$$K_S = \{e | \exists y, f(y \oplus e_y, x \oplus e_x) \oplus f(y, x) \oplus e_f = \mathbf{0}, \forall x\}. \quad (1)$$

Under strong attack model, the nonzero errors $e \in K_S$ can be used by the attacker to bypass the protection of the error detection code with the kernel K_S. In order to prevent such attacks, an AMD code should have a kernel K_S composed of only zero vector in $GF(2^n)$, $n = k + m + r$.

Definition 3.2: [22] A (k, m, r) error detecting code is called **Algebraic Manipulation Detection (AMD)** code iff $K_S = \{\mathbf{0}\}$, where $\mathbf{0}$ is the all zero vector in $GF(2^n)$, $n = k + m + r$.

For AMD codes, there are no undetectable errors (errors that are undetected with a probability of 1). For any y and e, the error masking probability can be computed as

$$\begin{aligned} Q_V(y,e) &= 2^{-m}|\{x \mid (y,x,f(y,x)) \in V, \\ &\quad (y \oplus e_y, x \oplus e_x, f(y,x) \oplus e_f) \in V\}| \quad (2) \end{aligned}$$

The security level of a code can be characterized by the worst case of error masking probability $\max_{y,e\neq 0} Q_V(y,e)$. A lower bound on Q_V for AMD codes can be found in [11].

Let $x = (x_1, x_2, \cdots, x_t), x_i \in GF(q), q = 2^r$. Let

$$A(x) = \begin{cases} \bigoplus_{i=1}^{t} x_i^{b+2} & \text{if } b \text{ is odd;} \\ \bigoplus_{i=2}^{t} x_1 x_i^{b+1} & \text{if } b \text{ is even and } t > 1; \end{cases} \quad (3)$$

and

$$B(x,y) = \bigoplus_{1 \le j_0 + j_1 + \cdots + j_{t-1} \le b+1} y_{j_0,j_1,\cdots,j_{t-1}} \prod_{i=0}^{t-1} x_i^{j_i}, \quad (4)$$

where $\prod_{i=1}^{t} x_i^{j_i}$ is a monomial of x of a degree at most $b+1$ and $\prod_{i=1}^{t} x_i^{j_i} \notin \Delta B(x)$ where $\Delta B(x)$ is defined as

$$\Delta B(x) = \begin{cases} \{x_1^{b+1}, x_2^{b+1}, \cdots, x_t^{b+1}\} & \text{if } b \text{ is odd;} \\ \{x_2^{b+1}, x_1 x_2^{b}, \cdots, x_1 x_t^{b}\} & \text{if } b \text{ is even and } t > 1; \end{cases} \quad (5)$$

Suppose $f(x, y) = A(x) \oplus B(x, y)$, it is easy to verify that the left hand side of the error masking equation $f(x \oplus e_x, y \oplus e_y) \oplus f(x, y) \oplus e_f = 0$ is always a non-zero polynomial of x of a degree up to $b+1$.

Theorem 3.1: [11], [12] Let $f(x, y) = A(x) \oplus B(x, y)$ be a q-ary polynomial with $y \in GF(q^s)$ as coefficients and $x \in GF(q^t)$ as variables, where $1 \le b \le q - 3$ and $q = 2^r$. Then the code V composed of all vectors $(y, x, f(x, y))$ is a (k, m, r) AMD code with $m = tr$, $k = (\binom{t+b+1}{t} - 1 - t)r$ and $Q_V = (b+1)2^{-r}$.

Remark 3.1: If b is even when $t = 1$, $A(x)$ can be chosen as x^{b+3} instead of x^{b+2}. In this case, $Q_V = (b+2)2^{-r}$.

Remark 3.2: When k is not a multiple of r, 0's can be appended to y before $f(x, y)$ is computed. The resulting AMD code will have the same Q_v as the AMD code with the AMD code with the same $f(x, y)$, for which k is a multiple of r.

Example 3.1: Let $t = b = 1$, then $m = r$ and $k = (\binom{t+b+1}{t} - 1 - t)r = r$. The encoding function $f(y, x)$ for the AMD code based on Theorem 3.1 is $f(y, x) = y \cdot x \oplus x^3$, where $x, y, f(y, x) \in GF(2^r)$. The resulting AMD code has $Q_V = 2^{-r+1}$.

If $t = 1$ and $b = 3$, then $m = r$, $k = (\binom{t+b+1}{t} - 1 - t)r = 3r$ and $f(y, x) = y_1 \cdot x \oplus y_2 \cdot x^2 \oplus y_3 \cdot x^3 \oplus x^5$, where $y_1, y_2, y_3, x, f(y, x) \in GF(2^r)$. For this code $Q_V = 2^{-r+2}$.

AMD codes for $t = 1$ have been discussed in [22], and details of AMD codes with $t > 1$ can be found in [11], [12], [23]. AMD codes based on different parameters used in this paper will be discussed in Section IV.

IV. Construction of Secure Flash Memory

Although the AMD codes defined in Section III have very high security level and can detect most of the injected errors with very low probability of missing an error, it has no ability to locate and correct the random or injected errors. Because the bit error rate is relatively high in MLC NAND flash, error control codes must be implemented besides AMD codes to detect and correct the random errors. Some linear codes such as BCH code and RS code have very good ability to detect and correct random and burst errors and they are often used in MLC NAND flash memories to improve the reliability [3], [2], [16], [21]. In this paper, we combine RS code and AMD code to construct a secure and reliable structure which can detect most of the malicious attacks and correct random errors.

RS code with symbols from $GF(q_{RS})$ can be defined by a set of three parameters (n_{RS}, k_{RS}, t_{RS}), in which k_{RS} and n_{RS} are the number of symbols before and after encoding respectively, and $t_{RS} = (n_{RS} - k_{RS})/2 = r_{RS}/2$ is the number of symbols which can be corrected among n_{RS} symbols. Symbols take their values in a Galois Field $GF(2^{m_{RS}})$, and are thus represented with m_{RS} bits. The parameter n_{RS} is bounded by $2^{m_{RS}}$ [24]. Through this paper, we use n_{RS}, k_{RS} to denote the length and the number of the information symbols in the RS code while t_{RS} is the number of errors which can be corrected by the RS code.

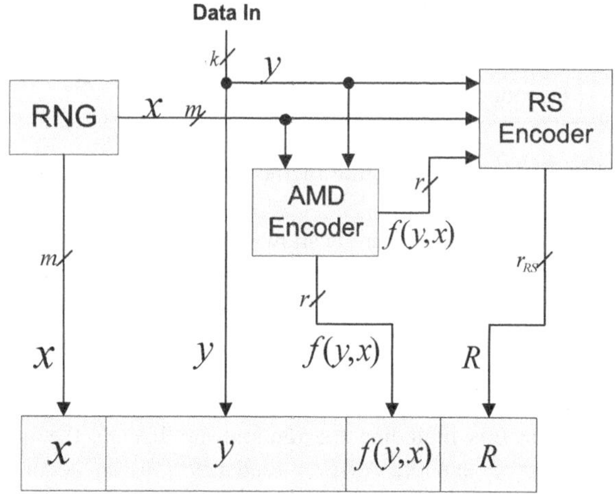

Fig. 3: Encoder structure of the proposed architecture

The encoding architecture based on the combination of RS and AMD code is shown in Figure 3. In this architecture, the **random number generator (RNG)** generates the random numbers $x_i \in GF(2^r)$ for the encoding of AMD code. (We note that the RNG module is already integrated in most of the modern cryptographic devices thus the proposed architecture needs no extra resource to build the RNG module in such cryptographic applications.) The AMD encoder then computes the AMD redundant bits $f(y,x) \in GF(2^r)$ with the random bits $x \in GF(2^m)$ and information bits $y \in GF(2^k)$. In this architecture, the AMD random number x and the redundancy $f(y,x)$ will also be part of the information bits for RS code such that the errors in x and $f(y,x)$ can also be detected and corrected. So the information part of RS code is $(x, y, f(y,x))$.

The random number x is generated and applied to the RS and AMD encoder before the information bits are read into the encoder module. When the information bits y are read into the encoder module, they are sent to the RS encoder and AMD encoder at the same time. When the information bits are all read into the encoder module, the AMD encoder will finish the encoding and generate the redundancy $f(y,x)$. Then $f(y,x)$ is sent to the RS encoder as a part of the RS information bits. So the encoding of AMD code and RS code can be processed in parallel, thus the architecture will need only several additional clock cycles for the AMD random number and redundant parts as compared with the architecture based on only RS code.

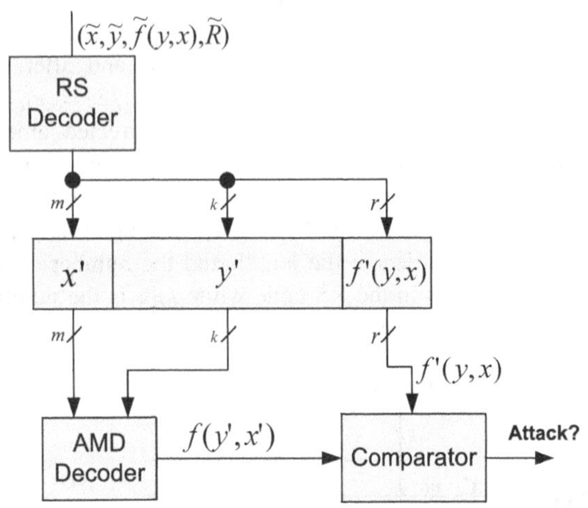

Fig. 4: Decoder structure of the proposed architecture

The decoder architecture is shown in Figure 4. The random number x' is decoded before the information bits in decoding process, thus the decoding of RS and AMD code can be implemented in parallel.

In the decoding process, the RS decoder will output the corrected (but may be still distorted due to the miscorrection) information bits including the random number x', the information part y' and the AMD redundancy $f'(y,x)$ according to the distorted inputs $(\tilde{x}, \tilde{y}, \tilde{f}(y,x), \tilde{R})$. The distortion is due to the possible miscorrection by the RS code. We note that if the information is not distorted, then $x = \tilde{x} = x'$, $y = \tilde{y} = y'$, $f(y,x) = \tilde{f}(y,x) = f'(y,x)$, $R = \tilde{R}$. The AMD encoder then generates $f(y',x')$ according to the recovered x' and y'. The comparator then compares the decoded $f'(y,x)$ and the newly generated $f(y',x')$, if they are not equal, then it means RS code cannot correct all the errors and miscorrection happened.

Apparently, if no more than $t_{RS} = 4$ byte errors happened then the RS decoder can recover all the symbols correctly. Then $x = x'$, $y = y'$ and $f(y,x) = f'(y,x)$, thus $f'(y,x) = f(y',x')$. If there are more than four byte errors in the code words, then the RS decoder can detect most of such situations and refused to correct the errors with the extra being miscorrected. Under such situation, $f(y',x') = f'(y,x)$ holds with a very small probability, which means the AMD code can detect most of the miscorrections.

After we implement RS and AMD codes in the architecture, the encoded message will be in the format $((x_0, \cdots, x_t), (y_1, \cdots, y_b), f(y,x), R)$. In which x_i are the random numbers generated by RNG, y_i are the information bits stored in the flash memories and $f(y,x)$ is the AMD redundancy. The AMD random number x_i, information bits y_i and the redundant part $f(y,x)$ are all in $GF(2^r)$. R is the RS redundancy part with $(x_0, \cdots, x_t)$, $(y_1, \cdots, y_b)$, $f(y,x)$ together as the RS input, where $x_i, y_i, f(y,x) \in GF(2^r)$.

A. Parameters of AMD Code

In the flash memory model we use in this paper, each section size is 512 bytes, or 4,096 bits, so the number of information bits k should be at least 4,096. We choose the length of the random number x_i to be 32 bits, thus $x_i \in GF(2^{32})$, $r = 32$. In this paper, we consider three alternatives:

1) If $t = 1$, according to Theorem 3.1, because the flash section size is 4096 bits, we can get $b = 128$. By (3) and (4), we have $A(x) = x^{131}$, $B(y,x) = \oplus_{1 \le j \le 129} y_j x^j$, $\Delta B(x) = \{x^{129}\}$.
2) If $t = 2$, $b = 14$, $x = (x_0, x_1)$, we have $A(x) = x_0 x_1^{15}$, $B(y,x) = \oplus_{1 \le j_0 + j_1 \le 15} y_{j_0 j_1} x_0^{j_0} x_1^{j_1}$, $\Delta B(x) = \{x_1^{15}, x_0 x_1^{14}\}$.
3) If $t = 3$, $b = 7$, $x = (x_0, x_1, x_2)$, then $A(x) = x_0^9 \oplus x_1^9 \oplus x_2^9$, $B(y,x) = \oplus_{1 \le j_0 + j_1 + j_2 \le 8} y_{j_0 j_1 j_2} x_0^{j_0} x_1^{j_1} x_2^{j_2}$, $\Delta B(x) = \{x_0^8, x_1^8, x_2^8\}$.

We have the AMD parameters of $t = 1, 2, 3$ discussed above and the maximum error masking probabilities Q_V for the corresponding codes estimated by Theorem 3.1 listed in Table I.

TABLE I: Parameters of AMD code

t	r	m	b	k	Q_V
$t = 1$	32	32	128	4,096	3.0×10^{-8}
$t = 2$	32	64	14	4,256	3.49×10^{-9}
$t = 3$	32	96	7	5,152	1.86×10^{-9}

I k is the number of maximum length of the AMD code, can be shortened to the size needed

II all the computation are in $GF(2^r)$

III m is the total length of the random number

From Table I and the definition of AMD code in Section III, we can see that trade-offs between security level and resource can be achieved by choosing different parameters of the code. For example, if we choose $t = 1$, then the extra area we need for the AMD redundancy and resources to compute $f(y,x)$ will be smaller, but the security level Q_V will also be lower. If we want a higher security level against advanced attacks, we will need larger t thus larger redundant area for AMD code and more complicated encoder and decoder circuit. At the same time, we can choose also larger r for AMD code for higher security level, but then the AMD code will be constructed over higher order Galois field thus more resources are needed.

In this paper, we will choose AMD code with $t = 1$ as an example and compare the result with the architecture based on only RS code. AMD encoder and decoder are actually the same. For $t = 1$, the AMD module needs two multipliers M_0 and M_1 to calculate x^j and $x^j y_j$ respectively. The AMD encoder architecture circuit for $t = 1$ is as in Figure 5. In Figure 5, the multiplier M_0 is used to calculate $x^2, x^3, \cdots, x^{131}$ and M_1 is used to calculate $y_j x^j$.

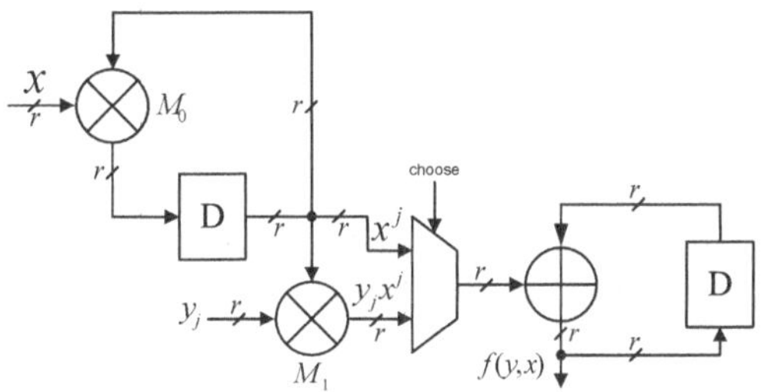

Fig. 5: AMD encoder structure for $t = 1$

For $t = 2$ and $t = 3$, we can use Horner's scheme to implement the AMD encoder and decoder. Or we can also compute x^j before the information bits are read into the system thus to save multipliers. The AMD encoder architecture circuit for $t = 2$ is as in Figure 6. In this architecture, the two multipliers M_0 and M_1 are used to calculate $x_0^2, x_0^3, \cdots, x_0^{15}$ and $x_1^2, x_1^3, \cdots, x_1^{15}$ before read the information bits. Then the multipliers M_0 and M_1 are used to calculate the $y_{j_0 j_1} x_0^{j_0} x_1^{j_1}$.

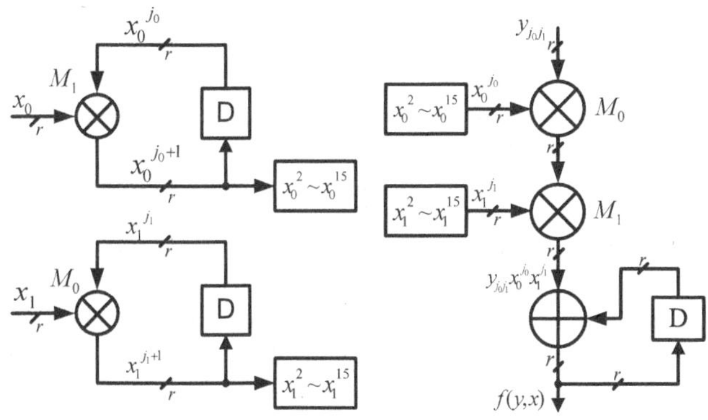

Fig. 6: AMD encoder structure for $t = 2$

B. Parameters of RS Code

In this architecture, the section size is 512 bytes in the MLC NAND flash memory model of Section II. We choose $t = 1$ for AMD code in this paper, so the size of the AMD random number and AMD redundancy are both 32 bits. RS code in the proposed architecture should cover not only the flash memory section, but also the AMD random number and redundancy at the same time, thus $m_{RS} \geq 9$. Higher m_{RS} means higher order Galois field and thus more resource, so we choose $m_{RS} = 9$ in this architecture, which means $n_{RS} = 511$. According to [21], we choose $t_{RS} = 4$ to make a balance between the reliability and resource. Thus the RS code in this architecture is a shorten $(511, 503, 4)$ code.

As described in Section IV-A, we choose $t = 1$ and $r = 32$ for AMD code in this paper, so the AMD random numbers and the redundancy are both 32 bits. The random number x and redundant part $f(y, x)$ are both appended four bits of 0 and then divided into four 9-bits parts. So the whole code can be written as $((x_{00}, x_{01}, x_{02}, x_{03}), (y_0, \cdots, y_{455}), (f_0, f_1, f_2, f_3), R)$. In which $x_{0i} \in GF(2^9)$, $y_i \in GF(2^9)$, $f_i \in GF(2^9)$. Thus the shorten RS code in this architecture is a $(472, 464, 4)$ code. In decoding, the decoder first recovers $(x'_{00}, x'_{01}, x'_{02}, x'_{03})$, then combine these data to get $x' \in GF(2^{32})$. Similar process to recover the $f'(y, x)$.

In this architecture, we use RiBM [25] algorithm which has extremely regular structure and thus is highly advantageous in VLSI layout to decode the RS code [16].

C. Clock cycles overhead

Because the AMD code is constructed over $GF(2^{32})$ and the RS code is constructed over $GF(2^9)$ in this architecture, these two codes need different number of clock cycles for encoding and decoding. In the encoding process, AMD encoder will need 128 clock cycles to compute the $x^j y_j (1 \leq j \leq 128)$ and extra three clock cycles for computing x^{131}. On the other hand, the RS decoder will need 456 clock cycles for the information part and 8 extra cycles to encode x and $f(y, x)$.

In decoding, the RS decoder first detects if the codewords are distorted and whether there are more than four errors using the syndrome. If there are no errors, the decoder outputs the messages directly. If there are less than four errors, the decoder will output the corrected codewords. If there are more than four errors, the decoder will be able to detect it with high probability or miscorrect the codewords with a small probability.

The decoding of AMD code and the decoding of RS code can be processed in parallel, thus no extra time overhead will be needed except for the decoding of x' and $f'(y, x)$, and the comparing of $f'(y, x)$ and $f(y', x')$.

V. Security Level and Hardware Complexity Comparisons

We run random error injection simulation to verify the security level of the proposed MLC NAND flash architecture based on the combination of RS and AMD code. In the simulation, we inject random errors into the $x, y, f(y, x)$ and R randomly. The t_{RS} is 4 in this design, so the RS code can correct any up to 4 byte errors. If we inject more than 4 byte errors, the RS decoder will detect most of them but miscorrect some. The miscorrected errors will be detected by the AMD code with a high probability. We injected 11 billion error patterns into the system and the simulation results show that if we randomly inject from 5 to 12 byte errors into the proposed architecture, about 4.092% will be miscorrected by RS code and most of the miscorrection will be detected by the AMD code with a probability of missing a miscorrected error as low as only 1.77×10^{-8}. This result is very close to the security level described in Table I.

The simulation results show that the proposed architecture based on RS and AMD codes has much higher security level than the architecture based on only the RS code. For the architecture based only on the RS code, even if the attacker just injects random errors distorting from 5 to 12 bytes randomly into the devices, the attacker can bypass the error detection and correction successfully with a probability about 4.092%. But for our proposed architecture, this probability is as low as 1.77×10^{-8}.

Different parameters of AMD code will cause different resource and time overhead and also different security level. For $t = 1$, $t = 2$ and $t = 3$, the time overhead and the number of multipliers are listed in Table II. The redundant bits in Table II include the random number x and the redundancy $f(y, x)$, so it's the sum of r and m shown in Table I.

TABLE II: Resource requirement of AMD code

t	Number of Redundant bits	Clock cycles overhead	Number of multipliers
$t = 1$ [I]	64	131	1
$t = 1$ [II]	64	0	2
$t = 2$	96	15	2
$t = 3$	128	9	3

[I] This architecture will need only one multiplier but more clock cycles

[II] This architecture will need two multipliers but no extra clock clocks

We note that for $t = 1$, we can compute all the x^j before reading y_j. In this case, we need only one multiplier but more clock cycles. Or we can also compute x^j while we are reading the y_j in parallel, then we will need one more multiplier but no extra clock cycles. We note that in this paper, we use the two-multiplier architecture which is shown in Figure 5 for $t = 1$ to build the proposed NAND flash encoder and decoder.

Actually, for $t = 2$ and $t = 3$, we can also decrease the clock overhead to zero by adding more multipliers in the architecture. From Table II we can see that higher security level will require more resources but need less clock cycles to finish the process. But usually, more clock cycles is not a big problem for AMD module because AMD code is always constructed over higher order Galois field than the RS code and both the encoding and decoding process for AMD code will need much less clock cycles than the RS codes.

Encoder and decoder architectures based on RS and AMD codes will cause different latency and area overhead. The encoder and decoder for the proposed RS&AMD architecture and the architecture based only on RS codes have been modelled in Verilog and synthesized in Cadence Encounter RTL Compiler with the Nangate 45nm Opencell library version v2009_07. The designs were placed and routed using Cadence Encounter. The latency, the area overhead of the encoders and the decoders were estimated using Concurrent Current Source (CCS) model under typical operation condition assuming a supply voltage of 1.1V and a temperature of 25 Celsius degree. The synthesis results for the encoder and decoder are shown in Table III. These results were all obtained based on same simulation conditions.

TABLE III: Synthesis Result of the Encoders and Decoders

Architecture	Latency (ns)	Gates	Area (um^2)
RS encoder	0.991	1,177	939.5
RS AMD encoder	1.934	10,231	8,164.6
RS decoder	1.023	60,659	48,406.1
RS AMD decoder	1.258	62,764	50,086.2

From Table III we can see that the proposed architecture based on RS and AMD code will require more resources than the architecture based on only the RS code. While the encoder for the AMD code constructed over higher order Galois field is more complicate than the RS code, the decoder of AMD is much simpler than the one of RS code.

VI. Conclusion

In this paper, we presented an architecture based on RS and AMD codes which can detect and correct up to four byte errors and detect strong attacks. Compared with the architecture based only on RS code, our architecture is more efficient for protecting NAND flash devices against malicious fault injection attacks.

The proposed architecture needs only 64 more redundant bits for every 4096 bits of the original flash and eight more clock cycles for the encoding and decoding compared to the original architecture based on the RS code.

We showed that the proposed architecture can provide both high security and reliability. Under the strong attack model, the chance for an attacker to conduct a successful fault injection attack is guaranteed to be as low as 3×10^{-8}. The simulation results show that under random fault injection attack, the miscorrection probability of RS architecture is 4.092%, and the proposed architecture will detect most of these miscorrections with the probability of missing a miscorrected error about only 1.77×10^{-8}. According to the simulation and synthesis results, we can see that our architecture can significantly improve the security level of the MLC NAND flash memories with only minor time and area overhead.

References

[1] Z. Wang, M. Karpovsky, and A. Joshi, "Nonlinear multi-error correction codes for reliable mlc nand flash memories," *Very Large Scale Integration (VLSI) Systems, IEEE*

Transactions on, vol. 20, no. 7, pp. 1221 –1234, july 2012.

[2] Y. Maeda and H. Kaneko, "Error control coding for multilevel cell flash memories using nonbinary low-density parity-check codes," in *Defect and Fault Tolerance in VLSI Systems, 2009. DFT '09. 24th IEEE International Symposium on*, oct. 2009, pp. 367 –375.

[3] W. Liu, J. Rho, and W. Sung, "Low-power high-throughput bch error correction vlsi design for multi-level cell nand flash memories," in *Signal Processing Systems Design and Implementation, 2006. SIPS '06. IEEE Workshop on*, oct. 2006, pp. 303 –308.

[4] C. Yang, Y. Emre, and C. Chakrabarti, "Product code schemes for error correction in mlc nand flash memories," *Very Large Scale Integration (VLSI) Systems, IEEE Transactions on*, vol. 20, no. 12, pp. 2302 –2314, dec. 2012.

[5] S. Skorobogatov, "Local heating attacks on flash memory devices," in *Hardware-Oriented Security and Trust, 2009. HOST '09. IEEE International Workshop on*, july 2009, pp. 1 –6.

[6] ——, "Optical fault masking attacks," in *Fault Diagnosis and Tolerance in Cryptography (FDTC), 2010 Workshop on*, aug. 2010, pp. 23 –29.

[7] ——, "Flash memory 'bumping' attacks," in *Proceedings of the 12th international conference on Cryptographic hardware and embedded systems*, ser. CHES'10. Berlin, Heidelberg: Springer-Verlag, 2010, pp. 158–172. [Online]. Available: http://dl.acm.org/citation.cfm?id=1881511.1881526

[8] M. Karpovsky, K. Kulikowski, and A. Taubin, "Robust protection against fault-injection attacks on smart cards implementing the advanced encryption standard," in *Dependable Systems and Networks, 2004 International Conference on*, june-1 july 2004, pp. 93 – 101.

[9] M. Karpovsky and A. Taubin, "New class of nonlinear systematic error detecting codes," *Information Theory, IEEE Transactions on*, vol. 50, no. 8, pp. 1818 – 1819, aug. 2004.

[10] K. Kulikowski, Z. Wang, and M. Karpovsky, "Comparative analysis of robust fault attack resistant architectures for public and private cryptosystems," in *Fault Diagnosis and Tolerance in Cryptography, 2008. FDTC '08. 5th Workshop on*, aug. 2008, pp. 41 –50.

[11] Z. Wang and M. Karpovsky, "Algebraic manipulation detection codes and their applications for design of secure cryptographic devices," in *On-Line Testing Symposium (IOLTS), 2011 IEEE 17th International*, july 2011, pp. 234 –239.

[12] ——, "Reliable and secure memories based on algebraic manipulation correction codes," in *On-Line Testing Symposium (IOLTS), 2012 IEEE 18th International*, june 2012, pp. 146 –149.

[13] A. Greg, F. Al, M. Duane, and B. Reaves, "Intel strataflash memory technology overview," Intel, Tech. Rep., .

[14] , "Slc vs. mlc: An analysis of flash memory," Super Talent Technology Corporation, Tech. Rep., .

[15] ——, "Choosing the right nand," Micron Technology, Inc., Tech. Rep., .

[16] B. Chen, X. Zhang, and Z. Wang, "Error correction for multi-level nand flash memory using reed-solomon codes," in *Signal Processing Systems, 2008. SiPS 2008. IEEE Workshop on*, oct. 2008, pp. 94 –99.

[17] "Nand flash 101: An introduction to nand flash and how to design it in to your next product," Micron Technology, Inc., Tech. Rep., 2006.

[18] *64Gb, 128Gb, 256Gb, 512Gb Asynchronous/Synchronous NAND Features.*

[19] "Tn-29-05: Ecc module for nand flash via xilinx spartan-3 fpga," Micron Technology, Inc., Tech. Rep., 2005.

[20] "Tn-29-06: Micron nand flash controller via xilinx spartan-3 fpga," Micron Technology, Inc., Tech. Rep., 2005.

[21] M. Mariano, "Ecc options for improving nand flash memory reliability," Micron Technology, Inc., Tech. Rep., 2012.

[22] R. Cramer, Y. Dodis, S. Fehr, C. Padr, and D. Wichs, "Detection of algebraic manipulation with applications to robust secret sharing and fuzzy extractors," in *Advances in Cryptology C EUROCRYPT 2008*, ser. Lecture Notes in Computer Science, N. Smart, Ed. Springer Berlin / Heidelberg, 2008, vol. 4965, pp. 471–488.

[23] Z. Wang and M. Karpovsky, "New error detecting codes for the design of hardware resistant to strong fault injection attacks."

[24] S. Lin and D. J. Costello, *Error Control Coding, Second Edition.* Upper Saddle River, NJ, USA: Prentice-Hall, Inc., 2004.

[25] D. Sarwate and N. Shanbhag, "High-speed architectures for reed-solomon decoders," *Very Large Scale Integration (VLSI) Systems, IEEE Transactions on*, vol. 9, no. 5, pp. 641 –655, oct. 2001.

SESSION

BIOMETRIC AND FORENSICS

Chair(s)

Prof. Nizar Al Holou

Fingerprinting Malware using Bioinformatics Tools Building a Classifier for the Zeus Virus

(Computer Security track, Virus Detection)

Jay Pedersen, Dhundy Bastola, Ken Dick, Robin Gandhi, William Mahoney
School of Interdisciplinary Informatics
College of Information Science and Technology
University of Nebraska at Omaha
Omaha, Nebraska
{jaypedersen, dkbastola, kdick, rgandhi, wmahoney} @unomaha.edu

Abstract— This paper describes an *exploratory research project which creates a classifier to distinguish artifacts containing content specific to a known computer virus, given a training set of samples of variants of that virus and using local alignments between the artifacts as its information source. A bioinformatics tool, BLAST, finds the local alignments between a digital artifact and a repository of representatives of the virus. The classification is driven by a comparison of the local alignments to determined alignment fingerprints of the virus representatives. Project methods include the creation of "synthetic DNA" representations of digital artifacts, representative selection for a set of computer viruses, alignment fingerprint creation for those representatives, and using the representatives, fingerprints and alignments in a classification scheme. The project examined Zeus Trojan viruses and had a 91% correct identification rate of verified Zeus viruses and a 3% false positive rate.*

Keywords: malware, classifier, virus

1. Introduction

In field of computer security, there is significant interest in understanding malware behavior and developing effective detection, prevention and recovery mechanisms [1]. Malware analysis typically involves reverse engineering compiled digital artifacts, configuration files, and metadata or foraging through other information. The results from such analysis provide clues for malware origin, behavior, locating other variants, signature patterns, and proper malware classification (e.g. trojan, worm, virus, zombie, fork bomb, bot, etc.).

In the field of bioinformatics, the Basic Local Alignment Search Tool (BLAST) tool discovers areas of local similarity between DNA or protein sequences [2][3]. These areas of similarity are known as local alignments. Biologic viruses have been detected by the local alignment of their biologic sequence to that of known virus sequences using BLAST [4][5].

The use of local alignments for comparing biologic sequences predates BLAST. Smith and Waterman in 1981 defined an algorithm for finding local alignments and described its usage for comparing biologic sequences [6].

Computer artifacts may be viewed as a sequence of byte values. Could local alignments detect similarities between a digital artifact and known computer viruses? Such similarities could be a strong indication of function similarity and virus content. The presented research tries to answer this question, using BLAST to determine local alignments between "synthetic DNA" representations of digital artifacts.

A synthetic DNA representation of a digital artifact is a sequence of DNA characters (A, C, G and T) [7] used to represent a digital artifact. It is considered synthetic as it represents the content of a digital artifact rather than biologic DNA. The synthetic DNA used in this research is created by a reversible translation of the byte sequence of a digital artifact. A DNA representation of a digital artifact is directly useable by BLAST. As early as 2000, research was conducted using BLAST and a synthetic DNA representation of journal articles to search for articles with particular keywords [8].

An existing method used to examine a digital artifact for virus content is the maintenance of "signatures" of known viruses and determining if a digital artifact has a matching signature. An example of this is comparing the MD5 signature (RFC1321) of a digital artifact to a database of MD5 signatures of known viruses. An example of an open source anti-virus detection engine using signatures is clamAV (http://www.clamav.net/lang/en/). A data mining approach to determining malware functionality in digital artifacts has been explored by Henchiri [9].

We hypothesize that that local alignment analysis of multiple variants of a virus will find the areas of similarity between them and that these areas will provide a 'fingerprint' of the virus. We also hypothesize that local alignment analysis will be able to detect variants of an existing virus made by making small or even very significant changes to an existing virus.

Consider the local alignments between a virus artifact and a modified version of that virus. Any unmodified portion will have a perfect local alignment and portions with relatively minor changes will have "gapped" local alignments.

A specific class of virus was chosen for examination – the Zeus Trojan virus [10], which is created from a malware kit that targets Windows-based computers to steal credentials such as banking information. The virus contains software which causes infected hosts to become part of a botnet. The kit contains a web interface for managing the botnet and a tool for creating Trojan binaries and related configuration files. Zeus was chosen because it is well-known and samples for analysis are readily available.

This research uses samples of the Zeus virus collected from the Zeustracker website [11], which tracks instances the Zeus virus. These samples are used for a training set and test set for a classifier which predicts if an arbitrary digital artifact contains Zeus virus content.

A general procedure for building such a classifier is presented. The procedure relies heavily on the local alignments returned by the BLAST tool as its information source for the similarities between artifacts.

A. Properties of Windows Executables

Windows executables are required to have a PE header by the operating system. This is a variable-length structure at the beginning of the file, taking several hundred bytes and containing bookkeeping information such as the location of code and data within the executable. Its presence must be accounted for as this area will have similarity in virus and non-virus executables.

Windows executables can be 'packed'. Packer programs take an executable and accomplish two tasks: reducing its size and obfuscating information inside of it. Any malware in these executables has a better chance of evading detection by anti-virus software due to changes made by the packing procedure. Malware authors use packers to hide the virus from detection and make it difficult to reverse-engineer. Popular packer programs include UPX, PECompact, ASPack, Petite, WinUpack, and Themida [1].

2. Bioinformatics Background

DNA is the biological blueprint used for building proteins and other cellular components. It is comprised of a long stretches of adenine (A), guanine (G), cytosine (C), and thymine (T) molecules, commonly referred to as "bases" due to their chemical nature. The seminal paper of Watson and Crick in April 25 of 1953 [7] described the molecular structure of DNA as a double helix. In double stranded DNA each strand runs anti-parallel to the other and each strand can be used as a template to construct the other strand using Chargaff's base pairing rule [13] which states that Adenine (A) will only pair with Thymine (T), and Guanine (G) will only pair with Cytosine (C).

DNA is represented computationally by character strings containing only the letters A, G, C and T. The representation includes only one of the strands; the other strand is implied and can be generated using the base-pairing rules.

BLAST is a widely used bioinformatics tool [2][3] that returns the set of similarities it finds between a query DNA sequence and a database of known DNA sequences. These similarities are called local alignments and each local alignment pairs a region within the query sequence to a similar region in a database sequence. Within these regions, every base is aligned to exactly one base in the other sequence or to a gap position inserted between bases in the other sequence. Gaps are introduced to represent deletions or insertions of bases, which may have occurred over time. Local alignments differ from global alignments which align the entire length of two sequences, rather than arbitrary areas within the sequences.

Local similarity comparisons have advantages over global similarity comparisons in studying functional and evolutionary relationships. For example, ape and human DNA have many areas of local similarity but are not globally similar. A given specimen can be inferred to have functional and evolutionary relationships with a known sample if it has strong local alignments to it.

It is hypothesized that analogous functional relationships exist between the variants of a computer virus and that these relationships can be detected by local alignments.

3. Methods

A. Convert Digital Artifacts into Synthetic DNA

This method provides a reversible conversion of the contents of an arbitrary digital artifact into a Synthetic DNA representation. This method was also used in previous research by the authors [14].

A digital artifact may be considered to be a sequence of byte values, with each byte being a sequence of four two-bit pairs. Each two-bit pair has four possible values 00, 01, 10 and 11 which can be mapped to the four DNA characters A, T, G and C. This mapping procedure generates four DNA characters for each byte in the digital artifact.

The following map was used in our research:

```
00 → T
01 → G
10 → C
11 → A
```

There are twenty-four possible mappings of bit values to DNA characters; each providing a consistent and comparable DNA representation. The mapping that was used has the property that the values for G and C and A and T are bit complements of each other. This was chosen to reflect the fact that G and C and A and T are paired biologically [7].

For example, the character "B" has ASCII character code of 66 which is 01000010 in binary and has the synthetic DNA representation "GTTC" based on the above mapping procedure. A file whose first two bytes are ASCII "BB" has a synthetic DNA representation starting with "GTTCGTTC".

Synthetic DNA is fully reversible to the original artifact. A reverse lookup table can be constructed which maps "GTTC" to its associated byte value of 66, and so on. A straight-forward reversal method is to process the synthetic DNA four characters at a time using a reverse lookup table to obtain the original byte values.

The cost of Synthetic DNA generation is linear with respect to the size of the input digital artifact.

B. Obtaining a Training Set and Test Set of Viruses

Two distinct sets of viruses are required: a training set for building a classifier and a test set to examine the accuracy of the classifier. Both sets should contain samples of all known virus strains. The procedure for obtaining these samples will be specific to the target virus.

C. Building BLAST databases and using BLAST to obtain local alignments

There are several implementations of BLAST. We chose NCBI's open-source BLAST software version 2.25 (ftp://ftp.ncbi.nlm.nih.gov/blast/executables/), which has tools for creating BLAST sequence databases and querying those databases to find local alignments.

NCBI's BLAST reports can return specified alignment attributes. The following attributes were examined:

Name	Description
qacc	"query accession" -- identification of query sequence
Sacc	"subject accession" -- identification of the similar sequence found in the BLAST database
qstart, qend, sstart, send	Start and end positions of the local alignment in the query and subject sequences
evalue	Expected number local alignments of this size in a BLAST database of this size [3]. This is a statistical measure of the likelihood that the local alignment is a 'chance occurrence'. A value near zero indicates low probability that the alignment is merely a chance occurrence.

It is possible to have NCBI BLAST return a filtered set of results. One option is to specify a small "maximum e-value" so that every reported local alignment is very unlikely to have occurred by random chance.

Tests were conducted examining the alignments of a randomly selected Zeus Trojan virus with a BLAST database containing representatives of the virus. The results indicated the bulk of reported alignments were small in size, where 98% reported areas smaller than 100 bytes in the original file. A maximum e-value of 10^{-300} resulted in a report where every local alignments representing at least 600 bytes of the original file was reported; and alignments representing as few as 158 bytes were also reported. We chose to focus on larger alignments by specifying a maximum e-value of 10^{-300}. This dramatically reduced the BLAST report size and the associated processing requirements. Because the e-value relates to BLAST database size [3], this e-value cutoff should be revisited as the BLAST database size increases. Our hypothesis is that alignments of more than one hundred bytes of the original file which represent entire subroutines of a virus are of the most interest in virus analysis.

To find all local alignments between a set of sequences, an "all versus all" BLAST operation can be performed. This is a query containing all sequences in the set against a BLAST database containing only sequences from the set. The result is a BLAST report of all local alignments between the set of sequences.

D. Pick virus representatives

The goal of this procedure is to choose representatives for viruses in the training set. The model of the training set is that it contains a number of strains of a virus. Viruses of the same strain should have local alignments to each other and alignments should form identifiable clusters. A representative of each strain can be chosen and used in a classifier. Digital artifacts with strong local alignments to a representative would likely be a virus of that strain. Using representatives in the classifier reduces the overhead associated with the classifier. Figure 1 visualizes this model.

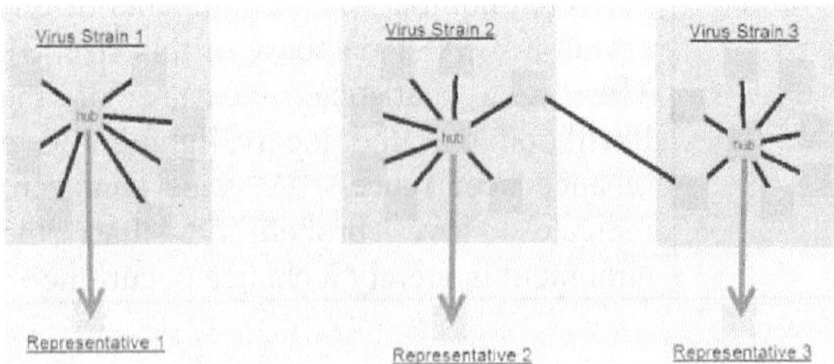

Figure 1. Hubs of virus strains chosen for representatives.

The first step determines the local alignments between the all viruses in the training set using an "all versus all" BLAST operation. An undirected graph [14] of the alignments is created where the nodes in the graph are the viruses in the training set and an edge indicates two viruses with at least one local alignment between them.

The method then proceeds iteratively. The first iteration determines the largest hub the graph, assuming it to be the hub of the largest virus strain and a suitable representative for the virus strain. That representative and all viruses in the training which closely align to it are removed from the graph, ending the first iteration. The following iterations repeat the steps of the first iteration using the reduced graph. Iterations continue until all viruses in the training set have a representative. The representatives are collected into a BLAST database that is used by the fingerprinting procedure and the classifier.

Procedure for choosing virus representatives, given a training set V of viruses:

1. Generate A, the "all versus all" BLAST report of V
2. U_0 = V (U_x are unrepresented viruses after iteration x)
3. Perform iterations 1 through k, where k is determined when $|U_i| = 0$ indicating that no unrepresented viruses remain

Procedure for iteration i:

1. A_i = alignments in A for the unrepresented viruses in U_{i-1}
2. $G_{i,=}$ the undirected graph of A_i, where nodes are viruses and edges indicate local alignment relationships
3. R_i = node in G_i with the largest degree, arbitrarily choosing between ties
4. DB_i = BLAST database of $\{R_1, R_2, \ldots, R_i\}$
5. BR = BLAST report of V against DB_i
6. C_i = set of viruses in BR with alignments to DB_i
7. $U_i = V \backslash C_i$, viruses without alignments to DB_i
8. $|U_i| = 0 \rightarrow k = i$; DB_k is the classification BLAST database; END

The cost of the procedure is dominated by the "all versus all" BLAST operation, but also includes the cost of the iterations which select representatives. The "all versus all" BLAST operation is equivalent to using BLAST once for each virus in the training set against a database of all training set viruses. BLAST searches are used to update the represented and unrepresented virus sets. This cost is significantly less than the "all versus all" blast operation, because the target BLAST database is much smaller. The generation of the graph of alignments and the processing of the graphs are linear with the size of the generated BLAST reports.

E. Obtain a training set and test set of benign executables

Two sets of benign executable artifacts are needed. The first set is used to determine expected local alignments between benign executables and the virus representatives. The second set is needed for testing the classifier to determine if any benign artifacts are incorrectly classified as viruses.

The method of obtaining benign executables was simply to extract a set of executables from a Windows 7 based machine which had been virus-checked using Kaspersky anti-virus software (http://usa.kaspersky.com). The set was taken from the "Program Files" and "Program Files (x86)" and included executables and DLLs and included both 32-bit and 64-bit executables and DLLs

F. Create the alignment fingerprints of the virus representatives

This procedure creates a map of the bytes of each virus representative, indicating which bytes align with virus samples and which align with benign executables.

Why track alignments to benign executables? Many viruses target Windows-based computers, as the Zeus Trojan virus does. Windows executables contain a PE header, a variable-length structure at the beginning of the file. The presence of this header creates similarity at the beginning of many Windows executables. Alignments between PE headers are expected and are not virus content indications. The rationale for tracking alignments to benign executables is that such alignments do not indicate virus content and should be ignored.

Procedure for determining the alignment fingerprints for all k representative viruses, given training set V of viruses and set B of benign executables.

1. DB = BLAST database of virus representatives
2. BR_V = BLAST report of the alignments from V to DB
3. BR_B = BLAST report of the alignments from B to DB
4. For each representative virus i
    a. $FP_{i,V}$ = map (fingerprint) of aligned bytes from sequences in V, obtained using BR_V
    b. $FP_{i,B}$ = map of aligned bytes from sequences in B, obtained using BR_B

The procedure to create a fingerprint F for representative i using BLAST report BR:

1. A_i = alignments in BR specific to representative i
2. F = set of byte numbers in alignments A_i, determined from the "sstart" and "send" attributes of each alignment

G. Create a virus classifier

The classifier decides whether an arbitrary digital artifact contains content from a target virus, given a BLAST database of representatives of the virus and alignment fingerprints for those representatives. The classifier's goal is to find alignments to areas which aligned more with viruses than benign executables. If such an alignment does not exist, we can assume that the object does not have virus content. The rationale is that such an alignment is a strong indicator of virus content.

The following is the classification procedure for arbitrary digital artifact X, given BLAST database DB containing k virus representatives and alignment fingerprints FPi,V and FPi,B for each virus representative i (i from 1 to k):

1. RESULT = FALSE
2. S = synthetic DNA representation of X
3. BR = BLAST report for the alignments from S to DB
4. For each reported alignment a in BR:
    - i = representative virus number (1 to k), (from the 'sacc' alignment attribute)
    - S = size of the alignment, in bytes
    - B = byte numbers in representative i that were aligned to (from 'sstart' and 'send' attributes)
    - B_V = count of bytes in B aligning to training set viruses, determined from $FP_{i,V}$
    - B_B = count bytes in B aligned to benign executable artifacts, from $FP_{i,B}$
    - If $(B_V - B_B)/S > 0.5$ then RESULT = TRUE; END

The cost of the procedure is dominated by the cost of the BLAST operation, but also includes the linear cost of creating the synthetic DNA (relative to the size of artifact X) and the linear complexity of examining the alignments returned from BLAST (relative to the number of local alignments returned).

4. Results

A. Obtaining Zeus Trojan viruses

The Zeustracker website maintains an archive of viruses which may be downloaded for examination. The viruses include but are not limited to variants of the Zeus Trojan virus. Zeustracker website administrators describe the archive as containing any artifact retrieved from a connection to a discovered Zeus botnet (i.e. a network of computers infected with malicious software and controlled as a group without the owners' knowledge). There is no guarantee that these artifacts are all Zeus Trojan viruses. To identify the Zeus Trojan viruses in the archive, Kaspersky antivirus software was used on a Windows 7 machine (Kaspersky Security Scan version 12.0.1.117 (a) using database update dated 08/20/2012 09:50 AM).

In May of 2012, an archive of 5467 digital artifacts was obtained from the Zeustracker website, with 351 identified as Zeus Trojans. These were used as the training set of Zeus virus Trojans.

In August of 2012, an archive of 6492 digital artifacts was obtained from the Zeustracker website, with 495 new Zeus Trojan viruses identified. These viruses were used as a test set for the classifier.

Each Zeus Trojan virus was identified as a 32-bit windows executable or a MS-DOS executable by the Linux "file" command. None of the viruses were identified as a 64-bit windows executables.

B. Picking Virus Representatives

The procedure for selecting virus representatives from a training set was followed. This resulted in 25 representatives being chosen for the 351 Zeus Trojan viruses in the training set. Iterations continued until each Zeus Trojan virus in the training set had an alignment to a chosen representative virus.

C. Obtain benign executables and DLLs

A set of benign executables and DLLs were selected for use in virus fingerprinting and classifier testing. The artifacts chosen were from one of the author's computers running Windows 7 in August 2012. The executables were verified as being benign by using Kaspersky antivirus software. Samples of both 32-bit and 64-bit executables and DLLs were obtained. There were a total of 1019 benign executable artifacts selected.

For virus fingerprinting, a set of 388 files were randomly chosen for a training set. This included 193 executables and 195 DLL files. Among the executables were 116 which were 32-bit and 77 which were 64-bit. Among the DLL files were 115 that were 32-bit and 80 which were 64-bit.

For classifier testing, the remaining 631 benign executable artifacts were used as a test set. This test set included 233 executables and 398 DLL files. The executables included 205 32-bit and 28 64-bit executables and the DLL files included 267 32-bit and 131 64-bit DLL files.

D. Create the alignment fingerprints of virus representatives

The procedure for creating alignment fingerprints of chosen representative viruses was followed.

The first 500 bytes of each representative were aligned to both Zeus Trojan viruses and benign executable artifacts. These are the expected alignments to the PE header of Windows. Beyond this, there were few other alignments from benign executables to the representatives.

The alignments from the training set viruses to the representatives showed that in almost all cases, there were two to four contiguous areas in each representative with alignments from viruses in the training set. A single representative had a large contiguous alignment covering nearly 100% of its content due to very strong similarity to another virus in the training set. This result indicated that there were relatively small bands of core content held in common between the viruses. These bands are considered the fingerprint of virus-specific content.

Figure 2 shows the alignment fingerprint of the seventh representative virus; which had a typical fingerprint. The first graph shows alignments to viruses in the training set and the second shows alignments to benign executables.

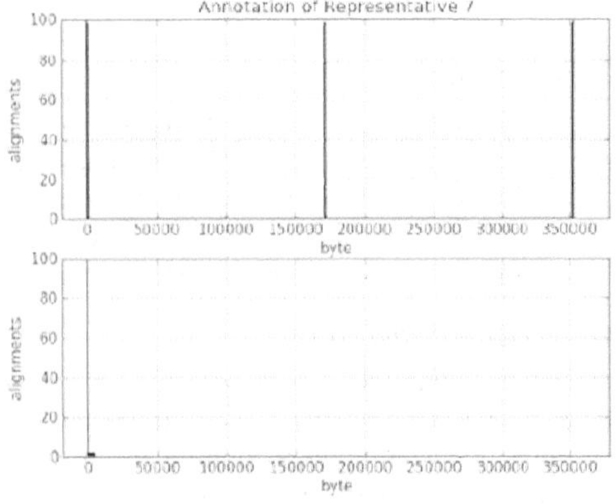

Figure 2. Alignment Fingerprint of Representative 7

The graphs show three bands of alignments to training set viruses and a single band of alignment to benign artifacts. The benign band is to the area from byte 1 to byte 500 which is the Windows PE header. The virus alignments bands include the PE header and bands around byte numbers 170,000 and 350,000. The virus alignments were to very limited areas of concentration in the executable. This suggests that the actual Zeus virus code which is common among the strains of Zeus viruses is relatively small compared to the size of the executable file that the virus is housed in.

E. Classification Results

Three sets of digital artifacts were used to test the classifier.

The first set contains 495 Zeus Trojan viruses collected from the Zeustracker website in August 2012 which were not in the training set viruses. This set is used to test for true positives and false negatives.

The second set is the remaining set of 631 benign executable artifacts that were not used in the alignment fingerprinting of the representative Zeus Trojan viruses. The set includes both 32-bit and 64-bit executables and DLL files. This set is used to test for true negatives and false positives.

The third set is a set of 100 digital artifacts that are not executable files. This include source code files in various computer programming languages, a few articles written in English and a few binary files including PNG images and Java ".class" files. This set is used to test for true negatives and false positives.

The results of testing the 495 identified Zeus Trojan viruses are as follows:

- 91.7% true positive rate – (454 /495) reported as having Zeus Trojan virus content
- 8.3% false negative rate – (41/495) reported as not having Zeus Trojan virus content

The following statistics were gathered concerning the local alignments for the 91.7% of test set viruses which were correctly identified.

- The number of alignments indicating virus content had a mean of 4.0 and standard deviation of 8.8. This indicates that typically several alignments which trigger virus identification.
- The number of representative viruses which were aligned to had a median of 4.0 and a standard deviation of 0.832. This indicates that multiple representatives which were typically aligned to.
- The lengths of the alignments indicating virus content had a mean of 869. The mean alignment case represents approximately 217 bytes in the original executable due to the four to one ratio of DNA characters to original bytes.

The results of testing the 631 benign executable artifacts are as follows: •

- 97.3% true negative rate – (614/631)
- 2.7% false positive rate – (17/631)

The results of testing the 100 non-executables are as follows:

- 100% true negative rate

5. Discussion

There were 8% (41 of 495) of the test set of viruses classified as not having virus content. In 36 of the 41 cases, the viruses had alignments only to the PE headers of the representatives. There are several possible reasons for this. They could represent new virus strains or virus strains missing from the training set or even objects misclassified as Zeus Trojan viruses. It is also possible that an executable was created using a packing method that had no representative in the training set. In two other cases there were alignments to virus content areas that accounted for less than half of the alignment and were ignored. This identifies a potential improvement in the classifier, which could view "large enough" virus content alignments as virus content indications, even when less than half the alignment size. In the final three cases, there were alignments to areas other than the PE header but were not fingerprinted as having Zeus virus content. These could be areas which would be fingerprinted as Zeus content by a rigorous annotation.

There were 3% (17/631) of benign executables classified as having Zeus Trojan virus content. This indicates that these benign executables aligned to fingerprinted virus content areas in the representatives. These could be areas which would be fingerprinted as benign by a rigorous annotation.

An improved procedure for picking representative viruses can be imagined that examines the alignment graph in a single iteration; determining all the hubs using graph processing techniques from social networking.

How would new strains of a virus be accommodated? One method of accomplishing this is to add the new strains to the training set and re-execute the procedures which would create an updated classifier.

A rigorous manual reverse engineering and annotation of all the viruses could generate an improved fingerprint compared to the fingerprints created through the procedures in this paper. The procedures presented here provide an automated method for virus fingerprinting, but are not guaranteed to be optimal.

6. Conclusions and Further Research

The high rate of detection of Zeus viruses in the test set and low rate of false positives for benign executables in the test set give evidence that local alignments may be effective in detecting computer malware such as viruses.

The procedures presented in this paper are not specific to Zeus Trojan viruses. Zeus viruses were chosen for examination because they are a well-known example of a computer virus with readily available samples. These procedures could be followed to build a classifier for other computer malware.

Online BLAST databases containing representatives of various computer viruses could be created. This would be analogous to the online BLAST databases of biological sequences which exist today. Such databases would allow researchers to examine arbitrary digital artifacts for similarity with a wide variety of known computer viruses.

The runtime properties of a computer executable could be monitored and examined with local alignments. The security related website "anubis" (http://anubis.iseclab.org) examines the runtime behavior of executables in a sandbox environment and provides reports of the observed behavior. Similar reports could be used as the source of a BLAST database of virus behaviors.

References

[1] Distler, Dennis, and Charles Hornat. "Malware Analysis: An Introduction." *Sans Reading Room*. Sans, 14 Dec. 2007.

[2] Altschul S, GishW, MillerW, Myers E and Lipman D, Basic local alignment search tool, 1990, J. Mol. Biol, Vol 215

[3] Pagni M, Jongeneel CV, Making sense of score statistics for sequence alignments, Briefings in Bioinformatics, 2001, Vol 2

[4] Papa A, Bozovi B, Pavlidou V, Papadimitriou E, Pelemis M, Antoniadis A, Genetic detection and isolation of crimean-congo hemorrhagic fever virus, Kosovo, Yugoslavia. Emerg Infect Dis. 2002;8:852–4

[5] Chisholm K, Dueger E, Fahmy N, Crimean-Congo Hemorrhagic Fever Virus in Ticks from Imported Livestock, Egypt, Emerg Infect Dis. 2012;18:181-2

[6] Smith T, Waterman M, Identification of common molecular subsequences. 1981, J. Mol. Biol. 147: 195–197.

[7] Watson JD, Crick FH, "Molecular Structure of Nucleic Acids: A Structure for Deoxyribose Nucleic Acid", *Nature, 1953, Vol* 171

[8] Krauthammer M, Rzhetsky A, Morozov P, Friedman C, Using BLAST for identifying gene and protein names in journal articles, Gene. 2000 Vol. 259(1-2), pgs. 245-52

[9] Henchiri O, A Feature Selection and Evaluation Scheme for Computer Virus Detection, ICDM 2006 Proceedings of the Sixth International Conference on Data Mining, pages 891-5

[10] Shankarapani M., Mukkamala S., Anatomy of Banking Trojans – Zeus Crimeware, Proceedings of the 6th International Conference on Information Warfare and Security (ICIW), pages 252-9, 2011

[11] https://zeustracker.abuse.ch

[12] Practical Malware Analysis, Michael Sikorski and Andrew Honig, No Starch Press, San Francisco, 2012

[13] Elson D, Chargaff E, "On the deoxyribonucleic acid content of sea urchin gametes".Experienti, 1952, Vol 8

[14] Pedersen J, Bastola D, Dick K, Gandhi R, Mahoney W, Malware analysis using bioinformatics tools, Proceedings of the 2012 International Conference on Security & Management (SAM2012), pages 493-9, 2012

[15] West D, Introduction to Graph Theory, 2nd Ed, Prentice Hall, 2001

Combination of Fingerprint and Password system

KyoungYul Bae and Hyun Byun
jbae@smu.ac.kr
Sangmyung University
20, Hongjimun2gil, Jongno-gu, Seoul, 110-743, Korea

***Abstract*- Growing remote access by mobile device and smartphone makes security importance to increase but these days password or pattern security system is too simple to be abused by unauthorized person. Cause of fake and falsify using biometrics can't provide perfect solution. In this thesis to solve this kind of problem we research how to improve security by consolidating finger recognization and password system**

I. INTRODUCTION

Thereby using smartphone and mobile device be more popular the more people utilize mobile device in many area such as education, news, financial. In January, 2007 Apple release i-phone it touch off rapid increasing in user of smartphone and it create new market and these broaden its utilization area. Smartphone use WiFi or 3G mobile radio communication network and it has a feature that can access to internet whenever and anywhere. Also using smartphone application people can search arrival time of public transportation in real time and application is used in mobile banking and stock trading[1].

Computer ' s function is replaced by smartphone so it involves important user's information such as financial and personal pictures, videos. Present smartphone security systems are not only too simple but the unlocking methods are spreading out covertly. I-phone is secured by using combination of number and character but USA ' s IT magazine Engadget reveal that it is easily unlocked by using combination with some part of number pad and buttons Android operation system is using pattern system and it is known as using 9 point dot so user can utilize various variable but according to Jonathan smith professor of University of Pennsylvania Android security system is easily unlocked by tracing fingerprint which remains on the smartphone screen. [2]

So both of Android and I-phone OS are vulnerable at security threat. Compared with problem of password and pattern finger recognition has advantage in security and possibility of loss. The reason why current using finger recognition smart phone, and device are not so popular is that there are many problem : not providing reasonable price, breaching human rights. in addition, finger recognition sensor is not providing reasonable price to customers but through continuous development of the smartphone and device, it will be more miniaturized and its price will fall.[3]

So once utilization of finger recognition is actively used in smartphone and if its utilization area broaden to financial transaction. Utilization of biometrics in smartdevice will be debated briskly. So in this thesis we will propose fingerprint numbering system which is combined fingerprint and password to fortify existing fingerprint recognition.

II. PASSWORD SYSTEM

At the password system user using their indentifier and password to certificate themselvs all of users ID(identifier) and password is storage in system and system compare entered ID and password with storage information. So system authorizes to access to the system or file only when ID and password are entered correctly. The initial password have saved ID and password at file and restrict authorization to access but cause of risk that exposing of administrator's password so new method is developed using Hash function. This method is by entering password and calculates it using one-way function. one-way function is it is easy to calculate to one direction but reverse calculating is impossible. when user enter ID and password with passing through the one-way function it is compared with stored information certify user. Currently the mostly be used method is SHA(Secure Hash Algorithm). SHA is developed by American of NIST(National Institute of Standards and Technology) in 19993. SHA1 is used in DSA(Digital signature algorithm) and in many internet application it is used as a default Hash algorithm.

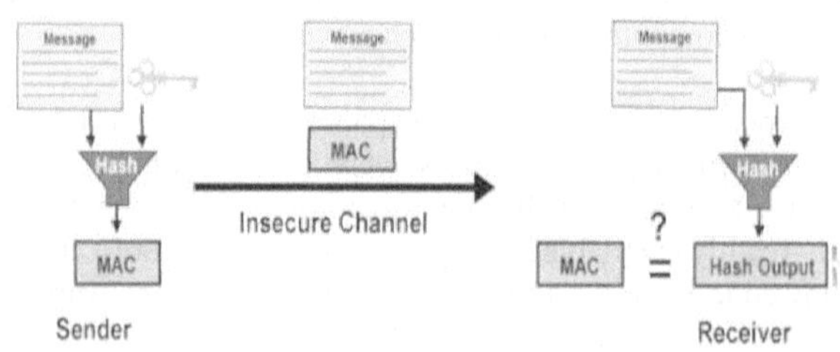

Fig. 1 Hash function block diagram

III. SECURITY THREAT OF PASSWORD SYSTEM

Password's security threat mean is users' password is exposed illegally. The attacker who wants to invade to system can know user's password as a next method. First the method of reading a system's password file. Password file contain user's password and ID so if it is exposed system and all of user's data be endanger. Thus password file limit normal user's access and give authority to only security administrator. But the most certain way is through the one-way function save the result with a ID then if password file be exposed system remain password safely. This method adapt one-way function to entered password then by comparing with the result and saved one system perform user certification Second attacker snatch information from the communication of the exchange between user and system. If the security administrator judge it has a high possibility that snatched by attacker then communicated password should be encrypted at entering place and be sent to comparing place. Third password is made carelessly by user it can be assumed easily. Actually user select the password as a related with them and common word which they usually using. For making password assumption user select password randomly or make it automatically at the system.

IV. FINGER RECOGNITION AND SECURITY THREAT

Fingerprint is formed by uplifted sweet gland and makes some flow. The lines that flow in various patterns across fingerprints are called ridges and the spaces between ridges are valleys.

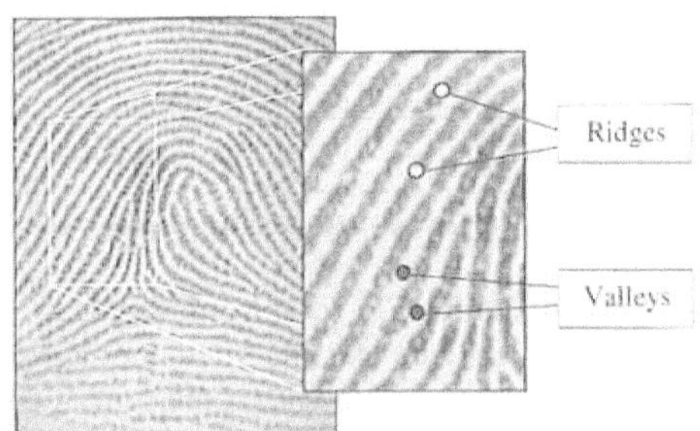

Fig. 2 Ridges and valleys on a fingerprint image

The minutia, which is created when ridges and valleys bifurcate or terminate, is important feature for matching algorithms.

The fingerprint pattern contains one or more regions where the ridge lines create special shapes. These regions may be classified into three classes: loop, delta, and whorl. Many fingerprint matching algorithms pre-align fingerprint images based on a landmark or a center point which is called the core[4] Fingerprint recognition using standardized fingerprint model.

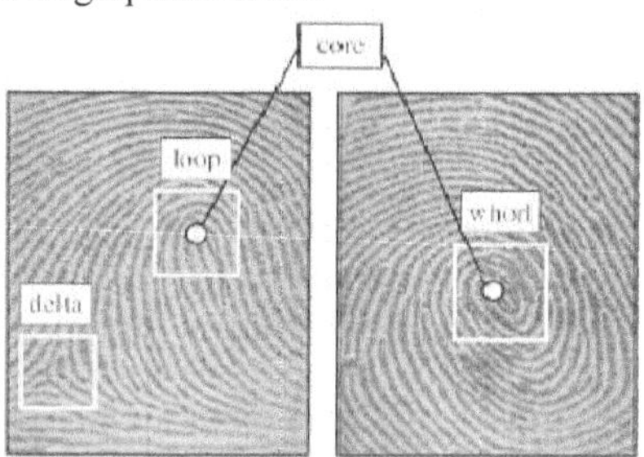

Fig. 3 Special regions (white boxes) and core points (small circles) in fingerprint images

But fingerprint recognition technology also can be falsified and forged so the security threat is still existed. Falsify and forge information is by imitating human's bio information so it has a similar bio feature. Recently creating bio technology improved rapidly so making a forge bio information is not hard to make anymore. Especially using silicon and gelatin it is possible to make a fake fingerprint that can't be distinguished from original fingerprint this kind of technology is drastically developing. The method to make a forge fingerprint is divided as a in case of be helped by user or not in case of helped by user is using material which can delicate description then make a mold and on the mold inject a silicon or gelatin to create forge fingerprint. The second method to make a forge fingerprint is using remained fingerprint. This method is first by using fine powder for catching fingerprint or an adhesive tape get a remained fingerprint. Collected fingerprint image is converted by high performance camera after then through image processing get rid of image's noises this image is printed at the film and attached to photosensitive PCB(printed circuit board). Cause of this kind of forge method.

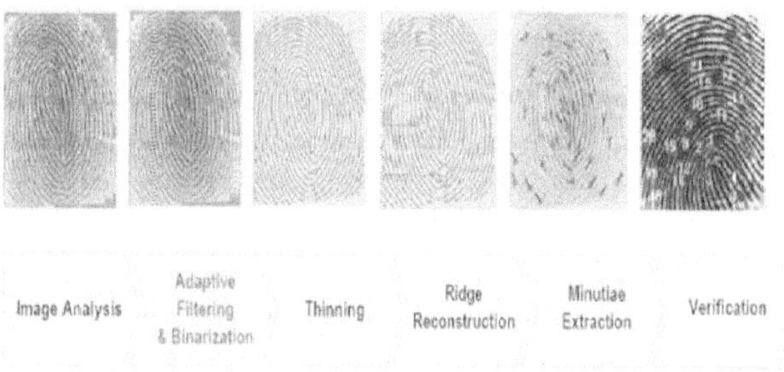

Fig. 4 Fabricate of fake fingerprint

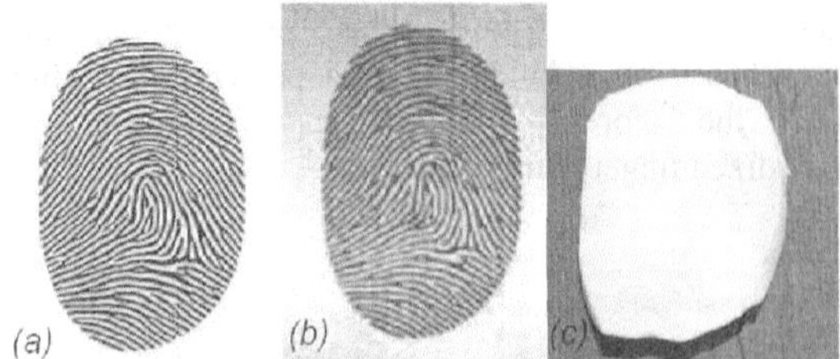

Fig. 5 Fabricate of fake fingerprint [4] (a) Reconstructed fingerprint image (b) fingerprinted on the PCB (c) fake silicon fingertip

V. AUTHORIZATION OF MOBILE USER

Google ' s android OS(operation system) use pattern recognition so instead of password some series of moving is entered so it prevent unauthorized user's access. This kind of pattern recognition method is almost similar with existing password method and it has lower security than password method mechanism. As shown in fig.6 at the android OS pattern is entered as a [1, 2, 4, 6, 9] also this kind of security mechanism can't enter incontiguous number such as [1, 9, 5] it should go through adjacent number so it proof that android pattern recognition have low security[5].

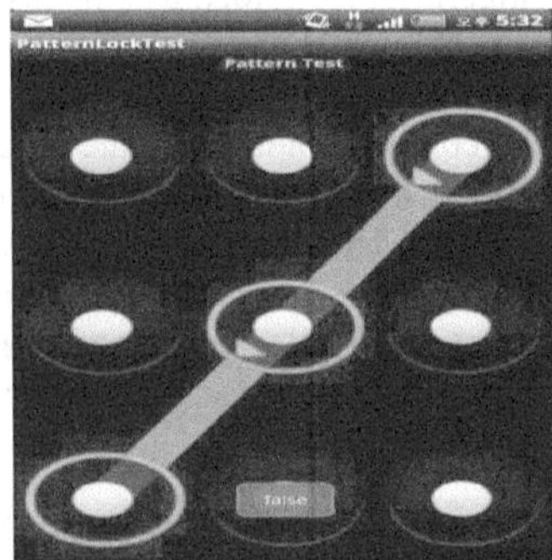

Fig. 6 Example of pattern recognition

In case of Apple's iPhone basically it needs 4 numbers of passwords but follow user's setting English capital and small letter so it is intended to enhance its security level but this kind of password is even though reinforced than 4numbers password still have password's problem iPhone user authorization password have a range of minimum 1 to maximum 9. Attacker by using this password range attempt to attack if attacker knows correct range of password then it more easily inferred.

Fig. 7 Example of iPhone user authorization

VI. FINGERPRINT RECOGNITION NUMBERING SYSTEM

Present usually using 4 number password entering is shown at Fig. 8. At Fig. 8 setted password [6, 2, 6, 3] have range from 0000 to 9999 so total it has 10000 ranges. So if attacker substitutes all kind of number of case then attacker can infer the password. These days the security problem about touch screen password is occurring and also the protocol on the network that entered password is send and not only vulnerable at application but also physical vulnerability is announcing. It has been worn when entering password at the smartphone fingerprint mark is still remaining on the screen so attacker can infer easily. By inferring the fingerprint mark on the touch screen to know what number is used for password and get a information about number is used The attacker try to change its arrange maximum in 4!=24 easily get a information also if someone watch for entering password in case of easy to enter the password it can be leaked easily.

1	2	3	1	2	3	1	2	3	1	2	3
4	5	6	4	5	6	4	5	6	4	5	6
7	8	9	7	8	9	7	8	9	7	8	9
cancel	0	correct	cancel	0	correct	cancel	0	correct	cancel	0	correct

Fig. 8 Example of numbering password

Consisted by 4 number of password has this kind of problem so we will replace existing 4number password and pattern system and consolidate with fingerprint recognition and password reinforce security. In original fingerprint recognition system there is only 10 number of cases but if numbering to fingerprint like Fig. 9 we can consist a password as a new method. Using proposed method user enter fingerprint as invested number to the finger. So attacker will have difficulty to collect all kind of fingerprint to forge and infer user's password.

standard number	Combination avaiable number									
1	1	2	3	4	5	6	7	8	9	10
2	1	2	3	4	5	6	7	8	9	10
3	1	2	3	4	5	6	7	8	9	10
4	1	2	3	4	5	6	7	8	9	10
5	1	2	3	4	5	6	7	8	9	10

Fig. 9 Example of numbering password

After fingerprint numbering, system can use the method of recognization of entering several fingerprint at the same time or enter fingerprint in regular sequence. In this thesis we adapt entering fingerprint in regular sequence and if in this system allow duplication when entering fingerprint. In case of allowing duplication a number of possible combinations is $\sum_{i=1}^{10} {}_{10}P_i$ and its total cases of number is 9,864,100. So by this method user retain security the other hand attacker will have a number of difficulties to conjecture and it is needed to obtain user's fingerprint thus this system will enhance user's security.

Table 1 Fingerprint numbering's number of casses

1 numbering	$\frac{10!}{(10-1)!} = {}_{10}P_1$	10
2 numbering	$\frac{10!}{(10-2)!} = {}_{10}P_2$	90
3 numbering	$\frac{10!}{(10-3)!} = {}_{10}P_3$	720
4 numbering	$\frac{10!}{(10-4)!} = {}_{10}P_4$	5,040
5 numbering	$\frac{10!}{(10-5)!} = {}_{10}P_5$	30,240
6 numbering	$\frac{10!}{(10-6)!} = {}_{10}P_6$	151,200
7 numbering	$\frac{10!}{(10-7)!} = {}_{10}P_7$	604,800
8 numbering	$\frac{10!}{(10-8)!} = {}_{10}P_8$	1,814,400
9 numbering	$\frac{10!}{(10-9)!} = {}_{10}P_9$	3,628,800
10 numbering	$\frac{10!}{(10-10)!} = {}_{10}P_{10}$	3,628,800
total	$\sum_{i=1}^{10} {}_{10}P_i$	9,864,100

When user enroll their fingerprint they can select what finger will have specific number or system suggest specific number of finger then user enter fingerprint corresponds to requested number of fingerprint proposed method in this thesis is can be used not only smartphone or mobile device but also utilized in financial trade area if related law is revised.

VII. CONCLUSION

This system is method not accept only one fingerprint but accept multiple finger in regular sequence. In this thesis we introduce the method in the environment of smartphone by using multiple numbered fingerprint enter to authorize user. Present smartphone authorization using pattern and password and fingerprint are exposed to high risk so if proposed system overcome delay time when user enter their finger to recognition device and relate to other biometric method it will have more concrete security. The problem should be solved after this research is reducing fingerprint's numbering time and hardware development should be preceded. If in the future using fingerprint public certification becomes popular. The fingerprint recognition in the smartphone will become important security issue so this thesis will utilize to fortify fingerprint recognition research

REFERENCES

[1] Korea Communications Commission ," 2011 the first half year , 'third 'smartphone utilization condition research announce Jul 2011.

[2] Digital times http://www.dt.co.kr/contents.html?article_no=2010102802010351747002]

[3] KyoungYulBae,HyunByun "Utilization of Fingerprint System in TheMobile E-Government" *WORLDCOMP'12*: July 16-19, 2012, USA

[4] Fake Fingertip Generation from a Minutiae Template, Javier Galbally, Raffaele Cappelli, Alessandra Lumini, Davide Maltoni , Julian Fierrez

[5] Le Hoang Thai and Ha Nhat Tam "Fingerprint recognition using standardized fingerprint model " *IJCSI International Journal of Computer Science Issues*, Vol. 7, Issue 3, No 7, May 2010

[6] Seung-hwanJu, Hee-suk Seo "Password Based User Authentication Methodology Using Multi-Input on Multi-Touch Environment" *korea simulation academy* Vol. 20, No. 1, pp. 39-49 (2011. 3)

A Biometric Authentication System That Automatically Generates Feature Points

Hiroshi Dozono[1], **Youki Inaba**[1], **Masanori Nakakuni**[2]
[1] Faculty of Science and Engineering, Saga University, 1-Honjyo Saga, 840-8502 JAPAN
[2] Information Technology Center, Fukuoka University, 8-19-1, Nanakuma, Jonan-ku, Fukuoka 814-0180 JAPAN

Abstract—*Recently, personal information in the mobile devices have been threatened as the popularization of mobile devices because of the lack attention to the information. The purpose of our research is to develop the reliable and convenient authentication system for mobile devices. In this paper, the development of the biometric authentication system, which generates feature points from freehand pattern and uses the points as the anchors for drawing pattern and points for detecting pen speed, is introduced using the experimental results.*

Keywords: Biometrics, Authentication, Touch panel, Mobile device, Tracing Authentication

1. Introduction

Recently, computerization of the information has proceeded very rapidly. Along with the computerization, the mobile devices, such as smartphones and tablets, are spread among people very rapidly. For example, about 70% of Japanese will possess smartphones as ubiquitous devices in 2016.

However, the owners of mobile devices do not take care of the security of the personal information which stored in the mobile devices. The development of the mobile devices targets the performance or usability, and security is trampled upon. For this problem, the authentication method that is flexible and convenient for the users is proposed. If the authentication method is not annoying and does not require special knowledge about security, the user will naturally use the authentication system, and will have consciousness to the security.

2. Authentication Methods using Touch Panel

As the popularization of the mobile devices such as smartphones and tablet devices, the devices which equipped with touch panel become widespread. And, these devices grow in usage and popularity with the people who are not familiar with the conventional computers. In these situations, a simple authentication method which uses a touch panel is desired.

As the authentication method using touch panels, the signature written on the touch panel is often used[1]. However, it is difficult to write identical signature on slippery touch panel especially for capacitive type panel that is recently equipped to almost all mobile devices. As another method, the authentication method which uses the knowledge factors in selecting the symbols or positions in the image is often used[2]. However, this method has a weakness for snooping.

Android devices use the lock screen which uses the knowledge factor with connecting the points displayed on the touch panel (Figure 1). However, the patterns which can be drawn are not flexible, and users tend to select simple patterns because the points are fixed. Thus, this method also has a weakness for snooping. For avoiding snooping, biometric authentication[3] is effective. Biometric authentication is classified into two types; biometric authentication using biological features and biometric authentication using behavioral features. As the biological features, the fingerprints, vein patterns and iris patterns are often used. They can achieve high accuracy. However, special sensor devices, such as fingerprint readers, are required for implementation. As the behavioral features, keystroke timings[4][5] and calligraphy of handwritten patterns or signature[1] are often

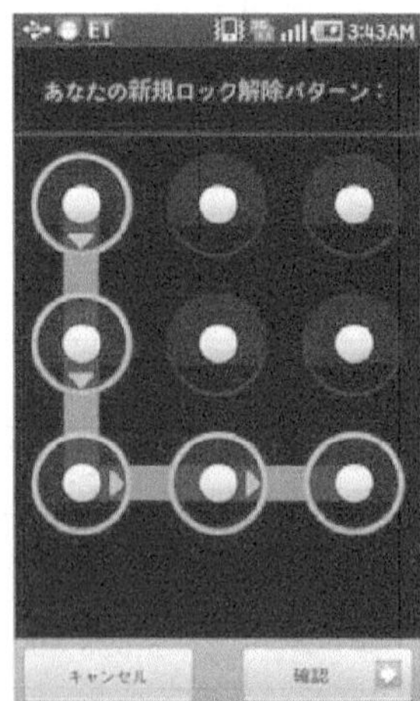

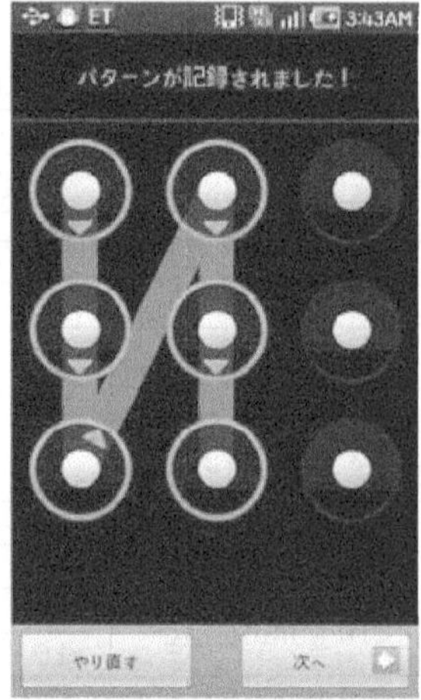

Fig. 1: Android lock screen

used. They can be obtained from conventional input devices. However, the accuracy of authentication is lower than that of biological features. At the same time, high accuracy is not always necessary for the devices that are used personally because authentication is used as the lock method just in case the device is stolen or possessed by malicious users. In this paper, the biometric authentication method which uses the biological features obtained from touch panel is proposed. We have proposed an authentication system using the behavior biometrics during drawing the symbol displayed in the touch panel[6]. This system uses pen speed and pen pressure at all sampling times as behavior biometrics, and marks 0.1 as Equal Error Rate (EER). However, capacitive type panel, which is mostly used recently, cannot detect pen pressure, and it requires much computational cost for matching all pen speeds and pen pressures at all sampling time. For this problem, we propose an authentication system which generates feature points automatically.

3. The System Which Generates Feature Points

At first, we developed a system which generates feature points. As the environments of development, Xcode 3.2.6 and iOS SDK 4.3 is used, and iPad is used as the target machine. As shown in Figure 2, this system generates feature points automatically from the freehand curving line. These

Fig. 2: The system which generate feature points

points are displayed on the touch panel during authentication to increase reproducibility of the registered curving line. By displaying the points without curving line, the pattern of connecting points is used as a knowledge factor for authentication. The pen speeds between the points are used as a behavior factor for biometric authentication. The integration of multi-modal biometrics is reported in [7][8], and the combination of knowledge factor and behavior factor is reported in [9].

The feature points are generated on the points which have large curvature factors of curving line. To detect both of shelving curve and sharp curve simultaneously, the curvature factors are calculated in long intervals and short intervals. The detection of feature points in short interval tends to generate dense points due to jiggling of the finger or touch pen. To avoid this problem, the dense points are integrated to one point.

Figure 3,4 shows the examples of generating feature points. In case 1, the feature points are successfully generated in both shelving curve and sharp curve. In case 2, the feature points generated closely during drawing circle twice are integrated

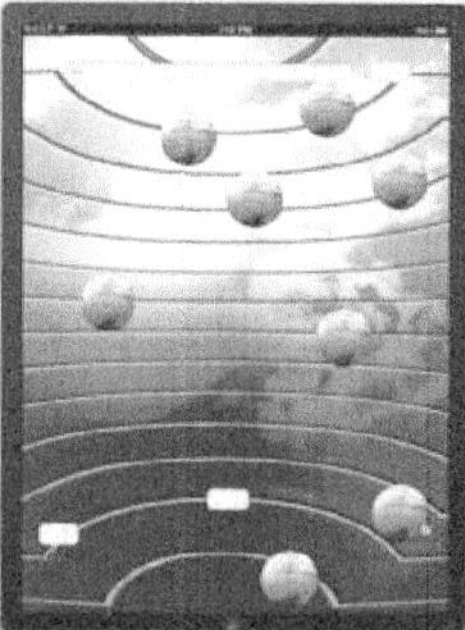

Fig. 3: Generation of feature points(case 1)

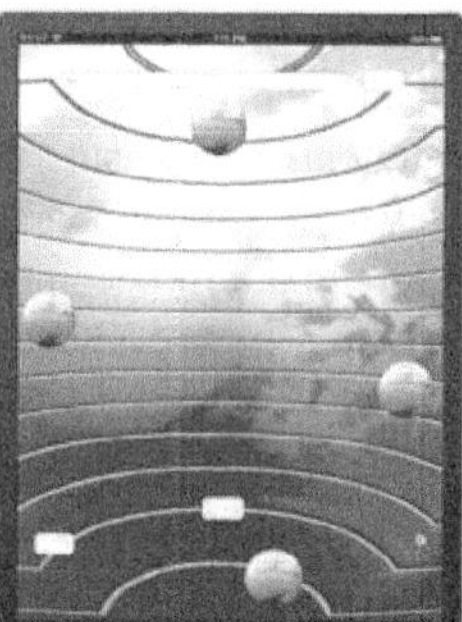

Fig. 4: Generation of feature points(case 2)

4. Authentication using Knowledge Factor

In this section, the results of authentication experiments using the connection pattern of feature points as knowledge factor are reported. The pattern is represented in the order of the connections of feature points. It faces the possibility of two problems. At first, the pattern may be guessed from the feature points displayed on the touch panel. Secondly, the user cannot remember the pattern from the feature points. The first problem is examined in this section. The settings of the experiment are as follows. 3 patterns of feature points shown in Figure 5 are registered by users. Ten users triy to guess the pattern from the feature points displayed on the screen. Table 1 shows the results. The number in the table denotes the number of successful users. No user can completely guess the patterns. And, only two users can guess the starting point of pattern C. From this experiment, the authentication using knowledge factor is secure enough. However, if the number of feature points decreases or the registered pattern becomes too simple, it may not secure. An algorithm which evaluates the security of registered pattern is required in practical use.

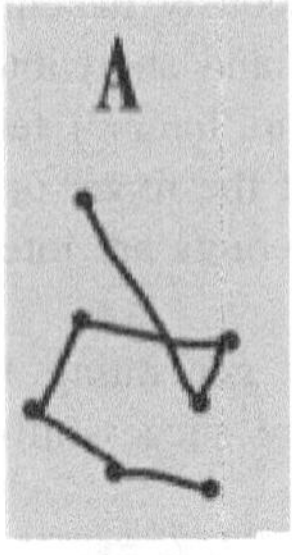

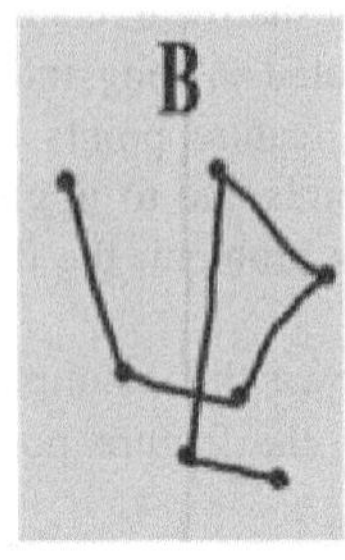

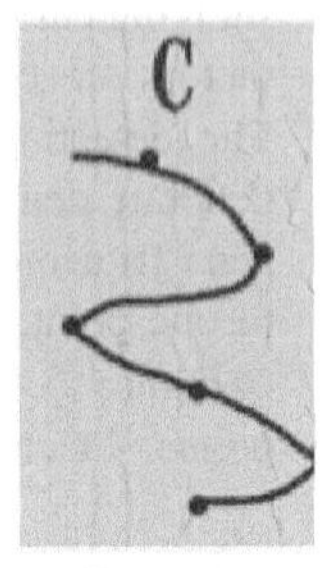

Fig. 5: Registered patterns of feature points

Table 1: Result of authentication experiment using knowledge factor

	A	B	C
Complete	0	0	0
Starting point	0	0	2

5. Biometric Authentication using Behavior Factor of Pen Speed

We have reported the biometric authentication using behavior factors of pen calligraphy of pen speed and pen pressure[6]. However, recent capacitive touch panel, which is equipped with almost all recent devices, cannot detect pen pressure. Considering the compatibility, the biometric authentication using pen speed is effective. However, it may be not secure enough as biometrics, thus the authentication using the knowledge factor of connecting patterns is simultaneously used. In [6], the distribution of the pen speed along the curving line is used as feature value. However, it requires large computation costs because the number of points tends to be large, and it may be problematic for mobile devices. In this paper, much simpler method is used. The pen speeds between the feature points are used as feature value. For each connection between feature points, threshold values for authentication are set, and authentication succeeds if all differences of pen speeds are less than the thresholds. As the behavior factor varies in each drawing, and the dispersion is different for each user, the threshold is set as $\alpha\sigma$ according to the variance σ^2 of the pattern that is traced three times in registration phase. The procedure of authentication experiment is as follows.

Step 1: Generation of Feature Points
The user, who is registered on the system, draws a curving line on touch screen. Then, the feature points are generated as mentioned in Section III, and the connecting pattern is registered for the user as shown in Figure 6. The name of the user is set in the text box on the top of screen for later analysis using the recorded data.

Fig. 6: Registration screen

Step 2: Registration of Behavior Factor of Pen Speed
The user traces the pattern on the touch screen which displays the feature points without curving lines in three times. Then, the averages and variances of pen speeds between the feature points are registered as a behavior factor of pen speed.

Step 3: Authentication
The user who is authenticated draws the curving line on the touch screen which displays the feature points without curving line. Then, the connecting pattern and pen speeds between the feature points are examined, and if both of knowledge factor and behavior factor meet the condition of authentication, the user is authenticated as true user.

Next, the experimental results using a behavior factor of pen speed are reported. As the indexes of evaluation, FRR and FAR are used. FRR is the False Rejection Rate, which is the rate of falsely rejecting the true user as false user. FAR is the False Acceptance Rate, which is the rate of falsely accepting the false user as true user. At first, the factor α

in the threshold value is set during the experiment of the authentication of the author as to achieve less than 10 % for FRR as shown in Table 2. To examine the effectiveness of behavior factor, the experiments are conducted with giving the knowledge factor of connecting patterns to all users. Thus, following results of experiments denote the security of behavior factor without knowledge factor.

Table 2: Result of authentication experiment using pen speed of author

	A	B	C
FRR	0.069	0.100	0.095

At first, experiments are conducted with showing the connecting pattern with straight lines displayed between the feature points as shown in Figure 7. 6 users A-F register the pattern, and for each calculation of FAR and FRR, more than 10 trials are conducted. Figure 8 shows the results.

Fig. 7: Authentication screen with lines

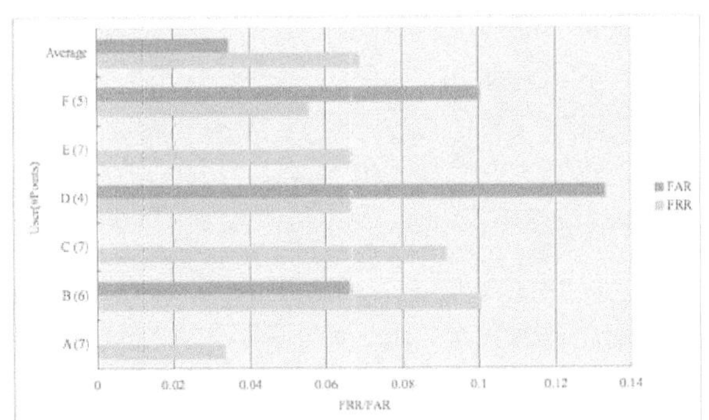

Fig. 8: Result of authentication experiment using behavior factor (1)

The number in brackets denotes the number of feature points. For all users, FRR becomes less than 0.1, and FAR is also small except user D. The EER is not calculated in these experiments. However, it will be more or less than 0.05 on average. Next, the experiments with showing the authentication process of true user to false users are conducted. In the practical case, the false user may snoop the pattern just before spoofing the true user, and can remember the curving line in authentication process. In these experiments, the lines connecting the feature points are not displayed on authentication screen as in Figure 9. Figure 10 shows the results. User A-F are not identical to those in the previous experiments. In this case, FAR becomes worse because the pattern is snooped. However, the average is less than 0.1, and EER will be more or less than 0.08 on average. In both experiments, FAR becomes larger for smaller number of feature points. Thus, an algorithm which evaluates the security of registered pattern is required also for behavior factor in practical use.

Fig. 9: Authentication screen without lines

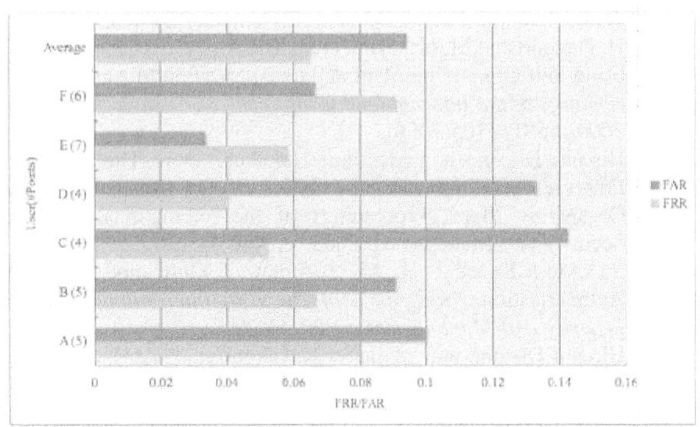

Fig. 10: Result of authentication experiment using behavior factor(2) - under snooping

These experimental results are the extreme case in which the connecting pattern is known by false users. In the practical use, the combination of knowledge factor and behavior factor will meet secure authentication.

6. Conclusion

In this paper, we propose the authentication which generates the feature points from the handwritten curving line automatically. The pattern of connecting feature points is applied to the authentication using a knowledge factor, and pen speeds between the feature points are applied to the authentication using a behavior factor. The effectiveness of both authentication is examined by experiments, and the combination of the authentication will accomplish secure system.

As the future work, the authentication accuracy should be more strengthened. In this paper, simple algorithm using threshold is applied. More sophisticated algorithm like neural network should be applied to authentication system. Recently, the cloud system using HTML 5 WEB applications is spread to mobile devices. The application of this method to WEB applications will achieve the security on cloud system.

References

[1] J. J. Brault and R. Plamondon: A Complexity Measure of Handwritten Curves: Modelling of Dynamic Signature Forgery, IEEE Trans. Systems, Man and Cybernetics, 23:pp.400-413(1993)

[2] Hiroshi Dozono, Takayuki Inoue and Masanori Nakakuni,et.al, Study of Biometric Authentication Method using Behavior Characteristics on Game Consoles, Proc. of SAM 2009, (2009)

[3] R. Bolle, J. Connell, S. Pankanti, N. Ratha, and A. Senior, *Guide to Biometrics, Springer*, 2004

[4] F. Monrose and A.D. Rubin: Keystroke Dynamics as a Biometric for Authentication, Future Generation Computer Systems, March(2000).

[5] H. Dozono and M. Nakakuni et.al, The Analysis of Key Stroke Timings using Self Organizing Maps and its Application to Authentication, *Proceedings of the International Conference on Security and Management 2006*, pp.100-105(2006)

[6] Hiroshi Dozono and Masanori Nakakuni, et.al: The Analysis of Pen Pressures of Handwritten Symbols on PDA Touch Panel using Self Organizing Maps, Proceedings of the International Conference on Security and Management 2005, pp.440-445(2005)

[7] S.Dokic,A.Kulesh,et.al, An Overview of Multi-modal Biometrics for Authentication, *Proceedings of The 2007 International Conference on Security and Management*, pp.39-44(2007)

[8] Hiroshi Dozono and Masanori Nakakuni,,et.al: An Integration Method of Multi-Modal Biometrics Using Supervised Pareto Learning Self Organizing Maps., Proc. of the Internal Joint Conference of Neural Network 2008,(2008)

[9] Hiroshi Dozono, Takayuki Inoue and Masanori Nakakuni, A study of the Graphical User Interfaces for Biometric Authentication System, Proc. of SAM 2012, (2012)

A Biometric Security Model with Identities Detection and Local Feature-level Fusion

S. Soviany[1], **C. Soviany**[2]
[1]T.C.T. Department, National Communication Research Institute (I.N.S.C.C), Bucharest, Romania
[2]IDES Technologies, Bruxelles, Belgium

Abstract - *The paper presents an innovative solution for biometric security systems design in order to enhance the identification applications performance and also to reduce their complexity. The proposed model is relying on a special kind of classifiers called detectors and it is suitable especially for various security requirements applications. The model also includes a local feature-level fusion for each of the integrated biometrics. The designed system is useful especially for medical database remote access control in which different users have different authorization levels, and their precise identification need more optimized solution (either from the execution time and recognition accuracy points of view).*

Keywords: detectors, hierarchical classifier, identification

1 Introduction

The modern approach in security system design is to integrate biometrics for preventing the unauthorized accesses to the critical resources such as medical databases or banking applications servers. However many of these applications have different performance and implementation costs requirements. On the other hand, although biometrics based applications are reliable security solutions for persons authentication, there are still challenges to be solved. One of the most critical issues is the identification accuracy. Many biometric security systems are better performing especially for the verification operational mode (in which the system is designed to validate the association between the pretended identity and the biometric credential) and not for the identification mode (in which the system has to guess who is a real person before accepting or rejecting his/her access, without any additional identification) [1][2].

We proposed an innovative approach for a more accurate identification system in which for the biometric data matching we applied special classifiers called detectors. They are trained for a few persons identification, and so the proposed method is more suitable for applications in which not all the enrolled users present the same misidentification risk. An example of application domain is the medical database remote access control, for users with different authorization levels.

The remainder of this paper is structured as follows. Section II presents the biometric system architecture. Section III describes the 1st stage in biometric data processing. The data classification stage is detailed in section IV. Experimental results which we achieved on the available data are presented in section V. Finally section VI concludes our paper and also proposes some further research areas to be explored on more biometric data sets.

2 The System Architecture

The biometric security system architecture is depicted in fig. 1.

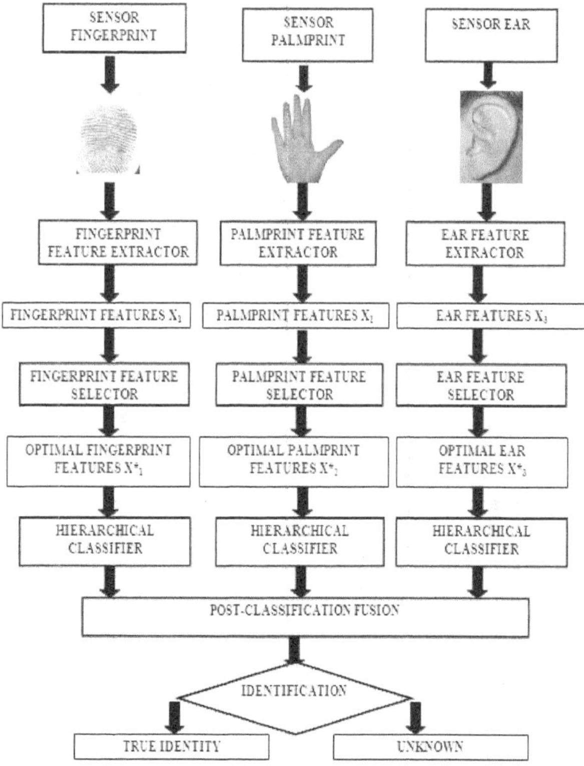

Figure 1: The biometric security system architecture

The biometric security system is relying on a multimodal architecture which integrates 3 biometric measures (fingerprint, palm print and ear). The basic systems functions, further detailed in the next sections, are the following: feature extraction, feature selection for dimensionality reduction and hierarchical classification. The final stage is the post-classification fusion which provides the identification decision for the real biometric system application.

The biometric data comes from 30 users of a medical database. We use 5 images per person per biometric measure (fingerprint, palm print and ear) leading to an overall biometric database which contains 450 images. From these images we generate the biometric templates datasets for the enrolled users within the feature generation and selection stage (Section III). In order to perform the biometric data classification providing the final identification decision (Section IV) we randomly divide the generated biometric datasets into 2 independent subsets: the 1st one is used for system training and the 2nd is used for system performance evaluation.

3 Feature Generation and Selection stage

3.1 Feature Extraction

For the feature extraction we apply a regional approach and also exploit the textural statistical properties of the acquired images (for fingerprint, palm print and ear, respectively). The overall process is depicted in fig. 2.

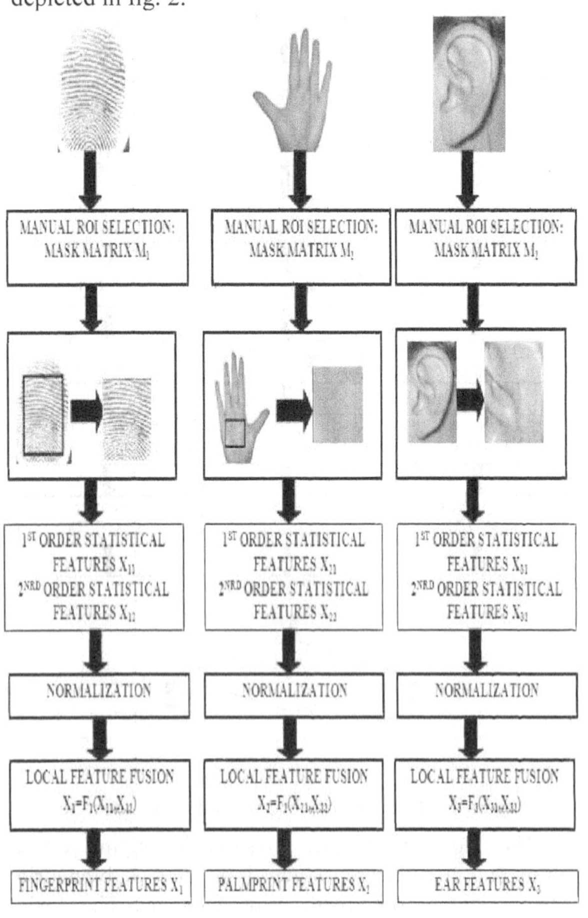

Figure 2: The feature generation step

Before proceeding in feature extraction step, we convert the color images in black-and-white images applying the procedure proposed by Bhattacharyya for iris texture analysis in [3].

Then we perform the manual Region of Interest (ROI) selection on each image, in order to further feature extract only from the regions containing the most useful information for the biometric identification. For each of the 3 biometrics we apply a mask matrix covering a rectangular region selected in the original images, according to:

$$M_k(i_k, j_k) = \begin{cases} 1, x_k \leq i_k \leq x_k + \Delta x_k, y_k \leq j_k \leq y_k + \Delta y_k \\ 0, \ otherwise \end{cases} \quad (1)$$

where x_k, $x_k + \Delta x_k$, y_k, $y_k + \Delta y_k$ are the rectangular area coordinates for the selected ROI (k=1 for fingerprint ROI selection, k=2 for palm print ROI selection and k=3 for ear ROI selection). The mask matrix has the same size like the original image (for fingerprint, palm print and ear, respectively).

In the main sub-step of this process we compute 2 sets of statistical textural features from the input ROIs. These features are related to the gray-levels distributions over the selected regions pixels [4]. We generate 2 feature vectors for each biometric containing the 1st and respectively the 2nd order statistical features:

- for fingerprint ROI: X_{11} (the 1st order statistical features) and X_{12} (the 2nd order statistical features);
- for palm print ROI: X_{21} (the 1st order statistical features) and X_{22} (the 2nd order statistical features);
- for ear ROI: X_{31} (the 1st order statistical features) and X_{32} (the 2nd order statistical features).

The 1st order statistical features evaluate the gray-level distribution in the input image [4]. They are relying on the 1st order histogram $P(I_k)$ for the fraction of pixels with gray-level I_k [4]. If N_k is the number of the possible gray levels for fingerprint, palm print and ear ROI images, then the 1st order statistical features derive from the following measures [4]:

- *moments:*

$$m_{j_k} = E\left[I_k^{j_k}\right] = \sum_{I_k=0}^{N_k-1} I_k^{j_k} \cdot P(I_k), \quad j_k = 1,2,\dots, k = \overline{1,3} \quad (2)$$

- *central moments*:

$$\mu_{j_k} = E[(I_k - E[I_k])^{j_k}] = \sum_{I_k=0}^{N_k-1} (I_k - m_{1_k})^{j_k} \cdot P(I_k), \ j_k = 1,2,\dots, k = \overline{1,3} \quad (3)$$

- *absolute moments*:

$$\widehat{\mu_{j_k}} = E[|I_k - E[I_k]|^{j_k}] =$$

$$\sum_{I_k=0}^{N_k-1} |I_k - E[I_k]|^{j_k} \cdot P(I_k), j_k = 1,2,\dots, k = \overline{1,3} \ (4)$$

- *entropy*:

$$H_k = -E[\log_2 P(I_k)] = -\sum_{I_k=0}^{N_{k-1}} P(I_k) \cdot \log_2 P(I_k), k = \overline{1,3} \quad (5)$$

The feature vectors X_{k1} (for the 3 integrated biometrics in our multimodal architecture) contain the following 1st order feature statistics computed from the previously selected ROIs: *mean* (m1), *variance* (the 2nd central moment μ_2), *skewness* (the 3rd central moment $\mu3$), *kurtosis* (the 4th central moment $\mu4$), the *first 4 absolute moments* ($\widehat{\mu_{j_k,j}}$, $j = \overline{1,4}$, $k = \overline{1,3}$) and *entropy*; therefore each of the 1st feature vectors will have 9 components representing the 1st order statistical features derived from the selected ROI image histograms.

The 2nd order statistical features are pixel-pairwise derived and are provided based on the co-occurrence matrix. Each element in a co-occurrence matrix C contains the probability of a certain gray-level for one pixel in the original image Im_k while another displaced pixel exhibit another gray-level, according to [5][6][7]:

$$C_{\Delta x_k,\Delta y_k}(i_k, j_k) = P\{Im_k(x_k, y_k) = i_k, Im_k(x_k + \Delta x_k, y_k + \Delta y_k) = j_k\}, \quad k = \overline{1,3} (6)$$

where the pixels displacements are Δx_k and Δy_k. We applied 6 gray-levels for the fingerprint data, 5 gray-levels for the palm print data and 4 gray-levels for the ear data resulting in 36 components for the fingerprint 2nd feature vector, 25 components for palm print and 16 components for ear.

The co-occurrence matrices allow to compute the following additional features [4]:

- *angular second moment:*

$$ASM_k = \sum_{i_k=0}^{N_k-1} \sum_{j_k=0}^{N_k-1} (P(i_k, j_k))^2, k = \overline{1,3} \ (7)$$

- *contrast:*

$$CON_k = \sum_{n_k=0}^{N_k-1} n_k^2 \cdot \left\{ \sum_{i_k=0}^{N_k-1} \sum_{\substack{j_k=0 \\ |i_k-j_k|=n_k}}^{N_k-1} P(i_k, j_k) \right\}, k = \overline{1,3} \ (8)$$

- *inverse difference moment:*

$$IDF_k = \sum_{i_k=0}^{N_k-1} \sum_{j_k=0}^{N_k-1} \frac{P(i_k, j_k)}{1 + (i_k - j_k)^2}, k = \overline{1,3} \quad (9)$$

- *entropy:*

$$H_{k,xy} = -\sum_{i_k=0}^{N_k-1} \sum_{j_k=0}^{N_k-1} P(i_k, j_k) \cdot \log_2 P(i_k, j_k), \quad k = \overline{1,3} \ (10)$$

So far the 2nd feature vectors X_{k2} have the following sizes: 40 for fingerprint, 29 for palm print and 20 for ear biometrics, respectively.

From the 2nd feature vectors X_{k2} we retain only the features which exhibit the lowest absolute values of the Pearson correlation coefficient in order to get **the least-correlated statistical features**: 10 features for fingerprint, 11 features for palm print and 9 features for ear. The apply correlation measure is given for the pixels pair (x_k,y_k) according to [4]

$$r_k(x_k, y_k) = \frac{\left[\sum_{i_k=0}^{N_k-1} \sum_{j_k=0}^{N_k-1} (i_k \cdot j_k) \cdot P(i_k, j_k)\right] - \mu_{x_k} \cdot \mu_{y_k}}{\sigma_{x_k} \cdot \sigma_{y_k}}, \quad k = \overline{1,3} \ (11)$$

where μ_{x_k}, μ_{y_k} and σ_{x_k}, σ_{y_k} are the mean and standard deviations, respectively, for the 2 pixels intensities. The new vectors are $X^*_{k2}, k = \overline{1,3}$.

The resulting feature sizes for all the integrated biometrics are given in table 1.

TABLE 1. FEATURE SPACES SIZES

Features sets for each biometric			
Biometric	***Size(X_{k1})***	***Size(X_{k2})***	***Size(X^*_{k2})***
Fingerprint	9	40	10
Palm print	9	29	11
Ear	9	20	9

We **normalize** the X_{k1} and X^*_{k2} components using the sigmoid function to provide a common numerical range for the statistical features:

$$f_{k,i}(X_{ki}) = \frac{1}{1 + exp(-A_{k,i} \cdot X_{ki} - B_{k.i})}, \quad k = \overline{1,3}, i = \overline{1,2} \quad (12)$$

The provided experimental data allowed us to use the following coefficients ranges:

- for fingerprint feature normalization: $A_{1,i} \in [2, 2.5], B_{1,i} \in [1, 1.5]$;

- for palm print feature normalization:
  $A_{2,i} \in [2,3.5], B_{2,i} \in [1.5,2]$
- for ear feature normalization:
  $A_{3,i} \in [1.5,2.5], B_{3,i} \in [1,2]$

Finally we applied a **local feature-level biometric fusion** by concatenating the 2 feature sets for each biometric (fingerprint, palm print and ear). The concatenation-based feature-level fusion needs more homogenous features, according to Jain and Ross [8] and this is why we previously normalized the features. The resulting feature vectors are X_1 (fingerprint biometric template with 19 components), X_2 (palm print template with 20 components) and X_3 (ear template with 18 components). This sub-step is shown in fig. 3.

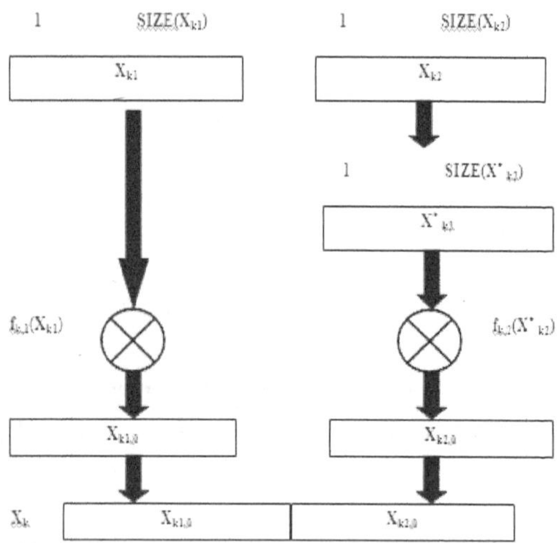

Figure 3: Local feature-level fusion

3.2 Feature Selection

We further apply a feature selection strategy because the biometric templates sizes are still too large. Our purpose is to reduce the feature space dimensionality to at most 10 features per biometric. Less features means less complexity classifiers for the biometric data, less training samples and also a reduced response time which is often an important requirement for the large-scale identification systems.

For feature selection step we apply the **forward-searching feature (sequential) selection** (FSFS) [4] and also we use as the performance criterion *1-NN (nearest-neighbor rule) classification error rate* because of its property to limit the classification error rate [10]:

$$\varepsilon^* \leq \varepsilon_{1-NN} \leq 2\varepsilon^* \cdot (1-\varepsilon^*) \leq 2\varepsilon^* \qquad (13)$$

where ε_{1-NN} is the error rate for the 1-NN classifier and ε^* is the optimal Bayesian classifier error rate.

The resulting optimal feature sets for each biometric are as following:

- for fingerprint data: 8 features instead of 19;
- for palm print data: 9 features instead of 20;
- for ear data: 10 features instead of 18.

4. Data Classification Stage

The classification stage is based on a hierarchical approach in which each of the 3 biometric data is processed within a multi-stage classifier (fig. 4).

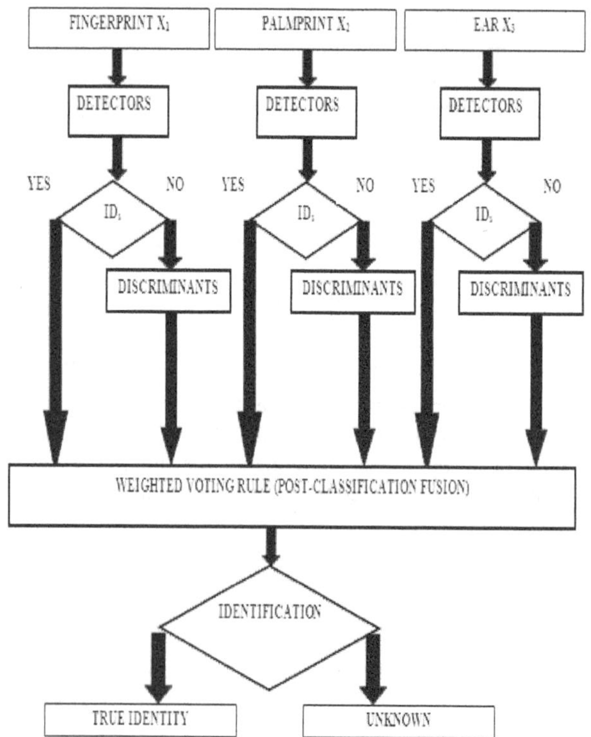

Figure 4: The classification stage

The 2 classification steps for each biometric are: *the detection step* providing decisions only on a few target identities and *the discrimination step* in which all the other identities have to be recognized if the detection failed on the first focused identities. Finally a *weighted voting rule* is applied to provide the most accurate identification decision.

4.1 Detection

In our biometric security application not all the medical database users have the same authorization level and also not all of them exhibit the same security risk in case of an identification error. This is the reason of applying a special kind of classifiers which are trained only for a few target identities. There are 3 most important users and therefore we trained 3 classifiers for their identities detections. Based on the available biometric data we found *that the Gaussian mixture models* fit very well to the identity detection goal. The basic model for each biometric detector is given by

$$p_k(X_k|I_i) = \sum_{j_{I_i}=1}^{n_k} p_k(X_k|j_{I_i}) \cdot P_{j_{I_i}}, i = \overline{1,3}, k = \overline{1,3} \quad (14)$$

where P_j are the mixture weights. We designed 3x3 detectors (one for each identity I_i and for each biometric (k=1 for fingerprint, k=2 for palm print and k=3 for ear biometric data, respectively). Also n_k is the mixture component numbers for each biometric detector. The unknown parameters of each Gaussian component are resulting from EM Algorithm (Expectation Maximization) [4][9][11][12].

The identification decision is relying on the following underlying function based on the Bayes rule:

$$g_k(X_k) = P(I_i) \cdot p_k(X_k|I_i) =$$

$$\frac{n_{Z,i}}{n_Z} \cdot \sum_{j_{I_i}=1}^{n_k} p_k(X_k|j_{I_i}) \cdot P_{j_{I_i}}, i = \overline{1,3}, k = \overline{1,3} \quad (15)$$

where $n_{Z,i}$ is the number of training biometric samples belonging to the person with identity I_i and n_Z is the overall training set size. The biometric detection rule becomes:

$$g_k(X_k) \geq \theta_{I_i} \Rightarrow Identity(X_k) = I_i i = \overline{1,3}, k = \overline{1,3} \quad (16)$$

no matter the other non-target identities.

4.2 Discrimination

The discrimination stage is performed if the 1st detection stage failed on their target identities. We trained the discriminant models only on the other N-3 enrolled identities (because at this point we already have decisions on the 1st 3 identities).

For our available biometric data we choose the following multi-class discrimination models: Naïve-Bayes, Parzen (with Laplace kernel instead of the Gaussian which was most used so far) and Quadratic, according to their behavior on the training datasets. Their learning curves are represented in figures 5 (for fingerprint data), 6 (for palm print data) and 7 (for ear data).

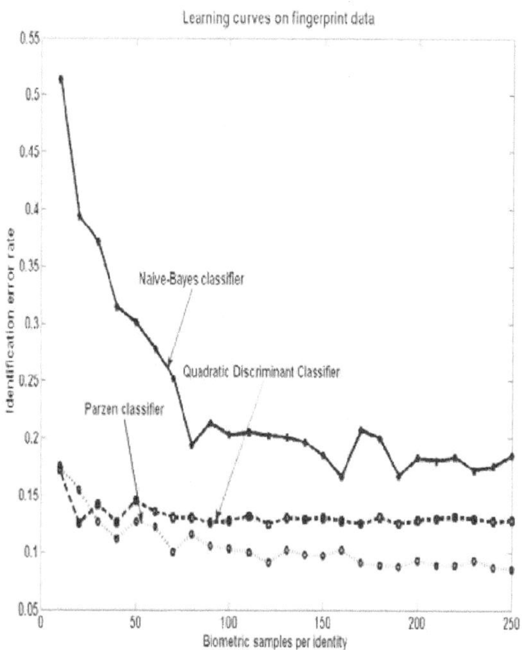

Figure 5: Learning curves for NBayes, Parzen and QDC classifiers on fingerprint data

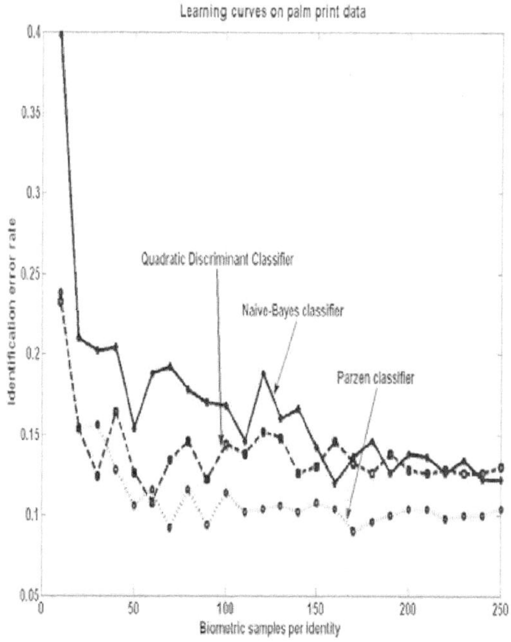

Figure 6: Learning curves for NBayes, Parzen and QDC classifiers on palm print data

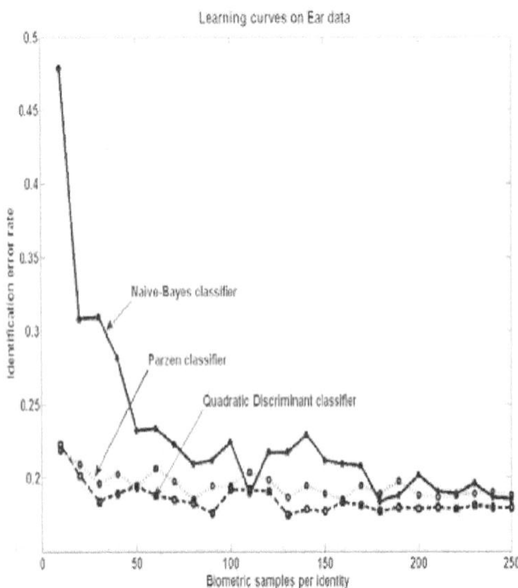

Figure 7: Learning curves for NBayes, Parzen and QDC classifiers on ear data

Parzen and QDC models exhibit the best behavior. We represented the classification (identification) error rate vs. the training biometric data set size. According to these learning curves, we finally choose Parzen classifier for fingerprint and palm print data and QDC model for ear biometric data.

4.3 The post-classification fusion rule

The final post-classification fusion rule is relying on a weighted voting scheme in which we maximize the best hierarchical classifiers contributions with the following weights updating iterative rule:

$$w(i+1) \leftarrow w(i) \cdot \eta(i) \tag{17}$$

in which $\eta(i)$ is the ratio between the detectors and discriminants performances (measured by their TPr, True Positive Rates) for each of the identification subsystems (fingerprint, palm print and ear).

5 Experimental Results

We evaluate the system performance on 10 experiments and averaging the achieved results. Each of the performed experiments consists in 2 persons authentication attempts for the remote medical database also using the 3 biometrics. The designed biometric security system performance is resulting from the ROC analysis while fixing the classifier operating points in order to provide an optimal trade-off for the 2 persons identification; one of these persons (identity I_1) has the highest authorization degree for using the medical database within the telemedicine application and the other is less authorized (identity I_2). Actually we compare the optimal operating points in 2 cases: with and without identities detection stage (figures 8 and 9, respectively). The classification system is trained with 50 samples per class (identity). Also for all classifiers we apply a rejection threshold of 5%. This rejection option reduces the influence of low-quality biometric templates on the overall biometric security system accuracy.

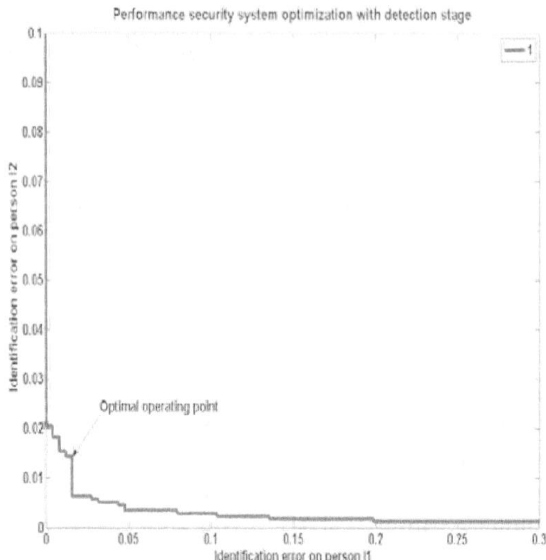

Figure 8: Optimal op.point fixing for the overall security system with detection stage

In Figure 8 one can see that the optimal op. point of the overall system provides an average identification error rate of 0.015 on 2 authenticating persons. Actually this performance indicator reveals the system capacity to find out the real identity, not the acceptance/rejection decisions correctness. In this evaluation we did not focus on the typical FAR (False Acceptance Rate) or FRR (False Rejection Rate) performance indicators. The values are already suggesting the detectors capabilities to improve the overall identification performance of the biometric systems.

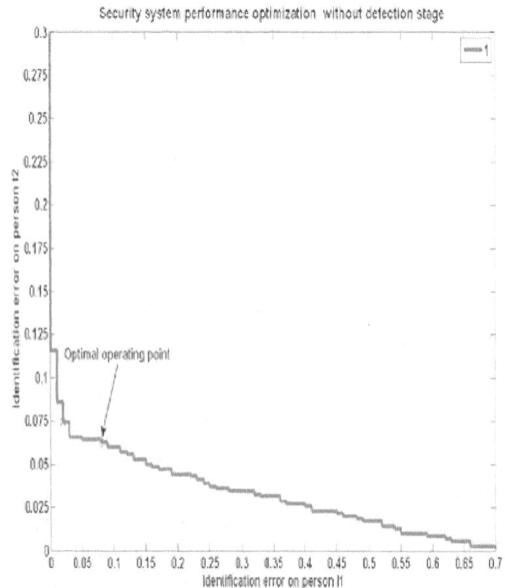

Figure 9: Optimal op.point fixing for the overall security system without detection stage

Without detection stage, the optimal operating point provides an average identification error rate of 0.067 on the same persons. This shows that the detection stage improved the identification process accuracy by almost 4 times. This improvement results from the detector basic principle, which is more focused to target class recognition (in this case, a certain person to be identified).

These results are achieved for a reduced feature number (between 8 and 10 features for the 3 integrated biometrics). Also the local feature-level fusion has a significant contribution to the identification performance.

6 Conclusions

The identification accuracy still remains an important challenge in biometric systems design. This is due to the computational complexity in exploring a huge searching space of possible identities (in large-scale identification). The multimodal biometric systems integrate more biometrics in order to enhance the accuracy and security, but there are still open issues regarding the integration levels, more specifically on the biometric fusion scheme (pre- or post-classification).

We approached these challenges for biometric identification systems through a multi-classifier hierarchical approach in which the biometric data matching is performed in 2 stages, detection and discrimination. This decision hierarchy significantly improves the identification accuracy although the users behavior has a non-neglecting influence on the overall system performance. On the other hand, the execution time should be considered while designing such biometric data classification systems.

Also we included a local feature-level biometric data fusion. So far the pre-classification or feature-level fusion was not implemented in many biometric systems because the different features sets are often incompatible. Also the biometric templates format is usually proprietary from security reasons. However, the pre-classification fusion should be considered for accurate biometric systems design because of its performance improvement. Combining the biometric data at an earlier processing stage enhances the identification accuracy by exploring more independent features sources from the same person.

Further research should be focused on the pre-classification fusion and its potential for performance improvement.

7 References

[1] Soviany S., Puşcoci S., Jurian M.: "A Detector-Discriminant Model for Biometric Security Systems", International Conference on Information Technology and Computer Networks (ITCN 2012), Viena, 10-12 november 2012.

[2] Soviany S., Soviany C., Jurian M.: "A Multimodal Approach for Biometric Authentication with Multiple Classifiers", International Conference on Communications, Information and Network Security (ICCINS 2011), Venetia, 28-30 november 2011

[3] Bhattacharyya D., Das P., Bandyopadhyay S.K., Kim T.: "IRIS Texture Analysis and Feature Extraction for Biometric Pattern Recognition", International Journal of Database Theory and Application, vol. 1, nr. 1, pp. 53-60, december 2008

[4] Theodoridis S., Koutroumbas K.: "Pattern Recognition" 4th edition, Academic Press Elsevier, 2009

[5] Eleyan A., Demirel H.: "Co-occurrence matrix and its statistical features as a new approach for face recognition", Turk J Elec Eng & Comp Sci, Vol.19, Nr.1, 2011

[6] Zucker S.W., Terzopoulos D.: "Finding Structure in Co-Occurence Matrices for Texture Analysis", Computer Graphics and Image Processing nr. 12, 1980

[7] Bino S. V, A. Unnikrishnan and Kannan B.: "Gray level Co-Occurrence Matrices: Generalisation and some new features", International Journal of Computer Science, Engineering and Information Technology (IJCSEIT), Vol.2, No.2, April 2012

[8] Jain A., Nandakumar K., Ross A.: Score Normalization in multimodal biometric systems, Pattern Recognition, The Journal of the Pattern Recognition Society, 38 (2005)

[9] Zhang David, Song Fengxi, Xu Yong, Liang Zhizhen: "Advanced Pattern Recognition Technologies with Applications to Biometrics", Medical Information Science Reference, IGI Global, 2009

[10] Devroye L., Gyorfy L., Lugosi G.: "A Probabilistic Theory of Pattern Recognition", Springer, 1997

[11] PerClass Training Course: Machine Learning for R&D Specialists, Delft, Netherlands

[12] Borman S.: "The Expectation-Maximization Algorithm. A short Tutorial", 2004

Framework for Next Generation Digital Forensics Models

Mohsen M. Doroodchi[1], **Amjad Ali**[1]
[1]Center for Security Studies, University of Maryland University College, Adelphi, Maryland, USA

Abstract - *Digital Forensics is a fairly new discipline, which due to the heavy overlap with the computer science and information technology is now categorized within the computer science field. On the other hand, the legal side of digital forensics is mainly coming from the traditional forensics procedures and the law. Therefore, the current models are modeling the process of digital investigation to be compliant with law and traditional investigations. In this work, we attempt to examine the forensics as a scientific discipline, in addition to the traditional view, and analyze the past and future trends of its models. Furthermore, key characteristics of a framework for next generation uniform models that are adaptable to computer science discipline are identified.*

Keywords: Digital forensics modeling; Digital forensics framework; Computer/network forensics;

1 Introduction

Digital Forensics is new discipline that involves understanding, recreating, and analyzing previously occurred events to extract court-presentable information. In [12], computer forensic is defined as: “the use of scientifically derived and proven methods toward the preservation, collection, validation, identification, analysis, interpretation, documentation, and presentation of digital evidence derived from digital sources for the purpose of facilitation or furthering the reconstruction of events found to be criminal, or helping to anticipate unauthorized actions shown to be disruptive to planned operations”. However, as a scientific discipline, digital forensics is still in developing stages lacking pedagogical models [1]. There is a need for rigorous and comprehensive model of forensics [9].

Supposedly, digital forensics should be driven by computer science theory in combination with law to provide evidence in the court of law. However, one of the immediate consequences of strong scientific support is standardization which digital forensics still lacks [10].

2 Digital Forensics Models overview

Many digital forensics models have been proposed and [13] provides a good overview of earlier versions of them. In another work by Carrier and Spafford, digital investigation analysis techniques are categorized based on something beyond investigator’s prior experiences and subjective preferences [18]. The notion of computer history, which is the sequence of states and events that have happened in a given time period, is used to categorize the analysis techniques. In this work, we examine some of the highlights of the digital forensics models.

Among the early models of digital forensics, the abstract digital forensics model provides a scientific approach to modeling [10]. It explores the development of the digital forensics process as an abstract model and not based on a particular technique designed for a particular digital resource. This model proposes nine steps for analysis as identification, preparation, approach strategy, preservation, collection, examination, analysis, presentation, and returning evidence. This model tracks the traditional forensic evidence collection strategy as practiced by law enforcement. One of the challenges of digital forensics has always been dealing with large data. The obvious solution is data reduction during investigation. In existing theory for locating a reduced set of data from a much larger data set, based on a search query, and to what extent they are appropriate for use in computer forensics, is addressed and a new method is proposed by focusing on areas of the data set where matches to a search query exist [11].

In [14], a model is proposed based on the theory that a computer is itself a crime scene, called the digital crime scene, and more than simply an object of physical evidence. Computers are analyzed in a manner similar to a body to identify additional pieces of evidence and the sequence of events that occurred inside of it. The model is called Integrated Digital Investigation Process and is based on the physical investigation environment to add credibility to the digital evidence analysis, which is challenged more than physical evidence in court. There are seventeen phases in this model which are organized into five groups of phases as readiness, deployment, physical crime scene investigation, digital crime scene investigation and review phases. Carrier later outlined the layers of abstraction in [15] addressing the digital forensics analysis from a scientific point of view and could be a legal requirement in the future. The objective was to approach the digital forensic tools produce results that have been successfully used in prosecutions, but lack designs that were created with forensic science needs. One problem in digital forensics is that acquired data is typically at a very low level in a raw format. Therefore, the data needs to be interpreted by the tool the level that is expected. This problem is known as Complexity Problem [15], and is solved by using tools to translate raw data through one or more layers of abstraction until it can be understood. For example, consider the contents of a directory from a file system image. Without proper tools and just by using the image, it is very hard to visualize the directory structure. In other words, the visual display of directory represents a layer of abstraction in the file system. Examples of non-file system layers of abstraction include ASCII codes, HTML files, Windows Registry, network packets, and source code. Therefore, each abstraction layer can be described as a function of inputs and outputs and a translation rule set. The rule set describes how the input data should be processed, and in many cases is a design specification of the desired object. The outputs of each layer are the data derived from the input data and a margin of error in two forms of Tool Implementation Error and Abstraction Error. It is predicted in [15] that as investigators use data reduction techniques to manage the increasing number of logs, network packets, and files, these "lossy" layers will introduce more errors into the final output and therefore must be clearly understood and documented.

In another work, the notion of "digital event" was introduced into the digital forensics based on the phases that are documented for investigating physical crime scenes [16]. Event is defined as an occurrence that changes the state of one or more digital objects. This event-based framework develops hypotheses by collecting objects that may have played a role in an event that was related to the incident.

The application of digital forensics methods into intrusion detection and network forensics was the start of network forensics in early 2000's. Later, National Institute of Standards and Technology (NIST) published a Guide to Integrating Forensics into Incident Response [17] in order to provide a more uniform framework for digital investigation.

3 Network Forensics

Network forensics evolved in response to the exponential growth of network intrusions to discover and attribute the source of attacks targeting the infrastructures. Network forensics is defined in [19], as monitoring network traffic to determine any anomalous traffic and ascertain whether it indicates any attack in that case will require further analysis. Network forensics investigator has to track back the attackers and provides sufficient evidence for persecutors. In other words, the investigator's goal is to start investigation from victim's system and network back to the source of attack in case of a network attack. Wei provided a conceptual model of network forensics system from six different perspectives as principle perspective, function perspective, architecture perspective, data objective perspective, timer perspective, and techniques perspective to formalize the network forensics procedure [4].

The network forensics frameworks are categorized into distributed systems-based, soft computing-based, honeypot-based, attack graph-based, formal method-based, and aggregation-based frameworks [19]. Several research challenges are listed in [19] for the different phases of network forensics among which perhaps the analysis and investigation are more critical. To analyze the available network data and arrive at a conclusion that meets the admissibility criteria in a court of law is a major challenge.

A logic-based approach is proposed in [3] for digital investigation of security incidents and its high level-specification language. The logic is used to prove the existence or non-existence of potential attack scenarios which, if executed on the investigated system, would produce the different forms of specified evidence.

Pilli, et. al., proposed a generic framework for network forensic analysis. What makes this model generic is the fact that it aggregates many of the phases available in previous digital investigation frameworks but builds on those phases which are specific to network forensics [5].

In [9], a list of several characteristics that a good network forensics tool should provide are listed such as comprehensive logging and capable of logging any level of abstraction, possession of automated metrics for recording and being able to define the boundary values for data capture, ability to record both before and after conditions of an event (cause and effect), the ability to model multi-stage attacks, and relating logged data to actual event.

The work presented in [6] is an attempt to address the processing of large amount of data using growing hierarchical self-organising maps (GHSOM) which is a machine learning algorithm applied to digital forensics. GHSOM is clustering data from network monitoring tools and subsequent visualization of network traffic is provided using different visualization techniques which is proven to be helpful for digital forensics investigator.

Contrary to the reviewed work above which attempted to provide comprehensive models, there are some models which particularly focus on certain techniques. For example, in [20], network forensics procedure was proposed within the framework of Intrusion Detection Systems (IDS). Even though this method seems to be very logical, it suffers from several difficulties such as the way IDS performing the task and collect the data based on the security policy which may not be totally inline with the requirements of collecting preserving forensic evidence. Another problem is in the way that IDS manages its information which is different from forensics systems related to chain of custody.

4 Ontology-based Forensics

In an attempt to reduce the theory-practice gap in digital forensics, ontological guidelines for digital forensics procedure are addressed in [1]. In this part, we first overview the ontology followed by ontology-based forensics systems and the future trend.

Ontology is a formal definition of concepts in a specific domain or area of knowledge. Therefore, Ontologies are used to define terms and relations among them. "Ontology is a term borrowed from philosophy that refers to the science of describing the kinds of entities in the world and how they are related [25]". Classes are of most importance in Ontologies, since they describe concepts in a specified domain. Class can have subclasses that represent concepts that are more specific than the super class [22]. In other words, Ontology is a specification of conceptualization. A conceptualization is an abstract, simplified view of the world that we wish to represent for some purpose. Every knowledge base, knowledge-based system, or knowledge level agent is committed to some conceptualization, explicitly or implicitly [23].

Ontology consists of a hierarchical description of important classes (or concepts) in a particular domain, along with the description of the properties (of the instances) of each concept. Web content is then annotated by relying on the concepts defined in specific domain ontology.

It is necessary to mention that complexity in knowledge presentation and definition will affect the ability to make trustful deductions in any case. So there should be a logical balance between the chosen ontology's ability to define structures and its ability to establish correct results in related domain.

Since digital forensics procedures are very complex and require simultaneous consideration of multiple factors, ontology-based forensics seems to be a good candidate for modeling such complexity. For example, in [21] for cyber-crime investigation, several factors are listed such as cyber-crime classification, collection of evidence in cyber space, and the applications of law to cyber-crime and need to be integrated within the cyber-crime case. For this purpose, the authors proposed a cyber forensics domain ontology for cyber-crime investigation that included several classes and subclasses such as cyber-crime, cyber case, criminal, cyber type, law, evidence, and etc. [21]. Each main class such as evidence class includes subclasses such as evidence-type, collection, etc. This ontology is used for data mining of cybercrimes to provide comprehensive objective information during the forensics investigation.

In another approach, the ontology classes are selected based on the four key elements of ubiquitous computing (UC), identification, location, sensing, and connectivity. Each of them then is identified by several main attributes or subclasses. For example, identification includes typically MAC address, IP address, email account, IM account, SIM card, and operating system [1].

Perhaps the DIALOG framework [7] would be the best combination of the above systems. According to this framework, the crime case ontology is the main ontology for description of cases which can be organized in a variety of ways. It specifies the crime cases into more specific ones such as Theft Case, Violent Case, Sexual Crime Case, Cyber Crime Case, and Non-Cyber Crime Case. Moreover, it drives the ontology of information, information location, and other ontologies. As an example, the Windows Registry is modeled in this work [7].

In an interesting work by Brinson, et. al., the ontology of cyber forensics discipline is driven. The model includes five layers hierarchical structure with the resulting final layer being specified areas for certifying and specializing [24]. The main two classes are technology and profession. The technology class includes the general abstract subclasses with the particular instances of each. For example, under software and operating system, two main subclasses of proprietary and open source are listed followed by different Windows OS's as well as variety of Linux blends. This part will be used in our proposed framework.

In a fairly recent work by Hoss and Carver [25], the authors proposed a method by combining ontologies and model weaving. In this interactive approach, users input forensic knowledge, query that knowledge, produce reports, and interconnect with existing forensic tools to upload data and/or perform further analysis. By applying ontological representation and reasoning combined with hypothesis testing, the forensic data and the search space could be narrowed.

In another recent work by Kota [26], ontology with dynamic instantiation was used for forensic analysis of emails. By limiting the domain of knowledge to emails, the author was able to generate some useful results and some domain specific questions related to email forensics have been successfully answered.

5 Framework for next-generation model

Digital technology is moving toward cloud-based and service-oriented architecture (SOA). It is obvious that digital forensics model should also be flexible to adapt to such trends. The first step perhaps is to make appropriate changes in dealing with evidence in a highly distributed environment. Developing a rigorous and uniform digital forensics model in such situations should be guided on each of the major components such as international, national, legislation, culture, and by the nature of each organization (e.g., by concrete procedural coverage of privacy issues between employer and employees) [2]. The proposed framework for next generation uniform digital forensics model should include both requirements and guidelines. The requirements should be carried out on two levels of security services and security mechanisms [2]. The model should start from services and maps into mechanisms. For example, access control as a security service level can be mapped as Access Control List (ACL). Therefore, the authors propose that increasing awareness and understanding of digital forensics in the service-oriented architecture (SOA) environment are essential for developing more rigorous and uniform digital forensics model.

The new framework should be adaptable to such technical changes that are happening around the world. It seems that with that massive data and cloud-based applications, the natural trend will be toward ontology-based and service-oriented digital forensics models. Such model obviously would be able to perform uniformly on local vs. cloud-based systems for computer and network forensics purposes.

Our proposed model is based on ontology of conceptual abstraction discussed in [8]. It also incorporates the ontology of current computer technology similar to the one driven in [24] to provide the ontological relationships between these classes.

The conceptual abstraction of [8] is a set of processes as a vector with two elements. The first vector element is techniques/methods/approaches/systems /tools and the second one is the legal principles which means that the digital forensics (and in [8] network forensics) includes a combination of techniques, methods, approaches, systems, and tools as well as particular legal principles and procedures. This abstraction can be used to drive the ontology of such fundamental components (i.e. techniques, methods, approaches, systems, and tools) and layout their interactions together as well as their corresponding legal principles. For example, the legal principles related to data are data originality, data integrity, and data continuity. When this ontology is combined with the ontology of current and available computer and communication technology provides the main framework which includes all the elements of digital forensics.

To summarize this model, we can list the following steps:

- Drive the environment's technology ontology using the model of [24]

- Drive the conceptual abstraction of such environment similar to [8]

- Combine the two ontologies to drive the overall ontology including the interaction between the technological components and the conceptual abstraction of the environment.

Similar to [25] and [26] an interactive model is used to dynamically instantiate the ontologies. The interactions are very similar to ontology query and response of [26] with the major difference of the capability of working with the entire evidence domain.

6 Future Works

A proposal of a novel model for digital forensics is given in this work. The main challenge is to develop practical tools for more efficient digital forensics analysis. For this purpose, a simple network of several client and servers running different applications and services in live mode is proposed to be built. Different standard digital crime cases will be planted. The ontology of such environment will be driven both for the abstract layers as well as the technologies used. The overall ontology will be used to find the possible criminal acts.

7 Conclusions

This work presents an overview of digital forensics models and concludes a novel framework for the future. The proposed model incorporates certain features of the past models to provide a new framework. In particular, the ontology of current computer technology in addition to abstraction layers of forensics science used to provide the structure of this model.

8 References

[1] Hai-Cheng Chu, Der-Jiunn Deng, Han-Chieh Chao, An Ontology-driven Model for Digital Forensics Investigations of Computer Incidents under the Ubiquitous Computing Environments, Wireless Personal Communications, Jan 2011, Vol. 56, Issue 1, p. 5-19.

[2] Denis Trček,; Habtamu Abie, Åsmund Skomedal, Iztok Starc, Advanced Framework for Digital Forensic Technologies and Procedures, Journal of Forensic Sciences (Blackwell Publishing Limited), Nov 2010, Vol. 55 Issue 6, p. 1471-1480.

[3] Slim Rekhis , Noureddine Boudriga, Logic-based approach for digital forensic investigation in communication Networks Computers & Security, Vol. 30, Issues 6–7, 2011, p.376–396.

[4] Ren Wei, On A Network Forensics Model For Infor mation Security, On a network forensics model for information security. In: Proceedings of the third international conference on information systems technology and its applications (ISTA 2004), June 15–17, 2004, Utah, p. 229–234.

[5] M. Kumar,M Hanumanthappa, T V Suresh Kumar, Network Intrusion Forensic Analysis Using Intrusion Detection System. Int. J. Comp. Tech. Appl., Vol 2, Issue 3, p. 612-618.

[6] E.J. Palomo, J. North, D. Elizondo, R.M. Luque, T. Watson, Application of growing hierarchical SOM for visualisation of network forensics traffic data, Neural Networks, Vol. 32, August 2012, p. 275-284 .

[7] D. Kahvedzic, T. Kechadi, DIALOG: A framework for modeling, analysis and reuse of digital forensic knowledge. Digital Investigation, 6, 2009.

[8] Ren Wei, Modeling Network Forensics Behavior, Journal of Digital Forensic Practice, Mar2006, Vol. 1 Issue 1.

[9] Sean Peisert, Matt Bishop, Sidney Karin, Keith Marzullo. Toward Models for Forensic Analysis. SADFE 2007. Second International Workshop on, 2007.

[10] M. Reith, C. Carr, G. Gunsch, An Examination of Digital Forensic Models. International Journal of Digital Evidence Fall 2002, Vol. 1 (3).

[11] B. Mangnes, The use of levenshtein distance in computer forensics. MS thesis, Gjovik University College. 2005.

[12] G. Palmer. A road map for digital forensic research. Report from the First DigitalForensic Research Workshop (DFRWS), Technical Report, November 2001.

[13] Mark M. Pollitt, An Ad Hoc Review of Digital Forensic Models, Proceedings of the 2nd International Workshop on Systematic Approaches to Digital Forensic Engineering (SADFE'07).

[14] B. Carrier and E. Spafford, Getting Physical with the Digital Investigation Process, International Journal of Digital Evidence Fall 2003, Vol. 2, Issue 2.

[15] B. Carrier, "Defining Digital Forensic Examination and Analysis Tools Using Abstraction Layers", International Journal of Digital Evidence Winter 2003, Vol. 1, Issue 4.

[16] B. Carrier and E. Spafford, "An Event-based Digital Forensic Investigation Framework", DFRWS 2004, Baltimore, MD.

[17] Kent, K., Chevalier, S., Grance, T. and Dang, H. " Guide to Integrating Forensics into Incident Response", Special Publication 800-86, Computer Security Division Information Technology Laboratory, National Institute of Standards and Technology, Gaithersburg, MD, 2006.

[18] B. Carrier, E. H. Spafford, Categories of digital investigation analysis techniques based on the computer history model. Digital Investigation Journal August 2006.

[19] E.S. Pilli, R.C. Joshi, R. Niyogi, Network forensic frameworks: Survey and research challenges, Digital Investigation. 7, 2010, p. 14 – 27.

[20] Ontology. Available at http://semanticweb.org/wiki/Ontology.

[21] H. Park, S-H Cho, and H-C Kwon, Cyber forensics Ontology for cyber criminal investigation. e-Forensics, Adelide, Au, 2009. LNICST 8.

[22] Natalya F. Noy, Deborah L. McGuinness, A Guide to Creating Your First Ontology, Stanford University,2001.

[23] Web Ontologies. http://www.freebase.com/view/user/narphorium/web_ontology

[24] Ashley Brinson, Abigail Robinson, Marcus Rogers, A cyber forensics ontology Creating a new appraoch to studying cyber forensics, Digital Investigation, 2006.

[25] Allyson M. Hoss and Doris L. Carver, Weaving Ontologies to Support Digital Forensic Analysis. IEEE Int'l conf. on Intelligence and Security Informatics, 2009. ISI '09.

[26] Venkata Krishna Kota, An Ontological Approach for Digital Evidence Search, International Journal of Scientific and Research Publications, Vol 2 (12), 2012.

SESSION

COMPUTER SECURITY I

Chair(s)

Dr. Cristina Soviany

Distributed Snort Network Intrusion Detection System with Load Balancing Approach

Wu Yuan, Jeff Tan, Phu Dung Le
Faculty of Information Technology
Monash University
Melbourne, Australia
{Tennyson.Yuan, Jeff.Tan, Phu.Dung.Le}@monash.edu

Abstract—**As we enjoy the conveniences that the Internet or computer networks have brought to us, the problems are getting larger, especially network security problems. A Network Intrusion Detection System (NIDS) is one of the critical components in a network nowadays. It can monitor and analyze activities of network users, and then uses knowledge of attack patterns to identify and prevent such attacks. It can minimize damages that will be caused by attacks. This paper uses Snort, which is one of the most commonly used NIDS in industry. The paper presents an approach of Distributed Snort NIDS, which can coordinate multiple sensors across the Local Area Network to optimize usage of computational resources. The approach implements a Balance Control System (BCS) for each subnet, which monitors CPU usage of a particular Snort NIDS and, when the Snort IDS's CPU usage is too high, delegates analysis work to lightly loaded IDS host.**

Keywords-Network Security; Network Intrusion Detection System; Snort; IDS; Distributed Snort NIDS; Load Balancing.

I. INTRODUCTION

According to FBI's Internet Crime Complaint Centre 2009 annual report that financial loss has doubled in 2009 compared with 2008 [5]. As importance of information security has increased significantly during recent years, the term of Intrusion Detection (ID) has become more and more important in current environment of computer and network systems. An Intrusion Detection System (IDS) is a piece of software program, which is able to monitor malicious activities or policy violations in a specific network or a computer system, and give particular reactions or alerts based on pre-set rules or knowledge database [18]. There are three major types of IDS: Network intrusion detection system (NIDS), Host-based intrusion detection system (HIDS) and Stack-based intrusion detection system (SIDS) [18]. In this paper, Network intrusion detection system is the one, which will be discussed. According to Ptacek and Newsham [17], the Network Intrusion Detection System is a particular type of IDS, which is used to monitor activities in network traffic and large numbers of hosts. Normally, the NIDS is connected to a network hub, switch or tap for gaining network access. The system also includes multiple sensors across the whole network to collect information. The sensors are often located in a Demilitarized Zone (DMZ) or at network borders. Snort is one good example of NIDS. According to Sourcefire [20], Snort is one of the most commonly used network intrusion detection system in industry, which is provided lots of advantages, such as, open source, lightweight and rule-based.

Currently, main issue we are facing is the system needs to spend more time to analyze each traffic pattern, because a database of knowledge of attacks patterns is getting obviously larger. Therefore, attackers may gain more time to perform some unauthorized or illegal activities in some components of a network. The ideal of Distributed Intrusion Detection Systems (DIDS) has been mainly used to increase efficiency of the NIDS, which distributes the IDS into different network segments to analyze and monitor network traffics in that specific network segment, or distribute the analysis work to a number of IDSs to increase the speed of traffic analysis. In this paper, we proposed a distributed Snort NIDS with load balancing mechanism, which can improve the performance of Snort NIDS to reduce the risks that may be brought by packets dropping in large network traffic environment.

The rest parts of this paper are organized as follow. Section 2 provides an overview of Snort NIDS technology. Then, an overview of existing distributed IDS approaches are discussed in Section 3. In Section 4, our proposed Distributed Snort NIDS (DSNIDS) model with load balancing mechanism is introduced. The evaluation and testing of our approach are presented in the following section (Section 5).

II. AN OVERVIEW OF SNORT NIDS

Snort NIDS is one of the most widely used and the most famous Network Intrusion Detection System (NIDS) [20][3]. It is an open-source application, which provides packet sniffing, packet logging, and intrusion detection, which search and scan each network packet's contents to match pre-set intrusion rules. Another advantage of Snort is that it is a lightweight NIDS, because it has a small footprint, and it has less system resources requirement compare with a normal NIDS. It uses rules to detect any anomalous behavior and malicious activities in a network. If any network packet breaches the intrusion rules, an alert will be triggered. The Snort NIDS is able to perform real-time packet logging and traffic analysis on Internet Protocol (IP) network by applying content searching and content matching. As mentioned above, the IDS can be configured to run in three modes, namely, sniffer mode, packet logger mode, and network intrusion detection mode [3]. According to Baker and Esler [3], the Sniffer mode allows the IDS to capture packets in the network, and display them on the console, and the Packet logger mode allows the IDS to log the packets to the disk. The network intrusion detection mode allows the IDS to analyze the network traffic against user pre-defined rules, and to perform actions that has defined in the rules. In our research, we are trying to improve the performance when the Snort NIDS is running at network intrusion detection mode.

A. Snort System architecture

Snort NIDS's architecture contains four main components:

- Sniffer: The sniffer is used to eavesdrop network traffic, which can be used in Network analysis and troubleshooting, performance analysis and benchmarking, and eavesdropping [3].
- Preprocessor: Pre-processor in the Snort NIDS applies raw network packets that are captured by the sniffer.
- Detection Engine: After the raw packets processed by all enabled pre-processors process packets, they will then be handled by detection engine. The detection engine analysis those packets against a set of rules, if any particular rule matches the payload or data of a packet, then the packet will be sent to alert processor [3].
- Alerting and Logging Component: alerting and logging component can save the alerts from the detection engine to a log file, or be sent to SNMP traps. An SQL database can be linked also [3].

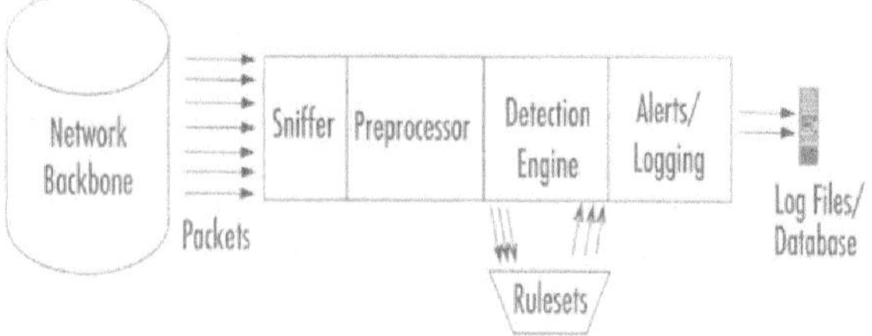

Figure 2.1 Snort NIDS architecture [3]

In the basic concept, the Snort NIDS is a packet sniffier, and it is designed to capture network packets, and a pre-processor will process them, and then these captured packets will be checked against a set of rules by a detection engine [3]. The figure above (Figure 2.1) shows a basic view of the Snort NIDS's architecture.

III. AN OVERVIEW OF DISTRIBUTED NIDS APPROACHES

Due to large network traffic on a broadcast LAN segment, and longer time consuming on packet analyzing in non-distributed IDS model, the IDS may drops large numbers of network packets, which gives a big opportunities for the anomalous behavior to be launched. Therefore, the non-distributed or centralized IDS model cannot satisfy current network and security environments. Distributing a number of Intrusion Detection Systems across the network is a way to significantly increase the capability of the intrusion detection system. In this section, two main Distributed Intrusion Detection approaches are discussed.

A. Early Prototype of DIDS

The concept and architecture of a Distributed Intrusion Detection Systems was created in 1991 at University of California by Snapp et al. [19]. In his DIDS architecture, the system contains three main components, DIDS director, host monitor and LAN monitor. The distributed monitors collect information, and send them to a centralized DIDS director to analyze. The host monitor is a kind of program, which is installed in each host computer. The monitor will analyze audit data in the host computer, and decide whether to forward the audit data to an expert system or the DIDS director to do further evaluation and analysis or not. Normally, critical information about the host computer is always sent to the centralized expert system or the DIDS director to evaluate. The LAN monitor is another component of this DIDS architecture. It is in charge of analyzing network traffic in one specific LAN segment. It can monitor network users' activities, network connection and the volume of the traffic. Same as host monitor, the LAN monitor also can identify and analyze some certain events, and all the security information are sent to the centralized expert system for further analysis. Finally, the last component of the DIDS architecture is the expert system, which is similar to an intrusion detection system like NSM, and SNORT. It is a rule-based system, and written in prolog. The expert system uses rules that are generated by Intrusion Detection Model (IDM), which describes the pattern of an intrusion from the audit data that are collected by the host monitors and the LAN monitors. There are six different levels in IDM, they are data level, event level, subject level, context level, threat level and security level, and each of those levels represents a performance of transformation from audit records.

Snapp et al. [19] develops an early prototype of a Distributed Intrusion Detection Systems. As the DIDS architecture distributed the monitors across the entire network, it can collect network information from different sources, and all those information is processed in the centralized expert system to prevent doorknob attack. However, As nowadays the number of rules is getting much larger, the system needs to spend much more time to analyze each traffic packet, and the prototype only distributes monitors across the network, and only uses one centralized expert system to analyze all information; therefore the overloaded IDS will drop some analysis and detection regularly, due to insufficient memory resources. It gives more chance to an attack to performance some damage activities [25].

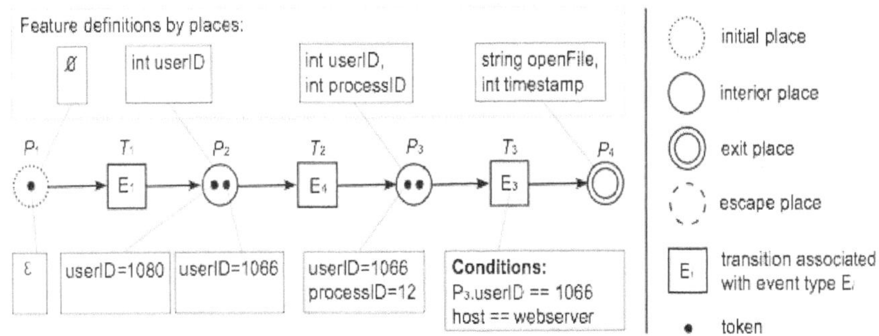

Figure 3.1 EDL Signature Example [25]

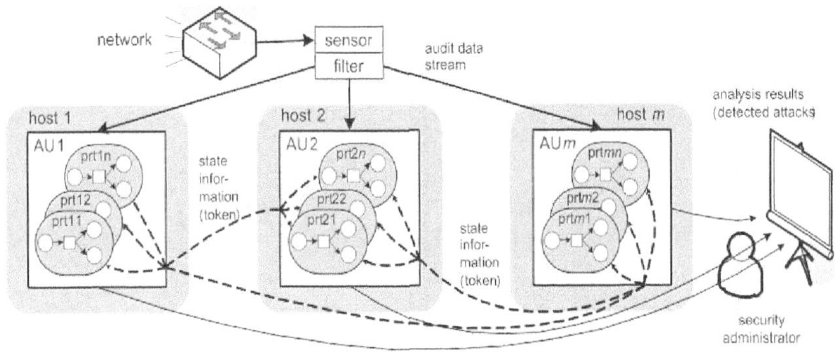

Figure 3.2 example of DIDS concept [25]

B. DIDS with Multi Step Signatures

The recent research by Vogel and Schmerl [25] has solved this problem, and significantly increased efficiency of a Distributed Intrusion Detection Systems by applying Multi Step Signatures, and arranging those signatures to different distributed IDSs. The approach uses Event Description Language (EDL) to define a multi-step signature. Figure 3.1 shows an example of an EDL signature; it consists of four places and three transitions. The place indicates the system states of an attack, there are four types of places: initial, interior, escape and exit. The transition represents changes of a state that are triggered by audit events.

In this approach, a sensor or monitor logs audit events, and then separate them into different event types. The signature will also be separate into some small parts of signatures, and all those small parts are then assigned to different analysis unit, which is based on availability of analysis units. A filter is in charge of discarding those audit data that is not relevant to event types to minimize the communication, and transfers those relevant audit data to certain distributed analysis units. The Figure 3.2 shows an example of this concept.

The research shows that this approach of Distributed Intrusion Detection Systems is 60 % faster than the centralized Intrusion Detection System. However, the research also indicates that analysis distribution is not well balanced.

IV. The Proposed Distributed Snort NIDS Model

Snort is the most famous and widely used Network Intrusion Detection System; however, when it faces large network traffic, it may drops amount of network packets depend on hardware configuration that may increase false positive rate on attacking detection. The idea of the DSNIDS model is to coordinate all distributed Snort NIDS sensors together, and optimizes all available computation resources. In this section, we present the design of our DSIDS approach from the network architecture, the load balancing mechanism, and the internal communication methods.

A. Network Architecture

The Network architecture of our Distributed Snort NIDS approach is based on one of Baker's basic Snort NIDS network architectures, which installs one Snort NIDS for each component or subnet of the network. The details of Baker's Snort NIDS network architectures are discussed in the chapter three. We design two network architectures for our approach, one of them has two Snort NIDS sensors, one for each sub-network, and another one has one Snort NIDS sensor and one Balancing Control System (BCS) for each sub-network. The choice between these two network architectures depends on budget for hardware configuration.

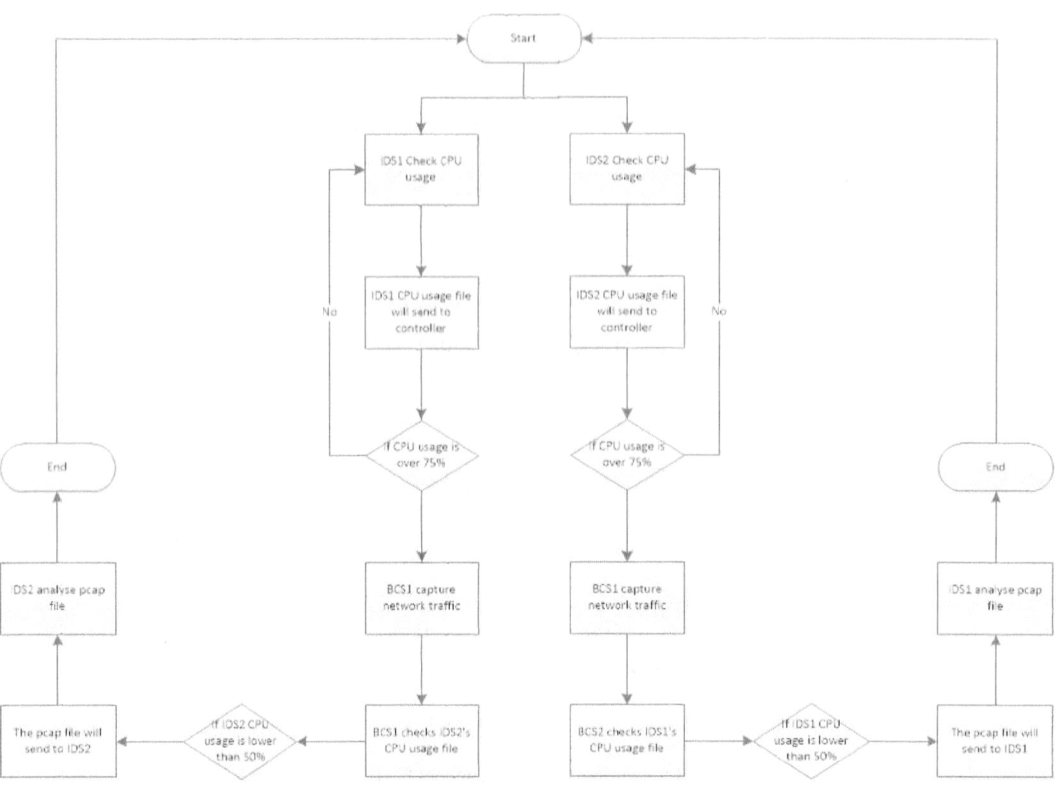

Figure 4.1 Flow chat of Load Balancing mechanism

B. Load Balancing Design

The Figure 4.1 illustrates the program processing flow of the mechanism. The program runs on each Snort NIDS sensor, and each BCS. A detailed list of processes of our mechanism is provided below:

1) Each Snort NIDS runs a program, which checks CPU usage of the IDS, and save it to a file.
2) The CPU usage file is then sent to the controller.
3) The BCS captures network traffic into pcap file (the BCS only capture 10 seconds of network traffic), when the CPU usage of its home network IDS sensor is over 75%.
4) The BCS runs a program, which will get the both IDS sensors' CPU usage files, and each BCS checks the CPU usage of its home network IDS sensor, if the usage is over 75%, and any of the IDS sensors in the network is below 50%. The BCS sends the pcap file to the idle Snort NIDS to analyze.
5) This process will restart every 10 seconds.

C. Internal Communication methods

From the Figure 4.2, we designed this private network to connect each Snort NIDS, each BCS, and a controller together, because exchanging CPU usage data and pcap files may use large amount of the network bandwidth, and it may affect performance of the packets capture. By using private network to connect these devices, data can be exchanged faster and more secure without too much security consideration.

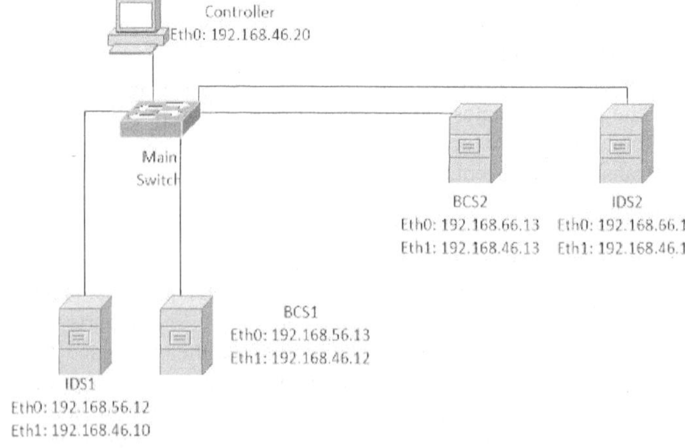

Figure 4.2 Load Balancing Design

V. EVALUATION OF DSNIDS APPROACH

This chapter presents the details of tests that we have done on the DSIDS approach. These tests illustrate performance improvement and benefits of our DSIDS approach with load balancing.

A. Traditional DSNIDS

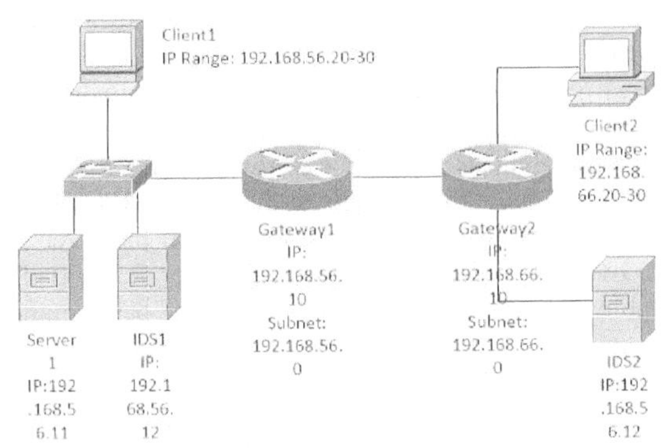

Figure 5.1 Traditional DSNIDS

Figure 5.1 shows the testing network architecture of the traditional DSIDS. Testing scenario is when there is a large volume of network traffic in 192.168.56.0 subnet, at same time client 2 uses FTP to transfer data to server 1 anonymously, which will cause IDS1 generates FTP anonymous user login attempt alert.

Test Details:

- Time: 5 mins.
- Total Number of FTP login attempted: 10 times
- Client 1 uses hping to generate large amoung of zero size UDP packets to keep IDS1 busy.

Test Results:

With large network traffic				
Test No.	Test 1	Test 2	Test 3	Test 4
No. of attacks detected	0	0	1	0
Without other network traffic				
Test No.	Test 1	Test 2	Test3	Test4
No. of attacks detected	10	10	10	9

Table 5.1 Traditional DSIDS

We performed eight times tests; four of them are with large network traffic. The testing result is shown in Table 5.1, and from the result we can see that when the network with large number of traffic, the Snort NIDS drops large amount of packets. This is caused by the size of the packets queue is over the buffer size of the IDS. During the test, we also found out that the IDS1's CPU usage reached 100% when the client 1 launched UDP flooding. However, the IDS2 still have plenty of resources are available. As we know, NIDS is hardware-sensitive, the testing results above is affected by limited resources, because we are running it as numbers of virtual machines.

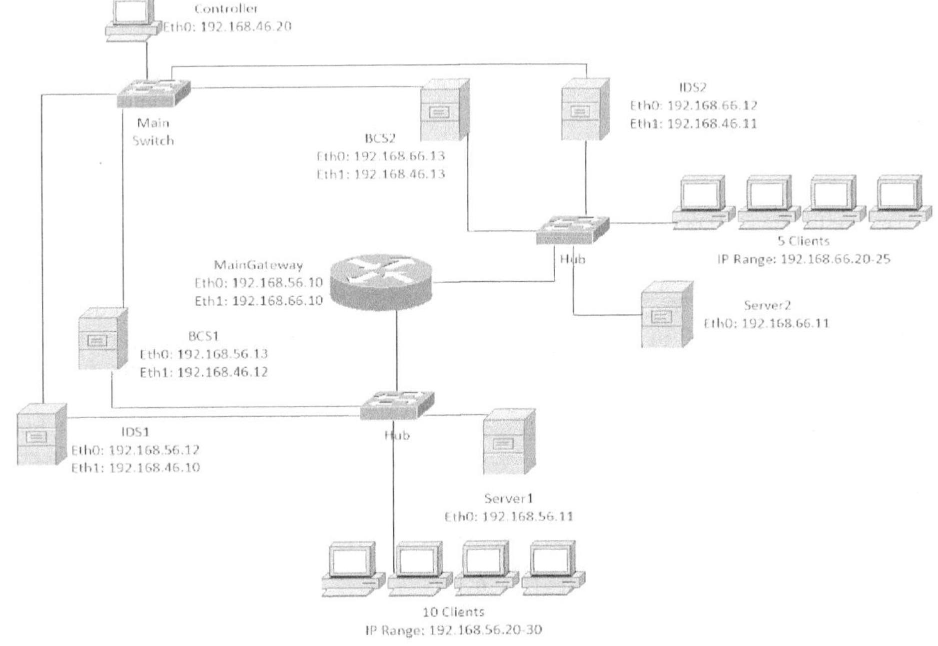

Figure 5.2 DSIDS Network Architecture with two BCS

B. The DSIDS Approach with Load Balancing

Our DSIDS approach with load balancing mechanism makes sure computation recourses are coordinated together. To achieve that, we designed an assistant system, namely BCS, which is used to capture the network traffics in one particular subnet when the IDS is busy, and then the network capture file sends to another free IDS to analyse. To test performance of our DSIDS approach, we create two testing environments. The first test uses our virtual network environment to test the performance of attacking detection in a small size LAN. The second test uses powerful cluster to run multiple snort sensors, and we give each of them a network capture file (each sensor gets different pcap file with different volume of network traffic) to analysis simultaneously. The test two is designed to show the performance of our approach, when there are multiple powerful snort sensors are available.

1) Test One – Small size network

The test one is applied on our virtual network environment to test the performance of attacking detection in a small size LAN (See Figure 5.2). However, due to limited computation resource, we only turned on one client machine for each subnet. The testing environment, and the IDS sensors hardware configuration are kept the same.

Testing Scenario: the client in the 192.168.56.0 subnet launches UDP flooding Denali of Service attack, which generates huge amount of empty UDP packets. At the same time, the client in the 192.168.66.0 subnet uses FTP to send file to server 1 anonymously.

Test Details:

- Time: 1 mins
- Total number of FTP logins: 6 times (Once per 10 seconds)

Test Results:

Testing for the DSIDS approach

	Test 1	Test 2	Test 3
Total Number of UDP packets	260459	254823	307122
Total Number of UDP packets IDS 1 detected	4569	3220	6789
Total Number of UDP packets IDS 2 detected	230971	250123	287962
Total Number of FTP login IDS 1 detected	0	0	0
Total Number of FTP login IDS 2 detected	5	4	6

Table 5.2 the DSIDS approach

From the Table 5.2, we can see that when IDS1 faces large amount of network packets, it drops large amount of network packets, as a result, the IDS 1 cannot detect any FTP anonymous login attempts. However, the BCS capture the network packets in the 192.168.56.0 subnet for 1 min, and store them into a pcap file. The pcap file then send to IDS 2 to analyze. As a result, the IDS 2 can detect almost all attacks.

2) Test Two – Multiple High Power Snort Sensor

The second test uses six nodes (See Table 5.3) in a Campus HPC cluster to run multiple snort sensors, and we give each of them a network capture file (each sensor gets different pcap file with different volume of network traffic) to analyze simultaneously. In this approach, the computational hosts are not exactly sensors: they do not capture packets, but only analyze them. The HPC cluster is a Sun (Oracle) Grid Engine cluster, which has over 3,300 cores over 200 execute nodes, and over 2.5 TB RAM available. Test Two is designed to show the performance of our approach, when there are multiple powerful snort sensors available purely for analysis.

Testing Nodes Details

Hostname	Architecture	No. of Cores	Total Memory
gn116	lx24-amd64	8	15.7G
gn152	lx24-amd64	8	15.7G
gn60	lx24-amd64	2	3.9G
gn62	lx24-amd64	2	3.9G
gn63	lx24-amd64	2	3.9G
gn65	lx24-amd64	2	3.9G

Table 5.3 Testing Nodes Details

Testing Scenario:

- Step one: We used the BCS to capture the network traffic ten times into ten pcap files, and the system listened for 5 mins each time. These pcap files contains different level of traffic volume, and different anomalous activities, such as UDP flooding, ICMP flooding, normal network traffic, large size of ICMP packets, FTP anonymous logins, etc. Then, these ten pcap files were arranged to the six nodes in the cluster, and run 10 Snort analysis jobs simultaneously.
- Step two: We double the numbers of pcap files to 20 by duplicating the pcap files from the step one, and then we assigned 20 Snort jobs to analysis these 20 pcap files simultaneously.
- Step three: We increase the numbers of pcap files to 100 by duplicating the pcap files from the step one, and then we assigned 100 Snort jobs to analysis these 100 pcap files simultaneously.

Testing Results:

- Step One:

Number of Done jobs	10
Number of failed jobs	0
Time Spent for all jobs done	22 mins 17.99 secs
Average job wall time	7 mins 52.45 secs
Maximum job wall time	20 mins 55.05 secs
Minimum job wall time	25.75 secs

Table 5.4 Step One Results

- Step Two:

Number of Done jobs	20
Number of failed jobs	0
Time Spent for all jobs done	23 mins 23.06 secs
Average job wall time	6 mins 21.21 secs
Maximum job wall time	20 mins 47.59 secs
Minimum job wall time	24.14 secs

Table 5.5 Step Two Results

- Step Three:

Number of Done jobs	100
Number of failed jobs	0
Time Spent for all jobs done	45 mins 4.54 secs
Average job wall time	5 mins 12.82 secs
Maximum job wall time	13 mins 11.82 secs
Minimum job wall time	18.86 secs

Table 5.6 Step Three Results

From the testing results above, we can see, the total time spent for six multi-core nodes to run 20 Snort jobs is almost similar to when the six nodes run 10 jobs, and we also can see that the average time spent on each job is shorter than when they run 10 jobs. This is because the jobs are allocated to free cores that can therefore execute the analyses at the same time. Therefore, if the network has multiple Snort machines with powerful multi-core hardware, and assuming they are idle, the BCS in our approach can assign more than one analysis jobs to each machine at same time, and each Snort machine can run these jobs simultaneously to achieve higher performance. From Test three we can see that 100 snort jobs did not run simultaneously, because the total time spent is much larger than maximum job wall time. This is due to insufficient computational resources. However, the Maximum job wall time and minimum job wall time are significantly less than previous tests.

VI. Conclusion

Our research presents an approach of Distributed Snort NIDS, which can coordinate multiple sensors across the Local Area Network to optimize usage of computation resources. However the approach is unable to drop abnormal network packets, and it can only give alerts to the system administrators. Due to the approach uses BCS to duplicate network traffic when a particular IDS's CPU usage is high, which causes some amount of network traffic may be analyzed more than once by multiple Snort NIDS sensors. To extend the research, a filter should be designed and developed to solve some network packets may be analyzed more than once by different Snort NIDS sensors, and improving the performance when facing large amount of traffic flow.

References

[1]. Abramson, D., Bethwaite, B., Enticott, C., Garic, S., Peachey, T., Michailova, A., et al. (2009). Robust Workflows for Science and Engineering. 2nd Workshop on Many-Task Computing on Grids and Supercomputers(MTAGS 2009). Portland.

[2]. Andrzej, G. (1991). Distributed operating systems: the logical design. London: Longman Group.

[3]. Baker, A. R., & Esler, J. (2007). Snort IDS and IPS Toolkit. Burlington: Syngress Publishing, Inc.

[4]. Chakrabarti, S., Chakraborty, M., & Mukhopadhyay, I. (2010). Campus Network Security Study of Snort-based IDS. International Conference and Workshop on Emerging Trends in Technology.

[5]. CyberInsecure.com. (2010, 03 16). Cybercrime Related Losses Doubled In 2009, Financial Losses Totaled 559.7 Million. Retrieved 06 1, 2012 from http://cyberinsecure.com/cybercrime-related-losses-doubled-in-2009-financial-lossestotaled-5597-million/

[6]. Denning, D. (1987). An intrusion-detection model. IEEE Trans. on Soft- ware Engg. , SE (13), 222-232.

[7]. Dineley, D., & Mobley, H. (2009). The Greatest Open Source Software of All Time. Retrieved 06 03, 2012 from InfoWorld, Inc.: http://www.infoworld.com/d/open-source/greatest-open-sourcesoftware-all-time-776

[8]. Dowell, C., & Ramstedt.P. (1990). The COMPUTERWATCH data reduction tool. 13th National Computer Security Conference, (pp. 99-108). Washington, DC.

[9]. Heberlein, L., Dias, G., Levitt, K., Mukherjee, B., Wood, J., & Wolber, D. (1990). A network security monitor. 1990 Symposium on Research in Security and Privacy, (pp. 296–304).

[10]. Hochberg, J. (1993). NADIR: an automated system for detecting network intrusion and misuse. Computers and Security , 12 (3), 235-248.

[11]. Javitz, H., & Valdez, A. (1991). The SRI IDES Statistical Anomaly Detector. 1991 IEEE Symposium on Research in Security and F'rivacy. Oakland.

[12]. Laing, B. (2000). How to guide-implementing a network based intrusion detection system. Reading: Internet Security Systems.

[13]. Ling, J. (2012). Campus Network Security Program Based on Snort Network Security Intrusion Detection System. Advanced Materials Research , 433-440.

[14]. Mukherjee, B., Heberlein, L., & Levitt.K. (1994). Network Intrusion Detection. IEEE Network , 8 (3), 26-41.

[15]. Monash University. (2010, 07 28). About the Monash network. Retrieved 05 30, 2012 from

Monash University: http://www.its.monash.edu.au/staff/networks/about/

[16]. Newman, R. C. (2010). Computer Security: Protecting Digital Resources. Sudbury: Jones and Bartlett Publishers.

[17]. Ptacek, T., & Newsham, T. (1998). Insertion, Evasion, and Denial of Service: Eluding Network Instrusion Detection. Secure Networks, Inc.

[18]. Scarfone, K., & Mell, P. (2007). Guide to Intrusion Detection and Prevention Systems (IDPS) . Gaithersburg: National Institute of Standards and Technology .

[19]. Snapp, S., Brentano, J., Dias, G., & Goan, T. e. (1991). DIDS(Distributed intrusion detection system)– motivation, architecture, and an early prototype. the Fourteenth National Computer Security Conference, (pp. 167–176).

[20]. Sourcefire, Inc. (2011, 12 7). SNORT User Manual. Retrieved 02 29, 2012 from http://www.snort.org/assets/166/snort_manual.pdf

[21]. Sourdis, I., & Pnevmatikatos, D. (2003). Fast, Large-Scale String Match for a 10Gbps Fpga-Based Network Intrusion. FPL , 2003, 880-889.

[22]. Softpanorama. (2012, 11 4). TCP Performance Tuning. Retrieved 10 20, 2012 from Softpanorama: http://www.softpanorama.org/Commercial_linuxes/Performance_tuning/tcp_performance_tuning.shtml

[23]. Tener, W. (1988). AI and 4GL: automated detection and investigation and detection tools. IFIP Security Conference.

[24]. Tener, W. T. (1986). Discovery: An expert system in the commercial data security environment. In IFIP Security Conference.

[25]. Vogel, M., & Schmerl, S. (2011). Efficient Distributed Intrusion Detection applying Multi Step Signatures. 17th GI/ITG Conference on Communication in Distributed Systems, (pp. 188–193).

[26]. Weir, J. (2012, 07 20). Building a Debian\Snort based IDS.

An Integrated Approach to Defence Against Degrading Application-Layer DDoS Attacks

Dusan Stevanovic and Natalija Vlajic
Department of Computer Science and Engineering
York University
Toronto, Canada
dusan@cse.yorku.ca, vlajic@cse.yorku.ca

Abstract—Application layer Distributed Denial of Service (DDoS) attacks are recognized as one of the most damaging attacks on the Internet security today. In our recent work [1], we have shown that *unsupervised machine learning* can be effectively utilized in the process of distinguishing between regular (human) and automated (web/botnet crawler) visitors to a web site. We have also shown that with a slightly higher level of sophistication in the design of some web/botnet crawlers, their detection could become particularly challenging, requiring additional vigilance and investigation on the part of the site's defense team. In this paper, we demonstrate an application of time series analysis in order to perform a further fine-tuned detection of suspicious visitors to a web site. Additionally, we propose a novel application-layer DDoS detection system that integrates the use of our combined unsupervised learning and time-domain web-visitor classifier with the use of standardized challenge-response tests. The system is aimed to ensure reliable detection of malicious (web/botnet crawler) visitors to a web site while being minimally intrusive towards regular (human) visitors.

Keywords—system security; distributed denial of service, DDoS detection and prevention, browsing behavior model

I. Introduction

Many of the traditional essential services, such as banking, transportation, medicine, government, education and defence, are increasingly offered by means of Web-based applications. Unfortunately, the inherent vulnerabilities of the Internet architecture provide opportunities for various attacks on the availability of these applications. Distributed Denial-of-Service (DDoS) is an especially potent type of attack on Web availability, capable of severely degrading the response-rate and quality at which Web-based services are offered. Given the scale of their potential implications on both the US industry and government, the FBI has recently identified cyber attacks - including DDoS attacks - as the fastest growing national security threat [2].

The most common way of conducting a DDoS attack is by sending a flood of messages to the target (e.g., a machine hosting a web site) with the aim to interfere with the target's operation, and make it hang, crash, reboot, or do useless work. An emerging and increasingly more prevalent set of DDoS attacks are the so-called application-layer or Layer-7 attacks that mimic a Flash Crowd event. A legitimate Flash Crowd event is a situation where some popular information emerges on a web site (such as a news story or a sports event), and many browsers (i.e., human visitors) attempt to access that information, thus creating a large demand/load on the server. An attacker can easily achieve a "Flash Crowd"-looking effect by performing an excessive number of seemingly legitimate actions on the target web application – such as database queries and transactions. From the logistics point of view, this kind of attack is typically executed by means of cleverly programmed crawlers instructed to perform a semi-random walk through the victim web site links, giving an illusion of a web site traversal conducted by a regular human visitor. Additionally, in order to hide their true identity, these smart DDoS-executing crawlers can resort to using spoofed user agent strings[1]. Since the signatures of such DDoS attacks look very much like a legitimate Flash Crowd event on a website, it is difficult to construct an effective metric for their mitigation, as well as to defend against them. Real-world examples of application-layer DDoS attacks that mimic Flash Crowd are reported in [3] and [4].

Now, the key tasks behind building a successful DDoS detection system that would defend against application-layer DDoS attacks that mimic a Flash Crowd event are: 1) to effectively distinguish between human and machine-generated web/HTTP sessions and, moreover, 2) in the group of machine-generated sessions to effectively distinguish between the sessions corresponding to benign vs. sessions corresponding to malicious crawlers.

Unfortunately, most real-world systems and techniques that are currently used to provide a defense against DDoS attacks are too generic and unsuitable for dealing with application layer DDoS attacks. Namely, on one side of anti-DDoS solution spectrum, there are rule-based and/or anomaly-detection firewalls and intrusion-prevention systems (IPSs). These devices/systems are generally effective in combating simple flood-type and 'off-the-shelf' forms of DDoS attacks. However, when dealing with more subtle and/or advanced

---

[1] A user agent string, part of the HTTP request packet, specifies the hardware/software (i.e., browser, crawler, Smartphone, tablet or others) used by the client to communicate with the server in the client-server communication.

forms of attacks, such as degrading application-layer attacks[2], their main drawbacks are:

a) Most firewalls and IPSs rely on the well-known and publicized attacks signatures in order recognize and defend against DDoS attacks. However, degrading application-layer DDoS attacks tend to be uniquely crafted for one/each particular web-site and thus do not conform to the 'generic' attack signatures. (For a good overview of "How Traditional Firewalls Fail Today's Networks" see a recent report by Dell SonicWall [5].)
b) Another drawback of traditional firewalls and IPSs is that they react with a 'delay' in blocking a malicious user (i.e., stopping a DDoS attack), as they need to be able to observe a user's behavior for a period of time before pronounce the user 'malicious'. In the case of degrading application layer DDoS attacks this delay may be significant.

On the other side of anti-DDoS solution spectrum are techniques that aim to distinguish between (malicious) automated visitors and regular human visitors to a web-site by relying on the so-called challenge-response tests (i.e., numerical and graphical puzzles), such as the well-known CAPTCHA. Although generally effective in accomplishing their task, the main drawbacks of this group of solutions are:

a) They are, often, annoying to human visitors, and therefore are rarely used for the protection of commercial web sites. (In a recent Scientific American article "Time to Kill-Off CAPTCHAs" [6], the author eloquently summarizes the commonly felt negative sentiment about CAPTCHA technology.)
b) They treat all automated crawlers equally – both the benign and malicious ones - by completely blocking their access to a web site.

In this paper, we propose an integrated machine-learning based anti-DDoS solution that aims to combine the best of both above mentioned approaches, while at the same time being effective in defending against application layer DDoS attacks with unique attack signature. Specifically, in Section II of this paper, we provide a general overview of our newly proposed anti-DDoS solution (see Fig. 1). In Section III we outline the main characteristics of the solution's first component – the SOM classifier – which is responsible for performing preliminary classification of visitors to a web site. We also present some of the most relevant experimental results derived using this classifier. (These results have been previously reported in [1].) In Section IV, we discuss the motivation behind employing the second-stage Time-Domain Analyzer, and present some key experimental findings pertaining to this analyzer. We close the paper in Section V by outlining the main directions for our future work.

II. Our Integrated Anti-DDoS System

An outline of our newly proposed multi-stage anti-DDoS system is provided in Fig. 1. The solution comprises an adaptable two-stage anomaly detection system – the first stage consisting of an SOM Classifier (described in more detail in Section III) and the second stage of a Time Domain Analyzer (described in Section IV). The main task of the SOM classifier is to categorize each visitor to a web site into one of the following four groups: human (benign) visitor, well-behaved automated visitor, malicious automated visitor, and unknown visitor. Visitors that exhibit clearly benign behavior (most human and well-behaved automated visitors) are granted uninterrupted access to the site. Visitors that are categorized as malicious crawlers or suspicious unknown visitors are immediately blocked from accessing the site. Finally, for visitors that are categorized as human, but in some aspects of their behavior resemble malicious crawlers, the system performs more detailed time-domain behavior analysis before resorting to the use of a challenge-response test (i.e., CAPTCHA). Clearly, any of these (human but suspiciously behaving) visitors that end up failing the challenge-response test will be denied further access/service.

Note that, in general, our system can be adapted to optimally operate for each particular web-site and its respective visitor population. In the case of some web-sites this may imply that the group of 'unknown visitors' be granted access to the site. For example, if the website being protected is an University website, web admin staff would likely allow benign known or brand new unknown search engine web crawlers to index their website. Alternatively, if the website being protected is an online content management application, with visitors that are exclusively users of the application, a web admin staff will likely chose to block everyone but human visitors since there is no need for search engines crawlers (and therefore public visitors) to index this type of a domain.

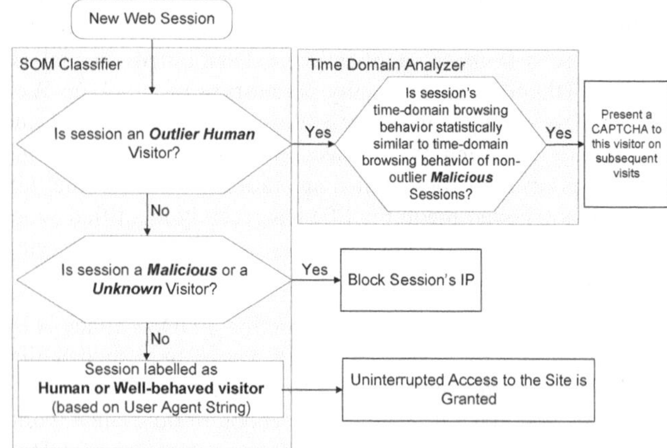

Fig. 1 The workflow of the real-time degrading application-layer anti-DDoS system

[2] In degrading Layer-7 DDoS attacks [23], attacker aims to partially degrade the victim's network response rate from the viewpoint of legitimate victim's clients, while in flooding or disruptive DDoS attacks, attacker aims to completely shot down the victim's network and prevent all legitimate clients from accessing it. Note also that in slow-rate DDoS attacks, attackers employ legitimate-looking network sessions that prevent the victim from detecting the attack. The flood DDoS attacks are much easier to detect since the network becomes completely unresponsive.

The main advantages of our solution presented in Fig. 1 over the existing anti-DDoS solutions are:

1) Unlike the systems that rely solely on the use of challenge-response tests, our solution makes a distinction between malicious and benign automated web visitors, and prevents only the malicious automated users from accessing a web site.
2) Through a customized machine-learning-based approach, the anomaly-detection component of our anti-DDoS system is able to identify (i.e., derive) attack signatures that are finely tuned to each particular web site. (I.e., the SOM network can be optimally trained for each particular web-site and its visitor population.) As a results, our system is far superior in dealing with degrading application-level DDoS attacks relative to the existing off-the-shelf firewalls and intrusion-prevention systems.
3) Our system resorts to the use of challenge-response tests only when there is a high certainty that a particular visitor to the site is malicious. Accordingly, the likelihood that a (benign) human user be exposed to (i.e., annoyed by) a challenge-response test is minimized.

III. SOM Web-Visitor Classifier

A. SOM Overview

The first stage of our anti-DDoS system deploys an unsupervised machine learning (i.e., neural network) classifier – the Self-Organizing Maps (SOM) [7]. The SOM algorithm was chosen mainly for the following reasons:

a) Its *topology preservation* ability, which implies that input samples that are close to each other in an n-dimensional space will also be close to each other in a 2D SOM map.
b) Its ability to produce natural clustering, i.e. clustering that is robust to statistical anomalies. This type of clustering is more effective in providing unbiased look and understanding of the underlying data set and, also, it is less sensitive to the presence of sporadic data outliers (i.e. presence of sporadically alterable features found in our dataset).
c) Superior visualization of high-dimensional input data in 2D-representation space. This was also important in our case since we were able to plot our 10-dimensional input data in 2D space for simple visual observation of cluster distributions.

B. SOM Classifier Experimentation

We performed our analysis of the SOM web-user classifier on two datasets: 1) a smaller web server access log from *www.cse.yorku.ca (CSE)* web domain and 2) a larger web server access log from www.*yorku.ca (YORKU)* web domain (see Table I). The purpose of performing our analysis on differently-sized datasets was to evaluate whether our analysis can be generalized to a significantly larger web domains with varied/different web visitors.

Table I Class distributions in the CSE and YORKU datasets

	CSE	YORKU
# of Human Sessions	53640	707854
# of Well-behaved Crawler Sessions	7607	9014
# of Malicious Visitor Sessions	287	860
# of Unknown Visitor Sessions	4042	3445
Total	65576	721193

As described in [1], for each web visitor session, we extracted the following features from the datasets: 1) Click number, 2) HTML-to-Image Ratio, 3) Percentage of PDF/PS file requests, 4) Percentage of 4xx error responses, 5) Percentage of HTTP requests of type HEAD, 6) Percentage of requests with unassigned referrers, 7) Number of bytes requested from the server, 8) Page Popularity index, 9) Standard deviation of requested page's depth and 10) Percentage of consecutive sequential HTTP requests. As shown in past research studies, namely [8], [9], [10], [11] and [12], these features are shown to be useful in distinguishing between browsing patterns of web robots and humans.

As described in [1], the session labels were generated by matching the user agent string of each visitor to a list of known user agent strings of browsers, well-behaved crawlers and malicious crawlers. The log analyzer maintains a table of user agent fields of all known (malicious or well-behaved) web crawlers and browsers. This table was built by compiling the data found on web sites [13], [14] and [15]. The details of the dataset labeling process are shown in Fig. 2. Note that we label all sessions that carry a user agent string of a known browser but access the robots.txt (operation performed only by crawlers) as malicious as well.

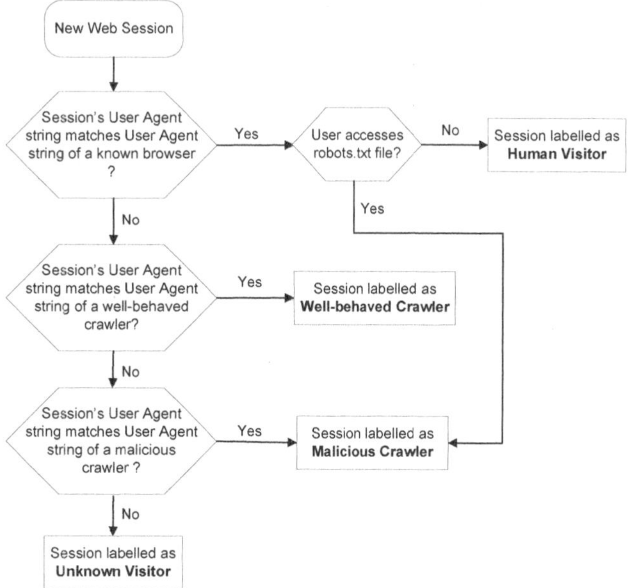

Fig. 2 The flow chart of our data labelling algorithm

From the clustering results, we were able to identify three distinct groups of sessions that could present a particular challenge for any Layer-7 anti-DDoS systems (from [1]):

1) Sessions that are labelled as malicious crawlers but 'behave' like humans – we refer to these sessions as *outlier malicious sessions* The position of these sessions in the SOM graph is shown in Fig. 3. Security staff administering a web site would be very much interested in taking a closer look at this group of malicious sessions. Namely, currently the only way of identifying these sessions as malicious is by looking at their user agent string. However, with an incrementally higher level of sophistication – e.g., just by employing a fake but legitimate-looking user agent string – these sessions would blend in with actual/regular human sessions and become virtually undetectable.
2) Sessions that are labelled as unknown visitors but 'behave' like humans – we refer to these sessions as *outlier unknown sessions*. The position of these sessions in the SOM graph is shown in Fig. 4. Security staff administering a web site would be very much interested in taking a closer look at this group of sessions since they carry unknown, suspiciously incorrectly crafted or even missing user agent string labels.
3) Sessions that are labelled as humans but 'behave' like malicious crawlers – we refer to these as *outlier human sessions*. The position of these sessions in the SOM graph is shown in Fig. 5. We speculate that security staff administering a web site would be particularly interested in detecting and analyzing this group of sessions. Namely, these are likely sessions corresponding to sophisticated human-like-behaving malicious crawlers that are attempting to disguise their identity by spoofing their respective user agent strings.

Note that we arrived at the similar results with both the CSE and the YORKU datasets.

IV. TIME-DOMAIN ANALYZER

The results of our study presented in [1] indicate that, even at the current level of web-crawlers sophistication, effective web-crawlers categorization is becoming an increasingly complex task. Accordingly, in order to effectively distinguish suspicious from truly malicious web sessions, we propose that another stage/component be added to our integrated anti-DDoS system – in particular, a stage that focuses on the time-domain behavior analysis of potentially suspicious visitors.

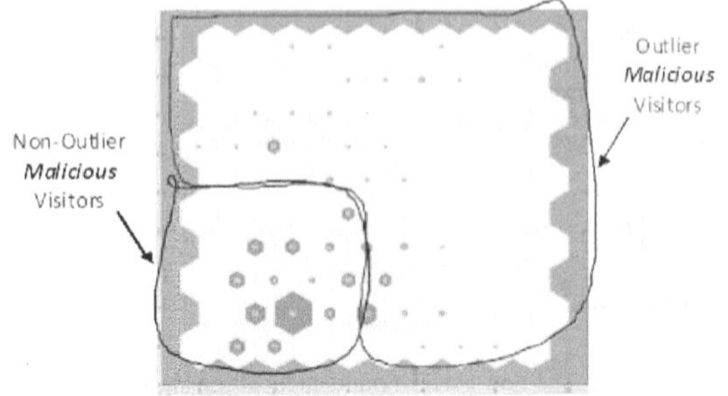

Fig. 3 Distribution of outlier and non-outlier malicious sessions in the SOM map

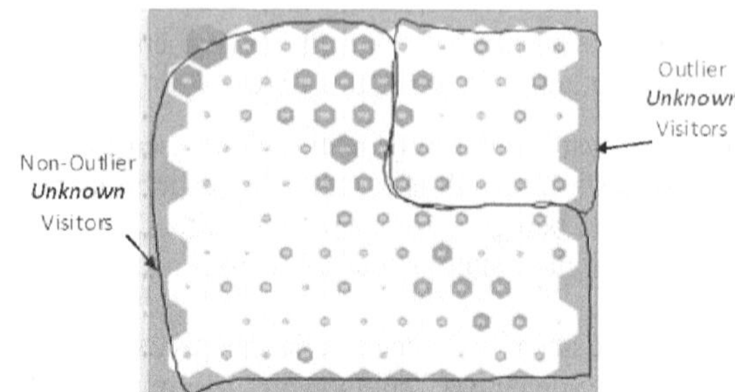

Fig. 4 Distribution of outlier and non-outlier unknown sessions in the SOM map

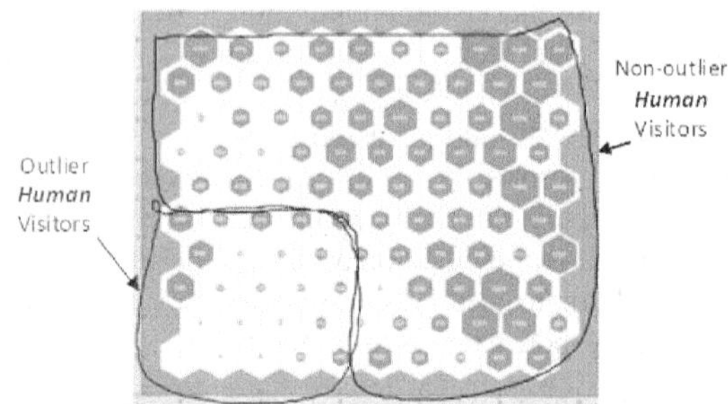

Fig. 5 Distribution of outlier and non-outlier human sessions in the SOM map

Here are the two simple illustrations as for how the inclusion of time-wise analysis may benefit the task of suspicious user classification:

- The time duration of a session is an important feature which has not been previously considered in our analysis or in the previous research works dealing with the issue of web-user classification. Namely, two sessions might comprise exactly the same number of accessed pages – looking at it as a simple number. However, it really matters whether all these pages are accessed as/in a rapid sequence, or over a longer period of time. Clearly, a rapid sequence access is likely to belong to a crawler, while longer sessions are likely to belong to humans (refer to Fig. 6).
- The time spent viewing each individual page is another important parameter to consider. Namely, crawlers are likely to spend the same amount of time 'viewing' each page, while the amount of time that humans spend viewing a page will likely be highly correlated to the contextual importance of that page relative to others – something an automated crawler is not able to comprehend/detect.

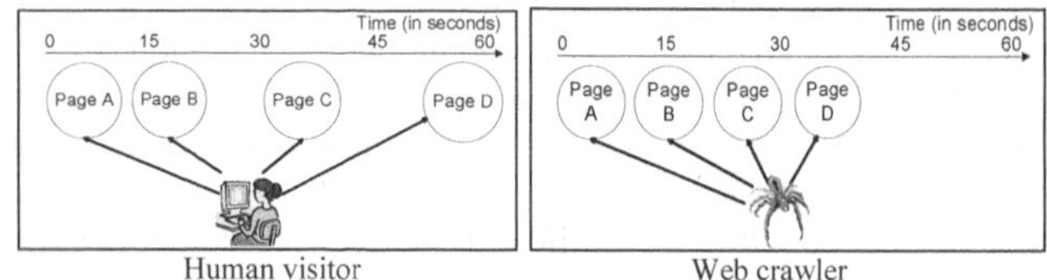

Fig. 6 Comparison of typical timing differences in web page access behaviour between a human visitor and a web crawler

A. Time-Domain Browsing Behaviour Model

In our time domain analyzer, we characterize the time-wise browsing behavior of a session based on the model presented in the recent study in [16]. In this study, authors state that the human browsing characteristics, such as page popularity, page viewing time and browsing session length (i.e., number of web pages visited in a session), can be modeled by a Markov model based on the three statistical distributions.

For instance, the web page popularity can be modeled by the following Zipf-Mandelbrot distribution function:

$$\Pr(W = i) = \frac{\Omega}{(i+q)^{\alpha}} \quad (1)$$

where $\Pr(W = i)$ is the access probability of page w_i, i is the rank/popularity of the web page, α ($\alpha > 0$) is the skewness factor, which characterizes the length of the tail of the distribution, and q ($q \geq 0$) is the plateau factor.

The page viewing time interval can be modeled by the Pareto's probability density function defined as shown in (2),

$$\Pr(V = v) = \frac{\alpha \cdot v_m^{\alpha}}{v^{(\alpha+1)}} \quad (2)$$

where v is web page viewing time, v_m is the minimum viewing time for all web pages and α is called the Pareto index.

Finally, the browsing session length can be modeled by the following Inverse Gaussian's distribution function:

$$\Pr(L = l) = \sqrt{\frac{\lambda}{2\pi l^3}} \exp\left[\frac{\lambda(l-\mu)^2}{2\mu^2 l}\right], l = 1, 2, \ldots \quad (3)$$

where L is the number of links that a visitor visits (i.e., follows) on a web site in a single session, average value of L, i.e. $E[L] = \mu$, variance $Var[L] = \mu^3 / \lambda$ and $\lambda > 0$ is the shape parameter describing the length of the distribution's tail.

Note that this human browsing behavior model employs a time-wise feature, i.e. page viewing time, but as well two additional features: 1) page popularity (which models users' page selection behavior) and 2) browsing session length (i.e. click number) which are not based in time-domain. Also, note that the latter two features were employed in our unsupervised study, and as discussed, these features are known to be very effective at distinguishing between human and machine-generated sessions.

In [17], the same authors show that under very specific conditions, such as small Botnet size and specific traffic characteristics, these type of malicious bots (that model their browsing behavior to mimic human-like behavior) could be detected. The work in [16] and [17] are one of the most recent works on the browsing behavior modeling, however it builds upon a number of other works and results (namely [18], [19] and [20]) produced during the last decade and a half.

B. Correlation Testing in our Time-Domain Analyzer

In order to evaluate the time-wise browsing behavior differences between visitor types, with significant level of confidence, our time-domain analyzer employs two nonparametric correlation tests:

1) Kolmogorov–Smirnov Test of 2 Independent Samples – a nonparametric statistical test that measures if there is a significant difference at any point along the two cumulative distribution functions (CDFs) between two samples which also implies that the two samples are derived from different populations.
2) Mann-Whitney U Test – a nonparametric statistical test that detects the significant difference between the medians of the two samples.

Specifically, both of these tests are employed to identify outlier human sessions that exhibit the browsing behavior (characterized in terms of the web page popularity rankings, page viewing times and number of pages visited during a session) that is not significantly different from the browsing behavior of non-outlier malicious sessions.

Note that our system could identify suspicious outlier human visitors even in the absence of any maliciously-labeled web session. In this scenario, the human visitors that are significantly different from non-outlier human visitors in terms of the three browsing behavior metrics would be asked to solve CAPTCHA puzzles by the system. Also note that these two tests apply different strategies to evaluate the differences between the given samples. By applying both techniques, we tend to provide a more holistic evaluation of the statistical differences between session types.

C. Experimental Results of the Correlation Tests

We experimentally evaluated the application of the correlation tests on the CSE and YORKU datasets from [1]. The web page popularity rankings, the web page visiting/viewing times and browsing lengths for outlier and non-outlier sessions in CSE and YORKU datasets were fitted to distributions in (1), (2) and (3), respectfully. The α and v_m parameters were derived by utilizing the method described in [21]. The μ and λ parameters were derived by utilizing the maximum likelihood estimation function provided with Matlab software package.

The results of applying the two correlation tests on the three metrics are displayed in Tables II-IV. In the case of Mann-Whitney U Test, the medians from the two samples are significantly different with 95% confidence if the obtained absolute value of the z-score is equal to or greater than 1.96. In the case of Kolmogorov-Smirnov Test 2, the empirical CDFs for the two samples are significantly different with 95% confidence if the Kolmogorov-Smirnov K-S statistic is greater than or equal to the so-called critical value of Kolmogorov-Smirnov Test of 2 Independent Samples – i.e., K statistic. Note that all of the results displayed in Tables II-IV are

TABLE II CORRELATION METRIC SCORES FOR WEB PAGE POPULARITY

Session Type Comparisons	Mann-Whitney z-score		K-S statistic / K statistic	
	CSE	*YORKU*	*CSE*	*YORKU*
Actual Human Visitors vs. Outlier Malicious Visitors	-5.38	45.55	0.36 / 0.015	0.534 / 0.03
Actual Human Visitors vs. Outlier Unknown Visitors	-14.53	19.1	0.22 / 0.044	0.25 / 0.038
Outlier Human Visitors vs. Actual Malicious Visitors	-36.2	69.14	0.36 / 0.029	0.34 / 0.014

TABLE III CORRELATION METRIC SCORES FOR WEB PAGE VIEWING TIME

Session Type Comparisons	Mann-Whitney z-score		K-S statistic / K statistic	
	CSE	*YORKU*	*CSE*	*YORKU*
Actual Human Visitors vs. Outlier Malicious Visitors	119.3-	27.77	0.62 / 0.016	0.36 / 0.03
Actual Human Visitors vs. Outlier Unknown Visitors	-14.7	2.86	0.22 / 0.046	0.1 / 0.04
Outlier Human Visitors vs. Actual Malicious Visitors	-23.48-	22.58	0.33 / 0.03	0.18 / 0.015

TABLE IV CORRELATION METRIC SCORES FOR BROWSING SESSION LENGTH

Session Type Comparisons	Mann-Whitney z-score		K-S statistic / K statistic	
	CSE	*YORKU*	*CSE*	*YORKU*
Actual Human Visitors vs. Outlier Malicious Visitors	-1.97	8.24	0.14 / 0.09	0.35 / 0.11
Actual Human Visitors vs. Outlier Unknown Visitors	-2.92	19.38	0.066 / 0.065	0.28 / 0.034
Outlier Human Visitors vs. Actual Malicious Visitors	8.43	16.98	0.28 / 0.1	0.3 / 0.058

significantly different in terms of both correlation metrics with 95% confidence.

We have made the following main conclusions from our results:

- **Non-outlier human vs. outlier malicious/unknown sessions.** The application of Mann-Whitney U and Kolmogorov-Smirnov 2 Independent Sample Tests show that there is a significant difference between the medians and distributions of the three statistical metrics between non-outlier human visitors and outlier malicious/unknown sessions. As such, these results have a great practical significance. Namely, they suggest that in the case that the outlier malicious or unknown sessions were marked by a spoofed browser-based user agent string – which would make them less 'obvious' and not as easily identifiable by the SOM algorithm – the use of time-domain analysis would provide for an effective way of distinguishing them from non-outlier (true) human sessions.
- **Non-outlier malicious vs. outlier human sessions.** The application of Mann-Whitney U and Kolmogorov-Smirnov 2 Independent Sample Tests show that there is also a significant difference between the medians and distributions of the three statistical metrics between non-outlier malicious visitors and outlier human sessions. These results may be an indication that the outlier human session, as identified by the SOM algorithm (see Section III), are not actually malicious but instead may be generated by legitimate human visitors that happen to exhibit non-typical human browsing behavior. Note also that these human visitors would not be CAPTCHA-ed by our anti-DDoS system.

V. FUTURE WORK

In our future work, we plan to include additional web logs from one or more non-academic public (or private) organizations. By analyzing a set of web logs from different organizations we aim to generalize the conclusions we have derived at this point in our research.

Also, we plan to evaluate the real-world DDoS bot, such as a Dirt Jumper [22], in a sandbox environment. The purpose of this task would be to evaluate how closely the actual DDoS bot's browsing behavior compares with the browsing behavior of actual human visitors and malicious crawlers.

REFERENCES

[1] D. Stevanovic, N. Vlajic, and A. An, "Detection of Malicious and Non-malicious Website Visitors Using Unsupervised Neural Network Learning," *Applied Soft Computing*, vol. 13, no. 1, pp. 698-708, Jan. 2013.

[2] B. Gerneglia. (2012, Mar.) Infosecisland. [Online]. http://www.infosecisland.com/blogview/20727-Cyber-Attacks-are-Fastest-Growing-National-Security-Threat.html

[3] K. Poulsen. (2004) FBI Busts Alleged DDoS Mafia. [Online]. http://www.securityfocus.com/news/9411

[4] H. N. Security. (2011, Oct.) Top DDoS attacks of 2011. [Online]. http://www.corero.com/en/company/news_and_events?item_id=4

[5] D. SonicWall. (2012) IDG Connect. [Online]. http://www.idgconnect.com/view_abstract/13111/how-traditional-firewalls-fail-today-networks-and-why-next-generation-firewalls-will-prevail?source=connect

[6] D. Pogue. (2012, Feb.) Scientific American. [Online]. http://www.scientificamerican.com/article.cfm?id=time-to-kill-off-captchas

[7] T. Kohonen, *Self-Organizing Maps*, 3rd ed. New York: Springer-Verlag, Berlin Heidelberg, 2001.

[8] D. Doran and S. S. Gokhale, "Web robot detection techniques: overview and limitations," *Data Mining and Knowledge Discovery*, pp. 1-28, Jun. 2010.

[9] A. Stassopoulou and M. D. Dikaiakos, "Web robot detection: A probabilistic reasoning approach," *Computer Networks: The International Journal of Computer and Telecommunications Networking*, vol. 53, no. 3, pp. 265-278, Feb. 2009.

[10] P. N. Tan and V. Kumar, "Discovery of Web Robot Sessions Based on their Navigation Patterns," *Data Mining and Knowledge Discovery*, vol. 6, no. 1, pp. 9-35, Jan. 2002.

[11] J. X. Yu, O. Yuming, C. Zhang, and S. Zhang, "Identifying interesting visitors through Web log classification," *Intelligent Systems*, vol. 20, no. 3, pp. 55-59, Jun. 2005.

[12] C. Bomhardt, W. Gaul, and L. Schmidt-Thieme, "Web Robot Detection - Preprocessing Web Logfiles for Robot Detection," in *In Proc. SISCLADAG*, Bologna, Italy, 2005.

[13] (2011, Aug.) User-Agents.org. [Online]. http://www.user-agents.org

[14] (2011, Aug.) Bots vs. Browsers. [Online]. http://www.botsvsbrowsers.com/

[15] (2012, May) User-agent-string.inf. [Online]. http://user-agent-string.info/

[16] S. Yu, Z. Guofeng, S. Guo, X. Yang, and A. V. Vasilakos, "Browsing Behavior Mimicking Attacks on Popular Web Sites for Large Botnets," in *proceedings of 2011 IEEE Conference on Computer Communications Workshops (INFOCOM WKSHPS)*, Shanghai, China, April, 2011, pp. 947-951.

[17] S. Yu, S. Guo, and I. Stojmenovic, "Can we beat legitimate cyber behavior mimicking attacks from Botnets?," in *IEEE INFOCOMM*, Orlando, Florida, 2012, pp. 2851-2855.

[18] L. Breslau, P. Cao, L. Fan, G. Phillips, and S. Shenker, "Web caching and zipf-like distributions: Evidence and implications," in *Proceedings of the INFOCOM*, New York, 1999, pp. 126-134.

[19] M. E. Crovella and A. Bestavros, "Self-similarity in world wide web traffic: evidence and possible causes," *IEEE/ACM Transactions on Networking*, vol. 5, no. 6, pp. 835-846, Dec. 1997.

[20] B. A. Huberman, P. Pirolli, J. E. Pitkow, and R. M. Lukose, "Strong regularities in world wide web surfing," *Science*, vol. 280, no. 5360, Apr. 1998.

[21] A. Clauset, C. R. Shalizi, and M. E. J. Newman, "Power-Law Distributions in Empirical Data," *SIAM*, vol. 51, no. 4, pp. 661-703, Nov. 2009.

[22] Prolexic. (2012, Mar.) Threat: Dirt Jumper v3. [Online]. http://unknown.prolexic.com/pdf/ProlexicThreatAdvisoryDirtJumper.pdf

[23] A. Asosheh and N. Ramezani, "Comprehensive Taxonomy of DDoS Attacks and Defense Mechanisms Applying in a Smart Classification," *WSEAS Transaction on Computers*, vol. 7, no. 4, pp. 281-290, Apr. 2008.

QR Code Steganography

Donny Jacob Ohana, and Narasimha Shashidhar
Department of Computer Science, Sam Houston State University, Huntsville, TX, USA

Abstract - *QR codes, also known as matrix codes, are basically two dimensional barcodes embedded with data that can be decoded quickly for information. In this work, we present a novel use of QR codes. We show that QR codes can be used for covert communication using steganography. We also show in complete detail how to build QR code symbols with a hidden payload and how to extract this hidden information in two ways: with and without a shared secret key. An interesting feature of our research is that we present a technique to convert innocuous QR codes into carriers for malicious messages and malware using simple, everyday tools and software. Communicating secret messages in plain sight creates a credible threat to our national security. We hope that our work brings this issue to light and enhances counter-terrorism education.*

Keywords: steganography; QR code; mobile QR code; malicious QR code; hidden QR code; QR code hacking, QR code steganography

1 Introduction

As industries become more technologically advanced, there are constantly new and exciting developments. Barcodes are one of those evolutions that have become a primary asset to business and advertisement. Generally speaking, barcodes are mostly seen in retail and grocery stores. These types of barcodes are usually one-dimensional. A more advanced barcode system is called Quick Response code; a two dimensional barcode commonly abbreviated as QR code. This type of code was created by Toyota in 1994 for tracking automotive information and depending on the version set, can store up 4,296 alphanumeric characters [8].

Quick response code is typically used for purposes such as freight tracking, commercial advertisement, embedded links to websites, and much more. However, there are risks to naively scanning QR codes which have been recently discovered. A fundamental risk revolves around the issue of malware. According to news articles, at the end of September 2011, Kaspersky Lab detected the first attempts of cybercriminals using malicious QR codes. By October of 2011, they further detected QR code symbols linked to malware for Android (OS) and J2ME (Java) [9]. Most prior research on QR codes is focused on the different application areas such as facial/pattern recognition, cryptography, secure authentication, and contextual feedback.

These studies are clearly more advanced applications than the simple and standard embedding of QR code information. There is minimal published research on malicious QR code symbols and virtually no published research on developing QR code symbols with hidden messages.

QR code manipulation technique: The most common QR code manipulation technique has been to embed QR code symbols with phishing links to websites containing viruses. By using this technique an attacker can utilize non-human readable symbols to gain sensitive information or monetary benefit. A far greater threat exists in the idea proposed in this paper: A terrorist or radical could utilize QR codes to hide secret information which can only be read by privileged members of the organization. It is important to note that by researching such methods of QR code manipulation, our nation's security can be strengthened and be better prepared to counter such techniques. Our contribution in this paper is twofold: firstly, to demonstrate the simple techniques one can use to generate steganographic QR codes and secondly to bring attention to this technique so that further research can be done to counter such covert communication channels.

This paper is organized as follows: Section 2 provides prior work on QR codes. Section 3 briefly outlines the framework of QR codes. Section 4 details the implementation and experiments done in this research work. Section 5 and 6 conclude the paper with some open questions, future work and discussion.

2 Related and prior work

In a study on physical access control based QR codes [2], researchers established a physical authentication method using a mobile phone and QR code. The OTP model, which is essentially a One Time Password authentication system, was also implemented into this research. Another authentication system was presented in [6] using a different protocol. This research proposed to use QR code password images that were sent via MMS (multimedia message). With this type of authentication system, a valid one time password could be used in a public or private setting. Another study [3] developed an authentication system using QR code as well. This type of framework was for a Single Sign On system (SSO). An SSO system allows for multiple services which are accessible from one protected account. However, they are susceptible to phishing attacks. The QR code used for this authentication method provided a secure system which protected against phishing and other hacking attacks. For instance, the root password is never revealed to support anti-phishing and a timestamp is embedded to expire upon scanning to prevent man-in-the-middle attacks and replay attacks.

2.1 QR codes and smartphones

Having discussed some different authentication methods, we now discuss how mobile phones are targeted for attacks. This is primarily because of the fact that most QR codes are now scanned with advanced mobile phones (smartphones). One study [4] showed how a camera phone could scan a QR code and certain information populated into specific locations of the device. It is unique how QR code images not only produce text, but the text can be linked for other uses. Since cell phones are becoming more advanced and are equipped with various barcode scanning applications, it is not surprising that they are being targeted for malware. One research article [7] showed how smartphones are attractive targets. Some people may ask why smartphones would be more likely to get attacked then a regular general purpose computer. The answer is simple. Smartphones can now be used for online banking, make purchases using digital currency, and store large quantities of sensitive information.

Another important thing to note about smartphones is that they function using an operating system much like a general purpose computer. Whether the mobile phone platform is Linux (Android), Windows, or Mac (iPhone), hackers may be able to make use of rootkits to eavesdrop on conversations, emails, and messaging services [7]. As we can see, QR codes can be used for a lot of good, but can also be used malicious intent. Recently, malicious QR code linking to malware on cell phones was detected by Kaspersky Lab [9]. Once the QR code was scanned, the cell phone would send numerous SMS messages that would charge the user money. One research study [1] showed the vulnerability of service set identifiers (SSID) using QR codes in Android phones. When the smartphone reads the specific QR code, the browser goes to a hacker's Webpage, downloads and installs a dropper. After the virus is installed, it deletes itself and activates the "Mobile AP" (Access Point) process.

3 QR code framework

In this section, we discuss the architecture of one-dimensional and two-dimensional QR codes and briefly outline how the encoding and decoding protocols work for QR codes.

3.1 Barcode architecture

Barcodes essentially contain variants that represent data in a machine-readable format by varying the widths and spacing of parallel lines. These types of barcodes are also known as one-dimensional codes. The benefit to these types of codes is that they are very resistant to degradation. For example, a warehouse that requires inventory control in a rough environment would benefit most from one-dimensional barcodes because of its resistance to damage. The reason for this is because there is little data spread over the height of the parallel lines. In contrast to one-dimensional codes, QR codes store data both vertically and horizontally which is why it is considered two-dimensional. As we see in Fig. 1, there are obvious differences between the two.

Fig. 1 Differences between one and two dimensional code

Currently, there are 40 different versions of QR codes. Version 40, the highest version, allows for up to 7,089 numeric data and 4,296 alphanumeric characters. In addition to the capacity storage, each codeword is 8 bits long and uses the Reed-Solomon correction algorithm with four levels (L, M, Q, & H) of error correction [8]. This implies that the higher the correction level, the less storage capacity there will be in the corresponding code. For example, if there is a version 40 QR code image with Level L correction error, then no more than 7% of the image can be distorted for the image to still be scanned properly. This would benefit companies that want to implement a custom logo on their QR image, in which the logo would introduce intentional errors and still scan properly. Additionally, if there was a smudge that covered 7% of the image, it would also scan properly. For QR code images intended to be used in environments where damage may occur, level H (30%) error correction is advised. This means that up to 30% of the image can be distorted for the image to still be scanned properly.

As shown in Fig. 2, all QR code images have the same architecture. The three large blocks in the corners of the image are called "Finder Patterns" for software applications to detect the QR code. The smaller blocks in the middle are called "Alignment Patterns" which create resistance to distortion from curved surfaces or tilted viewing. The "Timing Pattern" identifies the central coordinate of each cell. It is mainly used when the image is distorted and needs to be corrected. Once the alignment is settled and the image is processed, the data is then analyzed by the software to decode the message. When the message is stored, it uses binary numbers of zeros and ones that convert to black or white. This is also why it is considered a data matrix, which usually consists of square bits of information. Each square represents one bit; dark squares and light squares are either ones or zeros. For example if we were to represent the letter "A" using this method, the binary code would be "01000001". With the specified bits of code, there would be a total of 2 black squares and 6 white squares in a sequence or vice versa. That binary string translates to Hexadecimal "0x41" which is also the letter "A" in ASCII (base 16). All this is incorporated into the QR code symbol and decoded using an algorithm.

Fig. 2 QR code anatomy

3.2 QR code encoding and decoding

QR codes can be generated by anyone using free online generators or other software. For this reason alone, QR code scanning should be done with caution since there are no digital signatures or certificates required. A QR code symbol can easily be generated with website links, iTunes' links, mobile application links, SMS messages (text messaging), Wi-Fi (Wireless Fidelity) login information, contact information, and geo-locations. In order to create one of these QR code images, a QR code generator must be used. For instance, one article [10] provides the source code for a QR code generator using Google API (Google Chart Application Programming Interface). Other QR code generators are provided with certain smartphone applications or can be found free online. Several common ways to decode QR code symbols are to upload the symbol to a website, scan the symbol with a camera equipped cell phone, or scan the symbol with a webcam. In the past, some researchers have attempted to decode QR code symbols by hand, but the decoding algorithm is extremely complicated.

4 QR code steganography

In this section, we give a brief overview of steganography and how to build QR codes with steganographic content.

4.1 Overview

Steganography is the art and science of writing secret messages in such a way that aside from the sender and the intended receiver, no one even suspects the existence of the secret message. Notice that steganography goals are in contrast to the goals of cryptography because encrypted messages or images attract attention. In steganography, the mere suspicion of a hidden message existence is sufficient to declare the failure of the scheme, even if the hidden message cannot be deciphered. QR codes have been previously used to exchange encrypted content [12], but there is no such research that uses them for steganography in the same fashion as this research. Being able to hide secret messages within general QR code symbols creates endless possibilities for discreet communication through QR codes. The idea behind this research is to show how to communicate a secret message between the sender and the receiver using QR codes without arousing any suspicion. Additionally, we show two ways to extract the secret message from the QR codes: first, using a private shared key between the sender and receiver, and second, without a shared key. For the purpose of this experiment, we will show how person A (Adam) will communicate a secret message with person B (Bob).

4.2 Research scenario

Let us say Adam is an entrepreneur who works from home and sells merchandise from a personal website accessible to the public. Adam is also a prominent leader among a radical organization that promotes destruction. Bob, who is a member of Adam's radical organization, lives in another country but is an active participant. In order for Adam to communicate discreetly with Bob, Adam creates a QR code symbol with a general innocent message for the public and publishes it on his website (Fig. 3). Within this general message, Adam hides a secret message (Fig. 4) intended only for Bob. To anyone who scans and decodes this modified QR code (Fig. 6), the message will read as a discount coupon for consumers to purchase Adam's merchandise. Since Bob knows that the QR code is embedded with a secret message, Bob will use other methods to read the same code and get a different message. To do this, Bob can either use a shared private key that has been distributed to privileged members of this radical organization (Fig. 5), or Bob can use certain specialized techniques to extract the secret message. These two methods are illustrated in the following sections.

4.3 Experiment setup

To conduct our experiments we used the following tools:

- Mobile phone with a built-in camera for scanning bar-codes: HTC Evo Android OS smartphone with different bar-code scanning applications installed
- Computer running Windows 7 OS
- Free Online QR Code Generator [11]
- Image Manipulation Programs: GIMP 2.6 and Adobe Photoshop CS 5

To begin this experiment, a general innocent carrier message was created using a free online QR Code generator [11]. From the options menu, the code action was set for "Free

Formatted Text" with "QR Code" being the choice of code type. The block size was set to "10" in Pixels with the margin size in blocks set to "1". The image output was set for PNG (Portable Network Graphics) and the foreground/background colors remained standard black/white. Most important of all, the error correction level for the general message was set to "High" to enable us to embed the secret message (introduce distortion) and yet be able to decipher the original innocent message.

After the options were selected, a general innocent carrier message was entered into the text box and stated the following: *"Congratulations! You are a winner!!! Present this coupon code #54336 and receive 50% off anything in the store! Act fast! This coupon code expires soon!"*

The QR code symbol was then generated and verified (scanned) using various bar-code scanning applications on an HTC Android smartphone. The "general" QR code symbol can be seen and scanned in Fig. 3.

Fig. 3 General, innocent carrier message to the public with high error correction

Next, we created a secret message using the same format. This time, the error correction had to be set to low. The reason for the low error correction is so that the QR code symbol can be smaller in size. As long as the pixel size remained the same, using steganography in this sense was successful. The secret message was then entered into the free formatted text box and stated: *"BOMB PIN# 1234- wait for coordinates."* After the secret message was generated, it was tested and then edited using a free image manipulation program called GIMP, version 2.6. With the image file open, the three large square finder patterns were removed as well as the alignment pattern. This was done by creating a pixel mask from a specifically selected surface; the message portion of the QR code symbol. As we can see in Fig. 4, the secret message is considerably smaller than the general message and still has the same pixel size. Additionally, since the general message has a higher error correction level, there are more alignment patterns.

After the general message and secret message were created, they were all opened as separate layers in the GIMP workspace. A third layer was then created to generate a key, containing the missing finder and alignment patterns to the secret message. As shown in Fig. 5, a square key was created filling in the voided areas of the secret message. It is important to note that different message sizes using different error corrections will result in different key sizes. This was done using a magic selector and manipulating the layers. *Disabling the general carrier message:* A "pinstriped finder pattern" square was placed at the bottom left of the key, in order to disable the general message. This portion was created only after inserting the secret message into the general message, so that the key could properly be aligned. It is also important to note that if the key is even one pixel off, the message will not decode as a result of pattern change.

Fig. 4 Secret terroristic message with low error correction

Fig. 5 Private shared key

While viewing the secret layer and general layer simultaneously, the secret message layer was moved around until it blended into the general message perfectly and became undetectable, as shown in Fig. 6. At this point in time, the general message could still be scanned without any problems due to the high error correction.

Fig. 6 General QR code symbol embedded with secret message (undetectable)

Once the manipulated QR code was generated with both a general carrier message and an embedded secret message, it is ready to be used. At this point, Adam has now published a QR code symbol that contains an innocent consumer coupon message and a hidden terrorist message. For Bob to decode the secret message he has two options:

Option #1: Save the manipulated QR code symbol from the website and open it using Microsoft Paint or any general purpose image editing software. In this paragraph, we illustrate the process using MS Paint. Copy the "shared private key" using "transparency" selection. Finally, align the pinstriped finder pattern block with the general message's bottom finder pattern block, as shown in Fig. 7. After this is all said and done, the general message will be disabled and the secret message will be decoded instead. This method can also be used if a QR code is scanned from a public place and saved onto the mobile device.

Option #2: Save the manipulated QR code symbol from the website and upload it onto a QR decoding website [13]. Once the message is decoded, create a new general message by copying and pasting the general message into a free form text box [11]. Essentially, a new QR code symbol will be generated to compare the modified one. After the new symbol is generated and saved, it is opened with the modified symbol (separate image layers) using an image manipulation program. A pixel mask of the difference between the two is then created to show the secret message as in Fig. 4. The finder patterns and alignment pattern can then be placed to fill in the voided areas; the secret message is now readable. The advantage to this option is for when a shared key cannot be passed along. This option can also be implemented in a forensic setting.

Fig. 7 Secret message decoded using shared key (general message disabled)

Between the two options, option #1 could be used in a quick automated setting with a custom mobile application. Notice that option #2 as presented above allows Bob to retrieve the secret embedded message without a shared private secret key. Observe that this does not diminish the potency of our scheme. A steganographic scheme is said to have failed if anyone, besides the sender and the receiver, even suspects the existence of a hidden message. In this sense, we argue that is highly unlikely, at least at this time, that people have developed a sense of suspicion towards QR codes. One of our objectives in this paper is to bring this issue to light, and to demonstrate that indeed one ought to be suspicious of QR codes.

4.4 Result analysis

Our experiment proved to be successful in being able to convert a general purpose carrier QR code into one with a hidden payload. The general message, which was generated with high error correction, gave us an opportunity to hide a secret message so long as it did not exceed a surface area of 30%. By doing so, this allowed the general message to scan successfully at 100% despite the presence of hidden information. The secret message was then created with an overall smaller size but still had the same pixel size. This allowed for the secret message to blend in and become completely undetectable. Unless someone knows of the secret message, there is no possible way to look at the QR code and see any modifications. Additionally, the secret message can be hidden in more than one location. If and only if the key is aligned correctly, the general message easily becomes disabled allowing only the secret message to be retrieved when scanned. The code cannot be interpreted if the key is one pixel off because of sensitive alignment. To further show the capacity of this communication method, Fig. 8 shows one QR code generated with two hundred words and another generated with sixty words, which equates to the 30% error correction. As we can see, the pixel size remained the same in accordance with the experimental guidelines to allow us to embed the message. When the secret message content exceeded 30% of the host, it also exceeded 30% of error correction in size. Therefore, it is best to stay within the error correction ratios.

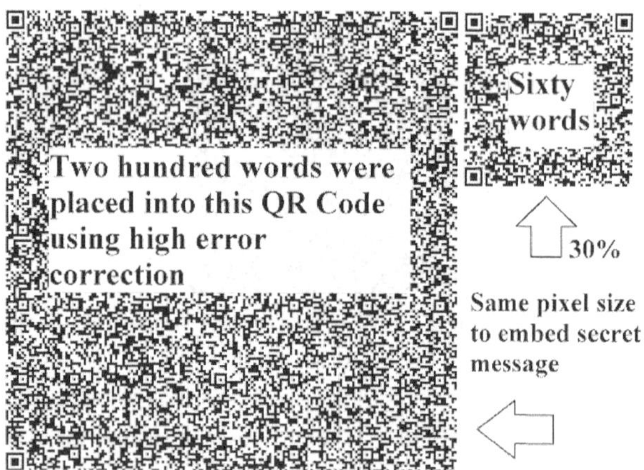

Fig. 8 Comparison of content capacity

Automating the process: In addition to the above experiment, we also performed the same steps using Adobe Photoshop CS5, which rendered an additional advantage as described. This software has the ability to save a pattern of image modifications into an executable script. Using this method, Adam could drop the selected files into the executable folder, and then the script would generate a modified QR code instantly. The same could be done on the receiver's end.

5 Future work

From a digital forensic, law enforcement, and Homeland Security perspective, there needs to be further research into developing protocols and applications that can process QR codes automatically and determine hidden layers; essentially an automated option #2 custom carver. It is very easy to bypass this hidden information when using forensic tools like FTK or Encase. At the very least, a method to flag the code as a mismatch should be implemented into forensic software.

6 Conclusion

As we can see, QR code implementation is rising in the areas of advertisement and business. This type of code has also become more apparent in personal use. Since there are readily available websites which allow anyone to generate QR code or embed a QR generator in their own website, it is important to learn what threshold two dimensional codes carry. Additionally, QR code symbols are growing in the public because cell phone technology is on the rise. Anyone who owns a smartphone can easily download a barcode scanner for free and use it to scan or create one/two dimensional barcodes. This is all vital to the longevity of QR codes containing secret messages because it is simply a common public icon. Therefore, no one would ever suspect there to be hidden information.

From a forensic standpoint, if a computer containing terroristic embedded QR code symbols was analyzed, the secret message would never be detected through indexing, hex string searches, regular expressions, or custom carvers. Additionally, the image would most likely be located, scanned, and discarded due to its mundane content. Since QR codes contain a large storage capacity, malicious message content could include terroristic plans, attack coordinates, links to landmark attractions, etc. On another note, this method could also be used by our government to communicate sensitive information to covert operatives. Based on the totality of the circumstances, this area of study should be researched and educated to strengthen our nation's security.

7 References

[1] W.B. Cheon, K.I. Heo, W.G. Lim, W.H. Park, and T.M. Chung, "The new vulnerability of service set identifier (SSID) using QR code in android phone," *Information Science and Applications,* pp. 1-6, Apr. 2011.

[2] Y.W. Kao, G.H. Luo, H.T. Lin, Y.K. Huang, S.M. and Yuan, "Physical access control based on QR code," *Cyber-Enabled Distributed Computing and Knowledge Discovery,* pp. 285-288, Oct. 2011.

[3] S. Mukhopadhyay, and D. Argles, "QR-SSO: Towards a QR-code based single sign-on system," *International Journal for Digital Society,* pp. 1-7, Sep. 2011.

[4] M. Rohs and B. Gfeller, "Using Camera-equipped mobile phones for interacting with real-world objects," *Proceedings of Advances in Pervasive Computing*, pp. 265–271, Apr. 2004.

[5] J. Rouillard, "Contextual QR code," *Computing in the Global Information Technology,* pp. 50-55, Aug. 2008.

[6] K.C. Liao, and W.H. Lee, "A novel user authentication scheme based on QR-code," *Journal of Networks,* pp. 937-941, Aug. 2010.

[7] B. Dixon, and S. Mishra, "On rootkit and malware detection in smartphones," *Dependable Systems and Network Workshops,* pp. 162-163, Jul. 2010.

[8] Y. Liu, J. Yang, and M. Liu, "Recognition of QR code with Mobile Phones," *Chinese Control and Decision Conference,* pp. 203-206, Sep. 2009.

[9] C. Purvis, "Don't scan that QR code," 2011, http://www.securitymanagement.com/news/hacker-says-%E2%80%98don%E2%80%99t-scan-qr-code%E2%80%99-009207

[10] X. Ding, "Build your own QR code generator with Google Chart API," 2011, http://www.onextrapixel.com/2011/10/12/build-your-own-qr-code-generator-with-google-chart-api

[11] Kerem Erkan, "QR Code and 2D Code Generator," 2011, *http://keremerkan.net/qr-code-and-2d-code-generator/*

[12] W.P. Fang, "Offline QR code authorization based on visual cryptography," *Intelligent Information Hiding and Multimedia Signal Processing*, pp. 89-92, Oct. 2011

[13] ZXing, "Decoder Online," 2011, http://zxing.org/w/decode.jspx

Dynamic Analysis of Malicious Code and Response System

Ajay Katangur[1], Vinay Chaitankar[1], Dulal Kar[1], and Somasheker Akkaladevi[2]
[1]School of Engineering and Computing Sciences, Texas A&M University-Corpus Christi, Corpus Christi, Texas, USA
[2]Department of Computer Information Systems, Virginia State University, Petersburg, Virginia, USA

ABSTRACT - *Malicious code detection and removal is critical to the security of a computer system. Virus scanners rely on a database of known signatures for viruses and malware for detection. This research paper presents novel methodologies and tools to detect any malicious code present on windows based machine dynamically, and can be used as a preventive measure to protect the system from being infected. Malicious code analysis can be static and dynamic. Dynamic code analysis has a greater edge over static code analysis as the instructions are analyzed at runtime. Thus polymorphic malware can also be detected. The work presented in this paper uses a newly designed dynamic code technique in conjunction with a developed minifilter driver for malware detection. It runs in a virtual environment to perform the analysis, thus making it impossible for malwares to detect the presence of the developed tool. The minifilter driver is used to monitor the windows API calls, registry changes and used to generate reports which are used to analyze a program as malware or normal. These reports can be analyzed to categorize a program as normal or malware.* The developed tool is tested using Symantec malware database and compared with other pre-existing tools to evaluate its effectiveness.

Keywords: Mini filter driver, Malware, Virtual Operating System

I. INTRODUCTION

A. Malicious code

Malicious code is a term used to refer to any code that can cause undesired effects, security breaches and potential damages to the software system without the users consent. A program or software is classified as malware based on the users intent rather than the features of it. Any harmful software cannot be considered as malware. For example, defective software can be legitimate and can still cause potential damage due to the presence of harmful bugs. Malware can be categorized into Viruses, Worms, Trojan horses, Attacker tools etc. [1, 6, 9]. Table 1 lists the various characteristics of malwares. Destructive malware [6] generally spreads through the web, email etc. A special category of malware called data-stealing malware exists. This type of malware intends to steal personal and confidential information of a person or an organization. Once this kind of malware gets successfully installed on the target machine, they can compromise the Intrusion Detection System or anti-virus programs protecting the system.

TABLE 1
DIFFERENTIATING MALWARE CATEGORIES

Characteristic	Self-contained?	Self-replicating?	What is its method of propagation?
Virus	No	Yes	User-Interaction
Worm	Yes	Yes	Self-Propagation
Trojan Horse	Yes	No	N/A
Tracking Cookie	Yes	No	N/A
Attacker Tools	Yes	No	N/A

Many factors may leave a system vulnerable to attacks. The most common being the exploits because of bugs in the operating system (OS) design, and the existence of over-privileged users (who can leave the system vulnerable to the malware by making wrong decisions).

B. Malicious Code Analysis

Malicious code analysis is used to refer to the process of determining the intent and nature of the malware sample. For a long time the malicious code analysis was a manual, time consuming and tedious task. Thus there was need for automated systems which could detect the presence of the malware and automatically act to prevent the malware from achieving its intended task.

The most important preventive measures for malware are the virus scanner, but these scanners rely on a database of known signatures for virus. Thus they are restricted to only known viruses and malware, but many new types of malware and viruses attack the computer systems every day. So there is a need for a better malware tracking solution. Whenever a new malware is found, its signature is written to the database of signatures, so that all systems infected with this malware can be easily fixed. Generally malware analysis is conducted by allowing the malware program to be executed in a restricted environment and by observing its actions. The actions of the program are analyzed using a debugger. This manual analysis is a time consuming and tedious task. Thus there is a need for automated analysis. This automation is generally achieved by executing the affected program in a virtual environment (VE) and recording the actions of the programs, and finally sending the recorded actions to the human analyst [1].

The existing automated malicious code analyzers have shortcomings. The most important among them is the failure of the analyzers because of the presence of detection routines within the malware [1, 3, 4]. The detection routines allow the malware to detect if the program is running in a VE. If so, the malware program acts in a different way, thus hiding its existence. Some malwares have the capability to check the existence of both hardware and software breakpoints, which can be used to detect the existence of a malware. Other problems with the automated malware analysis include the incapability of the tool to detect the complete interaction of the program with the system. Malware analysis can be static and dynamic.

1) Static Analysis: Static analysis is the process of analyzing the malware without actually executing it [3]. In this technique the binary code is converted into corresponding assembler level instructions as shown in Figure 1. After the transformation, control flow and data flow analysis techniques are implemented to draw a conclusion about the programs functionality [5].

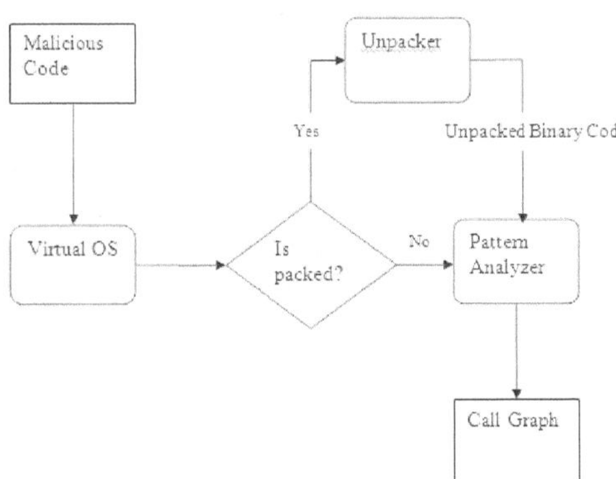

Fig. 1. Framework for Static Analyzer

Static analysis is faster in performance than dynamic analysis. One of the major disadvantages of static analysis is the ability of the malware to make use of binary obfuscation, which can be used to safely play with the control flow and data flow analysis. These obfuscation techniques are implemented with the help of opaque predicates and opaque constants [3]. It's not necessary that the code analyzed by the static analyzer is the code that will be actually executed. This is true in particular for the self-modifying programs that make use of polymorphism to hide their actual form.

2) Dynamic Analysis: In contrast to static analysis, the dynamic analyzers analyze the code when it is being executed as shown in Figure 2. The most important advantage of dynamic analyzer is; the instructions that are analyzed are the ones that are executed [2]. These tools provide security against the obfuscation techniques.

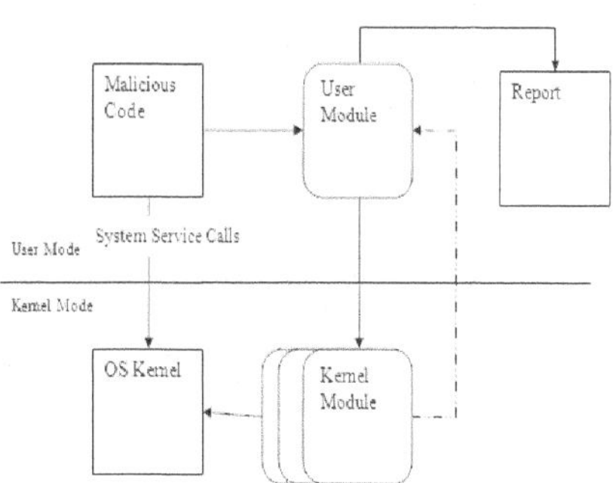

Fig. 2. A Dynamic Analyzer

Generally the analysis is conducted in a VE. Thus the risk of the system being damaged is reduced, because the VE image could be replaced with a new one [5]. One of the significant drawbacks of conducting the analysis in a VE is that the malware could determine that it is running in a VE and may change its behavior accordingly. VE detection tools are easily available [8]. These tools make use of CPU instructions to determine the existence of a VE. Some malwares can detect the VE t and change behavior accordingly to hide itself from the defensive system [8]. The work presented in this paper along with the developed tool examines the code in a VE along with a developed minifilter driver and dynamically detects any malicious code present. The minifilter driver is used to monitor the API calls, registry changes, and generate reports. These reports can be analyzed to categorize program as normal or malware.

II. MINIFILTER DRIVER

A. Analyzing a Executable

The main aim of this research is to analyze a given executable and generate a report of the changes made to the system by it. The analysis of the report is performed to decide if the executable is a malware or a normal program. This analysis looks into the list of open, modified, added and deleted files. It also considers changes made to the registry.

The executable is tested in a VE. The newly designed analysis tool has two main components. They are:

1. **Minifilter Driver**: The minifilter driver is used to dynamically monitor the activities of the program that is being tested. This driver can track the Windows API calls made by the program.
2. **Analysis Tool**: This tool works along with the driver. It makes use of the track report of the Windows API calls made by the program and generates a report for analysis. The report includes all the file and registry operations made by the program.

The minifilter driver is created using Windows programming with the Windows Driver Kit (WDK) [16]. The analysis component is developed using C and C++ code. Based on the reports generated by the analysis tool, the changes made by the program to the system are taken into consideration. An analysis is then performed to obtain at a decision of whether the program is malicious or normal.

B. Malicious Code Detection

Malicious code detection is the process of detecting various malwares that can cause potential damage to the system. Any defense technology can be separated into two components – a technical component and an analytical component. The technical component is a collection of program functions and algorithms that selects the data that will be analyzed by the analytical component. The analytical component serves as the decision-making entity. It assesses the data provided by the technical component using one or more algorithms and then issues a verdict about the data. The security program will then use the verdict to take action on the malicious program according to the security policy set in the security program. For example, a few of the possible actions that could occur based upon the verdict might be:

1. Notifying the user
2. Requesting further instructions from the user
3. Placing the file in quarantine
4. Blocking unauthorized program actions

Consider the following example code, which is extracted from the assembly code of Bagle virus [5], which is a widespread email-based virus. For ease of presentation and understanding, some simplifications have been made.

```
1   lea edi, ptr [ebp+0x4025]
2   mov edx, 0xef4013a0
3   mov ecx, 0x3ec5
    loop:
4           mov al, byte ptr ds[edi]
5                   sub al, dl
6           sub al, dh
7           xor al, cl
8           rol edx, cl
9           mov byte ptr ds[edi], al
10          inc edi
11          dec ecx
12  jnz loop
13  push edi
14  call 0x7c92a950
```

The key part of the sample code is a loop formed by instructions 4 through 12. The instructions preceding the loop (i.e., instructions 1 through 3) initialize the loop counter (*ecx*), starting address (*edi*), and another variable (*edx*). In the body of the loop a value is fetched from the data segment, performs a calculation based upon that value, and then finally stores the computed value back into the data segment. Following the loop, the program calls a library function that uses the newly computed values. The use of these values triggers the actions of the virus. Many different kinds of obfuscation transformations can be applied to this piece of code to affect mutations of the Bagle virus [5]. Existing techniques proposed by authors in [1, 3, 5, 9] would not be able to correctly identify mutated versions of the Bagle virus. In order to overcome these shortcomings the new novel techniques of detection in a VE using newly designed and developed minifilter drivers is considered.

C. Minifilter Driver

Minifilter: The filter manager is a kernel-mode driver that performs in accordance to a standard file system filter model. The ultimate goal of a filter manager is to provide the generic functionality that is required by file system filter drivers. This functionality is very useful for the third party driver developer to develop and write minifilters for the user applications [13]. The applications developed by minifilters are more robust and versatile [11].

Filter Manager Concepts: All Microsoft Windows OS based systems have a filter manager installed on them [12]. But the filter manager is turned into active mode only when a minifilter driver is loaded. The minifilter driver can register itself with the filter manager to perform filtering of a chosen set of I/O operations.

Load Order Groups: The "load order group" determines the position of a legacy filter driver position in the file system I/O stack relative to other filter drivers [14].

Altitude of a Minifilter: The *altitude* of a minifilter is the characteristic that identifies the position of a minifilter relative to other minifilters in the I/O stack when the minifilters are loaded [14].

Instance of a Minifilter: The attachment of a minifilter driver at a particular altitude on the file system stack is called an *instance* of the driver. Figure 3 shows the I/O stack with filter manager and three minifilter drivers [12].

Callback Routines of a Minifilter: A minifilter has the capability to filter all the three major I/O based operations. The three I/O operations are IRP-based I/O operations; fast I/O and file system filter (FSFilter) callback operations.

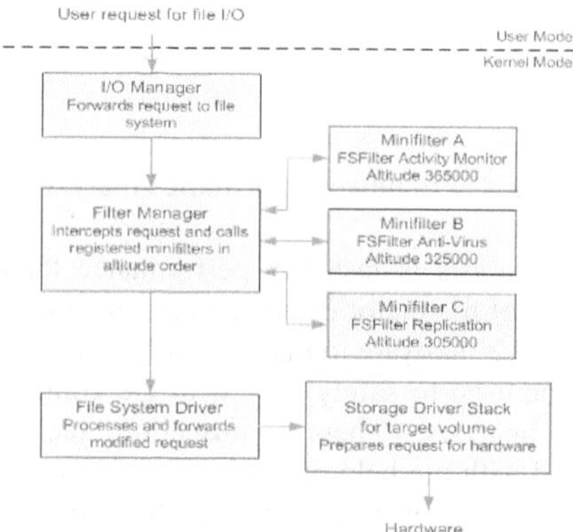

Fig. 3. I/O stack with filter manager and three minifilter drivers

Advantages of Minifilter Drivers: The advantages of minifilter driver over the existing legacy filter driver are:

1. Filter load order control is easy
2. Unloading a minifilter is possible
3. Ability to process only necessary operations

4. Kernel stack is used more efficiently
5. Code redundancy and Less complexity
6. New operations can be easily added
7. Can support multiple platforms easily
8. Better support for user-mode applications

III. SYSTEM DESIGN

A. Overview of the system

The use of a dedicated standalone system for testing the malware is not an efficient solution. The dedicated system can be reinstalled after each dynamic test run is performed, but this induces very high cost. In order to overcome the disadvantages of a standalone system, the new design utilizes a VE in conjunction with the developed minifilter drivers, thus limiting the effect of the malware only to the virtual machine (VM) but not the real system. In case of a virtual system, the infected virtual image is replaced with a new one. A major drawback of the virtual solution is that the malware may detect that it is running in a VE and may change its behavior accordingly.

The alternative solution to the above problem is the use of an emulator. A PC emulator is a piece of software that emulates the functionality of a real system including all the real time resources of a system. There is a subtle difference between an emulator and a VM. Virtual system executes a statically dominant set of instructions directly on a real system, whereas an emulator simulates all the instructions in software [4]. Also there is a very important difference between the speed of execution on a real time system and the speed of execution on a virtual OS. This difference can be used by the malware to judge whether it is being run on a virtual OS or a real system. This problem can be solved by using a minifilter driver which can redirect operations and makes a malware believe that it is not being run in a test, virtual or emulator based environment.

B. Information Analyzed

It is possible to classify the types of information that is captured during the analysis phase of the system. Many systems concentrate on the communication between the application and the OS. This includes intercepting system calls and hooking API calls.

There are tools that can be used to list all the windows processes running in a system. Generally these tools are implemented as OS drivers that can intercept the native windows calls. Thus they are invisible to the application that is currently on analysis. There are also tools that can intercept arbitrary user functions, including all windows API calls. This requires some rewriting of the target function. This could again be detected by a malware and thus it may act differently to overcome the detection.

In order to overcome the problem, virtual OS is used along with a minifilter tool. It has the capability of analyzing both the native windows calls as well as the windows API calls, at the same time being unidentified by the malicious code. Because of the use of the minifilter which has complete control over the system, the analysis being performed is more fine grain. This functionality is similar to the debugger but the technique does not make use of break points, which are known to create problems when used for analyzing malicious code. The reason being the software break points can be detected using code integrity checks and the malware could act accordingly [7].

The minifilter tool is used for analyzing windows executables, especially the files corresponding to the portable executable (PE) file format. In this technique the program is tested in a VE and the valid native windows calls and windows API are logged for analysis.

C. Analyzing the reports and decision making

Once a report is generated by the tool, analysis can be performed by the analyst. Based on the operations performed by the program as listed in the report, the analyst can classify a program as a malicious program or a normal program. For example, the following is the analysis of a sample report. The report is from Symantec Antivirus [10]:

Name: Auraax.c
Type: Worm
Infection Length: 27,136 bytes
Systems Affected: Windows 98, Windows 95, Windows XP, Windows Me, Windows Vista, Windows NT, Windows Server 2003, and Windows 2000.

Whenever the worm executes, it replicates itself and infects all the machines that are prone to it. It copies into the system files of a machine as follows:

%Program Files%\Microsoft Common\wuauclt.exe

Once a machine is infected, it creates several files on the infected machine. For e.g. the following files are created:

1. *%Windir%\Temp\rld[SINGLE NUMBER].tmp*
2. *%System%\config\systemprofile\Local Settings\History\desktop.ini*
3. *%System%\config\systemprofile\Cookies\index.dat*
4. *%System%\config\systemprofile\Local Settings\Temporary Internet Files\desktop.ini*

After the creation of files, the worm alters the following system processes:

1. *svchost.exe*
2. *explorer.exe*

The worm creates new entries into the windows registry along with modifying existing entries. These entries run every time the system boots. The worm also creates registry entries that have the capability to bypass the Windows firewall. The worm also searches the kernel drivers for .sys extension files for the purpose of modifying them. These files are generally overwritten with a root kit so that the worm can hide itself. The worm also modifies the host machine files to prevent the host from downloading new updates from Microsoft and other antivirus providers.

D. Testing Environment

The whole testing is performed on a virtual system. The developed tool's two major components are Minifilter Driver and Analysis Tool.

Once the minifilter is installed and the service is running, the program can be tested. Figure 4 shows the architecture of the developed tool.

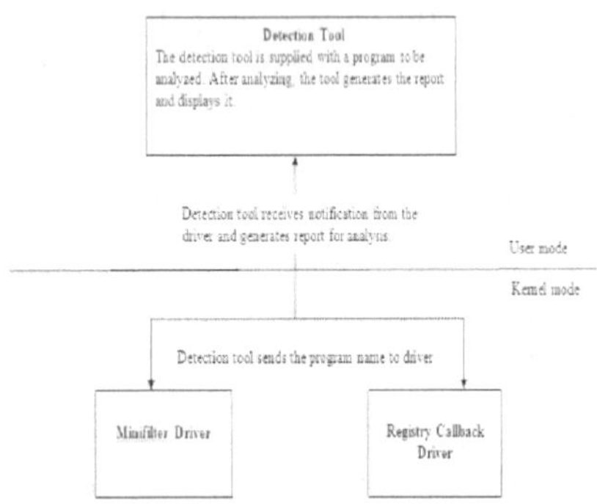

Fig. 4. Architecture of the Malicious Code Detection Tool

The testing is performed in the following steps:

1. First the program name is sent to the driver
2. Driver monitors process operations
    a. driver monitors the process creation
    b. drivers monitors the activity and redirect any operation
3. Driver monitors the exit of the process
4. Detection tool receives notification from the driver and generates report for analysis

Redirection using the detection tool: Redirection explains how the detection tool controls the malware by having greater control over the system. The following redirection schemes are used:

1. If a program wants to read an existing registry key:

HKLM\Software\Microsoft\Windows\TaskManager

Analyzer will let the program read the value and return to malware program.

2. Suppose malware wants to create a registry key

HKLM\Software\Microsoft\Windows\MalwareXXX

Analyzer will create a registry key as:

HKLM\Software\Analyzer Sandbox\Malware

The sub key will be:

HKLM\Software\Microsoft\Windows\MalwareXXX

The tool makes the malware believe that it is not detected by sending wrong registry keys. It monitors the creation and deletion of registry keys.

3. Whenever malware tries to read a registry key, Analyzer will first check the sandboxed key and if found will return the value from there, otherwise will let the operation continue as usual.

4. What happens if malware modifies any registry key? This operation will be considered as same to creation of key.

5. What happens when file operation is requested? It treats registry names as some file names and file paths.

E. Analysis Process

The analysis process is started by allowing the given program to execute in an emulated environment. When the program executes, all the OS services that are requested by the program are noted. Every action that involves communication with the environment requires some OS services, and it cannot directly interact with the hardware. In a windows OS environment, the application cannot directly interact with the windows native API. They are supposed to make use of the functions provided by the OS to interact with the OS services.

Malware writers make direct use of these native API to avoid any kind of DLL dependencies or confuse the virus scanners. This tool takes care of both Windows API function calls by an application and native API calls of an application, thus making the probability of a malware escaping the analysis very low. The tool will track which OS services are used by a program. This tracking requires us to solve two problems:

1. We must be able to track the execution of a malware process and also distinguish between the instructions executed by a malware process and the instructions executed by a normal process. This is very important because the emulated environment does not only run the instructions of the malware process, but also the native OS instructions and instructions of the other supporting processes.
2. We need to make sure that the native API call or a windows API call is invoked without any kind of modification to the malware sample.

The PDBR (Page Directory Base Register) can be used to track the execution of the instructions. For this purpose a tool a tool has been designed and developed to makes use of virtual OS and minifilter drivers for detection of malicious code. Figure 5 shows the detection tool in operation.

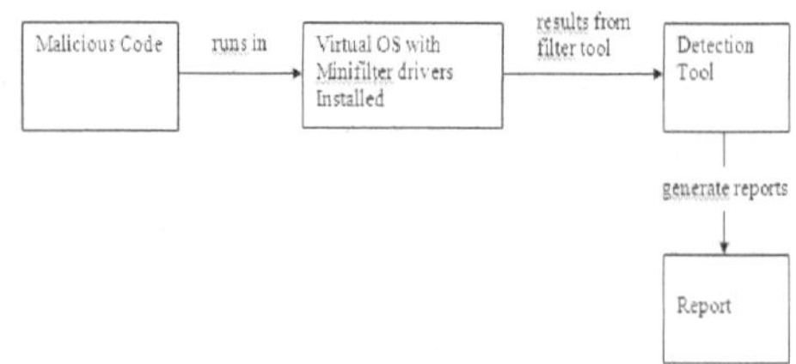

Fig. 5. Overview of the Malicious Code Analysis Tool

IV. RESULTS AND EVALUATION

To demonstrate the malware tool in successfully monitoring the actions of malicious code, the tool has been dynamically tested on currently existing malware samples. To evaluate the tools effectiveness, the results are compared against various anti-virus providers solutions.

The malware sample set is chosen from the Symantec's published list of the most prevalent malware samples [10]. A set of different malware programs that represent a good mix of different malicious code variants currently popular are chosen. From this pool, we choose one working sample for each malware type. All samples chosen for the experiments are run against the online virus scanner provided by Symantec and Kaspersky to verify their integrity. The detection tool was also able to recognize many viruses that are enlisted neither on Symantec's or Kaspersky's anti-virus list. The technical detail of malware includes the files, registry entries, processes and services affected by the malware. Generally these changes by a particular virus are not the same on different computers. The reasons can be that the malicious code chooses random file names or a name from a list of options that are not exhaustively covered by the malware description, or it can be a malware variant rather than the malware about which the virus scanner has published the technical details. Table 2 presents some malwares that are analyzed by the tool and compared to the results of the Symantec anti-virus list.

In Table 2 'P' refers to partial matches. The partial matches occur due to the malware dependency on the target system. Generally files are also dependent on the target system but the core files that are created or affected by the malware are always the same. 'Yes' represents malware infection and 'No' refers to no infection by malware. Also there are few malware samples listed in Table 2 for whom virus definitions are not found on the Symantec's anti-virus list. These viruses are successfully detected by the developed tool. Whenever some normal process is analyzed, the tool displays the changes made by the program to the system.

TABLE 2
MALPROBER TEST RESULTS

Malware Name	File	Registry	Process	Service
W32.Storm.Worm	Yes	P	P	P
W32.HLLW.Doo msjuice	Yes	P	P	P
W32.Sality.AE	Yes	P	P	P
W32.Qquzlzb.exe	No	No	No	No
W32.Srvcp.exe	No	No	No	No

The following steps describe the process of analyzing a program as malware or normal.

Step 1: The Malprober driver has to be installed first before any analysis can be performed.

Step 2: The Malprober service has to be started by going to the command prompt in the virtual OS and executing the command "`sc start malprober`".

Step 3: The command ""has to be executed after step 2 for testing the sample program and generating reports.

```
Malprober.exe srvcp.exe
```

Step 4: The Malprober tool automatically generates a report which contains the list of opened files, newly created suspicious files since the last scan, registry keys added, changed and deleted,. Figure 6 shows a report that is generated when a program is tested with the Malprober tool.

Step 5: Finally the analysis of report is performed. From Figure 7 it can be noticed that the program modifies the TCP/IP parameters. At the same time, it makes registry changes so that it can automatically get started every time the system boots.

A. Evaluation

The results obtained clearly show that the developed tool is successfully able to identify various categories of malwares as outlined in Table 2. The tool was successfully able to identify main categories of malwares, but due to space constraints a list of important malwares is provided in Table 2. The developed malware tool is able to detect W32.Sality.AE, W32.Qquzlzb.exe, and variants of polymorphic malwares which were not detectable by using the tool developed by duan et al. [4]. The TTAnalyze tool developed by bayer et al. [7] was either not successful in detecting the entire list of malwares provided in Table 1 as well as polymorphic malwares. From these results it is clearly evident that our new tool outperforms the TTAnalyze tool [7] and the tool by duan et.al. [4]

Fig. 6. Creation of Analysis Report

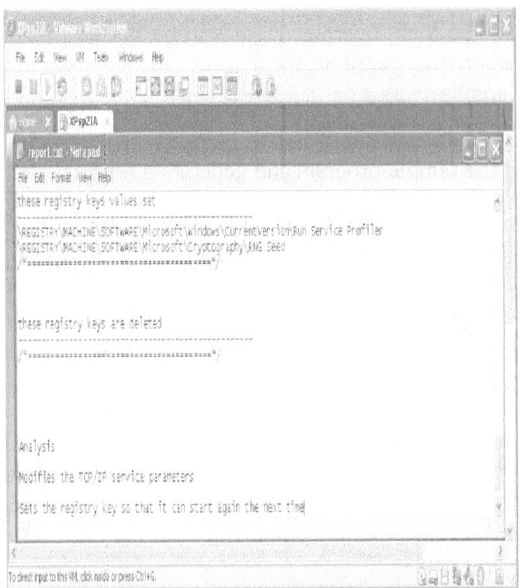

Fig. 7. Analysis Results

V. CONCLUSION

Because of the time gap between the vulnerability that comes into existence as a result of new malware and the point where a solution for the new malware is generated by the anti-virus provider, every new malware poses a serious threat to computer systems. The developed tool dynamically analyzes the behavior of an unknown program by executing the code in a VE using minifilter drivers. One of the main advantage is the report generated by the tool is simple and easy for an analyst to analyze. All the events are listed in chronological order, which makes it easy to understand. Because the analysis is performed in a VE, the overhead is less.

This dynamic tool makes use of a minifilter driver for tracking the security related OS events including Windows API functions and native kernel calls. Once a minifilter driver is provided with a program name, it notifies the tool about the activities of the program. The results successfully showed that this tool is able to identify the various categories of malwares provided by the Symantec database and also its ability to detect polymorphic malwares compared to previously available tools.

The tool can be improved to include more classified and detailed reports. It can be improved by creating a database to store the signatures of detected viruses and use this database whenever necessary.

REFERENCES

[1] U.Bayer, A.Moser, C.Krugel & E.Kirda, (2006) "Dynamic analysis of malicious code", *Journal in Computer Virology*, Vol. 2, No. 1, pp67-77.

[2] Fabrice Bellard, (2005) "QEMU, a fast and portable dynamic translator", *Proceedings of the annual conference on USENIX Annual Technical Conference*, pp41-46, April 10-15, 2005, Anaheim, CA.

[3] M. Christodorescu, S.Jha, (2003) "Static analysis of executables to detect malicious patterns", *12th Usenix Security Symposium*, pp169-186.

[4] H.Duan, Y.Guan, J.Zhang, (2008) "AMCAS: An Automatic Malicious Code Analysis System", *The Ninth International Conference on Web-Age Information Management (WAIM 2008)*, pp501-507, July 20-22, 2008, Zhangjiajie, China.

[5] M.Feng, R.Gupta, (2009) "Detecting virus mutations via dynamic matching", *The IEE International Conference on Software Maintenance (ICSM 2009)*, pp105-114, Sept 20-26, 2009, Riverside, CA.

[6] K.Kent, P.Mel, J.Nusbaum, (2005) "Guide to Malware Incident Prevention and Handling", *National Institute of Standards and Technology*, SP800-83.

[7] U.Bayer, C.Kruegel, and E.Kirda, (2006) "TTAnalyze: A Tool for Analyzing Malware", *15th European Institute for Computer Antivirus Research (EICAR 2006) Annual Conference*, April 2006, Hamburg, Germany.

[8] D.Quist, V.Smith, "Detecting the Presence of Virtual Machines Using the Local Data Table", *Offensive Computing* http://www.offensivecomputing.net/

[9] M. Rothman, V.Zimmer, "Virus Scanning of Input/Output Traffic of a Computer System" *United States Patent Application Publication*, Pub No. US 2005/0216759 A1.

[10] Symantec Auraax, Available from http://www.symantec.com/security_response/writeup.jsp?docid=2008-092409-4704-99&tabid=2

[11] Microsoft Filter Drivers, Available from http://www.microsoft.com/whdc/driver/filterdrv/default.mspx

[12] Microsoft Filter Manager, Available from http://msdn.microsoft.com/en-us/library/windows/hardware/ff541610%28v=vs.85%29.aspx

[13] Microsoft INF file, Available from http://msdn.microsoft.com/en-us/library/ms924764.aspx

[14] Microsoft Load Order Groups, Available from http://www.microsoft.com/whdc/driver/filterdrv/alt-range.mspx

[15] Microsoft Minifilter Architecture, Available from http://msdn.microsoft.com/en-us/library/ff541613(v=VS.85).aspx

[16] Microsoft WDK, Available from http://www.microsoft.com/whdc/DevTools/WDK/WDKpkg.mspx

Security Standards and Best Practices for Quantum Key Distribution

Carole Harper
Center for Cyberspace Research
Air Force Institute of Technology
Wright-Patterson AFB, OH 45433
001-937-255-3636 x4800
Carole.Harper@afit.edu

Michael R. Grimaila
Center for Cyberspace Research
Air Force Institute of Technology
Wright-Patterson AFB, OH 45433
001-937-255-3636 x4800
Michael.Grimaila@afit.edu

Gerald Baumgartner
Laboratory for Telecommunications Sciences
College Park, MD 20740
gbbaumg@gmail.com

ABSTRACT

Quantum Key Distribution (QKD) systems combine cryptographic primitives with quantum information theory to produce a theoretic unconditionally secure cryptographic key. However, real-world implementations of QKD systems are far from ideal and significantly differ from the theoretic model. Because of this, real-world QKD systems require additional practical considerations when implemented to achieve secure operations. In this paper, a content analysis of the published literature is conducted to determine if established security and cryptographic standards and practices are addressed in real world, practical QKD implementations. The research reveals that the published, real world QKD implementations examined do not take advantage of established security and cryptographic standards and best practices. Based upon an analysis of existing industry security and cryptographic standards and best practices, systems architecture guidelines are used to make recommendations for how these standards can and should be applied to establish a practical, secure, QKD system framework.

Categories and Subject Descriptors

Quantum Cryptography, Systems Engineering

General Terms

Industry Security Standards, Content Analysis, System Architecture

Keywords

Quantum Key Distribution (QKD)

1. INTRODUCTION

Classical cryptographic methods rely on the computing time necessary to solve difficult mathematical problems such as discrete logarithms and factoring large prime numbers to provide security. They work by ensuring the time cost verses benefit gained to break the algorithm does not make solving the problem feasible for an attacker [1]; however, increases in computer processing speeds over time have prompted newer and more sophisticated methods of encrypting and protecting data for purposes of information security.

The past few decades, research has yielded a new technology called Quantum Key Distribution (QKD) which utilizes several quantum mechanics principles in conjunction with cryptographic primitives as a way to provide theoretically unconditional security. The appeal of QKD is driven by the unconditional security it provides despite any advances made in computing power or mathematics. As QKD becomes a more viable alternative to existing cryptographic technologies, researchers have sought to determine just how much security a QKD system provides through both mathematic and experimental rigor. While this research has produced a great deal of important discoveries for the future of QKD, very little has been published investigating whether systems meet existing security standards.

To understand the security of a QKD system, an understanding of its fundamental principles is required. A QKD system claims to theoretically provide unconditional security by combining three key concepts. First, it utilizes a cryptographic primitive known as a one-time pad [2]. A one-time pad is a symmetric cryptographic algorithm that requires a random key the same length as the message to be encrypted and, provided the key is never reused, is the only information theoretically secure encryption primitive. Information theoretically secure means that it has been formally proven that knowing the encrypted or cipher text message in no way gives information regarding the unencrypted, or plain text [1]. Second, it employs a message authentication primitive, which utilizes a fraction of the key in a Universal 2-Hash function [2]. Third, the principle that makes QKD a truly unique system is the key distribution primitive which relies on Quantum Information Theory that prevents bits sent on a quantum channel from being copied or intercepted without notice [2]. BB84 [3], a now well known QKD protocol was proposed by Charles Bennett and Gilles Brassard in 1984. In the ideal BB84 protocol single photons are polarized in one of four potential orientations using two possible bases. The polarization of the photon is assigned based on the desired bit and basis to be sent. The process depicted in Figure 1 is:

1) Alice randomly selects a bit and basis and polarizes photons accordingly.

2) Alice sends the polarized photons to Bob.

3) Bob receives polarized photons through his own randomly chosen basis

4) Alice and Bob then communicate via public channel to reveal which basis they selected for each photon. Photons where matching bases were chosen are kept; photons where bases did not match are ignored.

5) Alice and Bob then perform error correction/verification and in an ideal system what they have left is a secure key [3].

QUANTUM TRANSMISSION															
Alice's Random Bits	0	1	1	0	1	1	0	0	1	0	1	1	0	0	1
Random Sending Bases	D	R	D	R	R	R	R	R	D	D	R	D	D	D	R
Photons Alice Sends	⤢	↕	⤡	↔	↕	↕	↔	↔	⤡	⤢	↕	⤡	⤢	⤢	↕
Random Receiving Bases	R	D	D	R	R	D	D	R	D	R	D	D	D	D	R
Bits as Received by Bob	1		1		1	0	0	0		1	1	1		0	1
PUBLIC DISCUSSION															
Bob Reports Bases of Received Bits	R		D		R	D	D	R		R	D	D		D	R
Alice Says Which Bases Were Correct			OK		OK			OK				OK		OK	OK
Presumably Shared Information (if no eavesdropping)			1		1			0				1		0	1
Bob Reveals Some Key Bits at Random					1									0	
Alice Confirms Them					OK									OK	
OUTCOME															
Remaining Shared Secret Bits			1					0				1			1

Figure 1 BB84 Protocol [8]

Unfortunately, real world implementations very rarely meet ideal conditions. These non-idealities often introduce potential vulnerabilities into the system that were not anticipated by researchers. Standards and processes are developed to govern implementation, address non-idealities and to determine whether a system meets security requirements. In the case of a system such as QKD where security is a main system function, it becomes absolutely essential to use security standard considerations when developing baseline architecture. This paper answers the question: Does existing QKD research consider security standards?

2. PROPOSED ANALYSIS

In this paper, we propose a formal content analysis to determine the presence of security considerations in published literature. The content analysis identifies concepts to be analyzed, content to be analyzed, and proposes coding criteria discussed in this section.

Content analysis is used to determine the presence of words or concepts within text. It allows a researcher to quantify the presence of such concepts formally or informally or as broadly or specifically as the researcher decides. A content analysis calls for a text to be broken down into manageable categories and then examined using one of the basic content analysis methods. The content analysis methods chosen for this research is conceptual analysis, which quantifies the presence, either implicit or explicit, of a specified concept within a text [4]. Additionally, systems architecture guidelines will be examined to determine their use in meeting security requirements and identifying shortfalls.

3. EXPERIMENT SETUP

The content to be analyzed is drawn from published QKD research papers. There have been a great many papers published on this topic. This research attempts to analyze a cross sampling of papers published from the 1980s to present time and does so by breaking the content into three main categories: earlier concepts for QKD implementation when less work had been done towards making it a commercially viable concept [3, 5], different possible implementations and uses [6, 7, 8], and known security vulnerabilities in practical QKD implementations [9, 10, 11, 12, 13].

The concepts to be analyzed were derived from IT security standards. There are many standards present to select from; however, for this research four main documents were used to develop the criteria. These four standards are chosen based on general applicability to both secure IT and cryptographic systems and to QKD. From the department of defense Trusted Computer System Evaluation Criteria [14], the Common Criteria [15], the Federal Information Processing Standards Publication 140-2 [16], and the ETSI QKD Standards [2, 17, 18, 19, 20] a top level list of minimum conceptual considerations were synthesized.

Coding is done based on a "met," "partially met," or "does not meet" basis. For example, the security requirement to authenticate will not be considered met or not met based on a detailed explanation of how authentication was accomplished in each set up examined. Instead, if the author makes mention of the need to have an authentication mechanism, the requirement will be considered met and annotated with an "x." If the requirement was explicitly met in its entirety the matrix be annotated with an "x*." The blank matrix is presented in Figure 2.

Once the initial content analysis is complete, a second comparison will be done with basic products developed using the Department of Defense Architecture Framework v2.0 (DoDAF v2.0) [21] to determine if results improve when developing systems architecture.

		Quantum Cryptography: Public Key Distribution and Coin Tossing	Experimental Quantum Cryptography	Quantum Key Distribution Over 122 km of Standard Telecom Fiber	Has Quantum Cryptography Been Proven Secure	How to Implement Decoy-State Quantum Key Distribution for a Satellite Uplink with 50 dB Channel Loss	Optical Networking for Quantum Key Distribution and Quantum Communications	After Gate Attack on Quantum Cryptosystems	Information Leakage via Side Channels in Freespace BB84 Quantum Cryptography	Time-Shift Attack in Practical Quantum Cryptosystems	Effects of Detector Efficiency Mismatch on Security of Quantum Cryptosystems
Orange Book ("Department of Defense Trusted Computer System Evaluation Criteria, 1983)	Criteria 1										
	Criteria 2										
	Criteria 3										
Common Criteria	Criteria 1										
	Criteria 2										
	Criteria 3										
Federal Information Processing Standards Publication 140-2, Security Standards for Cryptographic Modules	Criteria 1										
	Criteria 2										
	Criteria 3										
ETSI QKD Standards	Criteria 1										
	Criteria 2										
	Criteria 3										

Figure 2: Conceptual Analysis Security Standards Matrix

4. RESULTS AND DISCUSSION

It can be seen that while evidence of some security standards concepts can be found in the published literature, no papers revealed a definitive discussion or emphasis on the criteria. The best result only partially addressed approximately 23% of the standards body of knowledge and the worst result considered a mere 1%. None of the literature analyzed addressed any one security concept in its entirety.

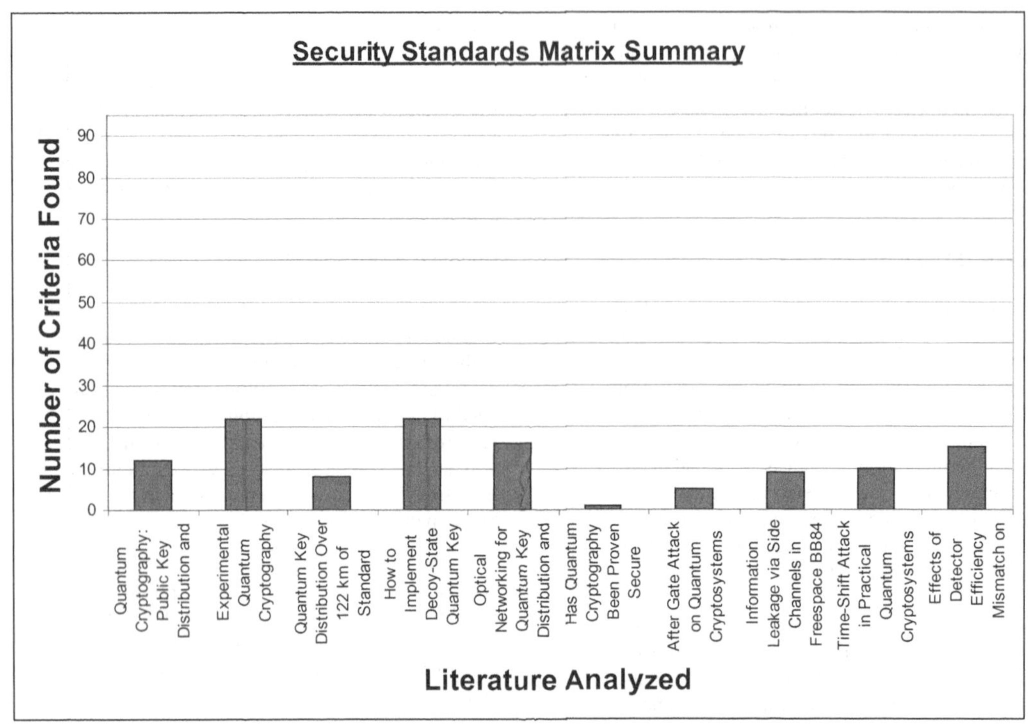

Figure 3: Security Standards Matrix Summary

For comparison, a basic notional top level systems architecture was developed. Using DoDAF v2.0 [21] guidelines an AV-1, AV-2, OV-1, SV-10, StdV-1, as well as a block diagram and use cases were built. Each view is designed to give a specific insight into developing a real-world QKD system.

The AV-1 or the first All Viewpoint provides context for the architectural description. Within the first All Viewpoint, key questions and goals to be met by development architecture are listed. Reviewing the purpose of QKD, several key questions should be addressed, and may be enumerated. The AV-2 or the second All Viewpoint, and the OV-1 or the Operational Concept Graphic help build a better picture of the system and architecture.

The SV-10 or the Systems State Transition Description describes system functionality by identifying response to events. This meets several key security conceptual requirements in multiple standards documents. The block diagram also identifies both information required by security standards as well as information required to answer the questions from the AV-1. Further, the block diagram implies several shortfalls in QKD security standards and guidelines particularly with regard to physical equipment used and interface descriptions. By developing Use Cases the architecture again identifies key system functions, responsibilities and parameters.

Finally, the StdV-1 or first Standards View forces the architect to address the very security standards used in the content analysis. It also identifies many more that may be relevant based on purpose, location and design choices of the QKD implementation.

After developing these architectural viewpoints, a conceptual analysis was performed to see if any improvement was found in the percentage of standards addressed. Results in Figure 4 show this architecture considers 84% of security concepts analyzed and indicates that architectural descriptions at a minimum force developers to consider existing standards and best practices.

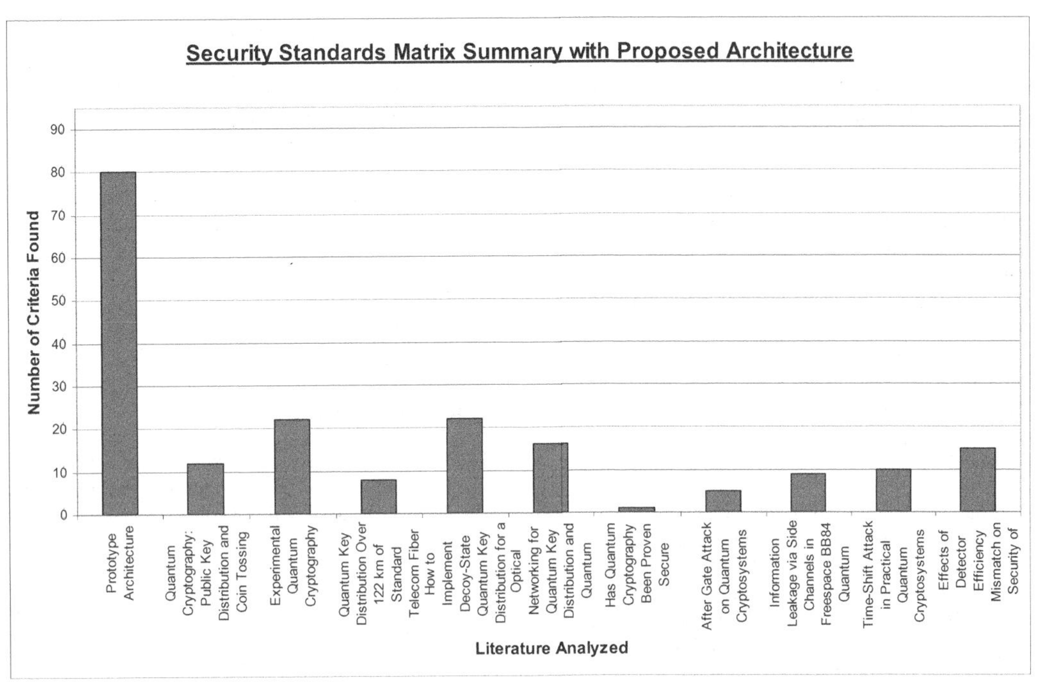

Figure 4: Security Standards Matrix Summary with Proposed Architecture

5. CONCLUSIONS

Initial findings show published QKD systems address partial security standards requirements peripherally, and do not directly consider them when discussing system implementation and security concerns. None of the papers surveyed displayed a definitive discussion of parameters found in the industry standards surveyed.

By conducting developing systems architecture using DoDAFv2.0 [21] guidelines, a prototype for system documentation and further research is developed. The views developed in this paper should be considered the minimum architectural models for security considerations and not a complete meta-model for analysis or security certification.

From a content analysis perspective, the scope of this paper is incredibly restrictive. Only analyzing 10 research papers against four standards is a relatively small sampling of content to review. A larger, more in depth sampling would hold greater meaning.

There are several recommendations for future research.

1) The limitations within the standards presented by this research be addressed further. The four standards analyzed above do apply and should be used when building a QKD system, but they are not a perfect fit. There are strengths and weaknesses within each criterion chosen. For example:

   a) The Common Criteria [15] are designed to be flexible and allow a range of security concerns to be looked at. They provide a methodology for evaluating the security of a system. As such, they are useful when developing and examining QKD. The Common Criteria, however, do not address the unique physical components or probabilistic security nature of QKD.

   b) FIPS 140-2 [16] as a federal cryptographic standard is very applicable to QKD, but will need to be tailored based on the implementation and use of the specific QKD system being evaluated, but FIPS 140-2, like the Common Criteria, does not address the unique nature of QKD security.

   c) As the ETSI [2, 17, 18, 19, 20] standards were created specifically for QKD modules, they are the most relevant. They address known parameters of the system and major components as well as discuss QKD specific protocols for key generation. However, they are not sufficient to evaluate the security of a system. The document provides needed discussion of security, but does not quantify the security or address how it should be validated.

2) Additionally, processes for dealing with multiple security levels within a QKD module should be defined. For example, the interface between the

quantum and classical modules in a QKD system must be carefully reviewed. For example, due to the nature of a QKD system the quantum module and some portions of the classical module should operate at a higher security level than other components within the system. Exactly how the security levels differ and what restrictions should apply as they are forced to interact needs to be addressed in detail. It is clear that the QKD standards that were reviewed do not adequately address this particular concern. However, since the purpose of the system is cryptographic key sharing, system architects must be keenly aware of the need to separate data from different security levels as this will drive the underlying component requirements and implementation constraints.

3) A formal methodology is needed to quantify the security of real-world QKD systems and components and provide for independent testing and validation. Standards could be developed that rigorously define the security within components, protocols and software used in QKD. For example, the laser that generates a single photon, the detector designed to detect a single photon, the configuration of the quantum channel are three main physical areas that are key to QKD security. The ETSI standards provide guidance as to how these should be implemented, but for independent validation, calibration, testing and other concerns, there may be additional standards that should be met. Developing a measurement framework and explicitly defining component and system parameters is a step that has begun to be taken, but must be developed further. There is an ongoing effort that began in September 2011 designed to provide a measurement framework. Metrology for Industrial Quantum Communications is attempting to define the operating parameters for photon emitters, quantum channels and photon receivers used in QKD [22]. This provides a start to developing independent verification and definition of security.

4) Future research should be conducted to utilize all existing applicable security standards for both cryptographic modules and trusted systems. This research is limited to four specific standards; however, there is a much larger body of knowledge that should be addressed in any practical attempt to develop QKD. These standards will need to be reviewed and tailored for the operation and configuration selected by each implementation.

5) The final recommendation derived from this research is to further develop a coherent integrated QKD architecture. A coherent and integrated architecture would utilize the industry security standards considered in this research as well as those omitted due to scoping limitations and help identify areas where standards fall short or need to be tailored for unique QKD concerns. Its formal process would generate a discussion of the future research concerns above and assist in testing and analysis of the many varied QKD configurations.

6. DISCLAIMER

The views expressed in this paper are those of the authors and do not reflect the official policy or position of the United States Air Force, Department of Defense, or the U.S. Government.

7. REFERENCES

[1] Trappe, Wade and Washington, Lawrence, Introduction to Cryptography with Coding Theory Second Edition, NJ: Pearson Prentice Hall, 2006.

[2] European Telecommunications Standards Institute. Quantum Key Distribution (QKD); Use Cases. ETSI GS QKD 008 v1.1.1, Sophia Antipolis Cedex – FRANCE, 2010

[3] Bennet, Charles H., and Gilles Brassard. "Quantum Cryptography: Public Key Distribution and Coin Tossing," Proceeding of the International Conference on Computers, Systems & Signal Processing. 1984.

[4] Busch, Carol, Paul S. De Maret, Teresa Flynn, Rachel Kellum, Sheri Le, Brad Meyers, Matt Saunders, Robert White, and Mike Palmquist. (2005). Content Analysis. Writing@CSU. Colorado State University Department of English. from http://writing.colostate.edu/guides/research/content/. Retrieved Mar 2012

[5] Bennet, Charles, Francois Bessette, Filles Brassard, Louis Salvail, and John Smolin, "Experimental Quantum Cryptography," Journal of Cryptology. (1992).

[6] Gobby, C. Z.L. Yuan, and A. J. Shields. "Quantum Key Distribution Over 122 km of Standard Telecom Fiber," Applied Physics Letters, 84: 3762-3764 (2009).

[7] Meyer-Scott, Evan, Zhizhong Yan, Allison MacDonald, Jean-Philippe Bourgoin, Hannes Hubel, and Thomas Jennwein. "How to Implement Decoy-state Quantum Key Distribution for a Satellite Uplink with 50-dB Channel Loss," A Physical Review, (2011).

[8] Chapuran, T E, P Toliver, N A Peters, J Jackel, M S Goodman, R J Runser, S R McNown, N Dallmann, R J Hughes, K P McCabe, J E Nordholt, C G Peterson, K T Tyagi, L. Mercer, and H. Dardy. "Optical Networking for Quantum Key Distribution and Quantum

Communications," New Journal of Physics, 11 (2009).

[9] Nakassis, Tassos, J.C. Bienfang, P. Johnson, A. Mink, D. Rogers, X. Tang, and C.J. Williams. "Has Quantum Cryptography Been Proven Secure?" Quantum Information and Computation, 6244 (2006).

[10] Wiechers, C, L Lydersen, C Wittmann, D Elser, K Skaar, Ch Marquardt, V, Makarov, and G Leuchs. "After-gate Attack on a Quantum Cryptosystem," New Journal of Physics, 13 (January 2011).

[11] Nauerth, Sebastian, Martin Furst, Tobias Schmitt-Manderbach, Henning Weier, and Harold Weinfurter. "Information Leakage via Side Channels in Freespace BB84 Quantum Cryptography," New Journal of Physics, 11 (3 June 2009).

[12] Bing, Qi, Chi-Hang Fred Fung, Hoi-Kwong Lo, and Xiongfeng Ma. "Time-shift Attack in Practical Quantum Cryptosystems," Quantum Information & Computation, 7: 73-82 (2007).

[13] Makarov, Vadim, Andrey Anisimov, and Johannes Skaar. "Effects of Detector Efficiency Mismatch on Security of Quantum Cryptosystems," A Physical Review, 78 (31 June 2008).

[14] Department of Defense. Department of Defense Trusted Computer System Evaluation Criteria. DoD 5200.28-STD. Washington, 15 August 1983.

[15] The Defence Signals Directorate and others, Common Criteria for Information Technology Security Evaluation. CCMB-2009-07-001, July 2009

[16] Information Technology Laboratory National Institute of Standards and Technology. Security Requirements for Cryptographic Modules. FIPS PUB 140-2, Gaithersburg, MD, 11 January 1994.

[17] European Telecommunications Standards Institute. Quantum Key Distribution (QKD); QKD Module Security Specification. ETSI GS QKD 008 v1.1.1, Sophia Antipolis Cedex – FRANCE, 2010

[18] European Telecommunications Standards Institute. Quantum Key Distribution (QKD); Security Proofs. ETSI GS QKD 008 v1.1.1, Sophia Antipolis Cedex – FRANCE, 2010

[19] European Telecommunications Standards Institute. Quantum Key Distribution (QKD); Components and Internal Interfaces. ETSI GS QKD 008 v1.1.1, Sophia Antipolis Cedex – FRANCE, 2010

[20] European Telecommunications Standards Institute. Quantum Key Distribution (QKD); Application Interface. ETSI GS QKD 008 v1.1.1, Sophia Antipolis Cedex – FRANCE, 2010

[21] Department of Defense. DoD Architecture Framework Version 2.0. Washington: GPO, 28 May 2009.

[22] European Metrology Research Programme, "Metrology for Industrial Quantum Communications," http://projects.npl.co.uk/MIQC/index.html, 15 February 2012.

Detecting the Insider Threat: Going beyond the Network Layer

Rita M. Barrios, PhD.
Computer Information Systems – Cyber Security
University of Detroit Mercy
Detroit, MI, USA
barriorm@udmercy.edu

Abstract

Intrusion detection is difficult to accomplish when utilizing the current detection methodologies when considering the database and authorized insiders. It is a common understanding that current methodologies focus on the network architecture, which is not an adequate solution when considering the insider threat. Recent findings suggest that many have attempted to address this concern with the utilization of various detection methodologies in the areas of database authorization, security policy management and behavior analysis yet have not been able to find an adequate solution to achieve the level of detection that is required.

While each of these methodologies has been addressed on an individual basis, there has been limited work focused on the collaboration of methodologies.

The research presented defines the development of a Database Intrusion Detection System (dIDS) framework by introducing a process and implementation method in a harmonious use of current methodologies to enable detection of the insider threat at the database level.

Keywords- Bayesian Belief Network; Database; Insider Threat; Intrusion Detection

I. INTRODUCTION

Detection of a data breach at the database level by an insider threat is an issue that has plagued the information technology community as far back as the mid 1970's. The research presented attempts to address the insider threat issue by presenting a novel approach to Database Intrusion Detection.

A. *Detection of Insider Threat*

Current intrusion detection approaches are unable to effectively identify misuse by authorized insiders at the database level. Existing intrusion detection methodologies are designed to identify anomalies and patterns of misuse at the host and network layer. The inability of these approaches to focus on misuse at the database level makes it extremely difficult to prevent the theft of data by the authorized insider.

As has been noted in recent research, the theft and exposure of the critical data components that resides in a relational database by the authorized insider is on the rise [10]. It is because of the authorized insider anomaly that are coupled with an increase in violations of trust, that has become known as the insider threat, which subsequently has given visibility to the need for an automated solution that enables the detection of this type of security breach [10], [20].

Finding those trusted entities that are capturing the confidential data components is a task that is difficult at best [10], [16]. Identification can encompass a complex decision making process on several levels of abstraction including an understanding of the daily non-threatening, functional actions of the users as identified in the usage logs and measuring those actions against the associated access control policies [7]. The challenge of maintaining information integrity within this limited contextual scope then becomes how identification can be successfully accomplished to distinguish between the dynamic and valid usages of the data components vs. the abuse situation.

With this challenge in mind, the primary objective of the research presented focused on a novel combination of established methodologies in data mining, policy identification and abuse identification in an attempt to identify inappropriate behavior. Additionally, there are two secondary objectives. The first being the creation of a supervised learning component of the dIDS to determine the validity of the 'normal' behavior and the latter is to develop the definition of the behaviors that were needed to identify, classify and respond to the introduction of new transactions to the system.

B. *Relevance of this Study*

When the theft of critical data components is successfully executed by the authorized insider within the organization, corporate trust begins to deteriorate among its consumer base as well as exposes the organization to various legal issues due to the violation of local, state and/or federal laws and regulations. Consequently, this situation will ultimately cause a negative impact on the profit margins for the targeted organization.

This phenomena has been realized in recent times where [12] reports that the data breach of T.J. Maxx (projected to be the largest data breach in history) is expected to see costs related to the breach to increase by more than 10 times the earlier estimate to a record of $4.5 billion. What this amounts to is about $100 per consumer record loss for each of the 45 million credit/debit card account numbers stolen over the 18-month period [12]. It is expected that the cost of the T.J. Maxx data breach to lower profits by $118 million in the first quarter of FY 08 [12].

The insider threat is considered significant. Statistics as presented in a study by [10], which had been conducted by the FBI in 2006 identified that approximately 52% of the respondents had reported unauthorized use of information resources by internal users along with 10% of the respondents unsure if they had been exposed. Further, judicial proceedings as presented by [29] as well as is documented in information systems industry publications as presented by [12] suggests that there is a significant degree of loss to those victim organizations where there has been an exposure of data as a result of the insider abuse anomaly. Reference [29] also presents a case where a senior database administrator (DBA) had pled guilty to stealing 8.5 million consumer information records over a five-year period, which subsequently had been sold by the rogue DBA for approximately $580k. Reference [29] further exposes the problem of the insider threat by presenting a case where the directors of admissions and computer center operations at a Manhattan college were indicted on charges of fraud after setting up an operation where people who had never attended the college paid between $3k and $25k to obtain forged academic transcripts.

Many researchers tend to focus on a single aspect of the overall solution. It is not clear as to why the merging of the two components of transaction validation and abusive activity validation has not been attempted even though many researchers do recognize the need for one [7], [14], [16], [17], [20].

C. Guide to the Paper

Section II presents a brief review of the literature. Section III presents a brief account of the methodologies that were employed to complete the presented research. Section IV presents the findings of the research while Section V concludes with a summary of the overall research and a brief discussion of future works.

II. Review of the Literature

A. Access Controls and the Insider Threat

Although the advancements in database access controls have made significant progress towards securing the data that resides in the database, there are still limitations of how much can be prevented when considering the insider threat phenomena given that the majority of the strides made thus far are focused on addressing the functions of proper authorizations. Since the insider is already authorized these methods will not prevent the theft and/or exposure of the data components when presented with the insider threat scenario [25].

B. Generalized Intrusion Detection Systems

Intrusion Detection Systems (IDS) have been a focused research subject in the area of information security for many. In recent years [3] and [5] as well as others began to present the foundational concepts in formalized research and publications. Because of the clarity presented in [5] research, the discussions presented in the following paragraph are centralized around his work however; the seminal works are identified as the basis for [5] study. It should be noted that the research presented in the [3] study follows the same presentation as [5] whereby the seminal works form the foundational concepts.

IDS can be defined as a system whose goal is to defend a system by raising an alarm when the decision is made that there has been a security violation, and addressed by the security officer [5], [18]. With this in mind, [5] and [3] as well as the seminal works in intrusion detection, identify two primary principles in the IDS model, anomaly detection and signature detection [18], [26]. Anomaly detection is defined as flagging all abnormal behavior as an intrusion [3], [18], [19], [26]. While Signature detection is defined as flagging behavior that is relatively, close in comparison of some defined, known pattern of an intrusion that has been previously defined to the IDS [3], [5], [18], [26].

C. Intrusion Detection Implementation

When implementing an IDS one must be concerned with its three primary components: the audit data, the detector model and the output that is presented to the security officer for follow up. The detector model and its underlying principles is the primary component of the system [3], [5], [8], [9], [18], [19], [21], [15], [28], [26]. Additionally, IDS are further categorized base on the type of intrusion that is recognized by the system. These categorizations include the following the Well-Known, the Generalized and the Unknown. The Unknown intrusion category is identified as a weak coupling between the intrusion and a system flaw. This in turn makes this category the most difficult to understand [5]. It is this last category, the Unknown Intrusion, which is the focal point of the presented research when coupled with the insider threat phenomena.

D. Database Intrusion Detection Systems

Historic as well as current research in the area of IDS and access control methodologies does not support the identification of intrusions at the database level [9], [7], [14], [17]. As [5] notes, the legitimate user can be most difficult to detect using standard audit trail data. If the access control methods are the focal point, a misconception that simply having the right levels of access applied to the data components as defined by [9] is sufficient to protect the data and furthermore these methods will function as a deterrent to the abusive behaviors. When taken into context of the legitimate user, standard forms of detection and access control often fall short in detecting the abusive behavior [9], [7], [14], [17].

Standard IDS authentication/authorization methods primarily reside at the networking and/or operating system level of the system. A false assumption is that because authorization and authentication is successful, that the entity is behaving in a trustworthy manner since the user has achieved database level access [14], [17].

To aid in the closure of this gap, research in the area of the authorized insider has started to take shape. As seen in the [10] study an attempt is made to identify the person making a request for information via usage of the DBMS audit logs in order to make a determination of whether the requestor is functioning within the boundaries of their specified security capacity as patterned in the historical database logs. Again, as presented by [20] an attempt is made at identifying suspect transactions via the usage of a quantitative measurement of transaction violations as had been mapped from the Database Management System (DBMS) audit logs in order to decide whether the requestor is making a 'legal' request [20]. However, both of these studies fall just short of proactively, dynamically and automatically identify the abusive use of the data components by the authorized insider.

As previously noted, [4] attempts to identify the unauthorized insider by constructing a Networked Bayesian Network (NBN) in an attempt to project the probability of an intrusion when critical data components are linked together within a transaction. The deficient factors identified in this study are that the authors' base assumption is that 50% of all insiders are attempting to breach the system, which leads the reader to conclude that the assumption is an unrealistic expectation of the study given that there are no documented references in the study that lends itself to this percentage. In addition, the authors of the [4] study realize that their proposed method is ineffective when it is applied to the authorized insider threat risk. The research put forth begins to fill the gap that exists between the concepts of malicious transaction and abusive action identification by expanding these concepts to incorporate the defined access control, security policies as well as the behavior of the authorized user.

III. Research Methods

The foundations of this study were focused on three primary facets. The first was the research proposed by [2] with their methodologies of mining association rules within a large set of data using the Apriori Hybrid Algorithm. The methodologies put forth by [19] in the area of utilizing the Stochastic Gradient Boosting and the Bayesian Belief Network algorithms to determine probabilities was the second pillar for this study. Thirdly, current methodologies utilized in the dynamic maintenance area of security policy, known as Digital Rights Management (DRM) served as the final pillar to secure the foundation of this research. Along with the novel approach to database intrusion detection that guided the presented research, a series of modified Intrusion Detection System heuristics has been presented to provide a solid foundation for the acceptance of the results of the approach. The following paragraphs outline how these objectives can be achieved with the utilization of the presented methodologies.

A. System Architecture Flow Diagram:

The architecture depicted in Figure 1 – System Architecture/Flow Diagram has been implemented. The process began with the Trusted User initiating a transaction. Whether the transaction is initiated via internal or external means has not been addressed but is considered in future work. Once the transaction has entered dIDS system, several processes were initiated to determine the probability of an intrusion. The results from the probability assessment were stored in the dIDS repository for future reference. These results were passed on to the entity responsible for the determination of whether an actual intrusion has occurred. At this time, the transaction continued on to its completion since this study was focused on intrusion detection and not intrusion prevention. Future work focuses on extending the work presented into the intrusion prevention.

B. The Association Rules:

As in most organizations, certain data components are dependent upon other data components. Often usage outside of the normal transactional scope is an anomaly in and of itself. It then makes sense if the selection of certain data components without their complimentary counterpart, one can reasonably conclude that an intrusion may be occurring. As [31] have reasoned, often times, in intrusion detection, the training data is developed utilizing a significant amount of expert information about the system and often times this domain knowledge is difficult to obtain. Continuing with the implementation of the [2] Apriori Hybrid Algorithm to mine the association rules, the difficulty of the domain expertise is greatly reduced. Following the acquisition of the training data, it is then subsequently used to identify known intrusions. These signatures must then be augmented on an on-going basis to capture unknown anomalies when the scope of the environment changes. As [29] points out, there is a direct relationship between the quality of the intrusion detection model and the quality of the training data obtained thru various data mining techniques. With this quality concern in mind, this research utilized an Apriori Hybrid Algorithm in order to determine the most appropriate data dependency signatures. Utilization of this type of algorithm is common during a data mining operations when obtaining a selection of relevant facts (data components) where the members have a high degree of correlation [2]. Once developed, the application of the algorithm to the TPC-C data occurs in order to determine which data components appear to be of significance for the processing environment of the prototype dIDS. Since the creation of the training data is a generic process, utilization of the algorithm to process the historical data in order to determine the data component significance is appropriate. As such, it is also appropriate to apply the training algorithm to a variety of input data following the definition of the components within the pool of information to develop newly identified association rules.

An unsupervised learning process was initially employed in a data-mining environment to establish the baseline rules, which developed the data association rules that established the behavior correlations. Rule associations algorithms are well researched as noted above. The Apriori Algorithm as implemented by [1] is said to be the most popular of these types of mining operations [13]. However, an extension to this algorithm as developed by [1], called the Apriori Hybrid was utilized in the development of the initial data signatures because of its wide acceptance within the data mining community. This is due in part to the algorithm's quality levels when mining user behavior, patterns of access and the assigned classifications from historical data [13]. Since the Apriori Hybrid Algorithm exploits the best features of both the Apriori and the AprioriTID in addition to being one of the most popular of the Association Rules algorithms as noted by [13], its foundational properties have been employed.

C. Determine the Probability of Intrusion:

As evidenced in historical and current research, fuzzy logic and/or neural networks have been successfully used to determine whether an intrusion has been encountered [7]. Since 'normal' behaviors are often known within the data processing environments and patterns of behavior can be established from the historical information, the utilization of a similar approach to the neural network IDS solution can be implemented utilizing the more defined decision tree methodology in a supervised learning process to determine the probability of an intrusion.

The data gathered was refined by utilizing the supervised Stochastic Gradient Boosting decision tree process to establish the probability of whether a given signature as created by the Apriori Hybrid Algorithm is considered an intrusion [19], [24].

It should be noted that the recommend practice as suggested by [24], is to perform both the Stochastic Gradient Boosting tree creation as well as a single tree. This is because the Stochastic Gradient Boosting method is more like a 'black box' methodology that is highly accurate however; it is difficult to visualize the relationships established during the process [24]. This recommendation of running both methods has been followed.

Once the prototype had been successfully built this same learning process was employed to account for new entities making requests for information. Upon the discovery of a new entity, the behavior signature repository was updated accordingly with relevant data.

D. Gather Current Security Policy Data:

Today, most organizations' view on publishing the policies modifications requires the updating of web pages, hard copy documents as well as applying any needed updates to the information systems via physical code modifications. Since a process so resource intensive can take weeks or even months to realize, often times, it is near impossible to determine if a violation of policy has occurred until sometime later. In recent times, the application of digital rights management systems (DRM) to allow for identity policy development and distribution is taking shape [30]. As [30] notes the ability to specify and manage the rights of an entity is one of the most important features of the DRM. Unlike standard authorization mechanisms, the DRM is meant to give specific rights to specific entities for a specific amount of time [30]. Bringing this notion of the DRM into context building a DRM-like repository allowed for dynamic, real-time policy.

E. Detection of Abusive Activities – Bayesian Approach:

Usage of the BBN was the most effective method of detection for this study following the building and training periods.

In [6] study, the Bayesian approach combined with a visualization component is defined to create an interactive intrusion detection system in an attempt to reduce the number of false positives presented in current intrusion detection systems. Again, in the [23] study, the Bayesian approach is applied to improve the effectiveness of the detection mechanism in the presented intrusion detection system for a mobile ad hoc network. [4] use the Bayesian approach to expand the independent environment variables often present in intrusion detection to propose a networked Bayesian Network to understand the correlation between these environmental variables which may be used to identify an intrusion within a relational database. Therefore, with the objectives of this research endeavor in mind and in keeping with current research, the probabilistic approach of utilizing the BBN where the conditional probability and the causality relationships between the variables as defined have been applied to the presented intrusion detection system in order to identify a possible breach. Since the dIDS does have knowledge of the acceptable behaviors, relevant security polices as well as the data dependencies, the BBN can make a reasonable assumption of the probability that an intrusion has occurred even when encountered with new information.

Implementation of the BBN took the path as presented in Figure 2.

F. Information Flow Overview:

The flow of information was as follows which is similar to the [4] study. Each of the contributing factors, which include environment, policy as well as data component combinations were given a conditional probability as outlined above. If the computed probability of the information request, (given the identified variables), fell within an acceptable range, the transaction was identified as not being an intrusion. However, if the probability fell outside of the acceptable range, the transaction was defined, as a potential intrusion where by further steps should be enacted in an attempt to make a determination as to whether or not the 'true' intrusion flag is accurate. These further steps include looking into the system to determine if there are any new applications as well as users accessing the system. Should this situation present itself where the dIDS encounters a 'new' entity, the signatures of the entity were stored for utilization in future detection processes. Should the system identify an actual intrusion, in addition to storing the intrusion signatures, the transaction was flagged as an intrusion that should be further examined.

It should be noted that in order to determine the most optimal thresholds, various probability thresholds were utilized. This aided in the determination of the level that the presented research is most effective with the goal being that the model should employ the most restrictive threshold possible while maintaining an acceptable level of detection.

G. Management of New Transactions:

'New' data was collected via the development of a non-functional (in terms of real dollars), simulated payment processing application, where the necessary data components was established and persisted in the targeted in a relational database schema. In addition, this subset of 'new' data was utilized to develop the intelligent features needed to enable the system to automatically identify the new entity and 'learn' from that new relationship for future reference.

The new information garnered from the use of this approach for intrusion detection also enabled the learning process to continue by which new rule associations and new user entities can be identified, validated and stored as needed in their respective repositories for later usage.

In order to generate a significant amount of data for the TPC-97 model, a data- generator software product was purchased under a research license via Red Gate Software, Ltd., a private limited company located in the UK. This software, called Data Generator, was specifically developed for the SQL Server environment to generate meaningful test data. To support this functionality, the TPC-97 model was implemented in the SQL Server 2008 Enterprise Edition environment followed by the generation of 1 million customer accounts as well as supporting order entry information, which included the customer order history using the primary keys of the schema's table objects.

Following the build of the baseline TPC-97 objects, the specific tables for the intrusion detection system were generated along with the incoming transactions. The policy and entity information was manually entered using standard INSERT statements of the SQL query language given that the data was not complex in nature. To support incoming transactions to the TPC-97 database, 925 random transactions were generated based on the policies of the database. The distribution of transactions has been identified in the data analysis section of Chapter iv.

Following the requirements definition of the experiment the Apriori Hybrid algorithm was implemented in the Java programming language and applied against the TPC-97 database to determine the most common patterns of data contained within the data. These patterns served as the baseline patterns used in the dIDS.

To begin the process, the generated transactions were sequentially read into the dIDS where an attempt was made to seek out any existing patterns previously identified as well as any policies that may be set in place to govern the transaction processing. If the policy and pattern were found within the signature repository, the transaction was identified as being proper. However, if only a portion or no information was gathered about the transaction, it was subjected to further scrutiny by first going thru the Stochastic Gradient Boosting algorithm to understand the probability of an intrusion based on the transactional statically defined components such as the data relationships and defined policies. If the transaction continued to be identified as an intrusion by exceeding the pre-defined threshold, the transaction was then subjected to the Bayesian Belief Net algorithm to determine the probability that an intrusion was occurring based on the uncertainty of the environment and the prior behavior of the requestor. Should the transaction continue to be identified as an intrusion, it was flagged as an intrusion then logged as such in the signature table to be used in the analysis of future transactions.

To support the learning component, if the transaction was not classified as an intrusion, it was also logged in the signature table along with the information to identify the transaction as a potential new signature.

Instead of using the network packet as the focus of the measurements as is done in network intrusion detection systems, the focus was directed towards the incoming transaction that are requesting database services. This insider entity was defined to take on the role of an authorized application user, a Database Administrator or an automated program that requests database resources. These roles were defined in the additional database objects that were built to support the intrusion detection system. No programmatic distinction was made during the development of the functional dIDS as to which entity was requesting the information meaning that the policy definitions were the driving force in the identification of the requesting entity.

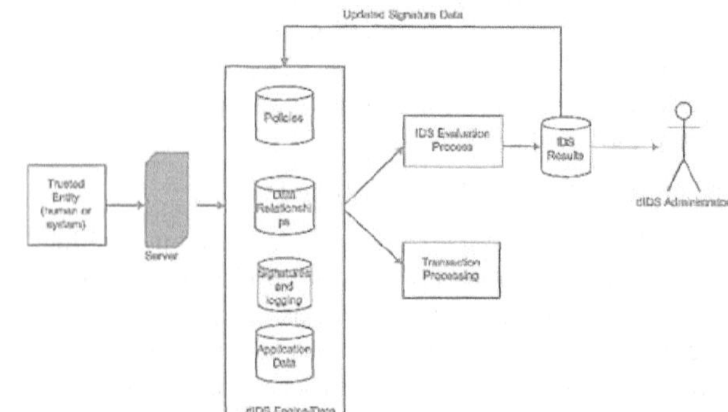

Figure 1 - System Architecture Diagram

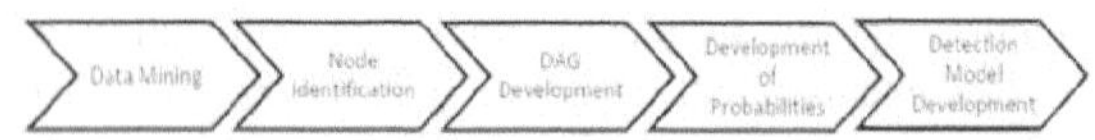

Figure 2 - BBN in Detection Model Development

IV. FINDINGS

Given that intrusion detection at the database level is a rather new concept, finding a relevant study to measure the presented research against was difficult at best. The [29] study was selected due to its similarities in methodology.

The metrics identified in the [17] were presented at a higher degree of abstraction that what was needed for this study. Therefore, the data identified in the study was extrapolated to a finer grain of detail, (the transaction), and is based on the data as presented in the original work in order to build the objective measurements that were to be achieved in the presented work. Given that [17] successful detection rate was identified as 38.38%, this also served as the threshold for successful detection in this study. The presented study achieved similar results as [17] that fell within the range of <61.62% for false responses and >= 38.38% positive responses overall. The extrapolated metrics that are based on the data presented in the [17] study has been identified in Table 1.

Additionally, where applicable, specific baseline measurement values identified of the [17] was adapted to the Information Assurance Directorate (IAD) – U.S. Government Protection Profile for Intrusion Detection Systems as described in the following paragraphs [17], [22].

The measurement of success applied to the functionality of the prototype Database Intrusion Detection System (dIDS) was based upon the security and assurance requirements identified in the IAD - U.S. Government Protection Profile for Intrusion Detection System for Basic Robustness Environments Version 1.1 June 2007 as issued by the National Security Agency (NSA). This directorate incorporated the Common Criteria for Information Technology Security Evaluation version 3.1 dated September 2006 [27]. Specifically, the measurements included qualitative measurements that relate directly to the accuracy of the detection model such as the following:

A. Coverage

Coverage is determined by the rate (c) by which the IDS can successfully identify an attack under ideal conditions. The original measurement as identified by [22] is concerned with measuring the number of unique attacks that can be detected. This measurement, in a signature-based system, is achieved by ascertaining the number of valid signatures (s) and mapping them to a standard naming schema. The entering transaction (t) is then measured against the known signatures to determine if the transaction exists within the signature baseline set t∃. If the transaction does in fact exist in the signature base, it is considered a valid request for information that meets the criteria of an authorized entity. If however, the signature does not exist, it is considered a successful realization of an anomaly and therefore counted in the measurement as noted in Equation 1. To support database intrusion detection in regards to the authorized insider, the measurement presented was adapted to focus attention on the rate by which the IDS can identify an anomaly that has been initiated by the authorized insiders with various levels of authorization. Therefore, only transactions that are initiated by the trusted user are considered in the measurement. This measurement achieved a rate of >= 38.38% as is indicated using the data presented in [17].

$$c = \Sigma(t \nexists s)/s \tag{1}$$

B. Probability of Detection

Determines the rate (d) of attacks detected correctly (b) by an IDS in a given environment during a particular period (T) in minutes [22]. As with the Coverage measurement, probability of detection assumes that various types of attacks were measured. Given that this study is focused on one type of attack, the measurement was adjusted to focus on the various levels of authorization of the information requestor as opposed to the various types of attacks. Given that the false positive rate is directly related to the detection rate, care must be given to ensure that equal scenarios are used in both measurements. This measurement, in accordance with the baseline set using the data as presented in [17] achieved a rate of measurement of >= 38.38% of attacks correctly identified.

$$d = \left(\frac{b}{t}\right) * T \tag{2}$$

C. Volume of Data

This measurement determines the difference in the amount of data (v) of the presented dIDS can manage when presented with a large volume of transactions as compared with the pre IDS implementation. While the data as presented in the NIST IR-7007 identify the number packets/second for the network IDS, when put into the context of this study, the transaction will be the unit of measure. Additionally, this measurement will identify the change of volume of data pre and post dIDS implementation in order to identify any latency issues that may arise.

Given that this measurement is very subjective to the environment in which the system runs, initially, the transactions set was processed without the implementation of the dIDS to determine the rate of processing using the maximum volume of data (m). This measurement was considered to be the baseline value that the rate of processing of the presented dIDS was compared with. Following the establishment of the baseline measurement, the same set of transactions was processed thru the presented implementation of the dIDS (i) to determine the change in the number of transactions that could be processed within this environment given the dIDS implementation. The pre and post IDS expressions used to calculate this measurement, m and i can be defined as follows:

m = Tpre/s where Tpre is the number of pre-IDS transactions and s is the elapsed processing time (in seconds) for the transaction set

i = Tpost/s where Tpost is the number of post-IDS transactions and s is the elapsed processing time (in seconds) for the transaction set

$$v = m - i \tag{3}$$

It was expected that the introduction of an IDS at the database level would cause additional latency in the transaction process. Pre-IDS resulted in a volume of data of 408.38 transactions per second. Overall the system performed as expected with the greatest latency observed at iteration 4 with 309.67 transactions per second or a difference of 98.71 transactions.

D. Adaptability Rate

These measurements determined the rate (a) by which the presented dIDS was able identify new, valid transactions (v) as well as new, authorized users (u). It was presented, as an aggregation of the two measurements, new user identification and new transaction identification where n is the total number of new transactions. It should be noted that because of new information introduced to the dIDS, there might be a higher rate of false positives obtained during the development of this measurement. The anticipated adaptability rate was achieved at >= 25% of new transactions identified.

$$a = (u + v)/n \tag{4}$$

All results presented are the results as produced from the automated system. The threshold values were manually modified in the code base as the iterations progressed during the testing phase. To test the policy change impact and to determine if the dIDS could recognize a change in permissions followed by an appropriate response, data in the policy tables were modified accordingly.

Using the generated data as noted previously, the Apriori Hybrid data mining Algorithm was then applied using the SPMF software as created by [11]. Overall, the result was the generation of 13199 patterns of data. Upon examination of the patterns it was noticed that those patterns where the support was <.8, created less meaningful information. Often patterns were generated that had no value in the intrusion detection process. To avoid this, the scope of pattern utilization was set at the support threshold of >= .8. This resulted in 14 common behavior patterns and 95 data patterns. From the 95 data patterns, 14 common fields were also identified as noted in Table 2. These patterns were then utilized as the baseline signatures of the dIDS system.

To support the incoming transaction set, 925 incoming transactions were generated using the Data Generator software. While the study presented here used 1/8 of the amount of input that [17] used, it was not deemed a significant concern since the study as presented is focused on the percentage of transactions in a set that can be identified as an intrusion not the volume of data. Additionally, the following results can further be inferred to account for a larger dataset.

Those patterns that were mined were determined to be the valid signatures while anything else was considered invalid. Using these valid signatures as the catalyst, both valid and invalid transactions were generated. Table 3 identifies the types of transactions that were generated for the input transaction set.

Analysis of the incoming transaction to determine the probability of intrusion began by identifying the tokens in the transaction. These tokens included the action of SELECT, INSERT, UPDATE, DELETE, the individual columns, the identity of the requesting entity and the tokens of the WHERE and SET clauses, if present. These tokens were then compared to the policy tables to determine if the tokens were contained in an existing policy. If the transaction could be validated based on the information in the policy tables, the transaction was deemed as a non-intrusion. If, however, the transaction could not be validated, the potential intrusion process began.

To begin the potential intrusion process, the incoming transaction was compared to the transaction logs of the database in an attempt to identify if the transaction should be considered a new, valid signature. If the transaction was not supported in the new signature identification process, the transaction was subjected to the potential intrusion detection process. This process began by taking into consideration the transaction as identified above while applying the Stochastic Gradient Boosting algorithm. Unlike the new signature identification process, logs did not support the transaction therefore, these factors were not considered in the probability of intrusion calculation. To refine the intrusion probability, if the transaction's probability of intrusion was computed by the Stochastic Gradient Boosting algorithm to be greater than the control threshold value, the transaction was subjected to further refinement using the Bayesian Belief Net algorithm. If the probability of this primary review was below the threshold, it was deemed as a non-intrusion event and added to the signature table as a validated signature. The same principles as identified for the Stochastic Gradient Boosting algorithm was applied to the application of the Bayesian Belief Net algorithm should the incoming transaction require further analysis. If this probability computation resulted in a value that was above the control threshold, the transaction was deemed an intrusion and logged to the intrusion table object to be used in the on-going signature identification process. There were six (6) iterations of the transaction cycle performed during the testing phase using the various threshold values as identified in table 4.

Table 1. Intrusion Detection Metrics [17].

Testing Area	Baseline Metrics
Coverage	38.38%
Probability of Detection	38.38%
Volume of Data	8368 input transactions

Table 2. Data Tables Volume of Data.

Table	Row Count
Customer	1,000,000
District	483,647
Item	100,000
Order Line	5,000,000

Order	1,000,000
Stock	500,000
Warehouse	5000
Red Gate Patterns	95
Transactions	925
Elements	14
Log Data	4385

Table 3. Input Transaction Set.

Function	Number	Type
Intrusions	51	Policy violations
	44	Global Select (SELECT *)
	51	Full Table delete (DELETE without a where clause)
	302	Invalid Update Statements
	144	Invalid Insert statements
Non Intrusions	333	All other input not identified as an intrusion

Table 4. dIDS Test Iterations.

Test	Threshold	Comment
0	.50	Baseline test
1	.75	Using .25 increments
2	.25	Using .25 increments
3	.35	Threshold refinement
4	.40	Proved to be the most optimum threshold
5	.45	Threshold refinement

V. Conclusions and Future Work

A. Conclusions

Based on the information provided to the dIDS model, the following conclusions have been drawn.

Identification of 'good' vs. 'malicious' transactions is greatly dependent upon the information contained within the transaction itself, the log information, the number of rows being impacted by the database request and the policies pertaining to the entity making the request and the behavior of the requesting entity. Without consideration of each of these components within the context of each other, it cannot be accurately determined if the authorized insider is behaving as expected.

The following table shows that when using the Stochastic Gradient Boosting algorithm alone, when compared to using both algorithms to reach a finer degree of analysis, is less effective than using both algorithms together in a single process when attempting to identify an intrusive transaction.

As can be seen in Table 5, using both algorithms within the same intrusion process, the number of false-positives was markedly reduced.

Several types of transactions were introduced to indicate a new entity; the system was able to identify the new entity as the testing iterations progressed regardless of what the threshold rate was set at. When policy changes were introduced, the system correctly identified the intrusion and non-intrusion state. These metrics are included in the calculation in Table 5.

Overall, the system presented as presented within this research proved very successful. As Table 7 identifies, each goal with the exception of the maintaining the latency factor at a steady rate was met. Further research in the area of maintaining or reducing the latency of a Database intrusion detection system is warranted.

As can be observed in the presented outcomes, to use one methodology in an attempt to identify the insider threat phenomena in the context of the database environment, that supports a reasonable probability measurement, cannot be considered a complete solution. The uncertainty of the requestor's prior behavior must take into consideration along with the complete set of data and environmental factors in order to reach the conclusion that the insider is behaving beyond the boundaries as stated within defined security policies.

Overall, the research presented proves that when the whole environment including behavior is presented, a reduction in the false positive rate can be expected with the increase in the probability of detection. This improvement allows for a more informed, rational decision about the intrusion that is based in evidence can be supported.

B. Future Work

The success of this research was based upon the research of many other researchers in not only intrusion detection but in the database technologies as well.

This research simply laid the foundations for future work to be investigated with respect to Database intrusion detection systems. To further the positive results this research presented, it can be expected that research in the following areas will build upon what has been presented in the preceding chapters.

As noted, the presented research was based upon current research in intrusion detection models. Some of these models are utilized at the network level while others are at the database level. While intrusion detection does aid in the discovery of potential intrusions, it still requires a manual decision to be made by an intrusion administrator as to whether the incoming database request can be definitively considered a non-intrusion event. This is most often accomplished by some form of human intervention.

Expansion of this study to move from an intrusion detection model to an intrusion prevention model allows for an expansion in the research area which enables the next generation of database security to be realized.

In the presented research, two algorithms were selected due to their successful predictive nature of static concerns as well as support for unknown information as demonstrated in the prior studies as presented in Section ii. The Stochastic Gradient Boosting and the Bayesian Belief Net algorithms are not the only types of algorithms that are available to support intrusion detection at the database level when considering the insider threat. With this understanding in mind, expansion of this study to consider other algorithms as well as how to perform a successful implementation is warranted in order to discover which combinations will produce the most effective result.

Finally, an area of research that one must consider when researching intrusion detection systems at the database level is in the area of cloud computing. More and more organizations are looking to include cloud computing in their technology stacks. With this move, it can be expected that the insider threat phenomena will grow given that the term 'insider' takes on a different meaning with the Cloud Service Providers (CSP) now being considered an inside entity. It can be expected that an increase in the number of intrusion events given the inherent weaker security of the environment. It is because of this environment that Database as a Service (DaS) will continue to present risks when considering the insider threat.

Table 5. Transactional (Intrusive) Comparison of Stochastic Gradient when used alone.

Test	Gradient	Gradient/Bayesian	Difference
0	335	131	204
1	360	94	143
2	334	229	105
3	372	198	174
4	360	144	216
5	378	180	198

Table 6. Reduction of False-Positives when both algorithms are used.

Test Iteration	Number of Intrusions	Number of Non-Intrusions	% Reduction in False-Positives
0	131	793	60.90
1	94	830	72.11
2	229	695	31.44
3	198	726	46.77
4	144	780	60.00
5	180	744	52.38

Table 7. Overall Outcomes based on the NIST IDS Metrics.

Metric	Goal	Actual	Observation
Rate of Coverage	>= 38.38%	62.92%	Mix of transactions generated exceeded expectations
Prob. Of Detection	>=38.38%	45.69%	Probability of Detection is greatly improved
Volume of Data	408.38 TPre/s	98.71 TPost/s	Transactions per second degrades a bit due to the extra processing needed
Adaptability	>=25%	33%	New transactions and users can be identified in an unsupervised model

ACKNOWLEDGMENTS

The author would like to thank Dr. Cannady, PhD. for his help in guiding the presented research.

REFERENCES

[1] R. Agrawal, T. Imielinski, T. and A. Swami, "Mining Association Rules Between Sets of Items in Large Databases," *Proc. ACM International Conference on Management of Data (SIGMOD 93)*, ACM Press., Washington DC, USA, 1993, pp. 207 – 216.

[2] R. Agrawal and P. Srikant, R. "Fast Algorithms for Mining Association Rules in Large Databases," *Proc. 20th international Conference on Very Large Data Bases,* Very Large Data Bases. Morgan Kaufmann Publishers, San Francisco, CA, 1994, pp.487-499.

[3] J. Allen, A. Christie, W. Fithen, J. McHugh, J. Pickel and E. Stoner, "State of Practice of Intrusion Detection Technologies," *Carnegie Mellon University/Software Engineering Institute Technical Report CMU/SEI-99-TR-028, 2000.*

[4] X. An, D. Jutla and N. Cercone, "A Bayesian Network Approach to Detecting Privacy Intrusion," *Proc.2006 International Conferences on Web Intelligence and Intelligent Agent Technology Workshop*, 2006, pp.73-76,.

[5] S. Axelsson, "Intrusion Detection Systems: A Survey and Taxonomy", *Department of Computer Engineering, Chalmers University of Technology*, Goteborg, Sweden, 2000, p. 27.

[6] S. Axelsson, "Combining a Bayesian Classifier with Visualization: Understanding the IDS," *Proc. ACM Workshop on Visualization and Data Mining For Computer Security* (VizSEC/DMSEC 04), ACM, New York, NY, 2004, pp. 99-108.

[7] S. Castano, M. Fugini, G. Martella and P. Samarati,."Database Security", ACM, Italy, 1994.

[8] H. Debar, M. Becke and D. Siboni, "A Neural Network Component for an Intrusion Detection System," *Proc. IEEE Computer Society Symposium On Security And Privacy*, 1993, pp. 240-250.

[9] D.E. Denning, (1987), "An Intrusion Detection Model", *IEEE Transactions on Software Engineering*. Vol. 13 No. 2, 1993, pp. 222-232.

[10] J. Fonseca, M. Vieira, and H. Madeira, "Online Detection of Malicious Data Access Using DBMS Auditing," *Proc. 2008 ACM Symposium on Applied Computing (SAC '08)*, ACM, New York, NY, 2008, pp. 1013-1020.

[11] P. Fournier-Viger, SPMF Software. [Computer Software Documentation], Available: http://www.philippe-fournier-viger.com/spmf/

[12] S. Gaudin, (2007, July, 23). Computer Crimes Charged In College Cash-for-grades Scheme, *InformationWeek,* Available: http://www.informationweek.com/story/showArticle.jhtml?articleID=201200429

[13] J. Hipp, U. Guntzer and G. Nakhaeizadeh, "Algorithms For Association Rule Mining — A General Survey and Comparison," *ACM SIGKDD Explorations Newsletter* Vol. 2 No. 1, 2000, pp. 58-64.

[14] Y. Hu, and B. Panda, "A Data Mining Approach For Database Intrusion Detection," *Proc. 2004 ACM Symposium on Applied Computing (SAC '04)*, ACM, New York, NY, 2004, pp. 711-716.

[15] K. Ilgun, R.A. Kemmerer and P.A. Porras, "State Transition Analysis: A Rule-based Intrusion Detection Approach," *IEEE Transactions on Software Engineering*, Vol. 21 No.3, 1995, pp. 181-199.

[16] A. Kamra, E. Bertino and G. Lebanon, "Mechanisms For Database Intrusion Detection and Response," *Proc. 2nd SIGMOD PhD Workshop on Innovative Database Research (IDAR 2008)*, ACM, New York, NY, USA, 2008, Pp. 31-36.

[17] A. Kamra, E. Tertzi, and E. Bertino, "Detecting Anomalous Access Patterns in Relational Databases," *The VLDB Journal*, Vol. 17 No. 5, 2007, pp. 1603-1077.

[18] S. Kumar and E.H. Spafford, "An Application of Pattern Matching in Intrusion Detection," *Technical Report CSD-TR-94-013*, The COAST Project, Dept. of Computer Sciences, Purdue University, W. Lafayette, IN; USA, 1994.

[19] G.E. Leipins and H.S. Vaccaro, "Anomaly Detection: Purpose and Framework, " *Proc. 12th National Computer Security Conference,* 1989, pp.495-504.

[20] G. Lu, J. Yi, and K. Lü, (2007). "A Dubiety-Determining Based Model for Database Cumulated Anomaly Intrusion," *Proc. 2nd International Conference on Scalable Information Systems (InfoScale '07)*, ACM International Conference Proceeding Series, Article 56.

[21] T.F. Lunt, A. Tamaru, F. Gilham, R. Jagannathan, C. Jalali, P.G. Newmann, H.S. Javitz, A. Valdes and T.D. Garvey "A Real-time Intrusion Detection Expert System (IDES)", Final Technical Report for SRI Project 6784, 1992.

[22] P. Mell, V. Hu, R. Lippman, J. Haines and M. Zissman, "An Overview of Issues in Testing Intrusion Detection Systems – NIST-IR7007, *National Institute of Standards and Technology*. Available: http://csrc.nist.gov/publications/PubsNISTIRs.html, 2003.

[23] A.H. Rezaul Karim, R. M. Rajatheva and K.M. Ahmed,"An Efficient Collaborative Intrusion Detection System for MANET Using Bayesian Approach". *Proc. 9th ACM International Symposium on Modeling Analysis and Simulation of Wireless and Mobile Systems (MSWiM '06)*, ACM, New York, NY, 2006, pp. 187-190.

[24] P.H. Sharrod, "TreeBoos: Stochastic Gradient Boosting, Available: http://www.dtreg.com/treeboost.htm, 2003.

[25] E. Shmueli, R. Vaisenberg, Y. Elovici, and C. Glezer, "Database Encryption: An Overview of Contemporary Challenges and Design Considerations", *ACM SIGMOD Record*, Vol. 38 No. 3, 2009, pp. 29-34.

[26] S. E. Smaha, "Tools for Misuse Detection," *Proc. Information Systems Security Association (ISSA '93)*, 1993,pp. 161-171 .

[27] United States of America (USA). (2007). "U.S. Government Protection Profile: Intrusion Detection System For Basic Robustness Environments," *National Security Agency (NSA)*, Version 1.7, 2007.

[28] H.S. Venter, M.S. Oliver and J.H.P. Eloff, (2004). "PIDS: A Privacy Intrusion Detection System" *Internet Research* Vol. 14 No. 5, Emerald Group Publishing, 2004, pp 360-365.

[29] J. Vijayan, "DBA Admits to Theft of 8.5m Records," *Computerworld*, Available: http://www.computerworld.com/action/article.do?command=viewArticleBasic&articleId=30 8611&source=rss_topic82, 2007.

[30] P.J. Windley "Digital identity," A. Randal & T. Apandi, Eds. O'Reilly, Sebastopol, CA, 2005.

[31] Z. Yu, J.J. Tsai and T. Weigert "An Adaptive Automatically Tuning Intrusion Detection System,". *ACM Trans. on Autonomous and Adaptive Systems*, Vol. 3, No. 3, 2008, Article 10.

SESSION

INFORMATION ASSURANCE

Chair(s)

Dr. Esmiralda Moradian

Java Design Pattern Obfuscation

Praneeth Kumar Gone
Department of Computer Science
San Jose State University
San Jose, California 95192

Mark Stamp
Department of Computer Science
San Jose State University
San Jose, California 95192
Email: stamp@cs.sjsu.edu

***Abstract*—Software reverse engineering (SRE) consists of analyzing the design and implementation of software, where, typically, we assume that the executable file is available, but not the source code. SRE has many legitimate uses, including analysis of software when no source code is available and probing code for security vulnerabilities. Attackers also use SRE to search for weaknesses in closed-source software and to hack software activation mechanisms, or otherwise change the intended function of software.**

There are many tools available to aid the aspiring reverse engineer. For example, there are several tools that recover design patterns from Java byte code or source code. In this project, we develop and analyze a technique to obfuscate design patterns. We show that our technique can defeat design pattern detection tools, thereby making reverse engineering attacks more difficult.

I. Introduction

Software reverse engineering (SRE) can be used to analyze executable files [14]. Examples of such analysis includes redocumenation of programs [3], code smell detection [8], renewal of software modules [19], migration of legacy code [4], translation of program from one language to another [17] and architecture recovery [2]. SRE is also used in software piracy, and other illegal activities.

Businesses spend an immense amount of time and money developing software. To protect their investment, it may be desirable to minimize the amount of information that rivals and attackers can gain through SRE. In this research, we propose and analyze techniques that make the recovery of high-level program design from Java class files more difficult. Specifically, our goal is to obfuscate design patterns.

In general, SRE of Java is much simpler than for programs that are compiled into native code. Java source code is compiled into machine-independent bytecode that can be executed by a Java Virtual Machine (JVM). This bytecode contains a great deal of information about the source code, making SRE of a typical Java class file a relatively easy task.

Software obfuscation is an anti-SRE mechanism that changes the structure of code, without changing its functionality. Many open source Java obfuscation tools are available [11, 25], including ProGuard [10], yGuard [29], SandMark [5], jarg [15], BebboSoft [27], and JavaGuard [28], as well as commercial tools such as Allatori [26], Zelix KlassMaster [30], and JShrink [7]. These obfuscation tools support a variety of obfuscation techniques, such as renaming classes, methods, fields and local variables to random strings, removing debugging information, removing dead code and constant fields, optimizing local variable allocation, and exception obfuscation.

However, existing obfuscation tools are not intended to perform design-level obfuscation. Obscuring the design requires changing the relationship between software system class components. Since design patterns use inheritance features, if we want to obfuscate such architectural-level information, we need to obscure the inheritance-level relationships between classes. Such obfuscation can be accomplished, for example, by removing interfaces or adding abstractions.

In this paper, we analyze a design obfuscation technique. We focus on the so-called Gang of Four (GoF) design patterns [12] and apply most of the design obfuscation techniques discussed in [20]. The effectiveness of the obfuscation is analyzed using existing design pattern recovery tools. Note that in [20], similar techniques are applied, but no testing is done to determine the effectiveness of the obfuscation on design recovery. The focus of [20] is on comparing the runtime performance of the obfuscated and unobfuscated code.

The remainder of this paper is organized as follows. In Section II, we discuss design patterns and pattern detection tools. Section III covers our approach to obfuscating design patterns. In Section IV we provide experimental results to illustrate the effect of our obfuscation on design pattern recovery. Finally, Section V concludes the paper and includes suggestions for future work.

II. Design Patterns

Software design problems are simplified by using design patterns. These design patterns are reusable and rely on object oriented (OO) techniques. In this paper, we focus on the 23 GoF design patterns [12].

The GoF design patterns are grouped into three categories, namely, creational, structural, and behavioral patterns. Next, we provide information on each of these categories, including a list of the specific GoF patterns belonging to each.

As the name implies, creational patterns deal with the creation of objects. Creational patterns serve to encapsulate the knowledge of a given object in order to create and hide the individual instances that represent how these objects are created. The five GoF creational patterns are AbstractFactory, Builder, FactoryMethod, Prototype, and Singleton.

Structural patterns are used to realize relationships between different entities. A structural pattern may be used, for example, when adapting an object or when creating a complex type from simpler types. The GoF structural patterns are Adapter, Bridge, Composite, Decorator, Façade, Flyweight, and Proxy.

Behavioral patterns solve design problems by creating a common communication and implementation between entities.

Communicating between entities includes mediating between classes, notifying the state of an object, and selecting different algorithms at run time. The GoF behavioral patterns are CoR (Chain of Responsibility), Command, Interpreter, Iterator, Mediator, Memento, Observer, State, Strategy, TemplateMethod, and Visitor.

For the sake of brevity, throughout this paper, we focus on the following four design patterns in detail: Builder, FactoryMethod, Decorator, and Mediator. The report [9] includes a detailed analysis for 12 of the GoF design patterns.

A. Builder

A Builder pattern can be used to create complex objects from smaller objects according to an algorithm or procedure. Figure 1 shows a UML diagram for a Builder pattern, as discussed in the following example.

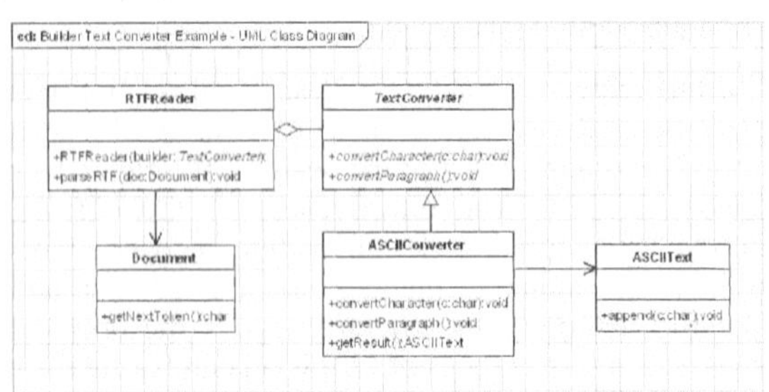

Fig. 1: UML diagram of Builder Pattern [6]

Example: Suppose a `Client` class calls the `main()` method that will initiate a `Builder` and `Director` class. A `Builder` class represents a complex object that needs to be built using other small objects and types. The `Director` receives this `Builder` class and is responsible for calling appropriate methods that create a complex object. A `Client` can call a respective `ConcreteBuilder` depending on the parameters defined to create different complex objects. An example would be a `TextConverter` that converts an RTF document to an ASCII document. An `RTFReader` class will be acting as a `Director`, where a `TextConverter` interface is a `Builder` interface and an `ASCIIConverter` is an implementation of `Builder`, i.e., `TextConverter`. An `ASCIIConverter` reads each character or string from an `RTFReader`, then converts and writes to an ASCII document by following the Builder pattern.

B. FactoryMethod

The FactoryMethod pattern solves the problem of creating objects without specifying an exact class initialization. Initiating different objects in the application could duplicate the use of code and might increase memory requirements. The FactoryMethod pattern defines a separate abstract method that can be overridden by all subclasses with the derived object used within the application [6].

Example: Consider a Factory Product with a Factory Interface that specifies generic behavior for products. The `Client` requests a product from the `ConcreteFactory` to initialize the `Product` variable which uses concrete products. `ConcreteProduct` is an implementation of the `Product` interface; there can be different implementations depending on the type of product. The UML diagram for this Factory Product example appears in Figure 2.

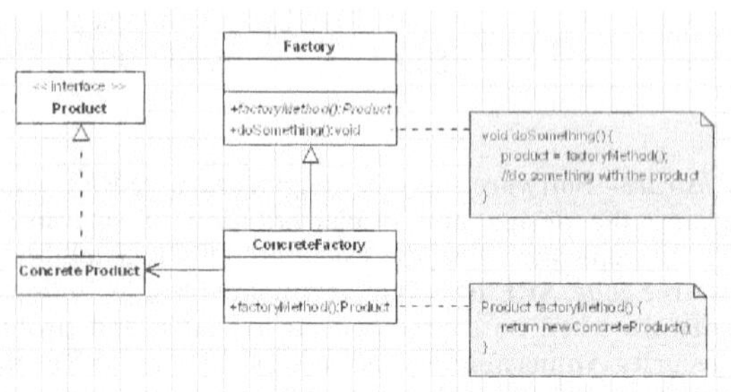

Fig. 2: UML diagram of FactoryMethod Pattern [6]

C. Decorator

A Decorator pattern is used to demonstrate the relationship, during runtime, between entities. In software development we can extend functionality of an object statically at compile time by using inheritance. However, in some situations we need to extend functionality dynamically during runtime.

Example: A graphical window used to create a `FrameWindow` class would decorate a `Window` class and a `FrameWindow` object would be created statically by the client program. This use of a `FrameWindow` needs to initiate different objects within the client program. A Decorator pattern can be used to create a `FrameWindow` dynamically, without creating objects in the client program. The UML diagram demonstrating this Graphical Window application, using a Decorator pattern, is shown in Figure 3.

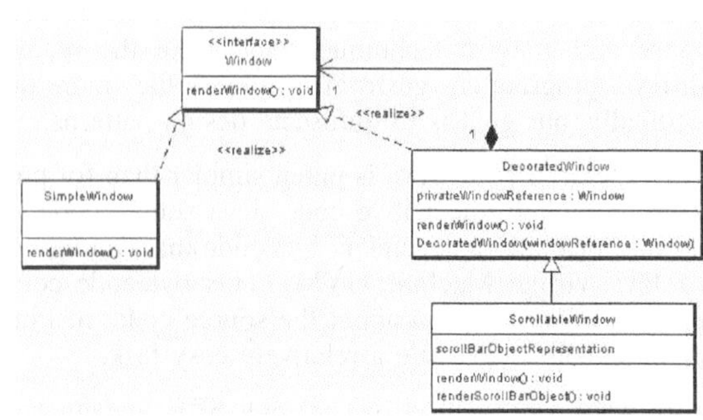

Fig. 3: UML diagram of Decorator Pattern [6]

D. Mediator

A Mediator pattern is a behavioral pattern that aids in the interaction of a large number of classes. A Mediator pattern can be used to remove tight coupling behavior. Figure 4, shows the UML diagram of a Mediator pattern, relevant to the following example.

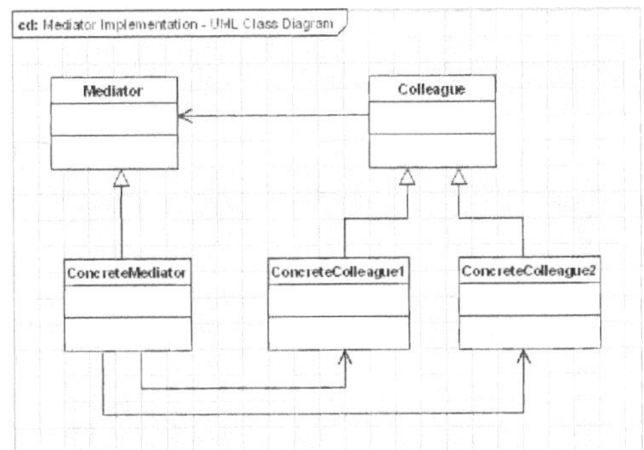

Fig. 4: UML diagram of Mediator Pattern [6]

Example: Consider the problem of developing a screen that contains different controls, that is, a case where various controls must interact with other controls. For example, if a button is pressed it must determine whether the data is valid in other controls. Therefore, in different applications these controls need to interact differently. To solve this problem we use a Mediator pattern that can be extended with different implementations.

E. Pattern Detection Tools

Design pattern detection is a reverse engineering technique that can aid in analyzing Java code. There are several pattern detection tools available, including Hedgehog [1], Reclipse [16], Pattern INference and recOvery Tool (PINOT) [23, 24], and Similarity Scoring [21, 22]. Next, we give a brief overview of each of these tools.

Hedgehog was developed using a pattern description language known as SPINE [1] (and hence the name). SPINE is a language similar to Prolog and contains typed first order logic for describing patterns; it is not currently available for download.

Reclipse is a reverse engineering tool for automatic pattern detection from Java source code. It uses UML 2.0 diagrams derived from source code to deduce the design. Reclipse provides graphical editors for structural and behavioral patterns. Detection of a specified pattern starts from detecting putative design pattern occurrences, or candidates. Dynamic analysis is used to confirm or reject candidates. Installation of this tool requires Eclipse IDE v3.6.1, and Eclipse Modeling Tools, version 3.6.1 [16], however, these versions of the software are no longer available.

In PINOT, Prototype and Iterator patterns are classified as language-provided patterns, since they are widely used and implemented in many languages. Classes that have inter-class relationships, such as Adapter and Façade, are identified as structure-driven patterns, while classes that differ in certain behavioral requirements, such as Singleton and Flyweight, are deemed behavior-driven patterns. Finally, GoF patterns such as Interpreter and Command are known as domain-specific patterns. PINOT focuses on detecting structure and behavior driven patterns [23].

Previous research has shown that PINOT has a significant false positive rate [13, 23]. Our results in Section III confirm these findings.

Similarity Scoring is a design pattern extraction tool available from [22]. The process of detection relies on building matrices from Java class files and comparing them to known matrices [21]. The name Similarity Scoring derives from the graph matching algorithms used in the tool. This pattern detection tool does not depend on behavioral characteristics. By considering only structural characteristics it is difficult to detect certain patterns, such as State and Strategy, which only differ in behavior.

PINOT and Similarity Scoring are currently available and employ very different approaches to pattern detection. Consequently, in this paper, we use these two algorithms to measure the success of our proposed design pattern obfuscation technique.

III. Design Pattern Obfuscation

This section describes the obfuscation techniques that we apply to the GoF design patterns. But first, we test the pattern detection tools discussed in the previous section (i.e., PINOT and Similarity Scoring) on unobfuscated code, and on code that has been obfuscated using the well-known Java obfuscation tools Proguard [10] and SandMark [5]. These results will serve as a point of reference when we apply analyze our obfuscation technique in Section IV.

A. Unobfuscated Pattern Detection

For this test, we used a package that contains all 23 GoF patterns, with many patterns appearing more than once. The number of patterns detected using both PINOT and Similarity Scoring are shown in Figure 5.

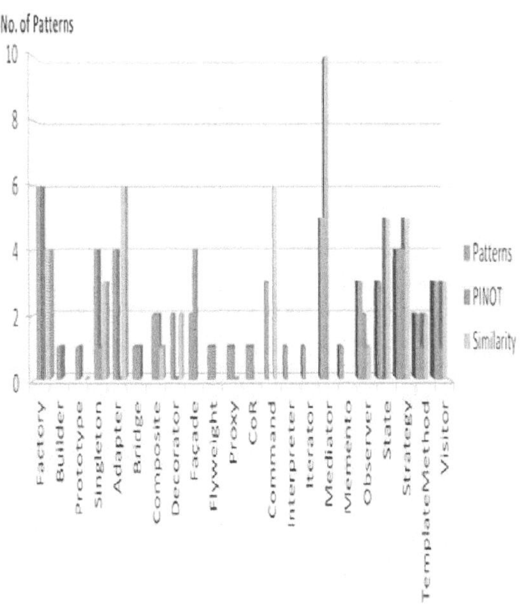

Fig. 5: Detected Patterns without Obfuscation

The results for PINOT show poor detection of creational patterns. For example, only one out of four Singleton patterns was detected. Also, PINOT had many false positives, as summarized in Table I.

TABLE I: PINOT False Positives for Unobfuscated Files

detected	actual	occurrences
Façade	Builder	2
Flyweight	Command	1
Strategy	AbstractFactory	1
Observer	Visitor	2
Mediator	Builder	1
Mediator	State	1
Bridge	Mediator	1

There were far fewer false positives using Similarity Scoring. With the exception of the false positives in PINOT, the results for Similarity Scoring and PINOT are comparable.

B. Obfuscation using Proguard and Sandmark

In this section we obfuscate the files considered in the previous section using two available obfuscators, namely, Proguard, and Sandmark. For Proguard, we test the obfuscated files using both PINOT and Similarity Scoring. However, for Sandmark we can only test the results using Similarity Scoring, since we cannot decompile the Sandmark obfuscated files, and PINOT requires the class files.

1) Proguard: Proguard is an opensource Java class file shrinker, optimizer, obfuscator, and preverifier [10]. The obfuscator option renames classes, fields, and methods, using meaningless names. For the test considered here, we only use the obfuscation option.

The results in Figure 6 show that PINOT and Similarity Scoring yield similar results on the Proguard obfuscated files as on the unobfuscated files. As with the unobfuscated files, PINOT produces many false positives; see Table II.

TABLE II: PINOT False Positives for Proguard Obfuscated Files

detected	actual	occurrences
Bridge	Mediator	1
Flyweight	Command	1
Factory	Memento	1
Observer	Visitor	2
Composite	Visitor	2

2) Sandmark: Sandmark is a tool developed for watermarking, tamper proofing, and obfuscation of Java bytecode [5]. The tool integrates a number of static and dynamic watermarking algorithms, a large collection of obfuscation algorithms, various code optimizers, and a tool to view and analyze Java bytecode. Here, we use the Sandmark obfuscation feature. In Sandmark, there are 39 different algorithms available to obfuscate Java bytecode. In our extensive experiments, we found that nearly all of the Sandmark obfuscation algorithms fail to obfuscate any design patterns. In fact, only three techniques—SplitClasses, Objectify, and OverloadName—were able to obfuscate any design patterns. The results for these three obfuscation techniques are summarized in Figure 7.

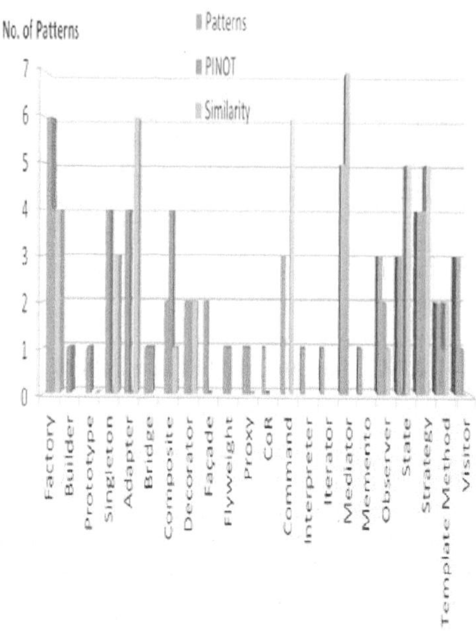

Fig. 6: Detected Patterns after Proguard Obfuscation

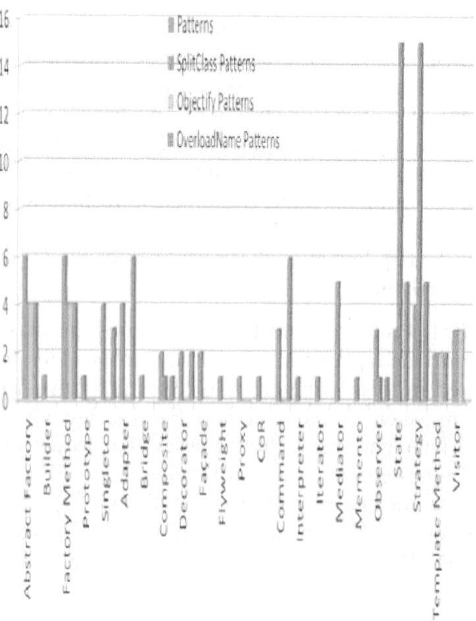

Fig. 7: Detected Patterns using Similarity Scoring after Selected Sandmark Obfuscations

C. Our Approach to Design Pattern Obfuscation

From the results in the previous section, it is clear that Proguard and Sandmark do not effectively obfuscate design patterns. Our goal is to develop a technique that can effectively obfuscate design patterns.

In [20], the authors consider design obfuscation based on class-coalescing, class-splitting, and type-hiding. Class-coalescing consists of combining two or more classes into a single class. At the extreme, we could replace all classes with a single class, effectively converting an OO program into a procedural program. Class-splitting consists of splitting one class into two or more classes. As with class-coalescing, class-splitting can have a major impact on program structure. Type-hiding introduces a number of Java interfaces that are implemented by existing classes, which can make the program structure more difficult to reverse engineer.

For our design pattern obfuscator, we employ class-coalescing and class-splitting. We are able to effectively hide design pattern information without employing type-hiding.

Next, we discuss the obfuscation we perform on the GoF design patterns. For the sake of brevity, we only provide details for the Mediator pattern. The discussion of the Mediator pattern below refers to the corresponding example presented in Section II. Many additional patterns are considered in the full report [9].

Obfuscating a Mediator pattern can be achieved using class-coalescing. Specifically, we remove the `Mediator` interface and replace `Mediator` references to respective mediator implementations. The example in Figure 8 illustrates the process, where the `Mediator` interface is removed and an `ApplicationMediator` is implemented as an ordinary class with all the necessary implementation. This `ApplicationMediator` is to be instantiated into a `Colleague` class All Mediators must be implemented and be used in respective `Colleague` classes.

Fig. 8: Obfuscate Mediator

D. Obfuscation of the GoF Patterns

The obfuscation techniques we apply to the 23 GoF design patterns are listed in the Table III. Note that "✓" denotes that the specified technique (i.e., class-coalescing or class-splitting) is applied, while "✗" implies the technique is not used.

TABLE III: Obfuscation Techniques

GoF Pattern	Obfuscation	
	Class-coalescing	Class-splitting
AbstractFactory	✓	✗
Builder	✓	✗
FactoryMethod	✗	✓
Prototype	✓	✗
Singleton	✗	✓
Adapter	✓	✗
Bridge	✓	✗
Composite	✓	✓
Decorator	✓	✓
Façade	✓	✗
Flyweight	✓	✗
Proxy	✓	✗
CoR	✓	✗
Command	✓	✗
Interpreter	✓	✗
Iterator	✓	✗
Mediator	✓	✓
Memento	✓	✗
Observer	✓	✗
State	✓	✗
Strategy	✓	✗
TemplateMethod	✗	✓
Visitor	✓	✗

IV. Results and Observations

In this section, we give results obtained using the design pattern obfuscation technique outlined in Section III. We consider two test cases, and for both we present design pattern detection results—using both PINOT and Similarity Scoring—before and after applying obfuscation. For the first test case, we also consider the effect of obfuscation on runtime performance. Additional test cases can be found in [9].

A. Test Case 1

The code used for this test case is the same as that considered in Section III. Figure 9 shows patterns detected using PINOT and Similarity Scoring. Note that the unobfuscated results in Figure 9 (a) are the same as those given in Figure 5

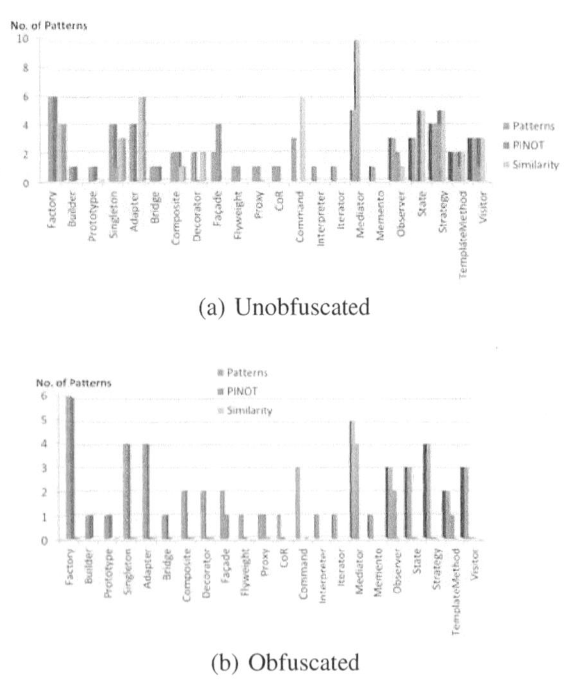

(a) Unobfuscated

(b) Obfuscated

Fig. 9: Test Case 1

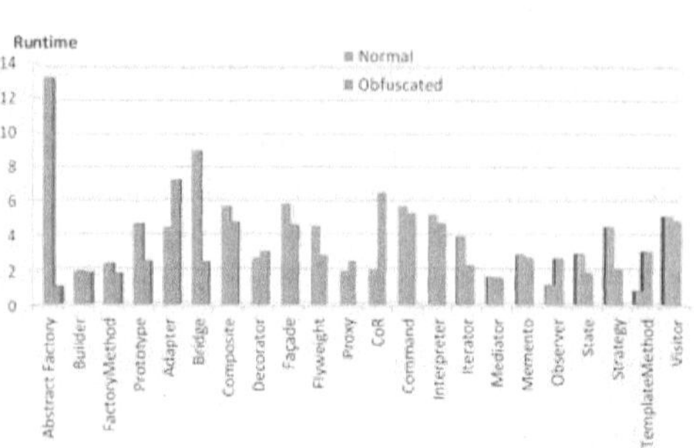

Fig. 10: Runtime Analysis

in Section III. We have reproduced the results here to illustrate the effectiveness of our obfuscation.

In Figure 9 (b), we see that Similarity Scoring was unable to detect any design patterns in the our obfuscated code. PINOT did detect a few patterns, but most of these are false positives; as we have seen previously, PINOT tends to produce a significant number of false positives. For example, the two Observer patterns detected by PINOT in Figure 9 (b) are both false positives that are actually Visitor patterns.

B. Runtime Analysis for Case 1

Runtime analysis for the individual patterns in Test Case 1 appears in Figure 10. Note that in some cases, obfuscation greatly improves runtime (e.g., AbstractFactory and Bridge). This improvement tends to occur when class-coalescing is used most heavily. Interestingly, class-splitting does not tend to cause an increase in runtime, as might be expected. Overall, the results in Figure 10 indicate that our obfuscation technique is likely to have no detrimental effect on the runtime performance of most code.

C. Test Case 2

For this test case we used GoF patterns from Grand's book [18]. These patterns make heavy use of object oriented structures, such as inner classes and multilevel inheritance. Figure 11 gives detection results for PINOT and Similarity Scoring, for both the unobfuscated code and after our obfuscation is applied. Again, we see almost no patterns detected by Similarity Scoring while most of the PINOT-detected patterns are false positives.

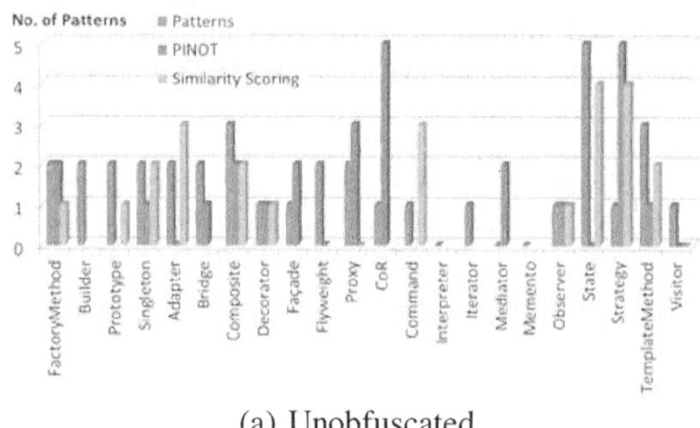

(a) Unobfuscated

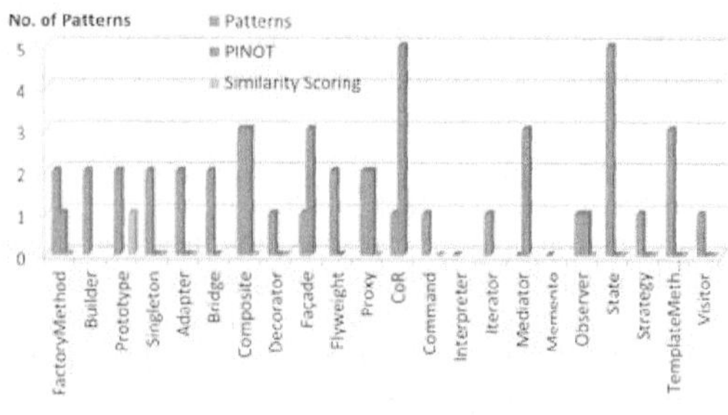

(b) Obfuscated

Fig. 11: Test Case 2

V. Conclusion and Future Work

In this paper, we showed that standard Java obfuscation tools have little effect on the ability to recover design patterns. We then discussed and tested an obfuscation strategy aimed at thwarting design pattern recovery. We provided test results showing that our technique is highly effective, and has no adverse effect on runtime performance. In this research, we focused on the 23 GoF design patterns, but our technique should be equally effective at preventing any high-level design recovery.

Our obfuscation technique employs class-coalescing and class-splitting. While this approach is highly effective, if could likely be further improved by including type-hiding, as suggested in [20]. Another area of future work is to improve the usability of the current tool, which is simply a proof-of-concept prototype.

References

[1] A. Blewitt, A. Bundy, and I. Stark (2001). Automatic verification of Java design patterns. *Proceedings 16th Annual International Conference on Automated Software Engineering*, (ASE 2001)

[2] G. Antoniol, et. al, (2001, November 15). Object-oriented design patterns recovery, *Journal of Systems and Software*, 59(2):181–196

[3] P. Benedusi, A. Cimitile, and U. D. Carlini (1992, November). Reverse engineering processes, design document production, and structure charts. *Journal of Systems and Software*, 19(3):225–245

[4] G. Canfora, et al (2000). Decomposing legacy programs: A first step towards migrating to client-server platforms. *Journal of Systems and Software*, 54(2):99–110.

[5] C. Collberg, SandMark: A Tool for the study of Software Protection Algorithms, Technical Report, Department of Computer Science, The University of Arizona, `http://sandmark.cs.arizona.edu/index.html`

[6] Design Patterns `http://www.oodesign.com/`

[7] Eastridge Technology, JShrink `http://www.e-t.com/jshrink.html`

[8] E. V. Emden and L. Moonen (2002, November). Java quality assurance by detecting code smells. In Ninth Working Conference on Reverse Engineering (WCRE 2002), Richmond, VA, USA, pp. 97–107

[9] P. K.. Gone (2012). Java Design Pattern Obfuscation. Master's thesis `http://scholarworks.sjsu.edu/etd_projects/242`

[10] E. Lafortune, ProGuard `http://proguard.sourceforge.net/`

[11] E. Lafortune, Proguard — Alternative shrinkers, optimizers, obfuscators, and preverifiers `http://proguard.sourceforge.net/index.html#alternatives.html`

[12] E. Gamma, et al, *Design Patterns: Elements of Reusable Object-Oriented Software*, Addison-Wesley

[13] G. Spanogiannopoulos (January 2007) An Analysis of Design Pattern Detection Using PINOT AND Similarity Scoring. York University `www.cse.yorku.ca/~spano/reports/report.pdf`

[14] H. A. Miller, et al, Reverse engineering: a roadmap, in Proceedings of Conference on the Future of Software Engineering, Limerick, Ireland, 2000, pp. 47–60

[15] H. Ohuchi, jarg — Java Archive Grinder `http://jarg.sourceforge.net/`

[16] M. von Detten, M. Meyer and D. Travkin, Reclipse — Reverse Engineering for Eclipse `http://www.fujaba.de/no_cache/projects/reengineering/reclipse.html`

[17] M. Ceccato, et al. (April 2010). Migrating legacy data structures based on variable overlay to Java, *Journal of Software Maintenance and Evolution*, 22(3):211–237

[18] M. Grand, *Patterns in Java: A Catalog of Reusable Design Patterns Illustrated with UML*, Wiley Computer Publishing, 1998

[19] E. Merlo, et al (1995). Reengineering user interfaces. *IEEE Software*, 12(1):64–73

[20] M. Sosonkin, G. Naumovich, and N. Memon (2003). Obfuscation of design intent in object-oriented applications, (DRM'03), *Proceedings of the 3rd ACM Workshop on Digital Rights Management*

[21] N. Tsantalis, et al (November, 2006). Design Pattern Detection Using Similarity Scoring, *IEEE Transactions on Software Engineering*, 32(11):896–909

[22] N. Tsantalis, et al, Design pattern detection `http://java.uom.gr/~nikos/pattern-detection.html`

[23] N. Sji and R. A. Olsson (2006), Recovery of design patterns from Java Source code, 21st IEEE/ACM International Conference on Automated Software Engineering `http://www.cs.ucdavis.edu/~shini/research/pinot/reverseJavaPatterns.pdf`

[24] N. Sji and R. Olsson, (2006) PINOT (Pattern INterference and recOvery Tool) `http://www.cs.ucdavis.edu/~shini/research/pinot/`

[25] Open Source obfuscators in Java `http://java-source.net/open-source/obfuscators`

[26] Smardec, Allatori Obfuscator `http://www.allatori.com/features.html`

[27] S. B. Franke, bb_mug a Java class obfuscator `http://www.bebbosoft.de/\#java/mug/index.wiki`

[28] T. Heit, JavaGuard bytecode obfuscator `http://sourceforge.net/projects/javaguard/`

[29] yWorks, yGuard Bytecode Obfuscator and Shrinker `http://www.yworks.com/en/products_yguard_about.html`

[30] Zelix, KlassMaster `http://www.zelix.com/klassmaster/features.html`

A Synthetic Solution Scheme for SOA Security Assurance

Bing Xu[1], Tianbo Lu[1,2], Xiaoqin Wang[3], Lingling Zhao[1], Xiaoyan Zhang[1], Wanjiang Han[1]
[1]School of Software Engineering, Beijing University of Posts and Telecommunications, Beijing, China
[2]Information Technology Research Base of Civil Aviation Administration of China,
Civil Aviation University of China, Tianjin, China
[3] China Software Testing Center, Beijing , China
lutb@bupt.edu.cn

Abstract - *Due to the changes of architecture, tradition security mechanism can't fulfill SOA security requirements. So it is the high time to design a comprehensive security assurance system of models and solutions that fulfill SOA and SOA-based applications' security requirement without hurting SOA's loose coupling and high scalability features. Based on the in-depth research of tiered SOA security, this paper provides a comprehensive solution and analyzes SOA security assurance on three levels: strategy, service solution, testing. Firstly this paper proposes a new security assurance model for the overall architecture, and then proposes a new framework as a practical application solution for modeling and evaluating reliability on single service, service pool and service composition. At last, compared with traditional application-oriented system integration testing, this paper proposes the strategies of integration test and test responsibilities division for SOA systems.*

Keywords- SOA security assurance; reliability; service pool; integration test

1 Introduction

With the continuous development of computer technology, environment confronted by modern enterprise becomes more and more complicated, where a loosely-coupled, cross-platform, and language-agnostic system is needed to coping with changes of the outside world rapidly. In order to solve such puzzle, more and more enterprises have noticed SOA (service-oriented architecture). SOA is a service-oriented architecture. In addition, it can strengthen agility of enterprise businesses and reduce development costs of enterprise information system. Major advantages of SOA can be summarized as: providing business centric better and faster, rapid flexibility, and reusability [1].

There is still not a comprehensive solution about SOA security. And such distributed computing methods as CORBA and DCOM can provide loose coupling to some extent, but they can't realize SOA better because of various limitations. However, it has become the set of some technologies which are best fit for realizing SOA because of maturity of web service standards and popularity of application [2]. It seems that there is an understanding in SOA field which can't be denied, namely it is unnecessary to change current software testing methods. However, it isn't the case. Change of testing methods is in bad need, and it is necessary to change many other things at the same time. Integration testing of SOA is particularly important because most tests are on single web services rather than sets of web service. In addition, safety issues can't be ignored, especially for e-commerce platforms. How to build safe networked transaction environment to ensure high confidentiality of transaction information in the network transmission process and not being threatened by such safety issues as forging, manipulation, and stealing etc., is an issue which must be considered for e-commerce platforms. E-commerce based on SOA conducts information exchange and completes electronic transaction on each heterogeneous platform with the use of XML technologies. At the time of information exchange, the following safety issues shall be considered: how to confirm accuracy of information exchange, identity of trading partners, and non-repudiation of transaction on platforms trusted by both parties.

The rest of the paper is organized as follows. Section 2 makes a research on tiered SOA security. Section 3 provides a security assurance model for the overall architecture. Section 4 proposes a new framework for modeling and evaluating reliability in web service system. Section 5 summarizes safety precautions. Section 6 proposes the strategies of integration test and test responsibilities division for SOA systems. Finally we draw a conclusion of this paper in section 7.

2 Tiered SOA Security

SOA security is reflected in the data safety of the SOA environment, the data is always in a different security level and facing security threats at every level. It can be summed up as following six security levels: transport layer security, message layer security, application layer security, data layer security, metadata layer security, management layer security. Transport layer security refers to the security of data in the point to point transfer by both sides. It is relatively easy to implement and there is already a series of transport layer security mechanisms. Message layer security refers to the security of passing data between service consumers and service providers. Now WS-Security protocols ensure security of data exchanging based on SOAP. Application security refers to the security of the data in the application logic processing. It can't achieve security assurance by Infrastructure transparent in this level. Data Layer Security refers to the security of the data encapsulated in service. It is crucial to protect the application related data in the stationary state. However, other data should also be taken into account in order to build a comprehensive and integrated security solution. The metadata layer security refers to the security of the public information in service. It needs to protect the definition of the service (WSDL document), port information, binding and protocol information, etc. Management layer security refers to the security of data being regulated. It includes preventing attacks on the management of infrastructure, preventing leakage of the authentication information or authorization information, preventing the abuse of service management permissions, etc.

No matter where the data is in the SOA environment, it always faces the following security problems: confidentiality, integrity, auditability, authentication management, authorization management, identity management, security policy management.Confidentiality is such a property that the data could not be acquired by non-authorized user or process, i.e., an eavesdropper or a non-authorized user can not view the secret message content. It can be ensured by typical encryption technology. It should be noted that confidentiality needs is different in transport layer and message layer. Integrity refers to the data has not been altered or damaged. The data received should be the same with the data source in a single message exchange, and this is mainly achieved by data signature mechanism. In multi-party interaction of the message, the data should not be changed in the transmission process, and it depends on the reliability of the transmission of the message. Auditability is a capacity which makes historical events relate to the perpetrators. Different systems may require different audit level. Some may only need a simple record, while some systems need to achieve non-repudiation, that is to say the initiator of the transaction can be identified as a unique entity. Authentication management's purpose is to prevent using the service by Illegals which includes process, module and external systems. This is the first line of defense in system security controls. Authorization management is assessed by identity information and access control policy information: Whether a user has permission to access specific categories of resources. Due to the distributed nature of the resources in the SOA environment, the distributed authorization management of accessing to services will be the key to success. Due to the openness of SOA, the traditional information systems security boundary is breaking. It should be taken into account that how to pass the identifier safely between different trust domains. The strategy refers to a series of rules to manage the entire computing system behavior. The strategy can be used to describe all aspects of security, and can be applied to the all the SOA entities, including service consumers, service providers and infrastructure. It should be considered that how to manage security and make a set of policies to achieve interoperability from different entities.

In addition to the above analysis of the safety issues, it also faces replacement messages, message replay, message injection, session hijacking and other security threats in the SOA message exchange. These security issues seriously affect establishing a reliable relationship between the cooperation partners, and therefore it needs to establish end-to-end security services between service providers and consumers.

3 S3R SOA Assurance Model

SOA is the architecture about how the services combine together, and software is an important component of the service. Currently, software assurance which focuses on security, insurance, reliability and survivability has become the core of security, forming a multidisciplinary discipline of software engineering and information security [3]. The concept of software assurance was first proposed by Marilyn S. Fujii [4] and received close attention of the U.S. government. U.S. Department of Homeland Security, National Security Agency, NIST and had some research results [5] [6] [7] [8] [9]. The study of the software assurance in China begun since 2007, and we proposed the S3R software assurance model first. Combined with the characteristics of SOA, we propose an improved model, as shown in Figure 1.

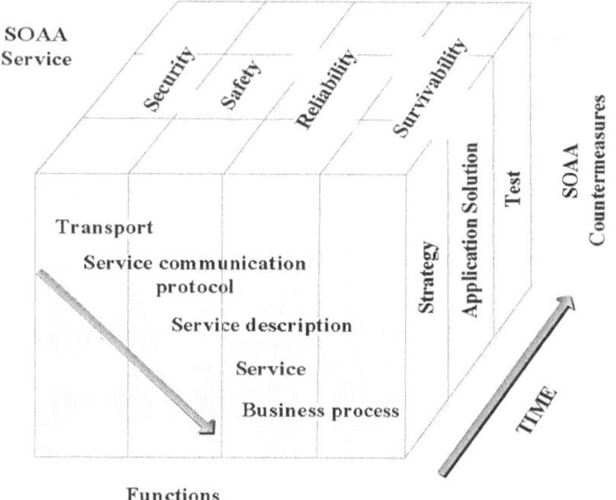

Figure 1. SOA Assurance Model

This model includes four dimensions: functions, SOA assurance (SOAA) services, SOAA measures, and SOAA time. There are five functions: transport, service communication, service description, service, business process, and each function can be divided by a fine granularity. Corresponding measures are different in different functions.

- Transport: It is a mechanism used to transfer the service request from the service user to the service provider and the response from the service provider to the service user.
- Service communication protocol: It is a negotiation mechanism through which the service provider can connect with the service user.
- Service description: It is a negotiation mode used to describe the service, how to call the service and what data is needed for successfully calling the service.
- Business process: It is a collection of services. In order to meet business requirements, it can be called in a specific order and a specific set of rules. There will be the concept that a business process can be composed by different granularity of services if the business process itself is seen as a service.

There is one key consideration for service users and providers that is the security of the processes of dealing with the service components during their development and distribution. Indeed, SOAA involves a shared responsibility among providers, service intermediaries, and customers containing three factors:

- Security: In the processes of the SOA design, development and testing, security threats are anticipated and addressed. The focus of both quality aspects (e.g., "free from writing off the end of the array") and functional requirements (e.g., "identity card number must be written in the police systematic database"), should be demanded.
- Integrity: The processes of creating and delivering service contain controls to strengthen the confidence that the functions achieve the goal the providers required.
- Authenticity: The service is real, not counterfeit and customers can use some methods to be sure that they own the real service.

4 Application Solutions

Figure 2 reflects a typical implementation frame of web service system. Actual physical structure is on the right side, including service portfolio flows on the top layer or logical layer and service (sets) (layers of middleware are omitted) on the bottom layer; basic implementation mechanism is on the left side.

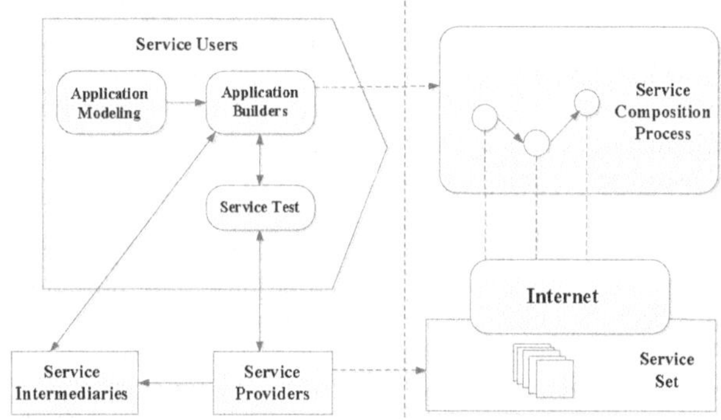

Figure 2. Typical Framework of Implementing a Web Services System

Modeling and evaluation process of SOA reliability are filled among the whole lifecycle, so a corresponding interlayer shall be added in the basic framework above as the support [10], as shown in the figure 3. The following are some newly-increased steps when compared with Fig.2:

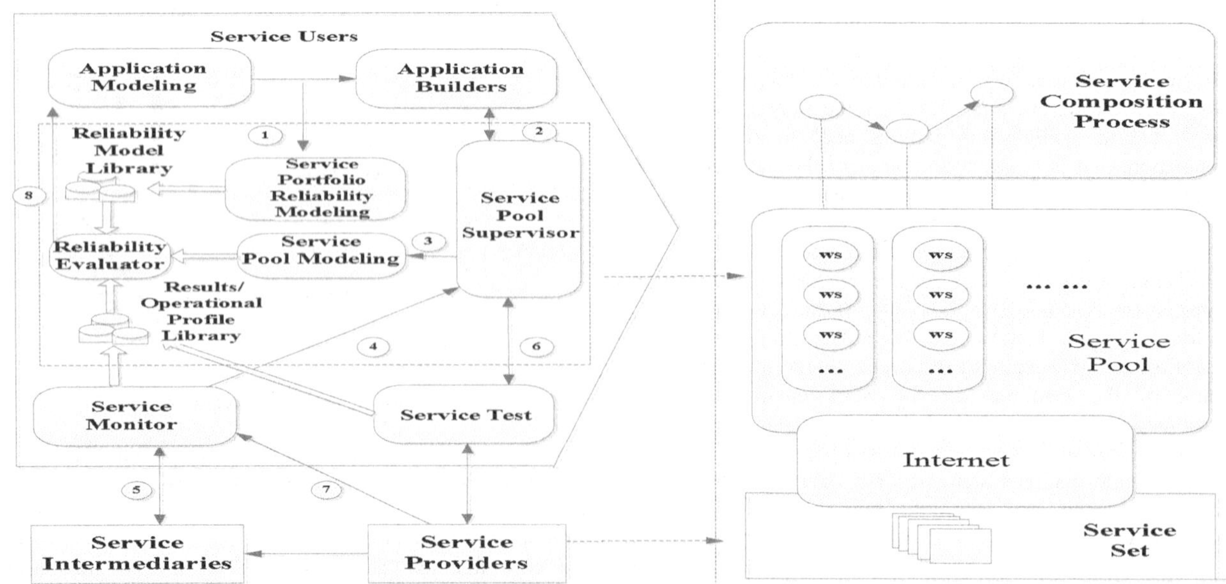

Figure 3. A New Frame Including Reliability Modeling and Evaluating Process

(1) Deliver constructed application model to the module charging reliability modeling of service portfolio. The module builds corresponding reliability models automatically or under manual intervention, which shall be stored in reliability model library. However, when application model changes, it may strike renewal of corresponding reliability models at the same time. Relative reliability models will be inserted when a portfolio of services are inserted into other service portfolios as a single service, and this can refer to Grassi's work [11];
(2) Look up services and invoke service testing functions in service intermediaries with application builder, whose transfers shall be charged by the service-pool supervisor;
(3) Service-pool supervisor is responsible for building and maintaining a service pool for each component in the service portfolio and submitting them to reliability modeling modules through composing them into conditions, and reliability can be calculated synchronously;
(4) Service-pool supervisor invokes service monitor to complete service seeking;
(5) Service monitor looks up services required in service intermediaries according to requirements of service-pool supervisor, and at the same time, service monitor shall check whether service intermediaries have renewed relevant services at regular intervals;
(6) Service-pool supervisor invokes testing processes for found services and stores testing results into testing results/ operational profile library. The service test is an external support technology. It started earlier and there are many results can refer to [12][13][14][15][16];
(7) Service monitor surveys running conditions of all services, which will submit monitoring and statistical results to testing results/ operational profile library for conservation;
(8) After the above tasks are completed, reliability evaluator can be invoked manually or triggered automatically, which can acquire reliability models and reliability data from reliability model library and testing results/ operational profile library, so as to complete reliability assessment of single services, service pools, service portfolios, and even the whole system, and assessment results shall be fed back to application modeling as bases for application modeling and service assembly.

5 Safety Precautions

Generally, there are several aspects of safety precautions aiming at safety issues confronted by each layer, including precautions in technology, management strategy, and educational training and improvement of safety awareness. Precautions in management strategy are supplementing defects discovered after design of safety system. For example, if there are defects in technology implementation, management strategy shall supplement them. However, the system may possess some potential threats with supplementary of management strategy, and educational training and improvement of safety awareness, the last layer of precautions, to is needed for supplementary. In this paper, precautions in technology are mainly concerned, so safety precautions in technology will be introduced mainly in the following, rather than other two layers of safety precautions.

In order to guarantee safety of SOA environment, it is necessary to adopt some new safety elements besides traditional safety technologies, such as data encryption technology, information signature technology, authentication technology, and licensing technology etc.

(1) XML Signature and Encryption

In order to guarantee safety of message exchange in SOA environment, confidentiality, integrity, and non-repudiation of SOAP information shall be considered, and mainly XML signature and encryption and WS-Security can solve safety technology of problems in these three aspects at present. Safety of traditional security mechanism communication layer is guaranteed with the use of SSL/TLS protocol, but it shall be implemented in SOA environment with the use of composite services units, which involves conditions of multiparty delivery of communication information. Furthermore, different parts of information contents may aim at different service providers, so it is inevitable to deal with information partially, which are solved by XML signature and encryption and WS-Security well.

(2) Single Sign-on

Generally, SOA environment is multi-domain, which is more complicated when compared with single-domain environment. A prominent problem in multi-domain heterogeneous environment is numerous users and widespread sources, especially service-oriented application. Widely researched single sign-on technology can solve identity authentication and identity management in the SOA environment well.

(3) Policy-based Access Control

Traditional access control frame couples safety logic and business application logic closely, with poor system flexibility, while service-oriented application needs a flexible way to carry out authorization management. Policy-based access control mechanism solves authorization management and strategic management in the SOA environment well. Flexible authorization policies can be formulated with the use of policy-based access control mechanism, so as to meet various access control demands of SOA environment.

6 SOA Integration Testing Strategy

Some modules in traditional testing can work alone, but whether they can work normally after connection is not been guaranteed. Issues that can't be reflected in partial process may be exposed on the whole situation, which may influence function realization. That is to say, the following issues shall be considered:

- Whether data passing through module interface will lose when each module is connected;
- Whether the predicted father function can be achieved through combining sub-functions;
- Whether functions of a module can have adverse effects on functions of another module;
- Whether global data structure has some problems;
- Whether errors of single modules can be enlarged through accumulation, to reach up to an unacceptable degree.

Therefore, it is necessary to conduct integration testing upon completion of unit testing, so as to find and to remove the above issues that may be occurred on module connection and to compose required software subsystem or system finally. It is the same to SOA testing. Unit testing of SOA conducts functional testing respectively towards each web service. At this stage, codes can be tested directly with the use of white-box testing, so as to find mistakes in programming inside modules and to guarantee that each web service can work normally. SOA emphasizes interoperation of web services in the framework, so integration testing shall be conducted upon completion of unit testing. The key to conducting integration testing towards SOA is testing information and communication errors that may be initiated among web services. Such communication errors may include: deletion, copying, delay, reordering, or false rumor of information.

6.1 SOA Integration Testing Contents

Integration testing of SOA mainly contains three role functions of SOA, namely release, binding, and finding, and asynchronous communication ability among web services, including functional testing and performance testing. In the following, functional testing and performance testing of SOA are analyzed generally.

Functional testing means testing functions of SOA system, mainly checking information errors possibly triggered at the time of interaction among web services, namely checking whether there are invalid operations in the calling process and web service can be invoked repeatedly. Invoking results of each service invocation includes success and failure. Generally, "failure" state is ejected through being translated into "abnormal" state in the system design and implementation where object-oriented thought is used widely. Customers shall deal with them further according to "abnormal" type and information after customer capture server ejects "abnormal" state. Abnormal state of web service system includes "abnormal system" and "abnormal customized definition". The former indicates abnormal core ejection of web service system, such as abnormal network and abnormal HTTP Server; the latter indicates abnormal customized definition in specifically implemented web services, which has nothing to do with the core of web service system. Only these specific services and customers using such services share common "abnormal" meaning. Therefore, three different service invocation result states shall be tested at the time of functional testing, as shown in the table.

TABLE I. FUNCION TESTING PLAN

Plan No.	Target Test Results	Client Input	Expected Output	Explain
1	Service call is success ful	Correct input parameters	Correct service results	No abnormal
2	Abnor mal user-defined	Wrong input parameters	Capture abnormal user-defined	System core normal, abnormal specific Web Service
3	Abnor mal Service call	Correct input parameters	Capture system abnor mality	Abnormal system core

Performance testing means the operation capacity of testing software in the integration system. It is impossible to provide software meeting functional requirements but not meeting performance requirements in real-time system. Performance testing can be generated in all steps during testing, but only when all compositions of the whole system are integrated, real performances of a system can be checked. One aspect of performance testing is pressure testing, mainly testing SOA system on several machines through operating several virtual users.

6.2 Integration Testing Strategy in SOA Development

(1) Integration Testing Strategy of Traditional Software

Three kinds of integration strategies are generally adopted in traditional software testing, namely top-down integration, bottom-up integration, and hybrid integration. Compile corresponding driver modules and stub modules as required and integrate step by step according to selected testing strategies. Complexity of software integration is greatly increased with the introduction, encapsulation, inheritance, and polymorphism of object-oriented development technology, and the above integration strategies are not proper again. What's more, integration strategies based on usage scenario are mostly applied in the integration testing of object-oriented system.

(2) Duty Allocation of SOA System Testing Duties

In the SOA system, web services of system-based basic modules are provided by service providers but SOA system is charged by web service users, namely developers of the SOA system, and they belong to different organizations under this circumstance, so its partition in testing responsibilities is different from traditional software testing. Specific partition in testing responsibilities is shown in the figure.

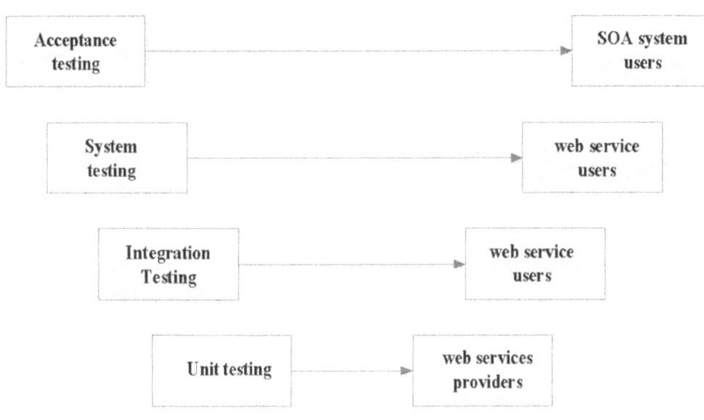

Figure 4. Duty Allocation of SOA System Testing Duties

Basic modules of SOA system are developed by web service providers, and codes are maintained by them, so unit testing shall be charged by web service providers naturally. However, web service users (developers of SOA system) are responsible for functional verification of web service. In addition, integration testing and system testing of SOA system are charged by the development team of SOA system. Acceptance testing is the same as that of traditional software development, which shall be solved by final users or personnel employed by final users.

(3) Preparations before Integration Testing – Test Single Web Service

Functional verification of web service can be conducted according to traditional black-box testing method, namely verify and confirm functions of single web service with the use of equivalence partitioning, boundary value analysis, cause-and-effect diagram, decision tables, orthogonal experimental design, and work flow according to web service's WSDL. Web service to be applied in the system may come from different web service providers, whose development level and coverage degree of unit testing are unexpected. Therefore, it is necessary to verify and to confirm single web service. And at the same time, in the testing on single web service, testers test a great quantity of illegal inputs not meeting WSDL requirements in detail with the use of black-box testing method, so that developers have relatively in-depth understanding on such web service, which lays solid foundation on positioning and ejection of issues in the following integration process. Testing single web service fully is also in favor of increasing developers' confidences on used web service, which simplifies the number of test cases in integration testing.

(4) Integration Testing Strategy

Among integration testing case design of SOA system, we choose testing strategies of scenario-based and top-down integration, whose design flow is shown in the figure.

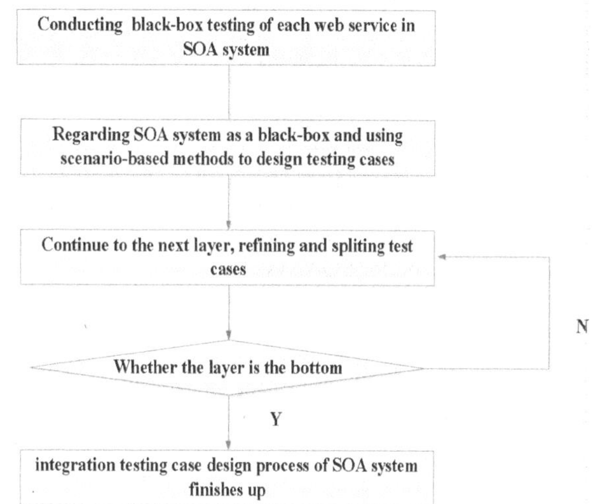

Figure 5. Integration Testing Case Design Process of SOA System

The integration strategy based on usage scenario can be adopted for the integration of SOA system. Each web service shall be integrated into the system successively according to different usage scenarios of users towards SOA system and framework of SOA system. Top-down strategy is adopted for the design of integration testing cases. SOA system is regarded as a black box, which provides certain functions for external users or other outside systems. Users input some parameters in the system interface, and the system may respond differently according to input parameters and show reaction results to external users through the system. In the design of integration testing cases, firstly, the above black-box testing methods (such as boundary value analysis method or equivalence partitioning method and so on) are comprehensively applied in the top layer of SOA, user input and system input are distinguished, and relevant testing cases are designed. Secondly, shielding of black box shall be removed layer by layer according to architecture design layer of the system, so as to show invocation relationship among web services layer by layer and to refine and divide corresponding testing cases further, till the bottom of web service. It has been found that testing cases designed with the use of such method are relatively complete, which covers various aspects of system function, tests invocation among web services completely, and is convenient for checking issues at the time of issues generated in the integration process.

7 Conclusion

As a new generation of application software architecture, SOA develops rapidly and is applied in various fields with loose coupling and high scalability features. It provides great convenience for application integration within the enterprise and between enterprises. But there is still a lack of a comprehensive solution for SOA security problems. this paper provides a comprehensive solution and analyzes SOA security assurance on three levels: strategy, service solution, testing. Firstly this paper proposes a new security assurance model for the overall architecture, and then proposes a new framework as a practical application solution for modeling and evaluating reliability on single service, service pool and service composition. At last, compared with traditional application-oriented system integration testing, this paper proposes the strategies of integration test and test responsibilities division for SOA systems.

Nowadays dynamic and uncertainty of software development is greatly improved, especially for service-oriented architecture. So it's important to work on empirical studies. The further research is to develop a security assurance tools integration platform to fulfill the requirement of test.

8 Acknowledgment

This work is supported by the following programs: the National Natural Science Foundation of China under Grant No.61170273; Open Project Foundation of Information Technology Research Base of Civil Aviation Administration of China (NO.CAAC-ITRB-201201); 2010 Information Security Program of China National Development and Reform Commission with the title "Testing Usability and Security of Network Service Software".

9 References

[1] Carey M J.SOA What? [J]. Computer, 2008, 3: 92-94.

[2] Bussler C. The fractal nature of web services [J]. Computer, 2007, 3: 93-95.

[3] FANG Bin-xing, LU Tian-bo, LI Chao. Survey of software assurance. Journal on Communications, 2009.30(2): 106-117.

[4] Marilyn S.Fujii. A comparison of software assurance methods. Proceeding of the software quality assurance workshop on Functional and Performance issues. Pages: 27-32,1978.

[5] National Research Council(NRC). Computer at Risk: Safe Computing in the Information Age[M]. Washington. DC. National Academy Press, 1991.

[6] National plan for information systems protection, the white house [EB/OL]. http://cryptome.org/cybersec-plan.htm,2000.

[7] [CYSEC05]Cyber security :a crisis of prioritization [EB/OL].http://www.nitrd.gov/pitac/reports/20050301_cybersecurity/cybersecority.pdf, 2005.

[8] Software 2015: a national software strategy to ensure U.S[EB/OL].http://www.cnsoftware.org/nss2report/NSS2FinalReport04-29-05PDF.pdf, 2005.

[9] National science and technology council. federal plan for cyber security and information assurance research and development[EB/OL].http://www.nitrd.gov/pubs/csia/csia_federal_plan.pdf, 2006.

[10] Lijun Wang, Xiaoying Bai, Rujuan Liu. Research on Service-oriented Software Reliability [J]. Journal of Chinese Computer Systems, 2009, (6) : 1031-1037.

[11] Grassi V, Patella S. Reliability prediction for service-oriented computing environments [J]. Internet Computing, IEEE, 2006, 10(3):43-49.

[12] Bai Xiaoying, Wang Yongbo, Dai Guilan, et al. A framework of contract-based collaborative verification and validation of web services [C]. The 10th International ACM SIGSOFT Symposium on Component-Based Software Engineering (CBSE), Boston, 2007, Lecture Notes 4608,256-271.

[13] Tsai Wei-tek, Chen Yinong, Paul R, et al. Adaptive testing, oracle generation, and test case ranking for web service [C]. Proc. Of the 29th Annual International Computer Software and Applications Conference (COMPSAC), Edinburgh, 2005, 101-106.

[14] Tsai Wei-tek, Bai Xiao-ying, Chen Yinong, et al. Web service group testing with windowing mechanisms [C]. Service-Oriented System Engineering (SOSE). IEEE International Workshop, 2005, 213-218.

[15] Cai Kaiyuan, Li Yongchao, Liu Ke. Optimal and adaptive testing for software reliability assessment [J]. Information and Software Technology, 2004, 46(15): 989-1000.

[16] Cai Kaiyuan, Jiang Changhai, Hu Hai, et al. An experimental study of adaptive testing for software reliability assessment [J]. The Journal of Systems and Software, 2008,81(8): 1406-1429.

Mandatory Access Control for Web Applications and Workflows

M. Fonda[1], **C. Toinard**[1], **and S. Moinard**[2]
[1]École Nationale Supérieure d'Ingénieurs de Bourges, 18020 Bourges Cedex, France
[2]QualNet, 24 route de Creton, 18110 Vasselay, France

Abstract--- *Despite the fact that mandatory protection has proven its efficiency for the Operating System level, mandatory access control is missing for Web-based applications. This paper proposes a novel approach of mandatory access control supporting both Web applications and Workflows. A general architecture includes a dedicated reference monitor that can be easily integrated into any Web server plus external components that ease the administration of the mandatory protection. An integration is proposed for the Microsoft IIS Web server. Although the proposed protection approach is not dedicated to Workflow environments, the experiments onto a real Workflow environment shows that it is possible to solve the problem of computing a safe mandatory policy. Indeed, our approach enables to compute and control the mandatory policy for a dedicated Web-based Workflow environment. A correctness approach is proposed showing that the protection safely enforces the required mandatory policy. Performance results show the low overhead of our solution. As far as we know, our solution is the first approach providing an efficient MAC solution that covers both Web-based applications and workflows.*

Keywords: Security, Web application, Workflows, Mandatory Protection

1. Introduction

The problem of integrating a mandatory protection at the application level is not new. It is a mean to control the access to classified information [1] and to reach a satisfying level of accreditation [2]. For example, the .Net framework supports mandatory protection. However, Microsoft does not provide any mandatory policy and the system administrators are not able to define a safe mandatory policy. Indeed, the problem of the mandatory protection is the complexity for defining a safe policy. In the context of Web environments, the general approach is either to ask the application developers to add controls within their code or to ask the administrator of the web servers to manage the access control. However, those two approaches are not safe since they are error prone and do not place the responsibility of the policy outside the scope of the developers and the system administrators.

This paper addresses the problem of designing a usable mandatory protection for Web-based applications. It proposes a general architecture including a reference monitor that controls the HTTP requests. This architecture includes additional components that ease the computation of the security contexts for the incoming requests and supports the computation of the required mandatory policy.

First, a section describes the problem of the mandatory protection for Web environments. Then, our mandatory model of protection is presented including rules between HTTP security contexts. The next section describes the general architecture supporting our model of protection. Experiments are presented for the QualNet workflow environments including a complete mandatory protection. For experimentation purpose, two dedicated Computer-aided process planning (CAPP) based on the Workflow environment of QualNet is protected. Related works are described and a conclusion defines the perspectives of our promising approach.

2. Problem definition

In a Web application without any centralization of the access control, developers must implement the access control for each Web page and resource they develop (See figure 1). Web applications such as workflow applications can easily contain hundreds of Web resources, so mistakes are easily made by the developers on the implementation of the access control. Developers may simply forget to implement the access control for some resources. Furthermore, it is difficult to know afterward the access control policy of a given Web site without studying all the code. Modifications of the access control rules are as well difficult, as it can imply to modify a lot of Web pages and inconsistencies may easily appear.

Any weakness in the access control policy of a Web application can allow attackers to access unauthorized functionalities of the application. That problem is presented by the OWASP as the eighth out of the ten most critical Web applications security risks [3]. In contrast with a Distributed Deny of Service (DDoS) that is impossible to solve [4] for opened Web applications, access control can be enforced and can guarantee integrity and confidentiality properties. To deal with those security properties, OWASP recommends to have a highly configurable role-based authorization policy that should deny all accesses by default.

The most common access control method on Web servers is the anonymous access method. In the anonymous access mode, all the users of the Web site are recognized by the Web server as the same user. Even if the application implements its own authentication system to differentiate the users, an access control is required to minimize the privileges of each user into the application. In practice, the notion of

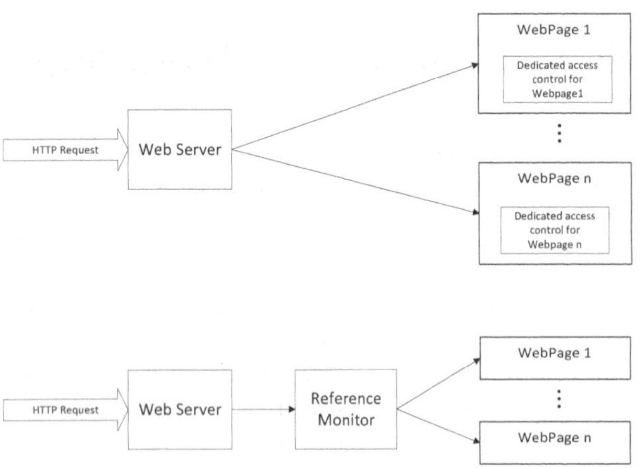

Fig. 1: Access control centralisation.

role eases the administration of the access control policy. However, current application environments such as .NET require the management of roles by the application developers. Finally, only mandatory access control can guarantee security properties related to confidentiality and integrity since it is the only approach that places the policy outside the scope of the developer and the system administrator i.e. the Web server administrator. But, a reference monitor, like presented in figure 1, is really missing to enforce a MAC policy preventing malicious HTTP requests from illegal accesses. Indeed, current approaches mainly run at the operating system or middleware levels and cannot analyze nor define access rules for the HTTP requests.

3. Mandatory Protection of the Web accesses

That section presents a novel protection language dedicated to the control of all HTTP requests incoming on the Web server. A protection rule is of two forms 1) $allow(Subject, Action, Object)$ and 2) $allow(Subject, Action, Object) : Conditions$. Our reference monitor compares the incoming Web requests with the MAC rules expressed using our language. If the HTTP request does not match with the MAC rules, then the HTTP access is denied by the mandatory protection (default-deny setup). Let us describe those two kinds of rules.

3.1 Elementary rule

A rule $allow(Subject, Action, Object)$ enables a Subject to carry out an Action onto the considered Object. This kind of rule supports elementary authorizations such as allowing a role to access a Web resource.

3.2 Extended rule

Extended controls use optional conditions within a rule $allow(Subject, Action, Object) : Conditions$.

The conditions permit to represent constraints between the application data e.g. data of the request, session or cache. Conditions allow a finer control especially when the notions of user and role are not sufficient. For example, the access can be allowed only if the amount of the bank balance of the user is positive by using a condition on the value of the balance data. Conditions can be expressed literally or as a piece of code. These conditions are evaluated by our reference monitor during the control of an incoming HTTP request.

3.3 Security contexts and Actions

Security contexts are required in order to designate the Subject and the Object. A security context is an extensible string including an unbounded number of elements in order to designate safely the considered entity. A subject designates the request while an object is a Web resource or a set of Web resources.

The security context of the subject, i.e. a user or a group of users, includes the user identifier, the role identifier, the application domain, the application identifier plus any other additional information. For example, the subject is designated with the string format $user : role : domain : application$. The notions of user and role are not always necessary to represent a subject context. A question mark represents an unknown user and/or role whereas an asterisk represents any known user and/or role within the Web application. These dedicated notations are useful to reduce the number of rules necessary to allow the access to the resources.

The security context of the object, i.e. a set of Web resources for the considered application, includes the relative path of the resource in the Web application tree. Regular expression can be used for designating more precisely a set of Web resources.

An action defines the considered access to the target object. An action defines execute/read/write/create/delete accesses.

3.4 Grammar

Listing 1 presents an extract of the grammar of the protection language, written in ANTLR (ANother Tool for Language Recognition). A policy file contains an unbounded number of $globalRule$. A $globalRule$ consists of a $rule$ plus an unbounded number of conditions.

```
policy : (globalRule '\r\n')*

globalRule : rule (' : ' Condition)*

rule : allow '(' subject ',' action ',' object ')'

subject : userIdentifier ':' roleIdentifier ':'
          appDomain ':' appIdentifier
```

Listing 1: ANTLR Grammar

4. Implementation of the MAC protection

Let us describe the implementation of our mandatory protection for the Windows/Internet Information Services (IIS)/.Net environment. Figure 2 shows an overview of the implementation, whose components are described in the following subsections, including a reference monitor plus external components such as the application adaptor and the policy generator. When an HTTP request arrives, an HTTP event handler runs the generator of the requested accesses that computes all the possible required rules corresponding with the incoming request thanks to the application adaptor. Then, the handler runs a decision engine that searches the requested accesses into the compiled format of the MAC policy. The policy generator solves the problem of computing a safe MAC policy. Indeed, computing a safe MAC policy, i.e. allowing the legal accesses while denying the illegal ones, generally remains an open problem. Our policy generator enables to solve this problem when the application formalizes the required accesses. In practice, Workflow models always formalize the access policy so our policy generator is able to compute a safe MAC policy without any assistance of the security officer.

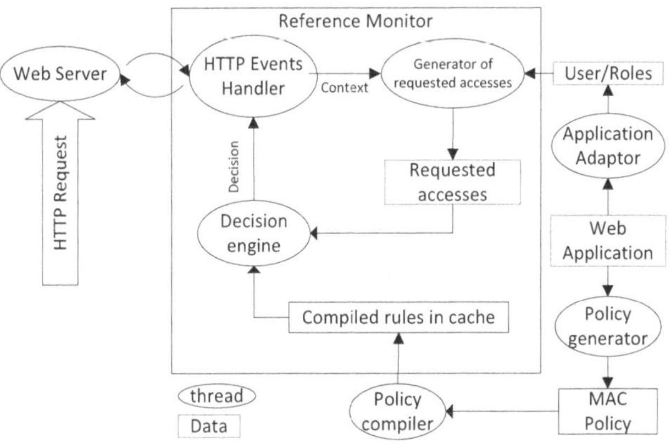

Fig. 2: Access control architecture

4.1 Reference Monitor

4.1.1 HTTP Events handlers

During the processing of an HTTP request, the ASP.Net framework runs a set of handlers for events such as *BeginRequest, AcquireRequestState,etc.* Our reference monitor is implemented as a set of handlers that extract information from the request and/or modify the context of the request in order to verify that the access satisfy our safe MAC policy. The handler *AcquireRequestState* runs all the components of the MAC reference monitor. *AcquireRequestState* is the first event for which the whole context of the request including the session state is accessible. The application adaptor (see 4.2.2) may need the session state to retrieve the user and roles of the incoming request. At that point, the handler has all the information it needs to generate the rules for the requested accesses (see 4.1.2) and runs the decision engine (see 4.1.3). That engine verifies that the requested accesses satisfy the MAC policy. When the decision engine denies the request, the handler sends back an error such as *You don't have enough rights to access this resource* and the requested Web page is not executed.

4.1.2 Generator of the requested accesses

Algorithm 1 describes the computation of the rules corresponding to the requested accesses for an incoming request. The decision engine will then use the requested accesses to verify that they match with the MAC policy. For the sake of readability, the presented algorithm does not consider the processing of the regular expressions used for the security contexts and the actions.

First, the type of action has to be defined. For example, if the incoming request concerns a Web page i.e. an aspx file, the requested action is an execution but for a jpg or pdf file it is a read action. Then, the generator of the requested accesses uses the application adaptor to retrieve the user and the roles associated with the current context. Furthermore, two cases are distinguished. If the user is unknown, it cannot have any role within the application. Therefore, there is only one requested access : an unknown user with unknown role requests the Action onto the Filepath.

In contrast, for a known user, several accesses can be requested. In fact, the user may have several roles within the application. For each of these roles, two access rules are generated :

- *any known user* with *the role* requests *Action* onto the object *Filepath.*
- *the incoming user* with the *role* requests *Action* onto the object *Filepath.*

Two additionnal rules can be added to the requested rules :

- *the incoming user* with *any role* requests *Action* onto the object *Filepath.*
- *any known user* with *any role* requests *Action* onto the object *Filepath.*

4.1.3 Decision engine

Algorithm 2 presents the decision mechanism. Its function is to decide whether the requested access, according to the Web context of the incoming request, satisfies the MAC policy.

The decision engine uses the previous rules defining the requested accesses (4.1.2) and looks for them into the compiled MAC policy. At the first matching, the decision engine authorizes the HTTP request that continues transparently. For an extended rule, the system checks the conditions. If the conditions are satisfied, the HTTP request is authorized. If none of the requested accesses have been found into the

```
Algorithm 1: Generation of all requested accesses
Input: Context, Filepath
Result: List of requested accesses
if Filepath is a Webpage then
    Action = "execute"
else
    Action = "read"
User = appAdaptor.getUser(Context)
Roles = appAdaptor.getRoles(Context)
if User is unknown then
    rule = generateRA("?","?",Action,Filepath)
    Add rule in RequestedAccesses
else
    foreach role in Roles do
        rule = generateRA("*",role,Action,Filepath)
        Add rule in RequestedAccesses
        rule = generateRA(User,role,Action,Filepath)
        Add rule in RequestedAccesses
    rule = generateRA(User,"*",Action,Filepath)
    Add rule in RequestedAccesses
    rule = generateRA("*","*",Action,Filepath)
    Add rule in RequestedAccesses
return RequestedAccesses

Data: AppDomain appD, AppIdentifier appI
Function generateRA(User,Role,Action,Filepath)
    subject = User:Role:appD:appI
    rule = allow(subject,Action,Filepath)
    return Hash(rule)
End Function
```

compiled MAC policy, the decision engine sends an error message and stops the request.

4.2 External components

4.2.1 Policy compiler

The purpose of the policy compiler is to get a MAC policy available into a textual format and produce a compiled version of the requested MAC policy. Using the grammar presented in 3.4, our compiler uses ANTLR to generate a parser in C#. An HTTP handler corresponding to the *Init* event runs that parser to produce the compiled version of the MAC policy.

The parser compiles the textual MAC rules into SHA-512 hashed rules. Those hashed rules reduce the overhead of the comparison carried out by the decision engine beside strings comparison (4.1.3).

4.2.2 Application Adaptor

The application adaptor ensures the reusability of the access control system. Indeed, it retrieves from the application the information about the user and its roles. In fact, the application adaptor retrieves the user and its roles from the context of an incoming request. That adaptor only has to provide two methods :

- getUser(requestContext ctx) must return a String representing the user associated with the incoming request.
- getRoles(requestContext ctx) must return a List of Strings representing the roles of the user related to the incoming request.

```
Algorithm 2: Decision mechanism
Input: Context, Filepath
Result: Boolean : authorized access ?
hashedRA = generateAllRA(Context,Filepath)
foreach access in hashedRA do
    if access is in hashedPolicy then
        if access has conditions then
            if conditions are verified then
                return True
            else
                continue
        else
            return True
return False
```

As described in algorithm 2, the decision engine performs a number of rule comparisons that is linearly dependent of the number of roles returned by the Application Adaptor. An efficient Application Adaptor must thus limit the number of roles it returns by providing only the roles that may give an access right for the requested object. The experiments, given in the sequel, show that it is possible to develop such an efficient Application Adaptor for a workflow environment. With such an improved Application Adaptor, the decision overhead is lower and the reference monitor faster.

4.2.3 Policy Generator

MAC protection faces the difficulty of defining a safe policy. While this problem generally remains unsolved, our approach proposes a policy generator for solving this problem. The policy generator takes into account the access model of the application (e.g. a workflow model that always define the access model) in order to compute the associated MAC policy.

The experiments show that a Policy Generator can be developed for a dedicated application such as a workflow system and a correctness test for the computed mandatory policy is available. The general idea is that each workflow defines the user and the roles accessing a resource i.e. a Web page. Thus, the policy generator will automatically transform the workflow access model into a MAC policy controlling the accesses to the Web pages.

5. Experiments

Let us describe the experiments and correctness tests performed on Intraqual Dynamic i.e. the workflow system provided by QualNet. Intraqual Dynamic is a full-Web workflow system based on Microsoft softwares. Since our solution controls the Windows/IIS/.Net environment, Intraqual Dynamic takes advantages of the proposed security enforcement. We performed the experiments on two different environments. Environment 1 is a copy of the application used by QualNet as its Computer-aided process planning (CAPP). Environment 2 is a large-scale CAPP environment used by one of QualNet's customer. The specifications of these environments are presented in table 1.

Table 1: Specification of the test environments.

	Environement 1	Environment 2
Users	25	548
Roles	13	45
Workflows	41	110
Web pages	116	587

5.1 Policy generator

In order to experiment the access control system on these environments, a mandatory policy is needed. A policy generator is proposed that computes the required mandatory policy according to the existing workflow model that defines for each user and role the allowed resources. IntraQual Dynamic stores these authorizations for each workflow within its database. Using this database and knowing the architecture of the workflows on the filesystem, the policy generator computes a policy file matching the accesses on the different workflows.

As the user management system of Intraqual Dynamic is fully role-based, the policy can be generated in two forms :

- the policy gives authorizations for each user on the resources they can access regardless of the roles.
- the policy gives authorizations for each role on the resources they can access regardless of the users.

Listing 2 presents an extract of the generated policy for the environment 1, using exclusively the roles.

```
1 allow(*:04 - Front end:Intranet:ERP,execute,/
      Modules/M22/et2/saisie22.aspx)
2 allow(*:05 - Administration:Intranet:ERP,execute,/
      Modules/M22/et2/saisie22.aspx)
3 allow(*:01 - Direction:Intranet:ERP,execute,/
      Modules/M87/et20/saisie87.aspx)
4 allow(*:00 - Everybody:Intranet:ERP,execute,/
      Modules/M84/et1/saisie84.aspx)
5 allow(*:01 - Direction:Intranet:ERP,execute,/
      Modules/M93/et1/saisie93.aspx)
```

Listing 2: Generated Policy

For example, the first rule authorizes any user in the role *04 - Front End* to execute the */Modules/M22/et2/saisie22.aspx* resource. In that case study, the generated policy using the roles containes 211 rules, whereas the one generated with users containes 574 rules. As expected, the roles permit to reduce the number of rules necessary on the application.

5.2 Execution of the reference monitor

Listing 3 gives the requested accesses generated by the reference monitor when the user *fonda* tries to access the resource */Modules/M84/et1/saisie84.aspx*. The user *fonda* has three roles in the application : the role "*00 - Everybody*", the role "*10 - Development*" and the role "*03 - Technical*". According to algorithm 1, it generates eight matching requested accesses.

```
allow(fonda:00 - Everybody:Intranet:ERP,execute,/          1
      Modules/M84/et1/saisie84.aspx)
allow(*:00 - Everybody:Intranet:ERP,execute,/              2
      Modules/M84/et1/saisie84.aspx)
allow(fonda:10 - Development:Intranet:ERP,execute          3
      ,/Modules/M84/et1/saisie84.aspx)
allow(*:10 - Development:Intranet:ERP,execute,/            4
      Modules/M84/et1/saisie84.aspx)
allow(fonda:03 - Technical:Intranet:ERP,execute,/          5
      Modules/M84/et1/saisie84.aspx)
allow(*:03 - Technical:Intranet:ERP,execute,/              6
      Modules/M84/et1/saisie84.aspx)
allow(fonda:*:Intranet:ERP,execute,/Modules/M84/           7
      et1/saisie84.aspx)
allow(fonda:*:Intranet:ERP,execute,/Modules/M84/           8
      et1/saisie84.aspx)
```

Listing 3: Generated requested accesses

The decision engine compares that list with the policy given in the listing 2. The decision engine finds that the requested access number 2 matches the rule number 4 of the mandatory policy. Thus, the access control system authorizes *fonda* to access the resource */Modules/M84/et1/saisie84.aspx*.

5.3 Performances

The aim of that experiment is to measure the execution time of the reference monitor and to detail its overhead, in order to bring out the most time-consuming component of the reference monitor.

5.3.1 Method

For that purpose, we compared the average execution time of several Web pages of the tests environments with and without the MAC system. We also measured the average execution time of the generator of requested accesses and of the decision engine with two different application adaptors :

- Simple application adaptor : it returns all the roles associated with the user.
- Efficient application adaptor : it only returns the roles that could allow access to the requested resource.

The measures were done using several StopWatch object, provided by the .Net Framework to perform time measures.

5.3.2 Results

Table 2 presents the results of the performance tests performed on both environments. These results show that for a complete policy, the overhead of our MAC system is under 10%.

Table 2: Performance tests results.

	Env 1	Env 2
Web page average execution time :		
With MAC (ms)	31.8	330.2
Without MAC (ms)	29.3	349.2
Average reference monitor execution time (ms):	2.5	19.0
Overhead (%)	8.5	5.8

$$Overhead = \frac{t_{MAC} - t_{without\ MAC}}{t_{without\ MAC}} (= \frac{349.2 - 330.2}{349.2} = 5.8\%)$$

When the size of the application increases, the overhead of the MAC protection decreases. Indeed, the execution time of the Web page increases more than the authorisation decision time. As a result, our MAC system fits with a large-scale application.

Table 3: Components execution time.

	Env 1	Env 2
Reference monitor global overhead :		
With Simple adaptor (ms)	2.5	19.0
With Efficient adaptor (ms)	2.2	17.0
Generator of the requested accesses overhead :		
With Simple adaptor (ms)	0.55	4.20
With Efficient adaptor (ms)	0.40	2.60
Decision engine overhead :		
With Simple adaptor (ms)	1.95	14.80
With Efficient adaptor (ms)	1.80	14.40

Table 3 shows that the decision engine is the most time-consuming component of the reference monitor as it represents about 80% of the execution time of the reference monitor.

$$\frac{decision\ engine\ overhead}{reference\ monitor\ overhead} = \frac{14.80}{19.0} = 0.78 = 78\%$$

Furthermore, the number of roles returned by the application adaptor (4.2.2) also have an impact on the decision time. The efficient application adaptor permits to gain about 11% on the execution time.

$$\frac{efficient\ execution\ time}{simple\ execution\ time} = \frac{17.0}{19.0} = 0.89 = 89\%$$

Further improvements must focus on the decision engine, for example by adding a cache system which will store the latest authorized accesses to reduce the decision time.

5.4 Correctness test

Since the policy generator enables to compute the required mandatory policy, a correctness approach is supported verifying that all the authorization rules expressed in the policy and only them are enforced. To ensure that the access control system is fully operational, no unexpressed authorization can be allowed.

5.4.1 Method

Algorithm 3 presents the process of the correctness test. Dealing with a list of users (each user is associated to a role), the process simply accesses each Web pages for each user modelized with a role. For each user, the process first logs in the application and navigates to all Web pages iteratively. Then, it navigates to the logout page and deals with the next user/role. The process detects a deny by parsing the HTML source returned by the Web server. In case of a deny, the HTML source only contains the generic error message sends back by the access control system (see 4.1.1). When the HTML source does not contain the error message, the access was authorized by the access control system.

Algorithm 3: Correctness tests

```
Input: Users, Roles, Filepaths
Result: A'_P, A_{\overline{P'}}, N_T
foreach User associated to a role do
    Log In as User
    foreach FilePath do
        NavigateTo(FilePath)
        N_T +=1
        if (access is authorised) then
            if (matching rule is in policy) then
                A_{P'} +=1
            else
                A_{\overline{P'}} +=1
    Log Out
```

5.4.2 Formal expression

The correctness of the access controller is formalized as follows.

Let N_P represents the number of rules in the policy P, R the number of roles and F the number of resources authorized by the policy.

Let C expresses the number of possible combinations i.e. the number of necessary tests to cover every cases. Let P' represents the extended policy i.e. the equivalent policy while developing the regular expressions present in P and N'_P the number of resulting rules. Because of the regular expressions, a rule can authorize accesses to several resources.

$$C = R * F; N'_P >= N_P \tag{1}$$

Let $A_{P'}$ expresses the number of accesses authorized by the reference monitor and verified i.e. the authorized access is in P', $A_{\overline{P'}}$ the number of accesses authorized by the reference monitor that are not in P' and N_T the number of tests really performed by the test process.

The conditions to ensure the correctness of the access control system are :

- The number N_T of tests performed must be equal to C the number of necessary tests to cover every case.
- The number $A_{P'}$ of authorized and verified accesses must be equal to N'_P the number of rules in the extended policy.

- The number $A_{\overline{P'}}$ of authorized accesses that are not in the policy must be zero.

Thus, the correctness is formalized as follows :

$$C_t = \frac{N_T}{C} = 1; C_r = \frac{A_{P'}}{N'_P} = 1; A_{\overline{P'}} = 0 \qquad (2)$$

5.4.3 Results

As the considered mandatory policy does not use any regular expressions, equation (1) becomes :

$$C = 13 * 116 = 1508; N'_P = N_P = 211$$

For the considered case study, the test program returns $A_{P'} = 211$, $A_{\overline{P'}} = 0$ and $N_T = 1508$. These values enable to verify the correctness of the access control system :

$$C_t = \frac{N_T}{C} = \frac{1508}{1508} = 1; C_r = \frac{A_{P'}}{N'_P} = \frac{211}{211} = 1; A_{\overline{P'}} = 0$$

These results show that the access control system enforces all the rules expressed in the mandatory policy and only them. No unexpressed authorization in the mandatory policy is allowed by the system. Consequently, the correctness method shows that the access control system satisfies the safe mandatory policy required by the workflow application.

6. Related works

Discretionary Access Control is known to be fragile [5]. Only Mandatory Access Control, such as proposed in SELinux [6], is able to guaranty security properties. However, MAC solutions are generally complex. For example, [7] proposes an architecture to provide an end-to-end access control over Web applications. They use SELinux and XSM policies to enforce a mandatory access control inside and between Virtual Machines. So, multiple MAC policies are requested using millions of rules. Moreover, they can not express high level security properties and do not cover the protection of the resources of a Web application.

Formal analysis [8] of workflows are proposed. However, they consider functional verifications and cannot analyze the threats coming from a Web implementation. A flow analysis [9] between Web pages provides a static analysis of the information flows between the Web resources. But, they do not control the flows between an HTTP request and the application resources. Role-based approaches [10] enable to control the accesses to the database tables and Web pages. Testing approaches [11] can detect SQL and PHP injections. However, they fail to detect illegal accesses to the resources of a Web application.

[12] proposes a language to ease the control of the information flows within a distributed architecture. However, that language does not support the control of Web applications accessing resources. Thus, current approaches poorly address the control of the Web applications. Moreover, they are complex and do not fit well with the workflow systems.

7. Conclusion

That paper proposes a novel approach of mandatory protection for Web applications. It addresses the difficulty of defining a mandatory policy. A dedicated language supports the formalization of the security requirements for the Web applications. A general architecture is proposed that eases the enforcement of the policy and the computation of a safe policy starting from a model of the Web application. A correctness approach enables to test the real Web application and to compute if the system is correct. The experiments on a complete workflow application show that our approach enables to solve the complexity of computing the required policy. The overhead is under 6 percent for a large policy. The correctness test shows that the protection is safe.

Future works deal with the usage of the PIGA approach [12] to enforce the protection of our Web reference monitor in order to prevent attacks on that component. Moreover, several improvements are under development such as an interface to ease the design of the mandatory policy when the model of application is not available and a cache of decisions to reduce the overhead of the protection.

References

[1] Relyea, H. and Library of Congress. Congressional Research Service. Security Classification Policy and Procedure, Executive Order 12958: The Clinton Administration Directive, Congressional Research Service, Library of Congress (1995)

[2] Guidance for Applying the Department of Defense Trusted Computer System Evaluation Criteria in Specific Environment, CSC-STD-004-85, 25 June (1985)

[3] OWASP *The Ten Most Critical Web Application Security Risks*, 2010

[4] Fischer, Michael J. and Lynch, Nancy A. and Paterson, Michael S., Impossibility of distributed consensus with one faulty process, J. ACM, volume 32, number 2, pp 374--382, ACM, New York, NY, USA (1985)

[5] Harrison, M.A., Ruzzo, W.L., Ullman, J.D., Protection in operating systems. Communications of the ACM, 19(8):461471, August (1976).

[6] Loscocco, P. Smalley, S., Integrating flexible support for security policies into the linux operating system. In 2001 USENIX Annual Conference (FREENIX 01), Boston, Massachusets, USA (2001)

[7] Hicks, B., Rueda, S., King, D., Moyer, T., Schiffman, J., Sreenivasan, Y., McDaniel, P., Jaeger, T., An architecture for enforcing end-to-end access control over web applications, Proceedings of the 15th ACM symposium on Access control models and technologies, SACMAT '10, 163--172, ACM, New York, NY, USA (2010)

[8] Kovács, M., Gönczy, L., Simulations and Formal Analysis of Workflow Models, In Proc. of the Fifth International Workshop on Graph Transformation and Visual Modeling Techniques. Electronic Notes in Theoretical Computer Science, 215--224, Elsevier (2006)

[9] Wu, Y., Offutt, Y., Modeling and testing web-based applications, Technical Report, Department of Information and Software Engineering, George Mason University, Fairfax, VA (2009)

[10] FARD, R.E., NEZHAD, R.K., Dynamic Workflow Management Based On Policy-Enabled Authorization, Journal of Information Technology Management, Volume XX, Number 4, 57--68 (2009)

[11] Wassermann, G., Yu, D., Chander, A., Dhurjati, D., Inamura, H., Su, Z.,Dynamic test input generation for web applications, Proceedings of the 2008 international symposium on Software testing and analysis, ISSTA '08, Seattle, WA, USA, 249--260, ACM USA (2008)

[12] Afoulki, Z., Bousquet, A., Briffaut, J., Rouzaud-Cornabas, J., Toinard, C., MAC Protection of the OpenNebula Cloud Environment, Proceeding of the Second International Workshop on Security and Performance in Cloud Computing, SPCLOUD 2012, to appear, June, Madrid, Spain (2012)

Decision Support for Assessment of IT-Security Risks

E. Moradian[1], **M. Kalinina**[1]
[1]Department of Computer and System Sciences, Stockholm University, Stockholm, Sweden

Abstract - *IT-security risks can have a great impact on organizations and can cause high financial damage. To address security issues and avoid problems, knowledge about risks is vital. Therefore, a risk assessment process, which addresses security of IT-systems, is essential. However, risk assessment methods based on qualitative or quantitative approaches involve some difficulties and limitations. Therefore, in this research, we propose a risk assessment method based on semi-quantitative approach. The method provides decision support for security experts during evaluation of IT-security risks and enables assessment of threats both at a detailed level and as a whole. Imprecise information is captured from expert judgment and expressed numerically in interval form. The method is applied to a scenario in order to demonstrate its usage. We utilize a decision tool to present the outcomes. Moreover, sensitivity analysis is performed to point out most critical values.*

Keywords: IT-Security Risks; Risk Assessment; Decision Support; Threat Tree; Imprecise information.

1 Introduction

A vast number of IT-systems handle sensitive information that can include research documents, financial transactions, and medical records. Almost all organizations have some form of digital service and, hence, can be exposed to security risks. According to Rodgers [1], security risk is the probability of sustaining a loss of a specific magnitude during a specific time period due to a failure of security system. Security risks in IT-systems can have a great impact on organizations, including damaged reputation, lost customers' trust, and can cause catastrophic outcomes in a form of high financial damage or bankruptcy. Systems are threatened by adversaries that have different reasons and a variety of motives for their actions. Criminals are interested in sensitive information that can be used, for example for making money, while terrorists target to destroy systems that handle critical infrastructure [2].

Risk management plays a key role in addressing security of IT- systems. Risk management process is necessary for threat identification and implementing adequate security level [3]. The purpose of risk management is to produce knowledge about relevant security characteristics of systems. Risk assessment is an essential part of effective risk management and aims to identify and determine risks by using relevant inputs [4]. Assessments approaches can be divided to quantitative, qualitative and semi-quantitative assessments depending on how the concepts of impreciseness and risk are perceived.

Quantitative assessment is based on the deterministic analysis or on the probabilistic analysis where values are determinate from statistical investigations and uncertainty is handled using probability theory. Thus, quantitative risk assessment is based on exact numeric values. However, such approach is not adequate, since it is not realistic to determine impact value of a threat and probability of threat in exact numbers. Qualitative assessment is based on qualitative expressions of expert's priorities and is used in the case of lack of numerical values. Hence, qualitative risk assessment uses non-numerical levels, such as "low", "medium", and "high". This, however, makes it difficult to compare and prioritize risks [4]. Semi-quantitative assessment uses the expert's judgment assigned in numerical values and uncertainty is handled using various methods, such as probability theory, and fuzzy theory. Of course, not all uncertainties can be handled by using semi-quantitative assessment. However, semi-quantitative assessment can capture the advantages of quantitative and qualitative assessments. Risk comparison can be performed based on risk values, as well as the results can be easier communicated to decision makers.

With respect to the above, in this research, we propose a risk assessment method, called Decision Support for Security Risk Assessment (DESSRA) that is based on semi-quantitative approach. DESSRA can provide decision support for security professionals during risk assessment process. In addition, it is possible to perform sensitivity analysis in order to determine the most critical values of the risks. Sensitivity analysis provides an opportunity for professionals to see how sensitive some of the risks are to changes of consequence and probability values.

The paper is organized as follows. Related work is discussed in chapter two. Chapter three provides a general description of risk assessment process. We describe interval decision analysis in chapter four. Chapter five describes the context of the DESSRA method, proposed in this research. We also present and explain the steps of the method. In chapter six, a scenario is presented. We demonstrate the application of DESSRA method with a scenario where assessment of IT-security risks is performed. The results are also provided. Chapter seven presents the conclusions from this work.

2 Related Work

Different methods for risk assessment have been proposed in the literature. A number of methods have been developed to support decisions of security specialists [5]. The application of a decision tree analysis to assess the cost-effectiveness of Man-Portable Air Defense Systems is described in [5]. The effects of implementing countermeasures to reduce the risk of a successful attack have been investigated by means of a decision tree analysis. In the paper, the decision tree analysis with a combination of sensitivity analysis have been assigned three especially important variables, namely, the economic losses, the probability of attempted attack and the cost of countermeasures. Winterfeldt and O'Sullivan [5] highlighted the drawback of the conducted analysis, the lack of possibility to assess the probability of an attack, and suggest expanding of standard methods in order to shift probabilities of attack.

Guan, et al. [6] applied the multi-criteria decision making methods to evaluate information security related risks. This multi-criteria decision-making approach has relied on Analytical Hierarchy Process in order to determine weights for the likelihood of the potential threat of each information asset. Authors [6] used the linguistic variables to express expert opinions on information risks, and then conduct impact analysis in the fuzzy environment [6].

In the context of emerging environmental threats, Linkov and Seager [7] suggested an approach that combines multi-criteria decision analysis, risk analysis and life-cycle assessment. The integrated framework enables decision making about emerging risks under uncertainty and is based on opinion from each distinct stakeholder or group of decision makers. Authors stated that the uncertainty regarding stakeholders' preferences may be managed through well developed methods of multi-criteria decision analysis [7].

Björkqvist *et al.* [8] propose an approach of evaluating risks associated with new district heating price structures. Authors suggested a risk premium assessment model that consist of two input modules, namely, risk premium estimation and probability assessments and, further, one output risk evaluation module from the previous modules. The probability assessment module is based on input the probabilities of different levels of risk factors. These probabilities of qualitative judgements of a decision maker are expressed in the form of intervals. Furthermore, the suggested evaluation methods are based on the methods of interval decision analysis, videlicet, expected risk premium level and cumulative risk profiles [8].

In this paper, we propose a DESSRA method that provides decision support for security professionals during risk assessment process. The proposed method elucidates how inputs of the imprecise information can affect the final outcome. The method enables assessment of the risks both as a whole and at a detail level — at each level of a threat tree. For this reason, we adopt decision analysis theory for risk assessment. The proposed method can facilitate decisions about risk response and selection of countermeasures.

3 Risk Assessment

Information security risks arise from the loss of confidentiality, integrity, and/or availability of information and reflect the potential negative impact on organizational operations [4]. Risk is a function of the probability that an identified threat will occur, and the consequence of that threat on the organization [9]. Risk assessment is a process of identifying and understanding risks through studying inputs, performing risk assessment, and defining the set of outputs [4]. Risk assessment process includes definition of risk factors and the relationships between the factors, as well as an assessment approach (quantitative, qualitative or semi-quantitative). Risk assessment implies asset valuation, threat assessment, vulnerability assessment, and risk determination. During risk assessment, a range of values for defined risk factors is specified [4]. Risk assessments support risk response decisions, such as "risk acceptance, avoidance, mitigation, sharing, or transfer", design decisions, and selection of security controls [4].

3.1 Asset Valuation

An asset is a valuable resource that must be protected from misuse by an adversary [10]. Some examples of asset can include information and resources related to information management, IT systems, security function, people, and network capacity [11]. To be able to perform risk assessment it is necessary to define value of an asset [12]. The overall value of asset can comprise following:

- security value of an asset, according to confidentiality, integrity, availability, and accountability security properties
- financial value, i.e., cost in the case of replacement and cost for operation and maintenance
- impact on organization in case an asset is compromised

The highest value, however, determines the overall value of an asset [12]. Asset valuation is an important input for threat modeling and, thus, for risk management [4], [9].

3.2 Threat Assessment

Threat is an indication that potential danger could negatively impact or damage the organization's objectives or mission [9]. Threat assessment includes identification of threats in relation to the identified assets, and threat analysis. During threat assessment following steps can be performed: define threat actions; build threat/attack trees; create likelihood scale; assign values of consequences. A threat involves threat agents, which are threat sources that have motive and may perform an action [9]. Threat agent can be any entity that jeopardizes security properties. Threat agents can be of three types:

- Human: includes malicious entity or accidental errors. Malicious entity can be criminal organization, individual, ideological organization, nation-state, etc.
- Technological: includes sensors, automated functions and processes, and networks.
- Environmental: These are related to natural threats such as fire, flood, tornado, and earthquake.

Threat motive is the driver of a threat agent, which can include financial winning, publicity, sabotage, and information superiority. A threat action is an event that exploits the weaknesses of a system [11]. Threat impact results in violation of security properties.

3.3 Vulnerability Assessment

Vulnerability is a weakness that can be exploited by a threat source and cause violation of security property of an asset [12]. The purpose of vulnerability assessment is to determine the nature and degree to which organizations, business processes, and systems are vulnerable to threat sources and threat events identified during threat assessment [4]. Vulnerability assessment can involve following activities:

- Vulnerability identification, which is associated with IT systems and the environments in which those systems operate [4].
- Determination of threat-vulnerability relationship that can be achieved by mapping threats to vulnerabilities or by utilization of threat scenarios
- Vulnerability rating that involves the vulnerability factors and the impact level on asset or system.

Different methods can be utilized to perform vulnerability identification, such as vulnerability scanning, penetration tests, and vulnerability catalogs.

3.4 Risk Determination

Risk determination implies evaluation and prioritization of risks to defined assets. Risks are determined based on inputs, such as the results from asset valuation, threat assessment and vulnerability assessment [12].

4 Interval Decision Analysis

One of the fundamental assumptions for the classical form of Bayesianism is that the decision maker's beliefs can be represented by a unique probability distribution [13]. Bayesian representation of degree of belief often requires conformity to statistical knowledge. In fact, decision makers have to deal with different information type: from comprehensive lack of knowledge about the events involved to the complete knowledge of the involved random processes.

Differences in the quality of information available in a variety of situation cannot be captured by single probability distribution [13]. The use of intervals to represent the degree of belief as one way to solve this problem was suggested by various authors. The attempt to formulate decision theory with interval information as a complete theory was made by Kyburg [14]. The decision theory with interval information presupposes that degree of belief is represented by probability intervals and the principle of maximizing expected utility by the principle of rationality. Interval representation of probabilities allows handling various types of information. The likelihood of various, uncertain eventualities may change by expansion or reduction of the interval. In the case of perfect information, interval would be reduced to a point; in the case of the lack of available information, the associated probability interval would be wider; in the case of comprehensive lack of knowledge, interval would be from 0 to 1 [14].

Interval decision analysis implies the use of decision analytical model with representation of uncertainty in interval forms. Interval decision analysis is based on research on vague or imprecise probabilities in interval form and also is extended through the use of utilities in the range of forms [15], [16], [17]. Besides expression of probabilities and utilities in the interval form, comparative constraints are used in order to define the preference of a decision maker. Possibility of assigning interval information enables carrying out a sensitivity analysis that leads to an interactive solution of the existing decision problem. The rule for discriminating between alternatives remains to select the alternative with the maximum expected utility or the minimum expected loss, but the commonly emerging problem is an overlapping expected losses. Additional stability analysis, such as interval contraction, is one way to handle this problem [18].

5 Decision Support for Assessment of IT Security Risks

In this research, we developed the DESSRA method for assessing IT-security risks. The method is presented and explained below and applied on the scenario in the next section. The proposed method is based on semi-quantitative approach and is compliant with the NIST 800-30. DESSRA enables determination of risks based on analysis of several threats and vulnerabilities. Threat assessment can be performed by utilizing threat/attack trees, which expose ways that adversary can take in order to achieve his goal. An example of a threat tree is depicted in Figure 1.

Fig. 1. Threat Tree

The root of the threat tree is the threat that has been defined during threat identification. Threat analysis comprises of hierarchical attack paths, as well as uncertainty of risk occurrences (also called threat likelihood or threat probability) and consequences. Probabilities of threat occurrence are identified at each level of the threat tree. Each child (threat action) has been assigned its own probability p_i. Last node of each branch in a threat tree assigned both probability p_j and value v_j, where value v_j is a product of consequence value and vulnerability severity. The vulnerability value for an asset can be acquired from, for example, vulnerability databases or expert judgment. The interval values for threat consequences can be adopted from, for example, NIST 800-30 standard [4], which is shown in Table 1.

TABLE 1
IMPACT SCALE

Qualitative values	Semi-Quantitative Values
Very High	96-100
High	80-95
Moderate	21-79
Low	5-20
Very Low	0-4

A threat action can be described as threat event that target an asset. The threat consequence can be seen as a security violation that results from the successful execution of the harmful event. Therefore, the threat can be considered as a set of branches and denoted by $\{\prod_i p_{ij}\ v_j\}$, where $\prod_i p_{ij}\ v_j$ is a product of probabilities p_{ij} and value v_j of treats in jth branch in the threat tree. Then, a risk value is defined as $\prod_i p_{ij}\ v_j$ for each branch j in the threat tree. In addition, the threat value, i.e., the value of the root threat can be calculated as follows:

$$\sum_j \prod_i p_{ij}\ v_j \qquad (1)$$

5.1 Method Steps

The method comprises of a number of steps. Initial inputs are provided by security professionals and are based on expert judgments. Therefore, the first step is to perform asset identification and valuation. After that it is essential to identify threats to each asset under review. An asset can be threatened by a variety of threats; a threat can threaten various assets.

During the next step it is important to collect information about identified threats and vulnerabilities for each asset. In order to perform threat assessment, threat/attack trees are built. Each branch of a threat tree represents a number of threats (threat actions). During this stage interval values of threat impact (consequence) and probability are assigned to the last nodes of a threat tree. Probabilities are defined for each threat node. The inputs to these probabilities can be based either on qualitative judgments of security expert, quantitative analysis of historic data or on combination of judgmental forecasting with historic data. The impacts' values can be based on impact intervals defined by NIST [4]. Furthermore, vulnerability severity is determined and interval values are defined for each asset. Values are added to each threat action that appears to be the last node in the branch and considered during risk value determination. Consequently, the risk value is a product of threat impact, threat consequence, and vulnerability value. Thus, the values of each branch in a threat/attack tree are defined.

The next step is to build a decision tree with alternatives, where each alternative is represented by a threat/attack tree. The threat value then can be obtained as a sum of risk values of each branch in a tree, i.e. it is possible to calculate the threat value according to $\sum_j \prod_i p_{ij}\ v_j$.

For the purpose of calculating the overall risk value, where asset value and risk value for each branch are included, we will use the following formula for each threatened asset included in the scope of the risk assessment:

$$A * \sum_j \prod_i p_{ij} v_j, \qquad (2)$$

where A is value of the threatened asset. A threat with the highest value will affect the system the most.

In addition, it is possible to perform sensitivity analysis in order to point out the most critical probability of each threat action and critical values of threat consequence. The result of the sensitivity analysis shows the most dangerous threat.

The proposed method allows performing both threat assessment and vulnerability assessment in an effective and holistic way. The DESSRA method can provide support for security specialists and facilitates security risk assessment at different levels of the organizational hierarchy, i.e. the organization level, business process level and system level. An important feature of the DESSRA method is that it gives the possibility to insert imprecise parameters in form of interval-valued probabilities at all levels of the threat tree and also interval valued consequences.

6 Scenario

In this section, we present a scenario in order to demonstrate the developed, in this research, DESSRA method for IT-security risks. Consider the following fabricated scenario. Organization "P&S" offers products and services to a wide range of customers. Customers can purchase products and view their orders and/or invoices online after they have been logged in to the website of organization "P&S". The valuable assets that need to be protected are: sensitive information, such as customer information, including financial information (orders/invoices); login session, network, web server, and backend database.

TABLE 2
ASSET VALUATION

Asset	Overall Value
Customer Information	10
Login Session	5
Network	10
Web Server	10
DB Server	10

To assure confidentiality, integrity, and availability of each asset, assets valuation is performed. Asset values, which are determined by security experts, are presented in Table 2. The system architecture consists of the front end web server and backend database server. The front end provides an interface to the customers. The backend contains all the data about customer, and data about products and services. The application connects to external SMTP server to send e-mail notifications to the customers. Welcome page is the first page customer meets. To be able to put an order and view invoices customers are required to register and login. To register customers need to provide personal information via registration page. To submit information 'Submit' function is used. To retrieve information 'Retrieve' function is utilized. The login procedure is as follows: the browser sends a request to login to the website with login information. The credentials are passed back to the backend database that verifies the credentials and sends a response to the web server. The web server displays the requested page if the verification of login credentials is successful; otherwise, an error message is displayed. In the case of successful request, web server sets session ID and a cookie. The data flow diagram is shown in Figure 2.

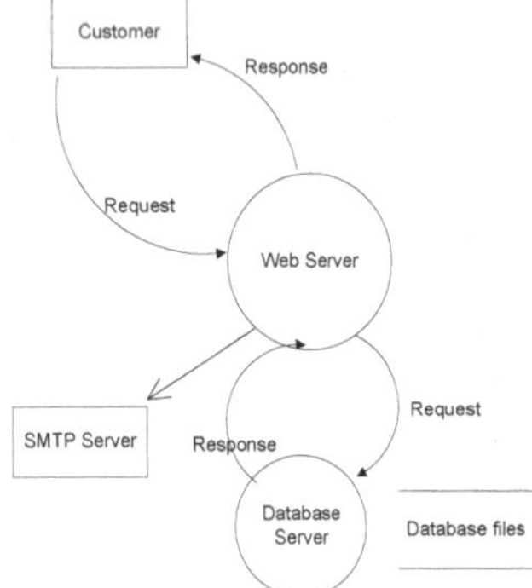

Fig. 2. Data flow diagram

Possible entry points of the adversary that have been considered are: user's login data, user's personal information, application, login sessions, system, process, access to backend database, and access to web server. In order to provide readability, three threats are discussed in this paper. The identified threats (Threat ID:1, Threat ID:2, Threat ID:3) show potential threat actions that threat agent might try to perform to attack the system. Threat source, possible intentions of the threat source, capabilities, threat actions, and the target (threatened asset) are considered during threat identification. Environmental threat sources are not considered. Vulnerability values are considered during risk value determination. In this scenario, the asset 'Customer information' is identified for the threat 'Gain Access to User Account'. Asset values have been taken into consideration during determination of the overall risk values.

The threat tree for the threat 'Gain Access to User Account' is presented in Figure 3.

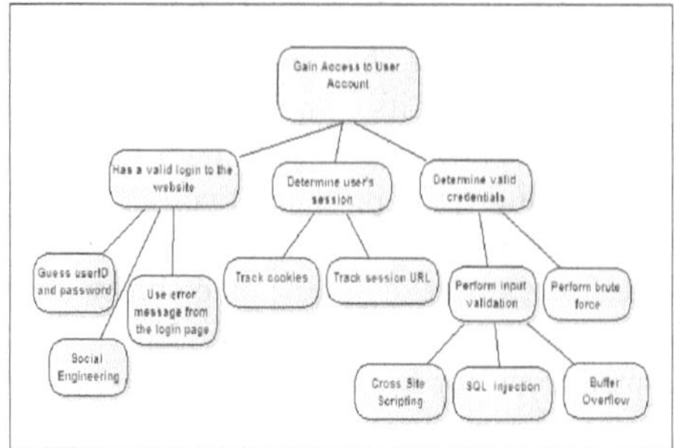

Fig. 3. Threat ID:1: Gain Access to User Account

Figure 4 shows the threat 'Prevent Access of Legitimate Users to the System'

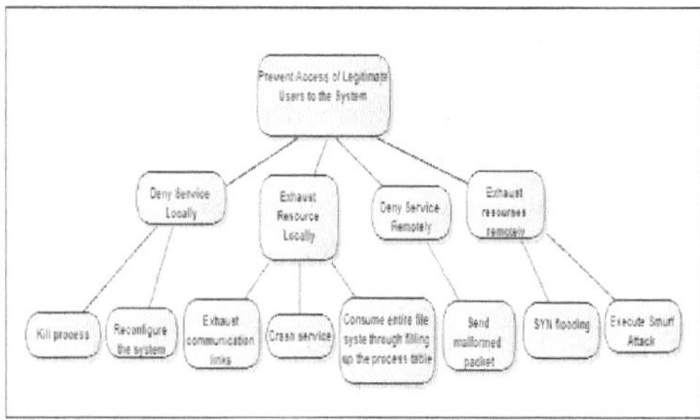

Fig. 4. Threat ID :2 : Prevent Access of Legitimate Users to the System

In Figure 5, threat tree for the threat 'Take over the traffic' is demonstrated.

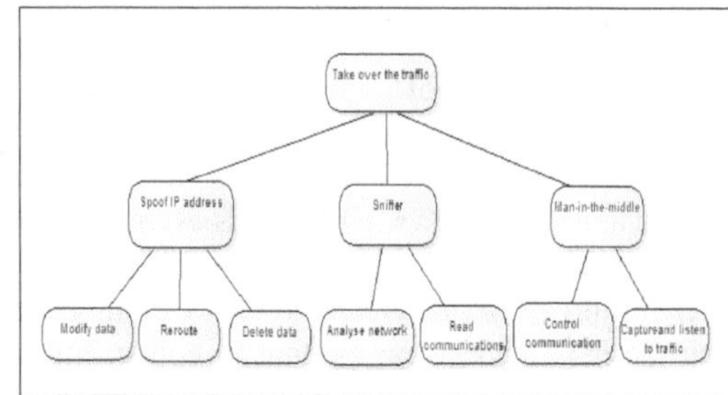

Fig. 5. Threat ID :3 : Take over the traffic

To perform risk assessment we utilize the decision tool, DecideIT [17]. The software DecideIT allows input of interval values, interval probabilities and qualitative statements such as "greater than" and "equal". Hence, it can provide support to a decision maker in the expression of varying degrees of imprecision. The decision tool is a combination of a developed set of evaluations algorithms and a user-friendly interface that display the decision problem and the evaluation results. The software is designed to be easily interpreted by a human decision maker. The set of algorithms [19], [20], [15] is based on the concept of contraction; the input's interval is compressed in a controlled manner in the direction of single point within this interval. Moreover, the tool enables performance of sensitivity analysis that is displayed by an interval tornado diagram. The interval tornado diagram allows displaying the individual sensitivities of probabilities and values in decision trees [16]. In the tornado diagram shown in Figure 8 and Figure 9, a red (dark) colored bar indicates negative influence and green (light) colored bar indicates a positive influence on the expected value.

In the scenario, the decision tree has three alternatives, represented by threat trees ID:1, ID:2, ID:3 with 25 mutually exclusive outcomes. The third alternative, threat ID:3, is shown in Figure 6.

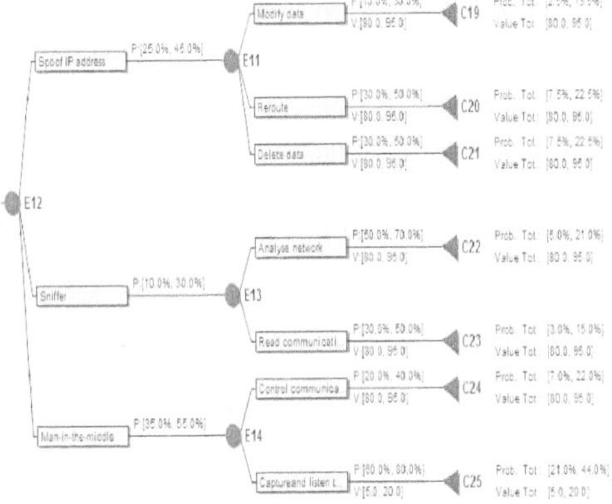

Fig. 6. Threat ID:3 in decision three

A pairwise comparison between two threats using interval contraction analysis shows the most dangerous threats. The outcome of interval contraction analysis between Threat ID:2 and Threat ID:3 also Threat ID:1 and Threat ID:3 are presented in Figure 7 and Figure 8 respectively.

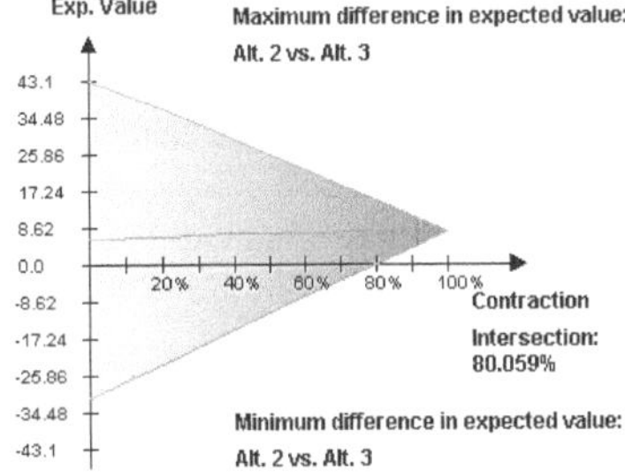

Fig. 7. Pairwise comparison between ID:2 and ID:3

From the contraction analysis presented in Figure 7, the threat, ID:3, is almost equally dangerous as threat, ID:2, although their respective overall risk values may overlap up to a contraction level of about 80%.

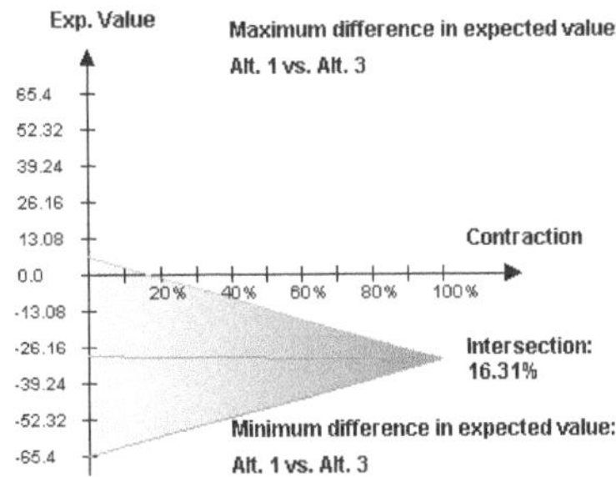

Fig. 8. Pairwise comparison between ID:1 and ID:3

On the contrary, from the contraction analysis shown in Figure 8, the threat, ID:3, is more dangerous than threat, ID:1, due to intersection of their respective overall risk values is only 16%.

Consequently, the conclusion can be drawn that the following two risks, which are 'Prevent Access of Legitimate Users to the System' and 'Take over the traffic are the risks with the highest impact on the system.

The application of sensitivity analysis is performed by using DecideIT tool in order to show the most critical values of identified threats (Threat ID:1, Threat ID:2, Threat ID:3) where the elements with highest impact on the system in focus are identified. The result is depicted in tornado diagram that displays a one-way sensitivity analysis of several variables (threat probabilities and consequences) within the same output.

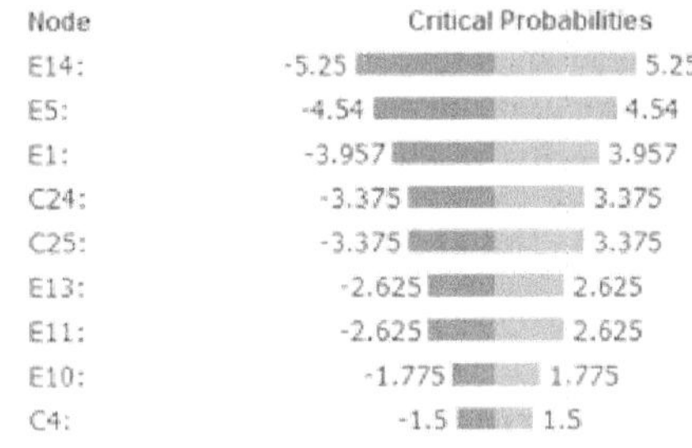

Fig. 9. Critical probabilities

As shown in the Figure 9, the most critical probabilities are E14 (Man-in-the-middle) and E5 (Determine valid credentials). Therefore, the probabilities variation will have the highest impact on the overall risk value.

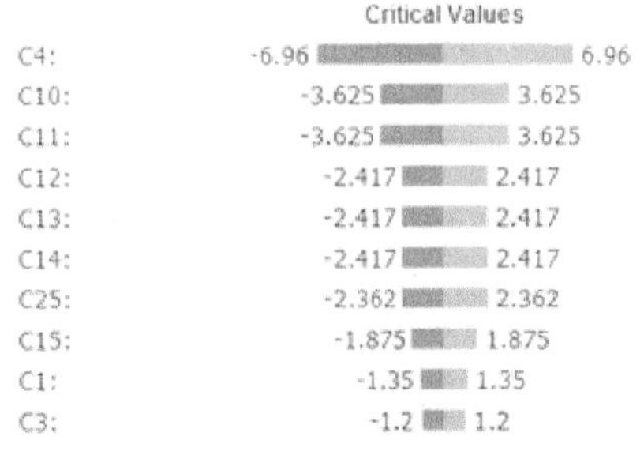

Fig. 10. Critical consequences

For consequences value variation, the uncertainty interval in the values of consequences C4 (Track cookies) and C10 (Kill process) as well as C12 (Crash communication links) and C13 (Crash service) mostly affect the overall risk values. The critical consequences are shown in Figure 10. The tornado diagram presented in Figure 9 and Figure 10 lets a security expert decide where to put the efforts in order to make more correct decision about the security risks countermeasures on a system. Based on the performed risk assessment results security professionals of organization "P&S" can make decisions about relevant risk responses, such as risk acceptance, mitigation, or avoidance, and also countermeasures.

7 Conclusions

In this paper, we propose a semi-quantitative approach for assessing IT-security risks. The DESSRA method is described in this research and demonstrated with a scenario. The method enables assessment of risks both as a whole and at the detail level, which means the threat is assessed not only in the root node but all possible threat branches in a threat tree are explored as well. Besides, such approach enables the comparison of large number of threats simultaneously. The inputs for risk assessment are captured from experts' opinions and expressed numerically, i.e., the imprecise information about probabilities and consequences are presented by interval values. We have utilized a decision tool to present the outcomes. The outcomes reveal most severe risks that can violate security properties of the threatened assets, including confidentiality, integrity, and availability. Thus, the proposed method can support decisions about risk response and selection of security controls in order to achieve secure design, and thus, secure the systems in focus.

8 Acknowledgment

This research was funded by the Swedish Research Council Formas, project number, 2011-3313-20412-31, as well as by Strategic funds from the Swedish government within ICT – The Next Generation.

9 References

[1] D. H. Rodgers, "Implementing a Project Security Review Process within the Project Management Methodology," SANS Institute, 2002.

[2] E. Skoudis and T. Liston, Counter Hack Reloaded A step-by-step Guide to Computer Attacks and Effective Defenses., 2 ed., Prentice Hall, 2006.

[3] J. Sherwood, A. Clark and D. Lynas, Enterprise Security Architecture A Business-Driven Approach, N-Y, CMP Books, 2005.

[4] Ronald S. Ross, "Guide for Conducting Risk Assessments (NIST SP - 800-30rev1)," The National Institute of Standards and Technology (NIST), Gaithersburg, 2012.

[5] D. von Winterfeldt and T. M. O'Sullivan, "Should WE Protect Commercial Airplanes Against Surface-to-Air Missile Attacks by Terrorists?," *Decision Analysis,* vol. 3, no. 2, pp. 63-75, 2006.

[6] B.-C. Guan, C.-C. Lo, P. Wang and J.-S. Hwang, "Evaluation of information security related risks of an organization: the application of the multicriteria decision-making method," in *IEEE 37th Annual International Carnahan Conference on Security Technology*, 2003.

[7] I. Linkov and T. P. Seager, "Coupling Multi-Criteria Decision Analysis, Life-Cycle Assessment, and Risk Assessment for Emerging Threats," *Environmental Science & Technology,* vol. 45, no. 12, pp. 5068-5074, 2011.

[8] O. Björkqvist, J. Idefeldt and A. Larsson, "Risk assessment of new pricing strategies in the district heating market: A case study at Sundsvall Energi AB," *Energy Policy,* vol. 38, no. 5, p. 2171–2178, 2010.

[9] T. R. Peltier, Information Security Risk Analysis, 2 ed., Boca Raton, Florida: Auerbach Publications, 2005.

[10] F. Swiderski and W. Snyder, Threat Modeling, Redmond, Washington: Microsoft Press, 2004.

[11] E. Moradian, A. Håkansson and J.-O. Andersson, "Ontology Based Patterns for Software Security Engineering," in *Advances in Knowledge-Based and Intelligent Information and Engineering Systems*, Spain, 2012

[12] M. Schumacher, E. Fernandez-Buglioni, D. Hybertson, F. Buschmann and P. Sommerland, Security Patterns Integrating Security and Systems Engineering, John Wiley and Sons, 2006.

[13] P. Gärdenfors och N.-E. Sahlin, Decision, Probability, and Utility, Cambridge University Press, 1988.

[14] H. E. Kyburg, "Rational belief," *Behavior and Brain Science,* vol. 6, pp. 231-275, 1983.

[15] M. Danielson och L. Ekenberg, "Development of algorithms for decision analysis with interval information," i *Conference on New Trends in Software Methodologies, Tools and Techniques: Proceedings of the Eighth SoMeT_09*, The Netherlands, 2009.

[16] M. Danielson, "Sensitivity Analyses in Interval Decision Modelling," *Engineering Letters,* vol. 1, p. 1, 2009.

[17] M. Danielson, L. Ekenberg, J. Johansson and A. Larsson, "The DecideIT Decision Tool," in *ISIPTA'03: Proceedings of the Third International Symposium on Imprecise Probabilities and Their Applications*, Lugano, Switzerland, 2003.

[18] L. Ekenberg, M. Boman and J. Linnerooth-Bayer, "General Risk Constraints," *Journal of Risk Research,* vol. 4, pp. 31-47, 2001.

[19] M. Danielson, "Generalized evaluation in decision analysis," *European Journal of Operational Research,* vol. 162, nr 2, pp. 442-449, April 2005.

[20] M. Danielson och L. Ekenberg, "Computing upper and lower bounds in interval decision trees," *European Journal of Operational Research 181(2),* pp. 808-816, 2007.

Creating Stronger Yet Easily Pronounceable Passwords

M. Barjaktarovic
Department of Computer Science, Hawai'i Pacific University, Honolulu, Hawai'i, USA

Abstract – This paper addresses the issue of secure passwords. Security is often a balance between usability and security. For example, strong passwords can be hard to remember. Computer users are forced by system administrators to change their passwords relatively frequently and to provide a strong password every time. This requirement can lead users to resort to various unsafe strategies, to name a few: reusing the same strong password for many accounts, changing just one simple thing in an existing password, providing a relatively simple password with just a few extra special characters (thus creating a rather weak password), and writing down passwords and storing them in insecure locations. This paper presents a strategy to create a strong password that is memorable with a rather small amount of effort.

I. Introduction

Historically, computer security and user satisfaction have always been in opposition; while users want more flexibility, ease-of-use and speed, system administrators want more secure systems. One of the ways to ensure stronger security is to mandate strong passwords that change frequently. However, if the requirement is too strict, the users will not be able to remember their passwords and will resort to recording passwords in convenient locations (such as their desk drawers where hackers can easily find the passwords), using the same passwords for all logins, and/or using quite simplistic passwords with just a few alterations that appear strong.

Passwords have been an issue for a long time [2]. The most common recommendation for creating strong(er) passwords is to use a mix of letters, numbers, and special characters, for example, to spell out the acronym of a sentence [10]. [11], [12]. There are also "convenient" password programs such as KeePass, discussed below.

A. KeePass Pronounceable Password Generator

KeePass Password Manager [4] is an open-source tool that promises to safely store passwords in one central location. The software is available under SourceForge. The page shows "107,803 downloads by March 2013, and 4709 recommendations, out of which 81% are positive." Negative evaluations on the tool page do not expose major flaws in the tool, but mainly complain of logistics, for example that KeepPass is a Windows and not a Unix tool. KeePass Password Manager's popularity has inspired various plugins, such as Web KeePass for the web and iPhone [5], KeePass Google Sync Plugin [6], KeePass Sync for synchronizing the password database online amongst different computers [7], and KeePass Pronounceable Password Generator (KPPPG) [3] discussed in this paper.

KeePass is designed to store passwords that users generate, and also offers the option to generate random passwords. The user specifies which character sets should be used (e.g. digits, upper-case letters, etc.) and KeePass randomly picks characters from that set. The user does not have to remember the passwords, since KeePass stores them; thus, passwords do not have to be memorizable. However, the user has to have access to the KeePass password file, which might be inconvenient (taking more time to look up passwords) and/or insecure, if the file has to be viewed remotely.

KPPPG works by substituting either numeric or "visually similar" patterns for particular characters. The following characters are substituted by default:

a=4 e=3 k=|< o=0 v=\/

b=8 g=6 l=1 q=9 w=\/\/

c=(h=|-| m=/\/\ s=5 x=><

d=|) i=!. n=/\/ t=7

KPPPG also allows substituting only numeric values, or only "look alike" characters. For example, the letter "a" can be substituted as a=4 or a=@. KPPPG numeric-only substitution is shown below:

a=4 g=6 o=0 t=7

b=8 i=1 q=9 z=2

e=3 l=1 s=5

KPPPG allows only look-alike substitution, shown below:

a=@ i=! o=0 t=+

c=(l=| s=$

This paper investigates if a KPPPG-like strategy would produce strong passwords. Our goal is to find the balance between user convenience and security. The substitution scheme has to be as easy as possible so that users can memorize their passwords, yet strong enough so that a password cracker like John the Ripper cannot crack the password.

In the first section of the paper, we propose a possible substitution scheme. KPPPG substitutes only one character, and has 0-3 possible substitutions for each letter. We hypothesize that the KPPPG strategy is relatively simple and proceeed to produce a more complex strategy. We discuss assumptions that we used to produce the substitution scheme. In the subsequent sections, we test our substitutions in various situations, from Webster dictionary words to real-life cracked passwords, and we find evidence to support our hypothesis. We also find various issues present in real-life password applications.

II. Enhanced Substitution Scheme

We propose to use more possible substitutions. For example, below is one possible pictographic representation of letters.

<table>
<tr><td>a = 4, &</td><td>A = /\, /-\</td><td>n = “</td><td>n = /\/</td></tr>
<tr><td>b = 8</td><td>B = |}, |3</td><td>o = 0</td><td>O = @</td></tr>
<tr><td>c = o</td><td>C = (, [</td><td>p = q</td><td>P = |*, |0</td></tr>
<tr><td>d = -|</td><td>D = |), |]</td><td>q = 9, p</td><td>Q = O_</td></tr>
<tr><td>e = 3</td><td>E = [-, {</td><td>r = i^</td><td>R = P\</td></tr>
<tr><td>f = |^</td><td>F = |+</td><td>s =5, ?</td><td>S = _/^</td></tr>
<tr><td>g = 6, q</td><td>G = [=</td><td>t =7, +</td><td>T = _|_</td></tr>
<tr><td>h = |-</td><td>H = |-|</td><td>u = y</td><td>U = |_|</td></tr>
<tr><td>i = !</td><td>I = |</td><td>v = ^</td><td>V = \/</td></tr>
<tr><td>j = ‘|</td><td>J = _|</td><td>w = ^^</td><td>W = \/\/</td></tr>
<tr><td>k = i<</td><td>K = |<</td><td>x = #, %</td><td>X = ><</td></tr>
<tr><td>l =1, |</td><td>L = |_</td><td>y = j</td><td>Y = \|/</td></tr>
<tr><td>m = ;;;</td><td>M = /\/\</td><td>z=2</td><td>Z = /_</td></tr>
</table>

Comma means alternative ways to express the character. For example, x can be represented as # or %.. Ideally, the user can pick which way suits them better, i.e. which way is more memorable for them.

The main idea behind our scheme is to “draw” pictographs of the letters. The main assumptions for the pictographic design are:

- | is a part of many English characters, so it is very convenient to represent many letters by using it. However, we do not want to overuse it; password crackers that recognize the repeating of single characters can recognize our scheme easily. Thus, some letters might not “look” as pictographic as possible.
- Some special characters, such as a or s, have very common substitutes, such as @ and $, respectively. We will use them at first, but suspect that we will try to either avoid them or use them differently.

Our substitution scheme will pick a random number of characters to substitute, from 0 to the password length. KPPPG allows only one character to be substituted, and we need to investigate if that is enough.

III. Testing Overview

Our testing algorithm can be summarized as follows: the user provides a password; our software substitutes 0-3 characters, encrypts the resulting password, and feeds it into the password cracking tool. We discuss each stage below.

A. Passwords

The words we use as initial passwords are obtained from a Webster dictionary word list of 234,936 single American English words, available from [1], as well as 3546 real-life cracked passwords supplied by the John the Ripper password cracking tool [8].

B. Character Substitution

At the moment, our tool substitutes only alphabet characters. If a password contains any other characters (for example, numbers or special characters), they are not converted, since numbers and special characters already help to make stronger passwords.

To provide some randomness in results, we provide four alternatives for each character. In order to keep it easily memorable for the user, substitution will not distinguish between lower- and upper-case letters. For example, letters “a” and “A” can be replaced by either 4, &, /\ or /-\. We reason that, if this weaker but more convenient substitution scheme works, it is not necessary to make it more complicated for the user. The actual code used is shown below:

```
char* table[26][4]= {                    \
"4",  "&",    "/\\",   "/-\\",   \
... mappings for all other letters ... }
```

If a letter does not have an obviously suitable, easily recognizable representation, (arbitrarily) -1 was substituted. Again, if this weaker but more convenient substitution scheme works, it is not necessary to make it more complicated for the user. It would be easy to change the “-1” wildcard to something else later, if it proves to be necessary. A summary of mappings used is shown below:

<table>
<tr><td>a, A:</td><td>4</td><td>&</td><td>/\</td><td>/-\</td><td>n, N:</td><td>;;</td><td>/\/</td><td>-1</td><td>-1</td></tr>
<tr><td>b, B:</td><td>d</td><td>|o</td><td>|}</td><td>|3</td><td>o, O:</td><td>0</td><td>@</td><td>-1</td><td>-1</td></tr>
<tr><td>c, C:</td><td>o</td><td>z</td><td>(</td><td>[</td><td>p, P:</td><td>q</td><td>|*</td><td>|0</td><td>-1</td></tr>
<tr><td>d, D:</td><td>-|</td><td>=|</td><td>|)</td><td>|]</td><td>q, Q:</td><td>9</td><td>p</td><td>O_</td><td>K</td></tr>
<tr><td>e,E:</td><td>3</td><td>G</td><td>[-</td><td>{</td><td>r, R:</td><td>i^</td><td>P</td><td>-1</td><td>-1</td></tr>
<tr><td>f, F:</td><td>|^</td><td>|+</td><td>-1</td><td>-1</td><td>s, S:</td><td>5</td><td>?</td><td>_/-</td><td>_/^</td></tr>
<tr><td>g, G:</td><td>6</td><td>q</td><td>[=</td><td>e</td><td>t, T:</td><td>7</td><td>+</td><td>_|_</td><td>-1</td></tr>
<tr><td>h, H:</td><td>|-</td><td>|-|</td><td>-1</td><td>-1</td><td>u, U:</td><td>y</td><td>|_|</td><td>-1</td><td>-1</td></tr>
<tr><td>i, I:</td><td>!</td><td>1</td><td>|</td><td>1</td><td>v, V:</td><td>^</td><td>\/</td><td>-1</td><td>-1</td></tr>
<tr><td>j, J:</td><td>'|</td><td>;</td><td>_|</td><td>_/</td><td>w, W:</td><td>^^</td><td>\/\/</td><td>-1</td><td>-1</td></tr>
<tr><td>k, K:</td><td>i<</td><td>c</td><td>|<</td><td>>|</td><td>x, X:</td><td>3</td><td>%</td><td>><</td><td>-1</td></tr>
<tr><td>l, L:</td><td>|_</td><td>1</td><td>-1</td><td>-1</td><td>y, Y:</td><td>j</td><td>\|/</td><td>\i/</td><td>W</td></tr>
<tr><td>m, M:</td><td>;;;</td><td>/\/\</td><td>-1</td><td>-1</td><td>z, Z:</td><td>2</td><td>/_</td><td>-1</td><td>-1</td></tr>
</table>

Some sites allow passwords with special characters and some (surprisingly) allow only letters and numbers. For example `mypassword*` is an unacceptable password on some sites (for example, the wireless AT&T customer support site [9]), because * is not allowed as a part of the password. For example, Figure 1 shows the screen resulting from trying an unacceptable password. Finding a substitution scheme that would circumvent this issue is a part of future work.

Figure 1 - An Example of Password Restrictions

C. Encryption

Passwords obtained by using our substitution scheme are encrypted using the Unix crypt(3) function on Linux distro CentOS 6. The man pages (i.e. Linux documentation) for crypt() state:

"crypt() is the password encryption function. It is based on the Data Encryption Standard (DES) algorithm with variations intended (among other things) to discourage use of hardware implementations of a key search.

Crypt() requirements are:

```
#define _XOPEN_SOURCE
#include <unistd.h>
char  *crypt(const  char  *key,  const
char *salt);
```

`key` is a user-typed password.

`salt` is a two-character string chosen from the regex set [a-zA-Z0-9./]. This string is used to perturb the algorithm in one of 4096 different ways. If salt is a character string starting with the characters "id" followed by a string terminated by "$," i.e. idsalt$encrypted, then instead of using the DES algorithm, id identifies the encryption method used and this then determines how the rest of the password string is interpreted. The following values of id are supported:

ID | Method
----
1 | MD5
2a | Blowfish (not in mainline glibc; added in some | Linux distributions)
5 | SHA-256 (since glibc 2.7)
6 | SHA-512 (since glibc 2.7)."

For example, string "nutmeg" encrypted with "vanilla" crypt(3) using DES and salt "Mi" is `MiqkFWCm1fNJI`. The same string encrypted with MD5 and the same salt is `$1$Mi$8BkU2WtOmHNQizHSZBrie..` For discussion on the strengths of various encryption and hashing algorithms and salts, please refer to [10], [11], or [12].

The String "nutmeg" used as a password on our CentOS 6 is showing an encrypted value in /etc/shadow file as `$1$AUJ8RqqI$bI51xVsKaEX6hUzOSnuPm/`:

```
root# useradd -m -d /home/test  test
root# passwd test
root# cat /etc/shadow
  test:$1$AUJ8RqqI$bI51xVsKaEX6hUzOSnuPm
  /:15784:0:99999:7:::
```

Obviously, our implementation of CentOS is using the MD5 algorithm with an 8-byte random salt and 22-byte hash. Although the CentOS 6 default encryption is SHA512, our /etc/login.def file shows that our CentOS is set to use MD5:

```
ENCRYPT_METHOD MD5
MD5_CRYPT_ENAB yes
```

Therefore, if we use the crypt(3) function with MD5 and a 2-byte salt, it should be a sufficient first-pass test for our scheme, since it is quite weaker than the 8-byte salt scheme used on real-life Unix. We can always increase the length of the salt to 8 bytes.

D. Password Cracking

We used the John the Ripper open-source password cracking tool [8]. The tool web site describes the tool as follows: "John the Ripper is a fast password cracker, currently available for many flavors of Unix, Windows, DOS, BeOS, and OpenVMS. Its primary purpose is to detect weak Unix passwords. Besides several crypt(3) password hash types most commonly found on various Unix systems, supported out of the box are Windows LM hashes, plus lots of other hashes and ciphers in the community-enhanced version."

IV. Implementation

The original user passwords are stored in the file test.txt and encrypted using the Unix crypt(3) function, as shown below.

```
user$ cat crypto.c
// Code to encrypt single words using MD5
// with 22-byte hashes
#define _XOPEN_SOURCE
#include <unistd.h>
#include <stdio.h>
//char *crypt(const char *key, const char
*salt);

void main() {
```

```
char password[]="12345678901234567890";
//char salt[] = "Mi";
char salt[] = "$1$Mi";
//char salt[] = "$1$12345678";
char str[20] = {0};

FILE* pFile;
pFile = fopen("test.txt", "r");
if (NULL != pFile) {
 while(fscanf(pFile,"%s",str) != EOF)
 {
   strcpy(password, str);
   printf("%s\n",crypt(password,salt));
 }
}
fclose(pFile);
}
```

Depending on how we choose to encrypt the passwords, we use different salts. `salt` "Mi" will produce a DES-encrypted password salted with string "Mi"; `salt` "$1"Mi" will produce a MD5-encrypted password salted with "Mi"; and `salt` "$1$12345678" will produce a MD5-encrypted password salted with "12345678."

We ran the code as follows:

```
user$ gcc -lcrypt crypto.c
user$ ./a.out > test
```

Finally, code was fed into John the Ripper:

```
user$ john test
```

The tool shows cracked passwords on the screen as soon as it cracks them. At the end of a (either successful or interrupted) cracking session, the tool provides statistics on total time spent and can show the cracked passwords:

```
user$ john -show test
```

V. Results

Various dictionary words and popular passwords from [1] and [8] were used as a starting point for generating easy-to-read (and hopefully stronger) passwords. Zero to three characters were modified to produce new passwords.

All new passwords were encrypted using our crypto.c code using MD5 with salt "Mi" (except test #3, which used an 8-byte salt) and tested against the password cracking tool John the Ripper [8].

Test #1: Used 23 Webster dictionary words shown below:

nutmeg	**aardwolf**	**Ababua**
password	Aaron	abac
A	**Aaronic**	**abaca**
a	**Aaronical**	
aa	**Aaronite**	
aal	**Aaronitic**	
aalii	**Aaru**	
aam	Ab	
Aani	aba	
aardvark	**Ababdeh**	

Surprisingly, the tool did not find all the words as easily as we expected. John the Ripper cracked 11 of these words in 2:04 minutes:

```
guesses: 11  time: 0:00:02:04 0.00% (3)
c/s: 36077  trying: 46370157.
```

The tool could not crack the bolded words for more than 60 minutes although they are common words in Hawaiian, Jewish and Middle Eastern cultures. John the Ripper is a current, internationally used tool made in the U.S.A, yet it did not seem culturally "savvy."

Therefore we decided to test our scheme with words that John the Ripper is guaranteed to easily crack. The tool comes with a list of most commonly used passwords as discovered by crackers [8]: "This list is based on passwords most commonly seen on a set of Unix systems in mid-1990's sorted for decreasing number of occurrences (that is more common passwords are listed first). It has been revised to also include common website passwords from public lists of "top N passwords" from major community website compromises that occurred in 2006 through 2010. Last update: 2011/11/20 (3546 entries)."

Test #2: Used 3546 passwords supplied with the tool.

It was no challenge for the tool:

```
guesses: 3540  time: 0:00:00:01 DONE
```

Test #3: Used 3546 passwords supplied with the tool encrypted using our crypto.c code with salt "$1$12345678."

It was still no challenge for the tool:

```
guesses: 3545  time: 0:00:00:06 DONE
```

Test #4: Used passwords obtained by modifying 3546 passwords supplied with the tool. Passwords were modified by substituting one character. One of the possible substitutions was randomly picked. We repeated the process for each character. For example, if the original password is "qwerty" possible new passwords and their hashes are shown below:

Original password and its hash:

qwerty 1Mi$HmT8hh85w.SUs1CNmVsOk0

One character substituted and the resulting hash:

pwerty 1Mi$lc55Jby2gR9cyAkbX80jG1
q-1erty 1Mi$rM6Tk9znD7iq4Q8xm8cUy1
qw3rty 1Mi$59jIjKEcFsrWX1sOiGJDY.
qweP\ty 1Mi$yQHPHG47wly0Qc/rQD7Xg/
qwer-1y 1Mi$Kup3ZsKkqLWhesV3r1WIw/
qwertW 1Mi$ZhbO62Q8M4MmXw9uIc1RF/

The tool cracked some passwords relatively easily. In 27 minutes it cracked 46 passwords:

```
guesses: 46  time: 0:00:27:31 0.00%
```

The list of 46 most easily cracked passwords is shown below. The left column shows the word that John the Ripper displayed as a cracked password. The right column shows our guess as to which original password the cracked password was obtained from. It did not take much effort to inspect the original passwords and see which single character was substituted. The character substituted is shown in bold. The passwords are sorted by the time it took to crack them, starting from the most easily cracked on the top:

Modified:	Original password:
jankee	**y**ankee
pun**c**in	pun**k**in
popey**3**	popey**e**
pupples	puppies
min**3**	min**e**
ren**3**	ren**e**
kin**q**	kin**g**
kall	**c**all
kc1n	kc1n
as**5**	ass
le**0**	leo
g@	go
soph**l**a	soph**i**a
matt**1**1	matt**i**1
carr**l**e	carr**i**e
paneet	(?)
p**l**ano1	p**i**ano1
p**l**anos	p**i**anos
b**u**ok	b**o**ok
ro**c**cie	ro**k**kie
ronn**1**e	ronn**i**e
ruth**1**e	ruth**i**e
s**c**ate	s**k**ate
scub**4**	scub**a**
s**c**unk	s**k**unk
dlitz	**b**litz
j**0**ker	j**o**ker
ga**d**y	ga**b**y
g**0**ld	g**o**ld
g**0**at	g**o**at
shell**3**y	shell**e**y
clipp**3**r	clipp**e**r
mim**l**	mim**i**
gr**3**en	gr**e**en
b**4**rry	b**a**rry
dosco	**b**osco
blac**c**	blac**k**
chr**1**s	chrls
d**0**ug	d**o**ug
j**4**ne	j**a**ne
m**G**	m**E**
fir**3**	fir**e**
fro**e**	fro**g**
f**y**zz	f**u**zz
m**1**mi	m**i**mi
5lip	**s**lip

Cracked passwords are short (4-6 characters) and contain very common words and names. The occurrences of "cracked" characters is shown in Table 1. Upon examining the cracked passwords statistics, the common denominator is that one character was substituted for another character using substitutions common in texting and misspelling.

Original	Substitute	Frequency	Commentary
i	l 1	12/46	personal names
e	3	7/46	
c / k	k /c	6/46	misspelling
o	0	5/46	common substitution
a	4	3/46	

Table 1 – Easy-to-crack Single Character Substitutions

Within about one hour the tool reported: `"302 password hashes cracked 20476 left."` The pattern of those passwords is very similar to what was shown in the table above. There are just some slight differences, for example cracked passwords include those where "7" is substituted for "t" such as:

7ech **t**ech

Our conclusion is that the tool "knows" how to recognize common and easily recognizable patterns such as names and very easily distinguishable words such as "scuba;" and will easily recognize such words if one letter is changed, especially if changed in a way that is rather common such as substituting "l" for "i."

The KPPPG rule is "Only one character may be replaced at a time but the replacement text can have more than 1 character." Therefore, our results prove that KPPPG strategy may not produce strong passwords.

Test #5: Used passwords obtained by modifying 3546 passwords supplied with the tool. Passwords were modified by substituting two characters. One of the possible substitutions was randomly picked for each character. We repeated the process for all combinations of two characters where the second character has a higher index in the string than the first character. For example if the original password is "password" some possible new passwords and their hashes are shown below. In order to save space, we show only one three-character substitution expansion :

Original password and its hash:
password 1Mi$F4UhtCfqS5RcHI13QBPMn1

One character substituted and the resulting hash:
p/\ssword 1Mi$W7NQDQqijnZsTotIF0I.l1

An additional character substituted and the resulting hash:
p/\5sword 1Mi$wEs/O/u5zp90cEMbbvfzB.
p/\s5word 1Mi$8tWoIQYYTBduX9VdDLeI70
p/\ss^^ord 1Mi$I.uq1XlmbCVDNBlq.fnWf/
p/\ssw-1rd 1Mi$hyagWmSrc3K3lBNjmcwog1
p/\sswoi^d 1Mi$tOi93u6JO65nbhrNOPL./.
p/\sswor=| 1Mi$LgXvX1iIGCn9Ej.nRhZ/U.

Even though 2 letter characters are substituted, some of the resulting passwords are still legitimate words or contain combinations of legitimate words, and thus were easily cracked. For example, the tool cracked the passwords shown below. The first column shows reported cracked passwords; the second column shows what we suspect was the original password from the tool-provided passwords; and the third column shows the word that we suspect the tool might have tried (suspected replaced characters are bolded). Again, the cracked passwords are short (4-6 characters) and contain very common words and names.

Cracked:	Original:	False original:
dust**3**r	**b**ust**e**r	duster
dybba		
ro**d!**n	ro**bi**n	rodin
b**l**t**o**h	b**i**t**c**h	bitoh
l**yo**y	l**uc**y	
tan**j4**	tan**ya**	**tanja**
bad**j**	**d**ad**y**	bady
dig**d**en	**b**ig**b**en	bigden
chloo		
bar**dl**e	barbie	bardie
doodie	**b**oo**b**ie	doobie
clng		
dyrns	bjrns	
r**0**n**1**	r**o**n**i**	ron1
5on**j**	**s**on**y**	sonj
co**c**o	**k**o**k**o	coco

The tool reported: `"1763 password hashes cracked, 58597 left"` within minutes. However, most of those cracked hashes are the original, unchanged passwords that contain numbers and special characters, such as "abc123," "x-files," "123456," or "!@#$%^."

An interesting side observation: as we were building our "substitution of two characters" code, our first draft of the code had a bug; it did not replace characters at the right location in the original string. However, by chance, it was still producing legitimate words or combinations of legitimate words. For example word "**b**u̲cks" was converted into "**d**ucks," which is correct; and then into "do̲cks" which is an incorrect substitution. However, "docks" is a legitimate word (and thus was easily cracked). This ability of English language to "flip" letters and still obtain legitimate words is quite interesting and requires further research.

Test #6: Used passwords obtained by modifying 3546 passwords supplied with the tool. Passwords were modified by substituting three characters. One of the possible substitutions was randomly picked for each character. We repeated the process for all combinations of two characters where the second character has a higher index in the string than the first character, and similarly for substituting the third character. For example, if the original password is "password" some of possible new passwords and their hashes are shown below. In order to save space, we show only one three-character substitution expansion.

<table>
<tr><td colspan="2">Original password and its hash:</td></tr>
<tr><td>password</td><td>1Mi$F4UhtCfqS5RcHI13QBPMn1</td></tr>
<tr><td colspan="2">One character substituted and the resulting hash:</td></tr>
<tr><td>|0assword</td><td>1Mi$bGEoJL8tdHlVfw3BObgYh/</td></tr>
<tr><td colspan="2">Two characters substituted and the resulting hash:|0a_/-</td></tr>
<tr><td>sword</td><td>1Mi$fbFm4McG1c1ZJ9GRE5cy70</td></tr>
<tr><td colspan="2">Three characters substituted and the resulting hash:</td></tr>
<tr><td>|0a_/-5word</td><td>1Mi$YoozW3ZXuuYdloBhMRY20.</td></tr>
<tr><td>|0a_/-s^^ord</td><td>1Mi$tjQ9gW58ioFEyTBPKTruP1</td></tr>
<tr><td>|0a_/-sw0rd</td><td>1Mi$ogigFwcedLEaQcwx3uE3x.</td></tr>
<tr><td>|0a_/-swo-1d</td><td>1Mi$U40jWPsIBvem.4Y3Nsusn1</td></tr>
<tr><td>|0a_/-swor-|</td><td>1Mi$n9ee0mCfnEsipBZZoLWhB1</td></tr>
<tr><td>|0as?word</td><td>1Mi$Jr5e9.b4aZV9Quxo9/lX3/</td></tr>
</table>

Finally, the tool could not crack the new passwords. In 10 days of running the tool, the tool reported "2904 password hashes cracked, 95117 left." However, the only passwords cracked are the originals with characters that were not substituted, e.g. legitimate words with added numbers or special characters, and all-numbers or all-special character words, and simple one-character substitutions such as:

piano**1** Michel**1** **6**iel
whale**1** good-luck

VI. Future Work

If our substitution scheme is used for applications which do not allow special characters as parts of a password, as mentioned in the "Implementation" section, users can still use our scheme but substitute numbers or other "allowed" characters. For example let us use a very simple (and unrealistic) password: `myP` which would be represented as `my|*` by our scheme, if only one character is substituted. However, if the site requesting the password does not allow special characters such as | and *, the user will be informed that the password is unacceptable. In that case we will have to substitute each special character; for example, by the digit below it on the keyboard. For example, on an English-based keyboard, it would produce the following substitution:

<table>
<tr><td>! = 1</td><td>(= 9</td><td>[= 16 10</td><td>,= 24 18</td></tr>
<tr><td>@ =2</td><td>) = 0</td><td>{ = 17 11</td><td>< = 25 19</td></tr>
<tr><td># = 3</td><td>_ = 10 a</td><td>] = 18 12</td><td>. = 26 1a</td></tr>
<tr><td>$ = 4</td><td>_ = 11 b</td><td>} = 19 13</td><td>> = 27 1b</td></tr>
<tr><td>% = 5</td><td>= = 12 c</td><td>; = 20 14</td><td>/ = 28 1c</td></tr>
<tr><td>^ = 6</td><td>+ = 13 d</td><td>: = 21 15</td><td>? = 29 1d</td></tr>
<tr><td>& = 7</td><td>\ = 14 e</td><td>' = 22 16</td><td></td></tr>
<tr><td>* =8</td><td>| = 15 f</td><td>" = 23 17</td><td></td></tr>
</table>

We picked this alternative substitution scheme because it is convenient, there is nothing to memorize for the special characters located above a non-special character on the keyboard. Users would still have to memorize other special characters, which is not easy. Perhaps we could substitute a short description of them, for example substitute "?" with "qm". We also allow space for technically inclined users to specify their numbers in hex. However this scheme might prove not to be secure, in which case a simple "shift" cypher can be used.

As expected, our letter substitution scheme shown in section III.B can always be improved. An interesting study would be to analyze texted messages to see what kinds of substitutions users are most likely to use.

Some letter substitutions are to be avoided, because they produce words that are legitimate. In the English language, it is is possible to "flip" letters and still obtain legitimate words. For example, the only difference between "ducks" and "bucks" is in the first letter. If letters b and d (often) can be switched to produce legitimate words, then they should not be substituted in our password enhancing scheme. Computational linguistics could help with finding "commonalities" in patterns between English words, and which letters are often easily switchable to produce legitimate words.

The KPPPG rules are openly published online, which makes them available to hackers and thus less than safe. Our substitution scheme is also in the public, published in a publicly accessible conference paper. It would be easy to add these rules to password cracking tools. We have not yet identified a way to stay in academia and circumvent the "open to the public" issue that is so ubiquitous in the security world.

VII. Conclusion

We did not expect John the Ripper, known as an excellent password cracking tool, to have difficulties with relatively simple and short English dictionary words which are rooted in non-Western cultures. It would be very interesting to try such words on other well-known password cracking tools such as Unicornscan.

It appears that a password with one or two characters substituted provides some level of protection if characters are substituted in a way that is not very common. Names and common substitutions have to be avoided because they are easily cracked as shown in Table 1. Also, the substitution strategy has to be such so that the resulting password does not contain legitimate word(s). KPPPG does not provide that.

Passwords with three (and possibly more) characters substituted using our strategy seem relatively strong, if they follow the guidelines below.

In general, the strategy for using our password enhancement scheme can be summarized as:

- avoid common substitutions using single characters, such as "3" for "e," or "1" for "i" or "l".
- substitute letters with patterns that ideally have at least 2 characters
- The final password must not look like a combination of legitimate words, and should not have numbers at the start or end of the password.

Overall, we still would advise to follow the recommended practice of creating a strong password as an acronym of an easy-to-remember sentence peppered with numbers and special characters.

References

[1] CSC, "Webster Dictionary of English Words," 1999. [Online]. Available: ftp://nic.funet.fi/pub/unix/security/dictionaries/English/Webster/.

[2] N. Provos, D. Mazieres, "A Future-Adaptable Password Scheme," in *Proceedings of FREENIX Track: 1999 USENIX Annual Technical Conference*, Monterey, CA, 1999.

[3] J. B. B. Engracia, "KeePass Pronouncable Password Generator," 15 8 2011. [Online]. Available: http://pronouncepwgen.sourceforge.net/.

[4] D. Reichl, "KeePass Password Safe - an open source password manager," SourceForge, 2 2013. [Online]. Available: http://sourceforge.net/projects/keepass/?source=directory.

[5] P. Jones, "Web KeePass," SourceForge, 11 2012. [Online]. Available: http://sourceforge.net/projects/webkeepass/?source=directory.

[6] Danyal, "KeePass Google Sync Plugin," SourceForge, 2 2013. [Online]. Available: http://sourceforge.net/projects/kp-googlesync/?source=directory.

[7] S. K. Mitch Capper, "KeePass Sync," Source Forge, 10 2012. [Online]. Available: http://sourceforge.net/projects/kp-googlesync/?source=directory.

[8] Openwall, "John the Ripper Password Cracker," 11 2011. [Online]. Available: http://www.openwall.com/john/.

[9] AT&T, "My AT&T Login," 3 2013. [Online]. Available: https://www.att.com/olam/passthroughAction.myworld?actionType=tech.

[10] R. T. M. Goodrich, Introduction to Computer Security, Pearson, 2011.

[11] W. Stallings, Cryptography and Network Security: Principles and Practice (6th ed.), Prentice Hall, 2013.

[12] S. Harris, CISSP Certification All-in-One Exam Guide, 5 ed., McGraw-Hill Osborne Media, Jan. 2010.

A Flexible Role-Based Delegation Model with Dynamic Delegation Role Structure

Zidong Liu[1], Weiqing Sun[2], and Mansoor Alam[1]
[1]Department of Electrical Engineering and Computer Science, University of Toledo, Toledo, Ohio, USA
[2]Department of Engineering Technology, University of Toledo, Toledo, Ohio, USA

Abstract - *As information systems became widely used by organizations and enterprises, resource sharing and collaboration of work have been pervasive. As a natural way to realize this, delegation has become the routine rather than the exception. However, traditional delegation models have encountered various issues in meeting the growing and diverse requirements. Some of them fail to provide sufficient delegation functionalities, while others are cumbersome to apply and manage practically. Therefore it is imperative to have a flexible delegation model that provides fine-grained control according to different scenarios. Meanwhile, such a model should be easy to apply and maintain. Therefore, we develop a flexible delegation model based on role-based access control which supports fine-grained delegation control at both role and permission levels. Moreover, the proposed model introduces a dynamic delegation role structure to deal with different types of delegation requests. Finally, a prototype was implemented to demonstrate the feasibility of the model.*

Keywords: Role-based access control, Delegation, Delegation model, Delegation role structure

1 Introduction

Nowadays, Role-based access control (RBAC) has become dominant in the access control domain and has been widely used by the majority of organizations, especially large enterprises, hospitals, and colleges due to its simplicity in the management of access rights [1]. In RBAC, individual users are grouped into roles that relate to their positions within an organization and assigned permissions to various roles according to their statures in the organization [2].

The basic idea of delegation is that some active entity in a system delegates authority to another active entity to carry out some functions on behalf of the former [3]. Delegation may occur in two forms: administrative delegation and user delegation. In administrative delegation, even though the administrative user does not possess certain rights, he/she can assign access rights to a user [4]. However, in user delegation, a user delegates the role or a subset of the role to another user to carry out a bunch of functions [4]. Rather than normal access right administration operations, which are performed centrally, delegation operations are usually performed in a distributed manner [5].

Due to the rapid growth of electronic commerce, the online information system has become the mainstream for large organizations. And all the resources required to carry out certain operations are barely local to the system where the user is logged in. In such cases, information sharing tends to be very dynamic and often ad hoc, and delegation is more often the rule than the exception [6]. Under these circumstances, the ideal delegation model should be flexible to cope with different delegation scenarios and reduce administrative costs. However, traditional delegation models have encountered various issues in meeting the diverse and growing delegation requirements. For instance, some existing approaches are focused on the theoretical models without the consideration of practical implementations and management costs.

This paper addresses the delegation issues surrounding user-to-user delegation. We introduce a flexible role-based delegation model. The objective of our model is to fulfill most delegation tasks in a flexible and cost-effective manner. In particular, our model introduces a delegation level decision making function so that delegations could be carried out at both role and permission levels. In addition, a dynamic delegation role structure is integrated into the model to meet the ever changing delegation requirements.

The rest of the paper is organized as follows. We present the related work in Section 2. Section 3 defines and explains the model in detail. Section 4 describes the implementation and evaluation of the model in a healthcare system. Conclusions and future work are presented in Section 5.

2 Related work

There has been much research work to address the delegation issues. The most famous one is RBDM0 (Role-Based Delegation Model 0), which is based on NIST's RBAC model. RBDM0 is the first attempt to model delegation of authorities which realizes a simple user-to-user delegation of roles. In particular, it formalizes the delegation model with total delegation, which means that each user in a delegation role delegates the total package of permissions embodied in that role. Meanwhile, it defines a can-delegate relationship to control the user-to-user delegation. It also deals with other delegation issues including revocation and multi-step delegation [3], [7].

RBDM1, the successor of RBDM0, adopts the formalization in RBDM0 and extends it to support hierarchical roles. Since the new model was introduced to support hierarchical roles, it also defines different semantics that impact the can-delegate relation [8].

RDM2000 (Role-Based Delegation Model 2000), an extension of RBDM0, was proposed to support delegation in the role hierarchy and multi-step delegation. It develops a rule-based declarative language to specify delegation policies and takes a different approach from RBDM0 to solve the delegation issues [9], [10]. But when a delegator wants to delegate a piece of role, none of the models above can provide a satisfactory solution since the unit of delegation in them is "role", and in many cases, it is necessary and useful to delegate only a subset of the permissions from a role.

While all the models mentioned above were focused only on delegation of roles, PBDM (Permission-Based Delegation Model) was developed to realize delegation based on permissions. It supports partial delegation by separating role sets, and a subset of permissions from a regular role is allowed to be delegated and a new delegation role is created with the set of permissions. PBDM is actually a family of models which extends RDM2000 to incorporate more features. It provides great flexibility in authority management [10], [11]. Although PBDM is a complete model, the controlled propagation on resources is not supported.

The RBDM model which uses sub-role hierarchies supports a variety of delegations. For example, administrators can easily control the permission inheritance behavior by using the restricted inheritance functionality. Roles are divided into a number of sub-roles based on the characteristics of job functions and the degree of inheritance [12]. However, like any other delegation model which is based on the role level, this model does not support permission level delegation.

Another extended RBDM model uses the characteristics of PBDM and the concept of sub-role hierarchies [13]. The advantages of both RBDM and PBDM models are thereby also available in this model. However, the role set in the model is divided into seven layers which add complexity to the realization.

With the development of information technology, traditional delegation models could not keep up with the needs of the ever-evolving information systems. It is a complex task to manage delegation and describe all the delegation requirements in a comprehensive model. Thus, delegation models themselves are extended to support new delegation characteristics [14]. And more and more delegation models were proposed by also taking account of specific delegation needs or organizational structures.

Based on the organizational hierarchies, the organizational supervised delegation model (OSDM) was proposed to identify users who must approve the delegation. The model targets at solving the problem in managing the complexity of the huge number of relations in traditional delegation models [15]. Event-Based Task Delegation aims to reason about the delegation events to specify the delegation policies dynamically to control and secure the delegation process. The model identifies two important issues for delegation, i.e., allowing delegation tasks to carry out, and having a secure delegation within a workflow [16]. RBAC with delegation in a workflow context (DW-RBAC) was proposed to address delegation and revocation in the workflow based systems because these systems have been criticized as being inflexible for the lack of support for delegation [17].

Administration cost is also an important factor in the delegation process; however, many delegation models are cumbersome and hard to apply in real world scenarios though incorporating various features.

In order to provide flexibility and reduce administration costs, the capability-based delegation model was proposed to achieve a higher level of collaboration in large-scale information systems. The approach to model delegation is to integrate a capability-based access control mechanism and map it to permissions as well as roles in each domain, and by means of the assignment of roles to capabilities, suitable permissions are automatically assigned to users [18].

3 A flexible role based delegation model

3.1 Dynamic delegation role structure

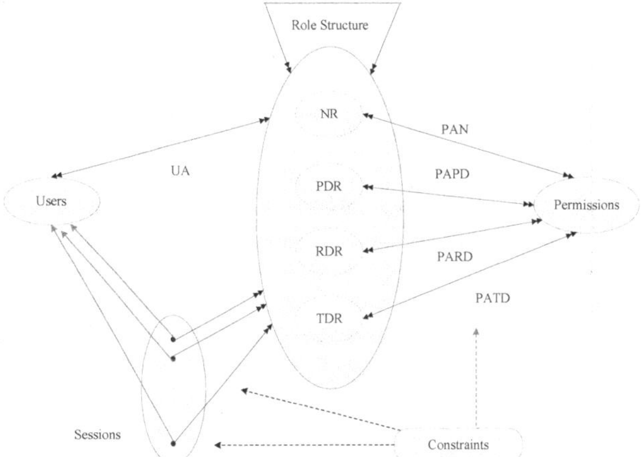

Fig. 1. A flexible delegation model with role structure.

A role in RBAC is the aggregate of responsibility and authority, to which the access to the object is permitted [19]. It is an intuitive way to realize delegation based on the existing role structure. A flexible delegation scheme is desired in many cases as we have mentioned above. Figure 1 shows our proposed model with the structured role sets. In the model, there are four layers of roles: normal roles (NR), predefined delegation roles (PDR), retained delegation roles (RDR) and temporary delegation roles (TDR). A role can be placed in one of the four layers by considering the different delegation scenarios. This leads to a partition of permission-role assignment (PA): permission-normal role assignment (PAN), permission-predefined delegation role assignment (PAPD), permission-retained delegation role assignment (PARD) and permission-temporary delegation role assignment (PATD).

NR is the set of normal roles which can also be used in delegation. PDR, RDR and TDR are the set of roles which can only be used in delegation.

PDR is defined in advance in order to fulfill the common delegation requests in the system. In other words, PDR contributes to the most common delegation scenarios. For instance, in distributed-computing environments, applications or users have to share resources and communicate with each other in order to get their jobs done. And it would be useful to support the delegation scenarios in which a user assigns a subset of the available access rights to another user. However, it is time-consuming to set up the temporary delegation roles for each such request. Therefore, it is more efficient to establish a set of predefined delegation roles for the system. Furthermore, in traditional information system, e.g., healthcare information system, inexperienced personnel such as intern doctors would be delegated typical tasks to be trained to be qualified for the job. A set of PDR would come in handy to fulfill the requirement.

Information is typically classified according to their security characteristics. Likewise, as shown in Table 1, we categorize permissions into three categories based on the information they have access to.

Table 1. Categorization of permissions and characteristics

Degree	Characteristics
Unconditional	Permissions which have access to confidential data
Conditional	Permissions which have access to secret data
Restricted	Permissions which have access to top secret data

Normally, a PDR is the sub-role of an NR based on the job functions. A PDR contains conditional permissions. With that, a PDR can be readily assigned to any member in a certain department.

However, the number of PDR should be limited. First of all, the number of conditional permissions of a certain role is limited. Second, in RBAC, a senior role inherits all the permissions from all its junior roles. If a PDR is derived from a senior role, chances are that the PDR is identical with one of its junior roles. In case of that, there is no need to set up a PDR role. Table 2 shows a possible scenario where a PDR and a junior role Assistant Doctor own the same permissions if the PDR is set up improperly in a healthcare information system. In particular, the permissions include create/view electronic patient records (EPR) and view prescription files (PR).

Table 2. Permissions of physician, assistant doctor and PDR

Roles / Permissions	Physician	Assistant Doctor	PDR
Create EPR	○	○	○
View EPR	○	○	○
Edit EPR	○	×	×
Delete EPR	○	×	×
View PF	○	○	○

Under this circumstance, Physician inheritances all the permissions of Assistant Doctor, PDR might be identical to role Assistant Doctor if the PDR is set up inappropriately.

Figure 2 illustrates a possible simple role hierarchy and their relationships. Vertically, the senior role holds all the permissions of the junior role, while horizontally, PDR 1 is the sub-role of the Senior role and PDR 2 is the sub-role of Junior role. It is possible that PDR 1 and the Junior role have the same permissions.

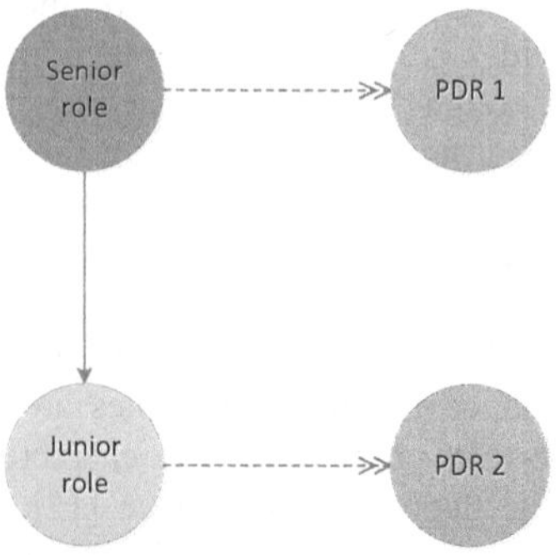

Fig. 2. Example of PDR roles in the role hierarchy.

For infrequent delegation requests, the TDR will be established. In our model, all the TDR roles will be stored in a dynamic buffer. It is used to deal with short-term delegation requests by realizing permission level delegations. When there is no suitable role to fulfill the delegation request, a TDR will be created using the PATD function. A temporary delegation role would be transformed into a retained delegation role (RDR) automatically once it has met certain usage rate and been proved secure under the surveillance of the delegation monitor. Otherwise it will be deleted after certain time period due to the lack of usage. RDR roles will be readily used to serve repeated delegation requests and therefore can reduce runtime overhead to create new TDR roles.

3.2 Delegation decision function

As discussed in Section 3.1, our proposed model provides four different delegation layers to cope with different delegation scenarios. However, there is a need to provide a systematic method to identify and select an appropriate layer from the role structure to fulfill the delegation requests. Therefore, we introduce the *Role_of_Delegation* function, which is in charge of selecting the appropriate delegation levels. It describes how the decision for the delegation level is made according to different delegation requests by taking users, operations and objects as input, and querying the current delegation role structure.

Role_of_Delegation: SESSIONS×OPS×PERS×OBS→ROLE or NULL

- ROLE: There is a suitable delegation role in the role structure for the delegation, and then the delegation will be executed at the role level.
- NULL: There are no suitable roles in the role structure, and in this case, the delegation has to be performed at the permission level, which means a partial delegation from a single or multiple roles is needed.

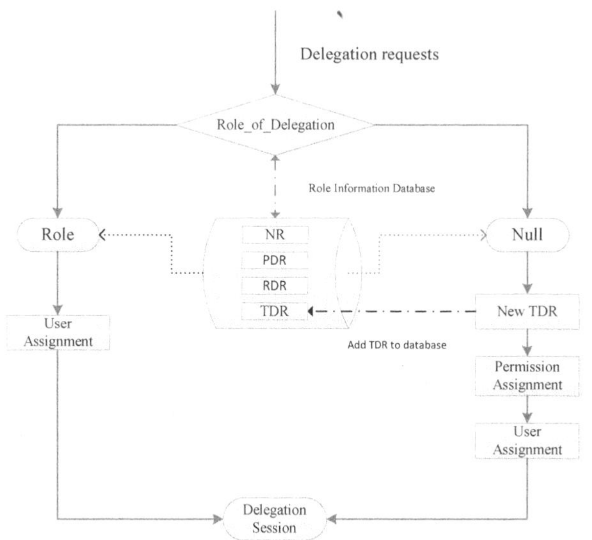

Fig. 3. Process flow-chart of the model.

Figure 3 shows the logical flow-chart for the model. The Role_of_Delegation function interacts with the role structure and checks if there is a suitable role for the request. If there exists such a role, the function will simply return it. Otherwise, the function returns NULL, and then a new TDR will be created and assigned with the permissions specified in the request. By this way, both role level and permission level delegations can be realized.

3.3 Multi-step delegation

Multi-step delegation is also an important delegation feature as it allows the delegated role memberships to be further delegated to other roles. Delegation depth denotes how many times the task has been delegated in a delegation chain. In multi-step delegation, the depth of the delegation chain is greater than one, and delegated permissions can be further delegated multiple times. Multi-step delegation is useful in a variety of organizations. For example, in healthcare information systems, unskilled delegatees like intern doctors or assistant doctors might not be able to handle the task independently, so the delegation has to be further delegated.

In traditional delegation models, permissions assigned to the delegation role are constant in the delegation chain. For example, Alice assigns a delegation role which could be her role or sub-role to Bob, and Bob further delegates the same role to Cathy. Although this arrangement simplifies the management, it is not flexible to handle certain delegation requests. For instance, a physician pays a visit to another hospital and delegates his/her role to the assistant. Later on, the assistant finds himself overloaded with other work and cannot fulfill the all the tasks alone, so he further delegates the role to an intern doctor who has time and skills to complete the task. However, due to the security policies, an intern doctor could not possess some of permissions. Usually, such a delegation request will be rejected and the assistant has to find another user to further delegate the entire privileges. However, it is possible that the delegation request be rejected again. In emergency situations, it will bring obstacles in carrying out the delegation in a timely manner.

In our model, the delegation chain is more flexible. The delegator may modify the delegation role to further assign it to the next delegatee. However, the subsequent delegator can only remove some of the original delegation privileges and further assign it to other users. For instance, Alice delegates her role to Bob; therefore a delegation chain is created. Later on, Bob further delegates the role to Eric; he can only re-delegate the role or a part of role. Such a scheme would be able to address the problem raised in the previous example, and in that case, the assistant is able to only delegate some of the physician's permissions to the intern and keep the rest; and the whole operation can be performed in a timely manner. Moreover, such a scheme is easy to implement in our model. Once the original delegation role is modified in the delegation chain, the proposed role structure and decision function would collaborate to make the appropriate delegation choice.

3.4 Delegation revocation

Since the proposed model supports delegation at both role level and permission level, multiple revocation schemes are supported to make the model robust and flexible, including timeouts and requiring the original member of the delegating role to revoke the delegation. Meanwhile, it is also possible to execute the revocation by revoking a user from the delegation role or removing a subset of permissions from that delegation role.

Furthermore, due to the structural delegation role sets, revocation schemes are also layered. Simple revocation schemes lay at the bottom level, while fine-grained control revocation schemes sit at the top. For instance, when a delegation role PDR is performing, it corresponds to a relaxed revocation scheme because it is considered as relatively secure. In this case, multiple revocation schemes are supported, such as grant-dependent revocation in which only the delegator is allowed to revoke the delegated privileges from the delegatees. In the meantime, noncascading revocation is supported which corresponds to multi-step delegation, in which the delegation between the second and the third user will not be revoked even when the first user revokes the delegation. For instance, in the multi-step delegation scenario, a PDR is delegated from Alice to Bob, and eventually transferred to Eric, the noncascading revocation is allowed in such a case. The revocation steps would be as follows.

1) Select the PDR which is delegated by Alice.
2) Remove the PDR in the first step of the delegation, in order to revoke the roles assigned to Bob.
3) The delegation chain from Alice to Bob is revoked.
4) Select the PDR which is delegated by Bob.
5) Remove PDR in the second step of the delegation, in order to revoke the roles assigned to Eric.
6) The delegation chain from Bob to Eric is revoked.
7) The entire delegation chain is revoked.

Even though Alice and Bob use the same PDR, the delegation chain has to be revoked step by step.

Noncascading and cascading revocation are both allowed if a PDR is used in the delegation. However, when the delegation request is from outside of an organization and a TDR is used, it would be considered less secure and the delegation should be under higher security supervision and demand a stricter revocation. Normally, once there are some abnormalities or when violations are detected, any user who has the privileges can revoke the delegation and the entire delegation role would be revoked. In this situation, if the delegation between the first user and the second user is revoked, the entire delegation chain will be revoked. Noncascading revocation is not allowed in delegations with a TDR. The revocation steps would be as follows.

1) Select the new created TDR which is delegated by the original delegator.
2) Remove the permissions associated with the TDR, which means to revoke the PATD function.
3) Remove TDR so as to revoke the roles assigned.
4) The entire delegation chain is revoked.

4 Implementation and evaluation

4.1 Implementation of the model

A prototype has been developed to verify the feasibility of the proposed model. It is based on the open source software OpenEMR (Open Electronic Medical Record) [20]. We chose it as our platform because it provides features such as electronic health records management, practice management, scheduling, and electronic billing. Meanwhile, it provides a set of predefined roles such as clinicians and physicians. However, OpenEMR does not have a delegation mechanism in its current version.

We designed the delegation server which handles the delegation requests and controls the delegation process based on the proposed model. We use PHP for the implementation of the prototype, and use MySQL to store all the delegation related data. OpenEMR uses phpGACL (Generic Access Control Lists) module to realize role-based access control [21]. And our delegation server makes use of functions provided by phpGACL to instantiate the delegation role structure. Delegation requests are submitted through the delegation request form as shown in Figure 4.

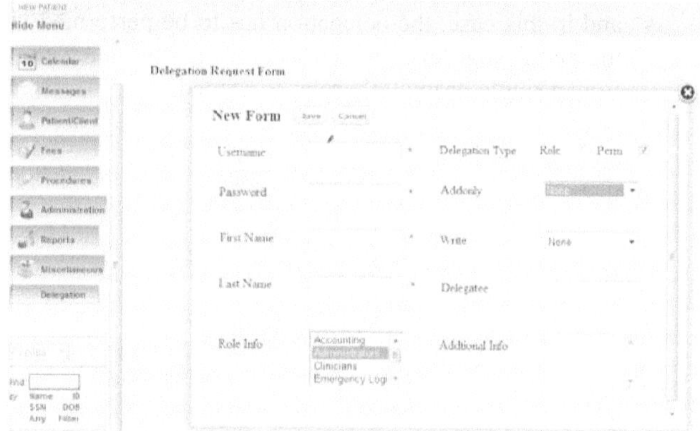

Fig. 4. Delegation request from.

In the delegation request form, the first four fields are used for authentication. "Role Info" is the role that the delegator currently holds. The delegator needs to specify whether he/she wants to delegate the entire role or just some of the permissions in the delegation type option. If the role delegation type is chosen, then the entire role will be delegated. If permission delegation type is selected, the delegator needs to specify the permissions and objects he/she wants to delegate. "Addonly" and "Write" are the two fields which store detailed operations associated with the objects. Upon the completion of the form, the delegation request will be sent to the delegation server. Then the delegation server will search the current delegation role structure for suitable existing roles for delegation. A TDR will be automatically created if no such role is identified.

The delegator can customize the permissions by manipulating the "Permissions" and "Objects" fields in the request form. In addition, the delegatee can be selected. Once the delegator submits the form, the delegation request will be sent to the delegation server for further processing.

Delegation server is the core component in the implementation. On the one hand, it accepts delegation requests, conducts checks and controls the execution of the delegation procedure based on the result of *Role_of_Delegation* function; on the other hand, it receives the feedbacks from Delegation monitor at the end of the delegation session, which includes useful information like whether the delegation is successful or not, what kinds of errors in case of failure, and so on. The feedbacks will be used to optimize the selection of delegation levels, delegation roles and delegatees. Each time the delegation task is fulfilled, the information about the delegation roles used in the process would be automatically stored or updated in the role set database.

Furthermore, the administrator monitors and manages all the delegation logs. All the denied delegation requests and all the unfulfilled delegation requests will be identified. By doing so, one can analyze the failed delegation or further realize a delegation scoring mechanism to select the best delegatee.

4.2 Evaluation of the model

In this Section, we simulate different scenarios in user-to-user delegation based on our prototype system to evaluate the functionality and performance of the model. Initially we set up a predefined delegation role Physician_intern which would be used when a physician delegated some permission to an intern doctor. The Physician_intern role consists of permissions (Documents (read), Medical history (read/write)).

Suppose that Alice is a physician in the hospital. And she wanted to delegate some permission to an intern doctor Bob by sending a delegation request which contained the permissions (Documents (read) and Medical history (read/write)). The authorization check will pass as there are no security violations. After that, the *Role_of_Delegation* function returned Physician_intern, which is exactly the desirable delegation role. Then the delegation session started. We name this delegation operation DO1.

Likewise, we changed the delegation role set by adding two more predefined delegation roles including Surgeon_assit and Surgeon_intern.

Then another physician Bill wanted to delegate a part of his permissions (Documents (read/write) and Medical history (read/write)) to the assistant Dan, he simply sent a delegation request message to the delegation server. Then the *Role_of_Delegation* function returned NULL, which meant there is no feasible delegation role under current circumstances. In this case, the system would create a temporary delegation role in which permissions the physician referred to were incorporated to perform the delegation task. When the physician's assistant logged in, the delegation module would notify Dan that the delegation role with the necessary permissions have been assigned in order to fulfill the delegation task. When the delegation session was expired, the delegation monitor would check if the task was fulfilled successfully. After that, the monitor would send a feedback to the delegation server and the temporary delegation role TDR1 would be saved in the temporary delegation role buffer. We call this delegation operation DO2.

Later, the same delegation request was issued by Alice to delegate the same set of permissions to her assistant, this time the *Role_of_Delegation* function returned TDR1, which indicated that the saved temporary delegation role created earlier in the role structure would work directly. In the prototype implementation, there is a delegation frequency for each delegation role. A temporary delegation role would become a retained delegation role once the frequency reaches 10. In the evaluation, we used the TDR1 for sufficient times so that it turned into a retained delegation role (RDR1). In this case, *Role_of_Delegation* returned RDR1 which was deemed to be more trustworthy. This time, the delegation operation is referred to as DO3. Table 3 shows the changes of the role structure between each of the delegation operations.

Table 3. Performance evaluation

Delegation Operations	Number of Roles				Request Fulfilling Time	
	NR	PDR	RDR	TDR	PBDM	Our Model
DO1	6	1	0	0	0.52s	0.56s
DO2	6	3	0	1	0.55s	0.38s
DO3	6	3	1	0	0.54s	0.39s

Initially, there are only 6 normal roles which were set up in advance, so the number of NR is constant. The numbers of RDR and TDR are dynamically changing due to the change of the delegation frequency. This evaluation showed the flexibility of our model because it can make appropriate delegation choices according to different delegation requirements. Meanwhile, the retained delegation role set in our model is dynamic as one temporary delegation role could be transformed into a retained delegation role while another could be removed from the temporary delegation role structure. By doing so, the model would be adaptive to the ongoing delegation requests.

Then we evaluated the multi-step delegation. This time Bill delegated the same task to his assistant Dan. However, Dan was not able to finish the task and he further delegated the task to Bob. In both steps of the delegation, *Role_of_Delegation* returned RDR1 because there was no modification in the delegation requests. After the user assignment indicated that the delegation would be performed at role level, the delegation session started.

In addition, we did a performance comparison between our model and a simple PBDM model implementation based on the prototype system. In particular, we implemented PBDM by disabling *Role_of_Delegation* so that delegation could only be performed at the permission level. In the evaluation, we gradually increased the number of roles to compare the efficiency between the two models. We monitored the simple delegation scenarios exactly as mentioned above and recorded the request fulfilling time which is the total elapsed time to fulfill the delegation request.

The results show that the request fulfilling time for PBDM is almost constant because each time a delegation contains a piece of permissions, a new temporary delegation role would be created, and the time is not affected by the number of roles in the role structure. Our model was slower than PBDM initially, because the number of roles was limited and most of the delegations had to be performed at the permission level, and our model had to call the *Role_of_Delegation* function for the delegation decision making. As the number of roles increased, the request fulfilling time of our model decreased because more and more delegation requests were being performed at the role level. The evaluation showed that our model is efficient and adaptive in typical delegation scenarios in a healthcare information system, and the model can help to accelerate the delegation decision making process by identifying the suitable delegation levels and roles automatically.

5 Conclusions and future work

This paper proposes a flexible delegation model in an effort to fulfill a variety of delegation scenarios. The dynamic role structure, as the key component in the model, enables delegation requests to be fulfilled at suitable levels automatically. The model has been shown to be effective and efficient through a prototype implementation and evaluation in a healthcare information system. However, there is still room for further improvement of our model. Multiple delegation and role-to-role delegation will be incorporated in order to support a wider range of delegation scenarios.

6 References

[1] D. F. Ferraiiolo, R. Sandhu, S. Gavrila, D. R. Kuhn and R. Chandramouli, "Proposed NIST standard for role-based access control," *ACM Transactions. On Information and System Security*, vol. 4, pp.224-274, Aug. 2001.

[2] J. Wainer and A. Kumar, "A fine-grained, controllable, user-to-user delegation method in RBAC," *Proc. The 10th Symposium on Access Control Models and Technologies*, New York, NY, June. 2005, pp 59-66.

[3] Ezedin Barka and Ravi Sandhu, "A Role-Based Delegation Model and Some Extensions," *Proc. The 23rd National Information Systems Security Conference,"* Dec. 2000.

[4] J. Crampton and H. Khambhammettu, "Delegation in role-based access control," *Proc. The 11th European Symposium on Research in Computer Security,* Berlin, Heidelberg, 2006, pp. 174-191.

[5] Qihua Wang, Ninghui Li and Hong Che, "On the Security of Delegation in Access Control Systems," Proc. The 13th European Symposium on Research in Computer Security, Berlin, Heidelberg, 2008, pp. 317-332.

[6] Longhua Zhang, Gail-Joon Ahn and bei-Tseng Chu, "A rule-based delegation framework for healthcare information systems," Proc. The 7th ACM symposium on Access control models and technologies, New York, NY, June. 2002, pp. 125-134.

[7] Ezedin Barka and Ravi Sandhu, "Framework for Role-Based Delegation Models," Proc. The 16th Annual Computer Security Applications Conference, Washington, DC, Dec. 2000.

[8] Ezedin Barka and Ravi Sandhu, "Role-Based Delegation Model/ Hierarchical Roles (RBDM1)," Proc. The 20th Annual Computer Security Applications Conference, Washington, DC, Dec. 2004, pp. 396-404.

[9] Longhua Zhang, Gail-Joon Ahn, and Bei-Tseng Chu, "A rule-based Framework for Role-Based Delegation," Proc. The 6th ACM Symposium on Access Control Models and Technologies, New York, NY, May 2001, pp. 153-162.

[10] Longhua Zhang, Gail-Joon Ahn, and Bei-Tseng Chu, "A rule-based Framework for Role-Based Delegation and revocation," ACM Transactions on Information and System Security (TISSEC), vol. 6, pp. 404-441, Aug. 2003.

[11] X. Zhang, S. Oh, and R. Sandhu, "PBDM: a flexible delegation model in RBAC," Proc. The 8th ACM symposium on Access control models and technologies, New York, NY, June 2003, pp. 149-157.

[12] HyungHyo Lee, YoungRok Lee, and BongNam Noh, "A new role-based delegation model using sub-role hierarchies," *Proc. The 18th International Symposium on Computer and Information Sciences (LSCIS 2003),* Antalya, Turkey, Nov. 2003, pp. 811-818.

[13] Dong-Gue Park and You-Ri Lee, "A flexible role-based delegation model using characteristics of permissions," *Proc. The 16th international conference on Database and Expert Systems Applications*, Berlin, Heidelberg, 2005, pp. 310-323.

[14] Meriam Ben-Ghorbel-Talbi, Frédéric Cuppens, Nora Cuppens-Boulahia, and Adel Bouhoula, "A delegation model for extended RBAC," *International Journal of Information Security*, vol. 9, pp. 209-236, June 2010.

[15] Nezar Nassar, Nidal Aboudagga, and Eric Steegmans, "An Organizational Supervised Delegation Model for RBAC," *Proc. The 15th international conference on Information Security*, Berlin, Heidelberg, Sept. 2012, pp. 322-337.

[16] Khaled Gaaloul, Ehtesham Zahoor, François Charoy, and Claude Godart, "Dynamic Authorisation Policies for Event-based Task Delegation," *Proc. The 22nd International Conference on Advanced Information Systems Engineering*, Berlin, Heidelberg, June. 2010, pp. 135-149.

[17] Jacques Wainer, Akhil Kumar, and Paulo Barthelmess, "A formal security model of delegation and revocation in workflow systems," Information Systems - IS, Vol. 32, pp. 365-384, May 2007.

[18] Koji Hasebe, Mitsuhiro Mabuchi, and Akira Matsushita, "Capability-based delegation model in RBAC," *Proc. The 15th ACM symposium on Access control models and technologies*, New York, NY, June. 2010, pp. 109-118.

[19] E.C. Lupu, D. A. Marriott, M. S. Sloman, and N. Yialelis, "A Policy Based Framework for Access Control," *Proc. The First ACM Workshop on Role-based Access Control"*, New York, NY, Dec. 1996.

[20] E. Helms and L. Williams, "Evaluating Access of Open Source Electronic Health Record Systems." *Proc. 3th International Conference on Software Engineering*, New York, NY, May. 2011, pp. 73-80.

[21] Mike Benoit, James Russell, and Karsten Dambekalns, *Generic Access Control Lists with PHP*, Sept. 2006.

A User-Centric Privacy-Aware Protection System

Li Yang, Travis Tynes
Department of Computer Science, University of West Georgia, Carrollton, GA 30118, USA

Abstract - *Nowadays it is increasingly important to protect private information from unintended and unauthorized use. Traditional access control models generally lack the support for privacy protection. Some studies have been done in the area of integrating privacy control with XML access control. However, often the focus is placed on organization-specific privacy policies. And how to handle user consent and user preferences are often not addressed. In this paper, we describe our approach based on XACML to integrating XML data access control and privacy control with user consent, preferences and break-glass access procedure considered. We also present a prototype system being developed in the context of health care systems to demonstrate the feasibility of our approach.*

Keywords: XML, Privacy Access Control, XACML, User Consent, User Preferences

1 Introduction

Privacy issues have recently gained a lot of attention, as consumers are increasingly concerned about how personal information is collected, stored and used. Computer systems where such private information is stored must provide some kind of protection mechanisms to ensure data security and privacy at the time of data request. There have been some research on integrating privacy requirements with access control models [2, 14, 15, 16, 3, 22, 12]. Privacy-based access control policies are different from traditional access control policies in that such policies have to stipulate not only who can/cannot access what, but also for what purpose under what condition, and what obligations the recipient has to fulfill.

In these models, in general, to guard users' private information, privacy-based access control policies have to be first specified, and later enforced at the time when a data request is issued. However, typically the policies involved in making access decisions are organization-wide policies, which are general policies that are domain or organization specific rather than data owner specific [1]. For instance, a hospital may have a policy stating no patients' personal information (such as name, address, among others) may be disclosed to third parties for marketing purpose. Data owner's consents or preferences are often not considered in these models. This strays from Westin's well-quoted definition of privacy: " the claim of individuals, groups, or institutions to determine for themselves when, how, and to what extent information about them is communicated to others" [20]. Individuals who gave out their personal information should have the right to state their privacy preferences and have them respected at the time of data requests[1]. We argue that such preferences or consents should always be respected so long they do not violate the business privacy principles of the organization.

However, one should also realize that there may be emergency situations where the general privacy policies and user preferences/consents have to be forgone to avoid unwanted consequences (e.g. in the health care domain, patient injury, or worse). An emergency or Break-Glass access procedure should be in place to allow personnel gain access to the needed data when normal access operations would not allow [9, 8].

In this paper, we propose to integrate individual user privacy preferences with general organization-specific privacy policies, and give a higher weight to user preferences when making an authorization decision to access private personal data in normal situations. A break-glass procedure is in place during emergency situations. We are in the process of completing a proof-of-concept system in the context of healthcare domain to demonstrate the feasibility of our proposal. In our system when a data request is issued, the request is checked against the general organizational privacy access control policies first, followed by a check against user preferences/consents. Only when the authorization decision from the general policies is not "deny" and the data owner has consented such an access, the requested data access can be granted. During emergency situations, both policies may be bypassed, and the request is granted, and necessary obligations will be fulfilled according to the break-glass procedure.

The remainder of the paper is organized as follows. Section 2 presents related work in privacy control and e-consent. Section 3 provides a detailed description of our approach. Section 4 describes the proof-of-concept system based on XACML we are working on. We conclude the paper and present future work in Section 5.

2 Related Work

There has been some work done in the area of privacy-centric access control [14, 15, 16, 2, 3, 21]. In [14], the authors proposed a family of Privacy Aware Role Based Access Control Models (P-RBAC) that extends the traditional Role-Based Access Control (RBAC) with support for expressing privacy-related issues, such as purposes, and obligations. In such models, a privacy policy can be expresses as (role, ((action, data), purpose, condition, obligation)), which can be interpreted as a role can perform the specified action on the data for the purpose under the condition and the obligation has to be fulfilled as well if the access is granted. Our access control model expands on theirs with the replacement of role with subject, as a subject may be a specific user or a role. In their work, they also presented a conflict resolution for two conflicting privacy policies. However, as they pointed out themselves, the resolution may not be general enough for dealing with conflict occurrence between more than two policies, which is more realistic. We leave the conflict resolution to the policy maker and assume if there are some present, the policy files should specify which one takes precedence (for instance, XACML has rule and policy combining algorithms such as deny-overrides, permit-overrides, first-applicable and only-one-applicable). In addition, their work focused on presenting a group of models that integrate privacy with access control and provide policy conflict resolutions. Their policies are organization-specific policies, which can be specified by policy writers who are familiar with their business privacy policies. In our work, we consider consent information as part of user preferences and present approaches to storing user preferences regarding their private data and respecting their preferences when an access decision is made. Finally, ours presented a proof-of-concept system to demonstrate the feasibility of the proposed access control model.

EXtensible Access Control Markup Language (XACML) [21] is a well-known 17 [17] XML Access Control Model standard. It aims at providing an application-independent core schema and namespaces to allow authorization policies to be expressed, shared and integrated across different applications. It provides a variety of features, such as support for various conditions, policy combination algorithms, and conflict resolutions. In the core XACML 2.0 [21] itself, it only specifies components that are central to any access control policies such as subjects, resources, actions, and conditions. In a separate document, Privacy policy profile of XACML v2.0 [18], purposes are explicitly described as an essential component for privacy-related control policies. Obligations are supported in XACML 2.0, though there are no standard definitions for what actions of an obligation has to fulfill. It is entirely left to each individual implementation. In our work, we used Sun's XACML Java implementation to implement our system [19].

Byun et al. [3] proposed a purpose-based data access control for privacy protection in hierarchical data. Their work focused on designing an attribute-based model to describe user intended access purposes. They did not consider obligations and implementation in the paper. Our work requires the user accessing the system to provide a purpose for which the access request is made, which is called action purpose in XACML. The system then tries to check if the user/role, object (resource), and action purpose match with the (subject, resource, resource-purpose) in the policies stored in the system and satisfy the predefined condition in the policies. The resource-purpose represents the purpose for which the data is collected. We do not further impose any attribute on the subject to facilitate a fine-grained purpose definition.

The idea of allowing users to set their privacy preferences essentially makes the data owners give consent for specifying what and how their personal data may be accessed. Consent management has been studied by various researchers [4, 11,7]. Most of the work focused on how to create, revoke, transfer and manage consent, which is specified by data owners. They generally do not consider general organization-wide policies. We consider both kind of policies in our design and give a higher weight to data owners' consent.

3 Our Privacy-Based Access Control Model

Traditional access control authorization models often represent an access authorization policy as (subject, object, action, permission), while context-aware access control authorization models [10] may extend the notion above with conditions, which results in a 5-tuple representation (subject, object, action, permission, condition). To integrate privacy protection into an access control model, it is essential to take into account the basic requirements for enforcing privacy, which are purposes and obligations. Purposes specify for what intention data is to be used, and obligations is what actions the subject has to perform once the access is granted.

Based on [14], we incorporate purposes and obligations in our privacy-based Access Control Model, in which an access authorization policy is represented as a 7-tuple *(subject, object, action, permission, condition, purpose, obligation)*, where

- *subject* represents an entity that is trying to make an access to an object in the system. A subject may contain properties that specify its id or role it belongs to. Unlike [14] in which entities are grouped into *roles* and access rights are specified on role , we extend the model by using *subject* to allow more fine-grained control. For instance, a patient may specify Dr. Jane Smith whose id is 3456 cannot access his drug information in our model;
- *object* refers to any resource that's to be protected in the system. In our research, we assume data is stored and represented as XML. The *object* part can be represented as an XPath expression;
- *action* is either read or write (while we only consider *read* at the moment)
- *permission* is either *permit* or *deny*.
- *condition* is provisions which must be met before access is allowed
- *purpose is for what purpose the object is collected (i.e. resource purpose in XACML)*
- *obligation* is the actions that have to be fulfilled after an access is granted or to be agreed on before an access is granted

```
<patients>
<patient>
    <id> p1234567</id>  <name>Jane Lee</name>
    <dob> January 12, 1955</dob>
    <room><number>5</number>  <bed>1</bed> </room>
     <illness>Angina</illness>
    <drug>
       <name>herapin</name>
       <daily_admin>30 U/Kg</daily_admin>
       <cost>$20.00</cost>
    </drug>
  </patient>
  <patient>
    <id> p7654321</id>  <name>Lee  Smith</name>
    <dob> October 12, 1975</dob>
    <room><number>5</number>  <bed>2</bed> </room>
    <illness>Angina</illness>
    <drug>
        <name>herapin</name>
        <daily_admin>30 U/Kg</daily_admin>
        <cost>$20.00</cost>
    </drug>
  </patient>
</patients>
```

Figure 1: an XML Document

For instance, given the data represented in XML(adapted from [5]) in Figure 1, we could have a privacy authorization policy specified as follows.

(*nurse, //drug, read, permit, owner_age>=18, research, notify(patient) & log*)

which is interpreted as "a nurse is allowed to read patients' drug information for research purpose if the patient is older than 17 years old, and the access has to be logged and the patient has to be notified".

A pure access authorization policy may be written byspecifying nulls for purpose, condition, obligation. For instance, the following policy,

(doctor, //drug, read, permit, null, null, null),

can be interpreted as "a doctor is allowed to read patients' drug information".

We assume that a policy writer will come up with all organization-wide policies either manually or using an authoring tool. How to assist policy writers to effectively specify all the policies is outside of the scope of this paper.

3.1 Consent Handling

In a privacy-aware environment, user preferences or consent are valued highly to protect personal information. For instance, a patient may choose as part of his/her privacy preferences what personal information can be disclosed to whom for what purpose. When an access authorization has to be made, it has to take into account user preferences. In our system, we collect and store such preference information in a database.

Unlike general policies, consent is more specific in the sense it is specified by a data owner on his/her data. For instance, a general policy stating no patients' personal *information (such as name, address, among others) may be disclosed to third parties for marketing purpose* can be applied to any patient. While a consent, *nobody can view his/her illness information for marketing purpose*, made by a patient whose id is "p1234567" can only be applied to the data of patient p1234567. Therefore, when storing consent, we have to make it clear that to whom it belongs. In our design, we store the unique id of the data owner along with the consent. For instance, Table 1 shows the consent table for the original XML document in Figure 1. The data shows patient whose pid="p1234567" chose to give user consent on her drug information if the roles are nurse or doctor and the access is for research or diagnosis purpose, while she denies access to her illness node by any role if the access is for marketing purpose. No consent was given by the patient whose id is "p7654321".

rid	pId	sub	obj	purpose	permission
1	p1234567	any	//patient/illness	marketing	deny
2	p1234567	doctor	//patient/drug	research	userconsent
3	p1234567	nurse	//patient/drug	research	userconsent
4	p1234567	doctor	//patient/drug	diagnosis	userconsent
5	p1234567	nurse	//patient/drug	diagnosis	userconsent
....	...	...		...	...

Table 1. A User Consent Table

3.2 Break-Glass Procedure

We employ a simple Break-Glass (BG) procedure to accommodate emergency situations where normal access control policies have to be overridden to gain access to data. A BG role and user account that have full access to the data are created. When user logs in using this account, he will bypass all the policies and user consent, and gain access to data. Such activity will be logged in the system and administrators will be notified.

3.3 Authorization Process

In this section, we describe the complete authorization process based on the framework of our system. Note that we used XACML as the policy specification language and its policy and rule combination algorithms for conflict resolution.

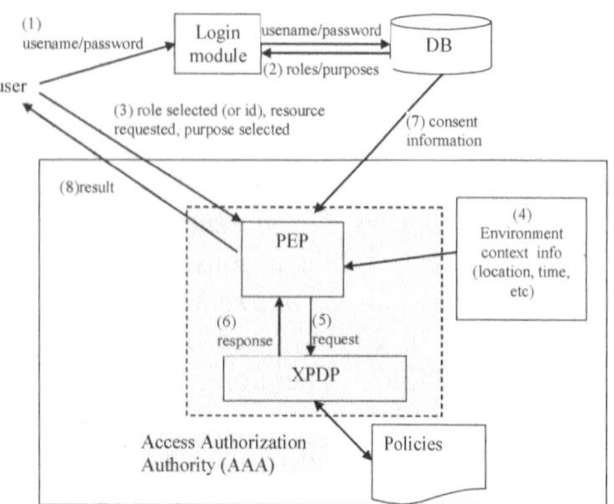

Figure 2: System Architecture

A user trying to access some sensitive data has to go through the following process to get permitted or denied to access the data.

1) The user provides user name and password to access the system.
2) If username and password are valid, the set of roles that the user participates in and the set of purposes associated with the roles are presented to the user.
3) The user may select the role he is taking on (or not do so in case he wants to access as himself) and the purpose of his access, and enters an XPath expression to represent the resource he/she is interested in.
4) The request tuple (role, resource, purpose) or (id, resource, purpose) is sent to the PEP (Policy Enforcement Point) along with any environment context information to form a request.
5) PEP then sends the request to XPDP (XACML Policy Decision Point) to let it make the final decision regarding whether or not the access to the node is allowed based on the policies stored in the policy files. The PEP and XPDP are called as **Access Authorization Authority (AAA)** in our system.
6) XPDP first checks in the policy files to see if there is any policy matching the requested resource and role/id and purpose. Based on the policies, a deny, not applicable (e.g. no matching policy is found), or permit decision will be returned to PEP. In the case of a BG role is submitted, it will issue an "permit" decision.
7) Based on the decision, PEP takes different routes to make the final decision.
   - If decision ="deny": regardless user preferences, the final decision is "deny". Here more general rules (policies in the policy files) take precedence over more specific rules (e.g. user preferences), as the policy maker has a more thorough and systematic view of the overall access control policies.
   - If decision ="not applicable": this indicates XPDP could not make a final decision solely based on the policy files. So PEP has to check user preferences and prune the original tree based on the consent information on the nodes. The nodes with user consent and match the xpath expressions will appear in the output. Any obligations will be fulfilled.
   - If decision= "permit",
     - If role="BG", requested data will be returned and administrators will be notified and this event will be logged
     - Otherwise, as the system respects user preferences, more specific rules (e.g. user preferences) take precedence over more specific rules (policies in the policy files). So PEP has to check user preferences and prune the original tree based on the consent information on the nodes. The nodes with user consent and match the xpath expressions will appear in the output. Any obligations will be fulfilled.

For instance, suppose a nurse tries to access patients' drug information for research purpose. A request tuple (nurse, //drug, research) will be formed and sent to the XPDP. If there is a matching policy:

(nurse, //drug, read, allow, (owner_age>=18), research, notify(patient) & log)

XPDP returns "permit" to PEP. When PEP gets the decision, it creates a temporary tree which contains the *id* node and the drug node and its sub-tree, then retrieves the consent information for each *id* in the temporary tree and prunes the tree to get a final result. In this example, since only the first patient has given consent, the first drug node should be returned as a result. And the obligations should be obeyed, which is to notify the parents and log the access event.

4 Implementation

The implementation is divided into two phases. In the first phase, we implemented a proof-of-concept system that demonstrates the viability of integrating privacy control and access control using the model we described earlier without the user preferences. In the current phase, we are integrating user preferences into the early prototype. To facilitate the development process, we used the XACML as the policy specification language, as it is a well-known OASIS standard and is designed to be application-independent and interoperable. We used the Sun's XACML implementation in Java [17]. The final system architecture can be found in Figure 2. All the components are written in Java.

To enable BG procedure, we specify a BG policy such as (BG, any, any, permit, null, any, notify(administrator)&log) as the first policy in the policy file and has the policy-combining algorithm as "first applicable" so that whenever a user with the BG account logs in and is mapped to a role BG, the BG procedure will take effect.

To enforce privacy protection, we need to specify the purposes and obligations in our model presented in section 3. XACML provides such concepts. We have implemented purpose per specifications in [18]. For instance the purpose "curious" can be written in XACML policy file as follows:

```
<ActionMatch MatchId="urn:oasis:names:tc:xacml:1.0:function:string-equal">
    <AttributeValue
        DataType="http://www.w3.org/2001/XMLSchema#string">
            curious
    </AttributeValue>
    <ActionAttributeDesignator
        AttributeId="urn:oasis:names:tc:xacml:2.0:action:purpose"
        DataType="http://www.w3.org/2001/XMLSchema#string" />
</ActionMatch>
```

Obligation is written in XACML policy file as well. For instance, to specify log the access regardless access is denied or permitted, the obligation can be written as follows:

```
<Obligations>
        <Obligation ObligationId="urn:xacml:2.0:westga:obligation:log-access-permit" FulfillOn="Permit" />
        <Obligation ObligationId="urn:xacml:2.0:westga:obligation:log-access-deny" FulfillOn="Deny" />
</Obligations>
```

5 Conclusion and Future Work

In this paper, we described an access control model that seamlessly integrates privacy issues such as purposes, obligations and user preferences. We also presented the architecture of the system that is currently in implementation that demonstrates the feasibility of the proposed model.

There are some open issues to be investigated in the future. For instance, we currently only implemented "logging" obligations, other complicated obligations such as notifying, and monitoring the usage of the digital objects need more sophisticated client side support.

6 References

[1] Steve Baker, Personalizing Access Control by Generalizing Access Control, SACMAT'10, 149-158, 2010.

[2] Elisa Bertino, Ji-Won Byun, and Ninghui Li, Privacy-Preserving Database Systems, Foundations of Security Analysis and Design III, FOSAD 2004/2005 Tutorial Lectures, LNCS 3655, Springer, 2005.

[3] Ji-Won Byun, Elisa Bertino, and Ninghui Li, Purpose Based Access Control of Complex Data for Privacy Protection, SACMAT'05, 102-110, June 2005.

[4] Enrico Coiera, Roger Clarke, E-Consent: The Design and Implementation of Consumer Consent Mechnisms in an Electronic Environment, Journal of the American Medical Informatics Association, Vol. 11, No. 2, 129-140, Mar./Apr. 2004.

[5] Ernesto Damiani, Sabrina De Capitani Di Vimercati, Stefano Paraboschi, and Pierangela Samarati, A Fine-Grained Access Control System for XML Documents, TISSEC, 5(2):169-202, May 2002.

[6] Ahmed AL Faresi, Duminda Wijesekera, Khaled Moidu, A Comprehensive Privacy-aware Authorization Framework Founded on HIPAA Privacy Rules, IHI'10, 637-646, November, 2010.

[7] Christine O'Keefe, Paul Greenfield, Andrew Goodchild, A Decentralised approach to Electronic Consent and Health Information Access Control, Journal of Research and Practice in Information Technology, Vol. 37, No2, 161-178, May 2005.

[8] Eric Helms, Laurie Williams, Evaluating Access Control of Open Source Electronic Health Record Systems, SEHC'11, 63-70, 2011.

[9] HHS Security Standards, http://www.hhs.gov/ocr/privacy/hipaa/administrative/securityrule/securityrulepdf.pdf, February 2003.

[10]R. J. Hulsebosch, A. H. Salden, M.S. Bargh, P.W.G. Ebben, and J. Reitsma, Context Sensitive Access Control, SACMAT'05, 111-119, June 2005.

[11] Qihua Wang, Hongxia Jin, An Analytical Solution for Consent Management in Patient Privacy Preservation, IHI'12, 2012.

[12] Jing Jin, Gail-Joon Ahn, Hongxin Hu, Michael J. Covington, Xinwen Zhang: Patient-centric Authorization Framework for Sharing Electronic Health Records, SACMAT'09, 125-134, 2009.

[13]Gustaf 13, and Mark Strembeck, An Approach to Engineer and Enforce Context Constraints in an RBAC Environment, SACMAT'03, 65-79, June 2003.

[14]Qun Ni, Dan Lin, Elisa Bertino, and Jorge Lobo, Privacy-aware Role Based Access Control, SACMAT'07, 41-50, June 2007.

[15]Qun Ni, Alberto Trombetta, Elisa Bertino, and Jorge Lobo, Conditional Privacy-Aware Role Based Access

Control, ESORICS'07, 72-89, 2007.

[16] Qun Ni, Elisa Bertino, Jorge Lobo, Carolyn Brodie, Clare-Marie Karat, John Karat, Alberto Trombetta: Privacy-aware role-based access control. ACM Trans. Inf. Syst. Secur. 13(3): (2010).

[17] OASIS website, http://www.oasis-open.org/home/index.php

[18] Privacy policy profile of XACML v2.0, http://docs.oasis-open.org/xacml/2.0/access_control-xacml-2.0-privacy_profile-spec-os.pdf

[19] Sun's XACML Implementation, http://sunxacml.sourceforge.net/

[20] A. Westin, Privacy and Freedom, New York: Atheneum, 1967.

[21] XACML 2.0 Core Specification, http://docs.oasis-open.org/xacml/2.0/access_control-xacml-2.0-core-spec-os.pdf

[22] N. Yang, H. Barringer, and N. Zhang, A Purpose-Based Access Control Model, In Proc. Of 3rd International Symposium on Information Assurance and Security (IAS), 143–148, 2007.

SESSION

CRYPTOGRAPHIC TECHNOLOGIES I

Chair(s)

Dr. Cristina Soviany

Performance Evaluation of Asymmetric Encryption Algorithms in embedded platforms used in WSN

Gustavo S. Quirino[1], **Edward David Moreno**[2], **and Leila B. C. Matos**[3]
[1]Department of Computer, IFBA, Barreiras, Bahia, Brasil
[2]Department of Computer, UFS, São Cristóvão, Sergipe, Brasil
[3]Department of Computer, IFS, Aracaju, Sergipe, Brasil

Abstract— *This paper presents the performance evaluation of asymmetric cryptographic algorithms oriented to embedded platforms used in Wireless Sensor Networks (WSN). The RSA algorithms, ECC and MQQ were evaluated on three different platforms: ARM, MSP430 and AVR Atmega128 platforms. We have used the processing time as evaluation criteria. We used the SimpleScalar tool, MSPsim and Avrora for our simulations analysis. The MQQ algorithm achieved the best results in most of the evaluated criteria. In the ARM platform, the MQQ algorithm obtained a processing time 230 times lower than the time of the RSA algorithm. The ECC algorithm has also shown effectiveness in the platforms evaluated, since in MSP430 platform was 4 times faster than RSA algorithm. Finally, we show that MQQ is a promising algorithm for embedded systems used in WSN, but the ECC algorithm is the most recommended by standardized and have already gone through safety testing.*

Keywords: Wireless Sensor Network, Public-key Cryptography, Performance Analysis.

1. Introduction

A Wireless Sensor Network (WSN) is composed of autonomous devices called sensor nodes that generally have low computational power, limited data transmission and power constraints. A WSN consists of sensor nodes that capture information from an environment, processing data and transmitting them through radio signals. WSNs are increasingly present in our days and can be found in environmental area (climatic measurements, presence of smoke), in health area (measurement of vital signs, temperature), home automation (motion sensor and image sensor) and other areas. Generally, WSNs have no fixed structure, and in many cases there is no monitoring station of sensor nodes during the operational life of the network, so a WSN must have mechanisms for self-configuration and adaptation in case of failure, inclusion or exclusion of a sensor node.

Security requirements of WSNs are similar to conventional computer networks, therefore parameters such as confidentiality, integrity, availability and authenticity must be taken into account in creation of a network environment. Due to limitations of WSNs, not all security solutions designed for conventional computer networks can be implemented directly in WSN. For a long time, it was believed that the public key cryptography was not suitable for WSNs because it was required high processing power, but through studies of encryption algorithms based on curves was verified the feasibility of that technique in WSN.

The cryptographic algorithm RSA [1] is currently the most used among the asymmetric algorithms, working from the difficulty of factoring large prime numbers. Standardized by NIST[1], this algorithm is widely used in transactions on the Internet. The Elliptic Curve Cryptography (ECC)[2], [3] was created in 80s, and are based on the difficulty of solving the discrete logarithm problem on elliptic curves. Despite its complexity the algorithm based on elliptic have been extensively studied in academia. Recently, the public key algorithm called Multivariate Quadratic Almost Group (MQQ) [4] was proposed in academia. Experiments performed in the FPGA and PC platforms showed that MQQ is faster than algorithms such as RSA and ECC [4], [5]. Algorithms involved in this study are asymmetric, but each one works with a specific encryption mode.

Many studies have evaluated performance of cryptographic algorithms in WSNs, but there is no standardization in the performance analysis. As stated by Margi [6] studies on performance evaluation of cryptographic algorithms for WSNs are often quite different in terms of methodology, platform, metrics and focus of analysis, making difficult a direct comparison among the obtained results. Thus, this paper describes a theoretical study of cryptographic algorithms such as RSA, ECC and MQQ as well as the performance analysis of these algorithms in embedded platforms used in wireless sensor networks.

This paper is organized as follows. Section 2 gives some background about asymmetric algorithms RSA, ECC and MQQ. Section 3 discusses on the simulation environment, describing details of platforms, simulators, compilers and cryptographic libraries that were used in implementation and simulation of algorithms. The section 4 shows the results of the performance evaluation. The section 5 brings the comparison of results between different platforms evaluated and compared with other works. Finally, some concluding

[1]U.S. Agency for technology that has a partnership with industry to develop and apply technology, measurements and standards. Further information: www.nist.gov

remarks and planning for future works are outlined in Section 6.

2. Asymmetric Algorithms

The IEEE 802.15.4 standard of 2011 defines parameters for low-range personal area networks (LR-WPANs). The first version of this standard was launched in 2003, and the second one [7] was appointed to be the standard communication protocol for WSNs. The encryption mechanism specified in IEEE 802.15.4 standard is based on encryption symmetric key. But according to Sen [8] recent studies have shown that it is possible to implement public key encryption using the right selection of algorithms and associated parameters, and optimization techniques for low power. In some cases the public-key cryptography shows similar efficiency or even greater than symmetric key encryption using smaller keys. According to Struik [9] is already proven that some public-key algorithms are suitable for hardware in WSNs.

2.1 RSA algorithm

In the introductory paper about RSA, [1] proposed a method to implement a public key cryptosystem whose security is based on the difficulty to factoring large prime numbers. Through this technique it is possible to encrypt data and to create digital signatures. It was so successful that today the RSA is the public key algorithm most used in the world. The RSA encryption scheme uses the fact that:

$$m^{ed} \equiv m(mod\, n) \tag{1}$$

for m integer. The encryption and decryption schemes are presented in Algorithms 1 and 2. The decryption works because $c^d \equiv (m^e)^d \equiv m(mod\, n)$. The safety lies in the difficulty of computing a clear text m from a ciphertext c = $m^e mod\, n$ and the public parameters n (e).

Algorithm 1: RSA Encryption

Input: RSA public key (n,e), Plain text m $\in$ [0, n-1]
Output: Cipher text c
begin
  1. Compute c = m^e mod n
  2. Return c.
end

Algorithm 2: Decryption RSA

Input: Public key (n,e),Private key d, Cipher text c
Output: Plain text m
begin
  1. Compute m = c^d mod n
  2. Return m.
end

The best known algorithm for factoring integers is the *general number field sieve* (GNFS), which takes time $O(e^{(\frac{64}{9})^{\frac{1}{3}}(n.log2)^{\frac{1}{3}}(log(n.log2))^{\frac{2}{3}}})$ for factoring an integer of n-bit. However, the best known quantum algorithm for this problem, the Shor algorithm runs in polynomial time. Unfortunately, this fact does not say much about where the problem is with respect to classes of non-quantum complexity [10]. For [11], problems of integer factorization (RSA) admit, in general, algorithms that run in sub-exponential time.

2.2 Elliptic curve cryptography (ECC)

The main idea of the algorithms based on curves is to build a set of points of an elliptic curve for which the discrete logarithm problem is intractable. According to [12] cryptosystems based on elliptic curves is an interesting technology because they reach the same level of security systems such as RSA, using minor keys, and thus consuming less memory and processor resources. This characteristic makes them ideal for use in smart cards and other environments where features such as storage, time and energy are limited.

In the mid-80 [2] and [3] proposed a method of cryptography based on elliptic curves ECC. According to creators of the ECC, an elliptic curve is a plane curve defined by the following equation:

$$y^2 = x^3 + ax + b \tag{2}$$

The procedure of encryption through elliptic curve analogous to ElGamal encryption scheme are described in the algorithm 3. The pure text m is first represented as a point M, and then encrypted by the addition to kQ, where k is an integer chosen randomly, and Q is the public key.

Algorithm 3: *ElGamal elliptic curve encryption*

Input: Parameters field of elliptic curve (p, E, P, n), Public key Q, Plain text m
Output: Cipher text (C_1, C_2)
begin
  1. Represent the message m as a point M in E (F_p)
  2. Select $k \in R^{[1,n-1]}$.
  3. Compute $C_1 = kP$
  4. Compute $C_2 = M + kQ$.
  5. Return (C_1, C_2)
end

The transmitter transmits the points $C_1 = kPeC_2 = M + kQ$ to receiver who uses his private key d to compute:

$$dC_1 = d(kP) = k(dP) = kQ, \tag{3}$$

and then calculating $M = C_2 - kQ$. An attacker who wants to read of M need to calculate kQ. This model algorithm have been extensively studied since according to [13] in recent years the ECC has attracted attention as a security solution for wireless networks, because the use of small keys and low computational overhead.

According to [14], a subgroup generated by a point which has order "r" with "k" bits gives $\frac{k}{2}$ bits of security, this value is related to the fact that the best algorithm for solving the discrete logarithm problem on an elliptic curve has complexity $O(2^{k/2})$. According to [15], unlike the case of the integer factorization problem, there are not algorithm of sub-exponential order known to the discrete logarithm problem over elliptic curves. The best known algorithm to date has exponential time.

2.3 Multivariate Quadratic Quasigroup (MQQ)

The cryptographic algorithms presented above have their security based on computationally intractable mathematical problems: computational efficiency of calculating the discrete logarithm and integer factorization [4]. In 2008, it was proposed a new scheme of public key called Multivariate Quadratic Quasigroup (MQQ) [16]. This algorithm is based on multivariate polynomial transformations of quasigroups quadratic and having the following properties [16], [4].

- Highly parallelizable unlike other algorithms that are essentially sequential.
- The encryption speed is comparable to other public key cryptosystems based on multivariate quadratic.
- The decryption speed is typical of a symmetric block cipher.
- Post-Quantum Algorithm

According to [17], [16] MQQ gives a new direction for the cryptography field and can be used to develop new cryptosystems of public key as well as improve existing cryptographic schemes. Furthermore, according to [16], [5] experiments showed that the MQQ in hardware can be as fast as a typical symmetric block cipher, being several orders of magnitude faster than algorithms such as RSA, DH and ECC.

A generic description for the scheme is a typical system multivariate quadratic $T \circ P' \circ S : \{0,1\}^n \rightarrow \{0,1\}^n$ where T and S are two nonsingular linear transformations and P'is a multivariate mapping bijective quadratic over $\{0,1\}^n$. The mapping $P' : \{0,1\}^n \rightarrow \{0,1\}^n$ is defined in the algorithm 4.

The algorithm for encryption with the public key is the direct application of the set of n multivariate polynomials $P = \{P_i(x_1, ..., x_n) | i = 1, ..., n\}$ on the vector $x = (x_1, ..., x_n)$, or is $y = P(x)$, can be represented as $y = P(x) \equiv y \equiv A.X$.

According to [18] the computational complexity of the MQQ algorithm is polynomial with degree of regularity D_{reg}, more precisely the complexity is: $O(N^{\omega D_{reg}})$, which basically consists in reducing complexity in an array of size $\approx N^{D_{reg}}$.

Algorithm 4: Non-linear mapping P'

Input: A vector $x = (f_1, ..., f_n)$ of n linear Boolean functions of n variable. We implicitly suppose that a multivariate quadratic quasigroup * is previously defined, and that n = 32k, k = 5,6,7,8 is also previously determined.

Output: : 8 linear expressions $P'_i(x_1, ..., x_n)$, i = 1,...,8 and n - 8 multivariate quadratic polynomials $P'_i(x_1, ..., x_n), i = 9, ..., n$.

begin

1. Represent a vector $x = (f_1, ..., f_n)$ of n linear Boolean functions of n variables $x_1, ..., x_n$ as a string $x = (X_1, ..., X_{n/s})$ where X_i are vector of dimension 8;

2. Compute $Y = Y_1, ..., Y_{n/8}$, where $Y_1 = X_1, Y_{j+1} = X_j * X_{j+1}$,for even j=2,4,...and $Y_{j+1} = X_{j+1} * X_j$, for odd j=3,5,...

3. Output (y)

end

3. Simulation Environment

Due the high cost of real sensor platforms and the possibility to evaluate many sensors through computer programs, it was decided to carry out the performance evaluation through simulations. The platforms used in this evaluation were ARM, MSP430 and AVR.

The SimpleScalar[19] simulator of ARM platform, the AVRORA simulator [20] of AVR platform and MSPsim [21] of MSP430 platform were used due to the large number of academic papers that use these tools in performance evaluations.

The MIRACL cryptographic libraries and RELIC were used in coding the algorithms RSA and ECC. The MQQ algorithm not changed since it does not rely on external libraries of ANSI C language. All algorithms were written in the same programming language (ANSI C).

3.1 Platforms

The embedded platform ARM consists of StrongARM which is a 32-bit RISC processor using 206MHz and 16KB of instruction cache using writeback strategy. The ARM platform is not widely used in WSN, but is the embedded platform most widely used today.

In the MSP430 platform, we used the MSP430F1611, which is integrated with Tmote Sky and TelosB sensors, has clocked at 8MHz, 48KB of ROM and 10KB of RAM [22].

The Atmega 128 platform is based on AVR architecture. This is an 8-bit microcontroller, contains 128KB of flash memory and 4KB of data memory [23]. In this evaluation, we considered a 16Mhz processor. This platform is widely used in WSN, including devices such as Mica2, MicaZ and IRIS.

3.2 Simulation Tools

The SimpleScalar simulator [24] is a computational architecture that models a virtual computer with CPU, caches (instruction and data), Random Access Memory (RAM) and the entire hierarchy of memories, and can simulate real programs running on such platforms. The gcc compiler and library MIRACL[25] were used in coding. According to [25] the Miracl library is reference from cryptographic tools providing facilities for implementation of algorithms for security applications in the real world. Furthermore, the available codes by Miracl are compact, fast and efficient, presenting high performance in any processor or platform. Studies by [26] [27] and [28] showed that codes based on Miracl get higher performance than codes based on other cryptographic libraries such as Crypto ++, LibTomCrypt, OpenSSL and GMP+Lydia. The code was turned into ARM by arm-linux-gcc[2] compiler.

In the MSP430 platform, the performance evaluation was performed using the simulator MSPsim [21] which measures the number of cycles spent by each function, making it easy to calculate the time of a simulation. The MSPsim is written in JAVA and simulates MSP430 family of processors, plus some sensor platforms. The gcc compiler and library RELIC [29] were used in coding, because the MIRACL library does not support this platform. The code was turned into MSP430 by msp-gcc[3] compiler.

In Atmega128 AVR platform, the performance evaluation was performed using the Avrora [20] simulator. The Avrora simulator returns among other information, the number of CPU cycles and throughput of simulated programs [30]. The codes were based on RELIC library and compile code in c language was made by avr-gcc[4] compiler.

3.3 Parameters and Load

The RSA algorithms, ECC and MQQ were evaluated on ARM platforms, MSP430 and AVR with the processing time as benchmark. The algorithms were written in the same programming language (C language) and subjected to charges of the same size. The message had a size of 44 bytes. The encrypted files by algorithms were identical, respecting the equivalence between key sizes, which can be viewed in Table 1.

The key generation was not part of this study because it was considered expensive for embedded platforms. The Table 1 shows that the security level obtained with the

[2]arm-linux-gcc: ARM compiler for code written in C language. More information on: http://www.gnuarm.com/

[3]msp-gcc: MSP430 compiler for code written in C language. More information on: http://mspgcc.sourceforge.net/

[4]avr-gcc: AVR compiler for code written in C language. More information on: http://www.nongnu.org/avr-libc/

Table 1: Equivalence of key size to RSA, ECC e MQQ [31] [16]

RSA	1024	2048	3072	7680	15360
ECC (Prime field)	192	224	256	384	521
MQQ 160	160	—	—	—	—

RSA-1024 algorithm is the same obtained with the ECC-192 (prime field) algorithm.

4. Architectural Evaluation

According to [32], different of NS2, that is a discrete event simulator, the SimpleScalar, MSPsim and Avrora are instruction level simulators. The operations of individual nodes are emulated, so it is not necessary to calculate the sample means. The data of processing time are separated by platforms.

4.1 ARM Platform

Considering the frequency of StrongArm processor in 206MHz and having the number of cycles of each algorithm, it was possible to calculate the time in milliseconds (ms). The Figure 1 shows that in the ARM platform, the processing time of RSA was slower than ECC and MQQ for all variations of key. The MQQ-160 had the best performance among the algorithms analyzed, since it had a time of 18.7 ms, against 305.8 ms of the ec-elg_p192 and 4302.8 ms RSA-1024. These data show that MQQ in the ARM platform is 16 times faster than ec-elg_p192 and 230 times faster than RSA-1024.

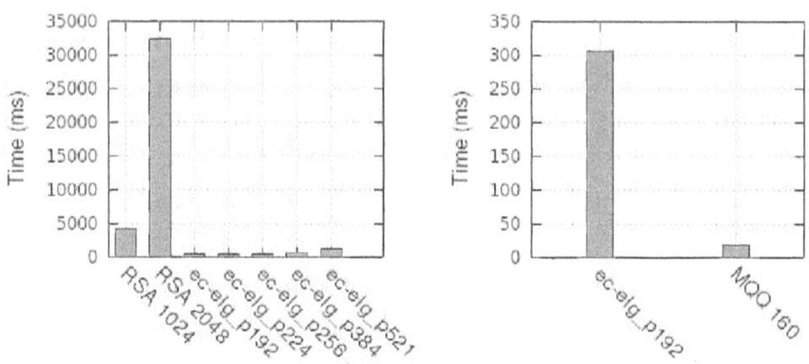

Fig. 1: Processing Time - ARM

4.2 MSP430 Platform

The compilation by msp-gcc generates a file with extension ".elf" that can be read by the MSPsim [21] simulator. In the case of RSA and ECC algorithm that were based on RELIC library, it was necessary to run a script available by the library, claiming the msp-gcc compiler and generates compiled files inside the folder "bin". The processing time of algorithms in seconds was calculated assuming an 8 Mhz clock. Is worth noting that most modern sensors, as TinyNode, uses MSP430 microcontroller with 16 MHz clock

[14]. Thus, the processing time for such sensors corresponds to half of the calculation presented here.

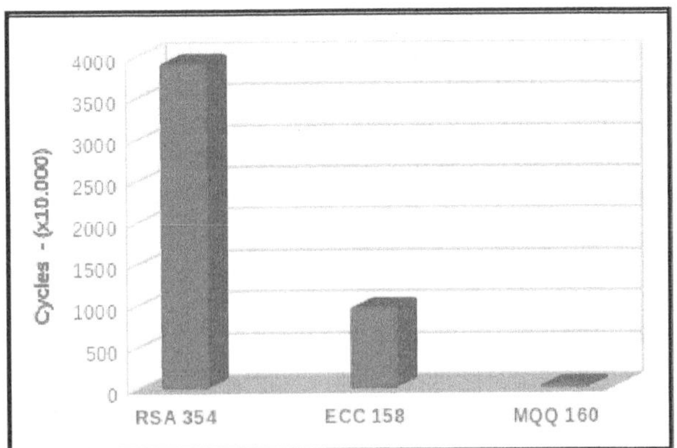

Fig. 2: Number of cycles in the MSP430 platform

The Figure 2 shows that the number of cycles of the RSA 354-bit algorithm was four times higher than the number of cycles of the ECC 158-bit algorithm. The MQQ 160-bit algorithm presented a number of cycles approximately 25 times smaller than the ECC 158-bit algorithm.

Table 2: Processing time on MSP430 platform

Algorithm	Time(s)
RSA 354	4,91
ec-elg_p158	1,22
MQQ 160	0,05

The processing time in seconds presented in Table 2 confirms again the best performance of the algorithm MQQ compared to RSA and ECC algorithms. Further, in accordance with Table 2, the processing time of the RSA 354-bit was approximately 300% higher than the processing time of the ec-elg_p158. The MQQ 160-bit algorithm had a processing time 98 times smaller than the time shown by the RSA 354-bit algorithm and about 24 times less than the processing time of the ec-elg_p158.

4.3 AVR Atmega128 Platform

In this section, we evaluated the implementation of MQQ-160 on platform AVR Atmega 128 with 8-bit processor. Due to restrictions of the platform, we compare the results obtained in the simulation of MQQ-160, with data from the literature with the ECC algorithm.

To simulate the code of MQQ algorithm in Avrora, was necessary to compile the code written in C using the avr-gcc compiler. In this compilation, the parameter "-mmcu=ATMEGA128" ensures that this code will be facing Atmega128 platforms. At the end, a binary file ".elf" is generated. The file ". elf" should be changed to ".od" through the avr-objdump tool[5] which forms part of the library avr-libc. This tool has the function of turning the assembler file in a text file supported by Avrora simulator.

[5]http://www.nongnu.org/avr-libc/

The work [33] evaluated the ECC algorithm on the AVR Atmega128 platform . The authors also used the Avrora simulator in performance evaluation. Considering the Atmega128 platform at 16 MHz, the data showed that the ECC 163 was executed in 6.94 s. The Figure 3 shows that the MQQ-160 was run in 0.21 s, which corresponds to a time about 33 times less than the processing time of the ECC-163 algorithm.

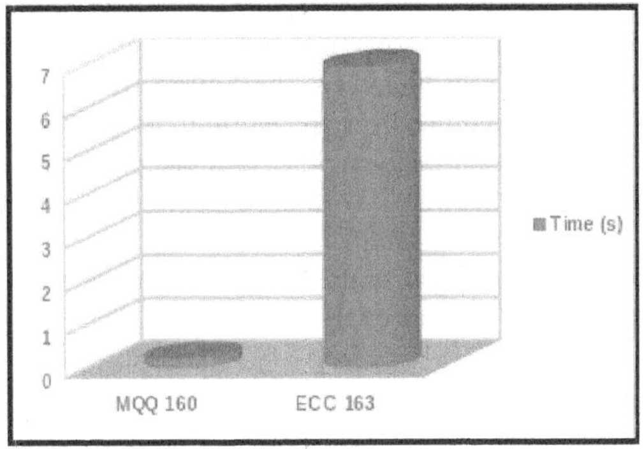

Fig. 3: Processing time on AVR Atmega128 platform

5. Comparative Analysis

The Table 3 makes a comparison between the times of cryptographic algorithms on ARM platforms, MSP430 and AVR. The data show that on all platforms, MQQ algorithm showed better results than the RSA algorithms and ECC. The shortest distance between the times of MQQ occurred in comparison with the ec-elg_p192 on ARM platform, where MQQ algorithm was 16 times faster. The ratio was higher in comparison with the RSA-1024 also on the ARM platform, where the MQQ algorithm presented a runtime 230 times smaller. The algorithm ec-elg_p192 proved be faster than RSA-1024 on all platforms, with the highest difference occurred in the ARM platform, where the ec-elg_p192 was 14 times faster.

The Table 3 also show that in the MSP430 platform, the MQQ-160 algorithm obtained a processing time 98 times better than the RSA-354 algorithm and 24 times better than the algorithm ec-elg_p158. Still in the MSP430 platform, the ECC algorithm was approximately 4 times faster than the RSA algorithm. In the AVR platform the MQQ algorithm was 33 times faster than the ECC algorithm. In this comparison the RSA algorithm showed the worst results on all platforms evaluated.

It can be seen from Table 4 that in general, the results obtained in this study, comparisons between RSA and MQQ are similar to those found in the performance reviews of the literature, that is, the performance outweighs MQQ several orders of magnitude the performance of RSA, and

Table 3: Comparison of processing time on the platforms ARM, MSP430 and AVR.

Platform	Algorithm	Time	Relationship (MQQ)	ECC vs RSA
ARM	RSA 1024	4431,8	230	14
	ec-elg_p192	314,9	16	–
	MQQ 160	19,2	–	–
MSP430	RSA 354	4,91	98	4
	ec-elg_p158	1,22	24	–
	MQQ 160	0,05	–	–
AVR	ECC 163 [33]	6,94	33	–
	MQQ 160	0,21	–	–

in most cases the ECC also outperforms the RSA. However, no authors compared the performance of MQQ with ECC, impeding a direct comparison between the results obtained in this study with the literature. The Table 4 was constructed by dividing the runtime of each algorithm by the number of bytes of messages used to encipher and decipher, so most of the data are in **"ms/byte"**, with the exception of data on the ARM platform, which are in **"cycles/byte"**. This conversion was performed to equalize the different message sizes used by authors who are part of this comparison.

Table 4: Analysis comparative with other works

Work	Platform	RSA	ECC	MQQ	Relationship (time)
[16]	TelosB	72540	–	48,4	1486,4
[34]	MSP430	111	–	1,13	98,23
[31]	ARM	0,08	0,3	—	3,75
[34]	ARM	0,88	0,06	—	14,6

Importantly, the primary datum of Table 4 is the ratio of processing time of algorithms, since the objective of this study was to compare the performance of cryptographic algorithms, and not between implementations of the same algorithm. The time differences between the implementations of the same algorithm are the result of own implementations, libraries, platforms, and other variables that can influence the runtime. As the time relationship between the algorithms, this work shows that it is not as large as found in other studies. [16] said the MQQ 160 on TelosB platform is about 1486 times faster than RSA 1024, but our comparison showed that this difference is approximately 98 times. [31] showed that the ARM platform, the RSA algorithm was faster than the ECC, but this study showed that the ECC on the same platform was 14.6 times faster than RSA.

6. Conclusion

Embedded systems are increasingly found in various applications, with emphasis on mobile devices, telecommunications, Wireless Sensor Networks(WSN) and general purpose applications. Critical issues in design and development of such systems are the runtime, physical size and power consumption, since the computing platforms have limited resources. The performance evaluation performed in this study took into account three different embedded platforms, where we compared the standard asymmetric algorithms (RSA) algorithms whose use in embedded systems is growing rapidly (ECC), in addition to promising (MQQ). Despite the ARM platform has not effectively be used in WSN, researches have been developed to enable the use of these devices on these networks, so the assessment platform that can serve as a basis for future research. The results showed that the ECC have reason to be widely used in WSN, as well as being faster than RSA, and this algorithm has been evaluated by cryptographers around the world, so it is an efficient algorithm and secure. The MQQ algorithm is promising, as it achieved excellent levels of processing time, but also due to its recent publication can not be considered truly safe.

As future work we plan to (i) study the key generation phase, since this analysis considered only the encryption and decryption processes, (ii) Studying of mathematical techniques which reduce the processing time of asymmetric algorithms for embedded platforms used in WSN, i.e. techniques which reduce the processing time of critical functions of algorithms, focusing on software, and (iii) more detailed studies of the safety level of MQQ algorithm.

References

[1] R. Rivest, A. Shamir, and L. Adleman, "A method for obtaining digital signatures and public-key cryptosystems," *Communications of the ACM*, vol. 21, no. 2, pp. 120–126, 1978.

[2] N. Koblitz, "Elliptic curve cryptosystems," *Mathematics of computation*, vol. 48, no. 177, pp. 203–209, 1987.

[3] V. Miller, "Use of elliptic curves in cryptography," in *Advances in Cryptology - CRYPTO Proceedings*. Springer, 1986, pp. 417–426.

[4] D. Gligoroski, S. Markovski, and S. Knapskog, "A public key block cipher based on multivariate quadratic quasigroups," *Arxiv preprint arXiv:0808.0247*, 2008.

[5] M. El-Hadedy, D. Gligoroski, and S. Knapskog, "High performance implementation of a public key block cipher-mqq, for fpga platforms," in *Reconfigurable Computing and FPGAs, 2008. ReConFig'08. International Conference on*. IEEE, 2008, pp. 427–432.

[6] M. S. Margi, M. Jr, and T. C. M. B. C. Barreto, "Segurança em Redes de Sensores Sem Fio," in *Simpósio Brasileiro em Segurança da Informação*, 2009, pp. 149–194. [Online]. Available: www.lbd.dcc.ufmg.br/colecoes/sbseg/2009/042.pdf

[7] D. Boyle and T. Newe, "Securing Wireless Sensor Networks: Security Architectures," *Journal of Networks*, vol. 3, no. 1, pp. 65–77, Jan. 2008. [Online]. Available: http://www.academypublisher.com/ojs/index.php/jnw/article/view/998

[8] J. Sen, "A Survey on Wireless Sensor Network Security," *International Journal of Communication Networks and Information Security (IJCNIS)*, vol. 1, no. 2, pp. 55–78, 2009.

[9] R. Struik, "Cryptography for highly constrained networks," in *NIST - CETA Workshop 2011*, 2011.

[10] S. R. Pereira, "O sistema criptográfico de chave pública rsa," Master's thesis, Universidade Católica de Santos, 2008.

[11] I. S. Torres, "Elliptical curve cryptography - segurança e privacidade em sistemas de armazenamento e transporte de dados," junho 2007, mSDPA, Univ. do Minho.

[12] I. Blake, G. Seroussi, and N. smart, *Elliptic Curves in Cryptography*, C. U. Press, Ed. Cambridge, 1999.

[13] F. Amin, A. H. Jahangir, and H. Rasifard, "Analysis of Public-Key Cryptography for Wireless Sensor Networks Security," *World Academy of Science, Engineering and Technology*, vol. 31, no. July, pp. 530–535, 2008.

[14] C. L. F. Gouvea, "Implementação em Software de Criptografia Baseada em Emparelhamentos para Redes de Sensores Usando o Microcontrolador MSP430," mestrado, Unicamp, 2010.

[15] J. Stapleton, *Information Security Management Handbook*, 6th ed. USA: CRC Press, 2012, ch. Elliptic Curve Cryptosystems.
[16] R. Maia, "Análise da viabilidade da implementação de algoritmos pós-quânticos baseados em quase-grupos multivariados quadráticos em plataformas de processamento limitadas." Master's thesis, USP, 2010.
[17] R. Ahlawat, K. Gupta, and S. Pal, "From mq to mqq cryptography: Weaknesses new solutions," in *Western European Workshop on Research in Cryptology*, 2009.
[18] J. Faugere, R. Ødegård, L. Perret, and D. Gligoroski, "Analysis of the mqq public key cryptosystem," *Cryptology and Network Security*, pp. 169–183, 2010.
[19] T. Austin, E. Larson, and D. Ernst, "Simplescalar: An infrastructure for computer system modeling," *Computer*, vol. 35, no. 2, pp. 59–67, 2002.
[20] B. Titzer, D. Lee, and J. Palsberg, "Avrora: scalable sensor network simulation with precise timing," *IPSN 2005. Fourth International Symposium on Information Processing in Sensor Networks, 2005.*, pp. 477–482, 2005. [Online]. Available: http://ieeexplore.ieee.org/lpdocs/epic03/wrapper.htm?arnumber=1440978
[21] J. Eriksson, A. Dunkels, N. Finne, F. Osterlind, and T. Voigt, "Mspsim - an extensible simulator for msp430-equipped sensor boards," in *European Conference on Wireless Sensor Networks (EWSN)*, Delft, The Netherlands, January 2007.
[22] C. P. L. Gouvea, "Implementação em Software de Criptografia Baseada em Emparelhamentos para Redes de Sensores Usando o Microcontrolador MSP430," *X Simpósio Brasileiro em Segurança da Informação e de Sistemas Computacionais*, pp. 531–538, 2010.
[23] J. Yang and M. Hua, "A popularizing movable environmental detection and regulating system based on smart home technology," in *Software Engineering and Service Science (ICSESS), 2012 IEEE 3rd International Conference on*. IEEE, 2012, pp. 165–168.
[24] T. Austin, E. Larson, and D. Ernst, "Simplescalar: An infrastructure for computer system modeling," *Computer*, vol. 35, no. 2, pp. 59–67, 2002.
[25] M. Scott, "Miracl–multiprecision integer and rational arithmetic c/c++ library," *Shamus Software Ltd, Dublin, Ireland, URL< http://www. shamus. ie*, 2003.
[26] N. Uto and D. Reis Jr, "Um survey sobre bibliotecas criptográficas com suporte à criptografia de curvas elípticas1," *Cad. CPqD Tecnologia*, vol. 1, no. 1, pp. 133–141, 2005.
[27] D. Pigatto, N. Silva, and K. Branco, "Performance evaluation and comparison of algorithms for elliptic curve cryptography with elgamal based on miracl and relic libraries," *Journal of Applied Computing Research*, vol. 1, no. 2, pp. 95–103, 2011.
[28] D. F. Pigatto, "Segurança em sistemas embarcados críticos - utilização de criptografia para comunicação segura," Master's thesis, USP, 2012.
[29] D. F. Aranha and C. P. L. Gouvea, "RELIC is an Efficient LIbrary for Cryptography," http://code.google.com/p/relic-toolkit/, 2012.
[30] S. Ben Othman, A. Trad, and H. Youssef, "Performance evaluation of encryption algorithm for wireless sensor networks," in *Information Technology and e-Services (ICITeS), 2012 International Conference on*. IEEE, 2012, pp. 1–8.
[31] I. Branovic, R. Giorgi, and E. Martinelli, "A Workload Characterization of Elliptic Curve Cryptography Methods in Embedded Environments," *ACM SIGARCH Computer Architecture News*, vol. 32, no. 3, 2004.
[32] P. J. Marron, S. Karnouskos, D. Minder, and A. Ollero, *The emerging domain of Cooperating Objects*. Springer, 2011.
[33] H. Yan and Z. J. Shi, "Studying software implementations of elliptic curve cryptography," in *Information Technology: New Generations, 2006. ITNG 2006. Third International Conference on*. IEEE, 2006, pp. 78–83.
[34] G. da Silva Quirino, "Analise arquitetural de algoritmos criptograficos assimetricos em plataformas embarcadas usadas em rssf," Master's thesis, UFS, 2013.

Implementing the ECC Brainpool curve generation procedure using open source software

V. Gayoso Martínez and L. Hernández Encinas
Information Security Institute (ISI), Spanish National Research Council (CSIC), Madrid, Spain

Abstract—*Elliptic Curve Cryptography (ECC) began to be used almost 30 years ago. Since then, ECC has been applied to an increasing number of fields (information encryption, digital signatures, integer factorization, etc.). However, one practical problem still arises when an organization decides to implement an ECC solution: what elliptic curve is the most adequate in the deployment scenario?*

This contribution analyses the most important features of the elliptic curve generation procedure defined by the ECC Brainpool consortium. In addition to that, this paper describes the Java application that we have implemented following the Brainpool specifications. This application can be used for generating new elliptic curves that fulfil the security requirements defined by Brainpool. Finally, we provide the test results offered by our implementation, so interested readers can understand how much time it takes to generate elliptic curves suitable for cryptographic purposes that conform to the Brainpool specification.

Keywords: Brainpool, elliptic curves, Java, public key cryptography.

1. Introduction

In 1985, Victor Miller [1] and Neal Koblitz [2] independently proposed a cryptosystem based on elliptic curves, whose security relies on the Elliptic Curve Discrete Logarithm Problem (ECDLP). Elliptic Curve Cryptography (ECC) can be applied to data encryption and decryption, digital signatures, and key exchange procedures, among others [3], [4].

Even though elliptic curve cryptographic protocols are well defined in standards from ANSI [5], [6], IEEE [7], [8], ISO/IEC [9], NIST [10], and other similar organisations, it is usually the case that the elliptic curve parameters that are necessary to operate those protocols are offered to the reader without a complete and verifiable pseudo-random generation process. Some of the most important limitations detected across the main cryptographic standards regarding the processes for generating elliptic curves suitable for cryptography are the following [11]:

- The seeds used to generate the curve parameters are typically chosen *ad hoc*.
- The primes that define the underlying prime fields have a special form aimed to facilitate efficient implementations.
- The parameters specified do not cover in all the cases key lengths adapted to the security levels required nowadays.

In this scenario, a European consortium of companies and government agencies led by the Bundesamt für Sicherheit in der Informationstechnik (BSI) was formed in order to study the aforementioned limitations and produce their recommendations for a well defined elliptic curve generation procedure. The group was named ECC Brainpool (henceforth simply Brainpool) and, apart from the BSI, some of the most relevant companies and public institutions that took part were G&D, Infineon Technologies, Philips Electronics, the University of Bonn, Gemplus (now part of Gemalto), the Institute for Experimental Mathematics (University of Duisburg-Essen), Siemens, the Technical University of Darmstadt, T-Systems, Sagem Orga (now Morpho, part of the Safram group), the Institute for Applied Information Processing and Communications (Graz University of Technology), and the Secure Information Technology Center - Austria (A-SIT).

In 2005, Brainpool delivered the first version of a document entitled "ECC Brainpool standard curves and curve generation" [11], which was revised and published as a Request for Comments (RFC) memorandum in 2010, the "Elliptic Curve Cryptography (ECC) Brainpool standard curves and curve generation" [12].

This contribution analyses the elliptic curve generation procedure as defined by Brainpool in [11] and [12]. Those specifications consist of the proper introductory sections, the step by step description of the elliptic curve generation algorithm, and the validation data that can be used for checking the correctness of any software implementation.

The rest of this document is organized as follows: Section 2 presents a brief mathematical introduction to elliptic curves. Section 3 describes the most important characteristics of the Brainpool specification. Section 4 includes a functional description of GCEC, the Java application developed by us in order to generate elliptic curves following the procedure defined by Brainpool. Section 5 provides an example of the elliptic curve generation process using GCEC. Section 6 details the results of the tests and offers information about the implementation performance. Finally, Section 7 summarizes the most relevant conclusions and provides additional comments about the security of the analysed procedure.

2. Elliptic curves

An elliptic curve E defined over a field $\mathbb{F}$ is a plane non-singular cubic curve with at least one rational point [13]. Such a curve is defined by the following equation, known as the Weierstrass equation in non-homogeneous form [14]:

$$E : y^2 + a_1xy + a_3y = x^3 + a_2x^2 + a_4x + a_6,$$

where $a_1, a_2, a_3, a_4, a_6 \in \mathbb{F}$ and $\Delta \neq 0$, being Δ the discriminant of the curve E [15]. Condition $\Delta \neq 0$ assures that the curve is smooth, i.e., there are no curve points with two or more different tangent lines.

The Weierstrass equation can also be described using homogeneous coordinates, producing the following equation:

$$Y^2Z + a_1XYZ + a_3YZ^2 = X^3 + a_2X^2Z + a_4XZ^2 + a_6Z^3.$$

The homogeneous version of the Weierstrass equation implies the existence of a special point, called the point at infinity, which is denoted as $\mathcal{O}$ and does not have a counterpart in the affine plane.

Regarding the points of an elliptic curve, it is possible to define the following operations:

- Point addition: $Q + R = S$.
- Point doubling: $Q + Q = 2Q$.
- Scalar multiplication: $k\,Q = Q + \cdots + Q$ (k times).

The set of points that satisfy the Weierstrass equation (plus the point at infinity), together with the point addition operation, fulfil the requirements to form a commutative group. This algebraic structure permits to use the elliptic curves in cryptography in a reliable way.

When working with finite fields of $q = p^m$ elements, where p is a prime number and $m \geq 1$, it is possible to obtain simplified versions of the Weierstrass equation. If the finite field is a *prime field* (and it is important to point out that the Brainpool procedure only uses prime fields), i.e. $\mathbb{F}_q = \mathbb{F}_p$, where $p > 3$ is a prime number, the equation defining the elliptic curve becomes

$$y^2 = x^3 + ax + b, \tag{1}$$

where $a, b \in \mathbb{F}_p$, and x and y are the affine coordinates of a point that belongs to the elliptic curve.

One of the elements that determine the cryptographic strength of an elliptic curve is its number of points, also known as the *cardinality* or the *order* of the elliptic curve. This value is formed by all the points that satisfy the elliptic curve equation plus the point at infinity $\mathcal{O}$.

If the field used to define the curve is a finite field, then the order of the curve is also a finite number. In a first approach to determine the cardinality of an elliptic curve, the Hasse theorem [16] states that the order of an elliptic curve defined over a prime field with q elements must fall inside the interval $[q + 1 - 2\sqrt{q}, q + 1 + 2\sqrt{q}]$.

Several algorithms have been proposed during last years to compute the number of points of an elliptic curve. The most well known procedures are the Schoof [17] and SEA (Schoof-Elkies-Atkin) [18] algorithms.

The Schoof algorithm was proposed by René Schoof in 1985, and it is a polynomial-time algorithm which uses the Frobenius endomorphism and division polynomials. Its time complexity is $O(\log^8 q)$, though using fast polynomial and integer arithmetic it can be reduced to $O(\log^5 q)$. It is recommended for elliptic curves of relatively small bit lengths.

The SEA algorithm is an improvement of the Schoof algorithm, with enhancements devised by Elkies and Atkin. This algorithm has a time complexity of $O(\log^6 q)$, though it can be reduced to $O(\log^4 q)$ using fast arithmetic.

In order to avoid some possible attacks, the number of points of an elliptic curve should have a small cofactor (typically 1, 2, 3 or 4) [13]. The *cofactor* is the additional factor that accompanies the large prime factor, so their multiplication matches the order of the curve. If the cofactor is 1, then the order of the elliptic curve is a prime number.

Table 1 provides a comparison between RSA and ECC key lengths, with data taken from [15] and [19], where the security level must be interpreted as the cryptographic strength provided by a symmetric encryption algorithm using a key of n bits. As it can be observed, the ratio between the key length in RSA and ECC clearly grows, which means that ECC is best adapted for applications where higher security levels are needed.

Table 1: Key length comparison of RSA and ECC.

Security level (bits)	RSA key length (bits)	ECC key length (bits)	Approximate ratio
80	1024	160-223	4.6:6.4
112	2048	224-255	8.0:9.1
128	3072	256-283	10.8:12.0
192	7680	384-511	15.0:20.0
256	15360	512-571	26.9:30.0

3. Main characteristics of the Brainpool procedure

3.1 Key length

In ECC, the term key length is interpreted as the number of bits needed to represent the prime number p. The key lengths allowed by Brainpool are 160, 192, 224, 256, 320, 384, and 512 bits ([12], page 6).

3.2 Seed generation

The seeds used in Brainpool are generated in a systematic and comprehensive way. These seeds have been obtained as the first 7 substrings of 160 bits each of the number $\pi \cdot 2^{1120}$ =*Seed_p_*160||...||*Seed_p_*512||*Remainder*, where || denotes the concatenation operator ([12], page 24).

3.3 Seed to candidate conversion

Brainpool uses SHA-1 ([12], page 22) during the process of finding candidates for the parameters p, a, and b given in formula (1). As the output of SHA-1 is 160 bits, and for different curves the length of the resulting parameters must be necessarily different, Brainpool performs a loop concatenating several SHA-1 outputs until the concatenated number has the proper bit length ([12], pages 22 and 24).

In addition to that, Brainpool uses two functions to generate the candidates, one for p and another for a and b. Those functions are very similar, in fact the only difference is that the most significant bit of a and b is forced to be 0 ([12], page 24). Given that another requirement states that the most significant bit of p must be 1 ([12], page 23), this implies that the values a and b generated are such that $a, b < p$.

3.4 Validation of parameters a and b

In Brainpool, once the algorithm has determined the value of p, it starts searching the proper values of the elliptic curve parameters a and b. When a candidate pair is found, the resulting curve is tested against the security requirements. In case the curve is rejected, both a and b are discarded, starting a new search for a proper pair ([12], page 25).

3.5 Cofactors

As it was mentioned in Section 2, in order to generate cryptographically strong elliptic curves it is necessary to compute the number of points of the elliptic curve and to determine if that value is a prime number, or if it has a small cofactor. In this regard, the Brainpool specifications only accept curves whose number of points is a prime number ([12], page 6).

3.6 Factorizations

Two of the security requirements defined by Brainpool imply the factorization of integers. In one case, it is necessary to factorize the value $q-1$, where q is the order of the elliptic curve, in order to avoid attacks using the Weil or Tate pairings. Those attacks allow the embedding of the cyclic subgroup of the elliptic curve into the group of units of a degree-l extension field of $\mathbb{F}_p$, where subexponential attacks on the Discrete Logarithm Problem (DLP) exist ([11], page 5).

In the other case, the specification requests to factorize the value d, which is the square-free factor of $4p - u^2$, where $u = q - p - 1$, so it can be checked that the class number of the maximal order of the endomorphism ring of the elliptic curve is larger than 10^7 ([11], page 5).

As the factorization of really big integers (such as those used in the aforementioned requirements) is a highly demanding computational task, it is recommended to use programs specifically designed for this mission that implement the latest advances in factorization.

4. GCEC application description

GCEC is a Java application that implements the Brainpool elliptic curve generation procedure as specified in [11] and [12]. GCEC consists of a single window panel, as it is shown in Figure 1.

Fig. 1: GCEC application executing the curve generation process.

In order to interact with the user, GCEC includes different elements such as combo boxes, buttons, and text boxes. Those elements are described next:

- Combo boxes:
  - *Length*: Length in bits of the prime number p that defines the underlying finite field.
  - *Cardinality*: Algorithm used to compute the number of points of the elliptic curve. In this version of GCEC the user can choose between two algorithms: Schoof [17] and SEA (Schoof-Elkies-Atkin) [18], introduced in Section 2. The implementation of both algorithms, developed by Mike Scott, is part of MIRACL (Multiprecision Integer and Rational Arithmetic Cryptographic Library), a C library offered by CertiVox as free software, and licensed under the FOSS (Free and Open Source Software) approved AGPL (Affero General Public License) terms [20].

    While the Schoof algorithm is coded into a single executable file (`schoof.exe`), the SEA algorithm requires three different executable files (`mueller.exe`, `process.exe`, and `sea.exe`) and a data file (`mueller.raw`) which contains the modular polynomials that are needed in the computations.

    In addition to outperform the Schoof algorithm when working with elliptic curves of significant key lengths, the SEA implementation is able to compute the value associated to the order of the curve modulo the prime numbers included in a input file and, when enough of those results are gathered by the algorithm, it can determine the order of the curve. This is an important feature that is used by GCEC to speed up the calculations, as it is not necessary to complete the computation of the cardinality of the curve if it is detected that the order is divisible by any number other than 1.

- *Factoring*: External program used for the factorization of integer numbers. In this version of GCEC the user can choose between two open source factoring applications: yafu v1.33 [21] and Msieve v1.5 [22]. The source code of both applications is accessible through their SourceForge repositories. According to its author, yafu is "an interactive command line utility for integer factorization. It implements multi-threaded NFS, SIQS, and ECM as well as P+1, P-1, SQUFOF, Pollard's Rho, and Fermat's method. It also contains a very fast implementation of the Sieve of Eratosthenes" [21]. Besides, Msieve is "a C library implementing a suite of algorithms to factor large integers. It contains an implementation of the SIQS and GNFS algorithms", in his author's own words [22].
  The reason for providing two different external factoring tools is that, when working with integers of more than 100 digits, the factorization time for any given integer may vary a lot between the two applications. Even for the same application, obtaining the factorization of two integers of the same bit length may differ substantially, as the internal routines of both applications are very sensitive to the nature of the specific number to be tested.

- *Text boxes*:
  - *Seed for P*: Initial seed that is used to compute the prime number p that defines $\mathbb{F}_p$.
  - *Seed for A & B*: Initial seed that is used to compute the curve parameters a and b.
  - Data: Output produced by the program.
- *Buttons*:
  - *Process*: Computes all the curve parameters using the seeds for p, a, and b.
  - *Stop*: Interrupts the computation without the possibility to continue the process.
  - *Save*: Stores the result of the computation in a file.
  - *Clear seeds*: Deletes the text boxes that contain the seeds.

Selecting a specific curve length automatically fills in the text boxes associated to the seeds for the parameters p, a, and b, so if the user wants to try the seeds provided by Brainpool it is not necessary to alter those values. On the other hand, if the user wants to try a different pair of seeds, he must enter the new values in the text boxes after clicking the *Clear seeds* button.

5. Generating an elliptic curve with GCEC

This section provides a complete example on how to generate an elliptic curve using GCEC.

After launching the application, the first step consists in setting the combo box options. In the example provided (see Figure 1), GCEC generates the Brainpool curve of 160 bits using the SEA algorithm and the yafu factoring application.

Once the user has clicked the *Process* button, GCEC starts with the computations, displaying information in the *Data* text box whenever new data is generated. A summary of the options selected by the user in the four combo boxes is shown in the *Data* text box (see Figure 1).

Clicking the *Process* button enables the *Stop* button (and, at the same time, the *Process* button gets disabled). If the user clicks the *Stop* button, the procedure is interrupted and the user is informed of that event in the *Data* text box (see Figure 2).

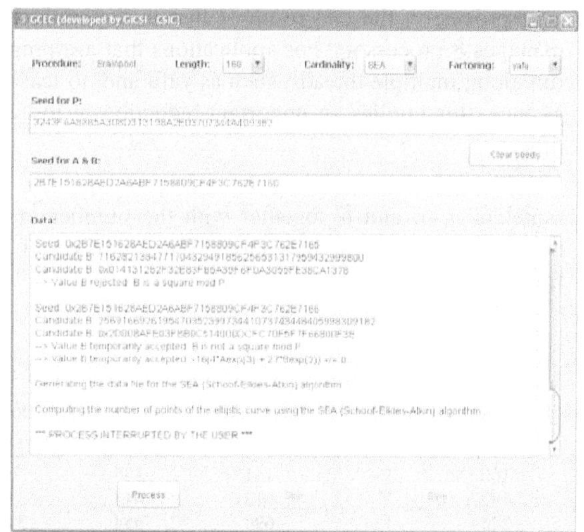

Fig. 2: Elliptic curve generation process stopped by the user.

Whenever GCEC finishes computing the elliptic curve, the *Stop* button is disabled and both the *Process* and *Save* buttons are enabled (see Figure 3).

Although the information displayed in the *Data* text box can be copied and pasted into any text editor, the user can store the result of the computation in an easy way by clicking the *Save* button, which pops up a dialog so the user can select the file where the information will be stored.

6. Tests and results

The tests whose results are presented in this section were completed using a PC with Windows 7 Professional OS

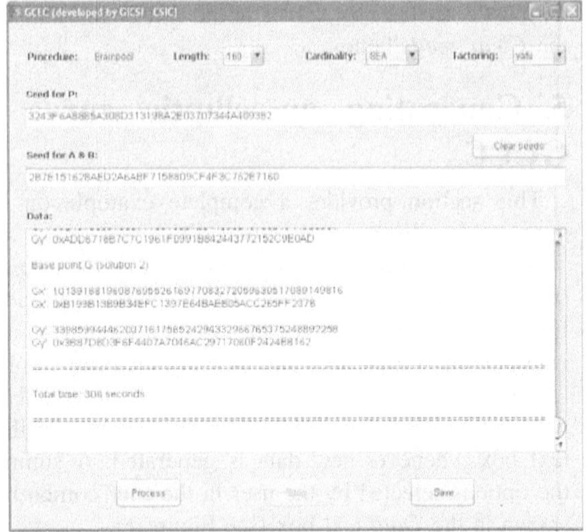

Fig. 3: Elliptic curve generation process finished.

and an Intel Core i7 processor at 3.40 GHz. As the i7 processor has 4 core processors and 2 logical processor per core processor, the end result is that the operating system manages 8 processors. For applications that are prepared to run along multiple threads, such as yafu and, to least extent, Msieve, this implies an important reduction of the working time.

Table 2 includes the number of candidates for the parameters p, a, and b, together with the number of elliptic curve point counting operations. The number of integer factorizations performed in all the tests is 2.

Table 2: Data summary regarding the Brainpool tests.

Bit length	Candidates parameter p	Candidates parameter a	Candidates parameter b	Point counting
160	1	151	135	76
192	1	613	643	332
224	1	694	654	342
256	3	995	948	504
320	2	1107	1121	556
384	6	2811	2845	1399
512	1	970	903	456

Table 3 includes the running time obtained when executing the GCEC application in the testing computer with the Brainpool sample curves. The term N/A stands for not available, in the sense that the test referred to was launched two months before this contribution was prepared and, at the time of writing these lines, was still in progress.

Figure 4 shows graphically the running time in seconds of the Brainpool tests with key lengths up to 384 bits. Besides, Figure 5 presents the running time for all the Brainpool key lengths.

Table 3: Computation time in seconds.

Bit length	yafu application	Msieve application
160	85	82
192	411	415
224	1115	1115
256	1745	1746
320	4514	10336
384	30969	51007
512	931211	N/A

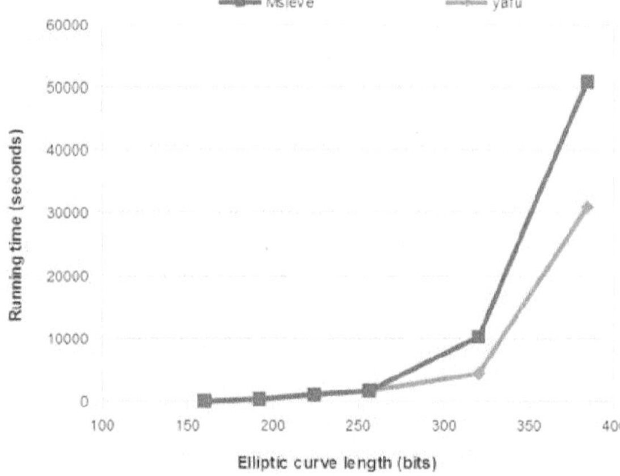

Fig. 4: Running time in seconds up to 384 bit lengths.

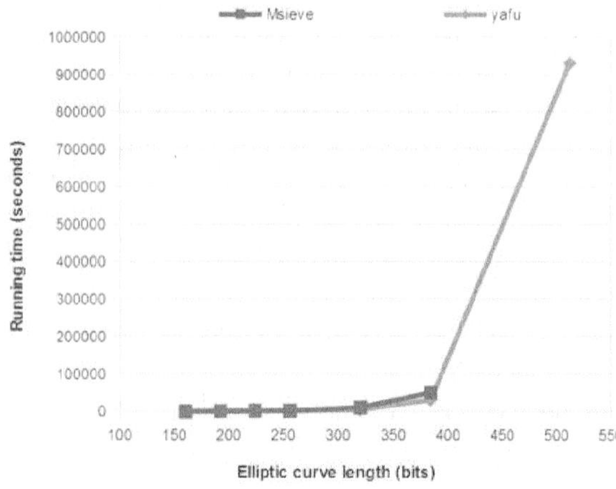

Fig. 5: Running time in seconds for all key lengths.

7. Conclusions

This report has analysed the elliptic curve generation procedure defined by Brainpool. In order to generate new elliptic curves that fulfil the security requirements of that organization, a Java application has been developed by us following the indications of the Brainpool specifications. In addition to that, the application can also be used for testing the sample elliptic curves included in those recommendations.

As it was expected, the execution time increases for bigger

key lengths (320, 384, and especially 512 bits). As it was mentioned in Section 2, a key length of 256 bits in ECC is equivalent to a key of 112-128 bits in a symmetric algorithm and of 2048-3072 bits in RSA, whilst a key length of 512 bits in ECC offers the same strength as a symmetric key of 192-256 bits and an RSA key of 7680-15360 bits.

For key lengths up to 256 bits, most of the computation time is dedicated by the program to execute the SEA algorithm. In comparison, for key lengths bigger than 256 bits, most of the time is devoted to factorize the integers of each test.

Regarding the comparison of Msieve and yafu, from the results of the tests it is clear that even though for small key lengths both programs offer a similar performance, when working with bigger key lengths (starting in 320 bits), yafu provides a significant improvement over Msieve when both applications are executed multi-threaded.

Acknowledgment

This work has been partially supported by Ministerio de Ciencia e Innovación (Spain) under the grant TIN2011-22668.

References

[1] V. Miller, "Use of elliptic curves in cryptography", *Lecture Notes in Computer Science*, vol. 218, pp. 417–426, 1986.

[2] N. Koblitz, "Elliptic curve cryptosystems", *Mathematics of Computation*, vol. 48 (177), pp. 203–209, 1987.

[3] V. Gayoso Martínez, L. Hernández Encinas, and C. Sánchez Ávila, "Elliptic Curve Cryptography. Java platform implementations", in *Proc. 23rd International Conference on Information Technologies (InfoTech-2009)*, 2009, pp. 20–27.

[4] V. Gayoso Martínez, L. Hernández Encinas, and C. Sánchez Ávila, "A Java implementation of the Elliptic Curve Integrated Encryption Scheme", in *Proc. WorldComp 2010 International Conference on Security & Management - SAM'10*, 2010, pp. 495–501.

[5] *Public Key Cryptography for the Financial Services Industry: The Elliptic Curve Digital Signature Algorithm (ECDSA)*, ANSI X9.62, 1998.

[6] *Public Key Cryptography for the Financial Services Industry: Key Agreement and Key Transport Using Elliptic Curve Cryptography*, ANSI X9.63, 2001.

[7] *Standard Specifications for Public Key Cryptography*, IEEE 1363, 2000.

[8] *Standard Specifications for Public Key Cryptography - Amendment 1: Additional Techniques*, IEEE 1363a, 2004.

[9] *Information Technology – Security Techniques – Encryption Algorithms – Part 2: Asymmetric Ciphers*, ISO/IEC 18033-2, 2006.

[10] *Digital Signature Standard (DSS)*, NIST FIPS 186-3, 2009.

[11] *ECC Brainpool standard curves and curve generation*, ECC Brainpool, 2005. Available: `http://www.ecc-brainpool.org/download/Domain-parameters.pdf`

[12] *Elliptic Curve Cryptography (ECC) Brainpool standard curves and curve generation*, IETF RFC 5639, 2010. Available: `http://tools.ietf.org/html/rfc5639`

[13] H. Cohen et al., *Handbook of elliptic and hyperelliptic curve cryptography*, Florida: Chapman & Hall/CRC, 2006.

[14] J. H Silverman, *The arithmetic of elliptic curves*, 2nd ed., New York: Springer-Verlag, 2009.

[15] D. Hankerson, A. Menezes, and S. Vanstone, *Guide to elliptic curve cryptography*, New York: Springer-Verlag, 2004.

[16] N. M. Katz and B. Mazur, *Arithmetic moduli of elliptic curves*, Princeton, NJ: Princeton University Press, 1985.

[17] R. Schoof, "Elliptic curves over finite fields and the computation of square roots mod p", *Mathematics of Computation*, vol. 44 (170), pp. 483–494, 1985.

[18] R. Schoof, "Counting points on elliptic curves over finite fields", *Journal de Theorie des Nombres de Bordeaux*, vol. 7, pp. 219–254, 1995.

[19] National *Recommendation for key management. Part 1: General*, NIST SP 800-57, 2007.

[20] CertiVox. (2012) MIRACL crypto SDK. [Online]. Available: `http://certivox.com/solutions/miracl-crypto-sdk/`

[21] B. Buhrow. (2010) yafu. [Online]. Available: `http://sourceforge.net/projects/yafu/`

[22] J. Papadopoulos. (2009) Msieve. [Online]. Available. `http://sourceforge.net/projects/msieve/`

Power and Electromagnetic Analysis Attack on a Smart Card Implementation of CLEFIA

Yongdae Kim[1], **Jaehwan Ahn**[1], **and Heebong Choi**[1]
[1]The Attached Institute of Electronics and Telecommunications Research Institute
P.O.Box 1, Yuseong, Daejeon, 305-600, KOREA
Email: {kimyd, jaehwan, gold}@ensec.re.kr

Abstract— *CLEFIA is a 128-bit block cipher developed by Sony Corporation in 2007. Since then, many papers related to security evaluations of CLEFIA have been published. However, these have mainly analyzed its mathematical weaknesses. In this study, we perform power and electromagnetic analysis attacks on a software implementation of CLEFIA. We implemented the CLEFIA algorithm with a 128-bit key length on a 8-bit AVR processor-based smart card. Our experimental results show that we successfully derived a 128-bit master key by attacking three rounds. We compare the results of using the two different side channel information (power and electromagnetic). In addition, we demonstrates the effectiveness of using a low-pass filter.*

Keywords: CLEFIA, Power Analysis Attack, Electromagnetic Analysis Attack, Smart Card

1. Introduction

Cryptographic modules that implement cryptographic algorithms play an important role in protecting secret information. However, power (electromagnetic) analysis attacks, which exploit the power (electromagnetic) consumption (emanation) variations of cryptographic procedures, have become a significant threat to cryptographic modules. Since the first power analysis attack published by P. Kocher et al. in 1999 [1], many cryptographic researchers have begun to investigate the vulnerability of cryptographic modules to power and electromagnetic analysis attacks when implementing cryptographic algorithms. There are many studies that have been done on various types of cryptographic modules and cryptographic algorithms including CLEFIA [1] - [8].

However, to the best of our knowledge, no work thus far has examined power and electromagnetic analysis attacks on CLEFIA. Most of the reported research has only focused on the classical cryptanalysis of the CLEFIA algorithm or different types of attacks, e.g. cache trace or fault attacks ([9], [3], [10],[11], [12], and [13]). In [8], X. Bai et al. introduced the first differential power analysis attack on the CLEFIA block cipher, but they reported only the simulation results of the attack.

In this study, we demonstrate a power and electromagnetic analysis attacks on a smart card implementation of CLEFIA. We use the Pearson correlation to find the linear relationship between power (electromagnetic) information and the power model [2]. We implement CLEFIA with a 128-bit key length on an 8-bit AVR-processor-based smart card.

In addition, we present a concrete method to retrieve a 128-bit master key by attacking three rounds. Our experimental results indicate that an actual software implementation of CLEFIA without any countermeasures is extremely vulnerable to power and electromagnetic analysis attacks. This constitutes the first contribution of a power and electromagnetic analysis attack upon an actual CLEFIA implementation.

The remainder of this paper is organized as follows. Section 2 describes the structure of CLEFIA and the key scheduling scheme. Section 3 presents the power and electromagnetic analysis attack on CLEFIA and the detailed steps to retrieve a master key by attacking three rounds. Section 4 gives our experimental results. Finally, Section 5 concludes the paper.

2. CLEFIA Algorithm

In 2007, Sony Corporation introduced a 128-bit block cipher, CLEFIA which is based on the 4-branch generalized Feistel network [14]. CLEFIA utilizes three different key sizes of 128, 192, and 256 bits. In this study, we focus on the 128-bit key length. The number of rounds for the 128-bit key length is 18, and each round has two different round keys. Therefore, CLEFIA-128 has a total of 36 round keys.

2.1 Structure of CLEFIA

Figure 1 shows the overall structure of CLEFIA encryption with a 128-bit key length. The 128-bit plaintext, P, and ciphertext, C, are divided into four 32-bit data; i.e., $P = P_0 \mid P_1 \mid P_2 \mid P_3$ and $C = C_0 \mid C_1 \mid C_2 \mid C_3$, respectively.

The 32-bit round keys and whitening keys are represented as $RK_i (0 \leq i \leq 35)$ and $WK_i (0 \leq i \leq 3)$, respectively. These keys are provided by the key scheduling component. Each round, r uses two round keys, $RK_{2r-2}, RK_{2r-1} (1 \leq r \leq 18)$. For example, the last two round keys are RK_{34} and RK_{35}.

As shown in Fig. 1, each round of the encryption process has two different F-functions, $F0$ and $F1$, which consist

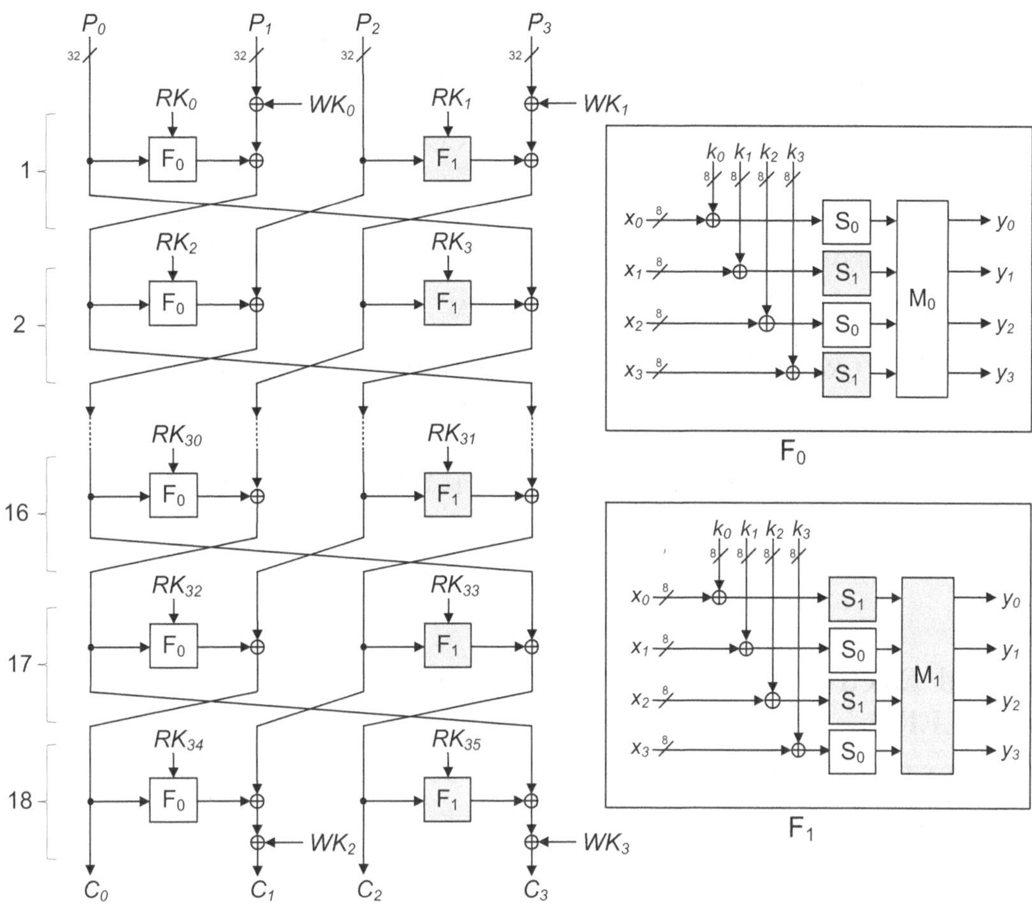

Fig. 1: Structure of CLEFIA encryption with 128-bit key length

of exclusive-or, two different S-boxes (S_0 and S_1), and two different multiplications (M_0 and M_1). We define the output of the F_0 and F_1 functions for the r-th round encryption operation as Y_0^r and Y_1^r, respectively.

In this paper, we also define the output of the r-th round encryption function as follows:

$$C^r = C_0^r \mid C_1^r \mid C_2^r \mid C_3^r. \quad (1)$$

Hence, the output of the r-th round of encryption is computed explicitly as

$$\begin{aligned} C^1 &= F_0(RK_0, P_0) \oplus WK_0 \oplus P_1 \mid P_2 \\ &\mid F_1(RK_1, P_2) \oplus WK_1 \oplus P_3 \mid P_0, \quad (2) \\ C^r &= C_1^{r-1} \oplus F_0(RK_{2r-2}, C_0^{r-1}) \mid C_2^{r-1} \\ &\mid C_3^{r-1} \oplus F_1(RK_{2r-1}, C_2^{r-1}) \mid C_0^{r-1} \quad (3) \\ &\text{(for } 2 \le r \le 17), \\ C^{18} &= C_0^{17} \mid C_1^{17} \oplus F_0(RK_{34}, C_0^{17}) \oplus WK_2 \mid C_2^{17} \\ &\mid C_3^{17} \oplus F_1(RK_{35}, C_2^{17}) \oplus WK_3. \quad (4) \end{aligned}$$

2.2 Key Scheduling

The key scheduling component of CLEFIA is composed of two parts: generating the 128-bit intermediate key, L, and round keys, RK_i. The intermediate key L is generated from 24 32-bit constant values, $CON_i(0 \le i \le 23)$, and a 128-bit master key. As a result, the intermediate value is determined by a given master key. Next, round keys and whitening keys are generated from the intermediate value as shown in Fig. 2.

The function Σ is called the *DoubleSwap* function and is defined as follows:

$$Y = X[7-63] \mid X[121-127] \mid X[0-6] \mid X[64-120], \quad (5)$$

where X and Y denote the input and output of the DoubleSwap function, respectively. Additionally, $X[a-b]$ denotes a bit string cut from the a-th bit to the b-th bit of X, and Σ^i denotes that the DoubleSwap function was applied i times.

$$
\begin{aligned}
WK_0 \mid WK_1 \mid WK_2 \mid WK_3 &= K \\
RK_0 \mid RK_1 \mid RK_2 \mid RK_3 &= L \oplus (CON_{24} \mid CON_{25} \mid CON_{26} \mid CON_{27}) \\
RK_4 \mid RK_5 \mid RK_6 \mid RK_7 &= \sum(L) \oplus K \oplus (CON_{28} \mid CON_{29} \mid CON_{30} \mid CON_{31}) \\
RK_8 \mid RK_9 \mid RK_{10} \mid RK_{11} &= \sum{}^2(L) \oplus (CON_{32} \mid CON_{33} \mid CON_{34} \mid CON_{35}) \\
RK_{12} \mid RK_{13} \mid RK_{14} \mid RK_{15} &= \sum{}^3(L) \oplus K \oplus (CON_{36} \mid CON_{37} \mid CON_{38} \mid CON_{39}) \\
RK_{16} \mid RK_{17} \mid RK_{18} \mid RK_{19} &= \sum{}^4(L) \oplus (CON_{40} \mid CON_{41} \mid CON_{42} \mid CON_{43}) \\
RK_{20} \mid RK_{21} \mid RK_{22} \mid RK_{23} &= \sum{}^5(L) \oplus K \oplus (CON_{44} \mid CON_{45} \mid CON_{46} \mid CON_{47}) \\
RK_{24} \mid RK_{25} \mid RK_{26} \mid RK_{27} &= \sum{}^6(L) \oplus (CON_{48} \mid CON_{49} \mid CON_{50} \mid CON_{51}) \\
RK_{28} \mid RK_{29} \mid RK_{30} \mid RK_{31} &= \sum{}^7(L) \oplus K \oplus (CON_{52} \mid CON_{53} \mid CON_{54} \mid CON_{55}) \\
RK_{32} \mid RK_{33} \mid RK_{34} \mid RK_{35} &= \sum{}^8(L) \oplus (CON_{56} \mid CON_{57} \mid CON_{58} \mid CON_{59})
\end{aligned}
$$

Fig. 2: Key Scheduling

3. Power and Electromagnetic Analysis Attack on CLEFIA

We use Pearson correlation as a distinguisher for the power and electromagnetic analysis attacks [2]. Because there are four whitening keys, we have to target more than one round key to retrieve a master key. In addition, we assume that an adversary knows the ciphertext. In this section, we describe in detail the steps of the attack.

3.1 Target Round Keys

3.1.1 RK_{35}

We adopted the Hamming weight model for the power model. To retrieve RK_{35}, the adversary calculates the Hamming weight using C_2^{18} which is known to him/her. Then, the adversary applies the attacks to derive four 8-bit round subkeys, namely, $RK_{35} = k_{35,0} \mid k_{35,1} \mid k_{35,2} \mid k_{35,3}$. Subsequently, the adversary extracts RK_{35} from the four 8-bit round subkeys, which are the primary target of the attacks.

3.1.2 RK_{34}

This round key can also be easily extracted from the Hamming weight calculated from the known value C_0^{18} as in the previous step.

3.1.3 $RK_{33} \oplus WK_2$

To extract RK_{33}, the adversary should know C_1^{17}, which is the input of the F_1 function in the 17-th round encryption operation. However, it is impossible to estimate C_1^{17} without knowing WK_2 as follows:

$$C_1^{17} = F_0(RK_{34}, C_0^{18}) \oplus C_1^{18} \oplus WK_2, \tag{6}$$

where C_0^{18}, C_0^{18} are already known to the adversary, and RK_{34} is retrieved in the previous step. From the F-function structure in Fig. 1, the following equation is satisfied in the 17-th round encryption operation:

$$F_1(RK_{33}, C_1^{17} \oplus WK_2) = F_1(RK_{33} \oplus WK_2, C_1^{17}). \tag{7}$$

The adversary calculates the Hamming weight from $C_1^{17} \oplus WK_2$, which can be retrieved easily from Eq. 6. Using the Hamming weight, the adversary can extract $RK_{33} \oplus WK_2$ (Eq. 7).

3.1.4 $RK_{32} \oplus WK_3$

Using the same method as above, the adversary can extract $RK_{32} \oplus WK_3$.

3.1.5 RK_{31}

The input of the F_1 function in the 16-th round is represented as

$$
\begin{aligned}
C_2^{15} &= C_1^{16} \\
&= C_0^{18} \oplus F_0(RK_{32}, C_0^{16}) \\
&= C_0^{18} \oplus F_0(RK_{32}, F_1(RK_{35}, C_2^{18}) \oplus WK_3 \oplus C_3^{18}) \\
&= C_0^{18} \oplus F_0(RK_{32} \oplus WK_3, F_1(RK_{35}, C_2^{18}) \oplus C_3^{18}).
\end{aligned} \tag{8}
$$

Because $RK_{32} \oplus WK_3$ and RK_{35} have already been retrieved in the previous attack, an adversary can calculate the Hamming weight from C_2^{15} to extract RK_{31}.

3.1.6 RK_{30}

An adversary can compute the relevant Hamming weight from C_0^{15}, which is determined by $RK_{33} \oplus WK_2$ and RK_{34}.

The round key, RK_{30}, can easily be extracted in the same way.

3.2 Retrieval of a 128-bit Master Key

From Fig. 2, it is easy to retrieve a 128-bit master key from the intermediate value, L, which is calculated from four round keys, such as $RK_{32}, RK_{33}, RK_{34}$ and RK_{35}. The four round keys can be extracted by attacking two encryption rounds. However, an attacker can only derive masked round keys, i.e., $RK_{33} \oplus WK_2$ and $RK_{32} \oplus WK_3$. If the attacker knows two more round keys, i.e., RK_{30} and RK_{31}, it is possible to retrieve the 128-bit master key.

3.2.1 RK_{33}

First, an adversary can calculate $\Sigma^8(L)[64-127]$ using RK_{34}, RK_{35}, and two constant values, CON_{58}, CON_{59}. Then WK_2 is determined as follows:

$$\begin{aligned} WK_2 &= K_2 \\ &= RK_{30} \oplus CON_{54} \oplus \Sigma^7(L)[64-95], \quad (9) \end{aligned}$$

where $\Sigma^7(L)[64-95]$ has the same value as $\Sigma^8(L)[71-102]$. Therefore, an adversary can unmask $RK_{33} \oplus WK_2$ using WK_2 and thus obtain RK_{33} (Fig. 3).

3.2.2 RK_{32}

In the same manner, we aim to retrieve WK_3 using all values known from the previous steps. From Fig. 2, we have the explicit relation $\Sigma^8(L)[32-63] = RK_{33} \oplus CON_{57}$. Therefore, an adversary can compute WK_3 as follows:

$$\begin{aligned} WK_3 &= K_3 \\ &= RK_{31} \oplus CON_{55} \oplus \Sigma^7(L)[96-127] \\ &= RK_{31} \oplus CON_{55} \oplus \\ &\quad (\Sigma^7(L)[96-120] \mid \Sigma^8(L)[57-63]). (10) \end{aligned}$$

Then, L can be computed from the four round keys $RK_{32}, RK_{33}, RK_{34}$ and RK_{35}. Finally, a 128-bit master key can be computed from L by inverting the generalized Feistel network.

4. Experimental Setup and Results

We performed power and electromagnetic analysis attacks on a software implementation of the CLEFIA algorithm. For the software implementation, we used an 8-bit AVR-processor-based smart card (ATMega 163). We did not implement any countermeasures in our target module.

4.1 Experimental Setup

We implemented the CLEFIA algorithm with a 128-bit key length on a contact smart card in a straightforward manner. In addition, we set the running frequency to standard external clock frequency of 3.57 MHz, and acquire power traces at 100 MSa/s using a 50-Ohm coaxial cable. We also capture the electromagnetic emanation at the same sampling frequency using a Langer LF-B3 EM probe with a Langer PA303 preamplifier. Futher, we utilize a low-pass filter (LPF) to investigate the influence of high-frequency noise for each side-channel information. Table 1 summarizes the details of our experimental environment.

Table 1: Experimental environment

Target Module	8-bit AVR-processor-based smart card
Digital Oscilloscope	LeCroy WaveRunner 6Zi
Sampling Frequency	100MSa/s
Probe (power)	Coaxial cable (50-Ohm)
Probe (electromagnetic)	Langer LF-B3
Low-pass filter	Mini-Circuits (DC-81MHz)
Sample Points	220000
Clock Frequency	3.57 MHz

Thus, the number of sample points for power and electromagnetic traces in each cycle is

$$\frac{100 \times 10^6 \text{ points/s}}{3.57 \times 10^6 \text{ cycles/s}} \simeq 28. \quad (11)$$

In this study, we target the last three round keys to retrieve a 128-bit master key. Hence, we capture power consumption and electromagnetic emanation while the last three rounds of encryption are processed. We can easily determine the range of the last three rounds from the traces by observing three distinct power (electromagnetic) patterns.

Because the running frequency of the smart card is low (approximately 4 MHz), we need a significant number of sampling points to measure power (electromagnetic) traces including the three rounds. Hence, a large amount of PC storage and time are required to collect sample points from the digital oscilloscope.

Therefore, we apply a resampling technique at 4MHz to reduce the number of sample points for each trace set. This method averages all the points in a cycle to produce one sample point. However, the electromagnetic traces roughly have the same number of +/- (positive and negative) sample points. Therefore, we first calculate the absolute value of the electromagnetic trace to prevent the average from tending to zero.

4.2 Experimental Results

Figures 4 and 5 show each of the resampled traces from our target module during the encryption operations of the 128-bit CLEFIA. Our target round keys are in the last three rounds, so the cropped traces shown in Figs. 4 and 5 correspond to the last three rounds.

Figures 6, 7, 8 and 9 show subkey retrieval results using each trace set. In the sub-figures labeled (a), the black line represents correlation peaks for the correct subkeys and gray lines show wrong key guesses. In addition, the sub-figures

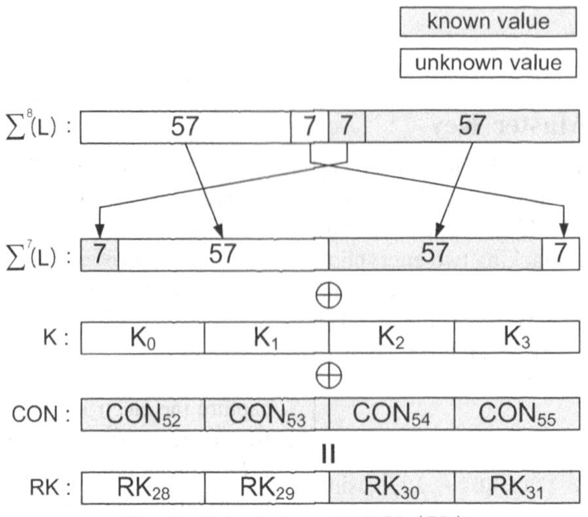

Fig. 3: Calculation of $WK_2(K_2)$

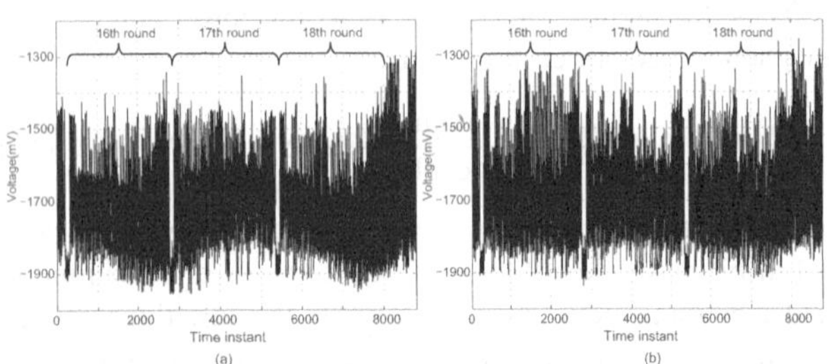

Fig. 4: Measured traces of the last three rounds encryption (a) Power trace, (b) Power trace with a LPF

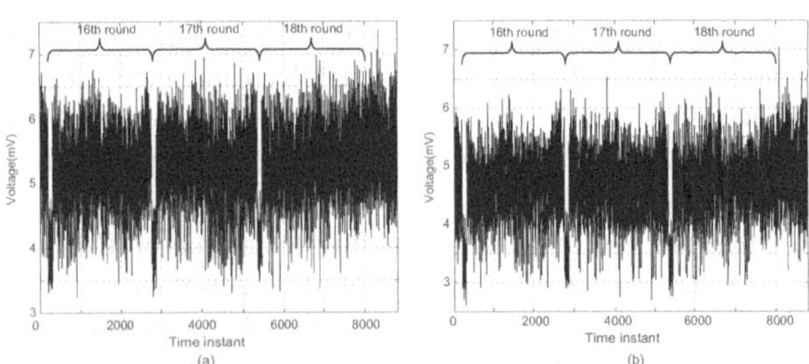

Fig. 5: Measured traces of the last three rounds encryption (a) Electromagnetic trace, and (b) Electromagnetic trace with a LPF

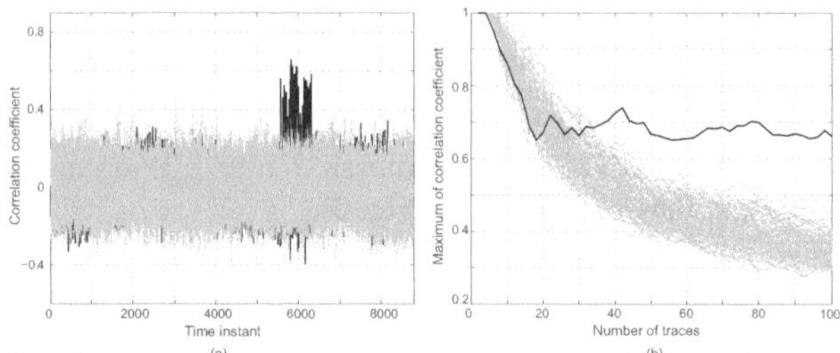

Fig. 6: Result of $RK_{34}[0-7]$ using power traces (a) Correlation coefficient using 100 traces, and (b) Transitions of correlation coefficient

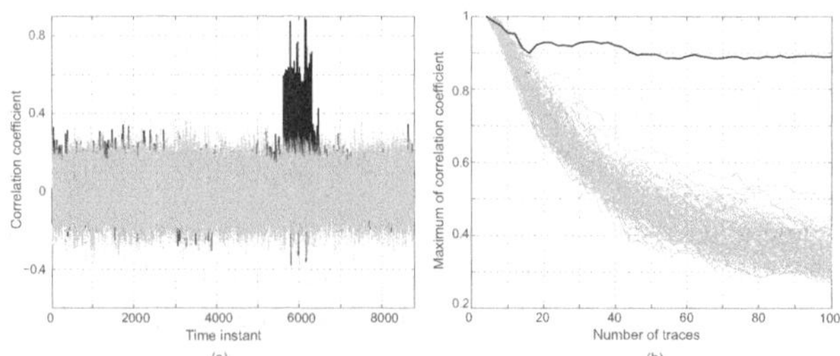

Fig. 7: Result of $RK_{34}[0-7]$ using power traces with a LPF (a) Correlation coefficient using 100 traces, and (b) Transitions of correlation coefficient

labeled (b) depict maximum of the correlation coefficient transitions according to the number of traces used in key retrieval. The results yield the minimum number of traces needed to discover the subkey. For example, we can extract $RK_{34}[0-7]$ with fewer than 40 power traces (Fig. 6 (b)).

Each of the round keys are composed of four 8-bit subkeys. Therefore, the total number of our target subkeys is 24, because each round has two round keys. We investigated the minimum number of traces to retrieve each of the subkeys. Figure 10 represents the classification rates of each trace set: power, power with a LPF, electromagnetic, and electromagnetic with a LPF. The horizontal axis indicates the number of traces for subkey extraction, and the vertical axis shows a classification rate in percentage computed as follows:

$$R_i = \frac{N_i^{ck}}{24} \times 100, \tag{12}$$

where R_i and N_i^{ck} denote the classification rate and number of correctly estimated subkeys using i traces, respectively.

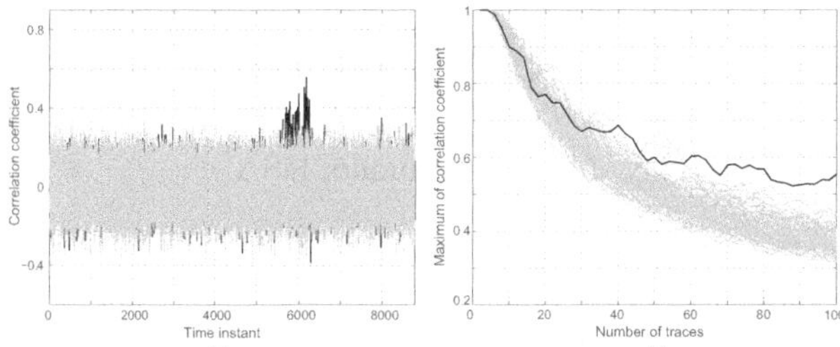

Fig. 8: Result of $RK_{34}[0-7]$ using EM traces (a) Correlation coefficient using 100 traces, and (b) Transitions of correlation coefficient

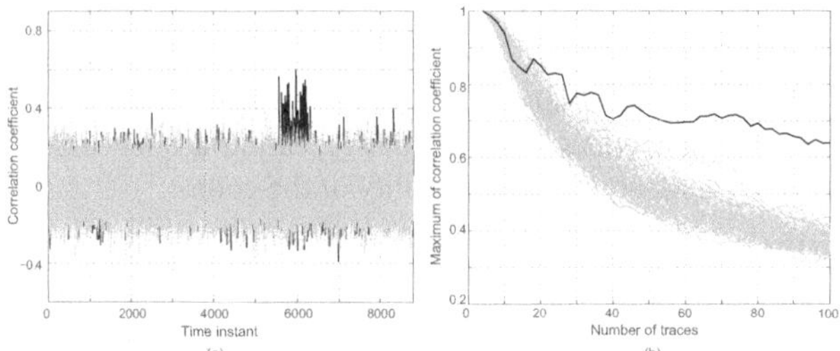

Fig. 9: Result of $RK_{34}[0-7]$ using EM traces with a LPF (a) Correlation coefficient using 100 traces, and (b) Transitions of correlation coefficient

If all 24 subkeys are successfully obtained, the classification rate is 100. As shown in the Fig. 10, the classification rate using the power trace with a LPF depicts the highest rate compared to the electromagnetic traces. We can assume that secret information leaks from the smart card can be easily detected by power consumption. However, the electromagnetic leakage often has more advantages when the adversary elaborately locate the position of the probe and utilize an electromagnetic shielding [4],[6]. In this paper, we don't use any the positioning system or tool to find the best spot for a measurement.

Moreover, the correlation coefficient can be increased by deploying a low-pass filter, especially when an adversary uses power traces. It is conceivable that the data-dependent components in power consumption have an extremely low frequency compared to electromagnetic emanation. Using a LPF in electromagnetic traces, the adversary could also have the ability to cutoff data-independent components which have high frequency. (Figs. 8 and 9)

5. Conclusion

In this paper, we presented power and electromagnetic analysis attacks on a software implementation of the 128-bit CLEFIA algorithm. We utilized the widely used the Pearson correlation as a distinguisher to find subkeys [2]. In addition, we presented a method to retrieve a 128-bit master key using the subkeys. We confirmed that a straightforward implementation of CLEFIA is vulnerable to power and

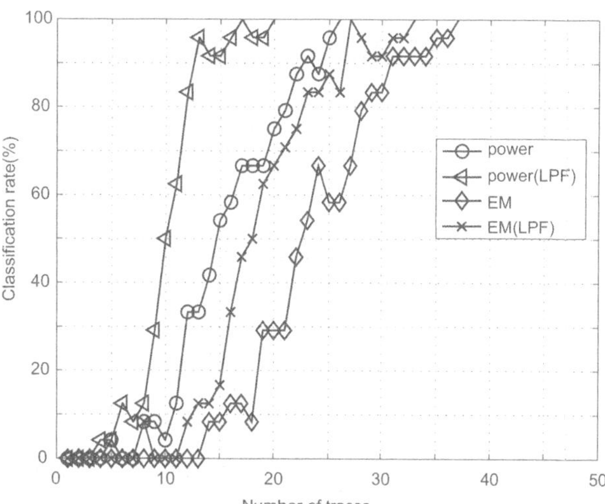

Fig. 10: Classification rates of each trace sets

electromagnetic analysis attacks. Our experimental results showed that an adversary can extract sufficient subkeys to retrieve a 128-bit master key by power traces with a low-pass filter using the lowest number of traces.

References

[1] P. Kocher, J. Jaffe, and B. Jun, "Differential power analysis," in *CRYPTO: Proceedings of Crypto*, 1999, pp. 388–397.

[2] Brier, Clavier, and Olivier, "Correlation power analysis with a leakage model," in *International Workshop on Cryptographic Hardware and Embedded Systems (CHES), LNCS*, 2004, pp. 16–29.

[3] J. Takahashi and T. Fukunaga, "Improved differential fault analysis on CLEFIA," in *Fault Diagnosis and Tolerance in Cryptography*, 2008.

[4] D. Agrawal, B. Archambeault, J. R. Rao, and P. Rohatgi, "The EM side-channel(s)," in *International Workshop on Cryptographic Hardware and Embedded Systems (CHES), LNCS*, 2002, pp. 29–45.

[5] S. Mangard, E. Oswald, and T. Popp, *Power Analysis Attacks: Revealing the Secrets of Smart Cards (Advances in Information Security)*. Springer-Verlag New York, Inc., 2007.

[6] E. Peeters, F.-X. Standaert, and J.-J. Quisquater, "Power and electromagnetic analysis: Improved model, consequences and comparisons," *Integration, the VLSI Journal*, vol. 40, no. 1, pp. 52–60, 2007.

[7] P. Kocher, "Timing attacks on implementations of diffie-hellman, RSA, DSS, and other systems," in *CRYPTO: Proceedings of Crypto*, 1996, pp. 104–113.

[8] X. Bai, L. Huang, and Y. Wang, "Differential power analysis attack on CLEFIA block cipher," in *International Conference on Computational Intelligence and Software Engineering*, 2009, pp. 1–4.

[9] H. Mala, M. Dakhilalian, and M. Shakiba, "Impossible differential attacks on 13-round CLEFIA-128," *Journal of Computer Science and Technology*, vol. 26, no. 4, 2005.

[10] C. Rebeiro and D. Mukhopadhyay, "Differential cache trace attack against CLEFIA," *IACR ePrint archive*, 2010.

[11] C. Tezcan, "The improbable differential attack: Cryptanalysis of reduced round CLEFIA," *Indocrypt*, pp. 1977–209, 2010.

[12] X. jie Zhao and T. Wang, "Improved cache trace attack on aes and clefia by considering cache miss and s-box misalignment," *IACR ePrint archive*, 2010.

[13] X. jie Zhao, T. Wang, and J. zhe Gao, "Multiple bytes differential fault analysis on clefia," *IACR ePrint archive*, 2010.

[14] Sony Corporation, "The 128-bit blockcipher CLEFIA algorithm specification," *[Online]*, 2007, available: http://www.sony.co.jp/Products/cryptography/clefia/download/data/clefia-spec-1.0.pdf.

Prime Base, Prime Moduli PRN Generator

Intelligence and Information Systems, Raytheon Company, Aurora, Colorado, USA

Contact Author - Palak Thakkar, 16800 E. CentreTech Parkway, Aurora, CO 80012
Palak.P.Thakkar@Raytheon.com, (720)-858-4260
Scott Imhoff, 16800 E. CentreTech Parkway, Aurora, CO 80012
Scott_Imhoff@Raytheon.com, (720)-858-4287
John Harms, 16800 E. CentreTech Parkway, Aurora, CO 80012
John_M_Harms@Raytheon.com, (720)-858-4677

IPCV'13

Abstract – *This paper presents an algorithm, which utilizes successive multiplications by a prime base and two stages of congruencing in order to generate a pseudorandom number (PRN) for use in encryption. The algorithm has advantages in one-way communication devices because only two prime numbers have to be known in order to decode the sequence. The efficiency of the algorithm stems from there being only a single multiplication tap. The code is determined by first generating the sequence in n of* $s_n = z^n (mod\ p)$ *where p and z are primes. Then* s_n *(mod 2) gives the binary sequence which can be used as a PRN code.*

Keywords: Linear Feedback Shift Register, Pseudorandom Number, Prime Base, Prime Moduli

1 Introduction

This paper presents a new, innovative, and efficient pseudorandom noise (PRN) generator. The PRN code bits are generated with successive multiplications using a prime base and two stages of congruence.

PRN codes are considered "pseudorandom" because the sequence appears to be random. PRN is not actually random as it is completely known at the time of modulation. PRN has several major characteristics: PRN must be deterministic, meaning that the subscriber station must be able independently generate the code that matches the base station code. PRN must have the statistical properties of white noise, so that it appears random to a listener without prior knowledge of the code. The cross-correlation between any two sets of PRN code must be small. The PRN code must also have a long period.

The problem with generating PRN codes is in order to correlate the arriving signal the receiver often needs to possess a long reference code along with complex circuitry. If there is any error in the code, the correlation inner product can peak at the wrong sample, or if decoding, the decoding can break down. Some PRN codes may contain repeating sequences, which can hurt the orthogonality of the code.

There is a theorem in number theory that says that if p is a prime and (z, p) = 1, then the period is p – 1 in the sequence $s(n) = z^n \bmod(p)$. Thus two examples are shown in Figure 1.

7^n(mod 13)	7^n(mod 17)
7	7
10	15
5	3
9	4
11	11
12	9
6	12
3	16
8	10
4	2
2	14
(1)	13
7	6
10	8
5	5
9	(1)
11	7
12	15
6	3
3	4

Figure 1: Two examples of how $s(n) = z^n \bmod(p)$ have period p-1.

A PRN code can be generated by taking the s(n) modulo 2. An example of this is presented in Figure 2. Here the PRN code is very short; however, we can generate longer PRN codes by using larger primes to get longer periods.

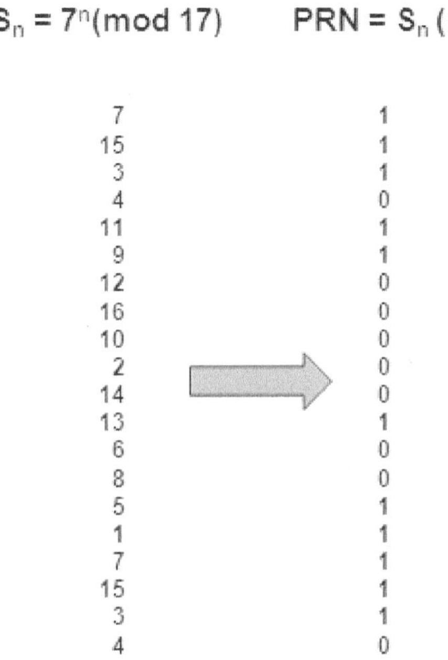

Figure 2. Apply the mod 2 operator to get a binary PRN code.

2 Linear Feedback Shift Registers

PRN generation is currently done by employing linear feedback shift registers (LSFR), powered by a transmitter clock. These shift registers are a row of cell initialized by a specified bit pattern. With each clock cycle, the contents of certain cells are extracted and submitted to a modulo-2 adder. The design of linear code registers can be described by the following polynomial:

$$1 + X^1 + X^2 + \cdots + X^i \quad (1)$$

The output is sometimes taken to be the contents of a particular cell, or the result of the modulo 2 addition. The problem of determining which cells should be tapped can be solved by considering the formal power series where the coefficients are the terms of the desired sequence. This power series must then be manipulated into a ratio of polynomials in lowest terms, where the coefficients of the denominator polynomial are the taps of choice.

LSFRs are used in PRN generation because of their ease of construction, long periods, and uniformly distributed output streams. One of the downsides of LSFRs is because they are linear, they lead to easy cryptanalysis.

An example of a LSFR is given in Figure 3.

3 Prime Base, Prime Moduli PRN Generator

The PRN generator proposed in this paper is summarized in Figure 4. The PRN code is generated by successive multiplications by a prime base and two stages of congruencing. The first congruence uses a large prime modulus and the second congruence uses a modulus 2 operation. Because the PRN code is completely determined by the prime base and first prime modulus, or a tuple, it is advantages for one-way communication in that very little information has to be retained by the receiver. The only piece of information that needs to be retained by the receiver is the tuple.

The PRN Prime Base, Prime Moduli PRN Generator along with the advantage of simplifying the information keeping also maintains good orthogonality by providing against the occurrence of repeating sub-sequences: In the first congruence stage there is a check to see if the product is congruent to unity in order to prevent the occurrence of a repeating sub-sequence.

Another important property of the Prime Base, Prime Moduli PRN Generator is by using a prime number as the modulus in the first stage of the congruence and another prime number for the base tends to increase the period of the sequence, allowing for longer orthogonal codes.

4 Results of Algorithm

Prime Base, Prime Moduli PRN Generator resulted in autocorrelation signal to noise ratios as high as 20.6 decibels. LSFRs typically have lower values. Using a typical LSFR of length 30, the SNR is 3.0 dB. Using the 3.0 dB as a measuring stick, Prime Base, Prime Moduli PRN Generator equals or exceeds 3.0 dB in 78.01% of cases for the first 100 prime bases and the first 300 prime moduli. Figure 5 shows the SNR plot for a typical LSFR. Figure 6 shows a case of when Prime Base, Prime Moduli PRN Generator exceeds the LSFR SNR.

5 Application of Prime Base, Prime Moduli PRN Generator

There are several identified applications of the Prime Base, Prime Moduli PRN Generator. The applications provided in this section are not exhaustive.

One important application is for the Federal Aviation Administration (FAA). The FAA can allow airport unique code with one way transmission to aircraft for better integrity, positioning, and ease of implementation to the fleet. The aircraft receives only information then can report through normal channels more accurate position, allowing aircrafts to fly closer to reduce airport congestion in the air space.

Another potential application is use in localized GPS accuracies and one way communication. Receivers would only need to know two prime numbers. The ability to send messages without complex and energy intensive devices would be useful for remote or rugged applications.

The algorithm would also be beneficial to increase the fidelity of secure banking between individuals and mobile devices.

6 Conclusion

The Prime Base, Prime Moduli PRN Generator uses single multiplication by a prime base and two stages of congruencing to generate each bit of PRN code, which allows for implementation using a single tap as opposed to multiple taps in other devices.

Because the PRN code is completely determined by the prime base and the first prime modulus, demodulation becomes easier in the case of one way transmission.

In order to remove the possibility of the occurrence of repeating sub-sequences, there is a check in the first congruence stage to check to see if the product is congruent to unity.

Finally, the Prime Base, Prime Moduli PRN Generator is able to increase the period of the sequence by using a prime number as the modulus in the first stage of the congruence and another prime number for the base. The increase in the period allows for longer codes.

7 References

Dudley, Underwood, *Elementary Number Theory*, 2nd Ed., W. H. Freeman and Company, 1978.

Kaplan, Elliot and Christopher Hegarty. *Understanding GPS: Principles and Applications, 2 ed.* Norwood: Archtech House, Inc., 2006.

Simon, Marvin K., Jim K. Omura, Robert A. Schulz, and Barry K. Levitt. *Spread Spectrum Communications Handbook, Electronic Edition.* McGraw-Hill Engineering, 2002.

Köhne, Anja, and Michael Wößner. "GPS Explained: Transmitted GPS Signals." *Kowama*. N.p., 19 Apr. 2009. Web. 01 Oct. 2012.

"Pseudo-Random Number Generation Routine for the MAX765x Microprocessor." *Maxim Integrated.* Maxim Integrated, 25 Sept. 2002. Web. 10 Feb. 2013.

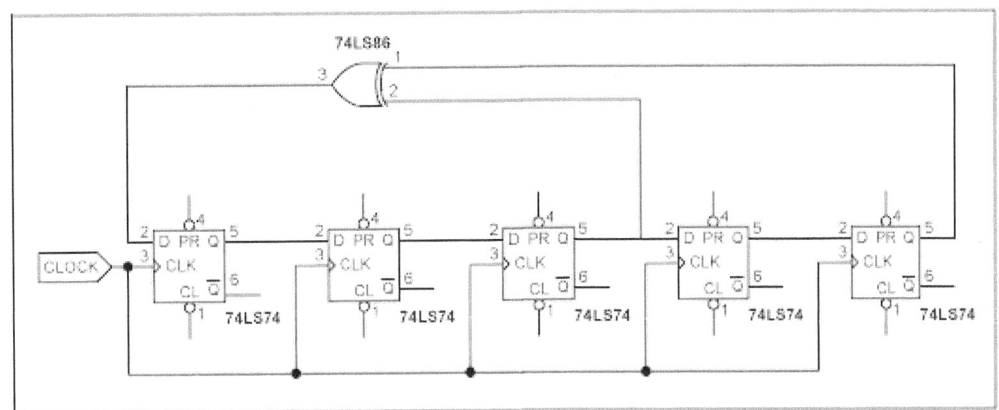

Figure 3: Typical LSFR

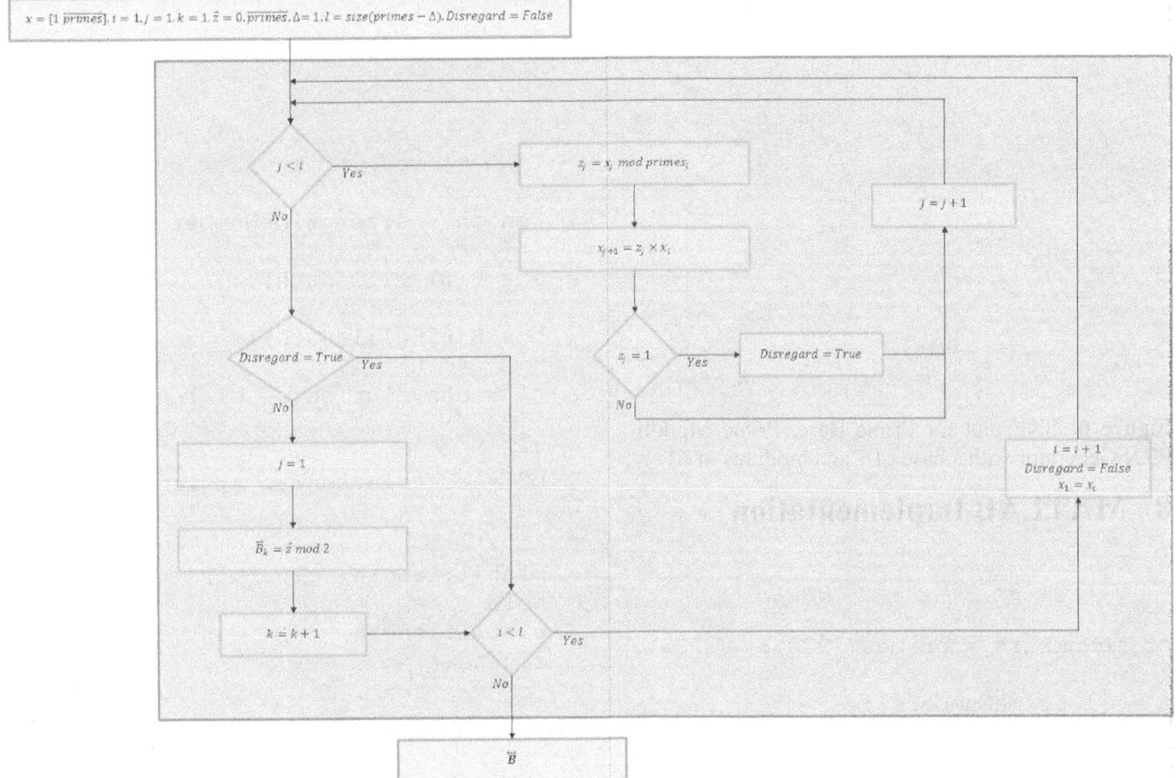

Figure 4: Prime Base, Prime Moduli PRN Generator algorithm

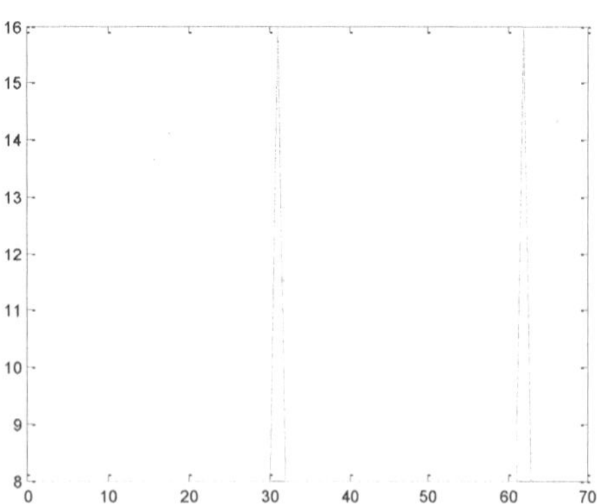

Figure 5: Typical LSFR plot

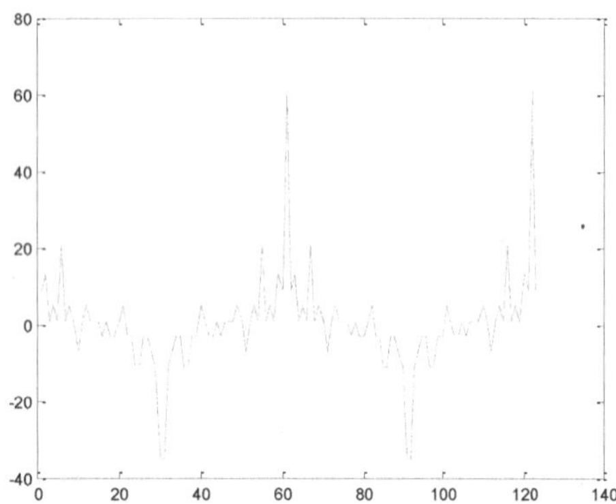

Figure 6: SNF plot for Prime Base, Prime Moduli PRN Generator with a base of 7 and modulus of 61

8 MATLAB Implementation

```
% Initialize variables
% Initialize the first n prime
numbers
primeNumbers = primes(7920);
% Initialize x
x = [1 primeNumbers];
% Create z array
z = zeros(1,size(primeNumbers,2));
% Choose a delta
delta = 1;
% Initialize counter variable
k = 1;
% Initialize loop size
l = size(primeNumbers,2) - delta;

% Generate PRNs
for i = 1:l
    % Reset disregard variable
    disregard = 0;
    % Reset x variable
    x(1) = x(i);
    % Create congruence series
    for j = 1:i-1
        z(j) = mod(x(j),...
        primeNumbers(i));
        x(j+1) = z(j) * x(i);
        if (z(j) == 1)
            % Disregard if series
            is repeating
            disregard = 1;
        end
    end

    if (disregard == 0)
        % Convert series to binary
        B(k,:) = mod(z, 2);
        % Increase counter variable
        k = k + 1;
    end
end

% % Determine Correlation
% Number of data points in
correlation
length = size(primeNumbers,2);
% First array
a = B(677,1:length);
% Second array
b = B(678,1:length);
% Convolution of two arrays
c1 = convolution(a, b, length);
% Convolution of one array with
itself
c2 = convolution(a, a, length);

% Plot Correlation
plot(1:length, c1, 'g')
hold on
plot(1:length, c2, 'm')
legend('cross
correlation','autocorrelation')
```

Verifiable Symmetric Searchable Encryption for Multiple Groups of Users

Zachary A. Kissel and Jie Wang
Department of Computer Science, University of Massachusetts Lowell, Lowell, MA, USA

Abstract— *We present an efficient method for providing group level hierarchical access control over keywords in a multi-user searchable encryption scheme under the Semi-Honest-but-Curious model. We achieve this using a shared global index stored on the cloud and efficient key-regression techniques on the client side. Our method extends the multi-user searchable encryption model of Curtmola et. al. [1] to multiple groups of users. Moreover, our method provides verifiability of search results, and we show that our system is non-adaptively secure.*

Keywords: Clouds, Cryptography, Search methods

1. Introduction

Cloud storage provides a convenient platform for users to store data that can be accessed from anywhere at anytime without maintaining a storage infrastructure. However, cloud storage is inherently insecure. To use storage services provided by a cloud, users would need to trust, at least implicitly, the provider. There have been attempts to alleviate the need for this trust through cryptographic methods. Trivially, one may encrypt each file before uploading it to the cloud. This approach, however, would significantly hinder searching over the data, causing a loss in critical functionality.

This is where Symmetric Searchable Encryption (SSE) comes into play. SSE allows users to offload search queries to the cloud, which is responsible for returning the encrypted files that match the search queries (also encrypted). Most previous work was focused on keyword search [2], [3], [4], [5], [6], [7], while some more recent work has considered searching on phrases [8].

Searching over encrypted data involves a number of encrypted files stored on an untrusted cloud. The client issues an encrypted search query to the cloud, and wants the cloud to return the results of the search query without learning the query itself. Moreover, the client wants assurance that the cloud is faithfully executing the search. When multiple users are present, data owners want control over who may search for which piece of information. Any mechanism for searching over encrypted data with multiple users must provide these security guarantees.

Early SSE systems typically use an index mechanism under the Honest-but-Curious (HBC) cloud model. This approach constructs an index of keywords contained in a document, encrypts the index in a special way, and associates the index with a document or a set of documents. The documents themselves are encrypted with a standard symmetric encryption algorithm. The encryption over the index is constructed in such a way that the cloud can successfully apply queries over the documents when given a piece of trapdoor information. Specifically, with the trapdoor, the cloud can determine which files contain the queried keyword. Some systems return a copy of the encrypted file, while others return just a list of document identifiers. In the later case, the client must request each file individually.

Our main contribution is the construction of an efficient multi-user searchable encryption system with group level hierarchical access control. We further demonstrate how to make our group membership dynamic while still preserving security. We achieve the security guarantees under the Semi-Honest-but-Curious (SHBC) model [2] (which includes the HBC model). In the SHBC model, the cloud honestly stores encrypted files of the data providers, executes a fraction of the search operations (or the whole operations), and returns the search results. The cloud, however, may try to learn the underlying plaintext of the encrypted data. SHBC is more realistic than HBC, for it allows a cloud to limit the amount of bandwidth and computating power when handling queries. This is at odds with the desires of the clients to have complete and accurate results. Hence, we add to the model that an SHBC cloud will respond to all queries even if it may not do so honestly. Thus, the users need to verify that the search results are accurate and complete. To meet this requirement we demonstrate a verification method for our system. Moreover, our system is both space and time efficient for the client as well as the cloud provider, and we show that our system is non-adaptively secure. Our work improves on existing searchable encryption work for one group of users [1] to multiple groups of users.

The paper is organized as follows: We describe previous work on searchable symmetric encryption in Section 2. In Section 3 we define a system model for searchable encryptions for multiple groups of users. We provide background information in Section 4 needed for constructing our system, which is presented in Section 5. We conclude the paper in Section 6 and provide proof in the appendix that our system is non-adaptively secure.

2. Previous Work

Research on encrypted search is either based on symmetric encryptions or asymmetric encryptions, first studied by, respectively, Song et. al. [5] and Boneh et. al. [9]. We will only consider symmetric searchable encryption in this paper.

Early approaches to the encrypted search problem made use of the Bloom filter [10], a probabilistic data structure used as an index for the keywords in each encrypted file. These include, for example, Goh's indexed based system [7]. The closely related system of Chang and Mitzenmacher uses a deterministic indexed based system, similar to a Bloom filter, for keyword search secure under the HBC model [6]. Goh's system supports extra features not presented in Chang and Mitzenmacher's system, and does so under a slightly weaker model of security.

These models, however, do not guarantee even a non-adaptive form of security. Non-adaptive security provides privacy when all search queries are issued at one time. It was not until the work of Curtmola, Garay, Kamara, and Ostrovsky [1] that a rigorous and exact security definition was given for SSE. They provided formal definitions for non-adaptive, respectively adaptive, indistiguishability notions and they showed a reduction to a form of non-adaptive, respectively adaptive, semantic security. Briefly, in non-adaptive security, privacy is only guaranteed when clients generate queries at one time. In the case of adaptive security, clients are guaranteed privacy even if they generate queries as a function of previous search outcomes. Until the work of Curtmola et. al. all systems were secure in the non-adaptive sense in the best case.

Tang et. al. [8] presented a two-phase protocol to handle phrase search over encrypted data. In the first phase, the cloud retrieves the document identifiers for documents that contain all the words in the phrase provided by the client, and returns the identifiers to the client. This phase relies on a global index shared among all documents in the cloud. In the second phase, the client sends a query and a list of document identifiers to the cloud. The cloud searches for an exact phrase match for each document in the per document index and returns to the client the actual encrypted documents that match the phrase. Their protocol, however, only provides security under the HBC adversarial model.

There were attempts to work on more realistic cloud models than the HBC model. In particular, Chai and Gong [2] studied verifiable symmetric searchable encryption under the SHBC model, which allows the client to verify that the cloud has returned the correct list of document identifiers. They achieved this through the use of tries [11].

3. Multi-User Searchable Encryption

Let $\mathcal{D} = \{D_1, D_2, \ldots, D_n\}$ denote a collection of n encrypted documents in the cloud storage, Σ the alphabet over which characters from strings are drawn, and $\Delta = \{w_1, w_2, \ldots, w_d\}$ a dictionary of d words drawn from Σ^*. We associate with each document in collection $\mathcal{D}$ an number we call the index. The function is denoted by id : $\mathcal{D} \to \mathbb{Z}$. Let $\mathcal{D}(w_i)$ denote the set of document identifiers that contain the word $w_i \in \Delta$, and $\mathcal{G} = \{g_i \,|g_i \subset \mathcal{U}\}$ an indexable set of groups of users from the set of users $\mathcal{U}$.

For cryptographic primitives we denote a symmetric encryption algorithm by the tuple $(G, \mathcal{E}, D)$, where G takes a security parameter and generates a key of the correct size, $\mathcal{E}$ is an encryption algorithm that takes a key and a message as input and outputs a cipher text; and D is the decryption algorithm of $\mathcal{E}$. In addition we rely on both Pseudo-random Permutations and Pseudo-random Functions. We also need a keyed hash function $\mathcal{F} : \{0,1\}^{\lambda} \times \{0,1\}^* \to \{0,1\}^z$, where z is some security parameter.

3.1 Model

Curtmola et. al. [1] defined a multi-user SSE (M-SSE) system as follows:

Definition 1: (Multi-User Searchable Symmetric Encryption (M-SSE)) MSSE is a collection of six polynomial-time algorithms MKeygen, MBuildIndex, AddUser, RevokeUser, MTrapdoor, and MSearch, where

- MKeygen (1^k) is a probabilistic key generation algorithm run by the owner O. It takes a security parameter k as input and returns an owner secret key K_O .
- MBuildIndex $(K_O, \mathcal{D})$ is run by O to construct indexes. It takes K_O and $\mathcal{D}$ as inputs, and returns an index $\mathcal{I}$.
- AddUser (K_O, U) is run by O whenever O wishes to add a user to the group. It takes K_O and a user U as inputs, and returns U's secret key K_U.
- RevokeUser (K_O, U) is run by O whenever O wishes to revoke a user from G. It takes K_O and a user U as inputs, and revokes the user's searching privileges.
- MTrapdoor (K_U, w) is run by a user (including O) to generate a trapdoor for a given word w. It takes a user U's secret key K_U and a word w as inputs, and returns a trapdoor $T_{U,w}$.
- MSearch $(\mathcal{I}_{\mathcal{D}}, T_{U,w})$ is run by the server S to search for the documents in $\mathcal{D}$ that contain word w. It takes the index $\mathcal{I}_{\mathcal{D}}$ for collection $\mathcal{D}$ and the trapdoor $T_{U,w}$ for word w as inputs, and returns $\mathcal{D}(w)$ if user $U \in$ G and $\perp$ if user $U \notin$ G.

We note that the group controlled searches presented in [1] only provides a single dynamic group. They showed that their system is non-adaptively secure, and that evicted users cannot perform a search, provided that they cannot collude with non-evicted users.

We extend this model to support multiple groups of users. Let $\mathcal{G} = \{g_i \,|g_i \subset \mathcal{U}\}$ be an indexable set of groups of users from the set of users $\mathcal{U}$. We associate with each group of users, g_i, a dictionary, Δ_i, of keywords allowed to be searched for. We further require that Δ_i contain all words in Δ_j for $j < i$. We define our extended model as follows:

Definition 2: (Hierarchical Access Controlled SSE (HAC-SSE)) Let $\mathcal{O}$ be the owner of a document collection $\mathcal{D}$ and $\mathcal{G}$ an indexable set of groups of users from the set of users $\mathcal{U}$. HAC-SSE is a set of polynomial time algorithms HKeygen, HBuildIndex, HAddUser, HRevokeUser, HTrapdoor, and HSearch, where HKeygen $(1^k, n)$ is the same as MKeygen (1^k).

- MBuildIndex $(K_O, \mathcal{D}, \mathcal{G}, \{\Delta_1, \Delta_2, \ldots, \Delta_{|\mathcal{G}|}\})$ is run by O to construct indexes. It takes, as input, the owner's secret key K_O, a document collection $\mathcal{D}$, the set of groups $\mathcal{G}$, and the set of dictionaries, $\{\Delta_1, \Delta_2, \ldots, \Delta_{|\mathcal{G}|}\}$. The function returns an index, $\mathcal{I}$, that forces the hierarchical access control.

- AddUser (K_O, U, g) is run by O whenever O wishes to add a user U to the group $g \in \mathcal{G}$. It takes the owner's secret key K_O, a user, and the group as input. The function then returns the group key to the user.
- RevokeUser (K_O, U, g) *(optional)* is run by O whenever O wishes to revoke a user U from group $g \in \mathcal{G}$. It takes the owner's secret key K_O, a user U, and a group g as inputs. The function then revokes the user's searching privileges.
- MTrapdoor (K_U, w) is run by a user (including O) to generate a trapdoor for a given word. It takes a user U's secret key K_U and a word $w \in \Delta_i$ as inputs, and returns a trapdoor $T_{U,w}$.
- MSearch $(\mathcal{I}_\mathcal{D}, T_{U,w})$ is run by the server S in order to search for the documents in $\mathcal{D}$ that contain word w. It takes the index $\mathcal{I}_\mathcal{D}$ for collection $\mathcal{D}$ and the trapdoor $T_{U,w}$ for word w in some dictionary Δ_g as inputs, and returns $\mathcal{D}(w)$ if user U belongs into a specific $g \in \mathsf{G}$ and $\perp$ if user $U \notin \mathsf{G}$.

For HAC-SSE to be secure we must have the following property satisfied:

Property 1: A user $u \in g_i$ can not, successfully, query for any word $w \in \Delta_j$ for all $j > i$ with more than a negligible probability.

4. Background

4.1 Key Regression

Our system relies on a construct by Fu et. al. called Key Regression [12], originally desinged to allow a content owner to manage dynamic group membership in a Content Distribution Network (CDN). The idea is that a content owner encrypts a document, for a group of users, with a key K_i at time i. All users belonging to the access group are given a member state stm_i, which allows them to derive the key K_i. At time j if a member of the group is evicted, then all documents will be re-encrypted with a new key K_j. All users remaining in the group are given a state stm_j which can be used to derive key K_j. They can now forget about stm_i. This can be done, due to the property of key regression that from state stm_j one can derive all previous states (and thus all previous keys). However, it is impossible for a user possessing state stm_j to accurately predict future states. We call $(i, \mathsf{stm}_1, \mathsf{stm}_2, \ldots, \mathsf{stm}_n)$ a publisher state. Formally, Key Regression [12] is defined as follows:

Definition 3: (Key Regression (KR)) A KR scheme consists of four polynomial time algorithms setup, wind, unwind, and keyder, where

- setup $(1^\lambda, n)$ returns a publisher state stp; where 1^λ (in unary) is a security parameter and n is an integer representing the number of evictions the system should support. This algorithm may be probabilistic.
- wind (stp) returns a tuple $(\mathsf{stp}', \mathsf{stm}_i)$, where stp' is the new publisher state and stm_i is the new member state. This algorithm may be probabilistic, and may return $(\perp, \perp)$ if the number of winds has exceeded the n used in setup.
- unwind (stm_j) returns the previous member state stm_i for $i < j$. If previous member states do not exist, the algorithm returns $\perp$.
- keyder (stm_i) returns a key K_i in some keyspace.

These algorithms can be based on the SHA-1 hash function, the AES symmetric cipher, the RSA public key cipher, and a generic construction based on any Forward-Secure Pseudorandom Generator. For our purposes we will simply use Key Regression as a black box.

4.2 Tries

Our keyword indexing mechanism uses a data structure called trie, devised by Fredkin in [11], It supports two main operations Insert and Search, both take a word $w \in \Sigma^*$ as input. A trie is a $|\Sigma \cup \{\$\}|$-ary tree, where each node of the tree is labeled with an element of $\Sigma \cup \{\$\}$. Moreover, a root-to-leaf path through the tree denotes a word $w \in \Sigma^*$, which is terminated by a special character $\$ \notin \Sigma$.

The Insert appends a \$ to the input w. Starting at the root node of the tree, we use w to create a path. The first time we reach a node that does not have the current corresponding letter in w, we add a subpath as a child to the current node. Moreover, we label this subpath appropriately with the remaining letters of w, terminating the path with a \$.

The Search function uses input w as a path through the tree. The function first adds a \$ to the path. If that path ends in a leaf, i.e., the path is a root-to-leaf path, the search is successful. Otherwise, the word does not exist in the dictionary.

In what follows we will denote a trie by T and a node by $T_{i,j}$, where i is the depth of the node and j the left to right placement of the node. We will denote the access to values stored in the node of T by $T_{i,j}[s]$, where s denotes the name of the field.

5. Construction of HAC-SSE and Security

Our system associates with each group $g_i \in \mathcal{G}$ a member state stm_i from a key regression system and a dictionary $\Delta_i \subset \Delta$. The dictionary Δ_i contains all the words in dictionary Δ_j for all $j < i$. Recall that in Key Regression, given a member state stm_i one can derive previous member states stm_j for all $j < i$. We will ensure that members of group g_i can search for any keyword in dictionary Δ_i, but not in dictionary Δ_k with $k > i$.

Our index structure, $\mathcal{I}$, is based on idea of secure trie [2]. The root to leaf paths through our trie, unlike the trie in [2], are secured in such a way that the hierarchical access policy is enforced. We insert into the trie the words in the set of dictionaries $\{\Delta_1, \Delta_2, \ldots, \Delta_{|\mathcal{G}|}\}$. Once this process is complete, we annotate the trie with the keys used to secure each letter along the root-to-leaf path. We start by annotating every root-to-leaf path in Δ_1 with K_1. Note that in a trie, a word is a root-to-leaf path. Starting at $i = 2$ we iteratively apply the following process for each word $w \in (\Delta_i - \Delta_{i-1})$. Walk through the trie according to w and look at each annotation. If the node is un-annotated, then annotate the node with key K_i (see Figure 1 for a completely annotated trie). We use a completely annotated trie for each dictionary Δ_i to

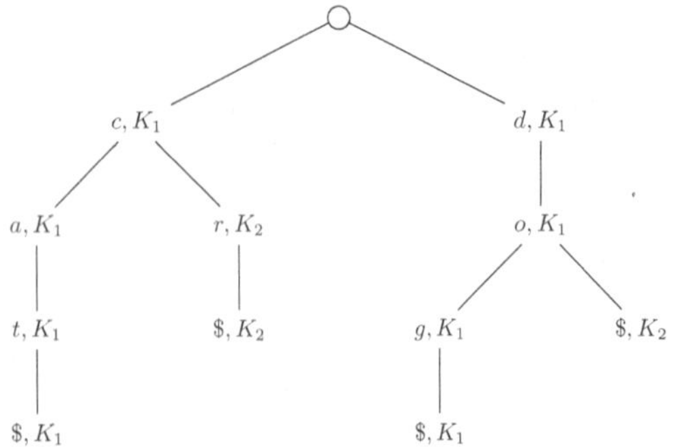

Fig. 1: An annotated trie for dictionaries $\Delta_1 = \{\text{cat}, \text{dog}\}$ and $\Delta_2 = \{\text{car}, \text{do}\} \cup \Delta_1$

generate a perfect hash table $\mathcal{H}_i$ with hash function h_i. Each entry in $\mathcal{H}_i$ contains a "Key Schedule" that represents what key is used to secure each node along the root-to-leaf path for the hash of the corresponding word. Finally, the trie is walked and each node is secured, using a keyed hash function, according to its key annotation. This new value is the hash of the value the node represents together with the hash of the path to the nodes predecessor. After a node is secured, the key annotation is removed (see Figure 2). Though we did not explicitly outline how, we note that every leaf node of the trie contains a list of document identifiers that denote the documents that contain the word specified by the given root-to-leaf path. The trie, which is the index $\mathcal{I}$, is then sent to the cloud.

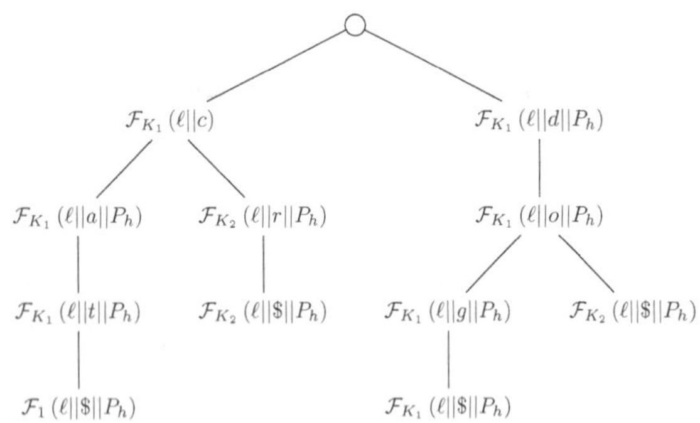

Fig. 2: Final trie based on Figure 1. The values P_h denotes the parents hash value and ℓ denotes the current nodes level.

When a user (call him Bob) $\in g_j$ wants to search for a specific word $w \in \Delta_j$, Bob looks up the appropriate entry $\mathcal{H}_j[h_j(w)]$, and determines the keys used to encrypt the root-to-leaf path specified by w. Bob then encrypts each character of w according to this "key schedule" and submits the encrypted query to the cloud. Upon receiving a query, the cloud uses the encrypted path to trace through the trie. If the cloud reaches a leaf node in the trie, then it returns the document identifiers to Bob; otherwise, it returns $\perp$ to Bob.

Placing our system in the formal model of Section 3.1 we achieve the system in Figure 3.

5.1 Security Guarantees of HAC-SSE

We first note that each document is encrypted separately. This means that nothing is leaked about the encrypted documents except their sizes. The privacy preserving queries are a collection of hashes of prefixes with confidentiality protected by the underlying hash function. The only information leaked by a query is the length of the query.

Turning our attention to confidentiality of the encrypted trie, we observe that each node contains a hashed value r_3. We know that, although it is improbable for an attacker to derive the original value from r_3, it is possible that the attacker will try to learn statistical information regarding r_3 when considering all the nodes in T. We show that this is impossible using the following theorem on the uniqueness of hash values in nodes of a trie [2].

Theorem 1 (Uniqueness of Node Values): Given a trie T of depth L with $C \geq \frac{|\Sigma|^{L+1}-1}{|\Sigma|-1}$, we have

$$\Pr\left(T_{j,q}[r_3] = T_{\hat{j},\hat{q}}[r_3] \,|\, (q,j) \neq (\hat{q},\hat{j})\right) \approx 1 - \left(\frac{2^z-1}{2^z}\right)^{\frac{C(C-1)}{2}} \quad (1)$$

Theorem 1 holds when the prefix path values for the nodes are computed with the same keyed hash function. While our system has $|\mathcal{G}|$ possible keyed hash functions, due to the construction of keyed cryptographic hash functions, the theorem still holds.

It is straightforward to see that Figure 3 satisfies Property 1, because no users, given a member state stm_i, can determine stm_j for any $j > i$ with more than a negligible probability.

We can further prove that our system is non-adaptively secure, stated in Theorem 2, by constructing search patterns appropriately. The detailed proof of this theorem is given in Appendix.

Theorem 2: The construction shown in Figure 3 is non-adaptively secure.

6. Adding Revocation and Verification

We extend our construction in Section 5 to include verification of search results and revocation of access. By adding verification we can place our system under the SHBC model. To do this we must modify MBuildIndex by augmenting the nodes of the trie in a fashion similar to the methods used in [2]. We also extend our model to contain a polynomial-time function MVerify to verify that the cloud has returned the results correctly. To add revocation of access we make use of the revocation method of Curtmola et. al. [1].

To add verification to our system we add a set, $\mathcal{B}$, of $|\mathcal{G}|$ bitmaps of size $|\Sigma|$ to every node of the trie construction algorithm given in Figure 3. We require that the bitmap $b_i \in \mathcal{B}$ represent all children reachable by a member of group $i \in \mathcal{G}$. Under step 5 for the BuildIndex algorithm we add verification tags to each node according to the algorithm given in figure 4.

HKeygen $(1^k, n)$ Set up a key regression system, $\mathcal{KR} = (\mathsf{setup}, \mathsf{wind}, \mathsf{unwind}, \mathsf{keyder})$. Set $\mathsf{stp} = \mathsf{setup}(1^k, n)$, construct the hierarchical dictionaries, $\Delta_1, \Delta_2, \ldots, \Delta_n$, and return $K_O = (\mathsf{stp}, \{\Delta_1, \Delta_2, \ldots, \Delta_n\}, \mathcal{KR})$.

MBuildIndex $(K_O, \mathcal{D}, \mathcal{G}, \{\Delta_1, \Delta_2, \ldots, \Delta_{|\mathcal{G}|}\})$

1) Create a full $|\Sigma|$-ary tree.
2) Set $(r_0, r_1, r_2) = (0, 0, 0)$ for every node, $T_{0,0}[r_1] = 0$, and $q_0 = 0$.
3) For each word $\mathbf{w} = (w_1, w_2, \ldots)$ in document D_i (where $1 \leq i \leq n$)
   a) Find an ℓ such that $w \in \Delta_\ell$, if one doesn't not exist skip the word.
   b) For $j = 1$ to $|\mathbf{w}|$
      i) Find a $q_j \in [q_{j-1} \times |\Sigma| + 1, (1 + q_{j-1}) \times |\Sigma|]$, where $T_{j,q_j}[r_1] = w_j$. If such a q_j can't be found, find a q_j such that T_{j,q_j} is empty and set $T_{j,q_j}[r_1] = w_j$ and $T_{j,q_j}[r_0] = \ell$.
   c) Find an appropriate $q_{j+1} \in [q_j \times |\Sigma| + 1, (1 + q_j) \times |\Sigma|]$ at level $j + 1$ such that $T_{j+1,q_{j+1}} =$ "\$". If one can not be found, find a q_{j+1} such that $T_{j+1,q_{j+1}}$ is empty and set its r_1 value to "\$" and r_2's value to ℓ. Where $\$ \notin \Sigma$. Add $\mathsf{mem} \leftarrow \mathsf{mem}||\mathsf{id}(D_i)$, since $\mathbf{w} \in D_i$ to node $T_{j+1,q_{j+1}}$.
4) From T build the set of perfect hash tables $\{\mathcal{H}_i | 1 \leq i \leq |\mathcal{G}|\}$.
5) For each node T_{j,q_j} in T
   a) If T_{j,q_j} is a leaf node, $\mathsf{mem} \leftarrow \mathsf{mem}||\mathcal{F}_{\mathsf{keyder}(\mathsf{stm}_1)}(\mathsf{mem})$.
   b) If T_{j,q_j} is not a leaf node, $T_{j,q_j}[r_3] = \mathcal{F}_{\mathsf{keyder}\left(\mathsf{stm}_{T_{j,q_j}[r_0]}\right)}(j||T_{j,q_j}[r_1]||\mathsf{parent}(T_{j,q_j})[r_3])$.
6) Pad all remaining r_3 fields in nodes with bit-strings of the same length as the other non-zero nodes of the trie. As well as clearing all values in r_0 and r_1.
7) Return $\mathcal{I} = (T, \{\mathcal{H}_i | 1 \leq i \leq |\mathcal{G}|\})$. The value, $\{\mathcal{H}_i | 1 \leq i \leq |\mathcal{G}|\}$ is given to the data owner and not the cloud.

HAddUser (K_O, U, g)

1) Parse K_O as stp.
2) If $1 \leq g \leq |\mathcal{G}|$, if not return $\perp$.
   a) set $\mathsf{newstp} = \mathsf{stp}$
   b) For $i = 1$ to g, $(\mathsf{newstp}, \mathsf{stm}) = \mathsf{wind}(\mathsf{newstp})$
3) Return $K_U = (\mathsf{stm}, \mathcal{H}_g)$.

HTrapdoor $(K_u, w = (w[1], w[2], \ldots))$

1) Parse K_u as $(\mathsf{stm}_g, \mathcal{H}_g)$.
2) Set $s = \mathcal{H}_g[h_g(w)]$ and $\mathsf{curstm} = \mathsf{stm}_g$, $\pi[0] = 0$, and $w[|w| + 1] =$ "\$".
3) For $j = 1$ to $|w| + 1$
   a) For $i = 1$ To $i < s[j]$, $\mathsf{curstm} = \mathsf{unwind}(\mathsf{curstm})$.
      i) If $\mathsf{curstm} = \perp$, return $\perp$.
   b) Set $\pi[j] = \mathcal{F}_{\mathsf{keyder}(\mathsf{curstm})}(j||w[j]||\pi[j - 1])$
4) Return the privacy preserving trapdoor $T_{u,w} = \pi$.

HSearch $(\mathcal{I}_\mathcal{D}, T_{U,w})$

1) Parse $T_{U,w}$ as $\pi[1 \ldots n]$ and set $q_0 = 0$.
2) For $j = 1$ to n
   a) Find a $q_j \in [q_{j-1} \times |\Sigma| + 1, (1 + q_{j-1}) \times |\Sigma|]$ such that $T_{j,q_j}[r_3] = \pi[j]$. If found, go back to top of loop, otherwise return $\perp$.
3) If T_{j,q_j} has no child, then return the document collection $T_{j,q_j}[r_2]$.

Fig. 3: A complete HAC-SSE system

To verify the results returned by the cloud we utilize the verification algorithm given in Figure 5. This algorithm is a slightly modified version of Verify in [2].

To handle the need for revocations in our basic system we again modify our construction. The idea is to use a traditional broadcast encryption system and a keyed pseudo-random permutation ϕ to manage group membership. Instead of sending trapdoor T_w to the cloud, we send $\phi(T_w)$. When the query arrives at the cloud, the cloud inverts the permutation (computes $\phi^{-1}(T_w)$) to recover the trapdoor T_w. To enable dynamic membership, this pseudo-random permutation is indexed by a key v. In [1] the value v is changed, via a broadcast encryption, each time a user leaves the system. In our system we will make use of a second Key Regression system. Recall that Key Regression allows for a content owner to share access to data with users. Moreover, it allows

1) For $y = 1$ To $|\mathcal{G}|$
   a) Set $T_{i,j}[r_4]$ as:

$$T_{i,j}[r_4] = T_{i,j}[r_4] || \mathcal{E}_{K_{\text{keyder}(\text{stm}_v)}}(b_y || T_{i,j}[r_3]) \quad (2)$$

Fig. 4: Modification to the BuildIndex algorithm to add verification support to the trie

HVerify $(w = (w_1, w_2, \ldots), \{\text{proof}_i | 1 \le i \le |w|\}, \pi)$:

1) Determine the key schedule s from the hash table $\mathcal{H}_g$
2) If the cloud responded positively we walk the list of proofs proof_t, For $t = 1$ to $r - 1$ we,
   a) Parse proof_t as $e_1 || e_2 || \ldots || e_{|G|}$
   b) Decrypt the the g-th entry in proof_t to obtain, $b_g || \sigma$. Where b_g denotes the children accessible from w_t and σ is the prefix signature for the node.
   c) If w_{t+1} is not one of the children listed in bit vector b_g or $\pi[t] \neq \sigma$, return false.
3) return true.

Fig. 5: The HVerify algorithm

a finite number of revocations of access. To add revocation to our system, as described in Figure 3, we modify, HSetup, HSearch, HTrapdoor, and define the routine HRevokeUser from the HAC-SSE model. We start by modifying HSetup to take an additional parameter that describes the maximum number or revocations, ρ, that the system should permit. The content owner, can now, run setup to initialize a new Key Regression system. The HSearch function should apply the inverse pseudo-random permutation, $\phi^{-1}_{\text{keyder}(\text{stm}_*)}$, to the trapdoor $T_{u,w}$. Where stm_* denotes the current member state. We modify the HTrapdoor algorithm to return the trapdoor, $T_{u,w}$, with the pseudo-random permutation $\phi_{\text{keyder}(\text{stm}_*)}$ applied. The revocation algorithm is designed to be run by the owner to revoke a user, u, from any group in the entire system. The algorithm appears in figure 6. We note here, that our

HRevokeUser (K_O, u, g):

1) Parse K_O as $(\text{stp}, \text{stp}^r)$
2) Run $(\text{stm}_*, \text{stp}) = \text{wind}(\text{stp})$ to obtain the next key material
3) Sent to the cloud and all users, except u, the new memberstate stm_*.

Fig. 6: The HRevokeUser algorithm

method for revoking access to searches relies on the trust that the cloud will not give away the key for the pseudo-random permutation.

6.1 Security Guarantees

We emphasize that revoked users are not able to issue successful queries after they are revoked. This is due to the assumption that a member state is not given to any user by the cloud. This directly implies that revoked users cannot generate a trapdoor, for they are unable to apply the correct pseudo-random permutation.

We now discuss the unforgeablility of verification tags in the system. In order for the cloud to successfully forge a verification tag it would need to be able recover at least one encryption key, since the cloud can not forge a valid encryption. Moreover, the cloud can not use a different verification tag from the tree as the hash of the prefix of the query is included in the verification tag, thus binding the verification tags to specific nodes.

7. Conclusion

We presented a secure SSE scheme with hierarchical access control for multiple groups of users under the SHBC model. Our system can support both addition and eviction of group members. One application of our system is tagging documents with security terms (e.g., *need-to-know*, *secret*, *top-secret*), and with efficient secure search that enforces the data hiding property. This data hiding property amounts to obscuring what documents are tagged with the *top-secret* designation. Another application is providing filters over search engine queries thus providing a child lock on Internet searches while still maintaining query privacy. Yet another application is providing protection for patient records allowing only certain classes of physicians to query for certain diseases or other medical tagging.

Future work in this area will be devoted to constructing both adaptively secure hierarchical access control system as well as investigating non-hierarchical access control systems. Additional future directions would be extending keyword searches to phrase searches, as well as other privacy-preserving queries over a search index.

Appendix

We prove Theorem 2 under the framework in [1]. We will use the following definitions.

Definition 4 (History, View, and Trace [1]): Let $\mathcal{D}$ be a collection of n documents, and Δ a dictionary. A *history* H_q is an interaction between a client and a server over q queries, which is denoted by $H_q = (\mathcal{D}, w_1, w_2, \ldots w_q)$.

An adversary's *view* of H_q under secret key K is defined by

$$V_K(H_q) = (\text{id}(D_1), \ldots, \text{id}(D_n), \mathcal{E}(D_1), \ldots, \mathcal{E}(D_n), \mathcal{I}, T_1, \ldots, T_q), \quad (3)$$

where $T_1, \ldots, T_q$ are a series of trapdoors and $\mathcal{I}$ is an index.

The *trace* of H_q is the following sequence:

$$\text{Tr}(H_q) = (\text{id}(D_1), \ldots, \text{id}(D_n), |D_1|, \ldots, |D_n|, \mathcal{D}(w_1), \ldots, \mathcal{D}(w_q), \pi_q), \quad (4)$$

where π_q is the search pattern of the user.

For our index we define the search pattern by creating a matrix $T_{q\times k}$, where every word in the dictionary Δ is of length at most k. Each entry $T_{i,j}$ in the matrix is a $q \times k$ binary matrix E, constructed in a way such that $E_{u,v} = 1$ if the jth letter of word i is the same as the uth letter of word v.

Proof of Theorem 2: We recall the definition of non-adaptive security from [1] and proceed to prove non-adaptive security of HAC-SSE. We describe a probabilistic polynomial-time simulator, $\mathcal{S}$, such that for all $q \in \mathbb{N}$, all probabilistic polynomial-time adversaries, $\mathcal{A}$, all distributions $L_q = \{H_q | \mathsf{Tr}(H_q) = \mathsf{Tr}_q\}$, where Tr_q is some q sized trace. Simulator, $\mathcal{S}$ can construct a view V_q^* such that $\mathcal{A}$ can not distinguish from a genuine view $V_K(H_q)$. Given that $\mathcal{S}$ is provided with $\mathsf{Tr}(H_q)$ for any $q \in \mathbb{N}$.

For $q = 0$, the simulator $\mathcal{S}$ constructs a V^* that is indistinguishable from $V_K(H_0)$ for any $H_0 \xleftarrow{R} L_0$. In particular, $\mathcal{S}$ generates $V^* = \{1, \ldots, n, e_1^*, \ldots e_n^*, \mathcal{I}^*\}$, where $e_i^* \xleftarrow{R} \{0,1\}^{|D_i|}$ for all $1 \leq i \leq n$ and $\mathcal{I}^* = T^*$. The simulator $\mathcal{S}$ generates a complete $|\Sigma|+1$-ary trie T^* of height $\max_{|w_i|}(w \in \Delta)$, and fills each node with a random number from $\{0,1\}^z$. The leaf nodes should be filled with a series of random numbers from 1 to n. We claim that V^* and $V_K(H_0)$ are indistinguishable. By a standard hybrid argument we must show that $\mathcal{A}$ cannot distinguish any element in V^* from the corresponding element in $V_K(H_0)$. This is true simply because the document identifiers in V^* and $V_K(H_0)$ are computational indistinguishable. It remains to argue that index $\mathcal{I}^* = T^*$ and $\mathcal{I} = T$ are indistinguishable and that the encrypted documents are indistinguishable. To see that T^* and T are indistinguishable, we note that every node in T^* are binary string in $\{0,1\}^z$ and the nodes of T are either a hash value from the set $\{0,1\}^z$ or a random binary string from $\{0,1\}^z$. In either case, the nodes are indistinguishable. In the case of the encrypted documents we observe that since $(G, \mathcal{E}, D)$ is a semantically secure encryption scheme, we conclude that e_i^* is indistinguishable from the associated encryption in $V_K(H_0)$.

For $q > 0$, simulator $\mathcal{S}$ constructs V^* as $V_q^* = \{1, \ldots, n, e_1^*, \ldots, e_n^*, \mathcal{I}^*, T_1^*, \ldots, T_q^*\}$, where $\mathcal{I}^* = T^*$ is a complete $|\Sigma|$-ary trie. Each value in the trie is drawn randomly from $\{0,1\}^z$. The trapdoors T_i^* are constructed as root-to-leaf paths through the trie. They are constructed in such a way that they have the correct length. Briefly, to get the correct length for word w_i the simulator inspects $E_{j,i}$. If $T_{j,i}$ is the zero matrix, then set $|w_i| = j - 1$. The trapdoors T_i^* are also constructed in a way such that they will lead to a leaf node that contains the appropriate document set. The encrypted documents as well as the document identifiers, are still indistinguishable for the same reasons as the case when $q = 0$. The index is likewise indistinguishable. The trapdoors are indistinguishable as they consist of a sequence of random values that are indistinguishable from the function used to create genuine trapdoors. Finally, we note that they are indistinguishable in length as well. This is because the search pattern of the trace provides the simulator with sufficient information to construct a trapdoor of the correct size.

We have thus described a polynomial-time simulator, $\mathcal{S}$, that can create a view indistinguishable from a genuine view for any polynomial-time adversary $\mathcal{A}$. This completes the proof.

In a straightforward manner, one can extend the proof to handle verification tags. To do this one must augment the trace, both genuine and simulator constructed, to contain the tags. To see that this does not change the proof above, we note that the verification tags themselves are the results of a semantically secure symmetric encryption system and thus are indistinguishable from random.

Acknowledgment

This work was supported in part by the NSF under grants CNS-1018422, CNS-1248380, and CNS-1247875. Any opinions, findings and conclusions or recommendations expressed in this material are those of the authors and do not necessarily reflect the views of the NSF.

References

[1] R. Curtmola, J. Garay, S. Kamara, and R. Ostrovsky, "Searchable symmetric encryption: improved definitions and efficient constructions," in *Proceedings of the 13th ACM conference on Computer and communications security*, ser. CCS '06. New York, NY, USA: ACM, 2006, pp. 79–88.

[2] Q. Chai and G. Gong, "Verifiable symmetric searchable encryption for semi-honest-but-curious cloud servers," in *IEEE International Conference on Communications, ICC'12*, June 2012.

[3] J. Li, Q. Wang, C. Wang, N. Cao, K. Ren, and W. Lou, "Fuzzy keyword search over encrypted data in cloud computing," in *Proceedings of the 29th conference on Information communications*, ser. INFOCOM'10. Piscataway, NJ, USA: IEEE Press, 2010, pp. 441–445.

[4] J. Wang, X. Chen, H. Ma, Q. Tang, J. Li, and H. Zhu, "A verifiable fuzzy keyword search scheme over encrypted data," *Journal of Internet Services and Information Security (JISIS)*, vol. 2, no. 1/2, pp. 49–58, 2 2012.

[5] D. X. Song, D. Wagner, and A. Perrig, "Practical techniques for searches on encrypted data," in *Proceedings of the 2000 IEEE Symposium on Security and Privacy*, ser. SP '00. Washington, DC, USA: IEEE Computer Society, 2000, pp. 44–.

[6] Y. Chang and M. Mitzenmacher, "Privacy preserving keyword searches on remote encrypted data," in *Proceedings of the Third international conference on Applied Cryptography and Network Security*, ser. ACNS'05. Berlin, Heidelberg: Springer-Verlag, 2005, pp. 442–455.

[7] E. Goh, "Secure indexes," Cryptology ePrint Archive, Report 2003/216, 2003, http://eprint.iacr.org/2003/216/.

[8] Y. Tang, D. Gu, N. Ding, and H. Lu, "Phrase search over encrypted data with symmetric encryption scheme," *2012 32nd International Conference on Distributed Computing Systems Workshops*, vol. 0, pp. 471–480, 2012.

[9] D. Boneh, G. D. Crescenzo, R. Ostrovsky, and G. Persiano, "Public key encryption with keyword search," in *Advances in Cryptology - EUROCRYPT 2004*, ser. Lecture Notes in Computer Science, C. Cachin and J. Camenisch, Eds. Springer Berlin / Heidelberg, 2004, vol. 3027, pp. 506–522.

[10] B. H. Bloom, "Space/time trade-offs in hash coding with allowable errors," *Commun. ACM*, vol. 13, no. 7, pp. 422–426, Jul. 1970.

[11] E. Fredkin, "Trie memory," *Commun. ACM*, vol. 3, no. 9, pp. 490–499, Sep. 1960.

[12] K. Fu, S. Kamara, and Y. Kohno, "Key Regression: Enabling Efficient Key Distribution for Secure Distributed Storage," in *Network and Distributed System Security Symposium (NDSS '06)*, 2006.

VERIFIABLE DYNAMIC MULTI-SECRET SHARING SCHEME

Aditya Nalwaya, P.D.Vyavahare, Manish Panchal
DEPARTMENT OF ELECTRONICS AND TELECOMMUNICATION ENGINEERING
S.G.S. INSTITUTE OF TECHNOLOGY AND SCIENCE, INDORE, INDIA
adityanalwaya@gmail.com, prakash.vyavahare@gmail.com, hellopanchal@gmail.com

***Abstract*—Secret sharing schemes are primarily used in cryptosystems for distributing shares of a secret among a set of entities in such a way that the secret can be reconstructed only with certain combination of shares. These schemes are mainly used in applications where there is no single trusted entity. In this paper we propose a Verifiable Dynamic Multi-Secret Sharing scheme with cheater detection mechanism. The proposed scheme has advantages of Lin-Yen's scheme in which each participant has only one secret share for reconstructing multiple secrets. In addition, proposed scheme does not require any secure channel between any participant and the dealer during secret share distribution phase. Analysis shows that the proposed scheme is as secure as the scheme which uses secure channel for distribution of share.**

***Index Terms*—Multi-Secret Sharing, Secret Key Distribution, Cheater Detection, Dynamic Multi-Secret Sharing.**

I. INTRODUCTION

In Cryptography key generation, its distribution with confidentiality and integrity are some of the major concerns. Since, how so ever complex encryption algorithm is applied to hide a confidential data, it will be of no use if the key is compromised by the opponent or lost somewhere by the owner or if the key gets corrupted. Therefore, for safe guarding such an essential cryptographic entity, a secret sharing scheme was proposed initially independently by Shamir [1] and Blakley [2] in 1979. Shamir's scheme is based on Lagrange interpolating polynomial whereas Blakley's scheme is based on the principle of linear projective geometry.

Both of these schemes split the secret key in n parts and distribute it among n participants such that the key can be reconstructed only if t of them contribute their shares. Some of the limitations of both the scheme are as follows:

1) Only one secret can be shared at a time.
2) Share of the participants are of no use after reconstructing secret for future addition secrets.
3) There is no mechanism to detect malicious participants.

Several multi-secret sharing schemes are proposed since the publication of [1] and [2] to enhance the efficiency of secret sharing scheme for the distribution and reconstruction of multiple secrets. Multi-Secret Sharing schemes (MSS) have been developed using strong mathematical structure such as those based one way-function [3], on polynomial equations [4], or on matrix projection [5] and many other.

In [4] Lin and Yeh proposed a method based on Lagrange's polynomial interpolation which is efficient and flexible multiple secret sharing scheme in which each participant has to keep only one secret share, which can be used to reconstruct different secrets. Further, if the group of secrets to be shared is updated each participants share is still unchanged. However, Lin-Yeh scheme cannot detect malicious participants. Various verifiable scheme have been proposed in the past [6-9] to overcome these limitations. However, they are computationally inefficient and require a secure communication channel during secret distribution phase.

In this paper we propose a scheme which is as efficient and flexible as Lin-Yeh scheme and is also verifiable in nature in terms of cheater detection. Another advantage of the proposed scheme is that it does not require any secure channel between the dealer and participants for distribution of shares during secret share distribution phase.

The rest of this paper is organized as follows. In the next section we review the Lin-Yeh scheme [4]. In section III proposed verifiable dynamic multi secret scheme is being presented. Security strength and performance comparison of the proposed scheme and its comparison with Lin-Yeh method is presented in section IV. Finally, the paper is concluded in section V.

II. REVIEW OF LIN-YEH'S DYNAMIC MULTI-SECRET SHARING SCHEME [4]

The Lin-Yeh method consist of three stages, namely (a) the system initialization stage, (b) pseudo secret share generation stage and (c) group secret reconstruction stage. Steps followed in each of these stage as presented in [4] are as follows:

A. System Initialization Stage

The System Authority (SA) is responsible for initializing various public parameters and selects their values which are as follows:

p : a large prime;
g : a primitive element over GF(p);
$h(.)$: a secure one-way hash function which accepts input of any arbitrary length and generates a fixed length output;
ID_j : an identifier with respect to the user U_j, for j=1,2,..., n, where n is the number of participants among which the secret is to be shared.

B. Pseudo Secret Share Generation Stage

Assume that SA wants to share k secrets $(S_i, 1 \leq i \leq k)$ group secret among n users. The SA performs the following steps to generate pseudo secret shares and distribute master secret shares among the participant.
Step 1: Choose distinct $x_j \in Z_p^*$ for j=1,2,...,n, as the master secret shares one corresponding to each participant j;
Step 2: Construct a polynomial $f_i(x)$ of degree (i-1), for i =1,2,....,k, as $f_i(x) = S_i + d_1x + ... + d_{i-1}x^{i-1}$ where $f_i(0) = S_1, d_1$ to d_{i-1} are randomly selected integers.
Step 3: For i = 1,2,....,k and j = 1,2,....,n, compute $V_{ij} = f_i(ID_j), c_{ij} = h_i(x_j) \oplus x_j, R_{ij} = V_{ij} - c_{ij}$ mod p; Here $c_{ij}{}^{'}s$ are pseudo secret shares and $h_i(x_j)$ denotes i successive applications of h to x_j.
Step 4: Deliver the master secrets x_j, for j=1,2,...,n, to each user U_j via secure channel and publish all R_{ij}.

C. Group Secret Reconstruction Stage

In order to reconstruct the lth group secret S_l, at least l participants out of n users must cooperatively perform the following steps with the group secret combiner:
Step 1: Each U_j, for j = 1,2,....,l computes his pseudo secret share as $C_{lj} = h^l(x_j) \oplus x_j$, and then sends it to the group secret combiner on secure channel.
Step 2 :Upon receiving all $C_{lj}^{'}s$, for j= 1,2,.....,l, the group secret combiner reconstructs the lth group secret.
$S_l = (\sum_{j=1}^{l}(C_{lj} + R_{lj}) \prod_{r=1,r\neq j}^{l} \frac{-ID_r}{ID_j - ID_r})$mod p.

III. PROPOSED SCHEME

The proposed scheme called as "verifiable dynamic multi-secret scheme" consists of two stages namely (a) System initialization and construction stage and (b) Verification and reconstruction stage. The steps followed in each stage are as follows:

A. System Initialization and Construction Stage:

Let $P = (P_1, P_2, ..., P_n)$ denote the set of n participants and ID_j be the identification of jth participant. Let k secrets to be shared be $S = (S_1, S_2, ..., S_k)$ and let D be the dealer who will compute and publish the share.

Various steps involved in construction of shares are as follows:-

1) D chooses two large prime number p and q and computes N=p*q.
2) Next D randomly chooses an integer g in the interval $[N^{1/2}, N]$ such that it is relatively prime to both p and q.
3) The dealer publishes (g, N). Each of the participant $j(1 \leq j \leq n)$ chooses an integer x_j in interval [2, N] as its own secret share and computes $R_j = g^{x_j}$ mod N.Then the participant sends R_j to the dealer on public channel.
4) The dealer must ensure that for any i and j $R_i \neq R_j$. If D finds that $R_i = R_j$ for some i and j then, D requests to participant j to send new R_j until D gets distinct values.
5) After getting unique values, D will publish (R_j, ID_j) for all j = 1, 2, 3...., n.
6) Next D will randomly choose an integer x_0 from interval [2, N] such that it is relatively prime to (p-1) and (q-1). Then D computes integer f such that, $x_0 * f = 1$ mod $\varphi(N)$, where $\varphi(N)$ is Euler's phi function.
7) Then D will compute $R_0 = g^{x_0}$ mod N and $I_j = R_j^{x_0}$ mod N, where j=1,2,....,n.
8) The Dealer then publish (R_0, f). Next, D choose another large prime number Q such that it is the greatest of all integers chosen so far and constructs a $(t-1)^{th}$ degree polynomial $f_i(x)$, $f_i(x) = S_i + d_1x + ... + d_{t_i-1}x^{t_i-1}$mod Q where $f_i(0) = S_i$.
9) For i = 1,2,...,k and j = 1, 2,....,n, dealer will compute $V_{ij} = f_i(I_j)$. The dealer randomly selects another integer a_0 and computes $E_0 = g^{a_0}$ mod N.
10) D will then compute $d_{ij} = R_j^{a_0 * i}$ mod N, $C_{ij} = d_{ij} \oplus I_j$ mod N, $R_{ij} = V_{ij} - d_{ij}$ mod Q.
11) Lastly the dealer publishes $(R_{ij}, E_0, Q, t_1, t_2, ..., t_k, C_{ij})$, for all values of i and j where t_i denote threshold value for i^{th} secret required during reconstruction.
12) For the addition of new secret at later stage step 8 to 11 are to be repeated.
13) For updating a secret we will add or subtract the difference of the existing secret and new secret to V_{ij}.

B. Verification and Reconstruction Stage

For reconstructing a secret $S_i(i = 1, 2.....k)$ any t_i number of participants out of n participants can contribute and reconstruct the secret. Verification for cheater detection is done as follows :

1) Each participant P_i will compute its pseudo share $I_j^{'} = R_0^{x_i}$ mod N, and where x_i is participants secret and sends it to secret combiner on public channel.
2) Now for verifying the validity of $I_j^{'}$ If $I_j^{'f} = R_j$ mod N, then $I_j^{'}$ is true otherwise it is false thus a cheater is detected.
3) Then participant computes $d_{ij} = E_0^{x_j * i}$ mod N and sends it to secret combiner on secure channel. For verifying it we use $C_{ij}^{'} = d_{ij} \oplus I_{ij}^{'}$ mod N, if $C_{ij} = C_{ij}^{'}$ then it is true otherwise the participant is a cheater.

Finally, Reconstruction is done using following Lagrange's interpolation.
$S_t = (\sum_{j=1}^{t}(d_{tj} + R_{tj}) \prod_{r=1,r\neq j}^{t} \frac{-l_r}{l_j - l_r})$mod p.

IV. ANALYSIS

A. Security Analysis

In this section we present the strength of the proposed scheme in various situations as given below:

1) If an attacker tries to guess x_0, and in turn derives I_j from it, still the secret V_{ij} is protected by d_{ij}.
2) If an attacker succeeded in getting secret share of participant from public information R_{ij}, then the problem

TABLE I
COMPARISION OF PROPOSED SCHEME WITH LIN-YEH SCHEME

Capability	Lin-Yeh Scheme	Our Scheme
Detection of malicious participant	NO	YES
Threshold value assigning flexibility	NO	YES
Dependent on security of other cryptographic function such as hash function	YES	NO
Secure channel requirement during share distribution	YES	NO

is equivalent to solving a discrete log problem which is known to be computationally hard.

3) If a malicious participant j tries to give false d_{ij} after giving the true value of I_j, he can still be easily caught while checking the equality of values C_{ij} and C'_{ij}.

B. Performance Analysis:

The performance comparison of the proposed scheme with the Lin-Yeh scheme is shown in Table I. Thus it can be seen that the proposed scheme has cryptoanalytical merits as compared to that of Lin-Yeh method. Further the proposed scheme does not require a secure channel during distribution phase.

V. CONCLUSION

In this paper we have proposed a Verifiable Dynamic Multi-Secret Sharing Scheme which is based on extension of Lin-Yeh scheme and intractability of discrete log problem solution. The scheme has the advantages of Lin-Yeh scheme with an additional feature of verification of given shares. The marginal increase in computational complexity is compensated by reduction in the cost of secure communication channel required during distribution phase. Also, the proposed scheme has the advantage of dynamically adding new participant and new secrets.

REFERENCES

[1] A. Shamir. "How to share a secret," *Communication of the ACM*, vol 22,pp.612-613, 1979.

[2] G. Blakley. "Safeguarding cryptographic keys," *Proc AFIPS 1979 Nalt Conf, New York: AFIPS Press*, pp. 313-317, 1979.

[3] J. He, E. Dawson. "Multistage secret sharing based on one-way function," *Electron. Lett.*, Vo1.30, pp. 1591-1592,1994.

[4] H. Y. Lin, Y. S. Yeh. "Dynamic Multi-Secret Sharing Scheme," *International Journal of Contemporary Mathematical Sciences*, vol.3, pp. 37 - 42, 2008.

[5] Li Bai. "A strong ramp secret sharing scheme using matrix Projection", *Proceedings of the 2006 International Symposium on a World of Wireless, Mobile and Multimedia Networks*, pp. 652-656, 2006.

[6] J. J. Zhao, J. Z. Zhang, R. Zhao. "A practical verifiable multi-secret sharing scheme," *Computer Standards and Interfaces*, vol. 29, pp.138-141,2007.

[7] Wang, Feng ;Gu, Li-ze ; Zheng, Shihui ; Yang, Yi-Xian X. ; Hu, Zhengming. "A novel verifiable dynamic multi-policy secret sharing scheme", *Advanced Communication Technology (ICACT), The 12th International Conference*, Vol: 2, pp: 1474 - 1479 2010.

[8] Qu, Juan ;Zou, Limin ; Zhang, Jianzhong. "A practical dynamic multi-secret sharing scheme", *Information Theory and Information Security (ICITIS)*, pp: 629 - 631, 2010.

[9] D Zhao, H Peng, C Wang, Y Yang, "A secret sharing scheme with a short share realizing the (t, n) threshold and the adversary structure", *Computers and Mathematics with Applications*, Vol 64, Issue 4, pp 611-615, August 2012.

[10] W. Diffie, M. Hellman, "New direction in cryptography", *IEEE Transactions on Information Theory IT-22 (6) (1976)644-654*

[11] Baek, J.; Chan Yeob Yeun, "Study on Secret Sharing Schemes (SSS) and their applications", pp: 40-45, 2011

SESSION

CRYPTOGRAPHIC TECHNOLOGIES II

Chair(s)

Drs. Gregory Vert
Levent Ertaul

Towards An Efficient Protocol for Privacy and Authentication in Wireless Networks

Clifton Mulkey, Dulal Kar, and Ajay Katangur
Texas A&M University-Corpus Christi
6300 Ocean Dr, Corpus Christi, TX 78412, USA
Email: dulal.kar@tamucc.edu

***Abstract*—We envision a scenario for security of wireless networks that include and integrate nodes of all different capabilities, including tiny sensors or similarly battery-powered, resource-constrained tiny nodes. However, the existing Wireless Protected Access (WPA) protocol may not be suitable for such resource-constrained, low-end nodes as the protocol could be too demanding since its existing authentication and privacy mechanisms can cause many inconveniences due their complexity in computation and key management. In this work, we propose an efficient protocol for authentication and privacy in wireless networks using identity-based encryption(IBE) techniques. Specifically, we propose an enhanced or extended version of the WPA protocol by incorporating IBE based authentication methods in the existing WPA protocol at the link layer level. The enhanced WPA protocol can be used for small and resource-constrained wireless devices to integrate them in existing wireless networks.**

Keywords*—*Elliptic curve cryptography, identity based encryption, wireless networks

I. Introduction

We envision futuristic wireless networks that allow seamless integration of all kinds of wireless devices to the network for secure communication. However, the inherent security risk on wireless networks that is often mitigated today by using the Wireless Protected Access (WPA) protocol [1] can be too demanding for some devices in terms of processing and energy requirements. We consider in this work to incorporate some enhancement of the existing WPA protocol to support as many devices as possible. While existing WPA enabled wireless devices must be able to communicate in secure manner using the existing WPA protocol, at the same time new, resource-constrained devices can be integrated to the network WPA protocol by adding efficient authentication mechanisms using identity based encryption techniques. This can extend operational life of a device and also can reduce hardware cost of a new device due less complex firmware needed to implement the new WPA protocol. Existing WPA authentication mechanisms require communication by the serving access point to some central authentication server every time a client makes a request for connection. Such dependency on a central server all the time can be problematic from the key storage and management point of view as well as the network's operational point of view where numerous devices need to be supported on a daily basis by the network.

To address the issues with the WPA protocol, a novel protocol using a form of asymmetric cryptography known as Identity Based Encryption (IBE) is proposed that allows integration of IBE to the existing WPA protocol. IBE uses Elliptic Curve Cryptography (ECC), which provides high cryptographic strength with a smaller amount of computation and smaller key size in comparison to traditional public key methods [2], [3]. This provides for a smaller communication, computation, and storage overheads for the protocol, and opens the door for the protocol to be used on resource-constricted devices. Because of these characteristics of IBE, this protocol can be managed by individual access points without the need for a central server for most of the time when they need to support such resource constrained devices. The overall contribution of this work is the design of such a protocol for wireless network privacy and authentication.

The remainder of the paper is structured as follows. Section II provides a review of previous research and background information in fields relating to IBE and wireless network security. Section III gives the design and details of the new wireless security protocol contributed by this work. Section IV contains the security and overhead analysis of the new protocol. Finally, Section V is the conclusion of this work and gives some topics that may be considered for future research in the area.

II. Background

A. Identity Based Encryption and Pairing Based Cryptography

Though the concept of identity based encryption was first introduced by Shamir in 1984 [5], it is pairing based cryptography (PBC) that has made modern IBE implementations possible. The first practical IBE cryptosystem using PBC was developed by Boneh and Franklin in 2003 [7]. The Boneh and Franklin scheme uses a pairing function known as the Weil pairing. This pairing performs the mapping, $G1 \times G1 \longrightarrow G2$, where $G1$ is a additive group of elliptic curve points, and $G2$ is a finite field. In general terms, a pairing function maps two elliptic curve points to an element in a finite field, known as the extension field. This function is usually represented by e, with $e(P, R) = k$, where P and R are points on an elliptic curve and k is an element of the extension field. In order for PBC and IBE to work, the pairing function e must have the bilinear property: $e(sP, tR) = e(P, R)^{st}$, where s and t are scalars.

The following example from [3] shows how this property may be used to share an encrypted message using IBE. First let us assume that we have a trusted party holding a secret s. The trusted party computes $R = sP$ and publishes R and P, which are points on an elliptic curve. Also assume that each party has already retrieved its private key d from the trusted server. The private key is sQ_x, where Q_x is an elliptic curve point representing that party's ID. Let us suppose Alice wants to generate an encryption key for sending data to Bob. She first determines Q_{Bob} using Bob's identity string and some known hash-to-point function. Next, she generates an elliptic curve point $U = kP$, where k is a random scalar. Finally, Alice generates a key using $e(kR, Q_{Bob})$ and sends this along with U to Bob. Assuming Bob has already retrieved his private key sQ_{Bob} from the trusted server, he can now determine the key generated by Alice calculating $e(U, sQ_{Bob})$. The following equation shows how Bob can retrieve the shared key using the bilinearity property.

$$\begin{aligned} e(U, sQ_{Bob}) &= e(kP, sQ_{Bob}) \\ &= e(P, Q_{Bob})^{ks} \\ &= e(ksP, Q_{Bob}) \\ &= e(kR, Q_{Bob}) \end{aligned} \quad (1)$$

Using similar methods, IBE and pairing functions can also be used to achieve authentication using signatures.

The security of pairing based IBE systems relies on the difficulty of either the Bilinear Diffie Hellman Problem (BDHP) or the Gap Diffie-Hellman Problem (GDHP) [8]. Besides the Weil pairing used in the Boneh and Franklin scheme, another pairing function known as the Tate pairing can also be used. The Tate pairing is often more computationally efficient than the Weil pairing [8].

Due to the small key sizes of ECC and the fact that IBE does not need a traditional public key infrastructure to operate, IBE has become a popular candidate for encryption and authentication in energy and resource-constrained devices such as in Wireless Sensor Networks (WSNs) [9], [10], [11]. In this work, we show that IBE security for wireless LANs can also be efficient enough for use with the growing number of resource-constrained mobile, hand-held, and tiny wearable devices.

B. Privacy and Authentication in Wireless Protected Access Protocol

The privacy specifications for the WPA protocol can be divided into two revisions. This first mode of privacy of the WPA protocol is WPA Temporal Key Integrity Protocol (WPA-TKIP) [1]. TKIP uses the RC4 stream encryption algorithm which encrypts data using a 104 bit key and a 24 bit initialization vector. The second mode of privacy specified by the 802.11i standard is WPA Counter Mode CBC Protocol (WPA-CCMP or WPA2) [12]. This form of WPA is more computationally intensive and is much more cryptographically secure as it uses the 128 bit AES algorithm in Cipher Block Chaining (CBC) mode.

WPA provides two different modes of authentication that can be used for wireless networks [1]. The two modes are known as Pre Shared Key (WPA-PSK) and Extensible Authentication Protocol (WPA-EAP). The simpler and more commonly used of the two is PSK mode. In PSK mode, network authentication is controlled by a master key. Any client that wishes to join the network is required to have this master key. As mentioned above, this master key is used to derive the session key used to encrypt frames between the access point and the client. This authentication mode is convenient for home and small office networks with a limited number of users. No central authentication server is required and a single access point can enforce access to the network. However, WPA-PSK does not scale well because of the need for every client to have knowledge of the same master password.

For larger networks involving multiple access points, WPA-EAP can be used. WPA-EAP requires a central authentication server with a database of credentials for authorized users. EAP uses upper layer protocols above the data-link layer to create a secure connection to the authentication server. In some EAP systems, digitally signed certificates are used to verify the access point, authentication server, or clients. Each client of an EAP network has its own set of credentials, so the system scales much better than PSK mode.

III. Protocol Design

A. Preliminaries

The specific pairing algorithm used in this work is the ηT pairing, which is the fastest known pairing over supersingular curves [11]. Particularly, we use a supersinglar curve defined over the ternary field $F_{3^{509}}$, given in [13]. The curve over this field is defined by $y^2 = x^3 - x + b$, where b is between -1 and 1. The modulus used for the field is the polynomial $x^{509} - x^{318} - x^{191} + x^{127} + 1$. This curve has an embedding degree of 6, which results in the extension field $F_{3^{509\times 6}}$. The order of the curve and the size of the extension field is large enough to provide 128 bit security, or about the same security level as 3054 bit RSA [13], [4]. A curve at this security level is chosen in order to match the standards of WPA2 and the NIST standards for the foreseeable future (beyond 2030) [4].

The following list defines the specific parameters that are involved in the design of the protocol and give the notations that will be used for the remainder of this work:

- E – an elliptic curve defined over $F_{3^{509}}$. Points in on the elliptic curve are denoted as being in the group $E(F_{3^{509}})$.
- e – a pairing function, which gives the following mapping:

$$E(F_{3^{509}}) \times E(F_{3^{509}}) \longrightarrow F_{3^{509\times 6}} \quad (2)$$

- s – the IBE master secret key that is known only to the access point. s is a 128 bit integer.
- P – a random point on the elliptic curve chosen by the AP. It is part of the public parameters of the IBE system.
- Q – another point on the elliptic curve. It is calculated as $Q = sP$ by the AP. Q is also a public parameter.
- g – a public parameter calculated as $e(P, P)$ by the AP.
- $H1$ – a hash function that converts a binary MAC address to a 128 bit integer.
- $H2$ – a hash function that converts an element of the extension field $(F_{3^{509\times 6}})$ to a 128 bit integer.

- Public Keys – The public key of each node involved in the protocol is a 128 bit integer calculated as $H1$(node MAC address). The public key for the access point will be denoted as a. The public key for each network client will be denoted as c_i.
- Private Keys – The private key of each device is an elliptic curve point calculated by the AP as $\frac{1}{s+h}P$, where h is the node public key. The value $\frac{1}{s+h}$ is calculated over the finite field $\mathbb{Z}_p$ where p is a 128 bit or larger prime integer. The private key for the AP will be denoted as A, ($A = \frac{1}{s+a}P$). The private keys for each client will be denoted as C_i, ($C_i = \frac{1}{s+c_i}P$).

B. Protocol Description

It is undesirable to use a master network password that is shared among users as in WPA-PSK. Instead, we want each client authentication to be independent of other clients. Independent authentication is also a part of WPA-EAP but it is done through upper layer methods. It can be achieved by the IBE protocol without the reliance on upper layer methods. To provide this functionality, IBE private keys will be generated for each network client and connections will be authenticated using this private key. IBE has the feature that private keys have an inherent authenticity in that the AP generates the private keys using the IBE master secret. In contrast, clients generate their own private keys in traditional public key cryptography systems, resulting in the need for certificate verification by trusted outside authorities [6].

1) Initial Connection: For the first time connection, we assume that user IDs and passwords are used. These user ID and password pairs can be stored on the AP until the client connects and receives its private key for the first time. Neither the temporary passwords or the IBE private keys need to be stored permanently on the AP.

Passing of passwords between an AP and a client for the purpose of authentication requires an encrypted channel since an wireless medium is vulnerable to eavesdropping. Accordingly, the following describes the steps to be taken in the protocol to provide privacy before any exchange of passwords for the first time authentication.

1) The AP periodically sends a beacon frame as specified in 802.11 protocol to make clients aware of its existence and security requirements.
2) A client wishes to connect to the AP. If the client does not have the parameters for the AP cached, it sends a probe request to retrieve the IBE parameters for the network.
3) The AP responds with a probe response containing the necessary IBE parameters: $\langle E, P, Q, g \rangle$
4) The client now begins the connection process. It sends an association request to the AP, indicating that it wishes to connect using the supported privacy method.
5) The AP sends an association response to the client, indicating the client can go ahead with session key generation.
6) The client generates two random 128 bit integers, w and t where t is the eventual session key. The client also calculates the AP public key, $a = H1$(AP MAC address). It is to be noted that the client already possesses the MAC address of the AP from the initial beacon frame.
7) The client then generates two more values: $M1 = w(Q + aP)$ and $M2 = t \oplus H2(g^w)$ ($\oplus$ denotes the xor operation). $M1$ and $M2$ are sent to the AP in an authentication management frame.
8) The AP retrieves the session key t by calculating $t = H2(e(A, M1)) \oplus M2$.
9) AP sends an authentication successful message back to the client. Although the client is not actually authenticated in a cryptographic sense, authentication frames are used to signal that the client has permission to join the network with the secure channel.
10) The remainder of the communication is encrypted using the shared session key and WPA-CCMP.

It is to be noted that the AP is able to successfully retrieve t because of the bilinearity property of the IBE pairing function:

$$\begin{aligned} e(A, M1) &= e\left(\frac{1}{s+a}P, w(Q + aP)\right) \\ &= e(P, Q + aP)^{\frac{w}{s+a}} \\ &= e(P, (s+a)P)^{\frac{w}{s+a}} \\ &= e(P, P)^w = g^w \end{aligned} \tag{3}$$

and

$$H2(g^w) \oplus M2 = t \tag{4}$$

It is to be noted that the preceding protocol steps only establish an encrypted channel between the AP and and the client. Once an encrypted channel is established between the AP and client, further steps are necessary to complete the mutual authentication process using User IDs and passwords first time. In the following, we describe the steps that are used only once:

1) The client and AP establish a secure connection in the same way as the unauthenticated protocol above.
2) The client sends the temporary user ID to the AP.
3) The AP looks up the user ID and password hash in its table and then sends the password hash to the client.
4) The client authenticates the AP by calculating the hash of its password and comparing it to the hash received from the AP. If the hashes match, the client proceeds to send the temporary password to the AP. Otherwise, the client terminates the connection by sending a disassociation frame.
5) After receiving the temporary password of the client, the AP calculates the hash. If the hash matches what is stored in its database, the AP proceeds. Otherwise, the AP sends a disassociation frame to terminate the connection.
6) The client and AP have now been authenticated. The AP calculates the new client private key: $C_i = \frac{1}{s+c_i}P$. The AP sends the private key to the client in an authentication success frame. The temporary user ID and password is also deleted from the database.

7) The client receives and saves its private key for future connections. The client also saves the public IBE parameters for the AP in order to avoid the need for another parameter probe request in the future. Normal data communication can now begin and is encrypted over the authenticated secure channel.

It is to be noted that by executing the preceding protocol steps, the client receives necessary IBE parameters to communicate with the AP without using the user ID and password.

2) Subsequent Connections: Once the client has performed the initial connection and authentication, all subsequent connections will be authenticated using the IBE private key. Since the IBE private keys are generated using the master secret that is held by the AP, both the client and AP can be authenticated to each other. Once the key setup steps are completed, a challenge and response mechanism is used to authenticate the client and allow it to connect.

The steps involved in the protocol are as follows:

1) The AP periodically sends beacon frames to make clients aware of its existence.
2) The client sends an association request to the AP, indicating that it already possesses its private key.
3) The AP sends an association response indicating that the client can go ahead with authentication.
4) The client generates a random 128 bit number p and calculates $p(Q + aP)$. The client sends $p(Q + aP)$ to the AP in an authentication request frame.
5) The AP receives the authentication request, generates a random 128 bit r, and calculates $r(Q + c_i P)$. The AP sends $r(Q + c_i P)$ back to the client.
6) The AP and the client simultaneously calculate the session key:
   - The client calculates $H2(e(C_i, r(Q+c_i P))^p)$
   - The AP calculates $H2(e(A, p(Q + aP))^r)$

   Both the client and the AP are able to securely share the 128 bit session key because of the relation:

$$\begin{aligned} e(C_i, r(Q + c_i P))^p &= e\left(\frac{1}{s + c_i} P, r(sP + c_i P)\right)^p \\ &= e(P, (sP + c_i P))^{\frac{rp}{s+c_i}} \\ &= e(P, P)^{rp} \end{aligned} \quad (5)$$

and

$$\begin{aligned} e(A, p(Q + aP))^r &= e\left(\frac{1}{s + a} P, p(sP + aP)\right)^r \\ &= e(P, (sP + aP))^{\frac{rp}{s+a}} \\ &= e(P, P)^{rp} \end{aligned} \quad (6)$$

7) Once the session key is calculated, the AP sends a random data payload to the client as a challenge.
8) The client receives the random challenge, encrypts it using the session key and WPA-CCMP, and returns it to the AP.
9) The AP also performs encryption on the challenge data using the session key. It compares the result to the challenge response received from the client to determine if the client has arrived at the correct session key. If the client does have the correct session key, it is authenticated and the AP sends an authentication success frame. Otherwise, the AP sends a disassociation frame to terminate the connection.
10) The client and AP can now commence normal data communication. All further traffic is encrypted using WPA-CCMP standards and the shared session key.

In this way, a client can achieve authentication while establishing a secure channel to the network. In this scenario, little or no user interaction is required on the client or AP side. The only requirement is that the client possesses the private IBE key that it was given during the initial connection. It should also be noted that no previous information about the client needs to be stored on the AP. All client information needed by the AP for this protocol can be calculated from the MAC address of the client.

C. Key Management and Changes

As mentioned above, adding new clients to an authenticated network will require some form of initial interaction. In the simplest case, a system administrator could be charged with generating user ID and random password combinations for each new client. For added security, the MAC address of the new client could also be obtained and stored along with the user ID/password. Temporary passwords should be stored as a SHA-224 hash in keeping with the NIST standard for 128 bit security [4]. For a single access point network, the password hashes and IDs can be uploaded to the AP via some secure channel. Since the temporary passwords are no longer needed after the first-time client connection and authentication, they can be automatically deleted to free up space on the AP. In this way, no central user database or authentication server is needed beyond the AP for a single access point network. However, for larger wireless networks with multiple access points, it may be desirable to have some kind of automated system with some centralized server for the setup and distribution of the initial temporary keys to the respective APs. Each AP can be configured to query the server during first time login, a process similar to a DNS query. It is important to note that this system would not have to be working at all times for the network to function.

For security reasons, it will likely be desirable to generate new master keys and IBE parameters on a periodic basis. In order to facilitate key changes and parameter changes efficiently a key timestamp mechanism is added to the protocol. With this mechanism, the AP stores one or more sets of old parameters. For each old set, only $\langle E, s, P \rangle$ need to be stored. During the initial authentication, the AP attaches a timestamp to the client private key. The client stores this timestamp along with its private key. Then, every time the client wishes to join the network, it sends its timestamp to the AP in the association request. The AP can use this timestamp to determine whether the requesting client possesses a private key generated with current parameters or with an old set. If the clients private key is current, the authentication steps proceed normally. If the timestamp shows that the private key was generated with an older set of parameters stored on the AP, the client will be allowed to authenticate using the old set of parameters. Once authentication is complete and a secure channel is established, the AP generates a new timestamp and client private key and sends it to the client. The client must then removed its old private key and store the new one. The client must also request and store the new set of parameters from the AP. If a client possesses a private key that is older than any set of parameters on the AP, it simply must be treated as a new user and go through the first-time authentication process.

All messages in key establishment and authentication can be passed using 802.11 management frames. For the development of the protocol, we assume a maximum transmission unit of 1500 bytes in keeping with the common Ethernet MTU [15]. The communication analysis in Section IV-B shows that this payload size is more than sufficient for all protocol messages that must be passed. In order to facilitate this IBE protocol, a 4 bit control code is added at the beginning of the data payload. The management frame type along with the control code is used to determine the protocol message type. Figure 1 shows the diagram for the frame format.

Beside the 4 bit control code, a 4 bit pad is added to the frame in order to achieve byte alignment.

IV. Protocol Security Analysis

In order to validate the new IBE wireless security protocol designed in this work, this section provides an analysis of protocol performance. It is assumed that the attacker has obtained or is able to obtain all information that is passed across the network including the MAC address of the AP and the MAC addresses of all clients. It is also important to realize that an attacker can easily spoof the MAC address of any client.

Many possible attacks exist for which this IBE protocol must be able to resist. Below is a description of likely attacks to the network and how this protocol proves to be resilient to these attacks.

- *Rogue AP* – As mentioned previously, an attacker could insert an AP that claims to be a part of the legitimate ESS. In this case, the attacker can easily obtain the public parameters $\langle E, P, Q, g\rangle$, and the IBE public keys corresponding to any MAC address. However, the rogue AP cannot obtain the master secret s, which is known only to authentic access points. Furthermore, the rogue AP does not have the database of temporary password hashes used for first-time authentication, so it will not be able to authenticate to itself to any first-time clients. For subsequent connection authentication, let us assume that the rogue AP possesses its own secret $k \neq s$, with which it has generated its own private key A_k. During the key generation phase of subsequent authentication, the client calculates:

$$e(C_i, r(Q + c_iP))^p = e(P, P)^{\frac{rp(s+c_i)}{s+c_i}} \quad (7)$$

However, the AP calculates:

$$e(A_k, p(Q + aP))^r = e(P, P)^{\frac{rp(s+a)}{k+a}} \quad (8)$$

Therefore, the rogue AP is unable to retrieve the correct session key.

- *Authentic client private key used with wrong MAC address* – If an attacker somehow manages to steal the private key, C_i, from a client without obtaining the client's MAC address, the IBE protocol will not allow the attacker to authenticate with the network. In this case, the MAC address used by the attacker will correspond to some public key $c_i' = H1(\text{attacker MAC address})$. During session key generation, the AP will calculate:

$$e(A, p(Q + aP))^r = e(P, P)^{\frac{rp(s+a)}{s+a}} \quad (9)$$

However, the client calculates:

$$e(C_i, r(Q + c_i'P))^p = e(P, P)^{\frac{rp(s+c_i')}{s+c_i}} \quad (10)$$

which does not result in the correct session key. Consequently, the client will not be able to correctly respond to the challenge from the AP and will be disassociated from the network.

- *MAC of an authentic client with an invalid private key* – In order for an IBE private key to authenticate correctly with the network, it must have been generated with the correct master secret s. Even if an attacker possesses the MAC of an authentic client, it cannot connect to the network with an invalid private key. Let us assume that the attacker has generated its own IBE private key, C_i' using the public parameters and some secret key $k \neq s$. During the session key generation phase, the AP calculates the same value shown in Equation 9. However, the client calculates:

$$e(C_i', r(Q + c_iP))^p = e(P, P)^{\frac{rp(s+c_i)}{k+c_i}} \quad (11)$$

which does not result in the correct session key. Again, the client will not be able to successfully respond to the authentication challenge from the AP.

- *Invalid MAC address and invalid private key* – The proof of security in this case clearly follows from the previous two cases.

- *Rogue/Hijacked Client* – We consider a scenario that an attacker may be able to capture a client that possesses an authentic IBE private key. Another scenario resulting in the same situation is an insider attack, where a previously authenticated user decides to attack the network using an authenticated client. In this case, the client will still be able to access the network, but will not be able to sniff traffic from any other clients of the network due to the randomly generated session keys.

In order to provide security once the secure channel between the AP and client has been established, the widely accepted WPA-CCMP (WPA2) protocol is used. The 128 bit AES encryption algorithm in cipher block chaining mode used for this protocol provides a security level recommended by NIST through the 2030 [4].

A. Storage Overhead

We analyze the data storage requirements for this IBE protocol on both access points and clients. Each access point must store the elliptic curve attributes for multiple different curves that are to be used in the protocol.

Once a particular curve is chosen the access point must also store IBE parameters for the operation of a specific instance of

Bytes	≤ 30	4 bits	4 bits	≤ 1499	4
	802.11 Header	Control Code	Padding	Protocol Payload	FCS

Fig. 1. IBE Protocol Frame Layout.

TABLE I. AP PARAMETER STORAGE REQUIREMENTS

Parameter	Bytes
E	1
s	16
P, Q	128 each
g	764
A	128
Total	1165

TABLE II. CLIENT PARAMETER STORAGE REQUIREMENTS

Parameter	Bytes
C_i	128
E	1
P, Q	128 each
$(Q + aP)$	128
Total	513

the protocol. Here we use storage sizes specific to the elliptic curve over $F_{3^{509}}$ used throughout this work. Since the curve is defined over a ternary field, each of the 509 ternary digits in the field are represented with 2 bits. Therefore, an element of $F_{3^{509}}$ is stored with 1018 bits. Furthermore, a point on an elliptic curve consists of (x, y), where x and y are both elements of the base field. To avoid the need for two field elements to be stored for each curve point, we can take advantage of the fact that an elliptic curve has two possible y values for a given x value. Using this information, we can simply store an extra bit that is used to choose between the two y values [11]. Using this method, an elliptic curve point can be stored with $1018 + 1$ bits, which rounds to 128 bytes. g, which is an element of $F_{3^{509 \times 6}}$ also requires 2 bits for each of its 3054 ternary digits. This results in a space requirement of 6108 bits which rounds to 764 bytes. Table I shows the parameters that must be stored on the AP.

In addition to the IBE parameters, the AP must obtain temporary user IDs and passwords for new clients from the central server and store them in its database. We assume that each user ID is 10 characters long. Along with the SHA-224 hash used to store passwords, a single ID/password combination requires 38 bytes. However, since these combinations are removed from the database after first-time authentication, there should never be a considerably large number of ID/passwords stored on the AP.

All other values needed in the operation of the protocol can be calculated on the fly by the access point. However, it would improve speed to cache some parameters that are commonly used. The first value that should likely be cached is the IBE private key for the AP, $\frac{1}{s+a}P$. This is simply a point on the elliptic curve, which requires 128 bytes. Another value to aid in computation is $(Q + c_i P)$ corresponding to recent or frequent clients. This is also an elliptic curve point. If storage is severely constrained, a method given in [11] can be used to further reduce the size of elliptic curve points.

As in the AP, the client must also store curve attributes for each available elliptic curve in the protocol. Beyond this, the client only needs to store its own private key, C_i, which is an elliptic curve point. All other values needed in the protocol can either be retrieved from the AP or calculated. However, to avoid excess communication, the client should also cache $\langle E, P, Q \rangle$. Furthermore, the client should store the point $(Q + aP)$ to reduce computation on future authentications. Table II gives a summary of parameters that need to be stored on the client.

B. Communication Overhead

Communication is the major cause for drainage of battery power. The IBE security protocol in this work has a relatively small communication overhead. Each protocol frame contains a control field that constitutes 1 byte, including padding. Only some of the protocol frames contain additional payloads, as described below. Since no upper layer protocols are used, there is no need for many frames to be transferred in order to establish upper layer sessions, such as TCP. The only point in the protocol in which a significant overhead is incurred is during connection setup.

The largest portion of data that must be transferred is the IBE public parameters, $\langle E, P, Q, g \rangle$. As shown in the above storage analysis, this constitutes a total of 1021 bytes, which can easily fit in one frame. These parameters are only sent when requested by the client via a probe request frame. In addition, clients can cache the parameters to reduce communication during subsequent connections.

The proposed IBE based protocol contains two phases: the initial authentication and subsequent authentications. The initial authentication includes the encrypted channel setup from the protocol without authentication, as well as 4 additional frames. These frames include payloads of the user ID, temporary password hash, temporary password, and the IBE client private key. The most significant payload in this set is the IBE private key, which is an 128 byte curve point. All other payloads will contain only a small number of bytes.

The authenticated key setup for subsequent connections requires a total of 7 frames to be exchanged. Of these 7, only 4 contain payloads: the 2 key setup frames and the 2 challenge-response frames. The key setup frames each contain a 128 byte elliptic curve points. The size of the challenge-response payload can vary, but needs to be at least 16 bytes in keeping with the 128 bit security level. All other frames contain only the control field.

The exchanges described above only take place once per connection. After the session key is established, all following messages transferred via WPA2-CCMP, which incurs 12 bytes of overhead per frame over unsecured 802.11 wireless Ethernet.

TABLE III. IBE COMPUTATION BENCHMARKS AT 656 MHZ

Operation	Iterations	Average Time (sec)
EC Addition	100000	3.791×10^{-4}
EC Point Triple	100000	2.34×10^{-5}
Multiplication over $F_{3^{509 \times 6}}$	10000	4.165×10^{-4}
Cube over $F_{3^{509 \times 6}}$	100000	3.603×10^{-5}
ηT Pairing	1000	1.07297×10^{-1}

TABLE IV. UPPER BOUNDS FOR COMPUTING EC SCALAR MULTIPLICATION AND EXPONENTIATION OVER $F_{3^{509 \times 6}}$

Operation	Time (3.0 GHz)	Time (656 MHz)
EC Scalar Multiplication	2.023×10^{-3} sec	3.258×10^{-2} sec
Exponentiation over $F_{3^{509 \times 6}}$	2.463×10^{-3} sec	3.662×10^{-2} sec

C. Computation Overhead

In order to estimate the time requirements of various computations used throughout this protocol, benchmark tests were conducted using IBE pairing code adapted from [13], [16]. This code is written in C++, with some inline assembly instructions included. The benchmark tests were conducted on a 32-bit Intel Core2 Duo processor at 3.00 GHz by forcing it run in single thread at 656 MHz. The code was built and run under Windows 7 with Microsoft Visual C++ 2008. Though the processor used is dual core, the benchmarking program was forced to run in a single thread. The elliptic curve and pairing algorithm benchmarked here is the same curve over $F_{3^{509}}$ and ηT pairing used throughout the development of this work. In order to achieve accurate timings, each basic operation was iterated multiple times and the average computation time was calculated from these iterations. Though the original source code from [16] was only used to estimate the calculation time of the ηT pairing, it was adapted for this work to time other primitive operations involved in the overall IBE protocol.

The processor clock of 3.0 GHz is likely higher than most mobile devices that use wireless networks. In order to obtain timings for a slower processor speed, the CPU scaling feature of the benchmarking computer was used. With the help of this feature, another set of benchmarks was conducted using the lowest configurable processor frequency of 656 MHz. The results of the same benchmarks conducted at this processor speed are shown in Table III.

Beside the ηT pairing, elliptic curve scalar multiplication and exponentiation over $F_{3^{509}}$ are the two other operations that play a large role the computation required for this IBE protocol. Using the benchmarks of the basic operations, the upper bounds for these two operations can be determined.

For the initial connection, the IBE protocol designed here has the advantage that the client does not have to calculate a pairing. This is important to save as much energy as possible for resource-limited devices. The client steps require a total of 2 elliptic curve scalar multiplications, 1 elliptic curve addition, and 1 exponentiation over $F_{3^{509 \times 6}}$. After the first connection, a and $(Q + aP)$ can be cached for future connections. Therefore, subsequent connections only require 1 elliptic curve multiplication and 1 exponentiation. The total time required for these operations is less than a single pairing calculation. As for the access point, 1 pairing calculation and 1 128-bit exclusive-or operation must be calculated. Beyond this, the client is not required to perform any more elliptic curve or IBE operations. The AP must perform one more elliptic curve scalar multiplication in order to compute the private key for the new client.

The subsequent connections with authentication require the most computation overhead of any phase of the protocol. This is due to the fact that IBE methods are used to authenticate both the AP and the client. Here we assume that the client has already cached $(Q + aP)$, since the first-time connection must have already taken place. Therefore, the client process involves a total of 1 elliptic curve scalar multiplication, 1 pairing calculation, and 1 exponentiation over $F_{3^{509 \times 6}}$. For the access point, we assume that neither the public key of the client nor the value $(Q + c_i P)$ is cached, since there is no guarantee that the AP has calculated these values before this point. Therefore, the AP process involves 2 elliptic curve scalar multiplications, 1 elliptic curve addition, 1 pairing calculation and 1 exponentiation over $F_{3^{509 \times 6}}$.

The total estimated upper bounds for each phase of the protocol are calculated using the benchmark results and the basic operations outlined above (Table IV). Tables V and VI show these results for the client and the access point, respectively. In order to provide a reference point for these time estimations, benchmarks were performed on the same machine for the commonly used RSA public key encryption method [14]. These benchmarks were performed using a 3072 bit modulus, which provides approximately the same security strength as the parameters used for this IBE protocol. The code for these benchmarks was developed by utilizing the standard OpenSSL library. Encryption and decryption are performed using a plaintext that is a random 128 bit number to simulate a session key. Table VII summarizes these results. The performance of the IBE protocol surpasses that of RSA in all areas except encryption. Furthermore, the RSA operations shown are only sufficient to share a session key. Further operations would have to take place in order to provide authentication. On the other hand, the IBE protocol is able to provide authentication within the same operations of key generation. These results show promise that this IBE protocol will be able to computationally outperform WPA-EAP protocols, which rely on upper layer encryptions mechanisms such as RSA.

V. CONCLUSION

Wireless networks are vulnerable by nature, and the growing use of these networks makes security increasingly important. Though the WPA wireless security protocol already exists and is widely used, improvements on this protocol can be made using more recent cryptographic techniques, which can make it feasible to integrate extremely resource-constrained devices to the network. With this in mind, this work provides the design and analysis of a new wireless security protocol using identity based encryption methods to provide privacy and authentication. This new IBE protocol provides improvements over current WPA-PSK and WPA-EAP authentication mechanisms. More specifically, this protocol does not require a master key to be shared among all clients of the network as in WPA-PSK. In regard to WPA-EAP, this protocol can eliminate the need for a central authentication server in a single access point network. Furthermore, this protocol distributes authentication among the access points of a large network, removing a possible performance bottleneck and ensuring that clients can almost always authenticate over

TABLE V. SUMMARY OF CLIENT COMPUTATION TIME BOUNDS

Protocol Phase	Basic Ops.	Time (656 MHz)
Unauthenticated Protocol	2 EC mult., 1 EC add., 1 exp.	1.022×10^{-1} sec
Auth. Protocol (First-time)	2 EC mult., 1 EC add., 1 exp.	1.022×10^{-1} sec
Auth. Protocol (Subsequent)	1 EC mult., 1 pairing, 1 exp.	1.765×10^{-1} sec

TABLE VI. SUMMARY OF AP COMPUTATION TIME BOUNDS

Protocol Phase	Basic Ops.	Time (656 MHz)
Parameter Generation	3 EC mult., 1 pairing	2.050×10^{-1} sec
Unauthenticated Protocol	1 pairing	1.073×10^{-1} sec
Auth. Protocol (First-time)	1 pairing, 1 EC mult.	1.399×10^{-1} sec
Auth. Protocol (Subsequent)	2 EC mult., 1 EC add., 1 pairing, 1 exp.	2.094×10^{-1} sec

TABLE VII. SUMMARY OF RSA COMPUTATION TIMES (3072 BIT MODULUS)

Operation	Iterations	Avg. Time (656 MHz)
Key Generation	60	23.82 sec
Encryption	6000	2.259×10^{-3} sec
Decryption	600	1.296 sec

only 1 hop. This reduces the role of a central authentication server drastically.

The IBE methods in this protocol use relatively small parameters, in comparison with traditional public key systems, while still providing a high level of security as recommended for use by NIST through the year 2030. It can be seen that these IBE techniques are more lightweight and computationally efficient than the commonly used RSA methods. Furthermore, this protocol does not rely on upper layer network protocols, so frame transmission is kept to a minimum during key set up and authentication.

REFERENCES

[1] D. Eaton, Diving into the 802.11i spec: A tutorial, EETimes News and AnalysisAvailable: http://www.eetimes.com/electronics-news/4143367/Diving-into-the-802-11i-Spec-A-Tutorial, Last Accessed: 30 August 2012.

[2] M. Anoop, Elliptic curve cryptography: An implementation tutorial, available: http://www.infosecwriters.com/text_resources/pdf/Elliptic_Curve_AnnopMS.pdf, Last Accessed: 30 August 2012 (May 2007).

[3] D. C. Kar, H. L. Ngo, C. J. Mulkey, Applied cryptography in wireless sensor networks, in: H. R. Nemati, L. Yang (Eds.), Applied Cryptography for Cyber Security and Defense: Information Encryption and Cyphering, IGI Global, 2011, pp. 146–167.

[4] Recommendation for key management - part 1: General, National Institute of Standards and Technology (NIST), available: http://csrc.nist.gov/publications/nistpubs/800-57/sp800-57-Part1-revised2_Mar08-2007.pdf, Last Accessed: 30 August 2012 (March 2007).

[5] A. Shamir, Identity based cryptosystems and signatures, in: Proceedings of Cryptology, Springer-Verlag, Berlin, Germany, 1984, pp. 47–53.

[6] M. Markovic, Data protection techniques, cryptographic protocols and pki systems in modern computer networks, in: 14th International Workshop on Systems, Signals, and Image Processing and 6th EURASIP Conference focused on Speech and Image Processing, Multimedia Communications, and Services, 2007, pp. 13 –24.

[7] D. Boneh, M. Franklin, Identity-based encryption from the weil pairing, SIAM Journal on Computing 32 (3) (2003) 586–615.

[8] The pairing based crypto lounge, available: http://www.larc.usp.br/~pbarreto/pblounge.html, Last Accessed: 30 August 2012.

[9] L. Oliveira, D. Aranha, E. Morais, F. Daguano, J. Lopez, R. Dahab, Tinytate: Computing the tate pairing in resource-constrained sensor nodes, in: Sixth IEEE International Symposium on Network Computing and Applications, (NCA), 2007, pp. 318 –323.

[10] P. Szczechowiak, M. Collier, Tinyibe: Identity-based encryption for heterogeneous sensor networks, in: 5th International Conference on Intelligent Sensors, Sensor Networks, and Information Processing (ISSNIP), 2009, pp. 319–354.

[11] X. Xiong, D. Wong, X. Deng, Tinypairing: A fast and lightweight pairing-based cryptographic library for wireless sensor networks, in: IEEE Wireless Communications and Networking Conference (WCNC), 2010, pp. 1–6.

[12] W. Stallings, Wireless Communications and Networks, 2nd Edition, Pearson Education Inc., 2005.

[13] J.-L. Beuchat, E. Lpez-Trejo, L. Martnez-Ramos, S. Mitsunari, F. Rodrguez-Henrquez, Multi-core implementation of the tate pairing over supersingular elliptic curves, Proceedings of the 8th International Conference in Cryptology and Network Security, 12-14 December, 2009.

[14] B. Schneier, Applied Cryptography, 2nd Edition, John Wiley and Sons, 1996.

[15] J. F. Kurose, K. W. Ross, The link layer and local area networks, in: Computer Networking: A Top-Down Approach, 4th Edition, Pearson Education Inc., 2008, Ch. 5, pp. 435 – 509.

[16] Multi-core implementation of the tate pairing over supersingular elliptic curves (source code), available: http://delta.cs.cinvestav.mx/~francisco/temp/Page-TatePairing2009/TatePairing-2009.html, Last Accessed: 07 May 2011.

A Robust User Authentication Scheme for Multi-Server Environment Using Smart Cards

Tien-Ho Chen[1], Hsiu-lien Yeh[2], Tseng-Yi Chen[1], Wei-Kuan Shih[1]
[1]Department of Computer Science, National Tsing Hua University, Hsinchu, Taiwan
[2]Institute of Information Systems and Applications, National Tsing Hua University, Hsinchu, Taiwan

Abstract - *Remote user authentication is a very important ingredient procedure for the network system service to authenticate whether a remote user is legal through any insecure channel. Recently, Hsiang-Shih proposed a dynamic ID based remote user authentication scheme for multi-server environment as an improved scheme over Liao and Wang's scheme, and asserted that their scheme can escape from masquerade attack, server spoofing attack, etc. In this paper, we show that Hsiang and Shih's scheme still suffers from the insider's attack and masquerade attack. To mend the problem, we offer a procedure to improve Hsiang- Shih's scheme. Our scheme is suitable for applications with higher security requirement.*

Keywords: Authentication, Dynamic ID, Multi-serve, Password, Smart card.

1 Introduction

With current network technologies, various business activities can be done in the Internet world, and how to assure the security of these activities in an insecure communication channel becomes the most important issue. In 1981, Lamport [12] proposed a password based remote user authentication scheme for servers to verify a remote user's identification, which is a good beginning for efficient applications of Internet systems. Later, many studies provided similar schemes [5,7,8,9,24] to enhance Lamport's method which verified the remote user by hash function and verifier table. For instance, Hwang's [9] scheme can authenticate passwords without passwords tables, which is able to avoid the attack of stealing verifier table from servers by the smart cards. In 2000, Lee and Chang [13] provided a scheme to verify remote users by user identifications and passwords in multi-server environment. After that, lots of studies [3, 11,13,14,17,18,20,21,22,23] have concentrated on the authentication improvement in multi-server environment. In 2004, Das et al. [4] proposed a dynamic ID-based remote user authentication scheme, providing a dynamic ID for avoiding ID-theft, which is the first dynamic ID-based user authentication. Later, Liao and Wang [16] proposed a similar secure dynamic ID based remote user authentication scheme for multi-server environment. The difference between [4] and [16] is that the latter's scheme used hashing functions to implement a robust authentication and could verify the remote user in multi-server environment but the former's used timestamp and [16]'s scheme. Recently, Hsiang and Shih[6] pointed out that Liao and Wang's scheme cannot resist insider's attack, masquerade attack, server spoofing attack, registration center spoofing attack, and provided an improvement scheme .

Unfortunately, we find that Hsiang and Shih's scheme is still vulnerable to an insider's attack, masquerade attack and server spoofing attack. To resolve these flaws, this paper proposes an improvement over Hsiang and Shih's scheme.

The remainder of this paper is organized as follows. Section 2 reviews Hsiang and Shih 's scheme. Section 3 shows the cryptanalysis of Hsiang and Shih 's scheme. Section 4 presents an enhanced security user authentication scheme for multi-server environment using smart cards. The security analysis is in Section 5. Finally, the conclusion is made in the Section 6.

2 Review of Hsiang and Shih's scheme

The notations used throughout this paper are summarized as follows:

TABLE I. NOTATIONS DEFINITIONS

Notation	Definition
U	The notation represents user
ID	The identity of U
PW	The password of U
S	The remote server
RC	The registration center
x	The permanent secret key of S
$h()$	A secure one-way hash function
=>	A secure channel.
→	A common channel.
$\|\|$:	String concatenation operation

In this section, we briefly review Hsiang and Shih's scheme [6]. There are four phases in Hsiang and Shih's scheme, namely: registration, login, verification and password change. Different phases work as follows.

2.1 Registration phase

This phase is a registration procedure for the user U_i to get a license from *RC*. Before the user accesses the service provider, he has to submit his identity ID_i and password PW_i to *RC*. Then, *RC* performs the license to U_i. The steps are as follows:

(1) *R1*: $U_i \Rightarrow RC$:$\{ID_i, h(b\oplus PW_i)\}$:

U_i selects a password PW_i and an arbitrary number *b*, computes $h(b\oplus PW_i)$ and then sends$\{ ID_i, h(b\oplus PW_i) \}$ to *RC* by the secure channel.

(2) *R2*: $RC \Rightarrow U_i$:$\{V_i, H_i, B_i, R_i, h()\}$:

After *RC* has received the message from U_i and decided to accept the user's application, *RC* calculates the results and sends $\{V_i, H_i, B_i, R_i, h()\}$ to U_i by the secure channel where

$T_i= h(b\oplus PW_i), V_i = T_i\oplus h(ID_i \| h(b\oplus PW_i))$, $A_i= h(h(b\oplus PW_i)\|r) \oplus h(x\oplus r)$, $H_i= h(T_i)$, $B_i= A_i\oplus h(b\oplus PW_i)$ and $R_i = h(h(b\oplus PW_i)\|r)$

(3) *R3*: Smart Card saves the data containing (V_i, H_i, B_i, R_i, $h()$, b)

2.2 Login phase

When U_i keys his identity ID_i, password PW_i and the server identity SID_j in order to login the service provider S_j, the smart card performs the following steps:

(1) *L1*: U_i *checks* $H_i^*=h(T_i)$

U_i's smart card performs the following computations:

$T_i=V_i\oplus h(ID_i\oplus h(b\oplus PW_i))$ and $H_i^*=h(T_i)$

Then the smart card checks whether H_i^* is equal to H_i or not. If yes, the validity of the user can be assured and proceeds to the next step; otherwise, it rejects the login request.

(2) *L2*: $U_i\rightarrow S_j$:$\{CID_i, P_{ij}, Q_i, D_i, C_0, N_i\}$

U_i generates a random nonce N_i and performs the following computations to send the message$\{CID_i, P_{ij}, Q_i, D_i, C_0, N_i\}$to the service provider Sj by a common channel.

$A_i = B_i\oplus h(b\oplus PW_i)$, $CID_i = h(b\oplus PW_i)\oplus h(T_i\|A_i\|N_i)$, $P_{ij}= T_i\oplus h(A_i\|N_i\|SID_j)$, $Q_i= h(B_i\|A_i\|N_i)$, $D_i=R_i\oplus SID_j\oplus N_i$, $C_o= h(A_i\|N_i+1\|SID_j)$

2.3 Mutual verification and session key agreement phase

After receiving the login request message $\{CID_i, P_{ij}, Q_i, D_i, C_0, N_i\}$, S_j executes the following to authenticate the user U_i:

(1) *V1*: $S_j\rightarrow RC$: $\{M_{jr}, SID_j, D_i, C_0, N_i\}$

S_j generates a nonce N_{jr} and calculates $M_{jr}=h(SID_j\|y)\oplus N_{jr}$, then sends the message $\{M_{jr}, SID_j, D_i, C_0, N_i\}$ to *RC* by a common channel.

(2) *V2*: *RC* checks $C'_0= C_0$

RC calculates $N'_{jr}=M_{jr}\oplus h(SID_j\|y)$, $R'_i=D_i\oplus SID_j\oplus N_i$ and $A'_i=R'_i\oplus h(x\oplus r)$ and gets $C'_0=h(A'_i\|N_{i+1}\|SID_j)$ to check whether C'_0 is equal to C_0. If yes, the validity of S_j can be assured.

(3) *V3*: $RC\rightarrow S_j$: $\{C_1, C_2, N_{rj}\}$

RC generates a random nonce N_{rj} and calculates $N'_{jr}=M_{jr}\oplus h(SID_j\|y)$, $R'_i=D_i\oplus SID_j\oplus N_i$ and $A'_i=R'_i\oplus h(x\oplus r)$ to get $C_1=h(N'_{jr}\|h(SID_j\|y)\|N_{rj})$, $C_2=A_i \oplus h(h(SID_j\|y) \oplus N'_{jr})$ then sends back the message$\{C_1, C_2, N_{rj}\}$ to S_j.

(4) *V4*: S_j: checks $C'_1= C_1$

S_j calculates $C'_1=h(N_{jr}\|h(SID_j\|y)\|N_{rj})$ to check whether C'_1 is equal to C_1 or not . If yes, the validity of *RC* can be assured.

(5) *V5*: S_j: checks $Q'_i= Q_i$

S_j calculates $Q'_i=h(B_i\|A_i\|N_i)$ where $A_i= C_2\oplus h(h(SID_j\|y)\oplus N_{jr})$, $T_i=P_{ij}\oplus h(A_i\|N_i\|SID_j)$, $h(b\oplus PW_i)=CID_i\oplus h(T_i\|A_i\|N_i)$ and $B_i=A_i\oplus h(b\oplus PW_i)$ to check whether Q'_i is equal to Q_i. If yes, the validity of user U_i can be assured.

(6) *V6*: $S_j\rightarrow U_i$: $\{M_{ij}, N_j\}$

S_j generates a random nonce N_j and calculates $M_{ij}=h(B_i\|N_i\| A_i\|SID_j)$ then sends back the message$\{M_{ij}, N_j\}$ to U_i.

(7) *V7*: U_i: checks $M'_{ij}= M_{ij}$ and $U_i\rightarrow S_j$: $\{K\}$

U_i calculates $M'_{ij}=h(B_i\|N_i\|A_i\|SID_j)$ and checks whether M'_{ij} is equal to M_{ij}. If yes, the validity of the server S_j can be assured, and then U_i calculates $K= h(B_i\|N_j\|A_i\|SID_j)$ and sends it to S_j.

(8) *V8*: S_j checks $K'= K$

S_j calculates $K'= h(B_i\|N_i\|A_i\|SID_j)$ and checks whether K' is equal to K or not . If yes, the validity of U_i can be assured, and the mutual authentication phase is completed.

(9) *V9*: $SK= h(B_i\| A_i\|N_i\|N_j\|SID_j)$

S_j and U_i compute $h(B_i\|A_i\|N_i\|N_j\|SID_j)$ as the *SK* (session key)

2.4 Password change phase

The user U_i can change his original password to *PW* new freely without the help from *RC*. The steps are as follows:

(1) *P1*: U_i inserts his smart card into the smart card reader, U_i enters ID_i and PW_i, then demands to change the password.

(2) *P2*: Smart Card: $H_i^* = H_i$

The smart card calculates $H_i^* = h(T_i\oplus (h(ID_i\|h(b\oplus PW_i)))$ and checks whether H_i^* is equal to H_i . If yes, U_i chooses a new password *PW* new .

(3) *P3:* Smart Card :$(V_{new}, B_{new}, R_i, h(), b)$

The smart card calculates $V_{new}=T_i\oplus(h(ID_i||h(b\oplus PW_{new}))$, $B_{new}=B_i\oplus h(b\oplus PW_i)\oplus h(b\oplus PW_{new})$ and replaces V_i and B_i with V_{new} and B_{new}, respectively

3 Cryptanalysis of Hsiang and Shih's scheme

In this section, we will show that Hsiang and Shih's scheme still cannot escape from masquerade attack, inside privilege attack, server spoofing and registration center spoofing attacks

3.1 Masquerade attack

Assume that an adversary Allen is a legal user of the system. He can masquerade as any legal user U_i to login the service provider S_j .He can forge the encryption message h(x $\oplus$r) and then pass authentication without U_i's password. A more detail description of the attack is as follows:

(1) Because Allen is a legal user of the system, he can obtain (V_{Allen}, H_{Allen}, B_{Allen}, R_{Allen}, $h($ $)$, b_{Allen}) from his smart card. Then, he can compute $h(x\oplus r)= B_{\text{Allen}}\oplus R_{\text{Allen}}\oplus h(b_{\text{Allen}}\oplus PW_{\text{Allen}})$, PW_{Allen} being Allen's password. And then, Allen eavesdrops U_i's message $\{CID_i, P_{ij}, Q_i, D_i, C_0, N_i\}$ which is transmitted to the service provider S_j, and eavesdrops S_j*'s* message $\{M_{jr}, SID_j\}$ which is transmitted to the registration center *RC* from S_j. Next, Allen computes $R_i=D_i\oplus SID_j\oplus N_i$ (as in *V2* and D_i, SID_j, N_i obtained from the message) $A_i=R_i\oplus h(x\oplus r)$ (as in *V2* and $h(x\oplus r)$ obtained from Allen) $T_i=P_{ij}\oplus h(A_i||N_i||SID_j)$ (as in *V5* and P_{ij}, N_i, SID_j obtained from the message) $h(b_i\oplus PW_i)= CID_i\oplus h(T_i||A_i||N_i)$ (as in V5).

(2) Allen can obtain B_i through $B_i = A_i\oplus h(b\oplus PW_i)$ (as in L2).

(3) Next, he can compute $\{CID'_i, P'_{ij}, Q'_i, D'_i, C'_0, N_A\}$ to cheat Sj and the registration center RC with a new random nonce NA where

$$A_i = B_i\oplus h(b\oplus PW_i)$$

$$CID'_i= h(b\oplus PW_i)\oplus h(T_i||A_i||N_A)$$

$$P'_i= T_i\oplus h(A_i||N_A||SID_j)$$

$$Q'_i= h(B_i|| N_A||N_i)$$

$$D'_i=R_i\oplus SID_j\oplus N_A$$

$$C'_0= h(A_i|| N_{A+1}||SID_j)$$

As a result, Allen can masquerade any user to attack the system

3.2 Inside privilege attack

Assume that Allen is a service provider S_j's system administrator; he can obtain the legal user U_i's data to attack the system. The description is as follows:

(1) Allen obtains the message $U_i\rightarrow S_j$: $\{CID_i, P_{ij}, Q_i, D_i, C_0, N_i\}$, $S_j\rightarrow RC$: $\{M_{jr}, SID_j, D_i, C_0, N_i\}$ and $RC\rightarrow S_j$: $\{C_1, C_2, N_{rj}\}$ from the server S_j or eavesdrops from the Internet.

(2) Allen calculates $R_i=D_i\oplus SID_j\oplus N_i$(as in *V2*), $A_i=C_2\oplus h(M_{jr})$ (as in V_3), $T_i=P_{ij}\oplus h(A_i||N_i||SID_j)$ (as in *V5*), $h(b_i\oplus PW_i)=CID_i\oplus h(T_i||A_i||N_i)$ (as in *V5*) and $B_i = A_i\oplus h(b_i\oplus PW_i)$ (as in *V5*)

(3) Next, Allen can get U_i's session key $SK=h(B_i||A_i||N_i||N_j||SID_j)$ and attack the system.

3.3 Server spoofing and registration center spoofing attacks

As mentioned above, if Allen can obtain the hash function *h*( ), he can also impersonate any service provider S_j to cheat U_i from outside. He just needs to follow the steps of section 3.2 to spoof U_i by impersonating S_j and getting U_i's session key $SK=h(B_i||A_i||N_i||N_j||SID_j)$. Hsiang and Shih's scheme is therefore vulnerable to server spoofing and registration center spoofing attacks.

4 An enhanced scheme

This section presents an enhanced remote user authentication scheme for multi-server environment using smart cards. This scheme has four phases in our enhanced scheme: registration phase, login phase, verification phase and password change phase. The proposed scheme is described below

4.1 Registration phase

This phase is a registration procedure for the user U_i to get a license from *RC*. Before the user wants to access the service provider, he has to submit his identity ID_i and password PW_i to *RC*. Then, *RC* performs the license to U_i. The steps are as follows:

(1) U_i=>RC:$\{ID_i, h(b\oplus PW_i)\}$

U_i selects a password PW_i and an arbitrary number b, computes $h(b\oplus PW_i)$ and then sends$\{ID_i, h(b\oplus PW_i)\}$ to *RC* by the secure channel.

(2) RC => U_i:$\{V_i, H_i, B_i, R_i, h()\}$

After *RC* has received the message from U_i and decided to accept *the* user's application, *RC* generates a random nonce *Ea* with Diffie-Hellman's method [5,10, 15] to calculate the remainder *Y* (where *p* denotes a prime number and *g* denotes a primitive root). The method is as follows:

- *RC* randomly chooses a large number E_a and sends U_i $Y = gEa \bmod p$.
- U_i randomly chooses a large number *b* and sends *RC* $N_i = gEb \bmod p$
- *RC* and U_i can calculate their key as $K = YEb \bmod p = g\ Ea\ Eb \bmod p$.

The steps are as follows:

$Y = gEa \bmod p$

RC then calculates the results and sends $\{Y_A, G, P, P^*, G^*, R_A, V_i, H_i, B_i, R_i, h()\}$ to U_i by the secure channel where $Y_A = Y \oplus h(b \oplus PW_i)$, $G = g \oplus h(b \oplus PW_i)$, $P = p \oplus h(b \oplus PW_i)$, $R_A = r_i \oplus h(b \oplus PW_i)$, $T_i = h(b \oplus PW_i)$, $V_i = T_i \oplus h(ID_i \| h(b \oplus PW_i))$, $A_i = h(h(b \oplus PW_i) \| r_i) \oplus h(x \oplus r_i)$, $H_i = h(T_i)$, $B_i = A_i \oplus h(b \oplus PW_i)$, $R_i = h(h(b \oplus PW_i) \| r_i)$ and r_i is an arbitrary number. P^* denotes another prime number and G^* denotes another primitive root, both of which are saved at the granted service servers.

(3) Smart Card saves the data:($Y_A, G, P, P^*, G^*, R_A, V_i, H_i, B_i, R_i, h(), b$).

4.2 Login phase

When U_i keys his identity ID_i, password PW_i and the server identity SID_j in order to login the service provider S_j, the smart card performs the following steps:

(1) U_i checks $H_i^* = H_i$

U_i 's smart card performs the following computations:

$T_i = V_i \oplus h(ID_i \oplus h(b \oplus PW_i))$ and $H_i^* = h(T_i)$

It then checks whether H_i^* is equal to H_i or not . If yes, the validity of the user can be assured and proceeds to the next step; otherwise, it rejects the login request.

(2) $U_i \rightarrow S_j$: $\{C_0, CID_i, D_i, P_{ij}, Q_i, RK, N_i, YC\}$

U_i generates a nonce Eb and performs the following computations to send the message

$\{C_0, CID_i, D_i, P_{ij}, Q_i, RK, N_i, YC\}$ to the service provider S_j by a common channel.

$Y = YA \oplus h(b \oplus PW_i)$, $g = G \oplus h(b \oplus PW_i)$, $p = P \oplus h(b \oplus PW_i)$, $r_i = R_A \oplus h(b \oplus PW_i)$ for calculating $N_i = gEb \bmod p$, $K = YEb \bmod p$, $R_K = r_i \oplus h(K)$, $D_i = R_i \oplus SID_j \oplus K$ And then, $A_i = B_i \oplus h(b \oplus PW_i)$ $CID_i = h(b \oplus PWi) \oplus h(T_i \| A_i \| N_i)$, $P_{ij} = T_i \oplus h(A_i \| N_i \| SID_j)$, $Q_i = h(B_i \| A_i \| N_i)$, $C_0 = h(A_i \| N_{i+1} \| SID_j)$

4.3 Mutual verification and session key agreement phase

After receiving the login request message $\{C_0, CID_i, D_i, P_{ij}, Q_i, RK, N_i\}$, S_j executes the following to authenticate the user U_i:

(1) $S_j \rightarrow RC$: $\{M_s, N_i, SID_j, D_i, R_K\}$

S_j generates the nonce NS and calculates $M_s = h(SID_j \| y) \oplus NS$, then sends the message$\{M_s, N_i, SID_j, RK\}$ to RC by a common channel.

(2) RC: $C_0^* = C_0$

RC calculates $K = N_i Ea \bmod p$, $r_i = RK \oplus h(K)$, $NS^* = M_S \oplus h(SID_j \| y)$, $R_i^* = D_i \oplus SID_j \oplus K$, $A_i^* = R_i^* \oplus h(x \oplus r_i)$ for $C_0^* = h(A_i^* \| K \| SID_j)$ to check whether C_0^* is equal to C_0 or not . If yes, the validity of U_i can be assured.

(3) $RC \rightarrow S_j$: $\{C_1, C_2, N_r\}$

RC generates nonce Nr and calculates

$C_1 = h(NS^* \| (SID_j \| y) \| N_r)$

$C_2 = Ai^* \oplus h(h(SID_j \| y) \oplus N_s^*)$ and then sends back the message$\{C_1, C_2, N_r\}$ to S_j.

(4) S_j: checks $C'_1 = C_1$

S_j calculates $C'_1 = h(NS \| (SID_j \| y) \| N_r)$ to check whether C'_1 is equal to C_1 or not . If yes, the validity of RC can be assured.

(5) S_j: checks $Q'_i = Q_i$

S_j calculates $A_i = C_2 \oplus h(h(SID_j \| y) \oplus NS)$, $T_i = P_{ij} \oplus h(A_i \| N_i \| SID_j)$, $h(b \oplus PW_i) = CID_i \oplus h(T_i \| A_i \| N_i)$, $B_i = A_i \oplus h(b \oplus PW_i)$, $Q'_i = h(B_i \| A_i \| N_i)$ to check whether Q'_i is equal to Q_i or not . If yes, the validity of U_i can be assured.

(6) $S_j \rightarrow U_i$: $\{C_3, YS\}$

S_j generates a nonce E_s for $YS = GE_s \bmod P^*$ (where P^* denotes a prime number and G^* denotes a primitive root) and calculates $C_3 = h(B_i \| N_i \| A_i \| SID_j)$, and then sends back the message$\{C_3, YS\}$ to U_i.

(7) U_i: $C'_3 = C_3$ and $U_i \rightarrow S_j$: $\{YC, T_c, C_4\}$

U_i calculates $C'_3 = h(B_i \| N_i \| A_i \| SID_j)$ to check whether C'_3 is equal to C_3 or not . If yes, the validity of the server S_j can be assured, and then U_i calculates $YC = GE_c \bmod P^*$, $M_K = YSE_c \bmod P^*$ and $C_4 = h(B_i \| YS \| A_i \| T_c \| SID_j)$ to send$\{YC, C_4\}$ to the server S_j at the time T_c (the current timestamp).

(8) S_j checks $C'_4 = C_4$

S_j checks $T_s - T_c < \Delta T$ at the time T_s (where T_s denotes the current timestamp and ΔT denotes the legal time interval for transmission delay), and then calculates $MK = YCE_s \bmod P^*$ and $C'_4 = h(B_i \| YS \| A_i \| T_c \| SID_j)$to check whether C'_4 is equal to C_4 or not . If yes, the validity of U_i can be assured, and the mutual authentication phase is completed.

(9) $SK = h(B_i \| YC \| A_i \| YS \| SID_j \| T_c) \oplus MK$

S_j and U_i compute Session Key $(SK) = h(B_i \| YC \| A_i \| YS \| SID_j \| T_c) \oplus MK$ as the session key SK for S_j and U_i communication

4.4 Password change phase

The user U_i can change his original password to new PW new freely without the help from RC. The steps are as follows:

(1) U_i inserts his smart card into the smart card reader

U_i enters ID_i and PW_i, and requests to change the password.

(2) Smart Card: $H_i^* = H_i$

The smart card calculates $H_i^* = h(T_i \oplus (h(ID_i \| h(b \oplus PW_i)))$ and checks whether H_i^* is equal to H_i or not . If yes, U_i chooses a new password PW new.

(3) Smart card:(V_{new} , B_{new} , R_i, $h()$, b}

The smart card calculates $V_{new} = T_i \oplus (h(ID_i||h(b \oplus PW_{new}))$, $B_{new} = B_i \oplus h(b \oplus PW_i) \oplus h(b \oplus PW_{new})$ and replaces V_i and B_i with V_{new} and B_{new}, respectively.

5 Security analysis

In this section, we will only discuss the enhanced security of our improved scheme. The others are the same as Liao–Wang's scheme and Hsiang and Shih's scheme [6, 16].

5.1 Resistance to masquerade attack

If the adversary Allen is a legal user, he cannot forge U_i's encryption message $h(x \oplus r_i)$ from the smart card containing(V_{Allen}, H_{Allen}, B_{Allen}, R_{Allen}, $h()$, b_{Allen}). for $B_{Allen} \oplus R_{Allen} \oplus h(b_{Allen} \oplus PW_{Allen}) = h(x \oplus r_{Allen})$. The random number r_{Allen} is a uniquely garbled character number for Allen only. Allen cannot pass authentication without knowing the user U_i's password.

5.2 Resistance to outsider impersonation attack

Assume that an adversary attacker Allen can obtain the transaction messages from anywhere, then he does not need to obtain the legal user U_i's data to attack the system. The description is as follows:

(1) Allen obtains the message $U_i \rightarrow S_j$:{C_0, CID_i, D_i, P_{ij}, Q_i, RK, N_i}, $S_j \rightarrow RC$: {M_s, N_i, SID_j, D_i, R_K}, $RC \rightarrow S_j$: {C_1, C_2, N_r}, $S_j \rightarrow U_i$: {C_3, YS } and $U_i \rightarrow S_j$: {YC,T_c,C_4} from the server S_j or eavesdrops from the Internet.

(2) Allen cannot calculate U_i's A_i from $R_i = D_i \oplus SID_j \oplus K$ and $A_i = R_i \oplus h(x \oplus r_i)$ for he does not know the private key K which only RC and U_i know. Allen' s attack will fail here.

Moreover, Allen cannot calculate A_i from $A_i = C_2 \oplus h(M_s)$ for he cannot obtain the hash function $h(\,)$.

5.3 Resistance to inside privilege attack

Assume that an adversary attacker Allen is a service provider S_j's system administrator. He cannot obtain the legal user U_i's data to attack the system. The description is as follows:

(1) Allen obtains the message $U_i \rightarrow S_j$:{C_0, CID_i, D_i, P_{ij}, Q_i, RK, N_i}, $S_j \rightarrow RC$: {M_s, N_i, SID_j, D_i, R_K } , $RC \rightarrow S_j$: { C_1, C_2, N_r }, $S_j \rightarrow U_i$:{C_3, YS} and $U_i \rightarrow S_j$:{YC,T_c,C_4} from S_j or eavesdrops from the Internet.

(2) Allen can calculate $A_i = C_2 \oplus h(M_s)$ by {C_2, M_s} and get $T_i = P_{ij} \oplus h(A_i|| N_i||SID_j)$,

$h(b_i \oplus PW_i) = CID_i \oplus h(T_i||A_i||N_i)$, $B_i = A_i \oplus h(b_i \oplus PW_i)$ and MK.

(3) Allen can only calculate $SK = h(B_i||YC||A_i||YS|| SID_j||T_c) \oplus MK$ at the time T_s but the user U_i is also communicating with S_j at the same time. If the SK is a uniquely exclusive session [1, 2, 19] at that time then Allen cannot attack by this session key. It is the same that even though Allen is RC's system administrator, he cannot obtain the legal user U_i's data to attack the system, for the session key can only be computed from S_j and U

6 Conclusion

We have analyzed Hsiang-Shih's user authentication scheme for multi-server environment using smart cards and some secure schemes which have been proposed for user authentication based on smart cards. Hsiang-Shih's scheme is more superior among the related user authentication schemes. However, we find that it is vulnerable to (1)masquerade attack, (2)inside privilege attack and (3)server spoofing (4)registration center spoofing attacks. The problems may render the scheme unsecured, because the attacker can successfully impersonate the legal user to login and use the server resources. Hence, we propose an improvement of Hsiang-Shih's scheme. The proposed scheme still does not need to maintain any verification table on the remote server. Further, it not only inherits the merits of Hsiang-Shih's but also enhances the security. Finally, the problem of masquerade attack, inside privilege attack and server spoofing and registration center spoofing attacks are completely solved under our scheme

7 Acknowledgement

We would like to thank the National Science Council of the Republic of China (Taiwan) for financial support of this research under contract numbers NSC 101-2221-E-007-128-MY2 and NSC 101-2219-E-007-007.

8 References

[1] G. Bollella, B. Brogsol, P. Dibble, S. Furr, J. Gosling, D. Hardin, M. Turnbull, R. Belliardi, D. Locke, S. Robbins, P. Solanki, and D. de Niz. ,The real-time specification for java, Addison-Wesley: November 2001. http://www.rtj.org/rtsj-V1.0.pdf.

[2] Harold W. Cain, Ravi Rajwar, Morris Marden, Mikko H. Lipasti, "An Architectural Evaluation of Java TPC-W," hpca, pp.0219, Seventh International Symposium on High-Performance Computer Architecture (HPCA'01), 2001

[3] C. Chang, J.S. Lee, An efficient and secure multi-server password authentication scheme using smart cards, IEEE. Proceeding of the International Conference on Cyber worlds, 2004.

[4] Manik Lal Das, Ashutosh Saxena, Ved P. Gulati, A dynamic ID-based remote user authentication scheme, IEEE Transactions on Consumer Electronics 50 (2) (2004) 629–631.

[5] W. Diffie and M. Hellman, "New directions in cryptography," IEEE Trans. Inf. Theory, vol. IT-21, no. 6, pp. 644–654, Nov. 1976.

[6] Han-Cheng Hsiang and Wei-Kuan Shih, Improvement of the secure dynamic ID based remote user authentication scheme for multi-server environment Compute. Stand. Interfaces doi:10.1016/j.csi. 2008.11. 002 (2008)

[7] M.S. Hwang and L.H. Li, A new remote user authentication scheme using smart card .IEEE Transactions on Consumer Electronics. v46 i1 . (2000)28-30

[8] T. Hwang,W.C. Ku, Reparable key distribution protocols for Internet environments, IEEE Trans. Consum. Electron. 43 (5) (1995) 1947–1949.

[9] T. Hwang, Y. Chen, C.S. Laih, Non-interactive password authentication without password tables, IEEE Region 10 Conference on Computer and Communication System, vol. 1, (Sept. 1990) 429–431.

[10] Antoine Joux, A One Round Protocol for Tripartite Diffie–Hellman, J. Cryptology (2004) 17: 263–276, doi: 10.1007/s00145-004-0312-y

[11] W.S. Juang, Efficient multi-server password authenticated key agreement using smart cards, IEEE Trans. Consum. Electron. 50 (1) (2004) 251–255.

[12] L. Lamport, Password authentication with insecure communication, Communications of the ACM 24 (11) (1981) 770–772.

[13] W.B. Lee, C.C. Chang, User identification and key distribution maintaining anonymity for distributed computer network, Comput. Syst. Sci. 15 (4) (2000) 211–214.

[14] L. Li, I. Lin, M. Hwang, A remote password authentication scheme for multi-server architecture using neural networks, IEEE Trans. Neural Netw. 12 (6) (2001) 1498–1504.

[15] I.-E. Liao, C.-C. Lee, M.-S. Hwang, A password authentication scheme over insecure networks, J. Comput. System Sci. 72 (2006) 727–740

[16] Y.P. Liao, S.S.Wang, A secure dynamic ID based remote user authentication scheme for multi-server environment, Comput. Stand. Interfaces (2007), doi:10.1016/j.csi.2007.10.007

[17] C. Lin, M.S. Hwang, L.H. Li, A new remote user authentication scheme for multi-server architecture, Future Gener. Comput. Syst. 1 (19) (2003) 13–21.

[18] T.S. Messergers, E.A. Dabbish, R.H. Sloan, Examining smart card security under the threat of power analysis attacks, IEEE Trans. Comput. 51 (5) (2002) 541–552.

[19] SH. Son, R Zimmerman, J Hansson," An adaptable security manager for real-time transactions", in Euromicro conference on Real-Time Systems, Stockolm, Sweden, 2000. 12th.

[20] W.J. Tsuar, C.C.Wu,W.B. Lee, A flexible user authentication for multi-server internet services, Networking-JCN2001LNCS, vol. 2093, Springer-Verlag, 2001, pp. 174–183.

[21] W.J. Tsuar, An enhanced user authentication scheme for multi-server internet services, Appl. Math. Comput. 170 (2005) 258–266.

[22] T.S.Wu, C.L. Hsu, Efficient user identification scheme with key distribution preserving anonymity for distributed computer networks, Comput. Secur. 23 (2004) 120–125.

[23] Y. Yang, S.Wang, F. Bao, J.Wang, R. Deng, New efficient user identification and key distribution scheme providing enhanced security, Comput. Secur. 23 (8) (2004) 697–704.

[24] S.M. Yen, K.H. Liao, Shared authentication token secure against replay and weak key attack, Information Processing Letters (1997) 78–80

Secure Wireless Fax Module

Shakeel Durrani, Imran Jattala
Horizon Technologies
Islamabad, Pakistan
shakeel.durranii@gmail.com, imran.jattala@gmail.com

Rida Ameer, Dr. Nassar Ikram
Horizon Technologies
Islamabad, Pakistan
rida.ameerr@gmail.com, dr_nassar_ikram@yahoo.com

Abstract— **Fax machine is still widely accepted as a legal document and a backup form of rudimentary communication. This acceptance has also left room for improvement/introduction of new communication mediums and techniques. This paper presents a secure fax module that uses GPRS/EDGE as its medium of communication. The system has two tier of encryption/security for securing all forms of data, first at the application layer (AES256) and second at the transport layer with TLS 1.1. The module is built on a customized PCB with a GSM modem; the central processor for the unit is C54x DSP. A secure fax management server with a static-IP processes all the required security information and registers each individual module against its public key, the Client Management System (CSM) connecting modules across the IP cloud. The system is cost effective commercial-off-the-self (COTS) based module and greatly reduces the operational expenditure (OPEX) by removing international termination cost for fax calls. This paper presents the complete SDLC for the secure fax module.**

Keywords: Wireless Fax, SDLC, Cybersecurity, Sierra Wireless Q2687

I. INTRODUCTION

The first commercial facsimile (fax for short) was introduced by Xerox in 1964 known as LDX (Long Distance Xerography) and later in 1966 launched 'Magnafax Telecopier', a device that could transmit a letter size document over a telephone line in six minutes [1]. Since then the paramount expansion of the Information Communication Technology (ICT) in the 21st century has led to more reliance on internet based communication and fax machines have slowly dwindled in numbers especially in small offices and home users. A host of PC applications are available that remove the requirement of having a standalone fax machine; such requirement has also been removed by ISDN [2]. Confidence on fax as rudimentary form of secure communication is still prevalent in government and military sector, to a certain extent in large organizations. Another predominant factor is that fax is treated as a legal document in majority parts of world, while other internet facilities (like email) do not enjoy such status.

This prerequisite has left room for sporadic introduction of secure fax machines and modules, such as ours. The use of 3G (or EDGE/GPRS) provides wireless connectivity to an old fax machine and simultaneously greatly reduces the OpEx (Operational Expenditure) of international faxing, avoiding international termination cost, as the fax is being transmitted via IP [3]. Secure fax modules also provide the comfort that legal documents are traversing over public wireless infrastructure in a secure manner. This paper is divided into three parts the first covers the hardware and firmware, the second covers the Client Management System (CMS) and the last being the testing and verification of the entire system.

II. WIRELESS SECURE FAX MODULE

The System Architecture or working model of the Wireless Secure Fax Module (WSFM) is given in Fig. 1.

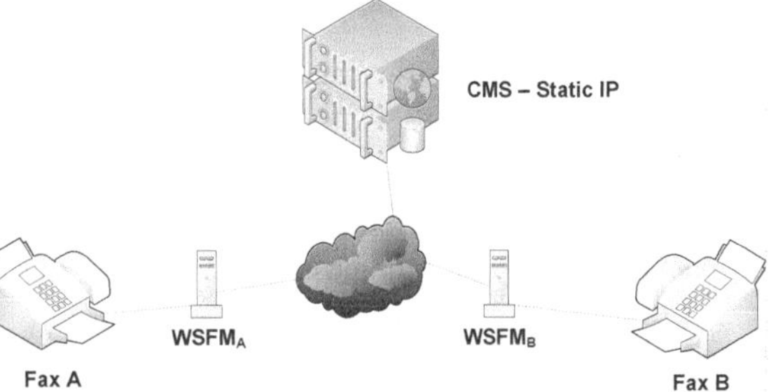

Fig. 1. Secure Fax - System Architecture

WSFM$_A$ and WSFM$_B$ are always connected (online) to the static IP server / CMS that host all clients' information. Fax machine A calls WSFM$_A$, a plain fax call (via RJ11). WSFM$_A$ receive the fax, encrypts it and forwards a request to the server via EDGE/GRPS (a TLS connection). The CMS connect the required module, acting as the super-node [4]. WSFM$_B$ receives the fax in secure mode via EDGE/GRPS and stores the fax within its SRAM.

WSFM$_B$ decrypts the file and calls the local fax machine B (via RJ11), which receives the fax in plain mode and prints it. An acknowledgement is sent back on the secure connection to fax machine A. CMS acts as a transparent connection between two Fax machines.

A. *Secure Fax Module*

WSFM is made of 4 different module controlled via a central processor (DSP) from Texas Instruments (TI) C54CST (Client Side Telephony). C54CST is an ultra-low power (50mW) processor that provides a host of telephony algorithm vital for the quick realization of the project [5]. Details of each module will be explained in subsequent paragraphs, followed by a system overview. The project was initially evaluated on a Spectrum Digital Starter Kit for Proof of Concept (PoC), a tailored down version of the final machine. Later customized PCBs were fabricated that included all the modules in the block diagram on a single multilayered PCB [6]. A fully functional Secure Fax Module was later tested extensively over the public GSM networks. The block diagram of the Wireless Secure Fax Module (WSFM) is given in Fig. 2.

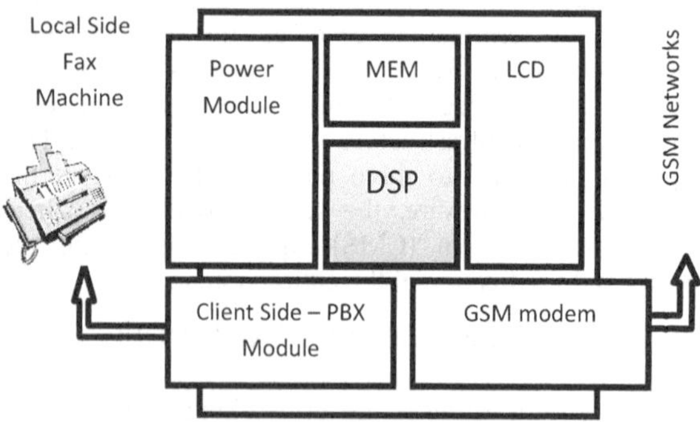

Fig. 2. Secure Fax Block Diagram

B. Hardware Overview

The power module was primarily based on regulators from Texas Instruments, while the ring voltages were generated via a customized transformer. The regulator used in the design fulfilled the current requirements with huge margins. The itemization of all regulated voltages is given in successive paragraphs.

1) Regulated Voltage 12VAC to 48VAC and 5VDC

The 12VAC to 48VAC setup was realized via a customized wound transformer with a 1:4 turn ratio providing 48VAC as Ring Voltage (1RN) for a single client side fax machine. The AC current after passing a DC rectifier is feed into 'TPS5430'. The regulator is used as per the OEM (Original Equipment Manufacturer) recommendation, provided in that datasheet of the regulator [7]. The Client Side PBX module also required a regulated 12VDC hence the output from the bridge was also feed into 'IC7812' which outputted the required voltage [8].

2) Regulated Voltage 5VDC to 3.3VDC and 1.5VDC:

Two 'TPS7301' were used with different networks to provide regulated outputs of 3.3VDC and 1.5VDC. The regulator was used in accordance with its datasheet [9].

3) LCD Control module:

3.5" touchscreen LCD was used for WSFM's User Interface (UI). The LCD screens were designed in Adobe Photoshop and ported to the LCD module in the required OEM format. The LCD was controlled via ATMEG128 and all the subroutine were written as per the OEM module. The LCD was interfaced to C54CST via an SPI interface, and a protocol was established between them based on a lookup table. The table was a transformation of characters to commands and acknowledgement.

4) Client Side PBX Module:

The initial design was based on the Project "The 89C51 PABX" [10]. The design used in WSFM was an abridged version, with customization as per the project requirements. Design borrowed from the original project, were 'Switching circuit', 'Tone Generator', and 'DTMF Decoder'; Acting as a mini exchange (PBX) with two RJ11 ports. One port is connected to the socket modem (for a landline solution), while the other line connects the WSFM and local side fax machine. The controller, 89C51, detects the hook and off-hook state on both lines. In case off-hook a dial tone is sent on the phone line and the exchange enters into a listening state, for DTMF. On detecting the phone number, the required information is passed on the GSM modem. The exchange provides the ring and the line voltages to the local side fax machine, hence providing the communication channel.

5) GSM modem:

The GSM modem is quad-band module from Sierra Wireless Q2687. The GSM module reduced the integration cycle of the project, as the firm provides a rich set of apps and key basic building blocks [11]. The development environment for the module is based on Eclipse, OpenAT, for an embedded ARM9 processor, which provides a user friendly environment.

C. Secure Fax Proof of Concept (PoC)

The PoC for the project was scheduled to be given on the Spectrum Digital starter kit. The PoC was divided into three phases; details of each phase are given below:

1) Phase I of PoC Development

Initially the printing and scanning of the fax were omitted from the PoC and a scanned copy of fax page was employed. The 14 algorithms within C54CST did not include soft G3 fax. Therefore the first task was to implement the G3 protocol. This was achieved within short period and commenced soft trials. A couple of troubling shooting sessions finally resulted in the successful transmission of a soft fax from terminal A to B via RJ11 (over a desktop PBX switch). Successful completion of Phase I trials enabled the project to move into Phase II.

2) Phase II of PoC Development

The primary goal of the second phase was the scanning and printing of the fax page on a local side fax machine using RJ11. The objective was to store a fax page within the SRAM on the starter kit and later have it printed on the same fax. Initially the project team had several issues, e.g. timing, scanning, and printing issues i.e. call dropping, half page scanning, printing garbage (all black lines, sending a single page and receiving multiple pages), printing half pages, etc. Finally after extensive troubling shooting with the help of a soft-fax programs (Putty fax) the exact timing and frame synchronization was achieved [12]. A plain fax was successfully scanned and printed on the local side fax machines. The same exercise was done in printing and scanning multiple fax pages.

3) Phase III of PoC Development

The GSM fax required the development of a Static IP server, to be explained in detail in the Client Management System (CSM) section. The GSM module sent a complete soft fax page (stored on the SRAM) via GPRS/EDGE using a TCP connection to the static IP server which successfully relayed the file to the destination WSFM. This was achieved using the development kit from Wavecom (now Sierra Wireless). The second part required the development of a secure protocol between client and server. The Sierra Wireless provides an OpenSSL API that made the client side development quicker and easier.

4) Prototype Development

The prototype phase was divided into three major components.

a) The functionality of individual modules,

b) Integration of all the hardware modules,

c) PCB designing, fabrication and assembly.

5) Individual Modules Functionality

All the modules mention in the block diagram were first made functional and tested individually. Module were tested on either there starter kits or evaluation modules. Certain parts were tested on breadboards, i.e. 48VAC with its customized transformer, others required the fabrication of two layer PCBs for functionality checking, i.e. LCD module. After successful functionality testing of each module an integration scheme was devised.

6) System Integration

Individual modules were integrated in a systematic way to the main DSP board either using their respective evaluation kits or making small two layer customized PCBs. After extensive troubleshooting and error removal 95% integration was achieved. The integrated lab prototype was tested extensive within lab environments on a Local PBX.

7) PCB Design, Fabrication and Assemble

All individual module schematics were put together into a single system schematics and a comprehensive Bill of Material (BOM) was generate for procurement of parts. The PCB was designed according to the specification of a CAD drawing for the WSFM casing. The casing was designed and fabricated prior to the designing of the PCB. The PCB designer also took into consideration optimized placement and routing, thermal management and stack management to produce the required 50 Ohm control impedance board [13]. A macro screenshot of the final PCB that shows a single top layer with components' silkscreen is given in Fig. 3.

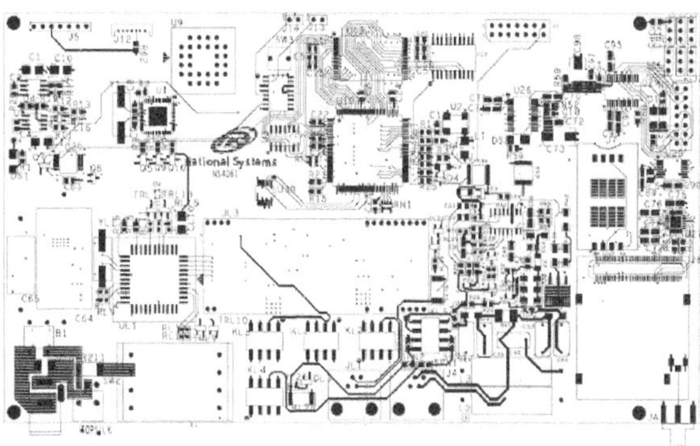

Fig. 3. PCB Top-layer Silkscreen

The final PCB is six layered with a single power and ground plane and was fabricated on FR4 with gold immersion. After fabrication and assembly the prototype was again tested for improved functionality. With a few errors and minor alterations and comprehensive troubleshooting, 100% functionality was achieved.

The PCB was redesigned, fabricated and assembled and only two recursive cycles resulted in an error free PCB. The new assembled PCB was again tested for functionality, which this time gave 100 percent functionality without a single glitch, as shown in Fig. 4.

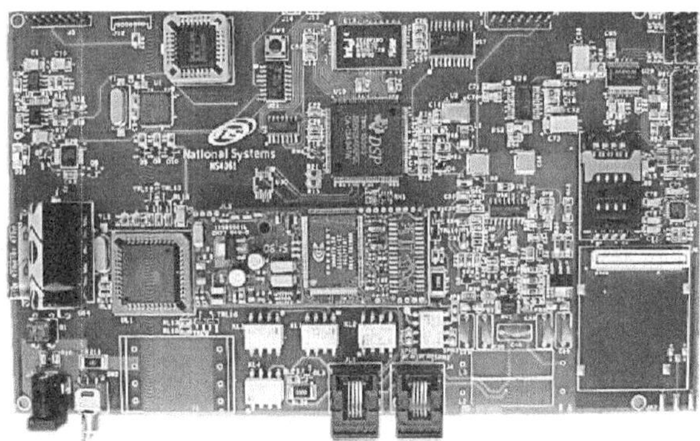

Fig. 4. Final PCB of WSFM

III. CLIENT MANAGEMENT SYSTEM

The Client Management System (CMS) was developed and tested on a Dell Edge Server T110, with a total of 500 simulated clients and later tested with four actual WSFM. The system comprised of a Fax & Crypto Management System (FCMS), Client Database (CD) and Client Management Application (User Interface). In order to improve performance and security each subsystem should be housed on a separate machine. The Certification Authority (CA) is on a separate x86 machine.

A. *Fax & Crypto management System*

The server was host on the internet with a static IP and all clients WSFM are connected to the server. The system uses two layer of security, first at the application layer and second at the transport layer. All communication between the client and server is secured first via TLS (based on OpenSSL 1.0.1-stable) [14]. OpenSSL is composed of two protocol layers, the SSL Handshake and Record Protocol. The Handshake is used to authenticate the server and the client, decide the cipher suite, generate the sessions and establish a trusted channel [15]. The machines currently use a self-signed certificate but a certification authority was also established however not tested. The application layer security uses AES256 and encrypts all data within the SRAM, fax page by page; the key exchange used is Diffie-Hellman [16]. The secure communication protocol within the TLS tunnel for transmission and reception is given in Fig. 5 & Fig. 6 respectively.

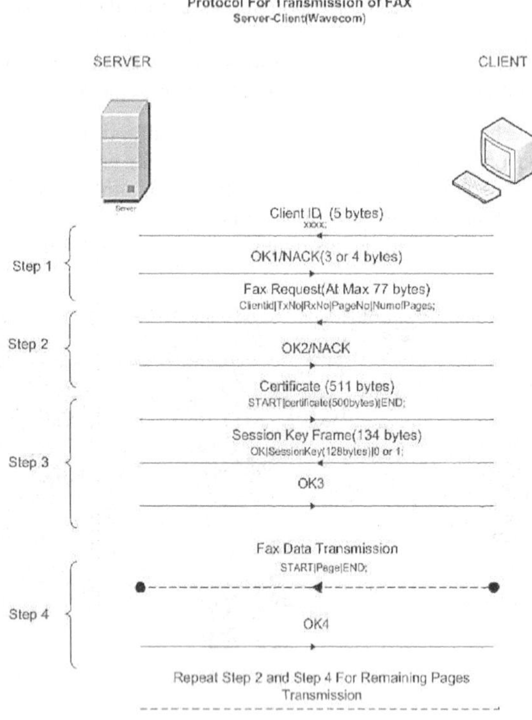

Fig. 5. Transmission of Secure Fax

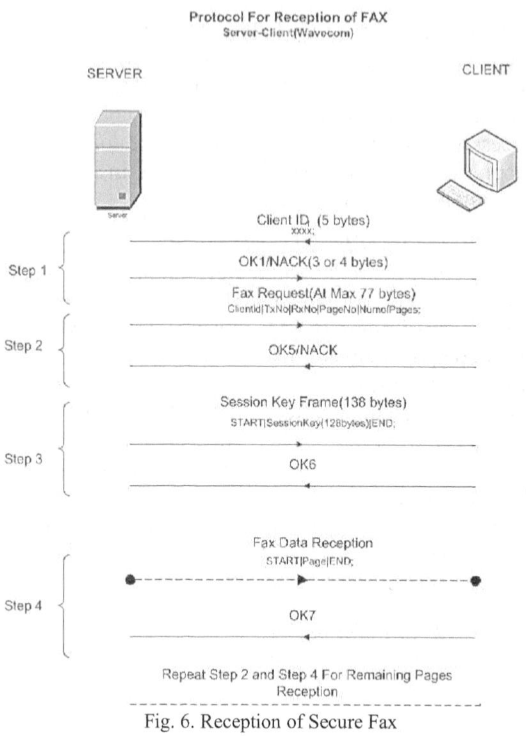

Fig. 6. Reception of Secure Fax

B. *Client Database (CD)*

The server keeps all client information encrypted within the database. An encrypted log of communication is also maintained in a separate database, the Syslog is also kept encrypted. Two tiered access control is put in place for the server; smart card and password based while biometrics can be integrated at a later stage [17]. Role based access control also reduced the risk of tampering of the server by lower tier operators [18]. The database does not manage or store fax data.

C. *Client Management Application (CMA)*

This application module allowed the system administrator and operators to manage all clients, add/register new clients, blacklist/revoke clients, retrieve Call Data Record (CDR), update security & software patches, and generate various reports for management purposes, etc. A single screenshot of the CMA for all connection-establishment is given in Fig. 7.

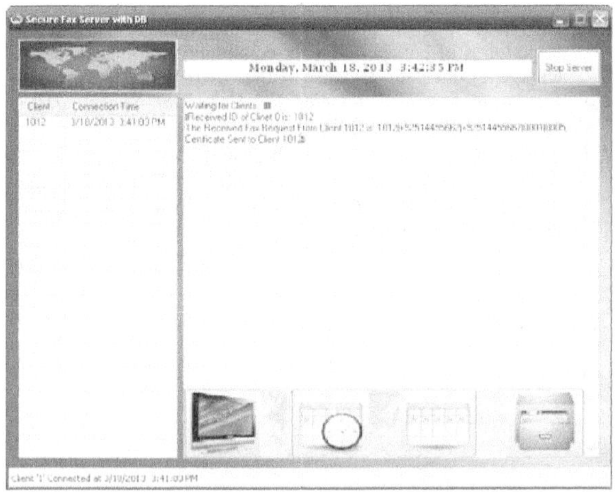

Fig.7. CMS' - Establishment of Fax Client Connections

D. Cybersecurity Perspective

In order to fulfill the CIA's Triad requirement of Confidentiality, Integrity and Availability comprehensively, the server also needs to be protected by a strong cyber and network security infrastructure. This may include DMZ protected within firewalls, Intrusion Prevention System (IPS), Unified Treat Management (UTM), security information event manager, etc. [19]. Strict security governance, policy and risk management is also critical to the infrastructure and overall protection. The level of the security controls depends on the criticality of the data/assets to be protected. The protection of the server is a separate topic/dimension and should be treated with an essential security perspective especially with the rise in recent cyber-attacks and level of sophistication [20].

IV. TESTING AND VERIFICATION

The complete system was tested extensively over three different GSM networks (communication service providers). AST (Accelerated Stress Test) was conducted on the module. This was achieved by putting the system under high stress by introducing an accelerating factor of continuous faxing within a short period of 6 hours, to produce 'number of fax(s)'-to-fail and finding an approximate Failure Probability for the module [21]. All the results showed that WSFM to be extremely successful machine with a single call lose in over 100 calls, resulting in 98 as the number of fax(s) to fail and a failure probability of 98 percent. All these results showed that fax module to be a reliable device. A comparative product analysis was not done due to non-availability of a similar device.

Calls errors if related to the local side fax machine were not included in the overall results i.e. fax paper jamming, printing error, etc. The WSFM only increases the duration of the call, which is the price to pay for the addition of a new security layer.

AST for the CMS was tested by simulating 500 parallel connections all sending similar fax data repeatedly. CMS was tested for continuous 5 days without any loss of fax data. In order to check the reliability of 'establishment of connections', random connection were made from 500 simulated module on/off with all security feature set enabled. The server was able to connect all 500 modules simultaneously. The results of the test are given in Fig. 7.

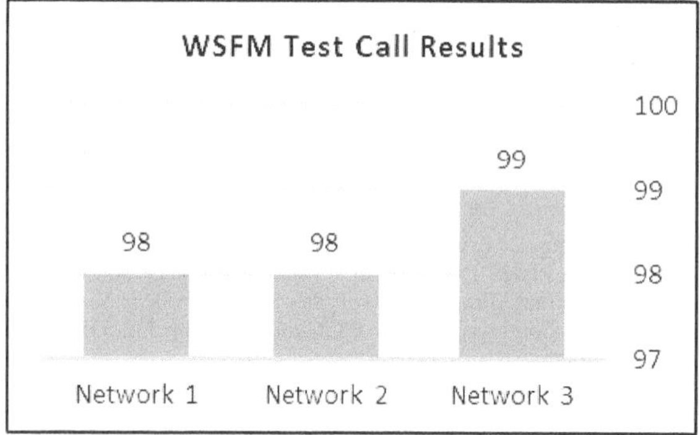

Fig.8. WSFM Test Call Results

V. CONCLUSION

The system presents a full functional secure fax machine module with a purpose developed Client Management System (CMS). A cost effective solution and reduces costs incurred from international secure faxing, along the lines of Fax over IP. The system is secured via an open source platform (OPENSSL) which is consistently studied, updated and patched for security vulnerability and threats. A second layer of security is provided for the security paranoid user. The module platform is custom built and extensively tested and produced the required results. The CMS was developed to provide a health user experience and optimized performance. The added advantage of the wireless module was the introduction of ubiquitous deployment and the removal of plain old telephone service (POTS) connection requirement. The system requires extensive international environments for it to be termed as an international compliant device.

REFERENCES

[1] J. X. Jiang, M. Harris Stanford, and Y. Xie, "Does it matter who pays for bond ratings? Historical evidence," *Journal of Financial Economics*, 2012.

[2] N. Gale, and P. Humphreys. "Making the Most of ISDN." *Communications Conference 1990: Electronic Communications in the 1990's-a New Era; Preprints of Papers*. Institution of Engineers, Australia, 1990.

[3] J. Baldwin, J. EwErt, and S. YamEn, "Evolution of the voice interconnect," *Ericsson Review*, no. 2, pp. 10–15, 2010.

[4] H. Xie and Y. R. Yang, "A measurement-based study of the skype peer-to-peer VoIP performance," in *Proc of IPTPS*, 2007.

[5] N.M. Anas, Z. Rahman, A. Shafii, M.N.A. Rahman, and Z.A.M. Amin, "Secure speech communication over public switched telephone network," *Asia-Pacific Conference on Applied Electromagnetics, 2005. APACE 2005.*, pp.20-21, Dec. 2005.

[6] K. Kucuk, M. Karakoc, A. Kavak, and H. Yigit, "Design and Hardware Implementation of a Novel Smart Antenna Algorithm Using TI DSPs," *2nd International Symposium on Wireless Communication Systems, 2005.*, pp.596-600, 5-7 Sep. 2005.

[7] S. Dhawan, D. Lynn, H. Neal, R. Sumner, M. Weber, and R. Weber, "Ideas on DC-DC Converters for Delivery of Low Voltage and High Currents for the SLHC/ILC Detector Electronics in Magnetic field and Radiation environments.," *Proceedings of the 12th Workshop on Electronics for LHC and Future Experiments (LECC 2006)*, pp.78–92, 2006.

[8] Puu-An Juang; Ching-Chih Tsai, "Characterization of an Asymmetric Disk-Type Ultrasonic Motor With Single-Phase Current Drive," *IEEE Transactions on Instrumentation and Measurement*, vol.58, no.9, pp.3122-3129, Sep. 2009.

[9] Kae Wong, D. Evans, "A 150mA Low Noise, High PSRR Low-Dropout Linear Regulator in 0.13µm Technology for RF SoC Applications," *Proceedings of the 32nd European Solid-State Circuits Conference, 2006. ESSCIRC 2006.*, pp.532-535, 19-21 Sep. 2006.

[10] M. Shakeel Malik, (2013, May 20), *The 89C51 PABX.*[Online]. Available: http://www.kmitl.ac.th/~kswichit/PABx/PABx.htm.

[11] J. Marais, and G.P. Hancke, "Design of a low cost video monitor store and forward device," *2012 IEEE International Instrumentation and Measurement Technology Conference (I2MTC)*, pp.165-170, 13-16 May 2012.

[12] P. Puech, E. Chazard, L. Lemaitre, and R. Beuscart, "DicomWorks Teleradiology: Secure transmission of medical images over the Internet at low cost," *29th Annual International Conference of the IEEE Engineering in Medicine and Biology Society, EMBS 2007.*, pp.6705-6708, 22-26 Aug. 2007.

[13] A. Amedeo, C. Gautier, F. Costa, and L. Bernard, "Signal Integrity Ensured Through Impedance Characterization of Advanced High-Speed Design," *2009 20th International Zurich Symposium on Electromagnetic Compatibility*, pp.249-252, 12-16 Jan. 2009.

[14] G. Brown, "PKE for sensitive mobile applications an implementation of TLS 1.0 (RFC 2246)," *IEEE Seminar on Secure GSM and Beyond: End to End Security for Mobile Communications, (Digest No. 2003/10059)*, pp.18/1-18/3, 11 Feb. 2003.

[15] Qu Bo, and Wu Zhaozhi, "Design and Implementation of SSL Secure Proxy for ARM Platform," *2011 International Conference on Internet Technology and Applications (iTAP)*, pp.1-4, 16-18 Aug. 2011.

[16] Eun-Jun Yooni and Kee-Young Yoo, "A new elliptic curve diffie-hellman two-party key agreement protocol," *2010 7th International Conference on Service Systems and Service Management (ICSSSM)*, pp.1-4, 28-30 Jun. 2010.

[17] A.K. Das, "Analysis and improvement on an efficient biometric-based remote user authentication scheme using smart cards," *Information Security, IET*, vol.5, no.3, pp.145-151, Sep. 2011.

[18] Ling Chuanfan, "Research on Role-Based Access Control Policy of E-government," *2010 International Conference on E-Business and E-Government (ICEE)*, pp.714-716, 7-9 May 2010.

[19] Li Jin, and Li Ya Chen, "Research of the campus E-government network security management," *2011 International Conference on E-Business and E-Government (ICEE)*, pp.1-4, 6-8 May 2011.

[20] D. Bunker, "Information systems management (ISM): Repertoires of collaboration for community warning (CW) and emergency incident response (EIR)," *2010 IEEE International Conference on Technologies for Homeland Security (HST)*, pp.216-221, 8-10 Nov. 2010.

[21] T. Tekcan, and B. Kirisken, "Reliability test procedures for achieving highly robust electronic products," *2010 Proceedings - Annual Reliability and Maintainability Symposium (RAMS)*, pp.1-6, 25-28 Jan. 2010.

Elliptic Curve Cryptography Coprocessor for Mobile Ad-Hoc Networks

Micho Radovnikovich[1] and Debatosh Debnath[2]
[1]Department of Electrical and Computer Engineering, Oakland University, Rochester, Michigan, USA
[2]Department of Computer Science and Engineering, Oakland University, Rochester, Michigan, USA

Abstract— *This paper investigates the design of an Elliptic Curve Cryptography (ECC) co-processor in an embedded system. The goal of this work is to create a general purpose module to greatly augment a network node's performance, thereby making it practical to implement secure ECC-based network protocols in potentially vulnerable ad-hoc networks. Specifically, the techniques presented here employ hybrid computing, where a CPU and several custom hardware modules are implemented together on the same chip. The proposed system was implemented on an FPGA utilizing Xilinx's MicroBlaze processor, and is compared to other implementations found in the literature.*

Keywords: elliptic curve cryptography, hybrid computing, ad-hoc networking, FPGA

1. Introduction

Elliptic Curve based cryptosystems [1] have been steadily gaining popularity in recent years, especially in embedded applications [2], [3]. ECC is a public key scheme that provides high security per key bit, and can achieve the same level of security as other public key systems like RSA with much smaller key sizes. To demonstrate this, Table 1 shows comparisons between various ECC and RSA key lengths that are approximately equivalent in security [4].

Table 1
SECURITY COMPARISON OF ECC AND RSA

ECC Key Size in bits	RSA Key Size in bits
163	1024
256	3072
384	7680
512	15360

ECC is well suited for embedded systems because the smaller key size saves both memory and communication bandwidth by avoiding having to store and transmit extremely long numbers. However, the field of embedded systems covers a vast area, with many different applications and design constraints. In the microprocessor realm of embedded systems, work such as [5], [6], [7] seek to improve ECC's performance on smaller processors for use in portable devices and other power-limited applications. They do this by optimizing the complexity of operations and clock speed to use less energy without compromising throughput. Other work in this area includes [8], which seeks to take advantage of the advancing technology of parallel computing architectures.

Reconfigurable logic such as Field Programmable Gate Arrays (FPGAs) is another domain of embedded systems where ECC is beginning to take root. In this approach, specialized hardware [9], [10], [11] is used to implement the algorithms, rather than using a general-purpose processor. Incredible performance, both in execution speed and power consumption, can be achieved using custom hardware, but this comes at the expense of less flexibility and larger circuits.

Yet another area of research is hybrid systems [12], [13], [14], [15], where microprocessors and specialized hardware are used together on the same device and communicate over a common data bus. Such a hybrid approach is taken in this paper, where the authors believe the best of both techniques can be utilized.

This paper addresses the development of a hybrid co-processor that can be used to dramatically improve the performance of an ECC-based ad-hoc network security system. The proposed system performs common computations in an ECC cryptosystem such as private/public key pair generation, multi-party key agreement, elliptic curve digital signature (ECDSA) generation and verification, and high bandwidth AES block cipher using a shared key. A higher level network computing node then communicates with the device through an API to access the functionality. It is envisioned that augmenting a network node with a fast, modular ECC co-processor will make realizing secure ECC systems become very practical in the near future.

In this system architecture, all the cryptographic computations are done on the hybrid embedded unit. Not only does this improve performance, but it is also more secure, since critical values such as the private key reside only on the embedded unit and cannot be accessed. The proposed coprocessor is implemented on a Xilinx Spartan 6 device using the Xilinx Embedded Development Kit (EDK). The software component of the system is implemented on a 32-bit MicroBlaze CPU, and the hardware components are implemented in custom VHDL modules.

The paper is organized as follows: Section 2 introduces the

fundamentals of ECC and defines the operations performed by the ECC coprocessor. Section 3 addresses the design of the individual components of the hybrid system. Section 4 presents performance results of the implemented system. Future extensions of the system are discussed in Section 5.

2. ECC Operations

2.1 Finite Field Arithmetic

Operations on elliptic curve points are defined over a Galois binary finite field [16]. This binary finite field, hereafter referred to as a 'Galois field', is notated by $GF(2^n)$, where all the field elements are represented by n-th order polynomials in some auxiliary variable z, and each coefficient of the polynomial belongs to the binary set $\{0, 1\}$. In addition, a binary field has an irreducible polynomial modulus $m(z)$. Any arithmetic operation on field elements must be performed mod $m(z)$. As such, fundamental arithmetic operations require a new definition. To demonstrate the arithmetic, consider the field $GF(2^4)$ where $m(z) = z^4 + 1$.

2.1.1 Addition

Suppose we want to add two elements $c_1(z) = z^3 + z + 1$ and $c_2(z) = z^2 + z$:

$$\left(z^3 + z + 1\right) + \left(z^2 + z\right) = z^3 + z^2 + \cancelto{0}{2z} + 1 \tag{1}$$

where the $2z$ term is eliminated since $2 \mod 2 = 0$. As shorthand, binary field elements are represented as binary numbers, where each digit corresponds to a coefficient of a z term. The example (1) is then written as $1011{+}0110 = 1101$. It can be seen that a binary field addition is simply a bitwise exclusive-OR operation. This operation is referred to as

$$\texttt{field\_add}(c_1(z),\ c_2(z)) \equiv c_1(z) \underset{b}{+} c_2(z)$$

2.1.2 Multiplication

Now consider multiplying $c_1(z)$ and $c_2(z)$:

$$\left(z^3 + z + 1\right)\left(z^2 + z\right) = z^5 + z^4 + z^3 + \cancelto{0}{2z^2} + z$$

Since the polynomial order of the result is larger than the field modulus, a modular reduction must be performed:

$$z^5 + z^4 + z^3 + z \mod (z^4 + 1) = z^3 + 1$$

This operation is referred to as

$$\texttt{field\_multiply}(c_1(z),\ c_2(z)) \equiv c_1(z) \underset{b}{\times} c_2(z)$$

2.1.3 Inversion

In order to divide in a finite field, the inverse element of the denominator must be computed, and then multiplied by the numerator. Define field inversion by

$$\overline{c(z)} = \texttt{field\_invert}(c(z))$$

where $\overline{c(z)}$ is the inverse element of $c(z)$, and satisfies

$$c(z) \underset{b}{\times} \overline{c(z)} = 1$$

Computing inverse field elements is significantly more expensive than the other finite field operations.

2.2 Point Operations

An elliptic curve is defined by

$$y^2 + xy = x^3 + ax^2 + b$$

where a and b are constants that define the shape of the curve. To use this in a cryptosystem, the curve is redefined over the Galois finite field using the arithmetic operations introduce previously:

$$\begin{aligned} & y(z) \underset{b}{\times} y(z) \underset{b}{+} x(z) \underset{b}{\times} y(z) \\ = {} & x(z) \underset{b}{\times} x(z) \underset{b}{\times} x(z) \underset{b}{+} a(z) \underset{b}{\times} x(z) \underset{b}{\times} x(z) \underset{b}{+} b(z) \end{aligned} \tag{2}$$

An elliptic curve in a Galois field contains a finite number of points that is called its order, denoted by N, plus one more point at infinity, denoted by P_∞. A point P on the Galois field elliptic curve is defined to be an ordered pair in affine ($\mathcal{A}$) coordinates (x, y) that satisfies (2).

To avoid expensive field inversions, the point operations are performed in Lopez-Dahab ($\mathcal{LD}$) projective coordinates $(X : Y : Z)$, which are then converted back to affine once the sequence of operations is finished. Using projective coordinates reduces the number of field inversions from hundreds down to two over the course of one point multiply operation. For detailed discussion of projective coordinates, the reader is referred to [17].

There are four operations that can be performed on elliptic curve points:

2.2.1 Point Negation

The point negation function is performed strictly in $\mathcal{A}$, and is defined by

$$P^* = \texttt{pt\_neg}(P) \equiv \begin{cases} x^* = x \\ y^* = x \underset{b}{+} y \end{cases}$$

where the input point $P = (x, y)$ and the negative point $P^* = (x^*, y^*)$.

2.2.2 Point Addition

Two distinct points on the elliptic curve can be added to obtain a third point, defined by

$$R = \texttt{pt\_add}(P, Q)$$

It is most computationally efficient to add a point in $\mathcal{LD}$ to a point in $\mathcal{A}$ to obtain the result in $\mathcal{LD}$. The point addition procedure is shown in Algorithm 1 [18]. This procedure assumes the curve parameter $a(z)$ is either 0 or 1. Many operations can be performed in parallel, so each line contains all the parallel operations performed at that step.

Algorithm 1: Point Addition

Input : A point in $\mathcal{LD}$ coordinates P and a point in $\mathcal{A}$ coordinates Q
Output: Another point $R = \texttt{pt\_add}(P, Q)$

if $P == P_\infty$ **then return** $R \leftarrow (Q_x : Q_y : 1)$
if $Q == P_\infty$ **then return** $R \leftarrow P$
$t_1 \leftarrow P_z \underset{b}{\times} Q_x, \quad t_2 \leftarrow P_z \underset{b}{\times} P_z$
$R_x \leftarrow P_x \underset{b}{+} t_1, \quad t_3 \leftarrow t_2 \underset{b}{\times} Q_y$
$t_1 \leftarrow P_z \underset{b}{\times} R_x, \quad R_y \leftarrow P_y \underset{b}{+} t_3$
if $R_x == 0$ **then**
  if $R_y == 0$ **then**
    return $R = \texttt{pt\_double}(Q)$
  else return $R \leftarrow P_\infty$
end
$t_3 \leftarrow t_1 \underset{b}{\times} R_y, \quad R_z \leftarrow t_1 \underset{b}{\times} t_1,$
$t_2 \leftarrow R_x \underset{b}{\times} R_x,$ **if** $a(z) == 1$ **then** $t_1 \leftarrow t_1 \underset{b}{+} t_2$
$R_x \leftarrow t_1 \underset{b}{\times} t_2, \quad t_1 \leftarrow R_z \underset{b}{\times} R_z, \quad t_2 \leftarrow R_y \underset{b}{\times} R_y$
$R_x \leftarrow R_x \underset{b}{+} t_2 \underset{b}{+} t_3, \quad t_2 \leftarrow R_z \underset{b}{\times} Q_x$
$t_2 \leftarrow t_2 \underset{b}{+} R_x, \quad t_3 \leftarrow t_3 \underset{b}{+} R_z$
$R_y \leftarrow t_2 \underset{b}{\times} t_3, \quad t_2 \leftarrow Q_x \underset{b}{+} Q_y$
$t_3 \leftarrow t_1 \underset{b}{\times} t_2$
$R_y \leftarrow R_y \underset{b}{+} t_3$
return R

2.2.3 Point Double

A single point in $\mathcal{LD}$ can be doubled to obtain another point in $\mathcal{LD}$, defined by

$$R = \texttt{pt\_double}(P)$$

The point doubling procedure for is shown in Algorithm 2 [18]. Just as in point addition, this algorithm is specific to the case where $a(z) \in \{0, 1\}$. The parallel operations are again grouped in each stage of the algorithm.

Algorithm 2: Point Double

Input : Elliptic curve point P
Output: Another elliptic curve point $R = \texttt{pt\_double}(P)$

if $P == P_\infty$ **then return** $R \leftarrow P_\infty$
$t_1 \leftarrow P_z \underset{b}{\times} P_z, \quad t_2 \leftarrow P_x \underset{b}{\times} P_x$
$R_z \leftarrow t_1 \underset{b}{\times} t_2, \quad R_x \leftarrow t_2 \underset{b}{\times} t_2, \quad t_1 \leftarrow t_1 \underset{b}{\times} t_1$
$t_1 \leftarrow P_y \underset{b}{\times} P_y, \quad t_2 \leftarrow t_1 \underset{b}{\times} b(z)$
$R_x \leftarrow R_x \underset{b}{+} t_2$
if $a(z) == 1$ **then** $t_1 \leftarrow t_1 \underset{b}{+} t_2 \underset{b}{+} R_z$
  else $t_1 \leftarrow t_1 \underset{b}{+} t_2$
$R_y \leftarrow R_x \underset{b}{\times} t_1$
$t_1 \leftarrow t_2 \underset{b}{\times} R_z$
$R_y \leftarrow R_y \underset{b}{+} t_1$
return R

2.2.4 Point Multiplication

Point multiplication is defined by

$$R = \texttt{pt\_multiply}(k, P)$$

where $k \in [0, \ldots, N-1]$ is a scalar coefficient less than the order of the curve, and P is the starting point to be multiplied. Point multiplication is performed by sequencing point additions and doubles until the desired scalar multiple of P is acquired. The sequence is determined by the bits of the binary representation of the coefficient. Every nonzero bit induces one point addition operation. Therefore, to lessen the number of required point additions, the non-adjacent form (NAF) of the coefficient is computed before the sequencing starts [18]. The point multiplication procedure is shown in Algorithm 3, and the NAF computation is shown in Algorithm 4.

2.3 Digital Signature

ECDSA was first proposed in 1992 by Rivest et. al. [19]. The signature generation and verification algorithms are shown in Algorithms 5 and 6, respectively. The function H can represent any cryptographically secure hash function.

3. Coprocessor Design

A diagram of the individual functions of the coprocessor is shown in Figure 1.

3.1 Microblaze Architecture

The functions on the software side of the coprocessor are implemented in a MicroBlaze C program, and the functions on the hardware side are implemented as custom VHDL

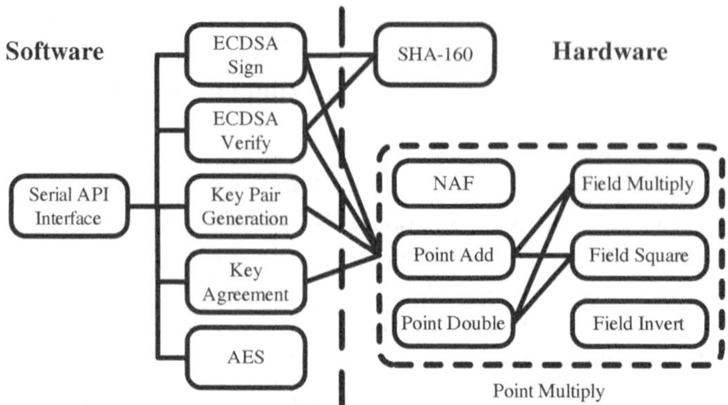

Fig. 1
DISTRIBUTION OF PROPOSED COPROCESSOR FUNCTIONALITY.

Algorithm 3: Point Multiplication

Input : Scalar coefficient k and start point P
Output: $R = \texttt{pt\_multiply}(k, P)$

$P^* \leftarrow \texttt{pt\_neg}(P)$
$K \leftarrow \texttt{compute\_naf}(k)$
$i \leftarrow 0$
while $K_i == 0$ **do**
  $i \leftarrow i + 1$
end
$R \leftarrow P$
$i \leftarrow i + 1$

while $i < N - 1$ **do**
  $R \leftarrow \texttt{pt\_double}(R)$
  if $K_i == 1$ **then**
    $R \leftarrow \texttt{pt\_add}(R, P)$
  else if $K_i == -1$ **then**
    $R \leftarrow \texttt{pt\_add}(R, P^*)$
  end
  $i \leftarrow i + 1$
end
return R

Algorithm 4: NAF Computation

Input : Binary representation of a scalar k
Output: Non-adjacent form of the scalar K

$i \leftarrow 0$
while $k > 0$ **do**
  if $k == 1 \mod 4$ **then**
    $K_i \leftarrow 1$
    $k \leftarrow (k/2)$
  else if $k == 3 \mod 4$ **then**
    $K_i \leftarrow -1$
    $k \leftarrow (k/2) + 1$
  else
    $K_i \leftarrow 0$
    $k \leftarrow (k/2)$
  end
  $i \leftarrow i + 1$
end
return K

modules. The entire system was developed using the Xilinx Embedded Development Kit (EDK). The EDK provides a simple environment to add Xilinx's MicroBlaze processor to hardware designs, and also simplifies laying out the architecture of the rest of the system.

MicroBlaze employs a Harvard architecture, where there are separate busses for data and instructions. The MicroBlaze program is stored directly in the block memory of the FPGA, and a dual port memory module is used to connect to the MicroBlaze over the instruction and data busses with independent memory controllers. MicroBlaze connects to hardware peripherals over a third bus known as the AXI peripheral bus.

The CPU communicates with the hardware components attached to the AXI bus via a register interface. The CPU writes to specific register addresses to transmit data to the hardware, and subsequently reads from specific register addresses to collect output data. Alternatively, dedicated FIFOs can be be attached to addressable memory to communicate with peripherals separate from the AXI bus. Figure 2 shows a block diagram of the MicroBlaze system architecture, laid out using the EDK.

3.2 Point Multiplication

The point multiplication module implements Algorithm 3 in the form of a finite state machine, following the flowchart

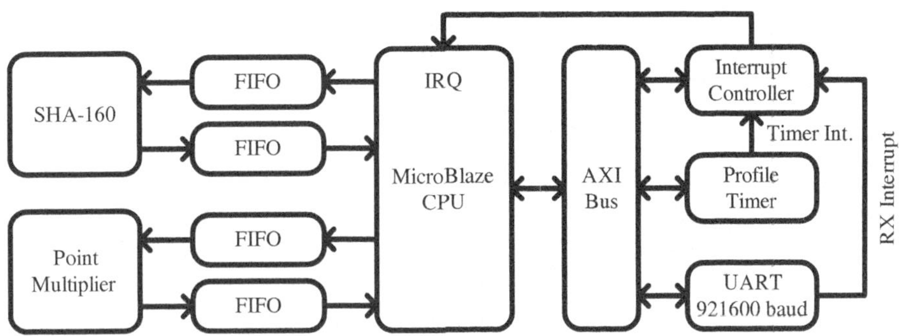

Fig. 2
LAYOUT OF THE FPGA HARDWARE ARCHITECTURE.

Algorithm 5: ECDSA Signature Generation

Input : Prime curve order N, generator point G, private key d, message m

Output: Signature integer pair (r, s)

1 Randomize $k \in [1, N-1]$
2 $P \leftarrow$ `pt_multiply`(k, G), treat P_x as an integer x
3 **if** $P_x == 0$ **then** go to 1
4 $r \leftarrow x$
5 $e \leftarrow H(m)$
6 $s \leftarrow k^{-1}(e + dr) \mod N$
7 **if** $s == 0$ **then** go to 1
8 **return** (r, s)

Algorithm 6: ECDSA Signature Verification

Input : Prime curve order N, generator point G, public key Q, message m, signature (r, s)

Output: 'Accept' or 'Reject'

if $r \notin [1, N-1]$ **then return** *'Reject'*
if $s \notin [1, N-1]$ **then return** *'Reject'*
$e \leftarrow H(m)$
$w = s^{-1} \mod N$
$u_1 \leftarrow ew \mod N$
$u_2 \leftarrow rw \mod N$
$P_1 \leftarrow$ `pt_multiply`(u_1, G)
$P_2 \leftarrow$ `pt_multiply`(u_2, Q)
$X \leftarrow$ `pt_add`(P_1, P_2)
if $X == P_\infty$ **then return** *'Reject'*
Treat X_x as an integer x
if $x == r$ **then return** *'Accept'*
else return *'Reject'*

illustrated in Figure 3.

The data transmitted from the MicroBlaze are the scalar k and the affine coordinates of the point to be multiplied P_x and P_y. After the multiplication is complete, and the resulting point is converted back into $\mathcal{A}$, the final affine point R is transmitted back to the MicroBlaze.

To take maximum advantage of parallel processing, the scalar multiplier is transmitted first such that the NAF computation can begin while the starting point's coordinates are still being received. In addition, the point addition and double modules take advantage of the parallel operations indicated in Algorithms 1 and 2.

The dominant function is field multiplication, which takes roughly twice as long to compute as a field square. Field additions are negligible to squares and multiplies since they are simply an exclusive-OR operation. Therefore, the critical path of Algorithm 1 is eight field multiply operations, whereas a serial implementation would also have to spend time computing five field squares. Likewise, implementing Algorithm 2 results in a critical path of four multiplies and one square, whereas a serial implementation would include four multiplies and five squares.

3.3 API Interface

The API is written as a C++ class that is used to communicate with the FPGA over a 921600 baud serial interface. It also manages the data it receives back from the FPGA. Each API function that interacts with the FPGA has a unique ID. The MicroBlaze waits for the first byte of an API transmission and checks its value to determine the type of function. If more data is to follow, it reads the appropriate amount, does the necessary processing, and then transmits back the required result. The class functions are:

3.3.1 GenerateKeyPair

This function has no data to transmit, but it triggers the FPGA to randomly generate a private key, compute the public key, and then transmit the public key point back.

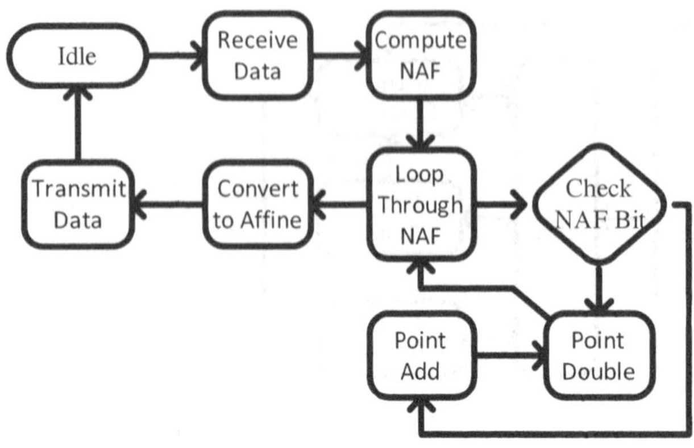

Fig. 3
POINT MULTIPLICATION FLOW DIAGRAM.

3.3.2 MultiPartyDH

The multi-party DH key agreement protocol implements the standard initially proposed in [20], appropriately interpreted to apply to ECC. This class function is run in response to receiving a list of partial keys from another network node during a key agreement process. Each partial key is transmitted to the FPGA to be point multiplied by the private key, and then returned. This function is also used to compute the final shared key at the last step of the procedure.

3.3.3 ECDSA Sign

This function transmits the variable length message to be signed to the FPGA. The FPGA computes the signature and returns the two signature values.

3.3.4 ECDSA Verify

This function transmits a received signature and the message and public key associated with it to the FPGA. The FPGA verifies the signature and returns whether it passed or failed.

3.3.5 SetAESKey

This function transmits an AES key for the FPGA to use for encryption and decryption.

3.3.6 AESCipher

This function transmits a message to be encrypted or decrypted by the FPGA, and receives back the ciphertext or plaintext, respectively.

4. Performance Results

This section presents experimental results from an implementation of the proposed system. For the experiment, the 233-bit National Institute of Standards and Technology (NIST) standard `secp233r1` elliptic curve is used [21]. On this curve, $m(z)$, $a(z)$, $b(z)$ and N are

$$m(z) = z^{233} + z^{74} + 1$$

$$a(z) = 1$$

$$b(z) = \texttt{0066 647EDE6C 332C7F8C 0923BB58 213B333B 20E9CE42 81FE115F 7D8F90AD}$$

$$N = \texttt{0100 00000000 00000000 00000000 0013E974 E72F8A69 22031D26 03CFE0D7}$$

where each bit of the hexadecimal representation of $b(z)$ corresponds to a power of z, and N is a prime integer.

4.1 Hardware Performance Measures

The point multiplication performance of the proposed hybrid system was compared to a pure software implementation on a MicroBlaze processor. The total execution time of each was measured with the MicroBlaze's profile timer, and includes the transfer of data to and from the MicroBlaze module through the FIFO interface. The recorded time benchmarks were obtained by averaging 10,000 uniformly generated random scalar multiplications of the generator point. The software implementation took an average of 751.5 milliseconds, and the hybrid system took an average of just 1.05 milliseconds, resulting in a speed gain of 716 times.

The hybrid system was implemented on a Xilinx Spartan 6 LX45 FPGA, and the resource usage is shown in Table 2. Table 3 compares the point multiplication performance of the proposed system to other similar implementations found in the literature. The system presented in [9] follows a very similar approach to the point multiply hardware as this paper, yet is 2.5 times slower. This difference is attributed to a slightly more advantageous use of parallelism, and the older Spartan 3 device used there.

The implementation in [22] is so much slower because the point multiplication is done in software, and passes individual field elements to hardware to implement the low level field arithmetic. This is a lot of data to transfer to and from the hardware, which ends up being the bottleneck of the system.

4.2 System Performance Measures

Each of the API's functions were run from a PC, and the computation time of each function was measured. Table 4 shows these timing results. The reported times represent the entire time from class function call to class function return, including any serial data transfer to and from the FPGA.

Table 2
HARDWARE SYNTHESIS RESULTS

Resource	Amount	Percentage
Slice Registers	9,729	17%
Slice LUTs	15,067	55%
Occupied Slices	5,439	79%
BRAM16 Blocks	32	27%

Table 3

COMPARISON OF POINT MULTIPLICATION PERFORMANCE

Design	Field Size	System Type	Time (ms)
This Paper	**233**	**Hybrid**	**1.05**
Morales-Sandoval [15]	163	Hardware	1.07
Muthukumar [9]	233	Hardware	2.28
Benaissa [22]	233	Hybrid	150
Malik [23]	160	DSP	63.4
Koschuch [24]	191	CPU	118
Van Ameron [6]	384	CPU	375

Table 4

API FUNCTION COMPUTATION TIMES

Function	Time
`GenerateKeyPair`	1.25 ms
`MultiPartyDH`	1.14 ms per partial key
`ECDSA_Sign`	2.14 ms (100 byte message)
`ECDSA_Verify`	3.35 ms (100 byte message)
`SetAESKey`	11.5 μs
`AESCipher`	720 μs (encrypt), 791 μs (decrypt)

5. Future Work

Currently, the system can easily be compiled to support different curves and field sizes, but they are through the use of VHDL generics. A good way to extend the system would be to control the field size dynamically, providing the user with control over the trade-off between security and computation speed, as was achieved by [15]. Future work will investigate the reconfigurability, making the hardware smaller and more efficient, and expanding the application of ECC to address the security issues inherent in ad-hoc inter-vehicle communication.

6. Conclusion

In this paper, an ECC system was designed for an FPGA that utilizes a combination of a Xilinx MicroBlaze CPU and several custom hardware modules. Results show the fundamental point multiplication operation runs over 700 times faster in the hybrid architecture system over a purely software implementation. Simultaneously, the design remains simple and flexible by using software to control the hardware modules and provide an interface to a higher level computer through an API. These results clearly demonstrate the capability of FPGAs to drastically increase performance of computationally expensive tasks, specifically for network security applications.

References

[1] N. Koblitz, "Elliptic curve cryptosystems," *Mathematics of Computation*, vol. 48, no. 177, pp. 203–209, January 1987.

[2] W. Qingxian, "The application of elliptic curves cryptography in embedded systems," in *International Conference on Embedded Software and Systems*, 2005.

[3] R. Duraisamy, Z. Salcic, M. Morales-Sandoval, and C. Feregrino-Uribe, "A Fast Elliptic Curve Based Key Agreement Protocol-on-Chip (PoC) for Securing Networked Embedded Systems," in *12th IEEE International Conference on Embedded and Real-Time Computing Systems and Applications (RTCSA'06)*, 2006, pp. 154–161.

[4] *An Elliptic Curve Cryptography (ECC) Primer*, Certicom Corp., June 2004, the Certicom 'Catch the Curve' White Paper Series.

[5] H. Wang, B. Sheng, and Q. Li, "Elliptic curve cryptography-based access control in sensor networks," *Int. J. Secur. Netw.*, vol. 1, no. 3/4, pp. 127–137, Dec. 2006.

[6] T. VanAmeron and W. Skiba, "Implementing efficient 384-bit NIST elliptic curve over prime fields on an ARM946e," in *Military Communications Conference, 2008. MILCOM 2008. IEEE*, Nov. 2008, pp. 1–7.

[7] T. Hasegawa and J. Nakajima, "A small and fast software implementation of elliptic curve cryptosystems over GF(p) on a 16-bit microcomputer," *IEICE Transactions on Fundamentals of Electronics, Communications and Computer Sciences*, 1999.

[8] P. Longa and A. Miri, "Fast and flexible elliptic curve point arithmetic over prime fields," *IEEE Transactions on Computers*, vol. 57, pp. 289–302, 2008.

[9] B. MuthuKumar and S. Jeevananthan, "Design of an efficient elliptic curve cryptography coprocessor," in *Advanced Computing, 2009. First International Conference on*, Dec. 2009, pp. 34–37.

[10] C. Ha, J. Kim, B. Choi, J. Lee, and H. Kim, "GF (2^{191}) elliptic curve processor using montgomery ladder and high speed finite field arithmetic unit," in *TENCON 2005*. IEEE, 2005, pp. 1–4.

[11] T. Kerins, E. Popovici, and W. Marnane, "An FPGA implementation of a flexible secure elliptic curve cryptography processor," in *Advanced Reconfigureable Computing*, 2005, pp. 22–30.

[12] M. Khalil-Hani, A. Irwansyah, and Y. Hau, "A tightly coupled finite field arithmetic hardware in an FPGA-based embedded processor core for elliptic curve cryptography," in *Electronic Design, 2008. ICED 2008. International Conference on*, Dec. 2008, pp. 1–6.

[13] X. Guo and P. Schaumont, "Optimizing the HW/SW boundary of an ECC SoC design using control hierarchy and distributed storage," in *Proceedings of the Conference on Design, Automation and Test in Europe*, 2009, pp. 454–459.

[14] S. Janssens and J. Thomas, "Hardware/software co-design of an elliptic curve public-key cryptosystem," in *Signal Processing Systems, 2001 IEEE Workshop on*, 2001.

[15] M. Morales-Sandoval, C. Feregrino-Uribe, R. Cumplido, and I. Algredo-Badillo, "A Run Time Reconfigurable Co-processor for Elliptic Curve Scalar Multiplication," in *2009 Mexican International Conference on Computer Science*. IEEE, 2009, pp. 345–350.

[16] R. Lidl and H. Niederreiter, *Finite Fields (Encyclopedia of Mathematics and its Applications)*. Cambridge University Press, 1996.

[17] H. Cohen and E. A. Gerhard Frey, *Handbook of Elliptic and Hyperelliptic Curve Cryptography*, ser. Discrete Mathematics and its Applications. Chapman & Hall/CRC, 2006.

[18] D. Hankerson, A. Menezes, and S. Vanstone, *Guide to Elliptic Curve Cryptography*. Springer Science and Business Media, LLC, 2004.

[19] R. L. Rivest, M. E. Hellman, J. C. Anderson, and J. W. Lyons, "Responses to NIST's proposal," *Commun. ACM*, vol. 35, no. 7, pp. 41–54, Jul. 1992.

[20] M. Steiner, G. Tsudik, and M. Waidner, "CLIQUES: A new approach to group key agreement," in *IEEE Distributed Computing Systems*, Amsterdam, 1998, pp. 380–387.

[21] *SEC 2: Recommended Elliptic Curve Domain Parameters*, Certicom Corp., Sep. 2000.

[22] M. Benaissa and M. N. Hassan, "A scalable hardware/software codesign for elliptic curve cryptography on PicoBlaze microcontroller," in *Circuits and Systems (ISCAS), Proceedings of 2010 IEEE International Symposium on*, 2010, pp. 2111–2114.

[23] M. Y. Malik, "Efficient implementation of elliptic curve cryptography using low-power digital signal processor," in *Advanced Communication Technology (ICACT), 2010 The 12th International Conference on*, 2011, pp. 1464–1468.

[24] M. Koschuch, J. Lechner, A. Weitzer, J. Großschädl, A. Szekely, S. Tillich, and J. Wolkerstorfer, "Hardware/software co-design of elliptic curve cryptography on an 8051 microcontroller," in *Proceedings of the 8th international conference on Cryptographic Hardware and Embedded Systems*, ser. CHES'06. Berlin, Heidelberg: Springer-Verlag, 2006, pp. 430–444.

Securing RTP packets using persistent packet key encryption scheme for real-time multimedia applications

Younchan Jung and Enrique Festijo
School of Information, Communications & Electronics Engineering
Catholic University of Korea, Bucheon-si, Gyeonggi-do, Korea 420-743

Abstract— *Most of the existing encryption methods use the same key to secure different RTP payloads during a given session. However, the use of the session key cannot guarantee protection against brute force attacks that can be done after transmission using the captured RTP data for the real-time multimedia streams. This paper deals with the packet key methods where Diffie-Hellman key exchange procedures repeat only for the RTP packets that are selected based on the key change rate. This paper proposes a persistent packet key encryption scheme that uses the same packet key for a certain period and changes the key for the next period. The key change schedule is controlled by the key change rate. The persistent packet key encryption scheme aims to improve latency for encryption and decryption compared with the full packet key encryption scheme where the packet key changes every packet. The main goal of this paper is to propose the packet key scheme that is significantly more secure than the session key scheme while satisfying the latency requirements for the real-time multimedia transmission.*

Keywords: Real-time Multimedia; Session Key; Key Exchange; Packet Key; Strength of Security

1. Introduction

The evolution of wireless handsets from simple mobile phones to smart devices has enabled to provide multimedia services across the Internet [1]. However, those trends of the wireless medium and mobile smart devices have made packet-sniffing and other digital attacks easy so that multimedia contents, including private information, may not be secure across the Internet. The VoIP (Voice over IP) is one of the leading real-time applications for this matter [2]. For example, real-time VoIP conversation may include private information that need to be secure from any forms of attacks. Thus, the need for end-to-end secure multimedia services is one of the important issues now in the Internet era, especially in real-time session.

The MIKEY (Multimedia Internet Keying) supports three different methods to set up an one-time session key: Pre-shared key, public-key and Diffie-Hellman key (DH-Key) [3]. The pre-shared key method and the public-key method are both based on key transport mechanisms, where the actual traffic-encrypting key generation key is securely delivered to the recipient(s). In the Diffie-Hellman method, the actual traffic-encrypting key generation key is instead derived from the Diffie-Hellman values exchanged between the peers. The DH-Key has the advantage of providing perfect forward security while pre-shared key suffers from scalability problems for larger user groups and public-key requires a public key infrastructure to handle the secure distribution of public keys.

The ZRTP, which defines a session key agreement protocol, relies on a DH-Key exchange per session to generate the session key [4], [5], [6]. The DH-Key agreement methods in MIKEY and ZRTP produce a relatively high computational workload because they use a discrete logarithmic algorithm. However, the scenario considered in this paper is that during an on-going session, the participants may decide to change from unsecure-mode to secure-mode. This requires on demand generation of a session key during a session period. The session key latency, which is required for the on-demand mode change, corresponds to the latency for the DH-key agreement. Such session key latency, which increases as the DH-Key size increases, should be less than several seconds for real-time multimedia applications. According to [7], the key size of 9 digits requires over 10 seconds to create a DH-key under the condition that the DH-Key computation runs on the user devices equipping with an Intel Pentium i7 CPU. This is the reason why such smart devices cannot use a session key of which the DH-key size is greater than 9 digits even though it is well known that DH-Key protocol is very hard to break if one chooses the value of key size as a sufficiently large number.

The use of the session key cannot guarantee protection against brute force attacks that can be done after transmission using the captured RTP data for the real-time multimedia streams. However, this paper intends to apply the DH-Key agreement procedure to the RTP packets that are selected based on the key change rate. This paper proposes a persistent packet key encryption scheme that uses the same packet key for a certain period and changes the key for the next period. This means that the propose packet key scheme uses a series of different packet keys during a given session. So, the the use of packet key will improve security strengths compared with the session key scheme where the same session key is continuously used during a session. Also, a packet key, which was once been generated can be applied to the next series of packets. This will reduce the latency burden to those packets because they do not need to invest time for the DH-key exchange. So, the main goal of this paper is to propose a packet key scheme that is significantly more secure than the session key scheme while satisfying the latency requirements for the real-time multimedia transmission.

In Section II, we discuss the background and related works for our proposed scheme. In Section III, we provide a detailed explanation for our proposed persistent packet key encryption scheme based on a Diffie-Hellman key exchange per packet in a real-time manner. Section IV verifies that our proposed scheme satisfies the requirements related to latency and security strength. Our conclusion is in Section V.

2. Background and Related Works

The real-time protocol (RTP) is used extensively in communication and entertainment systems that involve streaming media [8], [9]. For the purpose of securing RTP payloads, existing techniques use the SRTP (Secure Real-time Transport Protocol) [10], [11], [12]. It can provide security services such as encryption, message authentication/integrity and replay protection of RTP and RTCP traffic [13]. SRTP encryption consists of generating a pseudo-random keystream for each RTP packet and XORing the RTP data (excluding the RTP header) with the keystream. The SRTP specification provides guidelines for the key management system and mentions several standards but does not mandate a particular system. The same session key derived from ZRTP is applied to the whole RTP packets throughout a certain session. Fig. 1 shows a typical use of session key in which the payload of each packet is encrypted using RC4. As illustrated, a session key K_{ses} is used as the input for RC4 to generate a keystream KS_{ses}. Next, the same KS_{ses} will be XORed to the RTP packet payloads $P_{A,i-2}$, $P_{A,i-1}$, $P_{A,i}$, $P_{A,i+1}$, $\cdots$. Finally, encrypted RTP packet payloads $E_{KS_{ses}}(P_{A,i-2})$, $E_{KS_{ses}}(P_{A,i-1})$, $E_{KS_{ses}}(P_{A,i})$, $E_{KS_{ses}}(P_{A,i+1})$, $\cdots$ are produced. The Third Party (TP) can capture and record the encrypted packet stream. As an after-transmission attack, the TP may use the brute force approach to decrypt the encrypted packet stream. If the TP succeeds to decrypt any packet in the stream, it can decrypt the whole packets in the session. It is relatively easy for the TP to successfully decrypt just one packet throughout the whole session. This means that the use of session key has a weakness on security strength for the after-transmission attacks.

Differently from the session key encryption scheme, per-packet key has been proposed in [7]. The per-packet key scheme uses a Diffie-Hellman key exchange that occurs on a packet basis. Diffie and Hellman describe a means for two parties to agree upon a shared secret in such a way that the secret will be unavailable to eavesdroppers [14]. The basic idea of the key agreement is to apply the Diffie-Hellman key agreement procedure to each RTP packet. A Diffie-Hellman algorithm defines q as a prime number and α as a primitive

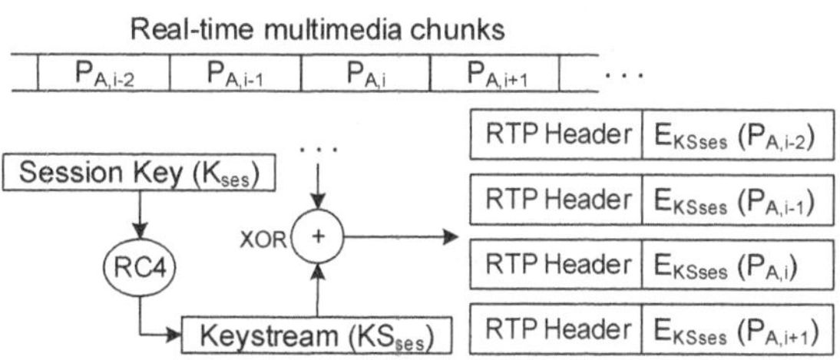

Fig. 1: Encrypting RTP streams using session key

root of the prime number q. Let us assume that Device A (D_A) and Device B (D_B) are communicating. As shown in Fig. 2, D_A selects a random integer $X_{A,i}$ and computes $Y_{A,i}$.

$$Y_{A,i} = \alpha^{X_{A,i}} \bmod q. \tag{1}$$

Similarly, D_B independently selects a random integer X_B and computes $Y_B = \alpha^{X_B} \bmod q$, which is given to user A. Then, D_A computes per-packet key $K_{A,i}$.

$$K_{A,i} = {Y_B}^{X_{A,i}} \bmod q. \tag{2}$$

The per-packet key $K_{A,i}$ is used to derived the per-packet stream key $KS_{A,i}$ via RC4 algorithm.

$$KS_{A,i} = \text{ RC4 } (K_{A,i}). \tag{3}$$

Then, the encrypted payload $E_{KS_{A,i}}(P_{A,i})$ is generated. Also, D_A includes $Y_{A,i}$ information into the RTP packet that has the encrypted payload.

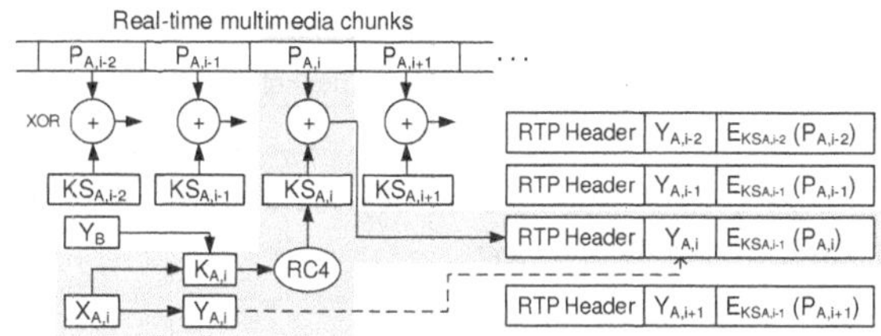

Fig. 2: Per-packet selective encryption (using packet key)

As shown in Fig. 2, the packet key scheme always uses a different key to encrypt each packet. A packet key, which was already been used, will never be reused throughout the whole session. This algorithm is similar to IEEE 802.11i protocol of which main feature is per-packet key derivation [15], [16]. The attractive feature of the packet key scheme is as follows. While the session-based key agreement mode operates the same session key throughout the whole session period, the packet key must be renewed every packet period of the multimedia RTP stream.

3. Proposed persistent packet key encryption scheme

Our persistent packet key encryption scheme is controlled by the parameter r_{KC}, which is defined as the probability of the packet key change at a single key change trial (we call r_{KC} as key change rate). As shown in Fig. 3, for each multimedia chunk, the sender generates a random number r_N and check if the number r_N is less than the key change rate r_{KC}. For the case that $r_N \leq r_{KC}$, the sender generates a new packet key, encrypts the packet and sends the encrypted packet. Otherwise (the case that $r_N > r_{KC}$), the sender encrypts the packet with the same packet key that has been already generated previously and sends the encrypted packet. Then, a certain number of packets will use the same packet key. The period during which they use the same packet key depends on the key change rate r_{KC}. A key change trial is given to each of the multimedia chunks $P_{A,i-2}$, $P_{A,i-1}$, $P_{A,i}$, $P_{A,i+1}$, $\cdots$. The key change trial means checking if the generated random number r_N is less than the parameter r_{KC}. For example, if the key change trial for the payload $P_{A,i}$ shows that r_N is less than r_{KC}, different packet key ($K_{A,i}$) will be used to encrypt the payload $P_{A,i}$. For the next payload ($P_{A,i+1}$), if the key change trial for the payload $P_{A,i+1}$ shows that r_N is greater than r_{KC}, the previous packet key ($K_{A,i}$) will be used to encrypt the payload $P_{A,i+1}$. Fig. 4 shows an example of a key change process where payloads $P_{A,1}$, $P_{A,4}$, $P_{A,8}$, $P_{A,11}$ and $P_{A,13}$ use different packet keys from their previous keys.

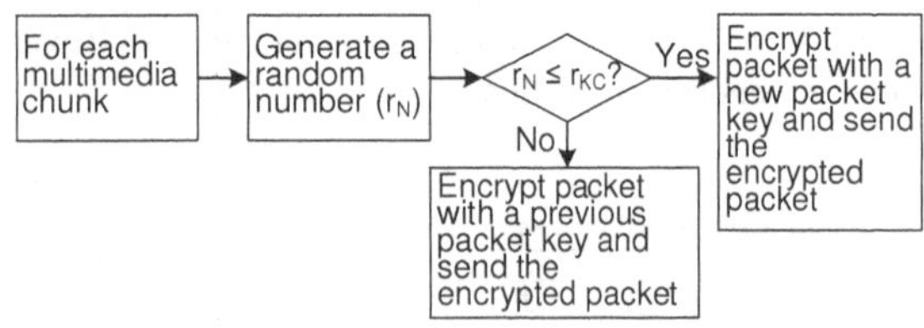

Fig. 3: Use of the same packet key for a series of packets based on the parameter r_{KC}

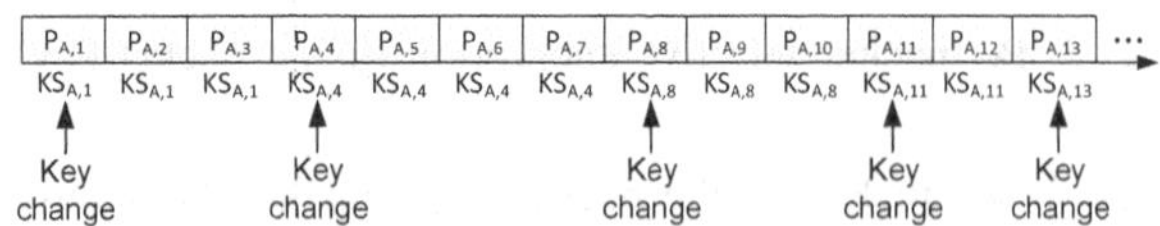

Fig. 4: Key change process

Fig. 5 shows how a packet key is persistently used in the real-time bi-directional multimedia stream. We also assume that using SIP (Session Initiation Protocol), D_A and D_B already entered the normal mode of operation for a real-time bi-directional unsecure multimedia session. Either D_A or D_B can initiate to enter the secure mode of operation for voice conversation by using the persistent packet key scheme. First, they agree on two global parameters and the key change rate, that is, q, α ($\alpha < q$) and r_{KC}. Thus, both D_A and D_B can share the values of the parameters α and q in Diffie-Hellman and r_{KC}. For each multimedia chunk to be sent from D_A to D_B, a random number r_N is generated. This random number r_N is used to check whether it is equal to or less than the key change rate r_{KC}. If r_N is equal to or less than r_{KC}, the payload will be encrypted by using a different key from previous one. However, if r_N is greater than r_{KC}, the payload will be encrypted by using the same packet key as the previous one.

Once the D_A and D_B share q, α and r_{KC}, D_A will generate the session secret value X_A and compute the corresponding blind key Y_A, using the same formula in equation 1. Similarly, D_B will generate a session secret value X_B and compute the corresponding blind key Y_B. D_A and D_B securely keep their secret values (X_A and X_B) and exchange session blind keys (Y_A and Y_B) to each other so that each side comes to know the counter side's session blind key. For the outbound chunk $P_{A,i}$, the generated random number r_N is checked whether it is less than r_{KC} or not. For the case of $r_N \leq r_{KC}$, the encryption process with a new key will be carried out as follows. The sender D_A will generate a packet secret value $X_{A,i}$ and compute the corresponding packet blind key $Y_{A,i}$, using equation 1. The sender D_A will then compute for the packet key $K_{A,i}$, using equation 2. This packet key $K_{A,i}$ will be used as an input key to RC4 to generate the keystream $KS_{A,i}$ as described in equation 3. This keystream $KS_{A,i}$ will be used to encrypt the RTP payload that is, $E_{KS_{A,i}}(P_{A,i})$. Then, D_A will transmit this encrypted payload along with the packet blind key $Y_{A,i}$. For the case of $r_N > r_{KC}$, the payload $P_{A,i}$ will be encrypted using the previous packet key. This means that the previous blind key $Y_{A,i-1}$ will be used as the current blind key $Y_{A,i}$. Also, the previous keystream $KS_{A,i-1}$ will be reused as the current keystream $KS_{A,i}$. So, the RTP packet will contain the blind key field of $Y_{A,i}$ ($Y_{A,i} = Y_{A,i-1}$) and the encrypted payload $E_{KS_{A,i}}(P_{A,i})$ ($E_{KS_{A,i}}(P_{A,i}) = E_{KS_{A,i-1}}(P_{A,i})$). When the RTP packet arrives at the receiving end (D_B), it checks the blind key contained in the RTP packet. For the case that the field of blind key contains $Y_{A,i}$ not equal to the previous blind key Y_{pre}, the D_B computes packet key $K_{A,i}$ using $K_{A,i} = {Y_{A,i}}^{X_B} \bmod q$. Then, the D_B derives the keystream $KS_{A,i} =$ RC4 ($K_{A,i}$). Using the keystream $KS_{A,i}$ the D_B can decrypt the encrypted payload $E_{KS_{A,i}}(P_{A,i})$, that is, $D_{KS_{A,i}}[E_{KS_{A,i}}(P_{A,i})]$. Then, D_B will store $Y_{A,i}$ as the previous blind key Y_{pre} and the keystream $KS_{A,i}$ as the previous keystream KS_{pre}. For the case that the blind key contained in the arrived RTP packet is equal to the previous blind key Y_{pre}, the D_B decrypts the encrypted payload using the previous keystream KS_{pre}, that is, $D_{KS_{pre}}[E_{KS_{A,i}}(P_{A,i})]$. Then, D_B will store $Y_{A,i}$ as the previous blind key Y_{pre} and the keystream KS_{pre} as

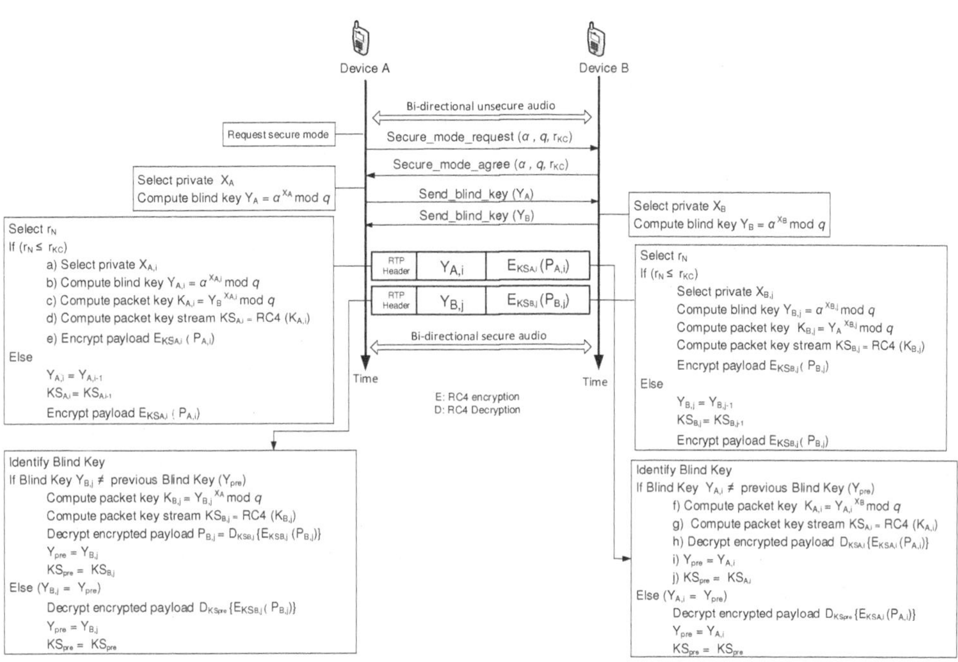

Fig. 5: Persistent Packet Key Scheme

the new previous keystream KS_{pre}. Since D_A and D_B need bi-directional communication services, as a sender, D_B will also send the encrypted payload $E_{KS_{B,j}}(P_{B,j})$ for the payload $P_{B,j}$ along with the packet blind key $Y_{B,j}$. Then, the receiving side D_A finally obtains the original payload $P_{B,j}$ ($P_{B,j} = D_{KS_{B,j}}[E_{KS_{B,j}}(P_{B,j})]$). A bundle of several payload may use the same packet key. The key change process along with a series of bundles is similar to the Bernoulli process with a success probability of r_{KC}.

4. Latency and security strength for the persistent packet key encryption scheme

4.1 Latency for encryption and decryption

Effects of encryption and decryption on end-to-end delay need to be investigated especially for real-time multimedia services. The packet key should be exchanged for the key-change packet that changes the packet key in the persistent packet key encryption scheme. For the purpose of measuring latencies needed to handle key-change packets, we implemented a testbed that consists of a video stream server that sends a video packet stream and a client that can receive the video packet stream. The video stream server and client independently run in an Intel Pentium R Dual-Core 3GHz CPU. The video sample we use is a short movie, that is, "movie.Mjpeg" of 4170 K bytes. The Mjpeg-encoded data are grouped into 100 ms packets, which results in a series of 500 RTP packets, each with a length of 1000 bytes. Using the testbed, for the packet key scheme, we measured latency of [a)+b)+c)+d)+e)] in Fig. 5 (delay for encryption) and that of [f) + g) + h)] (delay caused dominantly by discrete logarithmic computation, that is, the DH-Key agreement). We run eight sets of simulation for different q values: $q = 3, 4, \cdots, 10$. It is because the size of q corresponds to Diffie-Hellman key length. With these different key lengths we evaluate the latency time. Each point in Fig. 6 represents the average value of 500 measurements of [a)+b)+c)+d)+e)]. The results show that as the key size increases to 10 digits, the packet key latency will rise up to 30 seconds. This means that the packet key size should be limited below the 8-digit key in order that the latency level satisfies the maximum latency of 100 milliseconds.

In the persistent packet key encryption scheme, the average latency per packet depends on the key change rate r_{KC} as well as in the key size. Fig. 7 shows the average latencies, which correspond to 'experimental results in Fig. 6' $\times r_{KC}$. The five lines from graph are the results that come from the average latency of [f) + g) + h)] in Fig. 5. It is shown that latency varies depending upon the key size and the key change rate r_{KC}. We focused on the solid line with circles (key size = 7 digit) because this case shows the average latency of below 100 milliseconds for the r_{KC} value ranging from 5% to 100%. The average latency of 100 milliseconds is considered to be tolerable for normal multimedia devices.

The case of $r_{KC} = 100\%$ corresponds to the full packet key encryption scheme where a packet key always changes for each RTP packet. The solid line with circles in Fig. 7 shows decrease on average latency as the key change rate

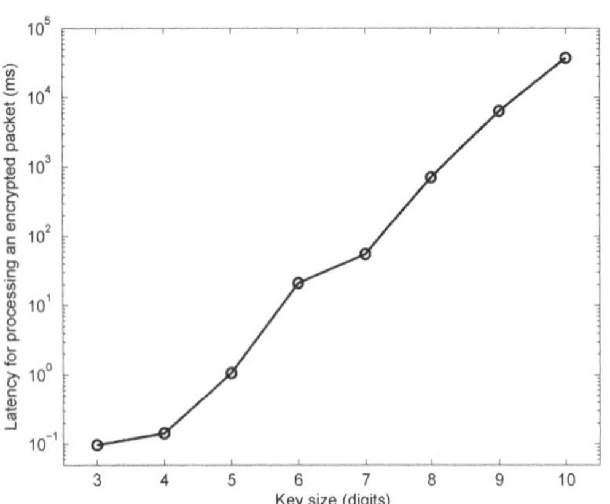

Fig. 6: Latency comparisons for different key sizes

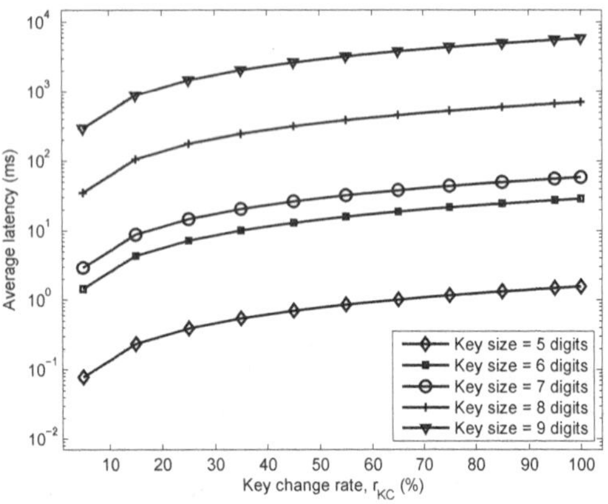

Fig. 7: Average latency for per-packet encryption

changes from $r_{KC} = 5\%$ to $r_{KC} = 100\%$ when a 7-digit key is used. For the case of $r_{KC} = 100\%$, average latency increases to 58.5 milliseconds. Meanwhile, average latency decreases to 3 milliseconds for the case of $r_{KC} = 5\%$. The case that $r_{KC} = 5\%$ means that average interval of key change is 20-packet period, that is, 0.4-second period considering that a packet period is 20 milliseconds. As a result, it is clear that our persistent packet key encryption scheme with the $r_{KC} = 5\%$ reduces latency by 55.5 milliseconds compared with the full packet key encryption scheme with $r_{KC} = 100\%$.

4.2 Analysis on security strengths

We aim to compare the different levels of security, which depend on key size. Given the prime number q, the attacker may try a brute force approach to search for the encryption key depending on the size of q. For the series of encrypted packets, the attacker will check if the decrypted data from the n_{bundle} packets match the original speech corresponding to them where n_{bundle} is defined as the number of packets in a bundle as a unit to decrypt. Because the enemy has no knowledge about the original speech, the enemy can only rely on checking whether the concatenated n_{bundle} payloads after decryption sounds like a noise or not. The confidence of the enemy will increase as the parameter n_{bundle} increases. The concatenated n_{bundle} payloads (160 bytes) correspond to the speech length of $n_{bundle} \times 20$ millisecond speech. For more comprehensible comparisons of strength of security, we compute months spent by the enemy to decrypt the unit length of speech, which corresponds to a bundle of n_{bundle} packets. For the persistent packet key encryption scheme, the exhaustive key search will require to try every value among $10^{(n_{bundle} \times \text{`}key\ size\text{'})}$ possible keys if all the n_{bundle} packets are encrypted with the different packet keys. However, the persistent packet key implies that the same packet key can be used to the different packets in the same bundle of the concatenated n_{bundle} packets. From the enemy's viewpoint, repeated use of the same packet key reduces the time it will take for the enemy to decrypt the concatenated n_{bundle} packets. Fig. 8 shows the number of possible keys among which the exhaustive key search have to try every value for the case that $n_{bundle} = 3$. The enemy begins with decrypting the tagged packet and proceeds to decrypt the second packet and the third packet consecutively. For the case that all the packet keys are different, the enemy is required to try $10^{(3 \times \text{`}key\ size\text{'})}$ possible keys with the probability $\frac{3!}{3!0!}(r_{KC})^3(1 - r_{KC})^0$. For the case that two out of three packet keys are different, the enemy is required to try $10^{(2 \times \text{`}key\ size\text{'})}$ possible keys with the probability $\frac{3!}{2!1!}(r_{KC})^2(1 - r_{KC})^1$. For the case that one out of three packet keys are different, the enemy is required to try $10^{(1 \times \text{`}key\ size\text{'})}$ possible keys with the probability $\frac{3!}{1!2!}(r_{KC})^1(1 - r_{KC})^2$. For the last case that three packet keys are same, the enemy is required to try $10^{(0 \times \text{`}key\ size\text{'})}$ possible keys with the probability $\frac{3!}{0!3!}(r_{KC})^0(1 - r_{KC})^3$. Then, the number of possible keys (N_b) required for the

For $n_{bundle} = 3$

Tagged packet	Second packet	Third packet	
D	D	D	⇨ $\frac{3!}{3!\,(3-3)!}(r_{KC})^3\,(1-r_{KC})^0$
D	D	S	⇨ $\frac{3!}{2!\,(3-2)!}(r_{KC})^2\,(1-r_{KC})^1$
D	S	D	
S	D	D	
D	S	S	⇨ $\frac{3!}{1!\,(3-1)!}(r_{KC})^1\,(1-r_{KC})^2$
S	D	S	
S	S	D	
S	S	S	⇨ $\frac{3!}{0!\,(3-0)!}(r_{KC})^0\,(1-r_{KC})^3$

S: Use the same key as the previous key
D: Use the different key from the previous key

Fig. 8: Number of possible keys for the exhaustive key search where $n_{bundle} = 3$

exhaustive key search can be expressed by the following general formula as a function of the parameters: n_{bundle}, r_{KC} and 'key size', that is, $N_b(n_{bundle}, r_{KC}, \text{'}key\ size\text{'})$.

$$N_b = \sum_{k=0}^{n_{bundle}} \frac{(n_{bundle})!}{k!(n_{bundle}-k)!} \times (r_{KC})^k (1-r_{KC})^{(n_{bundle}-k)} \times 10^{(k\times \text{'}key\ size\text{'})} \tag{4}$$

According to [17], the field-programmable gate array (FPGA)-based hardware implementation of a parallel key searching system for the brute force attack on RC4 encryption can achieve a key searching speed of around 10^7 keys per second. So, we assume the attacker uses a cipher (encrypted speech) breaking tool capable of 10^7 decryptions/second in RC4. This means that the enemy can try 10^7 possible keys per second. Fig. 9 shows average months to decrypt a unit of n_{bundle} packets as a function of the parameter n_{bundle} for our persistent packet key encryption scheme with the r_{KC} of 1%, that is, $\frac{N_b(n_{bundle},\ 0.01,\ \text{'}key\ size\text{'})}{10^7\times60\times60\times24\times30}$. It is shown that the persistent packet key encryption scheme with the r_{KC} of 1% can allow the attacker to decrypt the encrypted n_{bundle} packets by investing 2 days' effort if the key length exceeds 5 digits for the case $n_{bundle} = 4$ (80-millisecond speech from G.711 encoder). Fig. 10 shows

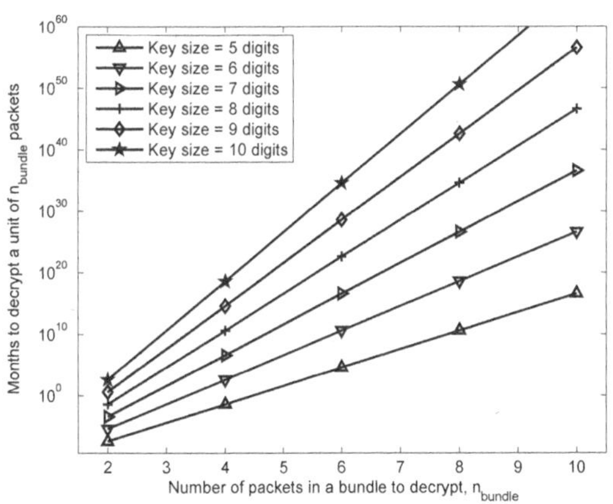

Fig. 9: Months to decrypt a unit bundle of n_{bundle} concatenated packets for different key sizes with the key change rate $r_{KC} = 1\%$

average months to decrypt a unit of n_{bundle} packets for the case that $r_{KC} = 5\%$, that is, $\frac{N_b(n_{bundle},\ 0.05,\ \text{'}key\ size\text{'})}{10^7\times60\times60\times24\times30}$. It is shown that even the persistent packet key encryption scheme with a 5-digit key size will prevent the enemy from decrypting the encrypted n_{bundle} packets by investing 24 months' effort for the case $n_{bundle} = 4$ (80-millisecond speech from G.711 encoder). Fig. 11 shows how many years it will take for the enemy to decrypt 30-second speech as a function of the parameter n_{bundle} for the persistent

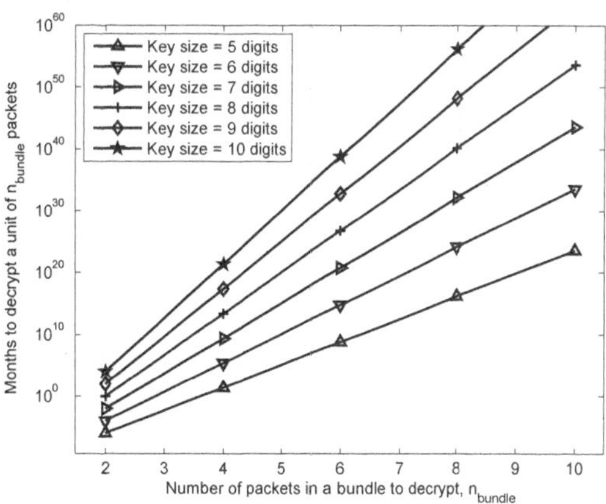

Fig. 10: Months to decrypt a unit bundle of n_{bundle} concatenated packets for different key sizes with the key change rate $r_{KC} = 5\%$

packet key encryption scheme with the key change rate $r_{KC} = 1\%$. The plots correspond to the results obtained from the formula $\frac{N_b(n_{bundle},\ 0.01,\ \text{'}key\ size\text{'})}{10^7\times60\times60\times24\times365} \times \frac{30}{n_{bundle}\times0.02}$ (we consider 20 millisecond packet period). It is shown that the persistent packet key encryption scheme with the r_{KC} of 1% does not allow the attacker to decrypt the 30-second concatenated packets (30-second speech) by investing one year's effort if the key length exceeds 5 digits under the condition that $n_{bundle} = 4$. Fig. 12 shows how many

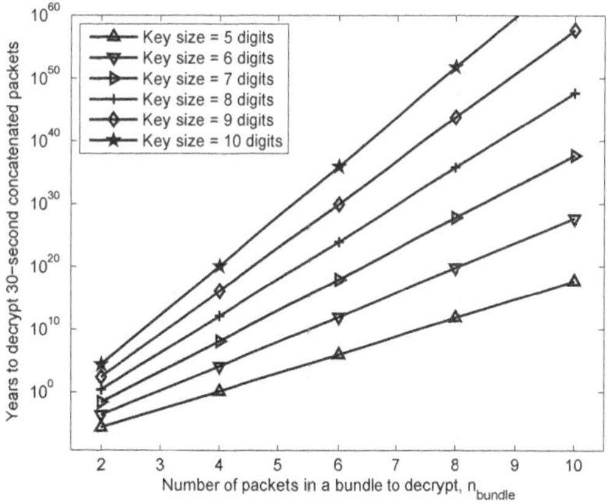

Fig. 11: Years to decrypt a 30-second speech as a function of the parameter n_{bundle} for different key sizes with the key change rate $r_{KC} = 1\%$

years it will take for the enemy to decrypt 30-second speech for the case that the key change rate $r_{KC} = 5\%$. The plots correspond to the results obtained from the formula $\frac{N_b(n_{bundle},\ 0.05,\ \text{'}key\ size\text{'})}{10^7\times60\times60\times24\times365} \times \frac{30}{n_{bundle}\times0.02}$. It is shown that the use of $r_{KC} = 5\%$ will prevent the enemy from decrypting the 30-second speech by investing 100 years' effort under the condition that $n_{bundle} = 4$ even though a 5-digit key is used.

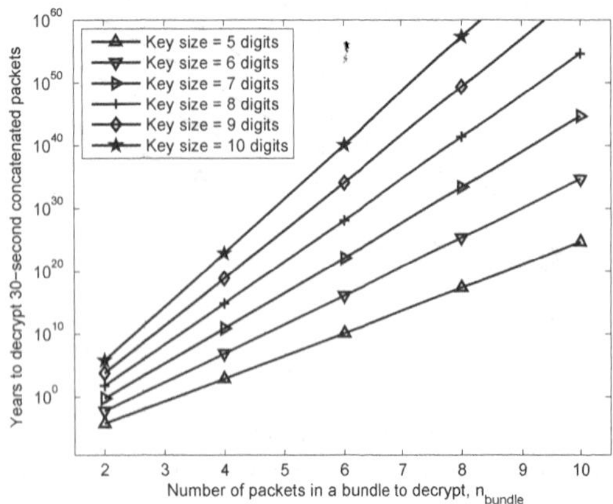

Fig. 12: Years to decrypt a 30-second speech as a function of the parameter n_{bundle} for different key sizes with the key change rate $r_{KC} = 2\%$

5. Conclusion

This paper proposed a persistent packet key encryption scheme that uses the same packet key for a series of packets and changes key for the next series of packets. The key change schedule is controlled by the key change rate r_{KC}. While existing encryption techniques use the same key to secure different RTP payloads during a given session, this paper dealt with the packet key methods where Diffie-Hellman key exchange procedures repeat only for the RTP packets that are selected based on the parameter r_{KC}. This paper first proved that the persistent packet key encryption scheme with the key change rate r_{KC} of up to 5% will significantly reduce latency for encryption and decryption compared with the full packet key encryption scheme with the r_{KC} of 100%. Secondly, this paper proved that the persistent packet key encryption scheme with key change rate r_{KC} ranging from 1% to 5%, is secure enough against after-transmission attacks. We found that our persistent 5-digit packet key encryption scheme will prevent the enemy from decrypting the encrypted concatenated packets in a unit bundle of 4 packets by investing 24 months' effort. We proved that it is almost impossible for the after-transmission attacker to decrypt the encrypted speech as the speech length increases and a negligible level of latency for encryption and decryption is achieved by the use of 5-digit packet key and $r_{KC} = 5\%$. As a result, we argue that our persistent packet key encryption scheme is an useful technique for secure real-time multimedia communications.

Acknowledgment

This research was supported by the Basic Science Research Program through the National Research Foundation of Korea (NRF) funded by the Ministry of Education, Science and Technology (2011-0015200).

References

[1] F. Almasalha, N. Agarwal, and A. Khokhar, "Secure multimedia transmission over rtp," in *Multimedia, 2008. ISM 2008. Tenth IEEE International Symposium on*, dec. 2008, pp. 404–411.

[2] S. Jelassi, G. Rubino, H. Melvin, H. Youssef, and G. Pujolle, "Quality of experience of voip service: A survey of assessment approaches and open issues," *Communications Surveys Tutorials, IEEE*, vol. 14, no. 2, pp. 491–513, 2012.

[3] J. Arkko, E. Carrara, F. Lindholm, M. Naslund, and K. Norrman, "MIKEY: Multimedia Internet KEYing," RFC 3830 (Proposed Standard), Internet Engineering Task Force, August, updated by RFC 4738.

[4] R. Pecori, "A pki-free key agreement protocol for p2p voip applications," in *Communications (ICC), 2012 IEEE International Conference on*, june 2012, pp. 6748–6752.

[5] R. Pecori and L. Veltri, "A key agreement protocol for p2p voip applications," in *Software, Telecommunications Computer Networks, 2009. SoftCOM 2009. 17th International Conference on*, sept. 2009, pp. 276–280.

[6] S. Puangpronpitag, P. Kasabai, and D. Pansa, "An enhancement of the sdp security description (sdes) for key protection," in *Electrical Engineering/Electronics, Computer, Telecommunications and Information Technology (ECTI-CON), 2012 9th International Conference on*, may 2012, pp. 1–4.

[7] Y. Jung, E. Festijo, and J. Atwood, "Securing rtp packets using per-packet key exchange for real-time multimedia," *ETRI Journal*, Recently accepted paper.

[8] A.-V. T. W. Group, H. Schulzrinne, S. Casner, R. Frederick, and V. Jacobson, "Rtp: A transport protocol for real-time applications," RFC 1889 (Proposed Standard), Internet Engineering Task Force, jan 1996, obsoleted by RFC 3550.

[9] F. Cheng, J. Luo, and J. Cao, "Research and implementation of real-time rtp streams monitoring in 3g voice quality system," in *Software Engineering and Service Science (ICSESS), 2012 IEEE 3rd International Conference on*, 2012, pp. 288–291.

[10] X. Zhang, H. Heys, and C. Li, "Energy cost of cryptographic session key establishment in a wireless sensor network," in *Communications and Networking in China (CHINACOM), 2011 6th International ICST Conference on*, aug. 2011, pp. 335–339.

[11] H. Roh and S. Jung, "Session key exchange and mutual authentication scheme between mobile machines in wlan based ad hoc networks," in *Information and Communication Technology Convergence (ICTC), 2010 International Conference on*, nov. 2010, pp. 482–483.

[12] M. Mohammed, A. Rohiem, and A. El-moghazy, "Confidentiality enhancement of secure real time transport protocol," in *Computer Engineering Conference (ICENCO), 2012 8th International*, 2012, pp. 43–48.

[13] M. Baugher, D. McGrew, M. Naslund, E. Carrara, and K. Norrman, "The Secure Real-time Transport Protocol (SRTP)," RFC 3711 (Proposed Standard), Internet Engineering Task Force, March, updated by RFC 5506.

[14] E. Rescorla, "Diffie-hellman key agreement method," RFC 2631 (Proposed Standard), Internet Engineering Task Force, jun.

[15] X. Xing, E. Shakshuki, D. Benoit, and T. Sheltami, "Security analysis and authentication improvement for ieee 802.11i specification," in *Global Telecommunications Conference, 2008. IEEE GLOBECOM 2008. IEEE*, 2008, pp. 1–5.

[16] R. Syahputri and S. Sriyanto, "Fast and secure authentication in ieee 802.11i wireless lan," in *Uncertainty Reasoning and Knowledge Engineering (URKE), 2012 2nd International Conference on*, aug. 2012, pp. 158–161.

[17] S. Kwok and E. Lam, "Effective uses of fpgas for brute-force attack on rc4 ciphers," *Very Large Scale Integration (VLSI) Systems, IEEE Transactions on*, vol. 16, no. 8, pp. 1096–1100, aug. 2008.

Using Secure Multi-party Computation when Pocessing Distributed Health Data

Anders Andersen
Department of Computer Science
Faculty of Science and Technology
University of Tromsø
9037 Tromsø, Norway

Abstract— *Patient related health data are typically located at different general practices and hospitals. When processing and analyzing such data, the provided infrastructure and toolset has to take into consideration legal, security and privacy issues. The combination of secure multi-party computations (SMC) algorithms, encryption, public key infrastructure (PKI), certificates, and a certificate authority (CA) is used to implement an infrastructure and a toolset for statistical analysis of health data. The general practices and hospitals are considered nodes in a computing graph, and at each node a sub-process performs the local part of the computation. The described approach tries to support a wide range of possible SMC algorithms and computing graphs.*

Keywords: SMC algorithms, Privacy, PKI, Health data.

1. Introduction

In this paper an infrastructure and a toolset for statistical analysis of health data is presented and discussed. It uses a combination of secure multi-party computations (SMC) algorithms [1], [2], encryption, public key infrastructure (PKI), certificates, and a certificate authority (CA) to manage the legal, security and privacy issues of such analysis. A coordinator that prepares the computation, and a set of sub-processes representing the parties in the multi-party computation. To send a message securely to a sub-process or the coordinator, the address and public encryption key of the receiver is needed.

In preparing the computation the coordinator creates a computing graph, and based on this a set of messages initiating the computation. The nodes in the computing graph are the coordinator and the sub-processes. The edges of the directed graph are the communication (messages sent) between nodes. A sub-process can only access or unwrap a limited part of the message it receives. The part it can access includes its input data and the address/key of the set of nodes it is forwarding its intermediate computational results to. The part of the message it cannot unwrap is encrypted with the public key of the receiver and is forwarded unchanged to the next nodes in the graph.

This approach will be evaluated in the context of the Snow SMSC (Secure Multi-party Statistical Computations) project. The Snow system [3] utilizes the mobile software agent approach. The system is deployed in health institutions and is used for data extraction for disease surveillance purposes. It extracts health data and performs data aggregation from general practices in Norway. In the Snow SMSC project the goal is to provide a toolset for statistical analysis of health data. Any medical research using health data is difficult because of the legal, security and privacy issues involved. This enforces a set of constrains upon the computations and their implementations. To address this, Snow SMSC will use the outcome of SMC research [4].

In [5], SMC for N institutions with values $x_1, \ldots, x_N$ who wish to evaluate a known function $f(x_1, \ldots, x_N)$ is subject to four constrains:

C1: The correct value $f(x_1, \ldots, x_N)$ is obtained and known to all institutions.

C2: No institution j learns more about the other institutions values $X_{-j} = \{x_n : n \neq j\}$ than it can deduce from x_j and $f(x_1, \ldots, x_N)$.

C3: No trusted third party—human or machine—is part of the process.

C4: *Semi-honesty*. Institutions perform agreed upon computations correctly using their true data. However, they are permitted to retain the results of intermediate computations.

For practical purposes, the zero information disclosure implied by C3 is a difficult implement efficiently [6]. In the context of the Snow SMSC project we will use the following relaxed constrain replacing C3:

C3 : No human or machine is allowed to have access to both the patient identifier i, and a data value x_i not previously known.

In [7] six requirements for secure disease surveillance are presented. These requirements includes what is special with health data and should be taken into consideration when performing such analysis. In [7] a secure multi-party computation protocol was developed to meet these requirements. However, in this paper we will focus on the four constrains presented above.

The implementation approach presented in this paper will consist of a combination of SMC algorithms and careful usage of encryption. The usage of public-key encryption is essential, but in many cases a combination of public-key and symmetric encryption should be used for performance reasons.

2. SMC in Snow SMSC

2.1 Computing graph and layered messages

A coordinator creates the computing graph for the computing processes. Each computing process is a sub-process of the overall computation. This relates to a MapReduce approach [8] where a coordinator performs the computation in a map and a reduce step. The map step divides a task and it inputs into a set of smaller sub-problems and distributes them to worker nodes. In the reduce step the answers from the sub-problems are collected and combined to the final result. However, in Snow SMSC (and in the case of many SMC problems) it is not always feasible to collect all the intermediate results at the coordinator. For some types of computations and data sets this might compromise the privacy of the patients. This is illustrated in the example below where a calculation of the mean value of some patient data is performed by forwarding the intermediate results to the next sub-process in a chain. This means that in Snow SMSC we have to support a wide range of computing graphs, and the tools and protocols developed in the project have to support this flexible arrangement.

The coordinator uses the computing graph to generate a set of layered messages. Each layer in these messages exposes the next edges in the directed graph. The computation is initiated by sending these messages to the first set of sub-processes. At each sub-process one layer of the received message is unwrapped exposing both the input data set for the calculation performed at this node, and the address/key of the next sub-processes in the computing graph. The calculation is performed using the input data set and local data available at this node. When the calculation is done the sub-process generates a set of messages forwarded to the next sub-processes in the computing graph. The data set included in these messages is based on the result of the performed calculation and a filter function. The filter function is used to ensure that a given sub-process is only forwarded data that it needs to perform its calculation. The filter function makes it possible for a sub-process to forward different data set to the next sub-processes in the computing graph. Local data at the node might also be updated when the calculation is performed.

2.2 Privacy

The privacy of the patients is a main concern in systems accessing personal health data. To maintain this privacy Snow SMSC has to ensure that constraints C2 and C3' (see above) are maintained [5]. This will be achieved with SMC algorithms [4], [2], encryption of data and messages, and a public-key infrastructure (PKI). SMC algorithms ensure that each participant performing a sub-process is unable to learn about the other participants input data and intermediate results. Public-key encryption (often in combination with symmetric key encryption) is used to ensure that data and messages are only visible to the intended receiver. And finally, a PKI and its certificate authorities (CAs) are used to ensure that the participants can use certificates to distribute and trust public keys. This enables public-keys as the tool to authenticate participants and maintain the integrity and privacy of the data exchanged.

2.3 Example: computation of the mean value

This is illustrated in a small example. The goal is to calculate the mean value of the values $x_1, \ldots, x_N$ from N participants. With the help of the PKI, its certificates, and CAs, the coordinator c has access to and can trust the public keys $P_1, \ldots, P_N$ of the N participants. The sub-process of each participant i will perform the calculation $r_i = r_{i-1} + x_i$. To achieve SMC, the coordinator starts the computation by sending a large random number r_0 to the first participant. Since each message is encrypted with the public-key of the receiver, only the first participant can see this message. Each participant i adds its value x_i to the sum and forwards the message to the next participant in the chain. Also this message is encrypted with the public-key of the receiver. This continues to the last participant N who performs the same task and forwards the message encrypted with the public-key P_c of the coordinator to the coordinator c. The coordinator subtracts the secret large random number from the sum and calculates the mean value m:

$$m = \frac{r_N - r_0}{N}$$

The computing path is generated at the coordinator c, and each participant only sees the next participant in the path. To achieve this the coordinator generates the following graph representation B_1:

$$\Big\{(A_2, P_2), \ldots \{(A_N, P_N), \{(A_c, P_c), n\}_{P_N}\}_{P_{N-1}} \cdots \Big\}_{P_1}$$

P_i is the the public key of i, where i is either one of the participants $1, \ldots, N$ or coordinator c. $\{\ldots\}_{P_i}$ says that the message (inside the curly braces) is encrypted with P_i. A_i and P_i are the address and public key of i. r_i is the intermediate sum at participant i. n is a large random and unique number (nonce) generated by the coordinator.

In the message forwarded to each participant the intermediate result of the computation r_i also has to be included. To the first participant the coordinator includes the secret large random number r_0. The message forwarded to the first participant will then be $\{r_0, B_1\}_{P_1}$. However, since B_1 already is encrypted with the public key of participant 1,

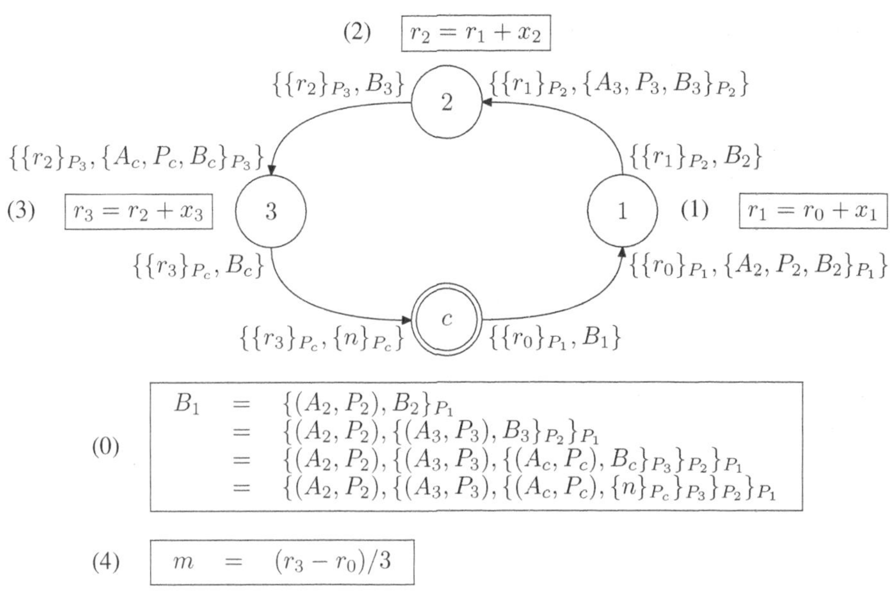

Fig. 1: Processing performed and messages sent and received when calculating the mean value with three participants 1, 2, and 3 and a coordinator c.

there is no need to re-encrypt that part of the message. Instead the message forwarded to each participant i will have the following structure:

$$\{\{r_{i-1}\}_{P_i}, B_i\}$$

Each participant can only see the part of the message that is encrypted with its public key. The rest of the message is treated as a data blob that is forwarded unmodified to the next participant. Any participant i can see the following received message:

$$\{\{r_{i-1}\}_{P_i}, \{(A_{i+1}, P_{i+1}), B_{i+1}\}_{P_i}\}$$

P_i is the the public key of participant i, and $\{\ldots\}_{P_i}$ says that the message-part (inside the curly braces) is encrypted with P_i. r_{i-1} is the intermediate result from the previous participant in the path. A_{i+1} and P_{i+1} are respectively the address and public key of participant $i + 1$, the next participant in the path. B_{i+1} is the data blob that participant i is going to forward unmodified to participant $i + 1$. Participant i performs the calculation $r_i = r_{i-1} + x_i$ and forwards the following message to the next participant A_{i+1} in the path:

$$\{\{r_i\}_{P_{i+1}}, B_{i+1}\}$$

The original message created by the coordinator specifies the computing graph (a path between the sub-processes in this example). Any participant i uses the address A_{i+1} to find the next node in the graph and the public key P_{i+1} to securely communicate the intermediate results to the next node in the graph. Figure 1 illustrates this example with a coordinator c and three participants 1, 2 and 3. The start of each edge in the directed graph illustrates how the senders sees the message it is forwarding. The end of the edge illustrates how the receiver sees the message. The difference between what the sender and receiver can see is due to the message part B_i that is encrypted with public key P_i of the receiver i. The coordinator encrypted B_i and only i has the private key that can decrypt B_i. The sender i has the knowledge about the intermediate value r_1 since it calculated it. After it was calculated, sender i encrypted it with the public key of receiver $i+1$. To summarize, at each node the following operations are performed:

(0) Coordinator c prepares and forward the message $\{\{r_0\}_{P_1}, B_1\}$ to participant 1. Both r_0 and n are large random numbers. B_1 is important since it specifies the computing path *and* includes the public keys needed to securely forward the intermediate results to the next participant.
(1) Participant 1 decrypts and interprets the received message and uses its content to perform the calculation and securely forward the message to the next participant. The part of the message that it cannot decrypt (B_2) is forwarded to the next participant unchanged.
(2) Participant 2 decrypts and interprets the received message and uses its content to perform the calculation and securely forward the message to the next participant. The part of the message that it cannot decrypt (B_3) is forwarded to the next participant unchanged.
(3) Participant 3 decrypts and interprets the received message and uses its content to perform the calculation and securely forward the message to the coordinator. Participant 3 do no necessarily know that the receiver

of its message is the coordinator. It uses the address and public key found in the message it received. The part of the message that it cannot decrypt (B_c) is forwarded to the coordinator unchanged.

(4) The coordinator decrypts and interprets the received message and uses its content, the stored value r_0, and the known number of participants, to perform the final calculation of the mean value m. Before the actual calculation is performed the coordinator will validate that the received nonce n matches the value it originally included in B_1.

3. A more generic approach to SMC

The example above illustrates a simple computing graph, a simple data set, and a simple algorithm. The computing graph is a simple path starting and ending at the coordinator. The data set is a single (intermediate) value updated based on local data at each sub-process. The algorithm at each sub-process is to add a local value to the received intermediate result. We will for now ignore the SMC algorithms and focus on a generic approach to represent and distribute the computation graph and the data set.

3.1 Supporting a wide range of graphs

As described above the coordinator initially generates the computation graph G. It is wrapped in the recursively encrypted blob that is unwrapped one layer at the time at each processing node using the private key of the node. In the generic approach each layer does not provide a single receiver of the intermediate results from the current node. It provides a set of receivers. A node i will receive and unwrap an input data set I_i and a set of data blobs B_i containing the necessary information needed to forward its intermediate results to the next set of processing nodes. I_i represents sufficient data to perform the calculation. It might be aggregated from a set of input messages containing a subset I_i' of the data. Node i forwards its intermediate results to M nodes. B_i contains the addresses/keys and the information for the receiving nodes:

$$\begin{aligned}\{&(A_{(i,1)}, P_{(i,1)}), B_{(i,1)};\\ &(A_{(i,2)}, P_{(i,2)}), B_{(i,2)};\\ &\vdots\\ &(A_{(i,M)}, P_{(i,M)}), B_{(i,M)}\}_{P_i}\end{aligned}$$

$(A_{(i,k)}, P_{(i,k)}), k \in \{1, \ldots, M\}$ is the address/key of the receiver k, and $B_{(i,k)}$ is the part of the received message that node i can not decrypt and it is forwarded to receiver k unchanged. Each node i will perform its calculation f using the received data set I_i and its local data set X_i:

$$R_i = f(I_i, X_i)$$

F is a filter function that removes data from a data set that should not be forwarded to a given node. $F(R, h)$ produces a new data set I_h' where all data that should not be available for node h are removed. In node i the intermediate results forwarded to node (i, k) is filtered like this:

$$I_{(i,k)}' = F(R_i, (i, k))$$

From node i all receivers (i, k) is forwarded the following message:

$$\{\{I_{(i,k)}'\}_{P_{(i,k)}}, B_{(i,k)}\}$$

In Figure 2 an example of a computation graph with a coordinator and the six participants 1, 2, $(1, 1)$, $(1, 2)$, $(2, 1)$ and $(2, 2)$ is shown. The coordinator has the following representation of the computation graph G:

$$\begin{aligned}G &= \{(A_1, P_1), B_1; (A_2, P_2), B_2\}_{P_c}\\ B_1 &= \{(A_{(1,1)}, P_{(1,1)}), B_{(1,1)};\\ &\quad (A_{(1,2)}, P_{(1,2)}), B_{(1,2)}\}_{P_1}\\ B_{(1,1)} &= \{(A_c, P_c), B_{(1,1,c)}\}_{P_{(1,1)}}\\ B_{(1,2)} &= \{(A_c, P_c), B_{(1,2,c)}\}_{P_{(1,2)}}\\ B_2 &= \{(A_{(2,1)}, P_{(2,1)}), B_{(2,1)};\\ &\quad (A_{(2,2)}, P_{(2,2)}), B_{(2,2)}\}_{P_2}\\ B_{(2,1)} &= \{(A_c, P_c), B_{(2,1,c)}\}_{P_{(2,1)}}\\ B_{(2,2)} &= \{(A_c, P_c), B_{(2,2,c)}\}_{P_{(2,2)}}\end{aligned}$$

$B_{(1,1,c)}$, $B_{(1,2,c)}$, $B_{(2,1,c)}$ and $B_{(2,2,c)}$ do not contribute to the representation of the computation graph. Typically they are unique nonces encrypted with the public key of the coordinator. They are used to validate that the computation has been following the specified paths in the computation graph.

At each step in the computation the following operations are performed:

(0) The coordinator c produces and filters the initial data set R:

$$I_1' = F(R, 1), \quad I_2' = F(R, 2)$$

Based on the graph representation G, the coordinator c generates and forwards the two messages M_1 and M_2 for the first two processing nodes in the graph. Each message contains the filtered data set encrypted with the receivers' public key and the information the receivers need to perform their tasks.

(1) Node 1 and 2 decrypts and interpret the received message and performs the following operation to create the intermediate results $I_{(i,j)}, i, j \in 1, 2$ forwarded to the next set of nodes in the computation graph:

$$I_{(i,j)}' = F(f(I_i, X_i), (i, j))$$

(2) Node $(1, 1)$, $(1, 2)$, $(2, 1)$ and $(2, 2)$ decrypts and interpret the received message and performs the following operation to create the intermediate results $I_{(i,j,c)}, i, j \in 1, 2$ forwarded to the coordinator c:

$$I_{(i,j,c)}' = F(f(I_{(i,j)}, X_{(i,j)}), c)$$

(3) The coordinator collects, decrypts and interprets the intermediate results from node $(1, 1)$, $(1, 2)$, $(2, 1)$

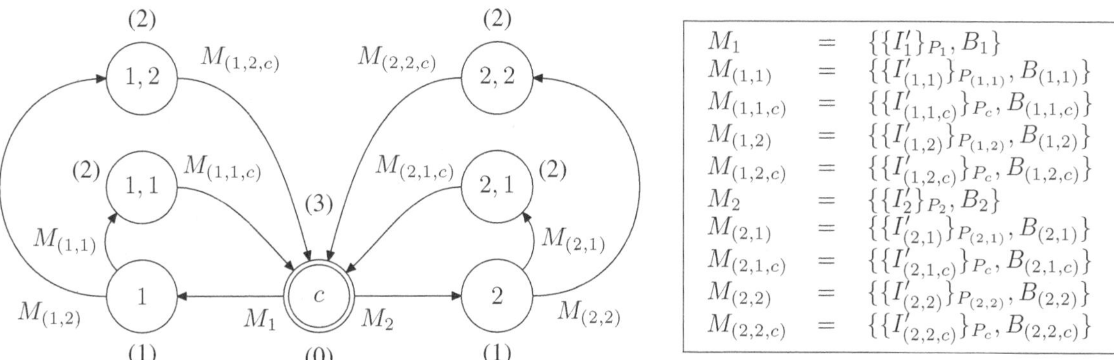

Fig. 2: The computation graph G with six participants and a coordinator c including the processing performed and messages transmitted in the computation.

and $(2, 2)$ in the computation graph. The intermediate results are then used to calculate the final results of the computation.

3.2 Authenticity and integrity

Above we have focused on the computation, communication and protection of data. Authenticity and integrity is also important in a system like this. The receiver of a message has to be assured that the message is received from an expected participant in the computation and that the message has not been altered with. Based on the above description of the system it is possible for ill-behaved nodes to generate messages that trigger a receiving node to perform the local calculation and disclose data in conflict with privacy concerns. To protect against such attacks each node signs every messages it forwards to other nodes. This signature is verified before the message is interpreted. It is verified both to check that the sender is who is claimed to be the sender and that the message is expected from the sender. The last verification is done against information found in the part of the computation graph unwrapped by the receiving node.

At node i a message M_i contains data blob B_1 encrypted with the public key P_i. Above we have seen that this data blob is a layered representation of the computing graph with address/key pairs and sub-layers of the graph. So far we have ignored that it also contains an identificator of whom you should expect to receive this message from. This identificator is verified against the signature of the message. Since B_i was generated and encrypted at the coordinator we can be ensured that the intention was that node i is expected to receive message M_i from the sender. For this to be valid B_i has to be signed by the coordinator. Message $M_{(1,1)}$ from Figure 2 with signatures can then be written like this:

$$M_{(1,1)} = \{\{I'_{(1,1)}\}_{P_{(1,1)}}, B_{(1,1)}\}_{S_1}$$

The meaning of D_{S_i} is that D is signed by i. $B_{(1,1)}$ is signed by the coordinator c:

$$B_{(1,1)} = \{\{1, (A_c, P_c), B_{(1,1,c)}\}_{P_{(1,1)}}\}_{S_c}$$

The trust we can establish from this is the following:

(i) Message $M_{(1,1)}$ originates from node 1 since it is signed by 1.
(ii) Message $M_{(1,1)}$ was expected to come from node 1 since the first element of $B_{(1,1)}$ is its identificator.
(iii) $B_{(1,1)}$ originates from the coordinator since it is signed by c.
(iv) $B_{(1,1)}$ is created for node $(1, 1)$ since it is encrypted with its public key. It can also be concluded that this was the coordinator's intention since the encrypted $B_{(1,1)}$ is signed by the coordinator.

Every message and data blob in this infrastructure are encrypted and signed as illustrated with message $M_{(1,1)}$ above. This ensures the authenticity and integrity of the messages and their content.

3.3 Progress and failure

In the example illustrated in Figure 2 each processing nodes is receiving a single message. The coordinator is however collecting the intermediate results from 4 different nodes. Before the coordinator can perform its final computation it waits for the intermediate results from all 4 nodes. In the generic case it is also possible that one of the processing nodes should receive input from more than one node. The calculation in a given node (and at the coordinator) is performed when the node has received *sufficient data* to perform the calculation. Sufficient data can mean *all possible inputs*, *a given number of inputs*, *a percentage of the possible inputs*, and all this in a combination with *timeout values* (to ensure progress by sacrificing the quality of the results). At a given node i the input data I_i to the calculation f should be interpreted as sufficient data to perform the calculation. This calculation is blocked until sufficient data is available. Table 1 lists some examples of sufficient data specifications where t is time since first input arrived, n is the number of inputs, and $|N|$ is the number of expected inputs. The meaning of the expression $t \to v$ is "when time t passes the timeout value v".

Table 1: Examples of sufficient data specifications.

Specification	Description
$t \leq 120 \wedge n = \|N\|$	Wait at most 120 seconds for all inputs. Otherwise abort.
$(t < 180 \wedge n = \|N\|) \vee (t \to 180 \wedge n \geq 0.75 \times \|N\|)$	Either wait less than 180 seconds for all inputs or wait 180 seconds and get at least 75% of inputs. Otherwise abort.
$(t < 60 \wedge n \geq 10) \vee (t \to 60 \wedge n \geq 8)$	Either wait less than 60 seconds for 10 inputs or wait 60 seconds and get at least 8 inputs. Otherwise abort.

It is possible for messages to get lost and nodes to fail, and the *sufficient data* specification can be used in algorithms to ensure progress even if this occurs. In some circumstances it is not possible ensure progress. A node that has not yet received any messages are not a part of the computation and have no roles in detecting such errors. A node that has received some input but not sufficient data to perform its calculation will abort the computation at a specified timeout time. It will then forward an abort message to the receivers it knows about. A node than receives an abort message will ignore it if it has sufficient data to perform the calculation. Otherwise it will aggregate the received abort messages in an abort message that is forwarded to the receivers it knows about. However, a node that receives an abort message might have to wait for a timeout before it can conclude that it should forward abort messages to its known receivers. It could be that it gets sufficient data later even if it receives an abort message at a state without sufficient data. In that case the abort message should be ignored.

3.4 From problem to computation

In this paper the SMC algorithms and how they are analyzed and approved are not discussed in details, but a short overview follows. When a statistical analysis is planned the algorithm, its computation graph and the handling of data, are presented for approval to the responsible authority. If this is granted the sub process activity for each node are distributed and configured and the layered representation of the computation graph is generated. The statistical analysis can then be performed. Both one-time and periodical statistical analysis exists. Disease surveillance is an example of an ongoing periodical analysis that is continuously performed at every node in the existing system.

4. Evaluation

The infrastructure and tool set described above are evaluated with an example. The purpose of this evaluation is to demonstrate its usability.

4.1 Pearson's r

The Pearson product-moment correlation coefficient (Pearson's r) measure of the correlation (linear dependence) between (n samples of) two variables x and y:

$$r = \frac{\sum_{i=1}^{n}(x_i - \bar{x})(y_i - \bar{y})}{\sqrt{\sum_{i=1}^{n}(x_i - \bar{x})^2 \sum_{i=1}^{n}(y_i - \bar{y})^2}}$$

In the case of m health institutions with s_j samples of x_{j_i} and y_{j_i} at each institution, r can be rewritten like this:

$$r = \frac{\sum_{j=1}^{m}\sum_{i=1}^{s_j}(x_{j_i} - \bar{x})(y_{j_i} - \bar{y})}{\sqrt{\sum_{j=1}^{m}\sum_{i=1}^{s_j}(x_{j_i} - \bar{x})^2 \sum_{j=1}^{m}\sum_{i=1}^{s_j}(y_{j_i} - \bar{y})^2}}$$

At each node j the following three intermediate results have to be calculated:

$$\begin{aligned} a_j &= \sum_{i=1}^{s_j}(x_{j_i} - \bar{x})(y_{j_i} - \bar{y}) \\ b_j &= \sum_{i=1}^{s_j}(x_{j_i} - \bar{x})^2 \\ c_j &= \sum_{i=1}^{s_j}(y_{j_i} - \bar{y})^2 \end{aligned}$$

We can then at the coordinator generate the following representation of the computation graph:

$$\Big\{(A_1, P_1), \{\{c, (A_c, P_c), B_{(1,c)}\}_{P_1}\}_{s_c}; \\ (A_2, P_2), \{\{c, (A_c, P_c), B_{(2,c)}\}_{P_2}\}_{s_c}; \\ \vdots \\ (A_m, P_m), \{\{c, (A_c, P_c), B_{(m,c)}\}_{P_m}\}_{s_c}\Big\}_{P_c}$$

From this graph the coordinator generates the following message to each health institution:

$$M_j = \Big\{\{(\bar{x}, \bar{y})\}_{P_j}, \{\{c, (A_c, P_c), B_{(j,c)}\}_{P_j}\}_{S_c}\Big\}_{S_c}$$

The initial mean values $\bar{x}$ and $\bar{y}$ can be securely calculated using an approach similar to the one discussed above in 2.3. At each health institution j the three intermediate results are calculated and the they are included in the following message to the coordinator c:

$$M_{(j,c)} = \{\{a_j, b_j, c_j\}_{P_c}, B_{(j,c)}\}_{S_j}$$

The coordinator validates the signatures (and nonces) of the received messages and when all input is received Pearson's r is calculated:

$$r = \frac{\sum_{j=1}^{m} a_j}{\sqrt{\sum_{j=1}^{m} b_j \sum_{j=1}^{m} c_j}}$$

4.2 Discussion

The computation in Pearson's r is a MapReduce. We have demonstrated that MapReduce based SMC algorithms can be implemented using our infrastructure and toolset. Earlier we have also demonstrated the implementation of other types of computation graphs and algorithms. The provided infrastructure and toolset supports a wide range of computing graphs and SMC algorithms.

In this paper we have ignored the details of the current Python based prototype implementation and we have not provided any code examples. This is done to keep the focus on the overall overview of the system and to avoid any implementation details. It is believed that the described system can be implemented using a wide range of programming languages, PKIs, crypto libraries and message systems. The current Python prototype demonstrates the main concepts and is one of the candidates for further development in a production system.

5. Conclusion

The privacy of the patients is granted by the combination of the SMC algorithms and the infrastructure and tool set discussed above. A PKI and public key encryption ensures confidentiality. Nodes not part in a computation has no access to any data or intermediate results, and nodes part in a computation only sees data and intermediate results explicit made available for them. When designing a computation it is now possible to focus on the SMC algorithm itself and not how to ensure confidentiality of data flowing through the system.

6. Acknowledgement

A special thank you to Johan Gustav Bellika who introduced me to this problem domain and the Snow SMSC project ideas. Also thank you to Yigzaw Kassaye Yitbarek for feedback and comments on this work.

References

[1] O. Goldreich, S. Micali, and A. Wigderson, "How to play any mental game, or a completeness theorem for protocols with honest majority," in *Proceedings of the nineteenth annual ACM symposium on Theory of computing*. New York: ACM, 1987, pp. 218–229.

[2] A. C. Yao, "Protocols for secure computations," in *Proceedings of the 23rd Annual Symposium on Foundations of Computer Science*. New York: ACM Press, 1982, pp. 160–164.

[3] J. G. Bellika, G. Aronsen, M. A. Johansen, G. Hartvigsen, and G. S. Simonsen, "The snow agent system: A peer-to-peer system for disease surveillance and diagnostic assistance," *Advances in Disease Surveillance,*, vol. 4, p. 42, 2007.

[4] S. Goldwasser, "Multi party computations: past and present," in *PODC'97, Proceedings of the sixteenth annual ACM symposium on Principles of distributed computing*. New York: ACM, 1997, pp. 1–6.

[5] A. F. Karr, "Secure statistical analysis of distributed databases, emphasizing what we don't know," *Journal of Privacy and Confidentiality*, vol. 1, no. 2, pp. 197–211, 2009.

[6] W. Du and Z. Zhan, "A practical approach to solve secure multi-party computation problems," in *Proceedings of the 2002 workshop on New security paradigms*. New York: ACM, 2002, pp. 127–135.

[7] K. E. Emam, J. Hu, J. Mercer, L. Peyton, M. Kantarcioglu, B. Malin, D. Buckeridge, S. Samet, and C. Earle, "A secure protocol for protecting the identity of providers when disclosing data for disease surveillance," *J Am Med Inform Assoc*, vol. 18, pp. 212–217, 2011.

[8] J. Dean and S. Ghemawat, "MapReduce: Simplified data processing on large clusters," in *OSDI'04: Sixth Symposium on Operating System Design and Implementation*, San Francisco, Dec. 2004.

SESSION

SPECIAL TRACK ON SYSTEMS ENGINEERING AND SECURITY

Chair(s)

Dr. Michael R. Grimaila

A New Quasigroup Based Random Number Generator

Matthew Battey
Computer Science Department
University of Nebraska at Omaha
Omaha, NE 68182

Abhishek Parakh and William Mahoney
Nebraska University Center for Information Assurance
University of Nebraska at Omaha
Omaha, NE 68182

***Abstract*—We propose a pseudo-random number generator based on qausigroups that meets the statistical analytic performance of those based on SHA-1, AES and RC4. We present the algorithm and heuristic results based on NIST-STS package.**

***Index Terms*—pseudo random number generator, quasigroup, block cipher, constrained resources**

I. Introduction

Pseudo random number generators (PRNGs) are essential to almost all digital systems. Random numbers are useful in games of chance: shuffling cards, altering the behavior of video game "enemies", etc. as well as for secure communications. PRNGs are deployed for creating digital signatures [1] [2], eliminating network congestion [3] [4], securing RFID communication [5] and facilitating cryptographic measures for key generation and even implementing stream ciphers. Unlike a true random number generator, PRNGs are defined by an algorithm.

The US Government, through the National Institute of Standards and Technology (NIST), is tasked with researching and recommending random number generators for use in governmental operations. The most recent recommendation is based on SHA-1, a hashing feedback algorithm [6]. However, the security of SHA-1 has been broken (theoretically), and NIST has recommended the move to another platform [7]. Although not implemented in major cryptographic suites, for the purpose of random number generation, NIST has identified SHA-2 and more recently SHA-3 successors to SHA-1 [6][8]. Similarly, ARC4 is used in many mobile devices, and it to has proven to be insecure [9].

Modern operating systems and development platforms offer PRNG algorithms as an included service. A survey reveals that Java and OpenSSL both implement the SHA-1 PRNG [10] [11] [12]; Microsoft.NET used SHA-1 prior to Windows 6.0 (Vista), but switched to an AES variant afterwards [13]; and Apple's MacOS and iOS devices rely on ARC4Random [14]. Software vendors tend to default to US government recommendations as a baseline for cryptographic tools.

II. Background - Quasigroups

A quasigroup is a mathematical construction very similar to a group. Although a mathematical group requires adherence to four axioms: closure, associativity, identity, and invertibility, Quasigroups need not conform to all four axioms, but rather require only closure and invertibility. Note, all groups are also quasigroups.

Consider some group G, containing $n = |G|$ elements. To abstractly identify members, we will assign each an ordinal from $(0...n-1)$. Next consider the mathematical operation $m \equiv a+b \mod n$. In this operation we see that the following axioms are met: closure, associativity, identity and invertibility. Interestingly, this group also defines exclusive-or, when $n = 2$. The number of combinations in this group (a, b) is n^2.

Next consider the following quasigroup definition which makes use of H an ordered tuple, each H_a is distinct:

$$H = (H_0, H_1, ..., H_{n-1})$$

$$\begin{aligned} &\forall\ a, b \in \mathbb{Z}, \\ &\quad 0 < a < n-1, \\ &\quad 0 < b < n-1, \\ &\quad \forall\ H_a \in \mathbb{Z}, \\ &\quad 0 < H_a < n-1, \\ &\quad a \neq b \Leftrightarrow H_a \neq H_b : \end{aligned}$$

$$m \equiv H_a + H_b \mod n$$

This quasigroup still remains closed and invertible, but has lost identity and associativity. The total number of permutations for this model is equal to the total possible permutations of H, $|H|! = n!$. Let us expand this model further by considering I also as an ordered tuple, identical to H in all characteristics save it is shuffled in another manner. $m \equiv H_a + I_b \mod n$ remains closed and invertible, but the total number of permutations has increased by a factor of the permutations of I, $|I|! = n!$, giving the total number of permutations as $(n!)^2$.

Quasigroups may be rationalized as nxn matrices, which have identical properties to Latin squares. In fact, all Latin squares are quasigroups. Naming these we say that an nxn Latin square is of order n. When such a realization is constructed, the number of quasigroups expands past $n!$. It has been shown that the number of possible Latin squares is given by $L_n = R_n n!(n-1)!$ (R_n being the number of reduced Latin squares of order n). Much work has gone into accurately calculating L_n, as there is no easy solution [15] [16]. As so many quasigroups exist, let us refer to the quasigroup operation as the symbol $\cdot$ for abstraction purposes. We will use the notation $m = a \cdot b$, indicating that m is the result of the quasigroup operation on a and b.

III. Quasigroups in Cryptography

The quasigroup allows us to make polyalphabetic substitutions, and have been in existence for more than four-hundred years. In 1585, Blaise de Vigenere constructed a Latin square of the same order as the target language (order 26 for English, etc.) [17]. He then proposed a key word that would select the cipher text (or pad-text in today's language). This cipher was considered unbreakable until 1863, when it was discovered that for a large enough plaintext the ciphertext demonstrated repetitions. Although this cipher received Vigenere namesake, Giovan Battista Bellaso had actually published the cipher 1553.

The matrix used for one-time pad (OTP) is also a quasigroup. Frank Miller first described this cryptographic system in 1882 [18], then again by Gilbert Vernal in 1917 [19] [20], where it was then patented. We know the OTP to have perfect security, as long as the pad is of the same length as the plain text, and is random, uniform and independent of the input.

Within the last decade, further research has gone into the polyalphabetic substitution properties of quasigroups. Gligoroski and Markovski (G&M) report cryptographic potentials of matrix quasigroups and suggest a stream cipher [21]. With this system the quasigroup remains secret and is pre-shared between communication partners. Priming the chain a seed is selected, and is published with the algorithm. This stream cipher takes the form $C_0 = s \cdot M_0, C_i = C_{i-1} \cdot M_i, i \geq 1$, which chaining each output byte to the previous. The strength of security is based on the order of the quasigroup selected, and the raw number of quasigroups to select from.

Then with Kocarev, Gligoroski and Markovski explore the potentials of removing the bias from poor PRNG systems by utilizing a quasigroup stream cipher to further randomize the data [22]. Here a weak random sequence generator such as libC's `random()` passed through G&M's stream cipher, with the goal of improving the data distribution of the driver. This method suffers in statistical evaluation however [23].

Satti and Kak envision a quasigroup cryptosystem for both data and speech in their paper [24]. Their research applies G&M's stream cipher to a number of practical inputs such as English text, constant values, and PCM audio data. They demonstrate success through autocorrelation techniques as well as propose systems for distribution of quasigroups and implementation in communication devices.

The authors of this paper explore the use of quasigroup block ciphers as well [25] [23]. In our research we sought to improve on the G&M stream cipher, producing a block cipher of increased strength. We compared encryption results to the Advanced Encryption Standard (AES) [26], via the National Institute of Standards and Technology's Statistical Test Suite [27] [28]. We utilized various input sources, including the text of Beowulf, the oldest known work of literature in the English language. We found that our algorithm met and in cases surpassed the statistical performance of AES.

IV. Algorithm

A. Quasigroup Block Cipher

Central to the proposed PRNG is the Quasigroup Block Cipher, which is defined as follows:

$$
\begin{aligned}
C_1 &:= K_i \cdot (K_i \oplus M_1) \\
\forall\, j &\in \{2, 3, ..., 16\}, \\
C_j &:= C_{j-1} \cdot (M_{j-1} \oplus M_j)
\end{aligned}
$$

Let C represent 128 bits cipher text (C_n a single byte in C), M 128 bits of plain text (M_n a single byte from M), K_i a key byte, $\cdot$ is the quasigroup operation and $\oplus$ is a bit-wise exclusive-or.

This algorithm is an improvement of the G&M stream cipher, which allows us to publish the quasigroup. For instance, if the quasigroup were publicly know for the G&M stream cipher, an attacker could take any C_j and C_{j-1} and compute M_j, effectively recovering the plain text by replaying the algorithm in reverse. In the improved algorithm each C_j is dependent not just on C_{j-1} and M_j but M_{j-1} as well. This prevents reverse auto-decryption, requiring the knowledge of a fully decrypted word to decrypt the following word.

Single-word keys would be very easy to brute-force attack, as most words are of order 2^8 to 2^{64}. Thus it is necessary to incorporate as many key bits as possible. Incorporation of multiple key words may be performed as follows:

$$
\begin{aligned}
&\bar{C}_{0'} := q(K_0, M), \\
&\bar{C}_0 := p(\bar{C}_{0'}, 1), \\
&\forall\, i \in \{1, 2, ..., |K| - 1\}, \\
&\quad \bar{C}_{i'} := q(K_i, C_{i-1}), \\
&\quad \bar{C}_i := \begin{cases} 0 \equiv i \mod 4, & p(\bar{C}_{i'}, 1) \\ 1 \equiv i \mod 4, & p(\bar{C}_{i'}, 3) \\ 2 \equiv i \mod 4, & p(\bar{C}_{i'}, 5) \\ 3 \equiv i \mod 4, & p(\bar{C}_{i'}, 7) \end{cases}
\end{aligned}
$$

Let K_i be a key byte from K, with $k = |K|$ denoting the number of bytes in K; $q(K_i, M)$ be the quasigroup block cipher (QGBC), $p(C, x)$ be a left bit-rotation by x bits. $\bar{C}$ represents an entire ciphertext block, and $\bar{C}_i$ is an incremental processing of $C = \bar{C}_{|K|-1}$ the final output.

Left bit-rotation is essential to the multi-word block cipher. This technique causes each bit in the output sequence C to be dependent on every bit in the input sequence M. The shift values of 1, 3, 5, and 7 were chosen based on their primeness and that they add to 16. If with $|K| = 32$ and $|M| = |C| = 16$ a full rotation is achieved (32 rotations, 8 rotations of 1, 3, 5, and 7 respectively). Later in the paper we discuss the security of the block cipher and show how the security of each C_j is improved through this rotation.

Figure 1, a S-P block diagram, depicts the one step in multi-byte key application of the block cipher. In this diagram, the S blocks represent the quasigroup $\cdot$ operation and the P block represents the bit rotation. An additional block, the $\oplus$ block, represents the exclusive-or substitution block.

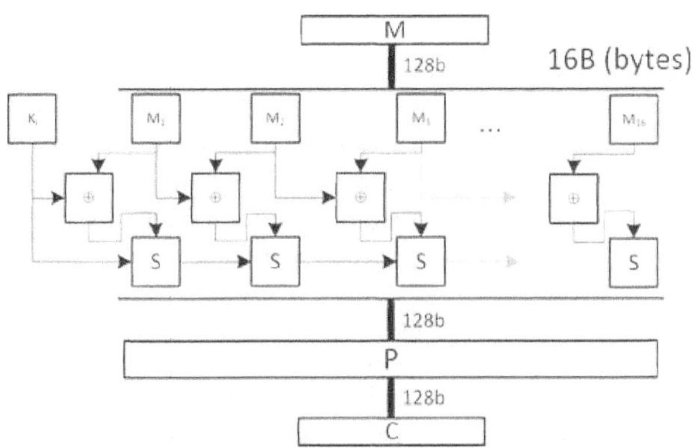

Fig. 1: Block Diagram: Multi-byte Key Quasigroup Block Cipher w/o cipher block chaining

Provided to demonstrate the QGBC graphically, fig 1 depicts how the 128 bit plain-text message block M is subdivided into 16 equal size 8-bit bytes. The diagram does not depict the looping behavior post P-block. This loop is described in the multi-byte algorithm above. Each of message byte is combined with the previous message byte ($\oplus$ *block*), and then polyalphabetically substituted (S-block) with either the previous cipher text C_{j-1} or the key K_i. Then in the P-block, the entire $C_{i'}$ sequence is rotated to become C_i, finally becoming C after the all bytes in K.

B. Feedback Generator

The quasigroup block cipher allows us to generate 128 random bits at a time. To generate more, we must construct a mechanism which is self-sustaining and statistically random. For this case, we deploy a feedback generator. The following steps occur in such a mechanism:

1) Select a random initialization vector (V)
2) Select a random Seed (i.e. K)
3) Select a plain text (M)
4) Calculate $O_1 = QGBC(V \oplus M, K)$ and report as first 128 bits
5) Calculate $\forall\ i \in \mathbb{Z}, 0 < x, O_x = QG(O_{x-1} \oplus M, K)$ and report as x^{th} 128 bits.

Here $QGBC(M, K)$ is the multi-byte quasigroup block cipher. This algorithm is depicted in figure 2. This feedback generator takes a random seed and initialization vector, and is self-sustaining from this point on.

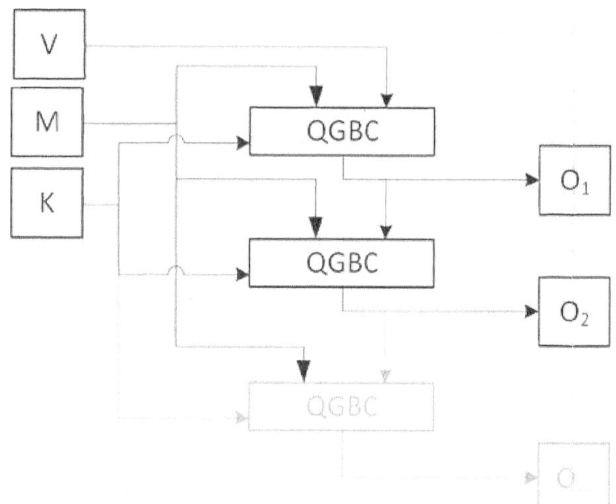

Fig. 2: Block Diagram: Feedback Generator for self sustaining PRNG

Figure 2 demonstrates the process of feeding back the previously generated random sequence O_{x-1}, while cipher-block-chaining it to the input M. To limit the amount of data required to seed our QGBC-PRNG system, we can choose $M = (K_0, K_1, ..., K_{15})$ and $V = (K_{16}, K_{17}, ..., K_{31})$. Nowadays, 256 bits of random data are simple to come by. We can use SHA-256 [6] as a source method to combine information such as the current time in seconds, and other data from the source system, like MAC addresses, memory consumption, TCP/IP address, etc. For the best hash possible, one should acquire at least 256 bits of source data.

C. Resource Optimization

Implementation of a quasigroup operation $\cdot$ can take many alternate forms. Previous implementations realize an entire nxn matrix and translate operands into column and row matrix indices to lookup the realized value. While this is very fast (a single two dimensional lookup), the method requires memory storage on the order of $O(n^2)$, calculation is $O(n)$.

However, there exists the possibility to trade memory for CPU operations. In such a case, the "$m \equiv H_a + H_b \mod n$" quasigroup series becomes very attractive. With this model two one-dimensional lookups are required, and a single operation calculating addition $\mod n$. Memory utilization is reduced from $O(n^2)$ to $O(n)$ and calculation remains $O(n)$ (the justification is given in the following section - *Processing Time*). Remember that n is the size of the finite field, which the quasigroup operates over. Practical implementations consider $n = 256$, allowing such an application to work with 8-bits as a single word. The memory required is 512 bytes compared to 65,536 bytes for a direct representation. The number possible quasigroups has been reduced from $R_n n!(n-1)!$ to $(n!)^2$, which is still a very large number $(256!)^2$.

D. Processing Time

First let us consider the cost in operations for the quasigroup block cipher. Let us consider this for a modern CPU with a random-access memory model. We will define the following costs:

c_m	Cost of memory retrieval
c_o	Cost of single byte $\cdot$ and $\oplus$
c_r	Cost of 128-bit rotation ($p(C,x)$)
$c_\oplus$	Cost of 128-bit $\oplus$

Modern processors can calculate $m = a + b \mod 256$ in a single step, for this reason we consider $\cdot$ and $\oplus$ to have equivalent cost. Thus recurrence for the quasigroup block cipher is given as:

$$T(q(K,M)) = 2|K||M|(c_m + c_o) + c_r$$

Substituting $|K| = 32, |M| = 16$ we see:

$$T(q(K,M)) = 2^{10}c_{m+o} + c_r$$

Now let us consider the feedback generator that incorporates cipher block chaining, thus the recurrence for each output block C becomes:

$$\begin{aligned} T(q(K,M)) &= 2|K||M|(c_m + c_o) + c_r + c_\oplus \\ &= 2^{10}c_{m+o} + c_{r+\oplus} \end{aligned}$$

As one may see, the time to produce each C is fixed, giving $T(C = q(K,M)) = O(c)$. Further the recurrence to produce m bits is:

$$\frac{T(C)m}{8|C|} = O(\frac{cm}{2^7}) = O(c'm) = O(m)$$

V. Evaluation

Common practice has the researcher compare the output of one PRNG to other well established PRNG systems. NIST has provided the public a suite of tests for this purpose. The Statistical Test Suite (STS)[27] evaluates variable length blocks of input data known as *m-bit blocks*, using more than eleven different standardized tests. Each test produces a result known as a *P-value*, which is the probability that the evaluated input is perfectly random. Further, the NIST team research lead to standard thresholds for each statistical test, so that a pass/fail grade could be assigned in addition to the calculated *P-value*.

The statistical test provided by the NIST-STS are:

Frequency (FREQ)
: This test focuses on the ratio of zeros to ones in the entire sequence. The test determines if the ratio is approximately equal. If this test fails, all subsequent tests will fail as well. Small P-Values (below 0.01) indicate the sequence is non random.

Block Frequency (BF)
: This test evaluates the ratio of ones and zeros in M-bit blocks. N partitions of size $\lfloor \frac{n}{m} \rfloor$ are evaluated. For blocks of $M = 1$ the results are equivalent to those of the Frequency test. Small P-Values (less than 0.01) indicate a large deviation from an equal proportion of ones and zeros in at least one of the blocks, and show the result to be non-random.

Runs
: This test determines the total number of runs in a sequence (where a run is a contiguous sequence if identical bits). The result of the test is an indication that the total number of runs in a sequence is expected for a random sequence. P-values below 0.01 indicate the sequence is non-random.

Longest Run (LR)
: The Longest Run test determines the longest run of ones with in M-bit blocks. The LR test determines if the longest run found is consistent with those found in a random string. Irregularities in the longest run of ones also indicates irregularities in the longest run of zeros. P-values less than 0.01 indicate the sequence is non-random.

Binary Matrix Rank (Rank)
: The test ranks disjoint sub-matrices within the entire sequence. Checks are performed to indicate linear dependence among fixed length substrings. The sequence is partitioned into $N = \lfloor \frac{n}{MQ} \rfloor$ blocks. Where M is the number of rows in each matrix and Q is the number of columns ($M\&Q$ are fixed to 32 in the STS). P-values less than 0.01 indicate the sequence is non-random.

Discrete Fourier Transform (FFT)
: The FFT test evaluates the peek heights of the Discrete Fourier Transform of the sequence. The test detects periodic features that would deviate from the assumed random model. Essentially, the number of peeks exceeding the 95% threshold is widely different from those at 5%. P-values less than 0.01 indicate the sequence is non-random.

Serial
: The Serial test has two variations. Both focus on the possibility of overlapping m-bit patterns within the entire sequence. As each m-bit block represents 2^m possible occurrences, the test determines the frequency of each. The test evaluates the frequency of all possible overlapping m-bit blocks, all (m-1)-bit blocks and all (m-2)-bit blocks. P-values below 0.01 indicate failure and non-randomness.

Approximate Entropy (AE)
: Like the Serial test AE focuses on the frequency of m-bit patterns across the sequence. The AE test refines the serial example by comparing the frequency of overlapping blocks of two consecutive lengths (m and $m + 1$) to the result for a random sequence. P-values less than 0.01 are considered failures, and non-random.

Cumulative Sums Forward & Reverse (CSF/CSR)
: This test determines the maximal diversion from zero of a random walk determined by the cumulative of adjusted digits in the sequence (0 becomes -1). Random sequences are expected to have a diversion near zero, thus great distances from zero indicate a heavy weighting of zeros or ones. The test is performed in both forward and reverse with regard

to the natural ordering of bits in the file. P-values less than 0.01 indicate the sequence is non random.

Each of the STS tests focuses on a different aspect of randomness through out the input sequence. Weighing any one test over the others could be a mistake, instead, some balance between the evaluations should be sought. The STS team points to the reason for this: First, they identify a Type I error (denoted as α, also known as the level of significance for a given test. The team chose P-values of 0.01 as significant for cryptographic work. Second, are Type II errors which they denote as β. β errors occur when a sequence is falsely identified as random, and there is no fixed value for this. One approach to reducing β errors is to elevate the significance of α, another is to increase the breadth of testing [28] [27].

A. Evaluation Process

Preparation for evaluation QGBC-PRNG involved selecting a set of well established PRNG systems. For comparison, we chose `arc4random` from Free BSD/MacOS X [14], Microsoft.Net's `RandomNumberGenerator` [29], OpenSSL `RAND` [12], and Java's `SecureRandom` [11]. These PRNG systems were chosen because each is well accepted by industry, including all major modern OS platforms (MacOS X, Linux, Windows, and Java). Further, `RAND` and `SecureRandom` are both implemented to conform with FIPS 180-4 [6], in which the NIST has specified the minimum requirements, for secure random number generation in US government cryptosystems. It should be noted that `RandomNumberGenerator` was operated on a system running *Windows 7*, and therefore utilized an AES based PRNG, instead of the SHA-1 system utilized in Microsoft systems prior to *Microsoft Vista* [13].

For each of the five PRNGs, we generated one-thousand (1000) sequences of random data, each containing 512 kilobytes (2^{22} bits). For each of these five-thousand files, we generated unique random seeds, so that each run would produce a unique sequence of data.

After generating the random outputs, each file was passed through the NIST-STS system. Table-I shows the configuration settings for NIST-STS, that were used. These values represent NIST-STS defaults, which we felt were adequate for our test.

Parameter	Value
Block Frequency Test - block length(m)	128
Non-overlapping Template Test - block length(m)	9
Overlapping Template Test - block length(m)	9
Approximate Entropy Test - block length(m)	10
Serial Test - block length(m)	16
Linear Complexity Test - block length(m)	500

TABLE I: Parameters for the NIST-STS test

B. Evaluation Results

We have captured the success rate of each of the five PRNG systems tested in Table II. QGBC-PRNG performs in the 99th percentile for all of the tests evaluated. Just as the STS performs statistical tests, the results should be considered statistically as well [27].

To evaluate the results we must look at the proportion of sequences passing a given test. It is suggested that the confidence interval for our test should be defined by:

$$\hat{p} \pm 3\sqrt{\frac{\hat{p}(1-\hat{p})}{m}}$$

where $\hat{p} = 1 - \alpha$ and m is the magnitude of the sample. We generated $m = 1000$ tests per PRNG system, $\alpha = 0.01$, thus the our confidence interval is $.99 \pm 3\sqrt{\frac{.\hat{9}9(.01)}{1000}} = .99 \pm 0.0094392$ or in other words the proportion should lie above 0.9805670. All of the QGBC-PRNG results scored well within the confidence interval.

	QGBC-PRNG	ARC4	OSSL	Java	MS.Net
AE	990	986	987	990	991
BF	990	993	988	993	997
CSF	985	990	985	988	989
CSR	987	993	987	986	989
FFT	993	985	983	988	987
FREQ	986	989	985	990	990
LR	995	987	995	989	994
Rank	994	988	992	992	989
Runs	986	986	995	991	990
Ser1	990	984	988	988	989
Ser2	988	984	988	985	993

TABLE II: NIST-STS Test Success Rates for 1000 Samples

The NIST-STS team does not provide guidance in interpellation of test success other than providing the definition for the confidence window of 98.0% to 100% success. Thus any system testing in this range is considered "acceptably random". Reviewing the test results showed that the commercially available PRNG systems pass the NIST-STS test suite as well, which should be expected, as these systems have been vetted through rigorous use. Therefore, it should be noted that even though the RC4 and SHA-1 based systems have been broken, they are still capable of passing the statistical tests. Additional inspection is required to demonstrate strength (see Security below). Also, cryptoanalysis of the QGBC-PRNG should be performed, but is outside the scope of this paper.

VI. Autocorrelation

Autocorrelation proves to be another successful examination of the randomness of a sequence. Like the *Cumulative Sums* test from the NIST-STS suite, autocorrelation works best when we evaluate adjusted bits (0 transforms to -1, etc.). While performing the evaluation, we may observe any adjusted sequence S. Thus autocorrelation may be defined by the following:

$$n = |S|$$

$$1 \leq i \leq n : r_i = \sum_{j=1}^{i} S_j + S_{n-j}$$

$$n+1 \leq i \leq 2n : r_i = \sum_{j=1}^{n-i} S_j + S_{j+(i-n)}$$

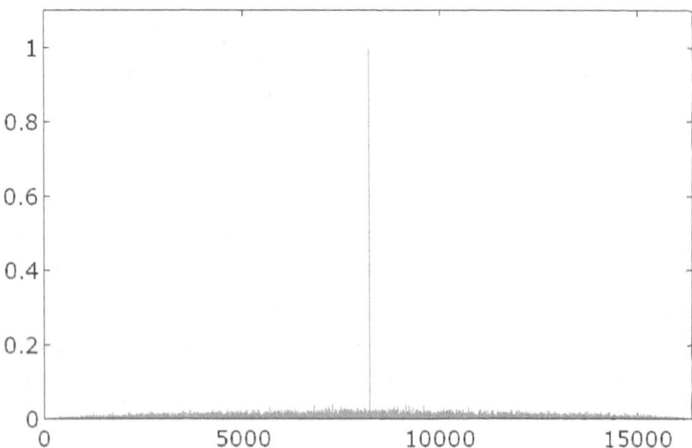

Fig. 3: Auto-correlation of QGBC-PRNG Output

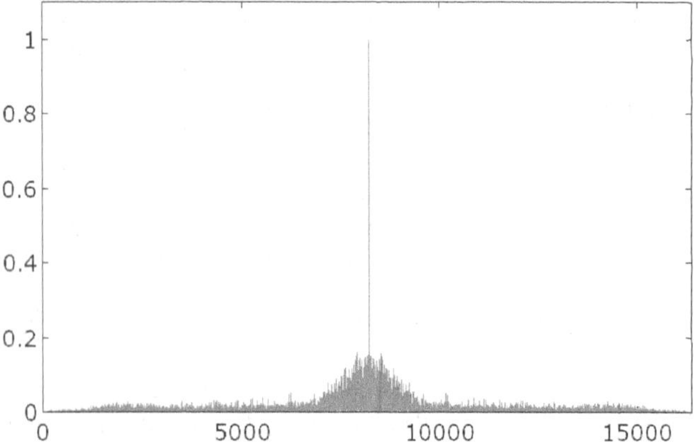

Fig. 4: Auto-correlation of Sample Audio PCM Data

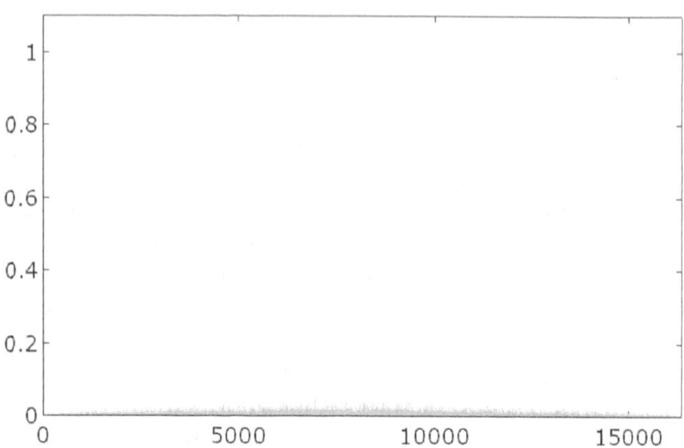

Fig. 5: Cross-Correlation of output from two different runs of QGBC-PRNG

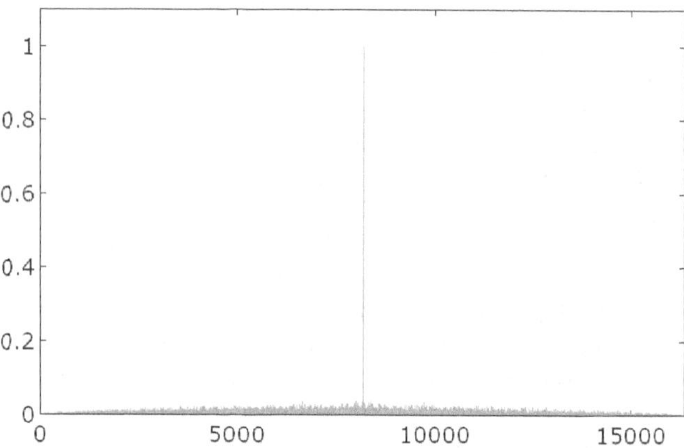

Fig. 6: Auto-correlation of Encrypted Audio

Autocorrelation procedure produces $2n$ data points. To examine randomness, we should consider the ratio between the number of data points $n = |S|$ and each correlation r_i. We examine the autocorrelation results for 2^{13} bits from QGBC-PRNG output (fig. 3), PCM data from sample audio file (fig. 4) [30], a cross correlation between two QGBC-PRNG outputs (fig. 5), and an OTP encryption of the sample audio using the QGBC-PRNG output as the pad (fig. 6).

Examination of an autocorrelation plot should show a single spike at n, where the sequence is directly correlated with itself. Peaks other than the n-spike indicate higher degrees of correlation showing repeating patterns.

Our results show that the QGBC-PRNG output (fig. 3) has a plot of a random data set, while sample audio PCM data does not (fig. 4). However, once we apply an OTP encryption to the sample audio, using the QGBC-PRNG output, we see that this sequence now matches the expected pattern for random data. This would suggest that we have inserted entropy into the audio sequence, providing for an acceptable encryption.

Finally, we should consider cross-correlation between outputs from the QGBC-PRNG with different seeding. Whenever an OTP encryption is applied, it is essential to use very different random sequences for each encryption application. This is an issue particular to OTP cryptosystems, as comparisons between runs with identical pads, will render both the pad and plain text. Figure 5 shows that the cross-correlation between two QGBC-PRNG output has very low correlation.

VII. Security of QGBC-PRNG

Let us consider 8-bit words ($n = 256$), and a 32 word (256 bit) key ($k = |K| = 32$) as input to a quasigroup block cipher. The probability of correctly selecting M_j given C_{j-1} and C_j is greater than or equal to $1 : 2^{16}$. Also, the probability of correctly selecting $M_1, M_2, ...M_j$ is given $C_1, C_2, ..., C_j$ is greater than or equal to $1 : 2^{16(j-1)}$. Further, using bit rotation (found in the QGBC cipher) and multiple K_i applications, guarantees that the probability of correctly selecting any one byte in the sequence to be $1 : 2^{16(j-1)}$. With a block size of 16 bytes, $j = 16$, thus the probability is greater $1 : 2^{240}$ for correctly selecting the sequence.

When cipher block chaining is used (as in the case of the feedback generator), the probability of correctly selecting a sequence of l blocks is greater than $1 : 2^{16(j-1)l}$, thus an output sequence of 32 bytes has a probability of $1 : 2^{480}$, a sequence of 64 bytes, $1 : 2^{960}$, and so forth. This leads us to conclude that an attacher would rather attempt to attack the input seed which has 256 bits. We can conclude that the QGBC-PRNG maximal strength is 2^{256}, making it key efficient.

VIII. Conclusion

The proposed QGBC-PRNG system is an efficient, low resource consuming algorithm, shown to be acceptably random by industry standard statistical analysis. We have shown the system to have linear processing time and consume a constant amount of memory.

Future work involves establishing the cryptanalytic results for the security of the proposed QGBC-PRNG.

References

[1] J. H. Cheon, N. Hopper, Y. Kim, and I. Osipkov, "Provably secure timed-release public key encryption," *ACM Trans. Inf. Syst. Secur.*, vol. 11, no. 2, pp. 4:1–4:44, May 2008. [Online]. Available: http://doi.acm.org.leo.lib.unomaha.edu/10.1145/1330332.1330336

[2] M. Naor and O. Reingold, "Number-theoretic constructions of efficient pseudo-random functions," *J. ACM*, vol. 51, no. 2, pp. 231–262, Mar. 2004. [Online]. Available: http://doi.acm.org.leo.lib.unomaha.edu/10.1145/972639.972643

[3] J. Lee and I. Yeom, "Avoiding collision with hidden nodes in ieee 802.11 wireless networks," *Communications Letters, IEEE*, vol. 13, no. 10, pp. 743 –745, october 2009.

[4] V. Bharghavan, "Macaw: A medium access protocol for wireless lan's," in *Proc. ACM SIGCOMM Conference (SIGCOMM '94)*, august 1994, pp. 212–225.

[5] Q. Tong, X. Zou, and H. Tong, "A rfid authentication protocol based on infinite dimension pseudo random number generator," in *Computational Sciences and Optimization, 2009. CSO 2009. International Joint Conference on*, vol. 1, april 2009, pp. 292 –294.

[6] NIST, "Secure hash standard (fips 180-4)," http://csrc.nist.gov/publications/fips/fips180-4/fips-180-4.pdf, March 2012. [Online]. Available: http://csrc.nist.gov/publications/fips/fips180-4/fips-180-4.pdf

[7] ——, "Nist brief comments on recent cryptanalytic attacks on secure hashing functions and the continued security provided by sha-1," 2004.

[8] ——, "Nist selects winner of secure hash algorithm (sha-3) competition," http://www.nist.gov/itl/csd/sha-100212.cfm, October 2012. [Online]. Available: http://www.nist.gov/itl/csd/sha-100212.cfm

[9] S. Paul and B. Preneel, "A new weakness in the rc4 keystream generator and an approach to improve the security of the cipher," *Fast Sfotware Encryption 2004 : Lecture notes in Computer Science*, pp. 245–259, 2004.

[10] S. I. Inc., "Cryptospec.html – sha1prng," http://docs.oracle.com/javase/1.4.2/docs/guide/security/CryptoSpec.html#AppA. [Online]. Available: http://docs.oracle.com/javase/1.4.2/docs/guide/security/CryptoSpec.html$\#$AppA

[11] Oracle/Sun, "Secure-random," http://docs.oracle.com/javase/6/docs/api/java/security/SecureRandom.html. [Online]. Available: http://docs.oracle.com/javase/6/docs/api/java/security/SecureRandom.html

[12] OpenSSL.org, "rand(3)," http://www.openssl.org/docs/crypto/rand.html. [Online]. Available: http://www.openssl.org/docs/crypto/rand.html

[13] I. Microsoft, "Cryptgenrandom function," http://msdn.microsoft.com/en-us/library/windows/desktop/aa379942%28v=vs.85%29.aspx. [Online]. Available: http://msdn.microsoft.com/en-us/library/windows/desktop/aa379942\%28v=vs.85\%29.aspx

[14] BSD, "Library functions manual – arc4random(3)," http://developer.apple.com/library/ios/#documentation/System/Conceptual/ManPages_iPhoneOS/man3/arc4random.3.html. [Online]. Available: http://developer.apple.com/library/ios/$\#$documentation/System/Conceptual/ManPages_iPhoneOS/man3/arc4random.3.html

[15] J. H. van Lint and R. M. Wilson, *A Course in Combinatorics*. Cambridge University Press, 1992.

[16] B. D. McKay and I. M. Wanless, "On the number of latin squares," *Annals of Combinatorics*, vol. 9, no. DOI 10.1007/s00026-005-0261-7, pp. 335–344, 2005.

[17] A. A. Bruen and M. A. Forcinito, *Cryptography, Information Theory, and Error-Correction*. John Wiley & Sons, 2011.

[18] F. Miller, *Telegraphic code to insure privacy and secrecy in the transmission of telegrams*. C.M. Cornwell, 1882.

[19] G. S. Vernam, "Secret signaling system - u.s. patent 1,310,719," US Patent, Sept 1919.

[20] ——, "Cipher printing telegraph systems for secret wire and radio telegraphic communications," *Journal of the IEEE*, vol. 55, pp. 109–115, 1926.

[21] D. Gligoroski and S. Markovski, "Cryptographic potentials of quasigroup transformations."

[22] S. Markovski, D. Gligoroski, and L. Kocarev, "Unbiased random sequences from quasigroup string transformations," *Fast Software Encryption: 12th International Workshop*, pp. 163–180, 2005.

[23] M. Battey and A. Parakh, "An efficient quasigroup block cipher," *Wireless Personal Communications*, pp. 1–14, 2012. [Online]. Available: http://dx.doi.org/10.1007/s11277-012-0959-x

[24] M. Satti and S. Kak, "Multilevel indexed quasigroup encryption for data and speech," *IEEE Transactions on Broadcasting*, pp. 270–281, 2009.

[25] M. Battey and A. Parakh, "Efficient quasigroup block cipher for sensors networks," *Proceedings of 21st International Conference on Computer Communication Networks (ICCCN 2012)*, 2012.

[26] NIST, "Fips-197 announcing the advanced encryption standard (aes)," 2001.

[27] A. Rukhin and et. al., "Sp800-22: A statistical test suite for random and pseudorandom number generators for cryptographic applications," NIST, Tech. Rep., 2010.

[28] J. Soto, "Statistical testing of random number generators," NIST, Tech. Rep., 1999.

[29] Microsoft, "Random-number-generator," http://msdn.microsoft.com/en-us/library/system.security.cryptography.randomnumbergenerator.aspx. [Online]. Available: http://msdn.microsoft.com/en-us/library/system.security.cryptography.randomnumbergenerator.aspx

[30] unknown, "Waveform audio format - 11,025 hz 16 bit pcm audio file," http://www.nch.com.au/acm/11k16bitpcm.wav. [Online]. Available: http://www.nch.com.au/acm/11k16bitpcm.wav

A Systems Engineering Approach for Assured Cyber Systems

Major Logan O. Mailloux, Dr. Brent T. Langhals, and Dr. Michael R. Grimaila
Air Force Institute of Technology, Wright-Patterson Air Force Base, Ohio, United States

Systems Engineering (SE) has gained favor as a means to tame the complexity of modern systems, specifically the design, analysis, and development of complex systems. This paper describes a SE approach for system assurance of modern Information Technology (IT) centric "cyber systems". In this paper, we discuss recent trends in information security towards the establishment of security patterns and identify key security patterns for the development of cyber systems. Specifically, this paper provides a cursory review of security patterns and highlights the utilization of key cyber patterns during the SE development process for a given cyber system. SE functional decomposition and system integration activities are described as they pertain to meeting formal system assurance claims resulting in secure and assured cyber systems.

Keywords—Systems Engineering; Security Patterns; Cyber Assurance

I. INTRODUCTION

Systems Engineering (SE) has gained favor as a means to tame the complexity of modern systems, specifically the design, analysis, and development of complex systems. The authors propose a SE approach for system assurance of modern Information Technology (IT) centric "cyber systems" that addresses cyber system complexity and security through established information security practices and fundamental SE processes. Specifically, this paper provides a cursory review of security patterns and highlights the utilization of key cyber patterns during the SE development process for a given cyber system. SE functional decomposition and system integration activities are further described as means to provide formal system assurance justification for cyber systems.

Section II describes the cyber security problem as it pertains to system complexity, while Section III provides a background of essential SE processes and principles used to tame system complexity. Section IV describes findings related to key security patterns, applicability within SE development processes, and justification of system assurance claims.

II. PROBLEM STATEMENT

The problem of IT security is so pervasive that "cyber security" has turned into a multi-billion dollar industry over the past decade. Recent public announcements from the highest levels in the U.S. government are quite telling on the subject. On February 12, 2013 President Obama issued an Executive Order which cited improving critical infrastructure cyber security as one of the most serious national security challenges the country faces [1]. Furthermore, while facing the most ominous Department of Defense (DoD) budget cuts since the cold-war, U.S. Cyber Command announced a colossal expansion plan from 900 to 4,900 personnel [2]. Perhaps even more telling, the private security firm Mandaint® released a comprehensive report *APT1* which details an extensive cyber espionage campaign conducted by the Chinese military against U.S. private firms [3].

Current cyber security approaches are failing in almost every area of interest from common operating system vulnerabilities to meticulously planned attacks against security software vendors. The cyber security problem is especially difficult because IT systems have deeply rooted design flaws, software bugs, weak assumptions, configuration issues, and various other deficiencies which result in vulnerabilities and weaknesses. The challenge is further intensified since these deficiencies can be introduced anytime in the system lifecycle from initial design and development to system fielding, configuration, and day-to-day operation. Modern cyber systems also fail because of unknown software issues, unexpected hardware failures, and unrealized operational and support system dependencies.

Principally, the cyber security problem is due to rising complexity—"the measure of how difficult a *system* is to understand, and thus to analyze, test, and maintain" [4]. Today's cyber systems are so complex that effectively designing and developing secure systems is exceedingly difficult bordering on nearly impossible. The beloved security engineer's Orange Book i.e., the DoD's 1985 Trusted Computing Evaluation Criteria correctly states the dilemma precisely: "the [cyber system] must be of sufficiently simple organization and complexity to be subjected to analysis and tests, the completeness of which can be assured" [5]. The elusive problem of providing secure and assured cyber systems is a significant cause of concern in the U.S. as a whole, and the DoD in particular.

III. BACKGROUND

This section provides a baseline of SE processes and principles to facilitate shared understanding of complex systems. The Defense Acquisition Guidebook (DAG) definition of systems engineering is provided for inspection:

> Systems Engineering. An interdisciplinary approach and process encompassing the entire technical effort to evolve, verify and sustain an integrated and total life cycle balanced set of system, people, and process solutions that satisfy customer needs [6].

The DAG definition identifies a three part interdisciplinary approach which addresses the entire solution space across systems, people, and processes. The holistic SE approach is particularly important when considering the cyber security

This work was supported by a research grant from the Air Force Research Laboratory (F4FBFV1297J001).

problem in operational environments where users and administrators are responsible for the operation, configuration, and maintenance of critical cyber systems. History has shown that people and processes are much more vulnerable than specific technologies. Consider for example, the devastating results of the Stuxnet worm against the Iranian Nuclear facility, Natanz. The facility was arguably one of the most protected facilities in the world, yet a single well planned cyber attack was able to cause untold damage through processes and personnel vulnerabilities [7].

The challenge for systems engineers is not only to support the entire technical effort to evolve, verify, and sustain systems but to completely understand the complex system under development. The International Council on Systems Engineering (INCOSE) handbook elaborates this concept:

> The SE process has an iterative nature that supports learning and continuous improvement. As the processes unfold, systems engineers uncover the real requirements and the emergent properties of the system. Complexity can lead to unexpected and unpredictable behavior of systems; hence, one of the objectives is to minimize undesirable consequences [8].

Systems engineers are therefore responsible to discover and facilitate shared understanding regardless of system complexity. To this end, the SE developmental process, commonly known as the V-model, is captured in Fig. 1 [9].[1] Note: The SE V-model will be referred to as the SE development process throughout this paper to more accurately capture its intended purpose.

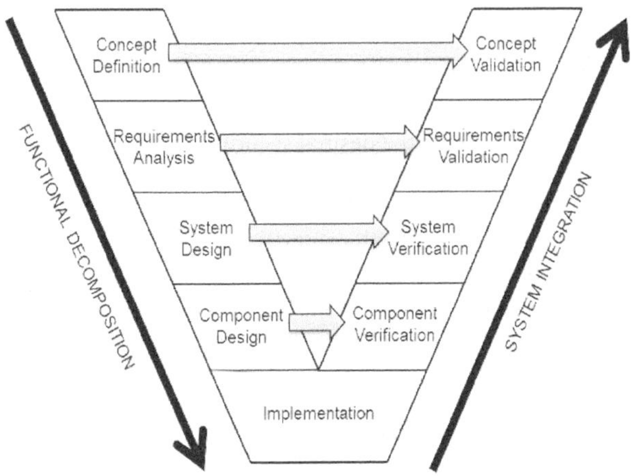

Fig. 1: The Systems Engineering Development Process

The goal of the SE development process is to make complex systems more readily understandable for users, developers and decision makers. The process demonstrates SE functional decomposition activities down the left side, system implementation at the bottom, and system integration activities up the right side. Although the process shows a linear progression, there are numerous iterations both vertically and horizontally within and across the various SE activities.

Functional decomposition is an essential SE tool to define, analyze, and understand complex systems. Functional decomposition products based on core mission requirements can provide great benefit for system users, developers, and decision makers. However, functional decomposition is also a challenging task; one that is often misunderstood, underutilized, and readily dismissed. As a general guideline, functional decompositions should be accomplished at the level of detail necessary for a given project, while addressing:

- Functional Requirements
- Inputs, Outputs, and Controls
- System Boundaries
- System Interfaces
- System Dependencies

Basic functional decompositions can be accomplished quickly using informal block diagrams or common work breakdown structures, while detailed decompositions can be accomplished through formal system architectures. Those associated with system development in the DoD should be familiar with the DoD Architecture Framework (DoDAF) which provides a detailed set of products for this specific task. Although the DoDAF can be somewhat cumbersome, it can yield great benefits when properly and proportionally utilized.

System implementation corresponds to the realization of the system under development by many specialized domain engineers. Components are built to specification in order to meet design criteria and higher level requirements. Implementation is typically accomplished over long periods of time across multiple assembly initiatives, which result in components ready for individual verification. Supply chain integrity is a critical part of the implementation, and a current focus item for DoD acquisition efforts.

System integration activities provide Verification and Validation (V&V) of specific components, system design, and system requirements against their respective functional decomposition activities. The overall purpose of V&V is to provide confidence to the user that the developed system will meet user requirements. Verification activities demonstrate that the implemented components, subsystems, and systems function as specified, while validation activities confirm the system operates as intended by the user.

SE V&V activities consist of assessment, test, and evaluation efforts which span the entire system development process in a continuous fashion. For example, requirements validation starts early on in concept definition, continues down into verification of individual components in the form of derived requirements, and ends with the validation of a fully integrated system against the original user system definition. Lastly, as with much of the SE development process, V&V activities are scalable from brief efforts to meticulously detailed efforts which can take months or years in some cases.

1. Although other common development models and processes exist, such as evolutionary acquisition and spiral development, the SE V-model was chosen because of its general acceptance in the SE community and clear linkages between decomposition and integration activities. Furthermore, distinct verification and validation activities readily lend themselves to the formalized 'justified confidence' requirements of system assurance claims as described in Section IV, parts C and D.

IV. RESEARCH

This section details the SE development process in conjunction with key security patterns to provide a baseline for secure and assured cyber systems.

A. Assessment of Security Patterns

For the software engineering community, design patterns are widely accepted to communicate object-oriented concepts and architectural structures. Because of their demonstrated benefits, other communities, such as the IT security community have attempted to develop equally effective security patterns. The seminal text for security patterns is "Security Patterns—Integrating security and systems engineering" by Schumacher et al. [10], while other publications of note are "Secure Design Patterns" by the Carnegie-Mellon Software Engineering Institute [11], a survey of security patterns by Yoshioka et al. [12], the online security pattern repository [13], and the open group security pattern technical guide [14]. Additionally, the First International Workshop on Cyberpatterns was hosted in 2012, which focused on attack-oriented security patterns [15]. Formally, a security pattern is defined as:

> Security Pattern. A security pattern describes a particular reoccurring security problem that arises in specific contexts, and presents a well-proven generic solution [10].

A strict interpretation of security patterns yields a growing, yet limited, set of results. However, given the broad nature of a pattern's stated purpose i.e., a well-proven generic solution to a reoccurring problem, there are many such security patterns available for review. Less formal security patterns exist in many formats captured as policy, standards, best practices, guides, processes, instruction manuals, checklists and many more, which ultimately result in a very large body of knowledge with significant depth.

From the practitioners' point of view, the key problem then becomes knowing when and where to apply the appropriate patterns. Therefore, the proposed SE approach for secure and assured systems highlights the utilization of key cyber patterns during specific points in the system development process. The key security patterns are introduced in Section B and fully described in Sections C and D.

B. Key Cyber Patterns for Cyber System Development

Key cyber security patterns were derived from the reviewed literature and categorized into the formalized SE developmental process as shown in Fig. 1. Because of overall similarity, concept definition and requirements analysis will be addressed together. System design will be addressed singularly, which supports the use of conventional IT enterprise architectures used in the design and operation of many IT centric systems. Component design and implementation activities will likewise be addressed together due to similarity of purpose.

1) Concept Definition and Requirements Analysis: Security patterns supporting system concept definition and requirements analysis are mostly related to high-level policy and risk management. These activities should not be discounted as they form the backbone of all cyber system security decisions. There are a number of critial issues at this level of system development which security patterns can aid. Key security patterns for consideration:

- Risk Management – conduct threat and vulnerability assessments, predict likeliness factors, calculate expected loss, prioritize results, plan/implement mitigation actions, and re-evaluate expected loss. Risk management is perhaps the single greatest concern for a cyber system under development.
- Asset Identification and Assessment – determine critical information and technologies, mission threads, core business processes, intellectual property, essential knowledge, personnel, and other crucial resources. This security pattern may be considered part of risk management proper; however, because of its importance we have specifically identified the security pattern as a uniquely important task. It also serves to prioritize security and assurance measures during the entire development process.
- Formalize Security Requirements – define and document the extent to which cyber security attributes are desired and/or required. Consider confidentiality, integrity, and availability, along with other security attributes specific to the system under development.

2) System Design: Security patterns supporting system design have grown out of enterprise level security, software, and network architectures used extensively by software and IT professionals for design and operation. While the practioners' architectures are focused more on building and operating cyber systems, the systems engineer's design architecture is focused more on understanding the system under development as discussed in Section III. Key security design patterns for consideration:

- Determine Appropriate Security Approach – select a scheme to achieve the desired security state i.e., approaches for deterrence, prevention, detection, and recovery. These decisions will heavily influence the system design and specific components.
- Security-Oriented Functional Decomposition – conduct decomposition using established security principles i.e., separation of duties, least privilege, and defense-in-depth.
- Separate Security Functionality – separate security functionality from other system functionality.

3) Component Design and Implementation: This grouping of security patterns is by far the largest, with many software and application specific security patterns available for consideration. These technology specific security patterns are generally applicable to very specific problems, although there are a number of very helpful objective-based security patterns such as "The Twenty Critical Security Controls" [16] and "Raising the Bar for Cybersecurity" [17]. Because of the abundance of security patterns available at this level, three types of security patterns are considered:

• Design Pattern Extensions for Security – security oriented extensions of longstanding object oriented software design patterns. These patterns provide great utility and ease of use for cyber system software implementers.

• Objective-Based – robust solutions to the broader cyber security problem. Generally, cover multiple security attributes and referred to as best practices.

• Application Specific – focused on the configuration and operation of cyber systems or security devices. Examples include firewalls, audit/logging, input validation, white listing, secure web applications, and many others.

Next, Section C briefly describes system assurance with respect to the SE development process, before entering a detailed discussion of the confluence of key cyber security patterns, the SE development process, and their contribution towards system assurance in Section D.

C. Systems Engineering Approach for System Assurance

Given the complex nature of modern cyber implementations and the current threat environment, system assurance is sometimes considered an unobtainable goal. Despite this bleak view, the National Defense Industrial Association (NDIA) recently published a comprehensive text for system assurance titled *Engineering for System Assurance*, which makes progress towards solidifying the practice. The definition of system assurance is provided for inspection:

> System Assurance. The justified confidence that the system functions as intended and is free of exploitable vulnerabilities, either intentionally or unintentionally designed or inserted as part of the system at any time during the life cycle [18].

Notably, NDIA describes 'justified confidence' with formal assurance claims including: context, assumptions, justification, evidence, and criteria which are used to formally answer the desired level of assurance for critical functional requirements.

The SE development process provides the flexibility to account for assurance claim context and assumptions early on while addressing justification, evidence, and criteria during system integration. SE functional decomposition and system integration activities can be used at each point in the development process to provide justified confidence through a formal and defined process. Each SE activity from concept definition to validation is scalable, which provides selectively robust support for critical system functions and their assurance claims. Specifically, SE system integration activities readily lend themselves to meeting assurance claims through defined V&V activities.

D. Detailed SE Process Activities for System Assurance

This section addresses each SE functional decomposition and system integration activities as they contribute towards cyber system assurance. A description of the relationship between the SE activity, key cyber security patterns, and formalized assurance claims i.e., context, assumptions, justification, evidence, and criteria is described. Because of inherent dependencies concept definition and requirements analysis will be addressed together.

1) Concept Definition & Requirements Analysis

As the starting point in the SE development process, concept definition and requirements analysis form the basis of all future decomposition and integration activities. Modern cyber systems face many common requirements problems, however, these problems are compounded by the additional challenges associated with cyber system complexity and security requirements. Further, all future assurance claim justification efforts will be accomplished against these formalized requirements.

The assurance claim is intended to define system assurance requirements, which take the form of confidence levels during concept definition and requirements analysis. With respect to assurance of cyber systems, concept definition and requirements analysis activities should result in both formalized security requirements and desired levels of assurance for functional requirements.

In cyber system development risk management is a critically important, yet a rather challenging task due to system complexity. For the cyber system developer, there is an overwhelming amount of information dedicated to IT risk management as it is a completely unique field of study. Fortunately, much of the conceptual material is similar in nature. Of note, the National Institute of Standards and Technology (NIST) produced an IT security framework which is rather verbose, but clearly articulated and detailed. NIST Special Publication 800-30 is an excellent place for the cyber systems engineer to start learning this vital security pattern [19]. A general rule of thumb is the level of security should be commensurate with an item's value as described in the asset identification and assessment security pattern.

Cyber system risk management must consider many difficult software issues, significant operational and support dependencies, and a hostile cyber threat environment that can change in a moment's notice. Because of the unbounded nature of risk management assessment and mitigation, the systems engineer should ensure baseline level of risk management is conducted, while providing additional detailed analysis where necessary to meet the user's needs. SE concept definition and requirements analysis activities coupled with risk management aid in the development of secure and assured cyber systems by appropriately addressing critical functions for cyber systems.

There are many very effective security patterns available for performing asset identification and assessment, especially as they pertain to risk. There is an expected overlap with risk management as asset identification and assessment are often cited as the first and second steps in the risk management process. However, in the cyber community asset identification and assessment is typically focused on physical asset inventory and does not adequately address the entire range of mission critical functions, information, and assets. This common shortfall supports why we have chosen to included this task as a uniquely important security pattern for cyber systems.

Within the DoD, Critical Program Information (CPI) has been a mainstay in program protection planning for identifying information and technology assets [20]. Criticality Analysis, and to a lesser extent Critical Mission Threads, are also methods widely employed in the DoD [6]. The purpose of these activities is simply to gain an accurate understanding of the resources—systems, people, processes—a system utilizes and prioritize their significance towards mission accomplishment. These prioritized critical functions and resources should then serve as the focus of system security and assurance efforts throughout the SE developmental process.

Formalized security requirements have recently been recognized as a necessary functional requirement for cyber system and not merely a support requirement. The distinction is significant and puts more attention on securing and assuring a system rather than falling into a security checklist mentality. The goal of the formalized security requirements is to consider and define what security attributes should be for critical functions in a cyber system under development. System assurance levels should be considered at this point in like manner. The direct link between formalized security requirements and desired assurance levels is a natural fit.

Security requirements are usually described in the context of the industry established security attributes: Confidentiality, Integrity, and Availability. For each core function of a cyber system, cyber security attributes should be enumerated. Typically, enumeration is done categorically in the form of "high, medium, low" or "extreme, urgent, high, medium, low" in a comparative fashion. The scale is subject to user preference and specific application. Two simple examples follow: 1. A command and control system may have an "urgent" data integrity requirement along with "high" availability and confidentiality requirements; and 2. An intelligence signal processing cyber system may have "extreme" confidentiality and integrity requirements, along with "medium" availability requirements.

Security professions often extend these core attributes with various other information security principles. For example, the core security attributes will often be extended with Identification, Authentication, and Non-Repudiation for secure communication functions. Furthermore, formalized security requirements specify the desired security principles and assurance levels for a system under development, which are also used during validation activities. Early SE functional decomposition activities are very helpful when paired with formalized security requirements to address the whole cyber system—systems, people and processes—security problem.

2) System Design

Once system requirements are established, design is the next step in providing an effective system. System design is where SE faces the challenge of realizing system-wide requirements in a functional design. In order to accomplish this task, systems engineers must first have a detailed operational and technical understanding of the subject domain(s). Second, systems engineers must study system functionality, inputs, outputs, controls, boundaries, interfaces, and dependencies. Additionally, there are many known and unknown complexity issues that may surface during system design activities. These issues will need to be addressed as they arise to assure the functionality of the system.

In general, SE should analyze and document system complexity through functional decomposition activities which typically result in a set of architectural products called views. These architectural views or products are scalable to a desired level of specificity, from conceptual block diagrams to detailed design architectures for the most complex systems. SE design activities fall right in line with providing assured systems through justifiable decision making to "build-in" smarter and more effective security solutions right from the start at less cost. System design decisions also need to be considered in a cost-benefit manner, with a clear understanding of the programmatic nature of large developmental efforts.

Appropriate security approaches should be selected to meet the overall security requirements. Often there is a mutually supportive overlap between security approaches as discussed in the security pattern literature. The security objective(s) will drive the security approach resulting in a mix of deterrence, prevention, detection, and response solutions. These approaches are tempered by the cost-benefit nature of risk management. Clearly articulating and applying security approaches for critical system functions directly supports assurance claims, contributing to a more stable system.

Recent trends are moving towards more cost-effective approaches of detection and response. It is often much simpler and quicker to rebuild a compromised system than attempt to prevent future compromises, which can be seen as impossible. There has also been a significant movement towards resilient and agile systems, which can self-recover from failures. System design is the optimal time to consider which approaches will be implemented for a given cyber system to meet the defined security and assurance requirements.

Separation of duties, least privilege, and defense-in-depth constitute the core of modern information security principles and should be considered throughout functional decomposition and specifically system design activities. As with selecting appropriate security approaches, applying core security principles builds towards a stable cyber system. In principle, this security pattern requires only a slight modification to existing SE functional decomposition practices. Considering key security principles during the design phase of a system is perhaps more of a basic practice and less of a documented security pattern, however, its importance cannot be overstated to solving the assured cyber system problem.

Separate security functionality should be considered and designed in whenever possible. This security pattern is often viewed expressly for software development efforts to separate security checks from object creation, however, this security pattern should be more broadly applied. For example, each security test or check should be considered separately from any system functional requirement. Separating security functionality has the benefit of clearly identifying security checks and reducing implementation complexity. Separate security checks should be enforced throughout system design and implementation wherever feasible given the appropriate risk management and cost-benefit considerations.

3) Component Design & Implementation

Although it is not the aim of this paper to discuss security patterns as they pertain to component design and implementation, there are a couple of interesting comments which should be made. First, because of the wide popularity of object oriented design patterns a rash of security-oriented extensions quickly arose. These design pattern extensions for security are very helpful for software engineers attempting to "build-in" security and should be applied wherever possible.

Second, there is essentially no limit to existing and potential application-specific security patterns, because they are tightly coupled to technological solutions for specific problems i.e., filtering on a firewall. There are literally thousands of application-specific security patterns available for review across many cyber security related problem sets. These security patterns should be investigated for a given application as many excellent ideas exist for securing cyber devices.

Third, because of the numerous application-specific patterns at the component level, consolidated security patterns have appeared. We've termed these objective-based security patterns which attempt to answer the broader cyber system security problem. Popular examples of objective-based security patterns are the SANS Top Twenty critical controls and the Australian DoD's top 4 mitigation strategies.

4) Component and System Verification

As system integration begins, there is a natural fit between component and system verification activities and system assurance goals. Verification activities can range from documentation reviews to detailed line by-line code reviews spanning days, weeks, or months. Formally, verification is described as "the purpose of the Verification Process is to confirm that the specified design requirements are fulfilled by the system" [21]. The prioritization of the cyber system verification activities should be driven by function criticality as described during functional decomposition activities. Fig. 2 shows the key cyber security patterns mapped to the SE development process for concept/requirements validation, system design verification, and component design/implementation verification.

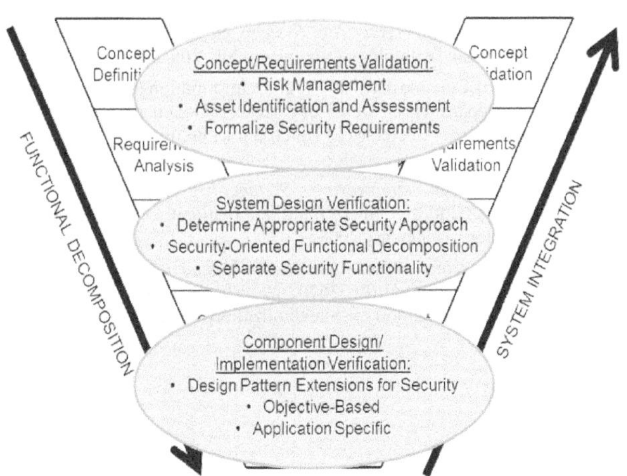

Fig. 2: Key Cyber Security Patterns

Revisiting the definition of verification, the systems engineer's goal is to "confirm that the specified design requirements are fulfilled" and should use whatever tools necessary to accomplish the task. A simple list of verification techniques includes: basic function testing, result comparisons, input/output sensitivity, parameter checking, structural code review, detailed code walkthrough, review of math/logic proofs, and detailed end-to-end input/output traces. This list is by no means exhaustive and meant merely as a starting point. Due to specific nature of verification activities and desired level of justification evidence, it is difficult to recommend specific verification activities for a given cyber system implementation. The author recommends reviewing cyber system verification activities and processes found in ISO/IEC 15288 [21], ISO/IEC 26702 [22], the DAG [6], and the INCOSE SE handbook [8].

As a pertinent aside, security measurement and evaluation of cyber systems is a highly debated subject. The effectiveness of current evaluation criteria and resulting formal measurement i.e., security audits are being called into question. It seems that despite significant effort put towards the development of thorough IT security criteria, they have not provided a sufficiently suitable solution to the cyber system assurance problem. This is evidenced by the weekly announcements of cyber security breaches, vulnerabilities, and the non-stop release of critical patches by major software developers.

5) Requirements and Concept Validation

During validation activities the entire technical effort described as systems, people, and processes should be evaluated to determine if it can meet the specified users' requirements. Formally, validation is described as: "the purpose of the Validation Process is to provide objective evidence that the services provided by a system when in use comply with stakeholders' requirements, achieving its intended use in its intended operational environment" [21]. The output of the validation activities should be a determination to what extent the systems meet's the desired capability.

SE validation activities tie closely to system assurance case evaluation methodology as described by NDIA's Engineering for Systems Assurance: "the purpose of an assurance case is to provide convincing justification to stakeholders that critical system assurance requirements are met in the system's expected environment(s)" [18]. SE validation activities significantly contribute to demonstrable proof that a particular system meets its documented purpose(s). There are some very helpful security patterns to assist in system validation as shown in Fig. 2 as previously discussed.

Some additional issues for consideration are system re-purposing and unexpected operational environments. System evaluation is typically only considered for the planned operational environment, despite a high likelihood of other possible implementations. Without a broader consideration, systems become immediately vulnerable when re-purposed or deployed in less than ideal environments. The system engineer must also consider that the system itself is always changing due to regular patching cycles, scheduled upgrades, operator rotations, and process improvement initiatives.

A basic list of SE validation activities consists of addressing: Key Performance Parameters (KPPs), initial assumptions, requirements traceability, concept review and requirements assessment (i.e., a document review addressing the stated purpose, requirements, and key functions), external validity (i.e., black box testing), and internal validity (i.e., white box testing). This list is by no means exhaustive and meant merely as a starting point for validation activities. It is difficult to recommend specific validation activities for a given cyber system implementation and the author recommends reviewing cyber system validation activities and processes found in ISO/IEC 15288 [21], ISO/IEC 26702 [22], the DAG [6], and INCOSE SE handbook [8].

Once the system is fully integrated, SE validation activities can justifiably determine if the system can meet the desired levels of assurance. The SE development process, particularly system integration, culminates in validation activities which are designed to provide objective evidence that user requirements are being meet. These same results can be leveraged to provide justified confidence in the desired system functionality for system assurance claims.

V. CONCLUSION

This paper presented a description of key cyber security patterns categorized to the SE development process. This paper further examined SE decomposition and integration activities, detailing their contribution to achieving cyber system security and assurance. SE V&V activities were examined and determined to provide sufficient justification to meet formal systems assurance claims. Specifically, verification can be used to directly support the justification, evidence, and criteria associated with formal assurance claims, while validation defines and supports the context, assumptions, justification, and criteria associated with these claims for cyber systems. In conclusion, this paper builds upon cyber security patterns and established SE process to provide assured cyber systems.

ACKNOWLEDGMENTS

Thank you to Mr. Rick Dove, INCOSE system security engineering working group chair, who provided helpful guidance towards the study of security patterns.

This work was supported by a research grant from the Air Force Research Laboratory (F4FBFV1297J001).

REFERENCES

[1] President Barack Obama. *Improving Critical Infrastructure Cybersecurity.* Executive Order, Office of the Press Secretary. 12 February 2013.

[2] Nakashima, Ellen. "Pentagon to boost cybersecurity force," The Washington Post, 27 January 2013. [Online]. Accessed: 23 February 2013. Available: http://www.washingtonpost.com/world/national-security/pentagon-to-boost-cybersecurity-force/2013/01/19/d87d9dc2-5fec-11e2-b05a-605528f6b712_story.html.

[3] *APT1 - Exposing One of China's Cyber Espionage Units,* Mandiant® [Online]. Accessed: 23 February 2013. Available: http://intelreport.mandiant.com/Mandiant_APT1_Report.pdf

[4] Definition of complexity is adapted from Information Technology—Security Techniques—Evaluation Criteria for IT Security, Part 1: Introduction and General Model, Third Edition. ISO/IEC 15408-1:2009(E). Switzerland: International Organization for Standardization, 15 December 2009.

[5] *Trusted Computer System Evaluation Criteria.* DoD 5200.28-STD. Washington: Department of Defense, 26 December 1985.

[6] Defense Acquisition University. *Defense Acquisition Guidebook, Chapter 4, Systems Engineering.* [Online]. Accessed: 11 October 2012. Available: https://acc.dau.mil/CommunityBrowser.aspx?id=490091.

[7] Langner's Stuxnet Deep Dive S4 Video. [Online]. Accessed: 3 March 2013. Available: http://www.digitalbond.com/blog/2012/01/31/langners-stuxnet-deep-dive-s4-video/.

[8] INCOSE System Engineering Handbook v. 3.2.2. INCOSE-TP-2003-002-03.2.2. San Diego, CA: International Council on Systems Engineering (INCOSE), October 2011.

[9] See [8]. Adapted from Forsberg, K., H. Mooz, H. Cotterman, Visualizing Project Management, 3rd Ed., J.Wiley & Sons, 2005.

[10] Schumacher, Markus., Eduardo Fernandez-Buglioni, Duane Hybertson, Frank Buschmann, and Peter Sommerlad. *Security Patterns: Integrating Security and Systems Engineering.* West Sussex, England: John Wiley & Sons, Ltd. 2006.

[11] Secure Design Patterns, Software Engineering Institute, Chad Dougherty et al., CMU/SEI-2009-TR-010, updated oct 2009.

[12] Yoshioka, Nobukazu., Hironori Washizaki, and Katsuhisa Maruyama. "A Survey On Security Patterns," *Progress in Informatics, National* Institute of Informatics, no .5, pp.35-47, 2008.

[13] *Security Patterns Repository Version 1.0.* [Online]. Accessed 22 January 2013. Available: http://www.securitypatterns.org/.

[14] Blakley, B. and Heath, C. et al.. Security Design Patterns. Technical Guide, G031. The Open Group, April 2004.

[15] Proceedings of Cyberpatterns 2012. Abingdon, UK. 9-10 July 2012.

[16] *Critical Controls for Effective Cyber Defense, Version 4.0.* SANS Institute InfoSec Reading Room. [Online]. Accessed 22 February 2013. Available: http://www.sans.org/critical-security-controls/cag4.pdf.

[17] Lewis, James A. "Raising the Bar for Cybersecurity." Center for Strategic & International Studies: Technology & Public Policy. 12 February 2013.

[18] National Defense Industrial Association (NDIA) Assurance Committee. 2008. *Engineering for Systems Assurance.* Arlington, VA: NDIA.

[19] National Institute of Standards and Technology. *Risk Management Guide for Information Technology Systems.* SP 800-30. Gaithersburg, MD: Information Technology Laboratory, July 2002.

[20] Department of Defense. Critical Program Information (CPI) Protection Within the Department of Defense, Change 1. DoD Instruction 5200.39. Washington: Under Secretary of Defense for Intelligence, 28 December 2012.

[21] *Systems and software engineering – System life cycle processes.* ISO/IEC 15288:2008(E). Switzerland: International Organization for Standardization, 31 January 2008.

[22] *Systems engineering – Application and management of the systems engineering process.* ISO/IEC 26702:2007(E). Switzerland: International Organization for Standardization, 15 July 2007.

SESSION

SECURITY APPLICATIONS

Chair(s)

Prof. Kathy Liszka
Dr. Milica Barjaktarovic

A Self-Protecting Security Framework for CDA Documents

G. Hsieh[1] and E.Nwafor[1]

[1]Department of Computer Science, Norfolk State University, Norfolk, Virginia, USA
[ghsieh@nsu.edu, e.c.nwafor@spartans.nsu.edu]

Abstract – *Clinical Document Architecture (CDA) is a standard for the exchange of electronic medical records. This paper describes a self-protecting security framework for protecting the security and privacy of CDA documents. The framework extends a CDA document with markups from XML based security standards including eXtensible Access Control Markup Language, XML Encryption, and XML Signature. This integrated structure uses a CDA document as the container while access control policies, digital signatures, and encrypted data are all embedded within the same CDA document in a fine-grained manner. The paper also describes an initial prototype implementation of this self-protecting security framework for CDA documents.*

Keywords: *e-Health, information security, HL7 CDA, XACML, XML Encryption, XML Signature.*

1 Introduction

Clinical Document Architecture (CDA) is a document markup standard that specifies the structure and semantics of a clinical document [1], [2]. It is a Health Level 7 (HL7) [3] standard approved by American National Standards Institute (ANSI).

A CDA document can include text, images, sound and other multimedia. CDA is based on XML. A Continuity of Care Document (CCD) [4], on the other hand, is a constrained form of CDA. The CCD is an implementation guide for sharing Continuity of Care Record (CCR) [5] patient data using the CDA. It contains a patient's health/healthcare summary such as administrative, clinical, and demographic information.

The CDA/CCD standards are designed to increase portability between systems because these documents can be used to exchange medical information in a platform-independent manner. In addition, these documents can exist as self-contained information objects for storing health/healthcare information.

To comply with national standards for protecting the privacy and security of individuals' electronic personal health information, such as those established by the Health Insurance Portability and Accountability Act (HIPAA) in the U.S., the CDA/CCD documents must be protected to ensure the confidentiality, integrity, and security of electronic protected health information [6]. Providing a user-friendly cost-effective security framework for the CCD/CDA document is very challenging because of the security and privacy requirements imposed by these regulations and business considerations. It is further complicated due to the need for sharing information among potential participants while maintaining confidentiality, integrity, authentication and access control.

In 2011, we proposed the idea for a self-protecting security framework for safeguarding CDA/CCD documents [7]. The concept of self-protecting security was derived from the security requirements and recommendations outlined in the ASTM E2369 - 05e1 Standard Specification for CCR [8].

The fundamental concept underlying this framework approach is the use of a variety of open standards that are commonly used for web services security [9], e.g., eXensible Access Control Markup Language (XACML) [10], XML Encryption (XML-ENC) [11], XML Signature (XML-DSIG) [12], and XML Key Management Specification (XKMS) [13], to specify or represent access control policies, results of encryption, digital signatures, and key management information, respectively.

These standards are extended and used in an integrated manner such that the access control policies, encrypted data, digital signatures, and key management information can all be embedded within a CDA document. In addition, these security mechanisms for confidentiality, authentication, authorization, and integrity control can be applied in a fine-grained manner, i.e., different parts of a CDA document can be protected with different access control policies, cryptographic algorithms or keys.

Overall, this framework approach is designed to provide self-protecting security for the CDA documents throughout their lifecycles and no matter where they reside: in transit or at rest, within or across organizational boundaries.

In this paper, we present our research results achieved since the publication of [7], with an emphasis on the detailed design and development of our first-iteration prototype software system for the proposed self-protecting security framework for CDA documents.

The remainder of the paper is organized as follows. In Section 2 we provide a brief overview of the self-protecting security framework for CDA documents. In Section 3 we describe the design and implementation of our first-iteration prototype software system for the security framework. We conclude the paper with a summary and discussion on future work in Section 4.

2 CDA Security Framework

The CDA self-protecting security framework is designed to help meet the ASTM security requirements and recommendations. It is adapted from a previously developed framework that was designed to be general purpose for protecting digital information of any type [14]-[17].

2.1 CDA Document Structure

The structure of CDA documents is very suitable for the embedded and fine-grained approach. A CDA document is wrapped by the <ClinicalDocument> element which can be used as the root element of the container for the security framework.

Many types of CDA elements can be candidates for fine-grained embedding and security protection. For example, if the <ClinicalDocument> element is chosen as the target for applying the embedding and security mechanisms, then the entire CDA document is protected. On the other hand, if multiple sections are chosen as targets for applying such mechanisms, then these sections are protected with possibly different policies and/or cryptographic algorithms/keys.

Furthermore, the fine-grained approach is facilitated (and also necessitated) by the concept of CDA context which defines the applicable scope of the assertions in the document. CDA context is set in the CDA header and applies to the entire document, and it can be overridden at the level of the body, section, and/or CDA entry.

For example, the <confidentialityCode> element is a contextual component of CDA, and can be used to express the confidentiality rules (*normal*, *restricted access*, or *very restricted access*) for the part of the document covered by the scope of this element. Multiple <confidentialityCode> elements can be used in the same CDA document to express different levels of confidentiality restrictions for different parts of the document.

2.2 Embedding XACML Policy

XACML [10] is an open standard established by the Organization for the Advancement of Structured Information Standards (OASIS). It specifies both an access control policy language and a request/response language. The policy language can be used to construct expressions that make up an access control policy that describes who can do what and when.

XACML can be used for controlling access to any type of resources, not just XML documents. It supports an architectural model of separating the policy decision logic from the policy enforcement logic. Three key logical functions are defined by XACML. A *Policy Decision Point* (PDP) is an entity that evaluates applicable policy and renders an authorization decision. A *Policy Enforcement Point* (PEP) is an entity that performs access control by making decision requests to a PDP and enforcing the authorization decisions returned by the PDP. The third XACML logical function, *Policy Administration Point* (PAP), is an entity that creates and manages access control policies.

The base construct of all XACML policies is a <Policy> which represents a single access control policy, expressed through a set of <Rule>'s. Each XACML policy document contains exactly one Policy root XML tag. A policy can have any number of Rules which contain the core logic of an XACML policy. The decision logic of most rules is expressed in a <Condition>, which is a Boolean function. If the condition evaluates to true, then the Rule's *Effect* (Permit or Deny) is returned. Otherwise, the Condition does not apply. XACML also provides another feature called *Target* which is basically a set of simplified conditions that must be met for a Policy or Rule to apply to a given request.

To support embedding, the standard XACML policy and response languages are extended to allow a <ResourceContent> element, which is already defined for the standard XACML request language, within a <Resource> element. The original content to be protected by this XACML policy is first encoded into the base64 format and the result is then encapsulated within the <ResourceContent> element.

2.3 Applying XML-ENC and XML-DSIG

The XML Encryption Syntax and Processing standard [11], established by the World Wide Web Consortium (W3C), specifies a process for encrypting data and representing the result in XML. If the data is an XML element or XML element content, the result of encrypting data is an <EncryptedData> element, containing the ciphertext, which replaces the element or element content (respectively) in the encrypted version of the XML document.

The XML Signature Syntax and Processing standard [12], also established by the W3C, specifies XML syntax and processing rules for creating and representing digital signatures. XML signatures can be applied to any digital content, including XML. An XML digital signature is represented by a <Signature> element. The enveloped mode of XML-DSIG is especially suitable for our embedded approach as the generated <Signature> element is inserted into the document (or element) for which the digital signature is applicable.

The XML-ENC and XML-DSIG mechanisms can be used together to encrypt and sign the CDA/XACML document in support of the embedded and fine-grained approach.

3 Framework Prototype Development

For feasibility study and experimentation purposes, we developed a prototype software system for the CDA self-protecting security framework.

This prototype software system is developed by leveraging the software base and development tools previously developed and used for the general-purpose framework prototype software system [14]-[17].

3.1 Code Base & Development Environment

For XACML related processing functions, we leveraged the source code from Oracle Sun' XACML Java Library, version 1.2 [18]. For XML Security related processing functions, we leveraged the source code from the Apache XML Security Java Library, version 1.4.3 [19]. Both packages are available through open source licenses.

We also use open source development tools, such as Apache Xerces-J, Xalan-J, Eclipse Java IDE as well as Apache Commons Library for Base64 encoding and decoding of the data objects.

The base code for the first-iteration prototype software system for the CDA security framework is derived from the code used for [15].

3.2 Prototype System Architecture

The major components of the prototype system are the extended PAP and PDP which can handle not only XACML, but also XML encryption/decryption and XML signature creation/verification. In the prototype implementation, the PEP and PDP are combined into one system making user request files directly accessible to the PDP System.

Figure 1 shows the architecture of the first-iteration prototype software system for the self-protecting security framework for CDA documents.

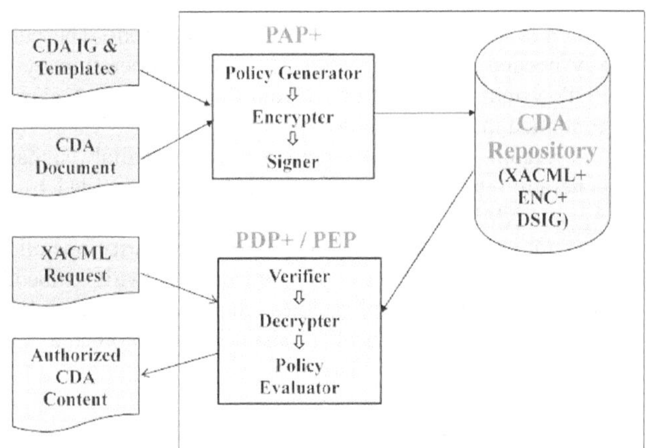

Figure 1. Prototype System Architecture.

To simplify the complexity for the PAP and PDP, we implemented only a fixed sequence of actions with respect to XML encryption and signature. Also, to simplify key management operations, we used a local Java KeyStore to store and retrieve cryptographic keys.

3.3 Prototype PAP

The PAP system accepts a CDA document as one input. A second input for the PAP is a user-defined CDA implementation guide or template that contains the specifications on how access control policies are to be generated based on the combination of confidentiality code, roles, and actions permitted. The output of the PAP system is an extended CDA document with embedded access control policies, digital signatures, and encrypted data (hiding the plaintext).

As shown in Figure 1, there are three major functional steps for the prototype PAP system:

1) The Policy Generator generates appropriate XACML policies and embeds them in the CDA document.
2) The Encrypter performs XML encryption operations and embeds the encrypted data in the CDA document replacing the plaintext.
3) The Signer performs XML digital signature generation operations and embeds the generated digital signature in the CDA document.

Figure 2 shows the user interface for the PAP system through which a user can choose to perform the following operations:

1) View a CDA document.
2) Generate embedded XACML policies.
3) Encrypt and digitally sign the CDA document with embedded XACML policies.
4) Select an implementation guide containing the desired security policy specifications.

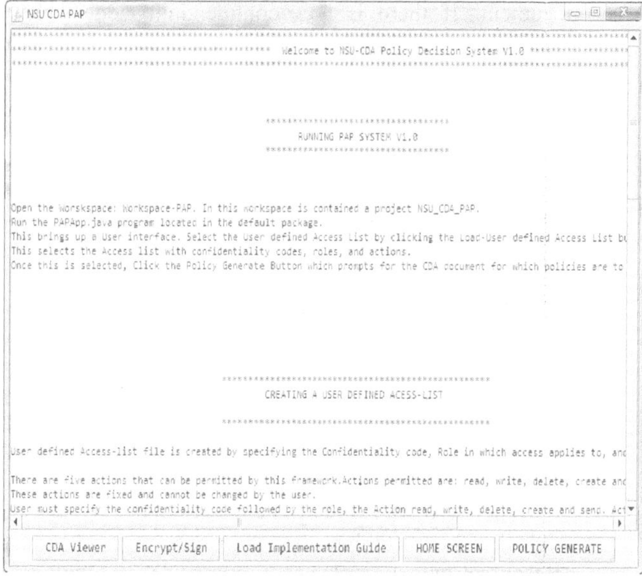

Figure 2. User GUI for Prototype PAP System.

3.3.1 XACML Policy Generation

As noted in [15], automatic generation of XACML policy is very challenging, and this view was concurred by [20]. Since the XACML policy language is designed to be general, it is extremely complex to design an automated XACML generator that can handle any types of policy requirements.

To constrain the complexity, we have designed the structure and syntax for an implementation guide to be used for specifying user-defined security policy requirements.

The implementation guide is a text file containing information on what actions (e.g., read, write, modify) are permitted for which roles (e.g., patient, physician, staff, family) for different levels of confidentiality code (e.g., high, medium, low, or none). An implementation guide can be created and modified by a user using any text editor.

Supplied with such an implementation guide as one input, the XACML Policy Generator can generate the appropriate XACML policy statements based on the (potentially multiple) <confidentialityCode> elements that are already contained within the CDA document (which is the second input for the policy generator), and the security policy specified in the implementation guide.

The first step is to automatically generate an XACML document with embedded, fine-grained access control policy statements and the content to be protected. This Policy is generated for each `<section>` contained in the CDA document based on the confidentiality code contained in the scope of the respective section. If a confidentiality code element is not specified for the section element, no policy is generated for that `<section>`. The policy generator leverages the code base provided by Sun's XACML Java Library.

To provide fine-grained access control, the XACML Policy Generator searches through the input CDA document for all <confidentialityCode> elements in the input CDA document. If there is no <confidentialityCode> element found in the input CDA document, the process stops as it is assumed that no security protection is required for the input CDA document.

A <Policy> statement is generated for each <section> contained in the input CDA document based on the confidentiality code applicable in scope to the respective <section>. If a confidentiality code element is not specified for the <section> element, no <Policy> is generated for that <section>.

On the other hand, if a <confidentialityCode> element is applicable in scope for the <section> element in the input CDA document, the XACML Policy Generator first generates a <Policy> element containing the appropriate XACML access control policy statements for the level of security specified by the applicable <confidentialityCode> element.

The XACML Policy Generator next embeds the original content within the <section> element into the <ResourceContent> element encapsulated within the <Policy> element. This <Policy> element is then used to replace the <section> element whose content has already been embedded into the <ResourceContent> element.

The XACML Policy Generator leverages the code base provided by Oracle Sun's XACML Java Library.

3.3.2 XML-ENC and XML-DSIG Operations

Our first-iteration prototype implementation does not provide the capabilities for users to specify how encryption and digital signatures are to be applied to the CDA document to meet their specific needs.

Instead, the current implementation uses a fixed approach to either encrypt the entire CDA document or all <ResourseContent> elements using the same encryption key(s).

To do so, the PAP performs the following steps using the encryption capabilities provided by the Apache XML Security Java Library.

1) Generate a symmetric key (using the AES algorithm) which will be used to encrypt the selected element content.
2) Generate a key, called key-encryption-key, to encrypt this symmetric key (using the triple-DES algorithm).
3) Encrypt the selected element content with the symmetric key to create the <EncryptedData> element which results in the element content being replaced by the <EncryptedData> element. The <EncryptedData> element also contains a <KeyName> element that contains a reference (alias) to the key-encryption-key.

The PAP then stores the value for the key-encryption-key under the alias name specified in the <KeyName> element into the local Java KeyStore.

The current implementation also takes a fixed approach for digital signature operations. The PAP only generates a single digital signature using the enveloped mode for the entire CDA document (with XACML access control policies and encrypted data already embedded). The generated <Signature> element is next embedded at the end of the content for the CDA document, i.e., right before the closing </ClinicalDocument> tag.

To do so, the PAP calls the EnvelopeSignature. getEnveloped() method. This generates a public key contained in the <KeyInfo> element and also a <KeyName> which is inserted into the <Signature> element. The public key needed for the signature verification operation by the PDP system can be retrieved from the <KeyValue> element contained in the <Signature>.

Again, the PAP performs the digital signature generation function using the capabilities provided by the Apache XML Security Java Library.

Once the PAP completes all these security operations, it stores the extended CDA document (with embedded XACML access control policies, encrypted data, and digital signatures) into a local repository for protected CDA documents.

3.4 Prototype PDP/PEP

The prototype PDP/PEP system accepts an XACML request as an input. Based on the request context, the PDP/PEP retrieves the applicable CDA document from the local repository for protected CDA documents.

The PDP/PEP system next performs three major steps as shown in Figure 1.

1) Verify the digital signature embedded in the retrieved CDA document.
2) Decrypt the ciphertext contained in the retrieved CDA document.
3) Perform the XACML policy evaluation function and return the authorized CDA content.

The output of the PDP/PEP system in response to the request context is the portions of the CDA content, if any, that are authorized for the request context. The authorized CDA content can be all, a subset, or none of the CDA document.

To simplify the implementation and operation, the prototype PDP/PEP system allows the user to directly specify the XACML request message. This is passed directly to the SimplePDP.java program which is the main program for the PDP/PEP system.

Figure 3 shows the user interface through which a user can choose to perform the following functions:

1) View a CDA document.
2) Verify the signature and decrypt the ciphertext(s) embedded in a CDA document.
3) Evaluate the embedded XACML policy.
4) Load a file containing an XACML request context.

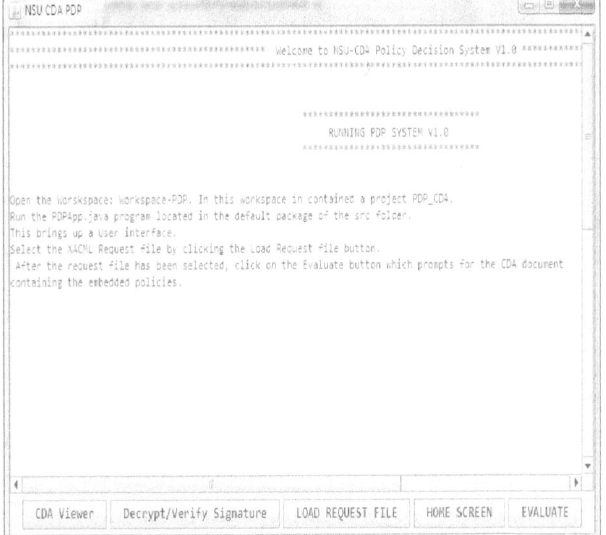

Figure 3. User GUI for Prototype PDP/PEP System.

Again, after receiving a valid XACML request message and successfully retrieving a valid protected CDA document, the PDP/PEP system first performs the digital signature verification operation using the <Signature> element embedded in the CDA document against the entire CDA document.

To do so, the PDP uses the signature verification function provided by the Apache XML Security Java Library by invoking the constructor in the Decryptandverify.java class. It also uses the public key value which is retrieved from the <KeyValue> element contained within the <Signature> element in the same CDA document to verify the signature of the CDA document. If the signature verification operation fails, then a deny decision (invalid signature) is returned to the requester. If the signature operation is successful, the signature element is removed from the runtime copy of the <ClinicalDocument> element.

The prototype PDP/PEP system next performs the XML decryption function to decrypt either the entire CDA document or each <ResourceContent> element for each XACML policy contained in the CDA document.

To do so, the PDP uses the decryption function provided by the Apache XML Security Java Library. It also uses the key name enclosed in the <KeyName> element within the <EncryptedData> element in the XACML policy as the alias to retrieve the necessary decryption key from the local Java KeyStore. If the decryption operation fails, then a deny decision (decryption failure) is returned to the requester.

Once the protected CDA document has been successfully signature-verified and decrypted, the PDP performs the XACML policy evaluation function to produce a response context.

For each XACML <Policy> contained in the <ClinicalDocument> element, a response is generated by the PDP system. Response generation is achieved by the SimplePDP.java class contained in the PDP package by evaluating the policy against the request context.

This response is used to determine if the protected content is authorized for the request context. If a <Response> contains a permit decision, then the <ResourceContent> element which contains the data content for which the access control policy protects, is decoded from its base-64 format and the result is used to replace the encompassing <Policy> element in the CDA document. After all the <Policy> elements have been evaluated and responses processed, the resulting CDA document represents the portions of the original CDA document, if any, that are authorized for the input request context. The resulting CDA document can be viewed through the user GUI for the prototype PDP/PEP system. It is also stored in a local repository.

Figure 4 displays a sample response CDA document produced by the prototype PDP/PEP system. The sample CDA document shows that two sections in the original CDA document are authorized for the request context, while a third section is denied access by its embedded XACML policy against the input request context.

```
<ClinicalDocument>
 <!-- CDA Header -->
<component>
 <StructuredBody>

    <component>
      <section>
        <text>"Text1"
        </text>
      </section>
     </component>

     <component>
       <section>
         <text>"Text2"
         </text>
        </section>
      <component>

      <component>
         <Response>
```

```
        <Result>
          <Decision>
             Deny
          </Decision>
          <Status>
            <StatusCode/>
          </Status>
        </Result>
      </Response>
    <component>

  </StructuredBody>
 <component>
 </ClinicalDocument>
```

Figure 4. A Sample Response CDA Document.

4 Summary and Future Work

In this paper, we present an overview of a framework for integrated secure embedded and fine-grained access control of CDA documents. It is designed to help meet the stringent security and privacy requirements for protecting CDA documents: end-to-end integrity and confidentiality, authentication and authorization (access control), and self-protecting security with security policy and information embedded within the same CDA document.

This framework leverages XML-based security standards such as XACML, XML Encryption, XML Signature, and XKMS. Thus, it benefits from the rich expressiveness, flexibility, extensibility, and general-purpose applicability of all these open standards. In addition, this framework supports fine-grained security protection which is necessary for protecting CDA documents such that sensitive information in certain parts of the documents can be accessed only by properly authenticated and authorized entities.

In addition, we provide a more detailed discussion on the design and implementation of the first-iteration prototype software system for the self-protecting security framework for CDA documents.

The prototype software system was developed by leveraging the open source Apache XML Security Java 1.4.3 Library, and Oracle Sun's XACML Java 1.2 Library. Through careful planning, design, and implementation efforts, we are able to integrate these packages together and provide the additional capabilities for embedding and fine-grained control.

Going forward, we plan to continue enhancing the capabilities, robustness, and effectiveness of the CDA self-protecting security framework, and the prototype implementation. We also plan to continue enhancing the integration and interoperation with CDA infrastructures such as software, tools, implementation guides and templates.

Furthermore, we plan to facilitate the development and deployment of such a framework, especially in cloud computing or healthcare exchange environments by exploring the advanced cryptographic and key management schemes, such as attribute-based encryption and secret key sharing schemes, that can be leveraged to enhance the flexibility, scalability, efficiency, and ease of use of the framework.

5 Acknowledgement

G. Hsieh's research was supported in part by U.S. Army Research Office, under contract no. W911NF-12-1-0081, and U.S. Department of Energy, under grant no. DE-FG52-09NA29516/A000.

6 References

[1] R. H. Dolin, L. Alschuler, C. Beebe, P. V. Boyer, D. Essin, E. Kimber, et al. "The HL7 Clinical Document Architecture, Release 2," in *J. Am Med Inform Assoc.*, vol. 13(1), Jan.-Feb. 2006, pp. 30–39.

[2] R. H. Dolin, L. Alschuler, C. Beebe, P. V. Boyer, D. Essin, E. Kimber, et al. "The HL7 Clinical Document Architecture," in *J. Am Med Inform Assoc.*, vol. 8(6), Nov.-Dec. 2001, pp. 552–569.

[3] Health Level Seven International. http://www.hl7.org. [Cited: May 21, 2013.]

[4] Product CCD – HL7Wiki. [Cited: May 21, 2013.] http://wiki.hl7.org/index.php?title=Continuity_of_Care_Document_(CCD).

[5] ASTM International. http://www.astm.org/index.shtml. [Cited: May 21, 2013.]

[6] HIPPA Security Rule. [Cited: May 21, 2013.] http://www.hhs.gov/ocr/privacy/hipaa/administrative/securityrule/index.html.

[7] G. Hsieh. "Towards Self-Protecting Security for e-Health CDA Documents," in *Proc. 2011 Int'l Conf. on Security and Management (SAM'11)*, Las Vegas, NV, 2011, pp. 637-643.

[8] ASTM E2369 – 05e1 Standard Specification for Continuity of Care Record (CCR). [Cited: May 21, 2013.] http://www.astm.org/Standards/E2369.htm.

[9] E. Bertino, L. D. Martino, F. Paci, and A. C. Squicciarini. Security for Web Services and Service-Oriented Architectures. Springer-Verlag, 2010.

[10] eXtensible Access Control Markup Language (XACML) Version 2.0. OASIS Standard Specification. 1 Feb 2006. [Cited: May 21, 2013.] http://docs.oasis-open.org/xacml/2.0/access_control-xacml-2.0-core-spec-os.pdf.

[11] XML Encryption Syntax and Processing. W3C Recommendation. 10 Dec 2002. [Cited: May 21, 2013.] http://www.w3.org/TR/xmlenc-core/.

[12] XML Signature Syntax and Processing (Second Edition). W3C Recommendation. 10 June 2008. http://www.w3.org/TR/xmldsig-core/. [Cited: May 21, 2013.]

[13] XML Key Management Specification (XKMS 2.0). Version 2.0. W3C Recommendation. 28 June 2005. http://www.w3.org/TR/xkms2/. [Cited: May 21, 2013.

[14] G. Hsieh, and M. Masiane. "Towards an Integrated Embedded Fine-Grained Information Protection Framework," in *Proc. 2011 Intl. Conf. on Information Science and Applications*, Korea, 2011.

[15] G. Hsieh, R. Meeks, and L. Marvel. "Supporting Secure Embedded Access Control Policy with XACML+XML Security," in *Proc. 5th Int. Conf. on Future Information Technology*, Korea, 2010, pp.1-6.

[16] G. Hsieh, K. Foster, G. Emamali, G. Patrick, and L. Marvel. "Using XACML for Embedded and Fine-Grained Access Control Policy," in *Proc. 4th Int. Conf. on Availability, Reliability and Security*, Japan, 2009, pp. 462-468.

[17] G. Hsieh, G. Patrick, K. Foster, G. Emamali, and L. Marvel. "Integrated mandatory access control for digital data," in *Proc. SPIE 2008 Defense + Security Conf.*, Florida, 2008, vol. 6973, pp. 697302-1 to 697302-10.

[18] Sun's XACML Implementation. [Cited: May 21, 2013.] http://sunxacml.sourceforge.net/.

[19] Apache Santuario – Apache XML Security for Java. http://santuario.apache.org/javaindex.html. [Cited: May 21, 2013.]

[20] B. Lang, N. Zhao, K. Ge, and K. Chen, "An XACML Policy Generating Method Based on Policy View," Proc. 3rd Intl. Conf. on Pervasive Computing and Applications (ICPCA 08), Oct. 2008, pp. 295-301.

Multi-Applications Secure Mobile Platform

Hao Zhao Sead Muftic
School of Information and Communication Technologies (ICT)
Royal Institute of Technology (KTH)
Stockholm, Sweden

Abstract

This paper describes the concept of Multi-Applications Secure Mobile Platform based on Javacard chip and applets stored in it. Javacard chip is used as pluggable secure module providing subscribers additional mobile services in mobile phones. Special security features of Javacard chip make multi-applications secure mobile platform a secure runtime environment for Javacard applets implementing various security functions. Various Javacard applets run simultaneously on the platform supporting various mobile security services. Multi-applications secure mobile platform is implemented by following our optimized design approach. It fully supports the functions of various mobile services with increased efficiency and optimal use of a Javacard chip space.

Keyworlds: *mobile services, Javacard multi-application secure platform, optimized design approach, Javacard applets*

1. Background and Introduction to the Research

Mobile phones are mainly used for making calls and transmitting messages since the first day they were invented. But situation has been changed. Mobile phones are more and more used as computation devices. Nowadays people spend more and more time with mobile devices not for making calls or transmitting messages, but for using functions offered by hundreds thousands of applications that are available online. Applications running in mobile devices, regardless whether Internet browser, E-books reader, game or an online air ticket booking toolkit, are all specially designed and implemented for users to receive services that are also specially customized for mobile platforms. Such services are called mobile services.

Mobile services are presented to subscribers through applications installed in mobile devices. These devices satisfy requirements for runtime environment for most applications and mobile services. But some mobile applications handle sensitive data and functions, such as payments, where financial data are used, healthcare, where private personal information is used, etc. For such applications the runtime environment that mobile phones provide is not secure enough. Currently the most popular smart phone platforms are Android derived from Google and iOS developed by Apple [1]. These two platforms have good native security mechanisms, but that is not enough. For example, Jailbreak of these systems can open some convenient functions for users, however it shuts down lots of system native security functions [2].

Javacard chips provide more secure runtime environment that is very hard to compromise. By using Javacard chips to store secrets and execute sensitive functions, mobile services using sensitive data and functions can be better supported.

In our research, mobile phone pluggable Javacard chip, for example micro SD card is used to provide secure runtime environment for applications (applets). A complete infrastructure to load, manage and use Javacard applets on a Javacard is established. It is structured in the form of a layered infrastructure that can be used by various mobile services providers to distribute and manage their applications (applets). This paper describes our approach of using applications in a multi-application platform represented by a Javacard chip to support mobile services.

2. Related Work

Jaemin Park, Kyoungtae Kim and Minjeong Kim from Terminal Application Development Team [3] performed research to implement security engine called Aegis in UICC SIM card [4]. The engine provides security functions to other applications in the same card. In their research, UICC SIM card is using Javacard chip. The work follows the concept of USSM proposed by ETSI [5]. Aegis is a Javacard applet in UICC SIM card providing security functions such as cryptography and certificates management. Other UICC applications call Aegis to perform security operations like encrypting/decrypting data, invoking certificates, generating and verifying signatures, etc.

The research team notices and emphasizes the multi-application platform of UICC chip. They investigate and practice the use of Javacard security functions and multi-application platform.

Compared with their work, our research investigates much broader set of characteristics of Javacard multi-application platform. We consider similar security applications in our research and various other applications are also designed and implemented. These applications are specially designed for mobile services addressed in our research. They invoke functions from each other so that they are combined together to perform more complicated functions to support external mobile services.

Our research proposes a flexible and open architecture. Therefore, open Javacard chip is used instead of the UICC SIM card that is strictly controlled by wireless network operators. Our work reflects more of the concepts of multi-application platform.

3. Methodology of the Research

Our research is based on existing standards and technologies. Smart card technology is used in our research and development for implementation. Knowledge of smart card is based on ISO/IEC7816 standards [6]. Furthermore, GlobalPlatform specifications [7] are followed with details about use of multi-application platform. Javacard technologies specifications of JCRE specifications [8], JCVM specifications [9], and Javacard APIs [10] specify the approach of developing Javacard applets and implementing multi-application platform from an implementation perspective.

Other standards specify provision of mobile services and functions. These standards are the guidelines that we follow when developing our Javacard applets. These standards include FIPS 201 PIV standard [11] and EMV standard [12]. Our own previous research results were also used for design Javacard applets. For example, our published paper *"The Concept of Secure Mobile Wallet"* [13] is used for design Wallet applet.

4. Mobile Services and Javacard Applets

In our research we address several mobile services for subscribers. These services are:

- *m-Identification*: m-ID provides reliable identity verification service to subscribers. Through m-ID service, subscribers can use their mobile phones to reliably identify themselves to other entities.
- *m-Payment*: m-Payment service allows subscribers to pay with their mobile phones. Payment methods include electronic cash and bankcards.
- *m-POS*: m-POS service is used by merchants. With m-POS service, merchants can use their mobile phones as POS devices to accept bankcard payments. Payment methods include electronic cash and bankcards.
- *m-Commerce*: m-Commerce services are commercial services for subscribers through mobile phones. These services include functions like mobile advertisements, coupons, discounts, gift cards, etc..

In this paper we describe software running in mobile phones for subscribers to use mobile services. Examples of GUIs for some of those mobile applications are shown in Figure 1 and Figure 2. Applications exchange messages with background servers and perform specific functions.

In our research, applications installed in Javacard chip are used to store secret data and perform mobile service functions. Other sensitive functions using secret data like cryptography are also implemented by these applications. Mobile phones require necessary data and invoke sensitive functions from Javacard chip. This approach prevents serious security concerns caused by loss of secrecy. The Javacard chip is used as mobile phone pluggable module. Mobile phones provide communication functions and display GUIs and results.

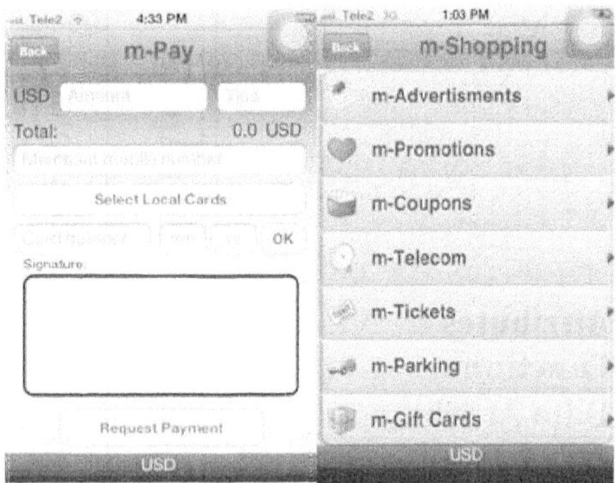

Fig. 1: m-Wallet Panel **Fig. 2:** m-Commerce Menu

The applications installed on Javacard chip are Javacard applets. We designed and implemented various Javacard applets to support our addressed mobile services.

5. Problems with Current Applets Design

Currently the standard approach of design a Javacard applet is to design a specific applet for a specific service. For example PIV applet follows FIPS 201 PIV standard [11] and EMV applet follows EMV [12] standard. According to the standards various data attributes and functions should be included in these applets. Table I shows part of data attributes of the applets and part of their functions.

Each applet contains all necessary attributes and functions. By this approach, our applets should be designed as what Table I shows. From Table I it can be noticed that some data attributes and functions are implemented multiple times in different applets. This duplication would not cause any problems with a single applet Javacard chip. However, if all of these applets were installed on one Javacard chip, the duplication would waste the space that is quite limited on a Javacard and slows down the efficiency. In addition, management of such applets is very complicated and they may even end up with inconsistent values. Once the value of an attribute is modified, all the copies of the attributes should be updated. Otherwise attributes inconsistent problem happens. This increases the difficulty of management of the applets.

In our research we plan to use one Javacard chip to run multiple applets supporting different mobile services. Therefore this design approach is not acceptable. Alternatively, we propose optimized approach to design and implement Javacard applets.

Table I: Data Attributes and Functions of Existing Applets

Attributes & Functions \ Applets	PIV Applet	EMV Wallet Applet	EMV POS Applet
Data Attributes			
First Name	✓	✓	
Last Name	✓	✓	
CHUID	✓		
Terminal ID			✓
Bank IBAN		✓	✓
Bank Account NO.		✓	✓
Authentication Certificate	✓	✓	✓
Private Key	✓	✓	✓
Functions			
fingerPrintVerification	✓		
cardHoderInformation	✓	✓	
readCertificate	✓	✓	✓
RSAPrivateKeyDecrypt	✓	✓	✓

6. The Concept of Optimized Multi-Applications Secure Mobile Platform

Multi-applications secure mobile platform is a concept of using and managing multiple Javacard applets in one Javacard chip to present mobile services to subscribers.

Javacard allows multiple applets to reside and run on one Javacard chip. These applets can provide functions to external entities simultaneously. This is implemented by the concept of logical channel [14]. Logical channel is the logical refection of the Javacard unique physical I/O channel. Javacard platform supports various logical channels and each logical channel is assigned to one applet. Each time only the selected logical channel occupies the physical channel. However, by switching logical channel different applet can be invoked alternatively. By this approach the applets work simultaneously from logical view.

Javacard multi-application platform supports another approach of using various applets. One Javacard applet can invoke functions from other applets on the same chip. On a Javacard platform, for security reasons, there is a firewall between two applets [14]. It prevents one applet to access data and functions of other applets. However, with a mechanism called Sharable Interface Objects [10], one applet can cross the firewall to invoke data and functions from other applets. SIO allows one applet to open parts of its functions to other applets without breaking the security mechanisms. Interfaces that are defined and authorized determine what data and functions are public. With SIO one single applet can invoke functions from other applets to perform more complicated functions than it can provide separately.

With such features we implemented multiple applets on one Javacard platform. We can use multiple applets' functions either through sending commands in sequence to different applets or through invoking one delegate applet. Either approach allows us to distribute data attributes and functions into separate, distinguish applet. Based on this idea we propose the approach of optimizing the design of our applets. With our design, every attribute and function is implemented only once, in one of our applets. The attributes and functions are distributed to different applets according to the nature of functions they support. For example, all functions and attributes related to security, like certificates and certificates verification, are implemented in a Security applet.

With optimized design approach, instead of one applet providing all data and functions, several applets are invoked together to support a mobile service. This approach avoids problems caused by duplication discussed earlier. We call this model optimized Multi-Applications Secure Mobile Platform. Figure 3 and Figure 4 show how the applets support mobile services under the standard design approach and using our multi-applications secure mobile platform.

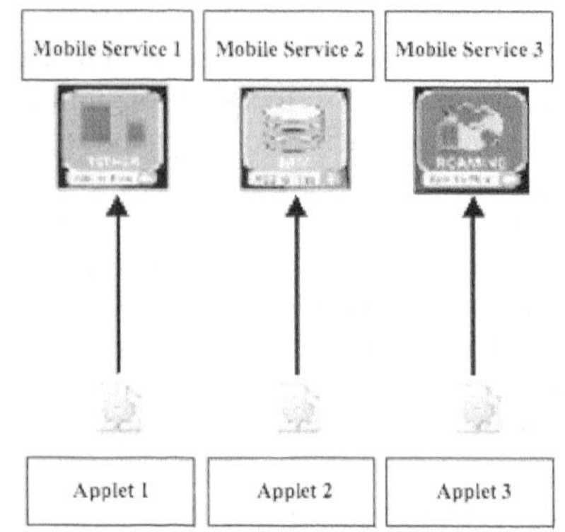

Fig. 3: Applets based on Standard Design Approach

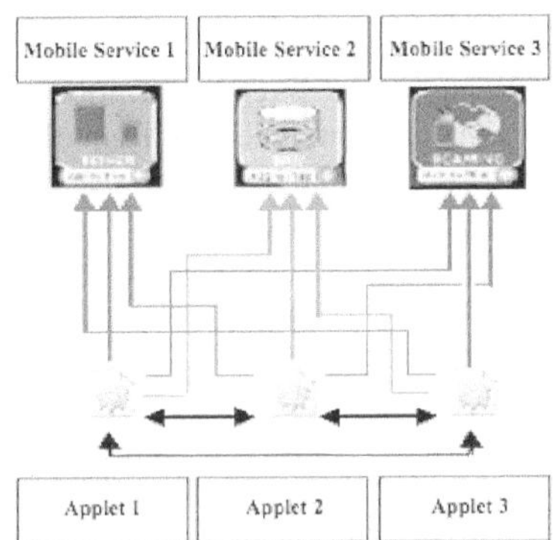

Fig. 4: Multi-Applications Secure Mobile Platform

Our multi-applications secure mobile platform uses as few applets as possible to support as many mobile services as possible. In order to achieve this goal, the following four criteria have been followed in our optimal design approach:

1. Supporting full functionality

All applets together contain all data and functions required by the targeted mobile services and applications.

2. Avoid redundancy

Every attribute and function should be implemented only once. Attributes and functions are structured into different logical groups according to their supported functionalities. These logical groups are finally implemented in different applets. No redundancy would happen.

3. Comply with existing standards

In our research we follow all existing relevant standards. This principle is also applied to the process of designing applets. The first step of our design is to structure data and functions that have been specified in relevant standards into the corresponding applet. The rest of data is then distributed into other applets.

However, criteria 3 should be followed by criteria 2 as much as possible, even if some standard is not completely followed. According to criteria 2, the attributes and functions should be structured into logical groups, based on their nature of supported functionalities. Take again certificate as an example: a certificate should be included in the Security applet since it is related to security functions. It should not be implemented in other applets even though it is specified in some standards specifying their own applets.

4. Support for multiple applications

Since functions and data are distributed into various applets, for each single applet it is not feasible to fully support a specific mobile service. Therefore, multiple applets should be combined together in order to perform functions needed to support some mobile service. Various applets work simultaneously and basic functions of one applet are invoked by other applets in order to implement more complicated functions. Functions and attributes are referenced from different applets to satisfy the requirements of mobile services. For that necessary interfaces in all applets to function smoothly and with mutual synchronization in multi-application module platform have also been designed and implemented.

Multi-applications secure mobile platform based on our optimal design approach increases the efficiency of the management and also use of applets. For example, in order to support mobile identification and mobile payments services, an X.509 certificate is required. According to the relevant standards for identification and payments, both identification applet and payment applet should contain an X.509 certificate. If the same issuer issues two certificates to the same user, the contents of the certificates are same. With the standard approach two copies of the same certificate are kept in two applets, what is not reasonable. However, with our optimized multi-applications secure mobile platform, the certificate is implemented only once and that is in the Security applet. Then, both identification and payment applets can use this certificate when necessary.

By following the optimal design approach, in our research, several applets have ben created and implemented. The attributes distributed in these applets are shown in Table II. In reference to Table I, it can be noticed that each attribute is only implemented in one applet, avoiding their duplication.

Table II. Data Attributes of the Optimized Applets

Applets / Attributes	Identification Applet	Security Applet	Wallet Applet	POS Applet
First Name	✓			
Last Name	✓			
CHUID	✓			
Terminal ID				✓
Bank IBAN			✓	
Bank Account Number			✓	
Authentication Certificate		✓		
Private key		✓		

7. Demo of the Implementation of Our Research Results

In the previous section we described design of our applets. In this section we describe a demo of our implementation. It is mobile payment service with electronic cash.

Hardware platform we use is iPhone 4 with iOS 5.1.1. Javacard is an ISO/IEC7816-2 [15] compliant standard smart card from Oberthur Technology [16].

The reader we are using to connect to the smart card from iPhone application is IDTech iSmart Mobile Smart Card Reader [17]. IDTech provides library to communicate with the Javacard applets from mobile applications.

In our research we implemented the complete system that supports secure mobile payment services. With the client application running in mobile phones, subscribers can perform payment transactions using electronic cash. In this paper we will not elaborate how the overall system works, including how the electronic cash represents real money and how it is transferred between merchants and subscribers. That is out of the scope of this paper.

In mobile phones we use mobile application providing GUIs to subscribers (shown in Figure 1) and exchanging information with the background system servers. This mobile phone application invokes functions from various applets in the Javacard chip in order to perform payment transactions. The whole process is grouped into 10 steps shown in Figure 5:

- Step 1: Mobile application requires subscriber's certificate from Security applet. Mobile application requires payment server's certificate and verifies it with authentication server;
- Step 2: Mobile application sends subscriber's certificate to the Payment Server. The server transfers subscriber's certificate to authentication server for ID verification;
- Step 3: Authentication server returns verification result. If the ID is ok payment server sends back verification result, transaction ID, encrypted transaction ID and session key. The session key is encrypted by subscriber's public key contained in certificate. Transaction ID is encrypted by session key. Payment server signs the package;
- Step 4: Mobile application verifies the signature of the package. If the signature is correct, mobile application encrypts payment amount received from the GUIs and transaction ID that is contained in the response from the server with a key shared between mobile application and the Wallet applet. Then mobile application sends encryption result, Key ID and encrypted package from server to the Wallet applet;
- Step 5: Wallet applet invokes Security applet to decrypt the session key with RSA private key. With the session key Wallet applet continues to decrypt the transaction ID contained in the respond package from payment server. Then Wallet applet uses the key shared with mobile application to decrypt the amount and transaction ID contained in the encrypted package generated by mobile application. Wallet applet compares the two IDs and if they are same, Wallet applet debits electronic cash with corresponding amount;
- Step 6: Wallet applet invokes subscriber's personal information including first name and last name from the Identification applet;
- Step 7: Wallet invokes Security applet to encrypt subscriber's personal information, transaction ID, debit amount, the remaining electronic cash value with session key, hashes the package and signs the hash value. Wallet concatenates encryption with signed hash value;
- Step 8: Wallet applet returns the result;
- Step 9: Mobile application transmits the complete package to the Payment Server;
- Step 10: Payment server decrypts data, verifies signature and verifies the authenticity of the data. If everything is correct, server updates the database and finally, Payment Server returns the transaction result to the mobile application.

Functions and the corresponding applets involved in this process are shown in Table III.

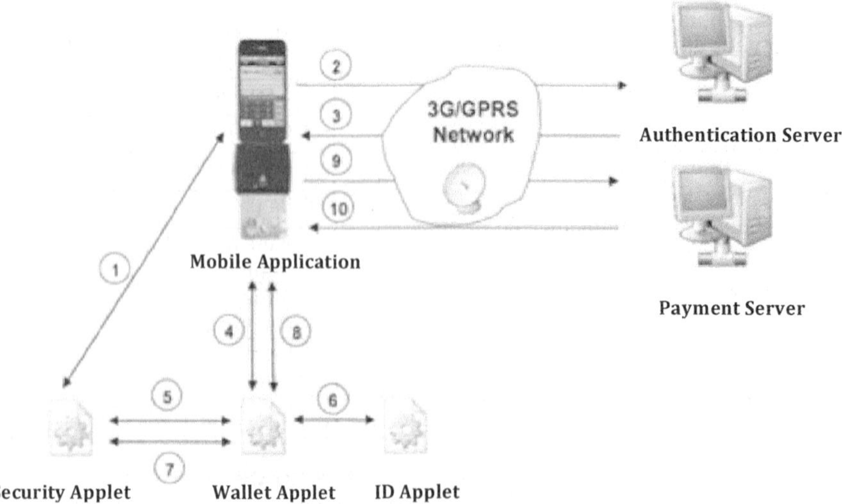

Fig. 5: Mobile Transaction Process

Table III: Functions and Applets for the Mobile Payment Process

Functions \ Applets	Wallet Applet	Security Applet	Identification Applet
getCertificate		✓	
decryptWithRSAPrivatekey		✓	
debitCash	✓		
Shareable *decryptWithShareKey*		✓	
Shareable *getPersonalData*			✓
Shareable *encryptData*		✓	
Shareable *hashData*		✓	
Shareable *signWithPrivateKey*		✓	

*Keyworld "Shareable" means the interface can be invoked by other applets.

From the demo it can be noticed that each applets provides corresponding functions and data attributes. By combined these functions and data, a complete secure mobile payment transaction is performed. There are no duplicates of data, unprotected values or redundancy in the process.

Following section shows part of the source code and pseudo code of our implementation:

Pseudo code for *Wallet* mobile application:

```
select m-Security Applet
read Subscriber's certificate
require payment server certificate
send payment request, subscriber's certificate to
payment server
verify payment server's certificate
if authentication result and response signature are
correct
       encrypt transaction ID, amount
       concatenate key ID, encryption result and
       response package
       select Wallet applet
       invoke debit function
else
       return error
if operation result is success
       send returned encrypted package to
       payment server
else
       return error
receive result from payment server
display the result
```

Pseudo code for the *Payment Server*

```
verifies customer's certificate by authentication
server
send certificate to customer
if authentication result is correct
        generate transaction ID
        generate session key
        extract customer's public key
        encrypt transaction ID with session key
        encrypt session key with customer's
        public key
        concatenate transaction ID, encrypted
        session key and encrypted transaction ID
       sign the package
       response with result
else
        return error
decrypt message from customer
verifies signature with customer public key
if signature is OK
       update database
       send success to customer
else
       return error
```

Pseudo code for *Wallet* applet

```
instance M-Security shareable interface object
instance M-ID shareable interface object
RSA decrypt session key
decrypt transaction ID
decrypt data from mobile application
if two transaction IDs are the same
    debit balance
    read customer first name and last name
    concatenate transaction ID, first name, last
    name, debit amount
    encrypt concatenated result
    hash concatenated result
    sign hash result
    concatenate encrypted result and signed
    hash result
    return result
else
    return error
```

m–Security Applet has shareable interfaces as follows:

```
public class MSecurityApplet extends
javacard.framework.Applet implements
MSecuritySharableInterface {

public interface MSecuritySharableInterface
extends Shareable {
public byte[] DESDecrypt(byte[]);
   //other interfaces
      .
      .
      .
}

public byte[] DESDecrypt(byte[] dataToDecrypt){
   //DES Decrypt
 }
public Shareable getShareableInterfaceObject(
AID clientAID, byte parameter) {
return (MSecuritySharableInterface) this;
 }
}
```

Wallet Applet invokes m–Security applet's functions:

```
private MSecuritySharableInterface securitySIO;

public MWalletApplet() throws Exception {

securitySIO=(MSecuritySharableInterface)JCSystem
.getAppletSharableInterfaceObject(MSecurityApple
tAID, (byte)0);
}
private void debit(byte[] amount){
   byte[] amountPlainValue=
securityISO.DESDecrypt(amount);
//other debit functions
 }
```

Wallet mobile application communicates with smart card in the following way:

```
T0Command *t0Command = [[T0Command alloc] init];
    ISO7816Command *resultCommand = nil;
    t0Command.classByte = 0x00;
    t0Command.instructionByte = 0xA4;
    t0Command.parameter1Byte = 0x04;
    t0Command.parameter2Byte = 0x00;
    t0Command.dataBytes = [self
hexStringToBytes:data];
    t0Command.lengthByte
=t0Command.dataBytes.length;
t0Command.expectedResponseLengthByte = 0;
t0Command.commandId = WRITE_CPU_CARD_COMMAND_ID;
resultCommand = [iSmartDevice
sendCommandToCPUCard:t0Command];
```

8. Conclusions

Mobile service is the trend of IT technology. Smart phones provide new and more convenient platform to provide mobile devices. However, these devices do not provide secure enough environment for running sensitive functions and storing sensitive data. Javacard applets store sensitive data and perform sensitive functions more securely. Javacard chip provides multiple applications platform where several Javacard applets work simultaneously. Our optimized design approach distributes functions and data into different applets. Multiple Javacard applets are combined together to support a mobile service. This model is called optimized Multi-Applications Secure Mobile Platform. Compared with the standard approach of Javacard usage, our optimized multi-applications secure mobile platform fully supports targeted mobile services, but with increased the efficiency of managing and usage of applets on Javacard platform.

9. References

[1] IDC, "*Android and iOS Combine for 91.1% of the Worldwide Smartphone OS Market in 4Q12 and 87.6% for the Year, According to IDC*", http://www.idc.com/getdoc.jsp?containerId=prUS23946013 (14 Feb. 2013)

[2] Vic Hargrave, "*To Jailbreak or Not to Jailbreak, That is the Question*", http://consumerization.trendmicro.com/to-jailbreak-or-not-to-jailbreak-that-is-the-question/ (21 May 2012)

[3] Jaemin Park, Kyoungtae Kim, Minjeong Kim, "*The Aegis: UICC-Based Security Framework*", Future Generation Communication and Networking, 2008, FGCN'08 Second International Conference, vol.1, pp.264-269, 13-15 Dec., 2008

[4] ETSI, "*Smart Cards: UICC-Terminal Interface: Physical and logical characteristics*", ETSI TS 102.221 V9

[5] ETSI, "*Smart Cards; USSM: UICC Security Service Module; Stage 1*", ETSI TS 102.266 V7.1

[6] ISO/IEC, Smart Card Specifications

[7] Global Platform, "*GlobalPlatform Card Specification Version 2.2*", [Online] Available: http://www.globalplatform.org/specificationscard.asp [Accessed: May.16, 2010]

[8] Sun Microsystems, "*Runtime Environment Specification*", JavaCard™ Platform V2.2.1

[9] Sun Microsystems, "*Virtual Machine Specification*", JavaCard™ Platform V2.2.1

[10] Sun Microsystems, "*Application Programming Interface*", JavaCard™ Platform V2.2.1

[11] NIST, "*Federal Information Processing Standard (FIPS 201): Personal Identity Verification (PIV) System*", [Online] Available: www.nist.gov [Accessed: Nov. 17, 2009]

[12] EMV, "*Integrated Circuit Card Specifications for Payment Systems*"

[13] Hao Zhao, Sead Muftic, Feng Zhang, "*The Secure Mobile Wallet*", Cutter IT Journal, Vol.23, No.7, July 2010, Page 32~35

[14] ISO/IEC 7816-4, "*Organization, security and commands for interchange*", ISO/IEC 7816-4

[15] ISO/IEC 7816-2, "*Cards with contacts — Dimensions and location of the contacts*", ISO/IEC 7816-2", ISO/IEC 7816-2

[16] Oberthur Tech., http://www.oberthur.com

[17] IDTech, http://www.idtechproduces.com/pro ducts/mobile-readers/136.html

Multi-Vendor PayWord with Payment Approval

A. Huszti
Faculty of Informatics, University of Debrecen, Debrecen, Hungary

Abstract— *One of the most well known micropayment scheme is the PayWord scheme. It is designed to be one-vendor, so if we apply it for multiple vendors, it does not protect against double spending. We extended the PayWord scheme, it supports shopping at multiple vendors without an on-line broker or an on-line secure database. The proposed credit-based system uses one hash chain, hence besides the secret signature key only the seed and a random value should be securely stored. Our scheme is analyzed in applied pi calculus, we prove that it fulfills payment approval, secure payment authorization, secrecy of payment information and unreusability.*

Keywords: PayWord, multi-vendor micropayment, payment approval, applied pi calculus

1. Introduction

In recent years electronic commerce has grown rapidly as Internet and web technologies have progressed. Usually content and service providers charge very small amount (e.g. less than a dollar), hence a special payment solution, called micropayment, is required. Compared to macropayment schemes, the computational time of micropayment schemes are less. Instead of public key cryptosystems, they use one-way, collision-resistant hashing extensively. One can find more information about micropayments in [11].

One of the most well known micropayment scheme is the PayWord scheme [7]. PayWord is designed to be one-vendor, so if we apply it for multiple vendors, it does not protect against double spending, *i. e.* the same amount can be spent at different vendors. There are three main categories of multi-vendor solutions with double-spending prevention. Some schemes require a broker (or a bank) being on-line, whenever a customer changes vendors [6], these are called semi-online systems. Some solutions expect an on-line database [5], that securely stores buyers' account information. This database is available for all vendors. Schemes from the third category use black lists [9], [10], meaning brokers maintain a list of users who did not pay for the products or services. In case of micropayment schemes financial and also computational costs should be minimized, involving an on-line broker or maintaining an on-line database increase expenses and black lists do not prevent the first violations.

Purchases made electronically call forth more disputes and charge backs than face-to-face ones. Frequent disputes result in penalty payments for vendors, hence vendors are concerned about minimizing the possibility of disputes. Payment approval might prevent a large number of conflicts. We have extended PayWord in order to achieve payment approval in [3], *i.e.* for each payment the user generates a proof of order information, the fact that he agrees to pay the requested amount of money for that product. After completing the payment phase the vendor is able to verify this proof. The obvious way would be to achieve payment approval to employ digital signatures, but this solution is computationally intensive for micropayments. Number of public key operations should be minimized, we applied message authentication codes (MAC) instead. Payment approval prevents misunderstandings between the user and the vendor that decrease number of disputes and charge backs.

We modified PayWord in a way, that it is applicable for multiple vendors without applying an on-line broker or database and we do not use blacklists either. Our scheme also provides payment approval. We did not increase the number of asymmetric key operations or the number of requisite asymmetric keys, we use only one hash chain, that requires two random values stored securely.

Electronic payment systems have critical security requirements, hence the design of their cryptographic protocol requires special care. Substantial evaluation should be provided in order to prevent flaws. Although there are several PayWord based scheme ([5],[6],[9],[10]), they do not give formal security evaluation. PayWord is formalized in spi calculus in [2] and we gave proof for payment approval, payment authorization in applied pi calculus with the help of ProVerif [4] in [3]. In case of the proposed scheme besides payment approval and payment authorization, we also provide proof for double spending detection with labeled semantics.

The paper starts with description of the PayWord extended with payment approval. In section 3, the proposed multi-vendor scheme is detailed. In section 4 we give the formal security evaluation starting with a short review of the applied pi calculus and the operational semantics we applied. In subsections 4.3 and 4.4 we give the formal model and security evaluation for our scheme. Finally, a conclusion is given. Further technical details of the proof are given in the Appendix.

2. Payment approval for PayWord

Let us review the extended PayWord micropayment scheme according to [3]. We have three participants: a user U, a vendor V and a broker B. The protocol consists of three phases: user-broker, user-vendor and broker-vendor relationship. We should emphasize that only the user-vendor relationship is short-term the others are assumed to be long-term. According to basic PayWord [7] user-broker and broker-vendor relationship could happen off-line. We consider the case when U registers on-line.

Let us describe the extended PayWord micropayment scheme in details. We employ digital signatures, where user's and broker's public and secret keys are denoted by K_U^+, K_B^+ and K_U^-, K_B^-, respectively. $\{M\}_{K_i^-}$ denotes a message signed by K_i^-, where $i \in \{U, B\}$.

User-Broker relationship

User U initiates a relationship with broker B by requesting an authorized PayWord Certificate. U transports his credit-card number and his public key K_U^+ on an authenticated encrypted channel.

$$1.\ U \to B : U, K_U^+$$

B digitally signs B, U, K_U^+ and E with key K_B^-, where E denotes the expiration date of the certificate. This certificate ensures any vendor that the amount will be paid-off before date E, since U is able to cover it.

$$2.\ B \to U : \{B, U, K_U^+, E\}_{K_B^-}$$

User-Vendor relationship

For achieving payment approval we have extended the basic PayWord scheme with vendor authentication. Secret MAC key is sent to the vendor encrypted. This solution does not increase the complexity significantly, since public key encryption should be run only once, at the beginning of the relationship.

Before shopping U generates a *payword chain*: $w_0, w_1, \dots w_n$. First U generates a random number w_n, then calculates

$$w_i = H(w_{i+1}),$$

where $i \in \{n-1, n-2, \dots, 0\}$. We call $w_1, \dots w_n$ paywords, w_0 is the root of the chain. U chooses the number n arbitrarily beyond the requested amount and generates a certificate containing the vendor's identification information V, his PayWord Certificate, the commitment w_0, the actual date D and the MAC key encrypted. This certificate is signed by the user's secret key K_U^-.

$$3\ U \to V : \{V, \{B, U, K_U^+, E\}_{K_B^-}, w_0, D, \{K\}_{K_V^+}\}_{K_U^-}$$

The vendor verifies U's signature by public key K_U^+, and B's signature by K_B^+, checks whether D is before E and stores w_0 with the user information.

Following U sends order information and a MAC proof for the vendor containing order information and a payword. Then the vendor sends the requested product on an encrypted channel without verifying the payword, we should mention that MAC verification happens after the user receives his product and sends the payment. In case of micropayments loosing the amount of one payment is not a large loss, if either the hash or the MAC verification is unsuccessful, then the vendor might decide to refuse other purchases. A payment is a pair of a payword and the corresponding index (w_i, i), where $i \in \{1, 2, \dots, n\}$. It is important that the user sends his paywords starting from w_1, the w_2 and so on.

$$4.1\ U \to V : OrdInf_1, Mac((OrdInf_1, w_1), K)$$

$$V \to U : Product_1$$

$$U \to V : (w_1, 1)$$

$$\vdots$$

$$4.n\ U \to V : OrdInf_l, Mac((OrdInf_l, w_l), K)$$

$$V \to U : Product_l$$

$$U \to V : (w_l, l)$$

Vendor V verifies the received payword w_i by applying i times the hash function on it, *i.e.* checks $H^i(w_i) = w_0$, in case of the first shopping, otherwise verifies w_i with the stored payword w_j, where $j < i$, *i.e.* checks $H^{i-j}(w_i) = w_j$. V also verifies correctness of the MAC value, with help of order information and the payword.

Vendor-Broker relationship

V sends all necessary information to B for the pay-off. V transmits the certificate generated by U, the last payword received from U and the corresponding index.

$$5.\ V \to B : \{V, \{B, U, K_U^+, E\}_{K_B^-}, w_0, D\}_{K_U^-}, w_l, l$$

B verifies the signature of user's certificate with K_U^+, checks whether identity information of the vendor received matches with V, the expiring date and validity of the payword, *i. e.* $H^l(w_l) = w_0$. If all verifications hold, then B pays the proper amount to V.

3. Shopping at Multiple Vendors

In this section we introduce our multi-vendor PayWord that provides payment approval.

Users in advance should decide about the vendors they would like to deal at and generate the hash chain. The hash chain is generated in a way that even if a vendor receives a hash value, he is not able to calculate other vendors' paywords. The user asks the broker to authorize his hash chain commitments. Broker's authorization proves that the user can cover his purchases. The system is credit-based, hence users are allowed to pay for as many as paywords posteriorly, as he used up. We do not need the broker to be on-line, since his authorization is necessary only during preparation and only once. Users are allowed to spend each payword only at the vendor that the corresponding commitment assigned to, the vendor can verify whether a payword is spent before or not, hence we do not need an on-line database, either.

We describe the modified scheme in details. Let us denote the vendors by $V_1, V_2, \ldots, V_j$, the user and the broker by U and B, respectively. The user possesses a (K_U^-, K_U^+) signature key pair for authentication, the broker also has a (K_B^-, K_B^+) signature key pair for generating a certificate verifying that U is able to afford his shopping and each vendor has a $(K_{V_i}^-, K_{V_i}^+)$ public key encryption key pair for key exchange. We would like to mention, that we did not increase the number of keys necessary for multiple vendor shopping comparing to the one vendor one.

We apply one payword hash chain per user, hence each user generates a random seed w_n and calculates hash values. The same hash chain is applied for all vendors, hence users need to generate another random value denoted by v. Both random values are kept secret and stored securely. The hash chain is generated as follows.

Each user should decide about the number of paywords he would like to spend at each vendor. Let us assume that U would like to spend k_i paywords at V_i, where $i = 1, \ldots, j$, hence $w_n = w_{j,k_j}$. In general

$$w_{i,l} = \begin{cases} H(Enc_v(w_{i+1,0})), & \text{if } l = k_i, \\ H(w_{i,l+1}), & \text{if } 0 \leq l < k_i. \end{cases}$$

Paywords $w_{i,k_i}, \ldots, w_{i,2}, w_{i,1}$ can be spent at vendor V_i, the corresponding commitment is $w_{i,0}$. Since the first payword U is able to spend at V_i depends on v - that is known only by U - V_{i+1} cannot calculate w_{i,k_i}.

User-Broker relationship

After generating the payword chain, U transports his credit-card number, his public key K_U^+, the list of vendors $V_1, V_2, \ldots, V_j$ and the list of commitments $w_{1,0}, w_{2,0}, \ldots, w_{j,0}$ on an authenticated encrypted channel to B.

$$1.\ U \rightarrow B : U, K_U^+, (V_j, w_{j,0}), \ldots, (V_2, w_{2,0}), (V_1, w_{1,0})$$

B digitally signs all data received, B and E with key K_B^-, where E denotes the expiration date of the certificate.

$$2.\ B \rightarrow U : \{B, U, K_U^+, E, (V_1, w_{1,0}), \ldots, (V_j, w_{j,0})\}_{K_B^-}$$

The certificate received from B is called PayWord certificate, and we denote it by C_U. The main difference between the one-vendor and multi-vendor solutions is that commitments are signed by the broker. Each vendor is able to verify all the paywords sent by the user with the help of these commitments. The system is credit-based, hence the user is able to spend a certain amount of money in advance and later, e.g. once a month, refunds it to the broker.

User-Vendor relationship

Users can spend his paywords at different vendors. U chooses a vendor V_i and generates a fresh symmetric encryption key KV_i. The user sends his PayWord certificate, the actual date and the encrypted symmetric key digitally signed.

$$3.\ U \rightarrow V_i : \{C_U, D, \{KV_i\}_{K_{V_i}^+}\}_{K_{U^-}}$$

The vendor verifies U's signature by public key K_U^+, the PayWord certificate by K_B^+. V decrypts the symmetric key KV_i and if D is before E, then stores $(w_{i,0}, 0)$, U and KV_i. User sends the corresponding order information and the proof of what he would like to buy and for what price. The proof is a MAC value generated with the hash of KV_i. Vendor sends the encrypted product, we might think of a song or an article. After receiving the product the user sends the next payword.

$$4.1\ U \rightarrow V_i : OrdInf_1, Mac((OrdInf_1, w_1), H(KV_i))$$

$$4.2\ V_i \rightarrow U : \{Product_1\}_{KV_i}$$

$$4.3\ U \rightarrow V_i : (w_1, 1)$$

V verifies whether the MAC value is valid, *i.e.* the proof received before is the MAC value of the proper order information and the payword. Paywords as hash values prove that they are fresh and originate from the user. V also verifies whether the hash value of the payword received equals to the one stored in his database. If all verifications are correct, then modifies the payword stored to the new one and updates the index.

$$\vdots$$

$$4.k_i\ U \rightarrow V_i : OrdInf_{k_i}, Mac((OrdInf_{k_i}, w_{k_i}), H(KV_i))$$

$$V_i \rightarrow U : \{Product_{k_i}\}_{KV_i}$$

$$U \rightarrow V_i : (w_{k_i}, k_i)$$

Vendor-Broker relationship

Vendor V_i sends the PayWord certificate, the payword stored with the corresponding index and the actual date to B.

$$5.\ V_i \rightarrow B : \{C_U, D, \{KV_i\}_{K_{V_i}^+}\}_{K_{U^-}}, (w_{k_i}, k_i), V_i$$

B verifies the user's PayWord certificate, checks its validity according to the date D and calculates $H^{k_i}(w_{k_i})$, whether it is $w_{i,0}$. If all values are valid, then B pays the proper amount to V_i.

4. Formal security evaluation

4.1 Applied pi calculus

Detailed description of this topic can be found in [1]. The calculus assumes an infinite set of names, an infinite set of variables and a signature. A signature $\sum$ is a set of function symbols, each with an arity.

$L, M, N, T, U, V ::=$	*terms*
$a, b, c, \ldots, k, \ldots, m, n, \ldots, s$	name
x, y, z	variable
$f(M_1, ..., M_l)$	function application

The grammar for processes is the following:

$P, Q, R ::=$	*processes*
0	null process
$P \vert Q$	parallel composition
$!P$	replication
$\nu n.P$	name restriction (new)
$if\ M = N\ then\ P\ else\ Q$	conditional
$u(x).P$	message input
$\overline{u}\langle N\rangle.P$	message output

We extend processes with active substitutions. We denote the substitution that replaces the variable x with the term M by $\{M/x\}$. With active substitutions we capture the knowledge exposed to the adversarial environment. For modeling multi-vendor PayWord scheme, we add a restriction to active substitution as follows: $\nu x.(\{M/x\}|P)$ that corresponds to $let\ x = M\ in\ P$.

4.2 Operational semantics

We give formalization for cryptographic primitives with the help of equational theory as follows:

Hash function, message authentication code. We represent a oneway hash function as a unary function symbol H with no equations. The absence of an inverse for H models the onewayness of H. Similarly we denote a oneway MAC function as a binary function symbol Mac, where the second argument corresponds to the secret key of MAC.

$fun\ H/1.$

$fun\ Mac/2.$

Symmetric encryption. We take binary function symbols $senc$ and $sdec$ for encryption and decryption, respectively, with the equation: $sdec(senc(x, y), y) = x$. Here x represents the plaintext and y the secret key.

$fun\ senc/2.$

$reduc\ sdec(senc(x, y), y) = x.$

Asymmetric encryption. In case of asymmetric encryption we have to generate a keypair, a public and a secret key. We have an unary function symbol pk for generating the public key, where the secret key is the argument. Similarly to symmetric encryption we represent asymmetric encryption and decryption with binary function symbols $aenc$ and $adec$ with the equation of $adec(aenc(x, pk(y)), y) = x$, where x denotes the plaintext and y is the secret key.

$fun\ pk/1.$

$fun\ aenc/2.$

$reduc\ adec(aenc(x, pk(y)), y) = x.$

Digital signatures. In order to formalize digital signatures that also employ secret and public keys we use function symbol pk for generating public keys, and binary function symbols $sign$, $checksign$. We interpret digital signatures with message recovery, meaning we have equation $checksign(sign(m, k), pk(k)) = m$, where m is the message and k is the secret key.

$fun\ pk/1.$

$fun\ sign/2.$

$reduc\ checksign(sign(m, k), pk(k)) = m.$

We define context $C[\_]$ to be an extended process with a hole. An evaluation context is a context whose hole is not in the scope of a replication, a conditional, an input, or an output.

Furthermore operational semantics is defined in terms of structural equivalence ($\equiv$), internal reduction ($\rightarrow$) and labeled reductions. Structural equivalence captures rearrangements of parallel compositions and restrictions and the equational rewriting of the terms in a process. Internal reduction defines the semantics of process synchronization and conditionals. While internal reduction rules are applied for executing a process without contact with its environment, labeled semantics enables us to reason about the interaction between processes and the environment. For detailed description we refer to [8].

4.3 Modeling Multi-Vendor PayWord

In this section we model our scheme in applied pi calculus.

The main process.

As a first step secret and public keys are generated and we issue identity numbers by applying function host for all participants. Identity information and public keys are made public.

$$
\begin{aligned}
\text{process} \triangleq\ & \nu ssk_U.\nu ssk_B.\nu esk_B.\nu esk_{V_1}.\ \ldots\ .\nu esk_{V_j}.\\
& \text{let } spk_U = pk(ssk_U) \text{ in let } spk_B = pk(ssk_B) \text{ in}\\
& \text{let } epk_B = pk(esk_B) \text{ in let } epk_{V_1} = pk(esk_{V_1}) \text{ in}\\
& \ldots\\
& \text{let } epk_{V_j} = pk(esk_{V_j}) \text{ in let } hU = host(spk_U) \text{ in}\\
& \text{let } hB = host(spk_B) \text{ in let } hV_1 = host(epk_{V_1}) \text{ in}\\
& \ldots\\
& \text{let } hV_j = host(epk_{V_j}) \text{ in } \overline{a}\langle hB, epk_B, spk_B\rangle.\\
& \overline{a}\langle hU, spk_U\rangle.\overline{a}\langle hV_1, epk_{V_1}, \ldots, hV_j, epk_{V_j}\rangle.\\
& ((!procU)\ |\ (!procB)\ |\ (!procV_1)\ |\ \ldots\ |\ (!procV_j))
\end{aligned}
$$

The user process.

Our user-broker relationship is managed on-line. We define several events. $UacceptsB$ event happens after authenticating the broker via asymmetric key decryption, $ValidCertificate$ proceeds if the certificate received from the broker is valid. $V_iReadytoPurchase$ runs at the beginning of the shopping process with V_i and $UV_iEndsPayment_{k_i}$ happens after transferring the k_ith payword.

$$\begin{aligned}\text{procU} \triangleq\ & \nu w_{j,k_j}.\nu v.\ \text{let } w_{j,k_{j-1}} = H(w_{j,k_j}) \text{ in}\\ & \text{let } w_{j,0} = H(w_{j,1}) \text{ in}\\ & \text{let } w_{j-1,k_{j-1}} = H(senc(w_{j,0}, v)) \text{ in } \ldots\\ & \text{let } w_{1,0} = H(w_{1,1}) \text{ in } \nu K.\\ & \overline{a}\langle aenc(sign((K, hU, hB), ssk_U), epk_B), hU\rangle.\\ & a(mes).\ \text{let } (n, = hU) = sdec(mes, K) \text{ in}\\ & \overline{UacceptsB}\langle hU, hB, K, n\rangle.\\ & \overline{a}\langle senc((CardInf, hU, n, w_{j,0}, hV_j,\\ & \ldots, w_{2,0}, hV_2, w_{1,0}, hV_1), K)\rangle.a(CU).\\ & \text{let } (= hB, = hU, E, = w_{j,0}, = hV_j, \ldots,\\ & = w_{1,0}, = hV_1) = checksign(CU, spk_B) \text{ in}\\ & \overline{ValidCertificate}\langle hU, hB, K, n\rangle.\\ & (V_j shop|V_{j-1} shop|\ldots|V_2 shop|V_1 shop)\end{aligned}$$

$$\begin{aligned}V_i shop \triangleq\ & a(s, = hV_i).\nu KV_i.\\ & \overline{V_i ReadytoPurchase}\langle hU, hV_i\rangle.\\ & \overline{a}\langle sign((CU, D, s, aenc(KV_i, epk_{V_i})), ssk_U)\rangle.\\ & \overline{a}\langle OrdInf_1, MAC((OrdInf_1, w_{i,1}), H(KV_i))\rangle.\\ & a(msg_1).\text{let } page_1 = sdec(msg_1, KV_i) \text{ in}\\ & \overline{a}\langle w_{i,1}\rangle.\\ & \ldots\\ & \overline{a}\langle OrdInf_{k_i}, MAC((OrdInf_{k_i}, w_{i,k_i}), H(KV_i))\rangle.\\ & a(msg_{k_i}).\text{let } page_{k_i} = sdec(msg_{k_i}, KV_i) \text{ in}\\ & \overline{a}\langle w_{i,k_i}\rangle.\overline{UV_i EndsPayment_{k_i}}\langle hU, hV_i\rangle\end{aligned}$$

The broker process. Event $BconnectstoU$ happens right before the broker establish communication with the user. $BacceptsU$ comes after authenticating the user via symmetric key decryption. Finally $BpaystoV_i$ proceeds if all data sent by vendor V_i is valid.

$$\begin{aligned}\text{procB} \triangleq\ & a(s, = hU).\text{let } sig = adec(s, esk_B) \text{ in}\\ & \text{let } (K, = hU, = hB) = checksign(sig, spk_U) \text{ in}\\ & \nu n.\overline{BconnectstoU}\langle hU, hB, K, n\rangle.\\ & \overline{a}\langle senc((n, hU), K))\rangle.a(mes).\\ & \text{let } inf = sdec(mes, K) \text{ in}\\ & \text{let } (CardInf, = hU, = n, w_{j,0}, hV_j, \ldots,\\ & w_{1,0}, hV_1) = sdec(mes, K) \text{ in}\\ & \overline{BacceptsU}\langle hU, hB, K, n\rangle.\\ & \overline{a}\langle sign((hB, hU, E, w_{j,0}, hV_j, \ldots,\\ & w_{1,0}, hV_1), ssk_B))\rangle.\\ & (V_j chargeoff|V_{j-1} chargeoff|\ldots\\ & |V_2 chargeoff|V_1 chargeoff)\end{aligned}$$

$$\begin{aligned}V_i chargeoff \triangleq\ & a(signMU, w_{k_i}, k_i, = hV_i).\\ & \text{let } (CU, D, x, y) = checksign(signMU, spk_U)\\ & \text{in let } (= hB, = hU, = E, = w_{j,0}, = hV_j, \ldots,\\ & = w_{1,0}, = hV_1)) = checksign(CU, spk_B) \text{ in}\\ & \text{if } H^{k_i}(w_{k_i}) = w_{i,0} \text{ then } \overline{BpaystoV_i}\langle hV_i, hB\rangle\end{aligned}$$

The vendor process.

$V_i AcceptsMU$ denotes the event that vendor V_i successfully authenticated the user via digital signature and the payword certificate is valid.

$V_i AcceptsPayment_l$ happens if the proof of payment approval and the lth payword are valid. $V_i RejectsPayment_l$ runs if the payword received is not valid.

$$\begin{aligned}procV_i \triangleq\ & \nu s.\overline{a}\langle s, hV_i\rangle.a(signMU).\text{let } (CU, D, = s, enckey) =\\ & = checksign(signMU, spk_U) \text{ in}\\ & \text{let } (= hB, = hU, E, w_{j,0}, hV_j, \ldots,\\ & w_{i,0}, = hV_i, \ldots, w_{1,0}, hV_1) = checksign(CU, spk_B)\\ & \text{in let } KV_i = adec(enckey, esk_{V_i}) \text{ in}\\ & \overline{V_i AcceptsMU}\langle hU, hV_i\rangle.a(OrdInf_1, proof_1).\\ & \overline{a}\langle senc(page_1, KV_i)\rangle.a(pw_1).\\ & \text{if } H(pw_1) = w_{i,0} \text{ then}\\ & \text{if } proof_1 = MAC((OrdInf_1, pw_1), H(KV_i)) \text{ then}\\ & \overline{V_i AcceptsPayment_1}\langle hU, hV_i\rangle.\\ & \ldots\\ & a(OrdInf_k, proof_k).\overline{a}\langle senc(page_k, KV_i)\rangle.\\ & a(pw_k).\text{if } H(pw_k) = pw_{k-1} \text{ then}\\ & \text{if } proof_k = MAC((OrdInf_k, pw_k), H(KV_i)) \text{ then}\\ & \overline{V_i AcceptsPayment_k}\langle hU, hV_k\rangle.\\ & \ldots\\ & a(OrdInf_{k_i}, proof_{k_i}).\overline{a}\langle senc(page_{k_i}, KV_i)\rangle.\\ & a(pw_{k_i}).\text{ if } H(pw_{k_i}) = pw_{k_i - 1} \text{ then}\\ & \text{if } proof_{k_i} = MAC((OrdInf_{k_i}, pw_{k_i}), H(KV_i)) \text{ then}\\ & \overline{V_i AcceptsPayment_{k_i}}\langle hU, hV_i\rangle.\\ & \overline{a}\langle signMU, pw_{k_i}, k_i, hV_i\rangle\\ & \text{else } 0 \text{ else } \overline{V_i RejectsPayment_{k_i}}\langle hU, KV_i, pw_{k_i}\rangle\\ & \ldots\\ & \text{else } 0 \text{ else } \overline{V_i RejectsPayment_1}\langle hU, KV_i, pw_1\rangle\end{aligned}$$

4.4 Security analysis

In this section we prove that our proposed scheme accomplish secure payment authorization, payment approval, secrecy of payment information and unreusability. First of all we recall security definitions given in [3], then we give a formal proof employing applied pi calculus. We also prove unreusability, *i.e.* double-spender detection employing labeled semantics.

Payment authorization. Payment authorization guarantees a proof for the vendor, that there is sufficient fund on the user's account. This proof or certificate is created by the broker.

Definition 4.1: We state that a payment scheme fulfills payment authorization if the following conditions hold:

1) Broker authentication: The consumer successfully authenticates the broker, it is indisputable that the certificate is authorized by the broker.
2) Consumer authentication: The broker successfully authenticates the consumer, it is indisputable that the consumer's account is questioned.
3) Certificate: There is a proof for the vendor, that the sufficient fund is available.

Secure payment authorization is achieved, if the certificate is undeniable.

Payment approval. Payment approval process generates a proof for the vendor that a consumer agrees to pay a certain amount of money for a particular product. We would like to emphasize requisiteness of vendor authentication, since if the consumer sends the proof to an adversary, then the adversary might be able to masquerade the consumer.

Definition 4.2: We state that a payment scheme fulfills payment approval if the following conditions hold:

1) Consumer authentication: The vendor successfully authenticates the consumer, it is indisputable that the proof originates from the consumer.
2) Vendor authentication: The consumer successfully authenticates the vendor, it is indisputable that the certificate is sent to the vendor.
3) Order information: The proof contains precise description of the product.
4) Price information: The proof contains the amount of money the consumer tends to pay.

Secure payment approval is achieved, if the proof is undeniable.

Secrecy of payment information. In case of payment schemes it is crucial that payment information such as credit card information should be kept secret.

Definition 4.3: We state that a payment scheme possesses secrecy of payment information, if confidential payment information is not revealed for adversaries.

Unreusability. Multi-vendor schemes should be protected against double spenders.

Definition 4.4: If the same coin is spent more than once, then the identity of the second spender should be detected.

Theorem 4.1: Our proposed multi-vendor PayWord scheme accomplish secure payment authorization, payment approval, secrecy of payment information and unreusability.

Proof: We give a proof for secure payment authorization and secrecy of payment information in the general case with the help of ProVerif. In order to prove payment approval ProVerif queries for a concrete case, when there are two vendors with $k_1 = 4$, $k_2 = 3$ are considered. Since the payment phase is the same for each purchase considering these queries is sufficient for us.

Our scheme fulfills *secure payment authorization*, since it provides an undeniable certificate: $sign((hB, hU, E, w_{j,0}, hV_j, \ldots, w_{1,0}, hV_1), ssk_B))$. Broker and consumer authentication are achieved, since the following queries return logical value true:

$query\ evinj\ :\ ValidCertificate(x,y,z,t) \implies evinj\ :\ BconnectstoU(x,y,z,t)$.

$query\ evinj\ :\ BacceptsU(x,y,z,t) \implies (evinj\ :\ UacceptsB(x,y,z,t) \implies evinj\ :\ BconnectstoU(x,y,z,t))$.

Our scheme possesses *secrecy of payment information*, since the following query returns true:

$query\ attacker : CardInf$.

Our scheme fulfills *payment approval*, since it provides a proof of order and price information for each purchase: $MAC((OrdInf_l, w_{i,l}), H(KV_i))$ and fulfills consumer and vendor authentication, since the following queries return true.

$query\ evinj\ :\ V1AcceptsPayment2(x,y) \implies evinj\ :\ V1ReadytoPurchase(x,y)$.

$query\ evinj\ :\ V2AcceptsPayment2(x,y) \implies evinj\ :\ V2ReadytoPurchase(x,y)$.

$query\ evinj\ :\ UV1EndsPayment2(x,y) \implies evinj\ :\ V1AcceptsMU(x,y)$.

$query\ evinj\ :\ UV2EndsPayment2(x,y) \implies evinj\ :\ V2AcceptsMU(x,y)$.

Our scheme fulfills *unreusability*. We consider a dishonest user, an attacker with the largest power, who intends to deposit the same coin twice either at the same, or at different vendors. We give a detailed proof in the Appendix. We show with labeled semantics that in case of an attack the identity of the double-spender is revealed. Active attackers with less power are handled similarly. ■

5. Conclusion and acknowledgment

We extended PayWord to support payments at multiple vendors. The proposed scheme is a credit-based, off-line solution, with minimal computational and storage costs. We also provided a detailed formal proof for payment approval, payment authorization, secrecy of payment information and unreusability in the applied pi calculus.

The publication was supported by the TÁMOP-4.2.2.C-11/1/KONV-2012-0001 project. The project has been supported by the European Union, co-financed by the European Social Fund. The author is also supported by the Hungarian National Foundation for Scientific Research Grant No. NK 104208.

References

[1] M. Abadi, C. Fournet, "Mobile Values, New Names, and Secure Communication", *28th ACM Symposium on Principles of Programming Languages*, pp. 104–115, 2001.

[2] L. Aszalós, A. Huszti, "Applying Spi-calculus for Payword", *Proceedings of ICAI'10 8th International Conference on Applied Informatics*, pp. 295–302, 2010.

[3] L. Aszalós, A. Huszti, "Payment Approval for PayWord", *D. H. Lee, M. Yung (Eds.): Information Security Applications - 13th International Workshop (WISA) 2012, ser. Lecture Notes in Computer Science, Berlin, Germany: Springer*, 2012, vol. 7690, pp. 161–176.

[4] B. Blanchet, B. Smyth, (2011), ProVerif 1.85:Automatic Cryptographic Protocol Verifier, User Manual and Tutorial, [Online]. Available: http://www.proverif.ens.fr/manual.pdf/.

[5] M. Hosseinkhani, E. Tarameshloo, M. Shajari, "AMVPayword: Secure and Efficient Anonymous Payword-Based Micropayment Scheme", *Proc. of International Conference on Computational Intelligence and Security (CIS)*, pp. 551–555, 2010.

[6] M. Payeras-Capella, J. L. Ferrer-Gomila, L. Huguet-Rotger, "An efficient anonymous scheme for secure micropayment", *Web Engineering, ser. Lecture Notes in Computer Science Berlin, Germany: Springer*, vol. 2722, pp. 80–83, 2003.

[7] R. Rivest, A. Shamir, "PayWord and MicroMint: Two simple micropayment schemes", *In Proc. of Security Protocols*, pp. 69–87, 1997.

[8] M. D. Ryan, B. Smyth, "Applied pi calculus", *In proc. of Formal Models and Techniques for Analyzing Security Protocols*, chapter 6, 2011.

[9] C. T. Wang, C. C. Chang, C. H. Lin, "A new micro-payment system using general payword chain", *In proc. of Electronic Commerce Research*, vol. 2, pp. 159–168, 2002.

[10] H. Wang, J. Ma, J. Sun, "Micro-payment protocol based on multiple hash chains", *In proc. of Second International Symposium on Electronic Commerce and Security*, vol. 1, pp. 71–74, 2009.

[11] W. Kou, *Payment Technologies for E-Commerce*, Berlin, Germany: Springer, 1998.

6. Appendix

Users' shopping processes:

$V_i shop\_ds \triangleq$ $a(s, = hV_i).\nu KV_i.$
$\overline{a}\langle sign((sign((hB, hU, E, w_{j,0}, hV_j, \ldots, H^{k+l}(w_{i,k+l}), hV_i, \ldots, w_{1,0}, hV_1), ssk_B)), D, s, aenc(KV_i, epk_{V_i})), ssk_U)\rangle.\overline{a}\langle OrdInf_1, MAC((OrdInf_1, H^{k+l-1}(w_{i,k+l})), H(KV_i)))\rangle.$
$a(msg_1)$.let $page_1 = sdec(msg_1, KV_i)$ in
$\overline{a}\langle H^{k+l-1}(w_{i,k+l})\rangle \ldots \overline{a}\langle OrdInf_k, MAC((OrdInf_k, H^l(w_{i,k+l})), H(KV_i)))\rangle.$
$a(msg_k)$.let $page_k = sdec(msg_k, KV_i)$ in
$\overline{a}\langle H^l(w_{i,k+l})\rangle \ldots \overline{a}\langle OrdInf_{k+l}, MAC((OrdInf_{k+l}, H^l(w_{i,k+l})), H(KV_i)))\rangle.$
$a(msg_{k+l})$. let $page_{k+l} = sdec(msg_{k+l}, KV_i)$ in
$\overline{a}\langle H^l(w_{i,k+l})\rangle$

$V_{i,i-1} shop\_ds \triangleq$ $a(s, = hV_i).\nu KV_i.\overline{a}\langle sign((sign((hB, hU, E, w_{j,0}, hV_j, \ldots, H^{k+l}(w_{i,k+l}), hV_i, H^{k_{i-1}}(Enc(H^{k+l}(w_{i,k+l}), v)), hV_{i-1}, \ldots, w_{1,0}, hV_1), ssk_B)), D, s, aenc(KV_i, epk_{V_i})), ssk_U)\rangle, \ldots, \overline{a}\langle OrdInf_k, MAC((OrdInf_k, H^l(w_{i,k+l})), H(KV_i)))\rangle.a(msg_k).$
let $page_k = sdec(msg_k, KV_i)$ in
$\overline{a}\langle H^l(w_{i,k+l})\rangle.a(r, = hV_{i-1}).\nu KV_{i-1}.$
$\overline{a}\langle sign((sign((hB, hU, E, w_{j,0}, hV_j, \ldots, H^{k+l}(w_{i,k+l}), hV_i, H^{k_{i-1}}(Enc(H^{k+l}(w_{i,k+l}), v)), hV_{i-1}, \ldots, w_{1,0}, hV_1), ssk_B)), D, r, aenc(KV_{i-1}, epk_{V_{i-1}})), ssk_U)\rangle.$
$\overline{a}\langle OrdInf_1, MAC((OrdInf_1, H^l(w_{i,k+l})), H(KV_{i-1})))\rangle.a(msg_1).$
let $page_1 = sdec(msg_1, KV_{i-1})$ in
$\overline{a}\langle H^l(w_{i,k+l})\rangle$

First we study the one vendor - double spender case. Let our evaluation context be: $C[\_] = \nu ssk_U.\nu ssk_B.\nu esk_{V_i}(\_|(!V_i shop\_ds)|(!procV_i))$ and our process is:
$P \equiv C[\overline{a}\langle hB, pk(ssk_B)\rangle.\overline{a}\langle hU, pk(ssk_U)\rangle.\overline{a}\langle hV_i, pk(esk_{V_i})\rangle]$. We show that $\varphi(P') \vdash (hU, KV_i, H^l(w_{i,k+l}))$, that gives the identity of the double-spender, its secret MAC key and the invalid payword. Let us consider the vendor's process only with event $V_i RejectsPayment_k(hU, KV_i, H^l(w_{i,k+l}))$ and deal with the following execution path:

$$P \xrightarrow{\nu b\_pk.\overline{a}\langle b\_pk\rangle} \xrightarrow{\nu u\_pk.\overline{a}\langle u\_pk\rangle} \xrightarrow{\nu v\_pk.\overline{a}\langle v\_pk\rangle} \xrightarrow{\nu x.\overline{a}\langle x\rangle} \xrightarrow{a(s,hV_i)} \xrightarrow{\nu y.\overline{a}\langle y\rangle} \xrightarrow{\nu z.\overline{a}\langle z\rangle} \xrightarrow{a(sign((sign((hB,hU,E,w_{j,0},hV_j,\ldots,H^{k+l}(w_{i,k+l}),hV_i,\ldots,w_{1,0},hV_1),ssk_B)),D,s,aenc(KV_i,pk(esk_{V_i}))),ssk_U))} \xrightarrow{a(OrdInf_1,MAC((OrdInf_1,H^{k+l-1}(w_{i,k+l})),H(KV_i)))} \xrightarrow{\nu v.\overline{a}\langle v\rangle} \xrightarrow{a(senc(page_1,KV_i))} \xrightarrow{\nu w.\overline{a}\langle w\rangle} \xrightarrow{a(H^{k+l-1}(w_{i,k+l}))} \ldots \xrightarrow{\nu f.\overline{a}\langle f\rangle} \xrightarrow{a(OrdInf_k,MAC((OrdInf_k,H^l(w_{i,k+l})),H(KV_i)))} \xrightarrow{\nu g.\overline{a}\langle g\rangle} \xrightarrow{a(senc(page_k,KV_i))} \xrightarrow{\nu h.\overline{a}\langle h\rangle} \xrightarrow{a(H^l(w_{i,k+l}))} \ldots \xrightarrow{\nu o.\overline{a}\langle o\rangle} \xrightarrow{a(OrdInf_{k+l},MAC((OrdInf_{k+l},H^l(w_{i,k+l})),H(KV_i)))} \xrightarrow{\nu p.\overline{a}\langle p\rangle} \xrightarrow{a(senc(page_{k+l},KV_i))} \xrightarrow{\nu q.\overline{a}\langle q\rangle} \xrightarrow{a(H^l(w_{i,k+l}))} \xrightarrow{\nu r.\overline{a}\langle r\rangle} P'$$

$P' \equiv \nu ssk_U.\nu ssk_B.\nu esk_{V_i}.\nu KV_i(\{(hB, pk(ssk_B))/b\_pk\} \mid \{(hU, pk(ssk_U))/u\_pk\} \mid \{(hV_i, pk(esk_{V_i}))/v\_pk\} \mid \{(s, hV_i)/x\} \mid \{sign((sign((hB, hU, E, w_{j,0}, hV_j, \ldots, H^{k+l}(w_{i,k+l}), hV_i, \ldots, w_{1,0}, hV_1), ssk_B)), D, s, aenc(KV_i, pk(esk_{V_i}))), ssk_U)/y\} \mid \{(OrdInf_1, MAC((OrdInf_1, H^{k+l-1}(w_{i,k+l})), H(KV_i)))/z\} \mid \{senc(page_1, KV_i)/v\} \mid \{H^{k+l-1}(w_{i,k+l})/w\} \mid \ldots \mid \{(OrdInf_k, MAC((OrdInf_k, H^l(w_{i,k+l})), H(KV_i)))/f\} \mid \{senc(page_k, KV_i)/g\} \mid \{H^l(w_{i,k+l})/h\} \mid \ldots \mid \{(OrdInf_{k+l}, MAC((OrdInf_{k+l}, H^l(w_{i,k+l})), H(KV_i)))/o\} \mid \{senc(page_{k+l}, KV_i)/p\} \mid \{H^l(w_{i,k+l})/q\} \mid \{(hU, KV_i, H^l(w_{i,k+l}))/r\})$

If there are two vendors, let our evaluation context be: $C[\_] = \nu ssk_U.\nu ssk_B.\nu esk_{V_i}.\nu esk_{V_{i-1}}(\_|(!V_{i,i-1} shop\_ds)| (!procV_{i-1})|(!procV_i))$ and our process is: $P \equiv C[\overline{a}\langle hB, pk(ssk_B)\rangle.\overline{a}\langle hU, pk(ssk_U)\rangle.\overline{a}\langle hV_i, pk(esk_{V_i})\rangle.\overline{a}\langle hV_{i-1}, pk(esk_{V_{i-1}})\rangle]$. We show that $\varphi(P') \vdash (hU, KV_{i-1}, H^l(w_{i,k+l}))$.

$$P \xrightarrow{\nu b\_pk.\overline{a}\langle b\_pk\rangle} \xrightarrow{\nu u\_pk.\overline{a}\langle u\_pk\rangle} \xrightarrow{\nu vi\_pk.\overline{a}\langle vi\_pk\rangle} \xrightarrow{\nu vi-1\_pk.\overline{a}\langle vi-1\_pk\rangle} \xrightarrow{\nu x.\overline{a}\langle x\rangle} \xrightarrow{a(s,hV_i)} \xrightarrow{\nu y.\overline{a}\langle y\rangle} \xrightarrow{a(sign((sign((hB,hU,E,w_{j,0},hV_j,\ldots,H^{k+l}(w_{i,k+l}),hV_i,H^{k_{i-1}}(Enc(H^{k+l}(w_{i,k+l}),v)),hV_{i-1},\ldots,w_{1,0},hV_1),ssk_B)),D,s,aenc(KV_i,pk(esk_{V_i}))),ssk_U)} \ldots \xrightarrow{\nu z.\overline{a}\langle z\rangle} \xrightarrow{a(OrdInf_k,MAC((OrdInf_k,H^l(w_{i,k+l})),H(KV_i)))} \xrightarrow{\nu v.\overline{a}\langle v\rangle} \xrightarrow{a(senc(page_k,KV_i))} \xrightarrow{\nu w.\overline{a}\langle w\rangle} \xrightarrow{a(H^l(w_{i,k+l}))} \xrightarrow{\nu p.\overline{a}\langle p\rangle} \xrightarrow{a(r,hV_{i-1})} \xrightarrow{\nu q.\overline{a}\langle q\rangle} \xrightarrow{a(sign((sign((hB,hU,E,w_{j,0},hV_j,\ldots,H^{k+l}(w_{i,k+l}),hV_i,H^{k_{i-1}}(Enc(H^{k+l}(w_{i,k+l}),v)),hV_{i-1},\ldots,w_{1,0},hV_1),ssk_B)),D,r,aenc(KV_{i-1},pk(esk_{V_{i-1}}))),ssk_U))} \xrightarrow{\nu t.\overline{a}\langle t\rangle} \xrightarrow{a(OrdInf_1,MAC((OrdInf_1,H^l(w_{i,k+l})),H(KV_{i-1})))} \xrightarrow{\nu u.\overline{a}\langle u\rangle} \xrightarrow{a(senc(page_1,KV_{i-1}))} \xrightarrow{\nu g.\overline{a}\langle g\rangle} \xrightarrow{a(H^l(w_{i,k+l}))} \xrightarrow{\nu h.\overline{a}\langle h\rangle} P'$$

$P' \equiv \nu ssk_U.\nu ssk_B.\nu esk_{V_i}.\nu esk_{V_{i-1}}.\nu KV_i.\nu KV_j(\{(hB, pk(ssk_B))/b\_pk\} \mid \{(hU, pk(ssk_U))/u\_pk\} \mid \{(hV_i, pk(esk_{V_i}))/vi\_pk\} \mid \{(hV_{i-1}, pk(esk_{V_{i-1}}))/vi-1\_pk\} \mid \{(s, hV_i)/x\} \mid \{sign((sign((hB, hU, E, w_{j,0}, hV_j, \ldots, H^{k+l}(w_{i,k+l}), hV_i, H^{k_{i-1}}(Enc(H^{k+l}(w_{i,k+l}), v)), hV_{i-1}, \ldots, w_{1,0}, hV_1), ssk_B)), D, s, aenc(KV_i, pk(esk_{V_i}))), ssk_U)/y\} \mid \ldots \mid \{(OrdInf_k, MAC((OrdInf_k, H^l(w_{i,k+l})), H(KV_i)))/z\} \mid \{(senc(page_k, KV_i))/v\} \mid \{H^l(w_{i,k+l})/w\} \mid \{(r, hV_{i-1})/p\} \mid \{(sign((sign((hB, hU, E, w_{j,0}, hV_j, \ldots, H^{k+l}(w_{i,k+l}), hV_i, H^{k_{i-1}}(Enc(H^{k+l}(w_{i,k+l}), v)), hV_{i-1}, \ldots, w_{1,0}, hV_1), ssk_B)), D, r, aenc(KV_{i-1}, pk(esk_{V_{i-1}}))), ssk_U)/q\} \mid \{(OrdInf_1, MAC((OrdInf_1, H^l(w_{i,k+l})), H(KV_{i-1})))/t\} \mid \{senc(page_1, KV_{i-1})/u\} \mid \{H^l(w_{i,k+l})/g\} \mid \{(hU, KV_{i-1}, H^l(w_{i,k+l}))/h\})$

Via active substitutions the identity of the second spender (hU) is revealed.

Social Networks Steganography using Unions of Lucas Sequences

N. Aroukatos[1], **K. Manes**[1], **K. Rigos**[1], **and F. Georgiakodis**[1]
[1]Department of Informatics, University of Piraeus, Piraeus, Greece

Abstract—*Since their introduction, social network sites such as Google+, Facebook, Linkedin and Twitter have attracted millions of users, many of whom have integrated these sites into their daily practices. The above networks assist their users to connect with each other based on shared interests, political views, or activities. Sites also vary in the extent to which they incorporate new information and communication tools, such as mobile connectivity, blogging, and photo or video sharing. The ability of photo sharing gives users the opportunity to use these services to exchange secret information using steganographic methods. In this paper, we examine these possibilities and we propose a unique and safe steganographic method using unions of Lucas sequences.*

Keywords: Steganography, LSB, Fibonacci, Lucas, Zeckendorf

1. Introduction

What makes social network sites unique is not that they allow individuals to meet strangers, but rather that they enable users to articulate and make their social networks visible. This can result in connections between individuals that would not otherwise be made. While social networks (SNs) have implemented a wide variety of technical features, their backbone consists of visible profiles that display an articulated list of "friends" who are also users of the system. Image files constitute an important feature of users' profiles. Most users usually upload a large number of personal images in their profiles. These images can be moments of their daily lives, pictures from holidays e.t.c. Theoretically, it will be easy for a SN user to exchange secret information with a member of the same SN and in many cases with a user outside the SN. The visibility of a profile varies by site and according to the user discretion. Many profiles on Facebook are crawled by search engines, making them visible to anyone. Facebook users who are part of the same "friend network" can view each other's profile, unless a profile owner has decided to deny permission to those in their "friend network". Structural variations around visibility and access are one of the primary ways that SNs differentiate themselves from each other. The public display of connections is a crucial component of SNs. The "friends" list contains links to each profile, enabling viewers to traverse the network graph by clicking through the friends lists. On the other hand, Google+ use Google+ Circles. Circles allow users to create and share information with groups of friends the same way as in their real life social circles. In the next chapters, we will present a unique steganographic algorithm using Unions of Lucas sequences, that can be used from SN users to exchange secret data.

2. Previous steganograpic methods

During the last decade [3] many scientific groups proposed methods that they use and/or extend the LSB (Least Significant Bit) method [1]. Each byte x from $n \times m$ 8-bit RGB image can represented by an 8-bit binary word $b_7 b_6 ... b_0$. According to the RGB model, each pixel of the image is encoded by 3 bytes, that is, 3 integers in the interval [0, 255]. Each byte x is encoded by an 8-bit binary word $b_7 b_6 ... b_0$, where

$$x = \sum_{i=0}^{7} b_i \cdot 2^i \quad \text{and} \quad b_i \in \{0, 1\}.$$

The 8th (rightmost) bit in this word holds less significant color information than the rest. This bit and, in many cases, a few bits more (e.g. the 7th or 6th) [4] can be replaced by a desired secret bit and so a new stegoimage is built bit by bit. The difference between the two images (the original and the stegoimage) is virtually indistinguishable by the human eye [2]. Of course, many steganalysis programs can detect and in many cases reveal the secret data. The limitations of capacity and secrecy motivated the researchers to develop and extend the LSB method by introducing new base systems other than the binary system.

In this direction, the Fibonacci method, presented in [10], uses the Fibonacci numbers to encode the pixel values of a given target image. The Fibonacci numbers are given by the linear recurrence relation

$$F_n = F_{n-1} + F_{n-2}, n > 1, \quad \text{with } F_0 = 0 \text{ and } F_1 = 1.$$

According to Zeckendorf's Theorem, every positive integer x can be uniquely represented as a sum of distinct, nonconsecutive Fibonacci numbers. This sum is called the *Zeckendorf representation* of x [6]. Equivalently, given that $F_k \leq x < F_{k+1}$, for some $k \geq 2$, we have that

$$x = \sum_{i=1}^{k} w_i F_{i+1},$$

where $w_i \in \{0, 1\}$, $w_k = 1$ and we never have $w_i = w_{i+1} = 1$. The sequence $w_n w_{n-1} \cdots w_1$ is a binary word with no consecutive 1's and it is called the *Fibonacci encoding* of x. Such binary words are called *Fibonacci words*.

Obviously, in order to encode all possible pixel values of an 8-bit RGB image, we only need the Fibonacci numbers up to 255, that is the sequence

$$(1, 2, 3, 5, 8, 13, 21, 34, 55, 89, 144, 233)$$

consisting of all F_n, where $2 \leq n \leq 13$. Consequently, each pixel value is encoded by a 12-bit Fibonacci word. In this way, we produce 12 bitplanes for embedding data and so we can increase the stego capacity.

For example, the number 39 has the Zeckendorf representation

$$39 = 0 \cdot 1 + 0 \cdot 2 + 0 \cdot 3 + 1 \cdot 5 + 0 \cdot 8 + 0 \cdot 13 + 0 \cdot 21 + 1 \cdot 34 + 0 \cdot 55 + 0 \cdot 89 + 0 \cdot 144 + 0 \cdot 233$$

and it is encoded by the Fibonacci word 000100010000.

Other scientific groups proposed (using the same main idea) other base systems using prime numbers [7], natural numbers [8] or other more "exotic" sets of numbers [9]. These methods have many benefits while they are easy to implement and work very fast. On the other hand, they have inevitable disadvantages. Once revealed to the public, they cannot provide secrecy to their future users. The reason is that the secrecy of these methods depends on the number set that is revealed.

3. A method using Lucas sequences and a Zeckendorf's Theorem extension

In this section, we present our proposed method, which improves the previously mentioned methods in two directions: Capacity and security. More specifically, increased steganographic capacity is achieved by introducing virtual bitplanes, via a suitable base system (Figure 1). This base system is not unique as in other methods, it is generated from a large set of possible choices, thus operating as an encryption-decryption key.

Consider the quadratic equation $x^2 - Px + Q = 0$, where P and Q are integers. The discriminant of this equation is $D = P^2 - 4Q$ and the roots are

$$a = \frac{P + \sqrt{P^2 - 4Q}}{2} \quad \text{and} \quad b = \frac{P - \sqrt{P^2 - 4Q}}{2}.$$

It also applies that $a + b = P$, $ab = \frac{1}{4}(P^2 - D) = Q$ and $a - b = \sqrt{P^2 - 4Q}$.

For $D \neq 0$, we define

$$U_n(P, Q) = \frac{a^n - b^n}{a - b} \quad \text{and} \quad V_n(P, Q) = a^n + b^n.$$

These sequences are called Lucas sequences [5]. We define the set

$$LU = \{1, 2, 3, 4, 5, 9, 11, 13, 17, 21, 33, 40, 43, 65, 85, 121, 129, 171\},$$

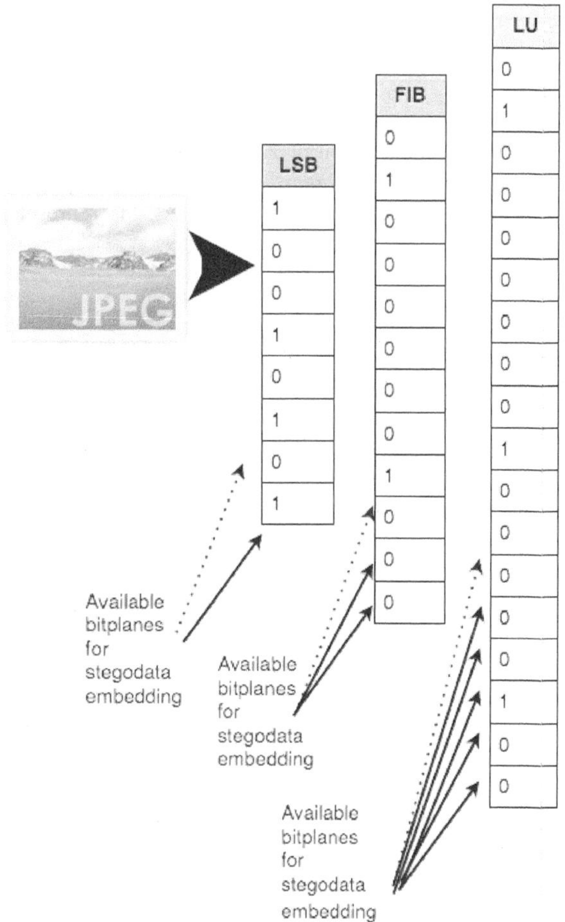

Fig. 1: Stegodata capacity for different methods.

that is,

$$LU = (U(1, -2) \cup V(3, 2) \cup U(4, 3)) \cap [1, 255],$$

where

$$U(P, Q) = \{U_n(P, Q) : n = 0, 1, 2 \ldots\}$$

and

$$V(P, Q) = \{V_n(P, Q) : n = 0, 1, 2 \ldots\}.$$

In general, the sets of the LU are selected using the following rule. We choose randomly from the many members of the Lucas sequences, until Union is "complete", that is, its members taken in ascending order form a sequence of integers in the closed interval $[1, 255]$ which satisfies the following Theorem.

Theorem 1: Let $(a_n)_{n \in \mathbb{N}^*}$ be a strictly increasing sequence of positive integers, with $a_1 = 1, a_2 = 2$ and $a_n + a_{n+1} \geq a_{n+2}$ and $n \in \mathbb{N}^*$. Then, every positive integer x with $a_n \leq x < a_{n+1}$, $n \in \mathbb{N}^*$, can be represented as a sum of different and nonconsecutive terms of the sequence (a_n), with the restriction that the term a_n appears in the sum.

This theorem is stated and proved in [9] and it can be considered as an extension of Zeckendorf's theorem.

According to our Theorem, given a sequence (a_n) satisfying the above requirements, any $x \in \mathbb{N}$ is represented as

$$x = \sum_{i=1}^{n} w_i a_i,$$

where $w_i \in \{0,1\}$, $w_n = 1$ and there is no $i \leq n-1$, such that $w_i = w_{i+1} = 1$. The number n is the unique positive integer satisfying $a_n \leq x < a_{n+1}$. Therefore, each representation corresponds to a unique Fibonacci word $w_n w_{n-1} \cdots w_1$, so that each $x \in \mathbb{N}$ corresponds to at least one Fibonacci word. By choosing the lexicographically greatest corresponding word, we define an encoding for the elements of $\mathbb{N}$. This is equivalent to applying recursively the restriction of the Theorem. The implementation for this is trivial and, therefore, the process of encoding and decoding each integer x is straightforward.

For example, the sequence $(1,2,3,5,7,9,11)$ is a sequence of length 7 which encodes all integers in the interval $[0,22]$. (Note that 22 is obtained as the maximum sum of nonconsecutive terms of the sequence, i.e., $22 = 11+7+3+1$.) Following the restrictions of the Theorem, the number 18 is represented as

$$18 = 11 + 7 \quad \text{or} \quad 18 = 11 + 5 + 2.$$

These representations correspond to the Fibonacci words

$$w = 1010000 \quad \text{and} \quad u = 1001010$$

respectively. Since w is greater than u, the number 18 is encoded by w.

So, every interger number in $[0,255]$ can be written as a sum of elements of the set LU.

For example, some representations of the number 55 are:

$$\begin{aligned}55 &= 1\cdot1+0\cdot2+0\cdot3+0\cdot4+0\cdot5+0\cdot9+1\cdot11\\ &+0\cdot13+0\cdot17+0\cdot21+0\cdot33+0\cdot40+1\cdot43\\ &+0\cdot65+0\cdot85+0\cdot121+0\cdot129+0\cdot171\end{aligned}$$

or

$$\begin{aligned}55 &= 0\cdot1+1\cdot2+0\cdot3+0\cdot4+0\cdot5+0\cdot9+0\cdot11\\ &+1\cdot13+0\cdot17+0\cdot21+0\cdot33+1\cdot40+0\cdot43\\ &+0\cdot65+0\cdot85+0\cdot121+0\cdot129+0\cdot171\end{aligned}$$

or

$$\begin{aligned}55 &= 1\cdot1+0\cdot2+0\cdot3+0\cdot4+0\cdot5+0\cdot9+0\cdot11\\ &+0\cdot13+0\cdot17+1\cdot21+1\cdot33+0\cdot40+0\cdot43\\ &+0\cdot65+0\cdot85+0\cdot121+0\cdot129+0\cdot171\end{aligned}$$

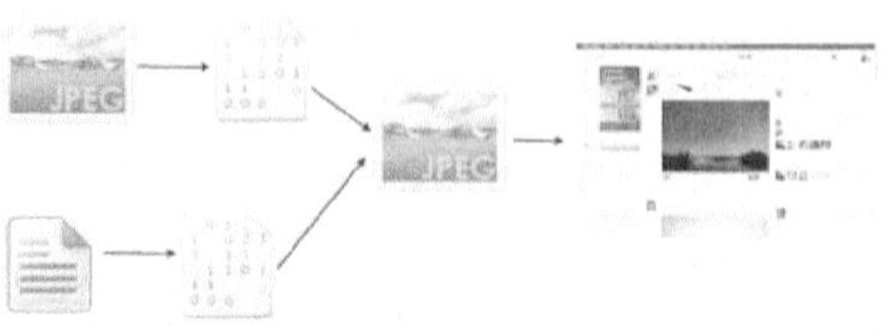

Fig. 2: Testing Procedure.

The above three sums are encoded respectively by the binary words:

$$000001000001000001_{LU}, 000000100010000010_{LU},$$

$$000000011000000001_{LU}.$$

As in the case of Fibonacci numbers, we use the

$$000001000001000001_{LU}$$

representation which is the lexicographically greatest. Obviously, the set LU can be defined as a union of different sets, for different values of P, Q. The user can generate a different set LU and share it with other users as an ecryption-decryption key.

4. Measures and results

We propose this method to use in SN for some reasons. Firstly, by using more bitplanes than previous methods, we can achieve higher stego data capacity. Secondly, by using randomly selected Lucas sequences, we generate each time a different set of LU numbers and this means more secrecy.

Next, we test our method in various SN and we investigate its effectiveness by applying well known image quality measures. The implementation of our method has been done by our own application (Crypto ver. 1.4). For testing purposes, we use some widely used test images such as lena, baboon, airplane, pepper as well as dozens of pictures taken by smartphones and SLR cameras.

To test the ability of SN to host stegoimages, we have built two user accounts in each service. We choose to test Facebook and Google+ while they are the most widely used. Our testing procedure is as follows: First we upload to a user account a large set of stegoimages of different dimensions (Figure 2) and then we download the images from another user account and make our measurements.

We use pictures of various resolutions (from 1200x1200 to 128x128) and various sizes (3Mbytes to 20 Kbytes). After many days of testing, we have the following conclusions:

In the case of Facebook, the algorithm for image resizing and reconstruction destorts our secret data, making the exchange of secret data worthless. In order to deal with this difficulty, we use small images (about 70-80 kb) and we alter

Fig. 3: Test1 and Test2 images.

Number of stego bits	PSNR (LSB)	PSNR (Fibonacci Numbers)	PSNR (Prime Numbers)	PSNR (Lucas Unions-average)
256	57.08	62.01	62.14	65.14
524	53.01	57.97	57.99	61.65
768	51.38	56.36	56.44	58.98
1024	50.16	55.14	55.31	57.02
1280	49.11	54.09	54.28	56.44
1536	48.04	53.03	53.23	55.54
1792	47.24	52.23	52.36	54.45

Table 1: Measures for Test1, Test2 images using 4 bitplanes (average).

only bits satisfying certain conditions involving their energy weight [11].

In Google+, when the image resolution and the image file size do not exceed a certain threshold, the downloaded stegoimage is exactly the same with the stegoimage that we have uploaded. For example, our test shows that a resolution of 512X512 pixel with file size about 100 Kb is safe.

We use two metrics, the Mean Square Error (MSE) and the Peak Signal to Noise Ratio (PSNR) to compare the previous steganographic methods with our method, using images with "qualified in Google+" image resoloution and size. The MSE is the cumulative squared error between the stegoimage and the original image, whereas PSNR is a measure of the peak error. Given two $m \times n$ monochrome images I and K, where one of the images is considered a noisy approximation of the other, the MSE is defined as:

$$MSE = \frac{1}{mn} \sum_{i=0}^{m-1} \sum_{j=0}^{n-1} [I(i,j) - K(i,j)]^2$$

and the PSNR is defined as:

$$PSNR = 10 \log_{10} \left[\frac{MAX_I^2}{MSE} \right],$$

where MAX_I is the maximum possible pixel value of the image I. When the pixels are represented using 8 bits per sample, this is 255. A lower value for MSE means lower image distortion, and as seen from the inverse relation between the MSE and PSNR, this translates to a high value of PSNR.

In the tables 1, 2 and in columns 2, 3, 4 and 5 we see the PSNR measurements for each method. We use 4 bitplanes for data embeding in Test1 image and 7 bitplanes in Test2

Number of stego bits	PSNR (LSB)	PSNR (Fibonacci Numbers)	PSNR (Prime Numbers)	PSNR (Lucas Unions-average)
256	38.86	48.28	54.05	58.82
524	36.02	44.19	49.44	53.95
768	34.46	42.56	47.78	52.11
1024	33.22	41.33	45.76	50.48
1280	32.18	40.28	45.21	49.26
1536	31.29	39.21	44.15	48.21
1792	30.63	38.41	43.20	47.14

Table 2: Measures for Test1, Test2 images using 7 bitplanes (average).

Fig. 4: Images Comparison(Original-LSB-Fibonacci-Prime-Lucas Unions).

image. We can see that our method improves the PSNR value of the stegoimage, when compared to the previous methods. In Figure 4, we can see the original image and the generated stego images of the methods LSB, Fibonacci, Prime, LU as they appear from left to right and top-down. We can observe that the LU method results in less image distortion, when higher bitplanes are also used for embedding.

5. Conclusions

As we see, Facebook and Google+ give us the ability to exchange with other users easily and freely our secret data using stegoimages that we have uploaded. Our method using Unions of Lucas sequences is an improvement over the previous steganographic methods which take advantage of different base systems. It is also very important the fact that our method gives us increased security, because the user can build his own Union of Lucas sequences and therefore generate in some sense a unique steganographic "key". On the other hand, much research and work must be done in order to apply our method in Facebook more efficiently. We must find a method to increase up to a satisfactory level the ability to retrieve the stego data from the downloaded stegoimage.

References

[1] Luo Xiangyang, Liu Bin and Liu Fenlin, 2005. Improved RS method for detection of LSB Steganography. Int. Workshop on Inf. Security and Hiding, Singapore.

[2] Cheddad A., Condell J., Curran K. and McKevitt P., Digital image steganography: Survey and analysis of current methods, Signal Processing, 90, pp. 727–752 (2010).

[3] Tanako S., Tanaka K. and Sugimura T., 2000. Data hiding via steganographic image transformation, IEICE Trans. Fundamentals, E83-A, pp. 311-319.

[4] Shao-Hui C., Tian-Hang Y., Wen Hong-Xun G. 2004. A variable depth LSB data hiding technique in images, Conference on Machine Learning and Cybernetics, Vol. 7, 26-29 pp. 3990-3994.

[5] Eric Weisstein, MathWorld, February 17, 2008 http://mathworld.wolfram.com/LucasSequence.html

[6] G.M. Phillips (2001), "Zeckendorf representation", in Hazewinkel, Michiel, Encyclopaedia of Mathematics, Springer, ISBN 978 - 1556080104 Picione.

[7] Sandipan D., Ajith A. and Sugata S., An LSB Data Hiding Technique Using Prime Numbers, The Third International Symposium on Information Assurance and Security, Manchester, UK, IEEE CS press (2007).

[8] Sandipan D., Ajith A., Sugata S., "An LSB Data Hiding Technique Using Natural Numbers", IEEE Third International Conference on Intelligent Information Hiding and Multimedia Signal Processing, IIHMSP 2007, Nov 26-28, 2007, Kaohsiung City, Taiwan, IEEE Computer Society press, USA, ISBN 0-7695-2994-1, pp. 473-476, 2007.

[9] Aroukatos N., Manes K., Zimeras S. and Georgiacodis F., Data Hiding Techniques in Steganography using Fibonacci and Catalan numbers, 9th International Conference on Information Technology - New Generations, Las Vegas, Nevada, USA (2012).

[10] De Luca, Battisti F., Carli M., Astola J., Egiazarian K., "A Fibonacci LSB data hiding technique", 14th European Signal Processing Conference, EUSIPCO 2006.

[11] Patsakis C. and Alexandris N., "Histographic Steganographic System", New Directions in Intelligent Interactive Multimedia Studies in Computational Intelligence Volume 142, 2008, pp. 67-73, Springer-Verlag Berlin Heidelberg.

Inter-Cloud Trust Model Security: Issues and Challenges

Dana Al-Tehmazi
Department of Computer Science, Ahlia University, Manama, Bahrain
d.altehmazi@gmail.com

Abstract - *Cloud Computing is a new networking technology, which provides a pool of highly scalable and easily accessible virtualized resources, such as development platforms or services, hardware, software, and is capable of hosting end user applications. A major concern in the Cloud is security; some agree that the Cloud is a secure and trusted system, while others seem to think differently. This paper will survey few major security issues and challenges for Cloud Computing, and investigate the trust models in the Inter-Cloud environment area.*

Keywords: Cloud Computing, Cloud Security, Trust Model, Inter-Cloud

I. Introduction

Cloud Computing is the new evolution wave in the Information Technology world in the recent decade which changes the concept of computing from physical model to virtual model. The Cloud is an Internet computing model, where data are hosted on virtual servers and located on the Internet. The Cloud concept is like Wide–Area–Networks (WAN) concept, because Cloud Computing is a collection of computer hardware or virtualizes network resources connected via a network over a geographic area. Cloud Computing network are commonly connected either through the Internet or special arrangements made with Internet Services Providers (ISPs) and it can be accessible from different devices by customer and end users. The major idea of Cloud Computing technology, is that Cloud Computing provides everything from platforms to power computing, and from infrastructure, applications, software, and business processes environments to personal environs.

This paper is organized as follows: Cloud Computing overview is introduced in section II, and Cloud security issues are mentioned in section III. In sections IV and V Cloud security challenges and surveying Inter-Cloud Trust Models are presented respectively. Conclusions are shown In section VI.

II. CLOUD COMPUTING OVERVIEW

A. Web Service Delivered Models

In this section, the Cloud web services and Cloud Computing architecture are discussed. Cloud web services offer a number of common services, such as Software-As-A-Service, Platform As-A-Service and Infrastructure As-A- Service.

1) Software As-A- Service (SAAS)

SAAS is a software delivery model in which applications are hosted by a vendor or service provider and made available to customers over the Internet [2,10]. SAAS helps to increase the availability of applications to global locations and ensures that all application transactions are logged for compliance purposes. The benefits of SAAS to the customer are include as simplified administration, automated update, patch management services, enterprise , wide cooperation, and global accessibility[2,5].

2) Platform As-A-Service (PAAS)

PAAS is an outgrowth of the SAAS application services delivery model. The PAAS service model makes all the facilities required to support the complete life cycle of building and delivering the web applications and services entirely available to developers on the Internet with no installation or software downloads for IT managers and end users. The client capabilities are browser based development tools. Some of these tools are Google Web Toolkit, Google Gears, and Google Gadgets. Windows Azure and Amazon Web Services (AWS) are examples of PAAS services [5,9].

3) Infrastructure As-A- Service (IAAS)

IAAS is the delivery model of computer infrastructure, typically it's a platform virtualization environment as a service. IAAS controls significant data center investments, services, and technology to deliver IT as a service to customers. IAAS suppliers manage the transition and hosting of selected applications on their infrastructure. Customers and users maintain the ownership and management of their applications in the cloud [2]. Rather than purchasing servers, data center space, network equipment and software. IAAS customers and users essentially rent the resources as a fully outsourced service [6]. Usually, the service is billed on a monthly basis similar to a utility company where the customer is charged only for resources utilized. Amazon Elastic Compute Cloud (EC2) and Windows Azure are good examples of IAAS [8].

B. Cloud Computing Architecture

Cloud Computing architecture is divided into two sections: the front end and the back end which are usually connected to each other through the Internet. The front end is the customer side that includes applications and clients computers that are required to access the cloud computing system. The back end which is the cloud side of the structure of the system represents the servers, computers and storages that make the cloud computing services [2,5,6]. The central administer server is monitoring traffic and client demands to ensure that everything is running efficiently. Cloud computing architecture, works as follows:

- The customer sends a service requests.
- The system then finds the accurate resources.
- Once the computer resources are found, the customer request is complete.
- Finally, the results of the service requests are sent to the customer [2,6,12].

Figure 1 represents the Architecture of Cloud computing [34].

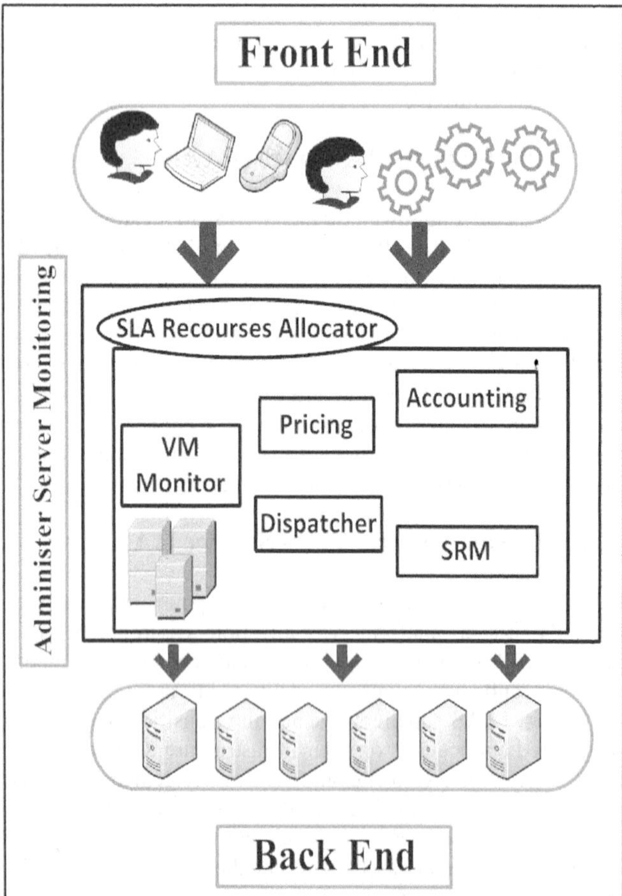

Fig. 1. Cloud Computing Architecture [34]

III. CLOUD SECURITY ISSUES

Security is a major issue in Information Technology business environment. Since customers and users shifted from Grid computing to Cloud computing in their business, many security issues emerged, which is a major concern for the Cloud provider due to the risk of losing customers [40]. The Cloud Computing is mainly built on virtualization environment, that increase more risk of securing the cloud. In this section, the virtual and physical security issues which effect the cloud services will be discussed.

A. Virtual Security issues:

The virtual environment area of the cloud computing is the most sensitive and important part of the cloud. This is because all the devices in the cloud are connected virtually through virtual networks that are running and managing the Information Technology (IT) infrastructures and virtual servers in the cloud. In virtualization technology, multiple Virtual Machines (VM's) can run on top of a single physical machine, and can run on any operating system within each VM's to manage the infrastructure. One of the main virtual security issues in the cloud are attacks on the network between VM's, and the trust between different VM's [3]. There are others problems, such as non-secure Apps and vulnerability in VM's, which allow any unauthorized access.

1) Network Attacks in Virtual cloud:

Running many different virtualization products increases the attackers (especially the hackers) perimeter. Higgins [4] demonstrated the way of how Amazon's cloud computing service (EC2), could be used to hack into other systems by using EC2 cloud service to allow a brute force attack, that will fire 400,000 passwords per second at a secured wireless network. Within a period of twenty minutes the system would had been attacked.

Moreover , the attackers hacked and shut down Sony's online customer networks in April 2011. Hackers used cloud based attacks to disrupt service to roughly 100 million users worldwide [4,12]. No one should forget the most serious threat by hackers which is the Distributed Denial of Services attacks (DDOS) [7].

2) Distributed Denial of Service (DDOS) Attacks:

This attack targets the networks and servers. It makes the network traffic and users being denied to access a certain Internet-based service in the cloud. In worst cases the attackers will use botnets to perform DDOS. In order to stop hackers of attacking the network, face blackmail is provided [21]. DDOS attacks should be considered as threats for cloud providers such AWS, Google Apps, and Microsoft Cloud. These scenarios show us that cloud computing network is still not secure, and this will drive us to non-secure applications.

3) Non-Secure Apps:

Cloud applications security is a complicated issue for organizations and customers if they ignore securing their data before deploying it in the cloud. They need to consider the new threats and attacks spread [31]. Non-Secure applications opens the doors for further threats that could result in attacking the cloud through the network and Application Programming Interface (API). Man in The Middle attack is one of the problems for non-secure apps. This attack works as eavesdropping. Here, the attacker creates independent connections with the victims and transmits messages between them to make them believe that they are talking directly to each other over a private connection when in fact the entire conversation is run and controlled by the attacker. Facebook application is prone to Man- In -The -Middle attack (MITM) on users' data [29].

4) Domain Name Server (DNS) Attacks:

It's easy for attackers to attack DNS in cloud computing when the users or customers try to call the server by name. Because, names are much easier to remember than Internet Protocol (IP) addresses, the attacker will create a temporary malicious cloud to fake the user or customers. Hence using IP address is not always feasible in DNS since customers will route malicious cloud. It may happen that even after all the DNS security procedures are implemented, security problems would exist based on the mode selected between the sender and the receiver[1].

B. Physical Security Issues

Physical security issues are the other part of the cloud computing security. Although the data is stored in the virtual server in the cloud, it must also be stored in physical locations within physical hardware. Physical security in the cloud represents the physical machines and storage in the datacenter. Physical security issues shows as a loss of physical control, human attacks, power failure, access control, and third party trust [41]. Those physical issues need to be protected also from any insider and outsider attackers. Usually the outside threats are easier to deal with than the inside threats because the outside attacks have been already prepared for through risk assessment plans. However, the internal physical security threats in cloud datacenter constitute the top risks in the cloud.

1) Loss of Physical Control:

The loss of physical access control occurs when the customers join the cloud either by keeping their applications in the cloud, or using cloud storage for saving their data. This loss of control results in issues and concerns for the customers, such as trust and privacy of their data in the cloud provider's datacenter, control over their data in the cloud, and legal restrictions by cloud provider [3,30].

a) Privacy and Data

With private, public and community clouds, customer's data may not remain in the same system. In other words, it will not be located in the customer premises any more. This raises multiple legal concerns [18].

b) Control over Data

Customers need to have a full control over their data, and not limited control and accountability within Public clouds such as (IAAS) implementation, and through (PAAS) operations. Customers need to have confidence that the provider will offer services with appropriate controls [3, 16].

c) Legal and Regulatory Compliance

It may be difficult or unrealistic for customers to utilize public clouds if their data need to be processed. This is a subject to legal restrictions or regulatory compliance. Customers should expect providers to build and certify their cloud to address the needs of regulated markets, and achieve certifications and trust confidentiality between customers and providers of the services. [3,19].

2) Human Attacks:

Human attacks happen when unauthorized personal tries to access the datacenter. This attack for datacenter could be man in the middle attack, or malicious insiders such as an employee of the datacenter. These kinds of attacks are examples of the cloud provider losing their significant control over securing datacenters and authorizing human attacker to enter their premises [13,14].

3) Power Failure:

In the event that the datacenter of cloud providers is faced with any kind of problems which causes power failure, and the providers do not have any disaster recovery plan, then the data in the cloud is at risk if it is not saved by the customer and user during the downtime. This give rise to the possibility of attackers accessing the servers through the man in the middle attacks [15]. Amazon's cloud services infrastructure faced a power failure issue in their datacenter in August 2011 where many people who were using AWS were affected by such an outage because all the services were disconnect [11]. Figure 2 shows the security issues discussed above.

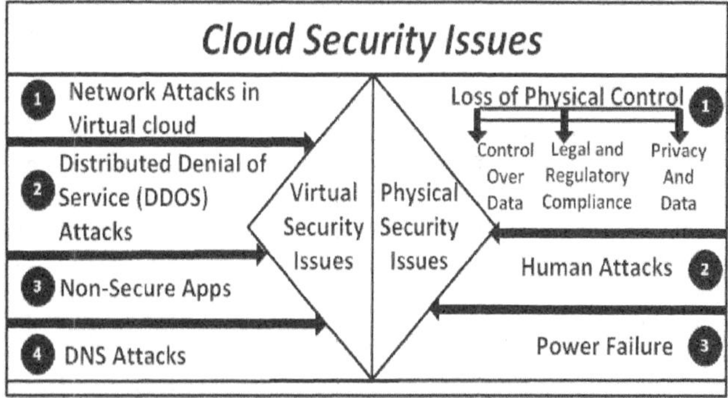

Fig. 2. Security issues in Cloud Computing.

IV. CLOUD SECURITY CHALLENGES

The concept of risk management is the heart of security and privacy. These two factors have become a critical element affecting security in business world and organizations for customers and cloud providers. As it was mentioned in section III, the cloud provider is facing a lot of security issues and they always try to mitigate leaks in their security system. This section will introduce some of cloud security challenges.

A. Trust Management:

Trust Management is one of the main challenges in cloud security. Trust is the factor which ensures the customer feels secure and safe. For the customer to trust cloud servicers, the cloud provider should satisfy the customer's security needs by reinforcing the safety and security in their data center. It is important to be able to assure the security of the data center. The key to establishing trust depends on choosing the right cloud computing model for the organization and the right place, and selecting the right model capacities with the right security mechanisms through Service – Level – Agreements (SLA) between customer and vendor [20]. The idea of trust management is based on having a mutual trust between providers and customers.

B. Transparency:

When a cloud provider does not expose details of their internal policy or technology implementation, customers must trust the cloud provider's security claims. Even so, customers and users require some insights by providers as to provide cloud security, privacy, and how incidents are managed [3,17].

C. Rapid Elasticity:

Rapid elasticity has become one of the security challenges in the cloud computing. Rapid elasticity has enabled many organizations and businesses to scale their operations up and down quickly to meet their demands. It has empowered organizations to cope with a variety of variations of demand such as regular patterns. An example of regular patterns would be running monthly financial reports [33]. The challenges which face rapid elasticity are monitoring, SLAs, attackers profiles (authenticated attackers), and infrastructure security. These challenges become risk that the provisioning process itself could simulate a DoS attack. For example, if the process of requesting resources are fully automated, and there is an application error or a logical failure in the provisioning process, this could drive to refine the requesting process. Finally, these frequent requests would fully utilize all the computing, memories, Central Processing Unit (CPUs), and storage resources within the cloud environment. When new customers initiate a service request, or existing customers wants to increase their allocations of resources and services, the private cloud environment would not be able to respond to these service requests. Hence, the cloud provider should manage and monitor requests to guarantee implementing the preset allocations and ensure that the limits of resources per customers are not breached without prior authorization. These allocations must be centrally configured and adjustable on each consumers basis for their maximum flexibility [33].

D. Virtualized Datacenter:

Virtualized datacenter is one of the cloud computing security challenges. Most of Cloud Computing customers run highly virtualized datacenters. While this technology has been a great enabler of standardization and, in some cases, has yielded savings, this is by far the case for most organizations when digging a bit deeper. The promise of virtualization was that through savings on physical hardware, rapid Return On Investment (ROI) would be realized. Unfortunately, cost has been driven up in many areas. On the hardware side many organization choose to invest in very expensive servers and expand their Storage Area Network (SAN) capacity. Previously, organizations only had Input/output (I/O) intensive and very critical workloads on SAN, but because of virtualization all workloads unexpectedly have consumed expensive SAN storage. In addition, software costs increased due to new technology along with licenses were introduced. Even though many physical servers were removed, administrative overhead still increased because a new technology was introduced that needed to be managed. In addition, all the virtualized workloads still needed to be patched and secured, and because deployment is easier in a virtual environment there were more servers than before. To keep virtualization intact, getting a better uniform management platform, right processes, and high levels of automation and orchestration are needed. Building the right solution that either leverages existing investments or builds a new highly efficient platform as an example Microsoft platform, can help customer reclaim some of the savings that were never realized during the virtualization era. The above concerns are some of cloud security challenges and there are other security challenges, which could be found in [32].

V. INTER-CLOUD

The vision and topology of Inter-Cloud is thought of as an analogy with the Internet itself in Transmission Control Protocol / Internet Protocol (TCP/IP) and the World Wide Web (WWW) data. In a world of Cloud Computing, content, Storage and computing is ubiquitous and interoperable in global network of Clouds known as the Inter-Cloud. Nevertheless, the Inter-Cloud faces many challenges other than solutions of concerning federation, security, interoperability, consumers, trust issues, legal issues, monitoring and Quality of Service (QoS). In the Inter-Cloud environment, overall security issues and requirements can be evaluated from the points of Cloud providers and consumers. Moreover, a provider that participates in both roles in a progressively complex and distributed Inter-Cloud environment has the need for a constant overview about security management components that guide future implementation and amendment within their Cloud system [27].

Inter-Cloud model has several techniques in the cloud computing, such as Inter-Cloud Exchange model, Inter-Cloud Trust model , Inter-Cloud Identity and Access Management with Security Assertion Markup Language (SMAL) and eXtensible Access Control Markup Language (XACML) Model.

A. Inter-Cloud Exchange Model:

Vij et al [22] explained the Inter-Cloud Exchange Model as much as a preferred alternative to each cloud consumers to establish connectivity and collaboration among themselves as P2P, which would not scale physically or in a business sense. Since Inter-Cloud Exchange provider will facilitate the negotiation, discussion and collaboration among disparate heterogeneous cloud environments, Inter-Cloud Root instances will work with Inter-Cloud Exchanges to solve the issues by acting as mediators for allowing connectivity. Subsequently the Inter-Cloud Root offers services such as Trust Authority, Naming Authority, Directory Services, and other root capabilities. Also its working similarly to DNS in the network.

Cloud providers rely on the Inter-Cloud Exchanges to manage trust. As part of the authentication and identification process for matching desired cloud resources, an individual cloud provider will need to signify the required Trust Zone value, such as Local Inter-Cloud Exchange domain or Foreign Inter-Cloud Exchange. Depending on the chosen Trust Zone value, one Inter-Cloud provider might trust another provider to use its storage resources but not to execute programs using these resources. Inter-Cloud Exchanges, in turn, will utilize the desired Trust Zone value as part of the matching preferences and constraints in order to identify matching cloud resources [39].

B. Inter-Cloud Trust Model:

Inter-Cloud Trust Model is a basic level model [38]. With regards to the Public Key Infrastructure (PKI) trust model, the Inter-Cloud Root systems will serve as a Trust Authority in the current trust architecture by issuing certificates in a fashion similar to the Certificate Authority (CA). These certificates must be utilized in the process to establish a trust chain between Inter-Cloud. As per the architecture of the CA, the Inter-Cloud Exchange will need to be the intermediate authority working with CA, to provide limited lifetime trust to the transaction at hand. From Inter-Cloud topology perspectives, Inter-Cloud Roots will provide static PKI CA root like functionality. On the other hand, Inter-Cloud Exchanges will be responsible for the dynamic "Trust Level" model covered on top of the PKI certificate based trust model. In general, the trust model is more of a domain-based Trust model. It distributes the cloud provider's computing environment into several trust domains and nodes. Same domains regularly are much more familiar with each other, they have a higher degree of trust for each other. Figure 3 illustrates the Inter-Cloud Trust Management Model [37].

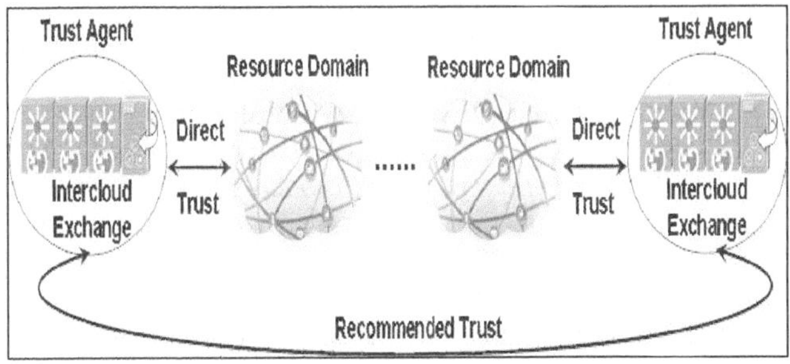

Fig. 3. Inter-Cloud Trust Management Model [37]

C. Inter-Cloud Identity and Access Management:

Gunjan et al [36] present Inter-Cloud Identity and Access Management (IdAM) with Security Assertion Markup Language (SMAL) and eXtensible Access Control Markup Language (XACML) model. Celesti et al [26] suggested that one of the key requirements to be successful is to effectively managing identities. In Inter-Cloud environment, the consumers support for federated identity management standards capabilities rely on prevail federation standards, such as SAML, Web Service (WS) Federation, and Liberty Identity Federation Framework (ID-FF) [24, 25].

The IdAM systems provide various services, such as User Provisioning, User Management, Authentication, Authorization, Role Engineering, Identity Data Integration, and virtualization.

To establish secure federated communication with another cloud provider, the service provider should first trust the other provider by requesting a trust token. The service provider sends two copies of secret keys to the other services provider. These encrypted keys are proof token of the trust services along with the encrypted requested token.

On the other hand, if the recipient cloud is affiliated with another Inter-Cloud Exchange, the Extensible Messaging and Presence Protocol (XMPP) server will send the message to the recipient's XMPP server hosted by the affiliated Inter-Cloud Exchange. This is essentially termed as XMPP federation. It represents the ability of two deployed XMPP servers to communicate and establish links between the servers. In the Inter-Cloud topology, a server accepts a connection from a peer only if the other peer supports Transport Level Security (TLS) and presents a digital certificate issued by a CA that is trusted by the server (*Trusted Federation)*.

In this instance, two cloud providers should have their own Inter-Cloud Root and Inter-Cloud Exchange and these should collaborate amongst each other to build the trust relationship. In this case, the Inter-Cloud Root system will serve as a Trust Authority and act as the Identity Provider to facilitate trust relationship as part of the Trusted Federation. Figure 4 represents the collaborations between Inter-Cloud Root and Inter-Cloud Exchange [22].

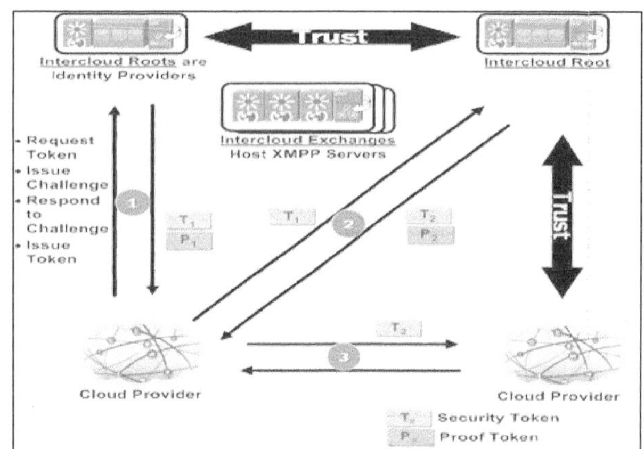

Fig.4.Inter-Cloud Root and Inter-Cloud Exchange Collaboration Scenario [22]

The other scenario is when collaboration between initiating cloud provider and recipient cloud provider is within the same Inter-Cloud Exchange. In this scenario, the Inter-Cloud Exchanges themselves will serve as a Trust Authority and act as the identity providers to mediate the trust relationship as part of the Trusted Federation. Figure 5 represent this scenario[37,39].

With regards to the level of authorization in the Inter-Cloud environment, the support of eXtensible Access Control Markup Language (XACML) compliant entitlement management is highly needed since XACML provides a standardized language and method of access control and policy administration. XACML has been standardized and defines both access control policy language requests and response language. The policy language is used to direct access control policies (who can do what and when). The request and response language expresses queries about whether a specific access should be allowed (needs) and describes answers to those queries (replies) [25].

After surveying the three trust models in Inter-Cloud, it became clear to the author that the best model to be used for implementing trust in cloud or Inter-Cloud is SAML Model. This is because the authentication assertions are used to make people prove their identities, in addition to the attribution of assertions to generate specific information about the customer and users, such as their email addresses or phone numbers. Finally the SAML Protocol defines the way that SAML act to get assertions using Simple Object Access Protocol (SOAP) over Hypertext Transfer Protocol (HTTP) [28].

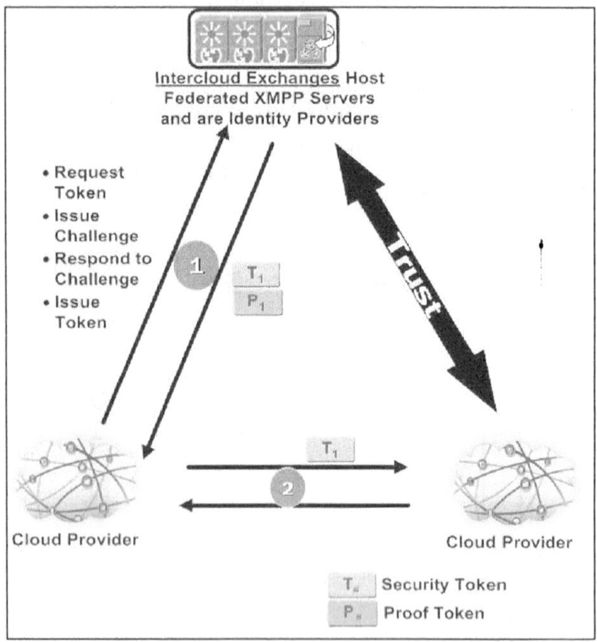

Fig. 5. Intra-Cloud Exchange Collaboration Scenario[39]

VI. CONCLUSIONS

Cloud computing requires some standardization system to ensure the security in the cloud environment and a third party certification to ensure that standards are met as per the requirements. Identity management is an early challenge that must be resolved since identification and authentication must be performed not only for customers and users, but also for resources as well within heterogeneous cloud environments. Apart from the Identity Management (IdM), solutions for the Inter-Cloud should be interoperable with current identity management systems in organizations in order to enable the outsourcing advance services such as user provisioning, access control, authentication, and certifications. This paper has addressed and surveyed some of the issues and challenges in cloud computing security while also discussing the three trust models in Inter-Cloud environment and selecting the best solution for solving authentication and trust security issues. Future work will concentrate on investigating the other security issues in the Inter-Cloud federation such as security issues for implementing trust relationship between platforms and infrastructures as services in the cloud computing, the Inter-Cloud exchange issues, the storage layer, and the data layer issues in the cloud. These issues related to security management of the Inter-Cloud environment.

REFERENCES

[1] Diana Kelley, “Cloud computing security: Routing and DNS security threats”, http://searchcloudsecurity.techtarget.com/tip/Cloud-computing-security-Routing-and-DNS-security-threats , June 2009.

[2] J. Rittinghouse, J. Ransome, Cloud Computing Implementation, Management , and Security, Florida, CRC Press, 2010.

[3] J. Winkler, Securing the Cloud: Cloud Computer Security Techniques and Tactics, Massachusetts, Syngress, 2011.

[4] Kelly Jackson Higgins, “Cloud-Based Crypto Cracking tool to be unleashed at black hat DC”, http://www.darkreading.com/authentication/167901072/security/encryption/229000423/cloud-based-crypto-cracking-tool-to-be-unleashed-at-black-hat-dc.html, January 10, 2011.

[5] T. Mather, S. Kumaraswwamy, and S. Latif, Cloud Security and Privacy An Enterprise Perspective on Risks and Compliance, California, O'Reilly Media, 2009.

[6] D. Sarna, Implementing and Developing Cloud Computing Applications, Florida, CRC Press ,2011.

[7] L. YANG, T. ZHANG, J. SONG, J. WANG, P. CHEN, "DEFENSE OF DDOS ATTACK FOR CLOUD COMPUTING", *IN PROC. THE 2012 IEEE 12TH INTERNATIONAL CONFERENCE ON COMPUTER SCIENCE AND AUTOMATION ENGINEERING (CSAE'12)*, CHINA, PP. 626-629, MAY 25-27, 2012.

[8] SKY TAP, BLOG, “DEMYSTIFYING SAAS, PAAS, AND IAAS”, HTTP://WWW.SKYTAP.COM/BLOG/DEMYSTIFYING-SAAS-PAAS-AND-IAAS, MARCH 22, 2011.

[9] R. Jennings, Cloud computing with windows Azure Platform, Indianapolis, Wiley Publishing, 2009.

[10] B. Melvin and J. Greer, Software as a Service Inflection Point, New York, iUniverse, 2009.

[11] Datacenter Dynamics, Inside the market, “Power outage brings down Amazon's cloud customers”, http://www.datacenterdynamics.com/focus/archive/2012/06/power-outage-brings-down-amazon%E2%80%99s-cloud-customers, Jun, 15, 2012.

[12] Amazon White Paper, "Introduction to Amazon Virtual Private Cloud", http://aws.amazon.com/about-aws/whatsnew/2009/08/26/introducing-amazon-virtual-private-cloud/ , pp. 6-8, Aug 26, 2009.

[13] R. Gellman, "Privacy in the louds: risks to privacy and confidentiality from Cloud Computing," World Privacy Forum, Feb. 2009.

[14] J. Szefer, P. Jamkhedkar, Y. Chen, R. Lee, "Physical attack protection with human-secure virtualization in data centers", *in Proc. The 2012 IEEE/IFIP42nd International Conference on Dependable System and Networks Workshops (DSN-W'12)*, Boston, pp. 1-6, June 25-28, 2012.

[15] C. MacLeod, "Is that a hacker next to you?", *IEEE Communications Engineer*, vol.5, no. 1, pp. 36 - 37, February-March 2007.

[16] L. Kaufman, "Data Security in the World of Cloud Computing," *IEEE Security and Privacy*, vol. 7, no.4, pp. 61-64 , August 2009.

[17] R. Bifulco, R. Canonico, G. Ventre and V. Manetti, "Transparent migration of virtual infrastructures in large datacenters for Cloud computing", *in Proc. The 2011 IEEE Symposium on Computers and Communications (ISCC'11)*, Kerkyra, pp. 179 - 184 , June 28 -July 1, 2011.

[18] Springer Link, "Privacy by Design: essential for organizational accountability and strong business practices", http://www.globalprivacy.it/Allegati_Web/57C2B8AA758546A0B76D5668F5CF5E16.pdf , 2010.

[19] J. Ruiter and M. Warnier, "Privacy regulations for Cloud Computing: compliance and implementation in theory and practice computers," Privacy and Data Protection: an Element of Choice, ch. 17, Springer, 2011.

[20] N. Coleman, M. Borrett, Cloud Security, Who do you trust?, New York, IBM Global Services, October 2010.

[21] W. Stallings, Network Security essentials Applications and Standers, New Jersey, Prentice Hall, 2011.

[22] D. Vij, D. Bernstein, "IEEE P2302TM/D0.2 Draft Standard for Inter-Cloud Interoperability and Federation (SIIF)", Institute of Electrical and Electronics Engineers, Technical Report IEEE P2302/D0.2, January 2012.

[23] SAML. Xml. Org, SAML Wiki Knowledgebase, "SAML Development", http://saml.xml.org/saml-specifications , July 1, 2008.

[24] S. Cantor, J. Kemp, D. Champagne, "Liberty ID-FF Bindings and Profiles Specification", *Liberty Alliance Project*, vol. 2.0, pp. 1-44,September12, 2004.

[25] OASIS, "eXtensible Access Control Markup Language (XACML) Version 2.0", http://docs.oasis-open.org/xacml/2.0/access_ control-xacml-2.0-core-spec-os.pdf , February 2005.

[26] A. Celesti, F. Tusa, M. Villari, and A. Puliafit, "Security and Cloud Computing: InterCloud Identity Management Infrastructure", *in Proc. The 2010 IEEE 19th International Workshop on Enabling Technologies: Infrastructures for Collaborative Enterprises (WETICE'10)*, Larissa, pp. 263-265, June 28-30, 2010.

[27] C .Priya, N. Prabakaran, "Security Management in Inter-Cloud", *International Journal of Emerging Trends and Technology in Computer Science (IJETTCS)*, vol. 1, no. 3, pp. 233-235, September-October 2012.

[28] Gluu Blog, "How Does SAML Work? IdP's & SP's", http://www.gluu.org/blog/how-does-saml-work-idps-sps/, December 19,2012.

[29] IT World Blogs, "Facebook's man in the middle attack on our data", http://www.itworld.com/it-managementstrategy/247344/facebooks-man-middle-attack-our-data , Feb5, 2012.

[30] Skatter tech, News Hub, "Sony Online Entertainment Shut Down, Account Information In Danger", http://skattertech.com/2011/05/sony-online-entertainment-shut-down-account-information-in-danger/, May 2, 2011.

[31] John Kinsella," 5 more key cloud security issues", http://www.csoonline.com/article/717307/5-more-key-cloud-security-issues?page=3 , Sep 26, 2012.

[32] Microsoft White Paper, "Datacenter Virtualization", http://social.technet.microsoft.com/Search/en-US?query=virtualization%20datacenters%20with%20author&refinement=90&beta=0&ac=5, pp. 1-27, June 2008.

[33] Microsoft TechNet, Wiki, "Cloud Security Challenges" , http://social.technet.microsoft.com/wiki/contents/articles/6651.cloud-security-challenges.aspx, , Jun 6, 2012.

[34] Christian Vecchiola, Dexter Duncan, and Rajkumar Buyya, "The Structure of the New IT Frontier: Part 2 – Market Oriented Computing", http://texdexter.wordpress.com/2009/12/21/cloud-computing/, December 21, 2009.

[35] D. Bernstein and D. Vij, "Intercloud Security Considerations", *in Proc. The 2010 IEEE Second International Conference on Cloud Computing Technology and Science (CLOUDCOM'10)*, Washington, pp. 537-544, Nov 30 – Dec 3, 2010.

[36] K. Gunjan, G. Sahoo, and R. Tiwari, "Identity Management in Cloud Computing –A Review", *International Journal of Engineering Research & Technology*, vol. 1, no. 4, pp. 1-5, June 2012.

[37] D. Bernstein and D. Vij, "Intercloud Exchanges and Roots Topology and Trust Blueprint", *in Proc. The 2011 International Conference on Internet Computing(ICOMP'11)*, Las Vegas, pp. 135-142, July 18-21, 2011.

[38] J. ABAWAJY, "ESTABLISHING TRUST IN HYBRID CLOUD COMPUTING ENVIRONMENTS", *IN PROC. THE 2011 IEEE 10TH INTERNATIONAL CONFERENCE ON TRUST, SECURITY AND PRIVACY IN COMPUTING AND COMMUNICATIONS (TRUSTCOM'11)*, CHANGSHA, PP. 118-125, NOV 16-18, 2011.

[39] D. Bernstein and D. Vij, "Intercloud Directory and Exchange Protocol Detail Using XMPP and RDF", in Proc. *The 2010 IEEE 6th World Congress on Services (SERVICES-1'10)*, Miami, PP. 431-438, July 5-10, 2010.

[40] A survey on security issues of federated identity in the cloud computing *(IEEE 4th International Conference on Digital Object Identifier: 10.1109/CloudCom.2012.6427513)*, Page(s): 532 - 565), 2012.

[41] Cloud security challenges *(Telecommunication Systems, Services, and Applications (TSSA), 2012 7th International Conference on Digital Object Identifier : 10.1109/TSSA.2012.6366028)*, Page (s) : 88 – 91) 2012.

SESSION

SECURITY MANAGEMENT, SECURITY EDUCATION, AND HARDWARE SECURITY II

Chair(s)

Dr. Andrea Huszti

Securing the bolts before the horse has bolted: A new Perspective on Managing Collaborative Assurance

Simon Reay Atkinson, *Fellow IET*, Seyedamir Tavakolitabaezavareh, David Walker, Li Liu, and Liaquat Hossain

Complex Civil Systems Research Group, Faculty of Engineering and IT, University of Sydney, Australia

Abstract – *We suggest that the bureaucratic response to leaks, e.g. wiki-leaks, has frequently been to add more controls in an effort to securitize the spaces in which the breach has occurred or may occur in the future. We argue that the result of these info/techno-socio controls is to create a socio-info/techno ecology less capable of problem solving. These coordinating rules and controls (CRC) take time / bandwidth to administer and, sometimes deliberately, make things difficult. Often, they do so by simultaneously creating a climate of fear, where adherence to process is rewarded and innovative dissent is punished. Controls may therefore impinge upon the collaborative social influence (CSI) networks necessary for innovation, adaptation and problem solving – so breaches may actually increase. We take a network perspective to security based upon ambidexterity between CRC and CSI networks and creating assuredness / trust to enable a secure and healthy organisational ecology.*

Keywords: coordination rule & control (CRC); collaborative social influence (CSI); problem-solving; ambidexterity; instrumentation

1 Introduction

This paper considers that healthy organisations have 'a critical capacity for solving problems', [1]. Warren and Warren [1] further identified three dimensions of *connectedness* (see also Thibaut and Kelley [2]): *identification* with the organisation (they referred to as neighbourhood); interstitial *interaction* within the organisation and existential *linkages* outside the organisation [3]. Warren and Warren [1] also considered integral neighbourhoods with close interstitial and good existential contacts and anomic neighbourhoods, where individuals have few interstitial or existential contacts. Backman & Smith [3] also reported that members (they called residents) of integral organisations were reported to be healthy and capable of organising for collective action (problem solving); whereas unhealthy, anomic organisations were unlikely to mobilize collectively or support each other.

We suggest that problem solving is indicative of both collaboration and shared awareness, see Mintzberg [4]. The ability to engage in efficient and effective collaborative work in the types of social networks described by Latour [5] rests not only on the experience of the people but on the availability and reliability of information. Enabling collaboration incurs costs in terms of technology, networking, and training of users. And coordination remains a necessary activity that is required for the group to complete its tasks. Similarly, breakdowns in collaboration (such as misunderstandings, failure to report, leaking, etc) can lead to delays and missed opportunities – all increasing the cost of collaborating and potentially offsetting its benefits. The political and organisational context in which collaboration takes place also influences individual performances and the group within the collaborative process. It can affect whether people collaborate to maximise group or individual outcomes [6]. Hence, Cohen et al [7] differentiate between 'cooperative-' and 'adversarial collaboration'.

A more 'normal' characteristic of *dynamic social* networks (DsNs) is of people working and collaborating in large-scale, dynamically reconfigurable networks across a range of organizations (commercial, civil and non-governmental), see Whitworth & de Moor [8]. In such situations, teams potentially consist of many members communicating and sharing information with each other across organisational and potentially national boundaries: the extent and sheer volume of this information can become too much for them to deal with efficiently, see Endsley et al [9]. In fact, it can reduce 'shared awareness' and so the trust individuals have in other collaborators and the associated technology. Dabbish and Kraut [10] showed that workers given a full view of a remote team-mate's activities were distracted from their own work. This problem will increase with the number of team members to be monitored, where monitoring itself can be a form of control in large-scale networks. Whereas this might be acceptable in a 'control tolerant' system [11], it is likely to lead to 'collaboration breakdown' in 'influence tolerant' regimes relying on the transfer of knowledge. For example, in the military domain, a study of watch-changes in naval operations revealed the need for better 'situation awareness' support for incoming personnel, see Endsley & Strater [12].

As information-technology (IT) has advanced, the social management of organizations has become more complex. Managers at all levels of the organization need both a deeper understanding of interactions between the individual, group, and organizational level and confidence / trust in the information and knowledge being exchanged [13]. An emphasis on IT and data rather than on social knowledge [14] has often led to internal competition even hyper-competition (by resource constraint) as a result of increased accessibility to information [15]. Consequently, managers need to become better at identifying the systems they are working with and 'managing the social capital via which [information] is both produced and shared' [16].

In dealing with complex systems, the division between management & control and leadership & influence becomes potentially more pronounced. Drawing on work by Alberts & Hayes [17] and Reay Atkinson & Moffat [18] we differentiate between *fidelity*, in terms of 'removing noise from an info/techno-socio system' (see Atlan & Cohen [19]) and 'agility', in terms of a socio-techno system's 'reflective capacity' (indicative of *fitness* see De Rosa [20]) to 'identify mutations (noise) as a vehicle for adaptation', see Atlan [21]. We suggest: *Management & Control may be a function of rules, time, bandwidth and fidelity, whereas Command & Leadership may be a function of influence, trust, collaboration and agility.* Note that while the word 'command' is often associated with strict rules and control mechanisms, it is being used here in the military sense, where it is roughly synonymous with leadership.

We consider, after He & Wong [22], that successful companies are constantly balancing between the *exploitative* (delivered *in time* by management & control) and the *explorative* (delivered *over time* through Command & Leadership). The balancing between management & control (the exploitative) and command & leadership (the explorative) to keep an organisation *in kilter* is known also as *ambidexterity* [22]. We consider that the ability to *dynamically balance* between the *exploitative* and the *explorative* is indicative of a systems ability to problem solve and, therefore, of its health.

In Section II we develop the methodology for modelling human terrains and *instrumenting* them. In Section III, we report on the results of human terrain modelling of a warship crew with implications for the private and public sectors. In Section IV we consider *ambidexterity* and we conclude by considering the need for organisations to retain their ability to problem solve in order to maintain a healthy working ecology in which dissent appropriately expressed may be considered as an expression of loyalty to be rewarded as opposed to leaking or whistle-blowing, to be punished. Organisations that do not leak, it is argued, tend to be able to problem solve and are therefore healthy places to 'be'. Whereas the reverse may be true of unhealthy organisations.

2 System Modelling & Instrumentation

Latour [5] maintains that 'if an anthropology of the modern world were to exist, its task would consist in describing in the same way how all branches of our government are organised'. The method developed in this paper builds on work by Buckley and Chapman [23] to allow researchers 'to formulate and pursue problems in their own terms' in order to develop an ethnography and ontology of a system to be modelled. This paper considers design and adaptation as a social system [24;25].

The Design Research Methodology (DRM) proposed by Blessing et al. [26;27]; informed by the Spiral Model proposed by Eckert et al. [28;29] is applied to model different organisations. The ethnographic process adopted conceptualises the question(s); develops the model; agrees the ontology; develops the ecology / human terrain; instruments the model (in simple terms calibrating the model so that it reflects what is being seen); falsifies model fitness by testing against the ontology / other criteria / questions and finally adapts the model and reflects upon its *fitness*. Interviews formed a central part of the ethnographic process, as they represent a key deductive methodology for providing evidence in support of a case and arguments deployed [30].

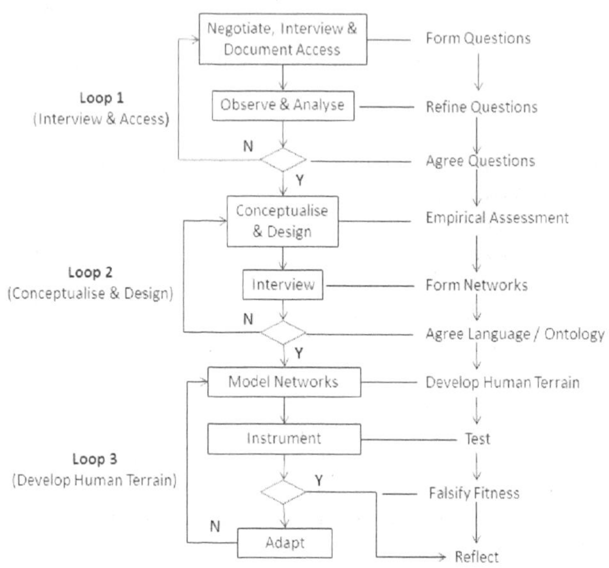

Figure 1: A methodology for dynamic network analysis [28, 29, 31, 32, 33]

The Dynamic Network Analysis tool consists of three loops:

Loop 1: three streams of semi-structured informal interviews were established. The first stream provided subject headings and research questions. The second stream provided the means of 'gaining rapport' with subject matter interviewees [34] and verifying the scope and nature of research. The third stream identified specific questions that may be researched.

Loop 2: Took these questions to conceptualise the design of models that might represent what was being identified and to begin forming the dyadic matrices [2; 35] necessary to design and build applicable networks. Loop 2 moved from a more deductive and qualitative approach in Loop 1 [36; 37] towards a more inductive and quantitative approach [38; 39], based upon data collection and the forming of networks. The second loop 'triangulated' data against observations, methods and modelling theorem to combine both quantitative and qualitative approaches [40].

Loop 3: the third loop took the dyadic matrices established and verified in Loop 2 to develop working models based upon the scenarios quantitatively and qualitatively described by Loops 1 and 2. Kitchenham et al [41] note although 'case studies cannot provide the scientific rigor of formal experiments, they can provide sufficient information to help judge if specific methods will benefit a project or an organisation'. Loop 3 develops, from scenarios, the means of network modelling relevant human terrain and instruments these models by testing them against interviewee's knowledge and expectations through a process of falsification [39].

Building on the Blessing and Chakrabarti [42] high level Design Research Methodology, a *process* for 'triangulating different sources' including: data sources (from interview and historical record); different evaluators (e.g. instruments developed); perspectives of the same data sets (through falsification of alternative network models) and methods (method triangulation) was established, see Patton [43]. This is a more sophisticated model than those considering only 'data sources' largely abstracted from 'open-ended interviews; focus interviews; structural interviews / surveys and observations (direct and participant) to establish convergence of evidence [30]. Like Denzin [40], we see triangulation as 'the use of multiple methods...[to] partially overcome the deficiencies that flow from one case study, one model, one investigation, one *instrument* or one method'.

Unlike Yin's [30] triangulation model that deals with the convergence of interviews, historical records and observations as independent inputs to create 'facts' or evidence, we consider these inputs as interactive and co-dependent. The evidential plays a role in qualifying and quantifying the five different sources of evidence and creating a believable narrative. The methodology adopted in this paper follows two *processes*: an *inductive*, reasoning approach of developing modelling theorems and falsifying them [38; 39] and a *deductive* approach of proving theorems through verification [36; 37]. The process enables the convergence and *synthesising* of evidence from multiple sources (interview and archives; instruments; shared perspectives; and human terrain models) so as to 'establish the facts'. To overcome the potential for a positivist / constructivist validation bias, identified by Lincoln & Guba [44] and Cho & Trent [45]. After Popper [39] and Forrest and Hofmeyr [46], 'falsification through negative logic' is applied.

Rowland [47] observed 'the differences from military trials and real combat can be an order of magnitude different'. Ford et al [48] built on 'joint composable object models', see Lutz et al [49], to consider a 'synthesised ontology of players and platforms'; 'resources as a thing that can do something, through the use of capabilities [e.g. tanks, humans, and software systems]; 'capability as a discrete piece of functionality that belongs to a resource' and 'a confederation as a set of resources'. Building on Ford et al [48] and ATL [50], this paper considers the role of 'instrumentation as a dynamic analysis tool' and instrumentation as:

> 'The ontological modelling of dynamic system ecologies so as to identify what has occurred at different combinations and scales in order to synthesise, *analyse*, *influence* and / or control future socio-info/techno and info/techno-socio phenomenon, strategies and processes' [33].

3 A Tale of Two Ships

Following the methodology set out in Section II, two identical Frigate Models were constructed. In one model, system identification had been undertaken to classify which of the five ship departments were *exploitative* (and more techno-socio/info [51]), coordination, rule and control (CRC) focussed [52] (such as the Navigation, Marine Engineering and logistics watch-keeping departments dealing with issues of control & management, in time) and those that were more *explorative* (more socio-info/techno [53]) Collaborative Social Influence (CSI) [54] focussed (such as planning and systems engineering departments and those dealing with command & influence, over time). Overall system Command & Influence and Management & Control network-models were developed in the Graphical Modeling System (GMS) [55] and applied using specially designed networks within the Change Prediction Method (CPM) [56; 57]. In broad terms, one Frigate model was constructed allowing for Reflective Capacity [33] within the explorative departments and individual nodes. In simple terms, not all the individuals / departments in this Ship were under control and observational reporting management type techniques (unless appropriate); whereas, in the other ship all individuals / departments were. The question being addressed through these two models was:

> 'Whether or not *noise* in the system, introduced by generating reflective capacity (in other words not having all individuals/ departments under control all of the time) contributed to shared awareness (seen also to be indicative of collaboration / CSI) and so improved problem solving'.

A method for identifying shared awareness when unique Bose-Einstein Networks formed (see Albert and Barabási [58]) was developed in CPM [33]. In these networks, 'any particular statistical distribution represents an outcome...they arise when quantum mechanical systems are considered [entangled] with classical systems' [59]. Such networks are fully aware and because of their 'powerful attractiveness' (described as 'Black Holes' by Moffat in Reay Atkinson [18]), such networks grow without the need for rules or formal organizations to set conditions, interpret them or enable collaboration'.

A number of different identical ship models were developed in CPM and tested through *instrumentation* by varying the number of identified linkages of one of the five Departments. This paper reports these results as they pertain to the calculated degree of control (Csy) being exercised on the system and system shared awareness ($SAsy$). In terms of ambidexterity, one Ship effectively balanced dynamically between the *exploitative* (by CRC) and the *explorative* (through CSI); whereas the other ship was driven entirely *exploitatively*. In other words, the *ambidextrous* model was considered potentially capable of both commanding & influencing *and* managing & controlling. It should be recalled, that each of the models tested had exactly the same number of linkages.

In design terms, Dahl [60], argues 'agents exert social influence [he defines power in terms of a relationship between people] through the manipulation of a base of resources, and resources like recognition, appreciation, and friendliness as well as economic rewards'. Wrong [61] saw people exercising mutual influence and control over one another's behaviour in all social interactions. He considered social influence to be: 'a particular kind of social relation without minimising what it continues to share with all social relations'. Meanwhile, Hickson et al [62] noted the division of social power analysis into two distinct paths from a 'social viewpoint', and Anderson

[63] concluded that they formed a 'convenient intersection between risk, trust and technology'. Felici [64], noting the 'complexity of trust' and that it was 'unfeasible to take a definitive model', suggested (after McKnight & Chervany [65]) a 'typology of trusts' which may (after Felici [64] and Hickson et al [62]) broadly align with structural; behavioural and relational divisions [33]:

Path 1) **Structural (more CRC)**: Consisting of *System Trust,* which exists to the extent that people trust the organisation and its technology to support people in their duties provided they are commensurate with the hierarchy, its structures, rules and identified sources of power; and *Dispositional / Transactional Trust* in which people are entrusted to behave in certain ways and to dispose of resources / agree exchanges provided they are commensurate with the hierarchy, its structures, rules and identified sources of power;

Path 2) **Behavioural (more CSI):** Consisting of *Trusting Behaviour* in which people are entrusted to behave reliably in certain ways based upon interpersonal behaviours, personal traits and accepted rules of conduct; and *Trusting Beliefs* in which people are entrusted to behave reliably in certain ways based upon a commonly held set of values, traditional ways of behaving and conducting themselves;

Relational (Ambidextrous) – between Path 1) and Path 2) / CRC and CSI: Consisting of *Situational [Aware] Decision Trust* in which people can be entrusted to behave reliably in certain ways based upon a systems hierarchy, its structures, rules and identified sources of power; and *Trusting Intention* in which people will behave reliably in certain ways based upon the common understanding of a systems hierarchy, its structures, rules and identified sources of power. In the *exploitative* series of ship models, it was possible by generating a large number of formal linkages applying a high degree of internal controls to generate a system capable of exercising a relatively high Systems Shared Awareness, of between 45-55 and 55-65%, see Figure 2. However, as calculated against the number of formal linkages provided the exploitative system's shared awareness was 'at best equal to and never more than the sum of its parts'. The sum of a system's parts is taken to be the total number of identified network links divided by the total theoretical number of possible links. We actually identify through this process more links than theoretically specified.

As one reduced the number of linkages, the model moved to a point at which it essentially collapsed to a position where it was capable of exerting a high degree of *interstitial* control but at significantly reduced system shared awareness – typically, at best, 20% of System Shared Awareness and less than 44% of the sum of its parts, Figure 2. The relationship between the two parts we consider as between a centrally coordinated organisation with its services being contracted out – as if the ship's command was relying on contracted staff to provide all its services, propulsion, logistics, weapons, etc. Two significant gaps are identified to have occurred, those of: Authority-Responsibility (between the Centre and the Contracted) and Responsibility-Authority (between the Contracted and the Centre), see (Purser & Cabana [66]). In terms of problem solving, the contractees can only comply with the contract and the centre has no real and tangible authority over them other than through the contract and the contracted company. The organisation (as a whole, incorporating the centre, contracted companies and contractees) is largely prevented from problem solving – in other words it is an unhealthy (and potentially unsafe) place to be. An example may be the unintended risks introduced to British Rail on radical privatisation in the 1990s and attributed as being the reasons behind the Paddington (1999) and Potters Bar (2002) fatal accidents. But there are also military ramifications regarding the increasing use of Private Military Companies (PMCs) to provide logistics support to Western armies.

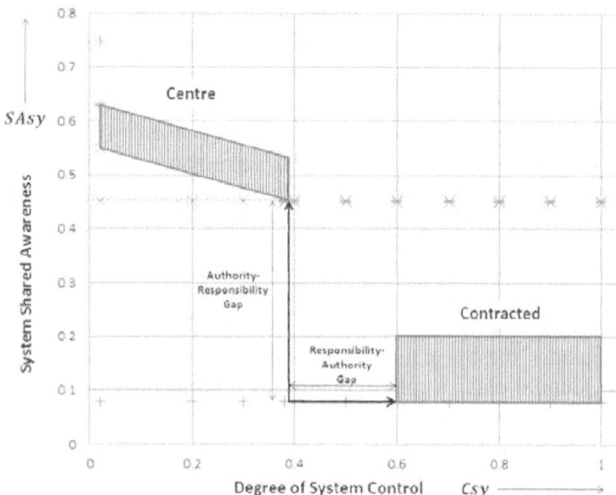

Figure 2: Centre and Contracted Vertical Polarisation

An alternative model was considered in which a single ship's company is maintained but one that achieves control through vertical polarisation – or *integration* – in which the different departments are essentially stood up as competing business units, as favoured by many accountancy consulting models applied widely in the private and public sectors, Figure 3. In this model, the centre comprising also the budget holders continues to exist in isolation of the newly defined and vertically integrated Business Units. Because ostensibly the Business Units remain part of the whole organisation, it is possible to *exploitatively* coordinate and train individual units to perform relatively well. That said, results from the Frigate models indicate that neither the centre nor the Business Units can achieved a shared awareness greater than or equal to the sum of their formal linkages.

In this example, a Responsibility-Authority gap exists between the Centre and Budget Holders and the Business Units. As example, investigations into the Deepwater Horizon Accident by the US National Commission [67] and the UK House of Commons [68] concluded, inter alia:

> The most significant failure at Macondo – and the clear root cause of the blowout – was a failure of industry management. Most, if not all, of the failures at Macondo can be traced back to underlying 'failures of management and communication'...within BP and other companies...and between BP and its contractors [67], and;

> We find some conflict in the reports from the HSE about bullying and harassment on rigs and the 'assurances' of the industry that 'sincere whistleblowers' will be 'heard and

protected'. It is important and necessary that the 'offshore safety culture' is 'cascaded' throughout the 'supply chain', from existing contractors at all levels, through to new-entrants on to the UK Continental Shelf [68].

We conclude there needs to be 'clarity on the identity and hierarchy of liable parties' to ensure that the Government, and hence the taxpayer, do not have to pay for the consequences of offshore incidents [68].

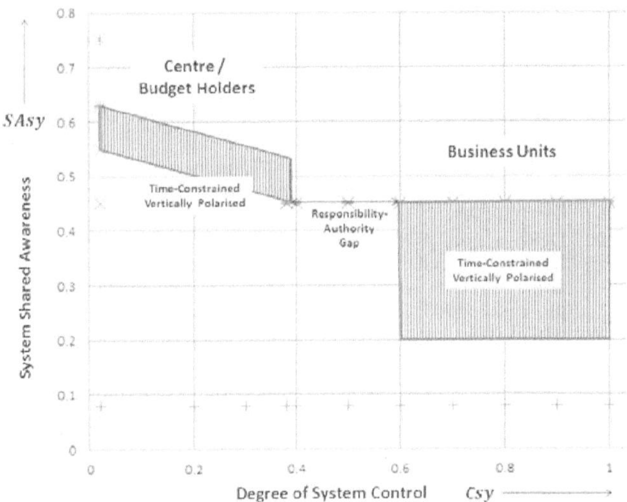

Figure 3: Centre and Business Unit Vertical Polarisation

In such cases, the contractor, business unit and budget holder appeared focussed, not on providing the best product for the company to market to the consumer but competing – through vertical polarisation – on service delivery, at best (cheapest) price, as in aspects of Value for Money (VfM). These type of arrangements also exist in government, for example the UK Ministry of Defence (MoD) which has been increasingly criticised by the UK National Audit Office (NAO) for its lack of financial awareness and concentration on vertically integrated arrangements such as Private Finance Initiatives (PFIs), usually at the expense and real risk of taxpayers, service personnel and public service employees [69]. The underlying issue to all these types of business models is that they may create *unhealthy* and even unsafe working ecologies (for example the crash of Royal Air Force Nimrod XV230 in Afghanistan, September 2006 [69]) in which problems can no longer be solved.

4 Ambidexterity

The final organisational construct revealed by this research, showed that the ambidextrous, *explorative* model combining both command & influence and management and control, CSI and CRC was time-varying [70; 71] and could adapt over time, Figure 4. Despite reducing the number of formal linkages, the organisation continued to adapt horizontally and, in actual fact, to generate between 12 and 20% more shared awareness than formally provided: it was more than the sum of its parts. As significantly, the U shaped time varying, shared awareness curve provided a safe setting (one can roll back to a stable equilibrium position) and give potential indication of organisational failure as one gets towards 60% System Control.

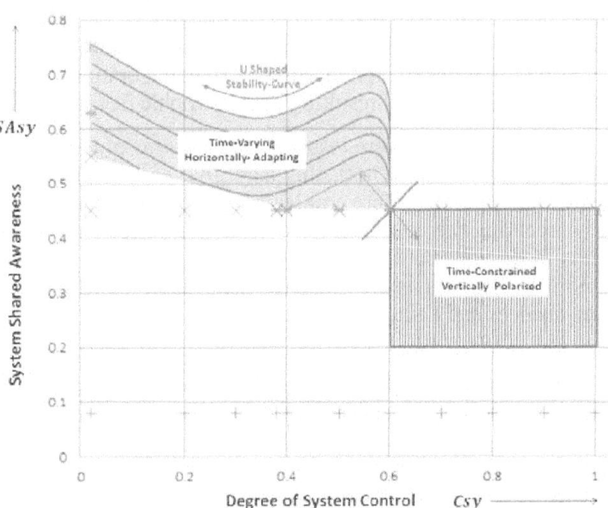

Figure 4: Ambidextrous Time-Varying/Horizontally-Polarised Organisation

There were some other significant differences in performance of this ship's company compared to the exploitative model. In the *ambidextrous* model, even if pushed into the time constrained, vertically polarised section, it was possible (with the restoration of reflective capacity in certain of its links) to restore the organisation to a time-varying and horizontally adapting being. This was not the case for the *exploitative* model – and it suffered catastrophic degradation on being pushed over the limit – it was irrecoverable. The other question raised, is 'what person would wish to be working in an environment subject to that degree of control, 60% or more?' Very tight control may be appropriate for activities where small deviations from a specification can cause catastrophic failure, such as deep-sea drilling, subterranean mining and space exploration, but such control comes at the expense of reflective capacity and organizational health. Organizations that employ tight control structures must therefore have the ability to recover into a reflective state. This reinforces the point that at all positions out to 60% control, the *ambidextrous* system remains capable of commanding & influencing (CSI) and managing and controlling (CRC). In other words, it is a time-varying, horizontally-adapting system capable of *healthily* problem solving, over time and dealing with issues, in time. The *exploitative* system can only solve the problems it is permitted to, in time, and cannot vary over-time. This organisation is inherently *unhealthy* and a place we would not / should not wish to place our people.

5 Conclusions

The response to many failures, e.g. the Nimrod Crash and at Macondo, has been to increase the controls and monitoring placed on people at different levels. This analysis suggests that the effects on potentially already *unhealthy* organisations have been the reverse of those intended. Instead of improving shared awareness, the excess of information and targets required as a form of control actually detracts from work [10] and so collaboration and shared awareness. We suggest that reducing collaborative assurance and shared awareness impacts negatively an organisation's ability to problem solve. *Ipso facto*, these *exploitative* type organisations become unhealthy and potentially risky places to be. Furthermore, one may fall into the vicious circle of failures; leading to more controls; leading to further erosion in trust and so collaboration; leading to more failure finally resulting in catastrophic degradation.

If organisations were *instrumented* in terms of their ability to problem solve (or not), this may give early indication of potential solutions before problems arise. This is what we mean by 'securing the bolt before the horse has bolted', which has less to do with putting in yet more bolts and, in actuality, is more to do with improving an organisation's *collaborative assurances* and ability to *problem solve*.

Finally, we conclude that a secure organisation is *ambidextrous* with high shared awareness and capable of collaboratively problem solving. It is this *ambidexterity* which allows the organisation to problem solve by commanding & influencing over time (CSI) and controlling & managing (CRC), in time. Successful *ambidextrous* and secure, *healthy* organisations, which *exploratively* learn from failure, may leak less. Our people secure the bolts in the first place.

6 Acknowledgment

The University of Cambridge, Engineering Design Centre and the Australian Defence Force.

7 References

[1] Warren, R.B., & D.I, Warren., *The Neighborhood Organizer's Handbook*, South Bend, Ind: University of Notre Dame Press. 1977.

[2] Thibaut, J.W., & H.H., Kelley, *The Social Phsychology of Groups*, New York, London: John Wiley, Chapman Hall, 1959.

[3] Backman, E.V., & S.R., Smith, "Healthy Organizations, Unhealthy Communities?" *Nonprofit Management & Leadership*, Vol. 10, no. 4, Summer, 2000.

[4] Mintzberg, H., D. Dougherty, J. Jorgensen, & F. Westley, "Some surprising things about collaboration - knowing how people connect makes it work better". *Organizational Dynamics*, Spring (pp. 60-71), 1996

[5] Latour, B., *We have never been Modern (Trans. C. Porter)*, Cambridge, MA: Harvard University Press, 1993.

[6] Johnson, H., & J. Hyde., "Towards Modeling Individual and Collaborative Construction of Jigsaws Using Task Knowledge Structures (TKS)". *Transactions on Computer-Human Interaction*, 10(4). ACM: NY. pp. 339-387, 2003.

[7] Cohen, A.L., D. Cash, & M.J. Muller., "Designing to support adversarial collaboration", in *In ACM Conference on Computer-Supported Cooperative Work*, ACM: Philadelphia, Pen, 2000.

[8] Whitworth, B., & A., de Moor, Handbook of Research on Socio-Technical Design and Social Networking Systems: Information science reference, New York, NY: Hershey, 2009.

[9] Endsley, M.R., B., Bolte & D.G., Jones., *Designing for Situation Awareness*, London & New York: Taylor & Francis, 2003.

[10] Dabbish, L., R., Kraut., "Controlling interruptions: Awareness displays and social motivation for coordination", in *ACM Conference on Computer-Supported Cooperative Work*: Chicago, USA, 2004.

[11] Blacker, K., Mills, R. and B. Weinstein., "People risk and those 'porous walls'". *Finance & Management*. September, Issue 114, 2004.

[12] Endsley, M.R., L., Strater., "Designing to Enhance SA in the CIC", in *Human Systems Integration Symposium*: Arlington, USA, 2005.

[13] Reay Atkinson, S., S. Lesher & D. Shoupe., "Information Capture and Knowledge Exchange: The Gathering Testing and assessment of Information and Knowledge through Exploration and Exploitation", in *14th ICCRTS: C2 and Agility*, CCRP: Washington, 2009.

[14] Bunge, M.A., "Ten Modes of Individualism - None of Which Works - And Their Alternatives". *Philosophy of the Social Sciences*, 30(3): p. pp. 384-406, 2000.

[15] Drucker, P., *Post-Capitalist Society*, New York: Harper Collins Publishers, 1993.

[16] Hossain, L., S., Reay Atkinson, M., D'Eredita, & Rolf.T., Wigand. "Towards a Mech-Organic Perspective for Knowledge Sharing Networks in Organizations". in *UK Academy for Information Systems*. Worcester College University of Oxford, 8-20th March, 2013.

[17] Alberts, D.S., & R. E. Hayes., *Understanding Command and Control*. DoD Command and Control Research Program, Washington: CCRP Publications, 2007.

[18] Reay Atkinson, S., & J, Moffat, *The Agile Organization*, Washington: CCRP Publications, 2005.

[19] Atlan, H., & I.R. Cohen., "Immune information, self-organization and meaning". *International Immunology*. Vol. 10, No. 6: p. pp. 711-717, 1998.

[20] DeRosa, J.K., A-M Grisogono, A.J. Ryan & D.O. Norman., "A Research Agenda for the Engineering of Complex Systems", in *IEEE International Systems Conference, SysCon 2008*, IEEE. p. pp. 15-22, 2008.

[21] Atlan, H., "Self-creation of meaning". *Physica Scripta*, 36:563, 1987.

[22] He, Z.-L., & P-K Wong, "Exploration vs. Exploitation: An Empirical Test of the Ambidexterity Hypothesis". *Organization Science*. Vol. 15, No. 4, July-August: p. pp. 481-494, 2004.

[23] Buckley, P., & M., Chapman., "The use of Native Categories in Management Research". *British Journal of Management*, 8: pp. 283-99, 1997.

[24] Luhmann, N., *Social Systems*, Stanford: Stanford University Press, 1995.

[25] Craig, R.T., "Communication Theory as a Field". *Communication Theory*. 9 (2), Ch 4.: pp. 119-161, 1999.

[26] Blessing, L., Chakrabarti, A. and Wallace, K. , "A Design Research Methodology". *In International Conference on Engineering Design*, ICED: Prague, 1995.

[27] Blessing, L., A. Chakrabarti., *DRM:* "A Design Research Methodology". *In Les Sciences de la Conception*: Lyon, 2002.

[28] Eckert, C., P.J. Clarkson, & M.K. Stacey., "The Spiral of Applied Research: A methodological view of an integrated design research". *In International Conference on Engineering Design (ICED)*, ICED: Stockholm, 2003.

[29] Eckert, C., M.K. Stacey & P.J, Clarkson., "The lure of the measurable in design research". *In 8th International Design Conference (Design 2004)*: Cavtat, Croatia, 2004.

[30] Yin, R.K., *Case Study Research: Design and Methods*, Los Angeles: 4th Edition, Sage Publications, 2009.

[31] Clarkson, P.J., C. Simons, & C.M. Eckert., "Predicting change propagation in complex design". *Journal of Mechanical Design*. 126(5): p. pp. 765-797, 2004.

[32] Wagner, S., & S., Reay Atkinson, "Operational Test & Evaluation (OT&E) of Vehicular-Socio CIED Networks (Afghanistan)". *In Australia Defence Trials Testing & Evaluation Organisation (ADTEO), DT899 Australian Protected Route Clearance*, ADTEO, Editor, AS-CDG-ADTEO: Canberra, Classified, 2011.

[33] Reay Atkinson, S., *Engineering Design Adaptation Fitness in Complex Adaptive Systems*, in *CUED EDC*, Cambridge University Engineering Department: Cambridge, UK, 2011.

[34] Leech, B.L., "Asking Questions: Techniques for Semistructured Interviews". *Political Science and Politics*. 35(4): p. pp. 665-668, 2002.

[35] Likert, R., "A Technique for the Measurement of Attitudes". Archives of Psychology, 140, 1932.

[36] Wittgenstein, L., Translated by F.P. Ramsey and C.K. Ogden, in Tractatus Logico-Philosophicus, Kegan Paul: London, 1922.

[37] Popper, K., *All Life Is Problem Solving*. London, New York: Routledge, 1999.

[38] Pólya, G., *Heuristic Reasoning in the Theory of Numbers*, in *Reprinted in: The random walks of George Pólya*, G.W. Alexanderson, Editor 1959 (2000), Mathematical Association of America: Washington, DC, 1959.

[39] Popper, K., *The Logic of Scientific Discovery* (published in German 1934) Berlin: Mohr Siebeck, 1959.

[40] Denzin, N.K., The Research Act: A Theoretical Introduction to Sociological Methods (3rd Ed), New Jersey: Prentice Hall, 1989.

[41] Kitchenham, B., L., Pickard & S.L., Pfleeger, "Case studies for method and tool evaluation". *Software*, IEEE. 12(4): p. pp. 52 – 62, 1995.

[42] Blessing, L.T.M., & A., Chakrabarti, *DRM, a Design Research Methodology*, Dordrecht; Heidelberg; London; New York: Springer, 2009.

[43] Patton, M.Q., *Qualitative Research and evaluation methods (3rd ed.)*. Vol. 3rd Edition. Thousand Oaks: CA: Sage, 2002.

[44] Lincoln, N.K., & E.G. Guba, *Naturalistic Enquiry*, Beverley Hill, CA: Sage, 1985.

[45] Cho, J., & A., Trent, "Validity in qualitative research revisited". *Qualitative Research*, 6(3): p. pp. 319-340, 2006.

[46] Forrest, S., & S.A. Hofmeyr., "Immunology as Information Processing". In *Design Principles for Immune System & Other Distributed Autonomous Systems*, L.A.Segel and I.R. Cohen, Editor, OUP. pp. 361-387: Oxford, 2000.

[47] Rowland, D., *The Stress of Battle*, London: HM Stationary Office, 2006.

[48] Ford, R., D. Martin, D., Elenius, & M., Johnson., "Ontologies and Tools for Analyzing and Synthesising LVC Confederations". In *Proceedings of the 2009 Winter Simulation Conference*, Eds R.R. M. D. Rossetti., Hill, B., Johansson, A., Dunkin, & R. G., Ingalls., 2009.

[49] Lutz, R., J., Wallace, A., Bowers, D., Cutts, P., Gustavson, & W., Bizub., "Common Object Model Components: A First Step Toward LVC Interoperability". *In Simulation Interoperability Workshop, 09S-SIW-031, Apr*, Simulation Interoperability, 2009.

[50] ATL. *Instrumentation*. 2007 [cited 2008 December]; Available from: http://www.atlab.com/index.php?ArticleID=75# (accessed December 2008).

[51] Reay Atkinson, S., A.M., Maier, N.H.M., Caldwell, & P.J., Clarkson., "Collaborative trust networks in engineering design adaptation". In *International Conference of Engineering Design, ICED11*: Technical University of Denmark, Lyngby, 2011.

[52] Walker, D., S. Reay Atkinson, & L. Hossian., "Counterinsurgency through Civil Infrastructure Networks". *Presented at The Second International Conference on Social Eco-Informatics (SOTICS) October 21 - 26*, SOTICS: Venice, 2012.

[53] Reay Atkinson, S., A. Goodger, N.H.M Caldwell, L. Hossain., "How lean the machine: how agile the mind". *The Learning Organization*, Vol. 19 Iss: 3: p. pp. 183 – 206, 2012.

[54] Walker, D., S., Reay Atkinson, & L., Hossain, "Collaboration Without Rules - A New Perspective on Stability Operations". *Presented at IEEE Cyber Conference, 14-16 Dec*, IEEE: Washington, 2012

[55] Zurcher, R., & R.N., Kostoff, "Modeling Technology Transitions". In *Paper produced on behalf of Office of Naval Research (ONR) Graphical Modeling System (GMS) Program*, US-DoD-ONR: Washington, 2004.

[56] Caldwell, N.H.M., & P.J. Clarkson, "CPM Software Prototype Tool User Manual Document". In *NECTISE, Draft 27042009, NECDSD0306A*2009, University of Cambridge Engineering Design Centre: Cambridge, 2009.

[57] Keller, R., C.M. Eckert & P.J. Clarkson., "Through-Life Change Prediction and Management". *In International Conference on Product Lifecycle Management*, 2008.

[58] Albert, R., & A-L. Barabási., "Statistical Mechanics of Complex Networks". Reviews of Modern Physics, Vol 74, 2002.

[59] van Aken, J., "Analysis of Quantum Probability Theory". *Journal of Philosophical Logic*. Vol. 14: p. pp. 267-296, 1985.

[60] Dahl, R.A., "The Concept of Power". *Behavioral Science*, 2:3, July: p. 201, 1957.

[61] Wrong, D.H., "Some Problems in Defining Social Power". *The American Journal of Sociology*. Vol. 73, No. 6 (May): p. pp. 673-681, 1968.

[62] Hickson, D.J., C. R., Hinings, C. A., Lee, R. E., Schneck & J. M., Pennings., "A Strategic Contingencies' Theory of Intraorganizational Power". *Administrative Science Quarterly*. Vol. 16, No. 2, (Jun): p. pp. 216-229, 1971.

[63] Anderson, A.M.F., "Classes of socio-technical hazards: Microscopic and macroscopic scales of risk analysis". *Risk Management*. 11: p. pp. 208 – 240, 2009.

[64] Felici, M., "Trust strategies and policies in complex socio-technical safety - critical domains: An analysis of the air traffic management domain". In *Proceedings of the 3rd International Workshop on Rapid Integration of Software Engineering techniques, RISE 2006, No. 4401 in LNCS*, Ed D. N. Guelfi, Buchs, Springer-Verlag: Geneva, Switzerland. p. pp. 51 – 65, 2007.

[65] McKnight, D.H., & N. L., Chervany, "Trust and distrust definitions: One bite at a time". in *Trust in Cyber-societies. No. 2246 in LNA*, Eds M. R. Falcone, Singh, & Y.-H., Tan, Springer-Verlag: Berlin, 2001.

[66] Purser, R.E., and S. Cabana., *The Self Managing Organization*. The Free Press, 1988.

[67] US-NC., "Deep Water:The Gulf Oil Disaster and the Future of Offshore Drilling". In *Report to the President by the National Commission (NC) on the BP Deepwater Horizon Oil Spill and Offshore Drilling*. Office of the President: Jan. Washington, 2011.

[68] UK-HoC., "UK Deepwater Drilling - Implications of the Gulf of Mexico Oil Spill". Government Response to the Committee's Second Report of Session: House of Commons (HoC) Energy and Climate Change Committee (ECCC). Fifth Special Report of Session 2010-11,15 Mar, 2011.

[69] UK-HoC., "The Nimrod Review - the Haddon-Cave Report". *Ordered by the House of Commons to be printed by the Stationary Office*. 28th October, 2009.

[70] Basu, P., A. Bar-Noy, R. Ramanathan & M. P. Johnson., "Modeling and Analysis of Time-Varying Graphs", in *http://arxiv.org/abs/1012.0260v1*2010, Cornell University Library: Ithica, New York, 2010.

[71] Bonnefoy, A.P., G. Bounova, O. de Weck, and R. J. Hansman., "Network Representations and Analyses of Engineering Systems". In *ESD Symposium June 17*, MIT: MIT Engineering Systems Division, 2009.

Anonymous Retrieval of k-NN POI in Location Based Services (LBS)

C. Asanya[1], and R. Guha[2]
Department of Electrical Engineering and Computer Science,
University of Central Florida, Orlando, Florida 32816, USA

Abstract— ***LBS is a type of location information service accessible through mobile device with the aid of mobile network and mobile device position. Through LBS users can receive information on nearest neighbor (NN) point of interest (POI). LBS need user location and data profile to customize these services. Due to privacy and security concerns, users may be reluctant sharing this information. Without this information, it will be difficult to customize these services. Previous solutions offered to process such queries anonymously either imposed too much computation on the user, involve costly transmission, or discloses too much database information. In this paper, we propose idea that allows user to specify and receive exactly k NN (number of POI desired) from LBS with lower transmission cost, minimal user computation, and minimal amount of database information disclosed. We propose two algorithms, first one returns approximate k NN, while the second returns exact k NN.***

Keywords: Privacy, Approximate K-NN, Exact K-NN, Less Communication.

1. Introduction

Location based services are information and entertainment services that are accessible by mobile users through GPS-enabled portable devices and mobile network. It operates by using geographical information of a mobile device [1] to provide real time information such as traffic, entertainment, etc. To effectively provide and customize these services, LBS providers need the location and data profile of a user.

However, users may wish to remain anonymous for various personal reasons. These concerns prompted research into ways to achieve quality of service needed in LBS and at the same time provide user privacy. Privacy requirement may vary between users based on the POI desired. However, the technique to provide this privacy are categorized into three [11]; Two-Tier Spatial Transformation, Three-Tier Spatial Transformation, and Cryptographic Transformation.

Two-tier spatial transformation provide direct communication between user and LBS. User privacy is usually provided through techniques like k-anonymity model which demand that every query from a mobile device be indistinguishable related to no fewer than k-1 respondents. For instance, for a user (Alice) to issue a query, there has to be other users beside Alice in the vicinity (cloaking region). With this condition satisfied, Bob (server) will be unable to distinguish who the query belongs to. As shown in fig 1, Alice issued a query for k=7. With k=7, Alice will be availed with the anonymity of the privacy technique. However, Alice has to wait for at least

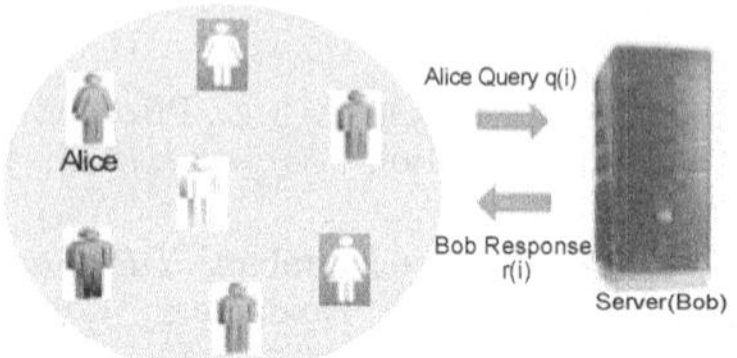

Fig. 1. Cloaked Region with 7 users

other k-1 user, which may not happen on a timely manner, and therefore could delay queries. Some two-tier transformations involve using a dummy location to issue query. Alice issue a query based on a phony location like a landmark, Bob responds to the landmark, Alice then retrieves its POI relative to the landmark.

Three-tier spatial transformations use a trusted central anonymizer. For example, Alice issue a query through a third party server, the server anonymizes Alice location before forwarding the request to the server. However, anonymizer provides not only a single point of attack [8], but also the user has to rely on the honesty of the trusted anonymizer.

Proposed by Ghinita et al, is a cryptographic transformation that does not require a third party intermediary. It is based on the private information retrieval (PIR) scheme that allows a user to retrieve information from a database without revealing the exact information retrieved. In [8], the database is treated as a X bit string represented as a matrix of size n, fig 2c. If Alice wants to retrieve the value represented by bit X_i, to preserve privacy, she sends an encrypted query $E(X(q(i)))$,where E is used for encryption. The server responds with a value $r(E(X(q(i))))$, which allows Alice to compute X_i. It returns a column to Alice as shown in fig 2b, thereby revealing more information than needed. [22], attempted to minimize the amount of information disclosed by combining PIR and oblivious transfer (OT) scheme to

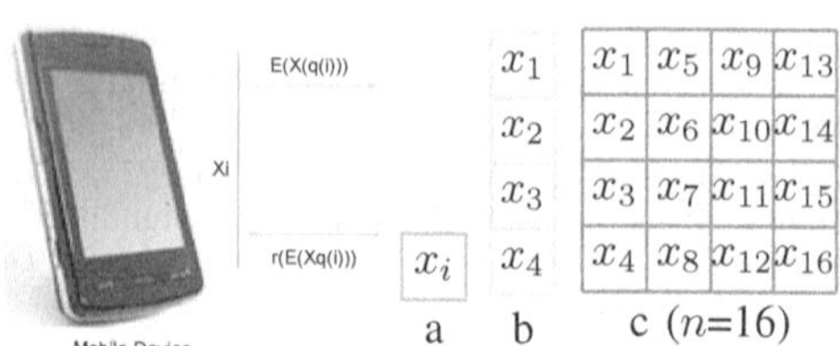

Fig. 2. User and Server Transaction

return NN as shown in fig 2a. However, the content of the cell is still more than the user requested. Remember that each cell of the matrix contains a listing of POI for a particular spatio region. If the LBS is established to make profit by charging per information retrieved, the LBS is disclosing more information than a user will be willing to pay for, or it is willing to give out for free. It also incurs a high transmission cost of at least $O(P_{max})$, where P_{max} is the number of POIs in a cell. Also the user has the responsibility of computing its NN from list of NNs. If user wants something different, for instance different gas station, another query has to be issued which results in another transmission and computation just to retrieve one NN.

To solve this problem, we propose a scheme, which will allow a user to specify k (number of information desired). User will then have k NN to choose from if so desired without issuing another query. This will allow the server to transmit only k nearest neighbor required by the user. It will also protect the server from giving out too many of its valued information. The communication cost is $O(k)$ compare to $O(P_{max})$ to $O(P_{max} \cdot \sqrt{n})$ incurred in the existing approach, and k is always less than P_{max}.

Our Contributions are:

1) We developed a method for finding k approximate nearest neighbor to avoid the overhead of transferring more object than necessary, thereby cutting down on the transmission and computation cost.
2) We also propose an improvement that utilizes the exact user location to find the exact k nearest neighbor without disclosing user location.
3) We also show that the transaction cost is much less than the comparable scheme.

The rest of the paper is organized as follows; Section 2 provides the problem formulation, and section 3 presents related works. Section 4 describes the architectural framework in our system, while 5 explains the implementation process. 6 Evaluates our protocol. Section 7 compares our scheme with existing protocol, while conclusion and future work is in 8.

2. Problem Formulation

This section provides definition for the k-NN problem set. Find the user location in Euclidean space and return k nearest neighbor to the user without compromising its location or divulging information requested.

2.1 Definition

Let p be data points of interest in Euclidean space represented as a square grid G of cells c. Let P_{max} be the maximum number of p in c. For a user u in location $l \in c$ wishing to obtain its nearest neighbor, let $k \in P_{max}$ represent the number of point of interest desired by the user in c. k-NN query returns to the user k data object in c whose distances from u are less or equal to the data objects $\in c \in G$.

2.2 Solution 1: (Approximate k NN)

For $p \in c \in G$, assign Hilbert value to p. For every $c \in G$, sort $p \in c$ according to their Hilbert value. Create R tree of k size node with index key, where k is the number of POI requested by the user. User finds the appropriate key based on its Hilbert value and use double PIR to retrieve its k NN.

2.3 Solution 2: (Exact k NN)

Server sends G and arbitrary point for each $c \in G$. User sends back k and its position relative to the arbitrary point in c. For each $c \in G$ server computes NN until k is reached. User retrieves k NN using double PIR.

3. Related Work

Most proposed privacy models in LBS use third party anonymizer which acts as intermediary between the user and the server, however, user location is usually known to the third party. Another form is K-anonymity that demands that location information contained in a message sent from a mobile user to a LBS should be indistinguishable from at least k-1 other messages. For the most part it does not protect information requested.

[9], offered a solution that uses spatio-temporal cloaking to transform each original message from a mobile node into a privacy protected message with the k-anonymity guarantee. The cloaking algorithm is run by the protection broker on a trusted server that anonymizes the message by cloaking the location information contained in the messages before forwarding them to the LBS provider(s).

[14], as in [9], allow each mobile node to specify the minimum level of anonymity desired as well as the maximum temporal and spatial resolutions it is willing to tolerate. For each query, user specifies its waiting interval tolerance, if within this interval other k-1 users issue a query, then all the queries will be combined into a single cloaking region, else the user query will be rejected.

Shin et al [6], proposed a profile based anonymization model. It generalizes both location and profile to the extent specified by the user. Location is generalized so that the generalized spatio-temporal region includes at least k-1 other users in the region and at the same time contains at least additional k-1 users with identical profiles of the user.

In [2], mobile nodes communicate with external services through a central anonymity server which is part of the trusted computing base. In an initialization phase, the nodes will

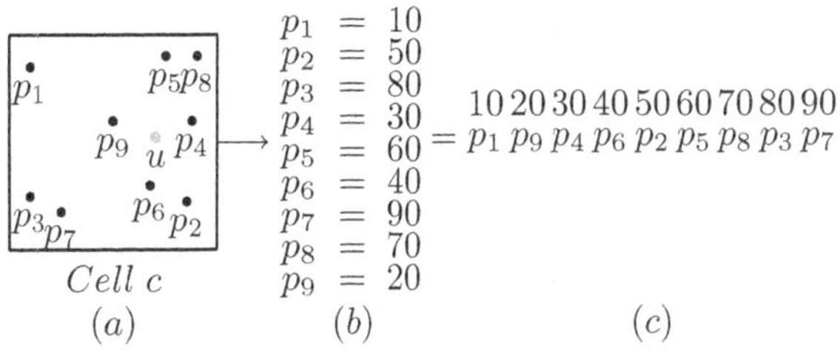

p_1, p_5, p_8, p_9, u, p_4, p_3, p_7, p_6, p_2 — Cell c (a)

$p_1 = 10$, $p_2 = 50$, $p_3 = 80$, $p_4 = 30$, $p_5 = 60$, $p_6 = 40$, $p_7 = 90$, $p_8 = 70$, $p_9 = 20$ (b)

$10\ 20\ 30\ 40\ 50\ 60\ 70\ 80\ 90 = p_1\ p_9\ p_4\ p_6\ p_2\ p_5\ p_8\ p_3\ p_7$ (c)

Fig. 3. Approximate k NN

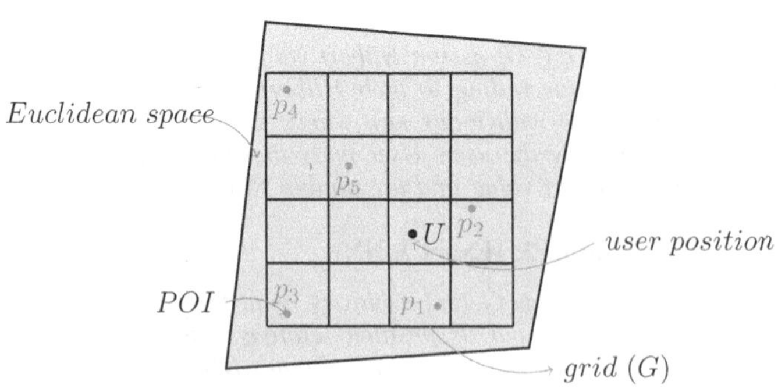

Fig. 4. Euclidean space with grid G

set up an authenticated and encrypted connection with the anonymity server. When a mobile node sends position and time information to an external server, the anonymity server decrypts the message, removes any identifiers, and distorts the position data according to the prescribed cloaking algorithms to reduce the re-identification risk.

One of the downside to the third party anonymizer is the possibility that the trusted server can turn into an adversary and therefore can compromise privacy.

Cryptographic approach was proposed to help eliminate third party, though some trusted third party scheme have used encryption, but user location is known to the third party. Encryption allow user to secretly retrieve information while keeping the server oblivious of the exact information retrieved. The server sends the user encrypted information of which only the user is able to decrypt.

In [7], a solution that uses a secure framework for protecting both the user's location information and user's usage profiles through oblivious transfer and homomorphic encryption was proposed. However, an intermediate proxy was introduced in the protocol to interact with the server and the user, which makes the privacy partly dependent on the proxy's honesty. A similar approach was proposed in [10]. It also requires third party. The server stored information is encrypted by using double oblivious transfer scheme to prevent server from knowing which information retrieved by the user.

Similar to our work is the approach used in Ghinita et al [8]. PIR scheme based on the Quadratic Residuosity Assumption (QRA) was used. The database is modeled as a string X of n-bit. User wishing to obtain bit X_i, will engage in the PIR protocol as described in section 4.1. From the list of POIs, user will be able to compute its NN. However, the protocol has some shortcomings. It reveals to the user more than what is required, and also has high transaction cost.

R. Vishwanathan, proposed an improvement that combined PIR and OT scheme. The scheme used a two phase protocol (PIR and OT) to minimize server returned information. However, it also reveals more objects than necessary, imposing on the user the task of calculating its NN from a list of NNs.

Neither of these two approaches was able to prevent the server from disclosing more database information than necessary, nor minimize user computation and transaction

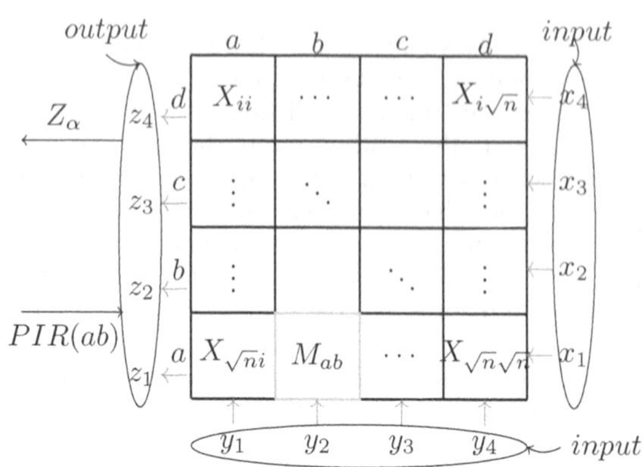

Fig. 5. Database Layout with user request and server response

cost. They also failed to offer user any choice in case a user is displeased with the information retrieved. For example, a user in a moving vehicle may receive NN that is already behind or may be logistically difficult to reach, user has to issue another query to obtain NN, while with our scheme user has k choices to choose from without issuing another query. In [23, 24, 25, 27 and 28], attempt was made to return k-nn, but it did not offer neither location nor data privacy. [26] proposed idea that returns only approximate k-nn, but depends on having other users within the cloaked region to be effective.

4. System Architecture

We used PIR protocol based on computational intractability of [3]. We also use dual encryption process as in [22], and [10]. We propose two algorithm to retrieve k-NN; the first returns approximate k-NN POI to the user with $O(log(k))$ computation, and $O(k)$ communication cost. The second returns exact K-NN.

4.1 PIR Framework

Private Information Retrieval (PIR) is a protocol that allows a user to retrieve information from a database without revealing the exact information retrieved. Different flavors have been proposed over the years [4]. The earlier PIR scheme requires replication of the database [13]. Kushilevitz and Ostrovsky introduced a computational private information retrieval ($cPIR$) that requires one database. We focused our work on Computational PIR applicable to one database tuple distribution structure as was introduced in [3].

$cPIR$ is based on the premise that there is no known function in polynomial bounded time that will allow a database of size n to distinguish a query for the ith bit and a query for the jth bit $\forall\ 1 \leq i, j \leq n$. The PIR scheme is such that for a database of n-bit string X from which a user wishes to obtain bit X_i while keeping secret index i from the database, it requires that the user queries divulge no information about i. *cPIR* as described in [3] relies on *Quadratic Residuosity Assumption (QRA)*.

QRA was used in cryptography by S. Golwasser and M. Bellare [15], and it states that, it is computational hard to find the quadratic residues in modulo arithmetic of a large composite number $N = q \cdot q'$, where q,q' are large primes. i.e, If N is a natural number, Define

$$\mathbb{Z}_{\mathbb{N}}^{*} = \{x | 1 \leq x \leq N, gcd(N, x) = 1\} \quad (1)$$

Let the quadratic residuosity predicate be defined as $Q_N(y) = 0$ if $\exists x \in \mathbb{Z}_{\mathbb{N}}^{*}$ such that $x^2 = y \ mod \ N$ and $Q_N(y) = 1$ otherwise. If $Q_N(y) = 0$ (i.e. y is a $square$ y), then y is said to be quadratic residue (QR), and if $Q_N(y) = 1$ (i.e. y is a $non - square$ y), then y is said to be quadratic non-residue (QNR). If

$$\mathbb{Z}_{N}^{+1} = \{y \in \mathbb{Z}_{\mathbb{N}}^{*} | (\frac{y}{N}) = 1\}, \quad (2)$$

is true, then half of the numbers in $\mathbb{Z}_{N}^{+1}$ are $\in$ QR, and half are $\in$ QNR. If q and q' are large enough $\frac{k}{2}$ bit prime, for every constant c and a family of computational bounded polynomial circuit $C_{k_0}(y)$ there exist an integer k_0 such that $\forall K > k_0$

$$Pr_{y \in \mathbb{Z}_{N}^{+1}}[C_{k_0}(N, y) = Q_N(y)] < \frac{1}{2} + \frac{1}{k^c} \quad (3)$$

If equation 3 holds, and for large enough k_0, the probability of differentiating between a QR and QNR is very small, i.e the server will be unable to unmask the information requested by user by attempting to find if $y \in QR$ or $y \in QNR$

4.2 k-NN Spatial Search

We implemented method similar to [5] and [12] to find k NN. It makes use of priority queue to keep track of the points. Readers interested in details can read [5].

4.3 Database Structure

Our scheme is implemented using the database structure as shown in figure 5. It is similar to [22] and [8]. It allows user to secretly retrieve nearest neighbor. It is of size n represented as a square matrix $M = \sqrt(n)$ x $\sqrt(n)$ indexed by X_i, for $(i = 1 ... \sqrt(n))$. Figure 5 shows database of n = 16.
X_i represent the section of the database corresponding to a cell in the Euclidean space as shown in figure 4. The contents of X_i is the POI found in the grid cell for POI from 1 to P_{max}, where P_{max} is the maximum number of POI in each cell. All X_i have equal number of POIs.

4.4 Space Partitioning

Figure 4 shows a Euclidean space enclosing POI's. A square grid G is super-imposed on top of the space. User location in the space is indicated by U, and p_1,p_2, etc. are the points in the space enclosed by the grid.

5. Implementation

The goal is to find k nearest neighbor POI without revealing user location, or the requested data profile. Recall that k is the number of nearest neighbor point of interest user wishes to retrieve from the server.

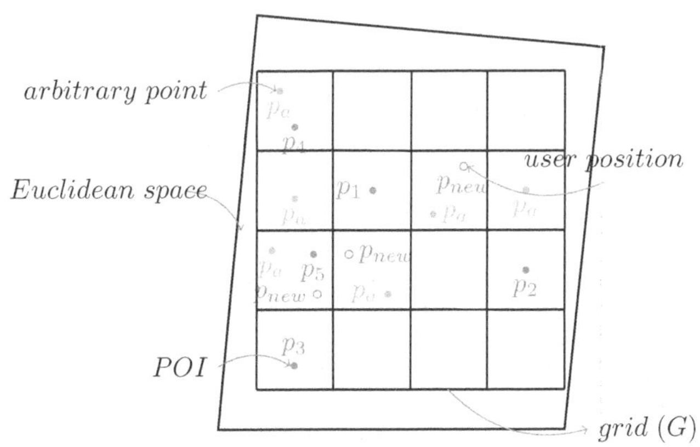

Fig. 6. Using arbitrary point to find exact user location

5.1 Approximate k-NN Algorithm

The database for the Approximate k-NN is mapped out to Hilbert curve ordering. Hilbert curve is useful for mapping between 2D and 1D space while still preserving locality. For instance, if (x, y) are the coordinates of a point within the unit square, and d is the distance along the curve when it reaches that point, then points that have nearby d values will also have nearby (x, y) values [29]. Simply put, if two POIs are close in the 2-D space, they are likely to be close in the Hilbert ordering, as well, therefore nearest neighbor to a user is the point of interest that has Hilbert value closest to that of the user [8]. To retrieve k NN POI, our algorithm follows the following steps;

1) Step 1: Server creates Hilbert ordering of the database in a matrix $M = \sqrt(n)$ x $\sqrt(n)$. Each object in M represents the POIs in cell c. Cells are padded to create cells of equal size, and the POIs are of equal bits. This will prevent the server from inferring the requested POI based on the size of the cell or amount of bit transferred. The POIs were sorted based on their Hilbert values. Figure 3a depicts a cell from a grid G of n cells. The cell has 9 POI from $p_1, \cdots, p_9$. All the points are assigned Hilbert values based on their distance to one other. Points with closer values are closer in space. For example, p_6 has H value of 40, p_4 has H of 30, while p_2 has H of 50.

2) Step 2, Initialization : User in location U initiates a query, and sends k to obtain its k nearest neighbor, server creates one level R-tree with nodes of size k, and indexed the nodes as shown in figure 8(a,b). Each index key is greater or equal to the left node which values are Hilbert. Server then sends the key to the user together with grid G. User finds the grid enclosing it and its Hilbert value.

3) Step 3, k-NN Protocol Procedure with double PIR: For a user wishing to retrieve k-NN, if, for instance user H value is 25, with the help of the index key, user will be requesting all the points belonging to the values which are to the left of index key 30 of figure 8b.
Let database D of size n be organized as a string of X elements in $s \times s$ matrix M, where $s = \sqrt{n}$. Let

M_{ab} figure 5 represent element X_{ii} that user wish to retrieve, and let figure 8c depicts the database entry for M_{ab}. User randomly generates modulus $\mathbb{N} = q \cdot q'$, with a query message $y = [y_1....y_s]$, and $x = [x_1....x_s]$, such that

$$y_b \in QNR,\ and\ \forall j \neq b, y_j \in QR, \text{ and}$$

$$x_a \in QNR,\ and\ \forall r \neq a, x_r \in QR$$

It then sends query $PIR(ab)$ to the server.

4) Step 4, Server Response: Server receives $PIR(ab)$ from the user. Server is unable to tell if y and x used for encrypting user query $\in QNR$ or QR due to the computational intractability of a large prime. Define

$$z_r = \prod_{j=1}^{s} w_{rj} \tag{4}$$

and

$$z_c = \prod_{r=1}^{s} w_{rj} \tag{5}$$

where z_r and z_c are vector. Let

$$Z_\alpha = z_r \times z_c \tag{6}$$

and $w_{rj} = y_j^2$ if $M_{rj} = 0$, otherwise $w_{rj} = y$ if $M_{rj} = 1$, for $j = 1....s$, and $w_{rj} = x_r^2$ if $M_{rj} = 0$, otherwise $w_{rj} = x$ if $M_{rj} = 1$, for $r = 1....s$.

Server runs PIR protocol on user request, it computes for every row and column equation 4, 5 and 6 and returns $Z = z_1....z_k$ with $O(k)$.

Since the user knows q and q', it will be easy to compute the following equation

$$\left(Z_\alpha^{\frac{q-1}{2}} = 1\ mod\ q_1\right) \wedge \left(Z_\alpha^{\frac{q'-1}{2}} = 1\ mod\ q_1\right) \tag{7}$$

if the above equation is true, then $Z_\alpha \in QR$ else $Z_\alpha \ni QR$. Therefore, M_{ab} computes to 0 if $Z_\alpha \in QR$ else, if $Z_\alpha \in QNR$ M_{ab} computes to 1. User does this for all the k objects requested and that is the k-NN. For a case where k = 3, and the user Hilbert value is 25, user will receive p_1,p_9 and p_4 as its nearest neighbor. User can then decide which one best suited its need.

Algorithm 1: (Approximate k-NN)

Input: grid size n, number of point of interest $POINumb$
Output: k NN point of interest p from p_1 to p_k
Procedure:

1) set the size of the grid; $cellNumb = n$, and $POINumb = P_{max}$;
2) **for** each grid c
   for $i = 1$ to p_{max}; p_1 to $p_{max} = hV$
3) Sort p in order of closeness
4) **for** each object p in c;
   if (hV for p_i from 1 to $p_{max} < hV$)
   for $p_i + 1$ from 1 to p_{max} - p_i; $*sortHV = p_i$;
5) **for** i = 1 to n
   for p = 1 to p_{max}
   for j = 1 to k ;**if** (j = k), key = hV[j];
6) **Client**
7) **for** each key
   if (chV $< key$), modulus $\mathbb{N} = q \cdot q'$;
   query message $y = [y_1....y_s]$;
   and $x = [x_1....x_s]$, such that
   $y_b \in QNR,\ and\ \forall j \neq b, y_j \in QR$, and
   $x_a \in QNR,\ and\ \forall r \neq a, x_r \in QR$
8) **Server** computes for every row and column
9) **for** j = 1 to s and r = 1 to s; **for** k times
   $z_r = \prod_{j=1}^{s} w_{rj}$ and $z_c = \prod_{r=1}^{s} w_{rj}$
   $Z_\alpha = z_r \times z_c$
   return $Z = z_1....z_k$;

5.2 Exact k-NN Algorithm

From figure 3a, the actual NN to the user is p_9,p_4 and p_6, but the server returned p_9, p_4 and p_1. To solve this problem we propose the second algorithm. The algorithm returned the exact k-NN by using exact user location to find its NN without compromising user privacy.

1) Server offline Phase: Server creates voronoi tessellation as in Ghinita et al using the set of POIs. It then super-impose a regular grid M of size $\sqrt(n)$ x $\sqrt(n)$ on top of the voronoi diagram, figure 7. For every cell c of the grid, it determines all voronoi cell intersecting it, and adds the corresponding POI to c. Cell c therefore contains all potential NNs of every location inside voronoi diagram intersecting it. For example in figure 7, cell $A1$ will contain $P1$ and $P3$, while $A3$ contain $P1$, $P3$ and $P4$. The cells are padded if necessary to create cells of equal size. All objects in M are of equal bits. Remember that number of bits for the POI can be of any size so long as they are consistent in M. For every cell c of the grid, server chooses arbitrary point P_a and maintains in an offline phase, and updates as necessary.

2) Initialization : When a user initiates a query to obtain its k-NN, server sends G and P_a for each cell in the grid. User finds the cell enclosing it, and calculates its distance $\pm d$ from P_a. User sends to the server $\pm d$ and k, representing its distance from P_a, and the number of information desired respectively. Server then add $\pm d$ to all the P_a in the grid to get P_{new}. This will ensure that the returned POI by the server is the exact K-NN to the user. The user location will now be $P_{new} = P_a \pm d$.

For each cell $c \in G$, server executes spatial search to find K-NN using P_{new}. The server does not know the location of the user nor its cell. Server only knows P_{new} figure 6, which can be located in any cell. Server stops execution of spatial search as soon as k-NN is found for the entire cell in the grid.

3) User Request : As was in the first case, If M_{ab} represent element X_{ii} user wish to retrieve, user randomly generates modulus $\mathbb{N} = q \cdot q'$, with a query message $y = [y_1....y_s]$, and $x = [x_1....x_s]$, such that

$$y_b \in QNR,\ and\ \forall j \neq b, y_j \in QR, \text{ and}$$

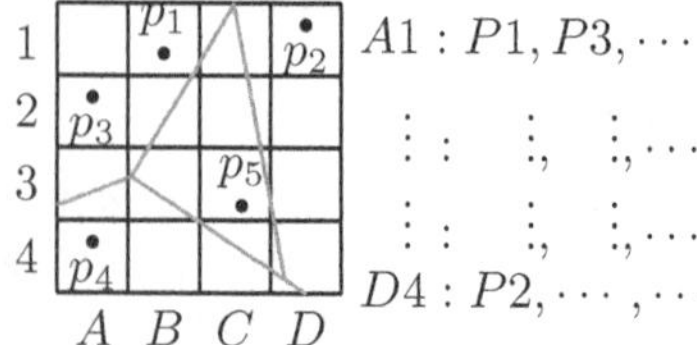

Fig. 7. Optimization

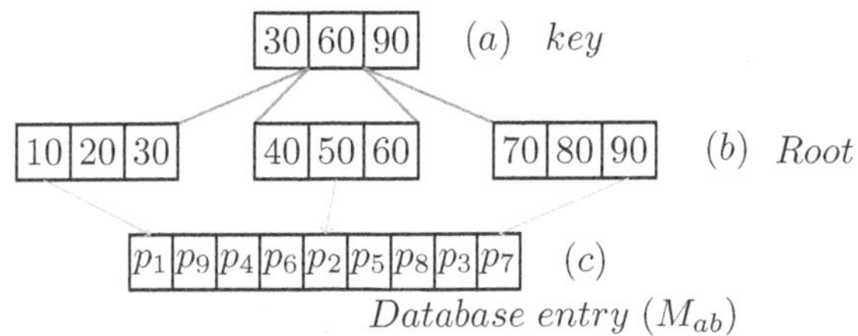

Fig. 8. Approximate NN for k = 3

TABLE I. BIT SIZE FOR N=100, AND POI PER CELL=15

	5	8	10	12	15
k NN	90	114	130	146	170
Previous Scheme 1	170	170	170	170	170
Previous Scheme 2	1250	1250	1250	1250	1250

$$x_a \in QNR,\ and\ \forall r \neq a, x_r \in QR$$

It then sends query $PIR(ab)$ to the server.

4) Server Response: Server receives $PIR(ab)$ from the user, but is unable to tell if y and x used to encrypt user query $\in QNR$ or QR due to the hardness of problem involving a large prime.

Server runs PIR protocol on user request. It computes for every row and column equation 4, 5 and 6 and returns $Z = z_1....z_k$ with $O(k)$.

Since the user knows q and q', it will be easy to compute equation 7. If equation 7 is true, then $Z_\alpha \in QR$ else $Z_\alpha \ni QR$. Therefore, M_{ab} computes to 0 if $Z_\alpha \in QR$ else, if $Z_\alpha \in QNR$ M_{ab} computes to 1. User does this for all the k objects requested and that is its k-NN.

Algorithm 2: (Exact k-NN)

Input: grid size n, number of point of interest $POINumb$
Output: k NN point of interest p from p_1 to p_k
Procedure:

1) **for** each grid c
   choose arbitrary point p_a;
2) **Client** in position U in grid c
   finds distance from p_a
3) **Server**
4) **for** each c; $P_{new} = P_a \pm d$;
5) **for** each $c \in G$; and **for** i=1 to k
   execute spatial search until k is reached;
6) **Client**
   modulus $\mathbb{N} = q \cdot q'$;
   query message $y = [y_1....y_s]$;
   and $x = [x_1....x_s]$, such that
   $y_b \in QNR,\ and\ \forall j \neq b, y_j \in QR$, and
   $x_a \in QNR,\ and\ \forall r \neq a, x_r \in QR$
7) **Server** computes for every row and column
8) **for** j = 1 to s and r = 1 to s;and **for** k times
   $z_r = \prod_{j=1}^{s} w_{rj}$; $z_c = \prod_{r=1}^{s} w_{rj}$
   $Z_\alpha = z_r \times z_c$; return $Z = z_1....z_k$;

6. Evaluation

Our goal is to show that our system incur less communication cost when transmitting nearest neighbor POI compare to other similar scheme. We also show that at the maximum user request our scheme is equal or less in communication cost to other comparable method.

6.1 Experimental Setup

The experiment was performed on a PC running Windows 7 with i5 processor and 2.30GHz CPU cycle with 3.85GB RAM. We used synthetic dataset of an independent and uniform distributed POI. We varied k from 5 to 15, and n from 100 to 144, and POI for each cell from 15 to 20. Each POI has 8 bits. Transmission payload is 50 bits. We implemented a 10MBits data transmission rate. We did not consider any propagation delay as we take the medium to be the same.

6.2 Results

Table I shows the transmission in bits for varying k up to P_{max}. As the table depicts, the payload transferred in our scheme (k-NN) increases as user request increase, as expected up to or less than the minimum for previous scheme. In the previous scheme, it is always the same regardless of user request. Table 11 shows the effect of increasing grid size n and P_{max} in a grid. As the table show, it has no effect on our scheme, while it increases for the previous method. Scheme 1 is the worst with a 36% increase, while scheme 2 has 19% increase. Figure 9a shows transmission cost for different k. Our scheme has lower cost when $k < P_{max}$, it catches up with PS1 as user request equals P_{max}. As figure 9b shows, as P_{max} increases, our scheme performs better.

7 Discussion and Comparison

In [8], server returns an answer set as shown in figure 2b. It will take $O(P_{max} \cdot sqrt(n))$ computation to retrieve NN. In [22], server returns are shown in figure 2a, which requires $O(P_{max})$ computation to retrieve NN. We were able to reduce the computation to $O(k)$ to retrieve k NN by returning only k NN to the user. There will be no need for user to compute and find its NN from the returned set as in [8] and [22] since server only returned what user requested. In the previous scheme, server has to re-issue another query to receive a different NN, while our scheme offered k choices at one snap shot. Our scheme also prevented server from disclosing too much database information by sending only what the user requested.

We also theoretically showed that server was unable to decipher user location, or request based on computational intractability of [3]. The transmission time is less than comparable scheme, unless for cases where $P_{max} < k$, then transmission time will be equal, since only p_{max} will be transmitted. Hilbert ordering and voronoi diagram creation are all done by the server in an offline phase. The largest piece of computation after user request is the NN search in algorithm 2, however it only runs k times.

TABLE II. BIT SIZE FOR N=114, AND POI PER CELL=20

	5	8	10	12	15	17	20
k NN	90	114	130	146	170	186	210
Prev Sch 1	210	210	210	210	210	210	210
Prev Sch 2	1970	1970	1970	1970	1970	1970	1970

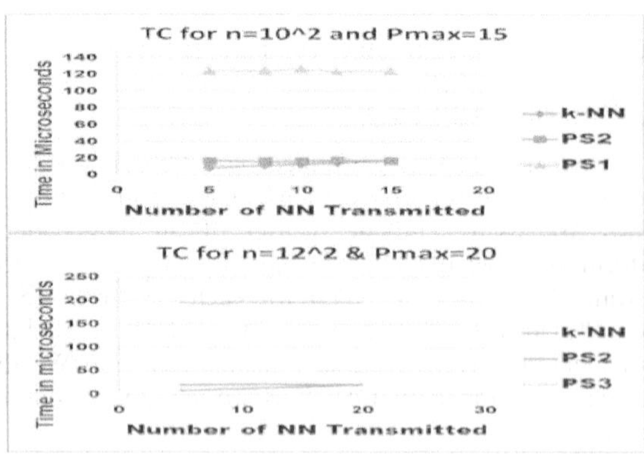

Fig. 9. Transmission Cost

8. Conclusion and Future Work

In this paper we proposed a new idea for finding k NN without the overhead imposed in some previous method. We were able to experimentally show that transmitting k NN has less communication cost. Requesting k NN is more efficient since it prevents query re-issue in the case of unsatisfied user. It provides opportunity for a user to make a choice without additional communication. By returning exact number of POI requested by the user, the protocol minimizes the number of objects returned in an answer set thereby reducing the transmission cost of sending the answer set to the user, also the user does not need to compute its NN, and user has more choice that does not require re-issuing of query to obtain next NN. In future we intend on using the parallel processing power of GPU to optimize our algorithm. We also intend on exploring a different way of reducing user computation when finding user distance from arbitrary point.

REFERENCES

[1] (2012, Jul.) Location based Service. [Online]. Available: http://en.wikipedia.org/wiki/Location-based_service

[2] M. Gruteser and D. Grunwald, "Anonymous usage of location-based services through spatial and temporal cloaking," in *Proc. ICMSAS 1st International Conference on Mobile Systems, Applications and Services Mobisys'03*, 2003, pp. 31–42.

[3] E. Kushilevitzr and R. Ostrovsky, "Replication is not needed: Single database, computationally-private information retrieval," in *Proc. IEEE 38th Annual Symposium on Foundations of Computer Science*, Oct.20-22, 1997, pp. 364–373.

[4] (2012, Sep.) Private information retrieval. [Online]. Available: http://en.wikipedia.org/wiki/Private_information_retrieval

[5] Derrick. (2007, Jun.) K-nn spatial search. [Online]. Available: http://blogs.msdn.com/b/devdev/archive/2007/06/07/k-nearest-neighbor-spatial-search.aspx

[6] H. Shin, V. Atluri, and J. Vaidya, "A profile anonymization model for privacy in a personalized location based service environment," in *Proc. IEEE ICMDM'08*, Newark, NJ, Apr.27-30, 2008, pp. 73–80.

[7] M. Kohlweiss *et al.*, "Efficient oblivious augmented maps: Location-based services with a payment broker," in *Proc. ACM 7th international conference on Privacy enhancing technologies PET'07*, Springer-Verlag Berlin, Heidelberg, 2007, pp. 77–94.

[8] G. Ghinita *et al.*, "Privacy queries in location based services: Anonymizers are not necessary," pp. 121–132, Jun.9-12, 2008.

[9] B. Gedik and L. Liu, "A customizable k-anonymity model for protecting location privacy," in *Proc. ICDCS International Conference on Distributed Computing Systems)*, 2004, pp. 620–629.

[10] R. Cheng and F. Zhang, "An improved privacy protocol in location based service," pp. 1–4, Dec.19-20, 2009.

[11] G. Ghinita, "Understanding the privacy-efficiency trade-off in location based queries," *ACM SPRINGL IRVINE,2008*, pp. 1–5, Nov. 2008.

[12] G. Hjaltason and H. Samet, "Ranking in spatial databases," in *Proc. 4th Symposium on Spatial Database*, Springer-Verlag, Berlin, 1995, pp. 83–95.

[13] A. Yamamura and T. Saito, "Private information retrieval based on the subgroup membership problem," pp. 206–220, 2001.

[14] B. Gedik and L. Liu, "Location privacy in mobile systems: A personalized anonymization model," in *Proc. ICDCS International Conference on Distributed Computing Systems*, Columbus, OH, 2005, pp. 620–629.

[15] S. Goldwasser and M. Bellare, *Introduction to Modern Cryptography*, Cambridge, MA, Aug. 1999. [Online]. Available: http://computing.unn.ac.uk/staff/cgmb3/projects/CryptLectureNotes.pdf

[16] M. Murugesan, W. Jiang, A. E. Nergiz, and S. Uzunbaz, "k-out-of-n oblivious transfer based on homomorphic encryption and solvability of linear equations," in *Proc (CODASPY)' 11*, San Antonio, TX, Feb.21-23, 2011, pp. 169–178.

[17] B. CHOR, O. GOLDREICH, E. KUSHILEVITZ, and M. SUDAN, "Private information retrieval," in *Proc. JACM'98*, vol. 45, New York, NY, Nov. 1998, pp. 965–981.

[18] Y. Huang and R. Vishwanathan, "Privacy preserving group nearest neighbour queries in location-based services using cryptographic techniques," in *Proc. GLOBECOM'10*, Dec. 6–10, 2010, Conference Publication, pp. 1–5.

[19] E. Magkos, D. Kotzanikolaou, S. Sioutas, and K. Oikonomou, "A distributed privacy-preserving scheme for location-based queries," in *Proc. WoWMoM'10*, Jun. 14–17, 2010, conference publication, pp. 1–6.

[20] A. Khoshgozaran, H. Shirani-Mehr, and C. Shahabi, "Spiral:a scalable private information retrieval approach to location privacy," Master's thesis, 2008.

[21] C. Sheedy, "Privacy enhanced protocols using pairing based cryptography," PhD. Eng. thesis, Dublin City University, Dublin, Ireland, Jan. 2010.

[22] R. Vishwanathan, "Exploring privacy in location-based services using cryptographic protocols," Ph.D. dissertation, Univ. of North Texas, May 2011.

[23] T. Hashem, L. Kulik, and R. Zhang, "Privacy preserving moving knn queries," in *Proc. In Proceedings of CoRR*, Apr.14, 2011.

[24] J. Bao *et al.*, "Efficient evaluation of k-range nearest neighbor queries in road networks," pp. 115–124, 2010.

[25] M. L. Yiu *et al.*, "Spacetwist: Managing the trade-offs among location privacy, query performance, and query accuracy in mobile services," in *Proc. ICDE '08*, May 2008.

[26] M. Y. Jang, S. Jang, and J. Chang, "A new k-nn query processing algorithm enhancing privacy protection in location-based services," in *Proc. IEEE 11th International Conference on Computer and Information Technology* ., Aug.31- sep 2, 2011, pp. 421–428.

[27] L. Hu *et al.*, "Enforcing k nearest neighbor query integrity on road networks," in *Proc. IEEE in Proceedings of the 20th International Conference on Advances in Geographic Information Systems SIGSPATIAL '12*, Nov.6-9, 2011, pp. 422–425.

[28] X. Huang, C. Jensen, and S. Saltenis, "Multiple k nearest neighbor query processing in spatial network databases," in *Proc. IEEE in Proceedings of 10th East European Conference, ADBIS '06*, Thessaloniki, Greece, Sep.3-7, 2006, pp. 266–281.

[29] (2013, Feb.) Hilbert curve. [Online]. Available: http://en.wikipedia.org/wiki/Hilbert_curve

Cyber-security Defense in Large-scale M2M System

Actual Issues and Proposed Solutions

Mohammad Fal Sadikin
DAI-Labor
Technische Universität Berlin
Berlin, Germany
mohammad-fal.sadikin@dai-labor.de

***Abstract*—Today's Machine-to-Machine (M2M) market is growing rapidly and it is estimated to be massively deployed in the years to come. However, the massive deployment of M2M solutions will introduce tremendous challenges in its communication requirements. One of them is in the field of cyber-security defense. This paper outlines our view on M2M communication for cyber-security, particularly our vision in mutual authentication between device and M2M Operator according to actual issues in common standardization bodies such as ETSI and 3GPP. We here present in detail such actual issues related to the extremely large-number of devices connected in the constraint nature of M2M system, affecting the burden of high communication process as well as high communication cost. Furthermore, we present our framework for cyber-security modeling and purpose the suggested solutions tailored to the issues in order to achieve the trust and cyber-security goal in the large-scale M2M realm.**

***Index Terms*— M2M security, attack modeling framework, cyber-security defense, IBAKE.**

I. Introduction

Machine-to-Machine (M2M) communication has recently become popular as smart solutions in wide area of applications (e.g healthcare, smart-grid, smart-cities, etc.). It has been foreseen in various projections [1] that M2M technology will be massively deployed in the years to come. As an example, WWRF estimates that there will be around 7 Trillion devices connected by 2017. In cellular context, Ericsson predicts that there will be more than 50 Billion devices connected in M2M realm based on ubiquitous internet access over mobile broadband by 2020 [2]. Nevertheless, the global enforcement of M2M technology introduces tremendous challenges in its communication requirements, particularly in the field of cyber-security defense.

One of the main challenges in providing trust and security mechanism in a large scale M2M scenario is the enforcement of mutual authentication between devices and M2M Operator or application providers. Such authentication aims at guaranteeing that only authorized devices, software and applications can participate in the communication system. In general we can further outline the specific authentication challenges in M2M scenario, which are:

1. The immense number of connected devices: The main challenge of the global deployment of M2M solution is how to provide security and privacy mechanisms such as authentication, integrity protection and encryption in massive realm. This introduces complex key management and distribution as well as the enormity higher of communication cost.
2. Limited devices capabilities: M2M realm typically incorporates with tiny device attributes, such as limited computational and processing capabilities, limited memory, low data rate and low power/battery capability. This hampers the deployment of well-known and powerful security enforcements such as cryptographic and authentication mechanism, as common mechanisms overburden the devices capabilities. Examples are:
   - Low data rate hampers the exchange of key and authentication messages such as in Authentication and Key Agreement (AKA), affecting massive congestion in overall communication system.
   - Limited memory as well as limited computational power and processing make it inefficient to enforce common security mechanisms such as storing, computing and processing strong cryptographic objects.
   - The use of powerful security processing mechanisms is typically parallel to energy consumption. On the other hand small devices commonly incorporate with limited battery power as it is constrained by such small size.
3. Unattended Devices: In M2M realm, devices are typically placed in unsupervised areas that make it easier to be compromised. Example scenario is the attacker might try to extract the Universal Integrated Circuit Card (UICC) from legitimate M2M device for performing malicious activity such as observe the credential of the communications [3].

This paper discusses our vision in enforcing M2M mutual authentication according to actual issues in common standardization bodies such as ETSI and 3GPP. In detail, we further study the possible adoption of Identity-Based Authenticated Key Exchange (IBAKE) [4] in the large-scale M2M realm, as well as purpose our practical solutions to analyze the vulnerability in order to achieve trust and cyber-security goal in large-scale M2M Communications.

The rest of this paper is organized as follows. Section II presents related work. In section III, we discuss the issues associate to Mutual authentication for M2M communications, analyze the security vulnerability, as well as discuss the suggested solutions. Section IV discusses possible group-based authentication model. Section V outlines our solution in attack modeling for cyber-security defense. Finally we conclude our vision and future works in Section VI.

II. Related Work

Although M2M security is currently one of the hottest research topics in internet communications, to the best of our knowledge, only a little studies focusing on cyber-security field. In this section we discuss various studies that have been done related to our work.

One of earlier works on introducing the complexity of trust relationships among the various M2M players is Broustis and Sundaram [3]. In this work, they present a high level overview of ongoing standardization efforts, reaching from the possible adoption of IBAKE for mutual authentication to group-based authentication for large scale M2M scenario. However, they didn't reveal their perspective related to the technologies adoption, including the vulnerability analysis, possible attack scenarios and the solutions as well.

A dynamic group-based authentication and key agreement (DGBAKA) Protocol for Machine Type Communications (MTC) was proposed in [10]. This paper presents a practical group-based authentication and key agreement for MTC roaming scenario. In such group-based protocol, each device shares a secret key as well as a group secret key with home environment and other devices within the same group.

In associate to comparative research of IBAKE and PKI method, Bai Qing-hai [12] analyze the comparative study of PKI and general IBE system in term of concept and structure as well as the strength and weakness. Nevertheless, this work did not study the comparative analysis associate to the constraint nature of M2M scenario as this is the fundamental study of selecting IBAKE protocol for the M2M scenario.

III. Mutual Authentication in M2M World

Today's communication provides various possible solutions for authentication method. However, most of the solutions might not be suitable for M2M communications especially considering the device and cost constraint of the M2M nature. One well-known solution is Public Key Infrastructure (PKI) mechanisms. Although PKI method is subject to common certificate and key distribution problems [9], such method has been proved as satisfying solution in various communication domains. However enforcing PKI method may not be suitable for the constraint nature of M2M communications. Here we outline the constraint of PKI system in the face of M2M communications:

1. The highly dependence on third party Certificate Authority (CA) service: In term of PKI system for large-scale M2M, this introduces a complex problem of certificate creation, distribution, verification and management which further introduce the need of extremely large scale of PKI system.
2. High CAPEX and OPEX: The need of large-scale PKI system further introduces extremely high computing, processing and communication cost.
3. The need of high memory, power and storage: PKI requires such need as each entity in communication system would need to compute, verify and store certificate and its signature. In contrary, M2M communication incorporates with tiny devices with particular constraint such as low memory, power and storage.
4. High bandwidth consumption: In common PKI method, there is a certificate management system that each certificate ought to be delivered to the corresponding entity. This means that each entity in the communication system demands more bandwidth capacity. M2M realm typically associates to the constraint nature such as limited or low bandwidth capacity. This might affect overwhelming delay in certificate management process.

Based on the constrained attribute of M2M realm, several standardization bodies such as ETSI and 3GPP are considering another authentication mechanism based on Identity Based Encryption (IBE) [5] called Identity-Based Authenticated Key Exchange (IBAKE) [4]. We here analyze the possible adoption of IBAKE in the next sections.

3.1. Mutual Authentication using IBAKE

Identity-based encryption (IBE) is a public-key encryption mechanism constructed based on elliptic curve cryptography (ECC), that enables to calculate a public key and the corresponding private key based on mathematical function of an identity. Thus the main distinction of IBE system that is different from other is that eliminates the use of certificate. In other word, the client only needs to fetch a set of public parameters and there is no need further communication to the third-party server after the fetching step.

Indeed, IBE is a prominent technology in M2M realm as a suitable solution to overcome the constraint nature of M2M communication, instead of PKI system adoption. This method doesn't require certificate creation, storage, distribution and management. Therefore, the communication cost is arguably more efficient as the need of power, memory and storage as well as bandwidth consumption are reasonably lower.

As illustrated in figure 1. The device and M2M Operator use IBAKE to perform mutual authentication and key agreement. In this scenario, both Device and M2M Operator must have trust relationship to a third-party entity so called Key Generation Function (KGF), represented by Public Parameter Server (PPS) and Private-key Generator (PKG). As explained in [5], PPS is IBE public parameters that include publicly-sharable cryptographic material, known as IBE public parameters, and policy information for an associated PKG. A PPS provides a well-known location for secure distribution of IBE public parameters and policy information that describe the operation of a PKG. While PKG stores and uses cryptographic material, known as a master secret, this is used for generating a user's IBE private key.

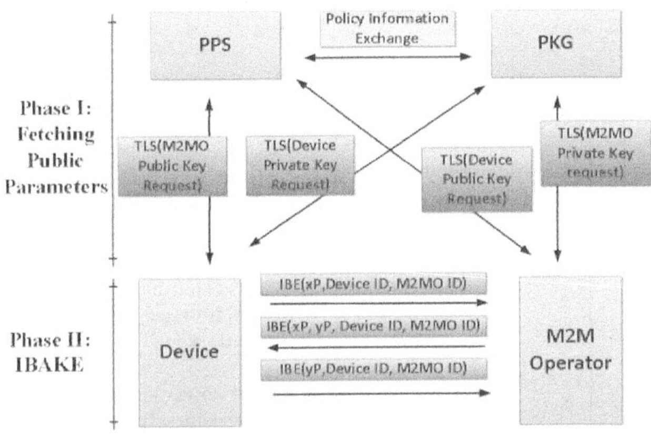

Fig. 1. Device authentication using IBAKE

In order to perform IBAKE handshake procedure, in Phase I: First of all both device and M2M Operator would need to fetch a set of public parameters from PPS and PKG, in order to further carry out asymmetric encryption and decryption process that is performed in the phase II. The public parameters here are a set of public key and private key of the corresponding entity in the mutual authentication. Each communication step in the phase I is transported over a secure protocol called Transport Layer Security (TLS). Such mechanism is enabled to enhance trust and security procedure such as to prevent eavesdropping and tampering by untrusted entity.

Once the set of public parameters is obtained, the IBAKE three-way handshake procedure is ready to be performed. As described in [4], IBAKE procedures in Phase II are conducted by exchanging three encrypted messages between the initiator and responder, in M2M scenario these are represented by device and M2M Operator. The detail exchanging message procedures are listed as follow:

1. The device and M2M Operator choose random x and y, respectively. In the first step of authentication process, the device computes xP using ECC, encrypts xP, the Device ID and M2M Operator ID using M2M Operator's public key, and includes this encrypted information in a MESSAGE_1 sent to the M2M Operator.
2. The M2M Operator, upon receiving the message, IBE-decrypts it using its private key, and obtains xP. The M2M Operator further chooses a random y and computes yP. The M2M Operator IBE-encrypts the device's identity (Device ID), its own identity (M2MO ID), xP, and yP using Device's Public Key. The M2M Operator includes this encrypted information in MESSAGE_2 sent to the Device.
3. The Device upon receiving and IBE-decrypting MESSAGE_2 obtains yP. Subsequently, the Device sends MESSAGE_3 to the M2M Operator, including IBE-encrypted Device ID, M2MO ID and yP. At this point, both the Device and the M2M Operator are able to compute the same session key as xyP.

In conclusion, this authentication mechanism is efficient and secure as the device and M2M Operator do not need to exchange their public key and private key to each other. Instead, KGF by means of PKG and PPS generate a pair of keys which are their corresponding public key and private key. Furthermore, each message in the three-way handshake procedure are encrypted by the public key of the addressed recipient, means that only the recipient can verify the message by decrypting it with their own private key. In other world, each message can only be decrypted either by M2M Operator private key or Device private key.

3.2. Security Analysis

This section discusses security issues using IBAKE in the face of M2M realm. First we discuss the possible passive eavesdropper and masquerade attack enabled by the large number of unintended devices. Afterward we present possible threats related to various Man-in-the-Middle (MITM) attacks.

3.2.1. Passive Eavesdropper and Masquerade as KGF Server

As standardized in IBE mechanism, IBAKE need to initially fetch a set of public parameters from third party KGF before performing the three-way hand shake procedure. In this case, there is no possible option for the device and the M2M operator other than ought to trust to the third party KGF which is protected using TLS. In other word, the security mechanism is highly dependent to TLS. However, TLS itself is well-known security technology shielded by various cryptographic options to protect application layer, and it is still a mainstay solution in wide area of internet applications. Nevertheless, such cryptographic options can only be enforced after the initial TLS handshake is successfully established. In other word, several credentials (e.g. server's identity, client's identity, etc.) are revealed during the initial handshake, as all those credentials are sent clearly as unencrypted messages. This event definitely allows a passive eavesdropper to observe the communications between client and KGF server, which then introduces opportunity to perform masquerade attack as KGF server. In M2M scenario, the threads become worst as the fact that there is no suitable protection mechanism tailored to large-number unintended devices. In such scenario, an attacker who impersonate as legitimate PPS or PKG can easily trick the unsupervised devices.

As explained in [5], there is a protection mechanism against masquerade attack for IBE communication. Here, IBE client software provides user interface that allow a user to visually determine whether connection to KGF servers is legitimate. This mechanism can help the user to stay aware and cannot easily be tricked to reveal their credential information to an adversary. Nevertheless, as discussed before, the clients in M2M realm are typically unintended devices without human intervention. This means that such solution is definitely not suitable in the face of M2M scenario. Furthermore, optional solution like facilitating M2M Network with detection system such as Intrusion Detection System (IDS), in order to oversee suspicious activities in the large-scale realm will affect the manifold higher of cost and introduce complex technical challenges. Therefore, such optional solution is arguably unrealistic for the constraint nature of M2M communications.

There is an on-progress work in [17], which intends to provide protection from passive eavesdropper; thereof it might be a suitable solution to prevent masquerade attack. In the on-progress work, the author defines a TLS extension which allows establishing encrypted TLS handshake with forward secrecy at the commencement of the handshake. However, this mechanism introduces an additional round trip communication between server and client affecting severe packet loss. In general, this circumstance may degrade the success rate of the communications. Severe packet loss will be definitely magnitude higher when considering the constraint nature of M2M world. Thus, this solution is arguably not feasible for M2M scenario particularly for critical applications (e.g. smart-grid, emergency services, etc.).

In this case, we mark this issue as further research work in the face of the most suitable solution to protect passive eavesdropper as well as masquerade as KGF Server specifically for the large-scale M2M communications.

3.2.2. MITM and DoS Against Key Exchange

This section outlines tangible threats of IBAKE over M2M realm related to Man-in-the-Middle (MITM) attacks and its derivation like Denial of Service (DoS) attack. Such threats are enabled by various apertures reaching from renegotiation feature in TLS to the possible chance for an adversary to issue forged certificates.

As published in [6], TLS is susceptible to a number of critical Man-in-the-Middle (MITM) attacks enabled by renegotiation mechanism. Renegotiation mechanism in TLS is a feature that allows session resumption to optimize the communication procedure, such as to save the computational time and cost by avoiding full cryptography processing on each update in the existing TLS connection (e.g. refreshing the keys, increasing the authentication level, repeatedly authentication attempt, etc.). Various MITM attacks have been demonstrated against HTTPS with variety of clients. The main issue in IBE standard is that IBE client must perform HTTP POST method to request a private key to PKG and verify the server certificate through HTTP over TLS (HTTPS). This means that private key communication procedure between device and PKG server are susceptible to MITM attacks as well.

Various possible MITM attacks over TLS have been published in [7][16], one of them is by injecting commands into an HTTPS session. Here, we outline in detail how the possible attack into HTTPS session is nevertheless possible to be conducted in the face of IBE private key communication in the M2M scenario.

As illustrated in figure 2. An attacker initially performs the MITM in step number (1) and (2), by holding TLS handshake session between legitimate device and PKG Server. In step (3), the attacker negotiates his or her own TLS Handshake instead of the holding session initiated by the legitimate device. In step (4), the PKG server sequential responds the attacker TLS handshake as the server cannot differentiate whether the message was requested from the legitimate device or from the

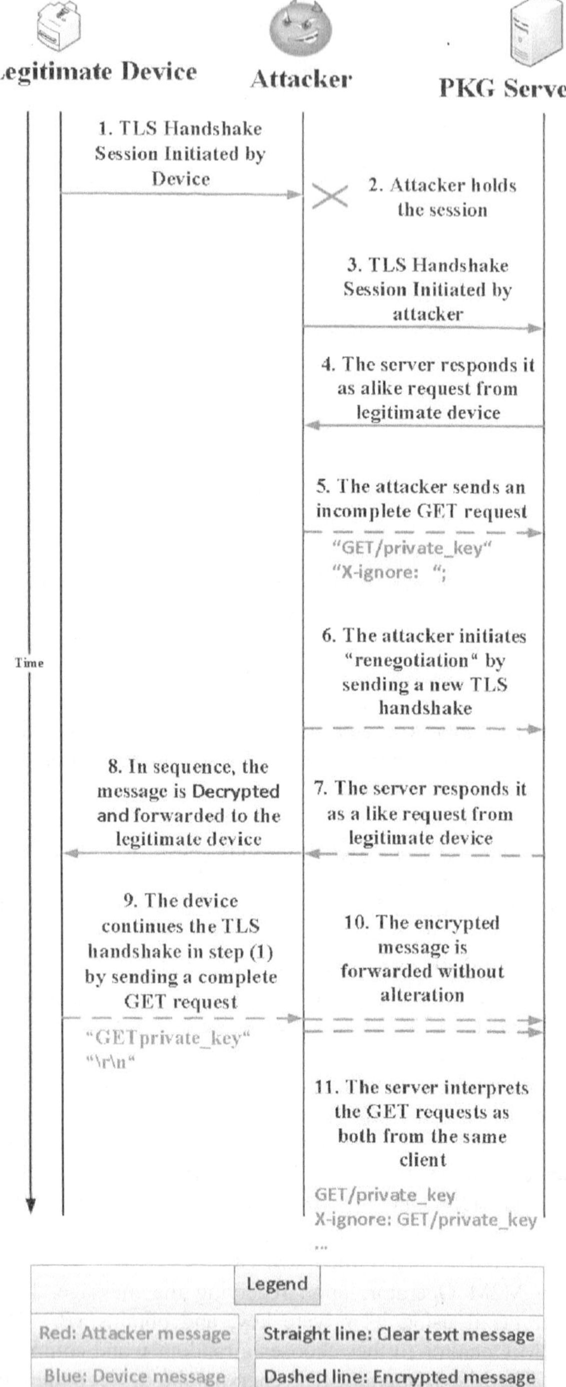

Fig. 2. MITM in the private key exchange

attacker. In step (5), the attacker sends an incomplete GET request to the PKG server; this step introduces a new chance to send renegotiation. Sequence in step (6), the attacker initiates the renegotiation by sending a new TLS Handshake. Again in step (7), the PKG server responds the Handshake request as it was recognized that the request was made from legitimate device. Henceforth the message is decrypted and forwarded to the legitimate device in step (8). In step (9), the legitimate device respond the forwarded message as it was recognized as the message from PKG server and as the sequence step initiated by the legitimate device in step (1). In this step, the device responds the forwarded message by sending a complete GET request. In step (10), the attacker forwards the message directly without alteration to the PKG server. Here the attacker has no chance to read the encrypted message. However, in step (11) the server interprets the GET requests both from device and attacker as the same requests from a legitimate device. The PKG server afterward link the legitimate device GET requests as sequence as GET request from the attacker. Therefore, it introduces a chance that the attacker requests will be authorized to perform further malicious activity.

Several solutions have been released for fixing the problem. However, there is no advanced solution other than simply disabling the renegotiation mechanism. On the other hand, disabling the renegotiation mechanism will introduce further problems (e.g. breaking the existing service, overburden in cryptographic processing, etc.), as the renegotiation feature was created to avoid such problems. Considering the constraint nature of M2M scenario, disabling renegotiation is certainly not a proper solution. Further solution has been proposed in RFC 5746 [11]. This solution offers a new TLS extension that cryptographically ties renegotiation feature to the TLS connections. This mechanism allows the server to differentiate renegotiation from initial renegotiation. Thus, it prevents negotiations from being spliced in the existing connections. Nevertheless, this solution further introduces a new serious threat for IBAKE communications in the M2M scenario. Here an attacker may attempt to splice an arbitrary renegotiation in to the TLS connection between legitimate device and PKG server. The server can thus detect the fake renegotiation by differentiating the cryptographic binding, and in sequence disables the TLS connection. This means that the attacker has just successfully performed Denial of Service (DoS) attack. Such attack prevents the private key exchange affecting the legitimate device or M2M Operator cannot decrypt and verify the authentication message. It is implied that DoS attack against mutual authentication between legitimate device and M2M Operator has been successfully done. Considering the critical M2M scenario like in Smart-grid application or emergency system, such attack introduces critical risks as it may cause serious damage.

MITM attack is indeed a serious problem, it is not only can be performed by exploiting renegotiation, but also can be done with various ways such as issuing forged certificates. Multiple studies have proposed various solutions that probably can be adopted for particular MITM protection. Most of them focused on the use of additional third-party. For example, Crossbear [13] uses third-party observers, which can detect and localize if there is a mismatch between the certificate reported by the client and the one from a given server. Perspectives [14] and Convergence [15] offer identical services that use network notaries to observe the certificate. While these solutions provide particular advantages, we strongly believe that the adoption of third party observers in the constraint nature of M2M world will introduce further problems such as communication overload, high operational cost, complex security procedure (e.g. certificate and key management). Furthermore, these solutions also introduce new privacy issue as the third-party observers actively oversee and process the communication credentials. In addition, as these solutions are essentially similar with IDS, the complexity of these solutions might introduce the same problems called false alarms (e.g. false positive and false negative). In this case we consider false positive as a worrisome problem that could harm the system. In this scenario a legitimate service may be treated as malicious activities which eventuate breaking the existing services. In general, adopting such solutions will introduce a complex challenges in associate to tackling such derivative problems.

Reflecting the characteristics of M2M communication, to the best of our knowledge, the most suitable solution to mitigate the MITM attacks is by preventing an adversary to actively eavesdrop credential information (e.g. server's ID, client's ID, unencrypted handshake messages, etc.). This mechanism can be established by defining a fully encrypted TLS handshake between clients and PKG server as early as possible, through initially perform a normal TLS handshake with anonymous PKG server and clients, then shortly renegotiate the new TLS Handshake with fully encrypted communications. Thus, such mechanism can protect the TLS connection against MITM attacks by confounding the adversary's chance to actively eavesdrop the credentials.

Nevertheless, defining the TLS communications with fully encrypted mechanism would need further investigation in term of communication burden. In this case, renegotiation is always required on each TLS session, which probably doubles the communication process, such as network delay improvements. Here we also mark this section as future study associating with the best solution to prevent MITM in the face of M2M realm.

IV. GROUP-BASED DEVICE AUTHENTICATION

In the introduction, we discussed one of the main challenges that the number of connected devices in the M2M world will soon be magnitude higher than the number exists today. Most of state of the art authentication mechanism can satisfy the actual communication requirements. Nevertheless, the case will be different in the large-scale M2M scenario which deals with tremendous number of devices. In such large-scale scenario, the operator will be overwhelmed by numerous numbers of authentication requests affecting massive congestion and network overhead.

Group-based Device Authentication (GDA) is an authentication mechanism that allows a group of devices to be authenticated as a single device. Therefore, such mechanism can significantly reduce the number of authentication messages between device and M2M Operator. In this section, we purpose our solutions which are Hierarchical Model and Chain Model, in order to enable mutual authentication between device and M2M Operator using IBAKE in Group-based methods.

4.1. Hierarchical Model

Hierarchical network model is a well-known solution in various area of communication system. Here we purpose hierarchical model for M2M group-based authentication by

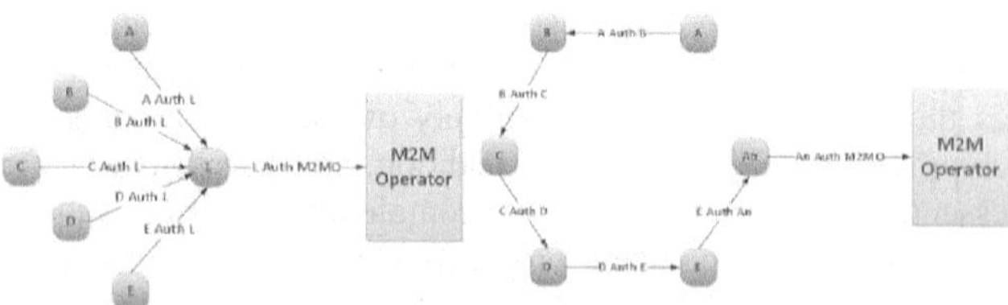

Fig. 3.a. and 3.b GDA based on hierarchical and chain model.

simply choosing a leader in particular group. A number of devices can be group based on particular parameters. For instance, all devices belong in the same home network will be grouped and authenticated as one entity or device.

As illustrated in figure 3.a. a leader performs mutual authentication with all devices in the group to build trust among them. In sequence, the leader also performs mutual authentication with M2M Operator. In this authentication scenario, a leader must be a device with exclusive specifications which are the most powerful device, well provisioned and well accessible to all entities in the nature of M2M system. Thus the leader has sufficient capability to fulfill a batch of mutual authentication requests both from its members and M2M Operator.

4.2. Chain Model

Chain Model can be considered as another solution instead performing the authentication in hierarchical manner. The advantage of this model is that there is no requirement for choosing a leader with particular specification. All devices in the group are threaded as equal. Instead, such model requires for choosing the anchor device which has better access to the M2M Operator as well as to the group members. Thus the anchor can easily perform mutual authentication to the M2M Operator without significant congestion.

As illustrated in figure 3.b. All devices perform mutual authentication to each other. In such scenario, each device supervises its neighbor so that an illegitimate device has no chance to perform mutual authentication to the legitimate group. Therefore only authorized device can participate in the communication system.

4.3. Authentication Messages and Security Consideration

We assume here that the M2M system use IBAKE which perform three-way handshake in each mutual authentication.

As implied in Table I. Both Hierarchical model and Chain model can significantly reduce the number of messages, especially the authentication messages between device and M2M Operator. Here an operator needs to exchange only a three-way handshake (3 messages) instead of exchanging 3n messages in the group with n devices. This is definitely critical factor that can avoid congestion and network overload caused by the overwhelmed requests in M2M Operator.

In the face of security consideration, both models are reliable as each device in the group is certainly authenticated. Therewith, it is feasible to authenticate a legitimate device which move and become a new member of a group. It is possible as long as such device can fetch a set of public parameters to KGF server. Therefore both models enable to

TABLE I. NUMBER OF AUTHENTICATION MESSAGES FOR HIERARCHICAL AND CHAIN MODEL

Number of Devices	Number of Authentication Messages	
	Group Network	Device-M2MO
5	12	3
15	42	3
(n) Devices	3(n-1)	3

ensure that each device participate in the M2M realm is an authorized entity.

Nevertheless, as same as other group-based authentication, both mechanisms are subject to various attacks on the issue of identity, such as Sybil Attack [8]. The main issue is that the M2M Operator cannot guarantee that each entity in such large-scale communication system is represented by a single identity. Here an identity has possible chance to masquerade as multiple identities. On the other hand, tackling this issue by providing manual attention in the large-scale M2M will be very costly. This section finally also introduces further study associate to mitigate such vulnerability.

V. ATTACK MODELING FOR CYBER-SECURITY DEFENSE

Attack Modeling is one of critical approach to evaluate the vulnerability, strengthen, as well as to protect the system from various threats. In the large-scale M2M system, such approach introduces a complex work and error prone. In addition, the complexity factor of M2M defense and preventing system could impact to the cost limitation of M2M realm. Here we present our framework which enables the efficient modeling as well as evaluate the security protection both in term of technical and economical aspect. One of our objectives is to speed up and eliminate the error prone of the complexity of M2M attack modeling. This framework is based on EMF [18] and GMF [19] technologies. However, distinct with SeaMonter [20], our framework focuses on security defense analysis [21].

Figure 4 illustrates our proposed model that enables to model the vulnerability based on attack tree. Furthermore such model also enables to model the countermeasure approach for evaluating the possible defense to strengthen the network.

Figure 5 illustrates an example of attack and defense modeling using our approach. Here we describe step by step possible DoS attack based on the vulnerabilities introduced in the previous section. We also depict all possible countermeasure based on defense tree approach which is illustrated as green branch-tree. Example here is method to prevent the Sybil Attack. One of the methods is by conducting movement observation for detecting the attack in mobile networks. In this case, the attacker device or identity will always appear moving together with the legitimate identity. Thus the attacker movement can be distinguished from the legitimate movement. Furthermore, in term of compromising the unintended device, the platform shows two possible approaches. Firstly by enforcing trusted devices that binds trusted certification authorities to specific device. Secondly, by installing alarm to the unintended devices, this approach is strongly believed can constraint the unintended devices from malicious activity.

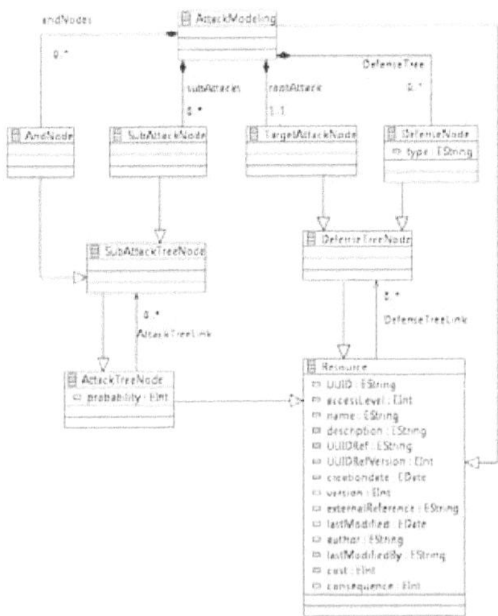

Fig. 4. Model of attack-defense tree.

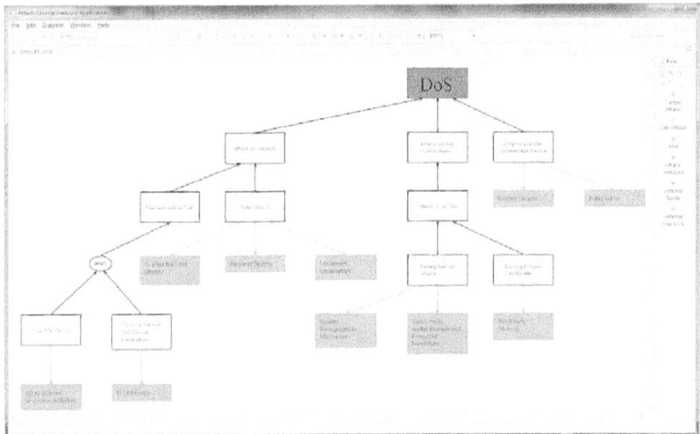

Fig. 5. DoS attack-defense modeling.

VI. Conclusion and Future Works

Although several standardization groups have initially published their perspective and solution for enforcing security mechanism in large-scale M2M communications, various issues are further introduced in their works.

Here we can conclude that IBAKE is prominent solution instead of adopting PKI system. Such solution is reasonably more appropriate with the constraint nature of M2M realm. Nevertheless, IBAKE system further introduces particular challenges which need further studies in term of cyber-security defense. There are various open issues related to MITM, Sybil Attack, DoS, etc.

Based on the conclusion, one solution is to develop intelligent attack modeling framework tailored to M2M system. Here the focus will be on autonomous operation that can help the operator to model and evaluate the vulnerabilities in order to achieve the strength of cyber-security defense.

References

[1] M. Dohler, T. Watteyne, and J. A. Zarate, "M2M: an emerging communication paradigm," Globcom, Tutorial, 2010.

[2] Ericsson White Paper, "More than 50 billion connected devices," February 2011. (Last retrieved in December 2012). http://www.ericsson.com/res/docs/whitepapers/wp-50-billions.pdf

[3] I. Broustis, G. Sundaram, S. Mizikovsky, and H. Viswanathan, "M2M Security, in M2M Communications: A Systems Approach", (editors: D. Boswarthick, O. Elloumi and O. Hersent), John Wiley & Sons, Ltd, Chichester, UK, 2012. doi: 10.1002/9781119974031.ch8.

[4] V. Cakulev, G. Sundaram, and I. Broustis, "IBAKE: Identity-Based Authenticated Key Exchange," RFC 6539, March 2012.

[5] G. Appenzeller, L. Martin, and M. Schertler, "Identity-based encryption architecture and supporting data structures," RFC 5408, 2009.

[6] M. Ray, S. Dispensa, "Renegotiating TLS," November 2009. http://extendedsubset.com/Renegotiating_TLS.pdf

[7] T. Zoller, "TLS & SSLv3 renegotiation vulnerability explained," 2011. http://www.g-sec.lu/practicaltls.pdf (Last retrieved in December 2012).

[8] J.R. Douceur, "The sybil attack," In Proc. the First International Workshop on Peer-to-Peer Systems (IPTPS), March 2002.

[9] C. Ellison, and B. Schneier, "Ten risks of PKI: what you're not being told about public key infrastructure," Computer Security Journal, v 16, n 1, 2000, pp. 1-7.

[10] Y. Zhang, J. Chen, H. Li, W. Zhang, J. Cao, C. Lai, "Dynamic group based authentication protocol for machine type communications," In Proc. 4th INCoS, 2012, vol., no., pp.334-341, 19-21 Sept. 2012.

[11] E. Rescorla, M. Ray, S. Dispensa, N. Oskov, "Transport layer security (TLS) renegotiation indication extension," RFC 5746. 2010.

[12] B. Qing-hai; , "Comparative research on two kinds of certification systems of the public key infrastructure (PKI) and the identity based encryption (IBE)," In Proc. CSQRWC, 2012 , vol., no., pp.147-150, 23-27 July 2012.

[13] R. Holz, T. Riedmaier, N. Kammenhuber, and G. Carle, "X.509 forensics: detecting and localising the SSL/TLS men-in-the-middle," In Proc. 17th ESORICS 2012, volume 7459/2012 of LNCS, pages 217-234, Pisa, Italy, September 2012. Springer Verlag.

[14] D. Wendlandt, D.G. Andersen, A. Perrig, "Perspectives: improving SSH-style host authentication with multi-path probing," In: Proc. USENIX 2008 Ann. Tech. Conf. ATC.2008.

[15] M. Marlinspike, Thoughtcrime Labs/IDS: Convergence (2011), http://convergence.io (last retrieved in December 2012).

[16] Y. Suga, "Countermeasures and tactics for transitioning against the SSL/TLS renegotiation vulnerability," In Proc. 6th IMIS, 2012, vol., no., pp.656-659, 4-6 July 2012.

[17] M. Ray, "Transport layer security (TLS) encrypted handshake extension," Work in progress, IETF Internet Draft. May, 2012. http://tools.ietf.org/id/draft-ray-tls-encrypted-handshake-00.txt (last retrieved in December 2012).

[18] Eclipse Modeling Framework Project (EMF), http://eclipse.org/modeling/emf/ (last retrieved in March 2013).

[19] Graphical Modeling Framework (GMF), http://www.ibm.com/developerworks/opensource/library/os-ecl-gmf/ (last retrieved in March 2013).

[20] P.H. Meland, D.S. Spampinato, E. Hagen, E.T. Baadshaug, K.M. Krister, K.S. Velle, "SeaMonster: Providing tool support for security modeling", NISK-2008 conference.

[21] S. Bistarelli, F. Fioravanti, P. Peretti, "Defense Trees for Economic Evaluation of Security Investments", In: ARES, pp. 416–423. IEEE Computer Society, Los Alamitos (2006).

SESSION

COMPUTER SECURITY II

Chair(s)

Dr. Rita Barrios

Pictorial Presentation of Computer Behavior and Fault Detection Automation Using Genetic Algorithm

Ali Mohammed Elsawwaf[1], **Ahmed Samir Eldessouky**[2]
[1]Faculty of Engineering, Ain Shams University, Abbassia, Cairo, Egypt
[2]Thebes Academy, Thebes Higher Institute of Engineering, Cairo, Egypt
ali_elsawwaf@yahoo.com, eldessouky_a@yahoo.com

Abstract - *In recent years, several approaches were developed to detect unknown malcodes including both worms and viruses using machine learning techniques. This paper introduces a novel algorithm to monitor the computer behavior through the computer counters. Pictorial presentation of the computer counters is adopted for both feature selection and online monitoring to detect the presence of both viruses and denial of service attacks. The proposed algorithm applies both genetic algorithm (GA) and best correlated record (BCR) in the calibration phase to identify a reference vector that represents the monitored counters during regular operation. A correlation technique is implemented in the monitoring phase to automate the process of computer fault detection at real time. The proposed algorithm has been tested on two different environments with different types of attack to evaluate its performance and validity. Results show that the system is able to early detect the attack with minimum false alarm rate.*

Keywords: Fault Detection; Pictorial Analysis; Machine Learning; Malecode Detection; Genetic algorithm.

1 Introduction

Detection of unknown malcodes including both worms and viruses is considered one of the most important activities in today's enterprises. Recent studies have proposed two approaches for the detection based on the use of machine learning (ML) techniques. First approach is based on extracting top byte N-grams [1-3] and Opcode N-grams [4-6]. Despite of its ability of detecting malicious files, it cannot detect faults due to remote attacks such as denial of service (DOS) attack and malcodes located in the memory. Second approach is based on monitoring computer's counters in order to detect the presence of the malicious effect [7-12]. While this approach does not prevent infection, it enables fast detection of an infection which may result in an alert.

Both approaches require labeling from an expert [11, 13] which is considered as a time consuming task. Whenever there is a miss-presentation of the numbers of examples to classes, which leads to imbalanced problem [13], the instances of the low represented classes tend to misclassify for most standard classifiers [14].

Pictorial analysis is an algorithm that presents any system parameters into a visualized picture. In addition, the algorithm incorporates human and computer interaction to select and adjust the visual representations for better feature and pattern selection. This way, the system normal operation can be monitored and any fault can be readily detected.

Pictorial analysis procedure was first presented by Grishin et al. [15, 16]. The approach is based on mapping multidimensional relations by transforming the initial data into artificial visualized pictures. The composed images should help the expert in decision making for fault detection and system diagnosis. The proposed algorithm presents the design and implementation of the pictorial analysis to monitor computers (personal or server machines) operation and early detect faults that may result from both benign and malicious programs. In addition, an automated mechanism is conducted to produce an alert as soon as a fault in the monitored computer is detected. The automation is performed based on two steps. Training step (calibration phase) comes first, in which a search for the best pictorial presentation of the monitored counters at normal operation is generated. The correlation step is the second step in which, online correlation between the trained image of normal operation and the current captured image of the computer counters is performed. The best correlated record and genetic algorithms are used for the first step.

The rest of the paper is organized as follows: section 2 describes the proposed algorithm, section 3 provides a case study to evaluate the proposed algorithm and section 4 describes the concluding remarks achieved.

2 Proposed detection algorithm

The proposed algorithm consists of four phases, pictorial representation; feature selection; calibration and correlation phase. This is shown in figure (1).

2.1 Pictorial representation phase

The system is trained to present computer counters as a visualized picture during the normal and abnormal operations. Color matrix representation is the most effective choice to make pictorial representation that will be used later in feature selection process [15]. Two colors (red and blue) are selected to represent the upper and lower boundaries of the dynamic range of each counter. Counters with values in between would have color change between the selected two colors.

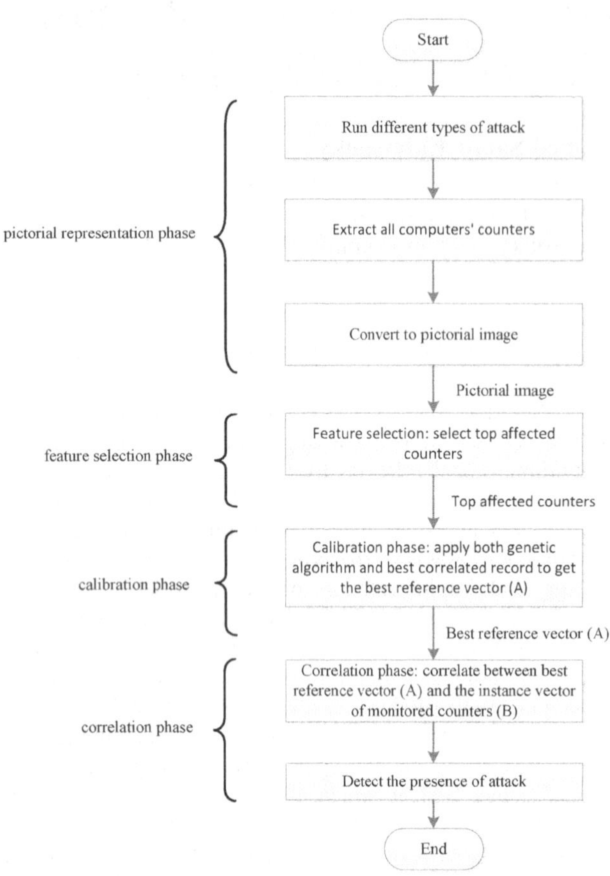

Fig. 1. Proposed detection algorithm

2.2 Feature selection phase

The large number of features presents a challenge, in which some of the features do not contribute to the accuracy of fault detection. Feature selection is the process of selecting the most affected counters in the dataset and discarding unaffected ones [11]. The goal of this phase is to find the common affected counters in order to generalize the detection of the unknown malicious activity effect. Feature selection reduces the dimensionality of the data and enables the correlation algorithm to operate more efficient. In addition, it minimizes the self-consumption of computer resources for monitoring operations. Two approaches can be adopted for feature selection, setting a predefined number of features to be monitored and hence, select the most affected counters, or define threshold level at which the counters that crosses the threshold level are selected while others will be neglected. The second approach is followed where the counters that were dramatically affected by computer's abnormal behavior were selected. Although Fisher score is the best tool for feature selection, it has major drawbacks. Correlations between features cannot be captured and thus several equivalent features might be selected. Here comes the advantage of pictorial presentation of computer counters. An expert can set proper criteria for feature selection and implement them through pictorial analyses. The criteria are formed such that counters that have dramatic color change (representing dramatic value change) will be selected.

In feature selection process, counters that have dramatic color change, as stated, will be selected. Other counters that have no color change, slight color change, or oscillating change in color during the full testing time will be excluded. Only one feature is selected among features with identical behavior.

2.3 Calibration phase

In automation process, and according to the different hardware configurations, installed services and applications on each server, it is required to perform system calibration. In this phase, all required services and applications on the monitored server are running and reaching their steady state (normal operation).

Based on this state, both of genetic algorithm and best correlated record are applied to get the best reference vector that will be used in the correlation process for the automation purpose. The first 100 instances of the steady state period represent the training set, from which a reference vector will be trained to provide maximum correlation with all other instances.

For genetic algorithm, the selected counters are coded into genes to represent one chromosome. The generation size is set to 100 individual and 80% of the population are allowed for crossover process. The mutation is performed on one randomly selected gene for one randomly selected chromosome each generation. The fitness function is selected to be the summation of the correlation between each individual in the generation and the 100 instance that represent the computer behavior at regular operation. The fitness function is as follow:

$$\text{Fitness} = \sum_{j=1}^{J} r \quad (1)$$

$$r = \frac{\sum_m \sum_n (A_{mn} - \bar{A})(B_{mn} - \bar{B})}{\sqrt{(\sum_m \sum_n (A_{mn} - \bar{A})^2)(\sum_m \sum_n (B_{mn} - \bar{B})^2)}} \quad (2)$$

Where:

r represents the correlation between two vectors,

A (represents the reference vector) ,

B (represents the sample instance of monitored counter),

$\bar{A}$ and $\bar{B}$ represent the mean value of the two vectors.

m and n are indices of two dimensional reference vectors (m represent the index of the time and n represents the counter index). In this case m=1(no dynamic presentation of the counter behavior) and n= ranges from 1 to the number of counters

J is the number of instances that represents the computer's normal behavior at steady state. In this case J=100.

2.4 Correlation phase

This phase, online monitoring and auto-fault detection using the correlation algorithm given by equation (2) is conducted.

3 Tests and Results

According to the variation of hardware specifications, it is expected to get more affected counters in case of testing the attacks on networks with low hardware specifications.

Hence, in order to have the optimal feature selection and attain generalization, two environments with different hardware configurations are described below.

Environment 1:

Total of six machines are connected as shown in figure (2). Three of them are client machines, (windows 7 32 bit& 64 bit, ubuntu 10.10), from which the attack will be launched. The server machines are: Microsoft active directory 2003(LDAP and DNS roles are installed), Microsoft SQL 2005 and IBM Domino 8.5 and sametime 8.0, this machine acts as both mail and web application server. Servers have low hardware specifications with memory within 776 MB to one GB, one processor, one logical partition, and network interface with 100 Mbps speed.

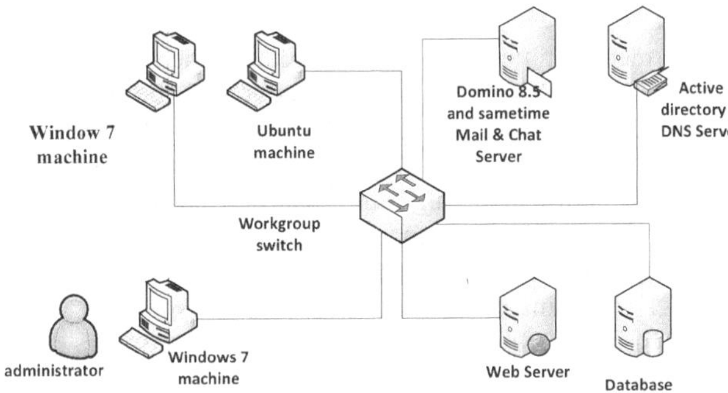

Fig. 2. Environment 1(E1), with low hardware specification.

Environment 2:

A total of five servers machines with much higher hardware specifications, four GB memory, four processors (two at least), two logical partitions at least, and network interface with a speed of one Gbps are connected as shown in figure (3). The network is divided into four controlled zones using a firewall. The Backend zone contains SQL Database server and Domino 8.5 Mail server. The demilitarized zone (DMZ) contains the Web server, IBM WebSphere Portal 6.0.1.3 and IBM HTTP server. The client zone contains the client PC from which the attacks will be launched. In addition there are more than 300 client's machines that have access to all of these servers. The last zone contains both primary and secondary active directory 2003, in which both of LDAP and DNS roles are installed.

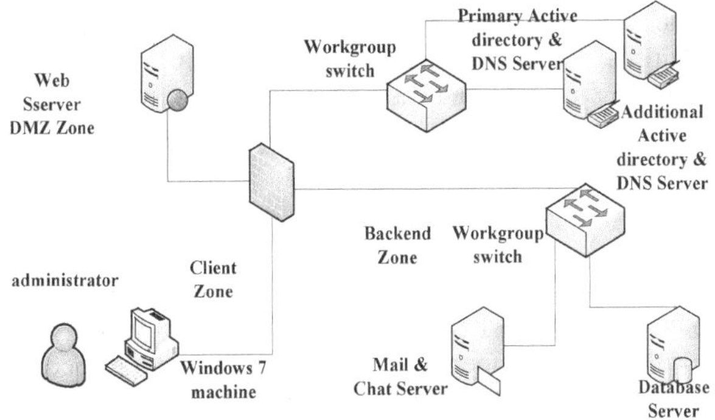

Fig. 3. Environment 2 (E2), with high hardware specification.

The counters of the following windows performance objects [22] are used: Cache, ICMP, IPv4, Logical Disk, Memory, Network Interface, Physical Disk, Process, Processor, System, TCPv4, UDPv4. In addition, it is possible to consider also counters that are completely related to running application on monitored server such as DNS. Monitoring the running application counters will be useful to determine the port number used in the attack. In case of Process object, only counters that are related to _Total, dns, idle, and System instances are selected. In case of Thread object, only counters that are related to _Total/_Total are selected.

Windows performance counter (WPC) tool is configured to measure the counters every second and store them in a tab separated log file. In case of automation, WPC will be configured to store its measurements in a central remote database server.

3.1 Case study 1:

To determine the best combination of features two set of experiments are performed. Network of environment 1(E1) was selected for the first experiment. UDP flooding, TCP flooding and virus simulator are activated and computer counters are monitored and converted to artificial picture. Pictorial analysis is performed in order to select the affected counters and exclude completely correlated counters.

Launching the attack:

The following attack scripts will be used in feature selection process.

- flood.pl (This PERL script provides a simple UDP flood generator [17]).
- Tcpflood.pl (This PERL script provides a simple TCP flooder [18]).
- Virus.bat (This file was downloaded from VX Heavens web site before it has been closed).

In each test, counters were monitored for 30 minutes as shown in table (1).

TABLE 1. LAUNCHING ATTACK SEQUENCE.

Time Period	activity
0-5 minutes	No (user activity, background application, launched attack)
5-10 minutes	Only background application and user activity (normal operation)
10-15 minutes	Background application, user activity and only virus simulator
15-20 minutes	Background application, user activity and only launching UDP flooding script
20-25 minutes	Background application, user activity and only launching TCP flooding script
25-30 minutes	No (user activity, background application, launched attack)

The algorithm shown in figure (4) will be used as a guide in feature selection process.

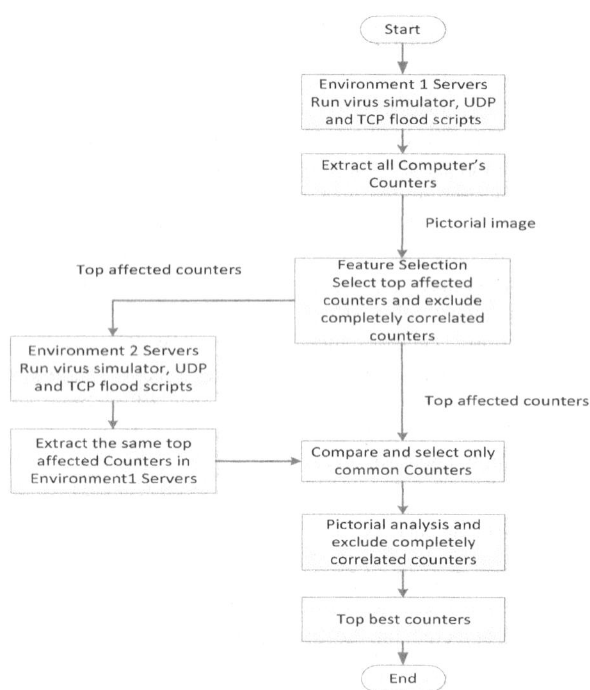

Fig. 4. Selecting the Top best counters

According to the algorithm explained in figure (4), it is clear that all counters of logical disk excluding (LogicalDisk\% Free Space and LogicalDisk\Free Megabytes) counters, are identical (completely correlated) to the physical disk counters as clearly noted by their pictorial presentation shown in figure (5).

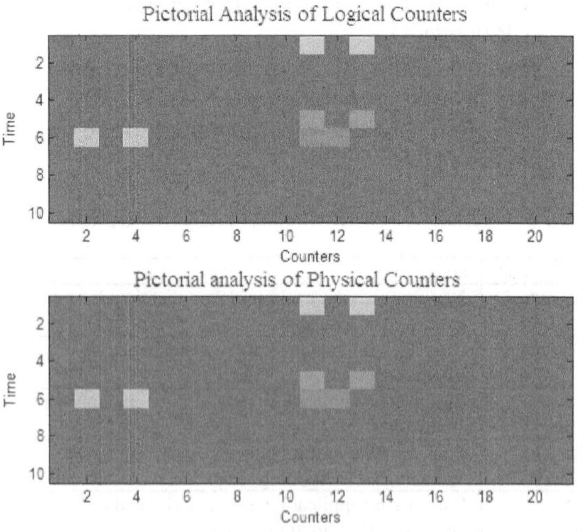

Fig. 5. Pictorial Analysis for Both Logical and Physical Counters.

The correlation for the physical and their corresponding logical counters equals one indicating the matching between their values during the test period. Hence the physical counters are excluded from the monitoring set.

Based on the first experiment, a list of 52 counters, as listed in table 2, were selected in case of DNS servers, while a list of 50 counters were selected in case of other servers, in which both of (\Process(dns)\IO Other Bytes/sec and \Process(dns)\IO Other Operations/sec) counters are related to DNS application only.

The same experiment was performed again using environment 2 (E2) with the same number of counters. The main purposes of this experiment are: (1) Study the effect of different hardware configuration on counters behavior, (2) Excluding unaffected counters.

Finally, a comparison between results of both environments E1&E2 was conducted and only common features were selected.

A list of 34 counters was achieved (shown in table 2) in case of monitoring DNS servers and 33 counters, excluding (\Process(dns)\IO Other Operations/sec) counter, are achieved in case of all other application servers such as web application and mail servers.

3.2 Case study 2:

To estimate the potential of the proposed approach to detect unknown faults, an additional experiment was performed with new attack tools. In this experiment, the top selected features in the case study will be monitored (number of counters nc = 33 or 34 in case of DNS servers). In addition, the process of fault detection is automated by applying both genetic algorithm and best correlated record, to identify the best reference of computer regular operation, and implementing the correlation mechanism.

The automation process is as follow:

- Use the first 100 instances of monitored system for Calibration Process.
- Perform training process to the reference instance that provides a maximum correlation with the first 100 instances (representing normal, no attack, and activity). Genetic algorithm and best correlated record are adopted for that purpose.
- The correlation between trained reference instance and real-time sampled instance is calculated according to equation (2).
- Finally the proposed approach is subjected to completely new attack tools that were not applied during feature selection phase; hence, the proposed algorithm is tested for generality.

The mean (μ) and standard deviation (σ) values for correlation during the normal operation and the system attack were calculated. The standard deviation shows the spread of the correlation around its mean value during both cases (normal operation and system attack). This would strongly reflect the false alarm rate (FAR) (alarm while no attack) and the miss rate (MR) (no alarm during attack). In addition, Fisher's score ranking (*R*) [10] is calculated according to equation (3):

$$R = \frac{|\mu_1 - \mu_2|}{\sigma_1 + \sigma_2} \tag{3}$$

Where (μ_1) and (μ_2) are the mean values of correlation for the normal operation and system attack respectively while (σ_1) and (σ_2) are the standard deviations for the normal operation and system attack respectively. Hence, the experiment with high *R* means that the band between the correlation during normal operation and system attack is wide with less probability of FAR and MR.

The following new attack tools are used for the test:

- HULK - Http Unbearable Load King [19]
  HULK is a web server denial of service tool written for research purposes.
- Pjam2 and pjam3 [20, 21]
  Pjam2 and Pjam3 are effective UDP packet flooders for windows however; Pjam3 is 50 times faster than pjam2 (up to 50mb/s). PJAM2 will be used in the implemented experiment.
- Generic.dx!bb3b and Generic.dx!bblv are inserted on the client machine.

The previous attack tools are used to run the following tests:

- Test1: attack web server (HTTP server) on port 80, TCP attack, using HULK tool.
- Test2: Attack server (HTTP server) on port 80, TCP attack, using PJAM2 tool.
- Test3: attack active directory server on port 389 (LDAP), TCP attack, using PJAM2 tool.
- Test4: attack primary active directory on port 53 (DNS), UDP attack, using both of Generic.dx!bb3b and Generic.dx!bblv.
- Test5: attack secondary active directory on port 53 (DNS), UDP attack, using both of Generic.dx!bb3b and Generic.dx!bblv.

For all five tests, Fisher's score (R) is calculated for both genetic algorithm and best correlated record methods to compare the effectiveness of both methods. For genetic algorithm, search process to find the best individual was set to stop as soon as the best fitness change is not improving over an epoch of 15 generation. The Best, average and worst fitness of the trained record verses generation is presented in figure (6). It shows that after 23 generations, the algorithm stopped the search process and the best fitness was settled after the 1st seven generations.
The output figures for test2, applying both genetic algorithm and best correlated record, are displayed in figures (7 and 8) for 33 counters.

The proposed algorithm proves that it is able to detect completely unknown TCP&UDP flooding from unknown attacks. Although the firewall was not able to stop any of the attacks, the proposed approach was able to identify that there was an attack.

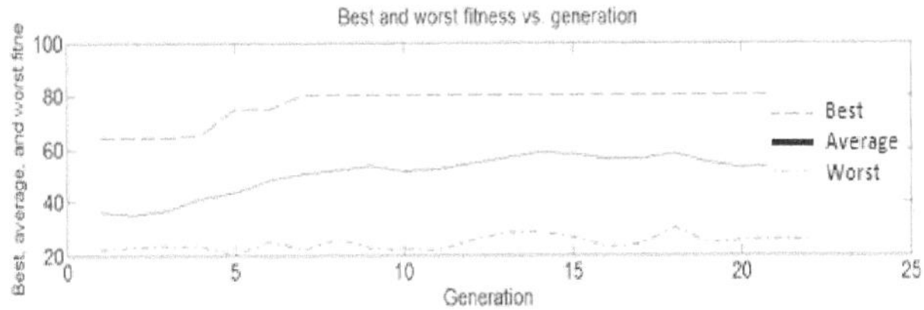

Fig. 6. Best, average and worst fitness of the trained record verses generation.

TABLE 2. SELECTED COUNTERS SETS HAVING 52 OR 34 COUNTERS FOR DNS SERVERS
(E1: Machines with low hardware specifications; E2: Machines with high hardware specifications); ✓ means affected; × means unaffected.

ID	Feature Name	E1	E2
1.	\Cache\Copy Read Hits %	✓	✓
2.	\Cache\Copy Reads/sec	✓	✓
3.	\Cache\Data Map Pins/sec	✓	✓
4.	\Cache\Data Maps/sec	✓	✓
5.	\Cache\Sync Copy Reads/sec	✓	✓
6.	\Cache\Sync Data Maps/sec	✓	✓
7.	\IPv4\Datagrams Received Delivered/sec	✓	✓
8.	\IPv4\Datagrams Received/sec	✓	✓
9.	\IPv4\Datagrams Sent/sec	✓	✓
10.	\IPv4\Datagrams/sec	✓	✓
11.	\LogicalDisk(_Total)\Avg. Disk Bytes/Read	✓	×
12.	\LogicalDisk(_Total)\Disk Read Bytes/sec	✓	×
13.	\Memory\Cache Faults/sec	✓	✓
14.	\Memory\Demand Zero Faults/sec	✓	×
15.	\Memory\Page Faults/sec	✓	×
16.	\Memory\Transition Faults/sec	✓	×
17.	\Network Interface(Broadcom NetXtreme Gigabit Ethernet)\Bytes Received/Sec	✓	×
18.	\Network Interface(Broadcom NetXtreme Gigabit Ethernet)\Bytes Sent/sec	✓	×
19.	\Network Interface(Broadcom NetXtreme Gigabit Ethernet)\Bytes Total/sec	✓	×
20.	\Network Interface(Broadcom NetXtreme Gigabit Ethernet)\Packets Received Unicast/sec	✓	✓
21.	\Network Interface(Broadcom NetXtreme Gigabit Ethernet)\Packets Received/sec	✓	✓
22.	\Network Interface(Broadcom NetXtreme Gigabit Ethernet)\Packets Sent Unicast/sec	✓	✓
23.	\Network Interface(Broadcom NetXtreme Gigabit Ethernet)\Packets Sent/sec	✓	✓
24.	\Network Interface(Broadcom NetXtreme Gigabit Ethernet)\Packets/sec	✓	✓
25.	\Process(_Total)\% Privileged Time	✓	×
26.	\Process(_Total)\% Processor Time	✓	×
27.	\Process(_Total)\IO Data Operations/sec	✓	✓
28.	\Process(_Total)\IO Read Operations/sec	✓	✓
29.	\Process(dns)\IO Other Bytes/sec	✓	×
30.	\Process(dns)\IO Other Operations/sec	✓	✓
31.	\Process(Idle)\% Privileged Time	✓	×
32.	\Process(Idle)\% Processor Time	✓	×
33.	\Process(System)\IO Other Operations/sec	✓	✓
34.	\Processor(_Total)\% C1 Time	✓	✓
35.	\Processor(_Total)\% DPC Time	✓	✓
36.	\Processor(_Total)\% Idle Time	✓	✓
37.	\Processor(_Total)\% Privileged Time	✓	✓
38.	\Processor(_Total)\% Processor Time	✓	✓
39.	\Processor(_Total)\C1 Transitions/sec	✓	×
40.	\Processor(_Total)\DPC Rate	✓	✓
41.	\Processor(_Total)\DPCs Queued/sec	✓	×
42.	\System\File Control Operations/sec	✓	×
43.	\System\File Data Operations/sec	✓	✓
44.	\System\File Read Operations/sec	✓	✓
45.	\TCPv4\Segments Received/sec	✓	✓
46.	\TCPv4\Segments Sent/sec	✓	✓
47.	\TCPv4\Segments/sec	✓	✓
48.	\Thread(_Total/_Total)\% Privileged Time	✓	×
49.	\Thread(_Total/_Total)\% Processor Time	✓	×
50.	\UDPv4\Datagrams Received/sec	✓	✓
51.	\UDPv4\Datagrams Sent/sec	✓	✓
52.	\UDPv4\Datagrams/sec	✓	✓

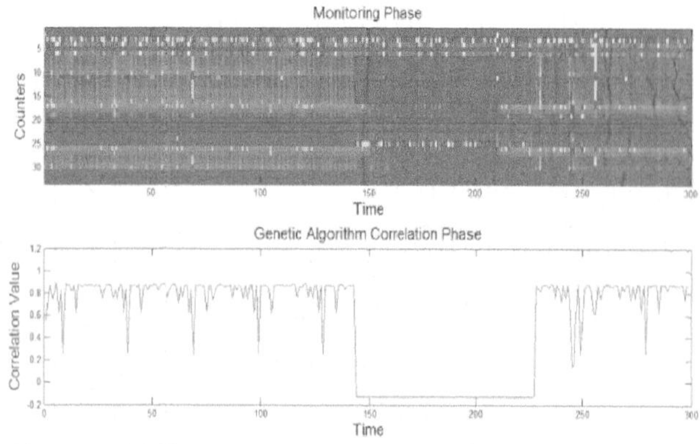

Fig. 7. Attack HTTP server, TCP attack (nc=33), using PJAM2 tool. $\mu 1$= 0.8034, $\sigma 1$= 0.1581, $\mu 2$= -0.128, $\sigma 2$= 0.0019, R = 5.8212 applying GA.

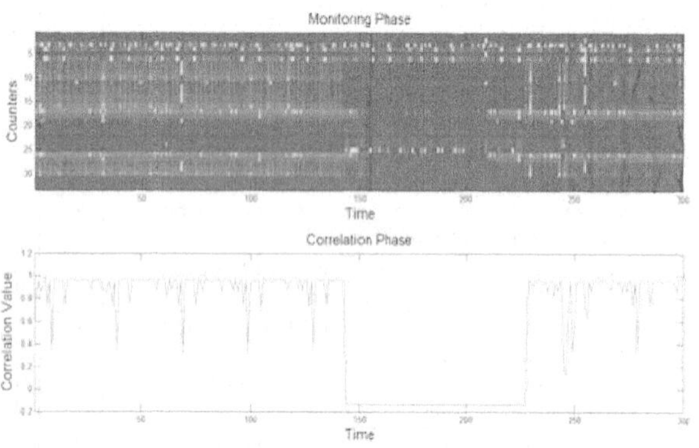

Fig. 8. Attack HTTP server, TCP attack (nc=33), using PJAM2 tool. ($\mu 1$= 0.9149, $\sigma 1$= 0.1406,$\mu 2$= -0.1399, $\sigma 2$= 0.0020, R = 7.4003 applying BCR).

According to results shown in table (3) and table (4), It can be noted that Fisher's score (R) improved with applying best correlated record as shown in figure (9).

TABLE 3. FISHER'S SCORE APPLYING GENETIC ALGORITHM (GA).

Test	# of counters	μ1	μ2	σ1	σ2	*R (GA 33/34)*
Test1	33	0.8483	0.6575	0.1993	0.5869	0.2743
Test2	33	0.8034	-0.128	0.1581	0.0019	5.8212
Test3	34	0.5714	0.002	0.1184	0.0194	4.1333
Test4	34	0.6687	0.1972	0.2004	0.0712	1.7361
Test5	34	0.2857	0.1315	0.2062	0.11	0.4875

TABLE 4. FISHER'S SCORE APPLYING BEST CORRELATED RECORD (BCR).

Test	# of counters	μ1	μ2	σ1	σ2	*R (BCR 33/34)*
Test1	33	0.8895	0.1846	0.0341	0.6138	1.08797654
Test2	33	0.9149	-0.1399	0.1406	0.002	7.396914446
Test3	34	0.8766	-0.0421	0.2002	0.0104	4.362298196
Test4	34	0.8662	-0.0549	0.2299	0.1015	2.77942064
Test5	34	0.7017	-0.062	0.5666	0.311	0.870214221

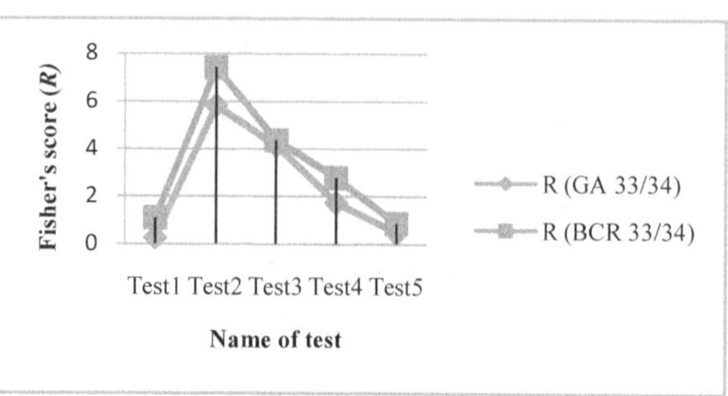

Fig. 9. Comparing R for GA and BCR.

3.3 Case study 3:

In this case study, we apply both genetic algorithm and best correlated record to study the impact of reducing the number of counters. The proposed algorithm proves that reducing number of monitored counters increase the total efficiency by increasing Fisher's score. Pictorial analysis for the 34 counters can help us to leave only one copy of identical counters. Upon pictorial analysis, it is found that there are pairs of five counters that are completely identical to each other as shown in table (5):

TABLE 5. CORRELATED COUNTERS

ID	Counter number & name	Identical Counter number & name
1	2.\Cache\Copy Reads/sec	5.\Cache\Sync Copy Reads/sec
2	4.\Cache\Data Maps/sec	6.\Cache\Sync Data Maps/sec
3	7.\IPv4\Datagrams Received Delivered/sec	8.\IPv4\Datagrams Received/sec
4	17.\Process(_Total)\IO Data Operations/sec	27.\System\File Data Operations/sec
5	18.\Process(_Total)\IO Read Operations/sec	28.\System\File Read Operations/sec

In addition, it is found that counter \Cache\Data Map Pins/sec is oscillating. As a result, six counters will be excluded. Fisher's score (R), for all different counters sets, is shown in figures (10 and 11). Applying best correlated record, it is found that (R) for counter sets having 27 or 28 counters is almost equal to counter sets having either 33 or 34 counters. In case of applying genetic algorithm, It is found that (R) for counter sets having 27 or 28 counters is almost greater than counter sets having either 33 or 34 counters.

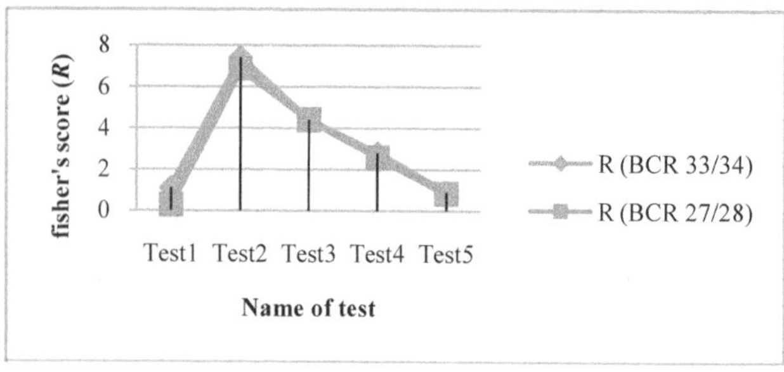

Fig. 10. Comparing R values for different Counter sets applying BCR.

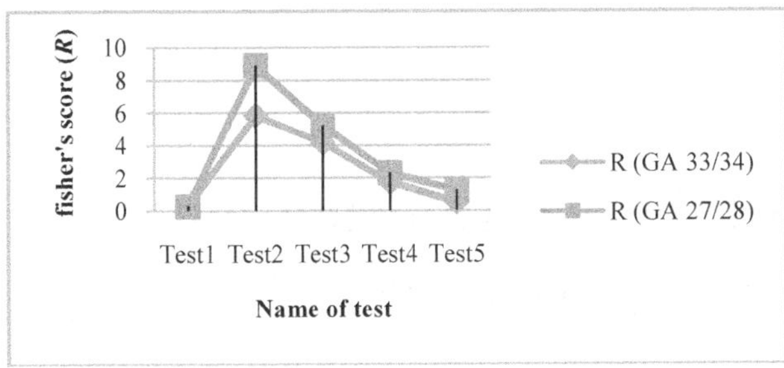

Fig. 11. Comparing R values for different Counter sets applying genetic algorithm (GA).

Comparing Fisher's score (R) for both genetic algorithm and best correlated record as shown in figure (12), it is found that genetic algorithm outperformed best correlated record.

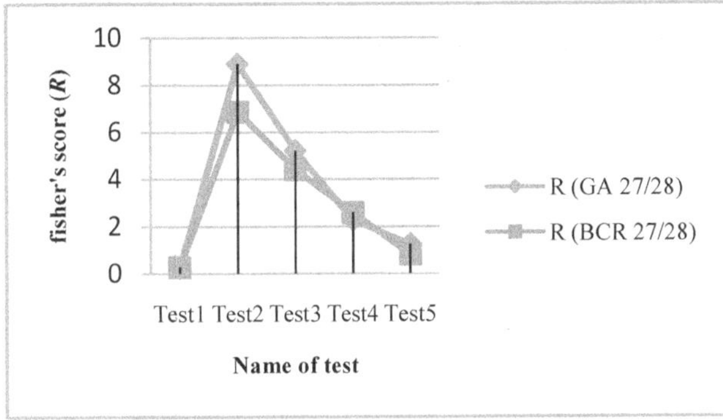

Fig. 12. Comparing R values for (33/34) Counters set applying genetic algorithm (GA) and best correlated record (BCR).

Accordingly, it is recommended to apply genetic algorithm and use the final counter set that contains 27 or 28 counters for both faster correlation process and reduced consumption in computer's resources.

4 Conclusion and future work

In the proposed approach, pictorial analysis is used as a significant tool to view and monitor the effect of abnormal behavior on server's machines. Using Pictorial analysis, it is possible to make feature selection correctly that will be deployed in the process of online monitoring. Response module wasn't implemented in this approach; however, monitoring module was the only implemented one.

The proposed algorithm proves its ability to detect completely new unknown attacks on servers sourced from clients' machine. In addition, the proposed algorithm overcomes the main disadvantages of conventional techniques. For algorithm verification purpose, two different environments with two different hardware configurations have been considered. A process of excluding unaffected counters has been carried out to improve the results of correlation and Fisher's score. In addition, the reduction of the monitored counters reduces the computational burden and reduces the consumption of the system resources.

The proposed approach is implemented at the level of the host. The system is considered a step towards an enhanced, proactive, and intelligent intrusion prevention system. As a future work, the proposed algorithm will be implemented at the network level applying more types of attacks.

5 References

[1] Abou-Assaleh T, Keselj V, Sweidan R: N-gram based detection of new malicious code. Proc of the 28th Annual International Computer Software and Applications Conference, IEEE Computer Society 2004, 41-42.

[2] D Krishna Sandeep Reddy and Arun K Pujari:] N-gram analysis for computer virus detection. Journal in Computer Virology, 2006, Volume 2, Number 3, Pages 231-239.

[3] Santos, I., Penya, Y., Devesa, J., Bringas, P.: N-Grams-based file signatures for malware detection. In: Proceedings of the 11th International Conference on Enterprise Information Systems (ICEIS), Volume AIDSS, pp. 317–320 (2009).

[4] Moskovitch R, Feher C, Tzachar N, Berger E, Gitelman M, Dolev S, Elovici Y: Unknown malcode detection using OpCode representation. European Conference on Intelligence and Security Informatics Heidelberg: Springer; 2008,204-215.

[5] Santos I, Brezo F, Nieves J, Penya YK, Sanz B, Laorden C, Bringas PG: Idea: Opcode-sequence-based malware detection. Proc 2nd International Symposium on Engineering Secure Software and Systems 2010, 35-42.

[6] Asaf Shabtai, Robert Moskovitch, Clint Feher, Shlomi Dolev and Yuval Elovici: Detecting unknown malicious code by applying classification techniques on OpCode patterns. Security Informatics, 2012, Volume 1, Number 1, 1.

[7] Robert Moskovitch, Dima Stopel, Zvi Boger, Yuval Shahar, Yuval Elovici: United States Patent Application 20070294768 - Method and system for detecting malicious behavioral patterns in a computer, using machine learning. Application 20070294768 Filed on January 29, 2007. Published on December 20, 2007.

[8] Robert Moskovitch, Nir Nissim, Dima Stopel, Clint Feher and Roman Englert, et al.: Improving the Detection of Unknown Computer Worms Activity Using Active Learning. Lecture Notes in Computer Science, 2007, Volume 4667, KI 2007: Advances in Artificial Intelligence, Pages 489-493.

[9] Robert Moskovitch, Dima Stopel, Zvi Boger, Yuval Shahar, Yuval Elovici: United States Patent Application 20080184371-METHOD AND SYSTEM FOR DETECTING MALICIOUS BEHAVIORAL PATTERNS IN A COMPUTER, USING MACHINE LEARNING. Application 20080184371 Filed on January 24, 2008. Published on July 31, 2008.

[10] Dima Stopel, Robert Moskovitch, Zvi Boger, Yuval Shahar and Yuval Elovici: Using artificial neural networks to detect unknown computer Worms. Neural Computing & Applications, 2009, Volume 18, Number 7, Pages 663-674.

[11] Moskovitch R, Elovici Y, Rokach L: Detection of unknown computer worms based on behavioral classification of the host. Computational Statistics and Data Analysis 2008, 52(9):4544-4566.

[12] Haruka MIMORIy and K^oki ABE: Detection of Unknown Computer Virus Variants Based on Computer Behavior. TECHNICAL REPORT OF IEICE.

[13] Moskovitch R, Stopel D, Feher C, Nissim N, Japkowicz N, Elovici Y: Unknown malcode detection and the imbalance problem. Journal in Computer Virology 2009, 5(4):295-308.

[14] Robert Moskovitch, Nir Nissim and Yuval Elovici: Malicious Code Detection Using Active Learning

[15] V. G. Grishin , A. S. Sula and Mihaela Ulieru (Pictorial analysis: a multi-resolution data visualization approach for monitoring and diagnosis of complex systems),Information Sciences Volume 152, June 2003, Pages 1-24.

[16] Dr.V.G.Grishin (View Trends Int.) Pictorial Methods with Applications to Monitoring, Diagnostics and Control in Industrial Processes.

[17] http://bugsec.googlecode.com/files/tcpflood.pl

[18] http://wiki.nil.com/UDP_flood_in_Perl

[19] http://packetstormsecurity.org/files/112856/HULK-Http-Unbearable-Load-King.html

[20] http://packetstormsecurity.org/files/26410/pjam2.exe.html

[21] http://packetstormsecurity.org/files/30530/pjam3.rar.html

[22] http://technet.microsoft.com/en-us/library/cc728167(v=ws.10).aspx

Correlation Analysis of Cyber Threat Information in Heterogeneous Security Systems

Jae-Kook Lee, and Chae-Tae Im
Applied Security Technology Team, Korea Internet & Security Agency,
Jungdaero 135, Songpa-gu, Seoul, 138-950, Korea

Abstract - *Recently The internet is widely used. As a result, cyber attacks are continuously changed and increased. Various security systems are used to protect internal network, servers and PCs. The KISA(Krcert/CC) operates a variety of security systems to prevent and protect against cyber attacks. For example, there are systems for detecting and preventing DoS/DDoS attacks, managing cyber threats, trapping spam emails, and preventing botnet damages. In this paper, we analyze cyber threat information that were detected through heterogeneous security systems. Then we propose a new correlation analysis method using gradient measurement for more effective monitoring. Finally we present results of continuity and redundancy of source IP address in several security systems.*

Keywords: Correlation Analysis; Intrusion Detection System(IDS); Intrusion Prevention System(IPS); Heterogeneous Security Systems; Computer and Network Security

1 Introduction

Increasing popularity of the Internet usage is causing many Distributed Denial-of Service(DDoS) attacks such as 7.7 DDoS in 2009 and 3.4 DDoS in 2011 in Korea. A DDoS, one of the simplest and most powerful cyber attacks is a big problem nowadays. Especially, DDoS attack is now getting a huge problem because the unspecified individuals(called zombie PCs) are used in loading malicious codes while attacking a single site or system. DDoS attack is directly related to targeted companies, institutions and even governments, security companies and users as well. Korea, on 4th of March. 2011., got assailed by large-scale cyber terrors is called DDoS. It was nearly ceased main functions of Korea because it got attacked from DDoS that about 40 websites, which were each kind of government agencies, national defenses websites of the army, the navy, the air force and U.S armed forces in Korea, and, the National Assembly, transportation, powerhouses, financial institutions, portal, shopping mall, security companies and including the Blue House, the official residence of Korean President. It can be called as a cyber-terror because essential agencies, such as the main government, national defenses, and basic facilities in Korea, got attacked[1].

In the past, DDoS attacks focused on exhausting the network bandwidth by generating a large amount of data. However, recent DDoS attacks are evolving from exhaustion of the bandwidth to exhaustion of resources of the application layer servers[2]. Figure 1 shows the distribution of packets for each attack type of 3.4 DDoS attack.

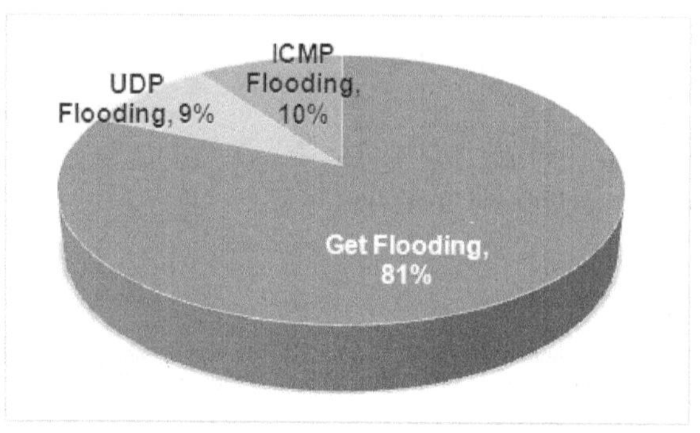

Figure 1. Distribution of the Types of Attack on 3·4 DDoS Traffic

As the pie graph shows, the 'HTTP Get Flooding' packets, which is intended to exhaust the server resources, took up the most at 81%. Only 19% of the total packets were generated by the attacks to exhaust the network bandwidth.

In addition to DDoS attacks, various types of attacks such as worms, viruses, Trojan horses and vulnerable scanning attacks are continuously occurring. To protect and prevent the intra-network, servers and PCs from these attacks, IDS and IPS are generally used. Moreover, heterogeneous security systems are used to respond to various intrusion incidents such as attack against vulnerable servers, and attacks that send a large volume of spam mails.

This paper analyzes the data acquired by systems implemented on Internet exchange network sections, set up and operated by the KISA(KrCERT/CC). Such systems include: DDoS attack response systems, virtual network scanning attack detection systems, Honeynet worm type malware acquisition systems, systems detecting the spam like malware by use of a virtual e-mail reception server and a virtual e-mail account, DNS sinkhole systems which block the infected PCs from accessing C&C to receive the attack and command control. We analyze threat information to determine the continuity of the attacks and redundancy of the attacking IP addresses detected by each system. And in this paper, we proposes a time series analysis method using the gradient to analyze the correlation of the data collection by the heterogeneous Internet security system.

2 Related Works

2.1 DDoS Attack Response System on the Internet Exchange Network(IX-DDoS Response System)

An IX(Internet eXchange) service is used to interchange the traffic among different ISPs (Internet Service Providers)[3]. The primary purpose of an IX service is to allow networks to interconnect directly, via the exchange, rather than through one or more 3rd party networks. The advantages of the direct interconnection are numerous, but the primary reasons are cost, latency, and bandwidth. Traffic passing through an exchange is typically not billed by any party, whereas traffic to an ISP's upstream provider is[4].

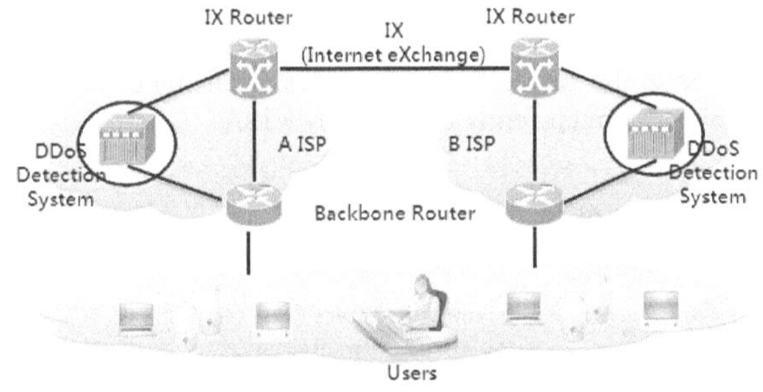

Figure 2. IX-DDoS Response System Architecture

The IX-DDoS response system is installed in the IX points to detect the DDoS attacks generated among the ISPs in order to respond quickly to the attack proliferated through the ISPs. Figure 2 shows the system diagram. It monitors the traffics between ISPs and filters which it detects as a DDoS attack so that only the normal traffics are transferred.

TABLE I. DETECTION LOG SAMPLE OF IX-DDOS RESPONSE SYSTEM

Time	Src. IP	Src. Port	Dst IP	Dst. Port	Detected Attack Name	Size(bytes)
2011-09-02 0:01:01	203.[illegible].163	1861	211.[illegible].10	80	TCP Connect DOS	60
2011-09-02 0:01:02	58.[illegible]30	0	211[illegible]50	0	ICMP DDoS(0303)	246
2011-09-02 0:01:02	119.[illegible].66	54452	121[illegible]45	80	HTTP Connection Limit Exhaustion Attack(By Slowloris)	60
2011-09-02 0:01:03	11[illegible]4.139	32769	21[illegible]100	123	UDP Destination-IP Flooding	90
2011-09-02 0:01:04	20[illegible]9.145	4633	211.[illegible].10	80	TCP Connect DOS	60

The attack log data detected by the IX-DDoS response system can segment the data into the attack occurrence time, source(attack) IP, source port, destination(target) IP, destination port, detected attack name, packet size, etc. as shown in TABLE Ⅰ.

2.2 Scanning Attack Detection System

A scanning attack detection system by KISA use to a virtual network to detect scanning attacks. A virtual network is a computer network that consists, at least in part, of virtual network links. A virtual network link is a link that does not consist of a physical (wired or wireless) connection between two computing devices but is implemented using methods of network virtualization. When an intrusion occurs, the virtual network analyzes it thoroughly and determines the intention, technique, and tools of the attack in order to strengthen security by analyzing new attack techniques and responding to them appropriately[4].

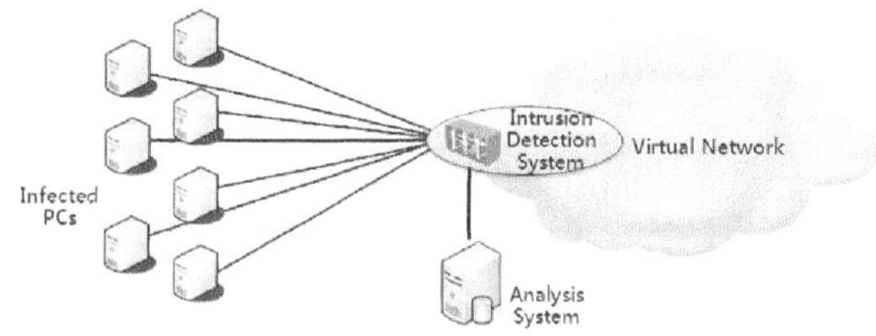

Figure 3. Scanning Attack Detection System Architecture

Recent developments in virtualization technology have enabled the network virtualization to be used widely. A virtual network scanning attack detection system forms a virtual network to detect attacks such as scanning attacks attempted on the virtual network from outside by taking advantage of the vulnerability of the specific service, and installs a system to detect the attack upstream of the network. Figure 3 shows the system diagram of a virtual network scanning attack detection system. It collects the log data of the detected scanning attack attempted from a PC infected by malware and operates a separate log analysis system to analyze the data.

TABLE II. DETECTION LOG SAMPLE OF SCANNING ATTACK DETECTION SYSTEM

Time	Src. IP	Src. Port	Dst. IP	Dst. Port	Detected Attack Name	Traffic(bytes)
2011-09-02 0:01:06	61.[illegible].1	1731	61.[illegible].168	135	Dcom_TCP_Sweep(MSBlaster Worm. Messenger..)	936
2011-09-02 0:01:11	203[illegible]77	4599	211[illegible]83	445	SMB Service sweep(tcp-445)	25606
2011-09-02 0:01:13	113.[illegible].57	80	210[illegible]88	48422	Host Sweep	2574
2011-09-02 0:01:15	61[illegible]46	20597	61[illegible]10	135	Dcom_TCP_Sweep(MSBlaster Worm. Messenger..)	3198
2011-09-02 0:01:15	61[illegible]81	2894	210[illegible]117	445	SMB Service sweep(tcp-445)	11036

The detected scanning attack log data shares a similar format with the IX-DDoS, including the attack detection time, source(attack) IP, source port, destination(target) IP, destination port, scanning attack name, and traffic volume as shown in Table Ⅱ.

2.3 Worm Type Malicious Code Detection System(Honeynet System)

A worm type malicious code detection system forms a network (honeynet) of vulnerable PCs that have not applied the security patches and installed the vaccine so that it will detect the worm type malware which is proliferated through the network. A worm type malicious codes(malwares) are programs that self-propagate across a network exploiting security or policy flaws in widely-used services[5]. The honeynet system operated by KISA then collects and analyzes the detected malware samples. Figure 4 shows the system diagram of a honeynet system.

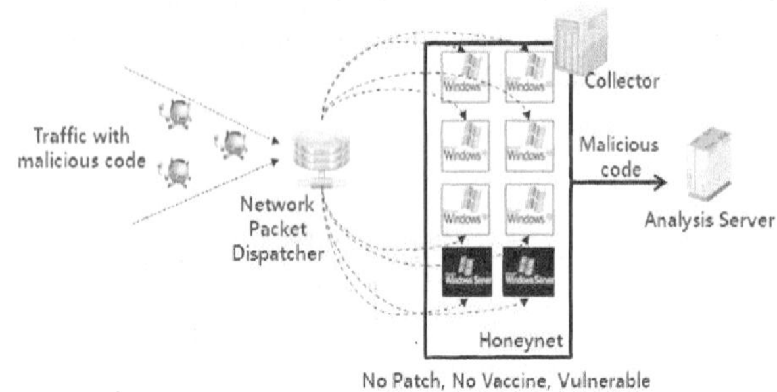

Figure 4. Honeynet System Architecture

The packet dispatcher divides the traffics flowing into the honeynet from outside and uniformly transfers them to vulnerable PCs of the network to prevent concentration of the traffic only to a PC. The worm type malware installed in a vulnerable PC is collected and transferred to an analysis server which analyzes the packet to obtain the IP address spreading the worm. The malware sample may also be used as the signature for vaccine.

2.4 E-mail Spam Trap System

E-mail services have become an important source of communication for millions of people all over the world. Due to this tremendous growth, there has been a significant increase in spam traffic. Spam messes up user's inbox, consumes network resources and spread worms and viruses[7]. Spam mails generated by Zombie PCs and e-mail worms have recently increased. According to the spam volume data by Symantec, spam mails occupy more than 60% of total e-mails[8]. The e-mail spam trap system is operated to respond to the continuously increasing spam mails. It collects and analyses the spam mail by a virtual e-mail server and blocks the spam[9]. Figure 5 shows a schematic diagram of an e-mail spam trap system. KISA analyzes the main body of the spam mail to determine the connecting site, sending IP address, and e-mail title to block the IP address used by the spam.

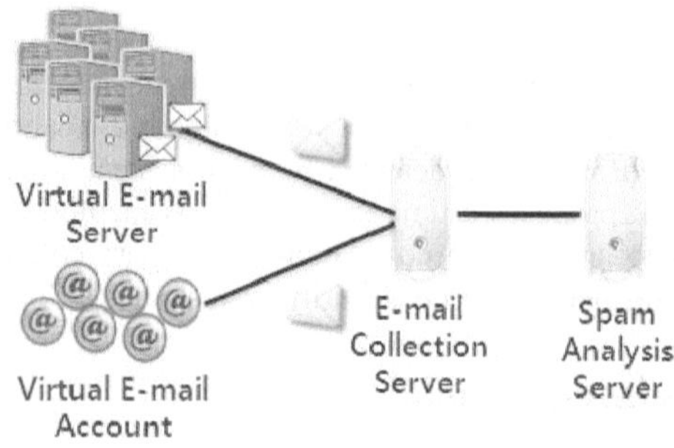

Figure 5. E-mail Spam Trap System Architecture

2.5 DNS Sinkhole System

One of the possible solutions against botnet attack is DNS sinkhole technique. It blocks zombies trying to connect to command and control(C&C) server by adapting simple configuration setting on DNS server. Especially, it is known to be most effective C&C based botnet detection technique[10]. A DNS sinkhole system detects the C&C servers controlling the infected zombie PC(bot) and blocks the C&C sent to the infected PC to prevent secondary damage. It delivers the sink hole network address instead of the actual network address when an infected PC attempts to access to a particular domain so that the packet will not actually be delivered to the server. Figure 6 shows a schema of the DNS sinkhole system currently operated by KISA.

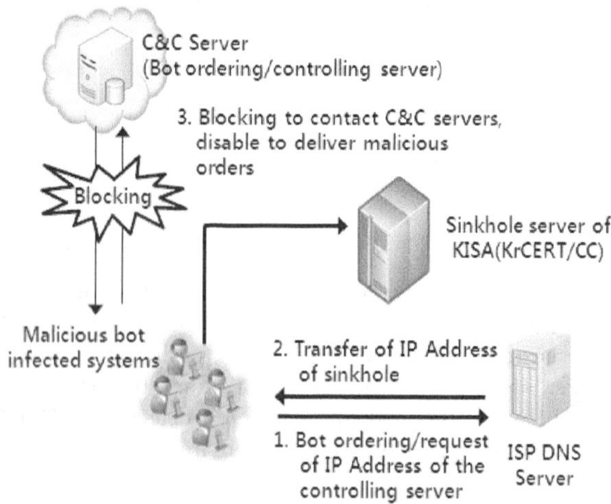

Figure 6. Operation Mechanism of DNS Sinkhole System

The system analyzes the packets that are transferred while it induces the infected PCs attempting to access a domain registered in C&C to the DNS sinkhole to check the IP of the infected PC.

3 Association Analysis Method of Security Data

3.1 Continuity and Redundancy Analysis of Attacking IP addresses

To study the correlation of the security information collected by the heterogeneous Internet security systems, we analyze continuity and redundancy of attacking IP addresses. The continuity analysis deals with how long an attacking IP address detected by each system attacks continuously, the redundancy analysis with how different security systems detect an attacking IP address By analyzing continuity, we can reverse track how long an infected system is left without being treated, and by analyzing redundancy, reverse infer the diversity of the attacks.

3.2 Time Series Analysis Using Gradient

When a correlating data is detected by the heterogeneous Internet security system, the data having the preceding relation to a specific attack can be observed or the detection log in another system can show the simultaneity of an arbitrary attack. Moreover, the data having the following relation to a specific attack can also be observed. To analyze the correlation of the data detected by various systems, this paper proposes the gradient according to the time series flow of each system.

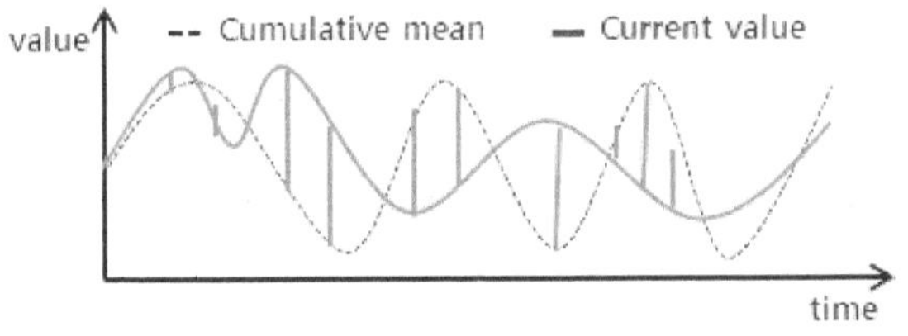

(a) Difference between the Cumulative Mean and Current Value in a Time Series

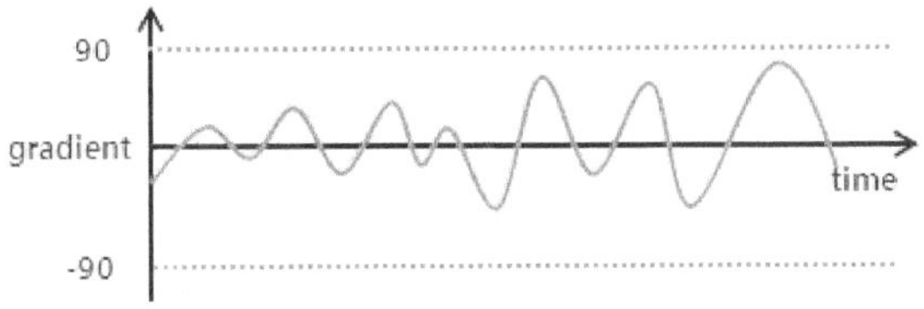

(b) Gradient Trend in a Time Series

Figure 7. Analysis of Data Correlation according to Gradient

First, the difference of the cumulative means and current measured values of the data acquired by the heterogeneous security systems can be checked by presenting them in a time series as shown in Figure 7 (a). To determine the level of the difference between cumulative means and current values, the slope is used. Assuming that the standard deviation is α and the difference between the cumulative mean and current value is β, change of the two values is expressed by the slope defined as the gradient.

A gradient is θ satisfying $\tan\theta = \beta / \alpha$ as shown in Figure 8. A time series using the gradient would be a graph shown in Figure 7 (b).

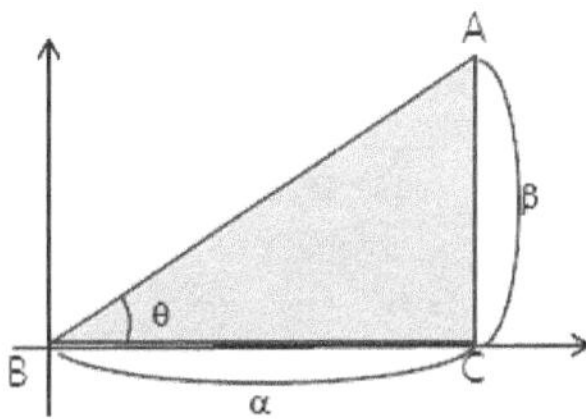

Figure 8. A Trigonometric Function for Gradient Analysis

$$\tan\theta = \beta / \alpha \quad (1)$$

α : standard deviation

β : cumulative mean - current value

Using the gradient, the difference between 0 and 0.5 would the same as that between 0 and 50 to be 45.

4 Experiments

For the analysis, this paper used data collected by the heterogeneous Internet security system for 24 hours from 00:00 to 23:59 on September 2, 2011. Table Ⅲ shows the number of data cases and attacking IPs (eliminating the redundancies) detected by each system.

TABLE Ⅲ. NUMBER OF DATA CASES AND ATTACKING IPs DETECTED BY SYTEMS

	IX-DDOS	TMS	HONEY	SPAM	SINKHOLE
# of detection	117,983	211,360	968	1,196,483	399,115
# of detected IP	26,292	11,434	271	42,600	22,605

IX-DDoS, TMS, HONEY, and SINKHOLE of Table Ⅲ are abbreviated as follows:

- IX-DDoS: IX-DDoS attack response system
- TMS: Scanning Attack Detection System
- HONEY: Honeynet system
- SPAM: E-mail spam trap system
- SINKHOLE: DNS sinkhole system

For the accumulated data needed for the time series analysis using the gradient, the data for 4 weeks in September 2011 were used.

4.1 Continuity Analysis of Attacking IP

To study the continuity of the attacking IP addresses detected by an IX-DDoS attack response system, Figure 9 shows the portion of continuing hours of attacking IP addresses determined by the detected attacking IP addresses at each hour.

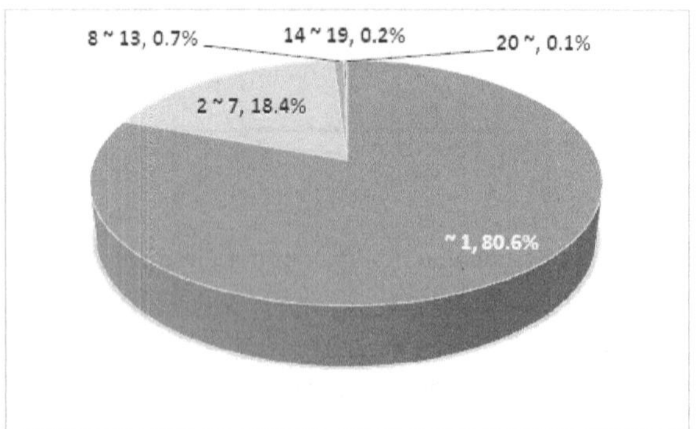

Figure 9. Portion of IPs at Each Attack Continuity Hours as Detected by an IX-DDoS Attack Response System

As shown in Figure 9, most of the attacks (80.6%) were one-time cases. However, attacks of 8 hours or longer were generated by 1% of PCs. (This paper assumes one IP address corresponds to one infected PC.) Some infected PCs even generated the attacks for 24 hours continuously.

To study the continuity of the attacking IP addresses detected by a virtual network scanning attack detection system, Figure 10 shows the portion of continuing hours of attacking IP addresses determined by 11,434 detected attacking IP addresses at each hour.

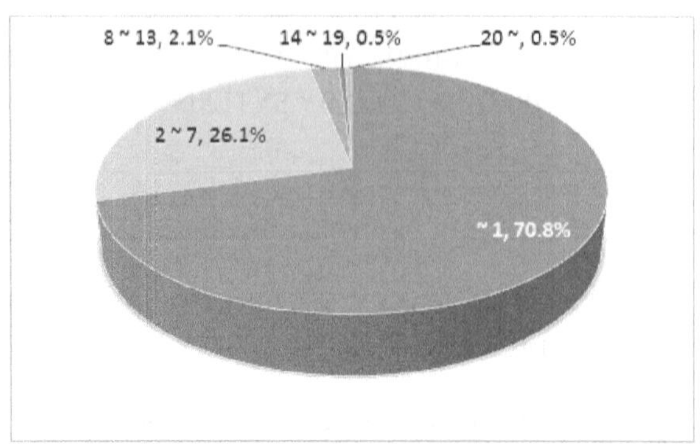

Figure 10. Portion of IPs at Each Attack Continuity Hours as Detected by a Virtual Network Scanning Attack Detection System

As shown in Figure 10, the portion of IP addresses attacking for 8 hours or longer was 3.1%, indicating that the scanning attacks lasted longer than the IX-DDoS attacks. It is probably because the scanning attacks use the vulnerable service of the attacked server to make other attacks.

968 IP addresses distributing the malware collected by the Honeynet worm type malware acquisition system were analyzed. The analysis indicated that most of the malwares were one-time distribution type. However, the portion of PCs vulnerable in the honeynet being infected by the worm type malware after they were initialized were significant at 5.7% in a 24-hour period as shown in Figure 11.

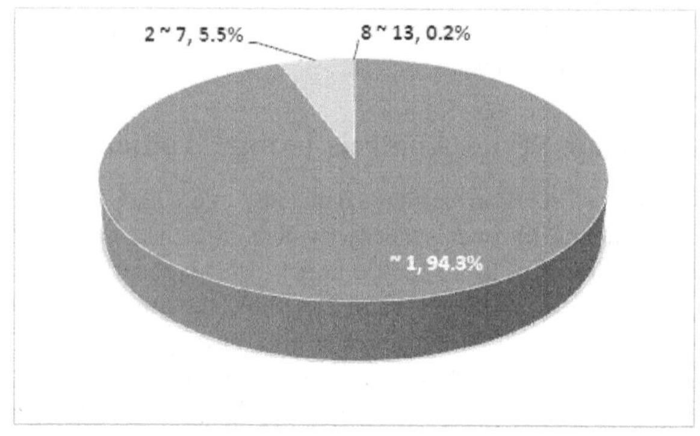

Figure 11. Portion of IPs at Each Attack Continuity Hours as Detected by a Honeynet System

To study the continuity of the attacking IP addresses detected by an e-mail spam trap system, Figure 12 shows the portion of continuing hours of attacking IP addresses determined by the detected attacking 42,600 IPs at each hour.

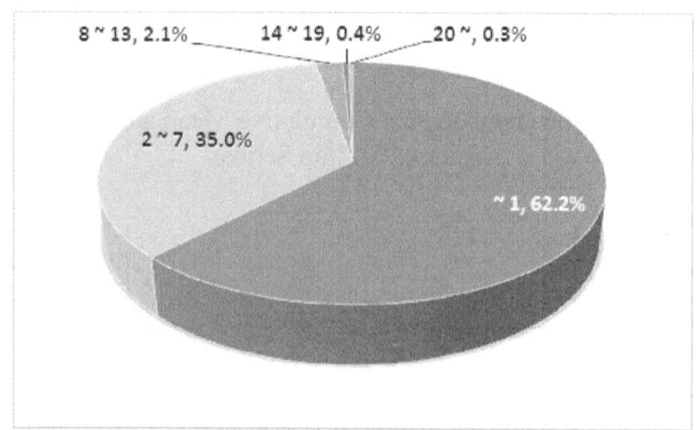

Figure 12. Portion of IPs at Each Attack Continuity Hours as Detected by an E-mail Spam Trap System

As shown in Figure 12, the portion was IP addresses attacking for 8 hours or longer was 2.8%, similar to that of the virtual network scanning attack detection system.

Lastly, 22,605 IP addresses detected by the DNS sinkhole system were analyzed. As shown in Figure 13,

24.2% of the attacking IP addresses detected by the DNS sink hole system attempted the access to C&C regularly for 8 hours or longer rather than one-time access unlike other systems. Inversely, it is evidence that the infected PCs were not properly treated.

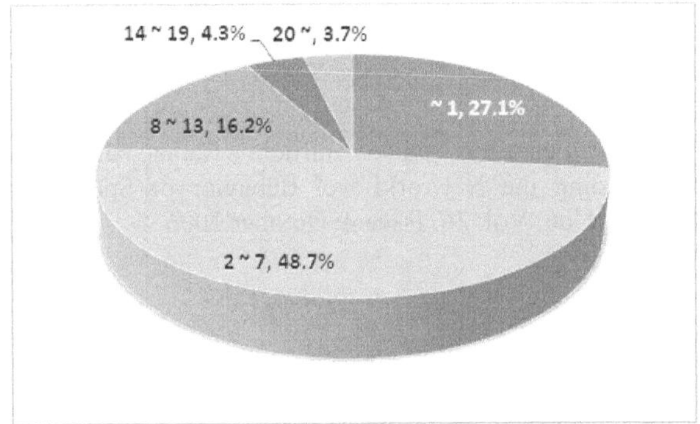

Figure 13. Portion of IPs at Each Attack Continuity Hours as Detected by a DNS sinkhole System

4.2 Redundancy Analysis of Attacking IP

To check if the attacking IP addresses detected by each system are redundant, the time when the attacking IP address was first detected by the heterogeneous system is checked.

TABLE IV. SAMPLING OF ATTACKING IPS AND TIMES DETECTED BY HETEROGENEOUS SECURITY SYSTEMS

IP	IX-DDOS	TMS	HONEY	SPAM	SINKHOLE
125.248.	9:07	X	X	21:37	9:21
222.189.	8:18	3:51	X	X	5:01
125.181.	19:40	X	X	20:23	0:01
200.206.	20:23	17:05	X	X	4:41
114.29.	3:35	X	X	19:43	X
58.226.	X	4:18	4:39	X	12:01
203.248.	5:39	X	X	X	8:01
210.182.	16:21	18:58	X	X	X
210.123.	X	X	X	13:01	8:01
219.241.	X	X	X	12:05	10:21
222.104.	14:30	X	X	X	8:01
85.94.	X	5:14	6:40	X	X
220.68.	X	15:56	X	X	9:31
218.159.	X	X	X	13:25	0:01
218.53.	X	X	X	10:11	8:51
58.87.	X	X	X	9:05	7:51
58.143.	X	X	X	9:54	10:01

Table VI shows the initial detection time of samples from 102,592 attacking IPs detected by the heterogeneous security systems between 00:00 to 23:59 on September 2, 2011. As Table VI shows, redundant IP addresses are shown in different network sections and in different systems installed for each purpose. Although, they are not many, 0.3% of PCs were detected by two or more systems. When the detection period was extended to 3 days from September 2, 2011 to September 4, 2011, the portion of attacking IP addresses detected by two or more systems increased to 4.4%. This indicates that some of the infected PCs attempted two or more different attacks over time. For security reason, the last parts of the IP addresses in Table VI are erased.

4.3 Time Series Analysis of Gradient

Figure 14 shows the graph of correlation analysis of number of attacking IPs detected by the IX-DDoS attack response system and virtual network scanning attack detection system. As the variance is large because the data occurred on the same day of the week and at the same time were accumulated during the month of September 2011, the graph still shows simultaneity of the data detected by both systems in some sections. In other words, two data were in support relation.

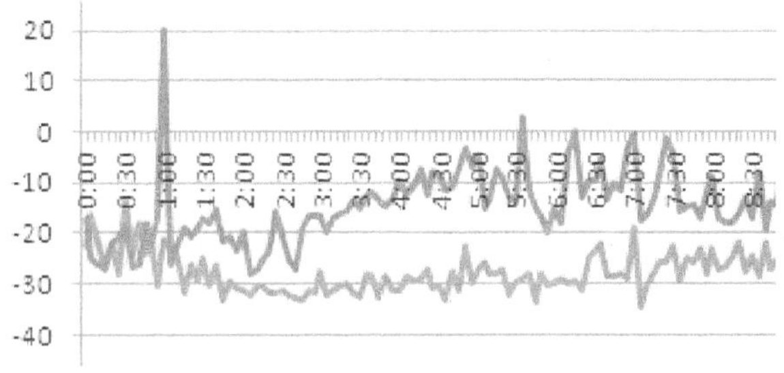

Figure 14. Analysis of Number of Detected Attacking IPs Detected by IX-DDoS and TMS

5 Conclusions and Future Works

The rapid development of the Internet infrastructure has enabled people to obtain necessary information at any time, it is also giving rise to many security threats. To protect the network and systems from these threats, various security systems are used. This paper analyzes the log data collected by the heterogeneous Internet security systems operated by KISA to study the continuity and redundancy of attacking IP addresses. Although most of the attacks were one-time cases, 24.2% of attacking IP addresses detected by the DNS sink hole system attacked for 8 hours or longer. This may indicate that the infected PCs were not treated, and attempted to access command from C&C. The analysis of redundancy of the attacking IPs detected by the heterogeneous security systems indicated that 0.3% of the PCs were detected by two or more security systems. Particularly, out of the 271 attacking IP addresses (redundancy eliminated) detected by the Honeynet worm type malware acquisition system, 111 IP addresses were previously detected by the virtual network scanning attack detection system.

This paper proposed time series analysis according to gradient in order to determine the spontaneity and precedence relationship of the data acquired by heterogeneous security systems. However, because of the limitation of the accumulated data, the testing could not be completed. In the future, we plan to carry out tests using the data accumulated for a specific period in order to verify the proposed technique.

6 References

[1] DongJoo HA, SangMyung CHOI, TaeHyung KIM and SeungYoun HAN, "Check Your Zombie Devices! : Analysis of the DDoS Cyber Terrorism Against the Country and Future Attacks on Various Devices," BLACK HAT ABU DHAB 2011, December 2011.

[2] Seong-Uk LEE, Change and Prospects of DDoS Attack Method, ISSUE REPORT, Vol. 2011-004, March 2011.

[3] A. Akella, A. Bharambe, M. Reiter, and S. Seshan, "Detecting DDoS attacks on ISP networks," PODS Workshop on Management and Processing of Data Streams, 2003.

[4] Peter Reiher, "A taxonomy of DDoS attack and DDoS defense mechanisms," ACM SIGCOMM Computer Communication, Volume 34 Issue 2, April 2004.

[5] N. Weaver, V. Paxson, S. Staniford, and R. Cunningham. A taxonomy of computer worms. In Proceedings of ACM CCS Workshop on Rapid Malcode (WORM'03), October 2003.

[6] Honeynet Project: Know Your Enemy: Defining Virtual Honeynets, http://www.koneynet.org, 2003

[7] Dhinaharan Nagamalai, "An In-depth Analysis of Spam and Spaammers," International Journal of Security and its Applications, Vol. 2, No.2, April 2009

[8] Spam Volume(Symantec), http://www.symantec.com/security_response/landing/spam/

[9] HyunCheol JEONG, HuyKang KIM, SanggJin LEE and JooHyung OH, "Study for Tracing Zombie PCs and Botnet Using and Email Spam Trap," Jounal of Korea Institute of Information Security and Cryptology, Vol. 21, No 3, June 2011.

[10] HaengGon LEE, SangSoo CHOI, YounSu LEE and HarkSoo PARK, " Enhanced Sinkhole System by Improving Post-processing Mechanism," LNCS, Vol 6485, 2010, pp469-480.

[11] Heung Youl YOUM, "Korea's experience of massive DDoS attacks from Botnet," ITU-T SG17, April 2011.

[12] Zhichun Li, Anup Goyal, and Yan Chen, " Honeynet-based Botnet Scan Traffic Analysis," Botnet Detection Advances in Information Security, Vol. 36, 2008, pp 25-44.

[13] David Watson and Jamie Riden, "The Honeynet Project: Data Collection Tools, Infrastructure, Archives and Analysis," WOMBAT Workshop on Information Security Threats Data Collection and Sharing, April 2008.

[14] Dwen-Ren Tsai and Chien-Ning Huang, " A Signature Exchange Model for Heterogeneous Intrusion Detection Systems," 43rd Annual International Carnahan Conference on Security Technology, October 2009.

[15] Nick Feamster and Anirudh Ramachandran, " Understanding the NetworkLevel Behavior of Spammers," SIGCOMM '06, Vol. 36, Issue 4, October 2006.

Towards a Service Migration Architecture for Service Availability

Yanjun Zuo
University of North Dakota, Grand Forks, ND, USA

Abstract - *This paper presents our work-in-progress towards system architecture to support service migration in a devastating attack scenario. In our design, service migration is a security mechanism that transfers critical services from a compromised platform to other clean, healthy platforms. The architecture is to ensure that critical services will be continuously provided even the underlying platform has been damaged. Any system with the specified design can provide a level of guarantee that the critical services will be available in spite of malicious attacks and security incidents. We specify the components of such service migration-based system architecture and describe the functions of those components.*

Keywords: Service migration, architecture, security, availability, critical service.

1 Introduction

Software intensive systems have been increasingly used in many high security and high integrity settings, including financial services, national defense, and healthcare, to cite a few. Due to their ultimate importance, critical systems are often the targets of malicious attacks. Even the best-designed systems cannot guarantee that well-organized attacks would never be successful. Given their crucial missions, it is important that those systems have the ability to adapt to the operating environment and continuously provide essential services to users even part of the systems has been compromised. From an engineering perspective, well-designed system architecture is the most fundamental factor in supporting a system's security functions to resist malicious attacks and to mask system faults.

In this paper, we propose architecture to equip a system with the ability to migrate the critical services from a severely compromised platform to other clean, healthy platforms in a devastating attack scenario. The idea is that even the underlying platform has been damaged, the critical services can still be provided on other healthy platforms if an effective migration mechanism has been put in place. From a user's perspective, service migration is transparent and the service is continuously available with little interruption. Conceptually, a service migration involves suspending the current service state on the old platform, moving the core service programs and trustworthy space to other platforms, and resuming where computation was left off on the new platforms. Migration has become the heart of the architecture of many safety-critical systems [1].

As compared with other survivability strategies, such as component/services redundancy and diversity [2-3], fault tolerance [4-5], and system reconfiguration [6-7], service migration is a viable solution to ensure that the most critical services are available in a security incident. Service migration is particularly effective in situations where damage to a system is so severe and very limited time is allowed to recover the damaged platforms without noticeably affecting service availability to users. In this research, we study the system architecture and essential components to support an effective service migration. We specify the main functions and properties of those components.

The rest of the paper is organized as follows. Section 2 discusses related work. The proposed system architecture and system components are presented in Section 3. We describe the data structures, functional specifications of the system components, and communications among them in detail. Section 4 concludes this paper.

2 Related work

System/service survivability has been an important topic in the research community. A set of techniques have been developed to improve a system's ability to survive malicious attacks and/or system failures. Although architectures for system and service survivability ([8-13], to cite a few) have also been proposed, we have not found any specific research which explicitly describes system design and specification to support an efficient service migration. We attempt to bridge this gap in this research by proposing service-migration based system architecture to provide a reasonable level of guarantee that a system can fulfill its mission in a timely manner in the presence of attacks, failures, or accidents. Next, we discuss some related work on service/process migration.

Service/process migration has been proven to offer substantial benefits for fault resilience, dynamic load balancing, and service availability. In [14], service migration is proposed as an effective approach for service placement for ad hoc or autonomic networks in a dynamic environment. Instead of solving continuously a large optimization problem requiring global information, moving the service position, based on local information, towards more effective positions would be a more viable solution. The authors develop a service migration policy for undirected tree topologies. It is shown that the information available at the current service node is sufficient for determining the direction towards nodes with monotonically decreasing service provision costs. The proposed policy moves the service continuously towards the optimal position in every step and reaches the optimal position through a shortest path migration trajectory. As the optimal position may change in a dynamic environment, the proposed policy adapts the service migration path continuously towards the currently optimal position.

In [15], a system for transparent process migration, called Zap, is proposed, which provides a thin virtualization layer on top of the operating system that introduces a Process Domain (pod) abstraction. The virtualization is integrated with a checkpoint-restart mechanism that enables processes within a pod to be migrated as a unit to another machine. A prototype is implemented in Linux that supports migration of unmodified applications without any kernel modification. In [16], a transparent mechanism is presented for commodity operating systems that can checkpoint multiple processes in a consistent state so that they can be restarted at a later time. An algorithm has been developed to record process relationships and save and restore shared states in a manner that leverages existing operating system kernel functionality. In [17], a reliable, flexible and efficient application checkpoint-restart is presented, which aims for inclusion in mainline Linux kernel. The approach is implemented in the operating system kernel and can detect resource leakage outside containers.

Different from the above research, our focus in this research is service-migration based system architecture. Our work complements the existing research by proposing system design for resisting malicious attacks and masking security damage. The main design objective of the proposed architecture is to make sure that the critical services are continuously provided even in a challenging environment.

3 System architecture to support service migration

The system we consider in this paper is a distributed system with an overall architecture as shown in Figure 1. The two control components are Proxy Server and Service Migration Manager. Each of them has a set of sub-components with specialized functions. The services provided by the system are hosted on a set of platforms. In the following sections, we first discuss the system specification in terms of those platforms and services offered by the system. Then, we discuss the functions of the two control components in facilitating an effective service migration.

3.1 Platforms and services

There are a set of platforms P_1, P_2, …, P_i, …, P_n distributed throughout the system to provide services to users. Each platform P_i represents a virtualized computing environment. Technically, it can be a single sever machine, a cluster of computers (e.g., a server farm), or a computing infrastructure in a cloud computing structure (the notation of Infrastructure as Service). P_i has both volatile and stable storage and can support a set of services as represented by its capability list, denoted as $Abi(P_i)$.

The system offers a different types of services S_1, S_2, …, S_n. Each S_j is provided through a set of service programs. Consider a cloud infrastructure operated by a financial institution such as a bank. The system offer multiple types of services such as online banking, stock trading, investment and mortgage management, and customer relationship management. For each type of service, there may be a set of service instances corresponding to different users (internal or external). We use $s_{j\text{-}1}$, $s_{j\text{-}2}$, …, $s_{j\text{-}m}$ to represent the m service instances of a service type S_j . For example, for an online banking service type, there may be several users who are conducting online banking activities. While all those users' operations are supported by the same set of service programs, each user application has its private data space. Each user application's data, the corresponding private memory space, and the underlying shared service processes form a service instance. To receive a service, a user must be authorized. After a successful authorization, an instance of the requested service (type) is created for the user. Each service instance is self-contained – the service processes and the user data can be referenced within the namespace assigned to the service instance. As we will see later, this type of encapsulation makes service migration easier from one platform to another. Some virtualization approaches are readily available such as Zap [15], OpenVZ [18], and Xen [19]. As a functional requirement, each service instance $s_{j\text{-}i}$ is executed only on one platform at any given time. Furthermore, each service type S_j is assigned a priority level $Priority(S_j)$ based on the functional specification under which the service is to be executed and on the significance of the service type. The priority of a service instance inherits the priority of its parent service type.

3.2 System control components

3.2.1 Proxy server

The Proxy Server provides an interface to users. Its behavior is represented as a finite state machine as shown in Figure 2. The Proxy Server contains two operating units and one data table (called Service Instance Registration Table (SIRT)). The first unit, the Authorization Manager is responsible for authorizing service requests based on user identities, service certificates, or other service credentials. Since authorization is not unique to service migration, our design does not specify any particular authentication approach that a system must use. Rather, any proven access control mechanism can be applied depending on the application under consideration. Once a user request for a service type S_j has been authorized, another unit, the Service Operation Manager checks the System Resource Database (SRD) to verify that there is a platform in the system that can provide the requested service. As shown in Figure 3, SRD maintains one entry about each platform P_i, including such information as the capacity list of P_i, i.e., $Abi(P_i)$ (the types of services that P_i can support) and resources available on P_i to provide services to users. Each platform P_i has limited resources in terms of memory storage, CPU cycles, and network connections and it can only support a limited number of service instances.

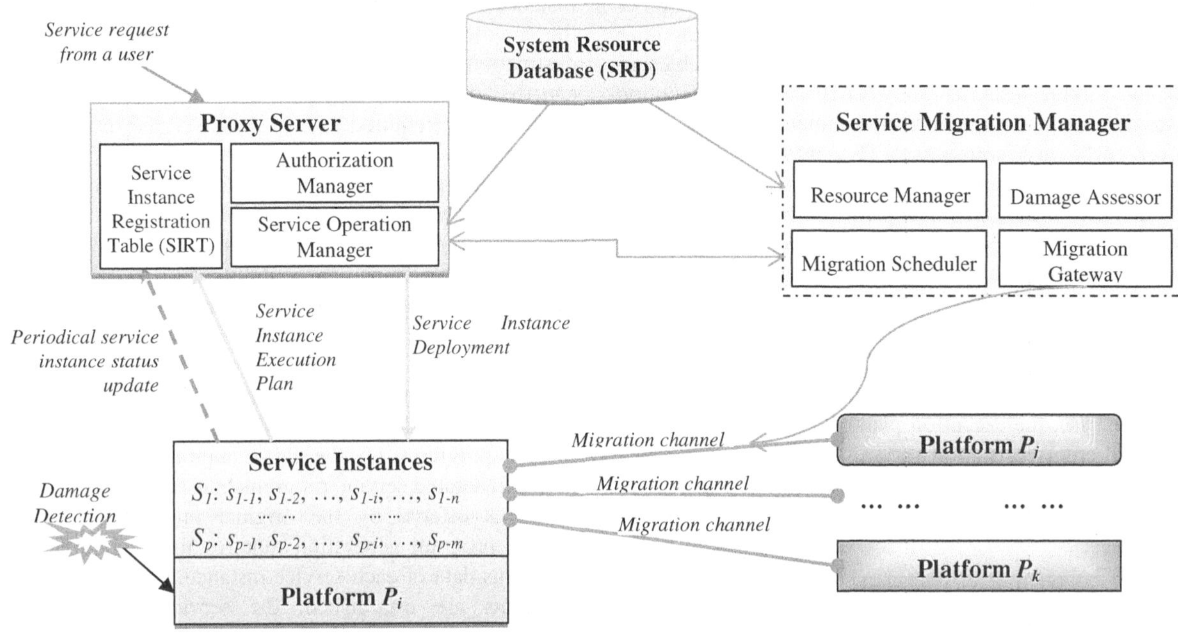

Figure 1: The Service Migration System Architecture

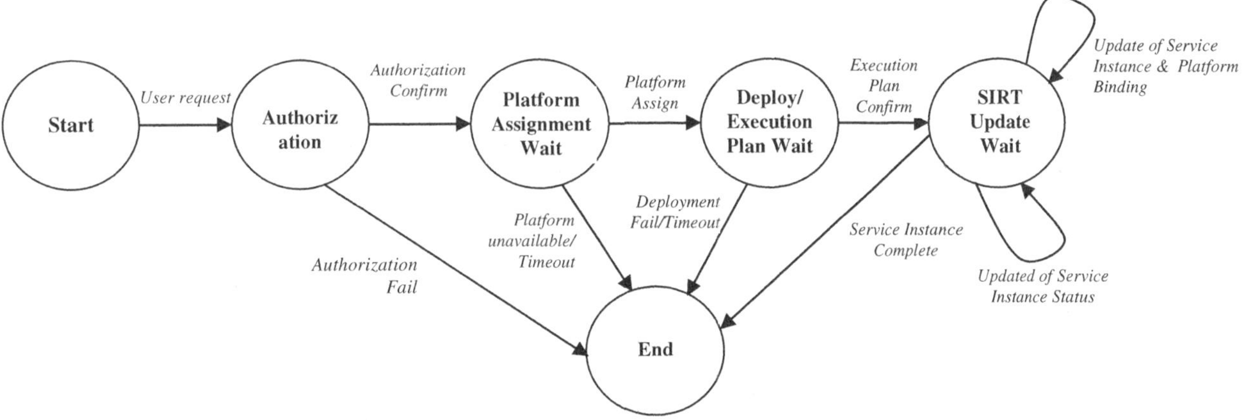

Figure 2: State Machine Representation of the Proxy Server

Platform P_i	Service Capability List $Abi(P_i)$	Resources Available

Figure 3: Scheme of System Resource Database (SRD)

Service quality is also a factor to consider when determining the platform load. For example, a platform in the financial institution's system may only be able to support up to 1,000 concurrent online trading service instances while maintaining a satisfied level of service quality. Any additional request for this type of service will go beyond the capacity of the platform and thus must be re-assigned to a different platform. If a platform P_i has been identified satisfying both the functional and resource requirements, the requested service will be assigned to be provided by P_i. Operationally, the Service Operation Manager sends a "Service Instance Deployment" message to P_i, instructing it to deploy and execute the requested service.

Upon receiving the service deployment message, P_i creates a new service instance $s_{j\text{-}k}$ (here we assume that the new service stance is the kth instance of service type S_j on the platform P_i). To customize services provided to different users, each service instance may be executed differently. P_i generates the corresponding execution plan and sends the plan to the Proxy server to be recorded in SIRT. An execution plan represents a concise description of how each service instance is executed. In its simple form, the execution plan includes the versions of the service programs and the algorithms (if any) to execute the service instance, the software signature of those programs, and other important parameters and variables to execute the service instance. As we will see, the execution plan provides important information about the execution details of each service instance. This information is very useful in re-generating the service programs in order to continuously execute $s_{j\text{-}k}$ on a new platform should the original service programs have been severely damaged (more will be discussed in Section 3.2.2). The Proxy Server creates a new entry for $s_{j\text{-}k}$ in SIRT to bind the service instance to the assigned platform. An entry in SIRT for $s_{j\text{-}k}$ is shown in Figure 4. Basically, the entry keeps track of the service instance (i.e., $s_{j\text{-}k}$), its service type (i.e., S_j), the platform on which it is executed (i.e., P_i), the execution plan of the service instance, and an initial empty execution service status. Afterwards, the status of the service instance, including important intermediate steps of the service execution, is periodically updated by P_i.

Service Instance $s_{j\text{-}k}$	Service Type S_j	Execution Plan of $s_{j\text{-}k}$ on P_i	Binding Platform P_i	Service Status Data

Figure 4: Scheme of Service Instance Registration Table (SIRT)

3.2.2 Service migration manager

The Service Migration Manager supervises the entire service migration process. Its behavior is represented as a finite state machine as shown in Figure 5. It contains four operating units: Damage Assessor, Migration Scheduler, Resource Manager, and Migration Gateway. The functions of those components are described next.

a) Damage assessor

A service migration is triggered by an event such as the detection of damage on a platform P_i. The Damage Assessor analyzes the collected incident data and decides whether the damage on P_i is severe enough so that a service migration is the best action to take given the current situation. If the faults are not severe and thus can be tolerated or masked (through mechanisms such as system/service redundancy, self-healing, or reconfiguration), the system's operations can be continued with a minimum level of delay. However, if the number of fault types is large or different actions/events must be taken following error detection, fault tolerance and damage masking become difficult. In the latter case, service migration is a viable solution for minimizing the impact of malicious attacks in order to continuously provide crucial services.

The damage assessment results suggest two types of migration for a service instance: (1) *a heavyweight migration*, or (2) a *lightweight migration*. A heavyweight migration should be applied if the underlying platform has been severely damaged but the main functions of the service programs are relatively tamper-free. Therefore, the service programs are still trustworthy. In this case, the entire service programs, along with the private spaces of the individual service instances, are migrated in one contained package. However, if the number of the service instances is too large for the destination new platform to handle (the capacity of a platform can be determined based on SRD), then multiple new platforms are required to host those service instances. In this situation, the individual service instance data (including their private namespaces and operating status) are migrated to different new platforms along with a copy of the service programs to each platform. On each of those new platforms, the service programs can continuously support the migrated sub-set of service instances. Different from a heavyweight migration, a lightweight migration is applied if the service programs on the compromised platform have also been damaged. Therefore, the entire service space is no longer trustworthy. In this situation, it is necessary to generate new service programs on the those migrated platforms. Those newly generated service programs must be able to provide the functions offered by the original ones. Technically, new service program generation requires the execution plan and the status data of each service instance. Once the new service programs are established, the service instances can be continuously executed. Service program generation and service set up on the new platforms will be discussed in more detail in *Section c)*.

b) Migration scheduler

Once a service migration is decided to be the best action to take, the Service Scheduler executes a function $Choose(P_i, s_{j\text{-}k}, P_k)$ to generate a feasible arrangement for each critical service instance $s_{j\text{-}k}$ with a high priority (e.g., $Priority(s_{j\text{-}i}) \geq L^*$, where L^* represents a threshold for high service priority) to be migrated from its current platform P_i to a new, healthy platform, say P_k. In the meantime, the service programs are halted on P_i, which consists of freezing service processes, recording global data (service configuration and state), recording the states of individual processes, and terminating the entire service programs. Due to limited resources and time constraints, other less critical services on the compromised platform P_i may be temporarily disabled and resumed after the damage is contained – a strategy to ensure that the most critical services will be guaranteed in a challenging environment.

A migration process is composed of three sub-actions: (1) migration preparation, e.g., saving the service programs and private data for each service instance in a resumeable image in a self-contained format with header, global data, internal process dependencies, and shared resources (e.g., task structure, open files); (2) service/data transfer, e.g., synchronizing data copies, withdrawing transactions, establishing recovery points, and disseminating the packed service programs and service instance data to the new platforms; and (3) service setup on the new platforms, e.g., resuming the service spaces and configuring the necessary service instance parameters. When a service instance is started on the new platform, a new namespace has to be created and its configuration/state will be restored. For the underlying

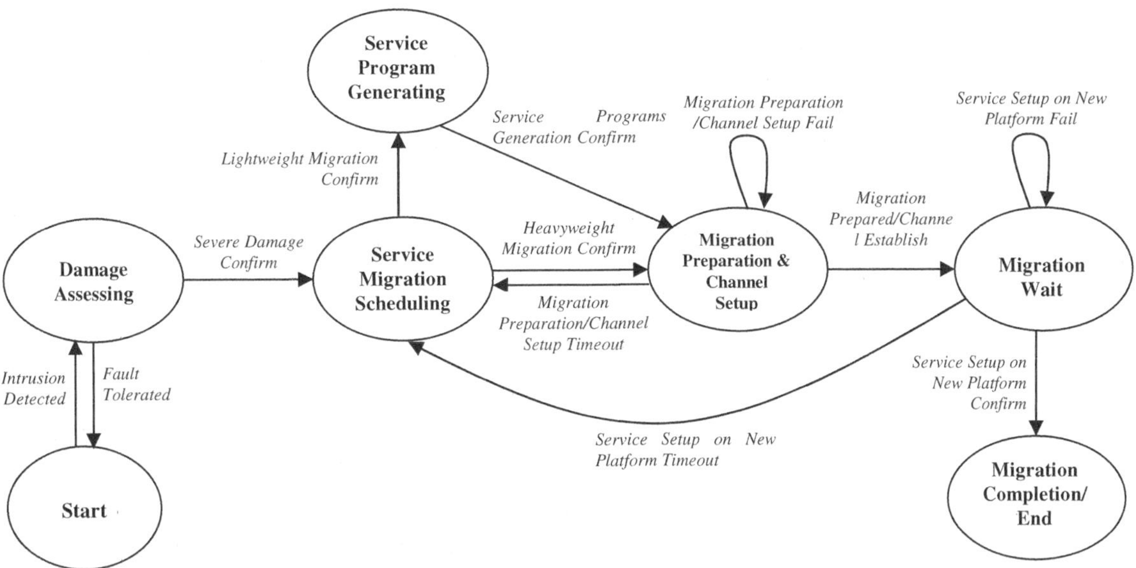

Figure 5: State Machine Representation of the Service Migration Manager

service programs, the inter-dependency relationships of individual service processes have to be re-established. To provide an ensured service migration, the system must preserve the invariants of process inter-dependencies on the new platform, maintain the consistence of memory contents, and ensure the integrity of transactions. The priority, response time, and throughput of each critical service instance must be ensured (or appropriately adjusted) during and after a service migration.

c) Resource manager

The Resource Manager manages migration related resources (e.g., the platforms that are capable of providing a particular type of service, the current capacities of those platforms), which are crucial for a timely scheduling plan for an effective service migration. When one service instance is migrated to a new platform, the Resource Manager must notify the Proxy Server of this re-binding between the migrated service instance and its new platform. Consequently, the Proxy Server updates the corresponding entry in SIRT. Other important functions of the Resource Manager include setting up the migrated services on the new platforms. More specifically, there are two main functions: (1) service program generation (in case of a lightweight migration); and (2) fuzzy data generation and recovery in case that some service data has been damaged. They are discussed in more detail next.

Service program generation As we mentioned earlier, a lightweight migration moves the execution plan and status data of a migrated service instance to a new platform without moving the service programs (which have been damaged). To continuously execute the service instances, new service programs must be generated and deployed on the new platform. In our design, service program generation is conducted by a software factory. As shown in Figure 6, the factory works like a software manufacturer: taking raw materials (supplied by the Resource Manager) – service functional specifications, execution plan of the service instances, and service quality and security requirements, and then assembling and producing a set of service programs to support the migrated service instances. The new service programs are then uploaded to the new platform, and they must provide the essential functions of those original service programs running on the old platform. The new software programs should have different implementations by applying such techniques as randomized code, obfuscation, and diversity. Therefore, the new software programs are not subject to the same type of attacks as the old ones. Afterwards, the execution of the service instances can continue from where they have been left.

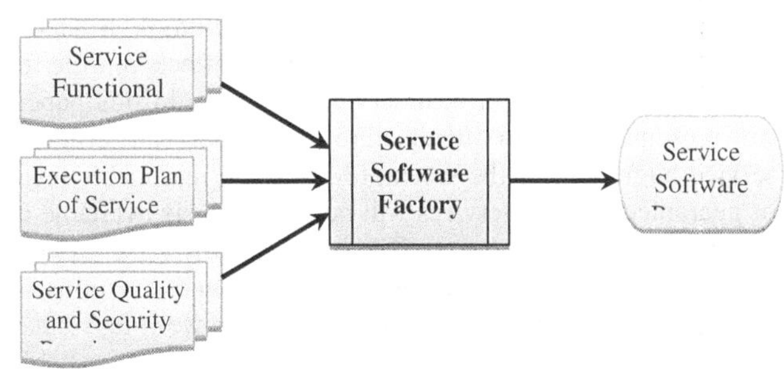

Figure 6: Functionality of a Service Software Factory

Fuzzy data generation and recovery Since certain data of a migrated service instance s_{j-i} may have been damaged, that data cannot be used on the new platform. Conducting a full cycle, offline data recovery may be difficult given limited time to make the service available. To deal with this situation, the Resource Manager must provide supplemental data by generating fuzzy data to support the continuous functions of s_{j-i}. Fuzzy data means that the data may not be accurate but are safe to use for a temporary time period to ensure the critical services are continuously available. In other words, fuzzy data is only meat to be used temporarily when the service instance is being executed on the new platform - as the critical functions must remain operational at all times. At a later time when the environment improves, an accurate recovery must be performed as soon as time and resources permit so that the fuzzy data items reflect exact values, not just acceptable values. Consequently, all transactions that have used approximate values have to take necessary corrective measures to ensure data integrity. Those operations are supervised by the Resource Manager since data is the most important resource for many services. Previous research [20-21] has demonstrated that fuzzy data can be generated in real time with a minimum level of delay.

d) Migration gateway

Service migration must be fast and secure. In our design, dedicated network communication channels have been set up among the platforms as preserved pathways for the purpose of service migration. Those channels are either established dynamically or pre-configured between two platforms. Since those channels are used only for transferring service packages from one platform to another and operating at a highly controlled model, they are relatively secure and efficient. The Migration Gateway is responsible for identifying and setting up those migration channels before or during a service migration. If necessary, this unit may act as an intermediate gateway to forward the migration data to the destination platform. There have been a set of techniques [22-23] available for configuring reliable connections among two nodes in a network.

4 Conclusions

In an attack scenario, service migration is a viable solution for minimizing the impact of attack effects in order to continuously provide critical services to users. In this paper, we presented system architecture to support an efficient service migration for the system to provide a reasonable level of guarantee that the services will be continuously available in a challenging environment. We have specified the system components and described their properties and functions in supporting an assured service migration. Our work lays out a foundation for further study in building survivable and reliable systems in high security and high integrity settings.

Acknowledgment

This material is based upon work supported by the US Air Force Office of Scientific Research (AFOSR) under Award FA9550-12-1-0131. Any opinions, findings, and conclusions or recommendations expressed in this publication are those of the author and do not necessarily reflect the views of AFOSR.

References

[1] Keromytis, A., Parekh, J., Gross, P. and Kaiser, G. (2003). "A Holistic Approach to Service Survivability", *Proc. of SSRS'03*, Fairfax, VA, USA.

[2] AlZain, M. (2012). "A New Approach Using Redundancy Technique to Improve Security in Cloud Computing", *Proc. of the International Conference on Cyber Security, Cyber Warfare and Digital Forensic*, pp. 230-235, Kuala Lumpur, Malaysia.

[3] Gashi, I., Popov, P. and Strigini, L. (2007). "Fault Tolerance via Diversity for Off-the-Shelf Products: A Study with SQL Database Servers", *IEEE Transactions on Dependable and Secure Computing*, (4) 4, pp. 280-294.

[4] Siozios, K and Soudris, D. (2012). "A Low-cost Fault Tolerant Solution Targeting to Commercial FPGA Devices", *Proc. of the NASA/ESA Conference on Adaptive Hardware and Systems*, pp. 46-53, Nuremberg, Germany.

[5] Mullner, N. and Theel, O. (2011). "The Degree of Masking Fault Tolerance vs. Temporal Redundancy", *Proc. of the IEEE Workshops of International Conference on Advanced Information Networking and Applications*, pp. 21-28, Biopolis, Singapore.

[6] Stunk, E., Knight, J. and Aiello, M. (2005). "Assured Reconfiguration of Fail-Stop Systems," *Proc. of International Conference on Dependable Systems and Networks*, pp. 2-11, Yokohama, Japan.

[7] Caporuscio, M., Marco, A. and Inverardi, P. (2007). "Model-based System Reconfiguration for Dynamic Performance Management," *Journal of Systems and Software*, (80)4, pp 455-473.

[8] Garlan, D., Cheng, S., Huang, A., Schmerl, B. and Steenkiste, P. (2004). "Rainbow: Architecture-based Self-Adaptation with Reusable Infrastructure," *IEEE Computer*, 37(10).

[9] Jiang, X. and Solihin, Y. (2011). "Architectural Framework for Supporting Operating System Survivability", *Proc. of IEEE 17th International Symposium on High Performance Computer Architecture*, pp. 456-465, San Antonio, TX, USA.

[10] Mikic-Rakic, M., Mehta, N. and Medridovic, N. (2002) "Architectural Style Requirements for Self-healing Systems," *Proc. of the First Workshop on Self-healing Systems*, pp. 49-54, Charleston, South Carolina, USA.

[11] Richards, M., Hastings, D., Ross, A. and Rhodes, D. (2007). "Design Principles for Survivable System Architecture", *Proc. of 1st Annual IEEE Systems Conference*, pp. 1-9, Honolulu, Hawaii, USA.

[12] Zhang, W., Liu, S. and Zhong, W. (2010). "Survivable Storage Architecture", *Proc. of Third International Symposium on Information Processing*, pp. 95-97, Qingdao, China.

[13] Medhi, D. and Tipper, D. (2000) "Multi-Layered Network Survivability – Models, Analysis, Architecture, Framework and Implementation: An Overview," *Proc. of DARPA Information Survivability Conference DISCEX 2000*, pp. 173-186, Hilton Head, SC, USA.

[14] Oikonomou, K. and Stavrakakis, I. (2006). "Scalable Service Migration: The Tree Topology Case", *Proc. of 5th Annual Mediterranean Ad Hoc Networking Workshop*, Lipari, Italy.

[15] Osman, S., Subhraveti, D., Su, G. and Nieh, J. (2002). "The Design and Implementation of Zap: A System for Migrating Computing Environments", *Proc. of 5th Symposium on Operating Systems Design and Implementation*, pp. 361-376, Boston, MA, USA.

[16] Laadan, O. and Nieh, J. (2007). "Transparent Checkpoint-Restart of Multiple Processes on Commodity Operating Systems", *Proc. of 2007 USENIX Annual Technical Conference*, pp. 323-336, Santa Clara, CA, USA.

[17] Laadan, O. and Hallyn, S. (2010) "Linux-CR: Transparent Application Checkpoint-Restart in Linux", *Proc. of the Linux Symposium 2010*, Ottawa, Canada.

[18] Web Site of OpenVZ, http://openvz.org, retrieved on March 14, 2013.

[19] Dragovic, B., Fraser, K., Hand, S., Harris, T., Ho, A, Pratt, I., Warfield, A., Barham, P. and Neugebauer, R. (2003). "Xen and the Art of Virtualization," *Proc. of the 19th ACM Symposium on Operating Systems Principles*, pp. 164-177, Bolton Landing, NY, USA.

[20] Zuo, Y and Panda, B. (2004). "Fuzzy Dependency and its Applications in Damage Assessment and Recovery", *Proc. of the 5th Annual IEEE Information Assurance Workshop*, pp. 350-357, West Point, NY, USA.

[21] Liu, Y. and Kan, X. (2007). "Fast Recovery of Real-time Database Based on Fuzzy Dependency", *Journal of Computer Applications*, (27)1, pp. 74-76.

[22] Akella, A., Shaikh, J., Seshan, S. and Maggs, B. (2004). "A Comparison of Overlay Routing and Multihoming Route Control", *Proc. of ACM SIGCOMM*, Portland, Oregon, USA.

[23] Hu, N., Mao, Z., Steenkiste, P. and Wang, J. (2004). "Locating Internet Bottlenecks: Algorithms, Measurements, and Implications", *Proc. ACM Conference on Applications, Technologies, Architectures and Protocols for Computer Communications*, Portland, Oregon, USA.

FAPA: A Model to Prevent Flooding Attacks in Clouds

Kazi Zunnurhain and Susan V. Vrbsky
Department of Computer Science
The University of Alabama
Tuscaloosa, AL 35487-0290
kzunnurhain@crimson.ua.edu, vrbsky@cs.ua.edu

Abstract- **Several schemes and a variety of intrusion detection systems are available in the market for DoS or flooding attacks. In this paper, we propose a model for the prevention of DoS attacks for clouds called FAPA (Flooding Attack Prevention Architecture). Based on the characteristics of attacks, our FAPA model uses a Learning Phase, Validation checking and Compatibility checking through its hypervisor to prevent flooding attacks. The central idea is to extract an extensive set of traffic behavior, which will describe the usual traffic flow for each session initiated by legitimate customers. Compatibility checking of the traffic from different customer sessions and associative rules will be used to find abnormalities. From those abnormalities, the system will automatically be aware of any phenomenon and precautions can be taken. Lastly, we show how our FAPA model can prevent different types of flooding attacks. Our goal is to design a model that allows a dynamic response that can adapt to prevent any type of flooding attack.**

Keywords- **Cloud security, DoS, Flooding attack, Hypervisor, Learning module**

I. INTRODUCTION

In the field of computation, there have been many approaches for enhancing the parallelism and distribution of resources for the advancement and acceleration of data utilization. Data clusters, distributed database management systems, data grids, and many more mechanisms have been introduced. Now cloud computing is emerging as the mechanism for high level computation, as well as serving as a storage system for resources. Clouds allow users to pay for whatever resources they use, allowing users to increase or decrease the amount of resources requested as needed. Cloud servers can be used to motivate the initiation of a business and ease its financial burden in terms of Capital Expenditure and Operational Expenditure.

There are three general layers that can be used to describe the services provided by a cloud system as shown in Figure 1: IaaS (Infrastructure as a Service), PaaS (Platform as a Service) and SaaS (Software as a Service). The infrastructure layer consists of all the hardware modules of the cloud. The platform layer contains the running applications on which the customers will obtain their virtual machines for desired computation. The software layer provides the actual computations requested by the customers. Cloud computing has been envisioned as the next generation architecture of IT Enterprise. It offers great potential to improve productivity and reduce costs. In contrast to traditional solutions, where the IT services are under proper physical, logical and personnel controls, cloud computing moves the application software and databases to large data centers. Unfortunately, the management of the data and services may not be fully trustworthy in a cloud, which poses many new security challenges which have not been well understood yet.

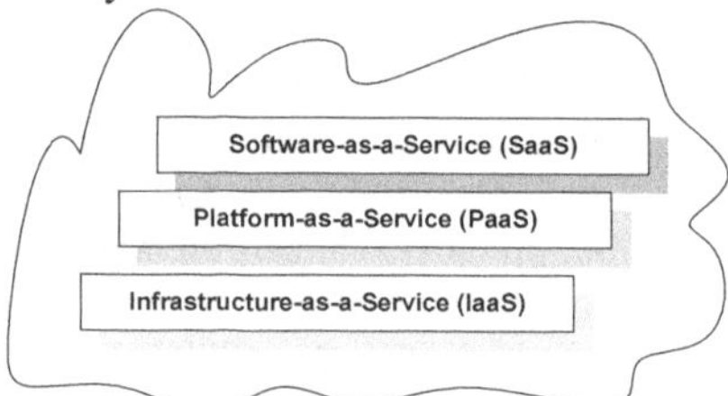

Figure 1: Principle Layers of a Cloud

Security is a vital issue for a distributed system where huge data processing and storage issues are a very common phenomenon. These kinds of systems are vulnerable to Denial of Service (DoS) attacks, also called flooding attacks. Because of their highly distributed nature, clouds and grids are very prone to Distributed Denial of Service (DDoS) attacks, occurs when a targeted system is attacked by multiple systems which themselves may have been compromised.

There are many different types of flooding attacks, but in general they all involve a victim receiving, processing and/or sending a large quantity of packets in response to the initial packets sent by an attacker. Dealing with this large number of packets depletes the victim's resources, causing legitimate requests to starve.

To address the threat of flooding attacks in clouds, our previous work in [6] we presented several possible ideas, one of which included the use of a hypervisor. In this paper, we present a model for preventing flooding attacks of clouds and provide specifics concerning the functionality of the hypervisor.

The remainder of this paper is organized as follows. Section II focuses on work related to DoS prevention and Section III describes different types of flooding attacks. Our FAPA (Flooding Attack Prevention Architecture) model and the role of each module in FAPA in preventing flooding attacks and blocking unauthorized access are presented in Section IV. Section V shows how the FAPA model prevents different types of attacks. Lastly, we draw conclusions in Section VI.

II. RELATED WORK

The four steps considered when responding to DoS attacks can be categorized into four types: Prevention, Detection, Response and Tolerance, and Mitigation [1]. Prevention of DoS attacks can take place by two types of filtering, either Ingress or Egress filtering. If a packet does not contain the IP address of the customer domain as the source address, then it could be filtered out in the outermost router of the customer domain, known as Egress filtering [7]. If packet dropping is possible inside the ISP domain, then it is known as Ingress filtering [12]. Thus, an inside attack could be prevented with Ingress filtering. However, now most research focuses on detecting and responding according to the attack, instead of blindly dropping the compromised packets.

Detection experts have developed many IDS (intrusion detection) systems [8], [9], [10], [11]. For these IDS systems, a system is built based on current scenarios of attack patterns and a developer's past experience and prediction knowledge [8],[9]. IDS might be rigid enough for any kind of attack along the network layers or transport layers, but if the attacker camouflages the IP packet and tries to intrude in the application layer, then few precautions can be taken. Also, some intrusion detection systems are modifiable and adaptable, but the extent to which these are limited. Sometimes the original code even has to be altered when the intrusion detection cannot perform well enough, which makes it difficult to keep up with network performance. This could be a problem in a cloud system.

In [2] Gil and Poletto proposed a scheme called MULTOPS to detect denial of service type attacks by measuring the ratio between the uplink and downlink packets. MULTOPS assumes that packet rates between two hosts are proportional during normal operation. If there is a significant disproportion between the packets going back and forth from a host or subnet, then it is a strong indication of a DoS attack. In clouds this IDS is not sufficient, because a cloud can be used as a computational device for a large and complicated program. Different modules of the program pass messages while functions call each other with the help of a SOAP message. This causes the ratio of packets to greatly increase and can even exceed the threshold of normal operations for that specific customer.

Lee and Stolflo [3] used data mining techniques to describe the patterns of system features and user behaviors in order to detect anomalies and intrusions. Rather than running a pattern matching algorithm along the command, they applied various types of algorithms, such as Link analysis, sequence analysis and classification type algorithms. The design is to make their IDS more general so that any kind of data can be fed into their system and statistical results can detect anomalies using association rules. All their data analysis takes place offline and their system does not filter until an anomaly is completely detected and an alarm has been generated. The flaw of this approach is that no effort is made to categorize the types of attacks. In a cloud system it is important to identify the types of malicious attacks to provide a dynamic solution on the fly to customers and to satisfy a proper SLA (service level agreement).

In [4], traffic which belongs to a DoS attack was detected by considering the high volume of traffic and then the correct drop probability was calculated to prevent the system from a flooding attack. In a cloud a more dynamic approach is required to accommodate any hardware malfunctions or increases in legitimate resource requests. Dropping legitimate requests can result in a loss of revenue and customer satisfaction.

Hybrid detection approaches [5] are also famous for their low false positives and high detection rate. Hybrid systems combine all the positive features of anomaly based and signature based detection models, such as the generation of association rules, and using data mining to construct features of the system and nature of the traffic. These types of systems are expensive and highly complicated during their implementation and not optimal in terms of cost for clouds.

Mitigation is an important aspect of clouds. An unusual phenomenon that occurs in a cloud and results in an increased cost must be investigated. For example, a usually long processing time for a general application that is not similar to the previous log history may cause increased charges, or the current account usage balance may dramatically increase suddenly for no apparent reason. A customer may charged for an application for which he is not the owner or a cloud user may be charged for using the cloud even though (s)he was not using the cloud at that specific time. An investigation should take place conducted by a neutral third party before charging the customer [13]. This third party investigation will proceed based on the log information and log records containing certain features in the provider's end [6]. If these features are ensured during the logging, then the actual cause of the interruption can be detected by the third party. However, such an investigation might take too much time. Instead, it is important to inform the third party on the fly, as soon as the alarm has been generated within the system.

III. Types of Flooding Attacks

There are various kinds of flooding attacks, including: ICMP flooding, UDP flooding, TCP SYN and indirect attacks. It is difficult for hackers to understand the infrastructure of a private cloud, so inside attackers are generally the first suspects for any kind of attacks in a private cloud. On the other hand, in a public cloud the flexible infrastructure of public clouds make them easy to penetrate and more vulnerable to outside attackers. We now describe different types of attacks and in Section V we will show how our proposed FAPA model can avert these types of attacks.

ICMP Flooding: One example of ICMP (internet control message protocol) flooding is a Smurf attack in which ping requests with a spoof source address are sent as a broadcast message. Many hosts then respond to the ping with an echo to the spoofed source address, which is the victim of the attack. For this type of attack in a cloud, the attacker is masked as an insider, because the spoof IP address can be a registered user of the cloud.

UDP Flooding/Spoof: A UDP (user datagram protocol) flooding attack can be initiated by sending a large quantity of packets, using UDP or TCP, to random ports on a remote host. In response to a packet received from a port, a distant host will check for an application listening at that port. Since no applications are listening at the random ports, the host will respond to the large quantity of packets by sending many ICMP Destination Unreachable packets, eventually resulting in it being unreachable by other clients.

In a UDP spoof, an attacker sends a UDP packet to a random port of the victim's system with a spoof source IP address. The attacker then continues to send additional packets. Eventually, the system tries to verify the spoofed IP address with its ACL (Access Control List) or legitimate user addresses, and finds nothing about the mentioned address. At this point, the attack has already committed its intentional task of occupying the resources of the system. Following this step, multiple packets are sent and the attacker is successful in occupying the total resources of the server.

Both ICMP flooding and UDP flooding can occur in clouds. A camouflaged attack unknowingly propagated from a cloud may compromise a legitimate user. Traditional solutions to prevent this type of attack require the use of additional hardware, a firewall or new devices. Requiring this additional hardware of a customer is not an acceptable solution in a cloud system.

Most of the communications in a cloud or grid take place in the transport layer of the network. In TCP/IP there are fewer layers with less overhead, smaller packets, and fewer redundant bits than the OSI model. With fewer bits, utilizing checksum becomes more complex. As a result, the TCP layers are more vulnerable to attacks and most of the intrusions consider these layers as a medium of transporting their illegal intension to reach the main unit. In a cloud computing environment, the main unit would include the cloud servers. Such an attack on a cloud system could be catastrophic.

TCP SYN flooding: A TCP SYN attack exploits the fact that total communication takes place through a three-way handshake protocol. A requester sends a SYN (synchronization) packet to the server, the server checks the packets and sends a SYN-ACK back to the requester and finally the requester sends an ACK back to the server to complete the communication path for transmitting further traffic. However, the attacker can send a very large number of SYN packets to the system and engage the system with a bulk amount of SYN-ACK packets, which engages the resources for a long time. These types of attacks are sometimes traceable if the attacker uses his own IP address and that IP address can then be blocked. This type of attack is known as a direct attack.

Indirect Attack: We must also consider what happens if the attacker uses some other handlers (zombies) to compel the attack. For example, the attacker machine (master) can command the handlers to send SYN packets to the victim machine with spoofed IP addresses. In this case, tracing the spoofed addresses of the handlers exhausts the system. Even if the system finds the handlers, it could be difficult for the administrators to find the actual attacker(s). While this scenario can occur in cloud systems, allowing the attack to continue in order to try to trace it back is not a feasible solution. The time taken to trace back the attacker could negatively affect the response time for the customer and the elastic nature of the cloud could allow a tremendous increase in packets.

Proxy servers can be deployed to filter packets with spoofed source IP addresses (indirectly for DoS), but all proxy servers have limitations. Usually the proxy servers are built for medium-sized industries and are capable of handling 15,000 requests/second for a total of 250,000 requests. This kind of system has to be adaptable and scalable to a large extent so that even the growth of requests in the system will not let the attackers penetrate the system. Since one of the characteristics of cloud computing is its scalability, deploying a proxy server may not provide the scalability needed by the cloud.

IV. FAPA MODEL

Though there has been much work on preventing DoS attacks, there is still no complete model for preventing DoS attacks in clouds. We introduce a model in this paper which is named FAPA (Flooding Attack Prevention Architecture), which contains different components that collaborate to prevent unauthorized intrusion or any kind of flooding attack. All these different components have different functions which we will describe in this section. The hypervisor is the composition of all these components. The role of the hypervisor is to learn the nature of the traffic packets, check its validity and schedule the tasks requested by the packets.

In our cloud system, the hypervisor is the core engine responsible for most of the message passing between different servers. While there may be some concern about centralizing multiple tasks around the hypervisor, the alternative is to distribute these tasks in the software layer, which may increase the likelihood of attacks. Instead, we propose to move higher level functionality to a lower level in order to increase security. In the next section we briefly describe the functions of our hypervisor.

A. Hypervisor

A hypervisor or virtual machine manager is an important component of a cloud system. A hypervisor allows multiple operating systems to run concurrently on a cloud. A hypervisor exists at the lowest level of the hardware. Since the hypervisor will be the kernel of the cloud system, it will be difficult for adversaries to intrude into the hypervisor [6], [14]. As attackers typically try to penetrate the system through the software layers, placing the hypervisor in the infrastructure layer provides additional protection. Currently, the only task a hypervisor performs in a typical cloud is the scheduling of resources, such as CPU, memory, disk I/O, etc., based on the requests from the customers. Our intension is to assign some additional tasks to the hypervisor in order to build a less vulnerable cloud system. We now identify cloud characteristics to determine the responsibilities of the hypervisor and to justify why the hypervisor should be the responsible component.

First, the traffic pattern in a cloud is not unique for all of its users. In other words, clients might have different patterns of usage or different times of day when they access the cloud. Therefore, there should be a module that has the self-learning capability to recognize a valid traffic pattern in order to authenticate all the users. Second, resource allocation should be flexible for each user during a given time span. For example, a user may need more CPU time or RAM during the day, while the same user needs less CPU or RAM at night time. In this regard the system also has to be scalable and dynamic for a cloud; in other words, balancing resources on the fly. Lastly and importantly, scheduling should utilize a separate module which establishes the initial connection between a user and the cloud system through an intermediary system. This is needed because direct communication could be misused due to the lack of knowledge of a new user or a simple mistake. We believe only the hypervisor should undertake all these three responsibilities: 1) learning behavior; 2) task of balancing resources to make the cloud more scalable and dynamic and 3) scheduling the resources based on the customer's requests by acting as an intermediary system. Satisfying these responsibilities would pose less of a security threat on a cloud system.

The first characteristic the hypervisor possess is a learning capability. There should be information about an application running in the system and the number of requests on a daily basis from a legitimate customer for that specific time period of the day. So for the same customer, if there is any discrepancy in the regular service pattern or if bulk amounts of requests start to arrive for the system to process, a third party can be engaged. The third party will conduct an investigation for this unusual phenomenon by comparing the log from previous records.

Second, the hypervisor should be scalable and highly dynamic. The hypervisor will not only count the number of SYN packets (requests) coming from the requester but also compare the rate of requests to the established TCP connections. It will facilitate the system's ability to detect attacks accurately on busy servers without false positives. This will also reduce the overhead of network administrators who spend time tuning the system to the network traffic.

Third, whenever a TCP connection request is placed, the hypervisor will commit the scheduling and also perform the handshaking. Similar to the scheduler in an operating system, which resides in the kernel of the OS, our hypervisor schedules tasks based on the register values collected from a strategy similar to that used by a File Allocation Table. The handshaking process of the hypervisor will proceed as follows. A request comes from the requester and the hypervisor will send a REQ-ACK to the requester and check if the source address is authenticated or not. If the source address is legitimate then it will send a CONN-REQ packet to the actual servers, which is based on a request for memory allocation, processing units or any file management servers from the cloud. If the system sends an ACK to the hypervisor, then upon receiving the ACK the hypervisor will send the requester a CONN-ACK and the direct connection between the requester and the server will be established through the hypervisor. In this way, if any attacker proceeds with a TCP SYN spoof IP address, then the spoof SYN-ACK will be handled by the hypervisor rather than directly engaging the resources of the cloud system. All these messages are accomplished by the hypervisor who is the sole coordinator of message passing between file servers and memory servers or a core processor. Much about this topology was discussed in our previous paper [6] where we depicted the major issues related to cloud security.

B. Learning Ability

Adapting the learning ability in the hypervisor requires extraction of various features from the incoming traffic in the system. The rate of traffic, volume, flow, etc. should be recorded and checked by the hypervisor to detect any kind of anomaly. Comparison with the normal traffic flow or user profile statistics in the cloud will detect any kind of intrusion. Suppose, $T_{in}(t)$ is the total traffic inflow in the system at time t, $T_{pr}(t)$ is the previous record traffic for that specific request usually flowing through the system at t, and T_{th} is the threshold traffic which will be determined based on the nature of traffic volume fluctuation for that specific t. An intrusion alert will be generated based on the overflow traffic volume, denoted as $T_{ov}(t)$.

Calculate, $T_{ov}(t) = T_{in}(t) - T_{pr}(t)$

if $T_{ov}(t) < 0$, then no traffic problems detected

else if $T_{ov}(t) > 0$;

then if $T_{ov}(t) > T_{th}$, {intruder alert in the system}

else "no action"

The intruder alert will propagate through the hypervisor by message passing. Every message is propagated by each module sequentially. Before raising the intrusion flag, the hypervisor will deploy a third party who is provided with the log table in order to investigate the issue within a specific (short) time frame. During a short span of time, no request will be processed from the requester and it will be queued. An unusual event may not be a flooding attack. For example, there could be a malfunction at the customer's end or a customer might have forgotten to stop his VM by mistake and kept it running for an unusually long period of time. After analyzing all these possibilities, if the third party determines there truly an attack, then based on the confirmation from the third party, a flag will be set indicating the intrusion. The hypervisor will pass the messages to its nearest servers notifying them of the intrusion and the servers themselves will be able to transfer this intrusion alert among their neighboring servers.

An important issue is how to make the system more scalable and dynamic during this kind of situation. We cannot assume that the intrusion detection method will completely check any kind of anomalies, because the adversary can inject a Trojan horse or logic bomb. A Trojan horse is a useful, or apparently useful, program or command procedure containing hidden code which will perform some unwanted or harmful functions when invoked. In a logic bomb, embedded code in some legitimate program is set to explode when certain conditions are met. For example, a logic bomb may be inside a regular message which does appears similar to the usual traffic pattern. After some time and based on some event, that logic bomb will be triggered inside one of the servers. Hence, to handle such kind of phenomenon, the system has to be highly scalable and dynamic.

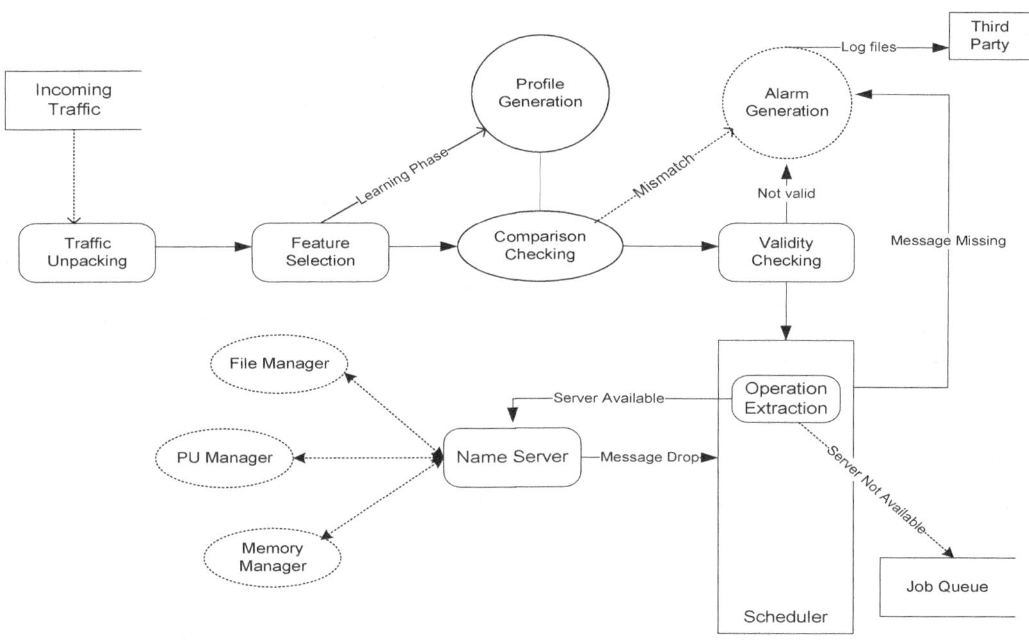

Figure 2: FAPA model

C. *Model Specifics*

Figure 2 illustrate the components and process flow of the FAPA model. First, as specified by the process flow, the incoming traffic will feed into the system and traffic unpacking will occur. Here by unpacking we mean the separation of the header information from the operation part of the traffic packet. The header information will contain all the infrastructure information, including the creation time, expiration time, type of request and security token for the validation of the message. Next, in the Feature Selection module, the infrastructure information stored in the header is checked to determine if it is an abnormal or a regular traffic pattern. If it is a usual type of traffic pattern, then it is directed towards the comparison checking module. If it is not a usual type, then it is forwarded to the Profile Generation module which has the task of storing records about the traffic. The finishing time of the operation is also used to determine if it is a legitimate packet.

The Comparison Checking module will verify the type, size and all infrastructure details with previously recorded information. Here the different columns of characters are merged into a single string and the string checking is performed. Specifically, assume the recorded information follows the NTFS multiple data streams system. The multiple data streams are independent executable modules and service modules containing access rights, encryption, and date and time information. All of these need to be checked while passing between the servers and the job queue. Based on the traffic scenario, dynamic rules are generated, classifiers applied and a link analysis performed for comparison checking to identify any abnormality in the traffic pattern. If this infrastructure information passes the comparison checking successfully then it is forwarded to the Validity Checking module, which will be done with the help of the security token. A bucket of security tokens will be organized to maintain continuous validation checking after extracting the body of the message from the header. The bucket of tokens is maintained in the Validation module which contains the unique identifiers of messages of a similar traffic type. If there is a mismatch with the traffic pattern anticipated by the profile generator, the validation module will not forward this message. Otherwise, the header information is extracted from the body and a decryption algorithm is applied in the validation module to retrieve the unique token number of each message. If the validation process fails, then an alarm message will be sent to the Alarm Generation module which executes the task of communicating with the third party by providing the detailed log for investigation.

If validation is successful, then the traffic is fed into the Scheduler. Here the requested operation will be extracted. Based on the type of request, the Scheduler will check the availability for that service in the fleet of servers (file manager, memory manager, process unit for complex computation, etc). If the specific type of server is not available, then the operation will be queued in the Job Queue storage. If it is available, then the operation will be appointed to the specific server via the Name Server. This Name Server has the task of coordinating all kinds of message passing between the servers and also with the scheduler (Figure 3). Hence, this server can also be considered as the monitoring server for message passing. If any missed message occurs in the system while executing jobs, then it will be detected and a "Drop Message" alarm will be generated by the Name Server. It will send this message to the Scheduler and the Scheduler will share this information with the Alarm Generator. Meanwhile, the Scheduler will also appoint another available server with the remaining task of the affected one via the Name Server, so that the remaining tasks of the attacked server do not starve.

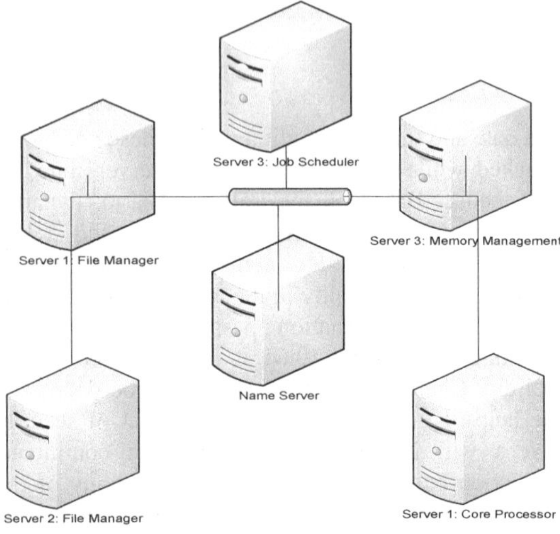

Figure 3: Messaging between servers

For any kind of alarm message received in the Alarm Generator module, a new tag will be issued by the scheduler itself. This tag will contain all the information about the time of the incident, and the infrastructure information about all the traffic packets at that specific time. These tags will be provided to the neutral third party in a progressive manner; which means based on the investigation of the third party, the logs will be provided without disclosing the provider's infrastructure information to the third party.

V. PREVENTING ATTACKS

In this section we discuss how our FAPA model prevents different types of flooding attacks.

A. ICMP and UDP Flooding/Spoofing

FAPA prevention: Unauthorized UDP packets will be detected in the Feature Selection module and the Comparison Checking module, and will not be sent to the scheduler.

Justification: The hypervisor is a communication mediator between the requester and the client. Whenever there is an unauthorized UDP packet the Feature Selection module will be able to verify unusual features, such as random ports of the client's application, unmatched header information or a dissimilar expiration period of that message. In the Comparison Checking module, all these features will point out the invalidity of this packet in the next phase (Validation Checking) before sending the packet for scheduling. Hence, the chance of sending ICMP packets by the Scheduler is eliminated prior to scheduling. Instead, the invalid messages are forwarded to the Alarm Generation module. The system will be saved from UDP flooding and the engagement of its resources. Also, the recorded information in the Profile Generation module will prevent the system from flooding due to these types of packets in the future.

B. TCP SYN flooding attack

FAPA prevention: The 3-way handshake protocol and third party evaluation of the log files can identify the invalid messages and can even identify their requester.

Justification: The TCP SYN attack follows the 3-way handshake protocol and waits for the SYN-ACK from the servers. In our system the hypervisor takes the responsibility of scheduling and coordinating 3-way handshaking. So whenever a requester sends a TCP request, the unpacking is done in the Feature Selection module and infrastructure information inside the TCP packet will determine its illegitimacy. Suppose the attacker somehow manages to create a valid SYN with the usual features and bypasses both the feature and comparison phase. In the validation phase, the system will check the previous records of this requester's TCP connection types, durations and creation request times etc. In this phase the TCP request will not be able to bypass the validation phase because this module checks all the previous TCP rates and SYN requests before forwarding the SYN to the scheduler. An unmatched TCP will be forwarded to the Alarm Generation module and will be analyzed by the neutral third party. Hence, the scheduler is again prevented from being flooded by SYN packets. Also, the third party will have sufficient log information to trace back to the requester who actually generated these SYN packets to flood the system.

C. Indirect Attack and Logic Bomb

FAPA prevention: The timer inside the Job Queue module will verify the validity of messages and identify an invalid request. Eventually an alarm will be generated so that the Alarm Generator module can broadcast this type of invalid message.
Justification: The hypervisor queues all these requests in the Job Queue module. If after a specific threshold time there is no match found for these types of messages or server requests, all these requests are forwarded to a neutral third party. Also, the Alarm Generation module will generate a broadcast message to notify all the working servers about these new types of invalid messages trying to flood the system. In the case of a Trojan horse or logic bomb, which will be triggered after a specific time, our monitoring device inside the scheduler will coordinate with the working servers and will provide feedback to the Alarm Generator.

FAPA is being design to circumvent any type of ICMP and UDP flooding, spoofing attack and TCP SYN flooding as either a direct one or an attack through handlers.

VI. CONCLUSIONS AND FUTURE WORK

A cloud is vulnerable to numerous types and different approaches of attacks. In this paper we propose a theoretical model (FAPA) to prevent DoS attacks. By considering different types of DoS attacks, we aim to make the cloud more dynamic and adaptive. To build a cloud with this capability requires the system to have a learning module that evolves over time, to balance resources to make the cloud more dynamic and to schedule the resources using an intermediary system.

In our future work, we will implement the tasks of the hypervisor to prevent DoS attacks in a cloud. The first step of our implementation phase will be to simulate the FAPA model in a private cloud. By simulating inside a private cloud it will be possible to detect the nature of the inside attackers and their ill intensions. Then we will try our model on a private cloud to verify the vulnerability from different types of DoS attack as an outsider.

For our first step, we have created a private cloud named FLUFFY in our research lab that will be used for the simulation. We also plan to compare the performance of our FAPA model to other strategies to measure the overhead required by FAPA. Based on the results of simulations, we will proceed to bring this model to reality.

REFERENCES

[1] B. B. Gupta, R.C. Joshi, Manoj Misra. "Dyanmic and Auto Responsive Solution for Distributed Denial-of-Service Attacks." Detection in ISP Network. *International Journal of Computer Theory and Engineering, Vol.1, No.1, April 2009.*

[2] T.M. Gil, M. Poletto, "Multops: a data structure for bandwidth attack detection," *in the proceedings of the 10th USENIX Security Symposium, Washington, DC, USA, 2001, pp23-38.*

[3] W. Lee, S.J. Stolfo, K. W. Mok, "A data mining framework for building intrusion detection models," *in the Proceedings of the 1999 IEEE Symposium on Security & Privacy, Oakland, CA, 1999, pp.120-132.*

[4] S. Floyd, S. Bellovin, J. Ioannidis, K. Kompella, R. Mahajan, V. Paxson, "Pushback Messages for Controlling Aggregates in the Network," draft-floyd-pushback-messages-00.txt, 2001.

[5] K. Hwang, M. Cai, Y. Chern, M. Qin(2007). Hybrid Intrusion Detection with Weighted Signature Generation over Anomalous Internet Episodes. *IEEE Transaction on Dependable and Secure Computing. 4(1) 41-55.*

[6] Kazi Zunnurhain, Susan V. Vrbsky. "Security in Cloud Computing". *Proceedings of the 2011 International Conference on Security & Management.*

[7]VMware. Virtual Appliance Marketplace. http://www.vmware.com/appliances/.

[8]Amazon Elastic Compute Cloud (Amazon EC2). http://aws.amazon.com/ec2.

[9] Meiko Jenson, Jorg Schwenk, Nils Gruschka, Luigi Lo Iacono. On Technical Security Issues in Cloud Computing. *IEEE International Conference on Cloud Computing 2009.*

[10] Andreas Haeberlen. A Case for Accountable Cloud. *Max Planck Institute of Software System (MPI-SWS).*

[11] Nils Gruschka and Luigi Lo Iacono. Vulnerable Cloud: SOAP Message Security Validation Revisited. *NEC Laboratories Europe Rathausallee 10 D-53757 Sankt Augustin (Germany), 2009 IEEE.*

[12] Mladen A. Vouk. Cloud Computing- Issues, Research and Implementations. *Proccedings of the ITI 2008 30th Int. Conf. on Information Technology Interfaces, June 23-26,2008, Cavtat, Croatia.*

[13] Michael Armbrust, Armando Fox, Rean Griffith, Anthony D. Joseph, Randy Katz, Andy Konwinski, Gunho Lee, Daviv Patterson, Ariel Rabkin, Ion Stoica and Matei Zaharia. A View of Cloud Computing. *Communications of the ACM, April 2010.*

SESSION

COMPUTER AND NETWORK SECURITY

Chair(s)

Dr. Youn Chan Jung

Mobile Root Exploit Detection based on System Events Extracted from Android Platform

You Joung Ham, Won-Bin Choi, Hyung-Woo Lee
School of Computer Engineering, Hanshin Univ., 411, Yangsan-dong, Osan,
Gyeonggi Province, 447-791, Rep. of Korea.
e-mail: you86400@hanmail.net, bindon@hanmir.com, hwlee@hs.ac.kr

Abstract—**Recently, the number of attacks by malicious application has significantly increased, targeting Android-platform mobile terminal such as Samsung Galaxy Note I/II and Galaxy Tab 10.1, etc. The malicious application can be distributed and installed on user's mobile devices through open market after masquerading as a common normal application. An attacker inserts malicious code into an application, which might threaten privacy by root exploit. Once the root exploit attack is successful, malicious code can collect and steal private data stored in mobile terminal, for example, SMS messages, contacts list and public key certificate for banking. To protect the private information from the malicious exploit attack, several response mechanisms such as malicious code detection, rooting attack detection and countermeasure method are required. To meet this end, this paper investigates mobile root exploits for Android based mobile devices. Based on that, this paper proposes countermeasure system that enables to extract and collect events related to root exploit attacks occurring from mobile terminal, which contributes to active protection from malicious mobile attacks.**

Keywords- Smart Mobile Device, Root Exploits, Detection, Malicious Application, Kernel Event, Android Platform

I. INTRODUCTION[1]

Recently, diversified attacks performed by malicious mobile application masquerading as an innocuous application have been growing high, targeting to a widely used Android platform based mobile device such as *Samsung Galaxy Note I/II* and *Galaxy Tab 10.1*, etc. An *exploit* is a piece of software, a chunk of data, or sequence of commands that takes advantage of a bug, glitch or vulnerability in order to cause unintended or unanticipated behavior to occur on computer software, hardware, or something electronic. Such behavior frequently includes such things as gaining control of a computer system[1]. In particular, *Android rooting* is the process of allowing users of smart phones, tablets, and other devices running the Android mobile operating system to attain privileged control (known as 'root access') within Android's subsystem[2]. Therefore, Android root exploit attack can expose a serious threat to privacy and security of the mobile user. In terms of *mobile root exploits*, an attacker inserts malicious codes into mobile application, which can collect and steal sensitive data from the user's mobile device, for example, SMS messages, contacts list and public key certificate for banking[3]. To prevent from spreading those malicious applications, it is necessary to examine a mobile root exploit running on Android-based mobile device and analyze their characteristics. Based on the analysis, this study is expected to provide effective countermeasures against the malicious rooting attack on android-based mobile device.

Firstly, this study investigates existing malicious applications running on a commercial mobile device to understand how it operates internally. Since Android malware using a exploit *RageAgainstTheCage* exploit[4] was discovered, *GinerBreak* exploit[5] based on *GingerBread* API has been analyzed and evolved into more advanced malicious root exploit module, named *GingerMaster*[6]. If applications infected by mobile root exploit module are installed and executed, private data stored in a mobile device can be leaked to remote attacker without user's awareness[7,8,9,10].

Security-related vulnerabilities were scrutinized on mobile devices against malicious application as a related works[11,12,13]. Especially, malicious application was implemented using the experimental exploit in [12]. It was demonstrated that the experimental malicious application could actually steal private data, particularly the user's public key certificate from inside of smartphone by mobile root exploit[14]. To cope with the security problem like this, our idea is the use of *system event monitoring by kernel daemon*. Daemon is created and installed on mobile device to collect events activated by system kernel while it runs in background. *Event log* consists of normal events as well as attack-type events[15]. Therefore, we propose a proactive countermeasure method against security-related vulnerability by collecting and extracting system events caused by mobile root exploit attacks done by malicious application.

This paper is organized as follows. Chapter 2 analyses the rooting process performed in Android platform mobile device and takes a look at an application that threatens the mobile device security by rooting attack. Chapter 3 investigates how the security information like private data and banking data are stolen by malicious application which is specially developed for experimental purpose. Chapter 4 presents experiment results obtained by running daemon process that is designed to gather system events coming from mobile device and cope with malicious attacks based on mobile root exploits.

II. ANALYSIS OF MOBILE EXPLOIT ATTACK

Android is an operating system based on Linux kernel. In Linux, root account has the highest level of authorization over the system, that is, root user can access all the files and programs inside the system. Rooting is a process that allows the users to gain root privileges over the Android system. To gain insight into attack mechanism for a currently used mobile device, this study analyses a rooting attack based on exploit discovered earlier. In addition, the study examines an internal structure of malicious application that appeared on the Android market more recently. Based on the analysis, this paper suggests security vulnerabilities of mobile terminals. Before progressing further, it would be useful to take a look at the rooting process performed by its own user without harmful intent.

A. Active Rooting Mechanism for Smart Mobile Device

Generally, the user is not allowed to attain root privilege over Android-platform mobile device since Android is an operating system based on Linux. However, after rooting an Android based mobile terminal, the users can do anything they want, for example, they can add and edit new fonts, improve system performance and modify the user interface as they want. Therefore, *active rooting* is performed

---

[1] Corresponding Author: Hyung-Woo Lee is with the School of Computer Engineering, Hanshin Univ., 411, Yangsan-dong, Osan, Gyeonggi Province, 447-791, Rep. of Korea. (e-mail: hwlee@hs.ac.kr). This research was supported by Basic Science Research Program through the National Research Foundation of Korea (NRF) funded by the Ministry of Education, Science and Technology (Grant # 2012R1A1A2004573)

with the goal of overcoming limitations that hardware manufactures pus on mobile devices, resulting in the ability to alter or replace system applications and settings by running specialized root exploit application[3].

There are a number of root exploit programs that allow users to acquire the root privilege over their own mobile device, such as *SuperOneClick*[16], *Universal Androot*[17], *Z4root*[18] and *Odin*[19] etc. These are good purpose rooting programs that help user gain admin privilege. For example, *SuperOneClick,* run on environment over 'Microsoft .NET Framework 2.0' or greater version, supports rooting and un-rooting for almost all of mobile devices. When rooting or un-rooting is carried out, the mobile device needs to be connected to PC.

The steps to install *SuperOneClick* and root the mobile device are as follows. First, connect an android device to PC via USB, and run the program. Second, click 'Root' button and then reboot the device. After rebooting, the user can see '*Superuser*' application that has been installed. Finally, if the user runs 'Superuser' program, the user gets root access. Other programs also can be executed similarly with this one.

When it comes to *Samsung Galaxy Tab 10.1,* rooting can be done in a passive way due to the change of internal system structure of device. By pressing volume down button and power button together, galaxy tab goes to recovery mode. After it enters recovery mode, start to execute exploit file for *Galaxy Tab 10.1*. Once exploit file runs, subsequent process would be same as mentioned above. *Superuser* application will be installed on the device. Once installed, the user is able to confirm whether rooting is successfully completed, via *adb* shell.

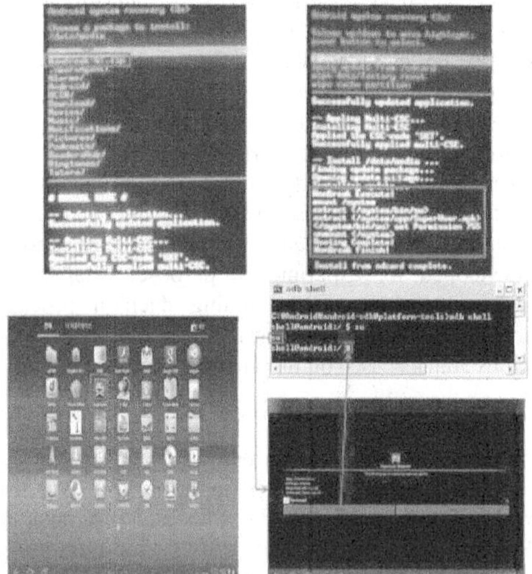

Fig. 1. Exploit Execution and Confirmation in Galaxy Tab 10.1

To root Galaxy Note I, '*Tegrak Kernel*'[20] is required to be installed. If users install *Tegrak Kernel* over the existing system, they can modify an internal system and install additional modules on it without affecting system files and functionalities of legal version of firmware. In order to install *Tegrak Kernel*, Samsung integrated USB driver must be installed first. Once *Tegrk Kernel* is installed, software *Odin* needs to be installed with maintaining connection between PC and *Galaxy Note I*. *Odin* is a program that enables the user to change system firmware. It is time to check version and build number of the device. Based on the version and build number, corresponding version of *Tegrak Kernel* needs to be installed using *Odin*. Kernel will be upgraded for *Galaxy Note I* through *Odin* as shown in fig. 2.

More specific steps are as follows. First step is to create Tegrak/update/ folder in sdcard of device. Second step is to copy *Tegrak-kernel-Build*.zip* file to the folder, and to execute it. After running *Odin*, the user needs to select *Tegrak-kernel-Build*.recovery.tar* in PDA in a tab that says 'PDA' and run it. Now the device goes to recovery mode. In recovery mode, the user can see *Tegrak kernel* rooting module installed on sdcard as shown in fig.3. This *Tegrak kernel* enables the user to root and un-root. It also provides the function to overclock processor inside the device for enhancing system performance.

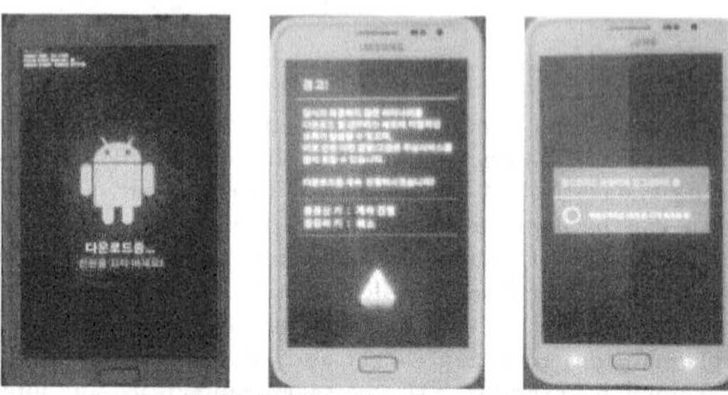

Fig. 2. Check Rebooting in mobile device

Fig. 3. Steps how to root using Tegrak Kernel in mobile device

B. Passive Rooting Mechanism for Smart Mobile Device

As mentioned in previous section, the role of rooting module is to allow users to root their own device. However, if the rooting module is misused, it can be harmful attacking tool. When a malicious attacker inserts it into mobile application, it can steal important private data from the mobile terminal. *RageAgainstTheCage* exploit[4] is one of well-known rooting codes used for this purpose. It can be embedded into malicious mobile application using C language based NDK module. If a malicious application containing *RageAgainstTheCage* exploit is installed and executed, it would copy malicious code to internal Android mobile device. That malicious code file is a binary executable file that had been produced by cross compiling. Once the malicious code is successfully copied, it makes a change to access permission of specific folder using *chmod* command. Subsequently, it invokes lots of processes by calling *fork()* over 400 times in Linux shell. At last, buffer will be overflown in Linux kernel. If Android based system kernel is not possible to run any process due to buffer overflow, Linux shell will be forced to terminate. At this moment, if malicious code gets access to shell, it can obtain root permission to access for kernel. Android 2.3 known as *GingerBread* has been updated to fix this security vulnerability problem caused by *RageAgainstTheCage* mechanism. However, new type of mobile root exploit named *GingerBreak* appeared targeting Android 2.3 *GingerBread*.

GingerBreak exploit[5] gains admin access permission after message hooking handled by 'init' process on Linux shell. *GingerBreak* exploit includes *su* file that has been modified from original one. If the *su* file is copied to system folder, the mobile terminal is considered to be rooted permanently. There are two types of rooting: *temporary* and *permanent* type of rooting. If device is temporarily rooted, system state will be recovered back as normal unrooted state after rebooting without need of separate recovery steps. On the contrary, permanently rooted device can be recovered back only through separate un-rooting process. As of *GingerBreak*, it roots the device permanently.

In terms of rooting process itself, *GingerMaster* exploit[6] is very similar to *GingerBreak*. However, it is known that *GingerMaster* steals much more information than *GingerBreak*. *GingerMaster* exploit takes advantage of the most recent root exploit against Android 2.3. And it was identified on August 2011 for the first time by evolution of existing *DroidKungFu* mobile application, which is repackaged into legitimate ones. Working mechanism and structure of *GingerMaster* is considered to be similar to that of *GingerBreak*. *GingerMaster* is one of extremely powerful malwares for Android 2.3 since it is not detected by existing virus scan tools. *GingerMaster* is concealed behind the general application. It is then installed and silently launches a service in a background. While the malicious service runs, it collects user's private data stored in mobile terminal and transmits the data to specific external server. More specifically, *GingerMaster* exploit can bury itself inside the device in a form of regular file named *gbfm.png*. In the meanwhile, it actually gains root privilege over the device. After getting root privilege, *GingerMaster* lets the mobile terminal connect to a remote C&C server, and silently download and install the malicious application without user's awareness. The malware installed through this process, will silently transfer internal information to outside.

Upon completion of rooting described earlier, the user is able to modify a basic system structure. In addition, the user can move key pad position and edit/delete/update applications installed in device as the user please.

On the other hand, rooted device is exposed to serious risk relating to security vulnerabilities like leakage of sensitive information, for example, contacts list, SMS messages contained in inbox and outbox, and web site accessing history etc. There are a number of malicious applications containing exploit to attack mobile terminal. In next section, we are going to take a look at those malwares.

C. *Malicious Application on Smart Mobile Device*

Various types of malicious apps targeting Android device have been seen and reported. Among them, several renowned types of malwares will be described here. First one is *DroidOS/Spitmo(SpyEye attack)*[21]. Malicious mobile exploit codes are hidden behind internet banking applications. If the user downloads the banking app, it leads to installing malware on mobile terminal. Once installation completes, the user is instructed to call a specific number, which charges user's phone bill with huge costs. If malicious codes are activated, *Trojan horse* will be installed on the system. Trojan horse can steal SMS related data and send those data to C&C server as attacker specified.

When a user browses to the targeted bank a message is injected presenting a 'new' mandatory security measure, enforced by the bank, in order to use its online banking service. The initiative pretends to be an Android application that protects the phone's SMS messages from being intercepted and will protect the user against fraud. Once the user clicks on 'set the application', they are given further instructions to walk them though downloading and installing the application.

To complete the installation, the user is instructed to dial the number '325000'; the call is intercepted by the Android malware and an 'alleged' activation code is presented, to be submitted later in to the 'bank's site'. Besides concealing the true nature of the application, this "activation code" does not serve any legitimate purpose. Once the Trojan has successfully installed, all incoming SMS messages will be intercepted and transferred to the attacker's Command and Control server (C&C). A code snippet is run when an SMS is received, creating a string, which will later be appended as a query string to a GET HTTP request, to be sent to the attacker's drop zone[21].

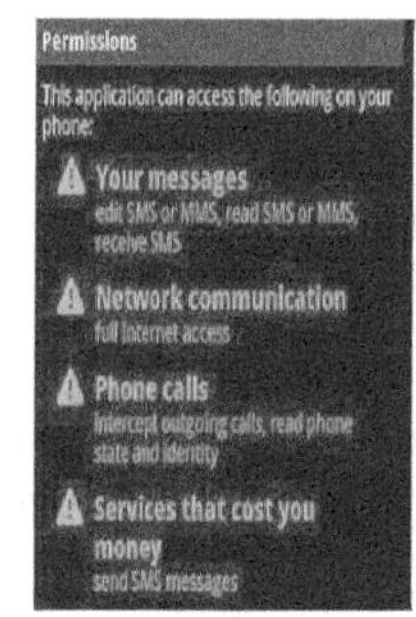

Fig. 4. DroidOS/Spitmo Trojan Horse(SpyEye)

Second, *DroidDeluxe*[22] is a malware that includes malicious code to acquire root privilege over the system. While it runs, it collects mobile device related information such as manufacturer name, model name, and device information, and then transmits the information to specific google account (UA-19670793-1). DroidDeluxe packages the *RageAgainstTheCage/Zimperlich* root exploit in an executable named password. When it runs, it will start the exploitation process in the background without user's awareness (to obtain the root privilege). If successful, it will then launch another embedded executable named special. This special program essentially changes the file mode of account-related files in the phone and makes them world-readable and world-writable. Once malicious app is executed, it makes a change to access mode of files that hold private information. The reason why it changes access mode of that file, it aims to get read/write-enabling permission for that file. As a result, important personal information might be stolen to outside.

Fig. 5. DroidDeluxe Malicious Application

Third, *BaseBridge*[23] exploits security weakness existing in older version of *Android* 2.3. *BaseBridge* exploit can be easily embedded into other legitimate apps. When an infected app is installed, the malware will ask users to upgrade it. If users choose to do so, it will install itself on another area of the phone with the name "com.android.battery". After the installation, a new prompt will ask the user to restart the app in order to run it. Once the app is restarted, the malware is activated. While app is executed, it connects to the remote server and sends IMSI(international mobile subscriber identity) and OS configuration information. Additionally, it silently transmits information associated with SMS. It also can erase the specific SMS message.

Finally, *CruiseWind* is an app that includes malicious code to relay the SMS[24]. *FlashServer* is forced to be installed on the system, which lets the system connect to the remote server. After connection is established, the *FlashServer* downloads XML file and keeps on sending a series of messages to a specific number as encoded in the file, which incurs considerable costs for phone bill. Moreover, the app can automatically delete message sent by malicious application to prevent from awareness. Besides from these apps, wide variety types of malwares exist by attacker using shell code such as *SimpleEpo, Hexbot* and *BullMoose* etc. *SimpleEpo* is a kind of Trojan app. *Hexbot* is capable of automatic insertion of java script containing malicious code into HTML file, which is provided by normal webserver. *BullMoose* with similar attacking pattern to *Hexbot*, is a mutated form of *Hexbot.* Following chapter describes detailed function and working process of the malicious app more specifically.

III. Analysis of Malicious Mobile Application

To gain insight into security-related vulnerability existing in mobile device, this paper developed experimental-purpose malicious app that steals private and banking information via rooting method. The malicious app was implemented, targeting most of the Android-platform mobile terminal.

A. Generate a GingerMaster-like Exploit : BinBreak

In this study, the malicious app was developed using a *GingerMaster-like* exploit(named it as a *BinBreak*). It collects private information stored in mobile device and sent to remote server. This study analyses security vulnerability for mobile terminal using experiment application.

As of *GingerMaster-like* exploit, once installed and executed, the application gains root access from kernel. Subsequently, it compresses a folder including public key certificate with compression tool named tar and then sends the compressed data to remote server. Furthermore, it stores contacts list and web accessing history in a *SQLite* format and sends them to remote server as well. Finally, it automatically starts recording and sends recorded file to remote server, if the device receives specific contents of SMS message.

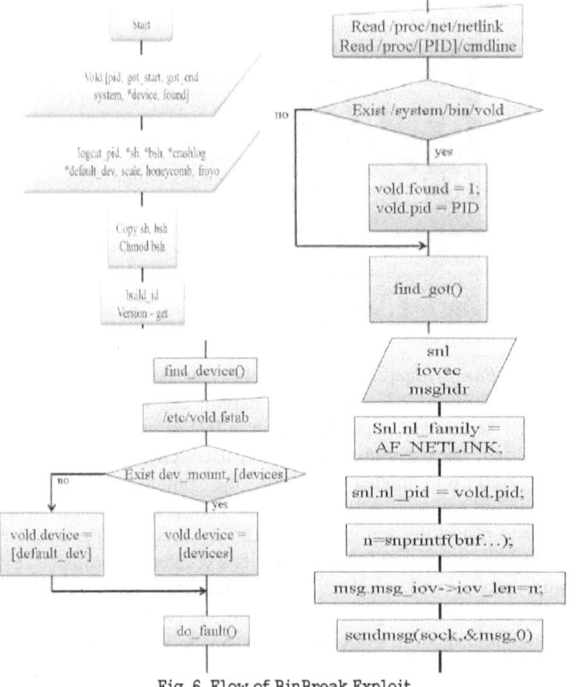

Fig. 6. Flow of BinBreak Exploit

Rooting process of *GingerMaster-like BinBreak* exploit is performed by spoofing *NetLinkMessage* via *Volume Daemon* running on Linux kernel in Android. When rooting process begins, firstly *BinBreak* searches and finds out PID of Volume Daemon. It can be accomplished by looking for each file named /proc/<PID>/cmdline, where PID means currently running processes' PID. Currently running process can be known from /proc/net/netlink file. Once identifying Volume Daemon's PID, malware retrieves device-related information from /etc/vold.fstable that is a file system table of Volume Daemon. With use of Volume Daemon's PID, socket connection is established. Finally, it sends specific message through the connection and gains root privilege.

B. Experimental-purpose Malicious App. : Andoku

In this study, malicious application named *Andoku* was developed using a *BinBreak* exploit for experimental purpose. It is designed to analyze security vulnerability of mobile device. *Andoku* application performs rooting process in conjunction with *Tegrak kernel.* In addition to this, *Andoku* has a functionality to check whether any internal data is leaked or not. For this purpose, *Andoku* is an application evolved from Sudoku which is one of popular games. If a user clicks 'Resume Game' button, a *BinBreak* exploit hidden behind *Andoku* application will be secretly executed as shown in fig. 7.

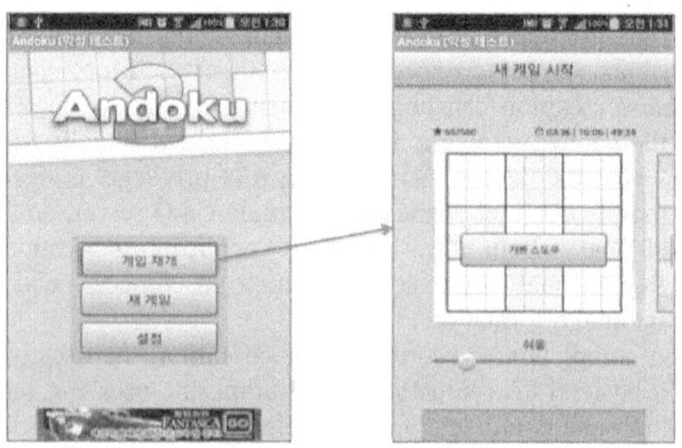

Fig. 7. Malware Andoku concealing BinBreak exploit

If a user installs and runs *Andoku* on his/her Android platform mobile device, a *BinBreak* module is invoked without user's awareness and it takes away root privilege over the system. Once gaining root privilege, malware steals private information such as contacts list, SMS messages and Internet accessing history. Furthermore, worse thing might happen when the user utilizes online banking service via mobile device. Banking confidential information like public key certificate will be compressed and sent to the remote server as specified by attacker. Fig.8 shows how *Andoku* collects, compresses private information and sends it to the external server, when *Andoku* runs.

Fig. 8. Private Information Compressing and Sending Module in Andoku

To compress data more efficiently, an additional class named ZipCompress has been developed as shown in fig. 9.

Fig. 9. Implementation of ZipCompress Class for Andoku

C. Private Information Leakage through Experimental Andoku Malware

Once *Andoku* is running, it can be observed that *ZipCompress* sends private information stored in device to outside. It is also eye witnessed that other information stored in SQLite is transferred to remote server.

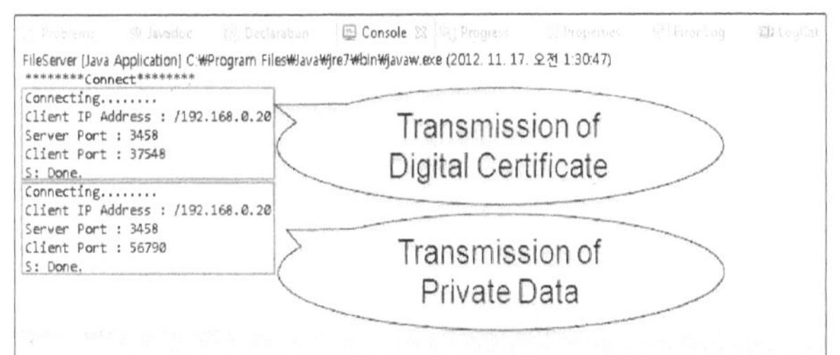

Fig. 10. Check the information transferred from user's device to remote server

Database is used to store and maintain various information such as names, phone numbers and web accessing histories generated while the user is using device. Therefore, important information including internet accessing history and contacts list are sent to external server without user's awareness if *Andoku* is executed. *Andoku* also has a function to send information about package currently running on the device.

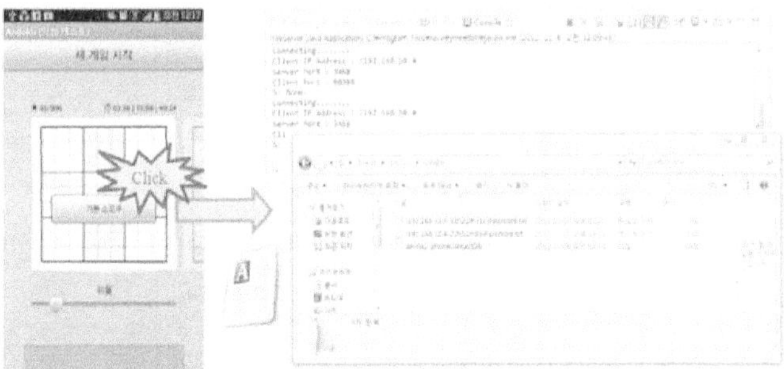

Fig. 11. Contacts list sent by Andoku

Another experiment was performed like this. If an application running on the mobile device was clicked, contacts list and web server accessing histories were sent to the remote server secretly, as shown in fig.12.

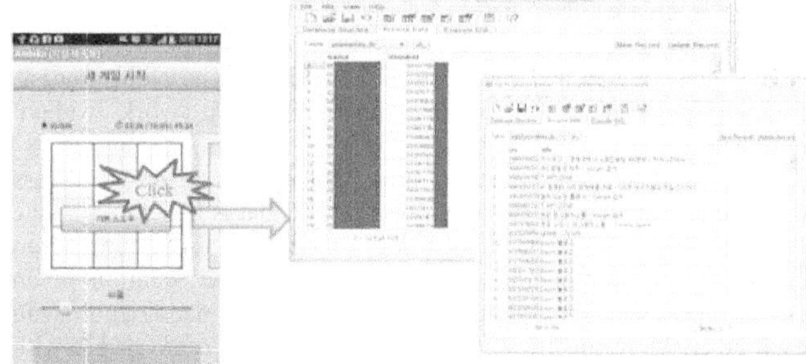

Fig. 12. Contacts list and Web Accessing Records sent by Andoku

Finally, it is eye witnessed that user's public key certificate was compressed and sent by *Andoku* to remote server. Data stored in SQLite DB also was transferred to outside.

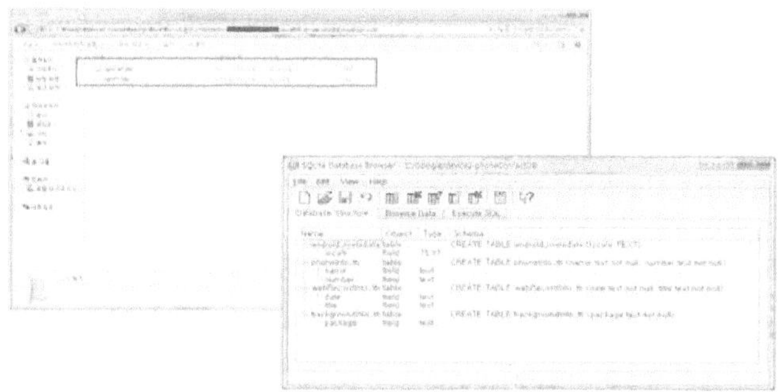

Fig. 13. Public Key Certificate Leakage and SQLite Table

From the experiments described above, it is clearly verified that Android platform mobile device has security vulnerabilities in case that it installs malicious app, which permits to secretly run exploit, attain root privilege illegally and transmit internal data to remote server outside. Therefore, it is required to study about proactive countermeasures against this rooting attack.

IV. ROOT EXPLOIT DETECTION AND RESPONSE SYSTEM

We propose countermeasures against mobile root attacks by analyzing malicious application's event activity caused by root exploits. The idea is to invoke *monitoring daemon* process at Android kernel in background. The purpose of daemon is to keep on monitoring services and processes running on the device and to investigate events collected and extracted from the system. To meet this goal, this study proposes internal structure of daemon process that is designed to extract events occurring from system. Next, this paper presents an implementation result on the proposed system. This study named the proposed application by '*PrintDaemon*' and suggested the effective way how to monitor events generated by malicious application and how to actively cope with this attacks.

A. System Event Extraction from Android Device

Daemon process in Android platform keeps running at kernel as background process as long as OS is up and running, since Android is an Linux based OS. Various daemons are widely used such as *nntpd* which is a daemon to deliver news to USENET, *fingerd* which is a daemon to display current login user information, *httpd* which is a web server for Linux, and *bootpd* which is a daemon to support being boot server.

There are many kinds of daemons. Before daemon starts, parent process is created first. Parent process invokes daemon as a child process and then parent dies. The child process invoked by parent creates new session and get a control as a leader. The child process, daemon is looping forever and doing its own work without termination.

To build daemon process, cross compile is required. Cross compile is a process of creating a target code that is generated in one computer and run in another one through the way of using compiler to cross compile a program. Cross compiler is good solution in an environment where host system and target system is incompatible with each other. More specifically speaking, our daemon is developed with NDK. By cross compiling, it can be applied to ARM processor.

For doing this, the first thing to do is install cross compiler using Sourcery G++ Lite for ARM to set a build platform to be GNU/Linux. A build platform means an environment where the compiler is actually compiled. In this environment, *daemon.c* is created and compiled by cross compiler. If compiling completes, background.png will be generated, which needs to be inserted into the folder of Android-based mobile device. Last thing to do is to change access mode of the file and run it. It is seen that new daemon process is added to kernel and is being executed in Android based device. With help of the daemon process, it is possible to collect and investigate information relating to services and processes performed in mobile device, which can help us detect anomalies that might happen in mobile device.

B. System Event Extracting and Logging System

The daemon process designed and implemented in this study enables the user to verify and retrieve services and processes running on inside of kernel in Android-based mobile device. If *PrintDaemon* application is executed, it invokes event monitoring daemon at kernel and the application is running in background. The background running application transfers event information to DB server in a log format whenever event occurs. DB server is implemented to collect and store the event data that comes from multiple devices. Those events information collected from the mobile device are used to detect any suspected event due to rooting attack.

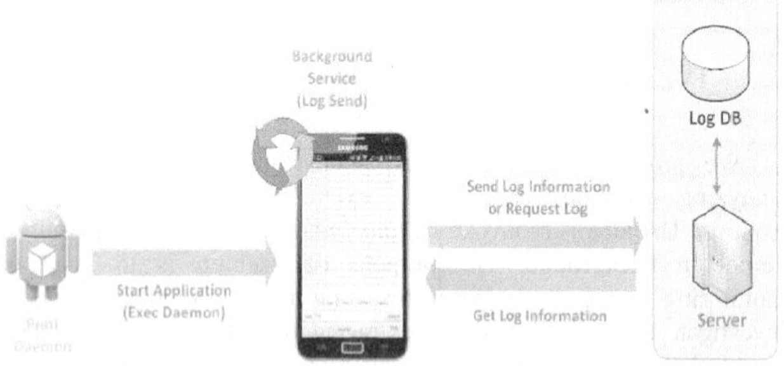

Fig. 14. Structure of PrintDaemon Application

PrintDaemon application was developed in Eclipse developing environment. The project implementing *PrintDaemon* is mainly composed of several folders and files as follows: (1) *src* folder containing Java source files, (2) *gen* folder containing R.java that holds mapping information between resource file and memory address, (3) *assets* folder storing resource files such as library files, binary files, and Android SDK, (4) *res* folder which stores image/layout/string, and (5) AndroidManifest.xml file that defines Activity/Service/Permission etc.

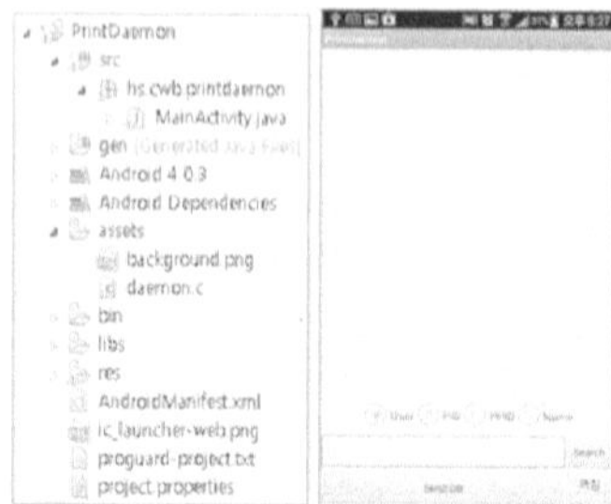

Fig. 15. Structure of PrintDaemon Android Project and Screen Display when running

While *PrintDaemon* is being executed, daemon process collects event data occurring in mobile device. The application also has functionality to retrieve data with user, PID, PPID, and name. Server and client are implemented as thread so that they can be operated on higher version of Android. If the user clicks Send DB button, the application sends current process related information to DB server, thus we can check the information. DB server is designed to retrieve and check the event for each mobile device. The information relating to event can also be retrieved with PID and PPID.

Fig. 16. Process Information Send

If toggle button is clicked, data transfer function to DB is activated. In this case, process information will be continuously transferred to DB server even if the application is terminated. When the application starts again, button status will be changed from on to off depending on whether the application is executed or not. Event monitoring application is implemented to display information on the main screen in the sequence of user, PID, PPID and Name. The information is stored in MySQL DB in the sequence of user, PID, PPID, USIZE, RSS, WCHAN, PC, and Name. In terms of data extraction, event data coming from malware will be extracted with user, PID, PPID and name.

Fig. 17. Process Information Send Search

C. Rooting Attack Event Detection

It has been demonstrated that the daemon proposed in this study is designed and implemented to check event data by monitoring events in background. *PrintDaemon* application invokes daemon process that collects and checks log data generated by main processes in the system. Furthermore, log data can be sorted by choosing user, PID,

PPID and name. Those functionalities are useful to extract and collect suspected events that might be generated by malicious app like *BinBreak-based Andoku* and various kinds of malwares masquerading as normal app. In case of using daemon based rooting attack event monitoring method, it is possible to implement the system to detect abnormal symptom that might be caused by rooting attack in the mobile device.

We gathered and compared the patterns of internal system event activated from mobile device. We can view the difference on the system event pattern as Fig. 18. In case of malicious application such as *Andoku*, we can see that more processes and events are activated from the malicious root exploit. Therefore it is possible for us to distinguish between the characteristics of root exploit and normal application. Fig.19 presents the screen in which rooting attack is successfully detected using data collected in DB server.

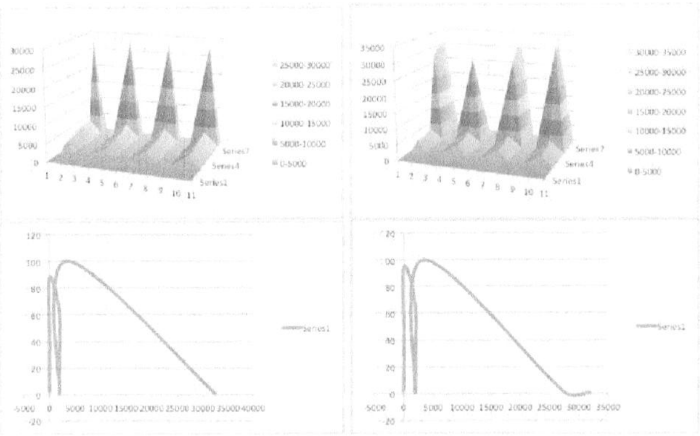

Fig. 18. System Event Pattern Comparison (Normal & Malicious App.)

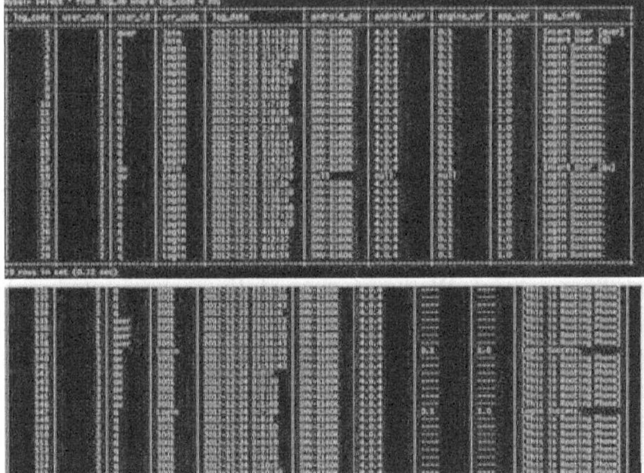

Fig. 19. Detection Result Screen for rooting attack to mobile terminal

V. CONCLUSION

We described various types of attacks to Android-based mobile devices with malicious mobile root exploit applications. Based on that, this study also proposed countermeasures to cope with it. First, root exploit attacks were investigated. Primary goal of rooting attack is to obtain root privilege illegally. Second, security vulnerability for mobile device was explored using exploit-infected malicious application specially developed for illegal purpose. It was observed that private information and banking data including public key certificate was successfully stolen by running malicious application in the mobile device. Third, countermeasure system was proposed. Proposed system mainly consists of two components: (1) proposed system keeps on monitoring while it runs on Android-based Linux kernel and (2) as a proposed system was operating in conjunction with the monitoring daemon, it collects information generated by processors and services running on mobile device. Moreover, it was designed to determine whether the mobile device is infected with malicious app or not. The proposed method utilizing event extracting daemon enables the user to detect whether mobile device is attacked by malicious code with exploit. To detect attacks much faster, future work will be carried out focusing on correlation analysis on event information generated by multiple devices.

ACKNOWLEDGMENT

This research was supported by Basic Science Research Program through the National Research Foundation of Korea (NRF) funded by the Ministry of Education, Science and Technology (Grant # 2012R1A1A2004573)

REFERENCES

[1] Exploit, http://en.wikipedia.org/wiki/Exploit_(computer_security)

[2] Android rooting, http://en.wikipedia.org/wiki/Android_rooting

[3] Rooting – is it for me? Some Q&A, http://www.androidcentral.com/rooting-it-me-some-qa

[4] Android Root Source Code: Looking at the C-Skills, http://intrepidusgroup.com/insight/2010/09/android-root-source-code-looking-at-the-c-skills/

[5] Egzthunder1, Root your Gingerbread Device With Gingerbreak, April 21, 2011, from http://www.xda-developers.com/android/ root-your-gingerbread-device-with-gingerbreak/

[6] GingerMaster: First Android Malware Utilizing a Root Exploit on Android 2.3, http://www.csc.ncsu.edu/faculty/jiang/GingerMaster/

[7] Android Developer Web Site, "Android.com. (2009, December 16). What is android?", Android Developer http://developer.android.com/guide/basics/what-is-android.html, 2009. 12

[8] Jill Duffy, "A Concise Guide to Android Rooting", pcmag http://www.pcmag.com/article2/0,2817,2393273,00.asp, 2011. 9

[9] Harron Q. Raja, "How to Root Your Android Phone/Device?", http://www.addictivetips.com/mobile/how-to-root-your-android-phone-device/, 2011. 1

[10] Derek Scott, "Rooting for Dummies : A Begineer's Guide to Rooting Your Android Device",(http://www.androidauthority.com/rooting-for-dummies-a-beginners-guide-to-root-your-android-phone-or-tablet-10915/), 2011. 3

[11] William Ench, "Defending users against smartphone apps: techniques and future irections," Proceedings of the 7th International Conference on Informatin Systems Security (ICISS'11), Vol.7, No.1, pp.47-70, Springer-Verlag, 2011.

[12] Iker Burquera, Urko Zurutuza, Simin Nadjm-Tehrani, "Crowdroid: Behavior-based Malware Detection System for Android," Proceedings of the 1st ACM workshop on Security and Privacy in Smartphone and Mobile Devices (SPSM'11), Vol.1, No.1, pp.15-26, 2011..

[13] Alexandre Bartel, Jacques Klein, Yves Le Traon, Martin Monperrus, "Automatically Securing Permission-Based Software by Reducing the Attack Surface: An Application to Android," Technical Report, University of Luxembourg, SNT, 2011.

[14] Won-Jun Jang, Sik-Whan Cho, Hyung-Woo Lee, Hong-il Ju, Jeong-Nyeo Kim, "Rooting attack detection method on the Android-based smart phone," International Conference on Computer Science and Network Technology (ICCSNT2011), Vol.1, No.1, pp.477-481, 2011.

[15] Event monitoring, Wikipedia, http://en.wikipedia.org/wiki/Event_monitoring

[16] SuperOneClick v2.3.3, http://forum.xda-developers.com/showthread.php?t=803682

[17] UniversalAndroot, http://lifehacker.com/5642797/universal-androot-roots-most-android-phones-no-pc-or-hacking-required

[18] Z4root, http://forum.xda-developers.com/showthread.php?t=833953

[19] Odin, http://forum.xda-developers.com/showthread.php?t=1738841

[20] Tegrak Kernel, http://tegrak2x.blogspot.kr

[21] First SpyEye Attack on Android Mobile Platform now in the Wild DroidOS/Spitmo attack is vurtually undetectable, http://www.mag-securs.com/Alertes/tabid/63/articleType/ArticleView/articleId/28778/First-SpyEye-Attack-on-Android-Mobile-Platform-now-in-the-Wild-DriodOS-Spitmo-attack-is-virtually-undetectable.aspx

[22] Security Alert: New Root-Capable DroidDeluxe Malware Found in Alternative Android Markets, http://www.csc.ncsu.edu/faculty/jiang/DroidDeluxe/

[23] BaseBridge: new Android malware has been busy, http://www.ubergizmo.com/2011/05/basebridge-new-android-malware/

[24] Mobile threat report Q4 2011, F-Secure, http://www.slideshare.net/fsecure/mobile-threat-report-q4-2011, 2011

ASNM: Advanced Security Network Metrics for Attack Vector Description

I. Homoliak, M. Barabas, P. Chmelar, M. Drozd, and P. Hanacek[1]
[1]Faculty of Information Technology, University of Technology, Brno, Czech Republic

Abstract— *In this paper we propose a method for the extraction of data from network flow and a contextual separation of partial connections using a set of network metrics that create a signature defining the connection behavior. We begin with the definition of the input dataset of captured communication and the process of extraction metrics from separated connections. Then we define the set of metrics included in the final behavioral signature. The second part of the article describes experiments performed with a state-of-the-art set of network metrics with comparison to our proposed experimental set. The paper concludes with the results of our experiments.*

Keywords: behavioral signature, detection, IDS, network metrics, security.

1. Introduction

There is considerable interest in developing novel detection methods based on new metrics for the description of network flow to identify connection characteristics, for examples to permit early identification of emerging security incidents, rapid detection of infections within internal networks, or instantaneous prevention of forming attacks. Buffer overflows continue to be one of the most common vulnerabilities prevalent today, dominating the field of undetected and most dangerous "zero-day" attacks. This factor has motivated researchers to create more or less sophisticated defenses addressing this threat. The first line of defense is based on memory randomization (ASR), which unfortunately makes the attack harder to achieve, but it is still possible to find a way of offsetting the current process address. The second line of defense is based on automated signature generation techniques that generate filters to block network traffic similar to an attack payload signature. Unfortunately, polymorphic attacks can evade these signatures, and hence subsequent research has focused on behavioral signatures that have favored the development of several data-mining methods defining sets of network metrics describing the attack vector by the features of its behavior. These methods use either the existing NetFlow standard or network traffic packets. Several previous research studies left NetFlow to create their own set of network metrics, which brought more information and context in analyzed connections. Recognizing the importance of the quality of network metrics for influence on successful detection, this paper proposes a new set of metrics with high detection and a low false positive ratio. It is expected that detection algorithms based on these new network behavioral metrics will outperform existing methods and will be applicable to a wider range of intrusion detection and prevention systems.

Our primary goal is to create a network based system for online defense against zero-day buffer overflow attacks in the production environment. We described the reduction of attack types to buffer overflow in a previous article [1]. The secondary goal of this research is (a) to design the architecture of a detection framework that will enhance the overall network security level with the ability to learn new behaviors of attacks without human intervention by using expert knowledge from Honeypot (or similar) systems; (b) to find the most suitable set of metrics that will successfully describe the behavior of attacks in network traffic and will significantly increase the detection rate and lower the false positive rate.

In our previous article [1] we proposed the idea of framework architecture that would be used for the detection of various network threats. The paper presented novel Automated Intrusion Prevention System (AIPS) which uses honeypot systems for the detection of new attacks and automatic generation of behavioral signatures based on network flow metrics. We have successfully experimented with the architecture of the AIPS system and have defined 112 metrics (recently updated to 167) divided into five categories according to their nature. These metrics are used to describe a properties of a detected attack, not upon the fingerprint of a common signature, but based on its behavior.

In this article we provide a definition of the method used for generating network behavioral signatures from a set of network security metrics – Advanced Security Network Metrics (ASNM) consisting of 167 metrics enhancing the ability of detecting potential attacks from network traffic.

The paper is organized as follows. Section 2 discusses related work in network security datasets and detection metrics. In Section 3 we describe a method used for signature generation and in Section 4 a description of metrics set. Section 5 presents experiments performed on two sets of metrics and Section 6 assesses the results of these experiments. Section 7 contains the conclusion of this paper.

2. Related Work

Since 1999, KDD'99[2] dataset, based on DARPA'98 IDS evaluation program, has been used for evaluating new intrusion detection methods based on analyzing network traffic. The training dataset consists of approximately 4.9 million single connection vectors, each labeled as either normal or attack, containing 41 features per connection record. The dataset is criticized [3] mainly because it does not seems to be similar to traffic in real networks, and also there are some critiques of attack taxonomies and performance issues. As a result, many researches have proposed new measures to overcome existing deficiencies.

DARPA IDS evaluation dataset [4] was created for the purpose of training and testing the intrusion detectors. However, in the dataset, all traffic was generated by software that is not publicly available and hence it is not possible to determine how accurate the background traffic inserted into the evaluation is. Also, evaluation criteria do not account for system resources used, ease of use, or what type of system it is.

The 2005 Moore sets [5] of data are intended to aid in the assessment of classification work. A number of data sets are described; each data set consists of a number of objects and each object is described by a group of features (also referred to as discriminators). Leveraged by a quantity of hand-classified data, each object within each data set represents a single flow of TCP packets between client and server. Features for each object consist of (application-centrist) classification derived elsewhere and a number of features derived as input to probabilistic classification techniques. In the classification, applications with similar dynamics are classified into the same class. A naive Bayesian classificator is used in the algorithm in which the Bayes formula is used to calculate posterior probability of a testing sample and selects the largest probability class as the classification result. A total of approximately 200 features of a network flow is used to train the model and a kernel-based function is used to estimate the distribution function [6]. The total accuracy is about 95% in the dimension of a flow number being correctly classified and 84% in the dimension of the flow size.

In our research, classifying IP traffic is crucial and it is important to include general classification techniques to our research for the classification of network attacks. The survey paper [7] reviewed state of the art work in the machine learning IP traffic classification in the period from 2004 to 2007. This paper created four categories of machine learning classification techniques, clustering approach, supervised learning, hybrid, and comparisons and related work approaches. Each category was reviewed according to a number of requirements divided to offline and real-time classification.

Auld et al., based on Bayesian method introduced in [6], proposed the Bayesian Neutral Network method [8]. Compared with the Bayesian method, it made the classification correct rate rise to 99% on data from a single site for two days, eight months apart.

In [9], a novel probabilistic approach was proposed that uses the Markov chain for probabilistic modeling of abnormal events in network systems. The performance of the proposed approach was evaluated through a set of experiments using the above mentioned DARPA 2000 data set. The proposed approach achieves high detection performance while representing a level of attacks in stages.

None of these approaches can be used in a real time evaluation of network traffic due to performance issues or high false-positive ratio. Only a little research has been done on creating new network metrics for the behavioral description of network attacks to raise the classification accuracy, which makes this area still attractive for researchers.

3. Method Description

In this section we provide the abstract description of a method used for the extraction of network connections and generation of attacks signatures.

3.1 Used notation

We will use capital letters as labels for a set or constants in most cases. Lower case notation will be used for an element label or for an index label. By notation $o[p]$ we mean the property p of the object o. The notation S^* or S^+ means the iteration of the set S or positive iteration of the set S, respectively. Notation A^B represents set A, which is a subset of set B. For example sets W^P and W^C denote semantically the same set, but these are constructed of different items at a different level of abstraction. In the first case items are a subset of set P and in the second case items are a subset of set C, respectively.

3.2 Principle of the method

The method of our approach is based on the extraction of various types of properties from each analyzed TCP connection. We suppose having all packets set $P = \{p_i\},\ i \in \{1, \ldots, N\}$, where N represents all packets count. The identification of each packet is represented by its index i. A packet p_i can be expressed as a tuple $p_i = (id, t, size, eth_{src}, eth_{dst}, tcp_{sport}, tcp_{dport}, tcp_{sum}, tcp_{seq}, tcp_{ack}, tcp_{off}, tcp_{flags}, tcp_{win}, tcp_{urp}, ip_{len}, ip_{off}, ip_{ttl}, ip_p, ip_{sum}, ip_{src}, ip_{dst}, data, ip_{tos})$. Symbols used in the packet tuple are described in Table 1.

TCP connection c is represented by tuple $c = (t_s, t_e, id_S, id_{SA}, id_A, id_{FA}, p_s, p_d, ip_s, ip_d, P_s, P_d)$. The interpretation of the symbols used in tuple is briefly described in Table 2. The source part of the TCP connection is the one with the initiation of the connection and the destination part is the opposite part of the connection.

The set of all packets can be interpreted also as a set of all TCP connections $C = \{c_1, \ldots, c_M\}$, where M is

Table 1: Symbols used in the packet tuple.

symbol	meaning
$id \in \aleph_0$	Id of the packet.
$t \in T$	Timestamp of the packet capture.
$size \in \aleph$	Size in Bytes of the whole Ethernet frame which wraps the IP packet.
$eth_{src} \in \{0,\ldots,2^{48}-1\}$	Source MAC address of the Ethernet frame.
$eth_{dst} \in \{0,\ldots,2^{48}-1\}$	Destination MAC address of the Ethernet frame.
$tcp_{sport} \in \{0,\ldots,2^{16}-1\}$	Source port of the packet.
$tcp_{dport} \in \{0,\ldots,2^{16}-1\}$	Destination port of the packet.
$tcp_{sum} \in \{0,\ldots,2^{16}-1\}$	TCP Checksum of the header.
$tcp_{seq} \in \{0,\ldots,2^{32}-1\}$	TCP sequence number of the packet.
$tcp_{ack} \in \{0,\ldots,2^{32}-1\}$	TCP acknowledgment number of the packet.
$tcp_{off} \in \{0,\ldots,2^{8}-1\}$	TCP offset and reserved fields together.
$tcp_{flags} \in \{0,\ldots,2^{8}-1\}$	TCP control bits.
$tcp_{win} \in \{0,\ldots,2^{16}-1\}$	TCP window field.
$tcp_{urp} \in \{0,\ldots,2^{16}-1\}$	TCP urgent pointer field.
$ip_{len} \in \{0,\ldots,2^{16}-1\}$	Size in Bytes of the whole IP packet with IP header.
$ip_{off} \in \{0,\ldots,2^{13}-1\}$	IP offset field.
$ip_{ttl} \in \{0,\ldots,2^{8}-1\}$	IP time to live field.
$ip_{p} \in \{0,\ldots,2^{8}-1\}$	IP protocol field.
$ip_{sum} \in \{0,\ldots,2^{16}-1\}$	IP checksum of the header.
$ip_{src} \in \{0,\ldots,2^{32}-1\}$	Source IP address of the packet.
$ip_{dst} \in \{0,\ldots,2^{32}-1\}$	Destination IP address of the packet.
$data \in \{0,\ldots,2^{8}-1\}^*$	Payload of the packet.
$ip_{tos} \in \{0,\ldots,2^{8}-1\}$	IP type of service field.

Table 2: Symbols used in the TCP connection tuple.

symbol	meaning
$t_s \in T$	Timestamp of the connection start.
$t_e \in T$	Timestamp of the connection end.
$id_S \in I$	Id of the first packet which contains SYN flag of TCP 3WH[1].
$id_{SA} \in I$	Id of the first packet which contains SYN, ACK flags of TCP 3WH.
$id_A \in I$	Id of the last packet which contains ACK flag of TCP 3WH.
$id_{FA} \in I$	Id of the packet p_i which contains FIN, ACK flags.
$p_s \in \{0,\ldots,2^{16}-1\}$	Source port of the TCP connection.
$p_d \in \{0,\ldots,2^{16}-1\}$	Destination port of the TCP connection.
$ip_s \in \{0,\ldots,2^{32}-1\}$	Source IP address of the TCP connection.
$ip_d \in \{0,\ldots,2^{32}-1\}$	Destination IP address of the TCP connection.
$P_s \subset P$	Source packet set of the TCP connection.
$P_d \subset P$	Destination packet set of the TCP connection.

the number of TCP connections, which we can identify in the P and N is the number of all packets in set P. The minimum packets count, which is necessary to identify the TCP connection, is three packets which are used to establish a TCP connection according to TCP specifications. These three or more packets must contain the same IP addresses (ip_{src}, ip_{dst}), ports (tcp_{sport}, tcp_{dport}) and fields tcp_{seq}, tcp_{ack} corresponding to a three way handshake specification stated in RFC 793[2]. The number of all TCP connections identified in P is $M \leq N/3$.

Then we define sliding window W_j^P as a subset of all packets set P:

$$W_j^P \subseteq P,\ j \in \{1+|C_s|,\ldots,M-|C_e|\}, \tag{1}$$

where M is the number of all TCP connections identified in P, index j is the position of the sliding window in the set of all TCP connections C and $|C_s|$, $|C_e|$ is the number of TCP connections found in the first half of the sliding window with an initial position $W_{1+|C_s|}$ and the second half of the sliding window with finite position $W_{M-|C_e|}$, respectively. It should be noted taht the sliding window W_j^P always represents continuous subset of packets bounded by a specified time interval t_{sw} in the time domain $T \subset \Re^+$ instantiated by timestamps with a floating point part. Interval t_{sw} represents a time bounded notation of the size of a sliding window W.

The next statement which we can proclaim about sliding window is that we can interpret it as subset of all TCP connection set:

$$W_j^C \subseteq C,\ W_j^C = \{c_I,\ldots,c_L\},\ I \leq L \leq M. \tag{2}$$

This notation of the sliding window we denote as the connection notation of the sliding window W_j^C. Note $L-I$ can be different for various positions of the sliding window for the same set C because of the time boundary of the sliding window, not boundary specified by n-connections. The next fact about each particular TCP connection c_k is an unambiguous association of c_k to particular sliding window W_j^C. We can interpret the start time t_s of the TCP connection c_k as a center of the sliding window W_j^P. We can also denote a shift of the sliding window $\Delta(W_j^P)$ is always defined by start time differences of two consecutive TCP connections in C:

$$\begin{aligned} \Delta(W_j^P) &= c_{k+1}[t_s] - c_k[t_s], \\ k &\in \{1+|C_s|,\ldots,M-|C_e|-1\}. \end{aligned} \tag{3}$$

Next we define the context of the TCP connection, which is a set of all connections in a particular sliding window W_j^C without an analyzed TCP connection c_k:

$$K_{c_k} = \{c_1,\ldots,c_n\} = \{W_k^C \setminus c_k\}. \tag{4}$$

Defined terms are shown in figure 1. In this figure the x axis displays time and in the y axis, TCP connections are shown in the order of their occurrences. Packets are represented by small squares and TCP connections are represented by a rectangular boundary of particular packets. A bold line and font is used for depicting an analyzed TCP connection c_k, which has an associated sliding window W_k and context K_{ck}. TCP connections, which are part of the

[2]URL http://www.ietf.org/rfc/rfc793.txt, page 30

sliding window W_k, are drawn by full line boundary and TCP connections, which are not part of this sliding window, are drawn by a dashed line boundary.

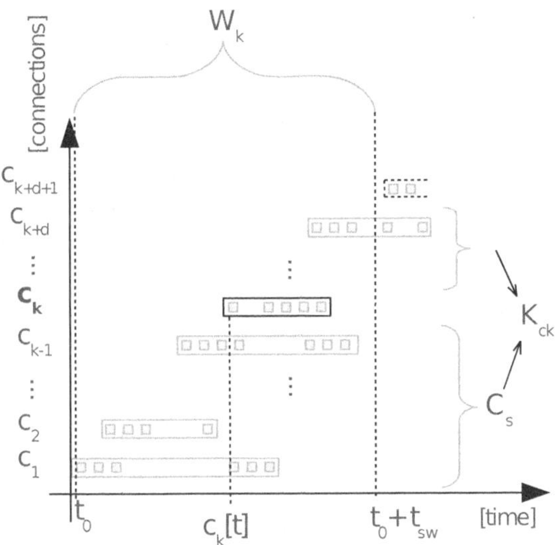

Fig. 1: Sliding window and context of the first analyzed TCP connection c_k.

3.3 Metrics extraction

We identify all TCP connections set C in a set of all packets P and next we perform metrics extraction for each TCP connection from a time bounded subset of C in the order of their beginnings. A time bounded subset is identified by C_B and is defined because a metrics extraction process is performed only for TCP connections with a complete context and this set states:

$$C_B = \{c_i\} \subset C,$$
$$\forall i : c_i[t_s] \geq \frac{t_{sw}}{2} \wedge c_i[t_s] \leq \left(p_l[t] - \frac{t_{sw}}{2}\right), \quad (5)$$

where $p_l \in P$ represents a packet with the latest timestamp.

The metrics extraction process is defined as an advanced process of signature computation from all packets of analyzed TCP connection and its context.

We define metric m as a tuple consisting of natural or real numbers or an enumerated set of finite symbolic literals:

$$m = (e_0, \ldots, e_n),\ n \in \aleph_0,$$
$$e_i \in \aleph \mid e_i \in \Re \mid e_i \in \Gamma^+,\ i \in \{0, \ldots, n\}, \quad (6)$$
$$\Gamma = \{a - z, A - Z, 0 - 9\}.$$

The input of the metrics extraction process is sliding window W_j^C, TCP connection c_k with metainformations of its associated packets. The output of the process is the set of all extracted metrics $M_k = \{m_1^k, m_2^k, \ldots, m_D^k\}$, where D is the number of all defined metrics and $m_i^k\ for\ i \in \{1, \ldots, D\}$ contains a tuple of values specific for analyzed input TCP connection c_k and its sliding window W_j^C.

3.4 Functions for metrics extraction

Metrics for a particular connection c_k are extracted by several functions with a very similar input, which in all cases, includes an analyzed TCP connection c_k. The other part of the input may be, in some cases, context K_{c_k} of the TCP connection c_k. There are exactly 30 functions used for metrics extraction and 7 of them uses the context of the TCP connection. Some functions return more than one metric when these can be directly extracted. Other functions are parametrized by various parameters as a direction of the TCP connection, order and type of polynomial, thresholds of the data size or packet count, etc.

One metric extraction function f declaration has the following form:

$$m^k = f(c_k, K_{c_k}, arg_1, \ldots, arg_n), \quad (7)$$

where m^k is the set of values of one defined metric m for input TCP connection c_k. K_{c_k} is context of input TCP connection and $arg_1, \ldots, arg_n$ are additional arguments of the function f.

4. Metrics Definition

All metrics were defined in order to describe properties, process and behavior of network attacks or legitimate TCP connections. By using these metrics we are able to identify an attack with a higher probability. For the purpose of the best relevant signature of the TCP connections we use 167 metrics as signature. These 167 metrics are in many cases, a result of reasonable parametrization of base metrics functions. Since our previous article [1] we have slightly changed the categorization of the set of all metrics and have defined several new metrics with an emphasis on the behavior of a TCP connection. New types of our metrics set are depicted in Table 3 with a number of them in each category. We decided to determine the naming of categories of metrics according to their principles, not according to static data representation. Vector and polynomial metrics from our previous article [1] were divided into behavioral and distributed metrics categories. The list of all metrics with regard to the categorization, is introduced in master's thesis [10].

4.1 Statistical metrics

In this category of proposed metrics statistic properties of TCP connections are identified. All packets of the TCP connection were considered in order to determine count, mode, median, mean, standard deviation, ratios of some header fields of packets or the packets themselves. This

Table 3: Distribution of Metrics.

metric	count
Statistical	50
Dynamic	32
Localization	8
Distributed	34
Behavioral	43

category of metrics partially uses a time representation of packets occurrences contrary to the dynamic category definition. Therefore, it includes particularly dynamic properties of the analyzed TCP connection, but without any context of it. Most of the metrics in this category also distinguish inbound and outbound packets of analyzed TCP connection. In total, 50 statistical metrics were defined.

4.2 Dynamic metrics

Dynamic metrics were defined in order to examine dynamic properties of the analyzed TCP connection and transfer channel such as speed or error rate. These properties can be real or simulated. Fourteen of the metrics consider the context of an analyzed TCP connection. The difference between some of the statistic and dynamic metrics from a dynamic view can be demonstrated on two instances of the same TCP connection, which performs the same packet transfers, but in different context conditions and with different packet retrasmitions and attempts to start or finish the TCP connection. There were 32 dynamic metrics defined in total. Many of them distinguish between inbound and outbound direction of the packets and consider statistic properties of the packets and their sizes as mentioned in statistical metrics.

4.3 Localization metrics

The principal character of localization metrics category is that it contains static properties of the TCP connection. These properties represent the localization of participating machines and their ports used for communication. In some metrics localization is expressed indirectly by a flag, which distinguishes whether participating machines lie in a local network or not. Metrics included in this category do not consider the context of the analyzed TCP connection, but they distinguish a direction of the analyzed TCP connection. We defined 8 localization metrics.

4.4 Distributed metrics

The characteristic property of distributed metrics category is the fact that they distribute packets or their lengths to a fixed number of intervals per unit time specified by a logarithmic scale (1s, 4s, 8s, 32s, 64s). A logarithmic scale of fixed time intervals was proposed because of a better performance of used classification methods. The next principal property of this category is vector representation. All these metrics are supposed to work within the context of an analyzed TCP connection. Altogether, we defined 34 metrics in this category which are a result of parametrization of 2 functions, which accepts parameters as unit time, threshold, direction and the context of an analyzed TCP connection.

4.5 Behavioral metrics

Behavioral metrics are a set of metrics based on the description of the properties directly associated with TCP connection behavior. Examples include legal or illegal connection closing, the number of flows at defined time intervals, polynomial approximation of the length of packets in a time domain or in an index of occurrence domain. Since our previous article [1] we have proposed new behavioral metrics:

- count of mutual TCP flows of participating nodes before an analyzed TCP connection bounded by a specified time interval. It considers the context of an analyzed TCP connection,
- count of new TCP flows after starting an analyzed TCP connection. It also works within the context of an analyzed TCP connection,
- coefficients of Fourier series in a trigonometric representation with distinguished direction of an analyzed TCP connection,
- standard deviation of time intervals between TCP connections going on the same ports and IP addresses,
- standard deviation of time intervals between TCP connections going on the same IP addresses,
- normalized products of the analyzed communication with $1, \dots, n$ Gaussian curves with regard to direction.

We defined 43 behavioral metrics. Most of them use the direction of the analyzed TCP connection and 6 of them consider the context.

5. Experiments description

The performance of our behavioral metrics was evaluated in comparison with discriminators suggested by [5]. The authors of this paper considered only TCP connections to perform extraction of discriminators in the same way we did. So there are equivalent conditions for performance comparison between our suggested metrics and discriminators suggested in the above mentioned work. There were 248 discriminators defined, including all items of vector types. Unlike their research we considered the whole particular vector metric as one. In their work, each TCP flow is described by three modes according to packet transmissions: idle, interactive and bulk. Many discriminators use these three modes as their input. The authors did not mention any explicit categorization of defined discriminators. The only possible categorization can implicitly follow from a direction of the TCP flow. We also performed a similar analysis of discriminators and metrics definition. We discovered that there is approximately 20% of discriminators' definitions principally similar or the same as in the metrics case. Unique properties of discriminators' definitions include, for example, the using of quartiles for a statistical analysis, analysis of selective acknowledgment of TCP, a number of window probe indication, pushed or duplicate packets etc.

A dataset CDX 2009 was used for these experiments, which was generated by Sangster et al. in [11]. This dataset is available from URL: https://www.itoc.usma.edu/research/dataset/. It contains data captured by NSA, data captured outside of the West Point network border (in TCP dump format) and snort intrusion prevention log as relevant sources for our experiments.

The CDX 2009 dataset was created during the network warfare competition, in which one of the goals was to generate a labeled dataset. By labeled dataset, the authors mean TCP dump traces of all simulated communications and snort log with information about occurrences of intrusions. Network infrastructure contained 4 servers with 4 vulnerable services (one per each server). These services with IP addresses of their hosted servers are described in Table 4. Two types of IP addresses are shown in this table:

- **internal IP** addresses – corresponding to snort log,
- **external IP** addresses – corresponding to a TCP dump network captured outside the West Point network border.

This fact has to be considered in the process of matching snort log entries with a TCP dump capture.

Table 4: List of CDX 2009 vulnerable servers.

service	OS	internal IP	external IP
Postfix Email	FreeBSD	7.204.241.161	10.1.60.25
Apache Web Server	Fedora 10	154.241.88.201	10.1.60.187
OpenFire Chat	FreeBSD	180.242.137.181	10.1.60.73
BIND DNS	FreeBSD	65.190.233.37	10.1.60.5

We noticed that specific versions of services described in [11] were not announced. Since this fact was not crucial for our research, it was of no concern to us.

It was discovered that the snort log can be associated only with data capture outside of the West Point network border and only with significant timestamps differences – approximately 930 days. We did not find any association between the snort log and data capture performed by the National Security Agency. We focused only on buffer overflow attacks found in a log from snort IDS and a match with the packets contained in the West Point network border capture was performed. It should be noted that buffer overflow attacks were performed only on two services – Postfix Email and Apache Web Server. An example of the buffer overflow snort log entry:

```
[**] [124:4:1] (smtp) Attempted specific command
buffer overflow: HELO, 2320 chars [**]
[Priority: 3]
11/09-14:22:25.794792
10.2.195.251:2792 -> 7.204.241.161:25
TCP TTL:240 TOS:0x10 ID:0 IpLen:20 DgmLen:2360
***AP*** Seq: 0x68750738  Ack: 0x24941B59
Win: 0xFDC0  TcpLen: 20.
```

We used IP addresses (5th row), ports (5th row), time of occurrence (4th row) and TCP sequence and acknowledgment numbers (7th row) as information to match the snort log entries with particular TCP connections identified in TCP dump traces.

Despite all efforts, there were exactly 44 buffer overflow attacks matched out of all 65, and these identified attacks were used as expert knowledge for the data mining process. In order to correctly match snort entries, it was necessary to remap IP addresses of the internal to external network because a snort detection was realized in the internal network and TCP dump data capture contains entries from outside the IP address space.

Buffer overflow attacks, which were matched with data capture, have their content only in two TCP dump files: *2009-04-21-07-47-35.dmp, 2009-04-21-07-47-35.dmp2*. Due to the enormous count of all packets (approximately 4 million) in all dump files, only two files were considered which contained 1 538 182 packets. We also noticed that network data density was increased in the time when attacks were performed. Consequently, we made another reduction of packets, which filters enough temporal neighborhood of attacks occurrences. In the result, 204 953 packets for next phases of our experiments were used.

The whole process of metrics and discriminators extraction with data mining comparison is illustrated in Figure 2. There are four segments and data flow direction from top to bottom depicted in the figure. Empty boxes represent data as input or output of some processes and filled ovals represent working components which perform some action. A working component takes input data and outputs output data. The upper segment represents the input of the whole experiment process and includes input data files: *CDX 2009 TCP dump files* and *CDX 2009 snort log file*. The *CDX 2009 TCP dump files* are the mutual input of both extraction processes. The input of expert knowledge (*CDX 2009 snort log file*) is directly provided to the metrics extraction process and is indirectly bounded to extracted discriminators after the end of metrics extraction process.

The left segment contains phases of discriminators extraction and the right segment contains the metrics extraction process with expert knowledge processing.

5.1 Metrics extraction process

The metrics extraction process of the right segment includes a process described in subsection 3.3. An all packets set P is represented by the input of *CDX 2009 TCP dump files*, which are imported into the database by a *DB importer* component. Next, an active component *Connection extractor* performs the identification of all TCP connections set C

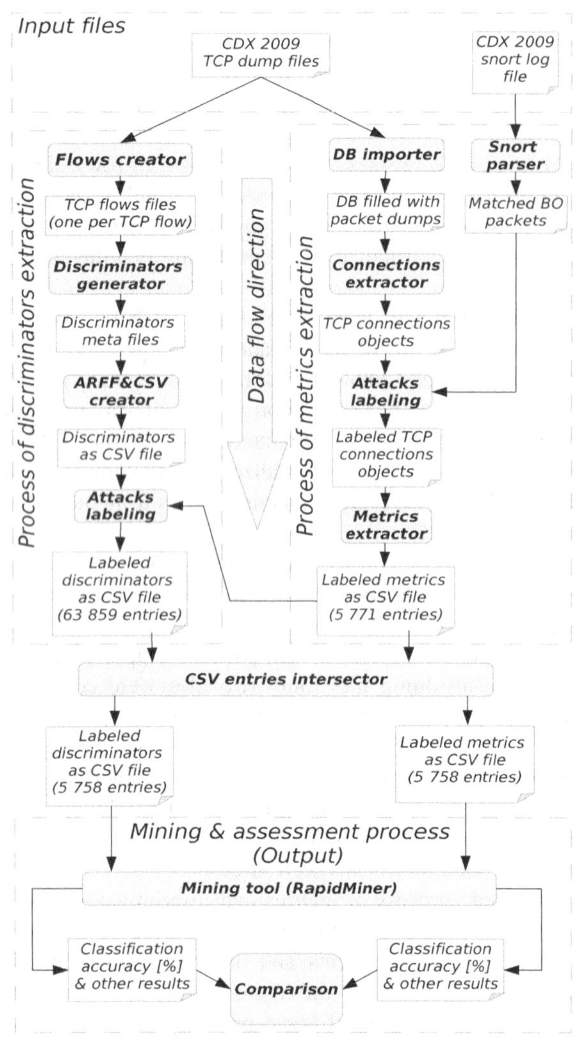

Fig. 2: The Process of metrics extraction and assessment.

in all packet set P. The extraction of TCP connections was followed by expert knowledge information processing, which means matching of extracted TCP connections with parsed snort log information. If a match occurred, the TCP connection is labeled as an attack by the *Attacks labeling* component. Then, metrics extraction is performed for each TCP connection in C by the *Metrics extractor* component and the result of this step are metrics values for each TCP connection object in CSV file. It should be noted that the metrics extraction process is independent of expert knowledge information.

5.2 Discriminators extraction process

The input of this process is the same as in the metrics extraction process. The component *Flows creator* performs the identification of TCP connections by netdude tool[3] and it creates a TCP dump file for each identified TCP connection. These TCP dump files are used as an input for *Discriminator generator* component, which performs extraction of discriminators for each identified TCP connection. This component performs equivalent operation as *Metrics extractor* component in the process of metrics extraction. It generates discriminators meta files which contain intermediate results of discriminators values. These meta files are processed and joined by the *ARFF&CSV creator* component into a CSV file. After this step, the attack TCP connections are labeled, which is performed by the the *Attack labeling* component.

5.3 Mining & assessment process

This process is depicted in the lower part of Figure 2. Before this process takes place, it is necessary to make an intersection between output CSV files of metrics and discriminators extraction processes, which is performed by the *CSV entries intersector* component. At the output of this step there are metrics and discriminators of the same TCP connections objects, so there are equivalent conditions for the data mining process. Two intersected CSV files with an equal number of entries are used as the input of the *Mining tool* component and output consists of classification accuracy and other results suitable for comparison.

It should be noted that we found 5 771 TCP connections by our TCP connections extractor and 63 859 TCP connections by the TCP demultiplexer from netdude framework which is used by discriminators extraction. The main reason is the fact that we consider only established TCP connections because only an established TCP connection can perform a buffer overflow attack. The intersection of metrics and discriminators outputs contains 5 758 objects and 44 of them represent attacks. This intersection was used in the data mining process and, therefore, they were adjusted by the same conditions for both metrics and discriminators outputs with the same TCP connections entries. Thirteen (13) established TCP connections were not found by the TCP demultiplexer. The discrimination extraction was performed using a source code available from the author's web[4]. The whole process of discriminators extraction itself was not described in [5], so we deduced it from a source code and README instructions. It was also necessary to debug some functionality of provided tools. During the preparation for discriminators extraction, there were some compatibility issues caused by old versions of dependencies. We finally used Linux Fedora 4 as the most suitable operating system for the necessary operation.

[3]URL: http://netdude.sourceforge.net/

[4]URL: http://www.cl.cam.ac.uk/research/srg/netos/nprobe/data/papers /sigmetrics/index.html

6. Result of Experiments

We analyzed joined outputs of metrics and discriminators extraction processes by the RapidMiner[5] tool. Our training model used the Naive Bayes classificator kernel. A stratified sampling with 5-cross fold validation for every experiment was performed. A feature selection component was used which tries to select the most relevant attributes for final model generation. We focused only on the accuracy evaluation of particular metrics and discriminators. Our experiments were adjusted for maximal classification accuracy of input data. The best results were merged from both input CSV files. In Figure 3 the best metrics and discriminators (over 99.43% overall accuracy) are shown, sorted by the overall accuracy. The names of discriminators consist of a number and label defined in [5]. The names of metrics are defined in [10]. The names of polynomial approximation metrics consist of 5 parts: polynomial metric label, method of approximation (indexes or time), order of polynomial, direction and coefficient index. Fourier coefficient metrics' names consist of the Fourier coefficient metric label, the goniometric representation, the angle or the module, the direction and the coefficient index. Gaussian products metrics' names are a compound of the Gaussian metric label, the number of Gaussian curves, the direction and the product index (e.g. *PolynomIndexes5OrdOut[1]*).

We can see that the best classification accuracy for the metrics sets was achieved by several polynomial approximation metrics. In most of these cases we achieved better results by the output direction, but we were also able to achieve interesting results with the input direction. A good performance was also achieved by Gaussian curves approximation and Fourier coefficients. The relevance in the case of standard deviation of packets length in the output direction (*sigPktLenSrc*) is also presented.

In the set of discriminators, the best results were achieved by an average segment size discriminator in the direction from client to server (*avg_segm_size_a_b*). It could be caused by the fact that the exploit's payload contains a huge amount of data necessary to perform application buffer overflow and these data are segmented. Another distinguished discriminator is the variance of bytes count in Ethernet or IP datagram in the destination direction (*var_data_wire_ab* and *var_data_ip_a_b*). This discriminator is equivalent to average standard deviation metric of packet length in the output direction and brings nearly equivalent results. Also, the average window advertisement in the input direction (*avg_win_adv_b_a*) holds relevant information potentially useful in the process of classification.

We have successfully increased the detection rate by 0.9% from the previous state-of-the-art classification method (99.0%) by extending the set of network metrics used for classification.

[5]URL: http://rapid-i.com/content/view/181/190/lang,en/

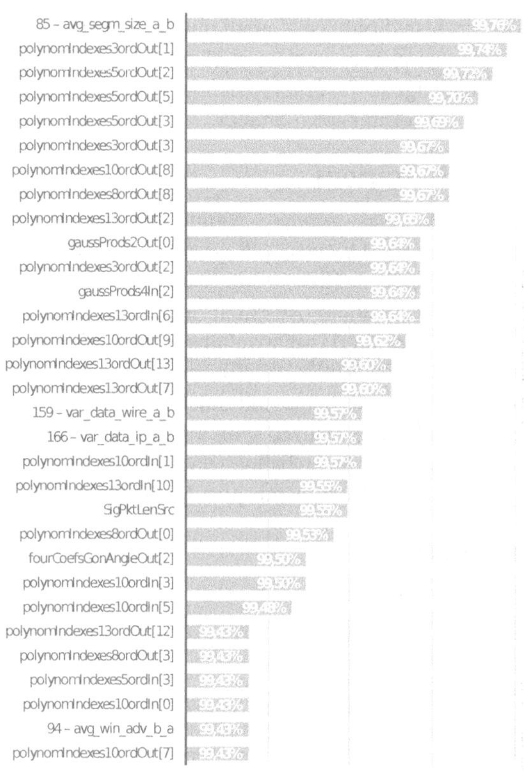

Fig. 3: List of metrics sorted by overall accuracy (over 99.43%).

7. Conclusion

In this paper, we focused on defining the process of extraction metrics from separated connections of captured network traffic and consequently focused attention on the experiments that proved the concept of a designed metrics set. In described experiments we achieved 99.9% accuracy of detecting buffer overflow attacks by combining an existing proposed metrics set with our solution. Accuracy is highly dependent on training samples parsed from captured network traffic. The training and testing samples may be biased towards a certain class of traffic. For example, valid communication (according to the separation to valid and attack connections) represents a large majority of the samples in the testing dataset[6] (approximately 99.24%). The reason to the high classification capability of fewer metrics is that classification of buffer overflow attacks was highly predicable due to the size of data in fragmented packets, which caused the overflow and the nature of a valid communication with a small number of fragmented packets.

Our future work focuses on extending the metrics set to achieve a more sufficient results in the detection of buffer overflow attacks. We plan to perform more experiments with actual metric sets. The efficiency of the current detection method was tested only on a small number of attacks. In the near future, we plan to create a public detection set that will create a challenge to the development of detection algorithms in order to detect unknown attacks.

Acknowledgment

This article was created within the research plan of the Security-Oriented Research in Information (MSM0021630528). This work was supported by the Operational Programme Research and Development for Innovations under the IT4Innovations Center of Excellence project (CZ.1.05/1.1.00/02.0070) and by the project Advanced Secured, Reliable and Adaptive IT (FIT-S-11-1). This project has been realized with a financial support from the Czech Republic state budget through the Ministry of Industry and Trade by research plan FR-TI1/037.

References

[1] M. Barabas, M. Drozd, and P. Hanáček, "Behavioral signature generation using shadow honeypot," in *World Academy of Science, Engineering and Technology*, ser. Issue 65, May 2012, Tokyo, Japan, no. 65. World Academy Science Engineering Technology, 2012, pp. 829–833.

[2] S. Stolfo, F. Wei, W. Lee, A. Prodromidis, and P. Chan, "Kdd cup knowledge discovery and data mining competition," 1999.

[3] S. J. Stolfo, W. Fan, W. Lee, A. Prodromidis, and P. K. Chan, "Cost-based modeling for fraud and intrusion detection: Results from the jam project," in *DARPA Information Survivability Conference and Exposition, 2000. DISCEX'00. Proceedings*, vol. 2. IEEE, 2000, pp. 130–144.

[4] C. Thomas, V. Sharma, and N. Balakrishnan, "Usefulness of darpa dataset for intrusion detection system evaluation," in *SPIE Defense and Security Symposium*. International Society for Optics and Photonics, 2008, pp. 69 730G–69 730G.

[5] A. W. Moore, D. Zuev, and M. Crogan, "Discriminators for use in flow-based classification," Technical report, Intel Research, Cambridge, Tech. Rep., 2005.

[6] A. W. Moore and D. Zuev, "Internet traffic classification using bayesian analysis techniques," in *ACM SIGMETRICS Performance Evaluation Review*, vol. 33, no. 1. ACM, 2005, pp. 50–60.

[7] T. T. Nguyen and G. Armitage, "A survey of techniques for internet traffic classification using machine learning," *Communications Surveys & Tutorials, IEEE*, vol. 10, no. 4, pp. 56–76, 2008.

[8] T. Auld, A. W. Moore, and S. F. Gull, "Bayesian neural networks for internet traffic classification," *Neural Networks, IEEE Transactions on*, vol. 18, no. 1, pp. 223–239, 2007.

[9] S. Shin, S. Lee, H. Kim, and S. Kim, "Advanced probabilistic approach for network intrusion forecasting and detection," *Expert Systems with Applications*, 2012.

[10] I. Homoliak, "Metrics for Intrusion Detection in Network Traffic," Master's thesis, University of Technology Brno, Faculty of Information Technology, Department of Intelligent Systems, 2011. [Online]. Available: in Slovak language, http://www.fit.vutbr.cz/study/DP/DP.php.en?id=13755&y=2011

[11] B. Sangster, T. O'Connor, T. Cook, R. Fanelli, E. Dean, W. J. Adams, C. Morrell, and G. Conti, "Toward instrumenting network warfare competitions to generate labeled datasets," in *Proc. of the 2nd Workshop on Cyber Security Experimentation and Test (CSETâĂŹ09)*, 2009.

Detecting Distributed SQL Injection Attacks in a Eucalyptus Cloud Environment

Alan Kebert, Bikramjit Banerjee, Glover George, Juan Solano
School of Computing
The University of Southern Mississippi
Hattiesburg, MS 39402, USA
Alan.Kebert@eagles.usm.edu

Wanda Solano
National Center for Critical Information Processing and Storage
National Aeronautics and Space Administration
Stennis Space Center, MS 39529, USA
Wanda.m.solano@nasa.gov

***Abstract*—Cloud computing environments offer malicious users the ability to spawn multiple instances of cloud nodes that are similar to virtual machines, except that they can have separate external IP addresses. In this paper we demonstrate how this ability can be exploited by an attacker to distribute his/her attack, in particular SQL injection attacks, in such a way that an intrusion detection system (IDS) could fail to identify this attack. To demonstrate this, we set up a small private cloud, established a vulnerable website in one instance, and placed an IDS within the cloud to monitor the network traffic. We found that an attacker could quite easily defeat the IDS by periodically altering its IP address. To detect such an attacker, we propose to use *multi-agent plan recognition,* where the multiple source IPs are considered as different agents who are mounting a collaborative attack. We show that such a formulation of this problem yields a more sophisticated approach to detecting SQL injection attacks within a cloud computing environment.**

Tracks: Computer Security (Hacking techniques and related issues, Intrusion detection systems, Malware analysis, Intrusion detection); Security Applications (Cloud computing security)

Keywords—cloud computing; Distributed Attack; Eucalyptus; SNORT; Havij; OSSIM; Multi-agent plan recognition

I. INTRODUCTION

Cloud computing offers new opportunities for software distribution, resource allocation, convenience, and information storage and security for users, but it also creates new opportunities for malicious users to penetrate security layers and damage, destroy or steal data of other users. One advantage that a cloud computing environment offers to malicious users is the ability to spawn multiple instances of cloud nodes that are similar to virtual machines, except that they can have separate external IP addresses. In this paper we demonstrate how this ability can be exploited by an attacker to distribute his/her attack, in particular SQL injection attacks, in such a way that an intrusion detection system (IDS) could fail to identify this attack. To demonstrate this, we set up a small private cloud using the Eucalyptus [10] cloud environment, established a vulnerable website in one instance, and placed an IDS (open source OSSIM [11]) within the cloud to monitor the network traffic. We found that an attacker, using a freely available SQL injection tool (Havij) could quite easily defeat OSSIM by periodically altering its IP address, i.e., by hopping from one instance to another in the cloud.

To detect such an attacker, we propose to use *multi-agent plan recognition* [1][2][4][5], where the multiple source IPs are considered as different agents who are mounting a collaborative attack. We show that such a formulation of this problem yields a more sophisticated approach to detecting SQL injection attacks within a cloud computing environment.

II. RELATED WORK

In the past, very little work has been done to study security issues and strategies in a cloud computing environment. A paper titled "Digital Forensics for Eucalyptus" [9] considered security vulnerabilities in a Eucalyptus cloud, and our work can be considered as an extension or a continuation of that work, since we not only address exploitation of some vulnerabilities of Eucalyptus cloud, but also how to detect a resulting attack, where existing IDS fail.

SQL injection continues to be a threat and is discussed in depth in "A classification of SQL-injection attacks and countermeasures" [3]. Although multiple methods exist to prevent or detect SQL injection attempts, these methods tend to focus on single actions. It can be difficult to differentiate a single action of an attack from normal traffic, so Security information and event management programs (SIEMs) try to correlate multiple activities with the plan of an attacker [6]. SIEM directives typically look for a pattern of activity from a single user to increase the reliability of an alert, but do not consider whether the actions of multiple agents have collectively achieved a malicious goal.

Multi-agent plan recognition [1][2][4][5] (MAPR) has been formalized and studied recently in abstract and theoretical settings, and to the best of our knowledge it has not been applied to any realistic cyber-security problem. Hence in this respect our work constitutes the first practical application of MAPR.

III. Description of Setting

In this section we describe how the various components of our system are set up, and how they operate. In succession, we will describe the Eucalyptus cloud setup that we used, the Havij SQL injection tool and the network traffic sniffer Snort, which is used as a sensor by the security event manager OSSIM to generate its alerts. Finally we describe how a simple strategy of switching source IP address can defeat OSSIM.

A. *Eucalyptus Cloud*

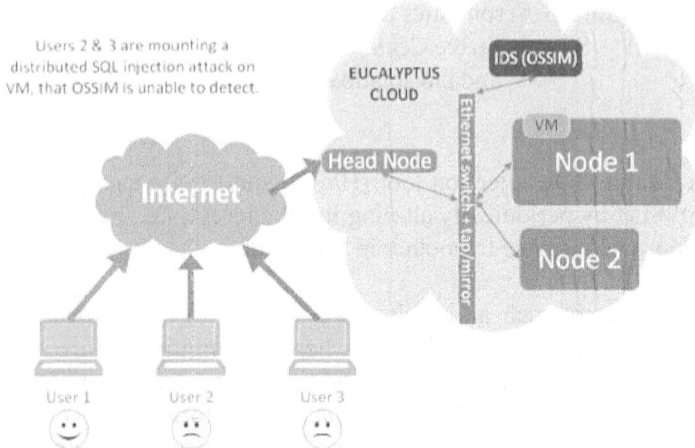

Fig. 1. The Eucalyptus Cloud Environment

The cloud environment on which this work is based is shown in Fig. 1. It contains three nodes, the head node – the manager of all communication with the external world – and two other nodes that offer various computational and storage resources to users. The communication between the head node and the other nodes are via an ethernet switch. An IDS (OSSIM) sniffs all packets passing through this switch. This gives OSSIM a vantage point to monitor any external attack on resources within the secondary nodes. In particular, we establish a vulnerable website within a VM in node 1. Fig. 1 also shows users outside the cloud accessing the cloud resources through the head node. Our attack computers were located outside the Eucalyptus cloud, but still able to compromise the database inside the cloud node.

B. *Havij*

In order to demonstrate an attack we used a program called Havij. Havij is a freely available SQL injection tool. SQL injection is the process of inserting arbitrary SQL code into a form whose input is queried against a SQL database. The form expects a user input, such as a username field on a login page, but if the text is not carefully sanitized a malicious user may place SQL commands into the field and cause the database to execute unintended commands. Havij facilitates this sort of activity by discovering the important field names needed for many SQL commands: database names, table names, and the columns of the tables. Havij can also reveal the contents of an unsecured database. It does this by first issuing a series of if-statements that test the length of field names, and then test the numerical value of the ascii characters representing individual characters of field names. Havij cannot ask the SQL database for the values directly, so it uses these comparisons to perform a binary search against a table of ascii numerical values. Each comparison will usually return zero immediately if false, but if true then an expensive MD5 benchmarking will be performed on a given string whose runtime will be reported to Havij. Based on this runtime, Havij can detect the binary outcome of the comparison. Fig. 2 shows a partial example of this process. The statements containing "`if (Length`" are part of a single binary search to determine the length (in this example 5) of the name of the database. The subsequent statements containing "`if (ascii(substring`" attempt to find the 5 characters one by one. The last statement of the form "`if (ascii(substring((database()),x,1))=y,BENCHMARK...`" that contains `=y`, marks the end of the process of finding the `x`th character. In this example, the 1st character has been determined to be "`d`" – the ascii character with code 100. The search for the 2nd character starts next, but is not completed in Fig. 2.

```
GET /?u=alan and if(1=1,BENCHMARK(26000,MD5(0x41)),0)

GET /?u=alan' and if(1=1,BENCHMARK(26000,MD5(0x41)),0) and 'x'='x

GET /?u=alan' and if(Length((database()))<32,BENCHMARK(32716,MD5(0x41)),0) and 'x'='x

GET /?u=alan' and if(Length((database()))<16,BENCHMARK(32716,MD5(0x41)),0) and 'x'='x

GET /?u=alan' and if(Length((database()))<8,BENCHMARK(32716,MD5(0x41)),0) and 'x'='x

GET /?u=alan' and if(Length((database()))<4,BENCHMARK(32716,MD5(0x41)),0) and 'x'='x

GET /?u=alan' and if(Length((database()))<6,BENCHMARK(32716,MD5(0x41)),0) and 'x'='x

GET /?u=alan' and if(Length((database()))=5,BENCHMARK(32716,MD5(0x41)),0) and 'x'='x

GET /?u=alan' and if(ascii(substring((database()),1,1))<79,BENCHMARK(32716,MD5(0x41)),0) and 'x'='x

GET /?u=alan' and if(ascii(substring((database()),1,1))<103,BENCHMARK(32716,MD5(0x41)),0) and 'x'='x

GET /?u=alan' and if(ascii(substring((database()),1,1))<91,BENCHMARK(32716,MD5(0x41)),0) and 'x'='x

GET /?u=alan' and if(ascii(substring((database()),1,1))<97,BENCHMARK(32716,MD5(0x41)),0) and 'x'='x

GET /?u=alan' and if(ascii(substring((database()),1,1))<100,BENCHMARK(32716,MD5(0x41)),0) and 'x'='x

GET /?u=alan' and if(ascii(substring((database()),1,1))=102,BENCHMARK(32716,MD5(0x41)),0) and 'x'='x

GET /?u=alan' and if(ascii(substring((database()),1,1))=101,BENCHMARK(32716,MD5(0x41)),0) and 'x'='x

GET /?u=alan' and if(ascii(substring((database()),1,1))=100,BENCHMARK(32716,MD5(0x41)),0) and 'x'='x

GET /?u=alan' and if(ascii(substring((database()),2,1))<79,BENCHMARK(32716,MD5(0x41)),0) and 'x'='x

GET /?u=alan' and if(ascii(substring((database()),2,1))<103,BENCHMARK(32716,MD5(0x41)),0) and 'x'='x
```

Fig. 2. Sample of (partial) tcpdump of a Havij attack formatted to be readable

Sometimes, perhaps due to delays in processing by the database, Havij receives non-zero runtimes for false statements that cause the binary search to go out of range or return a wrong length or character. This is usually inconsequential, as the search may be run again and comparing two searches allows the operator to fill in missing or wrong characters. In order to describe the database, Havij first runs these searches for length of the database name. Next it will perform binary search for that number of characters to determine the database name. Once it has the database name it can issue statements to determine the number of tables in the database. From there it will find each table name in a similar manner to the way it finds the database name, targeting the length of table names first and then each character of the table names. It may then do this for column names in each table, and then for data contained in the table. Once the structure of the database is known, a hacker may execute arbitrary commands by filling in the appropriate values.

Fig. 3 shows an attack where Havij has determined the length of the database's name to be 5, and then conducted 5 separate binary searches for the characters in the database's name, discovering the name "`dummy`". Fig. 4 shows an advanced stage of this attack where Havij has discovered the name of a table ("`users`") in the database "`dummy`", and used it to discover the three field names "`user`", "`email`" and "`password`". This attack can be manually continued through Havij, by selecting the columns in Fig. 4, and clicking "GetData", to reveal the contents of the table, potentially compromising sensitive data.

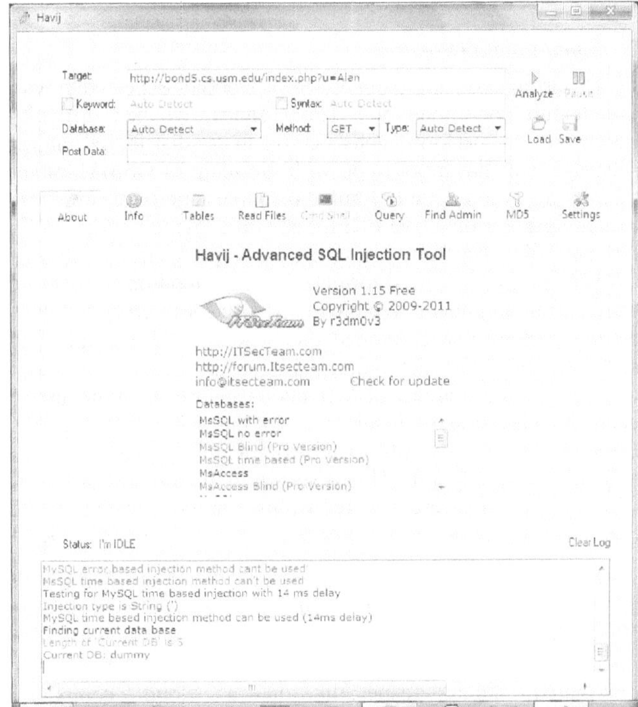

Fig. 3. Havij after finding the name of our database "dummy."

C. Snort

We decided to use the popular packet sniffer Snort to detect these attacks [8]. Snort compares the content of packets against a library of rules, and upon finding a packet whose contents match a rule, may raise an alert, log the packet, drop the packet, or perform some user defined function. With appropriate rules, Snort easily detects the Havij attack, but the functionality of Snort is greatly diminished by the large volume of alerts it raises. For example: our Snort rule library checks the packet content for the "`BENCHMARK`" command that Havij issues to check the results of its binary search. This causes Snort to alert hundreds of times for one Havij attack. This problem is worse if valid traffic can contain suspicious content. For example, the character "`'`" is often needed in SQL injection commands to end the query that is intended to run and allow the arbitrary commands to be inserted, but "`'`" may also be part of valid names like "`O'Reilly`". A snort rule that checks for "`'`" in the packet will alert on the name "`O'Reilly`" unless additional conditions are added to the rule. Each additional condition to reduce false positives makes the rule easier to defeat. This results in a tradeoff between reducing false positives and decreasing detection rate. Since Snort only considers one packet at a time, it is very difficult to avoid false positives. This is where SIEMs come in.

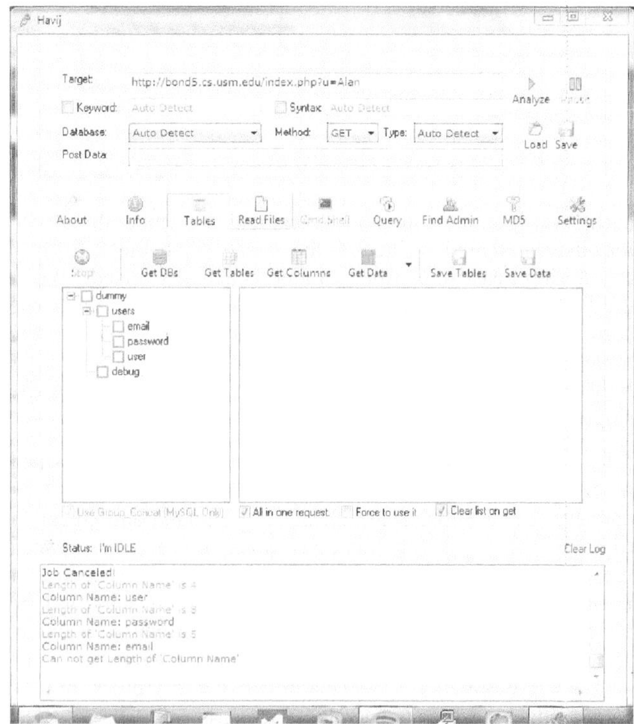

Fig. 4. Havij after identifying each column in the users table.

D. SIEM/OSSIM

SIEM stands for Security Information and Event Management. A SIEM uses tools like snort to detect various low level events, but interprets the results at a higher level before making alerts to the operator. Companies are increasingly using SIEM solutions to meet regulations and increase security [7]. We used the open source SIEM OSSIM for this project. OSSIM uses what its creators call a *correlation engine* to reduce false positives. The correlation engine relies on user created correlation directives to determine when to raise an alert. A correlation directive takes data from one or more sensors, like Snort, and tries to match them to patterns of malicious activity by organizing the data into correlation levels. The first level is always a single occurrence of a suspicious activity. Instead of alerting the operator immediately, the correlation directive moves to level two which will have a set of conditions and a timeout. If the conditions of level two are met before the timeout, the directive will elevate to level three and begin trying to meet a new set of conditions with a new timeout. The user defines how reliable

#	Alarm	Risk	Date	Source	Destination	Correlation Level
1	snort: "ET WEB_SERVER MYSQL Benchmark Command in URI to Consume Server Resources"	0	2013-02-08 14:12:39	131.95.171.124:49854	192.168.1.201:http	3
2	snort: "ET WEB_SERVER MYSQL Benchmark Command in URI to Consume Server Resources"	0	2013-02-08 14:12:39	131.95.171.124:49852	192.168.1.201:http	3
3	snort: "ET WEB_SERVER MYSQL Benchmark Command in URI to Consume Server Resources"	0	2013-02-08 14:12:39	131.95.171.124:49855	192.168.1.201:http	3
4	snort: "ET WEB_SERVER MYSQL Benchmark Command in URI to Consume Server Resources"	0	2013-02-08 14:12:39	131.95.171.124:49853	192.168.1.201:http	3
5	snort: "ET WEB_SERVER MYSQL Benchmark Command in URI to Consume Server Resources"	0	2013-02-08 14:12:38	131.95.171.124:49844	192.168.1.201:http	3
6	snort: "ET WEB_SERVER MYSQL Benchmark Command in URI to Consume Server Resources"	0	2013-02-08 14:12:38	131.95.171.124:49849	192.168.1.201:http	3

Fig. 5. Snort activations and correlation level 3

each level is in indicating an attack, and this value along with the user assigned value of the assets that the SIEM is monitoring determines when an alert is actually raised. While the Havij attack generates hundreds of lower levels alerts, the correlation engine raises only one alarm. Fig. 5 shows the directive accumulating multiple snort activations while the far right column displays the correlation level of 3 where the single alert is raised.

This directive generates an alert at level three. It is activated by Snort detecting the `BENCHMARK` command in the packet content. Upon initial detection of the command and elevation to level two, it looks for fifty activations in 6 seconds between the same source and destination IPs that activated level one. If it sees fifty activations before the timeout, an alert will be raised and it will elevate to level 3 where it attempts to collect 1000 activations in the next 10 seconds between the same source and destination IPs. This directive easily picks up on a Havij attack, which generates hundreds of `BENCHMARK` commands within a few seconds in order to perform the binary searches. The details of the directive appear in Fig. 6.

AV-FREE-FEED Web attack, web attack against DST_IP

Rules

Name	Reliability	Timeout	Occurrence	From	To
Web attack attempt detected	1	None	1	!HOME_NET	HOME_NET
Web attack attempt detected	5	600	10	1:SRC_IP	1:DST_IP
Web attack attempt detected	10	3600	1000	1:SRC_IP	1:DST_IP
Web attack attempt detected	10	3600	100000	1:SRC_IP	1:DST_IP

Fig. 6. The OSSIM correlation directive fired upon Havij attack

E. Simulating a Directive

Unfortunately, although OSSIM worked expectedly with the default conditions of a Havij attack, we had difficulty getting it to perform consistently in a distributed attack scenario. This has more to do with the setup of OSSIM, rather than its operation. Due to limited resources and time, we chose to simulate the directive of Fig. 6 with a python script and a tcpdump file. Tcpdump is a utility that captures traffic across a network in a widely used format. We used tcpdump to capture traffic from an attack. We then used a script to create a log of all the packets that contained the `BENCHMARK` command to simulate the snort activations. Using this data, our script counted up the number of activations before the timeout for each IP, elevating to level three in the same way that the OSSIM correlation would. An alert was then raised if enough activations were found. This is shown in the top part of Fig. 8, where 150 events were detected within 6 seconds leading to the outcome "`Attack Confirmed`".

Next, to simulate a distributed attack, we modified the IP addresses in the attack traffic so that after every 20 packets the IP would change, and these changes cycle within a set of 6 distinct IP addresses. This is a realistic simulation of a distributed attack, especially in a cloud computing environment, where a user can launch multiple instances with distinct IP addresses. By contrast, multiple VMs on a single machine do not acquire distinct external IP addresses (but they do acquire distinct internal addresses). After distributing the attack across the 6 distinct IP addresses, the script was still able to detect each attack, but since activations for any single IP address never exceeded the conditions, each distinct source IP remained at level two and raised no alarm. This is shown in the middle part of Fig. 8, where each source IP address was exonerated as "`False Alarm`". However, the total number of packets sent by any single IP address is not under 50 (as shown in the bottom part of Fig. 8 for the single source `137.24.100.201`), indicating that it is the temporal staggering of the packets that defeats level 2 of the directive, not a straightforward distribution of the packets among multiple sources which would make each source count fall under the threshold of 50 packets.

While a straightforward remedy to the above distributed attack scenario is to ignore the source IP addresses (which

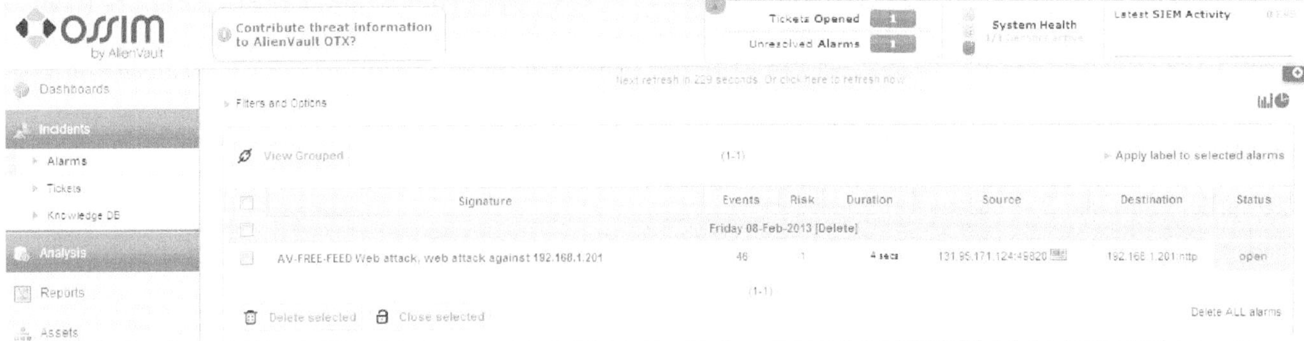

Fig. 7. The OSSIM correlation directive shown in Fig. 6 is the only incident/alarm that OSSIM fires upon Havij attack.

entails a simple modification of the directive of Fig. 6), it is conceivable that several independent nominal users could

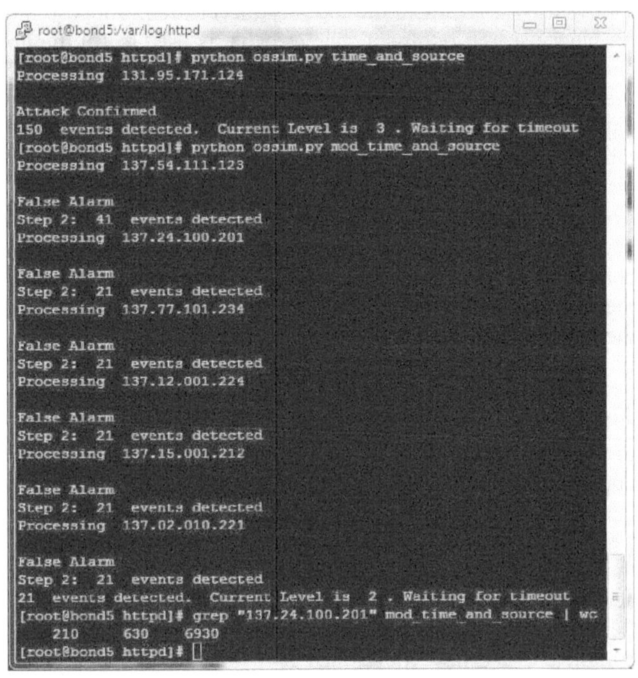

Fig. 8. Top: The attack from a single IP source, that raises an alert from the correlation angine. Middle: Attack spread across 6 source IP addresses. Events are detected but level 2 is not passed for any source, so no alert is raised by the correlation engine. Bottom: A single IP source sends more than 50 packets (210 packets) in all, showing that level 2 was defeated by temporal staggering of the packets.

actually be performing a similar pattern of activities, raising the possibility of false alarms. In general, for any directive expecting x activations within time t before raising an alarm, n activations could be spread over more than (n/x) IP addresses such that an IP address is not reused before t, where lowering x makes it harder to slip past but more likely to raise false alarms. We propose to delve deeper into the (distributed) activities themselves, than most IDSs do, to detect a malicious pattern.

IV. Multi-Agent Plan Recognition

Multi-agent plan recognition (MAPR) refers to the problem of explaining the observed behavior trace of multiple agents by identifying the (dynamic) team-structures and the team plans (based on a given plan library) being executed, as well as predicting their future behavior [1][2].

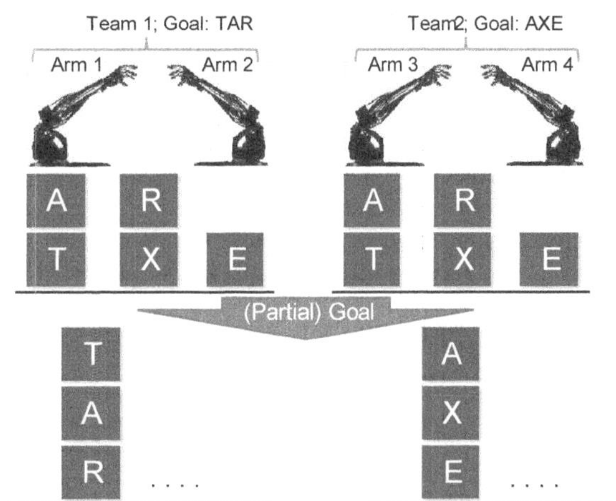

Fig. 9. Multi-agent blocks world example.

We first illustrate MAPR in a multi-agent blocks word domain, shown in Fig. 9, Fig. 10, and Fig. 11, using standard PDDL operators. In Fig. 9 we see two teams of robotic arms assemble (i.e., spell out) the goal words ``TAR'' and ``AXE'' from separate stacks, starting from the (not necessarily) same initial configuration. Fig. 10 shows the trace of 6 steps of activities of the 4 robotic arms available to the (remote) recognizer, who is not aware of the team-structure (i.e., the mapping of agent-id to stack-id). This assumption partly models the realistic incomplete information under which the recognizer must operate. While arms 1 and 2 appear to jointly assemble ``TAR'', and arms 3 and 4 appear to jointly assemble ``AXE'', arms 2 and 3 seem to assemble ``TAX'' as well, creating ambiguity for the recognizer. The key insight is to *partition* the trace into non-overlapping team plans, such that invalid teams (such as the supposed team of agents 2 and 3) fail to yield a complete partition hypothesis. In this example, agents 1 and 4 would be executing illegal plans individually,

Arm 1	Arm 2	Arm 3	Arm 4
(unstack R X)	(unstack A T)	(unstack R X)	(unstack A T)
(put-down R)	(put-down A)	(put-down R)	(put-down A)
(noop)	(noop)	(noop)	(pick-up X)
(pick-up A)	(pick-up T)	(pick-up A)	(stack X E)
(stack A R)	(noop)	(stack A X)	(noop)
(noop)	(stack T A)	(noop)	(noop)

Assembles TAR — Assembles AXE

Assembles TAX

Fig. 10. Trace of activities of 4 robotic arms, shown in Fig. 9

or building separate stacks as a team, neither of which yields a valid partition hypothesis. Fig. 11 shows a (non-unique) plan from the library, for start state in Fig. 9 and goal ``TAR'', in the form of a plan graph. This is a graph based on the partially ordered set of steps needed to achieve a goal from a start state, with added constraints for multi-agency: *role constraints* (which steps need to be performed by the same agent) and *concurrency constraints* (which steps need to be executed simultaneously; not needed in this illustration). The above illustration is adopted from a previous paper by the authors[2].

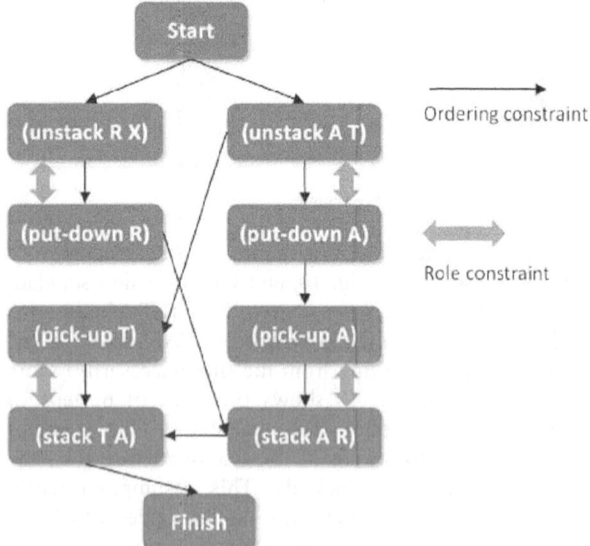

Fig. 11. A plan graph for the blocks world example.

V. Application of MAPR for Detection of Havij Attack

The SQL injection attack of Havij follows a pattern that can yield the abstract plan graph shown in Fig. 12.

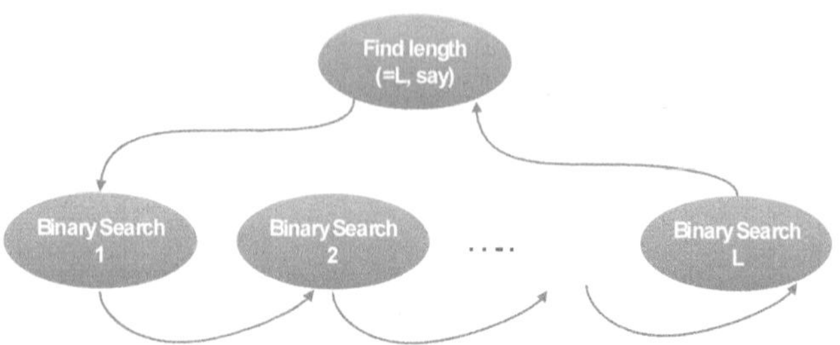

Fig. 12. Abstract plan graph corresponding to Havij attack

Here a binary search first finds the length of a certain field, say L. Then L binary searches are done in succession, followed by a return to the top (abstract) action. Suppose the ith binary search returns a character that is used to fill the ith character of a string s. Then the string $s[1:L]$ will be a part of the query used in the next search, e.g., after the name of a database is found this way, the queries to detect the names of tables in that database will include the name of the database already found. A string that differs by only a few characters from the database name used later should still be accepted because of the occasional false positives in the `BENCHMARK` command. This pattern repeats to find the names of tables in the database using the database name, and then again to find the column names in a table using that table's name.

A solution to the problem of limiting false positives while still detecting an attack that is spread across multiple agents is to use plan recognition. When a user switches IP addresses to appear as multiple users, the observable effect is indeed equivalent to there being multiple users. Hence, we can indeed treat this as a *multi-agent* plan recognition problem. Rather than relying on a single IP generating sufficient suspicious activity to raise an alert, a plan recognition algorithm searches input from all users to see if steps in a plan have been completed. We have developed and tested a simple Python script that finds the length command and then identifies the search result by finding the last "=" or equivalent symbol. It then looks for that number of binary searches using the `ascii` and `substring` commands. If it sees these actions it is reasonable to assume that a field name has been found whether spread across multiple agents or not.

We have tested our script on the same tcpdump file that was used with our simulation of OSSIM's correlation directive, where we showed successful camouflage of a Havij attack before. Fig. 13 shows the output of this script, not only detecting the attack despite distributed sources, but also revealing what the attacker has learned, viz., the words "`dummy`", "`debug`" and "`users`" that are names of actual entities in the database (see Fig. 4). Thus the ideas underlying

MAPR enable us to detect a SQL injection attack where a traditional IDS might fail in a cloud computing environment.

```
[root@bond5 httpd]# python planTest.py HA2.txt
Detected successful `length` search with result:  5
Detected successful `character` search with result:  d
Detected successful `character` search with result:  u
Detected successful `character` search with result:  m
Detected successful `character` search with result:  m
Detected successful `character` search with result:  y
Detected expected #character searches, with resulting word:  dummy
Detected successful `length` search with result:  5
Detected successful `character` search with result:  d
Detected successful `character` search with result:  e
Detected successful `character` search with result:  b
Detected successful `character` search with result:  u
Detected successful `character` search with result:  g
Detected expected #character searches, with resulting word:  debug
Detected successful `length` search with result:  5
Detected successful `character` search with result:  u
Detected successful `character` search with result:  s
Detected successful `character` search with result:  e
Detected successful `character` search with result:  r
Detected successful `character` search with result:  s
Detected expected #character searches, with resulting word:  users
[root@bond5 httpd]#
```

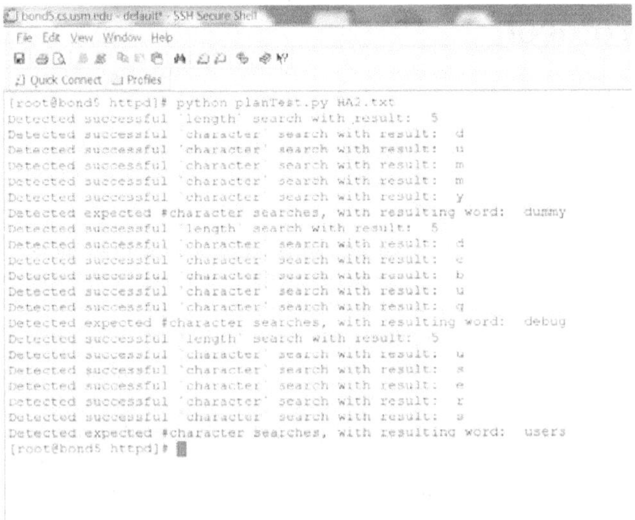

Fig. 13. Multi-agent plan recognition successfully detects Havij plan of Fig. 12 in the tcpdump, showing what the attacker has learned.

VI. CONCLUSIONS

In this paper we have argued that cloud computing environments offer opportunities for cyber-attackers to distribute their attacks, in particular SQL injection attacks, so as to defeat a traditional intrusion detection system. In such a scenario, we have demonstrated that the application of multi-agent plan recognition enables us to successfully detect a distributed SQL injection attack. Our deployment of MAPR toward cloud-computing security is currently limited to Havij-style SQL injection attacks only. However, the purpose of this paper is to demonstrate the feasibility of such a deployment in a realistic (instead of an abstract) scenario, rather than building a comprehensive suite of cyber-attack detection mechanisms. The latter is, in fact, a long term goal of this research.

A major limitation of the MAPR approach in detecting attacks is that the attack must follow a plan with multiple distinct steps. A brute force attack, for example, repeats the same action of attempting to log in many times until a login is guessed. This would be better handled by the correlation directives already in place. However, when there is a distinct plan it becomes easier to determine the validity of the attack, how successful the attacker was, and what the attacker is likely to do next by using the MAPR approach. Our experiment is also limited by the fact that our testing was performed against a simulated version of the OSSIM directive, which should perform the same way but this cannot be fully guaranteed. Also, running our test against log files does not test whether this method of detection is practical for examining larger volumes of traffic in real time.

In the future we would like to explore other types of increasingly complex cyber-attacks in the context of cloud computing and apply MAPR and evaluate its effectiveness in detecting such attacks. Even SQL injection attacks can be done in other (non-Havij) ways. Therefore our goal would require building (either manually or data mined from labeled data) a plan library for different variants of each kind of attack, for a range of different attack types. We plan to leverage our current setup to easily collect the required data to incrementally build a more comprehensive plan library.

VII. ACKNOWLEDGMENT

The authors thank the anonymous reviewers for feedback, and the NASA Office of Chief Technologist at NASA Stennis Space Center for support under the 2012 Center Innovation Fund.

REFERENCES

[1] B. Banerjee, L. Kraemer, and J. Lyle. Multi-Agent Plan Recognition: Formalization and Algorithms. In Proceedings of AAAI-10, pp. 1059–1064, Atlanta, GA, 2010.

[2] B. Banerjee and L. Kraemer. Branch and Price for Multi-Agent Plan Recognition. In Proceedings of the 25th AAAI Conference on Artificial Intelligence (AAAI-11), pp. 601–607, San Francisco, CA, 2011.

[3] Halfond, W. G., Jeremy Viegas, and Alessandro Orso. "A classification of SQL-injection attacks and countermeasures." In Proceedings of the IEEE International Symposium on Secure Software Engineering, pp. 65-81. IEEE, 2006.

[4] Hankz. H. Zhuo and Lei Li. Multi-agent plan recognition with partial team traces and plan libraries. In Proceedings of the 22nd International Joint Conference on Artificial Intelligence (IJCAI-11), pages 484–489, 2011.

[5] Hankz. H. Zhuo, Qiang Yang, and Subbarao Kambhampati. Action-model based multi-agent plan recognition. In Proceedings of NIPS 2012, 2012.

[6] Karg, . OSSIM, "Correlation engine explained.." Last modified 2004/02/01. Accessed March 5, 2013. http://www.alienvault.com/docs/correlation_engine_explained_rpc_dcom_example.pdf.

[7] Nicolett, Mark, and Kelly M. Kavanagh. "Magic Quadrant for Security Information and Event Management." Gartner RAS Core Reasearch Note (May 2009) (2011).

[8] Roesch, Martin. "Snort-lightweight intrusion detection for networks." In Proceedings of the 13th USENIX conference on System administration, pp. 229-238. 1999.

[9] Zafarullah, Z.; Anwar, F.; Anwar, Z., "Digital Forensics for Eucalyptus," Frontiers of Information Technology (FIT), 2011 , vol., no., pp.110,116, 19-21 Dec. 2011 doi: 10.1109/FIT.2011.28

[10] Nurmi, Daniel, Rich Wolski, Chris Grzegorczyk, Graziano Obertelli, Sunil Soman, Lamia Youseff, and Dmitrii Zagorodnov. "The eucalyptus open-source cloud-computing system." In Cluster Computing and the Grid, 2009. CCGRID'09. 9th IEEE/ACM International Symposium on, pp. 124-131. IEEE, 2009.

[11] Karg, D., and J. Casal. Ossim: Open source security information management. Tech. report, OSSIM, 2008.

A High-Throughput and Low-Complexity Secure Linear Network Coding Protocol

Majid Adeli[1] and Huaping Liu[1]
[1]School of Electrical Engineering and Computer Science, Oregon State University, Corvallis, Oregon, U.S.A.

Abstract—*A new scheme providing security against passive attackers in linear network coding is proposed. Throughput efficiency, low algorithm complexity, and high adaptability/applicability are the major design factors that are considered in this security protocol. A bijective permutation map defined over the code field is utilized to generate the randomness that is required for masking the plain information symbols. The input arguments of the permutation map are some of the plain data symbols and one random symbol that is chosen by the source node. It is shown that as long as the attacker does not have access to all the independent channels, he can not obtain any linear combination of the plain information symbols. Reducing data throughput by only one unit compared to the non-secure network code, and avoiding the use of complex transformations such as cryptographic algorithms or hash functions are the main advantages of the proposed security protocol.*

Keywords: Permutation map, secure linear network coding, throughput efficiency.

1. Introduction

Ensuring security and achieving throughput efficiency are two important and usually conflicting needs in most data networks. A common and well-established method of providing any level of data security is to use cryptographic algorithms [1]. When cryptographic approaches are used to secure a connection, many important issues need to be closely considered. Authentication of legitimate users; generation, management and secure distribution of proper keys; and establishment of initial agreements on the encryption/decryption parameters are some of the fundamental subroutines in cryptographic algorithms which often make the communication process complex and somewhat inefficient. Hence, providing security in data networks without going through the additional burden of conventional cryptographic schemes seems to be an appealing approach, and our goal in this paper is to do so. That is, using a light-weight auxiliary function along with a random symbol, a typical linear network code is converted to a snoop-proof code in this article.

Data networks can be generally classified in two categories: a) networks that are based on the traditional store-and-forward data routing algorithms; and b) networks in which network coding is used as the data routing protocol. In network coding based networks, each intermediate node has the ability to process its input data and relay the resultant processed symbols through its outgoing channels [2]. Hence, corresponding to each network node, a function whose input arguments are the node input symbols and its output arguments are the outgoing symbols leaving that node is considered. We call this function the *local encoding function*. Network codes can be broadly categorized into two main classes: linear network codes and nonlinear network codes. In linear network coding, the local encoding functions are linear, and since they are multi-input multi-output functions, the application of a local encoding function on the input symbols of a given node can be denoted by matrix multiplication. The matrix representing the network coding operation at a given node is called the *local encoding matrix*. Therefore, each intermediate node in linear network coding simply puts a linear combination of its input symbols on each of its outgoing channels [3]. The linear combination coefficients can be either chosen randomly from the code field by the intermediate node or they may be pre-assigned to each node by a supervisory entity in a centralized manner and based on the overall network topology. The former type of linear network coding is called random linear network coding, while the latter is known as centralized linear network coding [4]. Regrading the code linearity, it is shown that nonlinear network codes generally outperform the linear ones (e.g., [5], [6]); however, linearity makes the analysis and implementation of a network code much simpler while its performance is still acceptable. Therefore, in the literatures, linear network coding is considered as the more practical way of network coding.

1.1 Related Works

Same as any other data routing protocol, linear network coding should provide various aspects of data security such as privacy, integrity, and authentication before it is considered suitably practical for real applications. There are quite a few papers focusing on the subject of network coding security. Generally, one can categorize these works into two main classes: anti-passive-attack network codes and anti-Byzantine-attack network codes. In passive attacks (i.e., eavesdropping), the attacker may only "see" and possibly take a "copy" of the content of the original data packets. However, in Byzantine (active) attacks, the attacker can impersonate himself as a legitimate network node or he may compromise some of the genuine network nodes to execute his malicious intentions which can be injecting bogus and invalid data into the main data stream, blocking the data flow by not forwarding their received data, or manipulating the received data before forwarding it. Obviously, Byzantine attacks are more destructive than passive attacks and therefore the schemes that counteract this type of attacks in network coding are more complex than their counterparts challenging the passive attackers. Since the focus of this paper is anti-passive-attack schemes in linear network coding, in the following, we will have a brief review on some of the existing works in this particular field of secure network coding.

In [7], in addition to the regular global encoding coefficients, inclusion of an additional set of coding coefficients in each data packet is suggested. These "blocked coefficients" are chosen and encrypted by the source node while they are decrypted and used to decode the received data by the final destinations. This scheme uses a typical symmetric key cryptography algorithm to perform the encryption/decryption procedures while it keeps the linear network coding routines unchanged at the intermediate nodes.

Two schemes that provide weak security for linear network coding are proposed in [8]. They are designed to be bandwidth and throughput efficient as the second algorithm does not require enlarging the code field size or adding redundancy to the data packets.

In [9], a connection between strongly k-secure linear network coding and a secret sharing scheme called "strongly secure ramp secret sharing" is developed and based on this relationship, a generalization of strongly k-secure linear network coding is established. In this scheme, unlike many other algorithms with similar objectives, by increasing the number of independent wiretapped channels from k to $k+j$ for $0 \leq j < n-k$, the strong security does not break, instead the rate of secure transmission decreases by j symbols. An algorithm to construct such strongly k-secure linear network coding and an approach to convert a non-secure network code to a secure one are also proposed in this reference.

The issue of information-theoretic security against passive attackers in linear network coding and under a unicast scenario is considered in [10], where the optimal number of data symbols and the minimum number of noisy symbols in each data packet are derived. Their scheme also constructs a deterministic or random linear network code that achieves the calculated optimal transmission rate.

Use of Homomorphic Encryption Functions (HEFs) for encrypting the linear coding vectors at the source node is suggested in [11]. By utilizing HEF in this scheme, the source node is able to mix up the symbols of a coding vector with that of a plain data using a random permutation. The main idea is that based on a secret key which is only known by the source and the sink nodes, the order of the symbols in each packet (i.e., the symbols in the coding vector and the payload) is permuted. At the receiver side, after decoding the network coded data, the symbols are resorted back into the original order using the homomorphic encryption key in the decryption algorithm.

An interesting approach is outlined in [12] which utilizes MDS codes at the source node to information-theoretically secure the employed linear network code. In this scheme which stems from Ozarow-Wyner wiretap channel (see [13]), before running the linear network code at the source node, a wiretap code that is based on an MDS code is applied to the data. Assuming the eavesdropper has access to at most k linearly independent channels, it is shown that this scheme guarantees information-theoretic security as long as no linear combination of any k or less independent coding vectors lies in the vector space that is spanned by the rows of the MDS parity check matrix. The size of the network coding field and the procedure based on which the proper coding vectors are assigned to the network edges are also discussed in this reference.

The inner and outer capacity bounds for a multi-source multicast network using secure linear network coding are derived in [14]. The proposed quantitative definition of information leakage brings together all the security levels ranging from no security to complete security under one roof. Considering passive attacks as the threat model, the bounds derived in [15] are generalized in this work such that they fit both cases of weak and complete security.

In order to assure perfect security in multi-source multicast linear network coding, a necessary and sufficient condition on the global encoding vectors is derived in [16]. The threat model includes an eavesdropper who has full access to one predetermined subset of the network links at a time and the security goal is to prevent any information leakage. To this end, some randomness should be added to the original meaningful data, and it is shown that the sources of the randomness can be located at some nodes other than the ones that generate the meaningful data. It is essentially shown that there is no restriction on the locational distribution of the source nodes throughout the network. It is also proved that the random symbols can have any statistical distribution. In an earlier version of their work, the case of perfect security in single-source multicast linear network coding is considered in [17]. Their scheme suggests that based on a given feasible linear network code and the set containing all the possible subsets of the wiretapped links, a proper matrix is constructed at the source node. Using this matrix along with the insertion of some random symbols in the message vector, the original linear network code is transformed to a "secure code". In [18], same authors have shown the optimality of the r-secure linear network coding in terms of the throughput. In other words, it is shown that in their r-secure linear network code, the number of the meaningful symbols in each packet is maximal. The definition of perfect (complete) security is also expanded to the notion of imperfect security in which perfect security is a special case.

Security against passive attacks based on the network topology for linear network coding is studied in [19]. A unicast scenario in which the information transmission rate is one symbol per time unit and every node is equipped with a perfect random number generator is considered. Knowing the entire network topology, a spanning tree connecting the receiver to every other network node is established. It is shown that after performing the preprocessing phase, one symbol can be securely sent to the receiver as long as the eavesdropper does not tap into any link on the path connecting the source node to the receiver.

The idea of using maximum-rank-distance (MRD) codes in order to make the two processes of securing and designing a linear network code independent is considered in [20]. The scheme targets passive attacks in linear network coding and provides information theoretic security against wiretappers who have access to any limited-size subset of the network channels. Inspired by the work in [12] and [13], the security is obtained by defining a coset coding scheme over an extension of the network code field. It is shown that defining the maximum-rank-distance code over an extended field relaxes a fundamental independency restriction considered in [12].

Our goal in this paper is to design a security algorithm that is easily applicable to any available linear network code. The proposed scheme has to prevent information leakage to the eavesdropper while it maximally preserves the data throughput and system simplicity. The rest of this article is organized as follows. A short review on the employed notation, definitions, and assumptions is presented in Sec. 2. The problem being addressed is stated in Sec. 3, where the explanation of what the security algorithm is expected to provide as well as the factors that affect the scheme are delivered. Sec. 4 elaborates on the proposed scheme and describes how it satisfies all the requirements specified in Sec. 3. Comparison with the existing security schemes from different viewpoints is provided in Sec. 5 which is followed by a summary of this work in Sec. 6.

2. Notation, Definitions and Assumptions

A general data network is denoted by directed acyclic graph $G(V, E)$, where V is the set of network nodes and E is the set containing all the network edges (also known as channels or links). The sets $S \subset V$ and $R \subset V$, where $S \cap R = \varnothing$, denote the sets of source and sink nodes, respectively. Let $\mathbf{m} = (x_1, x_2, \cdots, x_n)^T$ be the original information vector, in which x_i is a plain information symbol that belongs to the code field $GF(q)$ with q being a prime power. Vector $\mathbf{m}$ which contains n i.i.d. plain symbols is generated by the source nodes and shall be entirely received by each sink node. Note that $\|S\| \leq n$, which implies that each source node in S generates at least one information symbol because otherwise it would be redundant and will be eliminated from the network. Since the proposed scheme does not depend on the locational distribution of the nodes in set S, for simplicity, all the source nodes are put together and the entire set S is considered as a single node called the *source node*. In networks that use linear network coding as the routing protocol, row vector $\mathbf{v}^l = (v_1^l, v_2^l, \cdots, v_n^l) \in GF(q^n)$, called *(global) coding vector*, is assigned to network edge $l \in E$, [3]. Therefore, the symbol flowing on each edge can be stated as the inner product of the corresponding coding vector and vector $\mathbf{m}$. Each edge can carry only one symbol per time unit. The data transmission is free of noise, fading and any type of interference. Such distortions exist in practical networks; however, they are assumed to be mitigated by other physical layer processes (e.g., channel coding) before recovering the network-coded data starts.

According to Max-Flow-Min-Cut theorem [21], in networks using network coding, each sink node should have access to n independent channels (or equivalently n independent coding vectors) in order to be able to decode the entire information vector $\mathbf{m}$ [2]. This condition (i.e., feasibility of a linear network code) is assumed to be satisfied in this paper. Two channels are considered statistically independent if their corresponding global coding vectors are independent.

3. Problem Statement and Threat Model

The goal is to securely send the information vector $\mathbf{m}$ from the source node S to each element of set R via network G with minimum overhead and low complexity. The security requirement mandates the algorithm to prevent any information leakage to the attacker. That is, the attacker who has access to at most $n-1$ independent channels should not be able to obtain any nonzero linear combination of the plain information symbols.

The required level of security should be achieved without using any cryptographic scheme. Avoiding conventional cryptographic algorithms considerably simplifies the transmission process. Additionally, we want to minimize the security overhead, which means that during each time slot, the scheme has to deliver as many meaningful information symbols to the sink nodes as possible. Note that since there are originally n plain information symbols in vector $\mathbf{m}$, the maximum throughput determined by Max-Flow-Min-Cut theorem in the non-secure case is n symbols per transmission.

4. The Proposed Solution

According to the discussion in Sec. 3, the three main requirements for the security protocol are i) no information leakage to the wiretapper, as long as the number of tapped independent channels is less than n; ii) minimum inflicted security overhead (maximum data throughput); and iii) low algorithm complexity. In the following, the proposed security scheme is described and it is shown that it meets all the design requirements.

4.1 Algorithm Description

In order to prevent the attacker from obtaining any linear combination of the components in information vector $\mathbf{m} = (x_1, x_2, \cdots, x_n)^T$, we substitute x_k in $\mathbf{m}$ with $\tilde{x}_k$ based on the following formulation.

$$\tilde{x}_k = x_k + \sum_{j=0}^{k-1} f^{(k-j)}(a + x_j) \qquad k = 1, \cdots, n-1, \quad \text{(1a)}$$

$$\tilde{x}_n = a + f\left(\sum_{i=1}^{n-1} \tilde{x}_i\right) \quad \text{(1b)}$$

In (1), $x_0 = 0$ and $f^{(m)}(\cdot)$ denotes m times composition of permutation function f with itself; for example $f^{(3)}(\cdot) = f(f(f(\cdot)))$. Also, symbol $a \in GF(q)$ is a uniformly distributed random symbol chosen by the source node. In Sec. 4.4, two different implementation approaches for permutation function f are explained. Hence, the source node sends out the secured information vector $\tilde{\mathbf{m}} = (\tilde{x}_1, \tilde{x}_2, \cdots, \tilde{x}_n)$ containing $n-1$ hidden meaningful information symbols.

The concealed information is recovered at the sink node in a step-by-step fashion. That is, after a sink node decodes its received symbols and obtains vector $\tilde{\mathbf{m}}$ (network de-coding), it executes the following *Extraction Algorithm*:

a) Recover the key (the noisy symbol a) by computing $a = \tilde{x}_n - f(\sum_{i=1}^{n-1} \tilde{x}_i)$.
b) Set $x_0 = 0$ and $i = 1$.
c) Recover the meaningful symbol x_i by computing $x_i = \tilde{x}_i - \sum_{j=0}^{i-1} f^{(i-j)}(a + x_j)$.
d) While $i < n-1$, increase i by 1 and repeat (c); otherwise exit the algorithm.

By following this recursive algorithm, all the meaningful information symbols are extracted from vector $\tilde{\mathbf{m}}$. Note that every operation such as addition, is defined over the code field $GF(q)$.

4.2 Security Analysis

To verify the algorithm security, let $r_k \triangleq \sum_{j=0}^{k-1} f^{(k-j)}(a + x_j)$ for every $1 \leq k \leq n-1$ and $r_n \triangleq \tilde{x}_n$. Considering the facts that 1) random symbol a has uniform distribution over $GF(q)$, 2) function $f(\cdot)$ is bijective, and 3) the plain information symbols are i.i.d with arbitrary distribution over the code field; one can infer that every argument $a + x_j$ $(0 \leq j \leq k-1)$ in r_k as well as symbol r_n is uniformly distributed over the code field. Moreover, for every two distinct plain information symbols x_i and x_j, there is

$$\forall d \geq 1 : \Pr\left(f^{(d)}(a + x)\right) = \Pr(a + x), \quad \text{(2a)}$$

$$\Pr(a + x_i) = \frac{1}{q}, \quad \text{(2b)}$$

$$\Pr(a + x_i, a + x_j) = \Pr(a + x_i)\Pr(a + x_j). \quad \text{(2c)}$$

Hence, $\forall 1 \leq k \leq n$, r_k is a summation of some mutually independent and uniformly distributed random variables. That is,

$$\Pr(r_k) = \frac{1}{q}. \quad \text{(3)}$$

For every plain information symbol x_k, the corresponding r_k (called *masking symbol*) depends solely on symbol a and all the plain information symbols that precede x_k; hence, x_k and r_k for every $1 \leq k \leq n-1$ are independent. This fact along with the result in (3) indicates that each original information symbol x_k is added to an independent and uniformly distributed random symbol in the proposed scheme. Adding the case of $k = n$ in which $\Pr(\tilde{x}_k = r_n) = \frac{1}{q}$, this fundamental noise-masking procedure is summarized below.

$$\Pr(\tilde{x}_k) = \Pr(x_k + r_k) = \frac{1}{q} \qquad 1 \leq k \leq n-1, \quad \text{(4a)}$$

$$\Pr(\tilde{x}_n) = \frac{1}{q} \quad \text{(4b)}$$

The results in (4) indicate that obtaining any individual entry of vector $\tilde{\mathbf{m}}$ does not give the wiretapper anything but uniform noise.

Assume the attacker has wiretapped $k < n$ independent channels and by taking a linear combination of the tapped symbols, he is trying to attain a linear combination of the plain information symbols. Let each row of matrix $\mathbf{B}_{k \times n}$ be a coding vector corresponding to one of the tapped channels. Let row vector $\mathbf{c}$ contain the arbitrary linear combination coefficients chosen by the attacker. The attack is modeled as

$$\begin{aligned} \mathbf{c} \cdot \mathbf{B} \cdot \tilde{\mathbf{m}} =& \mathbf{c}' \times (\tilde{x}_1, \tilde{x}_2, \cdots, \tilde{x}_n)^T \\ =& (c'_1, c'_2, \cdots, c'_{n-1}) \cdot (x_1, x_2, \cdots, x_{n-1})^T + \\ & (c'_1, c'_2, \cdots, c'_n) \cdot (r_1, r_2, \cdots, r_n)^T \\ =& L(\mathbf{m}) + L(\mathbf{r}). \end{aligned} \quad \text{(5)}$$

In (5), vector $\mathbf{c}'$ represents the arbitrary linear combination of the tapped independent coding vectors. As shown above, this linear combination can be decomposed into two parts: a) the arbitrary linear combination of the plain information symbols, denoted by $L(\mathbf{m})$; and b) the corresponding linear combination of the noisy symbols, shown by $L(\mathbf{r})$. To achieve the required level of security, it is sufficient to have $\Pr(L(\mathbf{r})) = \frac{1}{q}$, which means every arbitrary linear combination of the plain symbols is still masked by a noise component (called $L(\mathbf{r})$) with uniform distribution over the code field. To verify this, let us elaborate on vector $\mathbf{c}'$. We know $L(\mathbf{r}) = \sum_{i=1}^{n} c_i' r_i$. For every $c_i' \neq 0$ one has $\Pr(c_i' r_i | c_i') = \Pr(r_i) = \frac{1}{q}$. Therefore from the wiretapper's perspective, $L(\mathbf{r})$ is a summation of some mutually independent and uniformly distributed random variables. This results in uniform distribution for $L(\mathbf{r})$, i.e., $\Pr(L(\mathbf{r})) = \frac{1}{q}$. Hence, any arbitrary linear combination of the plain information symbols, $L(\mathbf{m})$, is masked with a uniformly distributed random symbol, $L(\mathbf{r})$, and therefore the security requirement is satisfied. In other words, neither any individual entry nor any linear combination of the entries of $\tilde{\mathbf{m}}$ reveals any information to the attacker.

4.3 Throughput Efficiency

Substitution of only one plain information symbol in the original information vector $(\mathbf{m})$ with one noisy symbol (a) is all the throughput reduction paid to ensure the data security in our scheme. This means instead of the maximum value of n symbols per time unit, the source node delivers $n-1$ meaningful information symbols to each sink node during each time slot. As described, conventional cryptographic security schemes do not require this substitution but they have much higher computational and hardware complexity. In our scheme, symbol a can be interpreted as the key which is securely hidden in the transmitted information vector $\tilde{\mathbf{m}}$; thus, each data packet carries its own key. This considerably simplifies the communication since the need for a trusted third party to execute the entire key management process is eliminated. It also enables the source node to change the key as frequent as it generates new packets (new information vectors) without imposing additional complexity to the system. In Sec. 5, we will discuss the throughput advantages of this scheme in greater detail.

4.4 Algorithm Complexity

Utilizing a light-weight permutation map instead of employing computationally expensive cryptographic algorithms in order to ensure data security considerably simplifies the transmission procedure. The permutation can be implemented as a look-up table with two rows and q columns, where q is the code field size. The input-output assignment is chosen randomly and any assignment is acceptable except identity relationship (i.e., $f(x) \neq x$). An example of a possible permutation map for $q = 11$ is shown in the following table.

Table 1: A Permutation Map Over GF(11) Realized as A Look-Up Table

x	0	1	$\cdots$	10
$f(x)$	3	8	$\cdots$	2

Another simple way of implementing the permutation map is an affine function with two constant parameters s and t where $s, t \in GF(q)$ and $s \neq 0$. To exclude the identity permutation case, we impose that if $t = 0$, then $s \neq 0, 1$. In other words, the permutation function $f(\cdot)$ is defined as

$$\begin{aligned} f : GF(q) &\to GF(q) \\ u &\mapsto su + t. \end{aligned} \quad (6)$$

with the above conditions on s and t. Note that the security does not depend on the privacy of function $f(\cdot)$, and therefore all the parties including the attacker may know this function.

5. Comparison with The Existing Schemes

As mentioned, in networks with conventional store-and-forward routing protocols, typical cryptographic approaches such as different modes of block or stream ciphers are usually used to encrypt the plain information at the source node and decrypt it at the authorized sink nodes. This requires execution of a series of routines such as key management (including generating, securely distributing and regularly verifying/notarizing appropriate keys), user authentication, security policy management (e.g., establishing initial agreements on the security parameters between the senders and receivers) as well as running encryption/decryption procedures [1]. These inhibiting factors are time consuming and use network resources such as bandwidth, power and hardware. Considering the fact that the proposed scheme eliminates these issues along with providing more freedom and flexibility in terms of security management and key renewal, the benefits of this protocol significantly outweigh the expense of reducing the throughput from n to $n-1$ meaningful symbols per time unit.

To summarize, the main advantages of this scheme over the cryptographic based approaches are as follows. a) It eliminates the need for the entire key management routines and enables the source node to generate its keys without supervision of a trusted third party. This can even yield to a higher security level since the number of parties involved in establishing a secure connection is reduced. b) The key information used to secure the content of a data packet is covertly embedded in the corresponding data packet; therefore, each packet safely and independently carries its own key information indicating that there is no need for sending the keys to the destinations in advance through a secret channel. c) It offers the capability of dedicating different keys to different data packets and changing keys as frequent as the source node generates new data packets. This is achieved without imposing additional delay or complexity to the system, or using network resources. d) It does not need a complex encryption/decryption module; instead, only a simple non-identity permutation map is used to generate the required randomness.

There are quite a few papers discussing security algorithms tailored for linear network coding, some of which targeting the same security goals as considered in this paper (e.g., [7], [9], [11], [17], [16], [12], [22], [20], [18], [10], [19]). These works assume that the attacker has access to at most $k < n$ independent edges. In order to prevent him from obtaining any linear combination of the plain information symbols, it is shown that $r \geq k$ symbols in vector $\mathbf{m}$ should be substituted with r uniformly distributed random symbols that are chosen by the source node. Therefore, in the secured information vector $\tilde{\mathbf{m}} = (x_1, x_2, \cdots, x_{(n-r)}, z_1, z_2, \cdots, z_r)$, the last r symbols are the substituted noisy symbols. After this step, the source node runs an invertible linear transformation on $\tilde{\mathbf{m}}$ and then sends out the resultant vector through the network. By applying the final transformation on $\tilde{\mathbf{m}}$, the source node avoids putting plain information symbols on some of its output edges. The linear transformation can be modeled by matrix multiplication. This way on each output edge of the source node there is a linear combination of the plain information symbols and some noisy symbols, yielding a uniformly distributed random symbol.

Let us denote this final transformation by matrix $\mathbf{T}_{n\times n} = [\mathbf{Q}_{n\times(n-r)}|\mathbf{P}_{n\times r}]$. To retain the security, it is necessary to include at least one noisy symbol in each outgoing linear combination. Therefore, the submatrix $\mathbf{P}_{n\times r}$ should not have any all-zero row. This condition excludes some of the possible choices for matrix $\mathbf{T}$ and requires the source node to take into account this constraint when it is constructing this matrix. Assuming the attacker has access to exactly k independent coding vectors, then the network is secure only if the attacker is unable to obtain any linear combination of the meaningful information symbols by linearly combining his wiretapped symbols. Let $\mathbf{C}_{k\times n}$ be the matrix whose rows are the k independent wiretapped coding vectors and let $\mathbf{A}_{1\times k}$ be the vector containing the linear combination coefficients chosen by the attacker. The attack may be modeled as

$$\mathbf{A}\cdot\mathbf{C}\cdot\tilde{\mathbf{m}} = \mathbf{A}\times[\Gamma_{k\times(n-r)}|\Delta_{k\times r}]\times (x_1, x_2, \cdots, x_{(n-r)}, z_1, z_2, \cdots, z_r)^T = d \quad (7)$$

For any arbitrary $\mathbf{A}$, in order to have at least one noisy symbol (i.e., z) participating in d, the rows of submatrix $\Delta_{k\times r}$ should be linearly independent and it requires $r \geq k$. The independency condition on the rows of $\Delta_{k\times r}$ imposes some additional limits on the assignment of proper coding vectors to the network edges. This makes the design and management of linear network codes, especially in the case of random linear network codes, more complex. On the other hand, the aforementioned existing approaches require at least k symbols to be substituted in the original information vector ($\mathbf{m}$), which means the throughput is at least decreased by k units.

Compared to the existing security schemes, the proposed approach has the following advantages. (a) It significantly improves the data throughput. With the proposed scheme, in each information vector (data packet) only one meaningful symbol is substituted by noise, as opposed to at least k substitutions in the existing counterparts. (b) There is literally no limitation on the coding vector selection in this algorithm while in previous works some of the coding vectors are improper and should be avoided in order to retain the required level of security. (c) It relaxes a fundamental assumption on the allowed number of wiretapped independent channels. In this scheme, the security is impenetrable as long as the attacker has not acquired *all* the n independent coding vectors while in the other works the security is broken as soon as the attacker acquires more than k independent channels. (d) Throughput is utterly independent of the number of the attacked channels as opposed to the previous schemes in which throughput is highly dependent on the attacker's ability such that by increasing the value of k from k_1 to k_2, in order to protect the security, the throughput at least drops from $n - k_1$ to $n - k_2$ symbols per transmission. In the presented protocol, as long as the attacker does not have access to *all* the independent channels, the throughput is equal to $n - 1$. (e) In this scheme, the need for deliberately designing, sharing, and applying an invertible linear transformation to the message vector prior sending it through the network is removed, and that is the case because every entry in vector $\tilde{\mathbf{m}}$ has already uniform distribution and maximum entropy. (f) The security concern existing in [23] is eliminated. In order to fully protect the key information (i.e., the noisy symbol a), the scheme in [23] imposes a constraint on the admissible coding vector set. In the scheme described in this paper, by concealing the key information in the secured information vector ($\tilde{\mathbf{m}}$), the restriction on the coding vector selection space is removed. Additionally, the use of simple permutation function as a replacement for the complex hash functions makes this algorithm much simpler than the scheme in [23].

6. Conclusion

An algorithm for securing data transmission in linear network coding is proposed. The main idea of this scheme is to mask each plain information symbol by a noisy symbol which has uniform distribution over the code field. To generate the required noisy symbols, a recursive algorithm in which a simple permutation function is the main building block is utilized. Only one noisy symbol along with some of the original information symbols is employed to produce the masking symbols. Two possible implementation approaches for the permutation function are also discussed. The comparison of the proposed approach with the existing schemes in terms of throughout efficiency and complexity demonstrates the capabilities and benefits of the projected security protocol.

References

[1] D. R. Stinson, *Cryptography: theory and practice,* 3rd edition, Chapman and Hall/CRC (Taylor & Francis Group), 2006.

[2] R. W. Yeung, S.-Y. R. Li, N. Cai, and Z. Zhang, *Network Coding Theory,* now Publishers Inc., 2006.

[3] S.-Y. R. Li, R. W. Yeung, and N. Cai, "Linear network coding," *IEEE Trans. Inform. Theory*, vol. IT-49, pp. 371-381, Feb. 2003.

[4] T. Ho, R. Koetter, M. Medard, D. Karger, and M. Effros, "The benefits of coding over routing in a randomized setting," *in ISIT'03*, Japan, Jun. 2003.

[5] R. Dougherty, C. Freiling, and K. Zeger, "Insufficiency of linear coding in network information flow," *IEEE Trans. Inform. Theory*, vol. IT-51, no. 8, pp. 2745-2759, Aug. 2005.

[6] A. Rasala-Lehman and E. Lehman, "Complexity classification of network information flow problems," in *41st Annual Allerton Conf. on Communication Control and Computing*, Monticello, IL, Oct. 2003.

[7] J. P. Vilela et al.,"Lightweigth Secuirty for Network Coding," in *Proc. IEEE Int. Conf. on Commun.*, Beijing, China, 2008, pp. 1750-1754.

[8] Y. Wei et al., "Efficient Weakly-Secure Network Coding Schemes against Wiretapping Attacks," in *Proc. IEEE Int. Symp. on Network Coding (NetCod)*, Toronto, Canada, 2010, pp. 1-6.

[9] K. Harada and H. Yamamoto, "Strongly Secure Linear Network Coding," *IEICE Trans. Fundamentals*, vol. E91-A, pp. 2720-2728, Oct. 2008.

[10] J. Wang et al., "Optimal Design of Linear Network Coding for Information Theoretically Secure Unicast," in *Proc. IEEE Conf. on Comput. Commun. (INFOCOM)*, Shanghai , China, 2011, pp. 757-765.

[11] P. Zhang et al., "P-Coding: Secure Network Coding against Eavesdropping Attacks," in *Proc. IEEE Conf. on Comput. Commun. (INFOCOM)*, San Diego, CA, 2010, pp. 1-9.

[12] S. Y. El Rouayheb and E. Soljanin, "On wiretap networks II," in *Proc. ISIT'07*, Nice, France, Jun. 2007, pp. 551-555.

[13] L. H. Ozarow and A. D. Wyner, "The wire-tap channel II," in *Proc. EUROCRYPT 84 workshop on Advances in cryptology: theory and application of cryptographic techniques*, Paris, France, 1984, pp. 33-50.

[14] T. Chan and A. Grant, "Capacity Bounds for Secure Network Coding," in *Proc. Australian Commun. Theory Workshop (AusCTW)*, Christchurch, New Zealand, 2008, pp. 95-100.

[15] R. W. Yeung, *A First Course in Information Theory*. New York, NY: Springer, 2002.

[16] N. Cai and R. W. Yeung, " A Security Condition for Multi-Source Linear Network Coding," in *Proc. IEEE Int. Symp. on Inform. Theory*, Nice, France, 2007, pp. 561-565.

[17] N. Cai and R. W. Yeung, "Secure network coding," in *Proc. ISIT'02*, Lausanne, Switzerland, Jul. 2002, page 323.

[18] N. Cai and R. W. Yeung, "Secure Network Coding on a Wiretap Network," *IEEE Trans. Inf. Theory*, vol. 57, pp. 424-435, Jan. 2011.

[19] K. Jian, "Security based on network topology against the wiretapping attack," *IEEE Wireless Commun. Mag.*, vol. 11, no. 1, pp. 68-71, 2004.

[20] D. Silva and F. R. Kschischang, "Security for Wiretap Networks via Rank-Metric Codes," in *Proc. IEEE Int. Symp. on Inform. Theory*, Toronto, Canada, 2008, pp. 176-180.

[21] R. Diestel, *Graph Theory*, 4th ed. New York: Springer-Verlag, 2010.

[22] J. Feldman, T. Malkin, C. Stein, and R. A. Servedio, "On the capacity of secure network coding," in *Proc. 42nd Annual Allerton Conf. Commun., Control and Comput.*, Sep. 2004.

[23] M. Adeli and H. Liu, "Secure Network Coding with Minimum Overhead Based on Hash Functions," *IEEE Communication Letters*, vol. 13, no. 12, pp. 956-958, Dec. 2009.

A practical study of the problems of current Internet routing tables

Arnav Ghosh, Bruce Hartpence, Daryl Johnson
School of Informatics,
Rochester Institute of Technology
Rochester, NY USA

Abstract - *The phenomenal growth of the Internet amazes even the creators of this worldwide network. Apart from the constantly changing data protocols and services that the Internet has to adapt to, the sheer volume of users has been one of the biggest challenges the Internet is coping with. This paper is directed towards the study of Internet scale routing tables in a lab environment to understand the dynamics of route processing by routers, and the effect of increasing the number of routing table entries on the overall performance of the router in terms of packet forwarding. This study is an effort to simulate an Internet scale network in the lab to shed light on some of the practical problems of the Internet routing table size and its performance and the security implications.*

1. Introduction

In the 1970s, an experimental network known as ARPANET was started to connect a few research universities and some government bodies. It was an experiment which never ended and has evolved to become the world's largest network; the Internet. The incredible achievement of the Internet is that it enables us to access information and data from all around the globe within seconds, in spite of traffic variations and departure from the original scope. The Internet as we know is a huge mesh, interconnecting networks all around the world. The meshed Internet architecture makes it inherently resilient to most network failures and is the strength of the Internet, making it tolerant to link failures, node failures and sometimes even network segment failures.

The Internet is based on Internet Protocol (IP) addressing which was first developed in 1980. IP addresses are logical addresses that make identification and communication possible across multiple networks. IPv4 addresses were initially divided into classful groups of A, B, C, D and E. Classful addressing and routing protocols meant that addresses in a particular class would be advertised to different networks across classful boundaries with the class specific subnet mask. This was inefficient and resulted in wastage of IPv4 addresses. In 1993, researchers came up with Classless Inter-Domain Routing (CIDR), which allowed networks belonging to a specific class being advertised with subnet mask of varying lengths. This was a great step and allowed efficient use of the IPv4 address space. CIDR was being widely used all around the world but as more and more IPv4 addresses were allocated, a hidden problem of routing table explosion emerged even though the routing table entries could be aggregated. Since CIDR allowed the propagation of IPv4 networks with any possible valid subnet masks, ISPs, enterprises, universities, etc started advertising their network block in smaller chunks rather than one huge network. For example, Apple Computer Inc. owns the entire 17/8 subnet and would advertise a single 17.0.0.0/255.0.0.0 block before the existence of CIDR. At present there are more than a hundred route entries in the 17/8 network which is advertised on the Internet which can be verified by using a publicly accessible router server at http://www.routeviews.org [13].

The sheer volume of users and nodes that are now connected to the Internet is the other important factor that has led to the huge increase in the current Internet routing table size. There are 1,966,514,816 Internet users as of June 30th, 2010 [15]. This means almost 1/3rd of the world's population are now connected to the Internet. The Internet has penetrated almost each and every country in the world. This wide spread geography of the Internet meant that large chunks of IP addresses would have to be broken down to cater the needs of individuals around the globe. This has led to the wide spread use of CIDR to break down classful addresses into smaller subnets to be distributed among various nations, ISPs, cities, businesses and homes. This exponential increase in the users and nodes connected to the Internet has eventually led to large number of advertised networks; meaning that the routers at the core of the Internet would have to keep all these advertised networks in their routing table and then make appropriate routing decisions. For each packet that a router has to route, it has to perform a route lookup and if the routing table is large, the route lookup can cause significant delay.

Border Gateway Protocol or BGP is the routing protocol of the Internet. BGP is a path vector routing protocol making complex routing decision based on various negotiated policies. If there are multiple routes to a single network, BGP selects the best route and places that particular route on the routing table. Since the Internet is a huge mesh there could be many possible ways to reach a particular network. The BGP Routing Information Base or RIB, is a table containing all possible routes to all the networks in use. From this table, the best possible route is selected. As of July 2010, the number of RIB entries in core routers of the Internet has reached more than 325000 [1]. The huge size of the RIB table is another significant problem that vendors are coping with. Processing such a large number of entries causes significant load on the routers and directly affects routing latency.

2. Problem Description

The unprecedented growth of the Internet has led to some fundamental routing problems. The routing table and the BGP RIB sizes have become enormous and continue to increase in size with each passing day. The global routing table size increases almost 16 percent annually compared to the RAM speed, which increases only 10 percent annually [7]. The routers at the core of the Internet make routing decisions after going through these large tables, which affects their efficiency. If a router reaches a point where it does not have the memory to store any more routes, it might simply crash or start behaving abnormally [2]. The presence of these large tables could also lead to new kind of Denial of Service or DoS attack.

The other issue with large routing and BGP tables is the time that it takes for these routers to converge. If a router crashes or there is a change in routing information for a large network segment, these routers have to process the new routing information, which takes significant amount of time even with enough memory and CPU cycles. Routers can only process a limited amount of information in a given interval of time. CPU cycles are allocated in a way that the new routing information does not overwhelm the router. This can cause a significant amount of down time. Vendors and ISPs have started to look beyond traditional routing architectures and many of them have started migrating to Multi Protocol Label Switching or MPLS which is a relatively new switching technology. In order to run a network with BGP, all core routers as well as the edge routers need to run BGP whereas when using BGP in conjunction with MPLS, only the edge routers need to run BGP, thus reducing routing load.

The vendors are trying hard to keep up with this growth but since the rate at which the Internet is growing is much higher than the rate at which hardware technology is progressing, they have started to realize that they could be eventually heading towards a dead end.

3. Hypothesis

Large routing tables affect the performance of routers and studying route lookup process on routers with large routing tables could enable us to generate a new exploitation technique to slow down the routing process on routers by forcing lookup of infrequently used routes.

This research will help in validating the hypothesis by thorough and in-depth study of routers with large routing information both in static and dynamic routing scenarios. Analysis of empirical data collected during the experiment using Cisco 2811 series routers will be used in this validation.

4. Related Work

This section presents a few related research ideas and results that are important to this study of current Internet routing tables. The Literature review has been broadly classified into two sections. The first section has previous research information about Internet routing instability and their causes. This section is important because it is directly related to this paper, which focuses on overloading routers to test their performance parameters. The second section deals with routers handling the route information and how they process routing tables. This section is important as this could have security implications.

The authors of papers [3] and [8] were among the first to research the various reasons of Internet routing instability. They pointed out that routing instability in the Internet could originate due to router configuration errors, link problems, lack of router resources, etc. Any one of these could cause routes to appear or disappear (route flaps), which could eventually lead to degradation of end to end performance of the Internet.

The authors of the paper [4] performed lab based analysis of a few commonly used routers from different vendors. The main goal of this research was to study the effects on a router when it is overloaded with excessive routing information, like large routing updates, large routing tables, etc. An incorrectly configured router could sometimes introduce a large amount of routing information into the Internet routing system. This could result other routers in the chain to crash or operate incorrectly and could eventually lead to cascading failures.

The authors tested a few routers from Cisco and Juniper Networks. They experimentally loaded the routers beyond the specified limit. Different routers running different firmware versions responded differently from each other, but the overall result proved that the routers would either stop responding to that particular peer which caused the problem, reset all BGP peers, or the particular interface would simply stop responding. Any of these would result in network disruptions and at some point would require manual intervention. The researchers were able to conclude that it is possible for routers to fail if they were inadequately equipped to handle large amount of routing information injected into the network.

This paper goes a step further in order to determine the effects an over loaded router has on routing traffic.

The authors of research paper [5] performed experiments in the AT&T backbone to understand the stability of BGP in the Internet. They wanted to establish a relationship between the popularity of prefixes and its BGP stability. Previous research had shown that BGP updates were very frequent and could cause traffic delivery problems. This research was the first one to understand the dynamics of the BGP updates. With this research, the authors were able to establish the fact that a few popular destinations were responsible for carrying majority of the traffic and had relatively stable routes. The majority of the BGP updates and instability are caused by unpopular destinations, which do not carry a lot of traffic.

The presentation [6] was a study to understand the Autonomous System or AS level dynamics of the internet traffic flow. This study also reinstated the fact that a small percentage of the AS level topology is used to send and receive majority of the traffic on the Internet.

The author of the paper [9] primarily focuses on the importance of service guarantee in networks. The author then explores the various DoS attacks, which are difficult to fight and could easily disrupt genuine network traffic. With real time traffic in the picture, Quality of Service or QoS is very important and the author concludes with the fact the DoS can impact and reduce the QoS offered by networks.

Following the lines of the papers [5] and [6], my research would try and determine whether the popular destinations that carry the majority of the traffic are routed faster than the other traffic and also determine whether a router arranges its routing table lookup in the order of most used prefixes.

My research would also look at the security implications of the way routers handle the routing table. As mentioned by paper [9], DoS attacks can degrade network performance; my research would try to establish whether it is possible degrade network performance by generating legitimate network traffic (similar to some DoS attacks) directed towards not so frequently used prefixes of the routing table.

5. Methodology

This research is Quantitative in nature. The research results and conclusions are based on data collected from the lab-based setup and often compared to real world data.

This research was completed in two phases. The first phase was directed towards studying the effects of loading the routers with large amounts of routing information. The focus of the second phase of this experiment was to understand how routers processes large amounts of routing information and whether it is possible to exploit this behavior of routers. The second phase of this research also focuses on determining whether frequently used routes are processed faster than others.

Each of the phases in turn has two distinct case studies based on the differences in setup. The first case study deals with experiments using only static routes to load the routers. The second case study deals with experiments using BGP as a routing protocol to load the routers.

Since the routers used in the experiments had only 256Kbytes of non volatile configuration memory, the generated configurations file, which had a size starting at 3.78 Mbytes, had to be copied to the running memory which was 256 Mbytes. TFTP was used to copy the configuration file to the running configuration memory using the following command: *copy tftp running-config*

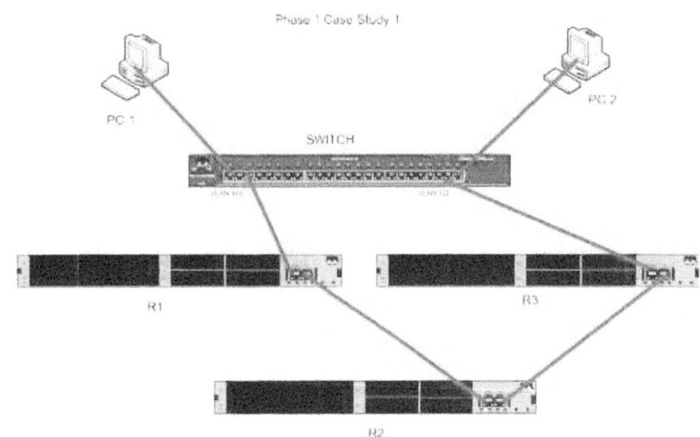

Figure 1. Phase 1 Case Study 1 network setup

Once the basic network connectivity was complete as shown in Figure 1, the respective devices were configured with appropriate IP addresses and connectivity from PC1 to PC2 was verified. Router R1 and R3 had default routes pointing towards R2 to simplify route processing on them. This configuration is called the base configuration for the devices where all the experiments would start. At this point a Perl script was used to generate a configuration file for router R2, which at the first instance of the experiment contained 60000 static routes pointing towards router R3, as shown below.

```
ip route 193.196.189.0 255.255.255.0 FastEthernet0/0 192.168.1.10
ip route 193.196.190.0 255.255.255.0 FastEthernet0/0 192.168.1.10
ip route 193.196.191.0 255.255.255.0 FastEthernet0/0 192.168.1.10
ip route 193.196.192.0 255.255.255.0 FastEthernet0/0 192.168.1.10
ip route 193.196.193.0 255.255.255.0 FastEthernet0/0 192.168.1.10
```

Once the file is copied to the running memory, the routers take significant amount of time to process this configuration file and actually use this. In this experiment I loaded the routers with static routes starting from 60,000 through 40,000 in 20,000 route increments. The time to process the configuration file at 60,000 routes was about 50 minutes. This value increased as the number of routes increased and while loading the router with 400,000 routes, the router required a total of 18 and 1/2 hours to process the file, which was copied into the running memory. During the period that the router slowly churns through the configuration file, it is almost non responsive and even the console connection to the router becomes non interactive.

Once the router R2 has processed the entire configuration and reaches a stable state to pass traffic, router R3 is configured to have 5 loopback interfaces with IP addresses randomly selected from the static routes configured on router R2. These 5 IP addresses become the destinations for which data is collected. The computer, PC2, is also used to collect data. Once the data is collected, the router R2 is reset to base configuration and the previous steps are repeated with 20,000 additional static routes maxing out at 400,000 routes.

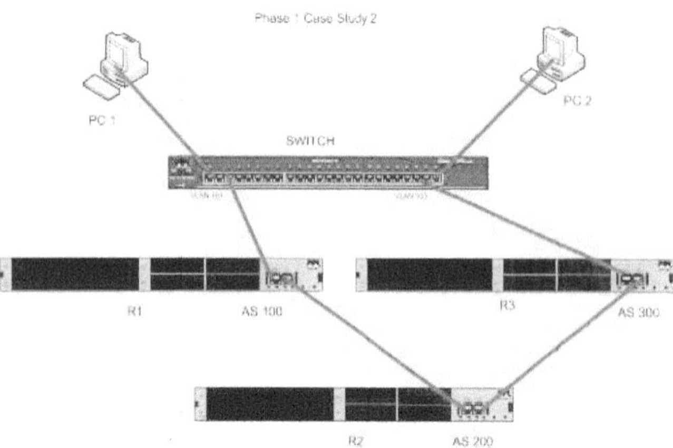

Figure 2. Phase 1 Case Study 2 network setup

Once the basic network connectivity is completed as shown in Figure 2, the respective devices are configured with appropriate IP addresses and connectivity from PC1 to PC2 is verified. Routers R1 and R3 have default routes pointing toward R2 to simplify route processing on them. This configuration is called the base configuration for the devices where all the experiments would start.

At this point a Perl script is used to generate a configuration file for router R3, which at the first instance of the experiment contained 60000 static routes. Once the router R3 has processed the entire configuration and reaches a stable state, eBGP is enabled on R2 and R3. This populates the routing table on R2 with large amount of BGP routes. Once router R2 has processed the entire configuration and reaches a stable state to pass traffic, router R3 is configured to have 5 loopback interfaces with IP addresses randomly selected from the BGP routing table on router R2. These 5 IP addresses become the destinations for which data is collected. Computer PC2 is also used to collect data.

Once data is collected, routers R2 and R3 are reset to base configuration and the prior steps are repeated with 20,000 additional static routes. The upper limit of this experiment is 200,000 BGP routes due to lack of memory on the routers.

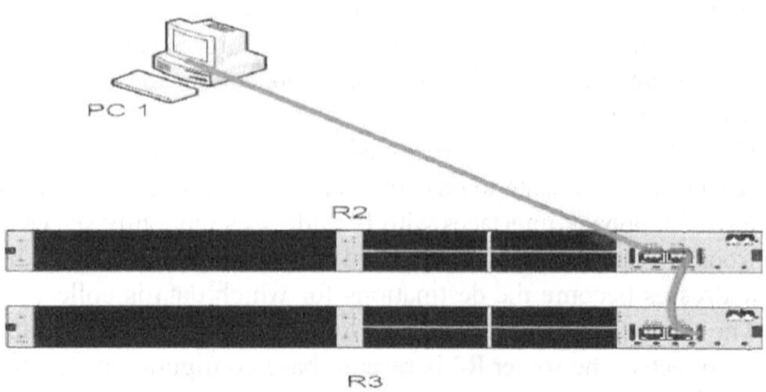

Figure 3. Phase 2 Case Study 1 network setup

Once the basic network connectivity is complete as shown in Figure 3, the respective devices are configured with appropriate IP addresses and basic connectivity from PC1 is verified. Router R3 has default routes pointing toward R2 to simplify route processing on it. This configuration is called the base configuration for the devices where all the experiments would start.

At this point the configuration file generated during Phase 1 containing 400,000 static routes is copied to router R2's running configuration memory.

Once router R2 has processed the entire configuration and reaches a stable state, the complete routing table from router R2 is captured on a text file as shown below.

```
R2#sh ip route
Codes: C - connected, S - static, R - RIP, M - mobile, B - BGP
       D - EIGRP, EX - EIGRP external, O - OSPF, IA - OSPF inter area
       N1 - OSPF NSSA external type 1, N2 - OSPF NSSA external type 2
       E1 - OSPF external type 1, E2 - OSPF external type 2
       i - IS-IS, su - IS-IS summary, L1 - IS-IS level-1, L2 - IS-IS level-2
       ia - IS-IS inter area, * - candidate default, U - per-user static route
       o - ODR, P - periodic downloaded static route

Gateway of last resort is not set

S    200.102.174.0/24 [1/0] via 192.168.1.10, FastEthernet0/0
S    200.85.157.0/24 [1/0] via 192.168.1.10, FastEthernet0/0
S    200.68.140.0/24 [1/0] via 192.168.1.10, FastEthernet0/0
S    200.51.251.0/24 [1/0] via 192.168.1.10, FastEthernet0/0
S    200.34.234.0/24 [1/0] via 192.168.1.10, FastEthernet0/0
```

With the entire routing table (400,000 routes) on a text file, I selected 50 IP addresses; every 8,000 (400000/50) routes from the routing table. These equally spaced IP addresses would form the test samples to determine the processing time of different routes positioned at different locations of the routing table.

Router R3 is configured to have 50 loopback interfaces with IP addresses previously selected from the routing table of R2. Data for all 50 IP addresses is collected from PC1, which directly connects to R2.

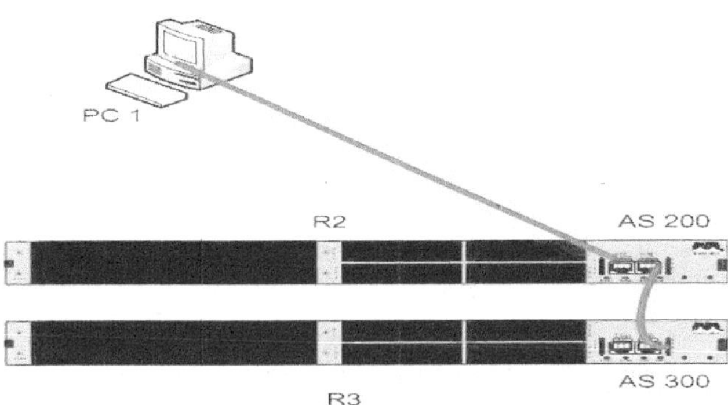

Figure 4. Phase 2 Case Study 2 network setup

Once the basic network connectivity is complete as shown in Figure 4, the respective devices are configured with appropriate IP addresses, and basic connectivity from PC1 is verified. Router R3 has default routes pointing toward R2 to simplify route processing. This configuration is called the base configuration for the devices where all the experiments would start.

At this point, the configuration file generated during Phase 1 containing 200,000 static routes is copied to the router R3's running configuration memory.

Once router R3 has processed the entire configuration and reaches a stable state, eBGP is enabled on R2 and R3. This populates the routing table on R2 with a large amount of BGP. This routing table is captured to a text file using the command shown below,

```
R2#sh ip route
Codes: C - connected, S - static, R - RIP, M - mobile, B - BGP
     D - EIGRP, EX - EIGRP external, O - OSPF, IA - OSPF inter area
     N1 - OSPF NSSA external type 1, N2 - OSPF NSSA external type 2
     E1 - OSPF external type 1, E2 - OSPF external type 2
     i - IS-IS, su - IS-IS summary, L1 - IS-IS level-1, L2 - IS-IS level-2
     ia - IS-IS inter area, * - candidate default, U - per-user static route
     o - ODR, P - periodic downloaded static route

Gateway of last resort is not set
B    193.187.122.0/24 [20/0] via 192.168.1.10, 1d00h
B    193.170.107.0/24 [20/0] via 192.168.1.10, 1d00h
B    193.153.88.0/24 [20/0] via 192.168.1.10, 1d00h
```

With the entire routing table (200000 routes) on a text file, I selected 50 IP addresses, every 4000 (200000/50) routes from routing table. These equally spaced IP addresses would form the test samples to determine the processing time of different routes positioned at different locations of the routing table.
Router R3 is configured to have 50 loopback interfaces with IP addresses previously selected from the routing table of R2. Data for the 50 IP addresses is collected from PC1, which is directly connected to R2.

6. Results

Data collected during the Phase 1 of this experiment was router memory, packet processing time and jitter. Router memory was a measure to check the load on the router with large routing tables and the *show ip route summary* command was used on the router to get this information. Traceroute was used to collect packet processing times and jitter value was collected using the tool iperf [15]. The packet processing time and jitter were used to determine network performance.

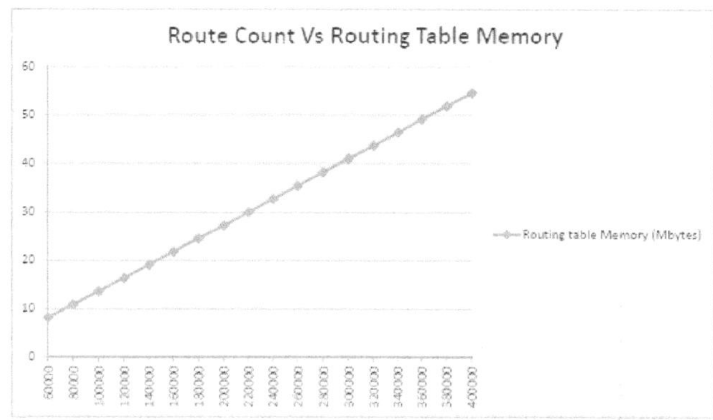

Figure 5. Phase 1 Case Study 1 Route count Vs Routing table memory

Figure 5 is a clear representation of the increasing memory usage with the increase in routing table size. This parameter displayed behavior as expected at the start of the experiment.

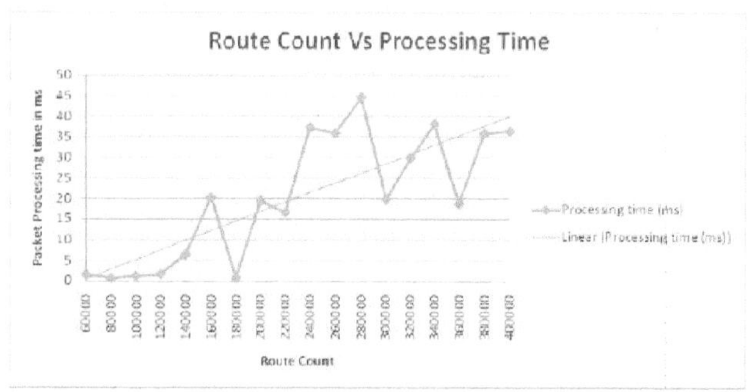

Figure 6. Phase 1 Case Study 1 Route count Vs Processing time

Figure 6 depicts the increasing trend of packet processing time with the increase in routing table size. At the start of the experiment, I had expected a more linear increase in the packet processing times. As seen in the graph, though the overall trend of packet processing time increases with the increase in routing table size, there are a few unexplained spikes in the packet processing time.

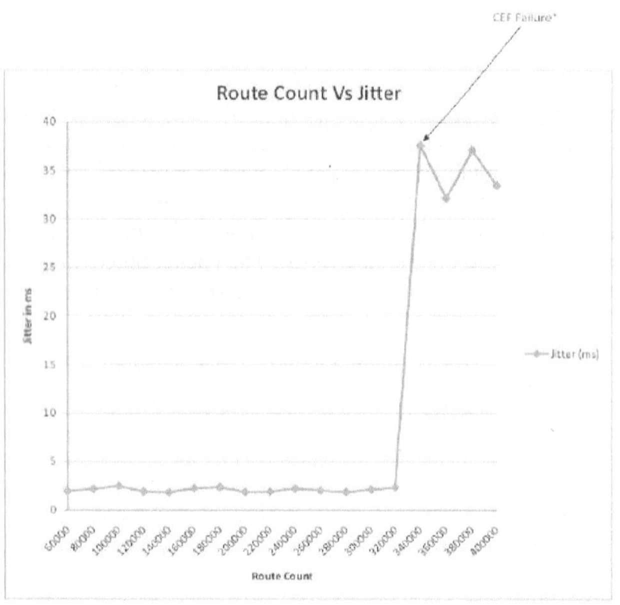

Figure 7. Phase 1 Case Study 1 Route count Vs Jitter

Figure 7 compares jitter to the increasing routing table size. The graph maintains a steady level until the routing table size reaches 340,000. At this point the router runs out of memory to incorporate the entire routing table into the Forwarding Information Base (FIB) table. The FIB table is used by the Cisco Express Forwarding (CEF) [11] mechanism, used by Cisco routers to speed up packet forwarding without having to perform traditional lookups. With the failure of CEF, the jitter value skyrockets from about 2ms to around 35ms. This in turn meant that packet delay variation had increased significantly now that the router had to go through the actual routing table before forwarding packets.

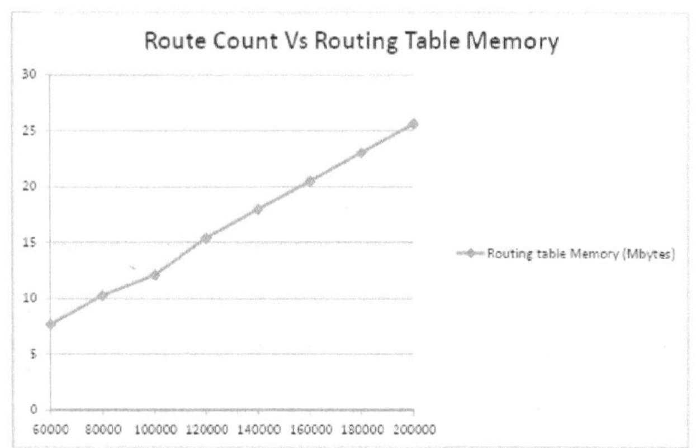

Figure 8. Phase 1 Case Study 2 Route count Vs Routing table memory

Figure 8 represents the increasing memory utilization with the increase in BGP routes. This increase is almost linear and indicates that the memory utilization of the router is directly proportional to the number of routes.

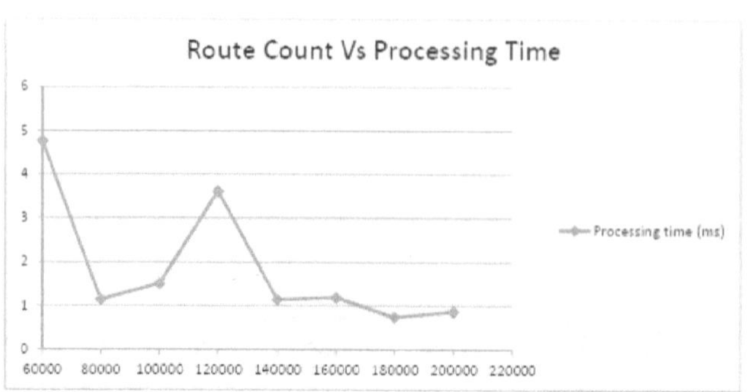

Figure 9. Phase 1 Case Study 2 Route count Vs Processing time

Figure 9 represents packet processing time against BGP route count. During the start of this experiment, I had expected the packet processing time to be fairly constant around the 1 – 2 ms second mark since this was the behavior shown during the static route testing until the 200,000 route mark. There were a few unexplained spikes in the packet processing time, but the overall trend is similar to the static route test at similar route counts. The packet processing time at 220,000 should have been theoretically infinite as the router was never able to process as many routes.

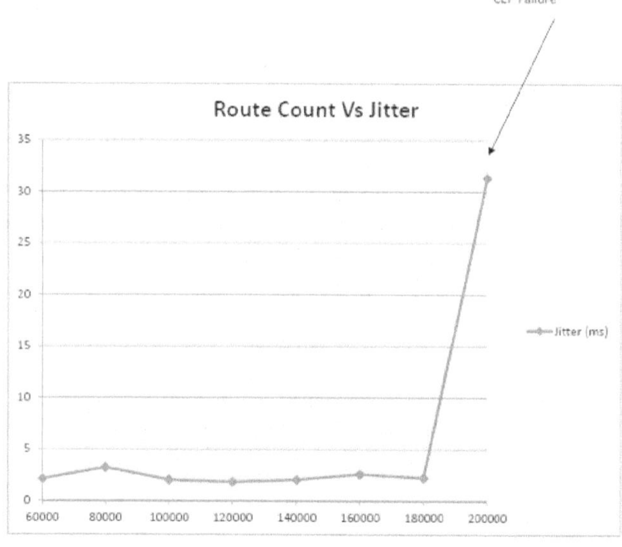

Figure 10. Phase 1 Case Study 2 Route count Vs Jitter

Figure 10 represents the jitter against the BGP router count. The jitter value can be seen to be fairly constant around 2 – 3 ms until about 180,000 – 200,000. Loading the router with 200,000 BGP routes is only possible by turning CEF (Cisco Express Forwarding) off. Similar to the static route case, once CEF is turned off the jitter value skyrockets to about 30 – 35ms.

Packet processing time was the only data collected during the phase 2 of this experiment. The data was collected at each of the 50 sample IP addresses.

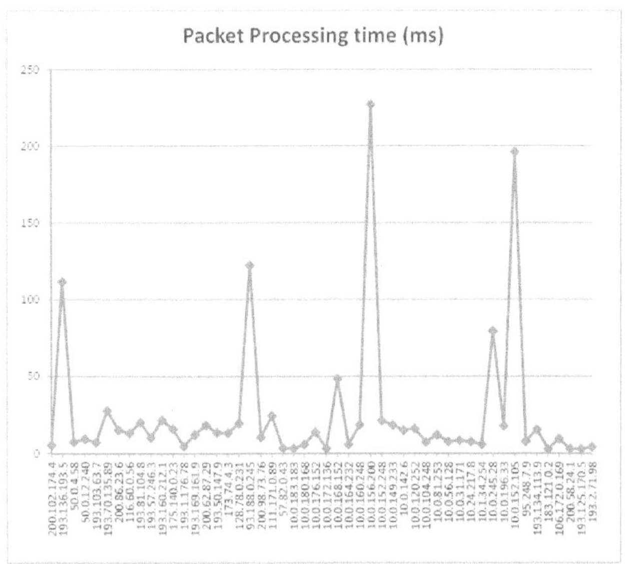

Figure 11. Phase 2 Case Study 1 Processing time samples

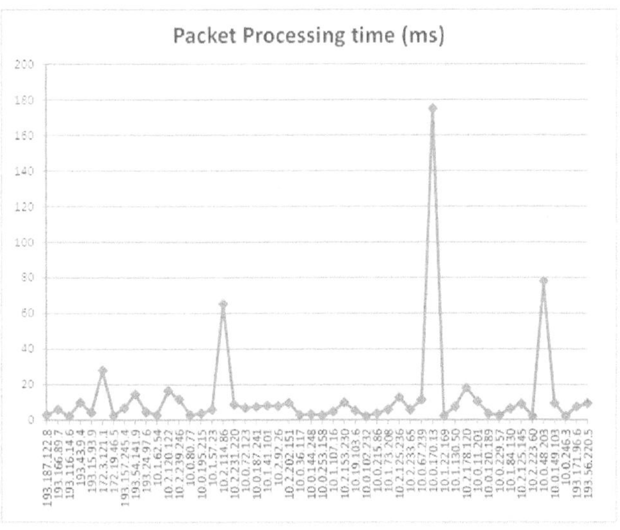

Figure 12. Phase 2 Case Study 2 Processing time samples

Figure 11 and 12 depicts the packet processing times for various IP address samples. The majority of the IP address samples have packet processing time around the 20 – 30 ms mark. In addition there are a few packets that have high packet processing times varying from around 50 – 230ms.

As an extension of phase 2 of this experiment, data was collected to determine whether the routers process frequently used prefixes faster than infrequently used ones. Figure 13 shows one such sample where a single IP address is traced in quick succession and the packet processing time at the router with the large number of prefixes is recorded.

```
IP 10.0.152.105

silvers@silvers-desktop:~$ sudo traceroute -I -n 10.0.152.105
traceroute to 10.0.152.105 (10.0.152.105), 30 hops max, 40 byte packets
 1  192.168.100.1  3.988 ms  3.740 ms  3.641 ms
 2  10.0.152.105  3.557 ms  3.481 ms  3.404 ms

silvers@silvers-desktop:~$ sudo traceroute -I -n 10.0.152.105
traceroute to 10.0.152.105 (10.0.152.105), 30 hops max, 40 byte packets
 1  192.168.100.1  1.823 ms  13.967 ms  13.876 ms
 2  10.0.152.105  13.793 ms  13.716 ms  13.638 ms

silvers@silvers-desktop:~$ sudo traceroute -I -n 10.0.152.105
traceroute to 10.0.152.105 (10.0.152.105), 30 hops max, 40 byte packets
 1  192.168.100.1  1.337 ms  5.368 ms  4.729 ms
 2  10.0.152.105  4.621 ms  4.541 ms  3.941 ms

silvers@silvers-desktop:~$ sudo traceroute -I -n 10.0.152.105
traceroute to 10.0.152.105 (10.0.152.105), 30 hops max, 40 byte packets
 1  192.168.100.1  3.543 ms  2.881 ms  2.786 ms
 2  10.0.152.105  2.700 ms  2.623 ms  3.294 ms
```

Figure 13. Data sample for consecutive traces

7. Observations

The important observation from phase 1 of this experiment was the fact that loading routers with enough routing information affects its performance and effectively the performance of the network. Figures 6, 7, 9 and 10 clearly depict this behavior.

The most important observation in the phase 2 of this experiment is the positioning of the samples in the routing table. As seen in the figures 11 and 12, the high packet processing times are not located just at the end of the routing table but also at the beginning of the routing table. At the start of this experiment, my assumption was that the router would take more time to process packets which had destinations at the end of the routing table since it would have go through more entries to reach there. The result of this experiment proved that the theory is wrong, and one possible reason could be that the router does not use the routing table in the sequence that is displayed when using the *show ip route command.* The other significant observation from the phase 2 of this experiment was the fact that the routers do not process frequently used subnets or destinations any faster than the ones which are not used as often. Successive lookups for the same destination in a quick succession of time yielded results which proved the hypothesis wrong.

8. Conclusions

The findings of this research conclude that large routing tables have a significant impact on the router performance. The other important conclusion is the uncertainty in predicting the behavior of routing table processing on a router.

Phase 1 of this research clearly indicated that increasing the routing table size on a router increases the packet processing times on the router. Post CEF failure, the jitter values also become fairly high indicating the performance degradation of the network. Based on this part of the research it can be concluded that it is very necessary to provision router correctly if we need good network performance. We should always keep in mind that Internet routing tables could be unstable at times and inject unusually large amounts of routing information to routers. In case the routers do not have enough memory and processor cycles to process these spikes, they would crash, causing large downtimes as these routers need a lot of time to stabilize and start processing packets after a crash or a reboot.

Phase 2 of the research indicated that predicting the route look up behavior is difficult. The routers do not process routes at the top of the table any faster than the ones at the bottom. Routes at the bottom of the routing table have processing time similar to ones at the top of the table. The other important conclusion from this research was that routers do not process frequently used routes faster than the routes which are not. This behavior of routers made it almost impossible to formulate an exploitation script to make use of the route processing procedure.

9. Future Work

This research can be further extended by using different routers models as well as routers from different vendors like Juniper Networks etc. This research was performed on a router which was not processing packets other than the experimental packets. A good next step would be to study routers with significant traffic other than the experimental traffic to take the study even closer to actual Internet routers.

Traffic generators and advanced visualization tools would enhance this study and could be used when this study is taken to the next step.

10. Acknowledgments

I would like to thank Professors Bruce Hartpence and Daryl Johnson for their ideas that helped me complete this study.

11. References

[1] http://bgp.potaroo.net/

[2] Elliott Karpilovsky, Jennifer Rexford, *Using Forgetful Routing to Control BGP Table Size*, ACM 2006.

[3] Craig Labovitz, G. Robert Malan, and Farnam Jahanian, *Internet Routing Instability*, Proceedings of the ACM SIGCOMM '97

[4] D.-F. Chang, R. Govindan, and J. Heidemann, *An empirical study of router response to large BGP routing table load*, in Proc. Internet Measurement Workshop, November 2002.

[5] Jennifer Rexford , Jia Wang , Zhen Xiao , Yin Zhang, *BGP routing stability of popular destinations*, Proceedings of the 2nd ACM SIGCOMM Workshop on Internet measurement, November 06-08, 2002, Marseille, France.

[6] Steve Uhlig, *AS-level traffic characteristics and their implications on traffic engineering, Measuring and modeling the Internet*, Louvain-la-neuve, Nov. 30 - Dec. 2, 2005.

[7] http://arstechnica.com/security/news/2008/01/internet-routing-growing-pains.ars/1

[8] Craig Labovitz, G. Robert Malan, and Farnam Jahanian, *Origins of Internet Routing Instability*, IEEE INFOCOMM, 1999.

[9] Philippe Owezarski, *On the Impact of DoS Attacks on Internet Traffic Characteristics and QoS*, IEEE INFOCOMM 2005.

[10] http://www.netdigix.com/servers.html

[11] http://www.cisco.com/en/US/tech/tk827/tk831/tk102/tsd_technology_support_sub-protocol_home.html

[12] http://openmaniak.com/iperf.php

[13] http://www.routeviews.org

[14] http://www.cisco.com

[15] http://iperf.fr/

SESSION

NETWORK SECURITY I

Chair(s)

Dr. Alan Kebert

Private Proximity Testing For Location Based Services

L. Ertaul, A Balluru, A. Perumalsamy

Math and Computer Science Department, California State University, East Bay
California, USA
Levent.ertaul@csueastbay.edu, aballuru@horizoncsueastbay.edu, aperumalsamy@horizoncsueastbay.edu

Abstract— **Over time privacy attacks on the Internet and Internet–attached systems have grown sophisticated and attacks have become more automated and can cause greater amounts of damage. Thus, a wide range of technologies and tools, complex protocols and applications are needed to counter the growing threat. This paper deals with the implementation and analysis of private proximity testing in the context of Location Based Services (LBS). The protocol states that Alice and Bob can investigate their proximity by exchanging set of encrypted messages via the server. The approach is novel since the server will not be able to track either Alice or Bob.**

***Index Terms*—Location Based Services, Proximity Testing, Privacy.**

I. INTRODUCTION

Location Based Services (LBS) are ubiquitous in today's applications. They are an indispensable component of our communication model as LBS has proven to be crucial not only for the companies but also for the consumers. Tracking and monitoring individuals, children and thieves and its uses in the law enforcement by police really has good implication on the society. In case of business as a vehicle tracking device or asset tracking component, LBS technology acts as a catalysts in the growth of industries especially telecommunication and transportation. However, as the system deals with confidential personal information like location, personal mobile number, concerning address, it becomes vital for the operator to offer adequate security for maintaining user's privacy [3, 4, and 10].

LBS, besides providing numerous services to consumers worldwide, they are also notorious in collecting user activity. This helps them target specific products at individuals which is a market proven strategy for increased growth. Vendors of many of the mobile applications often exploit the data that is collected by the use of their services. Location-based service advertising -- which ties in consumer locations with restaurants, retail shops and other locations through mobile devices -- will grow to over one-third of all mobile advertising in four years [14, 15 and 16].

According to a study by Pyramid Research [17], location-based revenue in the US is expected to climb from $2.8 billion in 2010 to $10.3 billion in 2015. By 2015, location-based advertising will be $6.2 billion, according to Pyramid Research. In 2010, location-based advertising was $588 million -- 18.5% of all mobile advertising. Location-based advertising will generate 60% of all location-based revenue in four years. Pyramid analyst Jan ten Sythoff believes that all forms of mobile advertising will grow. "However, local search will be the most important driver of location-based advertising revenues." Not only the developers of navigation applications will be changing their business model to fit into the local-search branch, but many different companies from different branches can also profit from the growth the of the local-search market – from start-ups like Poynt and Yelp, to the local business advertising from specialized portals like the Yellow Pages, to even the search engines that are specialized for a particular topic, like toptable or HotelBooker. The survey conducted by Pyramid shows the amount of revenue generated by the use of LBS.

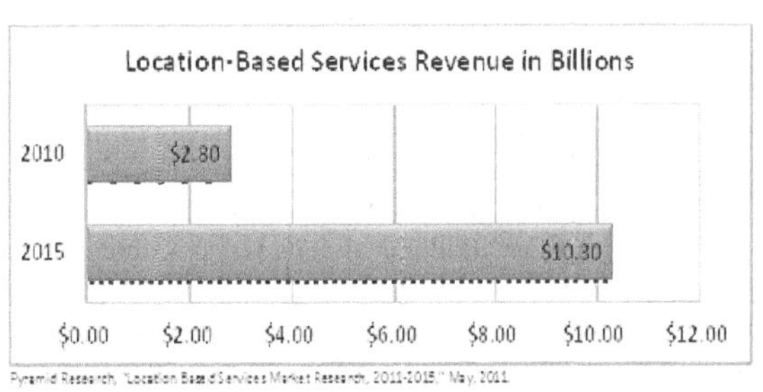

Fig 1.1LBS Services Revenue

The figure contrasts the revenue generated in 2010 vs. the projected estimate for the year 2015. It is observed that this amount is indeed staggering. This definitely suggests that data mining resulting from the use of LBS is a big boost to their revenues.

When is a person permitted to monitor someone by using LBS? Should the concerned person's consent is necessary? What about individual right and personal autonomy? What kinds of evidences are required to monitor a person? These are some of the questions that need to be answered before using LBS as monitoring a person can have psychological effect on the person being monitored. In case of monitoring criminals or suspects by police or security agencies the question of individual freedom came, as enforcing someone's freedom is not at all ethical when the person is only suspected of committing the crime. We notice a varying level of concern between male and female users. This is shown in Fig 1.2

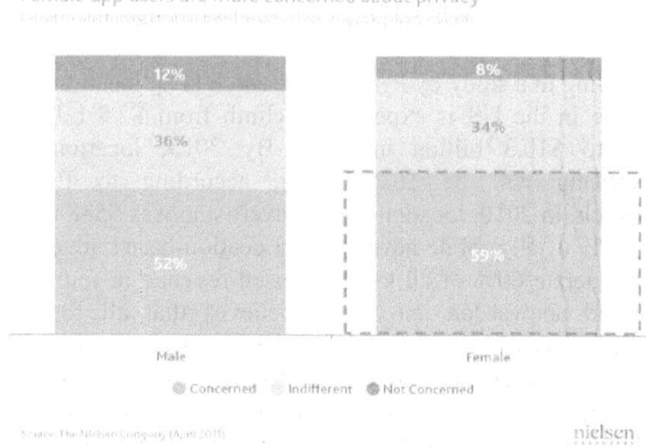

Fig 1.2 Level of privacy concern between male and female users

However, in the whole privacy and security issues of LBS, there are chiefly four points came as control, trust, privacy and security as legal, social, ethical and technological aspects. But all four are mutually exclusive as control decreases trust, trust enhances privacy, which needs security, and security again increases control.

Control (Legal) – Commonly GPS and other LBS devices are used to control and offer various types of services to the user. Personally it controls one's own direction of moving in guiding the right way. In case of child tracking, parents have exclusive right to look after their children, as it is not possible for the young ones to make their own decision. So it is their legal right to monitor their children thereby reflecting a sense of caring. In case of law enforcement, special laws provide legal rights to police or security departments to keep an eye on criminals or suspect.

Trust (Social) – In social life trust is the most essential part in human relationship. However, the use of LBS is being practiced in low trust conditions. Monitoring someone with the help of tracking system really affects personal relationship but as far as tracking criminals by cops or tracking children by parents are concerned, it is for the welfare of the individual & society.

Privacy (Ethical) – As a human being, everyone has the right to privacy or being free from intrusion or disturbances in one's personal life. But in case of LBS or any other telecommunication technologies dealing with transformation of various kinds of information, it becomes essential to provide adequate security to these kinds of data for not being misused by any unauthorized person. Tracking and monitoring someone without his/her consent is purely unethical so needs high level of security. But again as in case of law and order where tracking devices are used to monitor criminals becomes essential for the sake of society as a whole. Here, social security is counted higher than Individual safety and security.

Security (Technological) – Again for maintaining privacy, security system should be strong. Every technology has both positive and negative impact on human life and LBS also has shortcomings by locating accurate information data or even easily given access to unauthorized person. On one hand LBS enhances both national and personal security but create another problem for the privacy of individual by not providing a foolproof security system to that highly sensitive information stored in its database. For obtaining security, one needs to do a little compromise on his/her privacy but to what extent is a question. Fig 1.3 below shows is a survey conducted to gauge the concerns of various smart phone users and their use of LBS Despite the various concerns as posed by LBS, it is still considered as an invaluable tool for efficient communication. Following section will contrast the risks and benefits of LBS.

II. FAST ASYNCHRONOUS PRIVATE PROXIMITY TEST WITH AN OBLIVIOUS SERVER

There are a variety of Private Equality Testing protocols available [13, 14, and 15]. This protocol is a novel approach proposed and implemented by a team of researchers at the Stanford University. This protocol unlike its variant operates asynchronously, which implies that the two parties do not have to be online at the same time. In other words, it can be seen as a two party protocol at any instant of time where the interaction happens between a client and the server. In this setting, the server is responsible for not only handling the transactional requests but also performing some mathematical operations that will be discussed shortly.

The reason for making server more involved in this form of testing is to prevent dictionary attacks. This attack is possible if the application was a mere non-interactive message transferring between two parties exchanging only hash of their locations. The asynchronous setting allows a privacy-efficiency tradeoff due to the fact that the sender and receiver can each execute their half of the protocol with the server at arbitrary times. Specifically, a user might configure her/his device to participate in the protocol in the role of sender only when her location changes. Similarly, she/he might configure her device to participate in the role of receiver only when she explicitly checks the proximity testing application. For the sake of the explanation, Bob would be the sender side of the client application and Alice would be the receiver side of the application.

The protocol requires Alice and Bob to generate quantized location values which is representative of the center of the grid that they belong to. The protocol states that if their quantized locations match, Alice can know that they are in the same grid otherwise she can only know that Bob is in a different location than her location and nothing else. Bob does not learn anything in this process. It is assumed that the keys K_{ab}, K_b, K_a shared between Alice and Bob, Bob and the Server, Alice and server respectively are distributed using the concept of Social Keys[12].

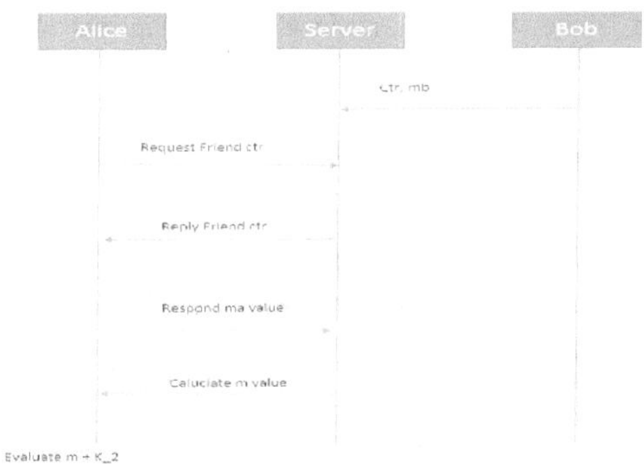

Fig 1.3 Private Proximity Testing

Application Set Up: The protocol generates 64 bits of quantized location data which is a function of the actual location of the client. It then generates three 64 bit parameters ***K_1, K_2*** and ***r*** using a secure pseudo-random function ***F (k, x)***, where ***K*** is the key for the secure pseudo-random function and ***x*** is the counter value that will be used to generate the pseudo-random number. Our implementation uses AES in ECB mode as the pseudo-random function [11]. There are three categories of messages that are exchanged in this protocol as shown in figure 1.3

Message 1: Bob computes the counter value as a function of time of day which is a 64 bit data. The counter (***ctr***) is incremented by one every time the pseudo-random function is called to generate ***K_1, K_2*** and ***r*** values. This is shown as follows:

$$K\_1 = F(K_{ab}, ctr + 1);\ K\_2 = F(K_{ab}, ctr + 1)$$

$$R = F(K_b, ctr + 1)$$

Bob then masks his quantized location ***Bt*** as ***Mb = r (Bt + K_1) + K_2*** and transmits this message along with the counter value. Server on receiving the counter value calculates r and stores it.

Message 2: This step is initiated by Alice when she desires to query about Bob. She first sends a query message to the server asking for Bob's counter value. The server looks up the request in its database and sends the counter value of the friend if it is fresh. On receiving the response from server, Alice then checks if the counter is fresh or not. If it is fresh, she calculates ***K_1, K-2*** using the pseudo-random function with the key she shares with Bob. Essentially, the ***K_1*** and ***K_2*** generated by Bob must match her values. She then masks her quantized location ***At*** by calculating ***Ma = At + K_1***. She then sends this value to server.
Message 3: Server on receiving the message from Alice calculates a value m as:

$$m = r * ma - m2$$

Alice receives this response and computes ***m + K_2***. If this yields a value of ***0***, it implies that Alice and Bob are close by or rather in the same grid. The value comes to be zero only if the quantized locations match. This is illustrated as below:

$$\begin{aligned} m &= r * ma - mb \\ &= r * (At + k1) - r * (Bt + k1) - k2 \\ &= r * (At - Bt) + k2 \end{aligned}$$

A non-zero value only implies that they are not close to each other and nothing else. Bob is not intimated about anything. He is not aware if anybody is looking for him. The following section will deal in detail regarding the various design decisions taken and the challenges faced. The performance and security of our implementation is also measured.

III. IMPLEMENTATION MODEL

Platform Details – We developed the protocol as a TCP/IP client server model on Java platform on Windows 7 operating system. Java's crypto library provided the AES based pseudo-random function. The key sizes were 128 bits. We have used JAVA SWT to implement the GUI for the application. The table below summarizes the platform details of our implementation.

Table 1.1 Implementation Platform Details

Runtime Environment	Java SE 1.6
Network Model	TCP/IP Client Server Model
Platform	NetBeans
GUI	Java SWT
Programming Language	Java
Operating Systems	Windows 7
Crypto Library	Javax.Crypto
Pseudo Random Function	AES – 128 bits ECB

Key sizes	128 bits
K_1,K_2,r,mb,ma,ctr sizes	64 bits

Message Formats – The client application communicates with the TCP client via messages in IP format. Each packet is of 25 bytes in size. For various messages following table 1.2 describes the transmission message format.

Table 1.2 Transmission Message Formats

Message Number	Packet Type	Description
Message A	3	The client queries for its friend's location data. If the requested friend's counter value is available, the server responds the same to Alice.
Message B	5	The client performs calculations and sends the same to the server. Expects a response with value m from the server.
Message C	7	The client wishes to update the location to the server and sends its counter and mb value.

The first byte of the messages sent from the client to the server denotes the packet type. All the messages contain the user ID of the initiator. The generic format of the message from the client to the server is as follows:

Table 1.3 Format of Client-Server Message

Packet Type	Client ID	Friend ID	Payload

All packets from the client have packet IDs of 3, 5, and 7. If a packet of any other ID is received, it is discarded.

Ideal Conditions vs. Assumptions– We have attempted to model various real life scenarios to a large extent; however, there is a scope of incorporating many more features to make the application more versatile. This section deals with the design decisions taken for the sake of the implementation and a possible solution that would be more suitable for real life application.

1. **Key Distribution** – Our application requires three secure 128 bit keys to be distributed K_{ab}, K_b, K_a which is shared between Alice and Bob, Server and Bob, and Server and Alice respectively. The secure distribution of these keys is vital for the security of this protocol since they are used to in the secure pseudo-random generator (AES) [11]. The level of security in this field will ensure to keep dictionary attacks at bay. In our implementation we have assumed that the keys have already been distributed securely and that all the parties know the keys required by each other. One of the ideal methods of key distribution will be the concept of Social Keys. SocialKeys embraces the idea that public keys must be associated with the digital identities that people widely own use, i.e., their social network accounts, rather than requiring the creation of new identities for cryptographic purposes. Although not novel in its approach, this may seem to be a more viable option as there is no involvement of a third party for maintenance of the keys. Instead various features of the Social Network are repurposed in order to achieve this. By offloading the establishment of trust between users to the social network, SocialKeys obviates the need for a "key manager". As a consequence, it is almost completely transparent to the user.

2. **User IDs** – On the same lines as the key distribution, the user IDs have been manually assigned to the users. It is given as an input when the application is fired up. Ideally, the user IDs would pertain to the social network user account since the key retrieval also happens from SocialKeys.

3. **Quantized Location Data** – The application requires generating quantized location data. This data is obtained by dividing an area of certain range into overlapping hexagonal grids as shown in the Fig 1.5. The grids are represented by the center of the grid. Users belonging to any one grid will have a quantized location that is referred to the center of the grid that they belong to. If Alice is in grid marked x and her friends in the same grid, then the protocol results in letting Alice know that they are in the same grid or not. Other users are not aware of anything. The use of quantized location further masks the actual location of the user and is way of representation of the location. This quantized location is represented by 64 bits of data [20, 21]. The grids themselves, ideally must be allowed for user configuration [5]. Fig 1.4 is as below.

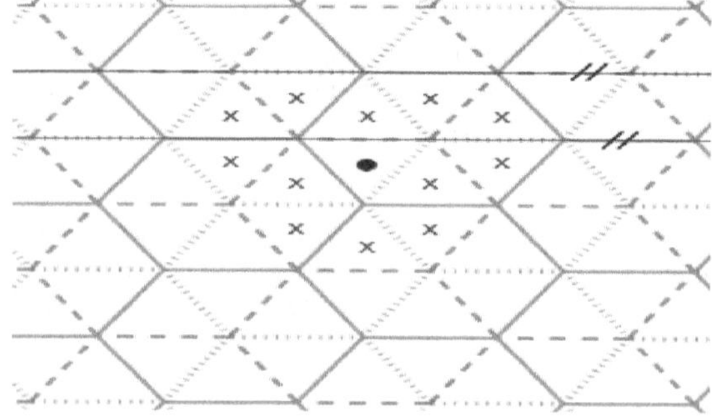

Fig 1.4 Grid structure for user configuration

However, in our implementation, we are randomly generating the quantized locations and feeding it to the application.

4. **Boundary Conditions** – The proximity testing allows applications to test for proximity besides equality. This allows users to determine the relative closeness even if they don't belong to the same grid. This is especially useful as it test for the boundary conditions. This is discussed at length in [1]. Based on the grid structure shown in Fig 1.4.However, in our application we would be testing for equality where in if the users are in the same grid, they are said to be close.

Performance Analysis – The protocol was executed on Windows environment with Intel core i3 with a processor speed 4 GHz. A very comprehensive study of the performance of the protocol was conducted. As noted by the authors of the protocols and in my research, I have concluded that the protocol is definitely an improvement over the synchronous version of the protocol. There are many reasons that contribute towards this agenda.

A. **Synchronous vs. Asynchronous mode of execution** – Unlike synchronous counterpart of this protocol, the clients after having updated their locations can go offline and be still probed for proximity by their friends while being offline. This reduces tremendous overhead on the communication network as there is no necessity of clients being connected to the server at all times.

B. **64 bits of data for communication** – This implementation requires 64 bits of data for representing data values of counter, AES generated random values, quantized location data, masked location data. A 64 bits of data representation was used as it is established for security purposes. Also the effective bytes per edge is still 8 bytes compared to 4 bytes if 32 bits of data was used. This is not as much of an overhead still.

C. **Delay Analysis** – The delay analysis is a crucial aspect of the protocol as it justifies the design decisions. The following table describes the delay analysis on the client side that updates its location data to server.

Table 1.4

Attempt #	Delay (milliSec)
1	358
2	258
3	263
4	308
5	297

The following table describes the delay analysis on the client side that queries the counter value of the friend from the server

Table 1.5

Attempt #	Delay (milliSec)
1	255
2	269
3	247
4	303
5	266

The above results are reflective for a setup of 2 client and one server system. However, based on the result, we can extrapolate the result that it may take about 2.5 seconds to 3 seconds on a computer with this environment to execute for about 100 friends. This can be established since the messages get multiplexed and sent as a package to the server and the same is received from the server. Hence there will be no more overhead in establishing connection with 100friends than it is for 1 friend.

Security – The security of a system is always under attack when there is an involvement of a party besides the participants of the application. In our case, as has already been stated, the server is involved in processing of some of the messages and computing values that help Alice determine proximity. Even though the quantized locations are masked, there are two possibilities of attacks that can be immediately seen.

First is the case when the server and Bob collude. If so, Bob can easily estimate Alice's location. Likewise, if Alice colludes with server, Bob's location can be estimated.

Challenges – There were many challenges that were encountered in the implementation of the protocol. Following is a list of few of them:

a. Configuring of the TCP/IP server
b. Determining the packet format for transaction.
c. Determining number of bytes for each field.
d. Assigning keys to various users.
e. Integration with GUI
f. Determining the mode of operation of AES function.

Screenshots: Following are some screenshots for the execution of the protocol. Figure below shows the scenario when Bob updates his location with server with an ID of 1000.

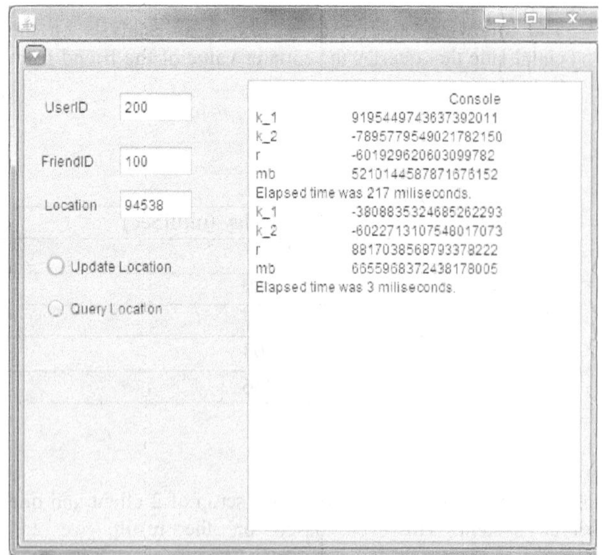

Fig 1.5 Result window for Location Update

Following is a figure that shows the execution of querying of location of Bob by Alice.

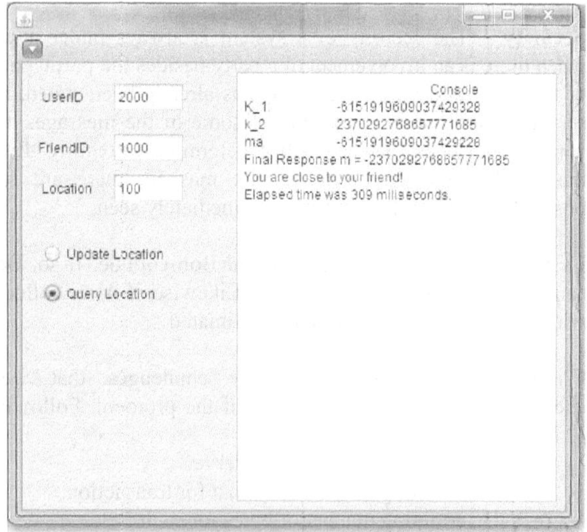

Fig 1.6 Result window for Proximity Testing

IV. Conclusions

Location-based social networks carry user-driven geographical information, and bridge the gap between real-world and online social media. In this paper we implemented Asynchronous proximity testing protocol without revealing actual location information of the user. This protocol does not leak any information about the secret value thus and preserves privacy of the user however there are still some issues to be resolved.

Instead using random number representation for the location data, a real time location data can be obtained from the LBS like Loopt, Google Latitude etc. Moreover session events can be developed to preserve previous activities and user can be requested to have login and password information because, If no session events are stored, So If server or client goes down will cause loss of data and new session should be started to run the system.

It is very important to ensure the privacy of the data. There has been extensive research in the field of providing security to many aspects of LBS services [19], [20].

References

[1] Narayanan, Thiagarajan, Lakshmi, Boneh, Hamburg, on Location Privacy via proximity testing, IEEE

[2] S. Jarecki, X.Liu, on Efficient Oblivious Pseudorandom Function IEEE, 2009

[3] R. D. Hopkins, R. Ho, I.E. Sutherland on Proximity Communications, IEEE, 2004.

[4] F.Olumofin,Tysowoski,Goldberg,Hengartner on Achieving Efficient Query Privacy for Location Based Services, IEEE, 2010

[5] C.Gentry, Fully Homomorphic encryption using ideal lattices, IEEE,2009

[6] M. Naor, B. Pinkas on Oblivious transfer and polynomial evaluation, IEEE, 1999.

[7] M. Raya, J.P Hubaux on The Security of Ad Hoc Networks, IEEE, 2005

[8] Rahman, S. Halles on A Distributed tust Model, New Security Paradigms, 2006

[9] Drost,R. Forrest, C. ; Guenin, B. ; Ho, R. ; Krishnamoorthy, A.V. ; Cohen, D. ; Cunningham, J.E. ; Tourancheau, B. ; Zingher, A.; Chow, A. ; Lauterbach, G. ; Sutherland, I on High Performance Interconnects, IEEE, 2005.

[10] Kuper A; Treu G; on Efficient proximity and separation detection among mobile targets for supporting location-based community services; ACM Digital Library, 2006

[11] J. Daemen and V. Rijmen, AES Proposal: Rijndael, AES Algorithm Submission, published and accepted in http://csrc.nist.gov/publications/fips/

[12] R. McGeehan, My Public Key (Facebook application) http://www.facebook.com/apps/application.php?id=7923770364

[13] F. Boudot, B. Schoenmakers, and J. Traore. A fair and efficient solution to the socialist millionaires' problem.Discrete Applied Mathematics, 2001

[14] R. Fagin, M. Naor, and P. Winkler. Comparing information without leaking it. Comm. of the ACM, 39:77– 85, 1996.

[15] S. Mascetti, D. Freni, C. Bettini, X. S. Wang, and S. Jajodia, "Privacy in geo-social networks: proximity notification with untrusted service providers and curious buddies," VLDB J.

[16] L. Siksnys, J. R. Thomsen, S. Saltenis, and M. L. Yiu, "Private and flexible proximity detection in mobile social networks," in Mobile Data Management, T. Hara, C. S. Jensen, V. Kumar, S. Madria, and D. Zeinalipour-Yazti, Eds. IEEE Computer Society, 2010.

[17] http://www.pyramidresearch.com/store/Report-Location-Based-Services.htm

[18] Data Analysis on Location-Based Social Networks, Huiji Gao and Huan Liu white paper.

[19] Analysis of a Location-Based Social Network, Chen Guanling, Computational Science and Engineering, 2009. CSE '09. International Conference, Aug. 2009

[20] M. Freedman, K. Nissim, and B. Pinkas. Efficient private matching and set intersection. In Proc. of Eurocrypt' 04, pages 1–19. Springer-Verlag, 2004.

[21] C. Hazay and Y. Lindell. Efficient protocols for set intersection and pattern matching with security against malicious and covert adversaries. In Theory of cryptography (TCC), pages 155–175, 2008.

DROP-FAST: Defending against DDoS Attacks using Cloud Technology

Rashad Aliyev[1], **Dongwon Seo**[2], **and Heejo Lee**[2]
[1]Department of Computer Science and Engineering, Korea University, Seoul 136-713, Republic of Korea
[2]Department of Computer Science and Engineering, Korea University, Seoul 136-713, Republic of Korea

Abstract—*DDoS attacks continue to be a major threat to network security. Several new types of attacks such as Layer-7 attacks (e.g., HTTP flood, Slowloris, RUDY, etc.) have emerged. We propose a novel DDoS defense mechanism called DROP-FAST. Our mechanism provides distributed DDoS defense utilizing multiple replicas of the protected server throughout a cloud infrastructure. DROP-FAST is dynamic and can adapt by controlling the number of replicas on cloud based on attack strength. Main server is isolated from network using replica servers. Service quality features such as response time, incoming traffic load, and load sharing are improved due to distribution of attack and replication of the main server throughout the cloud. We describe our mechanism in detail and discuss improvements made over previously existing related works. We set up an experiment that shows significant improvement of the traffic load on the main server as a result of utilizing DROP-FAST mechanism.*

Keywords: DDoS Attack, Cloud Computing, Load Sharing, Network Security

1. Introduction

Cloud systems are advantageous for utilization in the field of computer security due to their distributed nature. Cloud technology enables efficient resource management since more cloud resources can be allocated on demand. Absence of a specific location is a very useful feature of cloud systems. A single physical machine can be a host for several cloud services. Single cloud service can be distributed over several physical machines. It is very hard to understand the structure of the cloud network due to absence of information about the amount of resources available.

DDoS attacks are one of the main problems that need to be addressed in the field of network security and communications. Whether a particular system is vulnerable to DDoS attacks depends on the amount of computational resources available. The more resources the system has the more complex and larger attacks it can withstand. It is therefore straightforward that the system resources should exceed the power of the botnets used for the particular attack. Not knowing how strong an attack can be makes it difficult to prepare a stable and reliable defense method. Several cloud infrastructures existing today already have an exceeding resource capacity compared to most of existing botnets [1]. Therefore cloud systems need to be utilized for DDoS defense. In such a way, system resources can be shared among a large number of clients, making it more efficient and low cost.

Existing DDoS prevention solutions are either victim-based or network-based. Victim-based solutions suffer drawbacks such as necessity of oversized server resources (e.g., bigger servers, larger bandwidth). Network-based solutions have challenging drawbacks such as link congestion issue. Newly appearing types of attacks such as Layer-7 DDoS attacks (HTTP flood, Slowloris, RUDY, etc.) contribute to the difficulties with network-based approaches as well. Signature based solutions are utilized across various types of existing methods. Attack signatures are automatically shared among service providers [2]. Signature-based solutions are not strong enough due to the time consuming process of signature collection and analysis. CDN (Content Delivery Network) based approaches also exist. Solutions such as Akamai [3], and CloudFlare [4] are well known. As any CDN-based method they utilize cache servers. This means they are vulnerable to cache pollution attacks such as locality disruption attack, or false locality attack [5], [6]. Attackers might keep sending requests for unpopular data. This will pollute the cache stored in different locations within the systems topology leading to disruption of service and additional cost.

As a result of our study, we have come up with a distributed DDoS prevention mechanism utilizing cloud technology, DROP-FAST. Our approach is based on utilizing massive computing power of the cloud infrastructures, and distributed nature of the cloud allowing protection from DDoS attacks. The core concept is switching from centralized defense strategies to a distributed scheme via cloud. This is achieved by moving the battleground from the main server to the cloud. Providing a method for handling attacks using cloud infrastructure greatly improves defense possibilities and service stability. DROP-FAST is based on replicating the main server throughout the cloud infrastructure. Content of the replicated servers is kept synchronized with the main server. All clients are serviced through cloud allowing for a strong protection of the main server while providing fast and robust service. In order to achieve our goals, we have defined several requirements and principles.

Requirements:

1) Server response time improvement.
2) Filtering improvement.
3) Main server isolation from attackers.
4) Load-sharing utilization.
5) Attack traffic drop location improvement.
6) Service stability under a strong attack.

Principles:

- *Dynamic* in its ability to adapt based on attack strength.
- *Reactive* since defensive actions will be taken immediately after an attack is detected.
- *Optimized* since amount of resource to use and network locations for replicas to reside can be chosen.
- *Proactive* since replica servers are ready to be activated at all times.

Based on the principles described above we named our mechanism *DROP-FAST*.

Several works describing cloud-based defense systems exist [1], [7]–[9]. In Section II we shall discuss pros and cons of some of them. In Section III we describe the DROP-FAST mechanism and compare it with some previous works. We continue with a description of a simple experiment in Section IV and state our ideas for future work. The paper is finalized with a conclusion in Section V.

2. Related Work

Researchers acknowledge that modern protection tools and mechanisms already have the capabilities and power to scan almost any kinds of objects on various depth levels on the network [1]. The problem that has been noticed is the delay between the time a piece of malware is discovered and the time of protection being available. Cloud computing has been suggested for storing the latest protection solutions. Clients would be checking for updates from a single location on cloud. This type of strategy allows making use of the geographical location of clients and creating cloud instances closer to large groups of users. In our research we make use of the vast computing resources cloud infrastructures provide. We also try to choose the positions for the replica servers so that it is closer to large groups of clients. In such a way, a faster response time and better load sharing is possible.

Another important issue to consider is the availability of the cloud system itself. The cloud system could be a target for a DDoS attack just as any other computing system. The cloud system that happens to be under a DDoS attack will most probably request more computing resources. The reason is that any service provider would like to keep stable service even under attack. However this leads to financial loss due to high cost. Therefore, cloud providers resolve the issue by imposing limitations for clients. Service providers in their turn impose limits and define thresholds for users. With events such as flash crowds or when a valid client requests large amounts of data, the threshold is passed but it is not an attack. These cases were analyzed by researchers and alternate strategies such as load balancing and honeypot were suggested [7]. There is a need for the service providers to decide on the maximum amount of resources that they would like to be using at pick moments. This is necessary due to financial issues of each service provider. It is necessary to realize that even in that case a very large attack or a flash crowd may lead to demand of very large computing resources. Therefore, a threshold on the maximum amount of cloud resources to be used should be in place.

Cloud systems provide distributed infrastructure. This also applies to intrusion detection. It is possible to combine existing intrusion detection systems (IDS) and cloud infrastructures. This allows a better protection for all machines inside the cloud infrastructure as well as for the clients subscribed for the cloud service utilizing cloud-based IDS. Researchers have shown that combining IDS and cloud technologies shows significant improvements in attack detection rate, average packet analysis time, and process size [8]. The advantages gained by such an approach are immense. Nevertheless, these systems would suffer the same weaknesses as the IDSs that are being used. Once an attacker is able to bypass detection tools, it is a matter of time to get the service down. The reason is that the cloud instances are forwarding all of the received traffic to the main server. DROP-FAST prevents requests from bypassing the cloud instances and protects the main server.

Isolation of the protected server, improved response time, and better throughput are several criteria that need to be improved via usage of cloud computing. These goals have been achieved in a system called CLAD [9]. In the CLAD system protected server is completely isolated from the internet by cloud infrastructure. DNS settings are changed so that all requests are forwarded through at least one CLAD node. This allowed for better filtering and improved dropping location as well as response time and throughput. The system allows only for HTTP traffic to pass. Having filters on each CLAD node reduces the attack rate. This system is significant improvement for cloud-based DDoS defense solutions. However, the isolation is partial and the requests are still forwarded to the main server. DDoS attack on the main server is still possible. Therefore, in our mechanism we provide better protection by completely isolating the main server. DROP-FAST cloud instances are replicas of the main server. There remains no need to forward client requests since each replica can send a respond on its own.

3. DROP-FAST Architecture

We propose applying distributed defense against distributed attacks. Non-distributed attacks are handled well by modern defense systems. It is the distributed attacks which pose the main threat nowadays. DROP-FAST is based on the idea of providing efficient and secure service by distributing the load from one main server to an infrastructure of cloud based replicas of the main protected server. Fig. 1 describes the outline of the general structure that DROP-FAST provides.

As seen from Fig. 1 the given scheme isolates the main server from all users, malicious and valid. All users send their requests to the nearest cloud replica. There have been previous approaches allowing main server isolation [9]. The advantage of DROP-FAST is that requests are not forwarded to the main server but can be handled by the nearest cloud replica. Cloud replica is closer to the clients compared to the main server. This decreases the response time significantly. Server load decreases as well as a result of traffic distribution over the cloud replicas. The requests handled by the replicas do not need to be forwarded to the main server, thus allowing

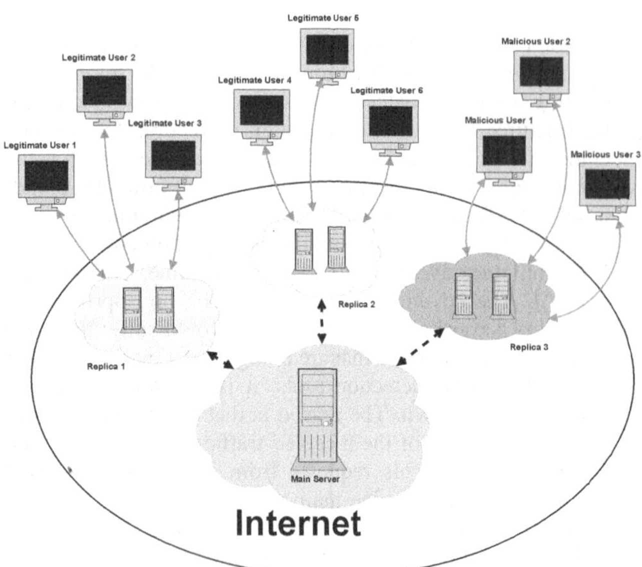

Fig. 1: DROP-FAST Architecture: Providing distributed service by replicating the main server throughout the cloud infrastructure

the main server to perform more efficiently. Several gateways can connect the main server with the internet and with clients depending on how large the network is. Therefore, appropriate locations can be chosen for placing the cloud replicas allowing the main server handle the requests coming from gateways connecting the server with parts of network without cloud replicas. Several issues should be handled in order for DROP-FAST scheme to work:

- Replication types
- Synchronization
- Load sharing
- Resource monitoring
- Security

3.1 Replication Types

Several types of replicating the main server on cloud exist. Various approaches could be applied based on the type and structure of data contained on the main server and contents. Short description of three main replication types is given.

3.1.1 Complete Copy

The main server is completely reproduced on the cloud replicas. All requests are handled by the cloud replica with no need of forwarding to the main server. Obviously, response time should be improved. DDoS risks are also greatly decreased because number of clients handled by each cloud replica is smaller than the number of clients that a single server would normally handle. Therefore, the total load is distributed among the cloud replicas. Since all requests are handled by cloud replicas directly, malicious requests do not reach the main server keeping it alive. The only communication between the replicas and the main server is synchronization of contents in order to keep data integrity. The main advantage is that failure of a single replica does not mean denial of service since other replicas would continue their service and main server would still be available.

3.1.2 Interest-based Copy

Replicas are partial copies of the main server. Both the main server and cloud replicas should be handling requests from clients. Depending on the content copied to the cloud replica, it will handle all the requests that it has the corresponding contents for, but forward the rest of the requests to the main server. Copying only part of the content makes it easier to synchronize and reduces the cost since the amount of necessary resources decreases. This approach might look similar to the CDN-based methods at the first glance. The main difference is that in CDN the contents of cache servers are determined by the frequency of requests from clients. Only the most popular data is stored. This opens up different attack channels such as cache pollution etc. We call this interest-based because we intend to copy only the content decided and agreed upon by the content providers. Content of cloud replicas would not necessarily change depending on what data is popular. This prevents cache pollution attacks. Advantage of using cloud systems is that a malicious user has no way of determining whether the data contained in the response packet is from the main server or cloud replica. The reason is that all the communication is done through the cloud replica. Nevertheless, an attacker might figure out what data is stored on the replica, leading to a possibility of an attack. Attackers could simply send huge amounts of requests only for the data residing on the main server. This would pose a serious threat if the attacker would launch an attack from all the locations where cloud replicas are placed. Therefore, the policy for choosing the data to be copied should be carefully analyzed and well planned. Due to risks stated above, we stick to the complete copy mechanism in our experiments.

3.1.3 Content Type-based Copy

The content could be divided into disjoint or partially joint sets or groups. This division can be carried out based on several criteria such as types of data (multimedia, documents, executable files, user files, etc.), or based on URL. Different cloud replicas would contain different portions of the data stored on the main server. URL splitting could be used if we decide to use content type-based copy mechanism. Different way of synchronization would be needed in case of using content type-based copy. There is a need to synchronize the cloud replicas between each other and the main server in order to keep data integrity.

3.2 Synchronization

Synchronization is a major concern in DROP-FAST. Same data should be available at different locations leading to unavoidable need of synchronization. We need synchronization in multiple directions. Modifications made on one of

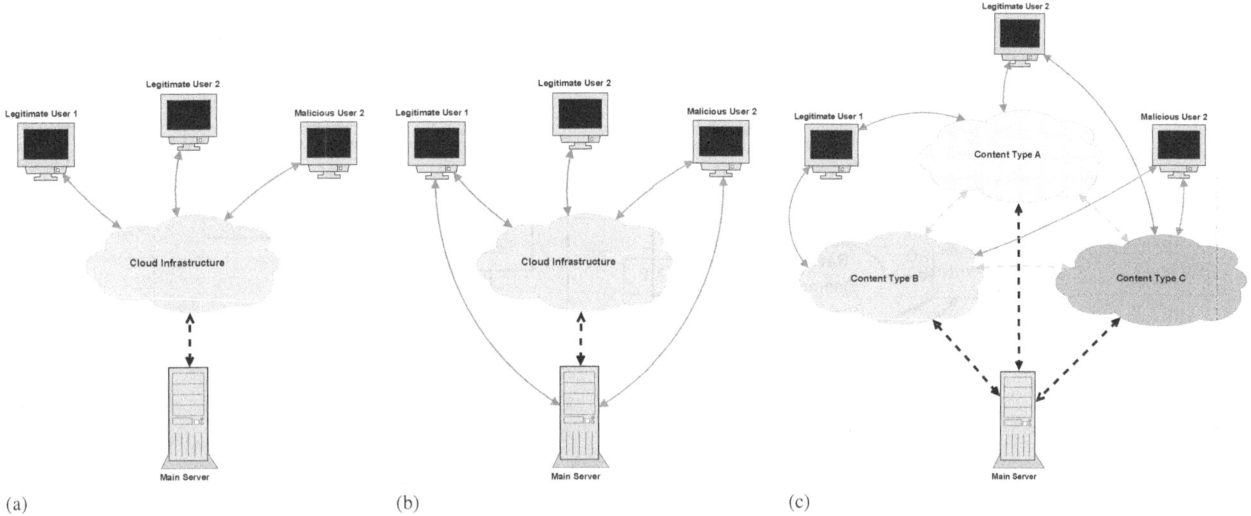

Fig. 2: Types of Content Copy: (a) Complete Copy (b) Interest-based Copy (c) Content Type-based Copy

the cloud replicas should be applied throughout the whole architecture including the main server. Various commercial software solutions are available for server synchronization. Modern synchronizations tools usually provide basic load sharing capabilities as well. For purposes of concurrent updates and distributed access to data making use of distributed file systems seems legitimate. Several free and commercially available tools for server synchronization exist.

3.3 Load Sharing

Depending on the network topology, each of the cloud replicas will be handling requests from a particular partition of the network. User behavior is hard to predict. Some parts of the network might have higher load compared to other parts. There is a need for strategy and policies in order to share the load and balance out the traffic to evenly divide it among closest replicas. Even though cloud infrastructures have large amounts of resources available, they cost money. It is a better choice to share the load among several replicas. Several load sharing and balancing approaches can be utilized. Most of the available methods are based on DNS configuration modifications or usage of multilayer switches.

3.3.1 DNS based Load Sharing

Load Sharing with Round Robin DNS is one of the straightforward ways of sharing that comes up to mind. BIND software should be used for this purpose. The idea is to simply rotate among several available IP addresses for the same domain name. The TTL (Time to live of DNS cache records) is set to relatively small values so that the A records (Address records linking a domain to an IP address) are renewed more often.

Round Robin is has low cost and is easy to implement. Nevertheless, there is no insurance in case of physical failure of one of the connected server machines. Caching problems might occur due to the need of having several requests per session. This will cause the DNS responses to the queries to cache and not being updated often.

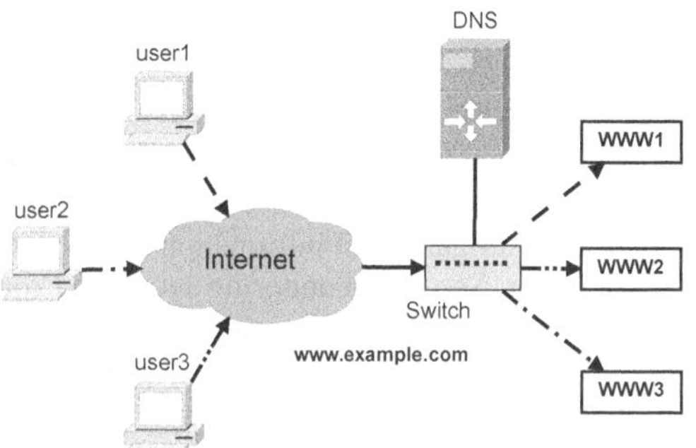

Fig. 3: Load Sharing using DNS Round Robin

In a systems such as DROP-FAST, where we try to share the load efficiently among several replica servers Dynamic Load Balancing [10] might be a better solution. For making use of this method we need to have some kind of resource monitoring to be in place on each of the replicas on the network. This is needed for determining the optimal decision of forwarding the traffic to the least busy server.

3.3.2 Switch based Load Sharing

Various network switches can manage the problem of load sharing and load balancing. Switches are able to automatically balance the traffic across several paths. Decisions as to which switch to use and what type of algorithms are utilized are specific to each case and network, they could change depending on the situation. Layer 7 switches could be used for performing load balancing on HTTP, HTTPS or TCP/IP traffic.

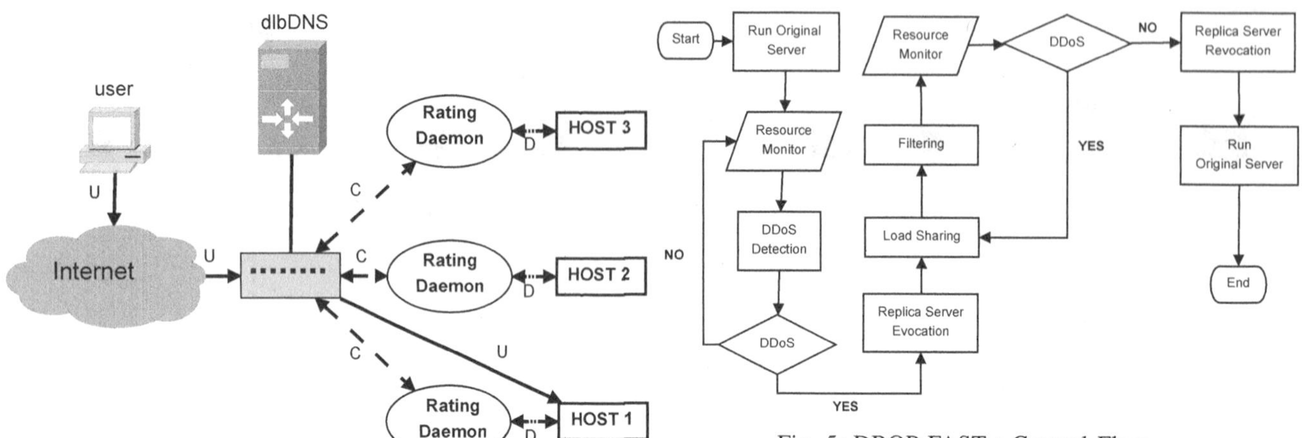

Fig. 4: Load Sharing using Dynamic Load Balancing (dlbDNS) : Path U - traced by user requests, Path C - communication between dlbDNS and rating daemons for locating the best server, Path D - process of updating server ratings by rating daemon

Fig. 5: DROP-FAST : Control Flow

3.4 Resource Monitoring

Resource monitoring is essential within the DROP-FAST mechanism. First, DROP-FAST needs it for implementing load sharing algorithms to gain load information from each individual replica server. Second, monitoring is needed for deciding whether the servers are under attack or not. Resources and network performance of the main server should be monitored in order to evaluate our ideas. Following metrics can be used:

Table 1: Criteria for Evaluation

Criteria	Unit	Description
Response Time	Seconds	Servers' Response Time
Server Load	Packets Per Second	Packet Rate of traffic reaching the main server
Response Sustainability	$\frac{N_{res}}{N_{req}}$	Ratio of number of responses and requests

Criteria in Table 1 and other metrics such as the CPU load or memory consumption information could be measured using existing software tools or writing some simple scripts. For evaluation purposes comparison between different states of the given system under evaluation should be given.

The DROP-FAST system has the following components:

- Main server (protected server)
- DROP-FAST core (DNS and monitoring functions, controls the whole mechanism)
- Clients (accessing the main server)
- Cloud replica servers (synchronized with the main server)

As you can see from Fig. 5 the flow starts with the main server running in a standalone mode.

3.4.1 Detection

Resource monitor is software running on the DROP-FAST core server. Performance of the main server is monitored by getting periodic reports from the main server or via port mirroring and analyzing the whole traffic of the main server from the network switch. Standard IDS should be used for detection purposes. The IDS should be capable of identifying DDoS attacks as well as flash crowd events.

3.4.2 Replica Evocation

In case of resource exhaustion above the given threshold limits or if an attack is detected by the IDS, DROP-FAST core server will send commands to replicas on cloud and evocate them. This process is simultaneous with the change in DNS configuration. DNS configuration should be changed using BIND or different methods depending on the load sharing strategy chosen. The clients are instructed through DNS to send their requests to the cloud replicas and not to the main server.

3.4.3 Resource Monitoring

DROP-FAST core and individual replica servers continue to exchange health status messages. While system is still loaded and is using all available resources the replicas continue to be active. Number of replicas increases as the attack gets stronger. Nevertheless, attacks might be strong and can lead to high cloud resource consumption and large number of replicas activating. Some clients or subscribers will suffer from high bills for cloud services. Therefore, we propose to put an upper limit on the maximum amount of cloud resources to be used. Threshold should be chosen by the subscriber.

4. Evaluation

In order to evaluate our idea, we have set up an experiment. We used the following configuration:

- Hardware:
    1) DROP-FAST core: Interl(R) Pentium(R) D CPU 3.20GHz / 2GB RAM

2) Main server: Inter(R) Core(TM)2 Duo CPU E6750 @ 2.66GHz / 4GB RAM
3) Replica: Inter(R) Core(TM) i5-2500k CPU @ 3.30GHz / 3GB RAM
4) Client: Sony VAIO, Inter(R) Core(TM)2 Duo CPU P8800 @ 2.66GHz / 4GB RAM
5) Switch: ipTIME SW2401

- Software: OS - Ubuntu 10.04 , Server - Apache/2.2.14 (Ubuntu), DNS - BIND9, Virtualization - VirtualBox
- Synchronization and Replication: Dropbox

The three machines have different roles in the experiment:

1) Main server: URL is server1.dropfast.com
2) DROP-FAST core: controlling center that governs the operation of the system
3) Replica server: URL is replica1.dropfast.com, runs two virtual machines

The content on the main server is saved under the Dropbox directory, so that any changes made on replicas or on the main server are effective throughout the infrastructure. Using Dropbox eliminates our need to take care of synchronization among the different servers.

The replica server is a host for two virtual machines running servers that listen on ports 8081 and 8082. The traffic is distributed randomly among the two replicas using JavaScript.

The DROP-FAST server acts as a control tower and listens for resource exhaustion messages from the main server. It also incorporates the DNS functions. For simplicity of the experiment we put a threshold of 100 KBps for signaling an attack[1]. Once the threshold is passed DROP-FAST alters the DNS configuration and redirects part of the traffic to the replica server. This leads to the load reduction on the main server side.

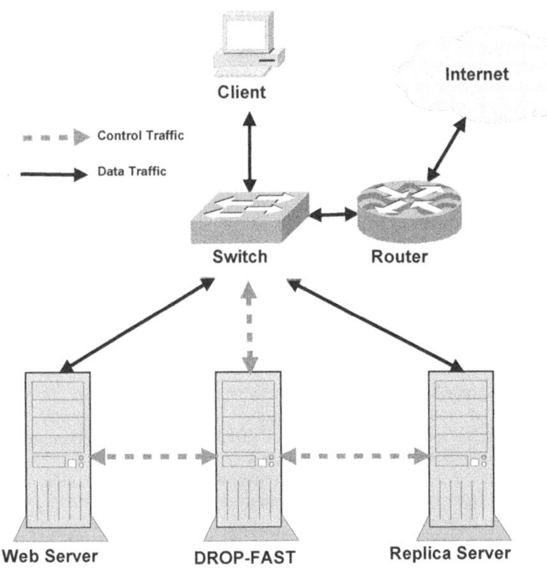

Fig. 6: Experimental Setup

[1]Threshold was chosen based on the attack tool that was used.

4.1 Modes of Operation

The system has two modes of operation:

1) Passive mode: system is operating under standard conditions with no attack or flash crowd event
2) Active mode: system is under attack or a flash crowd event occurs

In passive mode only the main server operates. DROP-FAST core runs and checks whether the incoming traffic is under the threshold value. The DNS records point to the main server with the URL server1.dropfast.com. All traffic flows in one direction only. Replica servers are not evoked.

The system switches to active mode when main server is under attack or a flash crowd event is detected. DROP-FAST core evokes the replica server hosting two web servers on virtual machines. DNS configuration is altered to enable traffic redirection to the replica server. Traffic is redirected based on load sharing policy. At this mode the traffic is distributed in several directions.

The experimental setup is schematically described in Fig. 6. The DROP-FAST core communicates with the main server and replicas internally as shown by the blue dashed arrows. This communication should not be visible externally and only the internal modules of the system must be aware of this communication. Insecure communication between the DROP-FAST core and the rest of the system poses a great risk to system security.

As a basic means of evaluation we measure the server load on the main server. First we monitor the main server load in the passive mode of operation to observe the incoming traffic rate. We then launch a HTTP flood attack. The server load is measured again to compare it to the load while the system was in passive mode. When main server is under attack DROP-FAST core changes the DNS configuration and the traffic is distributed between the main server and the replica server. One more measurement of the incoming traffic rate is made to check for any positive changes due to distribution of the load. You can see our results in Fig. 7.

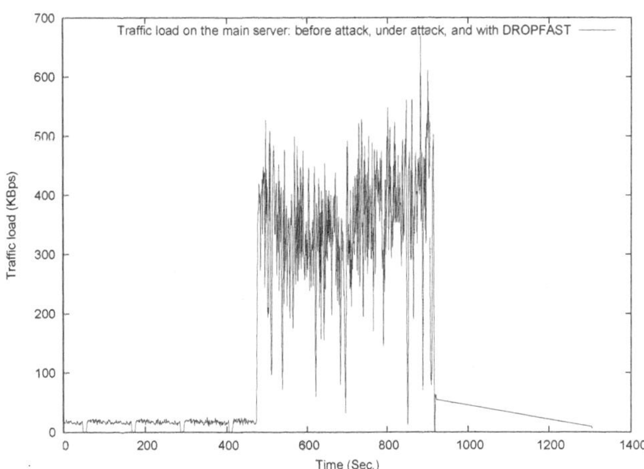

Fig. 7: Incoming traffic load on main server: passive mode, under attack, and active mode

The server load is stable while in passive mode. This means that no attack or anomaly is taking place. The system runs as intended and all the requests are handled by the main server. After 460 seconds a HTTP flood attack is launched. The load on the main server escalates quickly. This leads to DROP-FAST core activating the replica server and distributing the traffic. As a result of this action you can see how server load drops back to normal after approximately 900 seconds point.

Utilizing DROP-FAST made it possible to maintain normal response time even while under attack. Response time was monitored in passive mode, under attack, and in active mode. Results are presented in Fig. 8. Response time of main server is monitored while in passive mode. HTTP flooding attack is performed, hence rapidly increased response time is observed. Response time decreases rapidly as DROP-FAST is enabled.

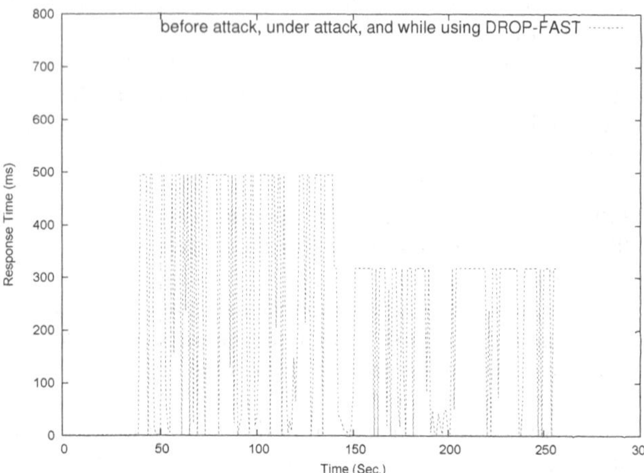

Fig. 8: Main servers response time: response time increases rapidly due to HTTP flooding at 40 seconds, response time remains high with lots of failed requests, response time reduces almost twice when DROP-FAST is applied.

It is important to note that we have performed a very basic experiment with only one replica server. The experiment was performed in a small lab network consisting of the three described computers only. The client accesses the servers via a Wireless LAN connection. Since the experimental topology is the possibly smallest one, it is impossible to make use of the advantage that is given by the use of best locations in network topology. We have only used one replica server running two virtual web servers. The system is stronger if more replica servers are available in advantageous network locations.

5. Conclusion

We have suggested a new approach to DDoS prevention using cloud technologies. We have stated several related works and elaborated on their pros and cons. Several important issues were discussed. These include but not limited to

- Replication methods,
- Synchronization,
- Load sharing,
- Resource monitoring,
- Security.

As a proof of concept we setup a basic experiment. Our network topology and network size are far from real internet like infrastructures. Nevertheless the results we have obtained suggest that DROP-FAST provides means to avoid DDoS by distributing the service. Experimental data shows improvement in server load and response time, proving viability of DROP-FAST mechanism. Experiments will be conducted to widen the idea further and apply the mechanism in real world networks.

In future, we plan to conduct further research in several directions:

1) Load Sharing: Develop sophisticated and efficient load sharing algorithm applicable to DROP-FAST.
2) Communication Protocol: Develop a secure and fast protocol to communicate among the main server, replica servers, and DROP-FAST core.
3) Topological Placement: Develop a method for optimal replica server placement decision for a given network topology.
4) Control Distribution: Develop a distributed control mechanism to substitute DROP-FAST core.

Acknowledgments

This research was supported funded by the R&BD Support Center of Seoul Development Institute and the South Korean government (WR080951).

References

[1] I. Muttik and C. Barton, "Cloud security technologies," *Information Security Technical Report*, vol. 14, no. 1, pp. 1 – 6, 2009. Malware.

[2] "Fingerprint sharing allience," tech. rep., ARBOR NETWORKS.

[3] E. Nygren, R. K. Sitaraman, and J. Sun, "The akamai network: a platform for high-performance internet applications," *SIGOPS Oper. Syst. Rev.*, vol. 44, pp. 2–19, Aug. 2010.

[4] I. CloudFlare, "An overview of cloudflare."

[5] Y. Gao, L. Deng, A. Kuzmanovic, and Y. Chen, "Internet cache pollution attacks and countermeasures," in *Proceedings of the Proceedings of the 2006 IEEE International Conference on Network Protocols*, ICNP '06, (Washington, DC, USA), pp. 54–64, IEEE Computer Society, 2006.

[6] M. Xie, I. Widjaja, and H. Wang, "Enhancing cache robustness for content-centric networking," in *INFOCOM, 2012 Proceedings IEEE*, pp. 2426–2434, March.

[7] "Availability challenge of cloud system under ddos attack," *Indian Journal of Science and Technology*, vol. 4, no. 6, pp. 2933 – 2937, 2012.

[8] H. Hamad and M. Al-hoby, "Article: Managing intrusion detection as a service in cloud networks," *International Journal of Computer Applications*, vol. 41, pp. 35–40, March 2012. Published by Foundation of Computer Science, New York, USA.

[9] P. Du and A. Nakao, "Ddos defense as a network service," in *Network Operations and Management Symposium (NOMS), 2010 IEEE*, pp. 894–897, April.

[10] V. C. Harish and B. Owens, "Dynamic load balancing dns," *Linux J.*, vol. 1999, Aug. 1999.

Simplified Network Traffic Visualization for Real-Time Security Analysis

Matthew Dean and Lucas Vespa
Department of Computer Science
University of Illinois Springfield
Springfield, IL 62703

Abstract—**Although traditional methods of network security analysis used in investigating network traffic and log files are essential to mitigating malicious network activity, these methods alone cannot keep up with constant increases in malevolent network traffic. Many visualization tools have been created as a supplement to traditional analysis and intrusion detection systems. Even though these tools are useful, each tool tends to have a niche use. Also, many network administrators fill dual roles as administrators and security analysts and have little time to learn different complex visualization tools. We therefore observe a need for a simple out-of-the-box solution for general network security visualization. We hope to fill this need with our tool called VNR, which in addition to its simplicity embeds transport layer data within visualizations allowing for better intra-host analysis. VNR can also be used for real-time or auditing purposes by configuring the amount of data visualized within specific time frames.**

I. Introduction

Malicious network traffic is increasing [1], including attacks on business networks, and also attacks originating from compromised hosts within networks. This increase in malicious behavior, along with other factors such as increasing network rates and increasing numbers of virtual and non-virtual hosts, makes a network security analyst's job very difficult. Traditional methods of network monitoring and log dissemination alone cannot keep up with demand for analysis. Alternative methods are required to aid in both real-time and log-based network security analysis.

Visualization tools [2], [3], [4], [5], [6] are a promising solution to the need for simplified analysis techniques, allowing analysts more freedom and a different perspective than traditional analysis. Many of these tools allow for several levels of data abstraction, permitting the user to drill down to packet level data if desired, or view high level visual data. There is a great deal of overlap between many visualization tools; however, each tool usually has some niche functionality.

As useful as network security visualization is to the analyst, there are some general problems that most visualization tools do not address. The following is a list of these problems, and possible solutions.

- *Problem*: Many analysts are not full time analysts, but rather admin/analysts who cannot devote their full attention to learning visual analysis tools, or for that matter, complex analysis techniques in general.
  - *Solution*: Create a basic, out-of-the-box visualization solution with functionality that is obvious to those with basic network knowledge.
- *Problem*: Many visualization tools utilize heavy abstraction, wherein, visualizations display only IP layer data if any data at all. Although this is useful for some analysis, transport and application layer data helps in detecting irregular behavior within single hosts.
  - *Solution*: Mix abstraction levels by embedding transport and/or application layer data across all visualized hosts, while still displaying IP layer host relationships.
- *Problem*: Grouping hosts based on internal/external status may focus an analyst's attention on external attacks. However, a great deal of malicious traffic may actually come from compromised hosts within a network, and internal IP ranges can be spoofed. These can be of greater concern than external attacks.
  - *Solution*: Treat all hosts equally in any graph-based visualization. Do not force groupings based on internal/external addresses.
- *Problem*: Many visualization tools are either too complex to visualize in real-time, or the amount of data visualized cannot be adjusted, such that real-time capture will yield useful analysis.
  - *Solution*: Simplify visualizations such that traffic can generally be process in real-time. Allow the user to adjust how many hosts will be displayed such that an accurate snapshot of current network traffic is visualized.

In this work we implement each of the above solutions in a network security visualization tool called VNR (Visualization of Networks in Real-time), a screenshot of which is shown in Figure 1. The visualizations and functionality of VNR need little explanation to those with fundamental network knowledge. VNR has basic grid and graph views which display IP layer relationships and transport layer information. Internal and external hosts are not forced to any locations or groupings. The visualizations are simple and old hosts fade from view by default, creating potential for real-time analysis. VNR also implements many traditional features such as details on demand and summary statistics.

The remainder of this paper is organized as follows. Section II presents related work in the area of network and security

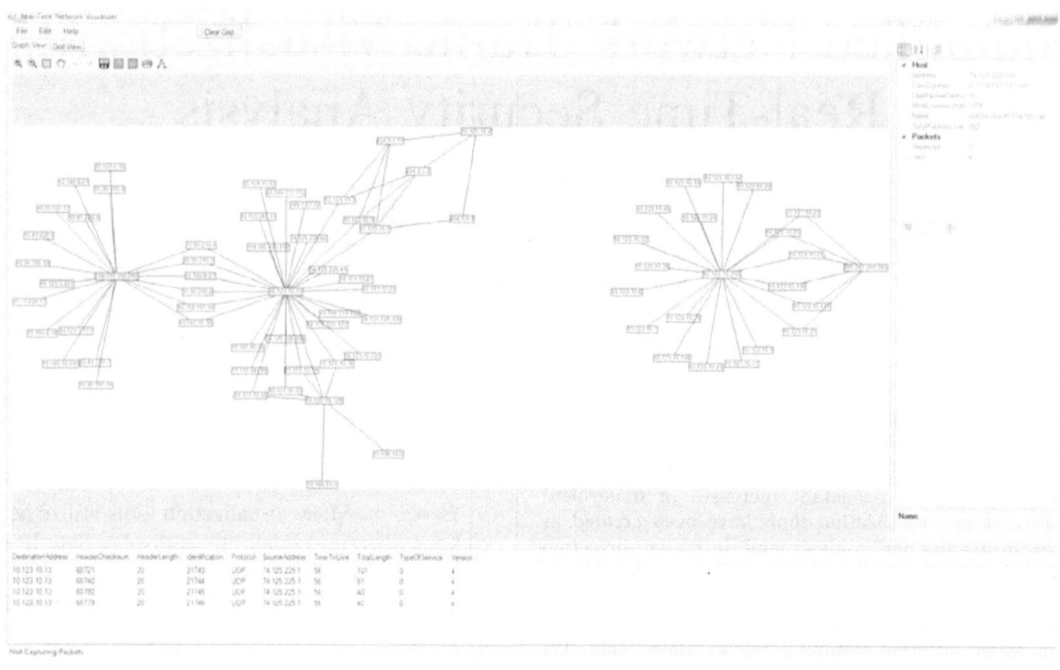

Fig. 1. VNR Screenshot

visualization. Section III summarizes VNR's design and basic functionality. Example uses of VNR for security and network analysis, and a further discussion of VNR are presented in Section IV. Conclusions are presented in Section V.

II. Related Work

A great deal of work has been done in the areas of visualization for networks [7], [8], [9] and security [10], [11], [12], [13]. Many tools for visualization have been produced, amongst which there is a great deal of overlap, with each tool having niche functionality. Most tools concentrate on visualizing trace files for better analysis, although some are designed for real-time analysis as well.

Specifically, in network visualization, TNV [4] displays a time-based matrix of host communications. TNV's matrix is detailed and gives the analyst many complex analysis tools. Several levels of granularity are displayed. Visual analysis of routing [5], [14] is another area of concern. BGPeep [5] is a visualization tool for BGP analysis. It presents a visual organization by IP space, using network address prefixes to categorize data. VisTracer [15] is a network tool to evaluate routing changes over time, and identify legitimate versus malicious route adjustments. Minarick and Dymacek [16] create a tool to use graphs to visualize netflow data. The graphs also include DNS name lookup and common port/service names for ease of understanding.

Even more specifically, network security visualization has been proposed to aid in the timely mitigation of network threats. Fligg et al [17] present an overview of network security visualization, specifically, the psychology of visualization and specific rules for efficiently utilizing particular space. Many visualization tools allow multiple levels of visual data abstraction, from high-level overviews to low-level details. TVi [18] reflects this functionality, implemented as a visual querying tool for network traces. Teoh et al [19] demonstrate how to perform visual analysis of log files as an alternative to traditional automated log analysis processes.

Because many visualization tools can help detect scans but not identify scan types, Muelder et al [20] create a methodology for further identifying scan characteristics, utilizing PortViz [3] and other tools. NFlowVis [21] uses a treemap visualization linked to attack alerts to analyze the validity of system alerts, as well as other analysis such as network service usage. Similar to NFlowVis, Garnet [6] uses a treemap to layout subnets, and then creates an attack graph which relates to the treemap. Musa et al [22] visualize Snort alerts in a 3D time-series graph. Netgrok [2] can visualize trace files by representing hosts in graph or treemap form.

III. VNR Overview

A. Overview

To facilitate easy evaluation of VNR's visualizations, two simple views are utilized, a grid view and graph view. Hosts communicating on the network are represented by a single element within each view. In grid view, these elements are cells, and each host is represented by a single cell. In graph view, the elements are vertices and each host is represented by a single vertex. Figure 2(a) shows the grid view and Figure 2(b) shows the graph view. Each view's output is simple to interpret allowing out-of-the-box analysis. Each element in either view displays multi-layer information about a host, allowing for intra-host analysis. Communicating hosts are connected by edges in the graph view.

Hosts are selectable and details for a selected host are displayed in the details pane, an example of which is shown

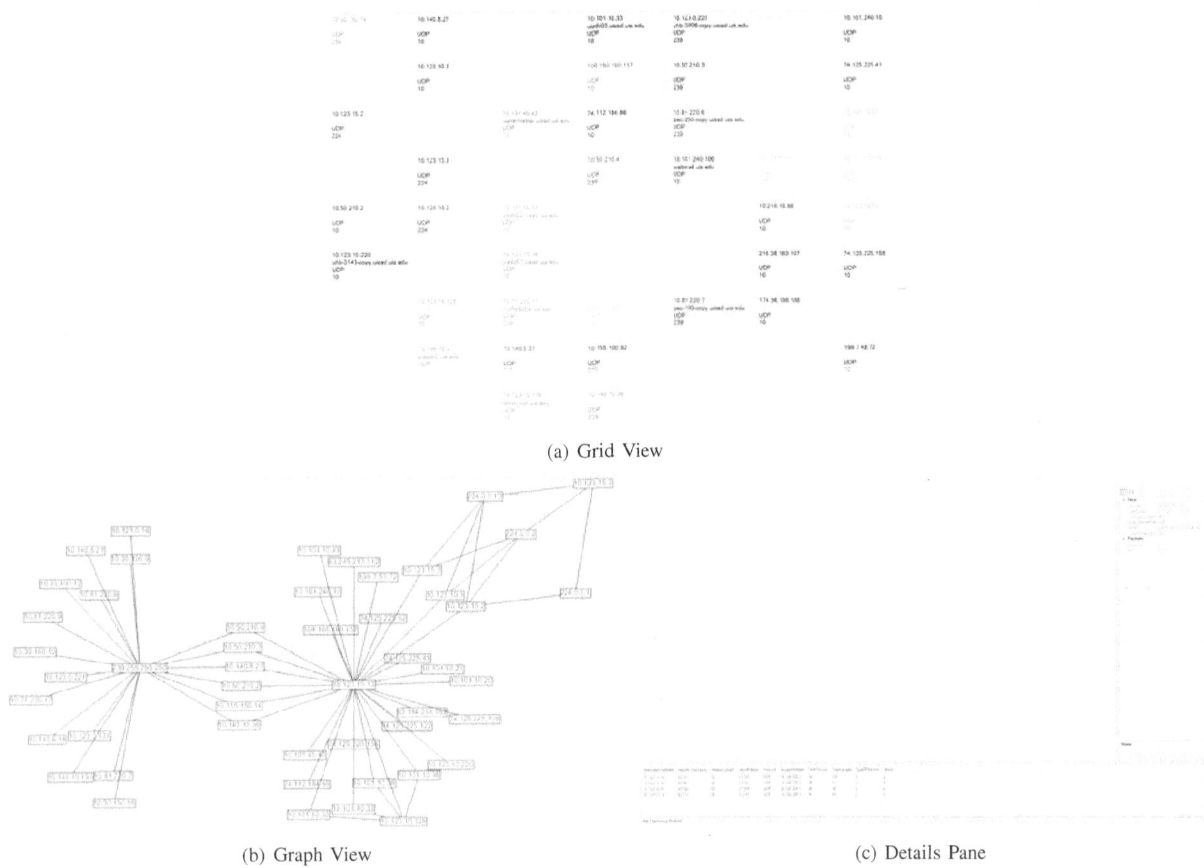

(a) Grid View

(b) Graph View

(c) Details Pane

Fig. 2. VNR Views

in Figure 2(c). Each view displays x currently communicating hosts, where x is configurable and has a default value of 100 hosts. The value of x can be adjusted depending on the level of real-time analysis desired. It should be noted that VNR is not strictly a real-time tool. By increasing x to a very large value, VNR can be used for auditing and trace file analysis with many hosts.

Packet capture in VNR is achieved using PCAP.Net [23], a Dot Net wrapper for the popular WinPCAP libraries [24]. Microsoft C# [25] is therefore used for the application development. Graph visualization is performed using Microsoft Automated Graph Layout (MSAGL) [26], developed by Microsoft research.

B. Views and Features

a) Grid View: The grid view is a collection of cell elements, one for each of the x most recently communicating hosts. The host information includes network IP, packet counts, current embedded protocol and other configurable information. The simple layout and efficient use of space in the grid view allows maximum intra-host information to be displayed. This view is therefore especially useful for analyzing the behavior of individual hosts. Clicking a host in the grid view will update the details pane with information for the selected host. Older hosts slowly fade from the grid if no new traffic is received from them.

b) Graph View: The graph view displays each host element (vertex), and also connects communicating hosts. The hosts present in the graph view are synced with the grid view. Clicking a host in the graph view displays details for the selected host.

c) Details Pane: Packet level and summary information are displayed for each host in the details pane. Some of the information displayed includes individual packets sent and received by the selected host and summary information such as the majority embedded protocol, the time the host first appeared, host name and size of communicated data.

IV. Discussions

Figure 3(a) shows what a simple NMAP network scan looks like in VNR. A quick appearance of a one-to-many host relationship demonstrates a scan of a subnet. Although, this is only one very obvious use of VNR, more subtle variations of this can help identify scans that might go undetected otherwise. Once a potential scan is visually detected, more information about individual hosts can be gathered from the grid view and details pane.

Figure 3(b) shows what a scan of an individual host looks like in the grid view. Typically, in the grid view, the protocol, port and other fields tend to seemingly remain static due to communications of one type. However, during a scan, some fields will look as if they are flashing. This demonstrates a

(a) NMAP scan of a network.

(b) NMAP scan of a host

Fig. 3. VNR Visualizations

rapid change in values which indicates a potential scan. The image in Figure 3(b) is created artificially from a base screen shot of the grid view. to demonstrate what this activity looks like. We had to create the image because it is impossible to take a screen shot while the screen is refreshing. A great deal of malicious activity shows up as rapidly changing fields in the grid view, and can be a starting point for detecting malicious activity. Other methods of detecting malicious behavior are also present in the grid view.

The visualizations in VNR can be used to identify many other types of scans and general malicious activity. Any information that rapidly changes within the header fields of two communicating hosts will be detected by an analyst using VNR. In addition, all many-to-few communication relationships will be exposed to the analyst. In addition, traditional packet level and summary analysis can still be utilized due to the details on demand ability of VNR. VNR can also be used for auditing of large recorded network trace files for non real-time analysis. This allows for a more detailed investigation of network behavior.

In the future, besides the ability to drill down to details, we will also include the ability to jump back to host level from the details level. For example, if an analyst clicks a host to view packet level details and subsequently notices a suspicious address in the recorded packets for that host, the analyst will simply be able to click on that suspicious address and the host associated with the address will become the selected host in the current grid or graph view. This will allow an analyst to easily follow audit trails in real-time or while analyzing trace files.

V. Conclusions

In this work we have presented VNR, a network security visualization tool with easy to understand visualizations. VNR displays information from multiple network layers simultaneously and can be used for real-time or log analysis. We have demonstrated the functionality of VNR and shown its usefulness for detecting malicious network activity. We believe that tools like the one presented in this work are an essential step in mitigating future network threats, and that VNR is a positive augmentation toward generalized use of network security visualization tools.

References

[1] M. Kowtko, "Securing our nation and protecting privacy," in *Systems, Applications and Technology Conference (LISAT), 2011 IEEE Long Island*, May 2011, pp. 1 –6.

[2] R. Blue, C. Dunne, A. Fuchs, K. King, and A. Schulman, "Visualizing real-time network resource usage," in *Proceedings of the 5th international workshop on Visualization for Computer Security*, ser. VizSec '08, 2008, pp. 119–135.

[3] J. McPherson, K.-L. Ma, P. Krystosk, T. Bartoletti, and M. Christensen, "Portvis: a tool for port-based detection of security events," in *Proceedings of the 2004 ACM workshop on Visualization and data mining for computer security*, 2004, pp. 73–81.

[4] J. Goodall, W. Lutters, P. Rheingans, and A. Komlodi, "Preserving the big picture: visual network traffic analysis with tnv," in *Visualization for Computer Security, 2005. (VizSEC 05). IEEE Workshop on*, October 2005, pp. 47–54.

[5] J. Shearer, K.-L. Ma, and T. Kohlenberg, "Bgpeep: An ip-space centered view for internet routing data," in *Visualization for Computer Security*, ser. Lecture Notes in Computer Science. Springer Berlin Heidelberg, 2008, pp. 95–110.

[6] L. Williams, R. Lippmann, and K. Ingols, "Garnet: A graphical attack graph and reachability network evaluation tool," in *Proceedings of the 5th international workshop on Visualization for Computer Security*, ser. VizSec '08, 2008, pp. 44–59.

[7] C. Kintzel, J. Fuchs, and F. Mansmann, "Monitoring large ip spaces with clockview," in *Proceedings of the 8th International Symposium on Visualization for Cyber Security*, ser. VizSec '11, 2011, pp. 2:1–2:10.

[8] C. Horn and A. D'Amico, "Visual analysis of goal-directed network defense decisions," in *VizSec '11: Proceedings of the 8th International Symposium on Visualization for Cyber Security*, 2011, pp. 1–6.

[9] S. S. Kim and A. L. N. Reddy, "Netviewer: a network traffic visualization and analysis tool," in *Proceedings of the 19th conference on Large Installation System Administration Conference - Volume 19*, ser. LISA '05, 2005, pp. 18–18.

[10] L. Nataraj, S. Karthikeyan, G. Jacob, and B. S. Manjunath, "Malware images: visualization and automatic classification," in *Proceedings of the 8th International Symposium on Visualization for Cyber Security*, ser. VizSec '11, 2011, pp. 4:1–4:7.

[11] A. Singh, L. Bradel, A. Endert, R. Kincaid, C. Andrews, and C. North, "Supporting the cyber analytic process using visual history on large displays," in *Proceedings of the 8th International Symposium on Visualization for Cyber Security*, ser. VizSec '11, 2011, pp. 3:1–3:8.

[12] R. Veras, J. Thorpe, and C. Collins, "Visualizing semantics in passwords: the role of dates," in *Proceedings of the Ninth International Symposium on Visualization for Cyber Security*, ser. VizSec '12, 2012, pp. 88–95.

[13] L. Harrison, R. Spahn, M. Iannacone, E. Downing, and J. R. Goodall, "Nv: Nessus vulnerability visualization for the web," in *Proceedings of the Ninth International Symposium on Visualization for Cyber Security*, ser. VizSec '12, 2012, pp. 25–32.

[14] S. T. Teoh, K.-L. Ma, and S. F. Wu, "A visual exploration process for the analysis of internet routing data," in *Proceedings of the 14th IEEE Visualization 2003 (VIS'03)*, ser. VIS '03, 2003, pp. 69–.

[15] F. Fischer, J. Fuchs, P.-A. Vervier, F. Mansmann, and O. Thonnard, "Vistracer: a visual analytics tool to investigate routing anomalies in traceroutes," in *Proceedings of the Ninth International Symposium on Visualization for Cyber Security*, ser. VizSec '12, 2012, pp. 80–87.

[16] P. Minarik and T. Dymacek, "Netflow data visualization based on graphs," in *Proceedings of the 5th international workshop on Visualization for Computer Security*, ser. VizSec '08, 2008, pp. 144–151.

[17] K. Fligg and G. Max, "Network security visualization," *IEEE Network Special Issue on Recent Developments in Network Intrusion Detection*, Apr. 2012.

[18] A. Boschetti, L. Salgarelli, C. Muelder, and K.-L. Ma, "Tvi: a visual querying system for network monitoring and anomaly detection," in *Proceedings of the 8th International Symposium on Visualization for Cyber Security*, ser. VizSec '11, 2011, pp. 1:1–1:10.

[19] S. T. Teoh, T. Jankun-Kelly, K.-L. Ma, and F. S. Wu, "Visual data analysis for detecting flaws and intruders in computer network systems," *IEEE Computer Graphics and Applications, special issue on Visual Analytics*, 2004.

[20] C. Muelder, K.-L. Ma, and T. Bartoletti, "A visualization methodology for characterization of network scans," in *Proceedings of the IEEE Workshops on Visualization for Computer Security*, ser. VIZSEC '05, 2005, pp. 4–.

[21] F. Fischer, F. Mansmann, D. A. Keim, S. Pietzko, and M. Waldvogel, "Large-scale network monitoring for visual analysis of attacks," in *Proceedings of the 5th international workshop on Visualization for Computer Security*, ser. VizSec '08, 2008, pp. 111–118.

[22] S. Musa and D. J. Parish, "Using time series 3d alertgraph and false alert classification to analyse snort alerts," in *Proceedings of the 5th international workshop on Visualization for Computer Security*, ser. VizSec '08, 2008, pp. 169–180.

[23] "Pcap.net," 2013, http://pcapdotnet.codeplex.com/.

[24] "Winpcap," 2013, http://www.winpcap.org/.

[25] "Microsoft visual studio express for windows desktop," 2013, http://www.microsoft.com/visualstudio/eng/products/visual-studio-express-for-windows-desktop.

[26] "Microsoft automatic graph layout," 2013, http://research.microsoft.com/en-us/projects/msagl/.

Challenges of Kerberos Variance with High QoS Expectations

Yoney Kirsal-Ever, Yonal Kirsal
School of Science and Technology
Middlesex University
London, UK
Emails:y.kirsal,y.x.kirsal@mdx.ac.uk

Alberto Polzonetti, Leonardo Mostarda
School of Science and Technology
University of Camerino
Camerino, Italy
Emails:alberto.polzonetti@unicam.it, leonardo.mostarda@unicam.it

Clifford Sule, Purav Shah, Enver Ever
School of Science and Technology
Middlesex University
London, UK
Emails:c.sule,p.shah,e.ever@mdx.ac.uk

***Abstract*—This paper presents modelling approaches for performability evaluation of high Quality of Service (QoS) of Kerberos servers which dynamically renew keys under pseudo-secure conditions in order to significantly reduce the chances of potential intruders. Since the proposed approaches involve temporary interruption to link/server access, it has implications in terms of performance degradation. Analytical methods are used to evaluate the cost in terms of the degradation of system performance. Unlike previous studies, the failures of the servers are considered together with link/server interruptions for renewals. Therefore the model presented considers the system for exact performability evaluation. In this study, the existing authentication protocols are considered in an unusual fashion. The performance degradations that may be caused by service interruptions are discussed with a new framework to model the interactions between the network and the authentication servers. Numerical results are provided in order to analyse the effects of renewal times, times between renewals and failures of the server.**

***Index Terms*—Kerberos Variance, Quality of Service, Performability Modelling, Wireless Networks**

I. Introduction

In order to meet increasing demands in secure computer communications, various security protocols have been developed. Kerberos is one of the commonly used mechanisms for authentication. It is based on Needham-Schroeder Authentication Protocol [15]. It utilises public key cryptography to provide authentication for client-server applications. Its implementations allow the introduction of additional algorithms for encryption and check summing. Clients (end users) and servers use digital tickets and cryptographic keys for identifying themselves to networks and secure communications. The Kerberos architecture is divided into two core elements, Key Distribution Centre (KDC) and Ticket Granting Service (TGS). The KDC stores authentication information and uses it to securely authenticate users and services while TGS holds digital tickets to identify the network clients and servers.

Each KDC stores a database of users, servers, and secret keys [11]. However, since the KDCs store secret keys for every user and server on a network, it is essential to do this with maximum security. If an attacker can gain administrative access to the KDC, he would have access to the complete resources of the Kerberos realm. Kerberos tickets are cached on the client systems. If an attacker gains administrative access to a Kerberos client system, he can impersonate the authenticated users of that system. In other words, the authentication service communicates with the TGS and then authenticates the client with a ticket. The TGS receives the ticket from the client and checks its validity and replies to the client with a new ticket. Client can use this ticket to request services. Since the TGS is not authenticated (i.e. it is assumed that it is trusted), a masquerading TGS (any client) can impersonate the TGS of the network [11]. In addition, Kerberos exhibits some other vulnerabilities widely reported in the literature [5].

The design of a new protocol description was considered in developing a specific authentication protocol [10] and provided authentication as part of a previously proposed framework [10]. This protocol combines the properties of Kerberos and Key-Exchange protocols together with a powerful intruder model. A new approach had been proposed to shut down external access to an enterprise network for a period of time to enable the distribution of randomly generated keys to users in a relatively secure way [11], [16]. This approach was based on the assumption that the main threat is from external sources, where internal sources can be controlled better. Renewing keys at various intervals while potential intruders are blocked out would inevitably work against intruders. Although the intruder had been given the power to attack, the protocol was successful in preventing replay attacks [11]. Increasing the decryption time of messages for an attacker is another way of attack prevention. Security protocols on distributed systems are time-sensitive. In the analysis of delayed decryption systems, timestamps play an important role. In [12], a new protocol is proposed based on the use of timestamps to delay decryption by potential intruders with delay decryption and time authentication properties. In addition to the proposed protocol, key renewal at reasonably secure environments is considered for increased security.

Frequent key renewal under pseudo-secure conditions approach is based on secure key distributions at various intervals. During key distribution, external access to the network is not allowed. The access restriction happens for short intervals [11], [12]. However, any link shut-down costs the network in terms of performance degradation. Therefore, it is essential to evaluate the impact of the proposed approach on system performance. For this purpose, an analytical model has been developed to evaluate the performability of the proposed approach in [11]. While key distribution times depend on network characteristics such as size, and speed, the intervals between key renewals can be determined by the mean values of decryption times. This way, before an intruder succeeds breaking an encryption to get a key, the key will be renewed in a secure manner [11], [12].

The rest of the paper is organized as follows: The related works and the Quality of Service (QoS) challenges in security environments are described in section II and III respectively. In section IV the necessity of considering security protocols for performability modelling is discussed. In section V the frameworks for performability model of Kerberos server is designed and presented. Conclusions and future work are provided in section VI.

II. Related Works

Throughout the last two decades, the multiplicity and complexity of authentication approaches have increased. In their research, Kirsal and Gemikonakli [12], proposed a framework [11] and a protocol script [10], in order to provide a design of a security solution for wireless local area networks (WLAN). Since the Kerberos Authentication Protocol is a trusted third party authentication protocol, its paradigms and entities were finalised for the proposed framework [11]. In this framework, both the protocol script and data containing the credentials of the legitimate entities of a particular WLAN environment are installed on each of the entities as well as TGS and KDC. The protocol in [10] adopted the challenge-response paradigm.

Furthermore, the proposed protocol was a timed model security protocol; it used timestamps to delay decryption of messages by intruders. An approach had been proposed to shut down external access to an enterprise network for a period of time to enable the distribution of randomly generated keys to users. Renewing keys at various intervals while potential intruders are blocked out would inevitably work against intruders [11]. In this previous study [11], the proposed approach was shutting-down external access to an enterprise network for a period of 140 seconds, to enable the distribution of randomly generated keys to users in a relatively secure way. This study was based on the idea that the main threat is from outside and it is relatively easier to control internal sources since the internal sources are known. Keys are renewed at various intervals while external access to the system is disabled. Also, an analytical model is developed in [11] to evaluate the cost in terms of performance degradation of the underlying network.

Since, a delay decryption mechanism was not used in that study, another protocol has been developed with a combination of Kerberos Authentication Protocol and Encrypted Key Exchange Protocol [10] with addition of the "delay decryption" property of the Kerberos Authentication Protocol. Tests carried out for this work and the network with shut-downs revealed that, the protocol in the previous study [11] increased the time taken to break the encryption.

III. Quality of Service Challenges

Quality of Service (QoS) refers to the ability of a network to provide better, more predictable service to selected network traffic over various underlying technologies, specifically wireless and mobile networks [13], [29], [30]. Wireless and mobile networks especially WLANs have gained widespread popularity mainly because of their low cost and relatively high data rates. Hence the need to address QoS issues becomes extremely important. In recent years, both the enterprises and users are demanding seamless time sensitive movement of information such as audio and video around a wireless communication systems. However interruptions that may be caused by the implemented security mechanisms can cause degradation of performance for the traffic in wireless communication. In addition interruptions in wireless and mobile systems cause the packet loss (order of the packets), latency, congestion and jitter which are the other important QoS challenges that needs to be considered in such systems [31]. Latency is the time delay occurred in speech by the end-to-end user communication system. In other words, latency creates delay in delivery of the packets in communication systems. The lower the latency, the better the QoS [1], [4]. To effectively transport the packets over the wireless media, mechanisms are required that ensure reliable delivery of packets with low and controlled latency. Hence the primary goal in the context of wireless and mobile communication, would be to provide less interruptions, dedicated bandwidth, controlled jitter and latency as well as improved characteristics in terms of packet losses. In general, it can be seen that greater levels of interruption introduce more delay and require lower network latency to maintain good QoS. Latency and/or delay also introduces other difficulties such as echo and talker overlap. The more information can be found in [13], [31]. The end-to-end interruption is therefore the major constraint and requires the delay to be reduced through a packet network. To support traffic reliably and enhance the QoS in WLAN, a network must therefore be able to provide packet forwarding latency, jitter, guaranteed network bandwidth and capacity for communication during periods of network congestion. In other words, to improve measures of quality of service in wireless networks, a network needs to maintain less interrupts and provide high performance considering low latency/delay and jitter with packet loss.

From the above discussion on QoS, it can be seen that enhancing of QoS in wireless networks is critical and challenging operation of a network. The evolution of the network based applications place more stress and require more complex algorithms and designs to support these challenges over WLANs.

IV. Necessity of Modelling Security Protocols for Performability Modelling

One of the main reason of service interruptions in wireless communication systems are the ones integrated in the implemented security mechanisms [3]. The wireless variants of existing protocols may prefer to shut the communication while the critical key exchange processes are taking place. That would introduce significant delays, and increased number of request awaiting for authentication. Furthermore certain types of communication may not be allowed before the authentication takes place.

System or server interruptions depend on the system's nature and can have different impacts on the system performance. The system may not support the on going process or the packet efficiently due to the interruptions hence performance may degrade. In order to overcome this problem, availability and performance of the system should be considered together [9]. From the designer and operator's point of view, it is necessary to take interrupts and factors which may delay the system to perform as usual (e.g. key exchange times) into account. Performability models are obtained by combining performance and availability models. They are used to combine performance and availability/reliability concerns in order to get more realistic results.

Composite performance and availability modelling considers two basic steps. The construction of the suitable model and the solution of the model are these steps. The proper modelling methodology which considers both performance and availability models together is called performability modelling and evaluation [18], [19]. Performability modelling and evaluation includes measures formulation, model specification, model construction, tool development, and application to wide variety of systems [18]. For evaluation of security mechanisms performability evaluation is the most realistic method, since considering the system from a pure performance point of view would ignore the interruptions which may cause QoS degradation severely.

In [17] a unified performability and reliability analysis by using Markov Reward model (MRM) is presented. The MRM approach leads to a separation of the performance and availability models of the system. The MRM approach is an approximate approach and most commonly used one. Probabilistic models, Queuing networks and Markov chains have been largely used in the design of complex systems and a variety of related applications have been employed to develop exact and efficient analytical models for performability evaluation of wireless and mobile communication systems. In this study existing performability evaluation methods are considered for evaluation of security mechanisms from a performance point of view. A new framework has also been discussed for modelling the interactions between the network and the authentication servers.

V. FRAMEWORKS

This section presents models for Kerberos servers suffering from potential KDC failures as well as key renewal protocols which requires the suspension of service.

In [3] a single Kerberos server suffering from potential KDC failures and used together with the Frequent Key Renewal protocol are considered. Allocation of jobs is usually done considering the availability of the Kerberos server. The values and the probabilistic distributions of the parameters used to develop the analytical models are mainly taken from literature [11], [12], [14]. The values of mean arrival and service rates are mainly application dependent.

Jobs arrive at the system in a Poisson stream at a mean rate of σ. The service times of jobs are distributed exponentially with mean $1/\mu$. The Kerberos server considered can execute jobs only during its operative periods, which means that during an operative period the processor is capable of its intended operation, whether working or idle. The Kerberos server is operative if it is not broken, or if the system is not shut. The the Kerberos server may suffer from failures and inter failure times are distributed exponentially with mean $1/\xi$. At the end of this period, the server breaks down and requires an exponentially distributed repair time with mean $1/\eta$. The distribution of time intervals between shutdowns are assumed to be exponentially distributed with given mean value $1/\delta$. When the system is shut, the server does not provide service to incoming request for an exponentially key distribution time which is given by $1/\varphi$. This system can be modelled as follows:

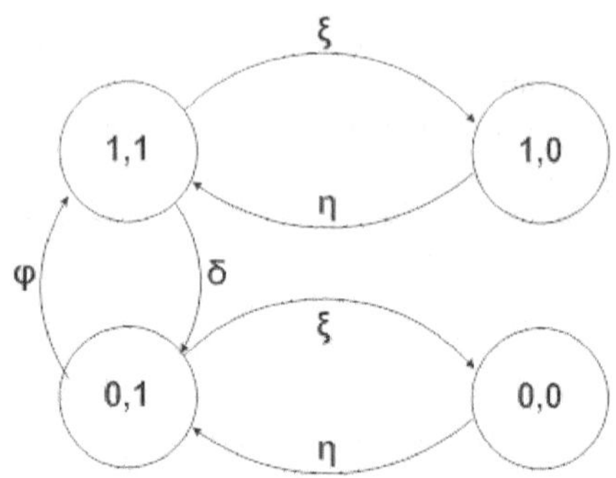

Fig. 1. State diagram for availability of standalone Kerberos authentication server

Please note that state $(0,0)$ represents the state where the server is broken and the system is shut, state $(1,0)$ the system is not shut but the server is broken. In the state $(0,1)$ the server is not broken but the system is shut since the key distribution takes place. Finally the state labelled as $(1,1)$ is the state where the server is operative since the system is not shut and the server is operative. As shown in Figure 1 there are no transitions between states (1,0) and (0,0), since system shutdowns are not required when the server is broken.

The system cinsidered state at time t may be described using a pair of integer valued random variable $I(t)$ and $J(t)$. $I(t)$ specifies the failure, repair, inter key distribution time and key distribution durations (states in figure 1), and $J(t)$ specifies the number of jobs in the system respectively. The operative states $I(t)$ in this case represents the assumed failed/shut and operative periods of the Kerberos authentication server. $Z = [I(t), J(t)]; t \geq 0$ is an irreducible Markov process on a lattice strip (a QBD process), that models the system. Its state space is $(0,1)$x $(0,1,\ldots)$. Similar models [3], [6], [7], [20], [21], [22], [23], [24] are analysed for exact performability evaluation of various Multi sever systems with single repairman and for both finite and infinite queuing systems for some repair strategies. It is possible to extend the exact solution methodology for performability evaluation for of Kerberos authentication servers.

Since the possible operative states of the Kerberos authentication server and the number of data arrivals are represented in the horizontal and vertical directions of the lattice respectively, the transition matrices can be derived as:

i. A is the matrix of instantaneous transition rates from (i, j) to state (l, j),$(i = 0, 1; l = 0, 1; i \neq l; j = 0, 1, \ldots)$, with zeros in the leading diagonal, caused by a change in the operative state. These are the purely lateral transitions of the model$Z$. A clearly depends on parameters ξ, η, δ and φ. The state transition matrices A and A_j can be given as:

$$A = A_j = \begin{pmatrix} 0 & \eta & 0 & 0 \\ \xi & 0 & \varphi & 0 \\ 0 & \delta & 0 & \xi \\ 0 & 0 & \eta & 0 \end{pmatrix}$$

ii. Matrices B and C are transition matrices for one step upward and one step downward transitions respectively [21], [24]. The transition rate matrices do not depend on j for $j \geq M$, where M is a threshold having an integer value [24]. The respective transition matrices are:

$$B = B_j = \begin{pmatrix} \sigma & 0 & 0 & 0 \\ 0 & \sigma & 0 & 0 \\ 0 & 0 & \sigma & 0 \\ 0 & 0 & 0 & \sigma \end{pmatrix}$$

$$C = C_j = \begin{pmatrix} 0 & 0 & 0 & 0 \\ 0 & 0 & 0 & 0 \\ 0 & 0 & \mu & 0 \\ 0 & 0 & 0 & 0 \end{pmatrix}$$

Following the Spectral Expansion solution, the steady-state probabilities of the system considered can be expressed as, where L can be finite or infinite depending on whether the case concerned is with bounded or unbounded queuing system, and N is the total number of operative states (four for the system in 1):

$$P_{i,j} = \lim_{t \longrightarrow \infty} P(I(t) = i, J(t) = j); \quad 0 \leq i \leq N, 0 \leq j \leq L \tag{1}$$

where L can be finite or infinite. Let's define certain diagonal matrices of size $(N + 1) \times (N + 1)$ as follows:

$$D_J^A(i, i) = \sum_{k=0}^{N} A_j(i, k);\ D^A(i, i) = \sum_{k=0}^{N} A(i, k)$$
$$D_J^B(i, i) = \sum_{k=0}^{N} B_j(i, k);\ D^B(i, i) = \sum_{k=0}^{N} B(i, k)$$
$$D_J^C(i, i) = \sum_{k=0}^{N} C_j(i, k);\ D^C(i, i) = \sum_{k=0}^{N} C(i, k)$$

and $Q_0 = B$, $Q_1 = A - D^A - D^B - D^C$, $Q_2 = C$. For both bounded and unbounded queuing systems, all state probabilities in a row can be defined as:

$$v_j = (P_{0,j}, P_{1,j}, \ldots, P_{N,j}) j = 0, 1, \ldots$$

Here, for a bounded system, j is limited by finite L. In this case, when the queue is full, the arriving jobs are lost. The matrices given above are used in the Spectral Expansion solution for both bounded and unbounded queuing systems.

The steady-state balance equations for unbounded queuing systems can now be written as:

$$v_0[D_0^A + D_0^B] = v_0 A_0 + v_1 C_1 \tag{2}$$

$$v_j[D_j^A + D_j^B + D_j^C] = v_{j-1} B_{j-1} + v_j A_j + v_{j+1} C_{j+1}; \quad 1 \leq j \leq M - 1 \tag{3}$$

$$v_j[D^A + D^B + D^C] = v_{j-1} B + v_j A + v_{j+1} C; j \geq M \tag{4}$$

and the normalizing equation is given as follows:

$$\sum_{j=0}^{\infty} v_j e = \sum_{j=0}^{\infty} \sum_{i=0}^{N} P_{i,j} = 1.0 \tag{5}$$

from Equation (4) one can write

$$v_j Q_0 + v_{j+1} Q_1 + v_{j+2} Q_2 = 0; j \geq M - 1 \tag{6}$$

Furthermore, the characteristic matrix polynomial $Q(\lambda)$ can be defined as:

$$Q(\lambda) = Q_0 + Q_1 \lambda + Q_2 \lambda^2 \tag{7}$$

λ and ψ are eigenvalues and left-eigenvectors of $Q(\lambda)$ respectively. Note that, ψ is a row-vector defined as

$\psi = \psi_0, \psi_1, \ldots, \psi_N$, $\lambda = \lambda_0, \lambda_1, \ldots, \lambda_N$ and $\psi Q(\lambda) = 0$; $|Q(\lambda)| = 0$.

Finally, for an unbounded system, when the stability condition is satisfied [6], one can obtain the general solution as:

$$v_j = \sum_{k=0}^{N} a_k \psi_k \lambda_k^{j-M+1}, j \geq M - 1 \tag{8}$$

and in the state probability form,

$$P_{i,j} = \sum_{k=0}^{N} a_k \psi_k(i) \lambda_k^{j-M+1}, j \geq M - 1 \tag{9}$$

where, λ_k $(k = 0, 1, \ldots, N)$ are $N+1$ eigenvalues that are strictly inside the unit circle[6] and a_k $(k = 0, 1, \ldots, N)$ are arbitrary constants which can be scalar or complex-conjugates. All the a_k values and the remaining v_j vectors can be obtained using the process in [2], [6].

From the $P_{i,j}$, a number of steady-state availability, reliability, performability measures can be computed quite easily. For example, mean queue length (MQL) can be obtained as:

$$MQL = \sum_{j=0}^{L} j \sum_{i=0}^{N} P_{i,j}$$

When the system in [3] is considered, the analytical model considered assumes an unbounded queue since incoming requests are not blocked. To show the effectiveness of the method presented, and to evaluate the performance of a Kerberos server with Frequent Key Renewal under Pseudo-Secure Conditions, numerical results are provided. Effects of Key Renewal periods are analysed as well as the effects of KDC failures. Figure 2 shows the MQL as a function of φ for various δ values. The other parameters are $1/\eta = 2$ hours, $1/\xi = 1000$ hours, $\sigma = 80 jobs/sec$, and $\mu = 200$ jobs/sec.

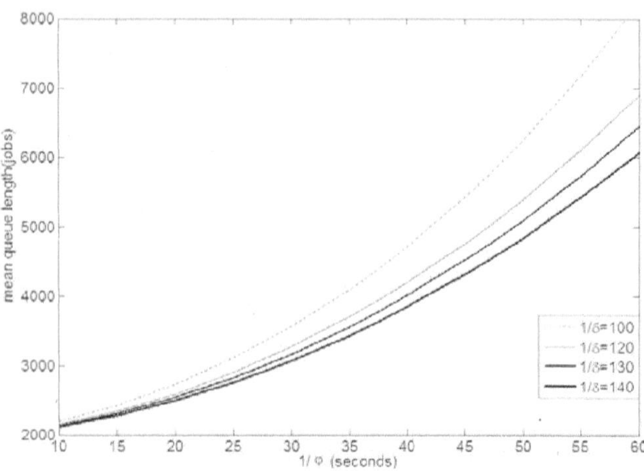

Fig. 2. Numerical results for stand alone Kerberos server

It is clear that as key distribution time increases, the mean queue length also increases. Also, effect of increasing the key renewal period $1/\delta$ decrease for greater $1/\varphi$ values. This is mainly because the effects of other factors such as failures and repairs become more significant while the key renewals do not take place quite often. In [7], [18], [19], [22], [20], [21], [23], [24], [25] and [26] some of the performability models are considered with the exact solution in the wireless and mobile systems. However the most of the previous research is focused on the standalone systems for performability evaluation of wireless cellular networks. In other words the existing studies do not consider the integration of the different networks (more than one process) for performability modelling. In the literature, it is shown that such an integrated system can be modelled as a two stage open queuing system for performance modelling [24], [27], [28], [29], and [30]. In addition the existing two stage open queuing system considers integration of various technologies for performance analysis with exact solution. In [20] and [21] similar modelling approaches are introduced for QoS evaluation of two stage open queuing systems. The models in [20] and [21] consider analytical methods for the performance and performability models of network memory server attached to a local area network respectively.

In order to obtain more realistic QoS measures in secure computer communication various security protocols have been developed. However performability modelling of security protocols considering behaviour of the server and impacts of interruptions has not been used in computer security. This can be done using the existing two stage open networks model used in [20], [21], [24], [27] and [28] with the model presented in [3]. An analytical framework is presented in this study as shown in figure 3.

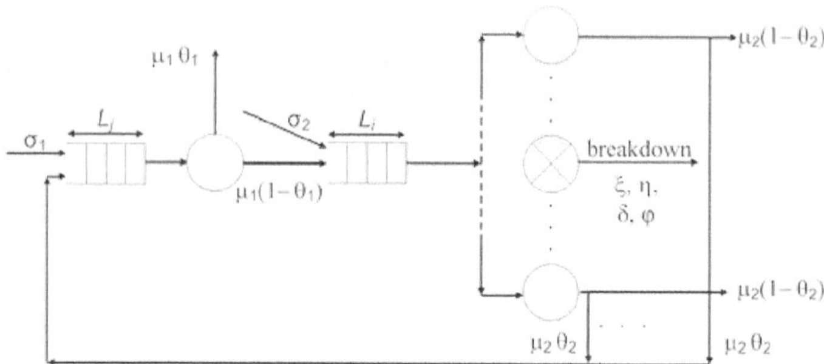

Fig. 3. Analytical framework for interaction of authentication server and network

Please note that when two random variables are used to represent the number of requests in each stage, similar to the studies in [7], [19], [22], [23], [24] and [25], the operative states of the servers cannot be incorporated. A three dimensional approach should therefore be employed similar to the studies in [8].

VI. Conclusions and Future Work

In this paper, we discuss secure communications with various security variants over Kerberos authentication protocol as an example to service interruptions in wireless communication systems caused by security measures. Frequent Key Renewal under Pseudo-Secure Conditions approach is based on secure key distributions at various intervals. During key distribution, external access to the network is not allowed. The access restrictions happen for short intervals [11], [12]. However, any link shut-down costs the network in terms of performance degradation. Therefore, it is essential to evaluate the impact of the proposed approach on system performance.

We provide some discussions on performance and availability evaluation of some security measures. In modern communications, due to high expectations and demand from the users, the communication systems cannot afford to have extensive delays, and interruptions due to security measures. In other words, we should not degrade the performance of the systems while we are trying to protect it. Therefore effects of security measures on overall network should be considered carefully. Kerberos authentication server with key renewal interruptions is an important case study in this sense.

In [3] a modelling approach for performability evaluation of Kerberos servers are considered which dynamically renew keys under pseudo-secure conditions in order to significantly reduce the chances of potential intruders. The proposed approach in [3] also involves temporary interruption to link/server access where it has implications in terms of QoS degradation. Hence in order to enhanced QoS of the security mechanisms in computer communication, the existing performance and availability modelling techniques used in the literature can be adapted to modelling of various security protocols considering the server behaviour as well as the characteristics of the networks. However it is necessary to extend these studies further in order to model the interactions between the underlying server and the incorporated network.

REFERENCES

[1] S. Balsamo, V. D. N. Persone, P. Inverardi, "A review on queueing network models with finite capacity queues for software architectures performance prediction", *Performance Evaluation*, vol. 51, issue 2-4, 2003, pp. 269-288.

[2] R. Chakka, "Spectral expansion solution for some finite capacity queues, *Annals of Operations Research*, 1998, 79, pp. 27-44.

[3] E. Ever, Y. Kirsal and O. Gemikonakli, "Performability Modelling of a Kerberos Server with Frequent Key Renewal under Pseudo-secure Conditions for Increased Security, *IEEE International Conference on the Current Trends in Information Technology (CTIT)* , Dubai Women College, December 2009, pp. 91 96.

[4] N. Baghaei, and R. Hunt, "Security Performance of Loaded IEEE 802.11b Wireless Networks ", *Computer Communications*, Elsevier, UK, vol.27 (17), November 2004, pp. 1746-1756.

[5] V. A. Brennen, "Kerbcros Infrastructure HOW TO", *CryptNET*, Guerrilla Technoogy Development, 2004.

[6] R. Chakka and I. Mitrani, "Heterogeneous Multiprocessor Systems with Breakdowns : Performance and Optimal Repair Strategies", *Theoretical Computer Science*, vol.125, 1994, pp. 91-109.

[7] E. Ever, Y. Kirsal and O. Gemikonakli, "Performability Modelling of Handoff in Wireless Cellular Networks and the Exact Solution of System Models with Service Rates Dependent on Numbers of Originating and Handoff Calls", *In IEEE Proceedings of International Conference on Computational Intelligence, Modelling and Simulation (CSSim 2009)*, September 2009, pp. 282-287.

[8] E. Ever, O. Gemikonakli, A.Kocyigit, E. Gemikonakli, "A hybrid approach to minimize state space explosion problem for the solution of two stage tandem queues", *Journal of Network and Computer Applications*, vol. 36, March 2013, pp.908-926.

[9] Y . Jiang, C. Lin, X. Shen, and M. Shi, "Mutual Authentication and Key Exchange Protocols with Anonymity Property for Roaming Services", *NETWORKING*, 2005, pp. 114-125.

[10] Y. Kirsal and O. Gemikonakli, "An Authentication Protocol to Address the Problem of the Trusted 3rd Party Authentication Protocols", *Novel Algorithms and Techniques In Telecommunications, Automation and Industrial Electronics, (CISSE 2006)*, 2007, pp. 523-526.

[11] Y. Kirsal, and O. Gemikonakli, "Frequent Key Renewal Under Pseudo-Secure Conditions For Increased Security in Kerberos Authentication and its Impact on System Performability", *Proceedings of the 3rd International Conference on Global E-Security*, University of East London (UeL), 2007.

[12] Y. Kirsal, and O. Gemikonakli, "Improving Kerberos Security through the Combined Use of the Timed Authentication Protocol and Frequent Key Renewal", *7th IEEE International Conference on Cybernetic Intelligent Systems (CIS2008)*, IEEE Press, 2008, pp. 153-158.

[13] G. Lowe, "Some New Attacks upon Security Protocols", *9th IEEE Computer Security Workshops*, Society Press, 1996, pp. 162-169.

[14] I. Mitrani, "Approximate Solutions for Heavily Loaded Markov-Modulated Queues", *Performance Evaluation*, vol.62 (1-4), 2005, pp. 117-131.

[15] R. M. Needham, and M. D. Schroeder, "Using Encryption for Authentication in Large Networks of Computer", *Commun. ACM*, ACM Press, vol. 21, 1978, pp. 993-999 .

[16] S. Schneider, "Verifying Authentication Protocols in CSP", *IEEE Trans. Sofw. Eng.*, IEEE Press, 1998, vol. 24, pp. 741-758.

[17] K. S. Trivedi, M. Malhotra, and R. M. Fricks, "Markov reward approach to performability and reliability analysis", pages 7-11, 1994.

[18] I. Mitrani, "Queues with Breakdowns, Performability Modelling: Techniques and Tools", Wiley, Chichester, 2001.

[19] K. S. Trivedi, S. Dharmaraja, and X. Ma, "Performability modelling of wireless communication systems", *International Journal of Communication Systems*, vol 16, 2003, pp. 561-577.

[20] O. Gemikonakli, G. Mapp, D. Thakker, and E. Ever, "Modelling and performability analysis of network memory servers", *Annual Simulation Symposium*, 2006, pp.127-134.

[21] O. Gemikonakli, G. Mapp, E. Ever, and D. Thakker, "Modelling network memory servers with parallel processors, break-downs and repairs", *Annual Simulation Symposium*, 2007, pp. 11-20.

[22] Y. Kirsal and O. Gemikonakli, "Performability Modelling of Handoff in Wireless Cellular Networks with Channel Failures and Recovery", *In IEEE Proceedings of* 11th *International Conference on Computer Modelling and Simulation (UKSim 2009)*, March 2009, pp. 544-547.

[23] Y. Kirsal, E. Ever, O. Gemikonakli and G. Mapp, "Critical Review of Analytical Modelling Approaches for Performability Evaluation of the Handover Phenomena in Mobile Communication Systems", *The Proceeding of IEEE* 11th *International Conference on Computer and Information Technology,* 2th *International Workshop on Dependable Service-Oriented and Cloud computing (DSOC 2011)*, September 2011, pp. 132-137.

[24] Y. Kirsal, O. Gemikonakli, E. Ever, and G. Mapp, "Performance Analysis of Handovers to Provide a Framework for Vertical Handover Policy Management in Heterogeneous Environments", *In 45th Annual Simulation Symposium,(ANSS'12)*, Orlando, FL, USA, March 2012, pp. 1-8.

[25] G.N. Gowrishankar, Sekhar, and P.S. Satyanarayana, "Analytic Performability Model of Vertical Handoff in Wireless Networks, *Journal of Computer Science*, 5(6), 2009, pp. 445-450.

[26] K.S. Trivedi, and X. Ma, "Performability Analysis of Wireless Cellular Networks, Symposium on Performance Evaluation of Computer and Telecommunication Systems (SPECTS 2002), 2002.

[27] T. Shensheng, and L. Wei, "Performance Analysis of the 3G Network with Complementary WLAN, *Global Telecommunications Conference GLOBECOM '05*, vol. 5, 2005, pp. 26362641.

[28] W. Xia, and, L. Shen, "Modeling and Analysis of Handoffs in Cellular and WLAN Integration *IEEE International Conference on Communications, ICC '07I*, pp. 385-391, June 2007.

[29] I. Saravanan, G. Sivaradje, and P. Dananjayan, "QoS provisioning for cellular/WLAN interworking, Wireless and Optical Communications Networks, 2006 IFIP International Conference, July 2006, pp. 50-55.

[30] W. Song, H. Jiang, W. Zhuang, and X. Shen, "Resource Management for QoS Support in Cellular/WLAN Interworking, *IEEE Network*, vol. 19, no. 5, Oct. 2005, pp.12-18.

[31] Z. Hua, M. Li, I. Chlamtac, and B. Prabhakaran, "A Survey Of Quality Of Service In IEEE 802.11 Networks, *In IEEE Wireless Communications Journals*, vol. 11, no. 4, 24 August 2004, pp. 6-14.

SESSION

NETWORK SECURITY II

Chair(s)

Dr. Levent Ertaul

Port Knocking- An Additional Layer of Security for SSH and HTTPS

Jigar A. Raval[1], **and Samuel Johnson**[1]
[1]Computer Center, Physical Research Laboratory, Ahmedabad, Gujarat, India

Abstract - *The availability of communication resources remote access of e-mails and data is increasingly required and desirable by users. This, however, implies security of user data and e-mails. The vulnerability of the system depends on the ability to scan the system for an open port and on the service running on the open port. Such open ports are entry points for attacks. Masking of open ports and services on the system, using port knocking technique, provides a simple and reliable method. Initially, during the port knock sequence all the ports remains closed, thus the services or open ports become invisible to any malicious port scan. After a valid port knock, a predetermined port is opened allowing access of predefined service. Thus port knocking technique adds an extra layer of security without any major changes to the application.*

In this paper, we discuss a complete practical approach of securing SSH and HTTPS (Web based email access) using available open source software. We wish also to share our experiences so that enterprise level secure systems can be deployed just by use of free and open source (FOSS) software.

Keywords: SSH security, HTTPS Security, IPtables, Port knocking

1 Introduction

Any system connected to the Internet can be scanned or probed to get detail of any open ports and associated services running on the respective open ports and then to exploit the vulnerabilities of the service to hack into the server. We normally need to connect to the respective service port for different requirements like to manage the system remotely, to remotely access of the data, to remotely access web based email. These open ports are entry point for the attackers. Looking with another angle, if the port is not open, it is difficult to exploit the service. Thus these open ports are the "Achilles heel" of the system.

For example, services like SSH, HTTPS (for this paper it refers to web email access) are running on a predefined well known port like 22, and 443. The default port is always open in the firewall so the service can be accessible over the network. When we use SSH, HTTPS services on standard well known port, we are likely to see brute force login attempts from different or same IP addresses. The SSH, HTTPS does not limit unsuccessful login attempts by itself. There are multiple ways to deal with problem. One good way is to use different non-standard port to hide the service to discover and use the service vulnerabilities to exploit the server. But using latest freely available tools like nmap[1] a complete scan of all the ports on the server will quickly reveal the open port and get the associated service detail like version of the service, running on the server. Then the hackers use the details, to find the vulnerabilities of the service and try to exploit the system using the service vulnerabilities. Another important point is to have a strong authentication mechanism. But this will not stop brute-force, dictionary attacks on the server. The other way is to configure the firewall (IPtables) and allow access of SSH/HTTPS from specific IP Address. However, it is difficult to open specific IP address if the legitimate user access request is coming from dynamically assigned IP address. IPtables can be further customized to stop brute force attacks but still we do not want to make system resources (CPU, Memory of server, and network) busy to deal with unnecessary traffic. Hence, there should be an appropriate security layer in place to protect from such system scanning, and unauthorized access attempts while keeping it accessible online to the trusted users. A good solution is to limit access of SSH, HTTPS services using a technique called - port knocking. The access to the SSH, HTTPS will be unavailable until there is some kind of secret port knock sequence. Then the port will be open for a certain time, and for specific IP address from where the correct port knock sequence observed. It may be relatively difficult for an attacker to find that the remote system uses the port knocking as there is no port open for entering the system. Even the system scan using nmap tool does not show open ports on the system.

Consider that for an attacker who does not know the knock sequence, in order to discover it requires massive brute force effort. That is, without prior knowledge of knock sequence, a simple two TCP port knock sequence (eg 5678, 4567) would require a scan of every combination of two ports in the range of 1-65535. The port would not open until the correct two port knock sequence received. That equates to attempt of a maximum of 65535^2 packets in order to obtain and detect a single successful opening. On the other hand, an authorized user would be able to open the port and access the system from any corner of the world.

In this paper, we have discussed port knocking technique, its implementation using IPtables, our experiment results and proposed a setup using all the available open source tools which adds an additional layer of security to secure SSH, Web email access using HTTPS with very less complexity on the server and client.

1.1 About SSH

The main purpose of SSH [2] is to securely transmit data over network connections using strong encryption and authentication methods. It is a replacement of non-secure Telnet, FTP and r-commands (rlogin, rcp, rsh). Many organizations now use SSH because of its features like secure remote login, secure file transfer, secure remote administration, secure remote-command execution, port forwarding (tunneling).

There are many methods/ways like Replay Attacks, Eavesdropping, Man-in-the-Middle Attacks, IP and DNS spoofing, an attacker might use to gain access of data in transit. SSH mitigate such attacks very effectively.

However, for strengthening SSH, we propose following steps, should be sufficient to protect SSH server and client, even if the number of attacks continues to rise.

(A) Run the service on non-standard port

(B) Defining restricted user access list

(C) Port Knocking [3,4] using IPtables [5]

1.2 About HTTPS

HTTPS (Hypertext Transfer Protocol Secure) is not a protocol in itself, rather it is a security add-on on top of HTTP using SSL/TLS. HTTPS URLs begin with "https://" and use port 443 by default, whereas HTTP URLs begin with "http://" and use port 80 by default. HTTPS is especially important over unencrypted/insecure networks such as Wi-Fi, cybercafé, etc, as anyone on the same network can do packet sniffing and discover sensitive information. Every thing in HTTPS message is encrypted, including headers and response/request.

To prepare a web server to accept HTTPS connection, the administrator must create a public key certificate, also known as the Digital Certificate. Digital Certificates forms the basis of secure HTTPS/SSL session. A certificate is simply a public key containing along with it an identity such as email id, organizations name, URL, It can not only be used for establishing the authenticity of the indentifying entity, but can also be used for encryption (using various key exchange techniques).

A certificate can be self generated and self-signed or a signed certificate can be bought from a Certificate Authority (CA). Both have their merits and demerits.

The organizations allow secure (HTTPS) email access through web based tool like SquirrelMail, TWIG within their own network and also from outside the network. There are many ways to break even HTTPS. Attackers can use vulnerabilities of web application to exploit and hack the server. For hardening web based email access using HTTPS, we propose following steps, should be sufficient to protect HTTPS server which provides web based email access even if the number of attacks continues to rise.

(A) Run the service on non-standard port

(B) Defining restricted user access list

(C) Port Knocking [3,4] using IPtables [5]

For experiment, we have configured latest version of Apache[14], PHP[15], Squirrelmail[13] on CentOS linux platform.

The remainder of this paper is organized as follows. The paper presents a port knocking technology briefly in Section II, followed by Section III presents the details about the implementation and result. Finally, Section IV presents concluding remarks and outlines future work.

2 Port Knocking

Port knocking is a technique that can be used to hide services that are running on a secure and hardened server. This is achieved by not opening the port until a correct sequence of knock packets are received by the server. The client attempts to initiate several three-way-handshakes and receives no reply. These connections attempts are monitored and recorded by firewall (IPtables). Initially, the server presents no open ports to the public and is monitoring all connection attempts. The client initiates connection attempts to the server by sending SYN packets to the ports specified in the knock. It is important to understand that port knocking is an added form of security, and not meant as a replacement for regular security maintenance. This process of knocking is what gives port knocking its name. The server offers no response to the client during the knocking phase, as it "silently" processes the port sequence. When the firewall (IPtables) decodes a valid knock, it opens a port for the specific IP address from where the port was knocked for a specific time. Following figures show how port knocking technique works:

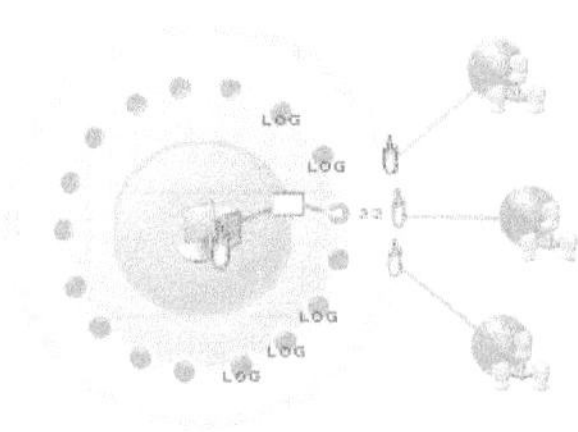

Fig. 1[3]. Default all the ports are blocked

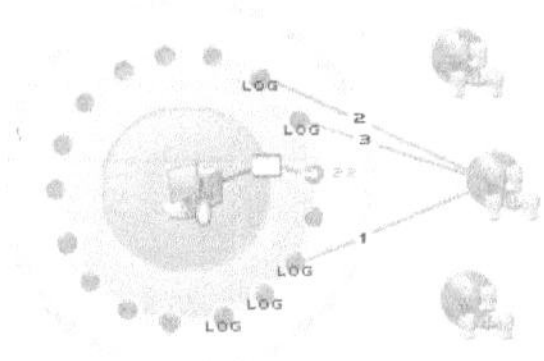

Fig.2[3] User knocks the required ports

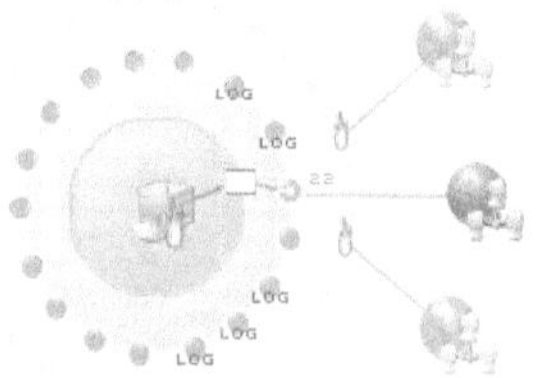

Fig.3[3] The system opens the defined port for specific host from where user has knocked the port

2.1 Pros and Cons of Port Knocking

The main benefit of port knocking is that it allows for stealthy authentication into a host without open ports. The method is stealthy because it is not possible to determine if the host is listening for knocks/requests. Since information is flowing as connection attempts, rather than packet data payload, it is unlikely that this method would be easily detected. The system is flexible, because existing applications such as SSH, which perform their own authentication, do not need to be changed, as port knocking is just an additional outer layer of security for the machine [4]. Consider that for an attacker who do not know the knock sequence, in order to discover it requires massive brute force effort. That is, without prior knowledge of knock sequence, a simple three TCP port knock sequence (eg 5678, 4567, 6789) would require a scan of every combination of three ports in the range of 1-65535. The port would not open until the correct three port knock sequence received. That equates to attempt of a maximum of 65535^3 (over 281 trillion) packets in order to obtain and detect a single successful opening. On the other hand, an authorized user would be able to open the port and access the system from any corner of the world. Modern port knock implementations are much more intelligent and mature, some use highly secure cryptographic hashes in order to defeat the most common attacks like packet sniffing and packet replay.

However, as with any security system, the disadvantage begins with the small inconveniences that must be endured while that system is in use. The use of the client imposes an overhead for each connection and users require instruction. Port knocking cannot be used to protect public services such as mail or web, as this would require everyone to know the knock. Thus, the public services should be relocated to a demilitarized zone (DMZ) and isolated from the hosts with sensitive information.

The implementation of any system that manipulates firewall rules in an automated fashion must be robust to prevent legitimate users and system administrators from being locked out. Also, if the service daemon crashes, the host access will not be available. Appropriate measures should be implemented to avoid such a scenario.

3 Experiment and Result

Our proposed setup solution comprises use of IPtables firewall which is built right into the Linux kernel. However, port knocking can be implemented using various methods. It could be implemented as a standalone daemon processes like knockd, fwknop, etc.. There also exists software to encrypt the entire knock sequence. However, it requires the use of dedicated software on both client and server side for the encryption and decryption process. To overcome these, we have not considered encryption in port knocking. We have configured IPtables with 'recent module' which requires initially single port to be knocked. However, it is possible to configure IPtables to sense multiple ports knocking in defined sequence. Hence, there is no specific daemon required to run on the server. Also, client does not require any specific software to knock the port. To avoid denial of service attack, we have also implemented rate control using IPtables.

3.1 Port knocking for SSH (An IPtables based approach):

We have implemented port knocking on the experiment server. We have separately installed latest SSH package. The new SSH is compiled in such a way that it does not display its version in nmap scanning or telnet command line access. This makes it more difficult for the attacker to find the SSH version and use the vulnerability for attacking the server.

To make the system/service more harden, we select the non standard port to run SSH. We have also taken other known security measures to protect the system i.e. allow only protocol version 2, allow only specific users, disable root login, etc.

We have implemented port knocking using IPTables. So, there would be no running service failed that could fail the access. By default, all the traffic is dropped by IPtables rules.

As per our needs, we have configured IPtables rules in such a way that it requires knock only one port and also avoid any extra utility on the client machine for knocking the port. The IPtables rules are written to open SSH port only for the specific IP address from where the port is knocked and keeps the port open for specific time period only. In other words, after knocking the ports, user must establish the session within the specific time period otherwise the IPtables rule drops the request and user should knock the port again to establish the SSH session. We have configured IPtables to log all the request of port scan, port knock and SSH. We have also tried to block some of the common attacks and force SYN packets check, Fragments packets check, XMAS packets check, drop all NULL packets etc.

In order to test the proposed setup, we have kept the system on the internet for more than a year. We have not observed a single unauthorized login attempt which was observed earlier while SSH service was running on well known port number 22. We have also observed that suppose the port is scanned and open for SSH session, at the same time if attacker scan the system using nmap the scan will display scan port either filtered or closed.

To analyze the server logs, we have developed web based software to analyze and display Monthly, Yearly SSH successful and failed login attempts by username, source IP address with IP Address geo-location. The software is developed on Linux using Java, Mysql and Apache-Tomcat. We have used GeoLite[6] freely available database to get geo-location of the IP Address. As mentioned, we have already rejected port 22 access attempt using IPtables. We have statistics of port 22 access attempts with source IP address and respective country. The statistics shows an average of 17 attempts on port 22 per day. Figure 4 shows day wise graphical representation rejected port 22 access attempts for the month of January 2013.

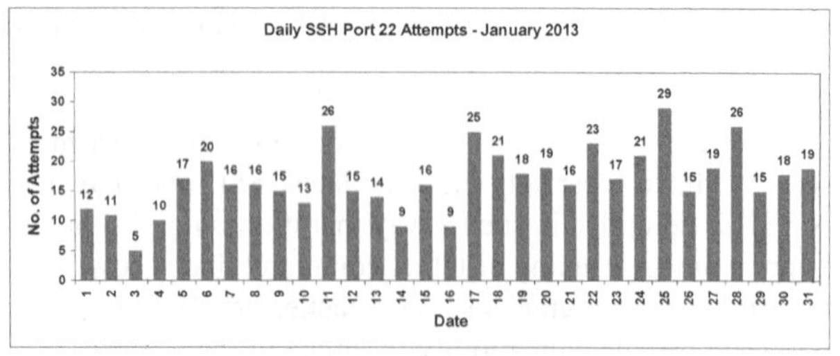

Fig.4 Dropped Port 22 Access Attempts-January 2013

Following table shows dropped port 22 access attempts (January 2013) of top five countries. Figure 5 also represents graphical representation for the same.

Sr. No.	Country	No. of Access Attempts
1.	China	199
2.	US	47
3.	Pvt. IP Address	42
4.	India	34
5.	Korea, Republic	27

Table 1 - Country wise dropped port 22 access attempts

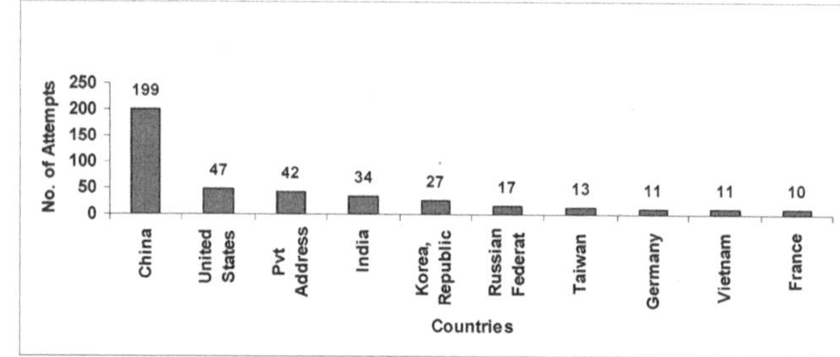

Fig.5 Country wise Dropped Port 22 Access Attempts

In the month of January 2013, there are total 244 number of successful and 18 number of failed (user has entered incorrect password) logins observed.

Sometimes Educational and Research institutes have a requirement to provide the access of Institute subscribed Library Journals/Paper from home/outside network to the students/scientists. To enable the access, we have experimented two mechanisms (1) SSH tunneling and (2) using freely available sshuttel[7] script which we customized as per our experimental need. We did experiment using both the mechanism on windows and linux client. It worked successfully and user could browse Institute subscribed Library Journals/Paper from home/outside Institute's network.

3.1.1 SSH tunneling

Below Figure 6 shows the experimental setup using SSH tunneling to access Institute's network and also to access Institute's Library subscribed journals over Internet.

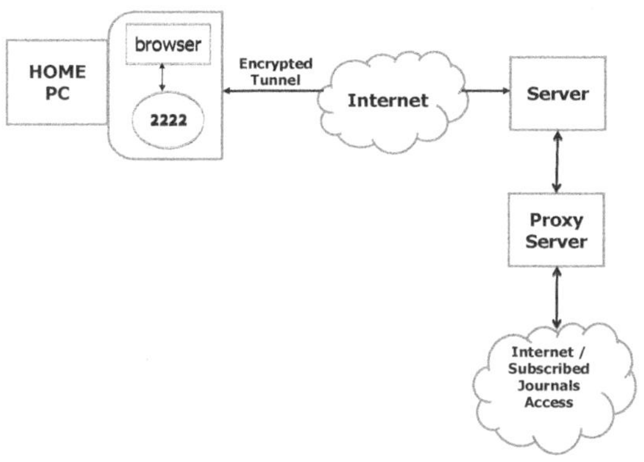

Fig.6 SSH tunneling

3.1.2 sshuttle[7] for Linux:

There is one open source Python based Linux tool/script available called sshuttle to establish SSH based VPN type tunnel. It creates transparent proxy server on local machine for all IP addresses that match 0.0.0.0/0. More specific defined IP addresses can also be used. We have modified the script as per our needs and repacked the whole bundle in a single Linux package file (RPM and DEB) called SSHVPN. Below figure 7 shows experimental setup to securely access Institute's network using sshuttle over Internet.

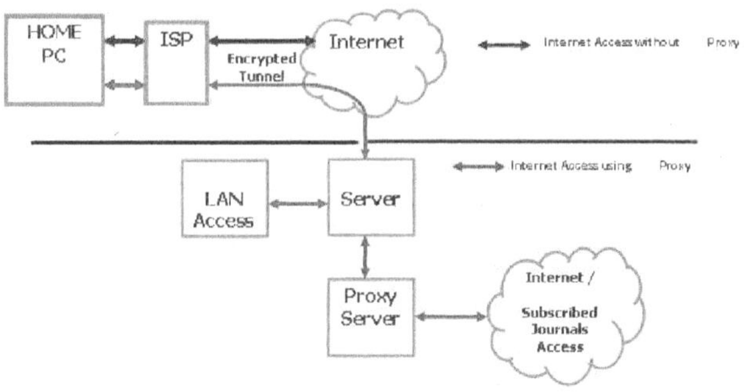

Fig. 7 SSH VPN using sshuttle

We have successfully tested the network access using our customized script from Linux client.

3.2 Port knocking for HTTPS (Web email access):

As explained earlier, the organizations also allow secure email access through web based (HTTPS) within their own network and also outside the network. To further secure from automated brute force password and other automated scripts attacks, we would also like to use port knocking for the web based email access. Now, the problem is that unlike SSH, HTTP is a stateless protocol. As a result, the port has to be kept open for the entire duration of mail access. For experiment, we have configured latest version of Apache[14], PHP[15], Squirrelmail[13] on CentOS linux platform. We have also taken care of basic security of Apache and PHP.

Solution 1:

A simple solution for the problem would be to designate another port which would close the HTTPS port. To automate the close port request, we modified the signout php page of webmail and incorporated the closing port knock. The closing knock port was chosen to be 80 (HTTP port) so that it is not readily visible in browser's address bar.

The solution was extensively tested and was working fine for users accessing mail from their home. However, a new problem arose, if the user was behind a NAT proxy. That is, if more than one user logs in from the same NATed Proxy IP, then the first one to signout will terminate the connection for all users since all 'appear' to come from the same IP address due to Network Address Translation in work behind the scene.

Now, since iptables do not provide a direct way to count the number of requests from same ip address, and take actions accordingly, the only choice we had in deploying this solution was to create a custom program that would monitor iptable's log and would insert or delete rules to allow or deny users. The script would make a note of number of IPs currently connected and would only delete the access rule when the last user from the same IP has quit. The drawback in this approach was that if that external program were to quit or terminate for some reason, then even legitimate users (irrespective of NAT) would be denied of mail access.

Though the problem of NAT would rarely occur, and though the workaround in that case would be to simply allow access for that organization temporarily, the inherent complications involved in dealing with this rare problem, the manual intervention required and dependence on an external program forced us to think of other possibilities.

Solution 2:

We analyzed access logs of the users' web based email access and monitor the duration of their webmail session and found that on average, a user typically spends only around five to fifteen minutes time while checking mail.

Based on that, we chose to close the port automatically after a predefined period of say thirty minutes. So as to not surprise the user by terminating the connection, a count down timer will also be displayed which would show the remaining time till port close. If the user wishes to extend the period, he/she shall again knock the opening port.

If in that duration, another user arrives from the same IP (using NAT) the time period of both the users will get extended.

3.3 Implementation

We have successfully tested both the solutions and found that solution 2 is more suitable without adding a layer of complexity. Since last two months, solution 2 is running on our test server. We have not observed any brute force login attempts, Denial of Service Attacks. We have also configured IPtables in such a way that if someone tries to scan the port, the system will automatically block the IP address for temporary defined time period. However, we are still doing further more experiments.

4 Conclusions and future work

Initially SSH was running on the well-known standard port 22. We have already set the Access Control List (ACL). However, we have observed many unsuccessful login attempts for login id like root, guest, mysql, admin, etc. from different IP sources. Some of the time we have observed unsuccessful brute of attack or Denial of Service attacks.

The multi layer security approach helps us to secure and harden the SSH service. We did experiment on the system with SSH and Port Knocking for more than one year. We have not observed any unsuccessful login attempt and brute force login attacks on the server. SSH with the above setup enable to economically, privately, effectively and safely access the system from public networks like internet.

We have also successfully tested open source - One Time Password (OTP) package on our server. To use this, user need to carry a pre-generated one time password list on a paper or a file. If it is lost/deleted than user can not communicate with the system. Hence, we would like to further study in detail for integration of OTP tool.

Although right now, we are doing experiment using timeout for HTTPS port knock session, in the future, we may instead use the external program based approach if it clears our rigorous testing process. In the near future, IPtables might itself contain branching logic so that we no longer be dependent on the external program.

No single piece of software can be complete security solution. To harden the system, we plan to enable Multi-Factor authentication and also to use available open source fail2ban utility which blocks the IP address for the certain defined time period for the defined unsuccessfully login attempts.

The experimental test setup will be useful to other organization to secure their SSH and web based email access services without any additional complexity on the server and client.

5 Acknowledgements

We thank Dr. A.D.K. Singh, Prof. V.K.B.Kota, Mr. Dholakia G. G., for providing their valuable suggestions and encouragement in establishing this system. We also thank our colleagues Mr. Alok Shrivastava, Mr. Hitendra Mishra, and Mr. Tejas Sarvaiya at the Computer Center and all the PRL users for their support and cooperation.

6 References

[1] NMAP- http://nmap.org

[2] SSH – http://www.openssh.org

[3] Port Knocking – http://www.portknocking.org

[4] M. Krzywinski, “Port Knocking: Network Authentication across Closed Ports”. SysAdmin 2003. Magazine 12: pp 12-17

[5] IPtables – http://www.netfilter.org

[6] GeoLite Database- http://www.maxmind.com/app/geolite

[7] Sshuttle- https://github.com/apenwarr/sshuttle

[8] S. Krivis, “Port Knocking: Helpful or Harmful? – An Exploration of Modern Network Threats”, GIAC Security Essentials Certification, 2004, unpublished

[9] Fwknop – http://www.cipherdyne.org

[10] S. Jeanquier, “An Analysis of Port Knocking and Single Packet Authorization”, MSc Thesis, Information Security Group, Royal Holloway College, University of London, 2006

[11] B. Maddock, Port Knocking: An Overview of Concepts, Issues and Implementations, GIAC Security Essentials Certification, 2004, unpublished

[12] R. deGraaf, C. Aycock M. Jacobson, “Improved Port Knocking with Strong Authentication”. ACSAC 2005, pp. 409-418

[13] SquirrelMail – http://squirrelmail.org

[14] APACHE – http://www.apache.org

[15] PHP – http://php.net

[16] Di Gioia P. , "Behind Closed Doors: An Evaluation of Port Knocking Authentication'. Donald Bren School of Information and Computer Sciences, University of California, Irvine 2004.

[17] Dr. Hussein Al-Bahadili and Dr. Ali H. Hadi "Network Security Using Hybrid Port Knocking" IJCSNS International Journal of Computer Science and Network Security, VOL. 10 No. 8, August 2010

Implementation of Boneh Protocol 3 in Location Based Services (LBS) to Provide Proximity Services

L. Ertaul, N. Shaikh, S. Kotipalli
Mathematics and Computer Science, California State University East Bay, Hayward, USA

Abstract* – In recent years, smartphones have taken over as the pocket technology of choice. More than a half of smartphone owners use a location based information service of some kind. And a core component of Location Based Services (LBS) is proximity testing of users. These services determine if two mobile users are close to each other without requiring them to disclose their exact locations. In this paper, we present Boneh Protocol 3 which supports private proximity testing by using location tags. We study the use of "location tags" generated from the physical environment in order to strengthen the security of proximity testing in Boneh Protocol 3. In this paper, we attempt to provide a realistic assessment of proximity testing for location-based services by implementing Boneh Protocol 3. We used Android platform for an implementation of Boneh protocol 3.

Keywords- Location Based Services; Smart Phones; Proximity Testing; Location Tags; Boneh Protocol 3.

1. INTRODUCTION

Mobile phones and the Internet have revolutionized the communication and lifestyle of people. Due to the growing number of smartphone users, location-based services are growing in popularity. An increasing number of mobile phones allow people to access the Internet where ever they are and whenever they want. From the Internet they can obtain information on places (city maps, restaurants, museums, hospitals). Such kind of restaurant search with respect to position and time can be done by use of LBS [1]. Thus, one can define Location Based Services as-

"Location Based Services are information services accessible with mobile devices through the mobile network and utilizing the ability to make use of the location of the mobile device" [2]

"A Location Based Services is a wireless IP (Internet Protocol) service that uses geographic information to serve a mobile user" [3]

There exist a number of LBS providing location sharing. This includes Google Latitude, Facebook places, Foursquare, Loopt, and a large number of smartphone applications [4], [5]. In recent years there has been considerable research on privacy in LBS. The fundamental problem seem to be that few people would like even their closest friends to know their location all the time, yet will allow distant acquaintances to know their location some of the time [5], [11]. These definitions describe Location Based Services (LBS) as an intersection of three technologies (*see figure 1*), such as the mobile telecommunication system and hand held devices, from Internet and from Geographic Information Systems (GIS) with spatial databases [13].

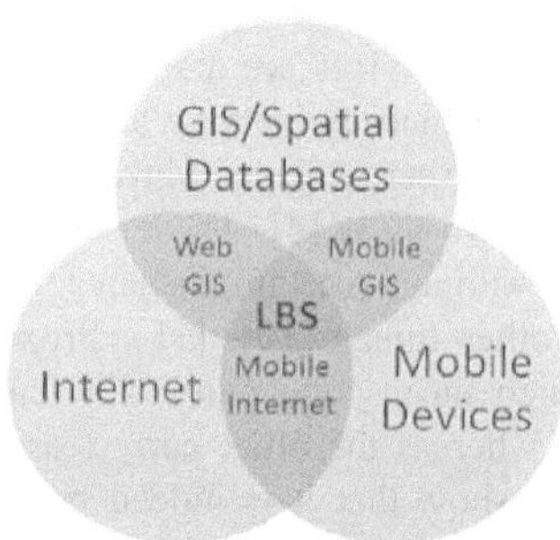

Fig.1. LBS as an intersection of technologies

The paper is organized as follows. The Security and Privacy Concerns in LBS are reviewed in Section 2 followed by Proximity Services and Private Set Intersection in Section 3 and 4. The Location Tags and Private Proximity Testing are discussed in section 5 and 6 and then protocol 1 and 2 are presented in section 7, 8. In section 9, the description of Boneh Protocol 3 is reported. To end with section 10 and 11, Implementation of Boneh Protocol 3 and its experimental results are presented respectively.

2. SECURITY AND PRIVACY ISSUES IN LBS

According to much of the research in location-based computing, privacy is an essential issue and the subject is often addressed in terms of how sensitive information is kept secured in the application [7]. A major privacy concern with the use of Location Based Services is the release to untrusted third parties of the user precise location information. This concern applies to proximity services as well [1]. One of the biggest concerns is that it can be possible to compile a very detailed picture of someone's movements if they are carrying a wireless device that communicates its location to network operators [6]. LBS providers must alleviate consumer privacy fears by implementing secure network and encryption technologies to curb illegal activity [6], [16].

2.1 Privacy Requirements

In general, privacy-preserving systems for LBS services are expected to satisfy some or all of the basic properties below [18].

- **Location Privacy:** The protocol does not reveal the (exact) user's location information to the LBS provider.
- **Identity Privacy (Untraceability):** The LBS provider is not able to find the identity of the user, based on the location information received during the user access [15], [18].
- **Tracking Protection (Unlinkability):** The LBS provider is not able to link two or more successive user positions [15], [18], [19].

2.2 Security Requirements

Access control in LBS involves satisfying some or all of the following security properties [20].

- **Mutual Authentication:** In order to protect themselves from spoofing attacks communication messages between system entities should be authenticated and integrity-protected [18], [20].

3. PROXIMITY SERVICES

Proximity based services are a special class of Location Based Services in which the service adaptation depends on the comparison between a given threshold value and the distance between two users [4]. These services inform users when they are within a certain distance of other people, businesses, or other things [10], [15]. Proximity testing is asymmetric which means one party will learn if the other party is nearby whereas the other party learns nothing [15]. In our paper we show that it is indeed possible to provide location functionality in a private manner. What this means is that a pair of friends will be automatically notified when they are nearby, but otherwise no information about their locations will be revealed to anyone.

Let us consider a application of proximity testing, keeping in mind that different applications require different proximity granularity [1].

- Alice and Bob are friends, and are serendipitously notified that they are shopping in the same mall. They meet and have a pleasant time together. Alternatively, Alice and Bob first meet online, but later decide to meet in person at a coffee shop. Alice arrives first and is notified when Bob arrives [1].
- Alice would like to get dinner with her friend Bob who travels a lot. Using privacy-preserving proximity testing, Alice can check if Bob is town before calling him. Note that for this application the proximity granularity is a wide geographic area [1].
- Bob, a student lands at his college airport and wants to check if anyone from his college is currently at the airport and can give him a ride to campus [1].
- Alice is a manager who wants to automatically record who is present at her daily meetings. However, her employees do not want their location tracked. Privacy preserving proximity testing over this well organized group allows satisfying both requirements [1].

3.1 Proximity Threshold

The distance threshold for proximity detection should not be globally fixed but instead configurable by each user. This is because a larger threshold is neither strictly worse nor strictly better than a smaller one, either from the security or the functionality perspective. With a larger threshold, the user is easier to locate but in case of a match their location is revealed less accurately [1].

4. PRIVATE SET INTERSECTION

Boneh protocol 3 is based on location tags and these are generated by 2 parties who wish to do the proximity test. Broadly speaking if these location tags have few in common, then we conclude that the parties are nearby and it there is no match, we understand that they live far away. In order to find the matching set of intersection, there are various methods proposed. In Boneh protocol, we use private set intersection proposed by Freedman, Nissim and Pinkaas [10].

5. LOCATION TAGS

A location tag is a secret associated with a point in space and time. It is a collection of location features derived from (mostly electromagnetic) signals present in the physical environment. Location tagging is a procedure to extract the tag from a point in space-time, together with a comparison or matching function [1], [17].

5.1 Properties of Location Tags

When compare the location tags, we need to compare two vectors that match approximately, fuzzy set intersection. Location tag is equal to vector and matching function i.e. space-time [15]. The two key properties are:

- ***Unpredictability***-Cannot produce matching tag unless nearby
- ***Reproducibility***-Two devices at same place & time produce matching tags (not necessarily identical) [17].

Location tags provide a different model for proximity testing. The main advantage is that since the location tags of the two parties need to match, spoofing the location is no longer possible, which stops online brute force attacks [1]. The main disadvantage is that users no longer have control over the granularity of proximity: the notion of neighborhood is now entirely dependent on the type of location tag considered [1], [17], [12].

6. PRIVATE PROXIMITY TESTING

In this section we analyse different ways to compute the proximity of Alice and Bob in terms of performance and accuracy. The obvious solution would be to calculate the distance between their positions and decide if the distance is lower than some threshold.

6. 1 Asymmetry

Proximity testing is asymmetric: one party will learn if the other party is nearby whereas the other party learns nothing [1].

The position of Alice along with a given range defines a circle, and the problem is to test if Bob is inside or outside the circle. Another solution is to approximate the area of the circle with cells of a grid. A position is then mapped to a cell, having a unique identifier, in the grid. Using this approach, proximity testing can be reduced to set inclusion as noted by others [5]. The way we detect when two friends are nearby is by dividing the plane [1], [13] into a system of 3 overlapping hexagonal grids. Cryptographic protocols for "Private Equality Testing" allow a pair of users to compare if they are within the same grid cell, but otherwise reveal nothing [1]. *See figure 2*

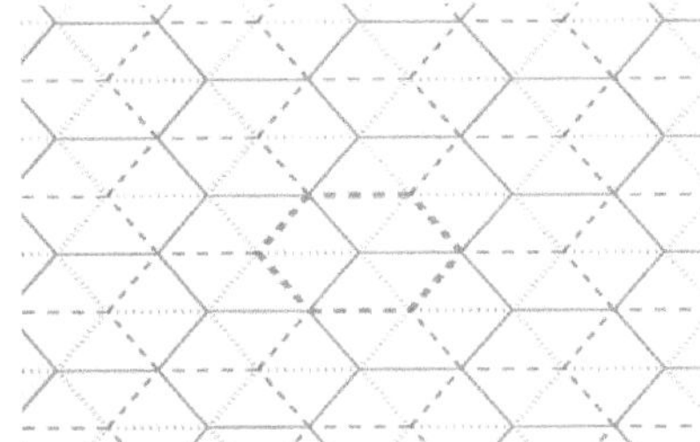

Fig.2. Three overlapping hexagonal grids. A blue grid cell is highlighted

7. PROTOCOL 1 SYNCHRONOUS PRIVATE EQUALITY TESTING

In this protocol the server is used only to forward messages between the two parties, and does not perform any computation. It is based on a mechanism of Lipmaa [27]. The protocol has the following characteristics:

- It is synchronous, i.e., both parties need to be online.
- Each party performs either 2 or 3 exponentiations.
- There are two rounds, namely Alice sends a message to Bob (through the server) and Bob responds to Alice
- Communication is about 40 bytes per edge per time interval using elliptic curves of size 160 bits (additional end-to-end encryption introduces a negligible overhead).

It is secure against arbitrary collusion assuming the hardness of the standard Decision Diffie-Hellman problem [1].

8. PROTOCOL 2 FAST ASYNCHRONOUS PRIVATE EQUALITY TEST WITH AN OBLIVIOUS SERVER

Our second private equality test is novel and requires far less communication and computation, but is only secure assuming the server does not collude with either party. The server learns nothing at the end of the protocol. The reason for the performance improvements is that this protocol uses three parties (Alice, Bob, and server) and is therefore able to rely on information theoretic methods such as secret sharing [1].

9. BONEH PROTOCOL 3

Boneh and team from Standford have proposed 2 versions of this protocol. Now let's look at the 1st version of the protocol. In this protocol, let's suppose Alice wants to know if Bob is near or not. So the protocol would work as follows :

- Alice generates a polynomial p from her set of location tags.
- Alice then sends the encrypted polynomial coefficients E(p) to Bob.
- Bob the calculates his own polynomial p(b) which his location tags and then encrypts it as E(p(b)).
- Then Bob picks random r on E(p) and computes E(r(p(b)) using polymorphic encryption.
- Then Bob sends Alice the permutation of encryptions computed in earlier step.
- Alice then decrypts it and outputs the nonzero decryptions as intersection of A and B.

This protocol has two disadvantages. First, it requires |A|.|B| modular exponentiations (E(p(b)) can be evaluated using Horner's rule [22] using O(|A|) modular exponentiations, and there are |B| such encryptions to compute). Second, it is only secure against semi-honest players. There is a version that handles malicious players, but it is significantly less efficient. More recent protocols can be more efficient [10], [22], [24], [25].

More importantly, revealing the size of the intersection can lead to security problems. For example, in our above example, Alice would come to know the intersection set (no of matching location tags) and she could resort to dictionary attack in case the threshold is very small. So to avoid the weaknesses pointed out in the version 1, the private threshold set intersection rule has been relaxed and version 2 has been developed on this basis. In version 2 protocol, neither of the parties will come to know about the intersection set. Instead one of the party that is seeking to know the proximity of its friend will come to know if set intersection has exceeded the threshold or not, but nothing other than that [5]. So this protocol will ensure the privacy between both the parties. The threshold value(t) and the number of location tags that needs to be generated (n) both are universal constants and if we could allow these values to change, there might be possibility of security issues (Brute-force attack) as mentioned in version 1 protocol. Now let's look at the protocol version 2 in detail [1].

- Alice generates its location tags using any of the generation techniques.
- Alice then uses one of the encoding techniques known, to convert her location tags into 'n' set of vertices say P {(p1, x1)(p2, x2)...... (pn, xn)}, where pi belongs F and xi belongs to F.
- Similarly Bob also generates his location tags using one of the generation techniques.
- He also encodes his location tags into a set Q{(q1, y1), (q2, y2).... (qn, yn)}.
- Alice constructs a polynomial p of degree n-1 defined by the points P using Lagrange's interpolation technique [26].
- Alice picks a random set of points R on polynomial, p such that R ∩ P = {} and |R| = 2(n-t), where n is the number of location tags and t is the threshold.
- Alice sends R points to Bob.
- Bob then tries to find a polynomial p' such that its degree is 2n-t of points (Q U R) that Bob has.
- If bob is able to find a polynomial through LaGrange interpolation. He outputs 1, which means Alice is nearby him.
- Otherwise he outputs 0 which means Alice is far away from Bob.

This protocol version is asymmetric because here only Bob learns about the Alice's proximity while Alice remains uninformed. If Alice also wants to test Bob's proximity, the protocol needs to be run from the other end. This above protocol produces accurate results of proximity and this can proved by the help of Berlekamp Massey algorithm as follows:

Suppose there are k pairs (xi, yi) over a field F and a degree parameter d, then if there exists a polynomial p that passes through at least (k+d)/2 of the points, BM outputs p otherwise BM outputs p. The proof of correctness now continues.

- **Case 1.** When Alice and Bob are nearby, there are at least t + 2(n - t) = 2n - t points on the polynomial. Substituting k = n + 2(n - t) = 3n - 2t and d = n, so will be able to find a polynomial
- **Case 2**. When Alice and Bob are far apart, this implies $|A \cap B| < t$. This means that there are fewer than 2n - t points on the polynomial p, and by BM theorem, Bob will fail to find an appropriate polynomial.

10. IMPLEMENTATION

This protocol can be better understood by looking at the following numerical example.

- *Let's assume Alice has values {91, 62,133}. She encodes them into set of points P = {(9,1), (6,2),(13,3)} where every entry is less than modulus 19.*
- *Alice then constructs a polynomial passing through the points of P by Lagrange interpolation, which is f(x) = 5*x^2+x+3 and picks 2(n-t) = 2(3-2) = 2 points and forms R.*
- *Let {4,5} be these points, then R = {(f(4),4), (f(5),5)} = {(11,4),(0, 5)}*
- *Bob gets R from Alice and let Bob's values be {62, 14, 27}, he then forms his Q using same encoding technique of Alice (lesser than modulus 19) into Q = {(6,2),(1,4),(2,7)}.*
- *Using Berlekamp-Massey algorithm [23] Bob supposed to find a 4th degree (2(3)-2). And since (Q U R) ∩ P is {(6,2)}, Bob is ouput 1 meaning Alice is nearby.*

We have implemented this protocol in Android platform as follows. We use separate emulators () for Alice and Bob and to run the application as show below. Android 2.2 (API level 8) for Alice (5556) and Bob (5554), and to run the application as show below. *See Figure 3and 4.*

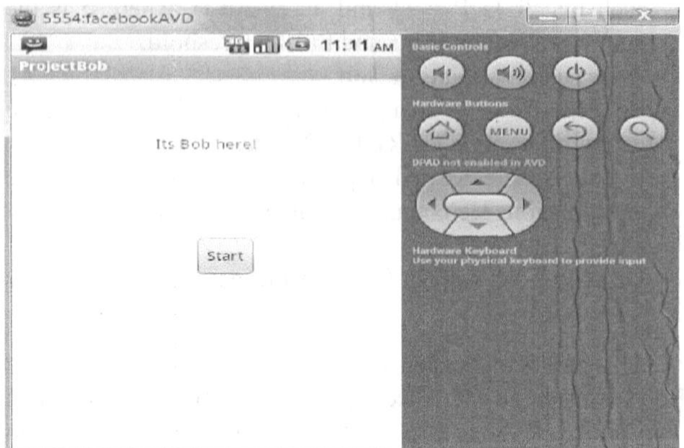

Fig.3. Start message from Bob

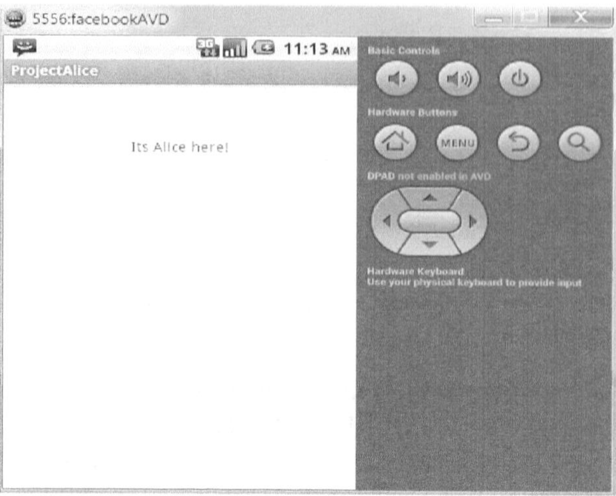

Fig.4. Message from Alice

SMSManager class of android package was used for sending and receiving messages between Alice and Bob emulators.

```
SmsManager sms = SmsManager.getDefault();
sms.sendTextMessage(phoneNumber,null, message, pi,
null);
```

- **Alice sends R to Bob**

```
SmsManager sms1 = SmsManager.getDefault()
sms1.sendTextMessage("5554",  null,  message,  null,
null);
```

We implemented a separate class for receiving SMS from other emulators as follows.

```
Object messages[] = (Object[]) bundle.get("pdus");
    SmsMessage SMS[] = new sms
Message[messages.length];
    for (int n = 0; n < messages.length; n++) {
        SMS[n] = Sms Message .createFromPdu((byte[])
messages[n])
}
```

- **To get the last message received from the inbox**

```
SMS[0].getMessageBody()
```

Once the message is received from Bob, Alice starts calculating the location tags. Since location tags are difficult to be calculated with the present hardware available, we used Random class of java for generating random numbers as follows.

- **For creating random P (Alice)**

```
Random rand = new Random();
for (int i = 0; i < N; i++)
{
    randP[i] = rand.nextInt(29 -11) + 11;
}
```

- **Here (29-11) is the range of the random numbers that can be created**

Then these location tags are encoded into vertices as follows.

```
for(int i = 0; i < N; i++) {
data[i][0] = (int) randP[i] / 10;
  data[i][1] = (int) randP[i] % 10;
  }
```

Then using LaGrange interpolation [26] of the matrices (constant and coordinate) are computed by substituting in a (n-1) degree polynomial as follows:

```
for (int i = 0; i < N; i++) {
     for (int j = 0; j < N; j++) {
   actualdata[i][j] = 1.0;
   for (int k = 0; k < j; k++) {
 actualdata[i][j] *= data[i][0];  } }
   constdata[i][0] = data[i][1];
}
```

Then coefficient matrix is calculated through computing matrix mathematics like determinant, transpose, inverse, multiplication of matrices. These were implemented using different java classes Matrix.java and MatrixMathematics.java respectively.

- **Finding determinant of matrix**

```
public static double determinant(Matrix matrix) throws
NoSquareException {
     if (!matrix.isSquare())   throw new
NoSquareException("matrix need to be square.");
     if (matrix.size()==2)
{ return (matrix.getValueAt(0, 0) * matrix.getValueAt(1,
1)) - ( matrix.getValueAt(0, 1) * matrix.getValueAt(1,
0));
}
double sum = 0.0;
for (int i=0; i<matrix.getNcols(); i++) {
       sum += changeSign(i) * matrix.getValueAt(0, i) *
determinant(createSubMatrix(matrix, 0, i));  }
return sum;
}
```

- **Calculating transpose of matrix**

```
public static Matrix transpose(Matrix matrix)
{
   Matrix transposedMatrix = new
Matrix(matrix.getNcols(), matrix.getNrows());
 for (int i=0;i<matrix.getNrows();i++) {
      for (int j=0;j<matrix.getNcols();j++) {
      transposedMatrix.setValueAt(j, i,
matrix.getValueAt(i, j));
   }}
   return transposedMatrix;
}
```

- **Matrix inverse**

```
public static Matrix inverse(Matrix matrix) throws
NoSquareException {
return (transpose(cofactor(matrix)).
multiplyByConstant(1.0/determinant(matrix)));
}
```

On running the application, the protocol gets triggered on Alice receiving a start message from Bob as show below. *See Figure 5.*

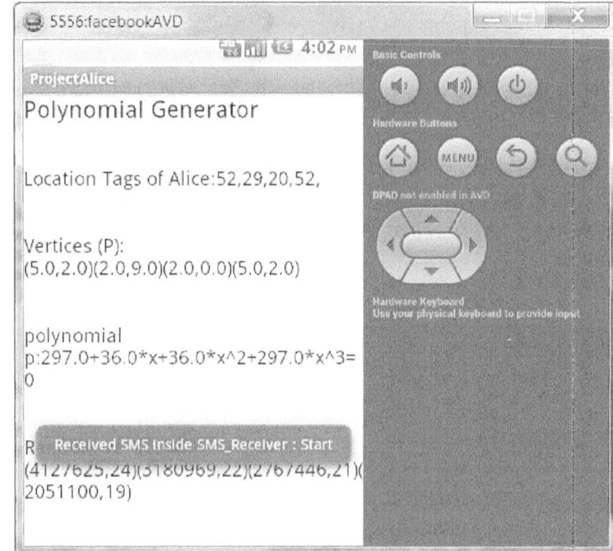

Fig. 5. Alice received a start message from Bob

Alice then proceeds with the protocol and finally sends R in a text message to Bob as follows. *See Figure 6*

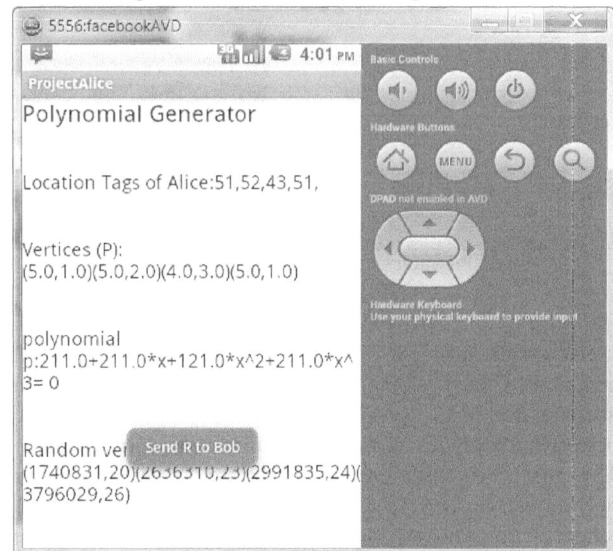

Fig.6. Alice then sends R in a text message to Bob

Bob in the meanwhile does the same processing to find Q and on receiving R from Alice will then try to find a polynomial that passes through 2n-t points. If he is successful, he outputs the following. However, if he is not able to generate a polynomial, he outputs the following. *See Figure 7,8.*

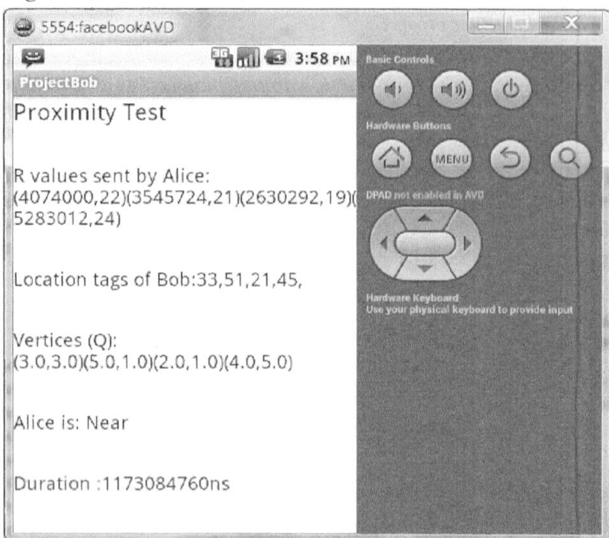

Fig.7. Bob is receiving R from Alice

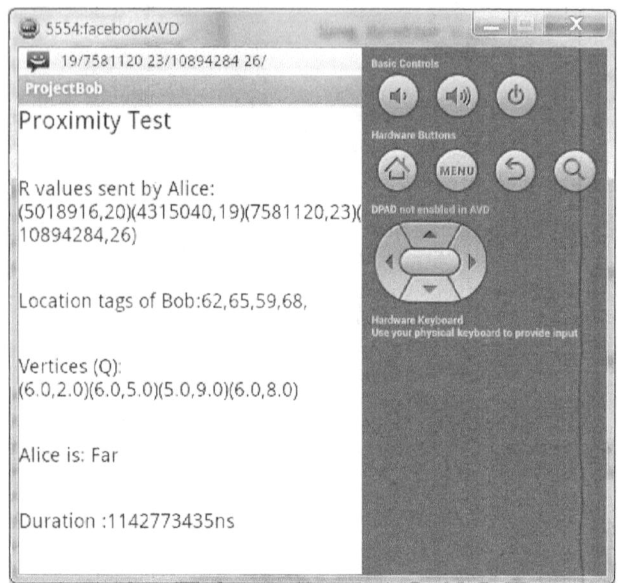

Fig.8. Proximity successful, Alice is near to Bob

11. RESULTS

When the protocol was run on Android platform with 2 emulators 1 each of Alice and Bob, it took 1.232 sec on an average for Bob to get the proximity of Alice. The performance of this protocol on android platform is good. The most time consuming parts of the protocol are the matrix operations like inverse & multiplication. This might take a longer time if the values of n & t are large. And this can be improved by implementing Strassen's algorithm for matrix multiplication which of order O(N ^ 2.8) or Coppersmith-Winograd algorithm of order O(N^2.3), when compared to the standard algorithm O(N^3). The performance of this protocol with multiple Bobs (Senders testing the proximity test of Alice simultaneously) can is represented graphically as follows.

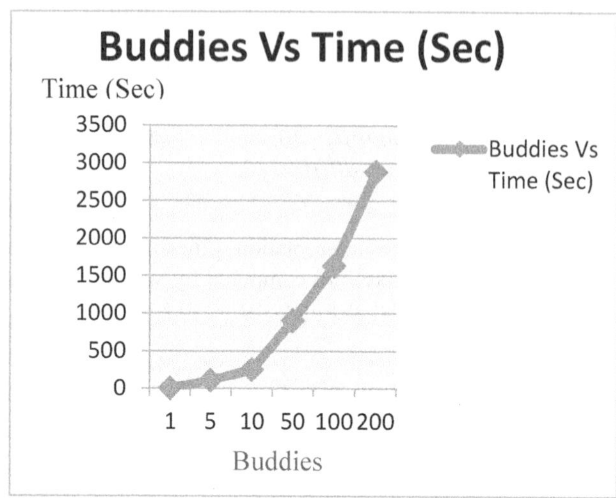

Fig.9. The performance of the protocol with multiples of Bobs

As the performance of this protocol is good in Android Platform but the main limitation is the ability of phone hardware to extract location tags. Currently the main viable method is using WiFi traffic; we showed experimentally that robust tags can be extracted within a few seconds.

On increasing the size of the location tags, the performance of this protocol is as depicted below:

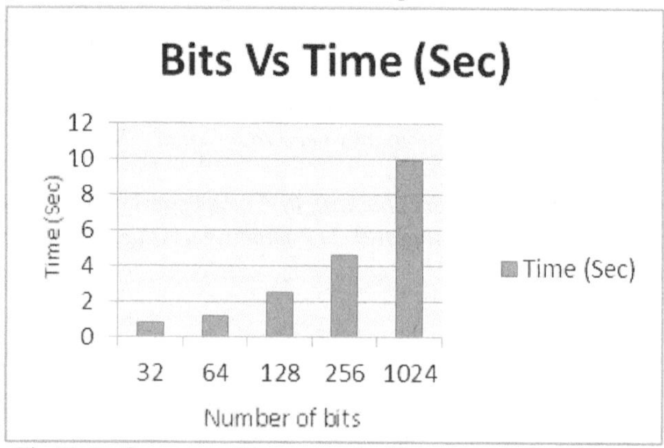

Fig.10. Performance of the protocol with increase in location tags

CONCLUSION

Location privacy is an important and growing concern in the real world today. In this paper we presented Boneh Protocol 3, a privacy preserving protocol for proximity service. We proved its correctness with respect to privacy preferences and we showed the results of an extensive experimental evaluation. Proximity is a checking for inclusion of one user's location inside another user's vicinity, offering users control over both location privacy and accuracy of proximity detection. We have implemented an actively secure protocol for proximity testing. Through the scenario that we targeted on Android Platform, from the results we have shown that it is feasible to execute the protocol on contemporary mobile devices through the android emulator. The protocol discussed in this paper doesn't use any cryptographic algorithmes. It merely uses encoding techniques to convert the location tags into vertices. So it remains a question unless it comes in to practical use.

REFERENCES

[1] A.Narayanan, N. Thiagarajan, M. Lakhani, M. Hamburg, and D. Boneh. Location privacy via private proximity testing. Network and Distributed System Security Symposium, NDSS, 2011.

[2] Virrantaus, K., Markkula, J., Garmash, A., Terziyan, Y.V., 2001. Developing GIS-Supported Location-Based Services. In: Proc. of WGIS'2001 – First International Workshop on Web Geographical Information Systems., Kyoto, Japan. 423–432, 2001.

[3] Open Geospatial Consortium (OGC), Open LocationServices.www.nttdocomo.com/corebiz/network/index.html Internet information on mobile networks, 2005.

[4] S.Mascetti, Claudio Bettini, Dario Freni, X. Sean Wang, X. Sean Wang, Sushil Jajodia. Privacy-Aware Proximity Based Services. Tenth International Conference on Mobile Data Management: Systems, Services and Middleware, 2009.

[5] J.Dam Nielsen, Jakob Illeborg Pagter, and Michael Bladt Stausholm. Location Privacy via Actively Secure Private Proximity Testing. Fourth International Workshop on SECurity and SOCial Networking, Lugano, 19 March 2012

[6] C. Steinfield. The Development of Location Based Services in Mobile Commerce. Technology Management for Reshaping the World. Portland International Conference, 2004.

[7] L. Barkuus, and Anind Dey. Location-Based Services for Mobile Telephony: a Study of Users' Privacy Concerns. 9TH IFIP TC13 International Conference on Human-Computer Interaction, 2003.

[8] FTC report recommends privacy practices for mobile platforms, developers, advertisers. http://www.techjournal.org/2013/02/ftc-report recommends privacy-practices-for-mobile-platfor ms developers-advertisers/, Feb 4th, 2013.

[9] S. Steiniger, Moritz Neun and Alistair Edwardes. Foundations of Location Based Services, 2006.

[10] M. Freedman, K. Nissim, and B. Pinkas. Efficient private matching and set intersection. In Proc. of Eurocrypt' 04, pages 1–19. Springer-Verlag, 2004.

[11] R. Baden, A. Bender, N. Spring, B. Bhattacharjee, and D.Starin. Persona: an online social network with user defined privacy. SIGCOMM Computer. Communication. Rev.,39(4):135–146, 2009.

[12] Brimicombe, A.J. (2009) GIS, Environmental Modeling and Engineering (2nd Edition) . CRC Press, Boca Raton, FL, USA. Proceedings GIS, Bahrain. 33-45, 2009

[13] Shiode, N., Li, C., Batty, M., Longley, P., Maguire, The impact and penetration of Location Based Services. In: Karimi, H. A., Hammad, A., ed. Telegeoinformatics. CRC Press, 349-366, 2004

[14] Sabine Ehlers. Mobile Proximity Services a VAS Research Series, research report from Berg Insight, publication date, January 2008.

[15] Mike Hamburg, Joint work with Arvind Narayanan, Narendran Thiagarajan, Mugdha Lakhani, Dan Boneh Location Services with Built--In Privacy, 2011

[16] Pravin Shankar, Yun-Wu Huang, Paul Castro, Badri Nath, Liviu Iftode. Crowds replace Experts: Building Better Location-based Services using Mobile Social Network Interactions, 2012

[17] D. Qiu, D. Boneh, S. Lo, and P. Enge. Robust location tag generation from noisy location data for security applications. In The Institute of Navigation International Technical Meeting, 2009

[18] Emmanouil Magkos (Ionian University, Greece). Cryptographic Approaches for Privacy Preservation in Location-Based Services, 2011.

[19] Blog of Arvind Narayanan,http://33bits.org/2011/02/14/cryptographic-approach-location-privacy proximity-testing/

[20] Saroiu, S., & Wolman, A. (2009). Enabling new mobile applications with location proofs. In 10th Workshop on Mobile Computing Systems and Applications ACM, 2009

[21] Boneh, D., & Franklin, M. (2001). Identity-based encryption from the Weil pairing. In Advances in Cryptology - CRYPTO 2001 (pp. 213–229). Springer

[22] A. Juels and M. Sudan . A fuzzy vault scheme. Designs Codes and Crytpography, 237-257, 2006.

[23] C. Hazay and K. Nissim. Effiecient set operations in presence f malicious adversaries. In Proc. of public key crypto (PKC) , volume 6056 of LNCS, pages 312-331, 2010

[24] S. Jarecki and X. Liu. Efficient oblivious pseudorandom function with applications to adaptive to and secure computation of set intersection.

[25] C. Hazay and Y. Lindell. Effiecient protocols for set intersection and pattern matching with security against malicious and covert adversaries.

[26] Jeffrey Hightower and Gaetano Borriella. A survey and taxonomy of location systems for ubiquitous computing. IEEE Computer, 34(8):57–66, August 2001.

[27] H. Lipmaa. Verifiable homomorphic oblivious transfer and private equality test. In Proc. of Asiacrypt,, 2003.

Privacy-Aware Proximity Based Service using Hide & Crypt Protocol: Implementation

L. Ertaul, B. F. Imagnu, S. Kilaru.
California State University, East Bay, Hayward, CA, USA

Abstract-Proximity based services are location based services (LBS) in which the service adaptation depends on the comparison between a given threshold value and the distance between a user and other (possibly moving) entities. While privacy preservation in LBS has lately received much attention, very limited work has been done on privacy-aware proximity based services. This paper describes the main privacy threats that the usage of these services can lead to, and explains the implementation of a privacy preserving protocol, Hide&Crypt. The use of simple and well-known encryption algorithms is also mentioned which is used to hide messages exchanged between users.

Index Terms- Hide&Crypt, LBS, SP-Filtering, Proximity-based services, Privacy-Aware LBS

1.Introduction

Location based services (LBS) are becoming popular thanks to the advances in positioning technologies and to the diffusion of mobile devices with data communication capabilities. Proximity based services are a special class of LBS in which the service adaptation depends on the comparison between a given threshold value and the distance between a user and other (possibly moving) entities. The so-called "friend- inder" services are an example: Alice would like to be alerted whenever her friend Bob is nearby, so that they could get in contact and possibly meet. The proximity service considered in this paper is a generalization of "friend-finder" in which each user is part of one or more possibly large and dynamically changing groups of users (called buddies) related to hobbies, sports, religious or cultural interests. Technically, a proximity query is a spatial range query on the database of moving buddies in which the range is defined by the circle centered at the issuer's location and having the proximity threshold as radius. [1][2][3][4][5].

A major privacy concern with the use of LBS is the release to untrusted third parties of the user precise location information. This concern applies to proximity services as well: Alice would like to use the proximity service without necessarily releasing her exact position to the service provider (SP). In some cases, she may even wish not to provide the exact location to the buddies, although she may be willing to reveal whether she is in proximity. For example, she may agree to let Bob know that she is in a neighborhood near Bob's location, but keep the specific address hidden from Bob. In practice, this may avoid the situation in which buddies can directly walk to other buddies, as the goal of the service is usually to enable communication that may only eventually lead to meetings in person. A solution to the above privacy concern can be to allow each user to specify certain minimum location privacy requirements both with respect to the service provider and to the buddies. Note that these are minimum requirements, and a system should be designed with the goals to (1) guarantee the satisfaction of the minimum privacy requirements, and (2) reveal as little location information as possible. This paper provides the design of proximity service protocol toward these two goals. Several LBS privacy preserving techniques have been recently proposed [1][2][3][4][5].

The rest of the paper is organized as follows. ***Section 2*** describes the services, the privacy preferences, the threats, and the evaluation metrics. In ***Section 3*** we illustrate the implemented protocol, Hide&Crypt and its formal properties. In ***Section 4*** explanation on the implementation of Hide&Crypt and in ***Section 5*** we report experiments, in ***Section 6*** we show screenshots from our implementation and finally in ***Section 7*** we conclude with a short discussion.

2. Proximity services and privacy concerns

In this section we first formalize the proximity services and the related privacy requirements. We then describe how these requirements may be violated, and how different techniques avoiding these privacy threats could be compared.

2.1. The proximity service

The proximity service informally described in the introduction can be more precisely defined by considering a typical service provisioning session: a user A sends her own location information, acquired via GPS or other techniques, and requests to be alerted whenever a buddy1 reports a location that is in proximity while it was not in proximity before, or vice versa is not anymore in proximity. Here, proximity is defined as being within a distance threshold given by A, denoted δ_A, i.e., A is interested in all the buddies B satisfying the following condition:

$$d(loc(A);loc(B))\leq\delta_A \qquad (1)$$

where d(loc(A); loc(B)) denotes the Euclidean distance between the reported locations of A and B. When (1) is true, we say that B is in the proximity of A. Since B may be different from A, this proximity relation may not be symmetric. In order to provide proximity service, it is convenient to have a service provider SP, especially when group sizes can be large and membership of the groups can dynamically change. Indeed, under these conditions, directly computing distances between A and every buddy can be extremely inefficient or even infeasible. Henceforth, we assume the existence of SP in providing proximity service.

With the presence of SP, and in the absence of privacy concerns, a simple protocol can be devised to implement the service: The SP receives from each user's automatic location updates and stores their last known positions, as well as the distance threshold δ_A for each user A. While in theory each user can define a different value δ_A for each buddy, in this paper, for the sake of simplicity, we consider the case in which each user defines a single value of δ_A. When the SP receives a location update, it may recompute the distance between A and each buddy (possibly with some filtering/indexing strategy for efficiency). If any proximity relation changes, A is notified. In a typical scenario, if B is in proximity, A may contact him directly or through SP; however, for the purpose of this paper, we do not concern ourselves as what A will do once notified.

2.2. User minimum privacy requirements

The privacy we are considering in this paper is location privacy, i.e. we assume that users are concerned about other persons obtaining information about their exact location at specific times. In the considered services, users may prefer the service provider to have as little information about their location as possible, and the buddies not to know her exact position, even when proximity is revealed. In general, the level of location privacy can be represented by the uncertainty that an external entity has about the position of the user, and this uncertainty can be formally represented as a geographic area in which no point can be ruled out as a possible position of the user. In principle each user could express her privacy preferences, by specifying for each other user (or class of users perceived as adversaries) a partition of the geographical space defining the minimal uncertainty regions that she wants to be guaranteed. For
example, Alice specifies that Bob should never be able to find out the specific building where Alice is within the campus, i.e., the entire campus area is a minimal uncertainty
region. The totality of these uncertainty regions can be formally captured with the notion of *spatial granularity*.

While there does not exist a formal definition of spatial granularity that is widely accepted by the research community, the idea behind spatial granularities is simple. Similarly to temporal granularity [6], a spatial granularity can be considered a subdivision of the spatial domain into a discrete number of non-overlapping regions, called granules. In this paper, for simplicity, we consider only granularities that partition the spatial domain. In principle, granules of the same granularity can have any shape and don't need to have the same size or shape. Each granule of a granularity G is identified by an index (or a label). We denote with G(i) the granule of the granularity G with index i.

Users specify their minimum privacy requirements via spatial granularities, with each granule being a minimum uncertain region. In the following of this paper we assume that each user specifies two granularities

$$G^{SP}{}_A \text{ and } G^U{}_A$$

defining the minimum location privacy requirements for SP and for any other user, respectively, as the two categories of potential adversaries. The two extreme cases in which a user requires no privacy protection and maximum privacy protection, respectively, can be naturally modeled. For example, if a user A does not want her privacy to be protected with respect to other buddies (in this case A can tolerate other buddies to know her location at the maximum available precision) then A will set $G^U{}_A$ to the bottom granularity $\perp$ (a granularity that contains a granule for each basic element, or pixel, of the spatial domain). Similarly, if A wants to impose the maximum privacy protection with respect to the SP, then A sets $G^{SP}{}_A$ to the top granularity T (the granularity that has a single granule that covers the entire spatial domain).

2.3. Privacy threats

In order to formally identify the privacy threats, it is crucial to first specify the assumptions about the available external knowledge and about the behavior of considered adversaries. In this paper we consider both buddies and SP (as well as external entities that may have taken control of one of them) as potential adversaries, and we assume the following: (a) there is no external knowledge on the location of users other than the one exchanged during the protocol, and (b) buddies and SP do not collude. The formal proofs of our results also assume that the involved entities are not malicious, in the sense that they follow the protocols defined in the service.

Observe the simple protocol described in Section 2.1; it is easily seen that even under the above assumptions the location privacy of users is at risk. When the SP is considered as a potential adversary, an SP-threat can be identified: Since the exact location of user A is stored by the SP, if $G^{SP}{}_A$ is not the bottom granularity, A's minimum privacy requirement is violated. When a buddy is considered as a potential adversary, a buddy-attack can be identified as follows. Suppose A is a buddy of B who sets a value of in a way such that the circular region of radius δ_B (centered at B's location) is properly contained in a granule of $G^U{}_A$. Then, if A happens to enter that circular region, the SP will notify B, and A's minimum privacy requirement would be violated.

2.4. Privacy protection performance

In the sequel, we present techniques to protect user privacy. The minimum goal of our techniques is to guarantee the satisfaction of users' minimum privacy requirements, which all of our protocols provide. However, there are three additional performance goals to be considered.

The first is based on the observation that more privacy is generally more desirable by users; we should strive to provide larger uncertainty region than the minimum ones given by the user. Hence, the first performance measure of the protection is the size of the uncertainty region. The larger the uncertainty region, the better.

The second performance goal is to minimize the system costs, including computation and communication. As we show later, there is a trade-off between the privacy level and the costs.

The third performance metrics is the service precision. Due to the user minimum privacy requirement, there may be uncertainty whether user B is actually in proximity of A. We take a conservative approach, namely when it's uncertain, we report to A that B is in proximity. The service precision is then defined as the percentage of times that B is indeed in A's proximity when alerted (based on the reported locations of A and B) among all the times A is alerted. Obviously, the higher precision, the better.

3. Privacy preserving Techniques

3.1 SP-Filtering

SP-Filtering[7] is a three-party protocol that computes the proximity of B to A with a certain approximation, guaranteeing the satisfaction of the minimum location-privacy requirements of both A and B.

The idea of the algorithm is that when a user A performs a location update, instead of providing her exact location to the SP, she sends a generalized location that is computed as a function of GU A and the granule G^{SP}_{A} (i) where A is located. More precisely, A sends to SP the location LA(i) that is computed as the union of the granules of G^{U}_{A} that intersects with G^{SP}_{A} (i). Formally

$$L_A(i) = \bigcup_{i' \in N | G^U_A(i') \cap G^{SP}_A(i) \neq \emptyset} G^U_A(i') \quad (2)$$

Each buddy B does the same when location is updated with LB(j) similarly defined, where j is the index such that the location of B is in G^{SP}_{B} (j). Then, the SP can compute, for each buddy B of A, the minimum and maximum distance between any two points of LA(i) and LB(j).We denote with d and D the minimum and maximum distance, respectively.

3.2 Hide&Crypt

Hide&Crypt works as follows. First, A computes the set S' of indexes of granules of GUB that intersects with the circle C centered in the location of A with radius δA. Then, in order to hide to B the cardinality of this set, A creates a new set S by adding to S0 some negative numbers. The aim of negative numbers is to increase the cardinality of S without affecting the result of the computation. The cardinality of S should be increased so that it is as large as the number SMAX that represents the maximum number of granules of GUB that intersect with any circle with radius δA. Note that SMAX can be computed off-line since its values depend only on GUB and δA. Then, A encrypts all the elements of S with an encryption function E and a private key KA and sends the result to B. User B encrypts again, using his private key KB, each element in the set he receives and sends it back to A together with the encryption of the index j such that B is located in GUB (j). Finally, A encrypts again EKB(i) using the key KA and checks if the result is contained in EKB(EKA(S)). Encryption function E is such that EKA(EKB(i)) ϵ EKB(EKA(S)) if and only if j ϵ S. Since negative numbers are not valid indexes, j ≥ 0, and hence j ϵ S if and only if j ϵ S'. Therefore A computes whether B is in her proximity or not.[7]

Protocol Hide&Crypt

Prerequisites: A and B are running the SP-Filtering protocol. User A knows G^{U}_{B}, a private key KA, the circle C centered in A's location with radius δ_A, and the value S_{MAX}. B knows a private key K_B, and the granule G^{U}_{B}(j)where B is located.[7]

Protocol:

1: A receives "B is possibly in proximity" from the SP.
2: A computes: S' = {jϵN s.t. G^{U}_{B}(j) n C≠ф
3: A computes: S'' as a set of SMAX-|S'| random negative numbers.
4: A computes: S = S' U S''
5: A sends "starting two-parties protocol $E_{KA}(S)$" to B
6: B sends $[E_{KB}(E_{KA}(S));E_{KB}(j)]^{1}$ to A

Note-[$E_{KB}(E_{KA}(S));E_{KB}(j)$]-hold true for any commutative symmetric encryption algorithm. ***We used Vernam Encryption algorithm for the implementation***

7: A computes: $E_{KA}(E_{KB}(j))$
8: if ($E_{KA}(E_{KB}(j))$ ϵ $E_{KB}(E_{KA}(S))$) then
9: A computes that B is in proximity
10: else
11: A computes that B is not in proximity
12: end if

4. Hide&Crypt Implementation

The process starts from User A which request to know if User B is in proximity or not by updating its location to the SP. The SP will then do some simple calculations and comparisons to notify User A whether User B is in proximity, not in proximity or might be in proximity.

In the last case, proximity is decided by secure communication between individual Users, not the SP.

A user updates its location in some interval of time or when they query the SP in order to know the proximity of their friends. SP uses the last known user location for proximity calculations.

In this implementation the granule of every individual user is represented 8 points which are calculated by the user itself using its own gps location using latitude and longitude. User's current location and the method used to calculate the 8 points that represent user's own location are kept secret of only the user. The SP is only provided with these 8 points from every user which updates their locations. The calculations done by the SP are completely based on these 8 points. For example, between the 8 points of User A and the last updated 8 points of user B.

The step-by step calculations used to create the eight points by user A for our implementation is as follows.

1. User A acquires its current latitude and longitude of his exact location. There are a lot of applications to get this information on mobile devices. Ex- Compass in Iphone, GPS Status in Android.
2. User A decides its minimum privacy distance, $\delta_{A.}$
3. $\delta_{A.}$ is changed to degrees of latitude and longitude, Ax and Ay respectively. Since 1^0 latitude = 69miles, 1^0 longitude = 53 miles.
4. Ax is added and subtracted to/from A's latitude, the same is done with longitude using Ay.
5. Choose two of the points results of Ax or Ay, but not one from each, from the four calculated location points in the previous step and add/subtract Ax or Ay to get locations the rest four points (add/subtract Ax if the two location points used are the sum/difference of Ax from A's current location and vice versa). As shown in Fig.1

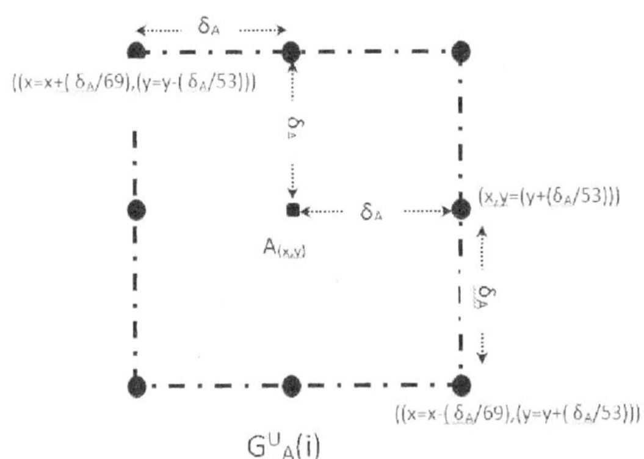

Figure 1. Granule of a user

After SP has acquired all the 16 points needed to calculate the proximity of B to A i.e. 8 points each calculated using their corresponding minimum privacy, δ_A and δ_B. SP will calculate the distance from every point of A to every point of B using simple calculation as shown below.

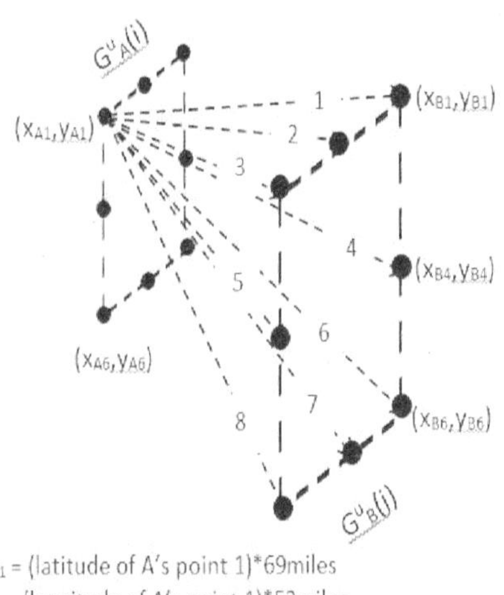

Figure 2. Calculating the distances between the granules of the two users

$$\text{Distance1}=\sqrt{(x_{A1}-x_{B1})^2+(y_{A1}-y_{B1})^2} \quad (3)$$

These 64 distance values will compare to each other to decide d and D.

d = the smallest distance from points of A to B.

D = the largest distance from points of A to B.

SP will decide the proximity based on the result of the comparison.

Case1.If, D≤ δ_A then "B is in proximity of A."

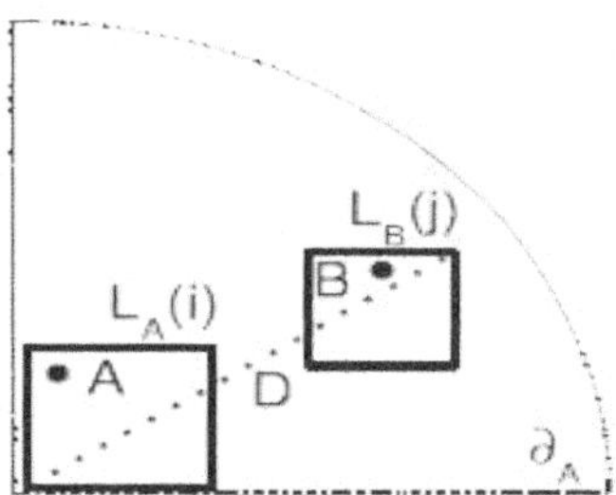

Figure 3. Case 1

Case 2. If d≥δ_A then "B is not in Proximity of A."

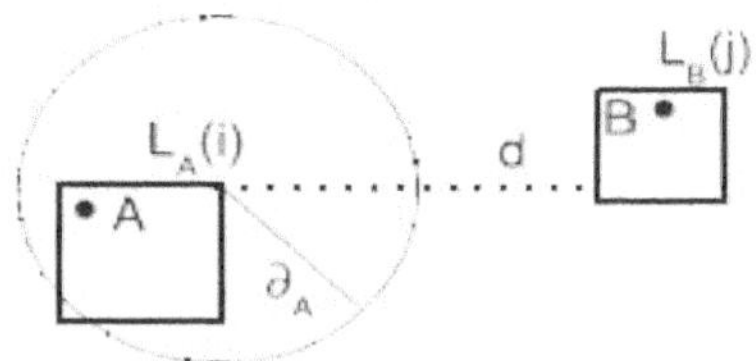

Figure 4. Case 2

Case 3.If d≤ δ_A≥D the "B might be in Proximity of A" where A and B communicate securely to decide proximity.

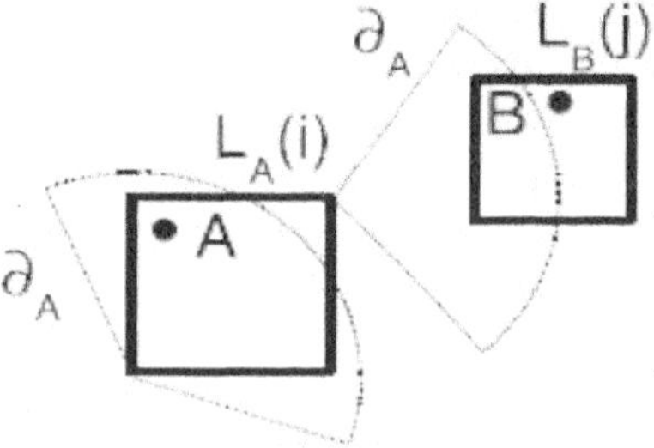

Figure 5. Case 3

If SP filtering results "B might be in proximity of A" then the SP divides the area, containing both A and B, into areas in the size of B's granule and index the divided areas. This table containing the indexes and their corresponding latitude and longitude values is sent to both users so that they can base the process of determining proximity through secure communication based on the same information (table).

The details of the preparation of this table are as follows. SP separate the minimum (min.) and maximum (max.) latitudes (Lat.) and longitude (Long.) from the 16 points that are sent from both users (8 from each) as shown in the Figure 6.

This area is divided to smaller squares starting from the point located at (max Lat., min Long.). Then each small area will be represented by the left top corner point i.e. the point with the largest latitude and lowest longitude among its four corner points.

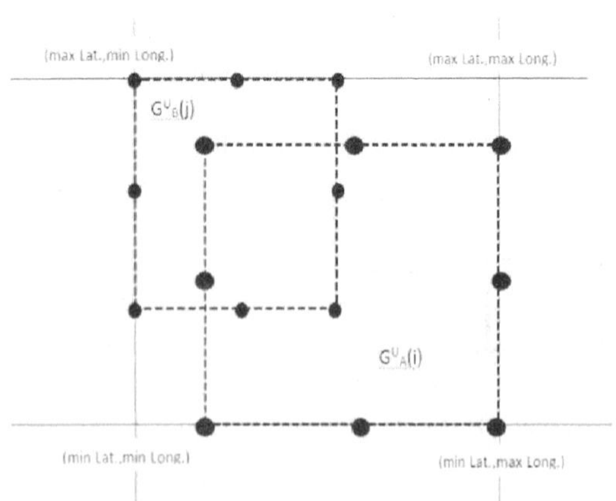

Figure 6. Calculating the coordinates

The latitude and longitudes of the individual cells will be calculated from the coordinate of the perivious cell except for the first one which is located at (max Lat., min Long.).The intervals for the latitude and longitude are calculated as follows.

Area 1= (max Lat.,min Long.)

Area 2=(max Lat,(min Long.+(δ_B/53)))

Area 3= ((max Lat.-(δ_B/69)),min Long.)

Area 4= ((max Lat.-(δ_B/69)),(min Long.+(δ_B/53))

The maximum number of cells resulted from the division of the whole area is,

Latitude m=(max Lat.- min Lat)/(δ_B/69).... (4)

Longitude n=(max Long.- min Long.)/(δ_B/5)... (5)

Number of cells= m*n....(6)

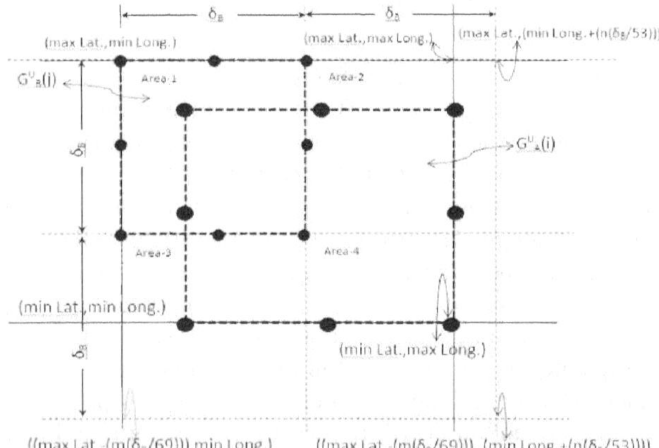

Figure 7 Dividing the area using the size of B's granule

Table 1.The indexed information

Index	m	n	Latitude	Longitude
Area1	1	1	max Lat.	Min Long.
Area2	1	2	max.Lat.-(m(δ_B/69))	min Long
Area3	2	1	max.Lat.-(m(δ_B/69))	min.Long.+(n(δ_B/53))
Area4	2	2	max.Lat.-(m(δ_B/69))	min.Long.+(n(δ_B/53))

After both users receive the table from Table 1 SP, proximity of B to A is decided by user A through a secure communication with B following the steps below.

1. User A will encrypt and send the indexes where its granule representing 8 points lie in using its secret key K_A, i.e. all the indexed areas 1,2,3,4, which is not always true.(two of them lie in area 1, three of them lie in area2,one lie in area3 and the last two lie in area 4)
2. B will encrypt the received message with its own secret key K_B and also encrypt and add the index of the area where it is located in and send all of it back to A.
3. A will encrypt the encrypted location of B and check with the other encrypted values. If a match is found then "B is in proximity of A" if not then "B is not in proximity of A".

Ex. Let B is located in indexed area 3 and $E_{KB}(3)$=p

$E_{KA}(1)$=a, $E_{KA}(2)$=b, $E_{KA}(3)$=c, $E_{KA}(4)$=d

$E_{KB}(a)$=w, $E_{KB}(b)$=x, $E_{KB}(c)$=y, $E_{KB}(d)$=z

$E_{KA}(1)$=a, $E_{KA}(2)$=b, $E_{KA}(3)$=c, $E_{KA}(4)$=d

1. E_{KA}(1,2,3,4)={a,b,c,d}........A sends to B
2. E_{KB}(a,b,c,d,3)={w,x,y,z,p}......B sends to A
3. E_{KA}(p)={y}.... A compare y with w,x,y,z

Since a match is found the "B is in Proximity of A."

5.Experimental Evaluation

We defined 5 levels of granularities for our experiment increasing in size as the level of granularity increase. The smallest and the largest size of granularities we considered are Level 0 which is 5milesX5miles square and Level 4 50milesX50miles as shown in Table 2.

Table 2. Five Level Granuluties

Parameter	Value
δ	5m,10m,25m,50m
Level of G^U Granularity	0,1,2,3,4
Avg number of buddies in a group	2,3,4,5

For simplicity reason we have forced all users to use the same minimum privacy requirement, δ for a given experiment.

Since hide&crypt protocol comes to action only when the "might be in proximity" condition happen, our experiments are on the same case too. SP-filtering calculations are simple and made by server so it is not included in this paper. Another think we held constant is the 128 bits encryption key generated using AES-CTR. Every user has fixed encryption key to use with Vernam Cipher.

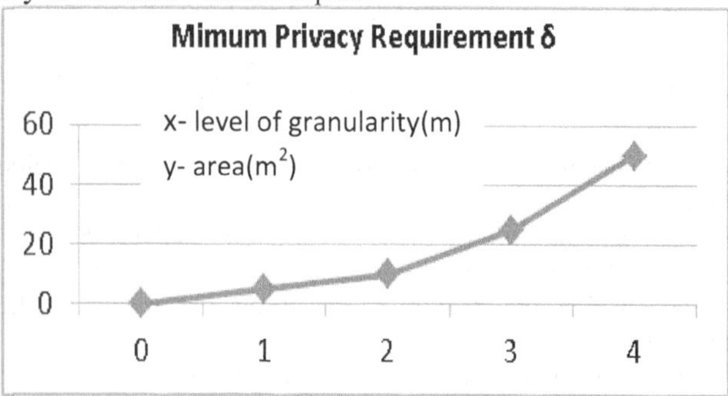

Figure 8. Minimum Privacy Requirements δ

As we can see from Figure 8 & 9 as δ increase the granularity of G^U increase exponentially making it cover a large area and cover many number of smaller granules the size of another user's granules, hence creating many indexes to be encrypted by users. This is shown in Figure 10.

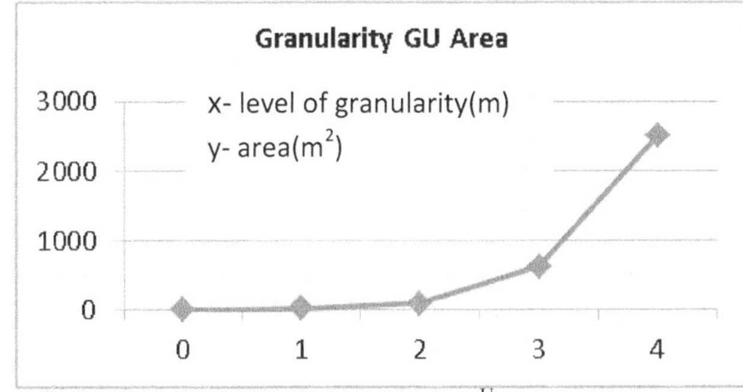

Figure 9. Granulity G^U Area

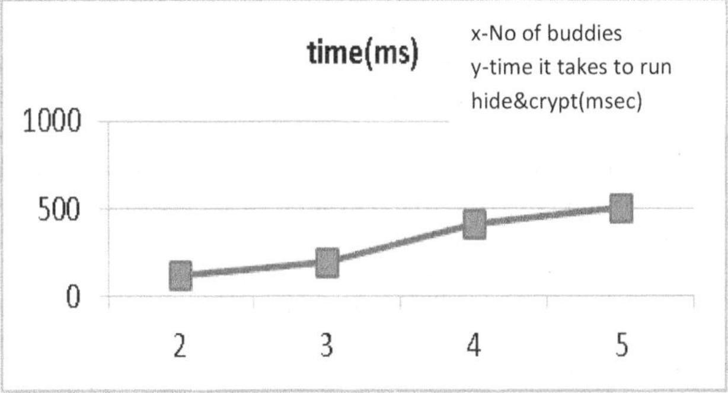

Figure 10. Total Time taken

6.Screenshots from Implementation

We used Dot Net, xml, html and javascript platform for our implementation.it is a web based program that works for all zipcodes in the USA. We used a tool in Visual Studio to change zipcodes into latitude and longitude.

Figure 11 shows the interface on which both users enter their zipcodes and their minimum privacy requirements to calculate their corresponding 8 representative points.

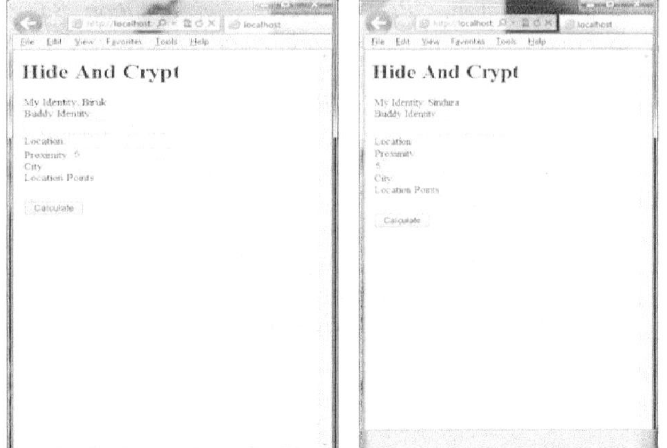

Figure11. Hide&Crypt Implementation Interface

The user calculated 8 points and the minimum privacy requirement are displayed in Figure12. This data is sent and proximity is determined by calculating the distances from each point of one user to each point of the other user. The smallest and largest values from these distances are selected and compared with the minimum privacy requirement of the user requesting the service for the decision. Proximity is decided by the SP and the message is sent to requesting user as shown in Figure 13.

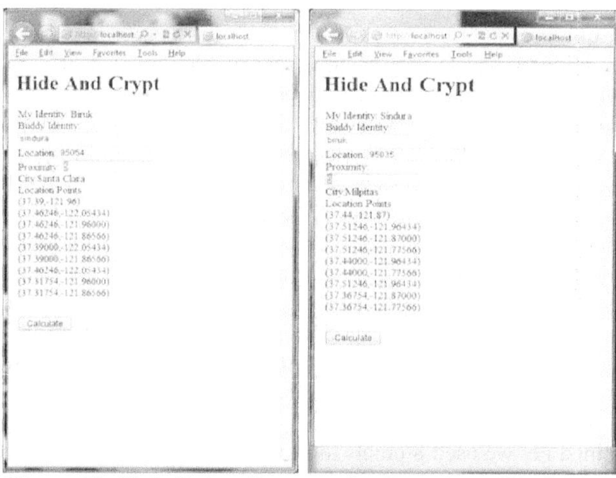

Figure 12. Eight Points Representing Location of Each User

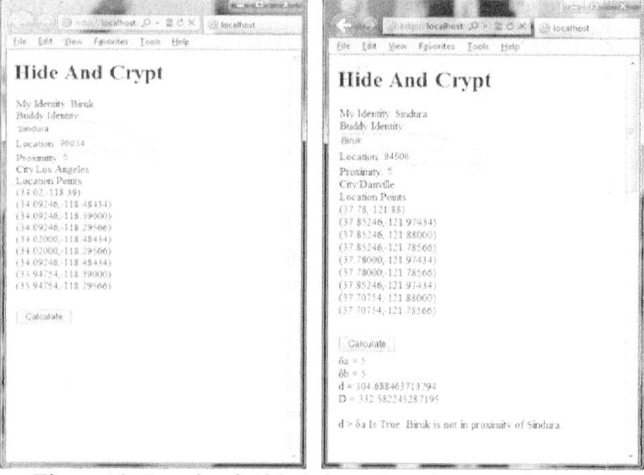

Figure13. Result of Hide&Crypt(Not in Proximity case)

In the case when one user might be in proximity of the other case, SP sends the index table as shown in Table 1 for both users. Then Hide & Crypt protocol starts communication between the two users. The process is described in detail in Section 4. Figure 14 shows the messages exchanged between the two users and the decision reached on proximity through this secure communication between them.

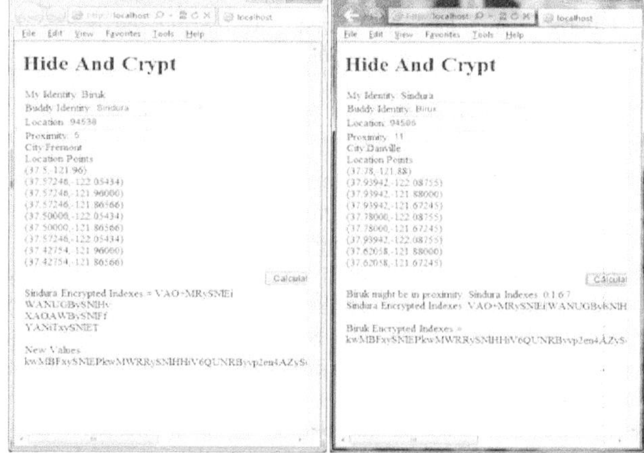

Figure 14. Encryption Process in Hide&Crypt

7.Conclusion

Hide&Crypt is very secure and reliable protocol. It uses simple and highly effective encryption algorithms for security. It does not reveal any information to a third party server, Service Provider or other buddy users about the exact location of service requesting user or vice versa.

Hide&Crypt seems to generate a lot repetitive calculations in the SP Filter but since SP Filter is a server provided by the Service Provider, computation is not time and resource consuming. But creating 8 points, generating new encryption key for every session and comparing ciphers and exchange of results between user devices might be power and resource consuming from which mobile devices are scares of.

Accuracy of this protocol depends on how granularity is defined i.e. we used 8 points to represent a granule, and when the minimum privacy requirement gets larger and larger these 8 points spread further from each other making the proximity determining calculations less and less accurate. But on the contrary it also gives users higher privacy when these points are far from each other making it much harder for attackers wanting to acquires users exact location. With additional methods of hiding users location and defining granules, this protocol's efficiency can be highly improved.

References

[1]. Bugra Gedik and Ling Liu. " *Protecting location privacy with personalized k-anonymity: Architecture and algorithms.* " IEEE Transactions on Mobile Computing, 7(1):1–18, 2008.

[2]. Gabriel Ghinita, Panos Kalnis, Ali Khoshgozaran, Cyrus Shahabi, and Kian-Lee Tan."*Private queries in location based services: anonymizers are not necessary*" In Proc. Of SIGMOD. ACM Press, 2008.

[3]. Panos Kalnis, Gabriel Ghinita, Kyriakos Mouratidis, and Dimitris Papadias. "*Preventing location-based identity inference in anonymous spatial queries.*" IEEE Transactions on Knowledge and Data Engineering, 19(12):1719–1733, 2007.

[4]. Sergio Mascetti, Claudio Bettini, Dario Freni, and X. Sean Wang. "*Spatial generalization algorithms for LBS privacy preservation*" Journal of Location Based Services, 2(1), 2008.

[5]. Hua] Man Lung Yiu, Christian S. Jensen, Xuegang Huang, and Lu. Spacetwist: "*Managing the trade-offs among location privacy, query performance, and query accuracy in mobile services.*" In Proc. of the 24th International Conference on Data Engineering. IEEE Computer Society, 2008.

[6]. Claudio Bettini, Xiaoyang Sean Wang, and Sushil Jajodia. "*Time Granularities in Databases, Temporal Reasoning, and Data Mining*". Springer, 2000.

[7]. Sergio Mascetti, Claudio Bettini ,Dario FreniDICo Universit`a di Milano, X. Sean Wang Department of CS University of Vermont, Sushil Jajodia CSIS,George Mason University, "*Privacy-Aware Proximity Based Services.*"

[8]. Canalys.com, "*Gps smart phone shipments overtake pnds in emea,*" November 2008. [Online]. Available: http://www.canalys.com/pr/2008/r2008111.html

[9]. ABI research, "*Location-based mobile social networking will generate global revenues of $3.3 billion by 2013,*August2008.[Online].Available:http://www.abiresearch.com/abiprdisplay.jsp?pressid=1204"*Stalk your friends withgoogle,*"2009.[Online].Available:http://features.csmonitor.com/innovation/2009/0/04/stalk-your-friends-with-google

[10]. S. Mascetti, C. Bettini, and D.Freni,"*Longitude: Centralized privacy-preserving computation of users' proximity.*" In *Secure Data Management*,2009,

[11]. P. Ruppel, G. Treu, A. Küpper, and C. Linnhoff-Popien"*Anonymous User Tracking for Location-Based Community Services,*" in *LoCA*, 2006, pp. 116–133.

[12]. L. Šikšnys, J. R. Thomsen, S. Šaltenis, M. L. Yiu,and O. Andersen, "*A Location Privacy Aware FriendLocator,*" in *SSTD*, 2009.

[13]. A. Amir, A. Efrat, J. Myllymaki, L. Palaniappan, and K. Wampler, "*Buddy Tracking - Efficient Proximity Detection Among Mobile Friends,*" in *INFOCOM*,2004,

[14]. C. A. Ardagna, M. Cremonini, E. Damiani, S. D. C.di Vimercati, and P. Samarati, "*Location Privacy Protection Through Obfuscation-Based Techniques,*" in *DBSec*, 2007,

[15]. M. Duckham and L. Kulik, "*A Formal Model ofObfuscation and Negotiation for Location Privacy,*" in *PERVASIVE*, 2005

[16]. M. Gruteser and D. Grunwald, "*Anonymous Usage of Location-Based Services Through Spatial and Temporal Cloaking,*" in *USENIX MobiSys*, 2003

[17]. M. F. Mokbel, C.-Y. Chow, and W. G. Aref, "*The New Casper: Query Processing for Location Services without Compromising Privacy,*" in *VLDB*, 2006

[18]. G. Ghinita, P. Kalnis, A. Khoshgozaran, C. Shahabi, and K.-L. Tan, "*Private Queries in Location Based Services: Anonymizers are not Necessary,*" in *SIGMOD.*2008, pp. 121–132.

[19]. A. Khoshgozaran and C. Shahabi, "*Blind Evaluation of Nearest Neighbor Queries Using Space Transformation to Preserve Location Privacy,*" in *SSTD*, 2007

[20]. K. Liu, C. Giannella, and H. Kargupta, "An Attacker'sView of Distance Preserving Maps for Privacy Preserving Data Mining," in *PKDD*, 2006, pp. 297–308.

[21]. T. Brinkhoff, "*A Framework for Generating Network-Based Moving Objects,*" *GeoInformatica*, vol. 6, no. 2,

SESSION

CYBERSECURITY EDUCATION

Chair(s)

Prof. George Markowsky

The 2013 NECCDC - Lessons Learned

G. Markowsky[1], D. Johnson[2], A. Moody[3], R. Soucy[4], and W. Stackpole[2]
[1]School of Computing & Information Science, University of Maine, Orono, ME, USA
[2]Department of Computing Security, Rochester Institute of Technology, Rochester, NY, USA
[3]Information Technologies, University of Maine, Orono, ME, USA
[4]Information Technology Service, University of Maine System, Orono, ME, USA

Abstract—*After having run the 2010 NECCDC at the University of Maine, we had an opportunity to run the 2013 NECCDC at the University of Maine. In the process, we rediscovered some lessons we had learned the first time along with a number of new lessons. We feel that the NECCDC and similar cyber defense competitions are very important for motivating students and for bringing the academic cyber defense community together. We are committed to making sure that the competitions are well supported and continue to improve. We also realized that our past system of basically having each hosting institution essentially build the competition from scratch does not contribute to keeping the competition of high quality and improving. This article serves as a how-to for staging the NECCDC or a similar competition.*

Keywords: A maximum of 6 keywords

1. The CCDC & The Regional Competitions

The Collegiate Cyber Defense Competition (CCDC) system was started in 2004 as a series of competitions designed to provide institutions with an information assurance or a computer security curriculum a competitive environment to assess their students' depth of understanding and operational competency in managing the challenges inherent in protecting computer networks and information systems. Today there are 9 regional competitions throughout the US which serve as qualifiers for the national CCDC competition held each year. The northeast region (NECCDC) was started by RIT in 2008 and represents the states of Connecticut, Maine, Massachusetts, New Hampshire, New York, Rhode Island, and Vermont. We have also had New Jersey schools that are part of the New York metropolitan area compete in the NECCDC. For more details see [1].

2. Some Basic Terminology

The participants at the NECCDC are grouped into teams. The following glossary describes the function of each team.

Blue The competing teams are referred to as the blue teams. Each blue team functions as if it were a company IT department and carries out a number of tasks.

Red The Red Team consists of individuals highly skilled in cyber attack. Their task is to stress test the technical skills and group dynamics of the blue teams by creating as much havoc as possible.

White The White Team consists of individuals with a strong background in information technology. Each blue team is assigned two members of the White Team who monitor that blue team, and act as their managers. They also ensure that the rules of the competition are being followed.

Black The Black Team consists of individuals highly skilled in networking and infrastructure. Their task is to build and monitor the competition network.

Inject A task blue teams are asked to perform during the NECCDC.

For an interesting perspective from someone who has served on the various teams, see [3].

3. The 2010 NECCDC

The Northeast Collegiate Cyber Defense Competition (NECCDC) was established in 2008 by the Rochester Institute of Technology (RIT), which also ran the 2009 NECCDC. The University of Maine first competed in the NECCDC in 2009. At that time, RIT indicated a strong preference for another institution to host the 2010 NECCDC. After some discussion, the University of Maine volunteered to host the 2010 NECCDC with support from RIT.

We modeled the 2010 NECCDC on the 2009 NECCDC. We kept the schedule used in 2009, which was based on the schedule used at the National CCDC. The competition begins on a Friday and runs from about noon to 7 PM. The next day the competition runs from about 9 AM to 7PM. The competition concludes on Sunday as it runs from 9AM to Noon. There is a keynote speaker and an awards luncheon starting at 1 PM.

For the 2010 NECCDC we used two buildings. There were no serious problems, but the few teams in the second building felt a bit out of the action. We resolved to hold future competitions in a single building.

In 2009, there were a number of teams that had agreed to come, but who did not show up for the competition. This was unfortunate, because RIT had turned some teams away thinking that they had a full slate of teams. We decided that for 2010 each team would have to pay a $750 entrance fee. To make this more palatable, we stipulated that all teams that showed up would receive a $750 travel grant. This scheme worked well and all nine teams who had indicated that they would participate showed up.

During the 2010 NECCDC there was little for the coaches to do. One vendor gave a talk about opportunities with his company, and the coaches met to decide on the venue for the 2011 NECCDC. One of the highlights of the 2010 NECCDC was that our winner, Northeastern University, went on to win the National CCDC the same year.

The 2010 NECCDC was the first cyber defense competition supported by the Department of Homeland Security. We were able to get a $10,000 grant from the Department of Homeland Security to help support the competition. Because of their experience with the NECCDC, the Department of Homeland Security now grants $15,000 to each of the regional competitions in addition to their support of the national competition.

In the 2010 NECCDC, the Red Team was captained by Daryl Johnson who captained the NECCDC Red Team from its inception and does so to this day. The Black Team was captained by Andy Moody and the White Team was captained by Tom Vachon and Ray Soucy.

4. The 2013 NECCDC

The 2011 and 2012 NECCDC competitions were hosted by Northeastern University. The physical location of the competition was the EMC training facility in Franklin Massachusetts. There were 19 schools interested in participating in the 2012 NECCDC, but there were only 12 openings. During the coaches' discussions it became clear that we would need to institute a qualifying round to select the schools that would be invited to the NECCDC. It was also decided that the next host would be required to organize the qualifying round of the competition. After some discussion the University of Maine received the opportunity to host the 2013 NECCDC. Based on our experience with the 2010 NECCDC, we came up with the following guiding principles for the 2013 NECCDC.

1) We would use a virtual competition for the qualifying round.
2) The competition would be held in a single building.
3) We would have a NECCDC Symposium for the coaches and others.
4) We would stress close cooperation between the Black, White and *RED* Teams in designing and running the competition.
5) We would select our keynote speaker from among our distinguished Red Team.
6) We would stress to the students that the NECCDC is not designed to be fair as a competition between the Blue Teams and the Red Team – the job of the Red Team is to provide challenges that the Blue Teams can use to distinguish themselves. In this sense, the more unfair the competition, the easier it will be to separate the truly great teams from the field.
7) We would provide a better scoring system along the lines discussed in [4].
8) We would provide more feedback to the Blue Teams.

We were able to accomplish all of the above goals for the 2013 NECCDC. We were extremely pleased as well by the fact that the winner of the 2013 NECCDC, RIT, went on to win the National CCDC.

5. Support for the Competition

Napoleon Bonaparte is famously to have said "an army marches on its stomach." This maxim applies to the NECCDC, and providing food for the competition is one of the major expenses. With 10 blue teams each having 8-10 people (counting coaches and alternates), the White Team with 25-40 people, the Red Team of 15-20 people and the Black Team of 4-8 people, plus visiting administrators, media and a scattering of other people, most meals have 150-200 people participating.

[2] shows the schedule for the NECCDC. On Friday, there are refreshments in the morning and lunch for all participants. We also had a dinner for the Red, White and Black teams, and snacks and beverages throughout the day for everybody. On Saturday we provided three meals for everyone, and on Sunday two meals. In addition, we provided constant snacks and beverages on all three days. The snacks and beverages cost about $1,000 for the event.

The competition received significant support from both Cisco and Dell. Cisco supplied all the networking gear, while Dell supplied 36 PCs (24 desktops and 12 laptops). Altogether we used 80 PCs of all types for the blue teams since each blue team received 8 computers. The computers for each blue team need to be identical. We wanted to have two spares of each computer so we needed 96 computers for the blue teams. Besides the 36 computers contributed by Dell, 48 computers came from the School of Computing and Information Science, and 12 came from the Mathematics and Statistics Department. There were, of course, additional computers used by the Black and White Teams. The Red Team members primarily used their own computers. We also needed to find identical printers for each of the teams. This complicated matters some since most of the clusters have heterogeneous collections of printers. Fortunately, we still had the printers we had purchased for the 2010 NECCDC.

There were several lessons that we learned this time around.

1) It is not a surprise, but collecting donations is harder than getting them.

- Bureaucracies have become more difficult to work with. This includes both university and company bureaucracies.
- Corporate donors like to use American Express cards so make sure you have some way to accept them.
- Do not get university development people involved in fundraising for the NECCDC because they will treat the donors as the property of the university and not the competition.

2) Start on the fundraising as early as possible.

The direct cost of the competition is somewhere between $20,000 and $25,000, so some fundraising is definitely required. To help with fundraising was one of the reasons that we created the NECCDC Foundation.

6. The Qualifying Round

At the 2012 NECCDC it was decided to create a qualifying round. After discussions with the Red Team Captain it became clear that the effectiveness of the Red Team decreased once the number of blue teams grew above 10. The Red Team was hampered by having to try all its exploits against every blue team. It was also clear that the qualifying round would have to be virtual since it would be too difficult and expensive to try to replicate the NECCDC for the qualifying round.

After some discussions with Dwayne Williams of the National CCDC and some searching, we were led to David Durkee and the Center for Systems Security and Information Assurance (www.cssia.org). With CCSIA's help we held the qualifying round and selected 10 teams to participate in the NECCDC from the 14 teams that signed up for the qualifying round. We are very grateful to David Durkee and CSSIA for their help with the qualifying round. We are also grateful to the NSF which supports CSSIA.

We learned a lot from running the qualifying round. First, we need to hold the qualifying round earlier in the year so as not to interfere with preparation time for the NECCDC. Second, you cannot just reuse NECCDC injects in a virtual qualifying round. Third, you need to plan better and allow more time if you want substantial red team activity.

One goal of the qualifying round is to determine which teams have the necessary base knowledge to be competitive in the NECCDC. To do this, there must be more injects per hour than in the NECCDC, but they need to be simpler because of the short time span of the qualifier. Examples of appropriate injects are demonstrating the ability to filter a packet capture and identify specific traffic or being able to write a description of a given technology from a security perspective.

7. Scoring

The national CCDC provides two scoring systems. The Scoring Engine (SE) is a system that simulates remote end-user traffic and awards points for successful service checks. The Inject Scoring Engine (ISE) is a web-based portal that provides on-line delivery of injects and allows each team to see the status of services externally. These two systems are indispensable tools and are distributed as virtual machines. For the 2013 NECCDC a new scoring system was tested to address concerns raised over the 2012 competition [4].

In previous competitions an effort was made to balance the various components of the final score. In practice, however, the aggressive and unpredictable SLA violation component of the Scoring Engine caused the service check points to completely dominate the final score rendering the inject score and the Red Team score largely irrelevant. For 2013 a weighted system was used: 40% service checks, 40% inject scores, and a 20% ranked score for Red Team activity. The scores were scaled in each category so that the top team in each category received 100%.

The specific weighting used is not as important as the idea that the knowledge and skills elements of the event are equally weighted in terms of assessment, and that the activity of the Red Team is a significant component of the final result.

A major concern with scoring for 2013 that should be addressed for future competitions is the need for a dedicated scoring manager, separate from the main judge. In the 2013 NECCDC having the main judge also be responsible for scoring resulted in a copy-and-paste error in a spreadsheet that swapped 3rd and 4th places.

There are a few areas for improvement in the scoring infrastructure. At present each team's ability to receive and submit injects is dependent on its network being functional. Consequently, injects might not be completed simply because of Red Team, or even the team's own activity. We recommend that each team receive a dedicated terminal to access the inject portal on a separate network.

We need a better system for collecting Red Team activity scores for Red Team activity to speed up scoring. We propose that a Red Team component be included in the Inject Scoring Engine that would provide the Red Team captain with direct portal access to submit incidents for approval.

The NECCDC needs to do a better job of providing teams with access to the details of their results along with explanations from the White Team on why points were awarded or deducted. As part of this goal for more feedback, we asked the White Team to take notes on their observations of each team. Some members of the White Team provided very good information, while others provided none. We recommend that future white teams receive an on-line training session to better explain their role and responsibilities.

A goal that was not realized due to time and man-power limitations, was the generation of a team-specific result packet which would include all injects, their scores, and feedback that could be used to prepare for future competitions. Other ideas for improvement include having the

Scoring Engine actually test connectivity and function of the services. This would include such things as login capability with password for services like SSH, or purchasing items at an appropriate price through the e-commerce system.

8. The Red Team

The 2013 NECCDC embraced the mantra *THE RED TEAM IS NOT THE ENEMY*. Since the purpose of the NECCDC is help to pick the strongest cyber defense team to represent the Northeast in the National CCDC, we want to ensure that the NECCDC stresses teams enough to differentiate clearly between the best team, the next best, etc. In short, the competition should be challenging enough and the scoring opportunities great enough to produce a clear scoring separation among the teams.

This year we included the Red Team in all phases of preparing and running the NECCDC. There was extensive consultation before the event and the Red Team Captain was included in all discussions and made significant contributions to the design of the NECCDC. The results of this year's competition were quite good with the NECCDC Champion winning the national title as well.

Collaboration between the Red Team and the White Team provides a "juicy" environment for the blue teams to experience, and for the Red Team to exploit. In a "real-life" environment, the defenders of such an infrastructure would likely not be aware of a zero-day vulnerability already in place in their infrastructure. The necessity for the blue teams to both discover and mitigate in-place exploits is an exercise that adds a real life element of stress to the competition.

The NECCDC is not a test of the Red Team's abilities. The Red Team is a partner in testing the blue teams' abilities. They are a component in the White Team's arsenal of tools to assess the blue teams. The back story used in the NECCDC is that each blue team is taking over for a removed, failed system administration team. Attackers could have been ingrained in the systems for months or years. This will *not* be reflected in any sitebook or documentation. That is one of the challenges for the blue teams. Such embedded advanced persistent threats (APTs) would have a good knowledge of the architecture of a system after weeks, months or even years of surveillance.

8.1 Blue Team Debriefing

The NECCDC is a wonderful testing exercise but it is also a great learning opportunity for the students. In the past the Red Team gave a single hour long debriefing to all teams at once from a very general perspective. Two years ago in response to a request by some struggling new teams, the Red Team meet with them before the collective debriefing and gave them some very specific feedback for their team. The response was overwhelming. The next year we eliminated the large debriefing and utilized the time to give individualized feedback to each team. The Red Team was split up into teams of two and each meet with two blue teams for about 20-30 minutes giving them some general and specific feedback and offered them a chance to ask questions. This has turned out to be an extremely valuable addition to the competition and was repeated at the 2013 NECCDC. The challenges of giving valuable feedback to the blue teams is another factor in limiting the number of teams competing at the NECCDC to 10.

8.2 Red Team Composition and Assignments

From its inception the NECCDC has been fortunate to have both a great collection of Red Team members and relative stability in the composition of the team. Several of the regulars on the Red Team are regular speakers at Black Hat and DefCon, have well-regarded books, and are the authors of widely used cybersecurity packages. Not all interested members are able to make every NECCDC so it is good to have a pool of high-quality professionals to draw from.

Each of the Red Team members needs to possess a strong knowledge and ability to exploit some portion of the infrastructure. Not everyone on the team must have an incredibly wide variety of penetration testing skills, even though having individuals with such breadth is certainly desirable. As long as the Red Team is well-balanced, and its members possess among themselves a reasonable set of skills to exploit and infrastructure, they should be effective.

A Red Team should have somewhere between 10 and 15 members to make sure that enough exploits are being deployed against the blue teams, but at the same time avoiding the chaos and confusion that would result from having too large a Red Team.

The skill sets necessary for a successful Red Team cross all fields: operating systems, Web services, network services, cryptography, database, etc. But not surprisingly, the most important trait is team work and camaraderie. No individual can "know it all" and during the time-crunched pressure of the NECCDC Red Team members must recognize their limits and know when to seek co-operation.

8.3 Attacking the Blue Teams

There are two philosophies of how to organize a Red Team for attacks on the blue teams. One can either assign individual to specific blue teams or one can assign individuals to handle particular types of attacks and to launch them against all blue teams. Assigning Red Team members to particular blue teams is simple, but leads to unbalanced results because the skills of the Red Team members are not uniform. The NECCDC exclusively uses the second approach and Red Team members select particular attacks that they must run against all blue teams. We feel that this is the best way to get results that can be compared.

This approach of aligning Red Team members by skills allows us to adhere to the Golden Rule that a successful exploit can be recorded only after it is attempted against all the blue teams. This ensures that all blue teams get the same Red Team attention and that no blue team gets "picked on." This also allows the Red Team to form sub-teams along the lines of reconnaissance, exploitation, persistence, and post-exploitation. The Red Team is also sub-divided by platform expertise. Each sub-team's success is passed to the next sub-team to take advantage. For the Red Team having access to the boardroom in the Red Team hotel for use over night has been invaluable.

The NECCDC Red Team has developed a reporting system that records and submits successful attacks. Exploits must be validated by the Red Team Captain before they are released to the White Team. The validation must confirm that the exploit has been tried against all blue teams, that the exploit can be scored, and that all necessary information has been recorded clearly. More information about creating and running a Red Team is available in [5]. Some thoughts about how to maximize the educational effectiveness of a red team can be found in [6].

9. The White Team

The White Team is responsible for judging the event. White Team members are assigned based on their experience and background to tasks such as proctoring a team room or assisting with scoring written deliverables from teams. Each White Team member should have a strong background in at least information technology.

The White Team Captain is in charge of the injects and making sure that tasks are delivered to the blue teams in a timely manner. Ostensibly, the Director of the competition is a member of the White Team, but there are so many things that must be tracked during the competition that the Director is focused on other things. One duty at the 2013 NECCDC that fell to the Director, was running the NECCDC Symposium.

There should be 2 White Team members per blue team. In addition there need to be an extra 2 to 4 White Team members available for other tasks. Add to that the White Team Captain and a separate, dedicated scoring manager and it is clear that a white team needs at least 26 people. Given that it is often the case that white team volunteers are not able to assist for the full three days of the competition, one should plan on having 30 or so people on the White Team.

So far we have not used blue team coaches for the White Team to avoid any questions about a team coach influencing the results. Cyber defense competitions differ from other competitions in that the coaches plan a minimal role during the competition. In particular, unlike sports, the coaches of cyber defense teams are actually capable of competing and influencing the outcome of the event. We are interested in getting the coaches more involved and having the NECCDC be more of an educational event. In the 2013 NECCDC we ran a symposium which addressed this concern to some extent. More remains to be done in this area.

A pool of laptops and desktop computers should be available for White Team members since there are often issues with them using their corporate laptops to run some of the White Team software such as IRC or Google Apps. The White Team must be prepared to handle complaints or concerns about individual or team misconduct. Over the course of the NECCDC we have had both individual disqualifications and team disqualifications. Fortunately, neither occurred in the 2013 NECCDC.

It is good to have some people play the part of "foolish" users on blue team systems. They would click on web links, try to log in to the systems and in general do things that may cause problems. We are considering fielding a separate team to do this or perhaps using some members of the White Team to carry out these tests.

10. The Black Team

The Black Team is responsible for setting up and maintaining the competition network. It must work closely with the White and Red Teams, and provide network monitoring sufficient to detect any transgressions of the rules. It must also provide maintenance support to the blue teams. This can include reimaging computers or dealing with hardware failures.

For both 2010 and 2013, the White Team and Black Team have been referred to as the Grey Team. The Black Team requires strong technical skill and experience in configuring and preparing the event infrastructure, but is also instrumental in introducing common security problems into the infrastructure for teams to locate and correct. Ideally, the Black Team has specialists in Windows, Linux, and networking, each with a security focus.

A black team should have a minimum of 4 people for the NECCDC. Since setting up the competition involves a lot of work, it is good if the Black Team can draw on some temporary help for moving equipment around and imaging computers. All members of the Black Team need to be team players and able to work in a dynamic and, at times, chaotic environment.

The Black Team should have a solid core group. Each member of the Black Team must be aware of the time commitment involved. Core members should be available to create images, direct setup and takedown as well as be available for all (or majority of) the competition weekend. There will be late nights and long days as well as some early mornings to get ready.

Effective and timely communication between the Red, Black and White Teams is essential to the smooth running of the event. In 2013 we used several IRC channels to facilitate that communication which worked quite well. In particular this cut down on the need for White Team members in the rooms to physically run up to the White Team room to ask questions or bring results back to the scorers.

11. Infrastructure

There are some non-trivial infrastructure requirements for hosting the NECCDC. First, there must be 10 good sized rooms for the blue teams. There should be a secluded room for the Red Team convenient to the competition, but not obviously visible to the blue teams. There needs to at least one operations room and a White Team Headquarters. It is helpful for there to be a separate Director's area for handling the media and visitors. This area can also provide room for scoring and other judging activities. There should also be a room that can be used for repairing hardware or working on competition infrastructure.

Blue team room size is important. There needs to be adequate room for the blue team, equipment and up to 2 White team members. Collaboration space should be provided within the blue team room as well. While White and Black team rooms can be different rooms it is best to have one room adequate for the combined White and Black teams.

As mentioned earlier, all blue teams must be supplied with the same exact computer systems, networking gear, peripherals, and supplies. This is to ensure fairness and to simplify staging the competition. We believe that having at least two spares of all systems used is sufficient for the NECCDC.

Some means of moving equipment in bulk is recommended, we used large carts capable of holding 4-6 systems (including monitors, keyboards and mice) for the 2013 NECCDC. Be sure to have a sufficient number of power cables, outlet strips and network cables for the competition. For the 2013 NECCDC we used approximately 150-200 network patch cords of various lengths and between 40 and 50 power strips. We also used about two dozen longer extension cords.

12. The Blue Teams

Experience has shown that the NECCDC is a highlight in the education of prospective cybersecurity professionals. Given the lack of a standard curriculum and detailed training guides for the cyber defense competitions, it is not always easy for prospective coaches and team members to put together an effective blue team. Blue teams must understand what a business inject looks like and also how the Scoring Engine works to successfully compete.

Some schools hold mock competitions that expose students to an environment very similar to the one provided in the NECCDC. Preparation and an understanding of the competition environment is likely to improve the performance of the blue team. Experience has shown that students who have taken a cyber defense techniques class will do better in the NECCDC than students who not had such a class. Such classes should prepare students both technically as well as teaching them the fundamentals of cybersecurity team work (see [16]).

Over the years, the Cybersecurity Education Session of the Security and Management Conference has covered many topics of interest to people interested in starting and running a blue team for cybersecurity defense competitions. Some papers of general interest include [7], [8], [9], [10], [11], [12], [13], [14], [15], and [16]. For a paper that discusses how keyloggers can be used in cybersecurity education see [17]. For a discussion of running cyber defense competitions in high school see [18]. Finally, for a discussion of references that can be used to teach SELinux see [19]. We hope to present more papers related to this in the current and future sessions of this workshop.

We note that so far, the NECCDC has not subsidized the expenses of blue teams at the NECCDC. Anyone planning to take a non-local team to the NECCDC needs to have at least $2,000 to cover the cost of transportation, hotels and meals on the trip.

13. The NECCDC Symposium

As noted earlier, we ran the NECCDC Symposium in parallel with the competition. The schedule for the competition is available at [20]. Space prevents us from going into more detail, but the Symposium was successful and produced some very good dialog among the coaches. We note that we were able to work the Symposium into one of the injects.

14. Publicity and Photo Releases

A goal of the NECCDC is to generate publicity for the purposes of attracting more students to the field. The 2013 NECCDC received coverage on all the local TV stations as well as in the local paper. More details will be available at [2] soon. We have traditionally required all participants to sign a photo release [21], which should actually be called a media release. The reason for this is that when the media comes it is not always clear who will and who will not in any photos or videos. To avoid any possible problems we have required a press release from everyone.

For the 2013 NECCDC we permitted a few students to come who did not sign a press release. Consequently, we found ourselves in a few difficult situations that required students to not be in photos. After some discussion among the coaches, it was decided that everyone participating in the NECCDC and any of its activities will have to sign a media release. If they choose not to, they will not be allowed to compete in any round of the NECCDC.

15. The NECCDC Foundation

At the 2013 NECCDC, it was decided by unanimous vote of the coaches to establish the NECCDC Foundation which would take ownership of the NECCDC competition. The NECCDC Foundation will ensure that the collective knowledge and experience related to running the NECCDC is passed on in an organized manner to each host school in turn. It will seek to get as many schools as possible involved in the process of preparing and staging the NECCDC, and it will help with some key items. The details are still being worked on, but here are some areas that the NECCDC Foundation will help with.

1) It will provide an orderly method for finding host schools.
2) In conjunction with the host school it will handle fundraising for the NECCDC.
3) It will try to raise funds so that eventually it can help schools support their blue teams.
4) The University of Maine Foundation will act as the initial 501 (c) 3 charitable institution for the NECCDC so that all contributions to support the event will be tax deductible.
5) The NECCDC Foundation will help organize the Qualifying Round.
6) The NECCDC Foundation will help provide the Red Team.
7) The NECCDC Foundation will help the host institution set up and prepare the Black and White Teams.

We created a temporary board of directors who will serve until June 30, 2013 at which time we will elect a more permanent board of directors. We hope to persuade the captains of the various teams to serve as advisors to the captains of the next host's teams if their help is needed. The details still need to be worked out, but this looks like a promising development in the history of the NECCDC.

As a final note, the coaches voted unanimously that any institution hosting the NECCDC will automatically have its Blue Team advance to the NECCDC. This is in compensation for all the extra work and distraction that the host institution needs to deal with.

16. The 2014 & 2015 NECCDC Competitions

In part because of the creation of the NECCDC Foundation and the promise of support in setting up the NECCDC, there was much more interest in hosting the NECCDC than has been true in the past. As a result of various discussions it has been determined that the 2014 NECCDC will be held at the University of New Hampshire in March 2014. We are glad to report that there is serious interest from at least two schools to host the 2015 NECCDC. We hope to have many schools host this event in the future so the burden is shared more widely and cybersecurity gets more support and exposure.

17. Conclusions

The NECCDC is a tremendously positive event in the preparation of the next generation of cybersecurity professionals and deserves widespread support. We have seen the positive impact on the students as a result of trying out, preparing and practicing for, and competing in the NECCDC. They acquire a great appreciation for the knowledge gained and the importance of cybersecurity to both our personal and business world. We hope that this paper has conveyed some of the excitement and promise of this event.

References

[1] The National CCDC website. [Online]. Available: http://www.nationalccdc.org/

[2] The NECCDC website. [Online]. Available: http://neccdc.net/

[3] Jeffrey C. Scaparra, "One Individual's Three Perspectives on the Collegiate Cyber Defense Competition," in *Proc. SAM'10*, 2010, pp. 307-313.

[4] George Markowsky, "Toward a More Perfect Scoring System for the NECCDC," in *Proc. SAM'12*, 2012, pp. 230-235.

[5] Daryl Johnson, "The Assembly and Provisioning of a Red Team," in *Proc. SAM'11*, 2011, pp. 530-534.

[6] Jeffrey C. Scaparra and Jeffrey R. Bullock, "Red Teaming for Education," in *Proc. SAM'11*, 2011, pp. 512-517.

[7] Patrick Engebretson, Joshua Pauli, and Joshua Bosma, "Lessons Learned from an Evolving Information Assurance Lab," in *Proc. SAM'10*, 2010, pp. 261-266.

[8] Jean Gourd, "Cyber Storm: The Culmination of an Undergraduate Course in Cyber Security," in *Proc. SAM'10*, 2010, pp. 300-306.

[9] Joshua Pauli and Patrick Engebretson, "A Cradle-to-Grave Approach to Retaining Students in Information Security Programs," in *Proc. SAM'10*, 2010, pp. 255-260.

[10] Nicholas Capalbo, Theodore Reed, and Michael Arpaia, "RTFn - Enabling Cybersecurity Education through a Mobile Capture the Flag Client," in *Proc. SAM'11*, 2011, pp. 500-506.

[11] Cory Cavanagh and Raymond Albert, "Goals, Models, and Progress towards Establishing a Virtual Information Security Lab in Maine," in *Proc. SAM'11*, 2011, pp. 496-499.

[12] Ronald Cheung, Joseph Cohen, Henry Lo, and Fabio Elia, "Challenge Based Learning in Cybersecurity Education," in *Proc. SAM'11*, 2011, pp. 524-529.

[13] Sonja Glumich and Brian Kropa, "DefEX: Hands-On Cyber Defense Exercises for Undergraduate Students," in *Proc. SAM'11*, 2011, pp. 487-493.

[14] Cory Cavanagh and Raymond Albert, "Implementation Progress, Student Perceptions, and Refinement of a Virtual Information Security Laboratory," in *Proc. SAM'12*, 2012, pp. 197-200.

[15] William D. Casper and Stephen M. Papa, "A Multi-Disciplined Security Engineering Education Approach," in *Proc. SAM'12*, 2012, pp. 243-248.

[16] Brandon Mauer, William Stackpole, and Daryl Johnson, "Developing Small Team-based Cyber Security Exercises," in *Proc. SAM'12*, 2012, pp. 213-217.

[17] Christopher Wood and Rajendra Raj, "Keyloggers in Cybersecurity Education," in *Proc. SAM'10*, 2010, pp. 293-299.

[18] Raymond Albert, George Markowsky, and Joanne Wallingford, "High School Cyber Defense Competitions: Lessons from the Trenches," in *Proc. SAM'10*, 2010, pp. 280-285.

[19] Linda Markowsky, "An SELinux Sourcebook for Cybersecurity Education," in *Proc. SAM'10*, 2010, pp. 248-254.

[20] 2013 NECCD Symposium Schedule. [Online]. Available: http://neccdc.net/wordpress/?page_id=99

[21] 2013 NECCD Media Release. [Online]. Available: http://neccdc.net/wordpress/wp-content/uploads/2013/02/NECCDCPhotoRelease2013.pdf

Experiences with the Promise and Potential of Service-Learning in an Online Information Security Curriculum

R. T. Albert[1] and R. E. Albert[2]
[1]Professional Management Division, University of Maine at Fort Kent, Fort Kent, ME, USA
[2]Academic Affairs, University of Maine at Fort Kent, Fort Kent, ME, USA

Abstract – *Service-learning has been reported as offering the promise of both enhanced educational experiences and valuable community services to various constituencies. More specifically, positive outcomes have been reported when service-learning components have been incorporated into information security courses. The effects of incorporation of service-learning into online information security curriculum have not been fully explored. The aim of this project was to elucidate such affects. A service-learning component for an online information security course was designed and implemented with support provided by the Maine Campus Compact and the Davis Educational Foundation. The purpose of this paper is to share the reported promise and potential of service-learning in information security curricula and report on experiences with transforming an online introductory information security course to include a service-learning component.*

Keywords: Service-learning, Information Security Education, Online Education, Cybersecurity

1 Introduction

The impacts and outcomes of service-learning are widely supported in the literature [12]. Research findings that have been reported shows significant positive effects on academic performance, values, self-efficacy, leadership, choice of a service career, and plans to participate in service after college [2]. Similar findings have been reported in the primary, secondary, and post-secondary education populations. Support provided by several national organizations such as the National Service-Learning Clearinghouse and Campus Compact aids in communication, sharing of resources, and the general evolution of service-learning in it numerous forms. Research on the effects of service-learning application to information security curriculum is growing and the results to date are promising. Focused research on the effects of service-learning activities in the context of online education are few.

The aim of this paper is to report on a project aimed at further elucidating the promise and potential of service-learning in an information security curricula and report on experiences with transforming an online introductory information security course to include a service-learning component.

The project was designed and implemented with support provided by the Maine Campus Compact and the Davis Educational Foundation.

2 Service-learning in Info. Security

Service-learning pedagogy, by nearly all accounts, can take the form of internships, externships, field experiences, as well as activities involving student provision of specialized planning, training, auditing, or research. Its malleability in being designed into a course based on the interests of students and the community organizations they serve is perhaps one of the greatest benefits it can offer. Motivation to learn and engage can be greatly increased if the experience is well designed. The adoption of service-learning has nevertheless been cyclical, with periods of increased adoption followed by periods of decreased adoption.

In their analysis of major national surveys, the Campus Compact organization reports that community-based, participatory educational experiences can positively contribute to students' academic performance and persistence [4]. Gonyea has reported that service-learning promotes deep/integrative learning and personal development among both first-year students and seniors [8]. It has also been identified in the National Survey of Student Engagement findings as one of six high-impact activities [1].

During the early 1990s when adoption of service-learning pedagogy was on the upswing, faculty members were limited in their ability to explore and engage in service-learning practice. The reason was the ill-defined role that such pursuits played in the evaluation and promotion process [4]. As promotion and tenure guidelines evolve to include recognition of service-learning efforts, either directly or indirectly as a form of scholarship, the prevalence of such pursuits will likely increase.

Innovative service-learning approaches in the information security domain have been designed, developed, and implemented with positive outcomes [6, 10, 11]. These efforts have been informed by past research and have made significant contributions in their own right. They have also approached the incorporation of service-learning into an information security course in a surprisingly wide array of ways.

Dark reported on successful outcomes associate with her project efforts to further the application of service-learning in partnership with a local educational cooperative and school corporations. According to Dark, increased civic responsibility and citizenship of students occurs by "exposing student to societal inadequacies where they can use the community service experience as a foundation for learning 1) about oneself, 2) the academic discipline, 3) real world skills and techniques, and 4) how the discipline, skills and techniques intersect with the social world around us" [6]. This was the case for both the exploration of ethics and information security risk assessment. Mikelic and Boras reported on the positive value service-learning presents to community partners and fostering a stronger relationship between the academic institution and community being served [11]. Many different forms of service-learning application exist. The application of some of these in the context of an information security curriculum have been explored and reported by Linke [10].

Linke explored and reported on the introduction of several different service-learning activities into the information security curriculum. The activities assigned to student groups focused on the following:

- Security Maturity Assessment aimed at students helping an organization determine their level of security maturity and where they could improve. Reported benefits of this activity include helping the community partner see where they ranked relative to other organizations, learn about best practices, and consider where they could improve.

- Security Planning aimed at students helping an organization in their security planning efforts. Reported benefits of this activity include helping community partners define security policies, standards and programs.

- Security Awareness Training aimed at students helping non-technical staff become more security aware. Reported benefits of this activity include helping end-users within the community partner organization develop a better awareness, understanding, and appreciation of appropriate information security practices.

- Security Product Research aimed at students helping an organization evaluate variants of a security tool and make a more informed decision about security product adoption. This activity was reported to be not as effective or beneficial as a security product evaluation.

- Security Product Evaluation aimed at students helping an organization to be more informed about the performance of security products based on evaluation of security audit results. Reported benefits of this activity include being able to perform evaluations outside of the community partner organization thereby avoiding the introduction of any threat to the community partners infrastructure or security privacy.

- IT Facility Audit aimed at students helping an organization audit a portion of their IT network. Reported benefits of this activity include being able to perform an audit based on the prescribed needs of the community by first performing the audit in a segregated laboratory environment prior to the conduct of the actual audit.

The findings reported in these studies informed the design and implementation of this project.

3 Project Description

Many working definitions of service-learning have been promulgated in the literature. For the purpose of this project the definition that was adopted asserts that service-learning is a method under which students learn and develop through active participation in thoughtfully organized service experiences that meet actual community needs, foster civic responsibility, and that are integrated into the students' academic curriculum or provide structured time for reflection, and that enhance what is taught in school by extending student learning beyond the classroom and into the community" [5]

3.1 Overview of Campus Compact

The Campus Compact organization aims to "educate college students to become active citizens who are well-equipped to develop creative solution to societies most pressing issues" [4]. Given that information security, in all its forms, is recognized by most as a "pressing" issue, the fit with this project was recognized as a good one. State level chapters of Campus Compact have coordinated the availability of funding for projects in support of their mission. Campus Compact has and continues to serve as a leader in the service-learning movement since its inception. Resources made available through their auspices proved to be very beneficial to be design and implementation of this project.

This project was designed from the principles, concepts, techniques and resources presented through participation in a state level Campus Compact service-learning workshop for University of Maine faculty. The problem based service-learning framework was selected for its potential to contribute to the creation of a learning environment that is rich, engaging, and in which students take ownership for their learning and help each other establish and meet high expectations.

Some of the key guiding principles include:

- Be purposeful. Know what you hope to achieve and be intentional about designing experiences that will aim for these goals.

- Give students meaningful work that engages them in learning. Avoid tasks that have one right answer.

- Believe in student potential and look for ways to help each of them succeed.

- Remember education is something done with students, not to them. Help students to take ownership for their learning.

- Remember learning is a process and it sometimes gets messy. The ability to tolerate uncertainty, accept challenge, and solve problems as they arise is an essential life skill [9].

3.2 Candidate Course Selection

The aim of the project, in accord with the guiding principles that were provided, was to redesign an existing course to include a service-learning component. Cos 206 Introduction to Information Security was selected from the online Information Security curriculum for its potential to reach the largest audience and achieve the greatest positive effect.

3.3 Course Service-learning Elements

The aim of the project, in accord with the guiding principles and resources provided, was to redesign an existing course to include a service-learning component. It was also essential for the redesign to reflect and build upon past research recommendations. The key difference being that the redesign target in this effort is an online course that is part of an online degree program. Other factors, including the mission of the university, specifically pertaining to the promotion of experiential learning and responsible citizenship, also influenced the design of the course. The selection of the key service-learning activity that was ultimately designed into the course was greatly influenced by past research.

Lincke, reported positive results for several different activities [10]. For example, a security awareness training activity in which students must prepare and present to a community audience to educate them, in non-technical terms, about security awareness. This particular activity also offered the advantage of not requiring a mid- to large-size community/corporate partner, a significant challenge for online students situated in rural regions.

A mandatory model of participation was used in which all students must participate. The service-learning activity was assigned as any other and carried a significant weight in determination of the final grade. The service-learning assignment consisted of the following components and timeline:

- By the end of the third week of the 16-week term students must complete and submit:
  - Planning Form
  - Partnership Agree
- By mid-term, students must complete and submit:
  - Interim-Service Reflection Essay
- By the end of the term, students must complete and submit:
  - Post-service Reflection Essay
  - Presentation of Experience
  - Faux Press-Release
- By the end of the term the community partner must complete and submit a student evaluation

The intention behind multiple points of student reflection was to further emphasize the importance of reflection in promoting an even deeper student understanding and appreciation of the value of the experience as reported in the literature [3]. Service-learning, when combined with appropriate opportunities for student reflection and engagement, has been linked to notable education contributions as far back as the early twentieth century.

> "Instruction in subject-matter that does not fit into any problem already stirring in the student's own experience, or that is not presented in such a way as to arouse a problem, is worse than useless for intellectual purposes. In that it fails to enter into any process of reflection, it is useless; in that it remains in the mind as so much lumber and debris, it is a barrier, an obstruction in the way of effective thinking when a problem arises." [7].

The emphasis on student reflection was therefore considered an essential design element. Other factors having more to do with appropriate instructional design also played a role in the success of this project.

3.4 Other Instructional Design Considerations

The instructional design process advocated by Campus Compact required the thoughtful consideration of several other key design factors, including:

- Creation of a preliminary plan and use of a step-wise refinement process
- Careful project management (including careful attention to effective communications, feedback, and liability matters)
- Building of student capacity to engage successfully
- Building a strong supportive sense of community (especially among students)
- Strategies for communication with community partners
- Effective assessment, reflection, and celebration of accomplishments

Careful attention to each of these during a series of workshop exercises helped ensure all instructional design elements were appropriate and effective.

4 Outcomes

Students reported very favorable experience in their post-service reflections. All students rated the experience highly, despite several having reservations based on their perceptions of information security knowledge in the general populace and on their own anxiety levels when faced with having to interact with a community partner. A sample of student comments follows:

"I have learned a lot … I have more sympathy for this issue because it is not addressed and stressed enough. Something that contributed to this was a recent suicide of a Canadian teen due to internet bullying. This opened my eyes to how little young people are educated on internet safety and cyber bullying…. My view of internet safety has grown drastically. I think I see myself as somebody who is willing to help others and help spread the word on information and internet safety… I established a good relationship with the Rec. Department and hopefully this project has opened possible project and future job opportunities with the organization."

"I have been humbled by the process and I have realized that the tiny bit of understanding I have in information security was useful… This project also gave me the opportunity to actively participate in something I enjoy doing. I was able to identify potential vulnerabilities and was able to help implement some counter measures. I definitely feel that my basic contributions made some difference."

"It helped to put in perspective the challenges small businesses have to maintain security measures within a small budget… After performing a basic preliminary assessment, it is easy to see the lack of understanding of security measures. Even the basic physical security measures are not put into to practice"

"My survey of … indicated only 6% of respondents always use a unique password for every website they visit. 80% responded with 'I have a few passwords that I reuse.' 12% even indicated that they use the same password for every website they visit. Another issue that made itself apparent was that 70% indicated that their passwords were generally less than 11 characters. Only 32% reported using multiple words in their passwords, and a whopping 58% reported using a variant of their own name in their passwords…These statistics had a large effect on my decision regarding which method of creating passwords to recommend in my project."

"I was dreading doing this service-learning project because I get really nervous when I talk to groups of people. I knew I had to do it, not only for my grade, but to actually share the information I know that some people don't… Before this class and project, I only had a little bit of knowledge about the importance of security. Now, I realize how many different things can happen to your information if you are not careful. I also learned that there are tons of ways to increase your security, but you are never actually absolutely safe… My ambitions are really high after this project."

"This experience has been different for me. This is the first time that I have had to do a presentation outside of a classroom. It was easy considering I knew the people, but teaching the information was difficult at the beginning. I believe that we all walked away with a better understanding…"

"Looking back at my attitude about the service-learning project, I would have to admit that I thought it was a terrible idea. I could not believe that we were being sent out into the community to provide a service as part of an introductory class… However, I am not as strongly opposed to it after doing the project. Since I have worked in the IT field, I understand that the best way to learn something or solidify what you have learned, is to teach it to someone else. It was very uncomfortable for me as most of my training and work experience has been on-line or over the telephone. This time, I would have to work face-to-face with a nonprofit group and teach them something outside of my specialty… I feel that the experience did change my initial attitude and was a beneficial project as I learned a great deal about information security concerns for end devices and was able to use that information to help others."

"Overall, my project went really well. My capstone experience wasn't exactly what I had planned or expected and I feel that it was a better experience for that… I was interested in using the National Cyber Security Alliance's Higher Education teaching guidelines to assist and teach a university community. Luckily, I knew some people at

Boston University that were pleased to have me down.... The group wound up being mostly staff members from the BU Medical Center so I added some additional content that highlighted HIPPA aspects of IT security... The best experience was having an opportunity to work with others outside of my current place of work."

Community partners similarly reported favorable experiences and outcomes in their final evaluations of student performance. A sample of community partner comments follows:

"[the student] was great. Very informative and helpful. Thank you for putting together this program."

"[the student] took her assignment seriously and helped our office staff to understand a security program more fully."

"[the student] has done a very good job. Presentation was great, all was prepared, very clean in appearance, sure of himself, answered all questions of the audience with no hesitation... Very informative"

"[the student's] presentation was very informative and well received by the staff. It prompted a good discussion among our staff about the prevalence of information security incidents and what is being done to minimize these."

5 Conclusion

Service-learning has been reported as offering the promise of both enhanced educational experiences and valuable community services to various constituencies. The outcomes of this project are consistent with the findings of past research in all respects. Positive effects are achievable in information security curriculum delivered via online modality provided appropriate attention is given to sound instructional design principles. Adherence to recommended practices, and appropriate use of service-learning resources widely available under the auspices of organizations such as the Campus Compact, greatly aid in the design and implementation of such instructional efforts. Additional research is warranted to further elucidate those factors that contribute most to improving the effectiveness of service-learning activities in online information security curricula.

6 References

[1] Association of American Colleges and Universities (2013). *National Survey of Student Engagement*. Retrieved May 15, 2013 from http://nsse.iub.edu/

[2] Astin, A. W., Vogelgesang, L. J., Ikeda, E. K., & Yee, J.A. (2000). "How Service Learning Affects Students: Executive Summary", *Higher Education Research Institute, UCLA*. Retrieved May 15, 2013 from http://heri.ucla.edu/pdfs/rhowas.pdf

[3] Bringle, R. G. & Hatcher, J. A. (1999). "Reflection in Service-learning: Making Meaning of Experience", *Educational Horizons, v77 n4 p 179-185*. Retrieved May 15, 2013 from http://www.usfca.edu/uploadedFiles/Destinations/Institutes_and_Centers/OSL/docs/Bringle_Making_Meaning_of_Exp.pdf

[4] Campus Compact website. Retrieved May 15, 2013 from http://www.compact.org/initiatives/integrating-service-with-academic-study/

[5] Corporation for National and Community Service (1990). National and Community Service Act of 1990. Retrieved May 15, 2013 from http://www.nationalservice.gov/pdf/cncs_statute.pdf

[6] Dark, M. J. (2004). "Civic Responsibility and Information Security: An Information Security Management, Service-learning Course", *Proceedings of the 1st Annual Conference on Information Security Curriculum Development*, pp. 15-19. Retrieved May 15, 2013 from https://www.cerias.purdue.edu/assets/pdf/bibtex_archive/2004-43.pdf

[7] Dewey, J. (1910) "*How we Think*" Published by D.C. Heath and Company

[8] Gonyea, R. M., et al. (2008). High impact activities. Retrieved May 15, 2013 from http://cpr.iub.edu/uploads/AACU_2008_high_impact_practices%20Kuh,%20Gonyea,%20Nelson%20Laird,%20Kinzie%20final.pdf

[9] Gordon, R. (Editor) (2000). "Problem-based Service-learning: A Fieldguide for Making a Difference in Higher Education 2nd ed.". Campus Compact for New Hampshire.

[10] Lincke, S. J. (2011). "Service-learning in Security". *Proceedings of the 15th Colloquium for Information Systems Security Education*, pp. 63-68. Retrieved May 15, 2013 from http://www.cisse.info/archives/category/16-papers?download=184:4-2011

[11] Mikelic, N. & Boras, D. (2006) "Service-learning: Can Our Students Learn How to Become a Successful Student?" *28th International Conference on Information Technology Interfaces* pp. 289-294. Retrieved May 15, 2013 from http://hnk.ffzg.hr/bibl/iti2006/106%20ICT%20in%20Higher%20Education/106-5-147-252.pdf

[12] National Service-Learning Clearinghouse (2004). "Impacts and Outcomes of Service-Learning in Higher Education: Selected Resources", Retrieved May 15, 2013 from http://www.servicelearning.org/instant_info/bibs/he_bibs/impacts_he

Visualizing Cybersecurity Events

G. Markowsky[1] and L. Markowsky[1]
[1]School of Computing & Information Science, University of Maine, Orono, ME, USA

Abstract—*The old adage "a picture is worth a 1,000 words" is relevant to cybersecurity because professionals must deal with large amounts of data in a very short period. It is also relevant to cybersecurity educators who must convey the complexity of cybersecurity events to students and to members of the general public who might have little or no background in cybersecurity. Fortunately, there are many fine tools now available for visualization and there will be more such tools in the future. This paper discusses some of the tools that are available and highlights some work that deserves to be better known by cybersecurity educators.*

Keywords: visualization, cyberattacks, DoS, honeypots, Wireshark, Netstat, cybersecurity event

1. Introduction

In 1983 Edward Tufte created a stir in the area of information display by publishing his book *The Visual Display of Quantitative Information* [1]. The book went through seventeen printings before a second edition came out [2]. Tufte's book sparked a lot of interest in graphic design and the visual display of information. Since then there have been quite a few books published in the area. Some examples include books by William Cleveland [3], [4], [5], and [6]. While computers have improved tremendously over the past several decades, humans have stayed pretty much the same, so it is important to follow well-established design principles when designing effective visualizations for people.

Cleveland [3, pp. 4-15] and [4, pp. 4-22] show some examples where inadequate visualizations of data helped exacerbate problems and where clever visualizations led to the discovery of new scientific effects. These examples are of value and will help most people concerned with visualization.

We use the term *cybersecurity event* to describe any event that has implications for the cybersecurity of an individual or organization. Examples of events are the installation of a rootkit, placing malware on a system, scanning a system and even an all-out denial of service attack (DoS). Some events give little indication that they are happening and detecting them might involve the cyber equivalent of finding a needle in the haystack. Other events, like a massive distributed denial of service attack are obvious to the people involved and might involve a massive number of rapidly changing IP addresses and massive numbers of packets.

2. Static and Dynamic Images

It would appear that for visualizing cybersecurity events, dynamic images (including video) would be preferable to static images. Static images, however, have several advantages over dynamic images.

1) They can be included on ordinary paper and made available in many formats.
2) They are often easier to study and absorb than a dynamic images.
3) They are easier to produce.
4) We have many tools available for annotating static images.
5) They are less resource intensive and less expensive to produce.

Well-designed static images can tell a lot about a dynamic event. The graphic drawn by Charled Minard showing the terrible fate of Napoleon's army when it invaded Russia is shown in Figure 1. Carefully studying Figure 1 can give even the casual student a lot of information about the Russian campaign. Edward Tufte [1, p. 40] has a high regard for this graphic and states that "it may well be the best statistical graphic ever drawn."

Drawing something like Figure 1 requires a great deal of design skill. Fortunately, many ideas are relatively straightforward and can be presented effectively with much simpler graphics. Figure 2 is a graphic that we used in [7] to highlight the frequency of social engineering attacks on supercomputing clusters. We used a graphic such as this one for each of the questions on our survey. We found this to be effective for communicating the results of our survey. Graphics such as Figure 2 are relatively quick and easy to generate. Of course, the ability to make videos easily extends our ability to capture dynamic events.

Not all information that one might wish to convey is numerical in nature. Some important cybersecurity threats such as *viruses*, *worms* and *trojans* are primarily behavioral in nature and cannot be easily represented using numerical techniques. The concept of a *trojan* is derived from the well-known story of the Trojan Horse, which is some 3,000 years old. To this day, it continues to inspire stories and paintings, some of which have been used to illustrate security related concepts, e.g., Figure 3 which once was displayed on the website *www.container-it.com*.

When people adapt classical ideas to modern security concerns, they often get some of the details wrong. For example, in Figure 3 the Greeks launch their attack during

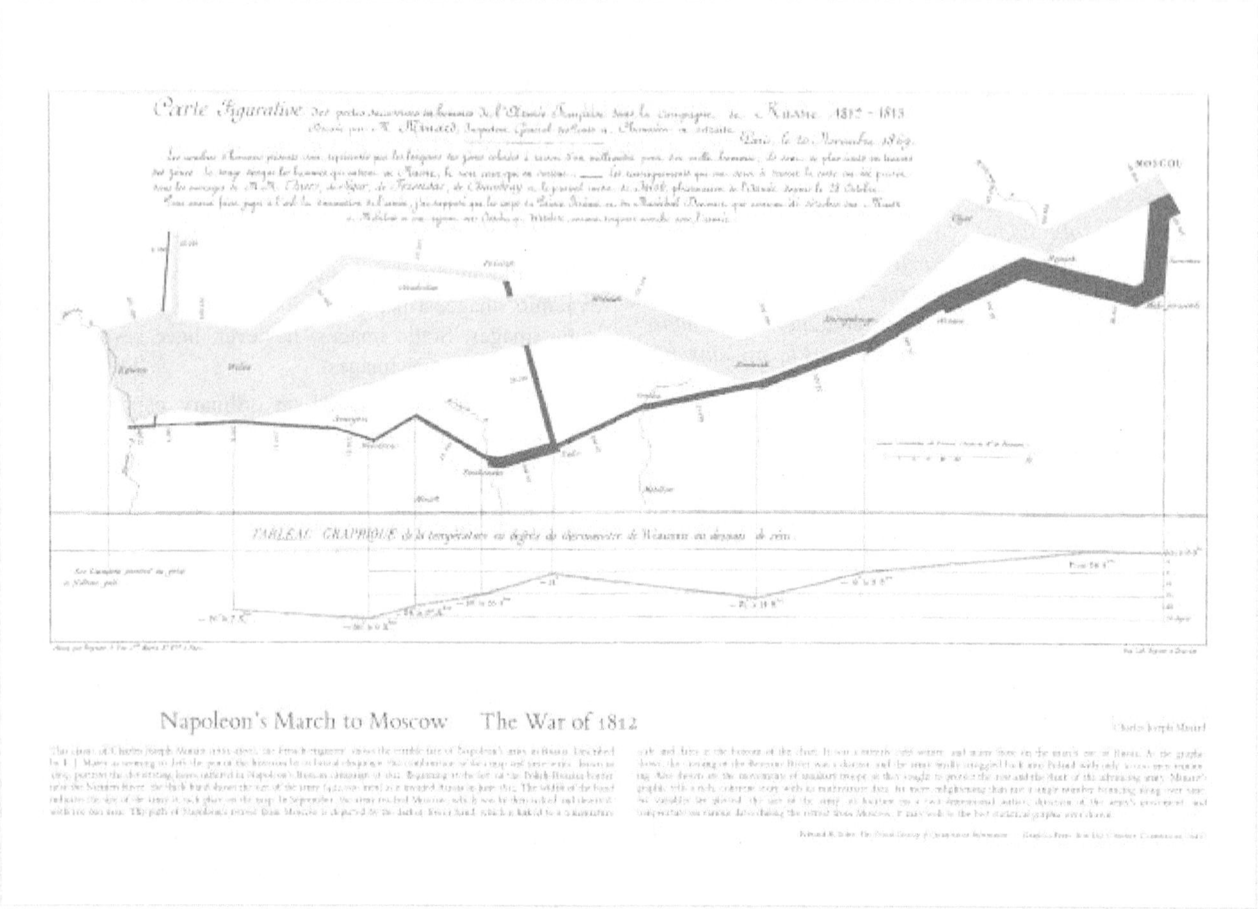

Fig. 1: A Static Image that Represents a Dynamic Event

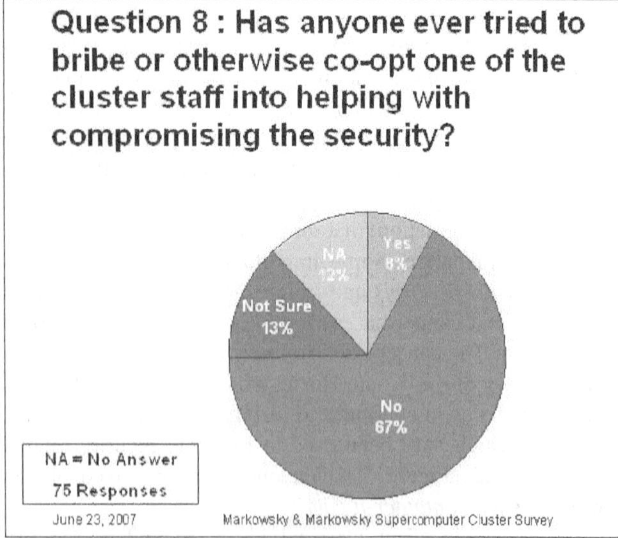

Fig. 2: The Likelihood of Insider Threats

the day, whereas it clearly had to be done at night. In [8] we discussed the image on the cover of the February 22, 2010 issue of *Information Week* shown here in Figure 4. Not only was the image a very poor representation of actual castles, it was actually a very bad way to apply the castle metaphor to the problems of cybersecurity. For better ways to utilize the castle metaphor for cybersecurity education see [8]. Some very compelling ways of visualizing complex firewall configurations is discussed in [9]. A sample image from [9] is shown in Figure 5. In [10] Sven Turpe discusses some general principles for designing cybersecurity visualization tools for developers.

3. Netstat

Netstat is a standard network information gathering tool that runs on all major computing platforms. Figure 6 shows a standard NetStat display. This display carries a lot of information for people who know how to read it. In [11] we discussed how to augment the NetStat display and produce variations that are easier for novices to understand. These versions might also help experienced users use NetStat more

Fig. 3: The Trojan Horse Cargo Container

Fig. 4: A Misleading Representation of a Castle

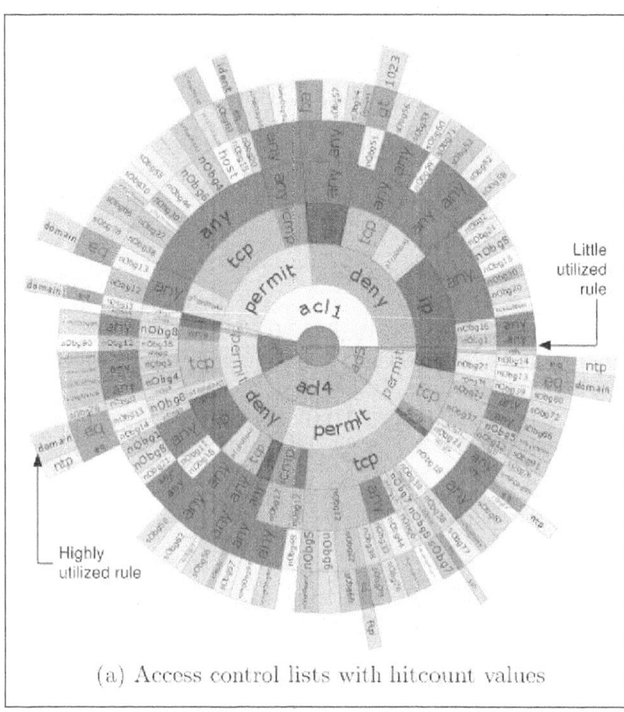

(a) Access control lists with hitcount values

Fig. 5: Visualizing Complex Firewall Rules

```
Active Connections

  Proto  Local Address          Foreign Address              State
  TCP    10.0.0.114:1177        STUDYSTORE:microsoft-ds      ESTABLISHED
  TCP    10.0.0.114:1269        w-client-lb:https            CLOSE_WAIT
  TCP    10.0.0.114:1399        ec2-107-20-249-77:https      CLOSE_WAIT
  TCP    10.0.0.114:6500        ec2-50-18-181-105:https      ESTABLISHED
  TCP    10.0.0.114:61199       sjc-not13:http               ESTABLISHED
  TCP    10.0.0.114:61280       v-d-la:https                 CLOSE_WAIT
  TCP    10.0.0.114:64201       vb-in-f103:https             ESTABLISHED
  TCP    10.0.0.114:64213       qa-in-f84:https              ESTABLISHED
  TCP    10.0.0.114:64215       lga15s28-in-f22:https        ESTABLISHED
  TCP    10.0.0.114:64422       lga15s28-in-f14:http         ESTABLISHED
  TCP    10.0.0.114:64423       lga15s28-in-f4:http          ESTABLISHED
  TCP    127.0.0.1:1030         NewtonII:5354                ESTABLISHED
  TCP    127.0.0.1:1243         NewtonII:27015               ESTABLISHED
  TCP    127.0.0.1:5354         NewtonII:1030                ESTABLISHED
  TCP    127.0.0.1:27015        NewtonII:1243                ESTABLISHED
  TCP    127.0.0.1:64225        NewtonII:64226               ESTABLISHED
  TCP    127.0.0.1:64226        NewtonII:64225               ESTABLISHED
```

Fig. 6: A Basic NetStat Display

effectively. Figure 7 illustrates the output of such a NetStat-Python combination.

Similar in style are two programs available for Windows machines called TCPview and Process Explorer. Screenshots of these programs can be seen in Figures 8 and 9. Both can be used to make valuable points about cybersecurity events.

4. Wireshark

Wireshark is a free protocol analyzer available from wireshark.org. It runs on all major computer platforms and is widely used by cybersecurity professionals. Simply running it, as illustrated in Figure 10, provides a user with a sense of how much traffice is seen by even a single computer. For

```
PORT: 135
    ('TCP', '0.0.0.0', '0.0.0.0', '0', 'LISTENING')
    ('TCPv6', '[::]', '[::]', '0', 'LISTENING')
PORT: 137
    ('UDP', '10.0.0.114', '*', '*', '')
    ('UDP', '192.168.56.1', '*', '*', '')
PORT: 138
    ('UDP', '10.0.0.114', '*', '*', '')
    ('UDP', '192.168.56.1', '*', '*', '')
PORT: 139
    ('TCP', '10.0.0.114', '0.0.0.0', '0', 'LISTENING')
    ('TCP', '192.168.56.1', '0.0.0.0', '0', 'LISTENING')
PORT: 445
    ('TCP', '0.0.0.0', '0.0.0.0', '0', 'LISTENING')
    ('TCPv6', '[::]', '[::]', '0', 'LISTENING')
PORT: 500
    ('UDP', '0.0.0.0', '*', '*', '')
    ('UDPv6', '[::]', '*', '*', '')
PORT: 546
    ('UDPv6', '[fe80::dc3:d544:ad26:ef9a%24]', '*', '*', '')
    ('UDPv6', '[fe80::58ef:5bcf:ebd6:a6db%10]', '*', '*', '')
```

Fig. 7: Using Python to Augment NetStat

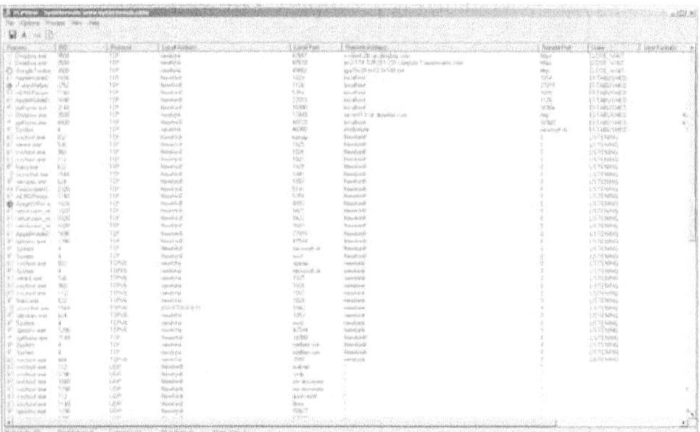

Fig. 8: A Screenshot of TCPview

Fig. 9: A Screenshot of Process Explorer

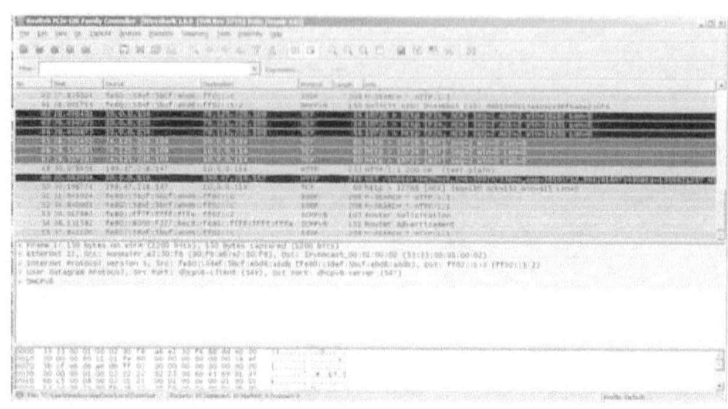

Fig. 10: A Basic Wireshark Display

Port	Protocol	State	Service	Version
139	tcp	open	netbios-ssn	
445	tcp	open	netbios-ssn	
1025	tcp	open	msrpc	Microsoft Windows RPC
1026	tcp	open	msrpc	Microsoft Windows RPC
1027	tcp	open	msrpc	Microsoft Windows RPC
1028	tcp	open	msrpc	Microsoft Windows RPC
1045	tcp	open	msrpc	Microsoft Windows RPC
5357	tcp	open	http	Microsoft HTTPAPI httpd 2.0 (SSDP/UPnP)
8093	tcp	open	http	Indy httpd 9.00.10 (.NET 1.0.2001.0; Acer Registration Service; greghsrw.exe)
47544	tcp	open	msrpc	Microsoft Windows RPC

Fig. 11: A Basic NMap Display

most effectiveness, a sequence of Wireshark screenshots can provide a compelling story of network activity.

5. NMap

NMap is a free security scanner available from nmap.org. Like Wireshark, NMap runs on all major computer platforms and is widely used by cybersecurity professionals. A basic display is shown in Figure 11. One of the nice features of NMap is its ability to produce a useful picture of a network's topology. A sample picture is shown in Figure 12. Figure 13 shows some of the memorable icons that NMap uses to describe the security rating of various systems and also icons that it uses to represent different operating systems. For maximum effectiveness a variety of NMap images can be combined to tell the story of a cybersecurity event.

6. The Radar Page

The "Radar Page" can be found at www.securitywizardry.com/radar.htm. It is shown in Figure 14. This page is designed for viewing in real time since many of the panels scroll. Nevertheless, static screenshots of this page are of great value in visualizing cybersecurity events. This page is so highly regarded that the Pentagon used it as a backdrop when briefing President George W. Bush on cybersecurity (Figure 15).

7. Honeypots

Honeypots are widely used to glean information about cyberevents. They are especially useful when organized

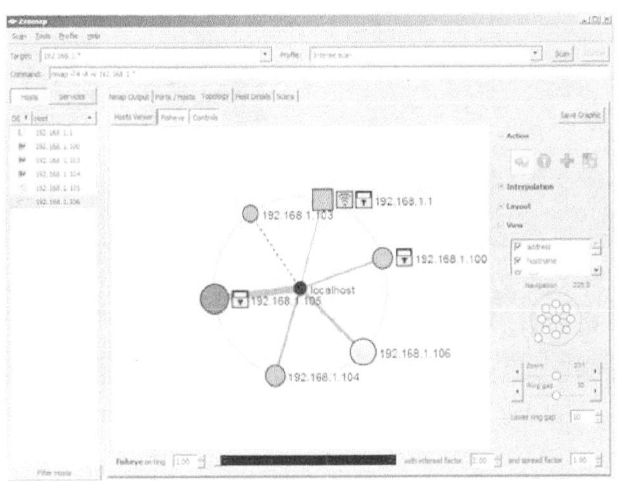

Fig. 12: An NMap Topological Display

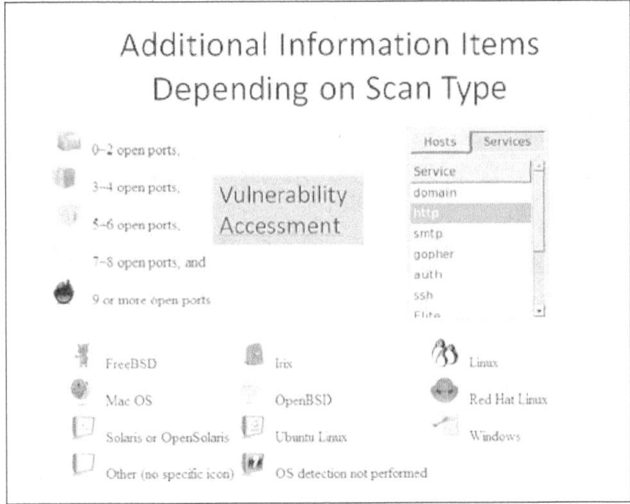

Fig. 13: NMap's Memorable Icons

Fig. 14: The "Radar Page"

Fig. 15: The Pentagon Showing Off for President Bush

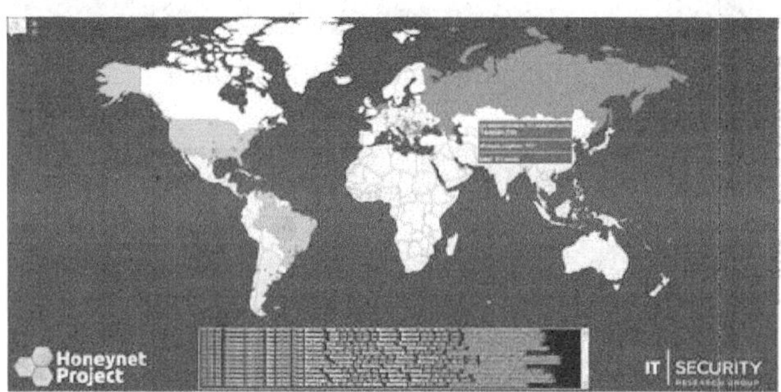

Fig. 16: Honeypots under Attack

into a distributed network that can collect data over a wide region. An interesting project of this sort can be found at www.honeynet.org. They have a web page at http://map.honeynet.org/ that displays what they call the "Honey Map." This map, which can be found at map.honeynet.org, provides a real-time indication of activity on the World Wide Web. A sample display is shown in Figure 16. There are periods when the map shows little activity. Of course, the map illustrates the activities on the World Wide Web that involve the honeypots operated by the project. This map is best viewed dynamically, although static screenshots also convey a lot of information to cybersecurity professionals.

8. Imaginative Displays

Figure 17 visualizes a distributed denial of service attack. It can be found at http://honeynet.org.au/?q=node/67. While a static image gives some flavor of the visualization, for best results we recommend that you view the video. A variant that can be found at https://code.google.com/p/logstalgia/ adapts the game of Pong to defend against a distributed denial of service attack. This is shown in Figure 18.

The visualizations in Figures 17 and 18 were produced using the Google Project tool called Logstalgia. More information about this tool is available at https://code.google.com/p/logstalgia/. Another interesting visualization project is called Gouse. It uses advanced

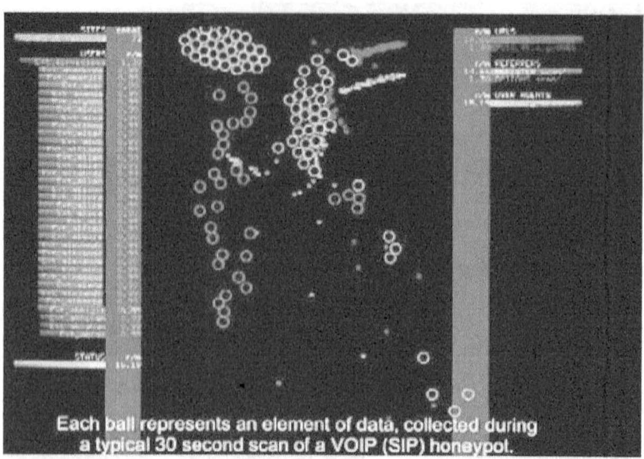

Fig. 17: Visualizing a DDoS Attack

Fig. 18: Adapting Pong to Defending Against a DDoS Attack

Fig. 19: A 3D Visualization of Cyberevents

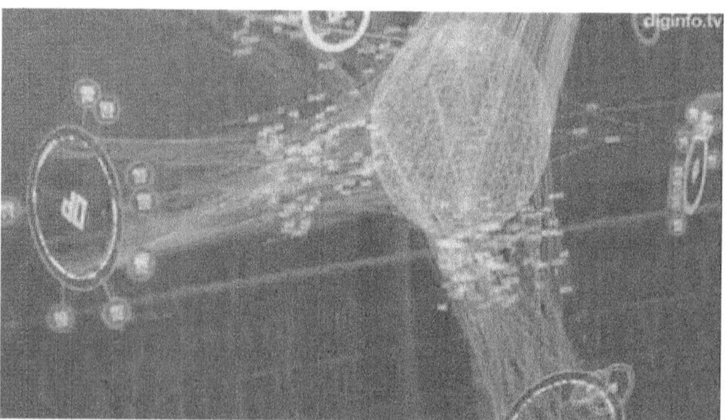

Fig. 20: A Closeup of a 3D Visualization System

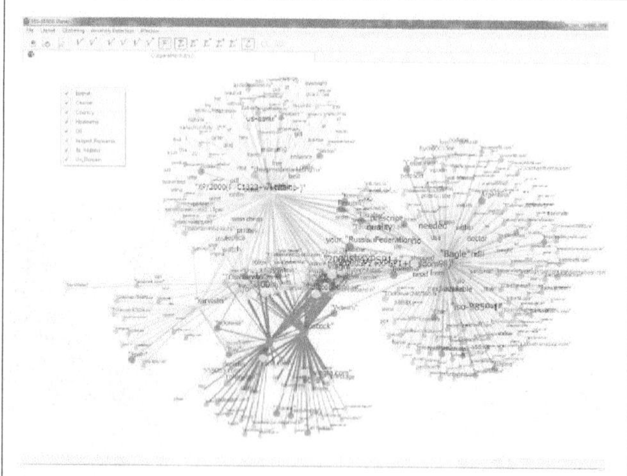

Fig. 21: Analyzing Spam Campaigns Launched by Botnets

techniques for software version control visualization. More information about this project can be found at https://code.google.com/p/gource/.

9. Three Dimensional Displays

Given the very dynamic nature of cybersecurity events, especially when dealing with cyber attacks, it seems clear that three dimensional visualizations might be very helpful. Daedalus, a tool that produces such visualizations, was produced by Japan's National Institute of Information and Communications Technology (NICT). More information about this project can be found at http://www.nict.go.jp/press/2012/06/06-1.html and also in [12]. Figure 19 shows the system in action. Using all three dimensions, the system clearly shows used and unused IP addresses. It is rightly assumed that activity involving unused IP addresses is suspicious and should be examined in more detail. Figure 20 shows a closeup of this system.

Another interesting use of three dimensional graphics can be found in [13]. Figure 21 from that paper shows how to analyze spam campaigns launched by various botnets.

10. Symposium on Visualization for Cyber Security

A wonderful source of cutting edge cybersecurity related visualizations can be found in the various Symposia on Visualization for Cyber Security. The website for this organization can be found at http://www.vizsec.org/. Their 2013 meeting, Visualization for Cyber Security (VizSec 2013) will be held on October 14, 2013 in Atlanta GA, USA in conjunction with IEEE VIS.

11. Conclusions

There are many promising tools that can produce very fine visualizations that can be of great help in communicating cybersecurity concepts to a wide range of audiences. We urge people to use the existing tools more widely and to add new visualizations for others to use.

References

[1] Edward R. Tufte, *The Visual Display of Quantitative Information*, Cheshire, CT, USA: Graphics Press, 1983.

[2] Edward R. Tufte, *The Visual Display of Quantitative Information*, 2nd ed., Cheshire, CT, USA: Graphics Press, 2001.

[3] William .S Cleveland, *Visualizing Data*, Summit, NJ, USA: Hobart Press, 1993.

[4] William S. Cleveland, *The Elements of Graphing Data*, Summit, CT, USA: Hobart Press, 1994.

[5] Antony Unwin, Martin Theus, and Heike Hofman, *Graphics of Large Datasets*, New York, NY, USA: Springer Science+Business Media, 2006.

[6] Nathan Yau, *Visualize This*, Indianapolis, IN, USA: Wiley Publishing, 2011.

[7] George Markowsky and Linda Markowsky, "Survey of Supercomputer Cluster Security Issues," in *Proc. SAM'07*, 2007, pp. 474-480.

[8] George Markowsky and Linda Markowsky, "Using the Castle Metaphor to Communicate Basic Concepts in Cybersecurity Education," in *Proc. SAM'11*, 2011, p. 507-511.

[9] Florian Mansmann, Timo Gobel, and William Cheswick, "Visual Analysis of Complex Firewall Configurations," in *Proc. VizSec'12*, 2012, pp. 1-8.

[10] Sven Turpe, "Point-and-Shoot Security Design: Can We Build Better Tools for Developers?," in *Proc. VizSec'12*, 2012, pp. 27-41.

[11] George Markowsky and Linda Markowsky, "Who's Knocking at Your Cybercastle's Gate?," in *Proc. SAM'12*, 2012, pp. 206-212.

[12] Daisuke Inoue, Koei Suzuki, Mio Suzuki, Masashi Eto, and Koji Nakao, "DAEDALUS-VIZ: Novel Real-time 3D Visualization for Darknet Monitoring-based Alert System," in *Proc. VizSec'12*, 2012, pp. 72-79.

[13] Orestis Tsigkas, Olivier Thonnard, and Dimitrios Tzovaras, "Visual Spam Campaigns Analysis using Abstrac Graphs Representation," in *Proc. VizSec'12*, 2012, pp. 64-71.

XSS Cookie Injection Covert Channel

Kyle Feeney and Daryl Johnson
Department of Computing Security
Rochester Institute of Technology
Rochester, NY USA
Email: kdf5506@rit.edu, daryl.johnson@rit.edu

Abstract—**This paper describes a method of covert communication by way of HTTP Cookie injection using Cross-site scripting into vulnerable website's. Website's susceptible to Cross-site scripting can be used as a medium for covert communication using Cookies as the message carrier between two or more nodes. Due to the necessity of Cookies in Web development and the format options of a Cookie, this covert channel offers a variation of implementation techniques which can achieve reasonably high data rates.**

I. Introduction

Research into covert channels is still fairly new and for that reason, defining a covert channel is difficult. Butler Lampson first used the term covert channel in his paper, The Confinement Problem [4] presenting techniques for safeguarding against information leakage in computing processes which may lead to other processes accessing the leaked data. It has sense been recognized that covert channels exist in many different technologies and are used legitimately and illegitimately. The Department of Defense's Trusted Computer System Evaluation Criteria (TCSEC) recognizes two types of covert channels: storage channels and timing channels. Storage channels include all vehicles that would allow the direct or indirect writing of a storage location by one process and the direct or indirect reading of it by another. Timing channels include all vehicles that would allow one process to signal information to another process by modulating its own use of system resources in such a way that the change in response time observed by the second process would provide information [1]. Although there are many different definitions for what constitutes a storage channel this implementation of a covert channel, based on the TCSEC definition, would be described as a covert storage channel.

Exploration in the area of HTTP Cookie covert channels is not new either. Past work includes Huba's HTTP Cookie Covert Channel using Google Analytic web Cookies [2]. These Cookies can be encoded to carry a predefined message which is passed to the web server in an HTTP request. Using a Man-in-the-middle style attack, a node can sniff traffic sent to the server and strip the Cookie content from the HTTP header and decode the message. The proposed covert channel in this paper will use Cross-site scripting to inject Cookies with encoded messages into website's which do not safely validate their form data. According to XSSed [6], one of the largest archives of Cross-site scripting vulnerable sites, there are over 45,000 website's listed which provides large a number of sites for this covert channel implementation.

II. HTTP Cookie

Though HTTP Cookies are a controversial topic due to tracking Cookies and Cross-site scripting exploits, they are largely misunderstood and are an integral part of the Web and serve an important purpose. HTTP is a stateless protocol, meaning the protocol does not save any information about its current state or the client and it's state is renewed with each invocation of an HTTP request. There arose a need to create a way for a website to save information about it's state such a session information or client information. This led to the advent of the HTTP State Management Mechanism [3] otherwise known as the HTTP Cookie or juts Cookie. Originally designed and patented by Lou Montulli in the early 90's. A Cookie contains small pieces of data passed from a website to a client's browser and depending on the browser it may also be stored on the client's file system. A Cookie can serve several purposes. It can be used to store information about user's preferences or browsing habits such as past website's visited. They can be used to collect information, otherwise known as tracking Cookies which obtain information such as the user's network address, location, and other information. Google Analytic's is an example of a tracking Cookie implementation. The most common use of Cookies is for storing user's login credentials. These different uses server the purpose of making Web browsing a more intuitive and enjoyable experience. Cookies are widely used and without them many of the popular website's would not work. For that reason, they offer an excellent vector for exploit.

The HTTP State Management Mechanism was originally documented in RFC2091 and later superseded by RFC2965 and again by RFC6265. An HTTP Cookie has 6 fields, 5 of which are optional. The number of optional fields leaves room for modifying and improving this covert channel in future development. The available fields include:

- Name - Required. The name given to the Cookie by the origin server.
- Expire - Optional. Specifies the date and time for which a Cookie should expire.
- Domain - Optional. Specifies the domain for which a Cookie is valid. This must always begin with a dot in a fully qualified format.
- Max-Age - Optional. Specifies the lifetime of a Cookie in seconds. It must be a non-negative integer. A zero

means the cookie should be discarded immediately. If specified along with Expire, the Max-Age attribute should take precedence.

- Path - Optional. Specifies a subset of URL's for which the Cookie applies.
- Secure - Optional. Indicates that securing the Cookie is in the best interest of the user agent.

According to RFC6265, the general implementation considerations for browsers should at least include:

- At least 4096 bytes per Cookie (as measured by the sum of the length of the Cookies name, value, and attributes).
- At least 50 Cookies per domain.
- At least 3000 Cookies total.

This covert channel will use HTTP Cookies as the message carrier. Therefore, these considerations are important as they will be used to derive the potential data rate this cover channel offers. This will be laid out in the Cover Channel Method.

III. Cross-site Scripting

Cross-site scripting, also referred to as XSS remains the largest vulnerability on the Web. According to Symantec, in 2007 over 84% of web exploits were related to Cross-site scripting attacks and still in 2012 Cross-site scripting remained the most common vulnerability on the web [6]. The vulnerability is typically the result of poor development and configuration. Website's which do not properly validate input on their form fields are susceptible to Cross-site scripting. An attacker can use JavaScript to manipulate the website to act differently than intended. One way to test for Cross-site scripting is to simply browse to a predefined website such a message board or Blog site and enter the following script as seen in an OWASP example [5].

```
<script type="text/javascript">
  var adr = '../evil.php?cakemonster=' + escape(document.cookie);
</script>
```

Fig. 1. Cookie Grabber Attack Example

This script will send the Cookie to the evil.php page where the PHP script can use it for whatever it wants. If the website accepts this as input, when the HTML is rendered it will not display what is in the script tags, however visiting users of the website will now have their Cookie information passed to an attacker. Because this vulnerability is so frequent, it makes for an excellent means for persisting our communication over the network.

IV. Method

The design of this covert channel is based on three entities. Firstly, the web server hosting a website which is vulnerable to Cross-site scripting. The server can either be owned by the communicating parties or it can be a third party server. Second is the sender which runs a simple Perl script to generate the message and encode it into a Cookies content field using the JavaScript **document.Cookie** property. This property acts as the **Set-Cookie** line in an HTTP header. Using this method, there is no perceivable difference between legitimate Cookies passed by the server and the ones we inject. Lastly, the receiver which runs a Perl script to parse all Cookies received and stored on the local file system. The receiver script then verifies whether a message exists and if it does it decodes the message. This method allows for bi-directional communication if both nodes are running the sender and receiver scripts. The figures below depict the message flow from sender to receiver and then from receiver to sender, respectively. The message is first encoded and injected by the sender. The receiver will refresh the page at a specified interval invoking an HTTP request. The Cookie is then passed to the receivers browser in the Set-Cookie header of the HTTP response. The receiver can now decode the message and acknowledge the message by injecting its own Cookie containing the Expire date of the original Cookie incremented by a single second causing the senders Cookie to be overwritten with the acknowledgement.

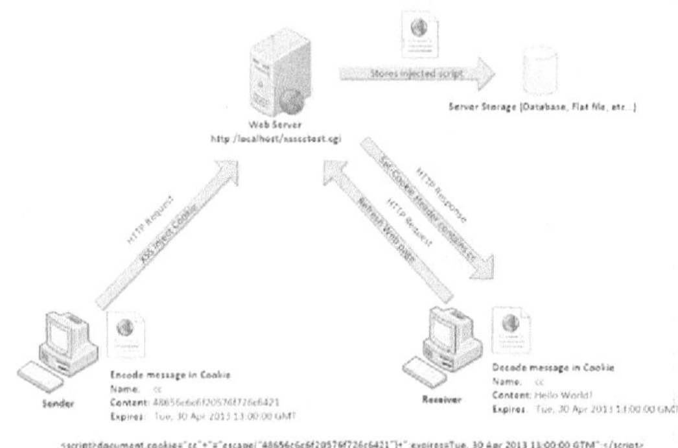

Fig. 2. Message from Sender to Receiver with Acknowledgment

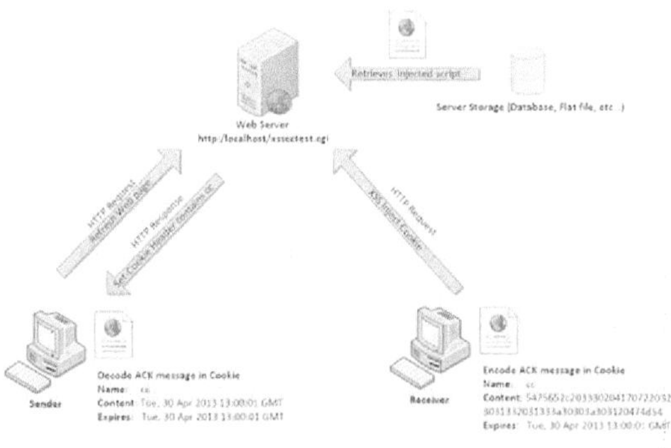

Fig. 3. Message from Sender to Receiver with Acknowledgment

In our case, we are not concerned with legitimate Cookies passed to the browser from the website, but those that were injected by the sender into the website's database using our Cross-site scripting attack. The Expire field of the Cookie tells the browser whether or not it needs to accept the new Cookie and overwrite the old. A browser will not accept two Cookies of the same name value from the same website instead it will overwrite an older one with one containing a later expire date. With this in mind, we can produce a TCP like communication between sender and receiver where the receiver acknowledges each Cookie received before the sender sends the next of the same name value. When the receiver gets a Cookie from the sender, the receiver could theoretically pass back the Expire date to the sender in the content field, telling the sender that it has successfully received that message. The sender can then increment the time on the next message in the Expire field and send the next message, again waiting for an acknowledgement. This way the sender and receiver can be assured the message is being passed in its entirety. If the sender receives an acknowledgement for a time less than the last messages Expire value than the sender can retransmit the message starting from the Expire value given by the receiver. This method presents a reasonable data rate but involves outside variables which can influence the data rate. Given the above example, the bandwidth, measured in bits per second, of a single message sent can be measured as such:

Given **S** representing the size of the Cookie in bytes. If **s** represents the number of seconds needed to inject the Cookie into the website, than **t1** represents the bit rate.

$$t1 = ((S * 8)/s) \quad (1)$$

As an example, a Cookie of max size 4096 bytes requiring 5 seconds to inject would have a bit rate of 6553bit/s for injecting the Cookie into a website.

$$((4096 * 8)/5) = 6553bit/s \quad (2)$$

If the receiver is set to automatically refresh the website at a specified interval of say 15 seconds, then **t2** can represent the download bit rate. Let **C** represent the size of our injected Cookie in bits and **n** represent the sum of all bits for additional Cookies passed by the website. Let **s** represent the time in seconds needed by the website to push the Cookies to the browser.

$$t2 = ((C + n)/(s + (15/2)) \quad (3)$$

As an example, if the injected Cookie was of max size 4096 bytes and no other Cookies were passed by the browser and we assume 5 seconds is required for the website to complete the HTTP response pushing the injected Cookie to the browser, than we would have a bit rate of 2621bit/s.

$$(((4096 * 8) + 0)/(5 + (15/2))) = 2621bit/s \quad (4)$$

The maximum theoretical throughput in bits per second can be calculated by subtracting **t2** from **t1**.

$$((4096*8)/5) - ((32768+0)/(5+(15/2))) = 3932bit/s \quad (5)$$

To effectively test this formula, both the sender and receiver modules should be automated. Currently, testing this theory requires manually injecting the scripts into the website while the receiver manually refreshes the page. Parsing the cookies is automated, however the receiver would need to manually inject an acknowledgement Cookie back into the website. Further development of this covert channel would include improving automation of both the sender and receiver modules.

V. Detection and Prevention

The implementation of this covert channel utilizing Cross-site scripting and HTTP Cookies does face some setbacks which have to be considered. Firstly, as the entire transmission relies on an Cross-site scripting vulnerable website as the channel medium and Cookies as the message carrier, it is critical that the sender and receiver agree on a vulnerable website to use, and that both the sender and receiver use a browser which has Cookies and Scripting enabled. From a security perspective, administrators can prevent this covert channel from being successful by disallowing Cookies to be pushed to the browser which can kill the message carrier portion of this channel. Furthermore, a well developed and configured website would prevent the sender and receiver from injecting scripts into its pages. This can be done by correctly validating data persisted through the website to its storage.

As previously defined, a successful covert channel hides the fact that two or more entities are communicating and that both the sender and receiver should not be identified even if the channel were to be. One flaw in this implementation is the use of injecting scripts into the website's form fields, which are then persistent on a storage medium of some sort. This means that the script itself resides local on the server in a database or flat file. This could also mean that the sender may be logged by the web server when data is posted to the website. The receiver or receivers however, can remain undetected because by merely visiting the page the receiver remains ambiguous to the server. Only a receiver who knows that a Cookie has been pushed to their browser and who knows how to decode the message would find the Cookie useful. Future development may include techniques for safeguarding the senders identity.

VI. Conclusion

In conclusion, though the detection and prevention techniques may hinder the success of this channel, it is still a viable covert channel if implemented correctly. Knowing that a sender may be logged we can use techniques such as spoofing an IP address to protect the senders identity. Enabling Cookies and scripting in the browser is a simple obstacle to overcome becuase it would be safe to assume the sender and receiver have access to the machines for which they are using for communication. Lastly, as noted covering Cross-site scripting; due to the number of Cross-site scripting vulnerable sites, there would be no shortage of communication mediums to choose from.

References

[1] *Nist department of defense trusted computer system evaluation criteria*, http://csrc.nist.gov/publications/history/dod85.pdf, CSC-STD-001-83, dtd 15 Aug 83.

[2] William Huba, Bo Yuan, Peter Lutz, and Daryl Johnson, *A http cookie covert channel*, Commun. ACM (2011), 1–4.

[3] D. Kristol and Montulli L., *Http state management mechanism*, Tech. report, Internet Engineering Task Force, February 1997, RFC2109 http://www.ietf.org/rfc/rfc2109.txt.

[4] Butler W. Lampson, *A note on the confinement problem*, Commun. ACM **16** (1973), no. 10, 613–615.

[5] The Open Web Application Security Project, *Cross-site scripting (xss) examples*, https://www.owasp.org/index.php/Cross-site_Scripting_(XSS), December 2011.

[6] XSSed, *Cross-site scripting (xss) information and mirror archive of vulnerable websites*, http://www.xssed.com/.

Composite Covert Channels through EVE Online

Ross Radford and Daryl Johnson
Department of Computing Security
Rochester Institute of Technology
Rochester, NY USA
{rer8936, daryl.johnson}@rit.edu

Abstract—***Online gaming has frequently been analyzed as a potential medium for covert communications. However, massively-multiplayer online role-playing games offer considerable advantages over other multiplayer game systems, allowing them to be manipulated for the purpose of leaking information with greater security and efficiency. This paper discusses the use of EVE Online for the construction of a covert channel combining aspects of both behavior channels and storage channels to hide the transmission of encoded data to another user.***

I. Introduction

Since the original definition of covert channels by Lampson [1], emergent networking technologies have been analyzed for their potential for the transmission of covert information. To a similar extent, new protocols using existing technologies are analyzed. However, while the protocols used by Internet games are old, the exponentially increasing complexity in many online games provides new opportunities to apply Lampson's methods of information leakage; opportunities which have not been extensively researched in recent years. That said, not all games are equal. While many online games provide the capacity to convey information, it is massively-multiplayer online role-playing games (MMORPGs) in particular that offer the best mix of traits for use in this role. As Johnson, Lutz, and Yuan [2] note, the communicants in an MMORPG can be extremely difficult to identify due to the use of a single central server and the large number (thousands or more) of users. Although the specific methods described here are not necessarily innovative, and are similarly limited as those described by Zander, Armitage, and Branch [3] and Deffenbaugh, Johnson, Yuan, and Lutz [4], their application to an MMO instead of a conventional multiplayer game circumvents a few of the issues associated with those media and drastically improves the security and deniability of the channel. For this paper, the game being used is EVE Online [5], a science fiction role-playing game with persistent elements that can be taken advantage of to produce a dual behavioral and storage covert channel. The primary concept is to use a behavioral channel to encode information on the Eve Online game servers, which will then serve as a storage channel for retrieval by another user. This allows the covert channel to take advantage of the difficulty of detection of behavioral channels, as well as the asynchronicity and reliability of storage channels.

II. Method

Eve's economy model revolves around the use of a variety of basic ore. The ore is mined from the environment and sold by the miners for a profit to be used by other players, who process them into minerals and then use the minerals to produce game items. This economy drives the game, and due to the prevalence of miners, a variety of ores can be cheaply purchased in large quantities using the currency a starting player is given. For a simple implementation of the channel, eight different varieties will be sufficient. The resources chosen will be the most common (and therefore cheapest) ores-Veldspar, Scordite, Pyroxeres, Plagioclase, Omber, Kernite, Jaspet, and Hemorphite. These can be purchased at any space station, allowing the user to quickly procure them and set up the channel.

When a player's spaceship leaves a space station and is in open space, the owner can jettison any or all of its cargo at any time. This jettisoned cargo forms a static cargo container next to the ship, and additional cargo can be placed inside. Each different type of item forms a separate listing within the container, with the quantity listed as well. This list has functions to sort by name (alphabetically), quantity, type, and several other factors that are not useful to this application. For example, a player could jettison 102 units of Veldspar, then add to the new container 101 units of Scordite, 101 of Pyroxeres, 98 of Plagioclase, 68 of Omber, 65 of Kernite, 69 of Jaspet, and 68 of Hemorphite. The resulting container, when sorted alphabetically, would appear thus:

Name	Quantity
Hemorphite	68
Jaspet	69
Kernite	65
Omber	68
Plagioclase	98
Pyroxeres	101
Scordite	101
Veldspar	102

If these quantities are used to look up the corresponding decimal entries in the standard ASCII table, and in the same order that they were read in (alphabetical by ore name), the simple message 'DEADbeef' is produced.

However, eight ASCII characters are insufficient bandwidth for a useful transmission. While eight different ore types is not a hard limit, as there are a total of 16 different ore types of increasing rarity in Eve and a single container can easily hold several hundred of each, the increasing in-game cost of each increasingly rare ore requires progressively more of the ingame currency to procure. One solution would be to buy a game time-card for $ 15 USD and sell it for in-game currency, which would provide more currency than this channel would ever require and would enable the use of all sixteen ore types for transmission. However, this method requires more of an initial time and resource investment in setting up the channel, and sixteen characters still provides very low bandwidth.

III. Multiple Containers

The solution is to use multiple containers, allowing an unbounded message length. By using the same eight ore types per container, the user can construct a sequence of eight-character messages that can be easily decoded by the receiver. The problem then is determining the order in which the message is to be read, since each cargo container lacks an identifying label. While the most straightforward solution would be to use an additional resource to numerically identify the container's placement in the sequence, there is another solution, and one which adds to the security of the channel. If all users involved in the channel have a single shared bookmark for the meeting place in space, then containers can be dropped with increasing distance from this bookmark. When another user approaches the bookmark, the order can then be determined based on the distance of each container from the starting point, as shown on their objects list in-game.

IV. In-Game Security

This method also increases the in-game security of the channel, since the containers now lack any intrinsic indication as to their order. If a third-party player should come across the meeting point while a message is in place, without knowing the starting point the sequence of the containers is unknown to them.

This occurrence is unlikely to happen in the first place, however, since avoiding detection is straightforward. Because Eve's universe is realistically-sized and detection range limited, it is virtually impossible for a player to randomly stumble across another player outside of the local area around an object of importance or the direct passage between two such objects. Unlike in most MMORPGs, this provides an added measure of security since the meeting point can be extremely remote. One user can travel into deep space, bookmark the location, then return to a space station and trade an item representation of the bookmark to other users of the channel. Since each space station is typically occupied by several dozen to several hundred active users, and no indication of the transaction is provided to other players, even an observer who knew such a transaction was occurring would be unable to identify the participants or even when or if it occurred at all. Once this transaction is complete and members of the channel have moved to the bookmark, it is extremely unlikely that another player will chance across it and be able to interfere with the channel.

Once the bookmark has been shared, no further in-game contact is required between the participants. When a message has been deployed, the cargo containers will persist for approximately an hour. Other users can approach the bookmark and read the contents without disturbing them, then leave. By logging out once reading the message, the player's ship disappears and has no need to return to populated space, since he will return to the same location when logging back in. The containers will self-destruct after their time limit, or the player who dropped them can reclaim the resources and remove the containers. The players do not need to interact with one another or even occupy the game world at the same time. Because they do not need to return to any populated area, they are safe from interaction with other players that could interfere with the operation of the channel.

However, because the cargo containers normally persist for only one hour, this requires an agreed-upon timeframe for meeting; otherwise the message will likely be lost before it can be read. Instead, the users involved can purchase secure containers, which are deployed in space and require a password to access. As with bookmarks, the password can be conveyed through the initial communication. These containers last for up to thirty days of inactivity, with this timer reset every time the container is accessed. With this method, a user can indicate that the message has been read by simply removing the resources from the container, and has up to a month after placement of the message to do so.

While this paper describes the encoding of plain ASCII text, there is no inherent requirement that this be the case. Each cargo container can store far more than 128 of each resource, limited only by the space in the cargo container and the number of ores being used. With 256 each of eight ores, well within limits, each ore type represents a byte, allowing the cargo container to store eight bytes of data. The overall message can be encrypted using any existing encryption algorithm before being split into eight-byte chunks and encoded through the cargo drop.

V. Real-World Security

The primary advantage of using an MMORPG such as Eve as the medium for a covert channel is that it is difficult to detect. The network traffic is all conducted between the client and a single server, rather than using peer-to-peer systems.

And unlike most conventional multiplayer games, which use a server supporting usually no more than 64 players, the number of clients connected to the primary Eve server system ranges from twenty thousand to fifty thousand at any given time [6]. Because the only actual in-game contact between the players is the initial, innocuous transaction of the bookmark, and even that is handled by the central server rather than peer-to-peer, not only does the network traffic appear entirely legitimate, but it cannot even be used to identify other participants in the network.

The details of the network, such as where and when the bookmark transfer will take place, any agreed-upon meeting times, and any encryption/decryption scheme in use for the data, can be determined weeks or months in advance by the participants. Because Eve Online offers a two-week free trial period, no initial investment or credit card info is even required, and new characters can be created (and bookmarks and cargo transferred from the old ones) every two weeks, eliminating the need for a paid subscription and decreasing the likelihood of a participant being identified based on their in-game account.

Because the channel, being behavior-based, cannot be identified on the basis of analyzing its network traffic, the most practical way to prevent the channel from being created is to simply deny the use of the game on the network altogether. While this is a practical solution in a corporate setting, it is not a viable option if the agency performing confinement is attempting to maintain a covert presence (such as during covert surveillance), as the blocking of game traffic will immediately indicate that an attempt at confinement is being performed. In this case, even with a man-in-the-middle attack to intercept the traffic, it will likely be difficult to detect the use of the channel, especially if the data is encrypted, as it will be indistinguishable from ordinary gameplay.

Lastly, the channel is highly secure on the client machine. No details of the drop are logged by the game, and even if key presses are being logged in real-time, the primarily visual and mouse-based interface hides the data being entered. Continuous screen capture could betray the encoding or receiving of a message, but would not provide sufficient information to decrypt it, or to identify the other participants. More importantly, visual detection is still contingent upon recognizing that the behavior seen on-screen, which even to an Eve player would not seem unusual, constitutes a covert channel. This detection method would of course require that screen-capture software be installed and active on the user's machine.

VI. Limitations

By this point it is apparent that there are some significant limitations to this covert channel. One is the limited bandwidth. Eight bytes per container is of limited utility, and is insufficient for transmitting programs or documents. While there is no limit on how many containers can be used, even with practice in the operation of the channel it may require as much as ten minutes to place ten cargo containers if using one character to indicate container order, or slightly more if the distance-from-bookmark method is used instead. Eighty bytes of data for ten minutes of work is insufficient to convey anything more data-intensive than a simple message.

This also implies a second issue, which is the requirement of manual encoding, reading, and decoding of data. While a variety of macro software schemes exist to automate the process of mining ore, a straightforward task, none exist which can read game data to the degree required to encode or read the data for the users. If such a method were developed, it could compromise the security of the covert channel, since it would permit a programmatic analysis of game data to detect the existence of the channel. As it stands, the obfuscation of game data within the network traffic and local memory, while making automation of these tasks difficult, aids in the security of the channel, but also makes it more complicated to use.

The third issue, and the most fundamental, is the reliance upon the game system. Eve Online offers, as mentioned earlier, a two-week trial period that eliminates the need for a paid subscription. However, it is still limited by factors such as game server downtime, and the need to install and run the game. As noted by Deffenbaugh, Johnson, Yuan, and Lutz[4], it is unlikely that a user will be able to use his own machine or install the software on a local machine within a secured environment. Because many companies and agencies, even those not ostensibly operating in a secure environment, block network ports associated with gaming, participation in the channel from within that environment is not possible.

VII. Conclusion

The development of this covert channel highlights how the evolving complexity and security of games can be adapted for the purpose of leaking information. While methods such as this are still limited by the need for local access to a high-performance game, which is not practical for many typical uses of covert channels, the same principles could be applied to other media. As cloud computing and remote data storage become more common, the core concept of using a behavioral channel to construct a storage channel in a remote and virtual medium, hiding the leakage of information but facilitating retrieval at any time and with no direct connection between users, becomes more relevant and deserving of further research. The same principle could potentially be applied to simpler programs than games, and if fully encapsulated within HTTP traffic could allow for a more easily deployed covert channel.

REFERENCES

[1] B. W. Lampson, "A note on the confinement problem," *Commun. ACM*, vol. 16, no. 10, pp. 613–615, Oct. 1973. [Online]. Available: http://doi.acm.org/10.1145/362375.362389

[2] B. Y. Daryl Johnson, Peter Lutz, "Behavior-based covert channel in cyberspace," *Intelligent Decision Making Systems*, pp. 311–318, 2009.

[3] P. B. Sebastian Zander, Grenville Armitage, "Covert channels in multi-player first person shooter online games," *Local Computer Networks*, pp. 215–222, September 2008.

[4] B. Y. P. L. Michael Deffenbaugh, Daryl Johnson, "A physical channel in a digital world," *SAM'12 - The 2012 International Conference on Security and Management*, p. 4, July 2012.

[5] Eve online. [Online]. Available: http://www.eveonline.com/

[6] Eve-offline. [Online]. Available: http://eve-offline.net/?server=tranquility

SSDP Covert Channel

Wesly Delva and Daryl Johnson
Department of Computing Security
Rochester Institute of Technology
Rochester, New York USA
wxd5947@rit.eu, daryl.johnson@rit.edu

Abstract—**A network covert channel provides a means of confidentiality with the intent to allow two nodes to communicate on a network with stealth. Simple Service Discovery Protocol is an Internet Protocol Suite that is capable of both discovering and advertising network services. This paper describes a method of using this discovery protocol as a means of sending covert messages between two nodes through steganography.**

I. Introduction

The National Institute of Standards and Technology defines a convert channel as an unauthorized communication path that manipulates a communication medium in an unexpected, unconventional, or unforeseen way in order to transmit information without detection by anyone other than the entries operating the convert channel [2]. Butler Lampson first used the term covert channel in his paper *A Note on the Confinement Problem* [4] where he addressed information leakage in computing processes and the possibility for other processes being able to access that data leakage.

Steganography is the process of hiding information inside any kind of message; therefore Network Steganography can be looked at as a covert channel [5]. By manipulating different fields that are unused or unrestricted you will be able to store a secret message, without losing the appearance of its authenticity. The goal of this covert channel is to send secret messages through SSDP with the method of blending the secret within the content of the protocol.

II. SSDP

The Simple Service Discovery Protocol, or SSDP, is a mechanism that allows a network client the capability to discover desired network services with little or no static configuration according to the RFC for SSDP [1]. This is accomplished by two functions: OPTION and ANNOUNCE, which is used with HTTP over multicast.

The OPTION function allows for a SSDP client to determine if a desired network service exists on the network [1]. The OPTION message is sent over a reserved multicast IP and port, which is 239.255.255.250 on port 1900. The SSDP server will always be listening and will always respond with one or more reply messages, if and only if the OPTION message matches the service. The ANNOUNCE function works similar to the OPTION function, in which the SSDP Server is used to announce the presence of its network service on the network.

In return, if the OPTION message request was successful, the SSDP server will send an HTTP 200 OK. The HTTP 200 OK would contain the entity-header fields that correspond to the request.

The purpose of SSDP was to build a protocol so that computer users would have an easy, quick, and dynamic way to discover services or resources without any prior knowledge. Therefore, SSDP only performs discovery and leaves any service description and/or negotiation to a higher layer service-specific protocol [1].

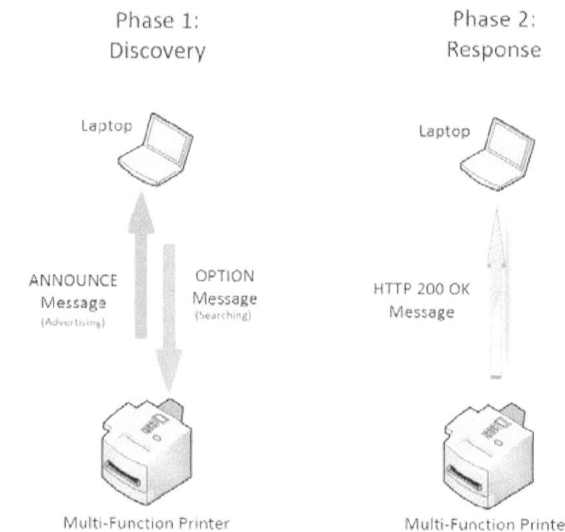

Fig. 1. SSDP Diagram

III. Text-Based Protocol

Network applications may use different methods of encapsulating data but one very common method found in IP protocols is text-based oriented representation [3]. This text-based oriented representation would transmit data as a line of ASCII text and terminate by a new line character. There are many protocols known to do this such as FTP, SMTP, and HTTP.

The main advantage of a text-based protocol is that it is easy for humans to read and write it out, which leads to a much simpler process when it comes to debugging it. The main disadvantage is that there is a lack of preciseness; therefore you can't instantly parse through and verify if something is valid; also using the wrong text encoding can become cumbersome and become error-prone as data begins to grow.

IV. SSDP Covert Channel

This covert channel is created for a one-way means of communication from Node A to Node B. We will refer to the two parties as sender and receiver. The sender and receiver applications were created with python to have the ability to generate, listen, and transmit SSDP packets over the network. The senders application will also have the ability to spoof an IP address to impersonate a fake request from a node that would be interpreted as the SSDP server or service provider. This is possible by using a security tool called Scapy, that is also written in python. Scapy is a powerful interactive packet manipulation program, that allows you to both forge or decode packets being send or received on the wire [6].

A. Mechanism

The receiver will first begin by generating a SSDP OPTION message, querying if a particular service is alive through a multicast. Within the OPTION message header, there will be a specific field that the sender will check to identify that a covert channel is ready to be initiated by the receiver. We will refer to this field as the identifier.

The sender is actively listening to the network traffic until it comes across a SSDP OPTION packet that contains the specific identifier. Once the identifier has been verified it will begin the process of transmitting a covert message. The sender would now extract the source address of the OPTION packet. The source information will be interpreted as the new destination for the covert message. The multicast address will be discard and the sender would spoof the IP address of a live host on the network as the new source address. With the new found information the sender will now generate a HTTP 200 OK message to symbolize a response from a SSDP server. Within the reply, the previous identifier will be stored within the header but a second identifier will be present that contains the encoded (ASCII to Hex) covert message. In the figures below, the NT field is the identifier in the SSDP OPTION message. In the SSDP HTTP 200 OK message the ST contains the first identifier and the EXT field contains the covert message.

```
Ethernet II, Src: Vmware_62:20:90 (00:0c:29:62:20:90), Dst: IPv4mcast_7f:ff:fa (01:00:5e:7f:ff:fa)
Internet Protocol Version 4, Src: 192.168.1.200 (192.168.1.200), Dst: 239.255.255.250 (239.255.255.250)
User Datagram Protocol, Src Port: scslao (2869), Dst Port: ssdp (1900)
Hypertext Transfer Protocol
  NOTIFY * HTTP/1.1\r\n
    HOST:239.255.255.250:1900\r\n
```

Fig. 2. SSDP OPTION

At this point the receiver would be listening and waiting for a HTTP 200 OK message. Once received it will check for the first identifier to verify that the message really came from the sender producing the covert message; once verified it will look for and extract the second identifier that contains the covert message. The receiver would now decode the message (Hex to ASCII) to reveal the message.

This covert channel is successful due the nature of this discovery protocol. SSDP has no obligation to perform any

```
Ethernet II, Src: Vmware_65:25:9e (00:0c:29:65:25:9e), Dst: Vmware_dc:92:64 (00:0c:29:dc:92:64)
Internet Protocol Version 4, Src: 192.168.1.254 (192.168.1.254), Dst: 192.168.1.200 (192.168.1.200)
User Datagram Protocol, Src Port: cnrprotocol (1096), Dst Port: ssdp (1900)
Hypertext Transfer Protocol
  HTTP/1.1 200 OK\r\n
    LOCATION: http://192.168.1.254:64178/psi/0.95\r\n
    CACHE-CONTROL: max-age = 1800\r\n
    SERVER: UPnP/1.0, Platinum UPnP SDK/0.4.7\r\n
    LOCATION: http://www.tty.com:3700/psi/0.95\r\n
    USN: uuid:d652f98e-d1fd-4f87-a5dc-70eb7daf7faf::urn:schemas-microsoft-com:service:OSInfo:1\r\n
    ST: urn:schemas-upnp-org:service:OSInfo:1ab\r\n
    \r\n
```

Fig. 3. SSDP HTTP 200 OK

additional service description and/or negotiation to any client or other server. If a requesting service is not found or packet was not understood it would simple ignore the message and not reply. This is what makes spoofing in this environment successful, while keeping the senders identity anonymous during the covert channel. Secondly, due to the fact that SSDP is a text-based protocol there is no standard or field required that all SSDP message must completely follow because its all based on each service provider. This allows for the implementer of this covert channel the ability to craft the packets header as they please to fix their covert channel.

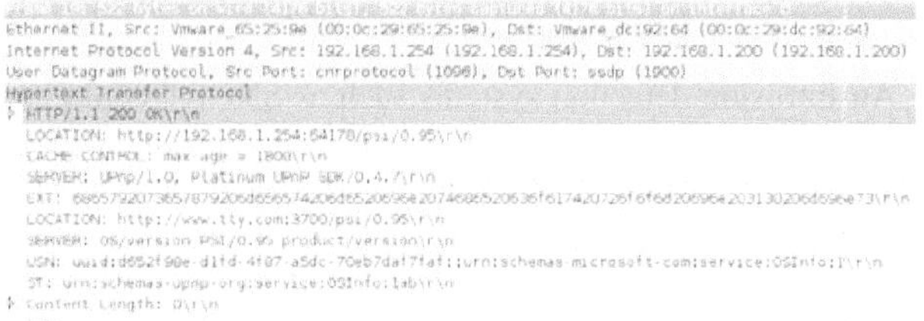

B. Type

Butler Lampson talks about how storage channels include all vehicles that would allow the direct or indirect writing of a storage location by one process and the direct or indirect reading of it by another [4]. This covert channel would be classified as a storage channel due to the fact that the covert message is being written within the SSDP header.

C. Throughput

An Ethernet frame has a max of 1500 bytes. When constructing a Ethernet frame there is a certain amount of overhead that must be defined; such as, the source MAC and IP address and the destination MAC and IP address. The source and destination port numbers must be present as while. In the SSDP protocol there is also a HTTP field that must be determine. The HTTP field is determine by how much data you want to be added, so that it can appear as a legitimate SSDP packet as show in figures 2 and 3. The collection of all the data above is what determines the size of the overhead. What cause it to vary is the amount of data within the HTTP field. The following is a break down of how much data can be sent through this covert channel:

OV = Overhead
CM = Covert Message
1 byte = 1 character
1500 bytes−OV bytes = CM bytes
Example: 1500 bytes−468 bytes = 1032 bytes

Fig. 4. Throughput Calculation

In the example above, 1032 bytes would equal 1032 characters for the covert message per set of SSDP packets sent.

D. Detection and Prevention

An Intrusion detection systems such as SNORT could have the capability to detect the presence of SSDP on the network. This is only useful if the presence of SSDP is prohibited on the network. Otherwise, there is no SNORT rule that will be able to detect anomalies in the header or payload due to the fact that SSDP is a text-based protocol and does not have universal fixed parameters. This makes it quite difficult for an IDS to detect a covert message based only on analyzing the context of the Ethernet frame. However, disabling a SSDP client and blocking port 1900 with a firewall can prevent this covert channel.

V. Conclusion

In a day and age where secrets must remain a secret, covert channels will continue to grow and be developed in new ways to send secrets. Simple Service Discovery Protocol provides a flexible method for sending covert messages. It can be very complex but it has the capability to be very simple depending on how the implementer would like to implement his/her covert channel. While detection is limited, there are still many more improvements to be made such as the timing of this covert channel and its different behaviors with network devices.

References

[1] Ting Cai, *Simple service discovery protocol/1.0*, http://tools.ietf.org/html/draft-cai-ssdp-v1-01.

[2] *Glossary of key information security terms*, http://csrc.nist.gov/publications/nistir/ir7298-rev1/nistir-7298-revision1.pdf.

[3] Olaf Kirch, *"black hats manual software security auditing, cracking, debugging"*, http://www.lst.de/okir/blackhats/.

[4] Butler W. Lampson, *A note on the confinement problem*, Commun. ACM **16** (1973), no. 10, 613–615.

[5] Raymond Sbrusch, *"network covert channels: Subversive secrecy"*, http://www.sans.org/reading_room/whitepapers/covert/network-covert-channels-subversive-secrecy_1660/.

[6] secdev.org, *Scapy*, http://secdev.org/projects/scapy.

SESSION

POSTERS

Chair(s)

TBA

Integrative Security for JavaEE Web Applications

Thorsten Kisner and Helge Hemmer
Management and Engineering
AHT GROUP AG
Essen, Germany
Email: {t.kisner,h.hemmer}@aht-group.com

Abstract—**Enterprise web applications have a inherent requirement on security components on different architectural levels. Common tasks are user authentication or access authorization to available functions and informations of the system. These tasks are implemented in security modules following a set of permission rules defining users, user groups and actions. Even there are some existing frameworks and libraries for web applications available helping to authenticate users, the authorization of users highly depend on individual business processes of each application. Granting or denying access to distinct web pages of an application fronted is in most cases not sufficient. With a fine granular role based access control model a permission control on single User Interface components like menu items or action buttons is a inherit requirement for advanced web applications. In this case a single level role model is not able to map the requirements of business processes needs to a security model. This can be done with multi level role models, but most of the common security concepts and libraries do not provide this without heavy modifications. This paper presents such a security framework which is optimized for web applications with an Enterprise Java Bean backend and Java Server Faces as a presentation layer and highly uses Context and Dependency Injection. All mentioned standards are part of the Java Enterprise Edition specification Java EE 6. The mentioned fine granular multi level role based access model is highly customizable and is provided out of the box with additional features. The security framework provides a tight integration with tools and concepts for different scopes ranging from menu creation, UI component authorization to page authorization. Advanced and wide scale enterprise applications benefit from the documentation tools provided for the security concept itself as well as different pre configured reports about the role based access control model. The framework is implemented in a Java library available with a GPL-licence for free download and it is currently in use for several enterprise web applications.**

I. Introduction and Related Solutions

Ambitioned approaches like Seam Security [1], Spring Security [2] (formally Acegi) or Apache Shiro [3] offer a lot of features out of the box. While Seam Security and Spring Security are focusing on Java EE web application development, Shiro is also designed to be used in a Java SE environment. All of these frameworks are a good choice in respect to their targeted environment(s). The individual optimization and extension of these frameworks is mostly done within closed source business projects or more academic focused works like in [4]. The AHTUtils security module is based upon the third version of Seam Security and extends it with additional data structures and concepts plus the option to combine security features from different scopes into single points of configuration. This realizes an orthogonal multi-level and fine granular role based access control model [5][6].

II. Applying AHTUtils-Security

A. Security concept

The core elements are `views`, `actions`, `use cases` and `roles`.

- A **view** is a single page identified by a unique JSF view identifier.
- Inside a view, the user can perform different **actions**.
- **use cases** can combine different views and actions.
- The privileges of a user are described by the granted **roles** in the system. A role can aggregate different use cases and actions or the aggregation of these defined in a use case.

Nesting roles are forbidden to reduce the complexity and error-rate in model-configuration [7]. The only relationship between an existing model and the proposed security model is the connection between `User` and `Role` (see example in Figure 1).

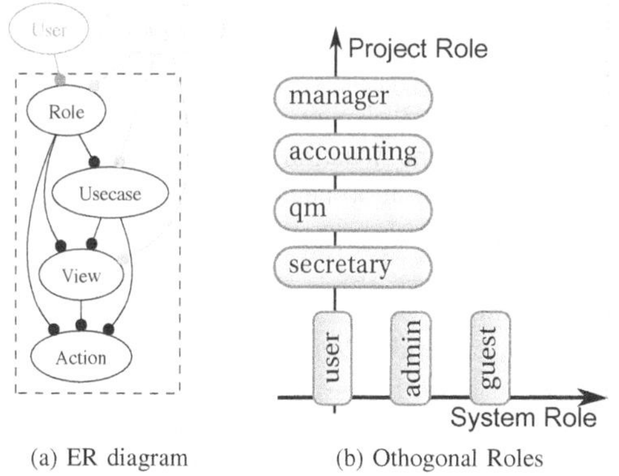

(a) ER diagram (b) Othogonal Roles

Figure 1: Security concept

Attaching a **role** to different **categories** allows the definition of independent role domains which can be described as a context specific orthogonal role concept. While all users belong to one or more *system role*, they may additionally belong to another context specific role domain (see Figure 1b.

B. Definition of security settings

The security settings are defined in XML files, at least the files `views.xml` and `roles.xml` are required. It can be enriched with tags for multi-language support or menu creation. For an example see Listing 1 and 2.

Listing 1: Example of roles.xml

```
<?xml version="1.0" encoding="UTF-8" standalone="yes"?>
<security>
  <category code="system">
    <roles>
      <role code="systemAdmin">
        <views>
          <view code="admin"/>
          <view code="adminUsers"/>
        </views>
      </role>
    </roles>
  </category>
</security>
```

Listing 2: Example of views.xml

```
<?xml version="1.0" encoding="UTF-8" standalone="yes"?>
<security>
  <category code="admin">
    <views>
      <view code="admin" public="false">
        <navigation package="my.web.admin">
          <viewPattern>
            /jsf/admin/admin.xhtml
          </viewPattern>
          <urlMapping>/admin</urlMapping>
        </navigation>
      </view>
      <view code="adminRoles" public="false">
        <navigation package="my.web.admin">
          <viewPattern>
            /jsf/admin/roles.xhtml
          </viewPattern>
          <urlMapping>/admin/system/roles</urlMapping>
        </navigation>
      </view>
    </views>
  </category>
</security>
```

C. Integrated URL rewriting

The `navigation` element of a `view` defines navigation specific settings. The location of related annotations automatically generated in a later stage (see Section II-D) is defined with the attribute *package*. Then, the user friendly URL defined in `urlMapping` maps the URL to a specific JSF view identifier `viewPattern`. The rewriting engine is pluggable, but currently *PrettyFaces* [8] is used.

The `urlMapping` allows additional arguments using the JSF Expression Language (JSF-EL) like `/admin/user/{id}`. In that case the expression would be mapped to the corresponding `viewPattern` with `?id=123` which can be evaluated with CDI injected `RequestParam`.

D. Type-safe security bindings

Type-safe security bindings can be achieved by Java annotations with `@Target` and `@Retention` CDI qualifiers. Their correct usage in the web application is enforced by the compiler and even CDI-capable IDEs warn the user if he wants to use a non-existing (maybe just due to a typing error) security binding.

Listing 3: Example or security binding for admin view

```
@SecurityBindingType
@Retention(RetentionPolicy.RUNTIME)
@Target({ElementType.FIELD,
        ElementType.TYPE, ElementType.METHOD})
public @interface ErpViewAdmin { }
```

A security binding can be attached to a `view` and enforces that the page rendered for users of roles to which this view is assigned. Depending on the current security context of the user, a forward is triggered to a login page or to an access-denied page. The concept is not limited to views, even methods in managed beans can be secured with these security bindings. If a button is attached to method call, this method can be annotated with `@RoleAdmin public void deleteNews()` and only members of the admin role are allowed to call this method.

E. Security in Facelet View Handler

Security roles can be easily applied by using AHTUtils security `view` tag as seen in Listing 4.

Listing 4: Security in Facelet View Handler

```
<?xml version="1.0" encoding="UTF-8"?>
<html>
  <h:head><title>JSF Hello World</title></h:head>
  <h:body>
    <h3>Example</h3>
    <p>Common content</p>
    <as:restrictTo role="role1">
      <p>Confidential content</p>
    </as:restrictTo>
  </h:body>
</html>
```

III. Conclusion and Future Work

Even complex security scenarios containing different levels of access like project- and system-related realms can be covered. Because it depends on the basic architecture of Java EE and JBoss Seam, experienced developers can easily get familiar with AHTUtils security. Available as a Maven artifact, adding it to projects is easy. Furthermore, a tutorial will be available on the project web presence soon.

References

[1] *Seam in Action*. Manning Pubn, 2008.

[2] Spring Source. Spring security. [Online]. Available: http://static.springsource.org/spring-security

[3] Apache Foundation. Apache shiro. [Online]. Available: http://shiro.apache.org

[4] M. C. Franky and V. M. T. C., "Cincosecurity: A reusable security module based on fine grained roles and security profiles for java ee applications," in *Proceedings of CIW 2011 : The Sixth International Conference on Internet and Web Applications and Services*, 2011.

[5] M. Benantar, *Access Control Systems: Security, Identity Management and Trust Models*. Springer, 2010.

[6] D. F. Ferraiolo, D. R. Kuhn, and R. Chandramouli, *Role-Based Access Control*. Artech House Inc., 2003.

[7] J. Fischer, D. Marino, R. Majumdar, and T. Millstein, "Fine-grained access control with object-sensitive roles," in *Proceedings of the 23rd European Conference on ECOOP 2009 — Object-Oriented Programming*, ser. Genoa. Berlin: Springer-Verlag, 2009, pp. 173–194.

[8] L. B. II, "Prettyfaces: Simplified jsf navigation, actions, and url-rewriting," in *Proceedings of JAX Conf 2012*, 2012.

HPA Lab: An Open-Source Educational Tool to Explore Host Protected Areas Under Linux

L. Markowsky
School of Computing and Information Science, University of Maine, Orono, ME USA

Abstract – *Disk areas, data streams, and CPU modes not normally seen by the user or operating system are vulnerable to abuse by hackers and might be used as vectors of a cyberattack. The Host (or Hidden) Protected Area (HPA) is one such hidden area. This poster discusses the vulnerabilities of these hidden areas and introduces HPA Lab, a new open-source education tool to explore HPAs under Linux.*

Keywords: HPA, host protected area, hidden protected area, data hiding, forensics, cybersecurity

1 Introduction: Hidden Modes, Streams, and Disk Areas

Hackers have learned to use CPU modes, data streams, and disk areas not normally seen by the user or operating system to hide and execute malware. Educational material and tools are needed to inform cybersecurity students, professionals, and researchers of hidden avenues that are vulnerable to the ever-growing threat of cyberattack. Hidden modes and areas that are vulnerable to hacker abuse include:

- System Management Mode (SMM)
- Windows Recovery Environment (WinRE) Partition
- Alternate Data Streams (ADSs)
- Device Configuration Overlays (DCOs)
- Host/Hidden Protected Areas (HPAs)

SMM is used legitimately for system maintenance. The operating system, which runs in Protected Mode, cannot handle all hardware events. For example, in order to handle power management on Intel-based laptops, a System Management Interrupt (SMI) is sent to the CPU, allowing firmware full access to all physical resources, including RAM and disk drives. Examples of SMM-based attacks have been published in the literature [1][2].

On some Windows Vista, Windows Server 2008, Windows Server 2012, Windows 7, and Windows 8 computers, a WinRE Partition contains the Windows Recovery Environment, which can be used to repair and restore a corrupt Windows system.

ADSs are used legitimately by NTFS (a proprietary Windows file system) to provide services for Macintosh clients, to store "summary" data, and to track changes to an NTFS volume [3]. Hackers have used ADSs to hide data and executables, which can then be run using at least five methods [4].

DCOs, introduced in the ATA/ATAPI-6 standard [5], enable computer manufacturers to assemble systems that appear to have hard drives of identical sizes even if the hard drives, in reality, have different sizes. "The DCO enables system vendors to purchase HDDs from different manufacturers with potentially different sizes, and then configure all HDDs to have the same number of sectors. An example of this would be using DCO to make an 80 Gigbyte HDD appear as a 60 Gigabyte HDD to both the OS and the BIOS" [6]. The "hidden" area then occupies the remaining 20 GB. Some rootkits hide in DCOs, a method known as "out-of-band concealment," in an attempt to conceal themselves from the end user's security software and from duplication by forensic investigators.

HPAs, introduced in the ATA/ATAPI-4 standard [7], are used by computer manufacturers to distribute recovery media without the use of separate CDs, which are easily lost by the end user, as well as for diagnostic utilities [8]. Like DCOs, HPAs have been used by rootkits for out-of-band concealment [9]. Although all hidden streams and areas are important in cybersecurity research and education, this poster focuses exclusively on HPAs.

2 Creation, Structure, and Hacker Abuse of HPAs

An HPA is created using the low-level ATA command SET MAX ADDRESS, which sets the maximum addressable sector of an ATA device. In hexidecimal notation, such a command (with six arguments) might be:

F9 04 00 00 00 00 40

If the maximum addressable sector is set to a value smaller than the true maximum sector of the device, then a "hidden" or "host protected" area has been created that extends from the first sector beyond the maximum addressable sector to the end of the disk. Once created, the low-level ATA commands IDENTIFY DEVICE and READ NATIVE MAX ADDRESS will return different values.

Low-level ATA commands cannot be sent directly to USB-connected drives such as USB-connected external hard drives and ATA disk drives mounted in external USB-connected enclosures. If a hidden area has been previously constructed on a USB-connected drive, then HPA-aware tools can be used, and the HPA is subject to abuse.

Many HPAs are formatted using BEER (Boot Engineering Extension Record) and PARTIES (Protected Area Run-Time Interface Extension Services), defined in

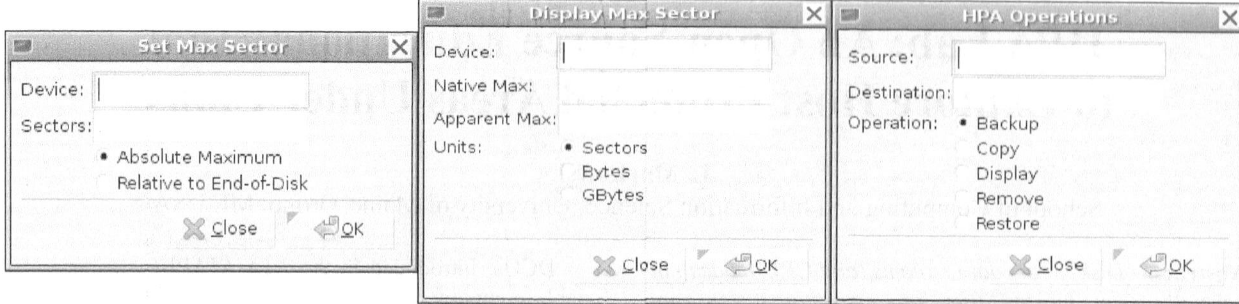

Figure 1. Three HPA Lab Dialog Boxes

the *Protected Area Run Time Interface Extension Services* document [10]. Because many major manufacturers format their HPAs using this standard, hackers can easily detect and make use of existing HPAs.

HPAs are used by hackers in an attempt to evade detection by security software and duplication by forensic investigators: "One way to subvert duplication is to place your rootkit so far off the beaten path that it might be overlooked ... For example, the Host Protected Area (HPA) is a reserved disk region that's often used to store diagnostic tools and system restore utilities" [11].

Countermeasures are now able to detect rootkits that attempt to hide in HPAs: "The current incarnation of tools like EnCase can see HPAs and DCOs without much of a problem. Thus, reserved disk areas like the HPA or the DCO could be likened to catapults; they're historical artifacts of the arms race between attackers and defenders" [12].

3 HPA Lab: A New HPA-Aware Tool for Educational Use

Although rootkits hiding in HPAs are no longer safe from detection and analysis software, the concept of out-of-band concealment is not well known to many cybersecurity students. HPA Lab is a new tool to give students hands-on experience working with HPAs. With HPA Lab, a student can create an HPA, display the native and apparent maximum addressable sectors of a disk, or choose from a variety of HPA operations on HPAs formatted using BEER and PARTIES. HPA Lab uses a GUI to extend the functionality of setmax and fiesta, two open-source command-line tools.

Setmax is an ATA-only command-line tool that can create or remove an HPA by setting the maximum sector number on the device. Setdisk cannot be used with USB-connected external drives or with ATA disk drives mounted in an external USB-connected enclosure. Examples of use include: "setmax --max M DEVICE", which will set the maximum sector number on the ATA DEVICE to M - 1; "setmax --delta D DEVICE", which will set the maximum sector number to D sectors below the end of the disk; and "setmax DEVICE", which will report the maximum accessible sector number.

Similarly, fiesta is a command-line tool for use with devices that are configured with an HPA using BEER and PARTIES that enables the user to:

- List the contents of a device's HPA.
- Backup the HPA data.
- Restore a previously saved image of the HPA.
- Copy an HPA to a second device.
- Remove an HPA from the device.

Much of the functionality of setmax and fiesta has been incorporated into the HPA Lab GUI. Figure 1 shows screenshots of three HPA Lab dialog boxes.

4 Acknowledgments

The author wishes to thank Dr. James Fastook and Dr. George Markowsky for their encouragement and support.

5 References

[1] L. Duflot, D. Etiemble and O. Grumelard, "Using CPU System Management Mode to Circumvent Operating System Security Functions," Proceedings of the 7th CanSecWest Conference, 2001.

[2] S. Embleton, S. Sparks and C. Zou, "SMM Rootkits: A New Breed of OS Independent Malware," SecureComm 2008, Instanbul, Turkey, September 2008.

[3] R. Means, "Alternate Data Streams: Out of the Shadows and into the Light," SANS Institute, p. 8, 2003.

[4] Ibid., pp. 14-15.

[5] P. McLean (editor), "Information Technology – AT Attachment with Packet Interface Extension (ATA/ATAPI-6), Revision 3b," February 2002.

[6] M. Gupta, M. Hoeschele and M. Rogers, "Hidden Disk Areas: HPA and DCO," International Journal of Digital Evidence, vol.5, no. 1, Fall 2006.

[7] P. McLean (editor), "Information Technology – AT Attachment with Packet Interface Extension (ATA/ATAPI-4), Revision 18," August 1998.

[8] IBM Hidden Protected Area: Access IBM Predesktop Area, International Business Machines Corporation, pp. 2-4, 2003.

[9] Kaspersky Lab Forum, "TDL/TDSS or other Doomsday Rootkit here (persistant) help!, persistant rootkit on Win7 x64," http://forum.kaspersky.com/index.php?showtopic=225465, accessed March 29, 2013.

[10] C. Stevens (editor), "Information Technology – Protected Area Run Time Interface Extension Services, Revision 3," September 2000.

[11] B. Blunden, "Anti-Forensics: The Rootkit Connection," Black Hat USA 2009 Conference Proceedings, p. 10, 2009.

[12] B. Blunden, "The Rootkit Arsenel: Escape and Evasion in the Dark Corners of the System," Jones & Bartlett, p. 538, 2009.

An Automatic Botnet Detection and Notification System in Taiwan

Lo-Yao Yeh, Yi-Lang Tsai, Bo-Yi Lee, and Jee-Gong Chang

***Abstract*—An automatic Botnet detection and notification system is developed by National Center for High-Performance Computing (NCHC) in Taiwan to efficiently inform users of malware infections on their computers. Due to the involvement with manual work in current notification flow, the notification time may last for 48 to 60 hours. By the aid of our notification system, the infected bot can be notified within 15 minutes (adjustable). As a result, our Botnet detection and notification system can effectively restrain the scale of Botnet.**

I. Introduction

Thanks to the high dense of information devices and computers in campuses, Taiwan is always an attractive object for hackers around the world. In order to constrict the rapid spread of Botnet, National Center for High-Performance Computing (NCHC) in Taiwan establishes wide-ranging honeynet systems in serveral universities around Taiwan such as NTU, NCTU, and NCKU. Our honeynet draws some 10,000 to 300,000 attacks per month including domestic and foreign bots. Our security operation center (SOC) located in Tainan issues approximately 500 infected notifications per day to campus network managers. For the ease of doing malware research and sharing attacking information, NCHC has developed a malware knowledge database [1]. A lot of malware information such as Top 10 attacking malware each day, malware distribution topology is available in the knowledge base. However, the current notification flow is cumbersome and involved with manual work resulting in longer notification time. Even worse, while bot masters launch attacks in holidays, the notification time may have a delay of 48 to 60 hours because of the off-duty days. It is worth to mention that the scale of Botnet highly depends on how long an infected bot can be notified and clean malwares.

In order to restrain the scale of Botnets, NCHC develops a comprehensive Botnet detection and notification system to efficiently inform users of malware infections on their computers. After installing our plug-in toolbar at Internet Explorer, an infection alarm will automatically pop up while the computer is attacking our NCHC honeynet. By the aid of our notification system, an infected bot can be notified within 15 minutes (adjustable) and then, the infected bot will clean malware in a short response time. Therefore, our detection and notification system can achieve the goal of suppressing the growth of Botnet.

L.-Y. Yeh, Y.-L. Tsai, and B.-Y. Lee are with the Network and Information Security Division as well as J.-G. Chang is with the Director office, National Center for High-performance Computing (NCHC), Tainan, Taiwan. (e-mail : lyyeh, yilang, boyi, changjg@nchc.narl.org.tw)

II. Honeynet Architecture

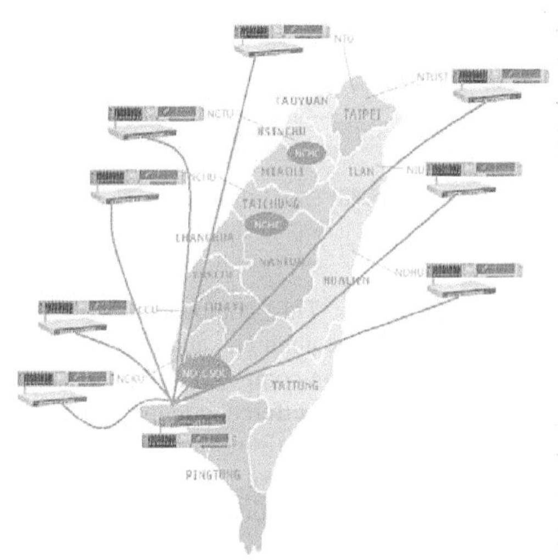

Figure 1. NCHA Honeynet Architecture around Taiwan

In order to lure various attacks, a set of trap systems with tons of vulnerabilities is established in campuses around Taiwan. Fig. 1 demonstrates the framework architecture of NCHC honeynet. Until now, our honeynet employs 3,000 IP addresses in various honeypots, including Windows, Linux and Android platform. Moreover, we also adopt low-interaction-based and high-interaction-based systems in honeypots for attracting different kinds of attackers. From 2010 to now, our honeynet systems have captured at least 25 billion attacks and 30 thousands different malwares in total [3]. On an average, 500 to 800 infected notifications per day are issued by our NCHC SOC to network administrators. Furthermore, we not only detect attacks but also analyze malwares [4] and abnormal traffic. Because there are some 30+ million connections and 50+ GB logs are recorded, our system takes advantage of Splunk software to manage the huge volume of traffic and logs.

III. Infection Notification Flow in Taiwan

To restrain the growth of Botnet, how to efficiently notify users about their infected computers is a vital step. In Taiwan, the notification flow of an infected computer is shown as Figure 2. In general, the notification flow is consisted by three components, detection divisions, information share organizations, and notification units. The responsibility of each component is discussed as follows.

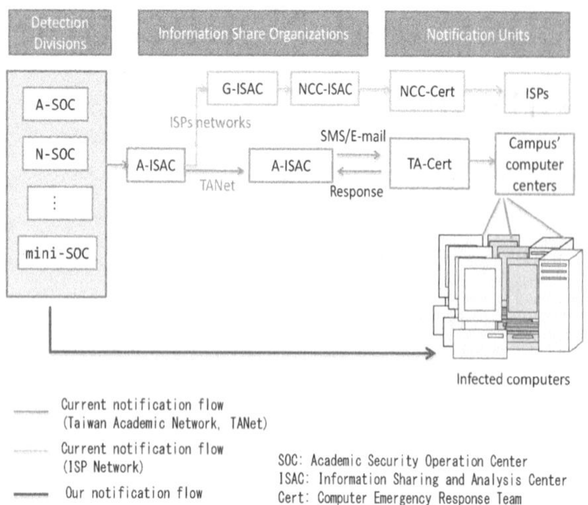

Figure 2. Infection Notification Flow in Taiwan

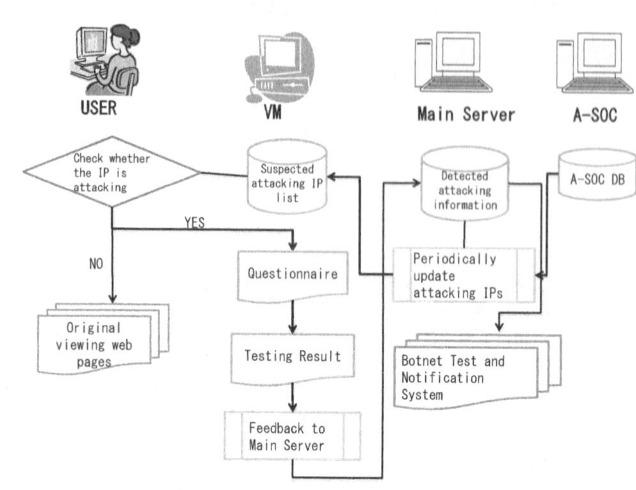

Figure 3. Notification System Architecture

- Detection Divisions: This component is in charge of detecting attacking computers and reports the IP addresses of the attacking computers to "Information Share Organizations." Due to different dominant realms, various security operation centers (SOC) coexist. For example, A-SOC manages the realms of Taiwan academic network (TANet), and N-SOC (National SOC) takes care of government service network.
- Information Share Organizations: The purpose of Information Sharing and Analysis Centers (ISAC) is to collect security sharing information, analyze threats and notify attacking behaviors to infected computers. In Taiwan, Academic ISAC (A-ISAC) is designed for academic campuses, Government ISCA (G-ISAC) focuses on government agencies, and National Coordinating Center ISAC (NCC-ISAC) administers the commercial ISP networks.
- Notification Units: To notify the owners of the infected computers, the network providers, campus network centers and ISPs, should serve as the notification units. For commercial ISP networks, NCC-ISAC informs NCC-CERT (Computer Emergency Response Team) of the IP addresses of infected computers, and then NCC-CERT asks the corresponding ISP who provides network service for the infected computers to halt the attacking behavior. Similarly, for academic network, TA-CERT (Taiwan Academic Network Computer Emergency Response Team) receives the infected IP addresses and then requests the corresponding network center in the university to deal with this attack.

Although the detection divisions always keep running 24 hours per day, the information share organizations and notification units usually come off duty off on the weekend. The traditional notification time may postpone for a few days, in particularly weekend or holidays, which facilitates the growth of Botnet. Therefore, we propose a novel notification system for slashing the notification time to effectively suppress the spread of Botnet.

A. *Notification System Architecture*

The architecture of our notification system is shown in Fig. 3. Based on NCHC honeynet and A-SOC (Academic Security Operation Center) database, our main server periodically updates attacking IP addresses to databases in VMs (virtual machines) and develops a website named "interaction-based Botnet Probing Test & Notification System" [2] for managing and querying information. In the future, this website is planned to be combined into one part of malware knowledge base. The functions of VMs are responsible for communicating with our plug-in toolbar installed in end users. For the sake of load balance, the number of VMs depends on how many users install our plug-in toolbars. As long as the user's IP address can be found in its corresponding VM's database, it is represents that the user's computer is involved with malicious attacks aiming to our honeynet. For further investigation, the toolbar then redirects the current browsing webpage to a questionnaire for gathering the infected syndromes. After filling out the questionnaire, our system will give the testing result and possible solutions to the user and then redirect back to the original viewing webpage. Figure 4 shows our notification homepage and plug-in toolbar which serves as the client-end terminal to regularly query its corresponding VMs on fifteen minutes basis. Moreover, users can launch instant detection, by clicking "Initiating" button, to check whether his/her computer has been infected or not. The "Dashboard" icon links to our notification homepage for looking up more information.

IV. Conclusions

Our automatic Botnet detection and notification system can effectively shorten the notification time for infected bots, ultimately resulting in the constraint on Botnet expansibility. This notification system can also collect the problems of infected bots for the advance analysis. In the future, we are starting

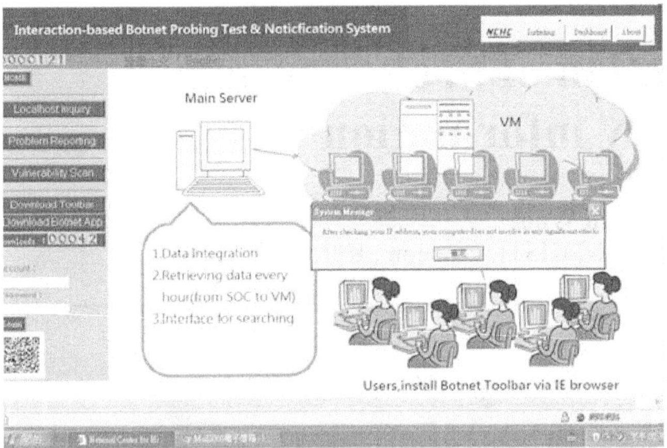

Figure 4. Homepage and Plug-In Toolbar

out adding new functions like malicious links comparisons, and client-end malware collection into our plug-in toolbar.

REFERENCES

[1] NCHC Malware Knowledge Base. http://owl.nchc.org.tw.

[2] Interactione based Botnet Probing Test & Notification System. https://140.110.96.12/botnet/eng/index.php.

[3] H.-D. Huang, C.-S. Lee, H.-Y. Kao, Y. L. Tsai, and J. G. Chang. Malware behavioral analysis system: Twman. In *IEEE Symposium on Computational Intelligence for Intelligent Agent*, 2011.

[4] Y.-L. Tsai, B.-Y. Lee L.-Y. Yeh, and J.-G. Chang. Automated malware analysis framework with honeynet technology in taiwan campuses. In *Proceeding of the 18th IEEE International Conference on Parallel and Distributed Systems (IEEE ICPADS 2012)*, 2012.

Design and Implementation of broker system for protect privacy information

Sung-Jun Kim[1], **Jun Woo**[1]
[1] Supercomputer Operation Team, NISN, KISTI, Daejeon , Korea

Abstract - *The Korean government has been enacted personal information act to protect privacy information. By this act, User's privacy information that stored in database must be encrypted[1]. Typical, to connect with web services and database, the database connection information must be stored on the web server. If already running database security solution's to protect database, the web server should be has permission to access databases in the security solutions. Due to the nature of web services, the information retrieved by access granted servers are not encrypted. In this paper, we proposed more secure web service connecting databases by eliminating connection information on web server and by limiting database query string. In proposed system, web servers did not know database server information. The User Information Broker(UIB) system has access policy which includes mapping information between web server and query.*

Keywords: privacy information, database security, broker

1 Introduction

KISTI supercomputing center is collecting personal information for billing and contract management. To protect privacy information, we are encrypting privacy information using database encryption solutions.

Web servers should be connecting DB server to access DB, so they must have connection information in local disk. If hacker intruding web server, he can be accessing all information in DB server using connection information.

In this paper, we are propose the method for requesting information to the DB via the query broker, instead of web server forwards the query to the DB directly. Therefore, there is no reason to store connection information to access DB in web server. So, if hacker intrude web server, there is no information related with DB server.

2 System Envrionments

Figure 1 show our system environments (AS-IS). We use DB encryption solutions to protect user privacy information. Also, we have many web servers that should be access to database server for retrieving user privacy information. It means that much vulnerability like DB connection information exploit possibility, exist in our environments.

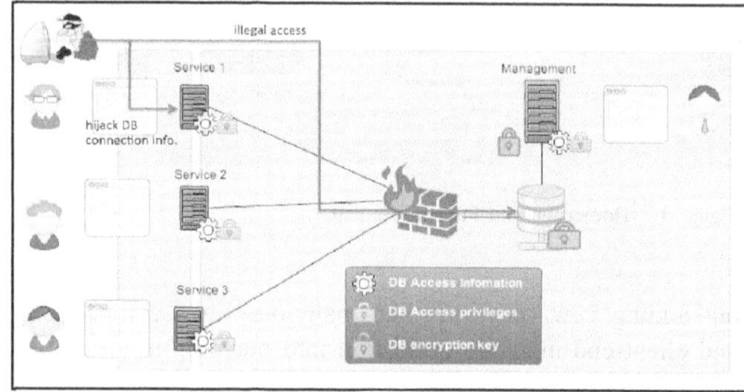

Figure 1. System Environment (AS-IS)

Figure 2 show our new system environments that eliminate DB connection information on web server side using our proposed query broker.

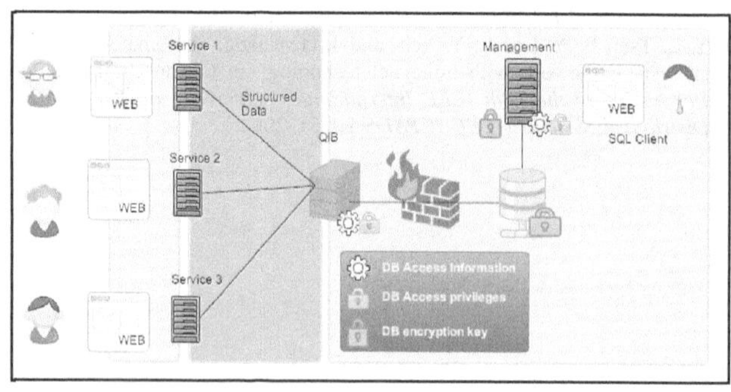

Figure 2 System Environment (TO-BE)

3 Module Design

Figure 3 is shown brief module operations flows of purposed system.

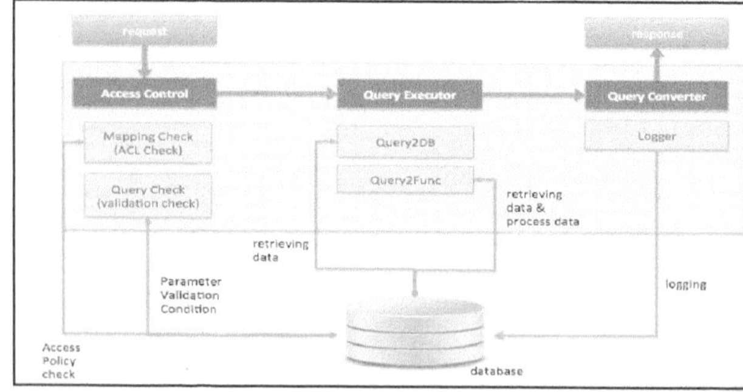

Figure 3. Module Diagram

3.1 Access Control module

This module is check privileges which the web server can be requesting that query. Using next three tables performs this operation. Additionally, there is a function of parameter validations check to avoid of abnormal behavior query result like SQL injection.

3.2 Query Executor module

This module executes SQL query requested by web server. It is consist two parts. One is query2db that is directly query to database, the other is query2func that is combined multiple query results. When it is possible to retrieve desired result set only using SQL statement, then query2db is used. In another case, query2func used. There is limitation of only use SQL statement to process statistics. Query2func is implemented by java to compute various data processing.

3.3 Query Converter module

It is converting XML format to result set returned from query executer. And then send XML message to web server as query result. Web server can be consisting of any format adapting their style.

4 Implementation

The message format examples between web server and query broker are shown as below. We don't consider encrypting messages between web server and broker system, because of both systems are located behind firewall.

4.1 Request Message example

Table 1 is a request message example. It means to requesting system_1 usage data for user_1 between 1 April , 2013 and 2 April, 2013. REQUEST_ID is web server's unique id, SERVICE_ID is web server's service id, QUERY_ID is pre-defined query id. In this example, it is specified query to retrieving user's system usage data given period. PARAMETERS have parameters to make WHERE clause of predefined query

Table 1. Request Message Example

```
<REQUEST_MESSAGE>
  <REQUEST_ID>12345</REQUEST_ID>
  <QUERY_ID>   101</QUERY_ID>
  <PARAMETERS>
    <PARAM>user_1</PARAM>
    <PARAM>system_1</PARAM>
    <PARAM>20130401</PARAM>
    <PARAM>20130402</PARAM>
  </PARAMETERS>
</REQUEST_MESSAGE>
```

4.2 Response Message example

Table 2 is the response of the previous request of query broker. RESPONSE_ID means corresponding response to the received REQUEST_ID. And RECORDs have result set of query execute. Each RECORD has one record of query result and have field name and values.

Table 2 Response Message Example

```
<RESPONSE_MESSAGE>
<RESPONSE_ID> 12345 </ RESPONSE_ID>
<RESPONSE>
<RECORED>
<COLUMN NAME='DATE'>20130401</COLUMN>
 <COLUMN NAME='SYS1'>90</COLUMN>
 </RECORED>
.. omitted ..
</RESPONSE>
</RESPONSE_MESSAGE>
```

4.3 Web interface

Figure 4 is show dashboard of web interfaces. It shows how many queries are processed per times and days. And, web interface can be defined new queries for requesting from web servers.

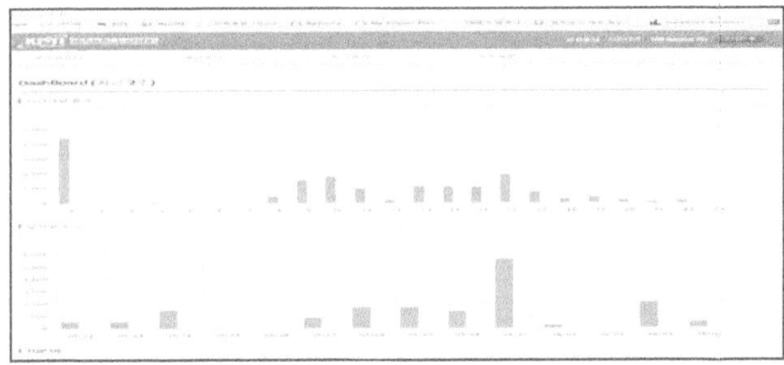

Fig. 1 Dashboard of Web Interface

5 Conclusion

In this paper, we purpose broker system for eliminating DB connection information on web servers. It is because of the feature of our environments. Our queries are not complex and relationship of tables is quite simple.As mentioned before, we already use DB security solutions to protect user privacy information in our DB. By using purposed system, we could be eliminating DB access information on web server, so reduce possibility of access to DB server through web server by hacker who is break into web server. Finally, we could be enhancement of security.

References

[1] Yang Hoon, Kim, "Design and Implementation of DB protection System through Critical Query Signagture," JKMS, vol.14.

SESSION

POSITION PAPERS + CRYPTOGRAPHY + MALWARE AND SPAM DETECTION + NETWORK SECURITY AND CYBER SECURITY EDUCATION

Chair(s)

Prof. Hamid Arabnia
University of Georgia

Feature Reduction for Optimum SMS Spam Filtering Using Domain Knowledge

Ala' Eshmawi and Suku Nair
Bobby Lyle School of Engineering
HACNet Labs
Southern Methodist University
Dallas, Texas 75275
aeshamwi,snair@smu.edu

***Abstract*—Most of the work done towards content-based SMS spam filtering has suggested the use of Bag of Words, word or character n-gram models, which can result on a huge number of features. In this paper, we study the possibility of using the minimal number of optimal features to classify SMS spam messages by introducing new features based on domain knowledge. Our experimental studies show that, by using our smaller set of features along with lighter models, the results achieved outperform BoW approaches that use dozens of features. The goal of our study is to enhance the performance of SMS classification when applied in a limited resource mobile devices.**

***Keywords*—SMS Spam; SMishing; BART; CART; Feature Selection; Classification Optimization**

I. Introduction

Spam messages are unsolicited messages that reach mobile users handsets without their consent. There are different types of these messages such as premium rate scams, advertisements and phishing messages. As reports show, SMS messages are becoming more popular for communication than emails in recent years [1]. This is mainly because SMS is considered safe, and mobile users have inherent trust on their mobile carriers. Unfortunately, spammers and fraudsters started to feed on such trust, by using SMS as their new attack vector. Moreover, email spams are not profitable for spammers the way SMS are [1]. As a result, the number of SMS spam is increasing 500% on a yearly basis [2], which led to the drastic rise in the number of phishing SMS [3].

The damage from SMS spam can be seen from two points of view. For the mobile user, besides wasting his/her time and device resources, it increases the possibility of him/her falling as a victim for one of the scams. On the other hand, the damage for the mobile operators can be devastating because spam messages endanger their reputation, and risk the trust the subscribers have put on them. Finally, spam wastes lots of the operator's network and financial resources.

The problem of classifying SMS spam is different than classifying email spam. The scarcity of SMS spam data compared to email's is one major difference. The reason is that mobile operators will not release SMS data because they are considered confidential. Unless donated voluntarily, these messages are hard to obtain. Moreover, SMS text is much shorter than email text, which makes the task of feature engineering more critical [4]. In addition, SMS messages are full of abbreviations and acronyms that are unique for texting and various languages. Furthermore, email and SMS are taking different paths to get to the user's smartphone. To understand this, and the impact of it on applicable solutions, consider the following scenario: An organization's email and phone directory was compromised by a group of phishers. The phishers are interested on finding credentials of the company's employees. By sending a phishing email to the employees, these phishers will have less hope in succeeding because phishing emails will pass through the company's mail server and will most likely be filtered out either in their mail server, or by the ISP. Whereas if they have decided to send a phishing SMS to all the employees, the company will have no measures to prevent such an attack, since each employee receives SMS through a different carrier. Figure 1, shows the difference between the email and SMS path

The need for content-base client side SMS spam filtration is inevitable to protect against spear phishing attacks, since these attacks can not be detected using the content-less (using the temporal and network data) solutions. Mainly because these attacks are sent to a specific group of people in low volume to harness information [1]. Moreover, with the limited resources of smartphones, the need to lightweight filtering is necessary, and thus the optimum number of features is required.

In our work, we study spam SMS messages, then use domain knowledge to introduce new features, and to find the optimum feature set for classification. We experimentally show that, by using the minimal number of optimal features, we achieve better results than using the high dimensional Bag of Words features. We then propose a distributed system for updating the compressed set of features to adapt with the latest SMS spam trends.

The paper is organized as follows: In section II, we describe the proposed approach in details. Then, in section III, we present the experimental results. After that in section IV, we discuss related work. Finally, we conclude in section V.

II. Approach

We propose a supervised learning approach where we divide the dataset into 80% for training and 20% for testing. We build different classification models using 10-fold cross validation on the training set, then use the models to test on

This work has been supported in part by a scholarship from King Saud University

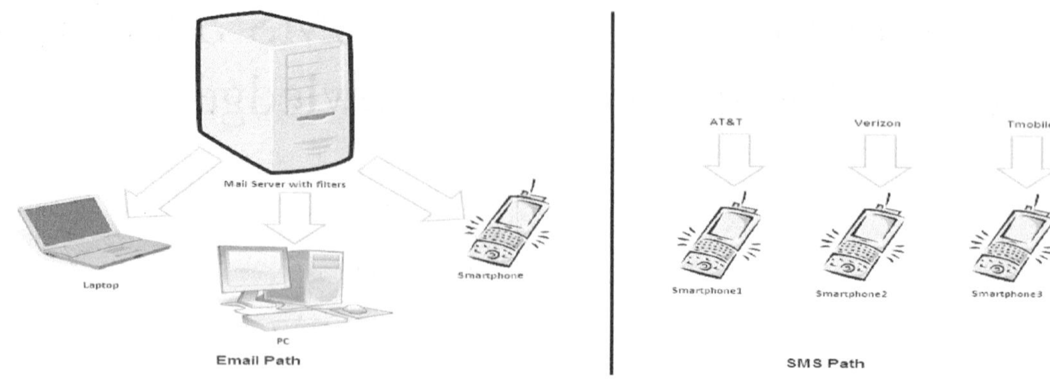

Fig. 1: Email path vs. SMS path

the remaining 20%. The goal is to show that the model built can generalize and to give the most honest results.

A. Corpus

We base our experimental studies on a publicly available SMS spam corpus [1]. The corpus has 5574 English SMS messages labeled as spam and ham. 86% of the messages are ham and the rest are spam. It was collected from various resources such as *NUS SMS, grumbletext and thesis*. The merging of the messages had lead to some duplicates and the required measures to remove these were taken. More details and comprehensive study of the collection can be found at [5].

B. Feature Engineering

According to [6], feature engineering is critical for the task of classifying SMS spam. Most of the work on that area, has suggested the use of either Bag of Words model or word, character n-gram models for classification features [7] [4] [8]. A known limitation of these models is the high dimensionality [9], which can affect the real time filtering, especially with the limited resources of mobile devices [10]. For that matter, we perform analysis on the text messages, based on observations, to extract features for SMS spam classification. Then perform an incremental study to test the significance of the proposed features. In the following, we list the features we used.

- Bag of Words (BoW): In Natural Language Processing, BoW model is used to represent documents, where all the words in the entire set are put together without regard to their order. The most frequent words can then be used as features in the term-document matrix. We use this model to setup a baseline for our experiments, and to study the benefits of adding new features. We created different datasets using the tm R package from [11], then experimented with term frequencies, binary occurrences and tf-idfs (term frequency inverse document frequency: a weight indicating the importance of the word in the dataset) of the words that occur most frequently in spam messages. The best results were achieved when using uni-grams with binary occurrence. Surprisingly, tf-idfs performed the worst with all classifiers.
- Part of Speech (POS) tags: In the area of Natural Language Processing, POS tagging is the task concerned with tagging words in a text with their part of speech, according to their definition or their context. It was used for text classification in [12] and in [13], and have proven to enhance the classification accuracy. We tagged the words in the SMS messages using the POS tagger from [14], to discover possible hidden characteristics of text messages. To compensate for the small number of words in the text messages, and the large number of POS tags, we reduced these tags into the main five ones: noun, verb, pronoun, modifier and wh-word. Then used the ratio of each of the five tags in each message as a feature. Thus we have the features: `nounRatio`, `verbRatio`, `pronounRatio`, `modifierRatio` and `wh-wordRatio` for each message. The mapping between the specific tags and the generic tags are as follow:
  - Any tag starting with VB → `verb`
  - Any tag starting with NN → `noun`
  - Any tag starting with JJ → `modifier`
  - Any tag starting with RB → `modifier`
  - Any tag starting with W → `wh-word`
  - Any tag starting with PR → `pronoun`
- The presence of a number: This feature was extracted after noticing that most of spam messages have either a phone number to call, or a code to reply with. These observations were supported by a recent report [3]. In this report 86% of SMS phishing scams used a phone number. `hasNumber`, is the feature indicating the presence of a number in a message.
- The presence of a link: This feature was extracted after noticing that a number of spam messages have a link to visit. Especially SMS phishing messages. In [3], 14% of spam messages include a URL. `hasLink` is the feature indicating the presence of a link.
- Misspelled words ratio: is the ratio of misspelled words in a message. Any word that does not appear in the English dictionary will be counted, then the

[1] http://www.esp.uem.es/jmgomez/smsspamcorpus/

ratio will be calculated by dividing the number of these words by the number of tokens in the message. This feature was extracted after noticing that spam messages are usually formal, and are using more correctly spelled words compared to ham messages. Also, some of spam messages use *word salad*, which is a set of random letters added to the end of the message to confuse filters [15]. `misspelledRatio` is the feature indicating the ratio of misspelled words in a message.

- Capitalized words ratio: is the ratio of capitalized words in a message. Any word with two or more letters where all capitalized will be counted. The ratio then will be calculated by dividing the number of these words by the total number of tokens in the message. This feature was extracted after noticing that spam messages are using capitalized words to catch users' attention. `capitalRatio` is the feature used to capture the ratio of capitalized words in a message. Figure 2, shows the different ratio of these features between spam and ham messages in the corpus.

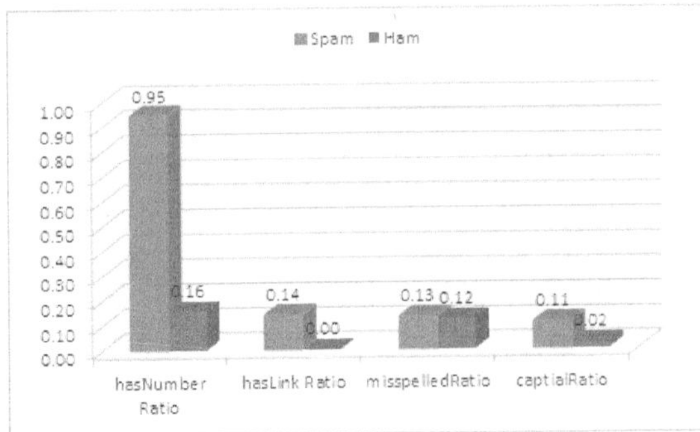

Fig. 2: The Ratio of Observed Features in SMS messages

As can be seen from the figure, `hasNumber` ratio is 80% higher in spam than in ham messages. Furthermore, none of the ham messages in this corpus included a link compared to 14% of the spam that included one, as indicated by the ratio of `hasLink` feature. The `misspelledRatio` is 1% higher in spam than in ham, while the `capitalRatio` is 9% higher in spam than in ham.

- Number of tokens: this feature indicates the number of tokens in a message. The average number of tokens in the corpus was 14 in ham compared to 22 in spam messages. This proves that spam messages are usually longer than ham. `tokNum` is the feature that indicates the number of tokens in a message. Table I summarizes the feature set.

C. Feature Selection

In this section we discuss the feature selection algorithms we run on the training data. But first we run an incremental study to see which of the features we propose enhance the results of the classification and which do not. We start by incrementally adding features to the baseline. Figure 3, shows the precision, recall and f-measure of adding different features to the BoW baseline.

Based on the results of this incremental study, we choose all features except for the misspelledRatio and POS tags to continue the experiments with. Although the use of POS tags was shown to enhance the results of classification in [13], it did not do that for this corpus. The reason might be that they have used a Korean SMS spam corpus and the language style differ from English. In the following subsections, we run feature selection algorithms on the entire training dataset without the misspelledRatio and the POS tags ratio.

To reduce the number of features in the dataset, and to run classification experiments with the optimum set of features, we propose two feature selection methods.

1) Info Gain Feature Selection: Here we run *Info Gain* feature selection algorithm from [16] on the training set, to choose the five most important features. The five selected features are ordered as follow:

1) `capitalRatio`
2) `hasNum`
3) `tokNum`
4) The term `call` binary occurrence
5) The term `text` binary occurrence

2) BART Feature Selection: Bayesian Additive Regression Trees (BART) [17], is a classifier that was reported to perform very well in detecting spam and phishing emails [18] [19]. One of BART capabilities is that it can be used for model-free feature selection by keeping track of the features that are used most frequently in the prediction process. The five features selected by BART feature selection are ordered as follow:

1) `capitalRatio`
2) `hasNum`
3) `hasLink`
4) The term `call` binary occurrence
5) The term `claim` binary occurrence

Table II, shows an example of both spam and ham messages with their corresponding selected feature values from both methods.

III. Experiments and Results

In this section we discuss the results of running classification experiments on different datasets, to assess the significance of the proposed features, and the significance of using only the selected features from both feature selection methods.

A. Evaluation Measures

To measure the accuracy of different classification models, we use precision, recall and f-measure. The higher the three measures are, the better the classification.

- Precision is the proportion of the predicted spam cases that were correct. It is calculated using the equation: $p = \frac{d}{b+d}$, where p = precision, d = The number of spam that are correctly predicted as spam, b = The number of ham that are incorrectly predicted as spam.

TABLE I: Features of the SMS Spam Dataset

No.	Feature	Value	Description
1-63	term binary occurrence	[0,1]	Binary value to indicate the presence of the term
64	hasLink	[0,1]	Binary value to indicate the presence of a link
65	hasNumber	[0,1]	Binary value to indicate the presence of a number
66	capitalRatio	[0...1]	Continuous value to indicate the ratio of capitalized words
67	misspelledRatio	[0...1]	Continuous value to indicate the ratio of misspelled words
68..72	POS	[0...1]	Continuous values to indicate the ratio of the five POS tags
73	tokNum	[0...[	Continuous value to indicate the number of tokens in a message

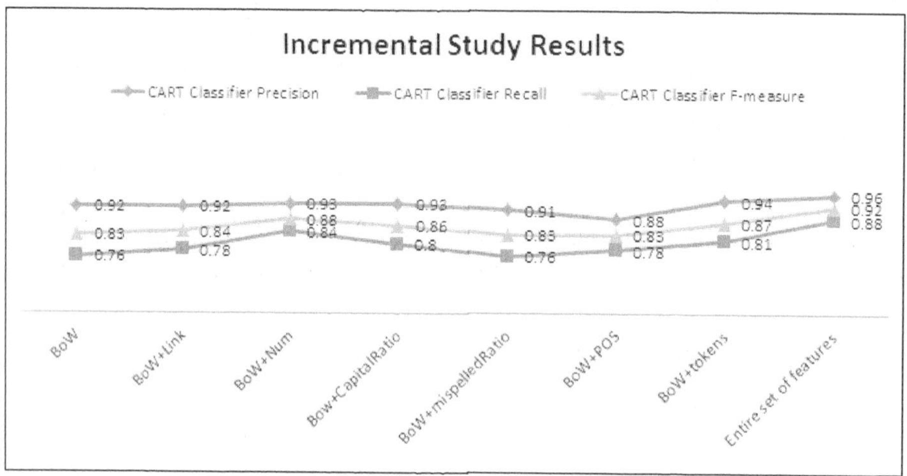

Fig. 3: Incremental Experiment Results

TABLE II: SMS Selected Feature Value Examples

SMS	Class	Features
WINNER!! As a valued network customer you have been selected to receive a $900 prize reward! To claim call 09061701461. Claim code KL341. Valid 12 hours only.	Spam	capitalRatio=0.04 hasNum=1 tokNum=27 hasLink=0 call=1 claim=1 text=0
Oh k...i'm watching here:)	Ham	capitalRatio=0 hasNum=0 tokNum=6 hasLink=0 call=0 claim=0 text=0

- Recall is the proportion of spam cases that were correctly identified. It is calculated using the equation: $r = \frac{d}{c+d}$, where r = recall, d = The number of spam that are correctly predicted as spam, c = The number of spam that are incorrectly predicted as ham.
- F-measure is the harmonic average of precision and recall. It is calculated using the equation: $fmeasure = 2 * \frac{p*r}{p+r}$, where *fmeasure* = f-measure, p = precision and r = recall.

To indicate the significance of the difference in performance between two classification results, we use the *z-score* test. For the difference to be significant, the *z-score* should exceed 1.96. It is calculated using the following equation: $z = \frac{abs(err_i, err_j)}{\sigma_d}$, where $\sigma_d = \sqrt{\frac{err_i(1-erri)}{ins} + \frac{err_j(1-errj)}{ins}}$, err_i and err_j are the f-measure for the two compared tests, and ins is the number of spam messages in the corpus.

B. Classification Setting

Our goal is to find the lightest classifier along with the least number of features for best classification performance and accuracy. To do that, we have experimented with a number of classifiers such as Support Vector Machine, Random Forest, Naive Bayes and CART. Table III, shows the results of running different classifiers on the selected features from the first method. As can be seen, *CART* has outperformed all of them.

Classification and Regression Trees *CART* [20], is a simple lightweight decision tree classifier, that meets the requirements for a client side lightweight SMS filtering. As shown in [19], it requires the least amount of memory and time compared to other classifiers. Thus, we choose CART for reporting the results of experiments on the following five datasets:

TABLE III: Different Classifiers on The Five Selected 1

	Training			Testing		
Classifier	**Precision**	**Recall**	**F-measure**	**Precision**	**Recall**	**F-measure**
Support Vector Machine	.76	.78	.77	.77	.79	.78
Random Forest	.91	.85	.88	.92	.83	.87
Naive Bayes	.86	.78	.82	.84	.75	.79
CART	.92	.87	.90	.91	.88	.89

- Baseline: This dataset includes the features from the BoW model, which are the binary occurrences of the 63 most frequent terms.
- Proposed: This dataset includes the features we have introduced based on our analysis of spam SMS messages.
- Combined: This dataset includes all the features from baseline and proposed datasets.
- Five selected 1: This dataset includes the five selected features from the first method (Using Info Gain).
- Five selected 2: This dataset include the five selected features from the second method (Using BART feature selection).

Figure 4, shows a simple decision tree built using CART with Five Selected 1 dataset.

C. Comparison Results

Table IV, shows the results of running CART on the five datasets. We report the results of classification on training and on testing to show that the built models can generalize. Hence, the following discussion will only consider the testing results since they were not involved in building the models and thus represent the honest results. As can be seen from the table, running CART on the proposed features alone has improved f-measure by 4% with *z-score*=2.01 and the addition of our proposed features to the baseline has improved the classification f-measure by 11% with a *z-score*=6.11 which is statistically significant. Thus, the proposed features addition is justified. Moreover, the results of running CART on the five selected 1 has improved the classification f-measure of the baseline by 9% with *z-score*= 4.7. Finally, the f-measure is 10% higher than the f-measure of the baseline, when running CART on the five selected 2 with a *z-score*=5.5, which is a significant improvement.

To evaluate the significance of each of the five features from the two methods, we conduct an ablation experiment, where we remove one feature after another according to their ranking order. Table V and table VI, show the results of ablation study on *Five Selected 1* and *Five Selected 2* respectively. We only report the results on the testing, since the results on training are almost the same. Notice that removing one feature after another has dropped the resulting f-measure drastically, which indicate the importance of each single feature of the five selected to the high classification results.

We compare the memory and time consumption of different experiments to test if the use of the selected features with CART does save time and memory. Table VII, shows the difference in memory consumption, represented by the number of leafs and the size of tree in the built model, and the time consumption, between different models built using different datasets. By introducing new features in the combined dataset, we notice that the memory and time consumption has dropped drastically. Which indicates better performance. Moreover, the use of the features from *Five Selected 1*, has decreased the memory consumption 25% less than the use of the combined and the proposed datasets. Finally, the use of the features from *Five Selected 2* has the best time consumption compared to all other datasets. All datasets perform better than the baseline in both time and memory performance. Note that, the time reported here is for running the experiments on an i5 core processor on a regular computer, and the benefit from saving parts of a second doubles when scaled to the mobile device. Though not reported here, the time for extracting only five features is far less than the time for extracting dozens of features.

IV. Related Work

Classifying SMS spam was studied in the literature from three different aspects: Content-base, content-less and access layer. Content-base classification considers the content of the message only, and can be deployed at the client side. In [6] [4] [5] and [7], the applicability of email classification methods to SMS was studied along with other classification techniques. Their studies show that content based SMS classification is in fact effective. A Bayesian filter was proposed in [8], that uses crowd sourcing and sender blacklisting to update the classifier. Furthermore, index based online SMS spam filtering was presented in [21]. Finally, in [13], they have studied the effect of stylistic features on filtering SMS spam.

Content-less classification using temporal and network features, to detect professional spammers, was studied in [2] and [22]. These techniques are applicable to servers where such data can be obtained. Moreover, byte distribution for spam and ham was used to detect SMS spam at the access layer of the mobile device in [23] and [24].

V. Conclusion

In our work, we studied the possibility of reducing the high dimensional features associated with the BoW model used for spam SMS classification. To achieve that, we introduced new features based on observations and on statistical analysis. Experimental results show that, adding these extra features to the BoW baseline, has increased the accuracy of the classification. We then ran feature selection algorithms to choose the optimal set of features, and the results of experimenting with only five optimal features surpassed the results of experimenting with the BoW dataset.

For future work, we intend to incorporate the findings of this research in a distributed system where the heavy lifting

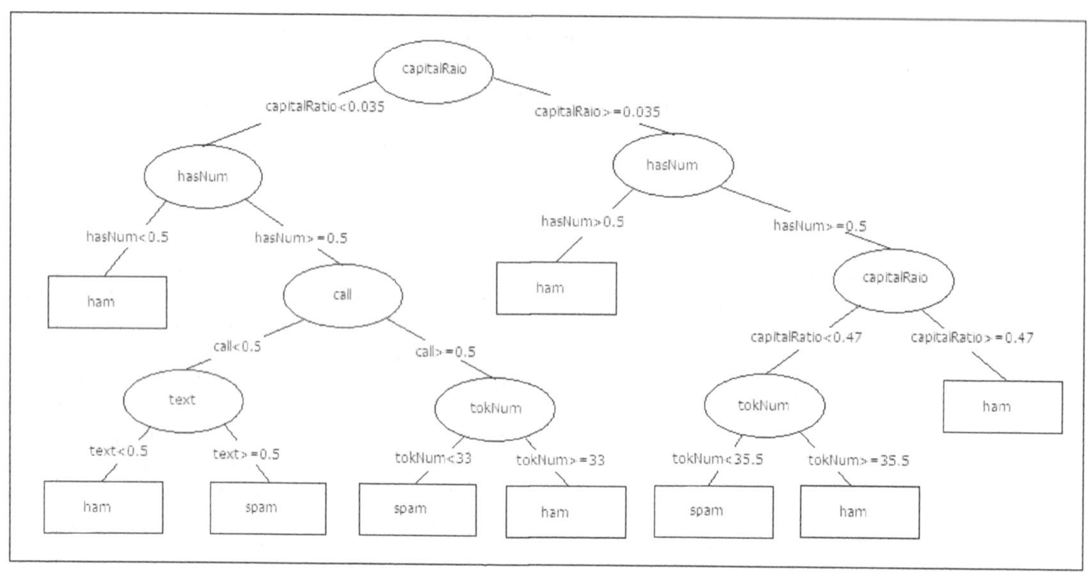

Fig. 4: CART Decision Tree with Five Selected 1

TABLE IV: Running CART with the five feature sets

	Training			Testing		
Dataset	**Precision**	**Recall**	**F-measure**	**Precision**	**Recall**	**F-measure**
Baseline	.92	.76	.83	.89	.71	.80
Proposed	.91	.81	.86	.93	.76	.84
Combined	.93	.88	.90	.92	.90	.91
Five selected 1	.92	.87	.90	.91	.88	.89
Five selected 2	.90	.87	.88	.90	.88	.90

TABLE V: Five Selected 1 Ablation Experiment Results

Feature Set	Precision	Recall	F-measure
All	.91	.88	.89
All-[capitalRatio]	.82	.74	.78
All-[capitalRatio+hasNum]	.76	.54	.63
All-[capitalRatio+hasNum+numTok]	.56	.59	.57
All-[capitalRatio+hasNum+tokNum+call]	.62	.17	.26

TABLE VI: Five Selected 2 Ablation Experiment Results

Feature Set	Precision	Recall	F-measure
All	.90	.88	.90
All-[capitalRatio]	.93	.61	.74
All-[capitalRatio+hasNum]	.96	.17	.28
All-[capitalRatio+hasNum+hasLink]	1	.15	.26
All-[capitalRatio+hasNum+hasLink+call]	1	.15	.26

TABLE VII: Memory and Time Consumption Comparison

Dataset	Number of leaf nodes	Size of the tree	Time for training	Time for testing
Baseline	52	103	8.42 seconds	0.02 seconds
Proposed	12	23	1.44 seconds	0.02 seconds
Combined	12	23	4.82 seconds	0.03 seconds
Five selected 1	9	17	0.92 seconds	0.02 seconds
Five selected 2	12	23	0.81 seconds	0 seconds

work of feature analysis and feature selection of new data is done in the server. Then, the resulting features will be conveyed to the mobile device to be used with a lightweight classifier. This is mainly done to adapt with new spam trends and to overcome the concept drift problem. Conversely, the mobile device should report back false positives and false negatives in a collaborative manner to enrich the data in the server and to enhance the system performance.

Acknowledgment

The authors wish to thank Dr Eduardo Blanco from UTD for his help and valuable comments, ideas and assistance to the writing and undertaking of the research summarized here.

References

[1] GSMA-Spam-Reporting-Service, "Sms spam and mobile messaging attacks introduction, trends and examples," GSMA, Tech. Rep., January 2011.

[2] I. Murynets and R. Jover, "Crime scene investigation: Sms spam data analysis," in *Proceedings of the 2012 ACM conference on Internet measurement conference*. ACM, 2012, pp. 441–452.

[3] GSMA-Spam-Reporting-Service, "Mobile messaging threat report," GSMA, Tech. Rep., September 2012.

[4] G. Cormack, J. Hidalgo, and E. Sanz, "Feature engineering for mobile(sms) spam filtering," in *Annual ACM Conference on Research and Development in Information Retrieval: Proceedings of the 30 th annual international ACM SIGIR conference on Research and development in information retrieval*, vol. 23. Citeseer, 2007, pp. 871–872.

[5] T. Almeida, J. Hidalgo, and A. Yamakami, "Contributions to the study of sms spam filtering: new collection and results," in *Proceedings of the 11th ACM symposium on Document engineering*, 2011, pp. 259–62.

[6] G. Cormack, J. Hidalgo, and E. Sanz, "Spam filtering for short messages," in *CIKM*, 2007, pp. 313–320.

[7] J. Hidalgo, G. Bringas, E. Snz, and F. Garca, "Content based sms spam filtering," in *Proceedings of the 2006 ACM symposium on Document engineering*, 2006.

[8] K. Indrapratha, P. Kumaraguru, A. Goyal, A. Gupta, and V. Naik, "Smsassassin: crowdsourcing driven mobile-based system for sms spam filtering," in *Proceedings of the 12th Workshop on Mobile Computing Systems and Applications*, 2011.

[9] C. Martins, M. Monard, and E. Matsubara, "Reducing the dimensionality of bag-of-words text representation used by learning algorithms," in *Proceedings of 3rd IASTED International Conference on Artificial Intelligence and Applications (AIA2003)*. Acta Press, 2003, pp. 228–233.

[10] A. Eshmawi and S. Nair, "Smartphone applications: Survey of new vectors and solutions," in *Proceedings of The International Conference on Computer Systems and Applications*. IEEE, 2013.

[11] I. Feinerer and K. Hornik, "tm - text mining package," http://tm.r-forge.r-project.org/, June 2012.

[12] J. D. M. Rennie, "Using part-of-speech information for transfer in text classification," 2003.

[13] D.-N. Sohn, J.-T. Lee, and H. chang Rim, "The contribution of stylistic information to content-based mobile spam filtering," in *Proceedings of the ACL-IJCNLP 2009 Conference Short Papers*, ser. ACLShort '09. Stroudsburg, PA, USA: Association for Computational Linguistics, 2009, pp. 321–324.

[14] I. Feinerer and K. Hornik, "opennlp: opennlp interface," http://cran.r-project.org/web/packages/openNLP/index.html, June 2010.

[15] S. J. Delany, M. Buckley, and D. Greene, "Sms spam filtering: Methods and data," *Expert Systems with Applications*, vol. 39, no. 10, pp. 9899 – 9908, 2012.

[16] M. Hall, E. Frank, G. H. B. Pfahringer, P. Reutemann, and I. Witten, "The weka data mining software: an update," *SIGKDD Explorations Newsletter*, vol. 11, no. 1, pp. 10–18, November 2009.

[17] H. Chipman, E. George, and R. Mcculloch, "Bart: Bayesian additive regression trees," Tech. Rep., 2006.

[18] S. Abu-Nimeh, D. Nappa, X. Wang, and S. Nair, "A distributed architecture for phishing detection using bayesian additive regression trees," in *Proceedings of eCrime Researchers Summit*. IEEE, 2008.

[19] ——, "Bayesian additive regression trees-based spam detection for enhanced email privacy," *ARES.*, pp. 1044–1051, March 2008.

[20] D. Steinberg and P. Colla, "Cart: classification and regression trees," *The Top Ten Algorithms in Data Mining, Chapman & Hall/CRC data mining and knowledge discovery series*, pp. 179–201, 1997.

[21] W. Liu and T. Wang, "Index-based online text classification for sms spam filtering," *Journal of Computers*, vol. 5, pp. 844–851, 2010.

[22] Q. Xu, E. Xiang, J. Du, J. Zhong, and Q. Yang, "Sms spam detection using content-less features," *IEEE Intelligent Systems*, vol. 99, 2012.

[23] M. Rafique and M. Farooq, "Sms spam detection by operating on byte-level distributions using hidden markov models (hmms)," in *Proceedings of the Virus Bulletin Conference*. VB, 2010.

[24] M. Rafique, N. Alrayes, and M. Khan, "Application of evolutionary algorithms in detecting sms spam at access layer," in *GECCO*. ACM, 2011, pp. 1787–1794.

Investigation of System Performance of Quantum Cryptography Key Distribution in Network Security

Mehrdad Sepehri Sharbaf
Senior IEEE Member
California State University Dominguez Hills
Computer Science Department
msharbaf@csudh.edu

Abstract

For the past decade progress in quantum cryptography changed the status of quantum key distribution (QKD) from laboratory to the practical innovation technology. Quantum cryptography is an emerging technology in which two parties can secure network communications by applying the phenomena of quantum physics. Quantum cryptography applies the uncertainty principle and the no-cloning theorem of quantum mechanics to provide ultra-secure encryption key distribution between two parties. Conventional secret-key cryptography techniques require the communication of a secret key prior to message exchange, and does not detect eavesdropping, and quantum principles can be used to detect eavesdropping probabilistically when it occurs. But there are challenges, and limitations to implement practical quantum cryptography such as detector performance for measuring photons, or optical sources which, enforce by the state-of-the-art components crucial for the system performance of quantum cryptography, and fiber optical distance range affect the system performance of quantum cryptography For that reason, the goal of this research is to investigate the system performance of quantum cryptography key distribution in network security, and this investigation develops a theoretical integrated research model or conceptual model framework concerning (figure 4) parameters which affect QKD system performance, and generates a key that affects by those variables.

To support the research the experimental data are performed, collected, and analyzed at MagiQ Technology in the Research & Development Lab. The rate of cryptography key or sifted key rate and the quantum bit error rate (QBER) are used to gauge the performance. The research presents a guideline to improve the system performance of the quantum cryptography.

Keywords-component; Quantum Crytography, QKD System Performance; System Conceptual Model; Quantun Bit Error

1.Introduction

Quantum cryptography concept developed by Charles H. Bennett and Gilles Brassard in 1984 (BB84) as part of research study between physics and information at IBM lab [9].This is the first known quantum distribution scheme. The quantum system is based on the distribution of single particles or photons, and the value of a classical bit encodes by the polarization of a photon [1]. According to [16] the key element of quantum communications is based on a quantum system which cannot only be in two states but also in a superposition of states, known as quantum bit ("qubit"). This system may be the two spin eigenstates of a particle, +1/2 and -1/2 or the polarization states of a photon. The two eigenstates are connected with the logic value "0" and "1", which mathematically are presented as:

$|0\rangle = |\downarrow\rangle \qquad |0\rangle = |\nearrow\rangle$

$|1\rangle = |\uparrow\rangle \qquad |1\rangle = |\nwarrow\rangle$

To illustrate the concept behind the quantum cryptography, let's define the photon.

A photon is an elementary particle of light, carrying a fixed amount of energy. Based on physical law, light may be polarized; polarization is a physical property that emerges when light is regarded as an electromagnetic wave (refer to figure 1).

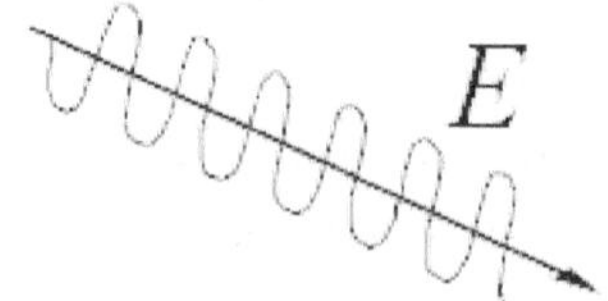

Figure 1. Light as an electromagnetic

According to [1] the direction of a photon's polarization can be fixed to any desired angle (using a polarizing filter), and can be measured using a calcite crystal (refer to Table 1).

Table 1. Polarization state pairs.

Basis	**State bit logic value**	**State bit logic value**	**Representation**
rectilinear	Horizontal (0°) →	Vertical (90°) ↑	+
Diagonal	45° ↗	135° ↖	X

According to [10, 1] the protocol BB84 uses 4 quantum states that constitute 2 bases. This encoding scheme is public knowledge. If Alice wants to transmit the conventional bit 0 or 1, she may choose to use + and consequently send out over the quantum channel →, ↑, or choose to use x and consequently send out ↗, ↖, If Alice is sending only ↑ and → to Bob, the coding system shall identify that Alice is using the base +. For example, if Alice sends sequence of photons: ↑, ↑, →, →, the binary number represented with these states is 1100. Now, if Bob wants to obtain a binary number sent by Alice, he needs to receive each photon in the same basis. In this case, this is + basis. For each conventional bit to be transmitted in the QKD protocol Alice will set differently oriented polarizes + or x uniformly random. If Alice sends random sequence of photons: ++xx++xxx++xx+, the binary number represented with these states is 10110011001110 Now, if Bob wants to obtain a binary number sent by Alice, He needs to receive each photon in the same basis. [19, 20] explain the procedure of BB84 protocol as follows (also shown in figure 2. Excerpted from http://www.idquantique.com).

Alice sends Bob a sequence of photons, each independently chosen from one of the four polarizations- vertical, horizontal, 45-degree, and 135-degree. For each photon, Bob randomly chooses one of the two measurements bases (rectilinear or diagonal) to perform a measurement, and records his measurement bases and results, and later Bob publicly acknowledges his results. [16] states that because a photon is an indivisible elementary particle, the QKD communications can not be passively tapped in the conventional sense so adversaries would need to undertake far more risky active attacks. However, the Heisenberg Uncertainty Principle ensures that any active attack will not permit an attacker to faithfully read the key transmission [12, 19, 20].

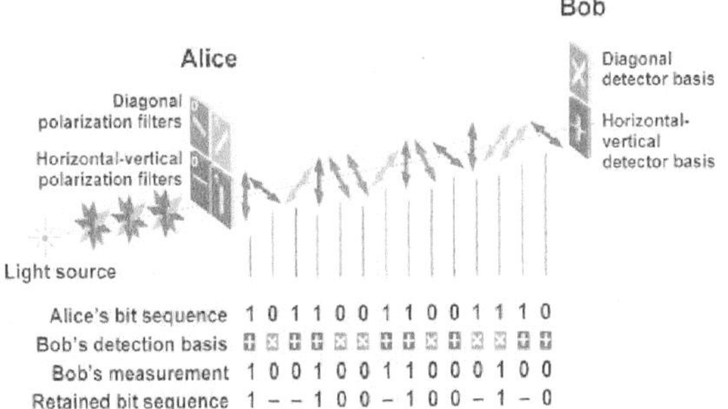

Figure 2. [idquantique]Principle of the BB84 protocol Quantum Key Distribution (QKD) Protocol Implementation

Figure 2 presents in schematic form the basic steps required for QKD, reading upwards from the bottom as is typical of networking protocol stacks, along with the current techniques implemented for each step [14, 17, 18, 27, 28]. The figure 10 represents in accordance with the conventions of network engineering, in which the physical layer is depicted at the bottom of the diagram and higher layers depend on the products of those beneath them. According to [9] at the physical layer or VPN/OPC interface receive these frame of raw key symbols, and then they perform QKD protocol (sifting, error correction, privacy amplification etc.). To elaborate in detail about QKD protocol, the explanation of each stage presented.

Sifting is the process whereby Alice and Bob window away all the obvious "failed qubits" from a series of pulses. Sifting allows Alice and Bob reconcile their "raw" secret bit streams to remove the errors. According to [9] at the end of this process, i.e. after a sift and sift response transaction- Alice and Bob discard all the useless symbols, and leaving only those symbols that Bob received and for which Bob's basis matches Alice's symbols. According to [9] some of the most common errors in sifting are: (a) Alice's source did not actually emit a photon; (b) that photon was lost in transmission; (c) Eve captured the photon and did not replace it; (d) Bob's detector did not fire when the photon hit it; (e) wrong basis symbols between Alice and Bob; (f) Multiple detection symbols in which more than one Bob's detector's fired. The Shannon's theorem (1949) [25] states that in any condition, the amount of information Bob has should exceed the information possessed by Eve, i.e. Bob must have more information on Alice's bits than Eve. If this is not the case, then the bits transmitted so far discarded and the previous steps are carried on again until this condition is satisfied.

Error correction is always probabilistic-unless all bits are revealed during the process. Error detection and correction allows Alice and Bob to determine all the "error bits" among their shared, sifted bits, and correct them so that Alice and bob share the same sequence of error-corrected bits. The process of error detection allows Alice and Bob to estimate the current Quantum Bit Error Rate (QBER) on the quantum channel between them, which can then be used as input for privacy amplification. Also to eliminate errors due to incorrect choices of measurement basis, errors induced by Eve eavesdropping, and errors due to channel noise, if any exists. Privacy Amplification is the process whereby Alice and Bob reduce Eve's knowledge of their shared bits to an acceptable level. As [9] states that privacy amplification depends on having an accurate estimate of the eavesdropping-free entropy sifted and error correction secret bit sequences. According to [12] privacy amplification is the fourth step which is applied to minimize the number of bits that an eavesdropper knows in the final key. According to [9] Alice and Bob must perform a final step in order to establish a perfectly secret key: this is the process of privacy amplification. The process of reconciliation results in a bit sequence which is common to Alice and Bob, but some of its bits may be known to an eavesdropper who has tapped the classical channel. To eliminate this "leaked" information, Alice and Bob must apply, in common, a binary transformation (usually, a random permutation) to their sequences, and discard a subset of bits from the result. The precise choice of transformation and the number of bits discarded, of course, determine the amount of secrecy of the final key. The objective of this step is to minimize the quantity of correct information which the eavesdropper may have obtained about Alice and Bob's common bit sequence. Privacy amplification uses Alice and Bob's key to produce a new, shorter key, in such a way that Eve has only negligible information about the new key. It's important fact that an incorrect estimate may lead to insufficient privacy amplification, and thus allow Eve to know more about the resultant "secret" bits than expected.

2. System Performance of Quantum Cryptography

The system performance of quantum cryptography or the over system range performance and throughput, are limited by detection efficiency, optical source efficiency, and fiber link loss [30, 31]. Also [13] argue about the limitation of detector efficiency on the system performance of quantum cryptography. Other scholars such as [27] discuss about backscattering limitation to the system performance of QKD, and [34] elaborate more about source efficiency, detector efficiency, and link loss related to the performance of QKD.
Also the scholars argue that the secure key generation rate of a quantum cryptography system is highly sensitive to the error rate due to eavesdropper [2, 4, 10, 12, 13, 32]. In the process of QKD BB84 Protocol implementation of the raw key creation is one of the important parameters to characterize the performance of QKD system [9, 11, 22]. The raw rate in the protocol is defined as:

$$Rate_{raw} = q\mu f \eta_d \eta_l \quad (1)$$

where q is a setup dependent coefficient, or where is the systematic factor, which is .5 for four state of BB84 protocol, μ is the mean number photons per pulse, f is the laser pulsing frequency, η_d is the photon's detection probability or the detector efficiency, and η_l is the transfer efficiency of the link or the transmission coefficient of the link between the active receiving station and Alice's detector. As it stated in this paper, sifting is the process whereby Alice and Bob window away all the obvious "failed qubits" from a series of pulses. Sifting allows Alice and Bob reconcile their "raw" secret bit streams to remove the errors. The sifted key rate is used to gauge the performance of the QKD [9, 13, 30]. The equation for sifted key rated can be expressed as:

$$Rate_{sift} = 1/2\mu f \eta_d \eta_l \quad (2)$$

Where the sifted key corresponds to the cases in which Alice and Bob made compatible choices of bases, hence its rate is half that of the raw key. For that reason [11] express that the raw rate is essentially the product of the pulse rate f_{rep}, the mean number of photons per pulse μ, the probability t_{link} of a photon to arrive at the analyzer and the probability η of the photon being detected:

$$R_{sift} = ½ R_{raw} = ½ q\, t_{link} f_{rep}\, \mu \quad (3)$$

The quantum bit error rate (QBER) which is also an important parameter to characterize the QKD system. It is used to gauge the performance of quantum cryptography [11, 12, 32, 33]. The QBER equation can be expressed as:

$$QBER = \frac{Fasle-Counts}{Total-Counts} = \frac{Fasle-Counts}{False-Counts+Correct-Counts} = \frac{N\ wrong}{N\ right+N\ wrong} = \frac{Rerror}{Rsift+Rerror} \approx \frac{Rerror}{Rsift} \quad (4)$$

The QBER is defined as the number of wrong bits to the total number of received bits.
According to [7] the QBER for the faint laser pulse QKD can be written as a sum of two main contributing factors:

$$QBER = QBERopt + QBERdet = P_{opt} + P_{noise}/P_{photon} = P_{opt} + P_{noise}/\mu\eta_d\eta_l, \quad (5)$$

where P_{opt} is the probability of a photon going to the wrong detector, and P_{nois} is the probability of getting a noise-count (mainly dark counts) per gating pulse window. For the phase-based

$$QKD: = P_{opt} = (1-V)/2 \quad (6)$$

where V is the interference visibility. Also [10, 11] present the QBER in different way as follows:

$$QBER = \frac{p_{opt}p_{phot} + p_{dark}}{p_{phot} + 2p_{dark}} \cong p_{opt} + \frac{p_{dark}}{p_{phot}} = QBER_{opt} + QBER_{det} \quad (7)$$

where p_{dark} and p_{phot} are, respectively, the probabilities of getting a dark count and a photon count and p_{opt} is the probability that a photon is detected by the wrong detector, due to the limited interference fringe visibility or due to poor polarization alignment. Equation (6) holds for a system implementing the BB84 protocol.
The probability of getting a photon count is given by:

$$P_{shot} = \mu\eta_t\eta_d \quad (8)$$

And

$$P_{dark} = n_{dark}\Delta t \quad (9)$$

where n_{dark} is the single photon avalanche diode(SPAD) dark counting rate (dark counts per second) and Δt is the detection time window. Based on that:

$$QBER_{det} = \frac{n_{dark}}{\eta_d}\frac{\Delta t}{\mu\eta_t} \quad (10)$$

$QBER_{det}$ is inversely proportional to the system's transmission efficiency.

Based on a thorough review of theoretical background, this investigation establishes the following questions:

Research Questions

R1: Does the detector affect to the QKD performance?
R2: Does the optical source affect to the QKD performance?
R3: Does the fiber optical distance range affect to the QKD performance?
R4: Is there a relationship between the rate of cryptography key or sifted key rate and the quantum bit error rate (QBER) to the performance of QKD?

Research Hypotheses

The hypotheses are derived directly from the research questions, and are posed in a format so that a determination can be made as to whether the data subsequently collected at MagiQ Technology R & D Lab, provides support for them or not.

H1: The detector does affect to the QKD performance.
H2: The optical source does affect to the QKD performance.
H3: The fiber optical range does affect to the QKD performance.
H4: There is a relationship between the rate of cryptography key or sifted key rate and the quantum bit error rate (QBER) to the performance of QKD.

Based on above research questions, and research hypotheses, this investigation develops a theoretical integrated research model or conceptual model framework concerning (figure 3) parameters which affect QKD system performance. Conceptual frameworks (theoretical frameworks) are a type of intermediate theory that attempt to connect to all aspects of inquiry (e.g., problem definition, purpose, literature review, methodology, data collection and analysis). Conceptual frameworks can act like maps that give coherence to empirical inquiry.

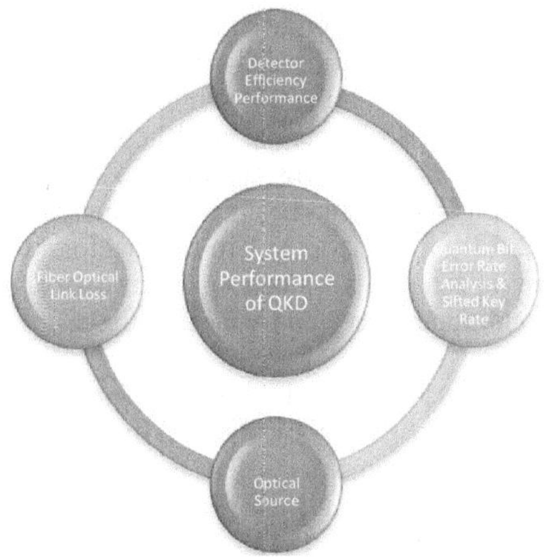

Figure 3. Conceptual Model

To build a commercial QKD system there are majors challenges such as interferometry, extra photons, single-photon detection, and distance limitation. To investigate performance of QKD, the research paper examines a typical QKD system consists of two parties (Alice, and Bob) exchanging weak optical signals through the quantum channel at MagiQ Technology in the Research & Development Lab (figure 4).

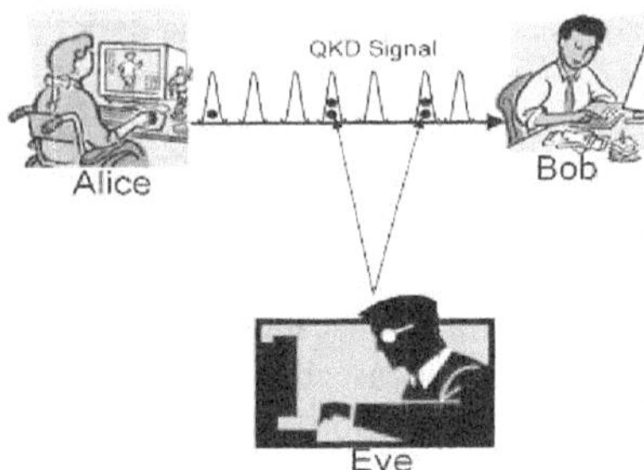

Figure 4

In real application, because of the limited availability of single photon sources, the research examines weak coherent pulses (WCP). The use of the WCP as compare to single photon source greatly simplified QKD apparatus, but WCP can contain more than one photon. If Alice uses weak coherent pulses (WCP), the probability of finding **n** photons in a pulse with the average photon number μ follows the Poisson statistics [33]:

$$P_{\mu}(n) = e^{-\mu}\mu^{n}/n! \quad (11)$$

Presence of multiphotons pulses creates a possibility of Eve's photon splitting attacks [33]. Using WCP increases vulnerability of the QKD system with the loss of the channel [32, 33]. In order to keep the link secure, Alice must maximize the difference between numbers of photons successfully deliver to Bob's detector, and the total number of the multiple-photon pulses. For that reason μ needs to stay low: (μ = η- is the channel transmittivity) to guarantee the security as the link distance (loss) increase [31, 32, 33]. In the case of zero channel loss, the optimization always takes place at μ=.5. This condition is accepted by most of the research groups [33, 34].

Also performance of a WCP QKD depends on the detector efficiency to detect the pulse, and dark current noise as well as the interferometer insertion loss, and the security model used through the choice of the mean photon numbers [30]. For that reason certain amount of errors can be accomplished by procedures known as error correction and privacy amplification. In this investigation the goal is to maximize the secure key rate under the theoretical conditions to reduce the probability of information leakage below predefined value. In this research it defines secure bit gain by G which is the probability of secure bit out of single initial pulse. The gain of the secure bits is dependent on the losses in the fibre link αL (where α denotes losses [dB/km], and L is the fibre length[km], quantum efficiency of the detector, visibility of interferometer V, and probability of the dark count of the detector P_{DC}. The first protocol Alice and Bob run is sifting. The sifted key contains errors. Alice and Bob have to run some error corrections protocol to estimate secure bits lost due to error correction. The protocol to define the requirement is Cascade [3, 21]. Based on numerical simulation cascade the raw bits are needed for the error correction, this can be done by work published by [3, 21, 33], where equation (12):

$$H = -f\left(e\log_2 e - (1-e)\log_2(1-e)\right)$$

The corrected sifted key is not completely secure due to privacy amplification. Alice and Bob have to run a privacy amplification protocol to establish the final secure key. This can be done by work published by [33] equation (13).

$$t = 1 + \log_2\left(\frac{1}{2} + 2e - 2e^2\right)$$

Based on additionally, quantum cryptography requires the use of privacy amplification to reduce, or eliminate, any potential information an adversary could have gained by interacting with the quantum transmission, privacy amplification increases security by combining several bits in the initial key to form each bit of the final key, reducing the length of the key in the process. This process becomes very inefficient as the error rate increases because the privacy amplification algorithm must essentially sacrifice exponentially many initial key bits in order to extract a single secure key bit.

Finally, the secure bit gain can be written as equation (14):

$$G = p_{sift}(1 - t - f \times H)$$

And Key Rate=Gain X Rep Pulse Rate

Figure 8. illustrates the procedures for the final secure key.

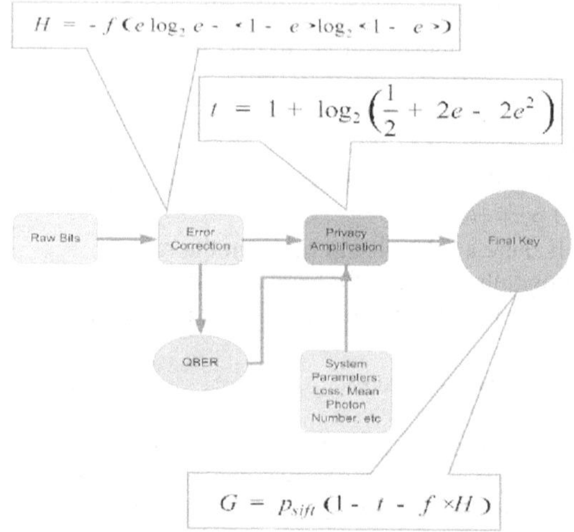

The final secure key depends to the system parameters such as mean photon number, loss ,detector efficiency, etc. The optimal mean number of photons can be found by maximizing G.

For the fixed detector temperature and transmission distance, optimization for the QKD can be achieved by increasing the strength of the optical signal sent by Alice. As μ is increased, Bob's detector's receives more photons, increasing the gain per pulse. But based on equation (14), the number of bits applied by error correction and privacy increases up as well which resulting in a decrease in gain. Figure 9 shows secure bit gain as a function of QKD transmission distance. As you see secure bit gain decreases as distance increase. It also suggests, an optimal value of μ does not depend on the detector operational parameters , but it is function of the link loss only Figure 9. [31, 15]

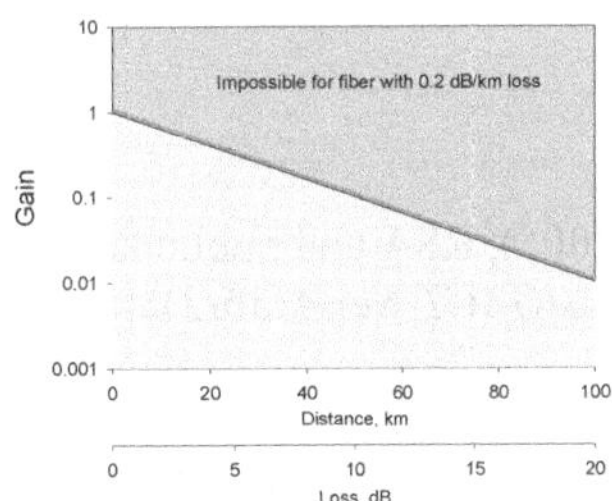

After μ optimization is performed, it needs to optimize the detector operational point in order to extract maximum performance from the system. For that reason it is essential to specify characteristic of the detector, such as quantum efficiency of the detector (QE), dark current probability (DC), and afterpulsing probability. Quantum efficiency of the detector (QE) is the probability of detector detects a true click from a single photon in given time slot. In another word , the quantum efficiency is the number of photons that can be detected as a photocurrent divided by the number of the incident photons. Based on definition, it's true click. Dark current probability is the probability of detector detects a false click containing no photon in a time slot. In another word, the dark current is a small current which flows when a reverse voltage is applied to a photodiode even in dark state. This is a major source of noise for applications in which a reverse voltage is applied to photodiodes. Based on definition, noise creates false click. Afterpulsing probability is the probability of getting a false click condition on the probability of getting click from previous time slot. The detector characteristics are effect to the system performance of QKD. For the system to detect reliable bit is a challenge. The quantum bit error is proportional to the ratio of the erroneous clicks in Bob's detector to the total number of photons registered. In real application QKD system, three main factors to the error count are: dark current in the detector (dark current probability, is the probability of detector detects a false click containing no photon in a time slot), and finite visibility of interferometer (probability of a detector misguided to a wrong detector), and afterpulsing probability which can be reduced by cooling down the detector. Also as link loss increases with distance, less photon arrive to Bob's detector. For that reason detector noise stays constant which that reflects to increase of QBER. As a guideline to improve the QKD system performance, a system designer could first to choose μ based on the known fibre loss, and then concentrates to optimize the system performance by adjusting detector parameters.

3. Conclusion:

It is possible to apply quantum cryptography key distribution to secure the bit communication at the current level of technology development. BB84 protocol can provide a secure communication link between Alice and Bob. The investigation of this research demonstrates that the system performance of QKD in network security affects by those variables which we discussed in our research questions. The research also provides guidelines for the optimization of QKD. There is a definite space for further improvement in photon collection efficiency, detector performance, and interferometer loss. By optimizing the system variables, a WCP QKD link can provide a stable secure communication against eavesdroppers.

4. Acknowledgement:

The author is grateful to Dr. Anton Zavriyev, Director of R & D in MagiQ Technology company for his technical advise, support, and help in this research paper.

5. References:

[1] Bennett, C. H., Bessette, F., Brassard, G., Salvail, L., & Smolin, J., "Experimental quantum cryptography". *Journal of Cryptology, 5(*1), 1992 p. 3-28.

[2] Bogdanski, J., Rafiei, N., & Bourennane, M. (2008). Five-user QKD over switched fiber networks. *Proceeding of SPIE Vol. 7092,* P. 70920k-1-8.

[3]BRASSARD, G. and SALVAIL, L., 1994, in Advances in Cryptology- *EUROCRYPT '93,* Vol. 765, edited by T. Helleseth (Berlin: Springer), p. 410.

[4] Bruss, D., Erdelyi, G., Meyer, T., Riege, T., & Rothe, J., " Quantum cryptography: A survey". *ACM Computing Surveys, 39(*2), 2007, p. 1-27.

[5] Buchmann, J., May, A., & Vollmer U., "Perspective for cryptographic long-term security". *Communications of ACM. 49(*9), 2006, p. 50-56.

[6] Coron, J. S., " What is cryptography?", *IEEE Security & Privacy Journal, 12(8), 2006, p. 70-73.*

[7] Curcic, T., Filipkowski, M. E., Chtchelkanova, A., D'Ambrosio, P. A., Wolf, S. A., Foster, M., & Cochran, D., "Quantum Networks: From Quantum Cryptography to Quantum Architecture", *ACM SIGCOMM Computer Communication Review*, Vol.34, No.5, 2004, pp. 3-8.

[8] Davis, J., "Information Systems Security Engineering: A critical Components of the Systems Engineering Lifecycle", *ACM SIGAda,* 2004, pp.13-17.

[9] Elliot, C., "Quantum Cryptography", *IEEE Security & Privacy Journal*, 2004, pp. 57-61.

[10] Gisin, N., Ribordy, G., Tittel, W., & Zbinden, H. (2008). Quantum Cryptography. *Review Moderns Physics, arXiv: quantum-ph/0101098v2*, p. 1-57.

[11] Gisin, N., & Thew, R. (2008). Quantum Communication. *Physics Review, arXiv:quant-ph/0703255v1.*

[12] Gumus E., Aydin, G., & Aydin M. (2007). Quantum cryptograhpu and comparison of quantum distribution protocols, *Journal of Electrical & Electronics Engineering, 8(*1), 2008.

[13] Jacobs, B., Hendrickson, S., Dennis M., & Franson, J. (2006). Quantum cryptography at 830nm in standard telecommunications fiber. *Poceeding of SPIE* Vol. 6244, p. 62440H-1-11.

[14] Khan M. M., Hyder, S., Pathan, M., & Sheikh, K. H. (2006). A quantum key distribution network through single mode optical fiber. *Proceeding of International Symposium on Collaborative Technologies and Systems.* p.13-19.

[15] Internet Resources:
http://www.magiqtech.com
www.idquantique.com

[16]Kartalopoulos, S. V. (2007). Quantum cryptography for secure optical networks, *Proceedings of IEEE ICC Conference,* p. 1311-1316.

[17] Li, X., & Zhang, D., "Quantum information authentication using entangled states", *IEEE Computer Society, International Conference on Digital Telecommunications*, 2006, pp. 64.

[18] Liu, S., Sullivan, J., & Ormaner, J. "A practical approach to enterprise IT security". *IEEE IT Professional Journal, 9(*3), 2001, p. 35-42.

[19]Lo , H. K., & Lutkenhaus, N. (2007). Quantum cryptography: from theory to practice. *arXiv:quant-ph/0702202v3*

[20]Lo H. K., & Zhao, Y. (2008) Quantum Cryptography. *Physics Review, arXiv:quant-ph/0803.2507v4*

[21]LUTKENHAUS, N., 2000, Phys. Rev. A, 61, 052304.

[22]Mayers, D. (2001). Unconditional security in quantum cryptography. *Journal of the ACM, 48(*3), p. 351-406.

[23]Mollin, R. A. (2005), RSA and public key cryptography. *ACM SIGACT News, 36(*2), p. 14-20.

[24] Rothe, J. (2002). Some facets of complexity theory and cryptography: A five-lecture tutorial. *ACM Computing Surveys, 34(*4), p. 504-549.

[25] Shannon, E. C., "Communication theory of secrecy system", *Bell System Technical Journal,* Vol.28, No.4, 1949, pp.656-715.

[26] Steane, M. A., & Rieffel, G. W., "Beyond bits: The future of quantum information processing", *IEEE Computer,* 2000, pp. 38-45.

[27] Subacius, D., Zavriyev A., & Trifonov, A. (2005). Backscattering limitation for fiber-optic quantum key distribution systems. *Applied Physcis Letter, 82*(1), p. 1-3.

[30] Teja, V., Banerjee, P., Sharma N. N., & Mittal, R. K. (2007). Quantum Cryptography: State-of-art , challenges, and future perspective, *Proceeding of the 7th IEEE International Conference on Nanotechnology*, p. 1296-1301.

[31] Trifonov, A., Subacius, D., Berzanskis, A., & Zavriyev, A. (2004). Single photon counting at telecom wavelength and quantum key distribution. *Journal of Modern Optics, Vol. 15*(9), p.1399-1415.

[32] Trifonov, A., Zavriyev, A., Subacius, D., Alleaume, R., & Roch J. F. (2005). Practical quantum cryptography. *Journal of Optical Society of America,* p. 13-21.

[33] Trifonov, A., Zavriyev, A.,(2004). Practical single photon source for quantum communications. *Journal of Optics B: Quantum and Semiclassical Optics. P. 25-29.*

[34] Trifonov, A., Zavriyev, A.,(2005).Secure communication with a heralded single-photon source. *Journal of Optics B: Quantum and Semiclassical Optics. P. 772-777.*

[35] Wang B. C., Kumavor, P., Yelin S. F., & Beal A. C. (20005). Multi-user quantum cryptography. *Proceeding of SPIE Vol. 6014*, p. 601416-1-12.

[36] Wootters, W. K., & Zurek, W. H., "A single quantum cannot be cloned". *Nature,* 299, 1982, p. 802.

Multi-disciplinary Approach to Cyber Security Education

Wendy A. Lawrence-Fowler
Department of Computer Science
The University of Texas-Pan American
1201 W. University Drive
Edinburg, Texas 78540
wfowler@utpa.edu

Abstract A multidisciplinary approach to cybersecurity education facilitates sound critical and analytic thinking and good communication. Students are introduced to a broader perspective and learn to think more openly and within alternative systems of thought. They are better prepared to recognize and assess assumptions, implications, and practical consequences.

Keywords: cybersecurity education, computer security education; forensics education, multidisciplinary education in security, security

I. INTRODUCTION

"We live in a world where a nation's security depends in no small part on the security awareness and practices of our agencies, firms, suppliers, schools, friends, neighbors, relatives and, well, all of us."[1] The increasing number of security breaches and threats to personal, organizational, and national safety have created a focus on cybersecurity. Today's security workload is outstripping the capacity of the current security workforce to meet the demand [2]. Personnel across all sectors are sought to fill the cyber workforce need[3]. A challenge is to identify the sorts of people and formal education that are needed to assure there is a highly skilled and creative workforce that can respond to the dynamic challenges of cybersecurity today and into the future. In response to the U.S. government/s recognition that "securing cyberspace is an extraordinarily difficult challenge that requires a coordinated and focused effort from our entire society – the federal government, state and local governments, the private sector and the American people"[4], NIST introduced the National Initiative for Cybersecurity Education (NICE). NICE serves as a national campaign to increase cybersecurity awareness, education, careers, and training across all sectors. Education is used as the vehicle preparing the general public, creating the workforce of tomorrow and keeping today's workforce up to date. To facilitate communication, NICE has developed the National CyberSecurity Workforce Framework (the Framework). The framework provides a common lexicon and a description of cybersecurity work in terms of categories and specialty areas. The categories group related specialty areas together. Each specialty area is defined by typical tasks and knowledge areas, skills and abilities (KSAs) required for work in the area[5].

For technology programs within educational institutions, emerging fields of study and practice in cyber security computer forensics, network security, software security, and critical infrastructure protection are increasingly important areas of interest [6]. The framework serves to guide curriculum decisions for both formal and informal education in cybersecurity.

This paper proposes that taking a multidisciplinary approach to security and more particularly cyber security results in graduates who can think more openly and within alternative systems of thought. They are able to recognize and assess assumptions, implications, and practical consequences.

II. CONTEXT FOR THE APPROACH

In 2007, The University of Texas – Pan American established an Intelligence Community Center of Excellence (IC CAE) in National Security Studies Program in collaboration with the U.S. Intelligence Community and funding from the Office of the Director of National Intelligence (ODNI). The purpose of the Center is to assure that professionals in the next generation of Intelligence Community are prepared with the appropriate skills and breadth of knowledge to be leaders in the national security challenges in the 21st century.

Focusing on the breadth of knowledge required to lead and recognizing that solutions to the current challenges in security demand the integration of human and technical resources, the UTPA IC CAE uses a multi-disciplinary approach to achieve substantial synergies in information assurance and analysis, risk assessment, management and leadership, as well as the application of technology. The IC CAE leads the discourse on national security across campus, identifying specific needs associated with bridging disciplines. To that end, the IC CAE manages an interdisciplinary Global Securities Studies and Leadership Program (GSSL) with an undergraduate minor, a graduate certificate and a Master's degree in Interdisciplinary Studies (MAIS). Its near-universal reach across the university curriculum is ambitious because it articulates skill and knowledge sets that reside in many of UTPA's departments. Existing courses are taught by current faculty in established departments. For example, a graduate level course in Computer

Security and Forensics in the Department of Computer Science is part of the core technology competency courses in the MAIS. When the course is offered, students in the course come from not only the MAIS, but also Masters programs in Computer Science (MSCS) and Information Technology (MSIT). While originally designed with a curriculum targeting a computer science audience, the content is delivered to take advantage of the synergies in understanding that can arise with analytical thinking and communication of diverse perspectives of a multidisciplinary audience.

III. THE GLOBAL SECURITY STUDIES PROGRAM

A. Overview of Master's of Interdisciplinary Studies(MAIS)

The MAIS degree prepares students for careers in Intelligence and National Security through focus on advanced research, effective cross-discipline team communication, and critical analysis. Given that jobs in government or private industry often require multidisciplinary cooperation, the GSSL MAIS prepares students to work with people from different backgrounds, abilities, and knowledge bases. This approach assures that students have the opportunity to gain the perspective of and proficiency in multiple disciplines, preparing them for careers in national security.

The program engages students and faculty in five of the five Primary Critical Skill Sets/Competencies areas of specialization: Information Technology Specialists, Political / Economic Specialists, Language Specialists, /Threat Specialists, Scientific/Technical Specialists. A number of general competencies for intelligence professional areas are also addressed: Analysis, Analytical Reasoning, Critical Thinking, Communications (oral and written), Research, developing rational conclusions and alternative solutions from ambiguity and limited data sets[7].

B. MAIS Curriculum

The GSSL MAIS consists of 36 semester hours of study, including a 12 hour core sequence, a 15 hour concentration in interdisciplinary studies and a 9 hour technical competency sequence. Through the core sequence the students learn how skill sets relate to the global context of intelligence and security work. The courses address competency skill areas including advanced research, problem solving, critical thinking, technical writing, and leadership. The core courses consist of Global Security, Open Source Research, Interdisciplinary Research and Analysis, and a practicum in Global Studies Security Studies. The interdisciplinary sequence addresses critical competencies required to understand the globalization of communication, societies, cultures, governments, businesses, and technology. The required courses include Culture and Communication, International Management, Cross Cultural Psychology, and Statistics.

The technology competency sequence provides students with the essentials of information technology and computer systems with a focus on information security. The three course sequence includes Information Security, Principles of Information Technology Systems, and Cyber Security and Forensics [7,8]. The first course is offered by the Department of Computer Information Systems located in the College of Business. The second two courses are taught in the Department of Computer Science in the College of Engineering and Computer Science.

IV. CYBER SECURITY AND FORENSICS COURSE FOR MULTIDISCIPLIANRY AUDIENCE

Using a variety of learning resources, the Computer Science course in Cybersecurity and Forensics introduces the foundations of cybersecurity and cyber forensics theory, policy and application. The goal of the course is to assure that students gain an understanding of the breadth and depth of cybersecurity and cyber forensics in both abstract terms and in the context of real systems. Readings, lecture, discussion, and thought experiments [9] are used to introduce the underlying formalisms and technologies in computer science that address challenges and potential threats to confidentiality, integrity, and availability. A laboratory component reinforces formalisms and technologies introduced in lecture and discussion. The labs support understanding through direct experience in applying knowledge in new situations [10,11,12]. Students are exposed to different types of tools, techniques, and procedures, as well as policy and legal issues and develop skills in the reduction of theory to practice and abstraction of practice to theory.

A. Course Objectives

Upon completion of the course, students are expected to (1) understand the basic theory and concepts of cyber security and privacy including policies, models, and mechanisms; (2) understand ethics, legal issues, and human factors associated with cyber security and forensics; (3) understand security vulnerabilities and be able to describe threats and risks; (4) be able to explain best practices in giving access to systems and networks and implement proper authentication techniques; (5) be familiar with cryptographic techniques, asymmetric key algorithms, and create certificates; (6) describe the requirements for a cyber forensic investigation and demonstrate an understanding of tools, techniques and procedures; and (7) be conversant in current security related issues in the fields of cyber security and cyber forensics.

B. Course Topics

The course begins with an overview of the security problem followed by an introduction of fundamental tools and techniques for addressing security. After providing a broad introduction to security, the course focus shifts to forensics. Course topics include: confidentiality, integrity and access policies; information flow and content (encoding and entropy); cryptography and ciphers; network security; malicious logic, vulnerability analysis ; strategic planning for security; law and legal issues; volatile and persistent data; forensics first responder activities; and hacking. Strategic planning for security is introduced as a scaffolding to provide a real-world context and supports the creation of connections between security topics.

C. Laboratory Component

The laboratory component of the course gives students practical experience with the concepts introduced in lecture and discussion. Each lab is designed so that students experience working with real world tools and real world problems. A broad array of commercial hardware and software, and open source tools are provided to develop solutions for problem based challenges involving confidentiality, integrity, access, and trust. Students identify and disable network attacks. They find hidden information, and they conduct forensic investigations using a systematic approach to evidence identification, preservation, analysis, documentation, and presentation following acceptable legal procedures and laws of evidence[10]. Additional lab exercises involve secure system design using covert channels and robust queues. [13].

Lab exercises are completed by interdisciplinary teams to encourage transfer of understanding and perspective across the spectrum of divergent bodies of knowledge held by course students and to address varying levels of comfort and skill in using technology.

D. AssessmentTechniques Used

Substantive and formative evaluations were given to both assess students learning and to help in making adjustments to content delivery. Students were given weekly assignments that included a set of readings and at minimum one deliverable. Deliverables varied by week, but consisted of one or more of the following: 1) short responses to issue specific questions used to measure understanding of the lecture and reading assignments, 2) lab results along self-assessment of success, and suggestions on improving the lab, 3) short essays on how a reading relates to past, current, or future experiences in global information security, 4) contribution to a lexicon for security, 5) identification of a resource and explanation of its value. The time in lab provided additional opportunities to gather feedback about content delivery and student learning.

Two larger learning exercises served as exams. The first was given midterm. Students were given two questions that required them to research specific security models and discuss their application. A third question served as a thought exercise requiring critical thinking and synthesis. The second served as a final and gave student the opportunity to choose one of two challenges. In the first challenge students were to build a forensic tool kit from existing open source resources and write a comprehensive user's guide on when, how and why to use each tool in acquisition, analysis and presentation during a forensic investigation. In challenge two, students were directed to read Cliff Stoll's book "The Cuckoo's Egg" and write a 7 to 10 page response to one of three prompts. Each of the prompts required analysis, synthesis, critical and creative thinking.

Finally, students completed UTPA's standard Student Evaluation of Teaching Form. Students were encouraged to submit comments in the section with open ended questions.

V. Discussion

Computers, the Internet, e-mail, wireless technology toys, and social networks are pervasive and a ubiquitous part of everyday life. The growth in digital details that are created, captured, and stored in more places than most people realize is exponential as is the growth rate of crimes in which cyber technology is the instrument of, the target of, or by its nature, the location where evidence is stored or recorded. The number of security breaches and threats to personal, organizational, and national safety and the increasing costs of security breaches have created a focus on cyber security[5,14,15,16] and a demand for qualified security professionals in both the private and the public sector[4,7]. Academic institutions respond by offering new courses in cyber security [16] and forensics [10].

A. Challenges to Leverage Potential Synergy

When the Cyber Security and Forensics course was chosen for the GSSL MAIS technology sequence, the delivery was designed as an elective course in the Master's of Computer Science and the Master's of Science in Information Technology (MSIT) programs offered by the Department of Computer Science. Students were expected to be familiar with, operating systems, data structures, programming languages, software application programming and hardware and had typically completed an advanced networking course. The course took a breadth first approach to introducing the fundamentals of computer security and forensics. Students experience theoretical concepts and their implementation. Reflective learning exercises were designed to empower students to link prior knowledge with new knowledge and develop a deep understanding of the complexity of cyber security and forensics theory and practice.

However, with the inclusion of this course in the GSSL MAIS, the demographic profile of students taking the course changes radically. Less than 3% of the students have undergraduate degrees in computer science and are pursuing a Master's degree in Computer Science. The remaining 97% of the students' program affiliations are split fairly evenly between the MSIT and the MAIS. Yet, of this group, only 8% have formal undergraduate training in information technology.

The new demographic includes students who have undergraduate degrees in accounting, computer science, criminal justice, early childhood education, economics, graphic design, information technology, political science, psychology, and sociology. The majority of MAIS students move directly from an undergraduate education in social and behavioral sciences to the MAIS graduate program. Similarly, a number of the MSIT students do not have formal backgrounds in computer science or information technology, but they find themselves working as professionals in information technology. Fortunately many of these students have extensive experience in either networking or management information technology systems. On occasion the class includes a Chief Security Officer from a banking institution or local government agency. This demographic shift among the students taking the course presents a number of challenges to the traditional delivery.

Recognizing that the essential body of knowledge for the domains of security and forensics are broadly distributed and include deep subdomains, the first challenge is to modify the course delivery to take advantage of the diversity in the new demographics body of knowledge. Given the IC CAE program goals, the five Primary Critical Skill Sets [5,6], and the UTPA GSSL program goals and curriculum, an approach to the topics is designed that recognizes that security issues do not rest solely in the domains of Computer Science and Information Technology[18].

Just as NICE has developed the Framework at the national level to provide a common lexicon for understanding categories and specialty areas for education of a cyber workforce, the diversity in students' program of study in this class demands the establishment of a common lexicon in security and forensics. This supports effective communication and facilitates sharing of perspectives and knowledge across disciplines. Students use a forum to provide profiles, including their backgrounds and expertise; their knowledge areas, skills, and abilities (KSAs). A wiki serves as a dictionary for terms and concepts. A second wiki serves as a repository for student contributed resource materials. These wikis create a framework for growing the Essential Body of Knowledge (EBT) [19]. Thus the diversity of academic training, perspectives and experience means that students are exposed to the breadth of knowledge that professionals should know to be conversant in the field of cybersecurity and more generally security. Students, at minimum, know the key concepts and terms to perform their work functions in security and they gain, at least, a basic familiarity with all of the key terms and concepts in the EBT [19].

Thought exercises are used throughout the lectures to provide an opportunity for students to think independently, discuss their thoughts in pairs, and share their ideas with the class. This think-pair-share approach also serves as the basis for work outside of class. Students reflect on concepts and present their thoughts on forums or in the form of short essays. These reflections serve as the basis for conversation and the opportunity to elaborate on ideas. This approach increases personal communication that is necessary to process, organize and retain ideas [20]. The approach takes advantage of the students' diverse knowledge base to expand individual perspectives on security and forensics topics.

The diversity among the students' skill levels in the use and the understanding of computing environments confirmed that labs, originally designed to expose students to the concepts introduced in lecture and discussion are too complex. The labs are modified so that students with minimal background in computing are able to complete the exercises and gain conceptual insight. In addition, interdisciplinary teams are created where each team has at least one individual with a strong background in information technology to assure success. The mix of team KSAs reinforces the development of strong analytical thinking and good communication.

Finally, there is strong interest and investment in information security at the institutional level. Taking advantage of the human capital resources in Privacy and Security and in the Division of Information Technology, Subdomain experts in network security and forensic investigation provide class and lab instruction and guidance. The University's Chief Security Officer along with recognized security experts from the health industry and intelligence community introduce strategic planning for security.

VI. Conclusion

This paper describes a Computer Science course in Cyber Security and Cyber Forensics offered at UTPA. The challenges of offering this course to a multidisciplinary audience lead to changes that leverage the diverse student knowledge base. During the course students learn, practice and gain understanding of concepts and develop the technical and leadership skills required of cyber security professionals. Hands-on lab exercises facilitate understanding of difficult concepts and procedures. Using both commercial and open source tools provides a rich environment. Using interdisciplinary teams facilitates the exchange of knowledge and understanding. Students see how complex the issues in cyber security and forensics are. Students gain an appreciation for true multidisciplinary nature of the field.

Acknowledgment

I would like to recognize Jennifer Garcia Avila for guiding us through EnCase, Ramon Herrera for providing expertise in network security Joe Voje for providing a strategic view for security, Dr. John Abraham for access to resource materials, Jeremy Miller in implementing many of the hands-on-labs and the UTPA IC CAE for coordinating the 2012 Cyber Security Symposium..

References

[1] Quote: Gnereal Keith Alexamder, DIRNSA, CSIS 2010.

[2] Williams, Robin, (2012). How to Plan for Your Cybersecurity Workforce. 26th Annual Conference Federal Information Systems Security Educator's Association, "Making Conncetions in Cubersecurity and Information Security Education" National Institute of Standards and Technology, Gaithersburg Maryland. March 9, 2013. Website: http://csrc.nist.gov/organizations/fissea/2013-conference/presentations/fissea_conf_2013_williams_workforce.pdf

[3] Irvin, Cynthia (2012). "Cyber Security Educaiton in a Time of Change" 21st USENIX Security Symposium, August 8-10, 2012 Bellvue WA, http://csrc.nist.gov/organizations/fissea/2013-conference/presentations/fissea_conf_2013_williams_workforce.pdf

[4] Bush, George. Forward to *The National Strategy to Secure Cyberspace, 2007*. http://www.whitehouse.gov/picpb/cyberspace_stratgey.pdf.

[5] http://csrc.nist.gov/nice/index.htm

[6] Stinikova, Elena and Ray Hunt. "Engging students through refelctive practice assessment within a software security lifecycle." 11-13 June 2012. *Proceedings of the 16th Colloquium for Information Systems Security Education*, Lake Buena Vista, FL. p. 136-141.

[7] Office of the Director of National Intelligence. United State of America. *United States Intelligence Community Centers of Academic Excellence (IC CAE) in National Security Studies, Guidance and Procedures, Program Plan for Fiscal Years 2005 – 2015*. April 2005.

[8] UTPA IGKNU GSSL website: http://portal.utpa.edu/utpa_main/daa_home/csbs_home/csbs_research/igknu_home/igknu_gssl/gssl_grad_deg. Accessed: 20 December, 2012.

[9] Young, William D. "Developng a blended computer security course." 11-13 June 2012. *Proceedings of the 16th Colloquium for Information Systems Security Education*. Lake Buena Vista, FL. p. 128-135.

[10] Chi, Hongmei, Edward L. Jones, Christy Chatmon and Deidre Evans. "Design and implementaiton of digital forensics labs." 22-24 November 2009. *Proceedings of the 12 IASTED International Conference on*

Computers and Advanced Technology in Education. St. Thomas, US Virgin Isalnds. http://www.famu.edu/cis/year2009-Chi-Jones-etal-CATE.pdf Accessed: 22 December 2012.

[11] Eckert, Ben. "Real-world security lab environment." 11-13 June 2012. *Proceedings of the 16th Colloquium for Information Systems Security Education*. Lake Buena Vista, FL. p. 122-127.

[12] Fulton, Steven and Dino Schweitzer. "A concept focused security lab environment." 13-15 June 2011. *Proceedings of the 15th Colloquium for Information Systems Security Education.* Fairborn. Ohio. p. 126-131.

[13] Bishop, Matt and Chip Elliot. "Robust Programming by Example." 9-10 June 2011. *Proceedings of the 7th World Conference on Information Security Education*. Lucerne, Switzerland. p. 23-30.

[14] Mecuri, R. 2003. "Analyzing security costs." *Communication of the ACM.* Vol. 46, no 6, pp 15-18.

[15] "Information security & data breach report, June 2012 update," June 2012. *Navigant*. https://www.privacyassociation.org/media/pdf/knowledge_center/2012_InfoSec_Data_Breach_Report_Navigant.pdf Accessed: July 22012.

[16] Armerding, Taylor, "The 15 Worst data security breaches of the 21st century." *CSO Security and Risk, February 2012*. http://www.csoonline.com/article/700263/the-15-worst-data-security-breaches-of-the-21st-century Accessed: February 2012

[17] Rigby, Steven "Teaching cybersecurity at the 'seams'." 13-15 June 2011. *Proceedings of the 15th Coloquium for Information Systsems Security*. Fairborn Ohio. p. 69-74.

[18] Nance, Kara L. and Brian Hay. "A breadth-first approach to computer security. 2-4 June 2008. " *Proceedings of the 12th Colloquium for Information Systems Security Education*. Dallas, TX. p. 139-146.

[19] Roth-Perreault, Ellen and Brenda Oldfield. "Strengthening the security workforce: a competency and functional framework for information technology security professionals." 4-7 June 2007. *Proceedings of the 11th Colloquium for Infomration Systems Security Education*. Boston, MA. p. 22-27.

[20] Pimm, D. (1987). *Speaking mathematically: Communication in mathematics classrooms*. New York. Routledge & Kegan Paul.

A Load Service Structure Using a P2P Network Based Reputation System in Ad-hoc Networks

Ming-Chang Huang
Department of Business Information Systems / Operation Management
University of North Carolina at Charlotte
mhuang5@uncc.edu

Abstract

Since hosts in an ad-hoc network moves dynamically, it is important how wireless hosts find other hosts securely and efficiently for load service purposes. This paper presents a method for load services in computer networks with a new reputation system to check available host reputation to avoid free-riding problems in P2P network file sharing. It uses databases for directory agents to save information provided by load-server agents and build protocols that how a host can find available hosts for load service and load transfer purposes when it moves to a new region. This includes how a directory agent builds its database, how a load-server agent provides its services, and how a load-client agent gets the services it needs. Fuzzy logic control method is applied to transfer loads for load balancing, instead of the fixed threshold level methods. The purpose of this new system structures is to provide efficient ways in building communication and accessing resources in ad-hoc computer network systems. This helps users to find data easily and securely.

Keywords: Load and Web Service, Ad-Hoc Network, Directory Agent, P2P network, Reputation System

Appropriate Track(s): Security Management, Network Security

1. Introduction

Computer networks can provide parallel computation and services. It is important that hosts send their loads to other hosts for certain function implementation through network transfer. With the increasing popularity of mobile communications and mobile computing, the demand for load services and load balancing grows. When a computer is overloaded or it needs special services from other computers, it may send requests to other computers for load transfer or load services. For example, a computer may need some jobs to be executed with higher quality of services or it needs some jobs to be done with a short period of time that its processor is too slow to perform the jobs; therefore, it may send part those jobs to other computers with higher speeds of processors. Since wireless networks have been wild used in recent years, how a host transfers its loads to other nodes has becomes a very important issue because not all wireless hosts have the ability to manipulate all their loads. For instance, a host with low battery power cannot finish all its jobs on time and should transfer some of them to other hosts. Currently, most of load balancing algorithms are based on wired network environments, it is important to find an efficient way for load service purposes.

Before a wireless host transfers its loads to other hosts or asks for load services from other hosts, it has to find available hosts using resource allocation algorithms. There are several resource allocation protocols been developed, for example, IEFT Service Location Protocol (SLP) [1] and Jini [2] software package from Microsystems. However, these protocols address how to find the resources in wired networks, not in wireless networks. Maab [3] develops a location information server for location-aware applications based on the X.500 directory service and the lightweight directory access protocol LDAP [4]; while it does not cover some important issues about the movements of mobile hosts, for example, how to generate a new directory service and how a host gets the new services, when a directory agent moves away its original region. In an Ad-Hoc network, system structure is dynamic and hosts can join or leave any time. Therefore, how to provide load services and how to find available hosts providing load services become importance issues in an Ad-Hoc network system.

To find a host which can fulfill the load service purpose, the requesting host also has to make sure that the host it is looking for has good reputation in load services. For good reputation hosts, they will have to share their resources as well besides just requesting resources from other hosts. It is called the "free-riding" situation if a host only requests resources from other hosts without sharing it resources to others. Measurement study of free-riding on Gnutella was first reported by [10] in 2000 which indicated that approximately 70% of Gnutella users did not share any files and nearly 50% queries were responded from top 1% peers. However, according to the most recently measurement study, the percentage of free riders rises to 85% [11]. It is very possible that a small number of peers who are willing to share information take most of the job loadings in P2P networks. As a result, the prevalence of free riders will eventually downgrade the performance of entire system and would make the system vulnerable [12].

This paper addresses a system structure for load services with reputation checking in wireless Ad-Hoc network systems using peer-to-peer concept [8, 9]. In Ad-Hoc network systems, hosts move dynamically without base stations for communication. The load service architecture provides special services upon requests from hosts and these services, e.g., include resource location services and load balancing services. A host may send its special requests to other hosts for load services or send its loads for load balancing. The requests include service types the host needs or the amount of loads to be sent to other hosts. For those special services, the host should define the conditions that other hosts may accept the services. For example, the request includes the price of job execution, the limit requirement of execution time, etc. Besides looking for the desired resources, the requesting host also check the requested host's reputation to avoid "free-riding" cases [7].

In this paper, Section 2 presents the system structure. Section 3 expresses the details of the method. Section 4 and section 5 illustrate the information format for databases, and the scalability respectively. The conclusion is in Section 6.

2. System structures

This section describes the structure used in the system. Basically, there are three components in my load service system – directory agent, load-server agent and load-client agent. A load-server agent provides load services that are queried by other hosts (load-client agents) which require load services. Load-server agents post the types of services periodically to their directory agents to update the services they can provide to load-client agents. A load-client agent is a host in the network, which may need some services performed by other hosts. It sends requests to its directory agents to ask for services from load-server agents when it is heavily loaded or it needs some special services, which it does not have the ability to perform. A directory agent forms groups for both load-server agents and load-client agents respectively and builds a database for service queries from load-client agents.

Figure 1 shows an example based on the architecture of my load service system. Figure 2 shows the structure of the reputation system (FuzRep) [7] which is used in the paper. Each directory agent has a query database, which stores all the query information from load-server agents. Load-server agents and load-client agents may join directory agents upon requests. In Figure 1, for example, Load-server Agent 1 and Load-client Agent 1 register with Directory Agent 1; Load-server Agent 2 registers with Directory Agent 1 and Directory Agent 2 at the same time. Load-client Agent 1 may send requests to Directory Agent 1 for querying load services and Directory Agent 1 checks its database and the reputation system to find fitted load-server agents and sends those available load-server agent addresses to Load-client Agent 1. The fitted load-server agents can be Load-server Agent 1, Load-server Agent 2, or both. Load-client Agent 1 can choose one of them based on its best convenience; or it can choose both of them for special purposes. Of course, it is possible that none of the load-server agents can be found.

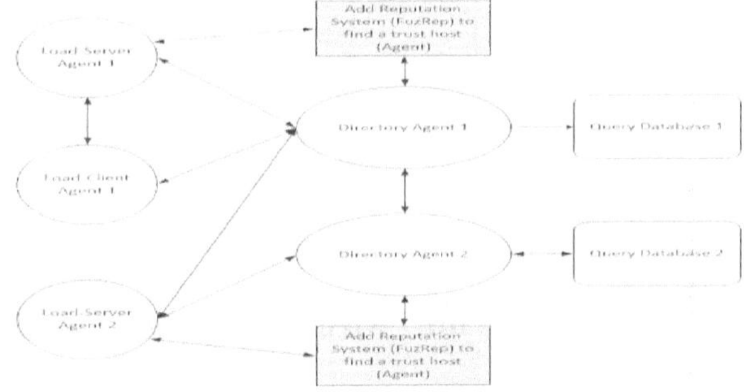

Figure 1: Load service system architecture with FuzRep Reputation System

FuzRep is a design of a fuzzy-based reputation system for P2P networks. It includes three techniques – reputation determination, selective polling, and service differentiation. This paper is going to describe how FuzRep works by revealing answers of the following questions.

- How to determine a peer's reputation level? What are the criteria? How to transfer a crisp score to a reputation level? How to maintain it?
- How and when to share the contribution information?
- How to encourage sharing and discourage free riding? How to differentiate the service level?

In FuzRep_M1, a peer's reputation is determined by its contributions to the communities. A peer saves transaction information into local transaction repository, including requesters' or providers' IDs, and accumulated contribution scores. The transaction repository is updated after every successful transaction. The initial local contribution score is set to zero originally for pre-unknown peers at their first interactions. A global accumulated contribution score is used to determine corresponding peer's reputation. It is built on two phase computes – personal reputation inference and global reputation deduction. Personal reputation inference simply fetches a peer's contribution score from its transaction repository. If a file provider chooses to determine a file request's reputation simply based on its experience, personal reputation inference fits that purpose. Otherwise, the file provider should run the global reputation deduction process using the selective polling reputation sharing process. [7]

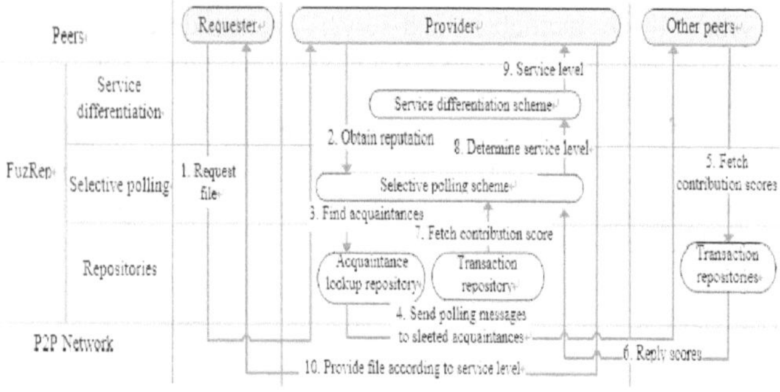

Figure 2. FuzRep architecture and operational processes

3. Algorithm for wireless ad-hoc load services

There are several issues considered when designing our system architecture, which includes, for example, how a directory agent asks a host to register with its database, the effects of the movement of mobile hosts to the join of load-server and load-client agents, and fault tolerance of the system. Below is the detail how hosts join or leave directory agents and how directory agents form their databases when they move.

It also describes how a load-client agent should pay load-server agents that it asks the services from and how hosts in the system gain tokens in order to pay the services it need. How to transfer loads between load-server agents and load-client agents is also mentioned in this section.

3.1 A directory agent asks hosts for registration

In order to collect load service information from other hosts and provide results for queries, a directory agent builds a query database. The information in the database includes the addresses of load-server agents which provide information, the service types, or the loads that load-server agents can accept. The host can be a desk computer or a laptop once it has the ability; for example, it has high-speed processors, enough power for communication, etc. The method how a directory agent asks for registration is discussed below.

1. A directory agent broadcasts a message to the other hosts within the range that its power can reach.
2. A host, which receives the broadcast message from a directory agent and is willing to register with the directory agent's database as a load-server agent, sends an ACK message to the directory agent for registration. The ACK message includes information, such as the service types it can perform and/or the loads it can accept, etc., provided by a load-server agent.
3. The directory agent keeps the ACK information in its query database and therefore builds a link from itself to the load-server agent sending the ACK message.
4. To check if a load-server agent is still available in the database, a directory agent periodically sends multicast messages to all the load-server agents, which have query information in its database. This purpose for this is for database information update because load-server agents might move away anytime. When a load-server agent receives a query message from a directory agent, it should send back a response to the directory agent to indicate that it is still existed in the directory agent's power range. If the directory agent does not get the acknowledgement from a load-server agent that has query information in the database, it deletes the information provided by that load-server agent from its database and therefore deletes the link between them. The Figure 3 demonstrates the steps how a directory agent builds its query database.

(1) A directory agent sends requests to hosts for registration.
(2) Hosts, which are willing to register as load-server agents, send ACKs back to the directory agent.
(3) The directory agent saves all the information in those ACKs to its database for future use.
(4) The directory agent also builds links between itself and its load-server agents.

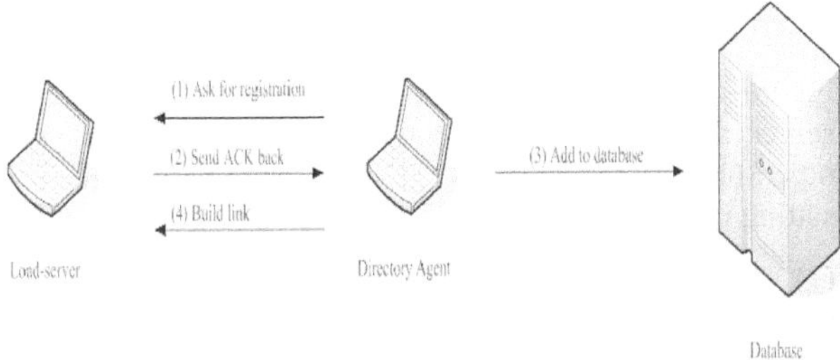

Figure 3: The procedures for a directory agent asks for registration

3.2 A host join directory agent's databases as a load-server agents

A mobile host may join directory agents' databases as a *load-server* agent when it has the ability to provide services, or it is lightly loaded and is willing to accept loads from other hosts. Not only a load-server agent may join a directory agent, but also it may join multiple directory agents. A load-server agent joins directory agent's databases in two ways.

Method 1: The first method is that it sends out messages to ask for registering with directory agents within its power range and waits for the replies from those directory agents. After receiving acknowledgements from directory agents, the mobile host registers with the databases of those directory agents by sending its address, the service types it can provide, and the amount of loads it can accept for load transfer. A mobile host can register with several directory agents at the same time; which means a mobile host can join several databases simultaneously.

Method 2: The second method, like the method in Section 3.1, is that a mobile host receives messages from some directory agents for requesting joining their databases. Thereafter, the mobile host may join those databases by replying acknowledgements (ACKs) back to those directory agents and the directory agents add the ACKs into their databases.

After the directory agents receive the ACKs from load-server agents, they build links between them. The following figure illustrates the procedures of Method 1 for a load-server agent to a directory agent database.

(1) A host sends request to directory agents for registering as a load-server agent.
(2) Directory agents send ACKs back to the host when they receive the request and allow it to join their databases.
(3) The host sends registration information to those directory agents once it receives the ACKs.
(4) Those directory agents add the information into their databases.
(5) The directory agents also build links between themselves and the load-server agent.

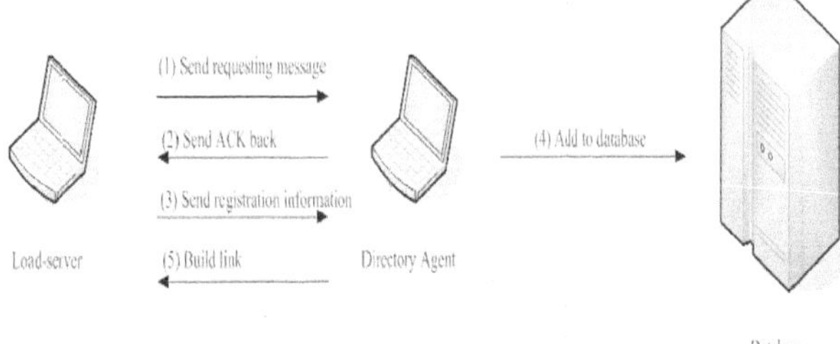

Figure 4: How a load-server joins a directory agent database for Method 1

3.3 Queries from load-client agents

A mobile host may join directory agents' databases as a *load-client* agent when it needs services from other hosts. Since directory agents broadcast their addresses periodically to ask for mobile hosts to register for services, a load-client agent can find the addresses of directory agents from those broadcasting messages. When a load-client agent needs load services, it sends queries to directory agents that it can contact and waits for the replies from them. The contents in these replies include the addresses of available load-server agents that can provide the services the load-client agent asks. The load-client agent may receive several replies from different load-server agents at the same time and it chooses the best-fit one. If it cannot find available load-server agents (without any reply from directory agents in a period of time), it waits for a certain period of time and sends queries again.

A load-client agent selects the best-fit load-server agent based on the service conditions it requests. For example, it may choose the one that satisfies the price the load-client agent asks. When a load-client agent selects the best-fit load-server agent, it directly sends service requirements or loads to the chosen load-server agent. Figure 5 shows the steps.

(1) A load-client agent sends query to directory agents to request services
(2) Directory agents apply the FuzRep reputation system to the requesting host for a free-rider check. Then the Directory agents search their database for the desired services requested by the load-client agent. Before the Directory agents send back searching information, they also apply the FuzRep reputation system to the load-server agents to avoid free-riding.
(3) Directory agents send replies back, which indicate the information they have in the databases.

(4) The load-client agent gets the services it needs from load-server agents.

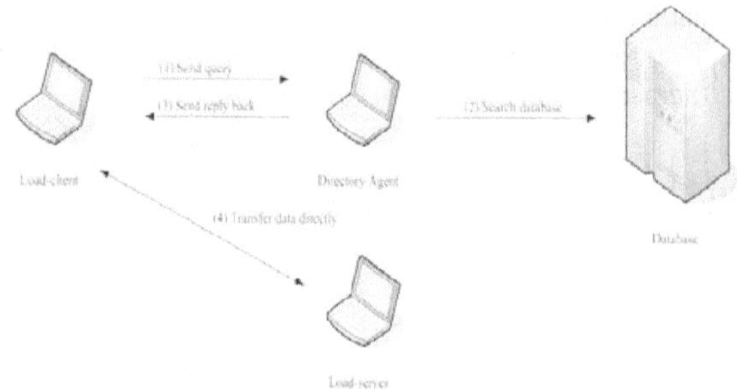

Figure 5: How a load-client agent sends queries

3.4 Movement of directory agents

When a directory agent moves to another region, it loses all the information in its database about load-server agents and its peer directory agents. How a directory agent notifies all the other agents about its movement becomes an important issue. There are two ways that other agents can detect the leave of a directory agent. The first is that the directory agent sends a message to notify other hosts about its movement. Hosts receiving the message will stop sending queries to this directory agent and remove the links between them.

The second method is to use the fact that hosts cannot detect the existence of a directory agent. Since load-server agents send update information to a directory agent periodically, load-server agents can notice that a directory agent does not exist in the region if hosts do not get the reply from that directory agent. For a load-client agent to detect the existence of a directory agent, if it does not receive any broadcast message during a period of time, then it deletes the link to that directory agent.

After moving to a new region, a directory agent sends messages to hosts in the power range it can reach to ask for hosts to join its database for load services as discussed in section 3.1. It may happen that some hosts do not have any directory agent to contact to once a directory agent moves away. Those hosts will keep sending messages to other hosts for finding new directory agents as described in section 3.2 and 3.3.

3.5 Movement of load-server agent

When a load-server agent moves to a new region, it may lose its original directory agents and it has to establish new links to its new directory agents as described in section 3.2. Once a directory agent does not receive update information from a load-server agent for a period of time, it deletes the information about that load-server agent from its database and therefore deletes the link between them.

3.6 An example

Figure 6 illustrates a flow how a directory agent, load-server agent, and load-client agent communicates each other. (1), (2), (3), (4), and (5) indicate the procedures for setting up the processes.

(1) A Directory Agent broadcasts join message to hosts.
(2) Load-Server Agent replies an acknowledgement to that Directory Agent to join the database.
(3) Directory Agent saves the information to its database.
(4) Load-Server Agent sends requests to Directory Agent for load services.
(5) Directory sends the address of Load-Server Agent if Load-Server Agent is suitable for load service.
(6) Load-Client Agent communicates with Load-Server Agent directly.

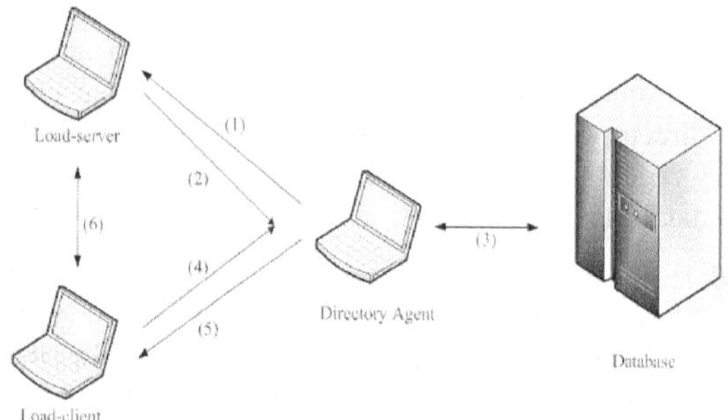

Figure 6: An Example for Communications between Agents

3.7 Load transfer

A host may transfer loads to other hosts when it is heavily loaded. Instead of using fixed threshold method to decide whether a host is heavily loaded, it uses fuzzy logic control method to improve the performance. First, the host finds an available host by sending service request as mentioned before. Once it finds a host that accepts its request for load transfer, it transferred its loads to the selected host. The amount of loads to be transferred is equal to half of the difference of loads between the load-client agent and the load-server agent. It is possible that there are several server load-server agents, which satisfy the request by a load-client agent. In order to reduce the distance and moving effect, a load-client chooses the load-server agent that is the closest one to it. Figure 7, for example, shows the power range that load-client agent C can reach and there are three load-server agents – S1, S2, and S3 – which satisfy the request from agent C. Since S1 is the closest one to C, it is chosen which C will transfer its loads to.

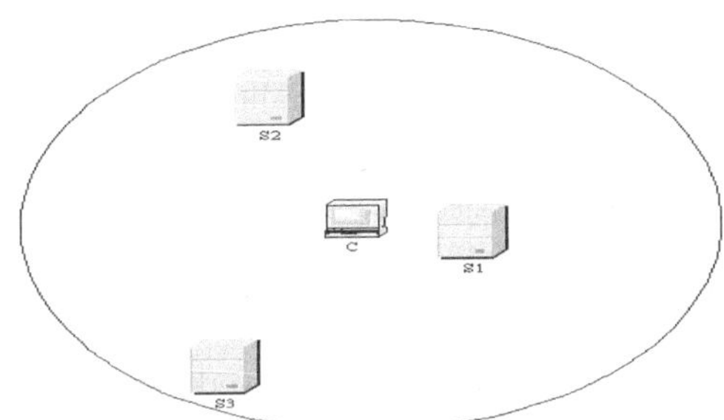

Figure 7: An example for a load-client agent to choose a best-fit load-server agent

The following steps show the details of load transfer.

(1) When a host detects that it is heavily loaded, it broadcasts a request message to hosts in its power range to ask for load transfer service. Instead of using fixed threshold levels to check if it is lightly loaded or heavily loaded, it uses fuzzy logic control [5] to check its queue status to improve the performance. This method is mentioned in [6, 7].

(2) Hosts, which receive the request, check their queue status using fuzzy logic control method, and returns ACKs, if they are lightly loaded, to the load-client agent that sent the request.

(3) When the load-client agent gets the ACKs from load-server agents, it chooses the load-server agent, which is the first one to send its ACK, for load transfer. That means that the load-client agent chooses the closest one in order to improve the performance.

(4) If there are no available hosts in the load-client agent power range, the load-client agent sends requests to its directory agents to look for the registered load-server agents for load transfer. Then it waits for the responses from its directory agents.

(5) The directory agents find available (lightly loaded) load-server agents when they receive requests from a load-client agent. Then, the directory agents send addresses of these available load-server agents to that load-client agent for load transfer. The load-client chooses the best host to transfer its loads to the selected host.

4. Service type format and service price

In the future, it is possible that hosts have to pay if they ask for service from other hosts. In this section, it discusses this situation and defines the service type format for load services and the price for each service. This format is for a directory agent to store the information in its database. Figure 8 shows the format that there are 4 fields in it – *address, service-type, number-of-tokens,* and *load.*

The *address* field is the address of a load-server agent, so that a load-client can directly connect to it. The *service-type* field indicates which kind of services that a load-server agent provides. The *number-of-tokens* shows the price of a service for a load-client to pay, and the *load* field shows the current load for a load-server agent. When a load-server agent provides load services to directory agents, it provides directory agents the information about the type(s) of services it can provides, the tokens (price) for a load-client agent to take the service, and the current load status and address for the load-server agent. A load-client agent can get the service only it matched the service type, and the price that the load-server agents ask, or it can find an available load-server agent for load transfer purpose if the load-server agent is lightly loaded and the load-client agent can pay the price.

address	*Service-type*	*Number-of-tokens*	*Load*

Figure 8: Service Type Format Stored

There are some assumptions in our architecture for hosts.

1. A load-client agent has to pay a load-server agent when it needs load services from that load-server agent.
2. When sending a request to a directory agent, a host loses tokens as the price for asking load service.
3. In order to increase the number of tokens and therefore increase the ability to ask for services, a host must try its best to gain tokens. There are two possible ways to implement it. First of all, a host can provide the services to other hosts to gain tokens. Secondly, a host should avoid sending useless requests to network to save tokens. This can be implemented by increasing the waiting time for a load-client agent to send requests. This also may avoid network congestion because the number of messages is reduced.
4. A load-client agent may find several available load-server agents for a particular request such that those load-server agents satisfy the requirements for the load-client agent. Then the client host has to choose the best-fit one.
5. If a host does not have enough tokens to find a load-server agent for load services, it should stop sending requests to its directory agents for asking load services until it can provide enough tokens.

The request message, which a load-client agent sends out when it needs a service, includes a price that the load-client agent can pay. The directory agent, which receives the message, finds available load-server agents by comparing the key words and the prices. For example, if a host needs a service with higher speed calculation, it sends requests to its directory agents. In these requests, the speed of the load-server agent's processor and the price the load-client agent can provide are included. Directory agents match these requirements to the information via the key words and the number of tokens in their database and therefore find the available load-server agents. The addresses of those load-server agents are sent to the requesting load-client agent. Upon receiving those addresses, the load-client agent chooses one available and sends jobs directly to that load-server agent. To choose an available load-server agent from those addresses by directory agents, the load-client agent may choose the one, which asks the lowest number of tokens for performing the requesting service.

5. Scalability

As the number of clients and servers in the network system increase, so does the burden to the system because of the increases of messages for service discovery and request. When a host joins or roams into a network, it sends out requests. If there are too many hosts that move too frequently, they may send many requests, which may cause the congestion of the network. Therefore, careful consideration of scalability issues is very important to the design of the protocols. In this system, number of tokens (the price to pay) is used to control the scalability of load-server agents registered with directory agents and load-client agents sending load service requests. For example, a client host cannot send requests to directory agents for services if it does not have enough tokens. It should provide its services to other hosts to gain enough tokens before it sends requests.

6. Conclusion

This paper introduces a new load service method in wireless ad-hoc networks using a reputation system to check nodes' reputation. Since the hosts in a wireless ad-hoc network can move anywhere by anytime, it is difficult for a host to find other host for load service or load transfer purposes. Several issues are discussed in this paper - how a directory agent asks for hosts to register as load-server agents, how a load-server agent registers in directory agents' databases, how a load-client agent finds available load-server agents when it need load services. Directory agents can find the available load-servers which provide services the clients need. Directory agents can also apply the FuzRep reputation system to check the clients and servers' reputation to load and services requests. This is to avoid free-riding situation in P2P network systems.

This paper also discusses a new concept that a host should pay the price when it needs services from other hosts in networks and how it works by using token as the price in the networks. The token concept is also used to control the scalability of networks and congestion control of network flow.

References

[1] E. Guttman, C. Perkins, J. Veizades and M. Day, "Service Location Protocol," Version 2, IEFT, RFC 2165, November 1998.

[2] J. Waldo, "The Jini Architecture for network-centric computing," Communication of the ACM, pp 76-82, July 1999.

[3] H. Maab, "Location-Aware Mobile Application Based on Directory Services," MOBICOM 97, pp 23-33.

[4] W. Yeong, T. Howes, and S. Kille, "Lightweight Directory Access Protocol," RFC 1777, March 1995.

[5] Ross, T. J., Fuzzy Logic with Engineering Applications, McGraw Hill, 1995.

[6] Huang, M., S. H. Hosseini, and K. Vairavan, "Load Balancing in Computer Networks," Proceedings of ISCA 15th International Conference on Parallel and Distributed Computing Systems (PDCS-2002), Special session in Network Communication and Protocols. Held in the GALT HOUSE Hotel, Louisville, Kentucky, Sep. 19 - 21.

[7] Ross, T. J., Fuzzy Logic with Engineering Applications, McGraw Hill, 1995.

[8] Andy Oram et al., "Peer-to-Peer:Harnessing the Power of Disruptive Technologies," Oreilly 2001.

[9] Stephanos Androutsellis-Theotokis and Diomidis Spinellis, "A survey of peer-to-peer content distribution technologies," *ACM Computing Surveys*, 36(4):335–371, December 2004. doi:10.1145/1041680.1041681.

[10] Adar, E., and Huberman, B. A. Free riding on Gnutella. *First Monday* 5, 10 (October 2000).

[11] Hughes, D., Coulson, G., and Walkerdine, J. Free riding on Gnutella revisited: the bell tolls? In *IEEE Distributed Systems Online* 6, 6 (June 2005).

[12] Ramaswamy, L. and Liu, L. Free riding: A new challenge to peer-to-peer file sharing systems. In Proceedings of 36th Hawaii International Conference on System Sciences (HICSS'03) (January 2003)

DES Based Educational Encryption System

Chadi Riman, Hicham H. Hallal
Fahad Bin Sultan University
Tabuk, Saudi Arabia
{criman, hhallal}@fbsu.edu.sa

Abstract

We present a simple encryption system that uses the main features of the Data Encryption Standard (DES) to be used mainly for educational purposes. The proposed Educational Data Encryption System (E-DES) is meant to facilitate the process of teaching cryptography and data encryption techniques in classrooms. The proposed cipher, which uses the same general Feistel structure, presents some improvements on the existing DES. It uses 1024 bit initial key and 128 bit data block size. In addition, the F function itself is modified n E-DES, where an AES like substitution is used to replace the DES substitution. Consequently, the proposed encryption system provides more security to the plain data by adding more diffusion through the encryption process. In addition, the sizes of the data block and the round keys ensure a high resilience to information leak (almost similar to AES).

Keywords: Cryptography, DES, AES, Data Encryption, Decryption, Information Security.

1. Introduction

Data Security is increasingly occupying more interest in the research work in both academia and the industry. The concern to preserve the security pyramid; confidentiality, integrity, and authentication, is always present and pauses continuous questions how to improve the existing techniques for data protection against ongoing attempts to breach them, and how to develop novel ones that cannot be breached. For decades, encryption has been one of the most reliable methods used to protect data confidentiality and integrity even since the old days of the Romans. Several encryption techniques (ciphers) have been proposed over the years following the need to protect more data, to reinforce existing techniques against successful attacks, and to cope with the advances in technology that make the development of a cipher that is immune against all types of attacks quite a tricky task. For the past few decades, the Data Encryption Standard (DES) [5] has been treated as the cipher to breach and to compromise. This was achieved mainly due to weaknesses in the cipher itself. DES was built based on a key of 56 bits. However, only 48 bits where effectively used in the F module of each round. On the other hand, the data block was set at 64 bits. This resulted in relatively easier (when almost exponential increases in computation power are factored in) attacks on the cipher.

Ultimately, DES was phased out and replaced by the Advanced Encryption Standard (AES) [5] as the standard for data encryption. However, the interest in the DES itself did not vanish as it had already become an integral part of the data security solutions of many industrial organizations. Consequently, the focus shifted to reinforce the DES cipher and to improve its resilience against cryptanalysis techniques and against attacks. In [5], Triple DES was introduced, where the same DES algorithm is applied repetitively on the data blocks to produce more resilient ciphered text. The cost for the increased security was primarily factored in the speed of execution while the man in the middle attack remained a threat. In [4] Enhanced–DES was proposed as an improvement on DES, where the difference was in randomizing the generation of the 56 bit round keys from the initial key. The rest of the cipher design remains intact. This can add to the diffusion of the ciphered data, but does not add to the key security since the 56 bit keys are still generated from the same initial key and they are still somehow correlated. In [6], a hybrid cryptographic algorithm that combines features from both Des and AES to produce a more resilient cipher. However, the main weakness that hampered DES remains in the proposed hybrid cipher since it uses the same data block and key size. Meanwhile, some work appeared recently, where the focus is on improving the AES cipher. The work in [1] describes an improved AES that features a modified S-box that can be generated dynamically from the cipher key. This makes the S-box changing in each round, which adds to the confusion associated with the ciphered text.

In this work, we propose a modified version of the Data Encryption Standard (DES), which uses an enlarged initial key and a larger data block. We propose to use a 1024 bit initial key, from which 16 independent 64-bit round keys are derived. The size of the proposed key provides immunity against brute force attacks even with actual computational resources. The 64 bit key are used completely in the rounds (without any omissions), which adds to the resilience within each round. On the other hand, a data block of 128 bits, similar to AES, provides efficient resistance against information leak (256 billion GB of data can be encrypted using a single key while DES ensured 32GB). In addition, we propose to use separate AES like S-boxes for substitution in the F function, which means more independence and diffusion in the production of the ciphered data.

The remainder of this paper is organized as follows. Section 2 presents an overview of the DES and AES encryption techniques. Section 3 describes the proposed E-DES cipher and details the encryption algorithm. Section 4 describes the decryption algorithm of E-DES. Section 5 presents a discussion on the efficiency of the E-DES cipher and its advantages. Finally, Section 6 concludes the paper and presents potential extensions of this work.

2. Overview of Encryption Standards

Introduced in 1977, the Data Encryption Standard (DES) is a symmetric block cipher that is based on the Feistel structure with a block size of 64 bits and a key size of 64 bits. Despite being compromised, DES is s till being used to provide data security by many sectors including the American Bankers Association's and in several security standards like the *IP Security Architecture* (IPSec) standard [9]. DES uses 16 rounds of a Feistel like encryption method to encrypt plain text. A key schedule is used to derive 16 keys for the successive rounds of encryption from the original key. The block diagram of one round of DES is shown in Figure 1.

Although DES uses a 64-bit key; 8 of these bits are only used for odd parity and do not count in the key length. The effective key length of DES is 56 bits which means 2^{56} possible different keys. A full 64-bit key has 256 times as many key combinations. In addition to the short key, the DES key schedule does not guarantee random keys for the 16 encryption rounds (The generated keys can be all-ones, all-zeros, or distinguishable patterns of ones and zeros [8]).

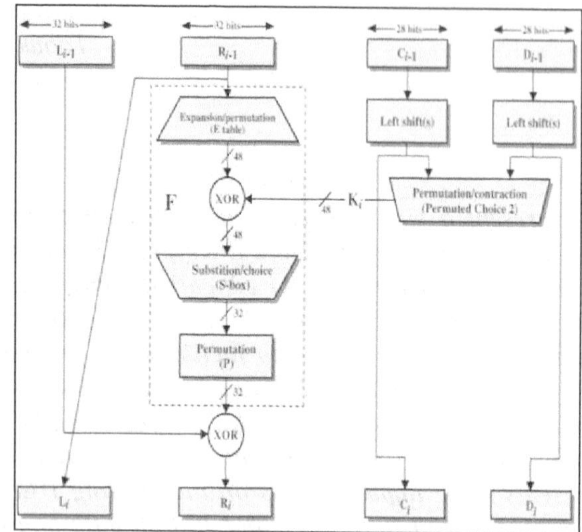

Figure 1. Depiction of one round of DES [5].

This made it possible for techniques based on differential and linear cryptanalysis [5] to attack the DES. Moreover, using a brute force key search seems not so difficult with the computation power levels in recent computer systems. Consequently, the Triple DES (3-DES) was introduced to solve the key problems of DES. In a typical implementation of the 3-DES cipher, the plaintext is encrypted with one key. The resulting cipher text is decrypted with another key, and, finally, the resulting text is encrypted again with the initial key (first key used). This implementation of the 3-DES uses two different keys. However, implementations with three different keys are also possible. Compared to DES, 3-DES offers a key length of 112 bits. This is an improvement of 2^{56} combinations over the 56 bit key. Although the problem of short key is solved with 3-DES, the problem with of (relatively) non random key generation remained in 3-DES but with a reduced effect. In addition, 3-DES is almost one third as fast as DES.

The Advanced Encryption Standard (AES), also known as the Rijndael cipher, was introduced in 2000. It uses 128, 192, or 256 bit key for encryption. This provides improvements of 2^{72}, 2^{136}, and 2^{200} over the 56 bit DES key, respectively. With longer keys, it became much harder to break the AES. In addition, AES compensated another shortcoming of the DES, the block size. AES encrypts blocks of 128 bits, which means it is more resilient against information leak (caused by repetitive blocks). Using DES, one can encrypt up to 32GB with a single key

[7]. On the other hand, AES allows 256 billion gigabytes to be processed with the same key before any leak can occur. Moreover, while DES uses the Feistel network, where the text block is divided into two halves before going through the encryption steps, AES applies a series of substitution and permutation steps to create the encrypted block.

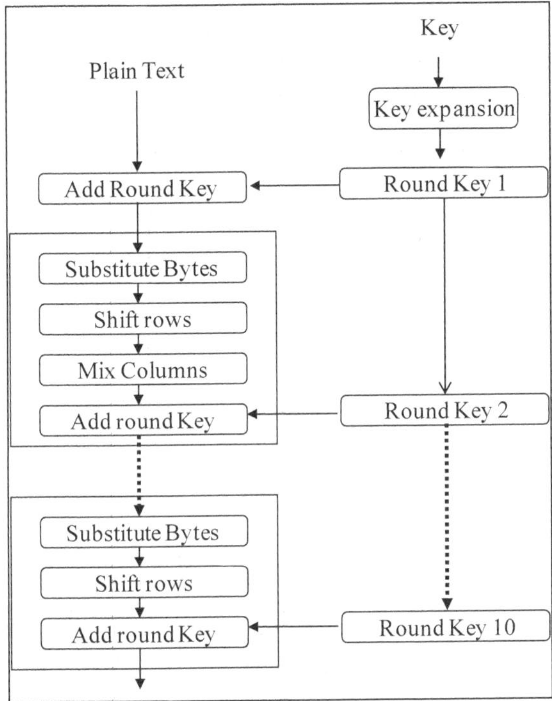

Figure 2. Block diagram of the AES cipher.

The following table [8], shows a summary of the comparison between the DES and the AES ciphers.

Table 1: DES vs. AES

	DES	AES
Key Length	56 bits	128, 192, or 256 bits
Cipher Type	Symmetric	Symmetric
Block (bits)	64	128, 192, or 256
Developed	1977	2000
Security	Proven inadequate	Considered secure
Possible Keys	2^{56}	2^{128}, 2^{192}, or 2^{256}
Time for brute force key attack	400 days	5 x 10^{21} years

3. The Educational Data Encryption System

We present E-DES, the Educational Data Encryption Standard as an enhancement of DES. The main changes proposed to implement E-DES include a larger key and block size, an improved F function in each round, an improved key schedule, and more complex permutation functions. In addition, the proposed cipher uses one of the components from AES, the substitution box; thus the name E-DES. In this section, we describe E-DES and detail its components.

Similar to DES, E-DES relies mainly on the Feistel Network with 16 rounds, where the first operation is application of the initial permutation of the plaintext. Then, each round consists of the sequence:

1. The permuted plaintext is split into two halves, left and right.
2. Right half text moves to the left without any manipulation, and left half is XORed with the output of a function F that takes round key and right half as inputs.

Finally, after 16 rounds are completed, the inverse initial permutation is applied to the produced text yielding the ciphered text block. This structure is illustrated in Figure 3.

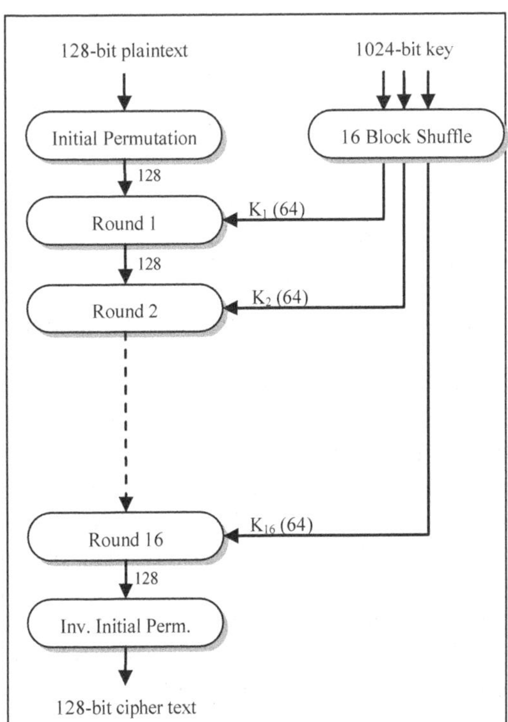

Figure3. General Encryption Structure

As mentioned earlier, E-DES uses a larger plain text block and initial key sizes. The plaintext block in E-DES is 128 bits and the initial key size is 1024 bits. In detail, the initial plaintext is divided into two 64 bit blocks, and each block is encoded separately. The cipher consists of 16 rounds: the first round is preceded with an initial permutation (IP) and last round is followed by an inverse initial permutation (IP^{-1}). The 1024 bit key is divided into 16 separate sub-keys for the 16 rounds, yielding sub-keys is of 64 bits each. The 16 keys, which are completely independent, are shuffled using a key permutation function before being distributed to rounds, which adds to the randomness of the sub key generation, thus making the recognition of round keys more difficult.

Then, each round i consists of:

1. Dividing text P_i into two halves right R_i and left L_i
2. Swapping right half input to left half output ($L_{i+1} = R_i$),
3. Performing XOR on the left half input with the function F, and sending result to right half output ($R_{i+1} = L_i \oplus F(R_i, K_i)$).

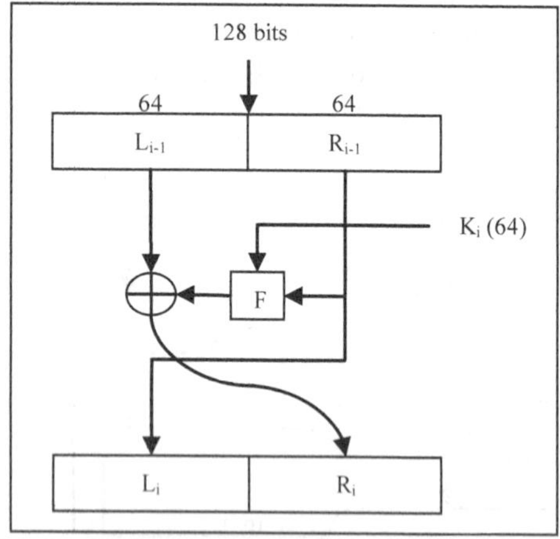

Figure 4: One Round Encryption Structure.

Figure 4 shows the general structure of each round in E-DES. As to the function F, it takes two inputs: the right half input of the text and the round key. F consists of a first permutation P1 on the text (right hand 64 bits of the text). The result is XORed with the Round Key (also kept at 64 bits). The output is treated as 8 blocks of 1 byte each. The 8 blocks are then shuffled and passed through 8 different AES like substitution boxes (S1 to S8). The results of the 8 Substitution boxes are merged again to 64 bits, and then passed to a second permutation P2, which leads to the final output of the F function. Figure 5 shows the complete structure of function F. The main difference between the proposed S-boxes in E-DES from the use of the S-box in AES is the independence between the different S-boxes proposed here for each 8 bit blocks.

Each substitution box, which takes 8 bits input and gives 8 bits output, consists of 16 rows and 16 column bytes. The left 4 bits of the input determine one row, and the right 4 bits determine one column. The byte intersection of the selected row and column is the output of the substitution.

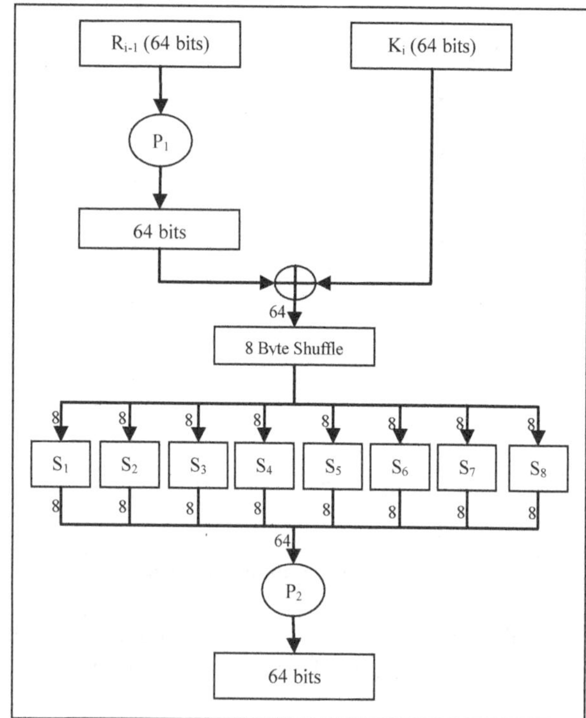

Figure 5: Structure of Function F.

4. Decryption of E-DES

As in the case of DES, decryption of E-DES is similar to encryption starting with cipher text. After Initial Permutation (IP), last round of encryption is applied to cipher text with the last round key. Rounds are visited in reverse order until the first round. Finally, inverse initial permutation is applied, and plaintext is completely retrieved. This is depicted in Figure 6.

Each round consists of dividing data into two halves right and left, swapping left half input to right half output ($R_{i-1} = L_i$), then performing XOR on right half input with a function F, and sending result to right half output ($L_{i-1} = R_i$ XOR $F(L_i, K_i)$). Figure 7 shows each round's structure.

5. Analysis

In this section, we discuss the main advantages of E-DES and its enhancement compared to DES. The first strong aspect of E-DES is the text block size which is 128 bits (64 bits on DES). Second, the initial key is 1024 bits (56 bits for DES), and the round keys are 64 bits (48 bits effective in DES). Third, round keys are derived independently from the original key, which is divided into 16 sub keys. The sub-keys are then permuted before being used for the respective rounds.

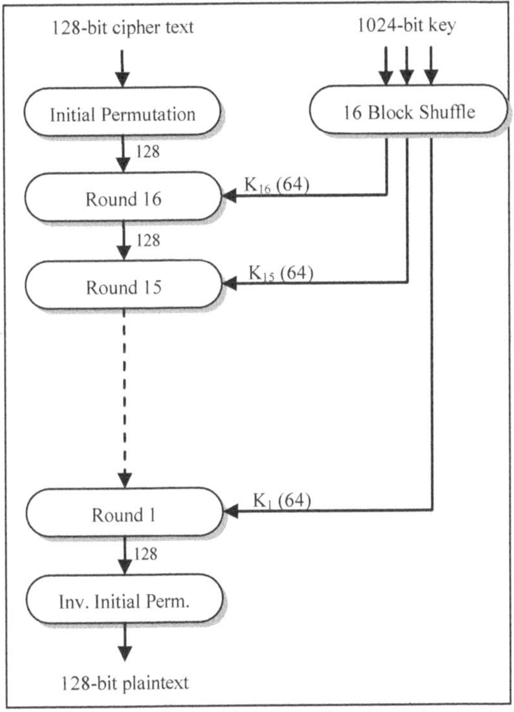

Figure 6: Overall decryption structure.

On the other hand, the function F itself features 8 independent one byte substitution boxes similar to AES compared to the 8, 6 to 4 bit, DES S-boxes. In addition, 8 byte shuffle (permutation) is performed in F before entering into the S-boxes.

In terms of implementation of E-DES, the algorithm via software is fairly simple, even simpler than DES, especially for the round key generation, which is fairly direct and simple since all sub-keys are independent. As is the case in AES implementation, the byte substitution in the S-boxes is fairly simple too. Finally the decryption algorithm is almost identical to the encryption, thus it is of the same complexity of the encryption algorithm.

From the security viewpoint, E-DES uses a data block size of 128 bit (16 bytes). This means it allows 256 billion gigabytes (2^{64} x 16) to be processed with the same key before any leak can occur. In the case of DES, the limit is 32GB.

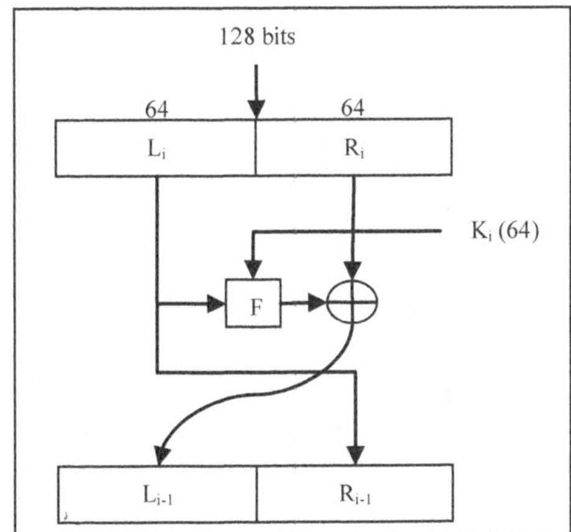

Figure 7: One Round Decryption Structure.

6. Conclusion

We presented E-DES, the educational data encryption system, which is a modification of the known DES with some improvements. The main features of E-DES are 128 bit data block size, a 1024 bit initial key, and more random key generation. In addition, E-DES uses an improved F function which takes 64 bit data and key blocks and applies AES like substitution boxes.

The proposed cipher shows an improvement over DES in two main areas: implementation is more straightforward and security is enforced with larger key and data block sizes.

Currently, a software implementation of the encryption algorithm has been completed and will be made available after the implementation of the decryption part is finalized.

Next, we are planning to produce a hardware implementation of the algorithm that can be useful to make it available in embedded and mobile systems.

References

[1] R. Hosseinkhani and H. Haj Seyyed Javadi. Using Cipher Key to Generate Dynamic S-Box in AES Cipher System, International Journal of Computer Science and Security (IJCSS), Volume 6 Issue 1, pp. 19-28, 2012.

[2] P. Kenekayoro. The data encryption standard thirty four years later: An overview. African Journal of Mathematics and Computer Science Research. Vol. 3(10), pp. 267-269, October 2010.

[3] K Ramesh Babu et al, International Journal of Computer Science & Communication Networks,Vol 2(2), 277-283

[4] R. Singh , A. Mishra and D.B. Ojha. An Instinctive Approach For Secure Communication – Enhanced Data Encryption Standard (EHDES), International Journal of Computer Science and Information Technologies, Volume 1 Issue 4, pp. 264-267, 2010.

[5] W. Stallings, Cryptography and Network Security, 4th Edition, Pearson Prentice Hall, 2006. ISBN13: 978-0131873162.

[6] M. Vishnu et al. Security enhancement of digital motion image transmission using hybrid AES-DES algorithm. 14th Asia-Pacific Conference on Communications, 2008. APCC 2008. PP.1-5.

[7] http://www.differencebetween.net/technology/difference-between-des-and-aes/

[8] http://www.cisco.com/web/about/ac123/ac147/archived_issues/ipj_4-2/goodbye_des.html

[9] W. Tuchman, A Brief History of the Data Encryption Standard, Internet besieged: countering cyberspace scofflaws. ACM Press/Addison-Wesley Publishing Co. New York, NY, USA, 1998, pp. 275–280. ISBN:0-201-30820-7

[10] C. Kaufman, R. Perlman and M. Speciner. Network Security: Private Communication in a Public World, 2nd Edition, Prentice-Hall, 2002. ISBN:0-13-046019-2

[11] C. Connel. An Analysis of NEWDES: A Modified Version of DES. Journal of Cryptologia, Volume 14 issue 3, pp. 217-223, July 1990.

[12] Zibideh, W.Y.; Matalgah, Mustafa M. "An optimized encryption framework based on the modified-DES algorithm: A trade-off between security and throughput in wireless channels", Radio and Wireless Symposium (RWS), 2012 IEEE, On page(s): 419 – 422.

[13] E. Schaefer. A simplified data encryption algorithm. Cryptologia, 20(1):77–84, 1996.

Android Malware Detection Using Library API Call Tracing and Semantic-Preserving Signal Processing Techniques

Seonho Choi[1], **Kun Sun**[2], **and Hyeonsang Eom**[3]
[1]Department Computer Science, Bowie State University, Bowie, MD 20715, USA
[2]Center for Secure Information Systems, George Mason University, Fairfax, VA 22030, USA
[3]School of Computer Science and Engineering, Seoul National University, Seoul, 151-744, Korea

Abstract - *We propose to develop a new malware detection mechanism for Android-based mobile devices based upon library API call tracing and signal processing techniques. By tracing and utilizing library API calls we can capture the intentions/behaviors of an application at a higher level. Also, signal processing techniques, such as a wavelet-based transformation, may have the advantage of enhanced flexibility, effective malware detection, reduced runtime overhead, and capability to detect hidden intrusive patterns compared to the other pattern classification techniques, and may enhance the detection capability even for evolving and varying malwares. A dynamic approach will be developed and investigated in this project.*

Keywords: Smartphone security, Android malware, dynamic analysis, anomaly detection, signal processing

1 Introduction

Android has become a popular mobile operating system for various devices including smart phones. However, its popularity and openness have made it a prime target for attackers. Source codes for various applications in Android platform may be easily obtained and used as a basis for developing malwares. It is reported that the percentage of malware infected applications in both the official and unofficial marketplaces are increasing rapidly []. However, most of the proposed malware detection techniques suffer from either the low detection rates or lack of flexibility (e.g., high false-positive rate and high false negative rate).

We propose to develop a new malware detection mechanism for Android-based mobile devices based upon library API call tracing and signal processing techniques. By tracing and utilizing library API calls we can capture the intentions/behaviors of an application at a higher level. Also, signal processing techniques, such as a wavelet-based transformation, may have the advantage of enhanced flexibility, effective malware detection, reduced runtime overhead, and capability to detect hidden intrusive patterns compared to the other pattern classification techniques, and may enhance the detection capability even for evolving and varying malwares. A dynamic approach will be developed and investigated in this project.

Even though Android is built based on Linux, the malware detection techniques developed for desktops may not be applied. Android has a different system architecture. At a lower level each application is encapsulated into a separate process and it is run by using the services provided by Linux kernel. Within each application, a virtual machine, known as a Dalvik Virtual Machine (DVM), provides a run-time environment for the Java components included in the application (app). All apps can contain both Java and native components. Native components are simply shared libraries that are dynamically loaded at runtime. The Dalvik virtual machine (DVM), a shared library named libdvm.so, is then used to provide a Java-level abstraction for the app's Java components. Application developers heavily make use of the objects and methods provided by the Java Library included in the DVM. To understand or grasp the intentions of the malwares, it will be more beneficial to trace/utilize the Java-level semantics that comprehend the behaviors of the Java components in the app rather than focusing on system call histories captured at the lower level.

Library API call traces may be utilized in detecting/identifying malwares. This will be carried out dynamically at run time after a training process to obtain a classifier. In this process, we will adopt and apply a signal processing technique, known as Wavelet Transformation (WT), after converting a sequence of library API calls (along with library object information) into a signal. We will develop a new semantic-preserving signal conversion technique combined with API clustering techniques.

A recent study of the performance comparison of existing Android malware detection systems indicates that such systems have shown great potentials to improve the accuracy of the detection. Although several interesting Android malware detection systems have been designed based on either signature-based or anomaly-based, they are still suffering from high false-positive rate or low detection rates. The following are some of the limitations of the traditional approaches based upon either signatures or anomaly detection:

- Ineffectivenes: It is prone to report a large number of false alarms because of its inability to quickly adapt to a legitimate behavior change.
- Inflexibility: In some of the approaches any slightly changes of attacks can affect the detection rate significantly.
- Difficulty in feature extraction: The intrusive patterns which are not easily visible may be hidden among the irrelevant and redundant features, which may make the feature extraction process miss them.
- Overhead: For example, the approaches based upon control flow checking suffer from scalability issues with a high overhead.

Wavelet transformation (WT) has been broadly known as a promising method for performing time-frequency analysis. Since wavelet indicates a small localized wave in time domain, any fast changes can be identified easily. The WT decomposes a data into different scales by calculating its correlation with a set of scaled and shifted versions of the chosen wavelet basis function, a process implemented by passing the data through multiple levels of high-pass and low-pass filters. This ability to preserve both time and frequency resolution has led to widespread use of the WT in many practical applications in Biology and Medicine. It is particularly well suited to local analysis of fast time varying and non-stationary signals. Thus, the merits of applying WT to our problem are (a) analyzing and capturing the time-varying nature of the library API call patterns in malwares and b) identifying appropriate characteristics that represent an app's hidden behavior.

2 Related Works

In signature-based malware detection systems malwares are detected by utilizing the sets of rules or policies [4, 8, 9, 12, 16, 24]. If an attack shows a signature exactly matching one of the known signatures, then it can be easily detected. However, this mechanism may not be effective against new malwares with unknown signatures.

In anomaly detection approaches machine learning algorithms are first used to obtain classifiers from the known malware behaviors [9, 14, 17, 18, 19, 20, 22]. Then, the classifier will be used at run-time to detect malwares. Although anomaly detection is able to detect new or evolved malwares more effectively compared to the signature-based approaches, it sometimes causes high false positive.

Malware detection techniques may also be classified into two different categories, static vs. dynamic. In static approaches the classifier or signatures will be obtained only from the apps' codes, which remove the necessity to collect the data by running the apps [1, 3, 5, 9, 11, 13, 23, 24]. These approaches have limitations. Metamorphic and polymorphic techniques may be applied to generate new signatures for the same virus. If polymorphic techniques are used, due to the encryption, it is difficult to generate the signatures; if metamorphic techniques are applied, all the codes will be obfuscated. In dynamic approaches, they obtain classifiers or signatures only based upon data obtained at run-time [6, 7, 10, 12, 14, 18, 19, 22]. They don't have limitations as in the static approaches, but it becomes critical how to design and conduct app running experiments to capture their behaviors or signatures in a comprehensive manner.

A few attempts were made to apply signal processing techniques to the design of intrusion detection systems for wired networks [15]. However, in our knowledge, applying signal processing techniques to malware detection on Android has not been attempted.

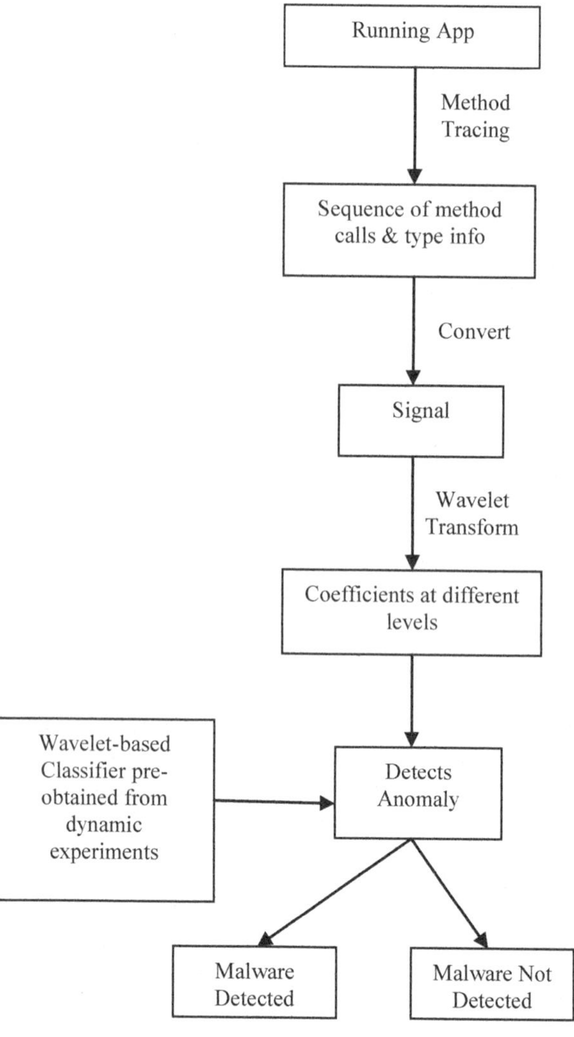

Figure 1: Overview of our scheme

3 Methodology and Plan

We will adop a dynamic approach to address the problem. The overview of the scheme is shown in Figure 1 and consists of the following components:

- Method tracing: method call information will be obtained from a running App code along with other class type information in which the method is implemented. We will utilize a fixed-window approach in obtaining and utilizing the sequence of method calls. The size of the window needs to be chosen carefully, which is one of the research issues in this project. Also, all the captured method calls may be used or a subset of them may be utilized.
- Conversion to Signal: A unique number will be assigned to each method name and a hierarchical class type name by using a semantic-preserving signal conversion technique to be developed in this project. This will convert the method call sequence into a signal to be analyzed further by utilizing the embedded semantic information.
- Wavelet Transform: We will apply WT to the signals obtained in the previous step. The resulting coefficients at different levels will be used for an incremental detection process.
- Classifier: This will be obtained by repeating the above processes for different Apps, some of them known to include malwares and the rest known to be free from malwares. The experiments should be designed and executed carefully to capture the behavior characteristics of the Apps thoroughly.
- Anomaly Detection: We will design an incremental detection algorithm which gives higher priority to low-level coefficients, and uses higher-level coefficients to improve the detection probabilities.

We will design and implement a dynamic solution approach for this problem.

3.1 Semantic-Preserving Signal Conversion

It would not be difficult to come up with new malwares by modifying known malwares. For example, the parts in the application that perform the core operations for the malware may be modified using different library objects , API calls, and/or using different orders. Or, various code obfuscation techniques may be utilized to disguise the malwares. It would be desired for our detection scheme to have the capacity to detect malwares even in such cases. For this purpose the following new technique will be incorporated into our scheme:

- Semantic-Preserving API (or class) clustering: we may capture the intentions of the App by utilizing the library API call history. There are similar API calls (e.g., reading from a file) in terms of their intentions. We will first create different API clusters. Each cluster will contain the similar API calls whose intentions may be close to each other. We will make use of these clusters in designing the semantic-preserving signal conversion technique. The main benefits of semantic based solution is to abstract the behaviors of the malwares, and to reduce the complexity of the detection by using the library API calls and reduce the number of false positives.

4 Conclusion

We propose a new solution approach for the malware detection problem in Adnroid evironment. It is based upon the semantic-preserving API clustering and signal processing technqiues. We finished automating the installation and execution of applications on Android phone, and we are in the middle of conducting a series of experiments to extract API tracing information for sets of malware-infected and normal apps.

5 Acknowledgement

This work was supported by US Army Research Office (ARO) grant W911NF1210060.

6 References

[1] D. Barrera, H. G. Kayacik, P. C. van Oorschot, and A. Somayaji. A methodology for empirical analysis of permission-based security models and its application to android. In *Proceedings of the 17th ACM conference on Computer and communications security*, CCS '10, pages 73–84, New York, NY, USA, 2010. ACM.

[2] A. Bose, X. Hu, K. G. Shin, and T. Park. Behavioral detection of malware on mobile handsets. In *Proceedings of the 6th internationalconference on Mobile systems, applications, and services*, MobiSys '08, pages 225–238, New York, NY, USA, 2008. ACM.

[3] E. Chin, A. P. Felt, K. Greenwood, and D. Wagner. Analyzing interapplication communication in android. In *Proceedings of the 9th international conference on Mobile systems, applications, and services*, MobiSys '11, pages 239–252, New York, NY, USA, 2011. ACM.

[4] A. Desnos and G. Gueguen. Android: From reversing to decompilation. Blackhat, 2011.

[5] F. Di Cerbo, A. Girardello, F. Michahelles, and S. Voronkova. Detection of malicious applications on android os. In *Proceedings of the 4th international conference on Computational forensics*, IWCF'10, pages 138–149, Berlin, Heidelberg, 2011. Springer-Verlag.

[6] B. Dixon, Y. Jiang, A. Jaiantilal, and S. Mishra. Location based power analysis to detect malicious code in smartphones. In *Proceedings of the 1st ACM workshop on Security and privacy in smartphones and mobile devices*, SPSM '11, pages 27–32, New York, NY, USA, 2011. ACM.

[7] W. Enck, P. Gilbert, B.-G. Chun, L. P. Cox, J. Jung, P. McDaniel, and A. N. Sheth. Taintdroid: An information-flow tracking system for realtime privacy monitoring on smartphones. In *Proceedings of the 9th USENIX conference on Operating systems design and implementation*, OSDI'10, pages 1–6, Berkeley, CA, USA, 2010. USENIX Association.

[8] W. Enck, M. Ongtang, and P. McDaniel. On lightweight mobile phone application certification. In *Proceedings of the 16th ACM conference on Computer and communications security*, CCS '09, pages 235–245, New York, NY, USA, 2009. ACM.

[9] A. P. Fuchs, A. Chaudhuri, and J. S. Foster. SCanDroid: Automated Security Certification of Android Applications. Technical Report CSTR- 4991, Department of Computer Science, University of Maryland, College Park, November 2009.

[10] P. Gilbert, B.-G. Chun, L. P. Cox, and J. Jung. Vision: Automated security validation of mobile apps at app markets. In *Proceedings of the second international workshop on Mobile cloud computing and services*, MCS '11, pages 21–26, New York, NY, USA, 2011. ACM.

[11] M. Grace, Y. Zhou, Z. Wang, and X. Jiang. Systematic detection of capability leaks in stock Android smartphones. In *Proceedings of the 19th Network and Distributed System Security Symposium (NDSS)*, Feb. 2012.

[12] H. Kim, J. Smith, and K. G. Shin. Detecting energy-greedy anomalies and mobile malware variants. In *Proceedings of the 6th international conference on Mobile systems, applications, and services*, MobiSys '08, pages 239–252, New York, NY, USA, 2008. ACM.

[13] S. Kim, J. I. Cho, H. W. Myeong, and D. H. Lee. A study on static analysis model of mobile application for privacy protection. In J. J. (Jong Hyuk) Park, H.-C. Chao, M. S. Obaidat, and J. Kim, editors, *Computer Science and Convergence*, volume 114 of *Lecture Notes in Electrical Engineering*, pages 529–540. Springer Netherlands, 2012.

[14] L. Liu, G. Yan, X. Zhang, and S. Chen. Virusmeter: Preventing your cellphone from spies. In *Proceedings of the 12th International Symposium on Recent Advances in Intrusion Detection*, RAID '09, pages 244–264, Berlin, Heidelberg, 2009. Springer-Verlag.-2792-2 50.

[15] Urbashi Mitra, Antonio Ortega, John Heidemann, and Christos Papadopoulos, "Detecting and Identifying Malware: A New Signal Processing Goal", IEEE SIGNAL PROCESSING MAGAZINE **110** pp.107-111, SEPTEMBER 2006.

[16] M. Ongtang, S. McLaughlin, W. Enck, and P. McDaniel. Semanticallyrich application-centric security in android. In *Proceedings of the 2009Annual Computer Security Applications Conference*, ACSAC '09, pages 340–349, Washington, DC, USA, 2009. IEEE Computer Society.

[17] A.-D. Schmidt, J. H. Clausen, A. Camtepe, and S. Albayrak. Detecting symbian os malware through static function call analysis. Number March2006, pages 15–22. IEEE, 2009.

[18] A. Shabtai and Y. Elovici. Applying behavioral detection on androidbased devices. In *MOBILWARE*, pages 235–249, 2010.

[19] A. Shabtai, U. Kanonov, Y. Elovici, C. Glezer, and Y. Weiss. "andromaly": A behavioral malware detection framework for android devices. *J. Intell. Inf. Syst.*, 38(1):161–190, 2012.

[20] P. Teufl, S. Kraxberger, C. Orthacker, G. Lackner, M. Gissing, A. Marsalek, J. Leibetseder, and O. Prevenhueber. Android market analysis with activation patterns. In *MOBISEC*, 2011.

[21] L. Xie, X. Zhang, J.-P. Seifert, and S. Zhu. pbmds: A behavior-based malware detection system for cellphone devices. In *Proceedings of the third ACM conference on Wireless network security*, WiSec '10, pages 37–48, New York, NY, USA, 2010. ACM.

[22] M. Zhao, F. Ge, T. Zhang, and Z. Yuan. Antimaldroid: An efficient svmbased malware detection framework for android. In C. Liu, J. Chang, and A. Yang, editors, *ICICA (1)*, volume 243 of *Communications in Computer and Information Science*, pages 158–166. Springer, 2011.

[23] W. Zhou, Y. Zhou, X. Jiang, and P. Ning. Detecting repackaged smartphone applications in third-party android marketplaces. In *Proceedings of the second ACM conference on Data and Application Security and Privacy*, CODASPY '12, pages 317–326, New York, NY, USA, 2012. ACM.

[24] Y. Zhou, Z. Wang, W. Zhou, and X. Jiang. Hey, you, get off of my market: Detecting malicious apps in official and alternative Android markets. In *Proceedings of the 19th Annual Network & Distributed System Security Symposium*, Feb. 2012.